FestWestEur-1958
Dewey: 94.2694
LC: GT4842.S75

Spicer, Dorothy Gladys. *Festivals of Western Europe.* 1958. Reprinted by Omnigraphics, 1994.

FolkAmerHol-1987
Dewey: 394.269
LC: GT4803.F651

Cohen, Hennig, and Tristram Potter Coffin. *Folklore of American Holidays.* Gale, 1987.

FolkWrldHol-1992
Dewey: 394.26
LC: GT3930.F651

MacDonald, Margaret R., ed. *The Folklore of World Holidays.* Gale, 1992.

GdUSFest-1984
Dewey: 394.6025
LC: GT3930.S41

Shemanski, Frances. *A Guide to Fairs and Festivals in the United States.* Greenwood, 1984.

GdWrldFest-1985
Dewey: 394.269
LC: GT3930.S431

Shemanski, Frances. *A Guide to World Fairs and Festivals.* Greenwood, 1985.

HolFestCelWrld-1994
Dewey: 394.26
LC: GT3925.T461

Thompson, Sue Ellen, and Barbara W. Carlson, eds. *Holidays, Festivals, and Celebrations of the World Dictionary.* Omnigraphics, 1994.

IndianAmer-1989
Dewey: 917.304
LC: E77.E117

Eagle/Walking Turtle. *Indian America: A Traveller's Companion.* John Muir Publications, 1989.

IntlThFolk-1979
Dewey: 790.2025
LC: PN1590.F47M47

Merin, Jennifer. *International Directory of Theatre, Dance, and Folklore Festivals.* Greenwood, 1979.

MusFestAmer-1990
LC: ML19.R3

Rabin, Carol Price. *Music Festivals in America.* Berkshire Traveller Press, 1990.

MusFestEurBrit-1980
Dewey: 780.794
LC: ML35.R14

Rabin, Carol Price. *Music Festivals in Europe and Britain.* Berkshire Traveller Press, 1980.

MusFestWrld-1963
Dewey: 780.79
LC: ML35.S87

Stoll, Dennis Gray. *Music Festivals of the World.* Pergamon, Macmillan, 1963.

NatlHolWrld-1968
Dewey: 394.26
LC: GT3930.D64

Dobler, Lavinia. *National Holidays around the World.* Fleet Press, 1968.

RelHolCal-1993
Dewey: 529.3
LC: CE6.K451

Kelly, Aidan, Peter Dresser, and Linda M. Ross. *Religious Holidays and Calendars.* Omnigraphics, 1993.

SaintFestCh-1904
Dewey: 299.932
LC: DR170.B7

Brewster, H. Pomeroy. *Saints and Festivals of the Christian Church.* 1904. Reprinted by Omnigraphics, 1990.

Holidays
and
Festivals
Index

Holidays and Festivals Index

Edited by
Helene Henderson
and
Barry Puckett

A Descriptive Guide to Information on More Than 3,000 Holidays, Festivals, Fairs, Rituals, Celebrations, Commemorations, Holy Days and Saints' Days, Feasts and Fasts, and Other Observances, Including Ethnic, Seasonal, Art, Music, Dance, Theater, Folk, Historic, National, and Ancient Events from All Parts of the World, as Found in Standard Reference Works. Includes Location, Date, Alternative Names, Cross References, and Indexes by Ethnic Group and Geographical Location, Personal Name, Religion, and Calendar.

Omnigraphics, Inc.
Penobscot Building
Detroit, MI 48226

Helene Henderson and Barry Puckett, *Editors*

Omnigraphics, Inc.

*   *   *

Matthew Barbour, *Production Coordinator*
Laurie Lanzen Harris, *Vice President, Editorial Director*
Peter E. Ruffner, *Vice President, Administration*
James A. Sellgren, *Vice President, Operations and Finance*
Jane Steele, *Vice President, Research*

*   *   *

Frederick G. Ruffner, Jr., *President, Publisher*

Copyright © 1995 Omnigraphics, Inc.

ISBN 0-7808-0012-5

Library of Congress Cataloging-in-Publication Data

Holidays and Festivals Index : a descriptive guide to information on more
   than 3,000 holidays / Helene Henderson and Barry Puckett, editors.
     p.   cm.
   Includes bibliographical references.
   1. Holidays—Indexes   2. Festivals—Indexes   3. Special days—
   Indexes.   I. Henderson, Helene.   II. Puckett, Barry.
   GT3925.H65   1995
   394.2'69—dc20   94-39351
                                         CIP

This book is printed on acid-free paper meeting the ANSI Z39.48 Standard. The
infinity symbol that appears above indicates that the paper in this book
meets that standard.

Printed in the United States of America

Contents

Introduction

One of the first things to attract the prospective *aficionado* to folklore is the realization that "it's a small world, after all"! It is entrancing that the myths and legends of the world, the customs and beliefs of the world, the festivals and celebrations of the world are so much more alike than different. A major reason for this lies in the fact that human beings tend to express themselves in similar ways as they pass through similar levels of culture. So, regardless of their racial or ethnic background or geographic locale, whether they flourished ages ago, a few centuries ago, or flourish today, if they count themselves as humankind, they will share deep-down similarities in spite of language, costume, and other superficial differences. People who don't understand scientific laws, and to some extent people who do, will honor the earth's ability to produce food, the reproductive capacities of plants, animals, and humans, as well as their own accomplishments in political and territorial struggles. And all punctuate humankind's passage from birth to adulthood to death.

It is through this fascination for a world community that one best approaches the *Holidays and Festivals Index* which is designed to ease our efforts to investigate it. Nor should one belittle such a fascination. It has been a major force driving some of the most important studies in the field of folklore: the "collective unconscious" of Carl Jung, the "hero with a thousand faces" of Joseph Campbell, the "golden bough" of James G. Frazer. Still, one's enchantment will deepen if he or she understands some principles about rites and festivals and celebrations before starting out.

Rites, festivals, and celebrations divide themselves into three parts: the genuinely traditional, the revived traditional, and the invented. It may seem surprising, but a genuine folk celebration usually generates far less effort and enthusiasm on the part of the participants than a revival or an artificially created holiday. In the United States, May Day is a genuinely traditional holiday, linked to other celebrations of spring and fertility across the world. As a nation we observe it a bit off-handedly and with a certain absence of stir. At some schools, girls used to decorate and dance about a phallic maypole and play games; somewhere people plant crops in exaggerated sexual garb to insure their fecundity; a few see it as a time to make predictions. But the majority of us simply acknowledge: "Oh yes, today's May Day" and go about our business.

Reviving or creating a celebration or festival involves more energy than simply acknowledging a traditional one. In his book, *The Nanticoke Indians—Past and Present*, C.A. Weslager reports that a number of years ago a group of Nanticoke Indians decided to hold a powwow every Thanksgiving, but had lost touch with the customs of their ancestors. The late anthropologist Frank Speck taught them some dances and songs and enlisted the help of some Delaware Indians from Oklahoma to participate as well. The excitement was great as these people learned what other Indians had done generations earlier to insure crops, be successful in war, and acknowledge rites of passage. They returned to their communities and with much ado reinvented a part of their culture. Even more excitement and energy may be produced if a festival becomes a tourist attraction and produces revenue. Mardi Gras, Carnival, and similar Shrove Tuesday rites were once genuine folk traditional events (and still are celebrated that way in many parts of the Roman Catholic world); however, in places like New Orleans or Trinidad, they have been steadily enlarged, evaluated, and promoted until now it takes an expert to tell what is truly traditional and what is simply commercial. Sometimes the whole festival becomes so involved it embraces a bit of everything. The eve of our New Year's Day (similar to other days when the calendar indicates a fresh start) has its perfunctory traditional side. Many of us suffer through or don't even bother with the routine party and the singing of "Auld Lang Syne" at midnight. Yet ballrooms and hotels across the country are able to promote the night, getting record crowds; Times Square is packed; and the next day bowl parades and football games are huckstered by television and the local chamber of commerce to be watched by millions.

One must also realize that a people do not need to understand a ritual to participate in it and to preserve it jealously. How many Americans know the difference between All Saints' and All Souls' or why in some communities there seem to be two "Halloweens" in a row? How many Chinese know why their years are given animal names? How many Latinos know why they celebrate General Zaragoza's defeat of the French on *Cinco de Mayo*? How many of us are aware of how St. Nicholas (Santa Claus), whose birthday is December 6, became associated with Christ's mass on December 25? Most people don't even know that our holidays begin, according to ancient custom, as the sun sets the evening before the actual day celebrated. Ritual, understood or not, does not die easily. Thus, square dances preserve old fertility steps, soccer and lacrosse are modern-day incarnations of village-to-village rivalries battled by whole communities on sacred days, and bullfights, even though they became professionalized by eighteenth-century Spanish slaughterhouse employees, still center on the killing of a male fertility symbol.

The time at which a festival or celebration takes place is subject to geography, calendar changes or differences, religious adaptations, and the like. It is because of climate that a celebration such as St. John's Day (June 24) in Sweden, which celebrates Midsummer on that date, is so much like Whitsunday (usually in May) in England. Similarly, the romantic implications of St. Valentine's Day (February 14, the day when the birds supposedly start mating) seems more appropriate to Italy than to North America. Then too, people with differing calendars conquered each other and intermingled their festivals, not always adjusting them neatly. As the Roman Catholic Church moved its messages northward across Europe, it absorbed a welter of pagan mid-winter rites, refocussing them on saint's days: in honor of Martin (November 11), Barbara (December 4), Nicholas (December 6), Lucy (December 13), Christ (whose mass date was set to coincide with the Roman mid-winter festival of the Kalends), New Year's (the mid-point of the twelve days of Christmas), Epiphany (January 6, Old Christmas Day with its Twelfth Night celebration) and even Plough Monday (late in January). Things we associate with Christmas itself—feasting, drinking, kissing under mistletoe, dancing, mumming, evergreens—are appropriate to these other days as well.

In 352, the council of Nicea ruled that another major Christian holiday, Easter, should be observed on the Sunday after the first full moon on or following the Vernal Equinox, a range of thirty-five days. But in October, 1582, Pope Gregory switched Europe from the solar Julian calendar to his solar Gregorian calendar by skipping ten days between the fifth and fifteenth. England did not comply for 170 years. The Eastern Church has continued to set Easter by the old calendar, while before the council acted many Christians celebrated Easter at the time of the Jewish Passover, eight memorial days beginning on the fifteenth day of Nisan, the seventh month of a lunar year. And Chinese-Americans celebrate their New Year according to a lunar calendar discarded many years ago. Under such circumstances it can be hard to tell what date any local group will use for a celebration.

If such glimpses into the confusions surrounding the world's holidays, festivals, and celebrations seem daunting, that's because they are. But these glimpses, and more detailed observations, introduce a reader to a truly amazing subject. And if one learns from using the *Index* that "it is a small world, after all," one also learns that it is a merging, reviving, and flourishing small world at that!

Tristram Potter Coffin
University of Pennsylvania

Preface

Holidays and festivals have been celebrated by people of all cultures from the earliest recorded times. Whether they mark seasonal cycles, spiritual milestones, or historical events, these celebrations and observances reveal the range and variety of human experience.

The Objective of the Work

Holidays and Festivals Index provides a guide to over 3,000 holidays, festivals, celebrations, commemorative days, feasts, and fasts held in over 150 countries around the world, as found in twenty-six of the best-known and most widely held dictionaries, encyclopedias, and other reference works on special days and observances. It is a companion to the *Holidays, Festivals, and Celebrations of the World Dictionary* (Omnigraphics, Inc., 1994), but covers substantially more events.

Criteria for Inclusion

The *Index* includes both secular and religious holidays, most of which continue to be celebrated. A number of ancient events are also indexed because of their continuing relevance in art and literature. Generally, an event is included if it holds cultural significance, whether localized in a single town or among nations; if its observance occurs on some regularly scheduled basis; and if it appears in the standard reference sources used. As a rule, commercial and trade events were not included.

In reviewing the reference works indexed, the editors found that sources often disagreed on such matters as the name or spelling of an event, or the date(s) on which it is held. In these cases, the editors have used the form of the name and date found in the majority of sources.

The Plan of the Work

The main text of the *Holidays and Festivals Index* is an alphabetical arrangement of events by name. Entries for each event include the geographic area(s) and/or peoples who celebrate it and the date(s) on which the event occurs. Alternate forms or foreign names of the holiday appear in parentheses immediately after the name of the entry. For example, "Christmas in Mexico" is rendered as "Christmas (Navidad)." "Navidad" also appears as a separate heading directing the user to "Christmas in Mexico." For events best known by their foreign names, cross references appear from the English to the foreign language name. Festivals are also grouped together alphabetically by such keywords as **art, autumn, dance, drama, Indian, music, powwow, spring, summer, theater,** and **winter.** Words such as **festival, international,** and **birthday of** have been transposed to the end of the holiday's name in order to list each entry by a keyword.

Sample Entry

Each numbered section in this sample entry designates an item of information that may be included in an entry. The sections are explained in the descriptive paragraphs following the sample.

---

① **Custer's Last Stand**

  ② **Named for:** George Armstrong Custer (1839-1876)

  ③ **Location:** Crow Reservation in Montana

  ④ **Ethnic or religious group:** Crow Indians

  ⑤ **Established:** June 25, 1876, Battle of Little Big Horn

  ⑥ **Date:** Observed with a pageant in late June

  ⑦ *AmerBkDays-1978,* 591, 593
    Chases-1993, 263
    HolFestCelWrld-1994, 182

---

① **Name of event.** The name of the holiday or festival. Foreign and/or alternate names follow in parentheses where applicable. A festival named for a person is alphabetized under the person's last name (for example, Lincoln's Birthday). An event named for a fictional character is alphabetized under the character's first name (for example, Tom Sawyer Days).

② **Named for.** The person or event for which the holiday is named or which the holiday honors. The entries for these types of holidays include the birth and death dates of the individual(s) celebrated, if known.

③ **Location.** Place(s) where the event is observed, according to the sources indexed.

④ **Ethnic or religious group.** Ethnic group(s) and/or religious denomination(s) that celebrate the holiday, according to the sources indexed.

⑤ **Established.** If sources indicate the first celebration of an event, that information appears under this heading. If the holiday commemorates a particular historical occurrence, the date and year of the historical event are given.

⑥ **Date.** The date(s) the holiday or festival is observed. Entries for movable events contain a chronological description of the date of observance.

⑦ **Sources with page numbers.** An alphabetical listing of abbreviated reference source titles, including date of publication, followed by the page number(s) on which the event appears in each source.

For major events that take place in many locales, such as Christmas and Easter, the editors have referenced the holiday in national and/or ethnic sections (**Location** and **Ethnic or religious** group). Where specific ethnic, religious and geographic information is available, ethnic and religious denominations are listed in alphabetical order by ethnic or religious group, then by geographic location.

Geographic locations for holidays and festivals reflect information in the sources indexed. These sources, published over the last 100 years, reflect the geographic realities of the era in which they appeared. Therefore, the reader will find events celebrated in both the Union of Soviet Socialist Republics (U.S.S.R.) and Russia as well as in Yugoslavia and Croatia. For this reason, the dates of the sources appear after their abbreviated titles. In instances in which countries have changed names, the editors have attempted to acknowledge the change. For example, an entry pertaining to Burma lists the location as "Burma; now Myanmar," whereas an entry pertaining to Myanmar reads "Myanmar; formerly Burma."

Indexes and Special Features

Ethnic and Geographic, Name, Religion, and Chronological Indexes follow the main index of the *Holidays and Festivals Index*. Other helpful features are a section explaining various calendars of the world and tables of state and national public holidays. An annotated bibliography features titles focusing on events in particular geographic areas and among certain ethnic groups and religions, as well as sources lending historical background and offering philosophical discussions.

Audience

The *Holidays and Festivals Index* is intended for use in elementary, middle and high schools and public libraries, as well as churches, synagogues, mosques, community affairs groups, and other organizations interested in learning about festive events.

Acknowledgements

The editors wish to thank our Advisory Board, including Linda Carpino of the Lincoln Branch of the Detroit Public Library, Richard Nagler of the Farmington Hills Public Library, Art Woodford of the St. Clair Shores Public Library, and especially Gail Beaver of the Huron High School Library in Ann Arbor and Jeff Tong of the Detroit Public Library, who evaluated the *Holidays and Festivals Index* during its formation. We hope their comments and suggestions have helped us to provide a comprehensive and useful guide. Laurie Lanzen Harris has offered her editorial expertise, guidance, and encouragement, for which we are deeply appreciative. We would also like to thank Frank Abate of Dictionary & Reference Specialists, Old Saybrook, Connecticut, for his valuable counsel. We also wish to recognize the assistance provided by the Main Branch of the Detroit Public Library and the Purdy-Kresge Library at Wayne State University, Detroit.

Suggestions

The editors welcome commentary and recommendations to enrich the value and usefulness of this volume.

Legal Holidays by State

The "standard six" holidays observed throughout the United States are:

New Year's Day	January 1
Memorial Day	last Monday in May (not celebrated in Alabama)
Independence Day	July 4
Labor Day	first Monday in September
Thanksgiving	fourth Thursday in November
Christmas	December 25

In addition, state offices throughout the United States are usually closed on Election Day, the first Tuesday after the first Monday in November. Veterans' Day, November 11, is observed in some manner by all the states.

The following list is of other legal holidays observed by the various states, Washington, D.C., and Puerto Rico. Under each the arrangement is by Gregorian calendar order.

Alabama

Martin Luther King, Jr. and Robert E. Lee birthdays	January, third Monday
Washington's Birthday	February, third Monday
Confederate Memorial Day	April, fourth Monday
Jefferson Davis' Birthday	June, first Monday
Columbus Day	October, second Monday
Fraternal Day	October, second Monday

Alaska

Martin Luther King, Jr. Day	January 19
Presidents' Day	February, third Monday
Seward's Day	March, last Monday
Alaska Day	October 18

Arizona

Martin Luther King, Jr. Day/Civil Rights Day	January, third Monday
Lincoln's Birthday	February, second Monday
Washington's Birthday	February, third Monday
Mother's Day	May, second Sunday
Father's Day	June, third Sunday
American Family Day	August, first Sunday
Constitution Day	September 17
Columbus Day	October, second Monday

Arkansas

Martin Luther King, Jr. and Robert E. Lee birthdays	January, third Monday

Washington's Birthday	February, third Monday
Christmas Eve	December 24

California

Martin Luther King, Jr. Day	January, third Monday
Lincoln's Birthday	February 12
Washington's Birthday	February, third Monday
Good Friday	Friday before Easter
Admission Day	September 9
Columbus Day	October, second Monday

Colorado

Martin Luther King, Jr.'s Birthday	January, third Monday
Washington-Lincoln Day	February, third Monday
Columbus Day	October, second Monday

Connecticut

Martin Luther King, Jr. Day	January, first Monday on or after January 15
Lincoln's Birthday	February 12
Washington's Birthday	February, third Monday
Columbus Day	October, second Monday

Delaware

Martin Luther King, Jr. Day	January, third Monday
Presidents' Day	February, third Monday
Columbus Day	October, second Monday

District of Columbia

Martin Luther King, Jr.'s Birthday	January, third Monday
Washington's Birthday	February, third Monday
Columbus Day	October, second Monday

Florida

Martin Luther King, Jr.'s Birthday	January 15
Robert E. Lee's Birthday	January 19
Lincoln's Birthday	February 12
Susan B. Anthony's Birthday	February 15
Washington's Birthday	February, third Monday
Good Friday	Friday before Easter
Pascua Florida Day	April 2
Confederate Memorial Day	April 26
Jefferson Davis' Birthday	June 3
Flag Day	June 14
Columbus Day and Farmers' Day	October, second Monday

Georgia

Robert E. Lee's Birthday	January 19
Martin Luther King, Jr.'s Birthday	January, third Monday

Washington's Birthday	February, third Monday
Confederate Memorial Day	April 26
Jefferson Davis' Birthday	June 3
Columbus Day	October, second Monday

Hawaii
Martin Luther King, Jr.'s Birthday	January, third Monday
Presidents' Day	February, third Monday
Jonah Kuhio Kalanianaole Day	March 26
Good Friday	Friday before Easter
King Kamehameha I Day	June 11
Admission Day	August, third Friday

Idaho
Martin Luther King, Jr.–Idaho Human Rights Day	January, third Monday
Washington's Birthday	February, third Monday
Columbus Day	October, second Monday

Illinois
Martin Luther King, Jr's Birthday	January, third Monday
Lincoln's Birthday	February 12
Washington's Birthday	February, third Monday
Casimir Pulaski's Birthday	March, first Monday
Good Friday	Friday before Easter
Columbus Day	October, second Monday

Indiana
Martin Luther King, Jr.'s Birthday	January, third Monday
Lincoln's Birthday	February 12
Washington's Birthday	February, third Monday
Good Friday	Friday before Easter
Columbus Day	October, second Monday

Iowa
Martin Luther King, Jr.'s Birthday	January, third Monday
Washington's Birthday	February, third Monday

Kansas
Martin Luther King Day	date set by governor
Lincoln's Birthday	February 12
Washington's Birthday	February, third Monday
Columbus Day	October, second Monday

Kentucky
Robert E. Lee's Birthday	January 19
Franklin D. Roosevelt Day	January 30
Martin Luther King, Jr. Day	January, third Monday
Lincoln's Birthday	February 12

Washington's Birthday	February, third Monday
Confederate Memorial Day & Jefferson Davis Day	June 3
Columbus Day	October, second Monday

Louisiana

Battle of New Orleans	January 8
Robert E. Lee's Birthday	January 19
Martin Luther King, Jr.'s Birthday	January, third Monday
Washington's Birthday	February, third Monday
Good Friday	Friday before Easter
Confederate Memorial Day	June 3
Huey P. Long Day	August 30
Columbus Day	October, second Monday
All Saints' Day	November 1

Maine

Martin Luther King, Jr. Day	January, third Monday
Patriot's Day	February, third Monday
Washington's Birthday	February, third Monday
Columbus Day	October, second Monday

Maryland

Martin Luther King, Jr.'s Birthday	January 15
Lincoln's Birthday	February 12
Washington's Birthday	February, third Monday
Maryland Day	March 25
Good Friday	Friday before Easter
Defenders' Day	September 12
Columbus Day	October 12

Massachusetts

Martin Luther King, Jr. Day	January, third Monday
Washington's Birthday	February, third Monday
Patriot's Day	April, third Monday
Columbus Day	October, second Monday

Michigan

Martin Luther King, Jr. Day	January, third Monday
Lincoln's Birthday	February 12
Washington's Birthday	February, third Monday
Columbus Day	October, second Monday

Minnesota

Martin Luther King, Jr.'s Birthday	January, third Monday
Washington-Lincoln Day	February, third Monday
Columbus Day	October, second Monday

Mississippi
    Robert E. Lee & Martin Luther King,   January, third Monday
        Jr. birthdays
    Washington's Birthday   February, third Monday
    Confederate Memorial Day   April, last Monday
    National Memorial Day and Jefferson   May, last Monday
        Davis' Birthday

Missouri
    Martin Luther King, Jr. Day   January, third Monday
    Lincoln's Birthday   February 12
    Washington's Birthday   February, third Monday
    Columbus Day   October, second Monday

Montana
    Martin Luther King, Jr. Day   January, third Monday
    Washington's and Lincoln's birthdays   February, third Monday
    Columbus Day   October, second Monday

Nebraska
    Martin Luther King, Jr. Day   January, third Monday
    Presidents' Day   February, third Monday
    Arbor Day   April, last Friday
    Columbus Day   October, second Monday

Nevada
    Martin Luther King, Jr.'s Birthday   January, third Monday
    Washington's Birthday   February, third Monday
    Columbus Day   October 12
    Nevada Day   October 31
    Family Day   November, Friday after fourth Thursday

New Hampshire
    Civil Rights Day   January, third Monday
    Washington's Birthday   February, third Monday
    Columbus Day   October, second Monday

New Jersey
    Martin Luther King's Birthday   January, third Monday
    Lincoln's Birthday   February 12
    Washington's Birthday   February, third Monday
    Good Friday   Friday before Easter
    Columbus Day   October, second Monday

New Mexico
    Martin Luther King, Jr.'s Birthday   January, third Monday
    Washington-Lincoln Day   January, third Monday
    Presidents' Day   February, third Monday
    Columbus Day   October, second Monday

New York

Martin Luther King, Jr. Day	January, third Monday
Lincoln's Birthday	February 12
Washington's Birthday	February, third Monday
Flag Day	June, second Sunday
Columbus Day	October, second Monday

North Carolina

Robert E. Lee's Birthday	January 19
Martin Luther King, Jr.'s Birthday	January, third Monday
Washington's Birthday	February, third Monday
Greek Independence Day	March 25
Good Friday	Friday before Easter
Halifax Resolves, Anniversary of signing of	April 12
Confederate Memorial Day	May 10
Mecklenburg Declaration of Independence, Anniversary of	May 20
Columbus Day	October, second Monday
Yom Kippur	September/October

North Dakota

Martin Luther King, Jr.'s Birthday	January, third Monday
Washington's Birthday	February, third Monday
Good Friday	Friday before Easter

Ohio

Martin Luther King, Jr. Day	January, third Monday
Washington-Lincoln Day	February, third Monday
Columbus Day	October, second Monday

Oklahoma

Martin Luther King, Jr.'s Birthday	January, third Monday
Washington's Birthday	February, third Monday
Jefferson Day	April 13
Oklahoma Day	April 22
Mothers' Day	May, second Sunday
Senior Citizens' Day	June 9
Cherokee Strip Day	September 16
Indian Day	September, first Saturday after full moon
Oklahoma Historical Day	October 10
Will Rogers' Day	November 4
Youth Day	Spring, first day

Oregon

Martin Luther King, Jr.'s Birthday	January, third Monday
Presidents' Day	February, third Monday

Pennsylvania
    Martin Luther King, Jr. Day   January, third Monday
    Presidents' Day   February, third Monday
    Good Friday   Friday before Easter
    Flag Day   June 14
    Columbus Day   October, second Monday

Puerto Rico
    Eugenio Maria de Hostos' Birthday   January 11
    Good Friday   Friday before Easter
    Jose de Diego Day   April 16
    Antonio R. Barcelo Day   April, second Sunday
    Luis Munoz Rivera Day   July 17
    Constitution, Day of the   July 25
    Jose Celso Barbosa's Birthday   July 27
    Santiago Iglesias Pantin Day   September, first Monday
    Columbus Day and Discovery Day   October 12

Rhode Island
    Martin Luther King, Jr.'s Birthday   January, third Monday
    Washington's Birthday   February, third Monday
    Rhode Island Independence Day   May 4
    Victory Day   August, second Monday
    Columbus Day   October, second Monday

South Carolina
    Martin Luther King, Jr.'s Birthday   January 15
    Robert E. Lee's Birthday   January 19
    Washington's Birthday   February, third Monday
    Confederate Memorial Day   May 10
    Jefferson Davis' Birthday   June 3

South Dakota
    Martin Luther King, Jr.'s Birthday   January, third Monday
    Native Americans' Day   October, second Monday

Tennessee
    Martin Luther King, Jr. Day   January, third Monday
    Washington's Birthday   February, third Monday
    Good Friday   Friday before Easter
    Columbus Day   October, second Monday

Texas
    Confederate Heroes Day   January 19
    Martin Luther King, Jr. Day   January, third Monday
    Washington's Birthday   February, third Monday
    Texas Independence Day   March 2
    San Jacinto Day   April 21
    Emancipation Day   June 19

Lyndon Baines Johnson's Birthday	August 27

Utah

Martin Luther King, Jr.'s Birthday and Human Rights Day	January, third Monday
Presidents' Day	February, third Monday
Pioneer Day	July 24
Columbus Day	October, second Monday

Vermont

Martin Luther King, Jr.'s Birthday	January, third Monday
Lincoln's Birthday	February 12
Washington's Birthday	February, third Monday
Town Meeting Day	March, first Tuesday
Bennington Battle Day	August 16
Columbus Day	October, second Monday

Virginia

Lee-Jackson-King Day	January, third Monday
Washington's Birthday	February, third Monday
Columbus Day and Yorktown Day	October, second Monday

Washington

Martin Luther King, Jr.'s Birthday	January, third Monday
Presidents' Day	February, third Monday
Columbus Day	October 12

West Virginia

Martin Luther King, Jr.'s Birthday	January, third Monday
Lincoln's Birthday	February 12
Washington's Birthday	February, third Monday
West Virginia Day	June 20
Columbus Day	October, second Monday

Wisconsin

Martin Luther King Jr. Day	January 15
Washington-Lincoln Day	February, third Monday
Columbus Day	October, second Monday

Wyoming

Martin Luther King, Jr.'s Birthday and Wyoming Equality Day	January, third Monday
Washington-Lincoln Day	February, third Monday

Legal Holidays by Country

The following list of legal holidays celebrated by the various countries of the world is arranged by Gregorian calendar order. The holidays for the former USSR, Czechoslovakia, and Yugoslavia have been included because many of them are still observed by the people, and because they are often referred to in literature.

For Jewish holidays and those Christian holidays based on the Christian liturgical calendar (Easter, Pentecost, etc.), we have given the range of months during which the day may fall. The more precise dates may be found in the Chronological Indexes. Some Christians still use the Julian calendar to determine all holy days, and therefore their dates for major feasts will be different.

The dates given for both Muslim holy days and holidays in Islamic countries are approximate since the exact date is only determined a few days before the actual event.

Asian festival dates fluctuate from country to country and may even be different in various parts of the same country because of the variety of traditions observed and calendars used. The dates given here are approximate. (See the section on Calendar Systems Around the World for a detailed explanation of calendar systems.)

Albania:
Anniversary Day	January 11

Algeria:
New Year	January 1
Labor Day	May 1
Independence Day	July 5
Revolution Day	November 1

Antigua and Barbuda:
New Year	January 1
Good Friday	Friday before Easter: March–April
Easter Monday	Monday after Easter
Labor Day	May 6
Whit Monday	Monday after Whitsunday: May–June
Queen's Birthday	June 8
Carnival	August 5-6
Merchant Holiday	October 7
Independence Day	November 1
Christmas	December 25–26

Argentina:
New Year	January 1
Maundy Thursday	Thursday before Easter: March–April
Good Friday	Friday before Easter

Malvinas Day	April 2
Labor Day	May 1
National Day	May 25
Flag Day	June 20
Independence Day	July 9
Death of San Martin	August 17
Discovery of America	October 12
Immaculate Conception	December 8
Christmas	December 25

Australia:

New Year	January 1
Australia Day	January 26; January 29
Good Friday	Friday before Easter: March–April
Easter Monday	Monday after Easter
Anzac Day	April 25
Christmas	December 25–26

Austria:

New Year	January 1
Epiphany	January 6
Easter Monday	Monday after Easter: March–April
Labor Day	May 1
Ascension Day	May 9
Whit Monday	Monday after Whitsunday: May–June
Corpus Christi	May 30
Assumption Day	August 15
National Day	October 26
All Saints Day	November 1
Immaculate Conception	December 8
Christmas	December 25–26

Bahamas:

New Year	January 1
Good Friday	Friday before Easter: March–April
Easter Monday	Monday after Easter
Whit Monday	Monday after Whitsunday: May–June
Labor Day	June 7
Independence Day	July 10
Emancipation Day	August 5
Discovery Day	October 12
Christmas	December 25–26

Bahrain:

New Year	January 1
National Day	December 16

Bangladesh:
- Shaheed Day — February 21
- Independence Day — March 26
- New Year — April 15
- May Day — May 1
- Jumatul Bida — May 5
- Dashami — October 10
- National Revolution Day — November 7
- Victory Day — December 16
- Christmas — December 25

Barbados:
- New Year — January 1
- Errol Barrow Day — January 21
- Good Friday — Friday before Easter: March–April
- Easter Monday — Monday after Easter
- Labor Day — May 1
- Whit Monday — Monday after Whitsunday: May–June
- Kadooment Day — August 5
- United Nations Day — October 1
- Independence Day — November 30
- Christmas — December 25–26

Belgium:
- New Year — January 1
- Easter Monday — Monday after Easter: March–April
- May Day — May 1
- Ascension Day — April–June
- Whit Monday — Monday after Whitsunday: May–June
- National Holiday — July 21
- Assumption Day — August 15
- All Saints Day — November 1
- Armistice Day — November 11
- King's Birthday — November 15
- Christmas — December 25–26

Belize:
- New Year — January 1
- Baron Bliss Day — March 9
- Good Friday — Friday before Easter: March–April
- Holy Saturday — Saturday before Easter
- Easter Monday — Monday after Easter
- Labor Day — May 1
- Commonwealth Day — May 25
- St. George's Caye Day — September 10
- Independence Day — September 21
- Colombus Day — October 12
- Garifuna Settlement Day — November 19

Christmas	December 25–26

Bermuda:

New Year	January 1
Good Friday	Friday before Easter: March–April
Bermuda Day	May 24
Queen's Birthday	June 17
Cup Match	August 1
Somers Day	August 2
Labour Day	September 2
Remembrance Day	November 11
Christmas	December 25–26

Bolivia:

New Year	January 1
Good Friday	Friday before Easter: March–April
Labor Day	May 1
Corpus Christi	May 30
Independence Day	August 6
All Saints Day	November 1
Christmas	December 25

Botswana:

New Year	January 1–2
Good Friday	Friday before Easter: March–April
Easter Saturday	Saturday before Easter
Easter Monday	Monday after Easter
Ascension Day	April–June
President's Day	July 15–16
National Day	October 1
Christmas	December 25–26

Brazil:

New Year	January 1
Good Friday	Friday before Easter: March–April
Easter Monday	Monday after Easter
Tiradentes Day	April 21
Labor Day	May 1
Corpus Christi	May–June
Independence Day	September 7
Nossa Senhora de Aparecida	October 12
All Saints Day	November 1
Proclamation of the Republic	November 15
Christmas	December 25–26

Bulgaria:

New Year	January 1
Liberation Day	March 3

Labor Day	May 1–2
Day of Bulgarian Culture	May 24
Days of Liberation	September 9–10
October Revolution Day	November 7

Burma (Myanmar):

Independence Day	January 4
Union Day	February 12
Peasants' Day	March 2
Armed Forces Day	March 27
Thingyan (Water Festival)	April 14–16
Myanmar New Year	April 17
Workers' Day	May 1
Martyrs' Day	July 19
Christmas	December 25

Cameroon Republic:

New Year	January 1
Youth Day	February 12
Good Friday	Friday before Easter: March–April
Easter Monday	Monday after Easter
Ascension Day	April–June
Labor Day	May 1
National Day	May 20
Assumption Day	August 15
Christmas	December 25

Canada:

New Year	January 1
Good Friday	Friday before Easter: March–April
Easter Monday	Monday after Easter
Victoria Day	May 20
Canada Day	July 1
Labour Day	September 2
Thanksgiving Day	October, second Monday
Remembrance Day	November 11
Christmas	December 25–26

Chile:

New Year	January 1
Good Friday	Friday before Easter: March–April
Easter Saturday	Saturday before Easter
Labor Day	May 1
Navy Day	May 21
Corpus Christi	May–June
St. Peter's and St. Paul's Day	June 29
Assumption Day	August 15
National Liberation Day	September 11

Independence Day	September 18
Army Day	September 19
Columbus Day	October 12
All Saints Day	November 1
Immaculate Conception	December 8
Christmas	December 25

China, People's Republic of:

Spring Festival (Lunar New Year)	February 15
Women's Day	March 8
Labor Day	May 1
Founding of the Communist Party of China	July 1
Birthday of the People's Liberation Army	August 1
National Day	October 1

Colombia:

New Year	January 1
Epiphany	January 6
St. Joseph's Day	March 14
Holy Thursday	Thursday before Easter: March–April
Good Friday	Friday before Easter
Labor Day	May 1
Ascension Day	April–June
St. Mary's Day	May 13
Corpus Christi	May–June
St. Peter's and St. Paul's Day	July 1
Battle of Boyaca	August 7
Assumption Day	August 19
Columbus Day	October 12
All Saints Day	November 1
Independence of Cartagena	November 11
Immaculate Conception	December 8
Christmas	December 25

Congo:

New Year	January 1
President's Day	February 5
Youth Day	February 8
Congolese Women's Day	March 8
Death of President Marien Ngouabi	March 18
Labor Day	May 1
Foundation of the National People's Army	June 22
Upswing of the Revolution	July 31
"Three Glorious Days" (Anniv. of the Revolution of August 1963)	August 13–15

Independence Day	August 15
Children's Day	December 25
Foundation of the Congolese Labor Party	December 31

Côte d'Ivoire (*see* Ivory Coast)

Cuba:

National Liberation Day	January 1
International Workers Day	May 1
National Rebellion Day	July 26
Beginning of War of Independence	October 10

Cyprus:

New Year	January 1
Epiphany	January 6
Green Monday	February 18
Greek Independence Day	March 25
Good Friday	Friday before Easter: March–April
Easter Monday	Monday after Easter
Greek Cypriot Independence Day	April 1
May Day	May 1
Kataklysmos	May 27
Assumption Day	August 15
Independence Day	October 1
Greek National Day	October 28
Christmas	December 25–26

Czechoslovakia (former):

New Year	January 1
Easter Monday	Monday after Easter: March–April
May Day	May 1
Liberation Day	May 9
Independence Day	October 28
Christmas	December 25–26

Denmark:

New Year	January 1
Maundy Thursday	Thursday before Easter
Good Friday	Friday before Easter
Easter Day	March–April
Easter Monday	Monday after Easter
Great Prayer Day	April 26
Ascension Day	April–June
Whitsunday	May–June
Whit Monday	Monday after Whitsunday
Constitution Day	June 5
Christmas	December 25–26

Ecuador:

New Year	January 1
Carnival	February–March
Good Friday	Friday before Easter: March–April
Labor Day	May 1
Pichincha Day	May 24
Simon Bolivar Day	July 24
Independence Day	August 10
Independence of Guayaquil Day	October 9
Columbus Day	October 12
Memorial Day	November 2
Independence of Cuenca Day	November 3
Christmas	December 25

Egypt:

Union Day	February 22
Sham-El-Nassim	April 11
Sinai Liberation Day	April 11
Labor Day	May 1
Bairam Holiday	May 6
Revolution Day	July 23
Armed Forces	October 6
National Liberation Day	October 23
Victory Day	December 23

Ethiopia:

Christmas	January 7
Epiphany	January 19
Adwa Day	March 2
Victory Day	March 6
Patriots Victory Day	April 6
Good Friday	Friday before Easter
Easter Day	April–May
Labor Day	May 1
Revolution Day	September 12

Finland:

New Year	January 1
Epiphany	January 19
Good Friday	Friday before Easter
Easter Day	March–April
Easter Monday	Monday after Easter
May Day Eve	April 30
Labor Day	May 1
Ascension Day	April–June
Whitsunday	May–June
Midsummer Eve	June 21
Midsummer Day	June 22

All Saints Day	November 1
Independence Day	December 6
Christmas	December 24–26

France:
New Year	January 1
Easter Day	March–April
Easter Monday	Monday after Easter
Labor Day	May 1
VE Day	May 8
Ascension Day	April–June
Whitsunday	May–June
Whit Monday	Monday after Whitsunday
Bastille Day	July 14
Assumption Day	August 15
All Saints Day	November 1
Armistice Day	November 11
Christmas	December 25

French Polynesia:
New Year	January 1
Good Friday	Friday before Easter: March–April
Easter Monday	Monday after Easter
Labor Day	May 1
Ascension Day	April–June
Whit Monday	Monday after Whitsunday: May–June
Bastille Day	July 14
Assumption Day	August 15
All Saints Day	November 1
Armistice Day	November 11
Christmas	December 25

Gabon:
New Year	January 1
Renovation Day	March 12
Easter Day	March–April
Easter Monday	Monday after Easter
Labor Day	May 1
Ascension Day	April–June
Whit Monday	Monday after Whitsunday: May–June
Liberation of African Continent Day	May 25
Assumption Day	August 15
Independence Day	August 16–18
All Saints Day	November 1

Gambia:
New Year	January 1
Independence Day	February 18

Good Friday	Friday before Easter: March–April
Labor Day	May 1
Assumption Day	August 15
Christmas	December 25–26

Germany:

New Year	January 1
Epiphany	January 6
Good Friday	Friday before Easter: March–April
Easter Monday	Monday after Easter
Labor Day	May 1
Ascension Day	April–June
Whit Monday	Monday after Whitsunday: May–June
Corpus Christi	May–June
Day of Unity	June 17
Assumption Day	August 15
All Saints Day	November 1
Day of Prayer and Repentance	November 20
Christmas	December 25–26

Ghana:

New Year	January 1
Independence Day	March 6
Good Friday	Friday before Easter
Easter Sunday	March–April
Easter Monday	Monday after Easter
May Day	May 1
Revolution Day	June 4
Republic Day	July 1
Christmas	December 25–26

Gibraltar:

New Year	January 1
Commonwealth Day	March 12
Good Friday	Friday before Easter: March–April
Easter Monday	Monday after Easter
May Day	May 1
Spring Bank Holiday	May 28
Queen's Birthday	June 17
Late Summer Bank Holiday	August 27
Christmas	December 25–26

Greece:

New Year	January 1
Epiphany	January 6
Shrove Monday	February–March
Independence Day	March 25
Good Friday	Friday before Easter

Easter Sunday	April–May
Easter Monday	Monday after Easter
Labor Day	May 1
Day of the Holy Spirit	May 26
Assumption Day	August 15
National Holiday	October 28
Christmas	December 25–26

Hong Kong:

New Year	January 1
Lunar New Year	February 14-16
Good Friday	Friday before Easter
Easter Day	March–April
Easter Monday	Monday after Easter
Queen's Birthday	June 15–17
Liberation Day	August 26
Christmas	December 25–26

Hungary:

New Year	January 1
Anniversary of Hungarian Revolution	March 15
Liberation Day	April 4
Easter Monday	Monday after Easter: March–April
Labor Day	May 1
Constitution Day	August 20
Christmas	December 24–26

Iceland:

New Year	January 1
Maundy Thursday	Thursday before Easter
Good Friday	Friday before Easter
Easter Day	March–April
Easter Monday	Monday after Easter
First Day of Summer	April 25
Labor Day	May 1
Ascension Day	April–June
Whitsunday	May–June
Whit Monday	Monday after Whitsunday
Republic Day	June 17
Shop & Office Workers Holiday	August 5
Christmas	December 25–26

India:

New Year	January 1
Republic Day	January 26
Good Friday	Friday before Easter: March–April
Labor Day	May 1
Independence Day	August 15

Mahatma Gandhi's Birthday	October 2
Christmas	December 25

Indonesia:

New Year	January 1
Prophet's Birthday	February 12
Nyepi Day	March 17
Good Friday	Friday before Easter: March–April
Ascension Day	April–June
Waisak Day	May 28
Independence Day	August 17
Christmas	December 25

Iran:

Revolution Day	mid-February
Iranian New Year	March

Iraq:

New Year	January 1
Army Day	January 6
Anniversary of the 1963 Revolution	February 8
First Day of Spring Festival	March 21
Day of FAO	April 17
Labor Day	May 1
National Day	July 14–17
Revolution Day	July 17
Day of Peace	August 8

Ireland, Republic of:

New Year	January 1
St. Patrick's Day	March 17
Easter Monday	Monday after Easter: March–April
June Holiday	June 3
August Holiday	August 5
October Holiday	October 28
Christmas	December 25–26

Israel:

Purim	February–March
Passover	March–April
Independence Day	April 30
Shavout	May–June
Jewish New Year	September–October
Yom Kippur	September–October
Sukkot	September–October
Simchat Torah	September–October
Hanukkah	November–December

Italy:
New Year	January 1
Epiphany	January 6
Easter Monday	Monday after Easter: March–April
Liberation Day	April 25
Labor Day	May 1
Assumption Day	August 15
All Saints Day	November 1
Immaculate Conception	December 8
Christmas	December 25–26

Ivory Coast (Côte d'Ivoire):
New Year	January 1
Good Friday	Friday before Easter: March–April
Easter Monday	Monday after Easter
Labor Day	May 1
Ascension Day	April–June
Whit Monday	Monday after Whitsunday: May–June
Assumption Day	August 15
All Saints Day	November 1
Peace Day	November 15
National Day	December 7
Christmas	December 25

Jamaica:
New Year	January 1
Ash Wednesday	February–March
Good Friday	Friday before Easter: March–April
Easter Monday	Monday after Easter
Labor Day	May 23
Independence Day	August 5
National Heroes Day	October 21
Christmas	December 25–26

Japan:
New Year	January 1
Traditional Bank Holiday	January 2–3
Adults' Day	January 15
Foundation Day	February 11
Vernal Equinox Day	March 21
Greenery Day	April 29
Constitution Day	May 3
National Holiday	May 4
Children's Day	May 5
Respect for Aged Day	September 15
Autumnal Equinox Day	September 24
Health and Sports Day	October 10
Culture Day	November 3

Labor Thanksgiving Day	November 23
Emperor's Birthday	December 23

Jordan:

New Year	January 1
Labor Day	May 1
Independence Day	May 25
Army Day	June 10
Accession of King Hussein	August 11
King Hussein's Birthday	November 14
Christmas	December 25

Kenya:

New Year	January 1
Good Friday	Friday before Easter: March–April
Easter Monday	Monday after Easter
Labor Day	May 1
Madaraka Day	June 1
Moi Day	October 10
Kenyatta Day	October 20
Independence Day	December 12
Christmas	December 25–26

Korea, South:

New Year	January 1–3
Folklore Day	February 15
Independence Movement Day	March 1
Arbor Day	April 5
Children's Day	May 5
Buddha's Day	May 21
Memorial Day	June 6
Constitution Day	July 17
Liberation Day	August 15
Thanksgiving Day	September 22
Armed Forces Day	October 1
National Foundation Day	October 3
Korean Alphabet Day	October 9
Christmas	December 25

Kuwait:

New Year	January 1
National Day	February 25

Lebanon:

New Year	January 1
Feast of St. Maron	February 9
Good Friday (Western)	Friday before Easter
Easter Day (Western)	March–April

Good Friday (Eastern)	Friday before Easter
Easter Day (Eastern)	April–May
Labor Day	May 1
Assumption Day	August 15
All Saints Day	November 1
National Day	November 22
Christmas	December 25

Lesotho:

New Year	January 1
Army Day	January 21
Moshoeshoe's Day	March 12
National Tree Planting Day	March 21
Good Friday	Friday before Easter: March–April
Easter Monday	Monday after Easter
King's Birthday	May 2
Ascension Day	April–June
Family Day	July 1
Independence Day	October 4
National Sports Day	October 7
Christmas	December 25–26

Liberia:

New Year	January 1
Armed Forces Day	February 11
Decoration Day	March 8
J.J. Robert's Birthday	March 15
National Redemption Day	April 12
Fast and Prayer Day	April 14
President Samuel K. Doe's Birthday	May 6
National Unification Day	May 14
African Liberation Day	May 25
Independence Day	July 26
National Flag Day	August 24
National Youth Day	October 29
Thanksgiving Day	November 2
W.V.S. Tubman's Birthday	November 29
Christmas	December 25

Libya:

British Evacuation Day	March 2; 8; 28
National Day	June 11
Italian Evacuation Day	July 23; September 1; October 7

Luxembourg:

New Year	January 1
Carnival Monday	February–March
Easter Monday	Monday after Easter: March–April

Labor Day	May 1
Ascension Day	April–June
Whitsunday	May–June
Whit Monday	Monday after Whitsunday
National Day	June 24
Assumption Day	August 15
All Saints Day	November 1
All Souls Day	November 2
Christmas	December 25–26

Malawi:

New Year	January 1
Martyrs Day	March 3
Good Friday	Friday before Easter: March–April
Easter Monday	Monday after Easter
Kamuzu Day	May 14
Republic Day	July 6
Mother's Day	October 17
National Tree Planting Day	December 21
Christmas	December 25–26

Malaysia:

Chinese New Year	February 15–16
Labor Day	May 1
National Day	August 31
Christmas	December 25

Malta:

New Year	January 1
Feast of St. Paul's Shipwreck	February 10
Feast of St. Joseph	March 19
Good Friday	Friday before Easter: March–April
Freedom Day	March 31
Labor Day	May 1
Commemoration of 7 June 1919	June 7
Feast of St. Peter and St. Paul	June 29
Assumption Day	August 15
Feast of Our Lady of Victories	September 8
Independence Day	September 21
Immaculate Conception	December 8
Republic Day	December 13
Christmas	December 25

Mauritius:

New Year	January 1–2
Thaipoosam Cavadee	February
Chinese Spring Festival	February 15
Maha Shivaratree	February

Independence Day	March 12
Ougadi	April 6
Labor Day	May 1
Ganesh Chaturthi	September 5
Divali	October
All Saints Day	November 1
Christmas	December 25

Mexico:

New Year	January 1
Epiphany	January 6
Constitution Day	February 5
Benito Juarez's Birthday	March 21
Maundy Thursday	Thursday before Easter
Good Friday	Friday before Easter
Easter Day	March–April
Labor Day	May 1
Anniversary of the Battle of Puebla	May 5
Independence Day	September 15–16
Columbus Day	October 12
Anniversary of the Revolution	November 20
Christmas	December 25

Morocco:

New Year	January 1
National Day	March 3
Labor Day	May 1
Green March Day	November 6
Independence Day	November 18

Mozambique:

New Year	January 1
Heroes Day	February 3
Women's Day	April 7
Labor Day	May 1
National Day	June 25
Victory Day	September 7
Armed Forces Day	September 25
Family Day	December 25

Myanmar (*see* Burma)

Namibia:

New Year	January 1
Good Friday	Friday before Easter: March–April
Workers Day	May 1
Ascension Day	April–June
Day of Goodwill	October 1

Human Rights Day	December 10
Christmas	December 25–26

Netherlands:
New Year	January 1
Good Friday	Friday before Easter: March–April
Easter Monday	Monday after Easter
Queen's Birthday	April 30
Liberation Day	May 5
Ascension Day	April–June
Whit Monday	Monday after Whitsunday: May–June
Christmas	December 25–26

New Zealand:
New Year	January 1–2
New Zealand Day	February 6
Good Friday	Friday before Easter: March–April
Easter Monday	Monday after Easter
Anzac Day	April 25
Queen's Birthday	June 3
Labor Day	October 28
Christmas	December 25–26

Nigeria:
New Year	January 1
Good Friday	Friday before Easter: March–April
Easter Monday	Monday after Easter
Labor Day	May 1
National Day	October 1
Christmas	December 25–26

Norway:
New Year	January 1
Maundy Thursday	Thursday before Easter: March–April
Good Friday	Friday before Easter
Easter Monday	Monday after Easter
Labor Day	May 1
Ascension Day	April–June
Constitution Day	May 17
Whit Monday	Monday after Whitsunday: May–June
Christmas	December 25–26

Oman:
Eid-Al-Fitr	1st Shawwal
Eid-Al-Adha	10th Dhu-l-Hijjah

Pakistan:
Pakistan Day	March 23

May Day	May 1
Independence Day	August 14
Defence Day	September 6
Anniversary of the death of Quaid-e-Azam	September 11
Iqbal Day	November 9
Birthday of Quaid-e-Azam	December 25

Panama:

New Year	January 1
Martyr Day	January 9
Carnival	February–March
Good Friday	Friday before Easter: March–April
Independence Day	November 3
Cry of Independence	November 10
Separation from Spain	November 28
Mother's Day	December 8
Christmas	December 25

Paraguay:

New Year	January 1
San Blas	February 3
Heroes' Day	March 1
Maundy Thursday	Thursday before Easter: March–April
Good Friday	Friday before Easter
Labor Day	May 1
Independence Day	May 15
Chaco Peace	June 12
Foundation of Asunción	August 15
Immaculate Conception	December 8
Christmas	December 25

Peru:

New Year	January 1
Good Friday	Friday before Easter: March–April
Labor Day	May 1
Independence Day	June 28–29
St. Peter & St. Paul	June 29
All Saints Day	November 1
Immaculate Conception	December 8
Christmas	December 25

Philippines:

New Year	January 1
People Power Day	February 25
Holy Thursday	Thursday before Easter: March–April
Good Friday	Friday before Easter
Labor Day	May 1

Day of Valor	May 6
Independence Day	June 12
All Saints Day	November 1
National Heroes Day	November 30
Christmas	December 25
Rizal Day	December 30

Poland:

New Year	January 1
Easter Monday	Monday after Easter: March–April
Labor Day	May 1
Constitution Day	May 3
Corpus Christi	May–June
Assumption Day	August 15
All Saints Day	November 1
National Day	November 29
Christmas	December 25–26

Portugal:

New Year	January 1
Shrove Tuesday	February–March
Good Friday	Friday before Easter
Easter Day	March–April
Liberation Day	April 25
Labor Day	May 1
Corpus Christi	May–June
National Day	June 10
Assumption Day	August 15
Republic Day	October 5
All Saints Day	November 1
Independence Day	December 1
Immaculate Conception	December 8
Christmas	December 25–26

Qatar:

Independence Day	September 3

Romania:

New Year	January 1–2
Workers Holiday	May 1–2
National Day	August 23–24

Saudi Arabia:

Eid-Al-Fitr	1st Shawwal
Eid-Al-Adha	10th Dhu-l-Hijjah

Senegal:

New Year	January 1

Confederal Agreement Day	February 1
Good Friday	Friday before Easter: March–April
Easter Monday	Monday after Easter
Labor Day	May 1
Ascension Day	April–June
Whit Sunday	May–June
Assumption Day	August 15
All Saints Day	November 1
Christmas	December 25–26

Seychelles:

New Year	January 1–2
Good Friday	Friday before Easter
Easter Sunday	March–April
Labor Day	May 1
Corpus Christi	May–June
Liberation Day	June 5
Independence Day	June 29
Assumption Day	August 15
All Saints Day	November 1
Immaculate Conception	December 8
Christmas	December 25

Singapore:

New Year	January 1
Chinese New Year	February 15–16
Good Friday	Friday before Easter: March–April
Hari Raya Puasa	April 16
Labor Day	May 1
Vesak Day	April–May
Hari Raya Haji	June 23
National Day	August 9
Deepavali	November
Christmas	December 25

South Africa:

New Year	January 1
Good Friday	Friday before Easter: March–April
Family Day	April 1
Founders Day	April 6
Workers Day	May 6
Ascension Day	April–June
Republic Day	May 31
Kruger Day	October 10
Day of the Vow	December 16
Christmas	December 25
Day of Goodwill	December 26

Spain:

New Year	January 1
Epiphany	January 6
St. Joseph's Day	March 19
Good Friday	Friday before Easter: March–April
Easter Monday (Barcelona and Mallorca only)	Monday after Easter
Labor Day	May 1
Corpus Christi	May–June
St. James's Day	July 25
Assumption Day	August 15
All Saints Day	November 1
Immaculate Conception	December 8
Christmas	December 25

Sri Lanka:

Tamil Thai Pongal Day	January 14
National Day	February 4
Good Friday	Friday before Easter: March–April
May Day	May 1
Special Bank Holiday	May 20–22; June 30
Christmas	October 14; December 12; December 25

Sudan:

Independence Day–New Year	January 1
National Unity Day	March 3
Christmas	April 4–6; December 25–26

Swaziland:

New Year	January 1
Good Friday	Friday before Easter: March–April
Easter Monday	Monday after Easter
King's Birthday	April 19
National Flag Day	April 25
Ascension Day	April–June
Public Holiday	July 22
Independence Day	September 6
Christmas	December 25–26

Sweden:

New Year	January 1
Epiphany	January 6
Good Friday	Friday before Easter
Easter Sunday	March–April
Easter Monday	Monday after Easter
Labor Day	May 1
Ascension Day	April–June
Whitsunday	May–June

Whit Monday	Monday after Whitsunday
Midsummer Day	June 21
All Saints Day	November 2
Christmas	December 24–26
New Years Eve	December 31

Switzerland:

New Year	January 1
Good Friday	Friday before Easter: March–April
Easter Monday	Monday after Easter
Ascension Day	April–June
Whit Monday	Monday after Whitsunday: May–June
Swiss National Day	August 1
Christmas	December 25–26

Syria:

New Year	January 1
Revolution Day	March 8
National Day	April 17
Labor Day	May 1
Martyrs Day	May 6
Christmas	December 25

Taiwan:

January 1	Founding Day of Republic of China
Youth Day	March 29
Tomb Sweeping Day	April 5
Dragon Boat Festival	May 28
Confucius' Birthday	September 28
National Day	October 10
Taiwan Retrocession Day	October 25
President Chiang Kai-shek's Birthday	October 31
Dr. Sun Yat-sen's Birthday	November 12
Constitution Day	December 25

Tanzania:

New Year	January 1
Zanzibar Revolution Day	January 12
CCM Day	February 5
Good Friday	Friday before Easter: March–April
Easter Monday	Monday after Easter
Union Day	April 26
International Workers Day	May 1
Peasants' Day	July 7
Independence Day	December 9
Christmas	December 25

Thailand:
New Year　　　　　　　　　　　January 1
Magha Puja　　　　　　　　　　January–February
Chakri Day　　　　　　　　　　April 6
Songkran Day　　　　　　　　　April 13
Visakha Puja　　　　　　　　　April–May
Coronation Day　　　　　　　　May 5
Asalha Puja　　　　　　　　　　June 26
Khal Phansa　　　　　　　　　　June 27
Queen's Birthday　　　　　　　August 12
Chulalongkorn Day　　　　　　October 23
King's Birthday　　　　　　　　December 5
Constitution Day　　　　　　　December 10
New Years Eve　　　　　　　　December 31

Trinidad and Tobago:
New Year　　　　　　　　　　　January 1
Good Friday　　　　　　　　　　Friday before Easter: March–April
Easter Monday　　　　　　　　Monday after Easter
Whit Monday　　　　　　　　　Monday after Whitsunday: May–June
Corpus Christi　　　　　　　　May–June
Labor Day　　　　　　　　　　June 19
Emancipation Day　　　　　　　August 1
Independence Day　　　　　　　August 31
Republic Day　　　　　　　　　September 24
Christmas　　　　　　　　　　　December 25–26

Tunisia:
New Year　　　　　　　　　　　January 1
Independence Day　　　　　　　March 20
Youth Day　　　　　　　　　　March 21
Martyr's Day　　　　　　　　　April 9
Labor Day　　　　　　　　　　May 1
Republic Day　　　　　　　　　July 25
Women's Day　　　　　　　　　August 13

Turkey:
New Year　　　　　　　　　　　January 1
National Sovereignty and Children's
　　Day　　　　　　　　　　　　April 23
Commemoration of Atatürk and Youth
　　Day　　　　　　　　　　　　May 19
Victory Day　　　　　　　　　　August 30
National Day　　　　　　　　　October 29

Uganda:
New Year　　　　　　　　　　　January 1
Liberation Day　　　　　　　　January 26

Good Friday	Friday before Easter: March–April
Easter Monday	Monday after Easter
Labor Day	May 1
Independence Day	October 9
Christmas	December 25–26

Union of Soviet Socialist Republics (U.S.S.R.) (former):

New Year	January 1
International Women's Day	March 8
Labor Day	May 1
Victory Day	May 9
Constitution Day	October 7
October Revolution	November 7

United Arab Emirates:

New Year	January 1
National Day	December 2
Christmas	December 25

United Kingdom:

New Year	January 1
Bank Holiday (Scotland)	January 2
St. Patrick's Day (N. Ireland)	March 17
Good Friday	Friday before Easter: March–April
Easter Monday	Monday following Easter
May Day Holiday	May 6
Spring Bank Holiday	May 27
Holiday (N. Ireland)	July 12
Bank Holiday (Scotland)	August 5
Late Summer Holiday (not Scotland)	August 26
Christmas	December 25–26

United States of America:

New Year	January 1
Martin Luther King's Birthday	January, third Monday
Washington's Birthday	February, third Monday
Memorial Day	May, last Monday
Independence Day	July 4
Labor Day	September, first Monday
Columbus Day	October, second Monday
Veterans Day	November 11
Thanksgiving Day	November, fourth Thursday
Christmas	December 25

Uruguay:

New Year	January 1
Epiphany	January 6

Holy Week	week before Easter: March–April
Labor Day	May 1
Battle of Las Piedras	May 18
General Artigas Birthday	June 19
Constitution Day	July 18
Independence Day	August 25
Columbus Day	October 12
All Souls Day	November 2
Christmas	December 25

Venezuela:

New Year	January 1
Epiphany	January 6
Holy Thursday	Thursday before Easter: March–April
Good Friday	Friday before Easter
Independence Day	April 19
Labor Day	May 1
Ascension Day	April–June
Corpus Christi	May–June
Carabobo Day	June 24
St. Peter and St. Paul	June 29
Independence Day	July 5
Simon Bolivar's Birthday	July 24
Assumption Day	August 15
Columbus Day	October 12
All Saints Day	November 1
Immaculate Conception	December 8
Christmas	December 25

Yemen Republic:

Labor Day	May 1
National Day	September 26

Yugoslavia (former):

New Year	January 1–2
Labor Day	May 1–2
Combatant's Day	July 4
Republic Day	November 29–30

Zaire:

New Year	January 1
Martyrs of Independence Day	January 4
Labor Day	May 1
Party Day	May 20
Fishermen's Day	June 24
Independence Day	June 30
Parents' Day	August 1
Youth Day	October 14

Three-Z Day	October 27
Army Day	November 17
Anniversary of New Regime	November 24
Christmas	December 25

Zambia:

New Year	January 1
Youth Day	March 12
Good Friday	Friday before Easter: March–April
Holy Saturday	Saturday before Easter
Labor Day	May 1
Africa Freedom Day	May 25
Heroes' Day	July 1
Unity Day	July 2
Farmer's Day	August 5
Independence Day	October 24
Christmas	December 25

Zimbabwe:

New Year	January 1
Good Friday	Friday before Easter: March–April
Easter Saturday	Saturday before Easter
Easter Monday	Monday after Easter
Independence Day	April 18
Workers' Day	May 1
Africa Day	May 25
Heroes' Day	August 11
Armed Forces Day	August 12
Christmas	December 24–25

Words Relating to Periods of Time

A descriptive listing of words related to periods of time is included below. Many of the words are adjectives in form, but also are commonly used as nouns, e.g., *the bicentennial of the U.S. Constitution.* All terms are defined in two separate lists: first by number referred to, then alphabetically.

Listed by number:

diurnal, per diem, quotidian   daily; of a day.

nocturnal   nightly; of a night.

nichthemeron   a period of 24 hours.

semidiurnal   twice a day.

hebdomadal   weekly; a period of 7 days.

semiweekly   twice a week.

biweekly   **1.** every 2 weeks. **2.** twice a week.

fortnightly   once every 2 weeks.

triweekly   **1.** every 3 weeks. **2.** 3 times a week.

novendial   a period of 9 days.

monthly, tricenary   **1.** relating to a period of one month. **2.** 30 days.

bimonthly   **1.** every 2 months. **2.** twice a month.

semimonthly   twice a month.

bimester   relating to a period of 2 months.

trimester   relating to a period of 3 months.

trimonthly   **1.** every 3 months. **2.** 3 times a month.

biquarterly   twice every 3 months.

biannual   twice a year (not necessarily at equally spaced intervals).

triannual   3 times a year.

semiannual, semiyearly, semestral   every half year or six-month period.

annual, solennial, quotennial, per annum   yearly; once a year.

biennial, biennium, biyearly, diennial   relating to a period of 2 years.

triennial, triennium   relating to a period of 3 years.

quadrennial, quadrennium, quadriennial   relating to a period of 4 years.

quinquennial, quintennial, quinquennium   relating to a period of 5 years.

sexennial, sextennial   relating to a period of 6 years.

septennial, septenary, septennium   relating to a period of 7 years.

octennial   relating to a period of 8 years.

novennial   relating to a period of 9 years.

decennial, decennium, decennary   relating to a period of 10 years.

undecennial   relating to a period of 11 years.

duodecennial   relating to a period of 12 years.

quindecennial   relating to a period of 15 years.

septendecennial   relating to a period of 17 years.

vicennial, vigintennial   relating to a period of 20 years.

tricennial, trigintennial   relating to a period of 30 years.

quinquagenary, semicentennial, semicentenary   relating to a period of 50 years.

centennial, centenary, centennium, centurial   relating to a period of 100 years.

quasquicentennial   relating to a period of 125 years.
sesquicentennial, sesquicentenary   relating to a period of 150 years.
bicentennial, bicentenary, bicentennium   relating to a period of 200 years.
tricentennial, tercentennial, tercentenary   relating to a period of 300 years.
quadricentennial, quatercentennial   relating to a period of 400 years.
quincentennial, quincentenary   relating to a period of 500 years.
sexcentenary   relating to a period of 600 years.
septicentennial   relating to a period of 700 years.
antemillenial, premillenial   relating to the period before the millenium.
millennial, millennium   relating to a period of 1,000 years; 10 centuries.
postmillenial   relating to the period after the millenium.
sesquimillennium   relating to a period of 1,500 years; 15 centuries.
bimillennial, bimillenary, bimillennium   relating to a period of 2,000 years; 20 centuries.
perennial   occurring year after year.
plurennial   lasting for many years.
aeonial   everlasting.

Listed alphabetically:
aeonial   everlasting.
annual   yearly; once a year.
antemillenial   relating to the period before the millenium.
biannual   twice a year (not necessarily at equally spaced intervals).
bicentenary, bicentennial, bicentennium   relating to a period of 200 years.
biennial, biennium   relating to a period of 2 years.
bimester   relating to a period of 2 months.
bimillenary, bimillennial, bimillennium   relating to a period of 2,000 years; 20 centuries.
bimonthly   **1.** every 2 months. **2.** twice a month.
biquarterly   twice every 3 months.
biweekly   **1.** every 2 weeks. **2.** twice a week.
biyearly   relating to a period of 2 years.
centenary, centennial, centennium, centurial   relating to a period of 100 years.
decennary, decennial, decennium   relating to a period of 10 years.
diennial   relating to a period of 2 years.
diurnal   daily; of a day.
duodecennial   relating to a period of 12 years.
fortnightly   once every 2 weeks.
hebdomadal   weekly; a period of 7 days.
millennial, millennium   relating to a period of 1,000 years; 10 centuries.
monthly   **1.** relating to a period of one month. **2.** 30 days.
nichthemeron   a period of 24 hours.
nocturnal   nightly; of a night.
novendial   a period of 9 days.
novennial   relating to a period of 9 years.
octennial   relating to a period of 8 years.
per annum   yearly; once a year.
per diem   daily; of a day.
perennial   occurring year after year.
plurennial   lasting for many years.

postmillenial   relating to the period after the millenium.

premillenial   relating to the period before the millenium.

quadrennial, quadrennium, quadriennial   relating to a period of 4 years.

quadricentennial   relating to a period of 400 years.

quasquicentennial   relating to a period of 125 years.

quatercentennial   relating to a period of 400 years.

quincentenary, quincentennial   relating to a period of 500 years.

quindecennial   relating to a period of 15 years.

quinquagenary   relating to a period of 50 years.

quinquennial, quinquennium, quintennial   relating to a period of 5 years.

quotennial   yearly; once a year.

quotidian   daily; of a day.

semestral, semiannual   every half year or six-month period.

semicentenary, semicentennial   relating to a period of 50 years.

semidiurnal   twice a day.

semimonthly   twice a month.

semiweekly   twice a week.

semiyearly   every half year or six-month period.

septendecennial   relating to a period of 17 years.

septenary, septennial, septennium   relating to a period of 7 years.

septicentennial   relating to a period of 700 years.

sesquicentenary, sesquicentennial   relating to a period of 150 years.

sesquimillennium   relating to a period of 1,500 years; 15 centuries.

sexcentenary   relating to a period of 600 years.

sexennial, sextennial   relating to a period of 6 years.

solennial   yearly; once a year.

tercentenary; tercentennial   relating to a period of 300 years.

triannual   3 times a year.

tricenary   1. relating to a period of one month. 2. 30 days.

tricennial   relating to a period of 30 years.

tricentennial   relating to a period of 300 years.

triennial, triennium   relating to a period of 3 years.

trigintennial   relating to a period of 30 years.

trimester   relating to a period of 3 months.

trimonthly   1. every 3 months. 2. 3 times a month.

triweekly   1. every 3 weeks. 2. 3 times a week.

undecennial   relating to a period of 11 years.

vicennial, vigintennial   relating to a period of 20 years.

Calendar Systems around the World: Julian, Gregorian, Jewish, Islamic, Hindu, Buddhist, and Chinese

A calendar is a means of reckoning time through the application of divisions—days, weeks, months, and years. Some of these divisions, such as months, originate in observations of phenomena in nature. Others, such as weeks, are quite arbitrary. In primitive times, people reckoned by cycles of the moon (months), but when a more convenient, shorter period was needed days were grouped, e.g., intervals between market days probably led to the use of the seven-day week. The originally Jewish seven-day week became a standard throughout Western civilization starting from the third century B.C.

The Day

The day is a fairly natural division, despite the variation in the length of sunlight through the year. The Babylonians introduced divisions of the day into twenty-four hours, but the length of hours varied through the year. Only with the development of accurate clocks, the demand for which was a byproduct of the interest in maritime navigation that came with the Renaissance, was the day given scientific regularity.

The Month

A lunar month, the period of a complete cycle of the phases of the moon, lasts approximately 29.5 days, is easy for all to recognize, short enough to be counted without using large numbers, matches closely with the female menstrual cycle and, given its relation to the tidal cycle, with the duration of cyclic behavior in some marine animals. Its simplicity and minimal ease of observation (if one discounts cloudy skies) led to its great significance, and it was widely used as the basis for calendars in many cultures. The length of each month varied according to the culture, e.g., the Babylonians alternated between twenty-nine- and thirty-day months, the Egyptians fixed them at thirty days, etc.

The Seasons

But the problem inherent in the use of a lunar calendar is that the cycles of the sun, not the moon, determine the seasons, the predictability of which is essential to the success of agriculture. The seasons could be determined by solar observation, either by measuring the cycle of the midday shadow cast by a stick placed vertically in the ground, or by sophisticated astronomical calculations. Either system resulted in a solar year of approximately 365 days, incompatible with the twelve 29.5-day lunar months that resulted in a 354-day year.

Civilizations attempted to reconcile lunar months with the solar year in varied ways. The most influential ancient effort was that of the Egyptian astronomers, working from precise mathematical observations and borrowing from Babylonian astronomy, who drew up the Roman calendar that Julius Caesar introduced.

Julian Calendar

Julius Caesar ordered the change of the reformed Roman lunar calendar to a solar-based one in 46 B.C. The intercalation of ninety days corrected a discrepancy that had been growing between the seasons and the months in which they had traditionally fallen. Prior to this intercalation, the Roman civic year had come to be about three months "ahead" of the seasons, so spring began in June. The year 46 B.C. was assigned 445 days to make the adjustment; it was called *ultimus annus confusionis*, 'the last year of the muddled reckoning.' The new calendar, based on the Egyptian solar calendar, provided for a year of 365 days with an additional day in February every fourth year. The addition of this leap year and day gives the Julian year an average length of 365.25 days—very close to the actual solar cycle. The Julian calendar (O.S., or Old Style) remained in civic use in the West for more than 1,600 years, is still the basis of the "Old Calendarist" Orthodox Christian liturgical calendar, and is used by all Orthodox Christian churches to determine the date of Easter.

Gregorian Calendar

By the late sixteenth century, the difference between the Julian calendar and the seasons had grown to ten days because the Julian year, averaging 365.25 days, was slightly longer than the actual length of a solar year, which, by modern calculation, is known to be 365.242199 days long. Fixed holy days began to occur in the "wrong" season, both for the church and for farmers, who used certain holy days to determine planting and harvesting. Pope Gregory XIII ordered the reform that deleted ten days from the year 1582; in that year, October 15 was the day after October 5. This change, coupled with the elimination of leap days in "century" years unless evenly divisible by 400 (e.g., 1600, 2000), corrected the calendar so that today only occasional "leap seconds" are needed to keep months and seasons synchronized. At first adopted only in Roman Catholic countries, the Gregorian (N.S., or New Style) calendar gradually came to be accepted throughout the West, and today has become the calendar used by most of the world, at least for business and government.

Jewish Calendar

In 358, Hillel II introduced a permanent calendar based on mathematical and astronomical calculations, eliminating the need for eyewitness sightings of the new moon with which the new month begins. Due to doubts as to when the new moon appeared, Biblical law stated that those living outside of Israel would observe two days rather than one for each festival, except for Yom Kippur, the Day of Atonement. The Talmud required that this custom continue even after the calendar was formulated. The Jewish era begins with the date of Creation, traditionally set in 3761 B.C.

Only slight modifications were made to Hillel's calendar, and it has remained unchanged since the tenth century. A day is reckoned from sundown to sundown, a week contains seven days, a month is either twenty-nine or thirty days long, and a year has twelve lunar months plus about eleven days, or 353, 354, or 355 days. To reconcile the calendar with the annual solar cycle, a thirteenth month of thirty days is intercalated in the third, sixth, eighth, eleventh, fourteenth, seventeenth, and nineteenth years of a nineteen-year cycle; a leap year may contain from 383 to 385 days. The civil calendar begins with the month of Tishri, the first day of which is Rosh Hashanah, the New Year. The cycle of the religious calendar begins on Nisan 15, Passover (Pesach).

The names of the months of the Jewish calendar were borrowed from the Babylonians. The pre-exilic books of the Bible usually refer to the months according to their numerical order, beginning with Tishri, but there are four months mentioned with different names: Nisan/Abib, Iyyar/Ziv, Tishri/Ethanim, and Heshvan/Bul:

Nisan: mid-March to mid-April
Iyyar: mid-April to mid-May
Sivan: mid-May to mid-June
Tammuz: mid-June to mid-July
Av: mid-July to mid-August
Elul: mid-August to mid-September
Tishri: mid-September to mid-October
Heshvan: mid-October to mid-November
Kislev: mid-November to mid-December
Tevet: mid-December to mid-January
Shevat: mid-January to mid-February
Adar: mid-February to mid-March

The intercalary month of Adar II is inserted before Adar as needed.

Islamic Calendar

The Islamic calendar, called *hijri* or Hegirian, is still strictly lunar-based. Moreover, the *actual* beginning of a month depends on the sighting of the new moon. Traditionally, if the sky is overcast and the new moon is not visible, the previous month runs another thirty days before the new month begins. However, the *practical* beginning of a month is according to astronomical calculations of lunar cycles. The Islamic era begins July 16, 622, the date of the hegira or flight into exile of the Prophet Muhammad from Mecca to Medina.

There are twelve Islamic lunar months, some of twenty-nine, others of thirty days; these yield 354 days in the Islamic year. The fixed holidays set in the Islamic calendar thus move "backward" about ten days each year in relation to the Gregorian calendar. In roughly thirty-six years, Ramadan, the Islamic holy month of fasting, moves back through the entire solar year. The Islamic day runs from sundown to sundown.

Other calendars were developed in Islamic countries for the sake of agriculture, which depends on a solar calendar. The Coptic calendar, a variation of the Julian, was used until recently, but is now limited primarily to use in Egypt and the Sudan, countries with large Coptic populations. The Turkish fiscal calendar, also Julian-based, was used in the Ottoman Empire. Nowadays, the Gregorian calendar is followed nearly everywhere for civic purposes, and the Islamic calendar determines only the days of religious observance. Saudi Arabia is one exception, and, at least officially, uses the Islamic calendar as the calendar of reference.

The names of the Islamic months are an ancient reflection of the seasons of the solar year:

Muharram: the sacred month
Safar: the month which is void

Rabi al-Awwal: the first spring
Rabi ath-Thani: the second spring
Jumada-l-Ula: the first month of dryness
Jumada-th-Thaniyyah: the second month of dryness
Rajab: the revered month
Shaban: the month of division
Ramadan: the month of great heat
Shawwal: the month of hunting
Dhu l-Qadah: the month of rest
Dhu'l-Hijjah: the month of pilgrimage

Hindu Calendar

Although each geographical region of India has had its own Hindu calendar, all are based on the Kali Yuga, the earliest time measurement system in India, dating from around 3000 B.C. Of the multitudinous regional Hindu calendars, used only for religious holidays, the majority divide an approximate solar year of 360 days into twelve months. Each day is 1/30th of a month, with the intercalation of a leap month every sixty months. Time measurements based on observations of the constellations are used along with the calendar. Each month is divided into two fortnights: *krsna* (waning or dark half) and *sukla* (waxing or bright half). In southern India, the month begins with the new moon. In other parts of the country, the full moon is considered to be the beginning of the month. (The Hindu Calendar Index is arranged so that the new moon begins each month.) Many references to the Hindu calendar (depending on the source) are given as follows: month, fortnight (either S = waxing or K = waning), and number of the day in that fortnight, e.g., Rama Navami: Chaitra S. 9.

The names of the Hindu months (with variant spellings) are given below, with the Burmese name for the month in brackets:

Chaitra or Caitra [Tagu]: March-April
Vaisakha [Kasone]: April-May
Jyeshta or Jyaistha [Nayhone]: May-June
Ashadha or Asadha [Waso]: June-July
Sravana [Wagaung]: July-August
Bhadrapada [Tawthalin]: August-September
Asvina [Thadingyut]: September-October
Karthika or Karttika [Tazaungmone]: October-November
Margashirsha or Margasirsa [Nadaw]: November-December
Pausha or Pausa [Pyatho]: December-January
Magha [Tabodwei]: January-February
Phalguna [Tabaung]: February-March

Buddhist Calendar

The Buddhist calendar originated in India and varies among different geographic locations, as does the Hindu calendar, with which it shares many common elements. The method for determining the date of the new year is not uniform among Buddhist sects. Theravada Buddhists (those primarily in Sri Lanka, Laos, Burma/Myanmar, Thailand, and Cambodia), using a Hindu calendar as their basis, calculate the months by the moon and the new year by the sun's position in relation to the twelve segments of the heavens, each named for a sign of the zodiac. The solar new year begins when the sun enters Aries, usually between April 13th and 18th. The lunar months alternate between twenty-nine and thirty days in length. The first lunar month is usually sometime in December, except for the Burmese Buddhist calendar, which begins in April (see Hindu Calendar for Burmese names). Periodically, the seventh month has an intercalary day, and an intercalary month is added every few years. Cambodia, Laos, and Thailand refer to the months by number. Tibetan Buddhists, whose calendar has been heavily influenced by the Chinese calendar, begin their new year at the full moon nearest to the midpoint of Aquarius. Mahayana Buddhists (those primarily in Tibet, Mongolia, China, Korea, and Japan) base their holidays on Buddhist, Chinese, or Gregorian calendars.

Chinese Calendar

The Chinese calendar, widely used in Asian countries, is based on the oldest system of time measurement still in use, with its epoch believed to be 2953 B.C. Part of the reason that the Chinese calendar has survived intact for so long is that, until the middle of the twentieth century, the document was considered sacred. Any changes to the calendar were tightly controlled by imperial authorities, and the penalty for illegally tampering with the time-keeping system was death. Until the rise of Communism in China during the twentieth century, the official calendar was presented to the emperor, governors, and other dignitaries in an annual ceremony. Since 1911, the Gregorian calendar has been in use for civic purposes.

The Chinese New Year takes place on the new moon nearest to the point which is defined in the West as the fifteenth degree of the zodiacal sign of Aquarius. Each of twelve months in the Chinese year is twenty-nine or thirty days long and is divided into two parts, each of which is two weeks long. The Chinese calendar, like all lunisolar systems, requires periodic adjustment to keep the lunar and solar cycles integrated, therefore an intercalary month is added when necessary.

The names of each of the twenty-four two-week periods sometimes correspond to festivals which occur during the period. Beginning with the New Year, which takes place in late January or early February, these periods are known by the following names: Spring Begins (New Year), the Rain Water, the Excited Insects, the Vernal Equinox, the Clear and Bright, the Grain Rains, the Summer Begins, the Grain Fills, the Grain in Ear, the Summer Solstice, the Slight Heat, the Great Heat, the Autumn Begins, the Limit of Heat, the White Dew, the Autumnal Equinox, the Cold Dew, the Hoar Frost Descends, the Winter Begins, the Little Snow, the Heavy Snow, the Winter Solstice, the Little Cold, and the Great Cold.

Comparative Table of Calendar Systems

The Gregorian calendar is based on the solar cycle of 365 days per year, while the Jewish, Hindu, and Burmese calendars are based on the lunar cycle of 29½ days per month. The first day of the lunar months depicted here is typically the day of the new moon. The lunar months can overlap with the Gregorian months near which they fall. This is reflected in the chart below. While the Burmese calendar is essentially identical to the Hindu, the names of the months differ and are thus represented below. An asterisk denotes the months in which the various New Years fall.

Gregorian Calendar	Jewish Calendar	Hindu, Jain, Buddhist and Sikh Calendar	Burmese Calendar
January*	Shevat	Magha	Tabodwei
February			
	Adar	Phalguna	Tabaung
March			
	Nisan	Chaitra*	Tagu*
April			
	Iyar	Vaisakha*	Kasone
May			
	Sivan	Jyeshta	Nayhone
June			
	Tammuz	Ashadha	Waso
July			
	Av	Sravana	Wagaung
August			
	Elul	Bhadrapada	Tawthalin
September			
	Tishri*	Asvina	Thadingyut
October			
	Heshvan	Karthika	Tazaungmone
November			
	Kislev	Margashirsha	Nadaw
December			
	Tevet	Pausha	Pyatho

Bibliography

Sources Indexed

AmerBkDays-1978
LC: GT4803.H36
Dewey: 394.2

Hatch, Jane M. *The American Book of Days.* 3rd ed., New York: H.W. Wilson, 1978. 1214 pp. Appendix. Index.

Contains over 700 entries pertaining to American holidays, festivals, and anniversaries organized by month. Selections reflect events in American history, including entries on each U.S. president and chief justice. There is at least one entry for every day of the year. Entries tend to be lengthy, averaging about 1,300 words. Each month begins with an essay recounting the origin of the month, ancient festivals observed, and the month's birthstone. Four essays comprise the appendix and cover ''The Calendar,'' ''The Era,'' ''The Days of the Week,'' and ''Signs of the Zodiac.''

Indexed entries dealing with observed holidays and festivals, over 250 in all, plus 18 ancient festivals gleaned from month essays.

AnnivHol-1983
LC: GT3930.G822
Dewey: 394.26

Gregory, Ruth W. *Anniversaries and Holidays.* 4th edition, American Library Association, 1983. 262 pp. Bibliography. Index.

Organized chronologically, this book offers over 2,600 short entries on religious and civic holidays and anniversaries marking notable people and events. The first and longest part of the book covers fixed days according to the Gregorian calendar. Months begin with an introductory note covering how the month was named, notable historical events or festivals occurring in the month, and flowers and birthstones associated with it. Entries are grouped together under each date by ''Holy Days and Feast Days'', ''Holidays and Civic Days'', and ''Anniversaries and Special Events Days.'' Movable days are listed in the second part and are organized by the Christian, Islamic, and Jewish calendars, followed by movable events observed according to the lunar calendar or other chronological criteria. The annotated bibliography describes 875 books related to holidays and anniversaries and is broken down by subject.

Indexed entries describing observed events, over 1,000 in all.

BkDays-1864
LC: DA110.C445
Dewey: 394

Chambers, Robert, ed. *The Book of Days: A Miscellany of Popular Antiquities in connection with the Calendar, including Anecdote, Biography, & History, Curiosities of Literature, and Oddities of Human Life and Character.* New introduction by Tristram Potter Coffin. 1862-64. Reprinted by Omnigraphics, Inc., 1990. 832 pp. in volume

I; 840 pp. in volume II. Illustrated. Index in volume II.

British tome organized chronologically and covering popular Christian festivals and saints' days; seasonal phenomena; folklore of the British Isles, especially items connected with the passing of time and seasons of the year; "Notable Events, Biographies, and Anecdotes connected with the Days of the Year"; "Articles of Popular Archaeology, of an entertaining character, tending to illustrate the progress of Civilization, Manners, Literature, and Ideas in these kingdoms"; and other miscellaneous items.

Indexed over 100 entries and descriptions of events within entries (each day of the year is considered an entry).

BkFest-1937
LC: GT3930.S75
Dewey: 394.26

Spicer, Dorothy Gladys. *Book of Festivals.* Foreword by John H. Finley. 1937. Reprinted by Omnigraphics, 1990. 429 pp. Appendix. Bibliography. Index of festivals.

The main part of the book is broken down into 35 chapters, each covering an ethnic or major religious (Hindu, Jew, and Muslim or Mohammedan) group or nationality. Groups were chosen on the basis of their representation in the United States. Geographic areas covered include Asia, Eastern and Western Europe, India, the Middle East, and the United States. Within each chapter, holidays and festivals are listed and described in chronological order. Part II of the book is devoted to discussions of the Armenian, Chinese, Gregorian, Hindu, Jewish, Julian, and Mohammedan calendars. Topics include rate of variation between the Julian and Gregorian calendars, dates of Easter computed between 1938 and 1950, and dates of major Jewish holidays computed between 1936 and 1951. The appendix is a glossary of religious and festival terms. The bibliography, with notes, organizes sources by ethnic group or nationality.

Indexed all entries, about 500 in all.

BkFestHolWrld-1970
LC: GT3932.I17
Dewey: 394.26

Ickis, Marguerite. *The Book of Festivals and Holidays the World Over.* Drawings by Richard E. Howard. New York: Dodd, Mead & Co., 1970. 164 pp. Index.

A selection of "holidays and festivals that are current and give promise of continuing indefinately," twelve chapters in chronological order cover customs and legends associated with New Year's, Epiphany, Lent, Holy Week, Easter, Advent, and Christmas, as well as over eighty winter, spring, summer, and fall festivals in nearly fifty countries.

Indexed all holiday and country main entries, over 150 in all.

BkHolWrld-1986
LC: GT3933 .V36
Dewey: 394.26

Van Straalen, Alice. *Book of Holidays around the World.* New York: E.P. Dutton, 1986. Illustrated. Appendixes. Index.

Brief datebook-style entries provide at least one observance or anniversary for each day of the year. Photographs and reproductions of literary illustrations and artwork punctuate nearly every page. Appendixes offer brief descriptions of Buddhist, Chinese, Christian, Hindu, Islamic, and Jewish calendars, followed by alphabetical listing of movable festivals and holidays.

Indexed entries covering observed events, over 300 in all.

Chases-1993
LC: D11.5.C49
Dewey: 394.26

Chase's Annual Events: the Day-by-Day Directory to 1993. Chicago: Contemporary Books, Inc., annual. Illustrated. Index.

Chronological guide provides over 10,000 brief entries on annual events, holidays, festivals, religious days, anniversaries, and national and state days. Special features include introductory section describing "banner" events of 1993, including important anniversaries to occur during the year; presidential proclamations issued from January 1, 1991 to June 20, 1992; a listing of national days throughout the world; various civil and religious calendars for the year; other miscellaneous information, including facts about the states and presidents, astronomical events predicted for the year, and major entertainment awards given throughout 1992.

Indexed entries on observed holidays and festivals, excluding promotional days and trade show types of events, about 1,000 in all.

DaysCustFaith-1957
LC: GR930.H29
Dewey: 291.36

Harper, Howard V. *Days and Customs of All Faiths.* 1957. Reprinted by Omnigraphics, 1990. 399 pp. Index.

Part One contains over 300 entries in chronological order that cover Roman, Jewish, and Christian religious festivals, saints' days and major secular holidays observed, especially in the United States. Part Two consists of chapters covering Jewish customs, major Christian holiday customs, including New Year's, words and expressions associated with various lore, and wedding customs.

Indexed over 100 entries pertaining to observed events.

DictDays-1988
LC: GT3925.D861
Dewey: 394.26

Dunkling, Leslie. *Dictionary of Days.* New York and Oxford: Facts on File, 1988. 156 pp.

Alphabetical listing of over 700 named days: local days, fictional days (such as *The Day of the Jackal* and Lewis Carroll's "unbirthday"), expressions (such as "hey-day" and "turkey day"), generic (e.g., Friday) and technical terms (e.g., sidereal day) as well as names of holidays and other observed events. Much cross-referencing. Emphasis is on providing general-interest etymological information on the name itself in addition to giving basic definition of the day's significance. Often gives Scottish and northern English dialectical forms. Many entries include relevant literary quotations. A special feature is a calendar that chronologically maps the days discussed.

Indexed entries covering observed events, over 420 in all.

DictFolkMyth-1984
LC: GR35.F98
Dewey: 398

Leach, Maria, ed. *Funk & Wagnalls Standard Dictionary of Folklore, Mythology & Legend.* New York: Harper & Row, 1984. 1236 pp. Index.

This first one-volume edition contains "a representative sampling," contributions from thirty-four anthropologists and folklorists of over 4,500 entries on animals, minerals, vegetables and objects, rituals, festivals and practices, songs, legends and games, and gods, monsters and other entities associated with the folklore and mythology of over 2,000 cultures, peoples, and countries and other geographical regions in the world. Over fifty longer essays surveying the folklore of various cultures and folkloric methodologies, themes and elements conclude with bibliographies. In addition, sources are occasionally inserted throughout in individual entries.

Indexed about 300 entries containing information on observed events.

DictMyth-1962
LC: GR35.J62
Dewey: 398.03

Jobes, Gertrude. *Dictionary of Mythology, Folklore and Symbols.* 3 vols. New York: Scarecrow Press, 1962. 1759 pp., plus 482 pp. Index (vol. 3). Bibliography.

Several thousand entries cover mythology, folklore, and symbols from around the world and from all religions, past and present. Includes names and their meanings, deities with their genealogy, function, attributes, emblems, behavior, depictions in art, and parallel deities; characters from novels and plays; animals, vegetables, and minerals with their symbolism, significance in dreams; Freemasonry, heraldry, the occult, religion, and mythology; constellations; significance of the parts of the body and body postures; festivals, holidays, and dances. Good cross-referencing. The third volume, the Index, contains symbols and abbreviations used, a table of Deities, Heroes, and Personalities, and a table of Mythological Affiliations (supernatural forms, realms, things).

Indexed entries pertaining to observed events, about 150 in all.

DictWrldRel-1989
LC: BL31.A24
Dewey: 291.03

Crim, Keith, ed. *Perennial Dictionary of World Religions* (originally published as *Abingdon Dictionary of Living Religions*). San Francisco: Harper & Row, 1989. 830 pp. Illustrations. Maps. Charts.

One hundred sixty-one scholars contributed over 1,600 entries on the world's major living systems of faith: deities, saints and other holy figures, religious sites, art and architecture, movements, sects, and societies, authors and texts, creeds, prayers, mantras, and spiritual practices. Some bibliograpy provided throughout in individual entries. Long survey article on each major religion. Good cross-referencing. Guide to abbreviations and pronunciation table. Listing of key entries pertaining to major religions.

Indexed entries covering observed events, over 100 in all.

FestSaintDays-1915
LC: BV43.U77
Dewey: 263.9

Urlin, Ethel L. *Festivals, Holy Days, and Saints' Days: A Study in Origins and Survivals in Church Ceremonies & Secular Customs*. 1915. Reprinted by Omnigraphics, Inc., 1992. 272 pp. Illustrated. Bibliography. Index.

Entries cover, in chronological order, major Christian festivals and saints' days in England and Europe. Some mention of ancient Roman and Greek festivals where they figure in the origins of current Christian feasts. Listing of liturgical colors and the festivals during which they are worn by clergy. English calendar of Christian festivals and saints' days.

Indexed all entries covering observed events, about 60 in all.

FestWestEur-1958
LC: GT4842.S75
Dewey: 94.2694

Spicer, Dorothy Gladys. *Festivals of Western Europe*. 1958. Reprinted by Omnigraphics, 1994. 275 pp. Index.

Major festivals in twelve western European countries described in over 250 entries. Some material duplicates or is revised from that found in the author's *The Book of Festivals,* described above. Table of dates for Easter and other Christian movable days from 1958 to 1988. Glossary of festival terms. Suggested reading list. Indexes of festivals by country and by names of festivals.

Indexed all entries.

FolkAmerHol-1987
LC: GT4803.F651
Dewey: 394.269

Cohen, Hennig, and Tristram Potter Coffin, eds. *The Folklore of American Holidays: A Compilation of More Than 400 Beliefs, Legends, Superstitions, Proverbs, Riddles, Poems, Songs, Dances, Games, Plays, Pageants, Fairs, Foods, and Processions Associated with Over 100 American Calendar Customs and Festivals*. Detroit: Gale Research Company, 1987. 431 pp. Indexes.

Chronologically arranged collection of lore associated with more than 100 holidays and festivals in the United States. Various ethnic, occupational and religious groups living in the United States are represented. The editors provide brief background information on events' history, followed by excerpts from written material describing actual observances of the event, as well as accompanying customs, legends, games, recipes, music, etc. Bibliographic information for each source follow the excerpts. Subject Index, Ethnic and Geographic Index, Collectors, Informants, and Translators Index, Song Titles and First Significant Lines Index, and Motif and Tale Types Index.

Indexed all entries covering observed events, over 100 in all.

FolkWrldHol-1992
LC: GT3930.F651
Dewey: 394.26

MacDonald, Margaret R., ed. *The Folklore of World Holidays.* Detroit: Gale Research Inc., 1992. 739 pp. Index.

Chronologically arranged collection of customs, legends, songs, food, superstitions, games, pageants, etc., associated with more than 340 festivals and holidays in over 150 countries. The United States and, for the most part, Canada, are not included. The editor provides a brief explanation of the holiday, followed by excerpts from written material describing actual observances of the event. Bibliographic information for each source follow the excerpts.

Indexed all entries, over 900 in all.

GdUSFest-1984
LC: GT3930.S41
Dewey: 394.6025

Shemanski, Frances. *A Guide to Fairs and Festivals in the United States.* Westport, CT: Greenwood Press, 1984. 339 pp. Appendix. Index.

Covers over 260 fairs and festivals held in the United States and American Samoa, Puerto Rico, and the U.S. Virgin Islands. Entries are arranged alphabetically by state and city, then by territory. Each entry provides a description of the festival's history, purpose, and idiosyncracies of observance. A state-by-state chronological listing of festivals follows the main text. Appendix lists festivals by type.

Indexed entries, excluding trade or commercial events and state fairs, over 90 in all.

GdWrldFest-1985
LC: GT3930.S431
Dewey: 394.269

Shemanski, Frances. *A Guide to World Fairs and Festivals.* Westport, CT: Greenwood Press, 1985. 309 pp. Appendix. Index.

Following the format of *A Guide to Fairs and Festivals in the United States,* this volume includes over 280 fairs and festivals held in 75 countries. A country-by-country chronological listing of festivals follows the main text. Appendix lists festivals by type.

Indexed all entries, excluding trade or commercial events, over 250 in all.

HolFestCelWrld-1994
LC: GT3925.T461
Dewey: 394.26

Thompson, Sue Ellen, and Barbara W. Carlson, eds. *Holidays, Festivals, and Celebrations of the World Dictionary: Detailing More Than 1,400 Observances from All 50 States and More Than 100 Nations. A Compendious Reference Guide to Popular, Ethnic, Religious, National, and Ancient Holidays, Festivals, Celebrations, Commemorations, Holy Days, Feasts, and Fasts, Supplemented by a Special Section on Calendar Systems, Tables of State and National Public Holidays, Special Indexes of Chronological, Cultural and Ethnic, Geographic, Historical, Religious, and Sports Holidays, and a General and Key-Word Index.* Detroit: Omnigraphics, Inc., 1994. 536 pp. Bibliography.

Entries describing more than 1,400 events held in over 100 countries are listed in alphabetical order by the first key word in the name of the event. Special features include listings of legal holidays by U.S. state and country; glossary of words relating to periods of time; discussion of major calendar systems around the world; and chronological, religious, and key-word indexes, as well as the following special subject indexes: ancient/pagan, calendar, folkloric, historic, promotional, and sporting events.

Indexed entries covering observed events, excluding commercial fairs, over 1,400 in all.

IndianAmer-1989
LC: E77.E117
Dewey: 917.304

Eagle/Walking Turtle. *Indian America: A Traveller's Companion.* Santa Fe, NM: John Muir Publications, 1989. 413 pp. Illustrated. Glossary. Bibliography. Appendix. Index.

Over 300 Indian tribes in the United States are listed and arranged by geographical region. Entries provide mailing address and location, phone numbers, public ceremony or powwow dates, visitor information, and historical background. The appendix offers chronological listing of Indian Moons according to tribe; powwow calendar for North America; Indian arts and crafts shows; Navajo rug auctions; museums with major American Indian collections; Indian-owned/operated museums and cultural centers, stores, rodeos, and community colleges; populations by state as of April 1980; reservations, rancherias and pueblos with population figures; and urban Indian centers in major metropolitan areas.

Indexed over 100 entries from text.

IntlThFolk-1979
LC: PN1590.F47M47
Dewey: 790.2025

Merin, Jennifer, with Elizabeth B. Burdick. *International Directory of Theatre, Dance, and Folklore Festivals.* Westport, CT: Greenwood Press, 1979. 480 pp. Bibliography. Appendix.

More than 850 festivals involving theater, dance or folklore in over 50 countries are covered. The United States is not included. Entries are organized by country and often contain mailing addresses, phone numbers, contact names, and dates of occurrence. Length of festival description varies from a few lines to a few paragraphs. Festival entries are followed by a country-by-country chronological listing of festivals, bibliography, an appendix listing the number of festivals in each country, and index of festivals by festival name.

Indexed all entries.

MusFestAmer-1990
LC: ML19.R3

Rabin, Carol Price. *The Complete Guide to Music Festivals in America: Classical, Opera, Jazz, Pops, Country, Folk, Bluegrass, Old-Time Fiddlers, Cajun.* 4th edition. Illustrated by Celia Elke. Great Barrington, MA: Berkshire Traveller Press, 1990. 271 pp. Index.

Covers more than 150 music festivals in 40 of the United States, territories, and Canada, arranged by type of music. Within each section, festivals are listed by the state in which they take place. Entries include a description of the event and addresses and phone numbers to obtain information on purchasing tickets and finding accommodations. Listing of music festivals by location, with maps. Suggested reading list. Index by name of festival.

All entries indexed.

MusFestEurBrit-1980
LC: ML35.R14
Dewey: 780.794

Rabin, Carol Price. *Music Festivals in Europe and Britain.* Stockbridge, MA: Berkshire Traveller Press, 1980. 163 pp. Index.

Over 90 music festivals in 21 European countries are described, arranged by country. Entries provide historical background, type of music offered, notable features and performers from past festivals, contact names, addresses and phone numbers for obtaining tickets and accommodation, and recommended attire and ticket price estimates. Listing of addresses and phone numbers of government tourist offices. Suggested reading list.

All entries indexed.

MusFestWrld-1963
LC: ML35.S87
Dewey: 780.79

Stoll, Dennis Gray. *Music Festivals of the World: A Guide to Leading Festivals of Music, Opera and Ballet.* London: Pergamon Press, Ltd., 1963. 310 pp. Illustrated.

Describes more than 50 music festivals in over twenty countries that run for at least eight days, feature performers known around the world, and show signs of continuing indefinately. Book is organized into thematic chapters containing essays discussing each event's special features and background and addresses for obtaining tickets. Index of festivals.

Indexed all entries, over 50 in all.

NatlHolWrld-1968
LC: GT3930.D64
Dewey: 394.26

Dobler, Lavinia. *National Holidays around the World*. Illustrated and designed by Vivian Browne. New York: Fleet Press Corporation, 1968. 233 pp. Bibliography. Index.

Covers over 130 national and independence days from over 130 countries. Written for a young audience. Entries are chronologically arranged and provide brief recounting of historical and political circumstances leading up to the observance of the day and a description of the nation's flag.

Indexed all entries.

RelHolCal-1993
LC: CE6.K451
Dewey: 529.3

Kelly, Aidan, Peter Dresser, and Linda M. Ross. *Religious Holidays and Calendars: An Encyclopaedic Handbook*. Detroit: Omnigraphics, Inc., 1993. 163 pp. Bibliography. Indexes.

Part One consists of chapters explaining the history and organization of calendars of the world: Babylonian, Hebrew, Greek, Christian, Islamic, Indian, Buddhist, Chinese, Egyptian, Roman, Julian, Gregorian. Part Two provides alphabetical listing by name of religious holiday, dates celebrated, and brief description of its history and current practice, if applicable. Monthly Index of Holidays. Religions Index. Master Index.

Indexed most of the nearly 300 entries.

SaintFestCh-1904
LC: DR170.B7
Dewey: 299.932

Brewster, H. Pomeroy. *Saints and Festivals of the Christian Church*. 1904. Reprinted by Omnigraphics, 1990. 558 pp.

Much of the book originally appeared as a series of articles published in the *Union and Advertiser* in Rochester, New York, which the author subsequently revised, adding more material to be published in the form reprinted in 1990. A yearbook of sorts of the Christian calendar, entries are arranged in chronological order, beginning with Advent. At least one saint or church feast is discussed for nearly every day of the year. Chronological list of the bishops and popes of the Christian church since St. Peter. Alphabetical list of canonized saints and others. General Index.

Indexed entries of the better-known saints and religious festivals, about 80 in all.

Other Sources

The following are sources dealing with holidays and festivals in particular geographic areas and among various ethnic and religious groups, books of special interest to teachers, as well as children and young adults, and texts offering historical background, critical analysis, philosophical discussion, and explanations of calendar systems around the world. A list of relevant journals and magazines follows.

Achelis, Elisabeth. *The Calendar for Everybody.* 1943. Reprinted by Omnigraphics, Inc., 1990. 141 pp. Index.

Traces the calendar from its beginning, relating little-known facts about our present calendar and presenting advantages to be gained from one that is newer and more simplified. Discusses the earth's time, the Egyptian, Julian, Gregorian, and world calendars.

Ahsan, M.M. *Muslim Festivals.* Holidays and Festivals Series. Vero Beach, FL: Rourke Enterprises, Inc., 1987. 48 pp. Illustrated. Glossary. Index.

Presents Islamic beliefs, holidays, and rites for young readers. Note on Islamic calendar. Chronological table of Muslim holidays by Islamic month. Further reading list.

Anderson, Mary M. *The Festivals of Nepal.* London: George Allen & Unwin Ltd., 1971. 288 pp. Illustrated. Bibliography. Index.

Author describes, in chronological order of occurrence, over thirty Hindu, Buddhist, and Nepalese festivals attended in Nepal, as well as legends and customs associated with them.

Anyike, James C. *African American Holidays: A Historical Research and Resource Guide to Cultural Celebrations.* Chicago: Popular Truth, Inc., 1991. 102 pp. Appendixes. Bibliography.

Covers holidays celebrated by slaves between the 17th-19th centuries as well as Martin Luther King, Jr.'s birthday observances, Black History Month, African Liberation Day, Juneteenth, Umoja Karamu (Unity Feast), and Kwanzaa. Appendixes include timeline of important dates in history and brief historical background on major holidays observed in the United States. List of related sources and organizations.

Ashby, Thomas. *Some Italian Scenes and Festivals.* New York: E.P. Dutton and Company, Inc., c1928. 179 pp. Illustrated. Index.

Describes several religious and folk festivals observed in Italy, while providing impressions of the landscape and peoples, as well as some historical background.

Asimov, Isaac. *The Clock We Live On.* Revised edition. Illustrated by John Bradford. London and New York: Abelard-Schuman, 1965. 172 pp. Diagrams. Index.

The scientist-science fiction writer explains the solar and lunar systems by which humans have learned to tell time. Surveys devices for keeping time, from ancient to modern clocks and calendars. Discussion of solar, lunar, Egyptian, Hebrew, Christian, Julian, Gregorian, and French Revolutionary calendars, and chronological eras.

Attwater, Donald. *The Penguin Dictionary of Saints.* Second edition revised and updated by Catherine Rachel John. London: Penguin Books, 1983. 352 pp. Bibliography. Glossary.

Covers, in alphabetical order, more than 750 saints. Scope is international. Includes obscure and early, as well as more popular and recent saints. List of emblems associated with saints. Chronological list of feast days.

Augur, Helen. *The Book of Fairs*. Introduction by Hendrik Willem Van Loon. Illustrated by James MacDonald. 1939. Reprinted by Omnigraphics, Inc., 1992. 308 pp. Index.

Traces the development of trade, customs, and social life in connection with fairs in history up to the 1939 World's Fair. Includes discussion of fairs and festivals in ancient Tyre, Athens, and Rome, the Kinsai Fairs in 13th-century Cathay, 13th-century France, 15th-century Belgium and Germany, medieval England, Ireland and Scotland, Russia, and the modern expositions.

Auld, William Muir. *Christmas Tidings*. 1933. Reprinted by Omnigraphics, Inc., 1990. 156 pp. Illustrated.

Describes legends, verse, and such historic liturgies as the Roman Breviary and the Missal.

———. *Christmas Traditions*. 1931. Reprinted by Omnigraphics, Inc., 1992. 179 pp. Index.

This history of Christmas surveys origins, antecedents, changes, and developments of the traditions through the ages. Covers ancient English carols, the yule log, the tree, bells, and more. Excerpts from literature, legends, and historical accounts.

Bailey, Carolyn Sherwin. *Stories for Every Holiday*. 1919. Reprinted by Omnigraphics, Inc., 1990. 277 pp.

Twenty-seven stories for young readers about 19 Christian and secular holidays observed in the United States. Arranged in chronological order, beginning with Labor Day.

Ballam, Harry, and Phyllis Digby Morton, eds. *The Christmas Book*. 1947. Reprinted by Omnigraphics, Inc., 1990. 260 pp. Illustrated. Appendixes.

Collection of articles and stories by such writers as Charles Dickens, Aldous Huxley, Washington Irving, Bram Stoker, and others on the subject of Christmas. Several holiday quizzes are included, for which the Appendixes provide the answers.

Bauer, Caroline Feller. *Celebrations: Read-Aloud Holiday and Theme Book Programs*. Drawings by Lynn Gates Bredeson. New York: H. W. Wilson Company, 1985. 301 pp. Index.

Education specialist offers 16 theme book programs dealing with holidays and such invented celebrations as National Nothing Day and Pigmania for teachers and other professionals working with primarily middle-grade children. Each program includes some prose and poetry selections, ideas for bulletin boards, recipes, activities and jokes, and lists of related books marked for various age groups.

Bauer, Helen, and Sherwin Carlquist. *Japanese Festivals*. Garden City, NY: Doubleday & Company, Inc., 1965. 224 pp. Illustrated. Index.

Essays on eleven major festivals. Chapters on food and flower festivals. Second half of book is a chronological arrangement of Japanese festivals. Back matter includes a pronunciation guide and summary of Japan's history.

Bauer, John E. *Christmas on the American Frontier, 1800-1900.* 1961. Reprinted by Omnigraphics, Inc., 1993. 320 pp. Illustrated.

Seventeen chapters cover such topics as "A California Festival of Good Will," "Down a Prairie Chimney," "Giving Christmas to the Indians," and more. Contains eyewitness accounts of frontier holidays.

Beezley, William H., Cheryl English Martin, and William E. French, eds. *Rituals of Rule, Rituals of Resistance: Public Celebrations and Popular Culture in Mexico.* Wilmington, DE: Scholarly Resources, Inc., 1994. 374 pp.

Fifteen papers presented by scholars at the Eighth Conference of Mexican and North American Historians in San Diego, 1990. Essays analyze popular culture, rituals, customs, and festivals in Mexico in the context of political and colonial power and domination.

Beier, Ulli. *Yoruba Myths.* Cambridge: Cambridge University Press, 1980. 82 pp. Illustrated.

The author and contributors present 41 myths from Nigeria about Yoruba deities, including Ogun and Oranmiyan.

Bentley, James. *A Calendar of Saints: The Lives of the Principal Saints of the Christian Year.* New York and Oxford: Facts on File Publications, 1986. 256 pp. Illustrated. Index.

Brief biographies of over 300 saints are provided. Inspirational quotes from saints preface each month and also appear throughout. Richly illustrated, over 300 paintings are reproduced.

Bettelheim, Judith, ed. *Cuban Festivals: An Illustrated Anthology.* New York: Garland Publishing, Inc., 1993. 261 pp. Illustrated. Index.

Scholars from various academic disciplines present essays on Cuban festivals: "The Afro-Cuban Festival 'Day of the Kings'," Fernando Ortiz; "Annotated Glossary for Fernando Ortiz's The Afro-Cuban Festival 'Day of the Kings'," David H. Brown; "Glossary of Popular Festivals," Rafael Brea and José Millet; "Carnival in Santiago de Cuba" and "Appendix: The Tumba Francesa and Tajona of Santiago de Cuba," Judith Bettelheim; and "Flashback on Carnival, a Personal Memoir," Pedro Pérez Sarduy.

Blackwood, Alan. *New Year.* Holidays and Festivals Series. Vero Beach, FL: Rourke Enterprises, Inc., 1987. 48 pp. Illustrated. Glossary. Index.

For young readers. Discusses ancient celebrations of the New Year in Egypt, Babylonia, and Rome, and among Celts. Explanation of the Jewish and Chinese calendars, the Muslim and Hindu New Year, the New Year throughout Asia, the New Year in the United States and Britain, and some mentions of customs in various European countries. Entries on St. Sebastian and St. Basil. Further reading list.

The Book of Easter. Introduction by William C. Doane. 1910. Reprinted by Omnigraphics, Inc., 1990. 246 pp. Illustrated.

Collection of Easter poems, stories, hymns, and essays from various sources including the Bible, and by writers such as Elizabeth Barret Browning, Walter Pater, Robert Browning, Alfred Tennyson, George Herbert, Thomas Hardy, and others. Reproductions of famous paintings relating to Easter by such artists as Rembrandt, Rubens, and Fra Angelico. Provides historic accounts and descriptions of customs and legends associated with Good Friday, Easter, and the Ascension.

Brand, John. *Observations on Popular Antiquities, Chiefly Illustrating the Origin of Our Vulgar Customs, Ceremonies, and Superstitions; with the Additions of Sir Henry Ellis.* London: Chatto and Windus, 1877. 807 pp. Illustrated.

Chronologically arranged discussion, with historical background, of over 60 holidays and festivals as observed in western Europe, especially England. Collection of lore on hundreds of items falling under such headings as sports and games, charms and omens, witchcraft and mythology, marriage, child-bearing, death, and drinking customs.

Bredon, Juliet, and Igor Mitrophanow. *The Moon Year: A Record of Chinese Customs and Festivals.* Shanghai: Kelly & Walsh, Limited, 1927. 522 pp. Illustrated. Bibliography. Index.

Chapters on the Chinese calendar, imperial ceremonies, and the many Chinese gods and cults associated with them, including a discussion of the rise of Confucianism, Taoism and Buddhism. A chapter is then devoted to each month of the Chinese year, describing the observance of festivals within each month.

Browne, Ray B., and Michael T. Marsden, eds. *The Cultures of Celebrations.* Bowling Green, OH: Bowling Green State University Popular Press, 1994. 244 pp.

Collection of 15 case studies from scholars working in areas relating to popular culture studies. Essays analyze various celebrations and forms of entertainment, including Shiite rituals, folk festivals in Australia, Lord Mayor's Procession, Columbus celebrations from 18th-20th centuries, and seasonal festivals in Manitoba.

Brumfield, Allaire Chandor. *The Attic Festivals of Demeter and Their Relation to the Agricultural Year.* Salem, NH: The Ayer Company, 1981. 257 pp. Notes. Bibliography. Glossary. Indexes.

Originally author's dissertation. Examines the festivals of Demeter in terms of their seasonal and agricultural context and importance. List of Athenian months. Glossary of Greek agricultural terms. General index and index of Greek words.

Buday, George. *The History of the Christmas Card.* 1954. Reprinted by Omnigraphics, Inc., 1992. 304 pp. Illustrated. Bibliography. Appendixes. Index.

Traces the rise of the Christmas card and discusses its forerunners, old Christmas card creators, children's cards, religious cards, and wartime Christmas cards. Appendixes list artists and designers, old Christmas card sentiment writers, and Christmas card publishers.

Buechler, Hans C. *The Masked Media: Aymara Fiestas and Social Interaction in the Bolivian Highlands.* The Hague, Netherlands: Mouton Publishers, 1980. 399 pp. Illustrated. Appendixes. Glossary. References. Indexes.

Anthropologist presents results of fieldwork on festivals, saints' fiestas, and other rituals among the Aymara people in Bolivia. Appendixes offer notes on musical instruments employed during different festivals throughout the year; a description of the Fiesta of the Skulls at the main cemetery in La Paz; comparative table of food and drink expenditures for sponsors of rural and urban festivals during the 1960s and 1970s; a fiesta sponsor's list of participants' contributions to and involvement with a fiesta held in Lamacachi; and a note on recent use of brass bands in Compi fiestas. Index of authors referenced. Index of subjects.

Burkhardt, V.R. *Chinese Creeds & Customs.* 2 vols. Hong Kong: The South China Morning Post, Ltd., 1953-55. Vol. 1, 181 pp. + index, i.-v.; vol. 2, 201 pp. + index, i.-ix. Illustrated. Appendixes. Bibliography.

Author describes customs and observance of more than twenty festivals and ceremonies in China, as well as legends, foods, objects, symbols, and fine arts, and discussion of the calendar. Appendixes include list of the 24 segments of the Chinese year, the ten celestial stems and twelve earthly branches, and a table of Chinese temples that lists each temple's locale, god(s) worshipped, and date founded.

Burland, C.A. *The Gods of Mexico.* New York: G.P. Putnam's Sons, 1967. 219 pp. Illustrated. Maps. Appendixes. Bibliography. Index.

Alphabetical listing of Aztec gods. Guide to pronunciation. Covers Aztec, Mayan, Toltec, and Olmec cultures, cities, calendar systems, deities, and religions. Aztec ceremonies and festivals described. Appendixes discuss Mayan, Aztec, and other Mexican codices and tlachtli, a ball game.

Campbell, Liz, comp. *1993 Powwow Calendar: Guide to North American Powwows and Gatherings U.S.A. and Canada.* Summertown, TN: The Book Publishing Company, 1992. 96 pp. Illustrated.

Lists, in chronological order, more than 400 powwows and other events observed by Native Americans in the United States and Canada. Entries include contact addresses and phone numbers.

Cantwell, Robert. *Ethnomimesis: Folklife and the Representation of Culture.* Chapel Hill: The University of North Carolina Press, 1993. 323 pp. Notes. Bibliography. Index.

Describes the Festival of American Folklife, held annually on the Mall in Washington, D.C., and discusses it as a cultural artifact that can yield insights on "festivity, identity, and memory."

Casal, U.A. *The Five Sacred Festivals of Ancient Japan: Their Symbolism & Historical Development.* Tokyo: Charles E. Tuttle Company, Inc., and Sophia University, 1967. 114 pp. Illustrated. Index.

Covers historical background, traditions, legends and myths, food, customs, and current observance of the New Year Festival, the Girls' Festival, the Boys' Festival, the Star Festival, and the Chrysanthemum Festival in Japan.

Cashman, Greer Fay. *Jewish Days and Holidays.* Illustrated by Alona Frankel. New York: SBS Publishing, Inc., 1979. 64 pp.

Describes for young readers the history of and traditions and customs associated with major

Jewish holidays, including the Sabbath. Sidebars depict foods and other items used during celebrations. Concludes with quiz on matching sidebar items with appropriate holiday.

Chun Shin-yong, ed. *Customs and Manners in Korea*. Part of the ten-volume Korean Culture Series. Seoul: International Cultural Foundation and Si-sa-yong-o-sa, Inc., 1982. 132 pp. Illustrated.

Scholars from various academic specialties contribute ten essays on Korean traditions and values, rituals and rites, mental health, literature and mythology. The essay ''Annual Ceremonies and Rituals,'' by Choi Gil-sung, discusses the timing, significance, and observance of various festivals throughout Korea. Kim Yol-kyu's ''Several Forms of Korean Folk Rituals, Including Shaman Rituals'' examines folk dance and festivals.

Coffin, Tristram P., and Hennig Cohen, eds. *Folklore in America: Tales, Songs, Superstitions, Proverbs, Riddles, Games, Folk Drama, and Folk Festivals with 17 Folk Melodies.* 1966. Reprinted by University Press of America, Inc., 1986. 256 pp. Source notes.

Presents numerous examples of folk tradition among more than thirty ethnic groups in the United States. Index of ethnic groups and geographic locations. Index of titles and first lines of songs. List of tale types and motifs.

Cohen, Hennig, and Tristram Potter Coffin. *America Celebrates! A Patchwork of Weird & Wonderful Holiday Lore.* Detroit: Visible Ink Press, 1991. 355 pp. Illustrated.

Drawing from oral history and newspaper and journal accounts, covers more than 200 traditions, legends, beliefs, superstitions, recipes, food, games, dances, poems, riddles, and music associated with over sixty religious, patriotic, commemorative, agricultural, ethnic, and folk holidays and festivals observed among various ethnic, regional, and occupational groups in North America.

Cole, William Owen, and Piara Singh Sambhi. *The Sikhs: Their Religious Beliefs and Practices.* London, Henley and Boston: Routledge & Kegan Paul, 1978. 210 pp. Illustrated. Maps. Glossary. Bibliography. Appendixes. Index.

Covers historical background, beliefs and practices of the Sikh faith, including discussion of founder Guru Nanak and others, scripture, places and style of worship, ethics, ceremonies, birth, marriage and death rites, and calendar of festivals. Appendixes cover the Rehat Maryada or guide to the Sikh way of life; prayers and meditations; population statistics; and explanation of the structure of the scriptural hymns, the Guru Granth Sahib.

Coleman, Lesley. *A Book of Time*. Camden, NJ: Thomas Nelson, Inc., 1971. 144 pp. Illustrated. Bibliography. Index.

Survey of ancient Sumerian, Babylonian, Muslim, Christian, Jewish, Egyptian, Roman, Julian, Gregorian, and French Revolutionary calendars and the proposed World Calendar. Includes discussion of timepieces, clockmakers, navigation, and some theories and literature dealing with time.

Cooper, Gordon. *Festivals of Europe.* 1961. Reprinted by Omnigraphics, Inc., 1994. 172 pp. Illustrated. Appendix. Index.

Traveller-oriented guide provides brief mentions or descriptions of over 1,000 festivals in 25 Western and Eastern European countries. Arranged alphabetically by country, festivals are discussed by type of event: agricultural, carnival, cultural, national, religious, sporting, trade, wine and food. Chapter offering travel hints. Directory of tourist offices for 24 countries.

Cosman, Madeleine Pelner. *Medieval Holidays and Festivals: A Calendar of Celebrations.* New York: Charles Scribner's Sons, 1981. 136 pp. Illustrated. Index.

Describes customs, activities, food and recipes, music, costume and decoration associated with twelve holidays from the 12th through the 16th centuries, mainly in England, France, Italy, and Germany: Twelfth Night, St. Valentine's Day, Easter, All Fool's Day, Mayday, Midsummer Eve, St. Swithin's Day, Lammas, Michaelmas, Halloween, St. Catherine's Day, and Christmas. Further reading list.

Couzens, Reginald C. *The Stories of the Months and Days.* 1923. Reprinted by Omnigraphics, Inc., 1990. 160 pp. Illustrated.

Explains how the months and days were named, telling stories about the Greek, Roman, Anglo and Saxon gods, goddesses, and emperors with whom they are associated.

Cowie, L.W., and John Selwyn Gummer. *The Christian Calendar: A Complete Guide to the Seasons of the Christian Year Telling the Story of Christ and the Saints from Advent to Pentecost.* Springfield, MA: G & C Merriam Company, Publishers, 1974. 256 pp. Illustrated. Index.

Introduction gives historical background on the development of the Christian calendar. Part one discusses each Christian holiday and Sunday of the liturgical year, from Advent to the 24th Sunday after Pentecost, discussing the scripture and/or festival associated with each day covered. Part two provides entries, in chronological order, on saints' day and feasts for every day of the Gregorian year. List of patron saints, in alphabetical order by saint. Glossarial index.

Cox, Harvey. *The Feast of Fools: A Theological Essay on Festivity and Fantasy.* Cambridge, MA: Harvard University Press, 1969. 204 pp. Appendix. Notes. Index.

Adapted from the William Belden Noble Lectures given by the author in 1968 at Harvard University. Theological examination of spiritual aspects of festivity and fantasy as practiced in Western cultures. Uses the medieval Feast of Fools and its eventual disappearance as a symbol for thesis that Western civilization needs a rebirth of ''the spirit represented by the Feast of Fools.''

Craig, Darrin, and Julie Craig. *The Festival Hopper's Guide to California & Nevada.* Third edition. San Jose, CA: Creative Chaos, 1991. 519 pp. Maps. Indexes.

Information on more than 450 festivals, fairs, rodeos, and arts and music events held in California and Nevada. Entries are organized by northern, central, and southern California, and Nevada, then chronologically within each region or state. Information provided within each entry includes a map, population of the town and festival attendance, average outdoor temperature during the time of the event, festival location, where to call for more information, and checklist of the event's features and existence of regulations, accommodations, and fees. Town index and festival index. List of festival coordinators and vendors with addresses and phone numbers.

————. *The Festival Hopper's Guide to the Rocky West.* San Jose, CA: Creative Chaos, 1991. 209 pp. Maps. Indexes.

Covers over 150 festivals, fairs, rodeos, and arts and music events held in Arizona, Colorado, New Mexico, Utah, and Wyoming. Entries are organized alphabetically by state, then chronologically within each state. Information provided within each entry is the same as in the book above. Town index and festival index. List of festival coordinators and vendors with addresses and phone numbers.

Crawford, Ann Caddell. *Customs and Culture of Vietnam.* Foreword by Henry Cabot Lodge. Illustrations by Hau Dinh Cam. Rutland, VT & Tokyo: Charles E. Tuttle Co., Publishers, 1966. 259 pp. Map. Bibliography.

In addition to providing a calendar and description of festivals and holidays, this book is a survey of mainly South Vietnamese geography, history, culture, religion, education, media, arts, medicine, agriculture, and industry against the backdrop of the Vietnam War. Customs, ceremonies, legends, and points of interest are also included.

Crippen, Thomas G. *Christmas and Christmas Lore.* 1923. Reprinted by Omnigraphics, Inc., 1990. 223 pp. Illustrated. Index.

Collection of customs, traditions, and legends relating to Christmas, drawn from chapbooks and pamphlets of the seventeenth and eighteenth centuries and from various books dealing with antiquities and legends.

Curtis, Mary I. *Why We Celebrate Our Holidays.* Illustrated by Jewel Morrison. New York and Chicago: Lyons and Carnahan, 1924. 148 pp.

Intended for a young audience, the author describes reasons for major observances of the year in the United States.

Dawson, W.F. *Christmas: Its Origins and Associations.* 1902. Reprinted by Omnigraphics, Inc., 1990. 366 pp. Illustrated. Index.

Arranged chronologically, covers the holiday's origin, its historical events, and festive celebrations during 19 centuries. Considers the evolving tradition in Britain and includes information on the celebration of Christmas in various lands.

Deems, Edward M., comp. *Holy-Days and Holidays.* 1902. Reprinted by Omnigraphics, Inc., 1968. 768 pp. Bibliography. Index.

Divided into two major sections—religious and secular holidays—both arranged chronologically. Covers events observed in the United States, Canada, and United Kingdom. For each holiday, the compiler presents an introductory essay, a selection of prose essays, sermons and speeches, an alphabetical list of "suggestive thoughts," and poetry pertaining to the occasion.

Denis-Boulet, Noële M. *The Christian Calendar.* Vol. 113 of the *Twentieth Century Encyclopedia of Catholicism.* Translated by P. Hepburne-Scott. New York: Hawthorn Books, 1960. 126 pp. Bibliography.

Provides historical background on how the Christian calendar evolved from earlier calendars. Discussion of the observance of Sunday, Easter, and other feasts. History of martyrologies. Calendar reforms through history and contemporary reform proposal of a world calendar.

Dillon, Philip Robert. *American Anniversaries; Every Day of the Year; Presenting Seven Hundred and Fifty Events in United States History, from the Discovery of America to the Present Day.* c.1918. Reprinted by Omnigraphics, Inc., 1991. 349 pp. + index, pp. i-xv.

Opens with a chronology of principal events during World War One and summary of armistice. Book is organized chronologically. At least one anniversary is given for each day of the year. Entries are anniversaries of historical events and people in politics and legislation, commerce and invention, arts and letters.

Dömötör, Tekla. *Hungarian Folk Customs.* Translated by Judith Elliott. Corvina, Budapest: Corvina Press, 1972. 86 pp. + plates. Illustrated. Map. Bibliography.

Brief survey of folk customs and beliefs, and their study in Hungary. Discussion of history and observance of seasonal, religious, and secular festivals, as well as birth, marriage, and burial practices.

Dossey, Donald E. *Holiday Folklore, Phobias and Fun: Mythical Origins, Scientific Treatments and Superstitious "Cures."* Los Angeles: Outcomes Unlimited Press, Inc., 1992. 231 pp. Appendixes. Bibliography. Index.

An expert on phobias and anxiety and stress disorders conducts informal survey of origins of various holiday customs—New Year's, St. Valentine's Day, St. Patrick's Day, Friday the 13th, Easter, April Fools' Day, Halloween, Thanksgiving, Christmas—while offering advice on dealing with holiday stress and anxiety. Appendixes include some folklore recipes, tips for cognitive refocusing and keying, and list of phobias and symptoms.

Drake-Carnell, F.J. *Old English Customs and Ceremonies.* New York: Charles Scribner's Sons; London: B.T. Batsford Ltd., 1938. 120 pp. Illustrated. Index.

Survey of religious, municipal (London), legal, commercial, military, school, marine, and royal ceremonies, customs and protocol relating to the House of Parliament, and rural festivals and traditions—such as the Furry Dance, Beating the Bounds, and Plough Monday—observed in England.

Duncan, Edmondstoune. *The Story of the Carol.* 1911. Reprinted by Omnigraphics, Inc., 1992. 253 pp. Illustrated. Appendixes. Bibliography. Index.

Surveys development of the forms and purposes of carols, as well as the days, feasts, pageants, and religious rites associated with them. Includes words and music to traditional carols. Appendixes cover brief biographical notes on relevant individuals, glossary, chronological table of development of carols, and list of manuscript carols held in the British Museum.

Dunham, Katherine. *Dance of Haiti.* Foreword by Claude Lévi-Strauss. Photographs by Patricia Cummings. Los Angeles: University of California, 1983. 78 pp. Glossary.

In a revised version of her thesis, the dancer-anthropologist surveys religious, social, and festive uses of dance in Haiti, including some commentary on dance and Lent, Mardi Gras, Holy Week, and Easter.

Dupuy, Trevor Nevitt, ed. *Holidays; Days of Significance for All Americans.* New York: Franklin Watts, Inc., 1965. 162 pp. Index.

Intended for elementary-school teachers. Brief essays from contributors to, and members of, the Historical Evaluation and Research Organization cover 27 patriotic holidays and commemorative days observed in the United States. Further reading list.

Eberhard, Wolfram. *Chinese Festivals.* Great Religious Festivals series. New York: Henry Schuman, 1952. 152 pp. Illustrated. Index.

Essays on observance and folklore associated with the New Year, Dragon Boat Festival, Mid-Autumn Festival, Spring Festival, Feast of the Souls, Sending the Winter Dress Festival, and the Weaving Maid and the Cowherd Festival.

Eddy, Lloyd Champlin. *Holidays.* Boston: The Christopher Publishing House, 1928. 304 pp. Index.

Day-by-day listing of holidays and birthdays worldwide, followed by chapters on various religious and secular events observed by a broad range of ethnic groups and religions.

Edidin, Ben M. *Jewish Customs and Ceremonies.* Illustrated by H. Norman Tress. New York: Hebrew Publishing Company, 1941. 178 pp. Bibliography. Index and Glossary.

A companion to *Jewish Holidays and Festivals* (see below), intended as an educational supplemental text, describes everyday customs as well as those associated with holidays and other important events, such as birth, bar and bat mitzvah, marriage, burial, and worship.

———. *Jewish Holidays and Festivals.* Illustrated by Kyra Markham. 1940. Reprinted by Omnigraphics, Inc., 1993. 66 pp. Bibliography. Index and Glossary.

Discusses history, significance and customs associated with Jewish holidays and anniversaries.

Eichler, Lillian. *The Customs of Mankind With Notes on Modern Etiquette and Entertainment.* Pen and ink drawings by Phillipps Ward. Garden City, NY: Garden City Publishing Company, Inc., 1924. 753 pp. Illustrated. Bibliography. Index.

One chapter on origins of holidays and customs accompanying them.

Eisenberg, Azriel. *The Story of the Jewish Calendar.* Wood engravings by Elisabeth Friedlander. London and New York: Abelard-Schuman, 1958. 62 pp.

A short story of two teenaged boys watching for the new moon prefaces a brief history of the Jewish calendar. Explanation of Jewish holidays and names of months and Sabbaths and their significance. Glossary of Hebrew terms and place-names.

Epton, Nina. *Spanish Fiestas (Including Romerías, Excluding Bull-Fights)*. New York: A.S. Barnes and Company, 1968. 250 pp. Illustrated. Map. Index.

Descriptions of Easter, Corpus Christi, midsummer, Christmas, New Year's, and Carnival celebrations throughout Spain, as well as Moors and Christians fiestas, and more than thirty other festivals, holy days, and romarías (pilgrimages) observed in Spain.

Falassi, Alessandro, ed. *Time Out of Time: Essays on the Festival*. Albuquerque, NM: University of New Mexico Press, 1987. 311 pp.

Collection of essays by Goethe, Hemingway and Aldous Huxley, and Victor Turner, Vladimir Propp, and other folklorists describing and analyzing festivals celebrated in Europe, North and South America, Africa, Asia, and Oceania such as the Palio at Siena, the Roman Carnival, bullfighting, Olojo Festival, Carnival at Rio de Janeiro, the Holy Ghost Festival in the Azores, and more.

Faris, James C. *The Nightway: A History and a History of Documentation of a Navajo Ceremonial*. Albuquerque, NM: University of New Mexico Press, 1990. 288 pp. Charts and figures. Notes. Bibliography. Index.

Anthropologist presents a study of recordings of the Navajo Nightway Ceremony and its stories, songs, beliefs, prayers and practices, including sandpainting. Charts and figures detail genealogies of medicine men who have led the Nightway, as well as specific elements of Nightways observed over the last 100 years.

Farmer, David Hugh. *The Oxford Dictionary of Saints*. Second edition. Oxford: Oxford University Press, 1987. 478 pp. Appendixes.

Covers, in alphabetical order, more than 1,000 saints venerated in the Christian church—mainly in Great Britian, but this edition also includes some Greek and Russian saints from Eastern Orthodoxy. Bibliographical sources conclude the entries. Appendixes include a list of English people who have been candidates for canonization and are associated with a popular cult; a list of patronages of saints; iconographical emblems of saints; places in Great Britain and Ireland associated with saints; and a calendar of feast days for saints.

Fergusson, Erna. *Dancing Gods: Indian Ceremonials of New Mexico and Arizona*. Foreword by Tony Hillerman. Albuquerque, NM: University of New Mexico Press, 1931. Sixth paperback printing, 1991. 286 pp. Illustrated. Index.

Describes history, meaning, and performance of religious and social dances and ceremonies observed among the Pueblo, Hopi, Navajo, and Apache peoples, including prayers, customs, and some historical background on each.

————. *Fiesta in Mexico*. Illustrated by Valentín Vidaurreta. New York: Alfred A. Knopf, 1934. 267 pp. + i-iv, index.

Account of travel to festivals throughout Mexico, including Pilgrimage to Chalma, Moors and Christians in Tuxpan, La Fiesta de Nuestra Señora de la Soledad in Oaxaca, Passion Play in Tzintzuntzan, Los Voladores in Coxquihui, a Yaqui Indian *Pascola,* Deer Dance, Coyote Dance, Los Matachines, Holy Week, Good Friday and Holy Saturday in Tlaxcala, Day of the Dead, All Saints' Day and All Souls' Day, Lent, Fiesta of Nuestra Señora de la Santa Vera Cruz, *El Viernes de Dolores* (fifth Friday in Lent) in Santa Anita, Christmas and Posadas. Also includes historical discussion of ancient Aztec, Christian, and secular celebrations.

Festivals in Asia. Asian Copublication Programme Series Two. Sponsored by the Asian Cultural Centre for Unesco. Tokyo, New York and San Francisco: Kodansha International Ltd., 1975. 66 pp. Illustrated.

For young readers. Describes, in chronological order, the New Year in Singapore, Festival of Fire (New Year) in Iran, Dolls' Day and Boys' Day in Japan, Bengali New Year in Bangladesh, the Water Festival in Burma, New Year in Cambodia, New Year in Laos, Sinhala and Tamil New Year in Sri Lanka, and Maytime in the Philippines, often through storytelling.

Fewkes, Jesse Walter. *Hopi Snake Ceremonies; an Eyewitness Account.* Selections from Bureau of American Ethnology, Annual Reports Nos. 16 and 19 for the years 1894-95 and 1897-98. Albuquerque, NM: Avanyu Publishing, Inc., 1986. Illustrated.

Reprint of two papers published in annual reports. Author describes ceremonies performed by the Hopi Snake Society during the 1890s.

———. *Tusayan Katcinas and Hopi Altars.* Introduction by Barton Wright. Albuquerque, NM: Avanyu Publishing, Inc., 1990. Illustrated.

Reprint of two texts by Fewkes, one an article, ''The Katcina Altars in Hopi Worship,'' that appeared in the Annual Report of the Board of Regents of The Smithsonian Institution for 1926. Both represent author's endeavor to describe and analyze kachina ceremonials among the Hopis, including the Powámû Ceremony.

Foley, Daniel J. *Christmas the World Over: How the Season of Joy and Good Will Is Observed and Enjoyed by Peoples Here and Everywhere.* Illustrated by Charlotte Edwards Bowden. Philadelphia and New York: Chilton Books, 1963. 128 pp. Index.

Customs and traditions associated with Christmas in over thirty countries around the world. Heavy coverage of Europe and Latin America.

———, ed. *Christmas in the Good Old Days: A Victorian Album of Stories, Poems, and Pictures of the Personalities Who Rediscovered Christmas.* 1961. Reprinted by Omnigraphics, Inc., 1994. 224 pp. Illustrated. Bibliography. Index.

Anthology of stories and poems written during the Victorian era by such authors as Louisa May Alcott, Washington Irving, Bret Harte, O. Henry, Charles Dickens, Hans Christian Andersen, Herman Melville, and others. Includes brief sketches on the authors.

Fowler, W. Warde. *The Roman Festivals of the Period of the Republic: An Introduction to the Study of the Religion of the Romans.* London: Macmillan and Co., Ltd., 1899. Reprinted in 1925. 373 pp. Indexes.

Describes the Roman calendar and Roman festivals of the Republican era in chronological order, from *Mensis Martius*, or March, to *Mensis Februarius,* or February. Chronological table of calendar festivals, according to the Republican calendar. Indexes of subjects, Latin words, Latin authors quoted, and Greek authors quoted.

Frazer, James George. *The Golden Bough: A Study in Magic and Religion.* One volume, abridged edition. New York: Collier Books, 1950. 864 pp. Index.

Numerous festivals are discussed in this classic work on legends, mythology, and religions all over the world, abridged in one volume.

Gaer, Joseph. *Holidays around the World.* Drawings by Anne Marie Jauss. Boston: Little, Brown and Company, 1953. 212 pp. Index.

Covers over thirty Chinese, Hindu, Jewish, Christian, and Muslim holidays, as well as United Nations Day. List of principal holidays in the United States.

Gaster, Theodor H. *Festivals of the Jewish Year.* New York: William Sloane Associates Publishers, 1953. 308 pp. Bibliography.

Presents origins of Jewish festivals and holy days, draws comparisons to other religious and ethnic holidays, and describes evolving nature of their observance throughout history.

Gaver, Jessyca Russell. *The Bahá'í Faith: Dawn of a New Day.* New York: Hawthorn Books, Inc., 1967. 223 pp. Index.

Surveys the development of the Bahá'í faith and its major prophets, beliefs, and laws and obligations. Discussion of observance of the Nineteen-Day Feast, New Year, and the Ridvan Festival.

Glassé, Cyril. *The Concise Encyclopedia of Islam.* Introduction by Huston Smith. San Francisco, CA: Harper & Row, 1989. 472 pp. Illustrated. Maps. Appendixes. Bibliography.

Over 1,100 entries cover people, places, texts, beliefs, rituals, festivals, and practices associated with the Islamic faith and its branches. Appendixes include historical synopsis of the Islamic world, maps of Mecca and description of the Hajj, schematic representation of branches of Islam, genealogical tables, and chronology.

Goldblatt, Joe Jeff. *Special Events: The Art and Science of Celebration.* Foreword by Linda Faulkner, Social Secretary to the White House during the Reagan Administration. New York: Van Nostrand Reinhold, 1990. 386 pp. Illustrated. Appendixes. References. Glossary. Index.

Guide to the special events industry, including social, retail, corporate and government events, meetings, and conventions. Provides techniques for budgeting, planning, and creating events such as theme parties, awards ceremonies, holidays, fairs, festivals, sporting events, and more. Appendix lists related books and organizations, and reprints the Flag Code.

Goldin, Hyman E. *A Treasury of Jewish Holidays: History, Legends, Traditions.* New York: Twayne Publishers, 1952. 308 pp. Illustrated. Index.

Examines Jewish festivals, explaining their meanings, describing customs and traditional beliefs associated with them, and telling the stories of their historical origins. Calendar of Jewish festivals from 1951 to 1971.

Green, Victor J. *Festivals and Saints Days: A Calendar of Festivals for School and Home.* Poole, Dorset, England: Blandford Press Ltd., 1978. 161 pp. Index.

Beginning with New Year's Day and following the calendar, the book covers over 30 secular, Christian, Jewish, Hindu and Muslim holidays observed in Britain. Also includes Independence Day and Thanksgiving in the United States. Further reading list.

Greif, Martin. *The Holiday Book: America's Festivals and Celebrations.* New York: The Main Street Press, 1978. 255 pp. Illustrated. Bibliography.

Lengthy entries cover, in chronological order, traditions, customs, and poetry associated with twenty major patriotic, religious, and commemorative holidays observed in the United States. Shorter entries discuss background and observance of twenty more special days.

Gupte, Rai Bahadur B.A. *Hindu Holidays and Ceremonials with Dissertations on Origin, Folklore and Symbols.* Calcutta and Simla: Thacker, Spink & Co., 1919. 285 pp. Illustrated.

The main text contains dictionary-style entries on Hindu festivals, days and places of worship and ceremony, and mythological and historical persons along with constellations associated with them. Brief glossary precedes main text with entries on animals and plants with folkloric significance.

Gutiérrez, Ramón, and Geneviève Fabre, eds. *Feasts and Celebrations in North American Ethnic Communities.* Albuquerque, NM: University of New Mexico Press, 1995. 200 pp.

Twelve essays analyze practices surrounding such events as funerals, holidays such as Halloween and Easter, folk festivals, and harvest rites among African Americans, Hispanics, Filipinos, West Indians, urban and rural Americans and gays throughout North and South America.

Gwynne, Rev. Walker. *The Christian Year: Its Purpose and Its History.* 1917. Reprinted by Omnigraphics, Inc., 1990. 143 pp. Appendix. Index.

Beginning chapters address the purpose and development of the Christian liturgical year. Discussion of Jewish holidays, as well as early Christians' observance of Jewish feasts and transformation of these into Christian feasts. Church calendar is explained, along with technical terms associated with it. History and description of observances of holidays and saints' days. Appendix includes liturgical colors and questions for review or examination.

Hacohen, Devorah, and Menahem Hacohen. *One People; The Story of the Eastern Jews: Twenty Centuries of Jewish Life in North Africa, Asia and Southeastern Europe.* Introduction by Yigal Allon. Translated by Israel I. Taslitt. New York: Sabra Books, 1969. Illustrated. 195 pp. Glossary. Bibliography.

Discusses history, folklore, beliefs and customs, ceremonies, and observance of holidays among Jews in Iraq and Kurdistan, Persia, the Caucasus, Bukhara, Morocco, Algeria, Tunisia and Jreba, Libya, Cyrenaica, Egypt, Syria, Yemen, Hadramaut, Aden, Turkey, Salonika, Bulgaria, and India.

Hamilton, Mary. *Greek Saints and Their Festivals.* Edinburgh and London: William Blackwood and Sons, 1910. 211 pp. Index.

Describes the observance of saints' days and other religious, as well as a few secular, holidays as celebrated in Greece, by the Greek Orthodox Church, and in Italy, Sicily, and Sardinia.

Hammerton, J.A., ed. *Manners and Customs of Mankind: An Entirely New Pictorial Work of Great Educational Value Describing the Most Fascinating Side of Human Life.* 4 vols. London: The Amalgamated Press, Ltd.; New York: Wm. H. Wise & Co., 193?. 1356 pp. Illustrated. Indexes.

Essays cover such topics as Animal Dances of the East, Midsummer Beliefs and Practices, and Food Taboos and Their Meaning, and are presented in no evident order. Subject headings under which essays are grouped are: Agricultural Customs; Children and the Young; Costume, Special Customs; The Dance; Death and the Disposal of the Dead; Education, Customs in; Etiquette and Conventions; The Family; Fetish and Fetish Worship; Folk Lore; Food and Food Gathering; Games and Amusement; Habitations; Law and Justice; Local Customs; Magic, Primitive; Marriage; Medicine and Treatment of the Sick; Miscellaneous; Music; Nature Lore and Superstitions; Naval and Sea Customs; Personal Adornment; Racial Manners; Religion and Religious Customs; Seasonal Customs; Sex Customs; Sport; Springtide; Summer; Taboo; War and Military Customs; and Witch Doctors and Witchcraft. Classified Index to Chapter Titles. General Index (including illustrations).

Hanawalt, Barbara A., and Kathryn L. Reyerson, eds. *City and Spectacle in Medieval Europe.* Minneapolis: University of Minnesota Press, 1994. 331 pp. Index.

Twelve papers from a conference at the University of Minnesota in 1991 explore various kinds of ritual and ceremony observed in medieval Europe, including liturgical rites in France, Holy Thursday in Spain, Midsummer in London, accounts of several festivals in medieval Castile, and more.

Handelman, Don. *Models and Mirrors: Towards an Anthropology of Public Events.* Cambridge: Cambridge University Press, 1990. Figures. Notes. Bibliography. Index.

Analyses of such festivals as the Palio of Siena, Christmas mumming in Newfoundland, observance of Jewish and state holidays in Israel and in Israeli kindergartens, and kachina dancers as well as other forms of public ritual play.

Hazeltine, Alice Isabel, and Elva Sophronia Smith, eds. *The Easter Book of Legends and Stories.* Illustrated by Pamela Bianco. 1947. Reprinted by Omnigraphics, Inc., 1992. 392 pp. Notes. Indexes.

Compilation of literature relating to Easter including biblical narrative, poems, plays, legends, and stories by such authors as Robert Frost, Emily Dickinson, A.E. Houseman, and others. Indexes of authors and titles.

Heinberg, Richard. *Celebrate the Solstice: Honoring the Earth's Seasonal Rhythms Through Festival and Ceremony.* Foreword by Dolores LaChapelle. Wheaton, IL: Quest Books, The Theosophical Publishing House, 1993. 199 pp. Illustrated. Notes. Bibliography. Index.

Discusses the celebration of winter and summer solstices and world renewal rites and myths throughout history around the world. Suggests activities for contemporary observance.

Helfman, Elizabeth S. *Celebrating Nature: Rites and Ceremonies Around the World.* Illustrated by Carolyn Cather. New York: The Seabury Press, 1969. 165 pp. Index.

Describes for young readers celebrations associated with the seasons from ancient times among Egyptians, Hebrews, Babylonians, Greeks, Romans, Ashanti, Yoruba, Ga, and Kikuyu peoples in Africa, New Guinea peoples, Thai people, Chinese, Japanese, Hindus, Saora people, Muslims, Incas, Mapuche Indians, Aztecs, and North American Indians, as well as observance of Christian holidays throughout the world. Pronunciation guide. Further reading list.

Hill, Errol. *The Trinidad Carnival: Mandate for a National Theatre.* Austin and London: University of Texas Press, 1972. 139 pp. Illustrations. Appendixes. Bibliography. Index.

Historical survey of Trinidad and the Carnival, calypso, and masquerades, including descriptions of observance from the 19th century. Argues that elements of the Carnival and its related traditions should be harnessed toward producing a national theater. Appendixes provide an example of calypso drama as well as a list of fifty renowned calypsos.

Hill, Kathleen Thompson. *Festivals U.S.A.* Foreword by Willard Scott. New York: John Wiley & Sons, Inc., 1988. 242 pp. Glossary. Index.

More than 1,000 art, drama, ethnic, music, food, and promotional festivals held in the United States. Organized by geographic region, then state. Estimated annual attendance provided for some entries. Information on event's date and location, foods served, admission price, accommodations, restaurants, and contact information provided within the entries, when known.

Hinnells, John R., ed. *The Penguin Dictionary of Religions.* Harmondsworth, Middlesex, England: Penguin Books, 1984. 550 pp. Maps. Bibliography. Indexes.

Over 1,000 entries contributed by 29 scholars cover deities, beliefs, people, places, texts, institutions, practices, rituals, and festivals associated with the world's religions, past and present. List of contents by subject area and contributer. Maps of Europe, ancient Near East and west Asia, Africa, the Indian Sub-Continent, Southeast Asia, Japan, China, Southwest Pacific and Australasia, North America, Mesoamerica, and Latin America. Substantial bibliography by subject area, cross-referenced with the entries. Synoptic index. General index.

Hobbie, Margaret, comp. *Italian American Material Culture: A Directory of Collections, Sites, and Festivals in the United States and Canada.* Westport, CT: Greenwood Press, 1992. 173 pp. Bibliography. Indexes.

Lists nearly 100 museum collections related to Italian American culture, over forty sites around the U.S. significant in Italian American history, and more than 100 religious, folk, agricultural, art, music, food, and commemorative festivals associated with Italian American material culture. Festival entries provide information on event's location, sponsor address and phone number, dates observed, estimated annual attendance and date first observed, and brief description of festival activities. Sponsor name index. Subject index.

Hodous, Lewis. *Folkways in China.* London: Arthur Probsthain, 1929. 248 pp. Illustrated. Bibliography. Index.

Author relates his travels to more than twenty festivals in China, covering history, lore, superstitions, customs, and foods. List of Chinese names.

Hole, Christina. *Christmas and Its Customs: A Brief Study.* Illustrated by T. Every-Clayton. New York: M. Barrows and Company, Inc., 1957. 95 pp. Bibliography. Index.

Discusses origins of the holiday, as well as garlands, gift-giving, carols, food, and legends and superstitions. Also covers Twelfth Night and the New Year.

————. *English Custom & Usage.* 1941-2. Reprinted by Omnigraphics, Inc., Detroit, 1990. 152 pp. Illustrated. Index.

Discusses the celebration of various holidays in England and examines the transformation of pre-Christian observances and rituals into Christian holy days.

Holweck, Frederick George. *A Biographical Dictionary of the Saints, with a General Introduction on Hagiology.* 1924. Reprinted by Omnigraphics, Inc., 1990. 1053 pp.

Covers thousands of saints—all those venerated in any Christian church, including those not officially canonized but with popular cult following. Brief bibliographical notices.

Hone, William. *The Every-Day Book; or, Everlasting Calendar of Popular Amusements, Sports, Pastimes, Ceremonies, Manners, Customs, and Events, Incident to Each of the Three Hundred and Sixty-Five Days, in Past and Present Times; Forming a Complete History of the Year, Months, & Seasons, and a Perpetual Key to the Almanack; Including Accounts of the Weather, Rules for Health and Conduct, Remarkable and Important Anecdotes, Facts, and Notices, in Chronology, Antiquities, Topography, Biography, Natural History, Art, Science, and General Literature; Derived from the Most Authentic Sources, and Valuable Original Communications, with Poetical Elucidations, for Daily Use and Diversion.* Introduction by Leslie Shepard. 2 vols. 1827. Reprinted by Omnigraphics, 1967. Vol 1., 1720 pp.; vol. 2, 1711 pp. Illustrated. Indexes.

Each volume presents a different collection of miscellany on holy days, festivals, and anniversaries from January 1 through December 31. Indexes of general subjects, Romish saints, poetry, flowers and plants, and engravings are found in both volumes. Bibliography of works by William Hone.

Hopkins, Lee Bennett, and Misha Arenstein. *Do You Know What Day Tomorrow Is? A Teacher's Almanac.* New York: Citation Press, 1975. Appendixes.

Guide intended to integrate chronologically presented information about people, places, and events with elementary-school curriculum. Each month contains brief explanation of its name and its flower and birthstone, representative poem, and descriptive listings in chronological order of events in history, anniversaries associated with notable people, holidays, admission days, and other events that occur on each day of the year. Appendixes include a reference bibliography for teachers and list of sources cited.

Hottes, Alfred Carl. *1001 Christmas Facts and Fancies.* 1946. Reprinted by Omnigraphics, Inc., 1990. 308 pp. Illustrated.

Facts and fancies, stories and legends gathered from author's personal experiences and obscure literature.

Howard, Alexander. *Endless Cavalcade: A Diary of British Festivals and Customs.* London: Arthur Barker Limited, 1964. 300 pp. Illustrations. Bibliography. Index.

Arranged in chronological order, over 360 entries describe at least one holiday, festival, civic event or custom for every day of the year, as observed in Britain.

Humphrey, Grace. *Stories of the World's Holidays.* 1924. Reprinted by Omnigraphics, Inc., 1990. 335 pp. Index.

Twenty stories for young readers describing the origins of commemorated historical events in the United States, England, France, Italy, China, Japan, Poland, Ireland, Czechoslovakia, and South America, arranged in chronological order. Suggested reading list.

Ickis, Marguerite. *The Book of Religious Holidays and Celebrations.* With drawings by Richard E. Howard. New York: Dodd, Mead & Company, 1966. 161 pp.

Covers Jewish holidays, Christian holidays, the New Year in the United States, Europe, Japan, China, India, Africa, and the Middle East. Includes legends, food, music, songs, prayers, symbols and emblems, and examples of programs and pageants. Discussion of plant lore. Further reading list.

Irwin, Keith Gordon. *The 365 Days.* Illustrated by Guy Fleming. New York: Thomas Y. Crowell Company, 1963. 182 pp. Maps. Index.

Discusses solar, lunar, and astronomical cycles, ancient calendars of Egypt, Babylon, Chaldea, Rome, and the Mayas. Traces origins and development from the Julian to the Gregorian calendars. Note on various calendars proposed in recent history. Section on dating the observance of Easter and Christmas. Discussion of carbon-dating and tree rings.

James, E.O. *Seasonal Feasts and Festivals.* 1961. Reprinted by Omnigraphics, Inc., 1993. 336 pp. Bibliography. Index.

Covers more than 100 season-based rituals, dances, plays, and festivals of the Palaeolithic era, vegetation cults, Egypt, Mesopotamia, Palestine, Hebrews, Asia Minor and Greece, Rome, Christianity, and medieval to eighteenth-century Europe. Examines Egyptian, Babylonian, Greek, Roman, Julian, and Christian calendars.

Janvier, Thomas A. *The Christmas Kalends of Provence.* 1902. Reprinted by Omnigraphics, Inc., 1990. 262 pp. Illustrated.

Relates tales about rites and celebrations of ancient feasts and festivals practiced in France.

Johnson, Margaret M. *Festival Europe! Fairs & Celebrations throughout Europe.* Memphis, TN: Mustang Publishing Co., 1992. 236 pp. Maps.

Tourist-oriented guide organized by region. Entries of over 700 festivals in 21 countries are in chronological order, from May to October. Includes descriptions of types of events held in each country. Addresses of tourist boards are provided.

Jones, T. Gwynn. *Welsh Folklore and Folk-Custom.* 1930. Reprinted by Suffolk: D.S. Brewer, 1979. 255 pp. Bibliography. Glossary. Index.

Collection of Welsh folklore regarding gods, ghosts, fairies, monsters, caves, lakes, magic, marriage, birth, and death. Recounting of some folk tales. Chapters 9-10 deal with customs concerning such holidays as May Day, Midsummer, Christmas, New Year's, Easter, Mari Lwyd, and others.

Kapoor, Sukhbir Singh. *Sikh Festivals.* Holidays and Festivals Series. Vero Beach, FL: Rourke Enterprises, Inc., 1989. 48 pp. Illustrated. Glossary. Index.

Background for young readers on Sikh religious beliefs, history, and ceremonies and festivals. Chronological table of holidays by Hindu month. List of Sikh gurus. Further reading list.

Kightly, Charles. *The Customs and Ceremonies of Britain: An Encyclopaedia of Living Traditions.* London: Thames & Hudson Ltd., 1986. 248 pp. Illustrated. Bibliography.

Book opens with a Calendar of Customs, listing events and holidays in chronological order. Next, in alphabetical order, more than 200 entries describe the observance and historical background of religious holidays, secular festivals, and other elements of social life. Practices associated with other types of events are discussed under such general headings as ''Bells and Bellringing Customs,'' ''Birth,'' ''Civic Customs,'' ''Coronations,'' ''Fairs,'' and ''Harvest Customs.'' Regional listing of events.

Kincade, Kathy, and Carl Landau. *Festivals of New England: Your Guided Tour to the Festivals of Connecticut, Maine, Massachusetts, New Hampshire, Rhode Island, and Vermont.* San Francisco: Landau Communications, 1990. 218 pp. Illustrated.

Covers more than 200 agricultural, ethnic, food and wine, marine, music, historical, art, and community festivals in New England in chronological order. List of festivals by state and by type of festival.

King, Noel Q. *Religions of Africa: A Pilgrimage Into Traditional Religions.* New York: Harper & Row, Publishers, 1970. 116 pp. Glossary. Index.

Discusses Ashanti, Yoruba, and others' religious festivals, ceremonies, and customs, such as the Egungun Festival and ceremonies for Yoruba deities, as well as birth, initiation, marriage, and death customs among various African ethnic groups. Notes on pronunciation. Good further reading list, including many works in English.

Krythe, Maymie R. *All About American Holidays.* New York: Harper & Row, 1962. 275 pp. Bibliography. Index.

Surveys historical background and contemporary observance of 51 religious days (Christian and Jewish), secular holidays, and patriotic anniversaries celebrated in the United States.

——. *All About the Months*. New York: Harper & Row, Publishers, 1966. 222 pp. Bibliography. Index.

Discussion, in chronological order, of how each month was named, anniversaries occurring within each month, lore and literature associated with the month, mention of ancient holidays and festivals, and each month's gem and flower.

Latsch, Marie-Luise. *Chinese Traditional Festivals*. New World Press, 1984. 107 pp.

Discusses seven major Chinese festivals and their changing significance through history. Festivals covered are New Year Lantern Festival, Pure Brightness Festival (Qing Ming), Dragon Boat Festival, Mid-Autumn Festival, Honoring the Kitchen God, and the Lunar New Year's Eve.

Lawson, E. Thomas. *Religions of Africa: Traditions in Transformation*. Religious Traditions of the World Series. San Francisco: Harper & Row, 1984. 106 pp. Illustrated. Glossary. Notes.

Surveys history and religious traditions of the Zulu and Yoruba peoples. Covers customs, legends, and ceremonies associated with birth, puberty, marriage, and death. Festivals described include Zulu/Shembe Festival, New Year's, and the New Yam Festival. Further reading list.

Levine, Donald N. *Wax & Gold: Tradition and Innovation in Ethiopian Culture*. Chicago and London: The University of Chicago Press, 1965. 315 pp. Illustrations. Maps. Glossary. Index.

Social scientist examines history, traditions, lifestyles, literature, art, and religion of Amhara people in Ethiopia. Festivals discussed include Meskel (Exaltation of the Cross), St. Michael's Day and other saints' days, Christmas, and Timqat (Epiphany).

Long, George. *The Folklore Calendar*. 1930. Reprinted by Omnigraphics, Inc., 1990. 240 pp. Illustrations. Index.

Arranged in chronological order, entries provide historical background for, and cover observance of, over forty holidays, festivals, ceremonies, and other events in Great Britain.

Long, Kim. *The Almanac of Anniversaries*. Santa Barbara, CA: ABC-CLIO, 1992. 270 pp. Bibliography. Index.

Timeline-like structure provides 25th, 50th, ... 500th anniversaries relating to notable events and people that will take place between 1993 and 2001. Within each year, anniversaries are given chronologically. Calendar Locator chart provides cross-reference of years and milestones.

Lord, Priscilla Sawyer, and Daniel J. Foley. *Easter the World Over*. Philadelphia: Chilton Book Company, 1971. 289 pp. Illustrated. Bibliography. Index.

Discusses origins of, and traditions, practices, rhymes, songs and music, fine arts, and food associated with, Easter, Holy Week, and Carnival or Mardi Gras in the Middle East, United States, Europe, Bermuda, the Caribbean, and South and Central America. Also covers the spring festivals of Ching-ming in China and Setsubun in Japan.

MacAloon, John J. ed., *Rite, Drama, Festival, Spectacle: Rehearsals Toward a Theory of Cultural Performance*. Philadelphia: Institute for the Study of Human Issues, Inc., 1984. 280 pp. Notes.

Papers from ten scholars in the humanities delivered at the 76th Burg Wartenstein Symposium, sponsored by the Wenner-Gren Foundation for Anthropological Research. Academic essays concerned with various cultural and performative implications of festival and ritual in literature and in actuality: "Liminiality and the Performative Genres," Victor Turner; "Charivari, Honor, and the Community in Seventeenth-Century Lyon and Geneva," Natalie Zemon Davis; "'Rough Music' in The Duchess of Malfi: Webster's Dance of Madmen and Charivari Tradition," Frank W. Wadsworth; "Borges's 'Immortal': Metaritual, Metaliturature, Metaperformance," Sophia S. Morgan; "Arrange Me into Disorder: Fragments and Reflections on Ritual Clowning," Barbara A. Babcock; "The Diviner and the Detective," Hilda Kuper; "A Death in Due Time: Construction of Self and Culture in Ritual Drama," Barbara G. Myerhoff; "The Ritual Process and the Problem of Reflexivity in Sinhalese Demon Exorcisms," Bruce Kapferer; "Carnival in Multiple Planes," Roberto Da Matta; and "Olympic Games and the Theory of Spectacle in Modern Societies," John J. MacAloon.

Madden, Daniel M. *A Religious Guide to Europe*. New York: Macmillan Publishing Co., Inc., 1975. 529 pp. Index.

Describes making pilgrimages to hundreds of shrines, sanctuaries, and other holy places in over 15 European countries, from Ireland to Turkey. Travel and accommodation information, as well as descriptions of secular points of interest are provided.

Marcus, Rebecca B., and Judith Marcus. *Fiesta Time in Mexico*. Champaign, IL: Garrard Publishing Company, 1974. 95 pp. Index.

Intended for young readers, describes the following holidays and festivals observed in Mexico: Day of the Dead, Our Lady of Guadalupe, Christmas, New Year's, Day of the Three Kings, St. Anthony the Abbot's Day, Holy Week and Easter, St. John's Day, Mexican Independence Day, Fifth of May, and the Twentieth of November. Pronunciation guide.

Martin, Pat, comp. *Czechoslovak Culture: Recipes, History and Folk Arts*. Iowa City, IA: Penfield Press, 1989. 176 pp. Illustrated.

Focus is on Czech-American culture, including traditions and stories carried over from Czechoslovakia. Essays on pioneer experiences, observance of holidays, including lengthy treatment of decorating Easter eggs, folk art, foods and recipes. Profiles of famous Czechs and Czech-Americans. A partial list of Czech festivals throughout the United States and tips on planning Czech festivals.

Megas, George A. *Greek Calendar Customs*. Athens: Press and Information Department, 1958. 159 pp. Illustrated.

Covers customs, beliefs, legends, food, and songs associated with over sixty saints' days, holidays, festivals, and agricultural activity in Greece (especially rural traditions), according to the seasons of the year.

Miles, Clement A. *Christmas in Ritual and Tradition; Christian and Pagan.* 1912. Reprinted by Omnigraphics, 1968. Illustrated. Notes. Bibliography. Index.

Part I deals with the Christian observance, examining Latin and European hymns and poetry, liturgy, popular customs, and dramas, pageants, and plays. Part II covers pre-Christian winter festivals and their surviving customs. Includes discussion of the Christmas tree, gifts, cards, and mumming, as well as over twenty saints' days and other holidays and festivals observed throughout the year in Europe.

Miller, Daniel, ed. *Unwrapping Christmas.* Oxford: Clarendon Press, 1993. 239 pp. Index.

Ten anthropological essays by scholars in various academic fields on the contemporary, and international, observance and meaning of Christmas: "A Theory of Christmas" and "Christmas against Materialism in Thailand," Daniel Miller; "Father Christmas Executed," Claude Lévi-Strauss; "The Rituals of Christmas Giving," James Carrier; "Materialism and the Making of the Modern American Christmas," Russell Belk; "Cinderella Christmas: Kitsch, Consumerism, and Youth in Japan," Brian Moeran and Lise Skov; "The English Christmas and the Family: Time out and Alternative Realities," Adam Kuper; "Christmas Cards and the Construction of Social Relations in Britain Today," Mary Searle-Chatterjee; "Christmas Present: Christmas Public," Barbara Bodenhorn; and "The Great Christmas Quarrel and Other Swedish Traditions," Orvar Löfgren.

Milne, Jean. *Fiesta Time in Latin America.* Los Angeles: The Ward Ritchie Press, 1965. 236 pp.

Organized chronologically, discusses over 80 festivals celebrated in Mexico, Central and South America. Concludes with list of festivals by country.

Mitter, Swasti. *Hindu Festivals.* Holidays and Festivals Series. Vero Beach, FL: Rourke Enterprises, Inc., 1989. 48 pp. Illustrated. Glossary. Index.

Background for young readers on Hindu beliefs, history, and festivals in and outside India. Note on the Hindu calendar and chronological table of Hindu holidays by month.

Monks, James L. *Great Catholic Festivals.* Great Religious Festivals series. New York: Henry Schuman, 1951. 110 pp. Illustrated. Index.

Discusses origins and Catholic observance of Christmas, Epiphany, Easter, Pentecost, Corpus Christi, and Assumption.

More Festivals in Asia. Asian Copublication Programme Series Two. Sponsored by the Asian Cultural Centre for Unesco. Tokyo, New York and San Francisco: Kodansha International Ltd., 1975. 66 pp. Illustrated.

For young readers. Describes, in chronological order, Tano Day in Korea, Eid-ul-Fitr in Pakistan, Lebaran in Indonesia, Hari Raya Puasa in Malaysia, Mid-Autumn Festival in Vietnam, Dasain in Nepal, Diwali Festival of Lights in India, Loy Krathong in Thailand, and the Buzkashi Game in Afghanistan, often through storytelling.

Mossman, Jennifer, ed. *Holidays and Anniversaries of the World.* Second edition. Detroit: Gale Research Inc., 1990. 1,080 pp. Glossary. Index.

Lists 23,000 brief entries on secular, religious, and historic holidays and special observances, and anniversaries of notable people and occurrences in chronological order. Perpetual calendar covers the years 1753-2100.

Murphy, Joseph M. *Santería: African Spirits in America.* Boston: Beacon Press, 1988. 189 pp. Notes. Glossary. References. Index.

Traces origins and presents beliefs, rituals, ceremonies, songs, gestures, foods, and herbs associated with the practice of the Santeria ("the way of the saints") religion, an Afro-Cuban outgrowth of the Yoruba religion in Nigeria, as observed by African Americans in New York.

————. *Working the Spirit: Ceremonies of the African Diaspora.* Boston: Beacon Press, 1994. 263 pp. Notes. Glossary. Bibliography. Index.

Describes history, significance, and performance of religious ceremonies, practices, music, and dances observed through vodou in Haiti, candomblé in Brazil, santería in Cuba and among Cuban-Americans, Revival Zion in Jamaica, and "the Black Church" in the United States, in attempt to show how all are connected to a common spiritual foundation.

Myers, Robert J., with the editors of Hallmark Cards. *Celebrations: The Complete Book of American Holidays.* Illustrations by Bill Greer. Garden City, NY: Doubleday & Company, Inc., 1972. 386 pp. Selected bibliography. Index.

Covers origins and observance of 45 religious, ethnic, and patriotic holidays in the United States, including dates of first observance, and summarizes another 14.

Nickerson, Betty. *Celebrate the Sun: A Heritage of Festivals Interpreted through the Art of Children from Many Lands.* Philadelphia/New York: J.B. Lippincott Company, 1969. 128 pp. Illustrated. Bibliography. Index.

Covers more than thirty holidays worldwide, as well as provides descriptions of such events as spring festivals, weddings, parades, processions, fairs, circuses, and side shows—all accompanied by over forty paintings by children around the world.

Olcott, Frances Jenkins. *Good Stories for Anniversaries.* Illustrated by Hattie Longstreet Price. 1937. Reprinted by Omnigraphics, Inc., 1990. 237 pp. Index.

Over 120 stories for children relating to holidays and events in the history of the United States, such as Inauguration Day, Bunker Hill Day, and pioneer days. Arranged chronologically by the school year.

O'Neil, W.M. *Time and the Calendars.* Sydney: Sydney University Press, 1975. 138 pp. Appendix. Bibliography. Index.

Examines Egyptian, Roman, Babylonian, Indian, Chinese, Meso-American, and Gregorian calendars, and the day, week, month, and year. Appendix gives names of the days in various languages.

Owen, Trefor M. *A Pocket Guide: The Customs and Traditions of Wales.* Cardiff: University of Wales Press, 1991. 136 pp. Illustrated. Notes. Index.

Discusses agricultural traditions, customs associated with the home and domestic life, Mari

Lwyd, St. Thomas's Day, Twelfth Night, Candlemas, St. David's Day, religious and communal observances and events, and eisteddfod from the nineteenth century to the present day. Historical survey of the study of folk customs in Wales. Selected reading list by chapter.

Ozouf, Mona. *Festivals and the French Revolution.* Translated by Alan Sheridan. Cambridge, MA: Harvard University Press, 1988. 378 pp. Notes. Bibliography. Index.

Historian examines the Revolutionary festivals observed between 1789 and 1799, and their role in the French Revolution. Discussion of Revolutionary calendar. Brief chronology of the Revolution.

Parise, Frank, ed. *The Book of Calendars.* New York: Facts on File, Inc., 1982. 387 pp. Index.

Summarizes the history and organization of the Babylonian, Macedonian, Hebrew, Seleucid, Olympiad, Roman, Armenian, Islamic, Fasli, Zoroastrian, Yezdezred, Jelali, Egyptian, Coptic, Ethiopian, Iranian, Afghanistan, Akbar, Fasli Deccan, Parasuram, Burmese and Arakanse, Chinese, Tibetan, Mayan, Julian, Gregorian, and Christian eras and calendars. Tables throughout convert the various ancient and multinational calendars to Julian or Gregorian dates or years. Dates of Easter provided from the year 1 through 1999. Calendar of Christian saints. Explanations of the French Revolutionary calendar and the Soviet calendar. Table depicts dates various regions in Europe celebrated New Year's Day.

Parke, H.W. *Festivals of the Athenians.* Ithaca, NY: Cornell University Press, 1977. 208 pp. Illustrated. Notes. Bibliography. Index.

Surveys, in order of Athenian month, religious festivals and ceremonies observed in ancient Athens. Explanation of the calendar. Calendar table of Athenian festivals. Map of Athens showing principal sanctuaries.

Parrinder, Geoffrey. *A Dictionary of Non-Christian Religions.* Philadelphia: The Westminster Press, 1971. 320 pp. Illustrated.

More than 2,400 entries provide A to Z coverage of people, deities, rites, locations, festivals, texts, philosophies, etc., associated with ancient and living non-Christian religions, including various African religions, Aztec, Bahá'í, Buddhism, Confucianism, Hinduism, Islam, Jainism, Judaism, Maori religion, Native American religions, Shinto, Sikhism, Taoism, Theosophy, Yoruba, Zoroastrianism, religions of ancient Rome, Greece, Babylon, Celts, Egypt, Inca, Maya, Scandinavia, and others. Cross-referencing. Lists of Egyptian, Chinese, and Islamic dates and dynasties. Further reading list.

Parry, Caroline. *Let's Celebrate! Canada's Special Days.* Toronto: Kids Can Press Ltd., 1987. 256 pp. Illustrated. Index.

For young readers. Entries cover more than 250 secular and religious holidays and festivals celebrated in Canada, including Muslim, Hindu, Chinese, Jewish, Bahá'í, Sikh, Jain, Buddhist, and Christian holy days. Entries are organized by season of the year and, in addition to discussion of the holiday's background, include riddles, games, poems, crafts, and other activities. Explanation of the calendar, as well as sidebars providing brief background notes on various religious and ethnic groups.

Patten, Helen Philbrook. *The Year's Festivals*. Boston: Dana Estes & Company, 1903. 270 pp. Illustrated.

One chapter each covers New Year's Day, Twelfth Night, St. Valentine's Day, All Fool's Day, Easter, May Day, Halloween, Thanksgiving, and Christmas. Discussion includes the general historical nature of observance, including customs, poems, songs, legends, often as represented in works of literature.

Perl, Lila. *Foods and Festivals of the Danube Lands: Germany, Austria, Czechoslovakia, Hungary, Yugoslavia, Bulgaria, Romania, Russia*. Illustrated by Leo Glueckselig. Cleveland, OH: The World Publishing Company, 1969. 287 pp. Index.

Discusses foods, festivals, and traditions in countries bordering the Danube River. Provides historical overview on the region and on each country's people and lifestyles, often stretching back to prehistoric times. Heavy coverage of foods prepared and consumed in each country, including recipes.

Pieper, Josef. *In Tune with the World: A Theory of Festivity*. Translated by Richard and Clara Winston. New York: Harcourt, Brace & World, Inc., 1965. 81 pp.

Philosophical essay discusses what festivity means from a predominantly Western and Christian orientation. Includes consideration of festivity in relation to art, labor, and modern commercialization of history.

Pike, Royston. *Round the Year with the World's Religions*. 1950. Reprinted by Omnigraphics, Inc., 1993. 208 pp. Illustrated. Index.

Chronologically arranged chapters covering customs, legends, and stories behind religious observances in ancient Rome and Greece, Europe, India, Tibet, China, Japan, and Ceylon, and among ancient Romans, Greeks and Egyptians, Jews, Christians, Hindus, Jains, Muslims, Buddhists, Incans, and Aztecs.

Purdy, Susan. *Festivals for You to Celebrate*. Philadelphia and New York: Lippincott Company, 1969. 192 pp. Illustrated. Bibliography. Index.

Holiday-related craft projects for group or individual celebrations. Thirty festivals of various religions and locales are discussed; emphasis is on holidays observed in the United States, and their origins and counterparts elsewhere. Activities subject index.

Rockland, Mae Shafter. *The Jewish Party Book: A Contemporary Guide to Customs, Crafts, and Foods*. New York: Schocken Books, 1978. 264 pp. Illustrated. Appendix. Index.

Traditional customs, foods, and activities associated with birth, bar and bat mitzvah, marriage, reunions, housewarmings, and holidays. Appendix provides explanation of Jewish calendar and table of holiday dates from 1978 to 2000.

Rodgers, Edith Cooperrider. *Discussion of Holidays in the Later Middle Ages*. New York: Columbia University Press, 1940. Reprinted by AMS Press, 1967. 147 pp. Bibliography. Index.

Examines holy days observed (or not observed), the Church's position on feasts, rules of observance, and nature of actual observance of religious holidays between 1200 and the Reformation.

Rosenau, William. *Jewish Ceremonial Institutions.* 3rd and revised edition. 1925. Reprinted by Omnigraphics, Inc., 1992. 190 pp. Illustrated. Index.

Adapted from a series of lectures given by the author at the Oriental Seminary of the Johns Hopkins University in 1901. Origin and purpose of the synagogue and explanatory commentary on its worship services and customs. Discussion of the Jewish calendar and observance of holidays and festivals at home and at the synagogue. Practices associated with birth, marriage, bar and bat mitzvah, divorce, mourning, and related laws and practices.

Russ, Jennifer M. *German Festivals & Customs.* London: Oswald Wolff, 1982. 166 pp. Illustrated. Appendixes. Bibliography. Indexes.

Origins and observance of over fifty religious, historical, and food festivals, pageants, and social customs and ceremonies. Includes rhymes, food, legends, and songs associated with events. Appendix lists legal holidays in the Federal Republic of Germany. Subject index. Index of names and places.

Sandak, Cass R. *Patriotic Holidays.* New York: Crestwood House, 1990. 48 pp. Index.

Covers sixteen patriotic holidays in the United States, and a handful of others elsewhere, for young readers. Further reading list.

Sanders, Paula. *Ritual, Politics, and the City in Fatimid Cairo.* Albany: State University of New York Press, 1994. 231 pp. Maps. Notes. Bibliography. Index.

Examines court ritual practices, ceremonial processions, and such festivals as the New Year and Nawruz, Ramadan, and the Festival of Breaking the Fast in fourth- and fifth-century Cairo in terms of social and political culture.

Santino, Jack. *All Around the Year: Holidays and Celebrations in American Life.* Urbana and Chicago: University of Illinois Press, 1994. 227 pp. Notes. Bibliography. Index.

Discusses origins and meanings of holidays observed in the United States, and customs, ephemera, and symbols associated with them.

Schauffler, Robert, ed. *Christmas: Its Origin, Celebration and Significance as Related in Prose and Verse.* New Foreword by Tristram Potter Coffin. 1907. Reprinted by Omnigraphics, Inc., 1990. 354 pp. Index.

Collection of prose and poetry, hymns and carols divided into sections on origins, celebration, and the significance and spirit of Christmas.

————, ed. *Memorial Day; Its Celebration, Spirit, and Significance as Related in Prose and Verse, with a Non-sectional Anthology of the Civil War.* 1940. Reprinted by Omnigraphics, Inc., 1990. 339 pp. Index.

Compilation of 140 stories and poems relating the significance of Memorial Day in the United States.

———, ed. *Mother's Day; Its History, Origin, Celebration, Spirit, and Significance as Related in Prose and Verse.* 1927. Reprinted by Omnigraphics, Inc., 1990. 380 pp. Index.

Collection of poetry and stories about mother-worship in pagan times, mother-love antedating Christianity, and some of the ancient customs and rites honoring mothers throughout the centuries. Suggestions for Mother's Day programs for school exercises also included.

Schaun, George and Virginia. *American Holidays and Special Days.* Illustrations by David Wisniewski. Lanham, MD: Maryland Historical Press, 1986. 194 pp. Bibliography. Index.

Alphabetical and chronological listings of holidays. List of dates states were admitted to the United States. Part I discusses the various calendars, names of the months and days of the week, movable days, and reasons for observance of special days. Part II consists of over sixty entries on holidays, festivals, and commemorative days observed in the United States in chronological order.

Schibsby, Marian, and Hanny Cohrsen. *Foreign Festival Customs.* Revised edition. New York: American Council for Nationalities Service, 1974. 74 pp.

Christmas, New Year's, and Easter customs, traditions, and recipes from over thirty immigrant groups to the United States. Discusses Thanksgiving and harvest traditions from Europe.

Sechrist, Elizabeth Hough. *Christmas Everywhere: A Book of Christmas Customs of Many Lands.* New revised and enlarged edition. Philadelphia: Macrae Smith Company, 1962. 186 pp. Illustrated.

For young readers. Stories and customs associated with Christmas in twenty locales around the world.

Secretariat, Bishops' Committee on the Liturgy, National Conference of Catholic Bishops [Gurrieri, John A.]. *Holy Days in the United States.* Washington, D.C.: United States Catholic Conference, 1984. 100 pp. Notes.

Description of history, meaning, and liturgical and popular observance of the six holy days of obligation, as well as saints' days, with discussion of American saints, and other special days, for Roman Catholics in the United States. Questions for discussion and suggested reading list conclude each chapter.

Sivananda, Sri Swami. *Hindu Fasts and Festivals.* India: The Yoga-Vedanta Forest Academy Press, 1983. 176 pp. Illustrated.

Explains religious significance and customs and observances of 27 popular Hindu festivals. Also discusses folklore surrounding eclipses and special days. Includes some Hindu prayers. Concludes with an essay on the "Philosophy of Idol Worship."

Snelling, John. *Buddhist Festivals.* Holidays and Festivals Series. Vero Beach, FL: Rourke Enterprises, Inc., 1987. 48 pp. Illustrated. Maps. Glossary. Index.

For young readers. Provides historical background on Buddha and discusses Buddhist festivals in Thailand, Sri Lanka, Tibet, and Japan, as well as brief notes on Buddhist observances in Asia, the United States, and Britain. Further reading list.

Speck, Frank G. *A Study of the Delaware Indian Big House Ceremony.* Dictated by Witapanóₓwe. Harrisburg: Pennsylvania Historical Commission, 1931. 192 pp. Illustrated. Appendixes. Bibliography. Index.

History and detailed explanation of the Big House Ceremony observed by the Delaware Indians, provided by Delaware Indian Witapanóₓwe to ethnologist Frank Speck. Witapanóₓwe's account is also transcribed in the Delaware language.

Spicer, Dorothy Gladys. *Folk Festivals and the Foreign Community.* 1923. Reprinted by Omnigraphics, Inc., Detroit, 1990. 152 pp. Bibliography.

Offers advice on administration and production gleaned from folk festivals organized during the 1920s that were attempts to bond recent immigrants with those born in the United States by fostering understanding and appreciation of cultural diversity.

———. *Yearbook of English Festivals.* 1954. Reprinted by Omnigraphics, Inc., 1993. 298 pp. Glossary. Map. Indexes.

Chronologically arranged descriptions of more than 200 English holidays, ceremonies, anniversaries, and local festivals and traditions. Map of England depicting regions and counties. Explanation of Julian and Gregorian calendars and their coexistence in parts of the country. List of movable Christian feasts dependent upon the date of Easter. List of liturgical colors, what they symbolize and when they are used. Table of dates of Easter for 1954 to 1984. Suggested reading list. Indexes by name of event, county, and region.

Spielgelman, Judith. *UNICEF's Festival Book.* Illustrated by Audrey Preissler. New York: U.S. Committee for UNICEF, 1966. 26 pp.

For young readers. Presents New Year in Ethiopia, Divali in India, Now-ruz in Iran, Hanukkah in Israel, Doll Festival in Japan, Posadas in Mexico, Sinterklaas in the Netherlands, end of Ramadan in Pakistan, Easter in Poland, Lucia Day in Sweden, Songkran in Thailand, and Halloween in Canada and the United States.

Spivack, Carol, and Richard A. Weinstock. *Best Festivals of North America: A Performing Arts Guide.* Third edition. Ventura, CA: Printwheel Press, 1989. Indexes.

Entries on over 150 classical music, chamber music, opera, dance, theater, film, jazz, folk music, bluegrass, ethnic, and children's festivals held in the United States, ordered by type of event, then state. Entries include information on points of interest, ticket prices, accommodations, and contact addresses and phone numbers. Index of festivals by name and state. Index of other attractions near festivals. Chronological Index by month.

Stepanchuk, Carol, and Charles Wong. *Mooncakes and Hungry Ghosts: Festivals of China.* San Francisco: China Books & Periodicals, 1991. 145 pp. Illustrated. Maps. Appendixes. Glossary. Notes. Bibliography.

Covers legends, history, foods, superstitions, poems, objects, and customs associated with such major Chinese holidays as New Year, Dragon Boat Festival, Mid-Autumn Festival, Clear

Brightness Festival, Feast of the Hungry Ghosts, Festival of the Cowherd and the Weaving Maiden, Tian Hou, Protectress of Seafarers, and Double Yang Day, as well as twelve holidays observed by national minorities in China. Appendix includes explanation of the Chinese calendar, listing of major festivals by the calendar, table of related symbols, notes on arranging food, pictorial glossary of symbols, Chinese character glossary, and chronology of dynasties.

Strassfeld, Michael. *The Jewish Holidays: A Guide and Commentary.* Illustrated by Betsy Platkin Teutsch. New York: Harper & Row, 1985. 248 pp. Index.

Each of eleven chapters deals with a holiday and its specific practices in depth. Appendixes on the Jewish calendar, laws pertaining to holidays, Torah reading list for the holidays, glossary of Hebrew blessings, glossary of Hebrew terms, and dates of holidays to the years 1999-2000.

Tannenbaum, Beulah, and Myra Stillman. *Understanding Time: The Science of Clocks and Calendars.* Illustrated by William D. Hayes. New York: Whittlesey House, 1958. 143 pp. Index.

Explanation for young readers of time and clocks, calendars, and other measuring systems used throughout history. Each chapter includes suggested experiments.

Thomas, P. *Hindu Religion, Customs and Manners, Describing the Customs and Manners, Religious, Social and Domestic Life, Arts and Sciences of the Hindus.* Second revised Indian edition. Bombay: D.B. Taraporevala Sons & Co., Ltd., 1948?. 161 pp. Illustrated. Glossary and Index.

Covers Hindu history and creation theories, the caste system, religious sects, beliefs and practices, philosophy, social and domestic life, superstitions, etiquette, dress and ornamentation, literature and languages, ceremonies, music, dance, the calendar and holidays, architecture, the fine arts, and courtship and love.

Thompson, E.P. *Customs in Common: Studies in Traditional Popular Culture.* New York: The New Press, 1993. 547 pp. Illustrated. Index.

Scholarly study of English working-class culture in the eighteenth and early nineteenth centuries. Includes examination of the historical contexts of such events as beating the bounds, the Horn Fair, and others.

Thornton, Willis. *Almanac for Americans.* 1941. Reprinted by Omnigraphics, 1973. 418 pp. Illustrated. Index.

A "Book of Days of the Republic," arranged chronologically, focuses on patriotic holidays and historical events in the United States.

Tiller, Veronica E., ed. *Discover Indian Reservations USA: A Visitors' Welcome Guide.* Foreword by Ben Nighthorse Campbell. Denver, CO: Council Publications, 1992. 402 pp. Illustrated. Maps. Appendixes. Index.

Travel-oriented information provided on more than 350 federal and state Indian reservations in 33 states, listed in alphabetical order by state. Entries include a brief profile on the reservation's land, population, and structure, its location and address, cultural institutes, special events (festivals, powwows, rodeos, etc.), businesses and organizations, accomodations, and special restrictions. Appendix I lists tribes alphabetically and gives their location. Appendix II is a powwow directory by state, then month.

Toor, Frances. *Festivals and Folkways of Italy.* New York: Crown Publishers, Inc., 1953. 312 pp. Illustrated. Appendix. Bibliography. Index.

Describes the author's observations of holidays, festivals and folk customs in Sicily, southern Italy and Sardinia, and Rome and its outskirts. Appendix includes notes on Italian festas, beliefs, folk arts, and folklore bibliography.

————. *A Treasury of Mexican Folkways: The Customs, Myths, Folklore, Traditions, Beliefs, Fiestas, Dances, and Songs of the Mexican People.* New York: Bonanza Books, 1985. 566 pp. Illustrated. Map. Notes. Bibliography. Glossary. Index.

Covers agricultural, religious, and folk festivals and ceremonies celebrated by the various peoples in Mexico, including dances, songs, folk arts, legends, riddles, and idiomatic expressions.

Trepp, Leo. *The Complete Book of Jewish Observance: A Practical Manual for the Modern Jew.* New York: Behrman House, Inc./Simon & Schuster, 1980. 370 pp. Illustrated. Index.

Covers Jewish prayers, practices, customs, and laws in addition to festivals and fasts.

Trimingham, J. Spencer. *Islam in West Africa.* London: Oxford University Press, 1959. 262 pp. Map. Appendixes. Glossary. Indexes.

Describes history, beliefs, practices, and observances of Muslim West Africans. Explanation of Islamic calendar, saints, social customs. Glossary-Index of Arabic and African terms. General index.

Tuleja, Tad. *Curious Customs: The Stories Behind 296 Popular American Rituals.* New York: Harmony Books, 1987. 210 pp. Bibliography.

Provides historical information and occasionally tongue-in-cheek observations on major American holidays as well as customs and superstitions surrounding various social activities including gestures, apparel, etiquette, eating, and mating.

Tun Li-Ch'en. *Annual Customs and Festivals in Peking.* Translated by Derk Bodde. Second edition (revised). Hong Kong University Press, 1965 (first edition, 1936). 147 pp. Illustrated. Bibliography. Appendixes. Index.

Originally written in 1900, this book describes over 100 annual events in Peking, arranged chronologically by Chinese month. Appendixes discuss the Chinese calendar and list units of measure, English equivalents of Chinese names, dynasties and emperors, and concordance of Chinese and Gregorian calendars from 1957-1984.

Turck, Mary. *Jewish Holidays.* New York: Crestwood House, 1990. 48 pp. Illustrated. Index.

Explanations for young readers of reasons for celebrating the holidays, ways in which they are observed, and food, blessings, and prayers associated with them. Brief further reading list.

Turner, Reuben. *Jewish Festivals.* Holidays and Festivals Series. Vero Beach, FL: Rourke Enterprises, Inc., 1987. 48 pp. Illustrated. Map. Glossary. Index.

Presents scriptural background for young readers on the Jewish feasts, along with customs and traditions, recipes and food, and activities associated with them. Sections explaining the Jewish calendar, including a calendar of festivals, and the Hebrew alphabet. Further reading list.

Turner, Victor, ed. *Celebration: Studies in Festivity and Ritual.* Washington D.C.: Smithsonian Institution Press, 1982. 318 pp. Illustrated.

This companion volume to the Smithsonian Institution's exhibition of celebratory objects is a collection of essays exploring such topics as objects used in festivals, celebrations as rites of passage, and political, economic and religious festivals. Events included within the discussions are Juneteenth, Penitentes, Trinidad Carnival, Incwala, Juggernaut, Dragon Boat Festival in China, Rama festivals in India, German-American Passion Plays in the United States, and more.

Von Grunebaum, Gustave E. *Muhammadan Festivals.* Introduction by C.E. Bosworth. New York: Olive Branch Press, 1988. 107 pp. Illustrated. Bibliographical notes and references. Index.

Provides historical background on Islam, as well as discussion of beliefs, prayers, saints, and worship services. Festivals covered are the pilgrimage to Mecca, Ramadan, Persian New Year, Mohammad's birthday, feasts of saints, and the death anniversary of Husain.

Walsh, Michael, ed. *Butler's Lives of the Saints.* Concise edition. Foreword by Cardinal Basil Hume. San Francisco: Harper & Row, Publishers, 1985. Index.

Abridgement of the four-volume *Lives of the Saints, or The Lives of the Fathers, Martyrs and other Principal Saints: Compiled from Original Monuments and other authentick records: Illustrated with the Remarks of judicious modern cricks and historians,* by Alban Butler, originally published in London between 1756 and 1759. The original contained nearly 1,500 entries. Later editions expanded to include 2,500. This edition provides biographical sketches and legends associated with one saint for each day of the year, in chronological order. List of patron saints.

Walsh, William S. *Curiosities of Popular Customs and of Rites, Ceremonies, Observances, and Miscellaneous Antiquities.* 1914. Reprinted by Omnigraphics, Inc., 1966. 1018 pp. Illustrated.

Dictionary-style coverage of Christian, Jewish, Islamic, Buddhist, Japanese, Chinese, Hindu, ancient, and secular holidays and feasts including entries on people, places, customs, and relics associated with them. Also contains entries on birthdays, the months, and various calendars.

————. *The Story of Santa Klaus: Told for Children of All Ages from Six to Sixty.* 1909. Reprinted by Omnigraphics, Inc., 1991. 231 pp. Illustrated.

Discusses the origin and development of the Klaus legend, mythological concepts absorbed by Christianity, the Three Kings, Twelfth Night customs, Father Christmas, and Christmas traditions and observances in various countries. Illustrations by artists of all times from Fra Angelico to Henry Hutt.

Ward, Barbara E., and Joan Law. *Chinese Festivals in Hong Kong*. The Guidebook Company, Ltd., 1993. 95 pp. Illustrated. Map. Glossary. Index.

Presents thirty Chinese festivals and ceremonies as they are observed in contemporary Hong Kong. Explanation of solar calendar and chart. Map of festival locations. Festival calendar, including table converting solar dates from 1992 to 2004.

Wasserman, Paul, ed. *Festivals Sourcebook: A Reference Guide to Fairs, Festivals and Celebrations in Agriculture, Antiques, The Arts, Theater and Drama, Arts and Crafts, Community, Dance, Ethnic Events, Film, Folk, Food and Drink, History, Indians, Marine, Music, Seasons, and Wildlife*. Detroit: Gale Research Company, 1977. 656 pp. Indexes.

More than 3,800 entries cover festive events in the United States and Canada. Organized by 18 subject areas, then alphabetically by state, entries list location, dates, contact name and/or address for more information, description of the event, and date event first occurred. Does not include widely celebrated holidays, such as the Fourth of July, or sports events, religious holidays, rodeos, county fairs, and beauty pageants. Chronological, Event Name, Geographic, and Subject Indexes.

Watson, Jane Werner. *A Parade of Soviet Holidays*. Illustrated by Ben Stahl. Champaign, IL: Garrard Publishing Company, 1974. 96 pp. Pronunciation guide. Index.

Aimed at a young audience, discussion of significance and celebration of more than twenty holidays and festivals, as well as other festive events, observed throughout the Soviet Union.

Webster, Hutton. *Rest Days; the Christian Sunday, the Jewish Sabbath, and Their Historical and Anthropological Prototypes*. 1916. Reprinted by Omnigraphics, Inc., 1992. 325 pp. Index.

The standard work on the origin of holy days and their religious and sociological development. Among topics covered are the tabooed days at critical epochs, the holy days, lunar superstitions and festivals, lunar calendars and the week, market days, unlucky days, the Babylonian "evil days," and the Shabattum.

Weiser, Francis X. *The Christmas Book*. Illustrated by Robert Frankenberg. 1952. Reprinted by Omnigraphics, Inc., 1990. 188 pp. Reference notes. Index.

Relates the story of the celebration of Christmas, from the beginning with its gospel and history, through the festivities of the Middle Ages, to the decline and eventual revival of Christmas customs in Europe and the United States. Ancient and familiar hymns are included, as well as a section on holiday breads and pastries.

———. *Handbook of Christian Feasts and Customs: The Year of the Lord in Liturgy and Folklore*. New York: Harcourt, Brace & World, Inc., 1958. 366 pp. Glossary. Index.

Part I discusses Christian significance of Sunday and other days of the week, ember days, and rogation days. Part II is organized according to the Christian calendar and presents description of major Christian feasts. Part III deals with the veneration of saints and Mary and provides some background on a few of the most popular saints.

Wernecke, Herbert H. *Christmas Customs Around the World.* Philadelphia: The Westminster Press, c.1959. 188 pp. Bibliography. Indexes.

Covers historical background, customs, and legends, holiday recipes, and pageants and programs. Describes observance of the holiday in over 60 countries on all continents.

Weslager, C.A. *The Delaware Indians: A History.* New Brunswick, NJ: Rutgers University Press, 1972. 546 pp. Illustrated. Maps. Appendixes. Index.

Survey of Delaware Indians' history, branches of the tribe, lifestyles and customs, and religious beliefs and practices, including discussion of such events as the Big House Ceremony. Appendixes include sources for maps of Delaware villages and reservations and an account of customs and manners pertaining to government, death, birth, marriage, science, and religion.

Westermarck, Edward. *Ritual and Belief in Morocco.* 2 vols. London: Macmillan and Co., Ltd., 1926. Vol. 1, 608 pp.; vol. 2, 629 pp. Map. Illustrations. Index.

Author presents results of on-site research, discussing peoples living in Morocco and their religions, beliefs and practices, saints, charms and superstitions. Calendar and agricultural rites and festivals are covered in vol. 2. List of tribes and locales. Index in vol. 2.

Wilson, Joe, and Lee Udall. *Folk Festivals: A Handbook for Organization and Management.* Knoxville: The University of Tennessee Press, 1982. 278 pp. Illustrations. Tables. Bibliography. Index.

Guide for folklore festival organizers covering such topics as administration, programming concepts, planning, publicity, and production. Part Two describes three folk festivals produced in the United States (Tucson, Meet Yourself Festival, Mississippi Valley Folk Festival, and Open Fiddlers' Contest), including an interview with a festival performer and samples of media releases and public service announcements.

Wright, A.R. *British Calendar Customs.* 3 vols. Preface by S.H. Hooke. London: William Glaisher Ltd., 1936. Vol. I, 212 pp.; vol. II, 272 pp.; vol. III, 333 pp. Illustrated. Index in Volumes I and III.

Volumes I-III cover popular customs, lore, superstitions, weather omens, and songs associated with holidays and festivals observed in England. Volume I deals with Christian movable holidays from Shrovetide to Corpus Christi, as well as other movable festivals and harvest customs. Volumes II and III survey nearly 100 secular and religious festivals occurring on fixed dates, presented in chronological order.

Wyndham, Lee. *Holidays in Scandinavia.* Illustrated by Gordon Laite. Champaign, IL: Garrard Publishing Company, 1975. 95 pp. Index.

Discusses ten holidays and festivals in Sweden, Norway, and Denmark for young readers. Pronouncing guide.

Young, Judith. *Celebrations: America's Best Festivals, Jamborees, Carnivals & Parades.* Foreword by Ray Bradbury. Santa Barbara: Capra Press, 1986. Series title: American Holidays: Volume One. 183 pp. Photos.

Arranged by region of the United States, then by season. Describes over 200 festivals in the United States and a few in Canada. Includes state maps, admission fee information, contact addresses, index of ethnic festivals by region, and index of Native American festivals by region.

Journals

African Arts. UCLA James S. Coleman African Studies Center, 1967-
African Studies. Witwatersrand University Press, 1921-
American Anthropologist. American Anthropological Association, 1899-
Anthropology and Archeology of Eurasia; a journal of translations from Soviet sources. M.E. Sharpe, Inc., 1962-
Asian Folklore Studies. Nanzan University, Nanzan Anthropological Institute, 1942-
British Federation of Festivals Yearbook. British Federation of Festivals, 1921-
Canadian Geographic. Royal Canadian Geographic Society, 1930-
Cavalcade of Arts & Attractions. BPI Communications, 1894-
Comparative Studies in Society and History. Cambridge University Press, 1959-
Dance Magazine. Dance Magazine, Inc., 1926-
Directory of North American Fairs, Festivals and Expositions (Amusement Business's Directory North American Fairs; until 1972, known as Cavalcade and Directory of Fairs). BPI Communications, 1888-
The Drama Review. MIT Press, 1955-
Ethnos. Folkens Museum, National Museum of Ethnography, Stockholm, Sweden, 1936-
Folklore. Folklore Society, 1878-
Folklore Forum. Folklore Institute, Bloomington, IN, 1968-
International Migration Review (International Migration Digest). Center for Migration Studies of New York, Inc., 1964-
Jewish Folklore & Ethnology Review. YIVO Institute for Jewish Research, 1978-
Journal of American Culture. Bowling Green Popular Press, 1967-
Journal of American Folklore. American Folklore Society, 1888-
Journal of Ethnic Studies. Western Washington University, 1973-
Journal of Folklore Research. Indiana University, Folklore Institute, 1964-
Journal of Latin American Lore. UCLA Latin American Center, 1974-
The Journal of Polynesian Society. Polynesian Society, Inc., 1892-
Journal of Popular Culture. Bowling Green State University, 1967-
Lore and Language. Centre for English Cultural Tradition and Language, 1969-
National Geographic. National Geographic Society, 1888-
Native American Directory. National Native American Co-Op, 1969-
Nigeria Magazine. Ministry of Culture and Social Welfare, Lagos, Nigeria, 1927-1988.
Western Folklore. California Folklore Society, 1942-
World's Fair. World's Fair, Inc., 1981-

Holidays
and
Festivals
Index

Ab or Av, Fast or Ninth of
See **Tisha B'Av**

Abbey Fair
  Location: Bethlehem, Connecticut
  Established: 1952
  Date: Two days in early August

  HolFestCelWrld-1994, 1
  RelHolCal-1993, 55

Abbots Bromley Antler Dance
See **Dance, Horn**

Abbotsbury Garland Day
See **Garland Day**

'Abdu'l-Bahá, Ascension of
  Named for: Abbas Effendi (1844-1921)
  Ethnic or religious group: Bahá'í
  Established: November 28, 1921
  Date: November 28

  AnnivHol-1983, 152
  HolFestCelWrld-1994, 1
  RelHolCal-1993, 58

'Abdu'l-Bahá, Birth of
  Named for: Abbas Effendi (1844-1921)
  Ethnic or religious group: Bahá'í
  Date: May 23

  RelHolCal-1993, 62

Aboakyer
See **Deer-Hunting Festival**

Abron
See **Christmas (Ghana)**

Abu Simbel Festival
  Location: Egypt: Abu Simbel temple
  Date: February 22 and October 22

  HolFestCelWrld-1994, 1

Acacia Day
  Location: Romania: Hanu-Conachi forest, Fundeni,
   Galati
  Date: First Sunday in May

  IntlThFolk-1979, 323

Acadian Festival
  Location: Canada: Caraquet, New Brunswick
  Ethnic or religious group: Acadian
  Established: 1962

  Date: August 5-15, ending on the Feast of the Assumption

  GdWrldFest-1985, 37
  HolFestCelWrld-1994, 2

Acadian Festivals
  Location: Canada: Maritime Provinces
  Ethnic or religious group: Acadian
  Date: Usually 3-4 days at the end of June; sometimes in
   July or August

  DictDays-1988, 1
  HolFestCelWrld-1994, 2

Acadiens, Festivals
  Location: Lafayette, Louisiana
  Ethnic or religious group: Cajun people
  Date: Third weekend in September

  HolFestCelWrld-1994, 2

Acorn Festival
  Location: Kule Loklo Miwok Indian Village, California
  Ethnic or religious group: Pomo Indians
  Date: Usually weekend after fourth Friday in September

  HolFestCelWrld-1994, 208
  IndianAmer-1989, 346

Adelaide Cup Day
  Location: Southern Australia
  Date: May

  DictDays-1988, 75
  HolFestCelWrld-1994, 139

Al-Adha al-zid al-kabir
See **Sacrifice, Feast of (Jordan)**

Admission Day
  Named for: Admission to the United States on December
   14, 1819
  Location: Alabama
  Date: December 14

  AmerBkDays-1978, 1102
  AnnivHol-1983, 160
  Chases-1993, 474

Admission Day
  Named for: Admission to the United States on January
   3, 1959
  Location: Alaska
  Date: January 3

  AmerBkDays-1978, 22
  AnnivHol-1983, 3
  Chases-1993, 54

Admission Day
  Named for: Admission to the United States on February
  14, 1912
  Location: Arizona
  Date: February 14

  AmerBkDays-1978, 180
  AnnivHol-1983, 24
  Chases-1993, 98
  DictDays-1988, 1
  See also **Gold Rush Days**

Admission Day
  Named for: Admission to the United States on June
  15, 1836
  Location: Arkansas
  Date: June 15

  AmerBkDays-1978, 558
  AnnivHol-1983, 80
  Chases-1993, 249

Admission Day
  Named for: Admission to the United States on September
  9, 1850
  Location: California
  Date: September 9

  AmerBkDays-1978, 827
  AnnivHol-1983, 116
  Chases-1993, 361

Admission Day
  Named for: Admission to the United States on August
  1, 1876
  Location: Colorado
  Date: First Monday in August

  AmerBkDays-1978, 714
  AnnivHol-1983, 101
  Chases-1993, 314
  DictDays-1988, 22

Admission Day
  Named for: January 9, 1788, ratification of the Constitution
  Location: Connecticut
  Date: January 9

  AmerBkDays-1978, 54
  AnnivHol-1983, 6
  Chases-1993, 60

Admission Day
  Named for: December 7, 1787, ratification of the
  Constitution
  Location: Delaware

  Date: December 7

  AmerBkDays-1978, 1080
  AnnivHol-1983, 157
  Chases-1993, 468

Admission Day
  Named for: Admission to the United States on March
  3, 1845
  Location: Florida
  Date: March 3

  AmerBkDays-1978, 231
  AnnivHol-1983, 32
  Chases-1993, 117

Admission Day
  Named for: January 2, 1788, ratification of the
  Constitution
  Location: Georgia
  Date: January 2

  AmerBkDays-1978, 20
  AnnivHol-1983, 3
  Chases-1993, 54

Admission Day
  Named for: Admission to the United States on August
  21, 1959
  Location: Hawaii
  Date: Third Friday in August

  AmerBkDays-1978, 768
  AnnivHol-1983, 109
  Chases-1993, 336

Admission Day
  Named for: Admission to the United States on July
  3, 1890
  Location: Idaho
  Date: July 3

  AmerBkDays-1978, 616
  AnnivHol-1983, 88
  Chases-1993, 276

Admission Day
  Named for: Admission to the United States on December
  3, 1818
  Location: Illinois
  Date: December 3

  AmerBkDays-1978, 1072
  AnnivHol-1983, 155
  Chases-1993, 463

Admission Day
  Named for: Admission to the United States on
    December 11, 1816
  Location: Indiana
  Date: December 11

  AmerBkDays-1978, 1094
  AnnivHol-1983, 158
  Chases-1993, 471
  DictDays-1988, 59

Admission Day
  Named for: Admission to the United States on
    December 28, 1846
  Location: Iowa
  Date: December 28

  AnnivHol-1983, 165
  Chases-1993, 484

Admission Day
  Named for: Admission to the United States in 1861
  Location: Kansas
  Established: Observed since 1877
  Date: January 29

  AmerBkDays-1978, 117
  AnnivHol-1983, 15
  Chases-1993, 77

Admission Day
  Named for: Admission to the United States on June 1, 1792
  Location: Kentucky
  Date: June 1

  AmerBkDays-1978, 510
  AnnivHol-1983, 74
  Chases-1993, 229
  DictDays-1988, 113

Admission Day
  Named for: Admission to the United States on April 30, 1812
  Location: Louisiana
  Date: April 30

  AmerBkDays-1978, 401
  AnnivHol-1983, 58
  Chases-1993, 185

Admission Day
  Named for: Admission to the United States on March 15, 1820
  Location: Maine
  Date: March 15

  AmerBkDays-1978, 257
  AnnivHol-1983, 37
  Chases-1993, 130

Admission Day
  Named for: April 28, 1788, ratification of the
    Constitution
  Location: Maryland
  Date: April 28

  AmerBkDays-1978, 393
  AnnivHol-1983, 58

Admission Day
  Named for: February 6, 1788, ratification of the
    Constitution
  Location: Massachusetts
  Date: February 6

  AmerBkDays-1978, 150
  AnnivHol-1983, 20
  Chases-1993, 88

Admission Day
  Named for: Admission to the United States on January
    26, 1837
  Location: Michigan
  Date: January 26

  AmerBkDays-1978, 113
  AnnivHol-1983, 14
  Chases-1993, 74

Admission Day
  Named for: Admission to the United States on May 11, 1858
  Location: Minnesota
  Date: May 11

  AmerBkDays-1978, 442
  AnnivHol-1983, 64
  Chases-1993, 204

Admission Day
  Named for: Admission to the United States on December
    10, 1817
  Location: Mississippi
  Date: December 10

  AmerBkDays-1978, 1091
  Chases-1993, 470

Admission Day
  Named for: Admission to the United States on August
    10, 1821
  Location: Missouri
  Date: August 10

  AmerBkDays-1978, 744
  AnnivHol-1983, 105
  Chases-1993, 324

Admission Day
Named for: Admission to the United States on November 8, 1889
Location: Montana
Date: November 8

AmerBkDays-1978, 1002
AnnivHol-1983, 143
Chases-1993, 435

Admission Day
Named for: Admission to the United States on March 1, 1867
Location: Nebraska
Date: March 1

AmerBkDays-1978, 224
AnnivHol-1983, 31
Chases-1993, 115

Admission Day
Named for: Admission to the United States on October 31, 1864
Location: Nevada
Date: October 31

AmerBkDays-1978, 972
AnnivHol-1983, 138
Chases-1993, 427
DictDays-1988, 81

Admission Day
Named for: June 21, 1788, ratification of the Constitution
Location: New Hampshire
Date: June 21

AnnivHol-1983, 82
Chases-1993, 258

Admission Day
Named for: December 18, 1787, ratification of the Constitution
Location: New Jersey
Date: December 18

AnnivHol-1983, 162
Chases-1993, 477

Admission Day
Named for: Admission to the United States on January 6, 1912
Location: New Mexico
Date: January 6

AmerBkDays-1978, 40
AnnivHol-1983, 5
Chases-1993, 57

Admission Day
Named for: July 26, 1788, ratification of the Constitution
Location: New York
Date: July 26

AnnivHol-1983, 97
Chases-1993, 307

Admission Day
Named for: November 21, 1789, ratification of the Constitution
Location: North Carolina
Date: November 21

AmerBkDays-1978, 1038
AnnivHol-1983, 149
Chases-1993, 449

Admission Day
Named for: Admission to the United States on November 2, 1889
Location: North Dakota
Date: November 2

AmerBkDays-1978, 984
AnnivHol-1983, 141
Chases-1993, 430

Admission Day
Named for: Admission to the United States on March 1, 1803
Location: Ohio
Date: March 1

AmerBkDays-1978, 194, 225
AnnivHol-1983, 31
Chases-1993, 115

Admission Day
Named for: Admission to the United States on November 16, 1907
Location: Oklahoma
Established: Observed since 1921
Date: November 16

AmerBkDays-1978, 1025
AnnivHol-1983, 148
Chases-1993, 443

Admission Day
Named for: Admission to the United States on February 14, 1859
Location: Oregon
Date: February 14

AmerBkDays-1978, 182
AnnivHol-1983, 24
Chases-1993, 98

Admission Day
  Named for: December 12, 1787, ratification of the
    Constitution
  Location: Pennsylvania
  Date: December 12

  AnnivHol-1983, 159
  Chases-1993, 473

Admission Day
  Named for: May 29, 1790, ratification of the Constitution
  Location: Rhode Island
  Date: May 29

  AnnivHol-1983, 72
  Chases-1993, 225

Admission Day
  Named for: May 23, 1788, ratification of the Constitution
  Location: South Carolina
  Date: May 23

  AnnivHol-1983, 70
  Chases-1993, 218

Admission Day
  Named for: Admission to the United States on November
    2, 1889
  Location: South Dakota
  Date: November 2

  AmerBkDays-1978, 989
  Chases-1993, 430

Admission Day
  Named for: Admission to the United States on June 1, 1796
  Location: Tennessee
  Date: June 1

  AmerBkDays-1978, 516
  AnnivHol-1983, 74
  Chases-1993, 230
  DictDays-1988, 113

Admission Day
  Named for: Admission to the United States on December
    29, 1845
  Location: Texas
  Date: December 29

  AmerBkDays-1978, 1163
  AnnivHol-1983, 165
  Chases-1993, 485

Admission Day
  Named for: Admission to the United States on January
    4, 1896

Location: Utah
Date: January 4

  AmerBkDays-1978, 27
  AnnivHol-1983, 4
  Chases-1993, 56

Admission Day
  Named for: Admission to the United States on March 4, 1791
  Location: Vermont
  Date: March 4

  AmerBkDays-1978, 233
  AnnivHol-1983, 33
  Chases-1993, 119

Admission Day
  Named for: June 25, 1788, ratification of the Constitution
  Location: Virginia
  Date: June 25

  AnnivHol-1983, 84
  Chases-1993, 264

Admission Day
  Named for: Admission to the United States on November
    11, 1889
  Location: Washington
  Date: November 11

  AmerBkDays-1978, 1015
  AnnivHol-1983, 145
  Chases-1993, 438

Admission Day
  Named for: Admission to the United States on June 20, 1863
  Location: West Virginia
  Date: June 20

  AmerBkDays-1978, 570
  AnnivHol-1983, 82
  Chases-1993, 258
  DictDays-1988, 130
  HolFestCelWrld-1994, 365

Admission Day
  Named for: Admission to the United States on May 29, 1848
  Location: Wisconsin
  Date: May 29

  AnnivHol-1983, 72
  Chases-1993, 226

Admission Day
  Named for: Admission to the United States on July 10, 1890
  Location: Wyoming
  Date: July 10

  AmerBkDays-1978, 650
  AnnivHol-1983, 91
  Chases-1993, 288

Admission Day, Kansas
  Location: Topeka, Kansas
  Date: January 29

  AmerBkDays-1978, 117

Admission Day, Nevada
  Location: Carson City, Nevada
  Date: October 31

  AmerBkDays-1978, 972

Admission Day, Oklahoma
  Location: Washington Cathedral, Washington, D.C.
  Date: November 16

  AmerBkDays-1978, 1025

La Adoracion de la Cruz
  See **Exaltation of the Cross (Paraguay)**

Adults Day (Seijin-no-hi)
  Location: Japan
  Date: January 15

  AnnivHol-1983, 9
  Chases-1993, 64
  FolkWrldHol-1992, 30
  HolFestCelWrld-1994, 311

Adults Day (Seijin-no-hi)
  Location: Japan: Sanjusangendo, Kyoto
  Date: January 15

  HolFestCelWrld-1994, 311

Advent
  Ethnic or religious group: Christian
  Established: About 6th century, Rome
  Date: Four-week season beginning Sunday nearest
    November 30 and ending December 24

  AmerBkDays-1978, 1059
  BkFestHolWrld-1970, 127
  BkHolWrld-1986, November 30
  DaysCustFaith-1957, 302
  DictWrldRel-1989, 5, 154, 175
  FestWestEur-1958, 79
  FolkWrldHol-1992, 573
  HolFestCelWrld-1994, 3
  RelHolCal-1993, 55
  SaintFestCh-1904, xiii

Advent
  Ethnic or religious group: Eastern Orthodox
  Date: Four-week season beginning Sunday nearest
    November 30 and ending December 24

  AmerBkDays-1978, 1060

  BkFestHolWrld-1970, 127
  DictWrldRel-1989, 175
  HolFestCelWrld-1994, 3
  RelHolCal-1993, 55

Advent
  Location: Austria
  Date: Four-week season beginning Sunday nearest
    November 30 and ending December 24

  FolkWrldHol-1992, 573

Advent
  Location: Germany
  Date: Four-week season beginning Sunday nearest
    November 30 and ending December 24

  BkFestHolWrld-1970, 128
  FestWestEur-1958, 79
  FolkWrldHol-1992, 573

Advent
  Location: Sweden
  Date: Four-week season beginning Sunday nearest
    November 30 and ending December 24

  FolkWrldHol-1992, 573

Advent
  Location: United States
  Date: Four-week season beginning Sunday nearest
    November 30 and ending December 24

  RelHolCal-1993, 55

Advent Sunday
  Ethnic or religious group: Christian
  Date: Sunday nearest November 30

  AnnivHol-1983, 169
  BkDays-1864, ii. 622
  Chases-1993, 219
  DictDays-1988, 2

Africa Day
  Location: Chad, Liberia, Mali, Mauritania, Zambia, and
    Zimbabwe
  Date: May 25

  AnnivHol-1983, 71

Africa Freedom or Liberation Day
  See **Africa Day**

African Methodist Quarterly Meeting Day
  Location: Wilmington, Delaware
  Ethnic or religious group: African Union Methodist Church
  Established: 1813
  Date: Last Saturday in August

  FolkAmerHol-1987, 263
  HolFestCelWrld-1994, 3
  RelHolCal-1993, 56

Age of Goibniu, Feast of
  Location: Ireland

  DictFolkMyth-1984, 374

Ages, Festival of the (Jidai Matsuri)
  Location: Japan: Kyoto
  Established: Commemorates both the founding of the capital city in 794 and Toyotomi Hideyoshi (1537-1598)
  Date: October 22

  AnnivHol-1983, 135
  HolFestCelWrld-1994, 161

Agonalia or Agonia (Feast of Janus)
  Location: Ancient Rome
  Date: January 9

  AmerBkDays-1978, 1,3
  DictFolkMyth-1984, 539

Agostinos, Fiestas
  See **Transfiguration of Christ, Feast of (El Salvador)**

Agricultural Days (Jordbruksdagarna)
  Location: Bishop Hill, Illinois
  Ethnic or religious group: Swedish-Americans
  Date: Two days in late September

  HolFestCelWrld-1994, 163

Agricultural Festival (Hadaga)
  Location: India: Maharashtra
  Date: September-October, Hindu month of Asvina

  FolkWrldHol-1992, 404

Agricultural Festival (Pola)
  Location: India: Maharashtra
  Date: July-August, Hindu month of Sravana

  FolkWrldHol-1992, 404

Agricultural Festival (Pola)
  Location: India: Poona and Sholapur, Maharashtra
  Date: August-September, Hindu month of Bhadrapada

  FolkWrldHol-1992, 404

Agricultural Festival
  Location: India: Satara District, Maharashtra
  Date: June-July, Hindu month of Ashadha

  FolkWrldHol-1992, 404

Agricultural Field Days
  Location: New Zealand
  Date: Three days during second week in June

  BkHolWrld-1986, June 9, 176
  HolFestCelWrld-1994, 105

Agriculture Day, National
  See **National Agriculture Day**

Agua, La Fiesta de
  Location: Peru: San Pedro de Casta
  Date: First Sunday in October

  FolkWrldHol-1992, 505
  HolFestCelWrld-1994, 3

Agwunsi Festival
  Location: Nigeria
  Ethnic or religious group: Igbo people
  Date: August-September

  FolkWrldHol-1992, 471
  HolFestCelWrld-1994, 3

Airborne Operations Day
  Location: Netherlands
  Established: September 20, 1944, Battle of Arnhem
  Date: September 20

  AnnivHol-1983, 121

Air Force Day
  Location: Canada
  Date: September 10

  DictDays-1988, 2

Airing the Classics (Double Sixth Day)
  Location: China
  Ethnic or religious group: Buddhist
  Date: Sixth day of sixth lunar month

  FolkWrldHol-1992, 351
  HolFestCelWrld-1994, 4

Air Races, National Championship
  Location: Reno, Nevada
  Established: 1963
  Date: September, three or four days ending second weekend after Labor Day

  GdUSFest-1984, 115
  HolFestCelWrld-1994, 4

Air Show, International
  Location: Canada: Abbotsford, British Columbia
  Established: 1962
  Date: Three days in August

  GdWrldFest-1985, 31

Ai-yá-g'ûk
  See **Asking Festival**

Ak-Sar-Ben Livestock Exposition and Rodeo
Location: Ak-Sar-Ben Field, Omaha, Nebraska
Established: 1928
Date: Nine days from late September to early October

GdUSFest-1984, 111
HolFestCelWrld-1994, 4

Akshya Tritiya
See **Undecaying Third (Hindu)**

Akwambo
See **Path Clearing Festival (Ghana)**

Alamo Day
Named for: March 6, 1836, American defeat of Mexican
army at the Alamo, a Franciscan mission at San Antonio
Location: Houston and San Antonio, Texas
Date: March 6

AmerBkDays-1978, 237
AnnivHol-1983, 34
Chases-1993, 121
DaysCustFaith-1957, 97
DictDays-1988, 2
HolFestCelWrld-1994, 4
See also **San Antonio, Fiesta; San Jacinto Day**

Alasita Fair ("Buy from Me" Fair)
Location: Bolivia
Ethnic or religious group: Aymara Indians
Date: January 24

AnnivHol-1983, 13
BkFestHolWrld-1970, 17
BkHolWrld-1986, January 24
Chases-1993, 73
DictFolkMyth-1984, 33, 342
FolkWrldHol-1992, 37
HolFestCelWrld-1994, 4

Alaska Day
Named for: Transfer of Alaska from Russia to the United
States on October 18, 1867
Location: Sitka, Alaska
Date: Three days in October

AmerBkDays-1978, 935
AnnivHol-1983, 134
Chases-1993, 413
DictDays-1988, 3
HolFestCelWrld-1994, 5

Alban Arthan
See **Yule**

Aldersgate Experience
Named for: Religious experience of Methodist leader John
Wesley (1703-1791)
Ethnic or religious group: Methodist
Date: Sunday nearest May 24

DaysCustFaith-1957, 127
RelHolCal-1993, 56

Alexandra Rose Day
Named for: Queen Alexandra (1844-1925), wife of King
Edward VII
Location: Great Britain
Date: A Saturday in June

DictDays-1988, 3
HolFestCelWrld-1994, 5

Algarve, National Festival of the
Location: Portugal: Vila Moura, Faro
Established: 1977
Date: Two days in August or September

Chases-1993, 364
IntlThFolk-1979, 314

Alholland Eve
See **Halloween**

Alice Springs Show Day
See **Regatta Day, Hobart**

Allen, Birthday of Richard
Named for: Richard Allen (1760-1831)
Location: United States
Ethnic or religious group: African Methodist Episcopal
Church
Date: February 11

DaysCustFaith-1957, 51
RelHolCal-1993, 63

Allerheiligen
See **All Saints' Day (Germany)**

Aller Heiligen Dag
See **All Saints' Day (Belgium)**

Allerkinder Tag
See **Holy Innocents' Day (Germany: Thüringia)**

All Fools' Day
Location: Mexico
Date: December 28

BkFestHolWrld-1970, 75
DictFolkMyth-1984, 36
FolkAmerHol-1987, 147
See also **April Fools' Day**

All-Halland Eve
  See **Halloween**

All Hallowmas or All Hallows' Day
  See **All Saints' Day**

All Hallows' Eve
  See **Halloween; Samhain**

Allied Landing Observances Day
  See **D-Day (France: Normandy)**

All Saints' Day
  Ethnic or religious group: Christian
  Established: Seventh century, Rome; in 835 Pope Gregory
    IV combined it with Samhain
  Date: November 1 in Western Churches; first Sunday after
    Pentecost in Eastern Churches

  AmerBkDays-1978, 978
  AnnivHol-1983, 140
  BkDays-1864, ii. 529
  BkHolWrld-1986, November 1
  Chases-1993, 428
  DaysCustFaith-1957, 280
  DictDays-1988, 3
  DictFolkMyth-1984, 36, 181, 573, 1056
  FestSaintDays-1915, 197
  FestWestEur-1958, 17, 47
  FolkAmerHol-1987, 309
  FolkWrldHol-1992, 541
  HolFestCelWrld-1994, 6
  RelHolCal-1993, 56
  SaintFestCh-1904, 470

All Saints' Day
  Ethnic or religious group: Anglican
  Date: November 1

  BkDays-1864, ii.529
  RelHolCal-1993, 56

All Saints' Day
  Ethnic or religious group: Church of England
  Date: November 1

  AmerBkDays-1978, 979

All Saints' Day
  Ethnic or religious group: Episcopalian
  Date: November 1

  AmerBkDays-1978, 978
  FolkAmerHol-1987, 312

All Saints' Day
  Ethnic or religious group: Inca people

  Date: November 1

  DictFolkMyth-1984, 1056

All Saints' Day
  Ethnic or religious group: Lutheran
  Date: November 1

  AmerBkDays-1978, 978

All Saints' Day
  Ethnic or religious group: Protestant
  Date: November 1

  AmerBkDays-1978, 978
  BkHolWrld-1986, November 1
  RelHolCal-1993, 56

All Saints' Day
  Ethnic or religious group: Roman Catholic
  Date: November 1

  AmerBkDays-1978, 978
  AnnivHol-1983, 140
  BkDays-1864, ii.580
  BkHolWrld-1986, November 1
  Chases-1993, 428
  FestSaintDays-1915, 194
  FolkAmerHol-1987, 312
  RelHolCal-1993, 56

All Saints' Day
  Location: Austria: Tirol
  Date: November 1

  DictFolkMyth-1984, 181

All Saints' Day (Aller Heiligen Dag)
  Location: Belgium
  Date: November 1

  DictFolkMyth-1984, 181
  FestWestEur-1958, 17
  FolkWrldHol-1992, 541

All Saints' Day (Kawsasqanchis, Our Living with the Dead)
  Location: Bolivia
  Date: November 1

  FolkWrldHol-1992, 541

All Saints' Day
  Location: England
  Date: November 1

  DictFolkMyth-1984, 181
  FestSaintDays-1915, 194

All Saints' Day (Kekri)
Location: Finland
Established: Kekri observed since at least 1754
Date: November 1

DictFolkMyth-1984, 573

All Saints' Day (La Toussaint)
Location: France
Date: November 1

DictDays-1988, 3
FestWestEur-1958, 47

All Saints' Day (Allerheiligen)
Location: Germany
Date: November 1

DictDays-1988, 3
FolkWrldHol-1992, 542

All Saints' Day
Location: Ireland
Date: November 1

DictFolkMyth-1984, 181

All Saints' Day
Location: Italy
Date: November 1

DictDays-1988, 3

All Saints' Day
Location: New Orleans and other cities in Louisiana
Date: November 1

AmerBkDays-1978, 979
DictDays-1988, 3
FolkAmerHol-1987, 312

All Saints' Day (El Día de los Santos)
Location: Mexico: Santa Cruz
Date: November 1

FolkWrldHol-1992, 542

All Saints' Day
Location: Mesilla, New Mexico
Date: November 1

FolkAmerHol-1987, 313

All Saints' Day
Location: Philippines
Date: November 1

FolkWrldHol-1992, 542

All Saints' Day
Location: Portugal
Date: November 1

DictDays-1988, 3

All Saints' Day
Location: Puerto Rico
Date: November 1

AmerBkDays-1978, 979

All Saints' Day
Location: Sardinia
Date: November 1

FestSaintDays-1915, 196

All Saints' Day
Location: Scotland
Date: November 1

DictFolkMyth-1984, 181

All Saints' Day
Location: South Carolina
Date: November 1

FolkAmerHol-1987, 313

All Saints' Day
Location: Spain
Date: November 1

DictDays-1988, 3

All Saints' Day
Location: Trinidad
Date: November 1

FolkWrldHol-1992, 543

All Saints, Festival of
See **All Saints' Day**

All Souls, Feast of
See **New Year's Celebration (Hindu people in Bali)**

All Souls' Day
Ethnic or religious group: Christian
Established: About 10th century
Date: November 2

AmerBkDays-1978, 980
AnnivHol-1983, 141
BkHolWrld-1986, November 2
Chases-1993, 429
DaysCustFaith-1957, 282
DictDays-1988, 3

All Souls' Day *(cont.)*
  DictFolkMyth-1984, 38, 184, 505, 842, 1051, 1052
  FestSaintDays-1915, 200
  FestWestEur-1958, 17, 47, 100
  FolkAmerHol-1987, 309
  FolkWrldHol-1992, 544, 548
  HolFestCelWrld-1994, 6
  RelHolCal-1993, 57
  SaintFestCh-1904, 472

All Souls' Day
  Ethnic or religious group: Anglican
  Date: November 2

  RelHolCal-1993, 57

All Souls' Day
  Ethnic or religious group: Eastern Orthodox
  Date: Three Saturdays before Lent and the day before
    Pentecost

  HolFestCelWrld-1994, 6
  RelHolCal-1993, 57

All Souls' Day
  Ethnic or religious group: Roman Catholic
  Date: November 2

  AmerBkDays-1978, 980
  BkHolWrld-1986, November 2
  Chases-1993, 429
  DaysCustFaith-1957, 282
  DictFolkMyth-1984, 38
  FolkAmerHol-1987, 314
  HolFestCelWrld-1994, 6
  RelHolCal-1993, 57
  SaintFestCh-1904, 472

All Souls' Day
  Location: Bavaria
  Date: November 2

  FestSaintDays-1915, 203

All Souls' Day
  Location: Belgium
  Date: November 2

  DictFolkMyth-1984, 1051
  FestWestEur-1958, 17

All Souls' Day (Le Jour de Morts)
  Location: Brittany
  Date: November 2

  AmerBkDays-1978, 981

  DictFolkMyth-1984, 842
  FestWestEur-1958, 47

All Souls' Day (El Día de Los Muertos)
  Location: Los Angeles, California
  Ethnic or religious group: Mexican-Americans
  Date: November 2

  HolFestCelWrld-1994, 7

All Souls' Day (Night of the Candle Ceremony)
  Location: Pala and Ricon Indian reservations near
    Oceanside, California
  Date: November 2

  AmerBkDays-1978, 981

All Souls' Day (Día de los Angelitos)
  Location: Colombia
  Date: November 2

  FolkWrldHol-1992, 544

All Souls' Day
  Location: Ecuador
  Date: November 2

  HolFestCelWrld-1994, 7

All Souls' Day
  Location: El Salvador
  Date: November 2

  HolFestCelWrld-1994, 7

All Souls' Day
  Location: England: Shropshire and Cheshire
  Date: November 2

  HolFestCelWrld-1994, 6

All Souls' Day
  Location: French West Indies
  Date: November 2

  HolFestCelWrld-1994, 7

All Souls' Day
  Location: Great Britain
  Date: November 2

  AmerBkDays-1978, 981
  BkHolWrld-1986, November 2
  DictFolkMyth-1984, 1052

All Souls' Day
  Location: Greece
  Date: November 2

  FestSaintDays-1915, 201

All Souls' Day (Il Giorno Dei Morti)
  Location: Italy
  Date: November 2

  AmerBkDays-1978, 981
  FestWestEur-1958, 100
  FolkWrldHol-1992, 544
  HolFestCelWrld-1994, 7

All Souls' Day
  Location: Macao
  Date: November 2

  HolFestCelWrld-1994, 7

All Souls' Day (Día de los Muertos, Day of the Dead or Festival of Hungry Ghosts)
  Location: Mexico
  Ethnic or religious group: Roman Catholic
  Date: October 30-November 2

  AmerBkDays-1978, 981
  BkFest-1937, 231
  Chases-1993, 428
  DictDays-1988, 28
  DictFolkMyth-1984, 963
  FolkWrldHol-1992, 545
  HolFestCelWrld-1994, 6
  IntlThFolk-1979, 278

All Souls' Day
  Location: Acoma Pueblo, New Mexico
  Date: November 2

  FolkAmerHol-1987, 314

All Souls' Day (Their Grandfathers Arrive from the West, or from the Dead, Feast)
  Location: Cochiti Pueblo, New Mexico
  Date: November 2

  AmerBkDays-1978, 981

All Souls' Day
  Location: Laguna Pueblo, New Mexico
  Date: November 2

  FolkAmerHol-1987, 314

All Souls' Day
  Location: Santo Domingo Pueblo, New Mexico
  Date: November 2

  AmerBkDays-1978, 982

All Souls' Day
  Location: Taos Pueblo, New Mexico

  Date: November 2

  AmerBkDays-1978, 982

All Souls' Day
  Location: Zuñi Pueblo, New Mexico
  Date: November 2

  AmerBkDays-1978, 982
  FolkAmerHol-1987, 313

All Souls' Day
  Location: Northern Marianas
  Ethnic or religious group: Chamorros people
  Date: November 2

  FolkWrldHol-1992, 548

All Souls' Day (Día de Finados, Day of the Dead)
  Location: Portugal
  Ethnic or religious group: Roman Catholic
  Date: November 2

  AnnivHol-1983, 141
  FestWestEur-1958, 185
  HolFestCelWrld-1994, 7

All Souls' Day
  Location: Romania
  Date: November 2

  DictFolkMyth-1984, 184, 505

All Souls' Day (Il Giorno dei Morti)
  Location: Sicily
  Date: November 2

  AmerBkDays-1978, 981
  BkHolWrld-1986, November 2
  FestSaintDays-1915, 202
  FestWestEur-1958, 101
  FolkWrldHol-1992, 545
  HolFestCelWrld-1994, 7

All Souls' Day
  Location: Uruguay
  Date: November 2

  HolFestCelWrld-1994, 7

All Souls' Eve
See **All Souls' Day**

Almabtrieb
See **Mountain Pasture, Return from**

Aloha Week
  Location: Hawaii
  Established: 1946
  Date: September-October

  GdUSFest-1984, 41
  HolFestCelWrld-1994, 7

Alpabfahrten
  Location: Switzerland
  Date: September-October

  HolFestCelWrld-1994, 7
  See also **Alps, Procession to the**

Alpaufzug
  See **Alps, Procession to the**

Alpenfest
  Location: Gaylord, Michigan
  Date: Third week in July

  HolFestCelWrld-1994, 8

Alphabet Day (Han-gul)
  Location: Korea
  Established: Since 1446, when King Sejong (1397-1450)
    oversaw the invention of the Korean alphabet
  Date: Early October

  Chases-1993, 404
  BkHolWrld-1986, October 9
  FolkWrldHol-1992, 509
  HolFestCelWrld-1994, 133

Alps, Procession to the (Alpaufzug)
  Location: Switzerland: Appenzell and elsewhere
  Date: Late April or May

  BkHolWrld-1986, April 17, 176
  FestWestEur-1958, 229
  HolFestCelWrld-1994, 7
  See also **Alpabfahrten**

Altura Do Espirito Santo
  See **Holy Ghost, Feast of the (Roman Catholic people in**
    Ponta Delgada, Sao Miguel Island, Azores, Portugal)

A-Ma, Feast of
  Location: Macao
  Date: April

  AnnivHol-1983, 173
  HolFestCelWrld-1994, 199, 200

Amalaka Ekadashi
  Ethnic or religious group: Hindu
  Date: February-March, 11th day of waxing half of Hindu
    month of Phalguna; marks the beginning of Holi

  RelHolCal-1993, 57

Amarnath Yatra
  Location: India: Amarnath cave with sacred ice lingam in
    the Kashmir Himalayas
  Date: July-August, full moon day of Hindu month of Sravana

  Chases-1993, 314
  HolFestCelWrld-1994, 8

Amateur One-Man Shows, National Meeting of
  Location: Poland: Zgorzelec
  Date: October

  IntlThFolk-1979, 301

Amateur Stages, Belgrade Review of Experimental
  Location: Yugoslavia: Belgrade, Serbia
  Date: Mid-May

  IntlThFolk-1979, 383

Amateurs to Their City
  Location: Yugoslavia: Belgrade, Serbia
  Date: October 20, Liberation Day of Belgrade

  IntlThFolk-1979, 381

American Indian Day
  See **Native American Day**

American West, Festival of
  Location: Utah State University, Logan, Utah
  Established: 1972
  Date: Nine days in July-August

  GdUSFest-1984, 189

America's Cup
  Location: Newport, Rhode Island
  Established: 1851
  Date: August 22, held whenever a challenger comes forth,
    usually every three to four years

  AmerBkDays-1978, 771
  Chases-1993, 339
  HolFestCelWrld-1994, 9

America's Discovery Day
  See **Columbus Day (Honduras)**

Anant Chaturdashi
  See **Fourteenth Day of Bhadrapada, Eternal Anniversary of**

Anastenaria
  Named for: Honors St. Constantine and St. Helen
  Location: Greece: Agia Serres and Langada
  Date: May 21-23

  HolFestCelWrld-1994, 9

Ancestors, Festival of
  See **Double Ninth (China)**

Ancestry Day
  Location: Haiti
  Date: January 2

  AnnivHol-1983, 3
  Chases-1993, 54

Anchorage Fur Rendezvous
  Location: Anchorage, Alaska
  Established: Officially instituted in 1936, but occurred earlier
  Date: Ten days in February

  AnnivHol-1983, 173
  GdUSFest-1984, 7
  HolFestCelWrld-1994, 10

Anden Paaskedag
  See **Easter Monday (Denmark)**

Anden Pinsedag
  See **Whit Monday (Denmark)**

Andersen Festival, Hans Christian
  Named for: Hans Christian Andersen (1805-1875)
  Location: Denmark: Odense
  Established: 1965
  Date: July-August, one month long

  GdWrldFest-1985, 73
  HolFestCelWrld-1994, 133

Andersen's Birthday, Hans Christian
  See **Children's Book Day, International**

Andorra National Festival
  Named for: September 8, 1278, treaty of independence
  Location: Andorra
  Date: September 8

  AnnivHol-1983, 115
  FolkWrldHol-1992, 474
  HolFestCelWrld-1994, 10
  NatlHolWrld-1968, 160

Andrzejki
  See **St. Andrew's Eve (Poland) and (Polish-Americans in Ohio)**

Animals, Blessing of the
  See **St. Anthony the Abbot of Egypt, Feast of (Christian)**

Anjar Festival
  Location: Lebanon: Anjar
  Established: 1973
  Date: First two weeks in September

  IntlThFolk-1979, 262

Anjin Matsuri
  Named for: Commemorates William Adams (1564-1620), who shared knowledge of English ships and navigation with the Japanese
  Location: Japan: Yokosuka
  Date: April

  AnnivHol-1983, 173

Anjou Festival
  Location: France: Angers, Maine-et-Loire
  Established: 1975
  Date: July-August

  IntlThFolk-1979, 98

Anklopfnächte
  See **Knocking Nights**

Annandag Påsk
  See **Easter Monday (Sweden)**

Annapolis Valley Blossom Festival
  Location: Canada: Nova Scotia
  Date: Last week in May

  BkFestHolWrld-1970, 89

Ann Arbor May Festival
  Location: Ann Arbor, Michigan
  Established: 1894
  Date: Four days in late April or early May

  MusFestAmer-1990, 86

Anniversary Day
  See **Australia Day**

Anno Novo
  See **New Year's Day (Portugal)**

Annunciation of the Blessed Virgin Mary
  See **Annunciation, Feast of the**

Annunciation of the Lord
  See **Annunciation, Feast of the**

Annunciation, Feast of the
  Named for: The angel Gabriel's announcement to the Virgin Mary (first century B.C.-first century A.D.) that she would

Annunciation, Feast of the *(cont.)*
give birth to Jesus Christ
Ethnic or religious group: Christian
Established: Since 5th century in the Eastern Church; 7th century in the Western Church
Date: March 25 (moves to April 1 if March 25 occurs within Holy Week)

AmerBkDays-1978, 4, 284
AnnivHol-1983, 42
BkDays-1864, i. 417
BkHolWrld-1986, March 25
Chases-1993, 140
DaysCustFaith-1957, 86
DictDays-1988, 4, 85
FestSaintDays-1915, 56
FestWestEur-1958, 6, 213
FolkWrldHol-1992, 188
HolFestCelWrld-1994, 11
RelHolCal-1993, 57
SaintFestCh-1904, 146

Annunciation, Feast of the
Ethnic or religious group: Anglican
Date: March 25

BkDays-1864, i.417
RelHolCal-1993, 57

Annunciation, Feast of the
Ethnic or religious group: Eastern Orthodox
Date: April 7 (O.S.); March 25 (N.S.)

AmerBkDays-1978, 285
RelHolCal-1993, 57
SaintFestCh-1904, 146

Annunciation, Feast of the
Ethnic or religious group: Episcopalian
Date: March 25

AmerBkDays-1978, 285

Annunciation, Feast of the
Ethnic or religious group: Lutheran
Date: March 25

AmerBkDays-1978, 285
RelHolCal-1993, 57

Annunciation, Feast of the
Ethnic or religious group: Roman Catholic
Date: March 25

AmerBkDays-1978, 285

BkDays-1864, i.417
Chases-1993, 140
RelHolCal-1993, 57

Annunciation, Feast of the (Notre Dame de la Prospérité)
Location: Belgium
Date: March 25

FestSaintDays-1915, 59
FestWestEur-1958, 6

Annunciation, Feast of the (Lady Day)
Location: England
Date: March 25

BkDays-1864, i.417
DaysCustFaith-1957, 86
DictDays-1988, 4, 85
FestSaintDays-1915, 59
HolFestCelWrld-1994, 11

Annunciation, Feast of the (Lady Day)
Location: Finland: Lapland villages
Date: March 25

BkFestHolWrld-1970, 62

Annunciation, Feast of the (Notre Dame de Mars)
Location: France
Date: March 25

BkDays-1864, i.417
FestSaintDays-1915, 59

Annunciation, Feast of the
Location: Germany
Date: March 25

FestSaintDays-1915, 59

Annunciation, Feast of the
Location: Greece
Date: March 25

FolkWrldHol-1992, 188

Annunciation, Feast of the
Location: Italy
Date: March 25

FestSaintDays-1915, 59

Annunciation, Feast of the
Location: Liechtenstein
Date: March 25

AnnivHol-1983, 42

Annunciation, Feast of the (Varfrudagen; Marie Bebådelsedag; Lady Day; and Våffla or Waffle Day)
Location: Sweden
Ethnic or religious group: Lutheran
Established: 1593
Date: March 25

BkHolWrld-1986, March 25
FestWestEur-1958, 213
FolkWrldHol-1992, 188
HolFestCelWrld-1994, 11

Año Nuevo
See **New Year's Day (Spain)**

Anthesteria (Day of Flowers)
Location: Greece
Date: May 1

BkFest-1937, 150

Anthesteria
Named for: Honored Dionysus
Location: Greece: Athens
Date: February-March; 11th-13th day of Greek month of Anthesterion

DictFolkMyth-1984, 64
HolFestCelWrld-1994, 11

Anthestiria Flower Festival
Location: Cyprus: Paphos
Date: Early May

IntlThFolk-1979, 84

Anthony Day, Susan B.
Named for: Susan B. Anthony (1820-1906)
Location: United States
Date: February 15 or August 26

AmerBkDays-1978, 184
AnnivHol-1983, 25
Chases-1993, 100
DictDays-1988, 115
HolFestCelWrld-1994, 326

AN tOIREACHTAS
Location: Ireland
Ethnic or religious group: Gaelic
Established: Music festival since 1897
Date: October-November

IntlThFolk-1979, 237

Antrosht
See **Mother's Day (Ethiopia: Gurage Province)**

Anul Nou
See **New Year's Day (Romania)**

Anzac Day
Location: Australia, New Zealand, and Western Samoa
Established: April 25, 1915, landing at Gallipoli, Turkey; observed since 1920 in Australia and New Zealand
Date: April 25

AnnivHol-1983, 56
BkHolWrld-1986, April 25
Chases-1993, 180
DictDays-1988, 4
HolFestCelWrld-1994, 12

Aoi Matsuri
See **Hollyhock Festival (Japan: Kyoto)**

Apache Fair
Location: San Carlos, Arizona
Ethnic or religious group: Apache Indians
Date: Weekend nearest Veterans Day, November 11

IndianAmer-1989, 275

Apache Maidens' Puberty Rites
Location: Mescalero, New Mexico
Ethnic or religious group: Mescalero Apache Tribe
Established: 1911
Date: July 4

HolFestCelWrld-1994, 12

Apache Tribal Fair
Location: Near Show Low, Arizona
Ethnic or religious group: Apache Indians
Date: First weekend in September, including Labor Day

IndianAmer-1989, 278

Apo Festival
Location: Ghana: Tanosu
Ethnic or religious group: Akan people
Date: Uncertain; annual planting festival

FolkWrldHol-1992, 225

Apokreos (Carnival)
See **Mardi Gras (Greece)**

Apple and Candle Night
See **Halloween (Wales)**

Apple Blossom Festival
  Location: Canada: Annapolis Valley Region, Nova Scotia
  Established: 1933
  Date: Five days in late May or early June

  Chases-1993, 221
  GdWrldFest-1985, 44

Apple Blossom Festival, Shenandoah
  Location: Winchester, Virginia
  Established: 1924
  Date: Thursday through Saturday nearest May 1

  AmerBkDays-1978, 403
  Chases-1993, 184
  GdUSFest-1984, 202
  HolFestCelWrld-1994, 315

Apple Blossom Festival, Washington State
  Location: Wenatchee, Washington
  Established: 1920
  Date: April or May

  AnnivHol-1983, 173
  BkFestHolWrld-1970, 89
  Chases-1993, 185
  HolFestCelWrld-1994, 362

Apples, Feast of
  See **Samhain**

Appomattox Day
  Named for: Appomattox, Virginia, where the Civil War
   ended on April 9, 1865
  Location: Appomattox, Virginia
  Date: April 9

  AmerBkDays-1978, 333
  Chases-1993, 159
  HolFestCelWrld-1994, 13

April Fair
  See **Seville Fair**

April Fools' Day
  Established: Late 16th century in France
  Date: April 1

  AmerBkDays-1978, 314
  AnnivHol-1983, 46
  BkDays-1864, i. 460
  BkFest-1937, 17
  BkFestHolWrld-1970, 75
  BkHolWrld-1986, April 1

  Chases-1993, 148
  DaysCustFaith-1957, 92
  DictDays-1988, 3, 100
  DictFolkMyth-1984, 36, 470
  FestSaintDays-1915, 58
  FestWestEur-1958, 34
  FolkAmerHol-1987, 147
  FolkWrldHol-1992, 223
  HolFestCelWrld-1994, 13

April Fools' Day
  Ethnic or religious group: Jewish
  Date: April 1

  FestSaintDays-1915, 58

April Fools' Day (April Noddy Day in northern England)
  Location: England
  Established: 18th century
  Date: April 1

  AmerBkDays-1978, 314
  AnnivHol-1983, 46
  BkDays-1864, i.462
  BkFestHolWrld-1970, 75
  DaysCustFaith-1957, 93
  DictDays-1988, 3
  DictFolkMyth-1984, 36
  FolkWrldHol-1992, 223

April Fools' Day (Poisson d'Avril)
  Location: France
  Established: Late 16th century
  Date: April 1

  AmerBkDays-1978, 314
  AnnivHol-1983, 46
  BkDays-1864, i.460
  BkFestHolWrld-1970, 75
  BkHolWrld-1986, April 1
  DaysCustFaith-1957, 93
  DictFolkMyth-1984, 36
  FestWestEur-1958, 34
  FolkAmerHol-1987, 147
  FolkWrldHol-1992, 223
  HolFestCelWrld-1994, 13

April Fools' Day
  Location: Germany
  Date: April 1 and 30

  BkFestHolWrld-1970, 75
  DictFolkMyth-1984, 36
  FolkAmerHol-1987, 147
  FolkWrldHol-1992, 223

April Fools' Day
  Location: Italy
  Date: April 1

  BkFestHolWrld-1970, 75
  DictFolkMyth-1984, 36

April Fools' Day
  Location: Macedonia
  Date: April 1

  FolkWrldHol-1992, 223

April Fools' Day (Mexico)
  See **All Fools' Day**

April Fools' Day
  Location: New Zealand
  Date: April 1

  FolkWrldHol-1992, 223

April Fools' Day
  Location: Norway
  Date: April 1 and 30

  BkFestHolWrld-1970, 75
  DictFolkMyth-1984, 36
  FolkAmerHol-1987, 147

April Fools' Day
  Location: Portugal
  Date: April 1

  BkFestHolWrld-1970, 75
  DictFolkMyth-1984, 36

April Fools' Day
  Location: Scandinavia
  Date: April 1

  FolkWrldHol-1992, 224

April Fools' Day (Huntigowk Day)
  Location: Scotland
  Date: April 1

  AmerBkDays-1978, 314
  BkDays-1864, i.461
  BkFestHolWrld-1970, 75
  BkHolWrld-1986, April 1
  DictFolkMyth-1984, 36
  FestSaintDays-1915, 58
  FolkAmerHol-1987, 147
  FolkWrldHol-1992, 224

April Fools' Day
  Location: Spain
  Date: April 1

  BkFestHolWrld-1970, 75
  DictFolkMyth-1984, 36

April Fools' Day
  Location: Sweden
  Date: April 1

  BkFestHolWrld-1970, 75
  DictFolkMyth-1984, 36
  FolkWrldHol-1992, 224

April Fools' Day
  Location: United States
  Date: April 1

  AmerBkDays-1978, 314
  AnnivHol-1983, 46
  BkFest-1937, 17
  FolkAmerHol-1987, 147

April Noddy Day
  See **April Fools' Day (England)**

Arab League Day
  Named for: Formation of the Arab League on March 22, 1945
  Location: Jordan
  Date: March 22

  AnnivHol-1983, 41
  Chases-1993, 138

Arafa
  See **Sacrifice, Feast of (Iran)**

Aranya Shasti
  See **Shasti, Festival of (Hindu Rajputanan women in Bengal, India)**

Arbor Day (Israel)
  See **B'Shevat**

Arbor Day
  Named for: Observed on the anniversary of death of Sun Yat-sen (1866-1925)
  Location: Taiwan
  Date: March 12

  Chases-1993, 127
  See also **Double Tenth Day; Sun Yat-sen Day**

Arbor Day (Tree Festival Day)
  Location: Tunisia
  Date: Second Sunday in November

  AnnivHol-1983, 144
  Chases-1993, 441

Arbor Day
  Location: United States
  Established: Legal holiday in Nebraska since 1872, for
  birth of day's founder, Julius Sterling Morton
  (1832-1902)
  Date: April 22 in Nebraska; usually observed last Friday
  in April elsewhere in the U.S.

  AmerBkDays-1978, 366
  AnnivHol-1983, 57
  BkFestHolWrld-1970, 86
  BkHolWrld-1986, April 24
  DictDays-1988, 5
  GdUSFest-1984, 109
  HolFestCelWrld-1994, 13
  See also **Bird and Arbor Day**

Archery Festival (Sur-Kharban)
  Location: Siberia
  Ethnic or religious group: Buryat people
  Date: Spring

  FolkWrldHol-1992, 227

Arena di Verona
  See **Opera Festival, Verona (Italy: Verona, Veneto)**

Argungu Fishing Festival
  Location: Nigeria: Argungu
  Date: February

  BkHolWrld-1986, February 10, 176
  HolFestCelWrld-1994, 14

Århus Festival Week (Århus Festuge)
  Location: Denmark: Århus
  Established: 1965
  Date: Nine days from first Saturday through second
  Sunday in September

  Chases-1993, 355
  GdWrldFest-1985, 71
  IntlThFolk-1979, 91
  MusFestEurBrit-1980, 37

Arikara Celebration
  Location: White Shield, North Dakota

  Date: Second weekend in July

  IndianAmer-1989, 52

Arles Festival
  Location: France: Arles, Bouches-du-Rhone
  Date: July-August

  IntlThFolk-1979, 99

Armed Forces Day
  Named for: Commemorates 1973 war against Israel
  Location: Egypt
  Date: October 6

  HolFestCelWrld-1994, 14

Armed Forces Day
  Location: Liberia
  Date: February 11

  AnnivHol-1983, 23

Armed Forces Day
  Location: New York, New York
  Date: Third Saturday in May

  AmerBkDays-1978, 455

Armed Forces Day
  Location: United States
  Established: 1949; formerly Army Day
  Date: Third Saturday in May

  AmerBkDays-1978, 454
  AnnivHol-1983, 67
  Chases-1993, 208
  DaysCustFaith-1957, 137
  DictDays-1988, 5
  HolFestCelWrld-1994, 14

Armed Forces Day
  Location: United States military installations
  Date: Third Saturday in May

  AmerBkDays-1978, 454

Armed Struggle Day, Commencement of the
  Named for: Rebellion against Portugal that began on
  February 4, 1961
  Location: Angola
  Date: February 4

  AnnivHol-1983, 19

Armindini
  See **May Day (Romania)**

Armistice Day
  Named for: Armistice between Allied and Central powers achieved on November 11, 1918
  Location: Belgium, France, French Guinea, Saint Pierre and Miquelon, and Tahiti
  Date: November 11

AnnivHol-1983, 145
BkFest-1937, 128
BkHolWrld-1986, November 11
Chases-1993, 438
HolFestCelWrld-1994, 357

Armistice Day (United States)
  See **Veterans' Day**

Army Commemoration Day (Rikugun-Kinenbi)
  Location: Japan
  Date: March 10

BkFest-1937, 197

Army Day
  Named for: June 30, 1871, agrarian reform movement; formerly Revolution Day
  Location: Guatemala
  Date: June 30

AnnivHol-1983, 86
Chases-1993, 270

Army Day
  Location: Iraq
  Date: January 6

AnnivHol-1983, 5

Army Day
  Location: Mali
  Date: January 20

AnnivHol-1983, 11

Army Day, Peking
  Location: China: Peking
  Date: August 1

AnnivHol-1983, 101

Art, Biennial of Children's
  Location: Poland: Poznan
  Date: Odd-numbered years in June

IntlThFolk-1979, 296

Art, International Encounter of Contemporary (France: La Rochelle, Charente-Maritime)
  See **Arts, Festival of International Contemporary (France: La Rochelle, Charente-Maritime)**

Art, International Festival of Popular
  Location: Tunisia: Carthage, North Tunis Region
  Established: 1962
  Date: Odd-numbered years in July-August

IntlThFolk-1979, 358

Art and Antiques Fair, Old
  Location: Netherlands: Delft
  Established: 1948
  Date: October-November

GdWrldFest-1985, 140

Art and History, Festival of
  Location: France: Valencay, Indre
  Established: 1974
  Date: Sundays in July and August

IntlThFolk-1979, 126

Art and History, Festival of
  Location: France: Saint-Aignan, Loir-et-Cher
  Established: 1970
  Date: Thursdays, Saturdays, and Sundays in August

IntlThFolk-1979, 23

Artemis Karyatis, Feast of
  Location: Ancient Greece: Karyai
  Date: Annual

DictFolkMyth-1984, 571

Art Fair, Native American
  Location: Suquamish, Washington
  Ethnic or religious group: Suquamish Indians
  Date: Mid-April

IndianAmer-1989, 215

Art Festival, Academic Youth
  Location: Poland: Swinouscie
  Established: 1966
  Date: June

IntlThFolk-1979, 296

Art Festival, Grant Wood
  Named for: Grant Wood (1892-1942)
  Location: Stone City-Anamosa, Iowa
  Date: Second Sunday in June

  HolFestCelWrld-1994, 123

Art Festival, International
  Location: Cyprus: Limassol
  Established: 1966
  Date: 10 days in July

  IntlThFolk-1979, 82

Art Festival, National Foundation
  Location: Republic of Korea: Chinju
  Date: November 1-5

  GdWrldFest-1985, 127

Artigas Day
  Named for: José Gervasio Artigas (1764-1850)
  Location: Uruguay
  Date: June 19

  AnnivHol-1983, 81

Artisans, Day of the
  Location: Mexico
  Date: December 4

  AnnivHol-1983, 156

Artistic Festival of the Damascus International Fair
  Location: Syria: Damascus
  Established: 1956
  Date: 20 days in July

  IntlThFolk-1979, 356

Artistic Weeks, Budapest
  Location: Hungary: Budapest
  Date: September-October

  IntlThFolk-1979, 199
  See also **Music Weeks, Budapest**

d'Art Lyrique et de Musique d'Aix-en-Provence, Festival International
  See **Opera and Music, Aix-en-Provence International Festival of (France: Aix-en-Provence)**

Artpark
  Location: Lewiston, New York
  Established: 1974

  Date: Last week in June to mid-August

  MusFestAmer-1990, 97

Arts, Banff Festival of the
  Location: Canada: Banff, Alberta
  Established: 1971
  Date: Early June to late August

  GdWrldFest-1985, 28
  IntlThFolk-1979, 59
  MusFestAmer-1990, 158

Arts, Big River Festival of
  Location: Australia: Grafton, New South Wales
  Date: One week in May-June

  IntlThFolk-1979, 9

Arts, Birmingham Festival of the
  Location: Birmingham, Alabama
  Established: 1951
  Date: Two weeks in April-May

  Chases-1993, 175
  GdUSFest-1984, 3
  HolFestCelWrld-1994, 32
  MusFestAmer-1990, 20

Arts, Festival of Asian
  Location: Hong Kong
  Established: 1976
  Date: Last two weeks in October

  GdWrldFest-1985, 107

Arts, Festival of International Contemporary (Recontres Internationales d'Art Contemporain)
  Location: France: La Rochelle
  Established: 1972-73
  Date: Two weeks in June-July

  IntlThFolk-1979, 109
  MusFestEurBrit-1980, 89

Arts, Festival of Native
  Location: Fairbanks, Alaska
  Date: Three days in late February

  Chases-1993, 110

Arts, Festival of the
  Location: Australia: Adelaide, South Australia
  Established: 1960
  Date: Even-numbered years in February-March

  GdWrldFest-1985, 8
  HolFestCelWrld-1994, 2
  IntlThFolk-1979, 19, 21

Arts, Festival of the
  Location: Oklahoma City, Oklahoma
  Established: 1967
  Date: Six days in late April

  Chases-1993, 173
  GdUSFest-1984, 146

Arts, Festival of the
  Location: Southern Vermont Art Center, Manchester, Vermont
  Established: 1929
  Date: Early June through mid-October

  GdUSFest-1984, 194

Arts, Festival of Traditional
  Location: France: Rennes, Ille-et-Vilaine
  Established: 1974
  Date: March

  IntlThFolk-1979, 121

Arts, Flagstaff Festival of the
  Location: Flagstaff, Arizona
  Established: 1966
  Date: Four weeks in July

  HolFestCelWrld-1994, 107
  MusFestAmer-1990, 23

Arts, Holiday Festival of the
  Location: Canada: Neepawa, Manitoba
  Established: 1966
  Date: July

  IntlThFolk-1979, 63

Arts, International Festival of
  Location: Monaco: Monte Carlo
  Established: 1970
  Date: July-August

  GdWrldFest-1985, 136
  IntlThFolk-1979, 279

Arts, International Festival of the
  Location: International Peace Garden, Dunseith, North Dakota, and Manitoba, Canada
  Established: 1969
  Date: Six weeks during June and July

  Chases-1993, 247
  GdUSFest-1984, 134

Arts, Lakefront Festival of the
  Location: Milwaukee, Wisconsin

Established: 1962
  Date: June

  Chases-1993, 253
  GdUSFest-1984, 213

Arts, Northam Festival of the
  Location: Australia: Northam, Western Australia
  Date: June-July

  IntlThFolk-1979, 29

Arts, North Queensland Festival of
  Location: Australia: Innisfail, Queensland
  Established: 1966
  Date: Three weeks in December

  IntlThFolk-1979, 18

Arts, Orange Festival of the
  Location: Australia: Orange, New South Wales
  Date: One week in April during even-numbered years

  IntlThFolk-1979, 10

Arts, Perth Festival of the
  Location: Scotland: Perth, Perthshire
  Established: 1971
  Date: Last two weeks in May

  IntlThFolk-1979, 187

Arts, Salisbury Festival of the
  Location: England: Salisbury, Wiltshire
  Date: September

  IntlThFolk-1979, 175

Arts, Shiraz Festival of
  Location: Iran: Shiraz; formerly Persepolis
  Established: 1966
  Date: August-September

  IntlThFolk-1979, 228

Arts, Summer Festival of the
  Location: Canada: St. John's, Newfoundland
  Established: 1967-68
  Date: Month of July

  GdWrldFest-1985, 41
  IntlThFolk-1979, 65

Arts, Winchester Festival of the
  Location: England: Winchester, Hampshire
  Established: 1976
  Date: July

  IntlThFolk-1979, 180

Arts and Crafts Show, Eight Northern Indian Pueblos Spring
   Location: DeVargas Mall, Santa Fe, New Mexico
   Date: April 19-20

   IndianAmer-1989, 286

Arts and Crafts Show, Annual Eight Northern Indian Pueblos
   Location: San Juan Pueblo, New Mexico
   Date: July 18-20

   IndianAmer-1989, 287, 312

Arts and Culture, World Black and African Festival of
   Location: Varies
   Established: 1966
   Date: Uncertain; held 1977, 1981

   IntlThFolk-1979, 6

Arts and Music, Frejus Forum of (Forum des Arts et de la Musique)
   Location: France: Frejus, Var
   Established: 1978
   Date: July

   IntlThFolk-1979, 106

Arts and Pageant of the Masters, Festival of the
   Location: Laguna Beach, California
   Established: 1932
   Date: 45 days in July and August

   GdUSFest-1984, 18
   HolFestCelWrld-1994, 14

Arts Colony, Inspiration Point Fine
   Location: Eureka Springs, Arkansas
   Established: 1950s
   Date: June to second week in July

   MusFestAmer-1990, 166

Arts en Belgique, Europalia Festival des
   Location: Belgium: Brussels
   Date: Every other autumn

   IntlThFolk-1979, 45

Arts Festival
   Location: Florida
   Ethnic or religious group: Miccosukee Indians
   Date: December, the week after Christmas

   IndianAmer-1989, 239

Arts Festival
   Location: Atlanta, Georgia
   Established: 1954

   Date: Nine days in May

   GdUSFest-1984, 38

Arts Festival, Braintree District
   Location: England: Braintree, Essex
   Established: 1972
   Date: Six weeks in April-May

   IntlThFolk-1979, 156

Arts Festival, Christchurch
   Location: New Zealand: Christchurch
   Established: 1965
   Date: Even-numbered years in March

   GdWrldFest-1985, 143
   IntlThFolk-1979, 285

Arts Festival, Dawlish
   Location: England: Dawlish, Devonshire
   Established: 1954
   Date: Last two weeks in June

   IntlThFolk-1979, 159

Arts Festival, Dogwood
   Location: Knoxville, Tennessee
   Established: 1956; current version since 1961
   Date: 17 days in April

   Chases-1993, 151
   GdUSFest-1984, 174

Arts Festival, Dublin
   Location: Ireland: Dublin
   Established: 1970
   Date: March

   IntlThFolk-1979, 232

Arts Festival, Europalia
   Location: Belgium
   Established: 1969
   Date: Odd-numbered years in September-December

   HolFestCelWrld-1994, 100

Arts Festival, Gorey
   Location: Ireland: Gorey, County Wexford
   Date: Summer

   IntlThFolk-1979, 234

Arts Festival, Hong Kong
   Location: Hong Kong
   Established: 1972-73
   Date: January-February

   GdWrldFest-1985, 105
   HolFestCelWrld-1994, 143
   IntlThFolk-1979, 198

Arts Festival, Jyvaskyla
  Location: Finland: Jyvaskyla
  Established: 1956
  Date: Several days in May-July

Chases-1993, 250
GdWrldFest-1985, 76
IntlThFolk-1979, 95

Arts Festival, Kalakshetra
  Location: India: Madras, Tamil Nadu
  Established: 1936
  Date: December-January

IntlThFolk-1979, 215

Arts Festival, L.G. Harris
  Location: England: Stoke Prior, Worcestershire
  Established: 1960
  Date: Even-numbered years during the second week in
  October

IntlThFolk-1979, 176

Arts Festival, Maidment
  Location: New Zealand: Auckland
  Date: April-May

IntlThFolk-1979, 285

Arts Festival, New Directions in the Performing
  Location: Canada: Hamilton, Ontario
  Established: 1976
  Date: Even-numbered years in summer or autumn

IntlThFolk-1979, 70

Arts Festival, Reykjavik
  Location: Iceland: Reykjavik
  Established: 1970
  Date: 16 days in June during even-numbered years

GdWrldFest-1985, 108
IntlThFolk-1979, 201

Arts Festival, Rhymney Valley
  Location: Wales: Rhymney Valley District
  Established: Caerphilly Festival since 1963; current version
  since 1975
  Date: Last two weeks in October

IntlThFolk-1979, 190

Arts Festival, Singapore
  Location: Singapore
  Established: 1978

  Date: Three weeks in December

GdWrldFest-1985, 159

Arts Festival, Summerscape-Huntington Summer
  Location: Huntington, New York
  Established: 1961
  Date: Late June to late August

MusFestAmer-1990, 214

Arts Festival, Three Rivers
  Location: Pittsburgh, Pennsylvania
  Established: 1960
  Date: 17 days in June

Chases-1993, 234
GdUSFest-1984, 163

Arts Festival, Utah
  Location: Salt Lake City, Utah
  Established: 1977
  Date: Five days in late June

GdUSFest-1984, 191
HolFestCelWrld-1994, 352
MusFestAmer-1990, 141

Arts for Young People, Festival of Performing—Round Up
  Location: Australia: Perth, Western Australia
  Date: Five days in February

IntlThFolk-1979, 30

Arts Series, Wave Hill Performing
  Location: Bronx, New York
  Date: September to May

MusFestAmer-1990, 114

Arts Week, Creative
  Location: Canada: Gimli, Manitoba
  Established: 1970
  Date: Last full week in August

IntlThFolk-1979, 62

Asarah be-Tevet (Fast of 10th of Tevet)
  Ethnic or religious group: Jewish
  Date: December-January

Chases-1993, 54, 481
HolFestCelWrld-1994, 15

Ascension Day
  Named for: Ascension of Jesus (c. 6 B.C.-c. 30 A.D.) into
  heaven
  Ethnic or religious group: Christian

Ascension Day *(cont.)*
   Established: About 68 A.D.
   Date: May-June, fortieth day after Easter Sunday

   AmerBkDays-1978, 422
   AnnivHol-1983, 169
   BkFest-1937, 135
   BkHolWrld-1986, May 21
   Chases-1993, 214
   DaysCustFaith-1957, 135
   DictFolkMyth-1984, 49, 1156
   DictWrldRel-1989, 65
   FestSaintDays-1915, 113
   FestWestEur-1958, 64, 165, 215
   FolkAmerHol-1987, 68, 193
   FolkWrldHol-1992, 280
   HolFestCelWrld-1994, 15, 24, 126
   RelHolCal-1993, 58

Ascension Day
   Ethnic or religious group: Eastern Orthodox
   Date: May-June, fortieth day after Easter Sunday

   AmerBkDays-1978, 422

Ascension Day
   Ethnic or religious group: Episcopalian
   Date: May-June, fortieth day after Easter Sunday

   AmerBkDays-1978, 422

Ascension Day
   Ethnic or religious group: Lutheran
   Date: May-June, fortieth day after Easter Sunday

   AmerBkDays-1978, 422

Ascension Day
   Ethnic or religious group: Roman Catholic
   Date: May-June, fortieth day after Easter Sunday

   AmerBkDays-1978, 422
   DictFolkMyth-1984, 79

Ascension Day (Vičak or Vijak, Festival of Fortune)
   Location: Armenia
   Date: May-June, fortieth day after Easter Sunday

   AnnivHol-1983, 183
   BkFest-1937, 25
   DictFolkMyth-1984, 1156
   RelHolCal-1993, 121

Ascension Day (Belgium)
   See **Holy Blood, Procession of the**

Ascension Day
   Location: Denmark
   Date: May-June, fortieth day after Easter Sunday

   DictFolkMyth-1984, 79

Ascension Day (Beating the Bounds)
   Location: England
   Date: May-June, fortieth day after Easter Sunday

   DaysCustFaith-1957, 135
   DictFolkMyth-1984, 79
   FestSaintDays-1915, 113
   FolkWrldHol-1992, 280
   HolFestCelWrld-1994, 15
   See also **Holy Thursday (Church of England)**

Ascension Day (Himmelfahrstag)
   Location: Germany
   Date: May-June, fortieth day after Easter Sunday

   BkFest-1937, 135
   DictFolkMyth-1984, 79
   FestWestEur-1958, 64
   FolkWrldHol-1992, 280
   HolFestCelWrld-1994, 15

Ascension Day
   Location: Italy
   Date: May-June, fortieth day after Easter Sunday

   FestSaintDays-1915, 116

Ascension Day (Festa del Grillo, Cricket Festival)
   Location: Italy: Florence, Tuscany
   Date: May-June, fortieth day after Easter Sunday

   BkFestHolWrld-1970, 105
   BkHolWrld-1986, May 21
   FestSaintDays-1915, 116
   FestWestEur-1958, 97
   HolFestCelWrld-1994, 126

Ascension Day
   Location: Netherlands
   Date: May-June, fortieth day after Easter Sunday

   FolkWrldHol-1992, 280

Ascension Day (Quinta-Feira da Espiga, Ear of Wheat Thursday)
   Location: Portugal
   Date: May-June, fortieth day after Easter Sunday

   FestWestEur-1958, 165

Ascension Day
   Location: Romania
   Date: May-June, fortieth day after Easter Sunday

   FolkWrldHol-1992, 280

Ascension Day
   Location: Sicily
   Date: May-June, fortieth day after Easter Sunday

   DictFolkMyth-1984, 80

Ascension Day (Kristi Himmelsfärdsdag)
   Location: Sweden
   Date: May-June, fortieth day after Easter Sunday

   FestWestEur-1958, 215
   FolkWrldHol-1992, 281
   HolFestCelWrld-1994, 15

Ascension Day (Banntag)
   Location: Switzerland: Basel
   Date: May-June, fortieth day after Easter Sunday

   HolFestCelWrld-1994, 24

Ascension Day
   Location: United States
   Ethnic or religious group: Pennsylvania Dutch people and German-Americans
   Date: May-June, fortieth day after Easter Sunday

   FolkAmerHol-1987, 193

Ascension of Christ
   See **Ascension Day; Holy Thursday (Church of England)**

Ascot, Royal
   Location: England: Berkshire
   Established: Horse race since 1711
   Date: Four days in mid-June

   HolFestCelWrld-1994, 277

Asdvadzahaidnootyoon
   See **Epiphany (Armenia)**

Ashokashtami
   Location: India: Lingaraja Temple, Bhubaneshwar
   Ethnic or religious group: Hindu
   Date: March-April, eighth day of waxing half of Hindu month of Chaitra

   RelHolCal-1993, 59
   See also **Juggernaut**

Ashura
   Ethnic or religious group: Muslim
   Established: Seventh century

Date: 10th day of Muharram, the first Islamic month

   AnnivHol-1983, 170
   BkFest-1937, 237
   Chases-1993, 270
   FolkWrldHol-1992, 369, 370
   HolFestCelWrld-1994, 15
   RelHolCal-1993, 59

Ashura
   Ethnic or religious group: Sunni Muslims
   Date: 10th day of Muharram, the first Islamic month

   FolkWrldHol-1992, 369
   HolFestCelWrld-1994, 15
   RelHolCal-1993, 59

Ashura
   Location: Iran; formerly Persia
   Date: 10th day of Muharram, the first Islamic month

   BkFest-1937, 237
   RelHolCal-1993, 59

Ashura
   Location: Morocco
   Date: 10th day of Muharram, the first Islamic month

   FolkWrldHol-1992, 369

Ashura (Shiite Muslims)
   See **Husayn Day**

Ashura
   Location: Turkey
   Established: Commemorates Noah's leaving the ark on Mount Ararat
   Date: 10th day of Muharram, the first Islamic month

   BkFest-1937, 237
   HolFestCelWrld-1994, 15
   RelHolCal-1993, 59

Ashura
   Location: West Africa
   Ethnic or religious group: Hausa people
   Date: 10th day of Muharram, the first Islamic month

   FolkWrldHol-1992, 370
   HolFestCelWrld-1994, 15
   See also **New Year (West Africa)**

Ash Wednesday
   Ethnic or religious group: Christian
   Established: About fourth century

Ash Wednesday *(cont.)*
Date: February-March, fortieth day before Easter Sunday

AmerBkDays-1978, 162
AnnivHol-1983, 169
BkDays-1864, i. 240
BkFest-1937, 299
BkFestHolWrld-1970, 47
BkHolWrld-1986, February 26
Chases-1993, 109
DaysCustFaith-1957, 64
DictDays-1988, 6, 92
DictFolkMyth-1984, 82, 535
FestSaintDays-1915, 48
FestWestEur-1958, 194
FolkAmerHol-1987, 93
FolkWrldHol-1992, 120
HolFestCelWrld-1994, 16
RelHolCal-1993, 58
SaintFestCh-1904, 115

Ash Wednesday
Ethnic or religious group: Anglican
Date: February-March, fortieth day before Easter Sunday

DictFolkMyth-1984, 82

Ash Wednesday
Ethnic or religious group: Church of England
Date: February-March, fortieth day before Easter Sunday

AmerBkDays-1978, 163

Ash Wednesday
Ethnic or religious group: Eastern Orthodox
Date: February-March, fortieth day before Easter Sunday;
  Lent begins the Monday before

AmerBkDays-1978, 162
HolFestCelWrld-1994, 16

Ash Wednesday
Ethnic or religious group: Episcopalian
Date: February-March, fortieth day before Easter Sunday

AmerBkDays-1978, 163
DictFolkMyth-1984, 82

Ash Wednesday
Ethnic or religious group: Lutheran
Date: February-March, fortieth day before Easter Sunday

AmerBkDays-1978, 163

Ash Wednesday
Ethnic or religious group: Protestant

Date: February-March, fortieth day before Easter Sunday

AmerBkDays-1978, 162
BkFestHolWrld-1970, 47
DictFolkMyth-1984, 82

Ash Wednesday
Ethnic or religious group: Roman Catholic
Date: February-March, fortieth day before Easter Sunday

AmerBkDays-1978, 162
BkDays-1864, i.240
BkFestHolWrld-1970, 47
BkHolWrld-1986, February 26
DaysCustFaith-1957, 65
DictDays-1988, 6
DictFolkMyth-1984, 82
FestSaintDays-1915, 48

Ash Wednesday
Location: Austria
Date: February-March, fortieth day before Easter Sunday

DictFolkMyth-1984, 82

Ash Wednesday
Location: England
Date: February-March, fortieth day before Easter Sunday

BkDays-1864, i. 240
FolkWrldHol-1992, 120

Ash Wednesday
Location: France
Date: February-March, fortieth day before Easter Sunday

DictFolkMyth-1984, 82

Ash Wednesday
Location: Germany
Date: February-March, fortieth day before Easter Sunday

DictFolkMyth-1984, 82

Ash Wednesday
Location: Greece
Date: February-March, fortieth day before Easter Sunday

DictFolkMyth-1984, 82

Ash Wednesday
Location: Iceland
Date: February-March, fortieth day before Easter Sunday

FolkWrldHol-1992, 120
HolFestCelWrld-1994, 16

Ash Wednesday
  Location: Italy
  Date: February-March, fortieth day before Easter Sunday

  DictFolkMyth-1984, 82

Ash Wednesday
  Location: Spain
  Date: February-March, fortieth day before Easter Sunday

  BkFest-1937, 299
  DictFolkMyth-1984, 82
  FestSaintDays-1915, 49
  See also **Burial of the Sardine (Entierro de la Sardina)**

Ash Wednesday
  Location: United States
  Date: February-March, fortieth day before Easter Sunday

  AmerBkDays-1978, 163
  FolkAmerHol-1987, 93

Ash Wednesday Eve
  See **Mardi Gras**

Asking Festival (Ai-yá-g'ûk)
  Location: Alaska and the Yukon
  Ethnic or religious group: Eskimos

  DictFolkMyth-1984, 83

Ass, Feast of the
  Location: Northern France
  Established: Medieval Constantinople
  Date: January 14

  BkDays-1864, i. 112
  DictFolkMyth-1984, 84
  FestSaintDays-1915, 254
  HolFestCelWrld-1994, 17

ASSITEJ—Association Internationale du Theatre pour l'Enfance et la Jeunesse
  See **Theatre for Children and Young People Congress and Festival, International Association of**

Assumption, Feast of the
  Named for: The "assumption" of the Virgin May (first century B.C.-first century A.D.) into heaven
  Ethnic or religious group: Christian
  Established: Fourth century in Jerusalem; since seventh century in the Eastern Church; sixth century in the Western Church
  Date: August 15

  AmerBkDays-1978, 755

  AnnivHol-1983, 107
  BkFest-1937, 172
  BkFestHolWrld-1970, 109
  BkHolWrld-1986, August 15
  Chases-1993, 330
  DaysCustFaith-1957, 206
  DictDays-1988, 6
  DictFolkMyth-1984, 886, 1065
  FestSaintDays-1915, 169
  FestWestEur-1958, 15, 47, 184, 203
  FolkAmerHol-1987, 257
  FolkWrldHol-1992, 270, 419
  HolFestCelWrld-1994, 17
  IndianAmer-1989, 288, 321
  IntlThFolk-1979, 335
  RelHolCal-1993, 59

Assumption, Feast of the
  Ethnic or religious group: Anglican
  Date: August 15

  HolFestCelWrld-1994, 17

Assumption, Feast of the
  Ethnic or religious group: Coptic Church
  Date: August 15

  FestSaintDays-1915, 172

Assumption, Feast of the
  Ethnic or religious group: Eastern Orthodox
  Date: August 15

  AmerBkDays-1978, 755, 756
  BkHolWrld-1986, August 15
  HolFestCelWrld-1994, 17
  RelHolCal-1993, 59

Assumption, Feast of the
  Ethnic or religious group: Greek Orthodox
  Date: Begins August 6 and lasts nine days

  FestSaintDays-1915, 172

Assumption, Feast of the
  Ethnic or religious group: Roman Catholic
  Date: August 15

  AmerBkDays-1978, 755
  BkHolWrld-1986, August 15
  DaysCustFaith-1957, 206
  DictDays-1988, 6
  FolkAmerHol-1987, 257
  HolFestCelWrld-1994, 17
  RelHolCal-1993, 59

Assumption, Feast of the (Naltësimi i Virgjereshës)
  Location: Albania
  Date: August 15

  BkFest-1937, 8

Assumption, Feast of the (Haghoghy Ortnovtyoon or Navasard Armenian Grape Festival, Blessing of the Grapes)
  Location: Armenia
  Date: Sunday nearest August 15

  BkFest-1937, 27
  BkFestHolWrld-1970, 109
  BkHolWrld-1986, August 25, 179
  DaysCustFaith-1957, 207
  FestSaintDays-1915, 172
  FolkWrldHol-1992, 419
  HolFestCelWrld-1994, 36

Assumption, Feast of the (Maia-Hemelvaart Dat)
  Location: Belgium
  Date: August 15

  BkFest-1937, 46
  BkFestHolWrld-1970, 109
  FestWestEur-1958, 15

Assumption, Feast of the (Festival of Virga Jesse)
  Location: Belgium: Hasselt, Limburg
  Date: Third and fourth Sundays in August every seven years

  BkFest-1937, 46
  FestWestEur-1958, 15

Assumption, Feast of the (Nossa Senhora dos Navegantes, Our Lady of the Navigators)
  Location: Brazil: São Paulo
  Date: August 15

  FolkWrldHol-1992, 419
  HolFestCelWrld-1994, 17

Assumption, Feast of the (Bogoroditza)
  Location: Bulgaria
  Date: August 15

  BkFest-1937, 72

Assumption, Feast of the (Tintamarre Celebration)
  Location: Canada: Maritime Provinces
  Ethnic or religious group: Acadian people
  Date: August 15 and Sunday nearest August 15

  FolkWrldHol-1992, 419
  HolFestCelWrld-1994, 17

Assumption, Feast of the
  Location: England

Date: August 15

FestSaintDays-1915, 173

Assumption, Feast of the
  Location: Ethiopia
  Date: 16-day fast in August

  FolkWrldHol-1992, 419

Assumption, Feast of the (L'Assomption)
  Location: France
  Date: August 15

  BkFest-1937, 127
  BkHolWrld-1986, August 15
  FestWestEur-1958, 47
  HolFestCelWrld-1994, 17

Assumption, Feast of the
  Location: France: Queven
  Date: August 15

  HolFestCelWrld-1994, 17

Assumption, Feast of the (Koimesis tees Theotokou)
  Location: Greece
  Date: August 15

  BkFest-1937, 152
  FestSaintDays-1915, 172

Assumption, Feast of the (Nagyboldag Asszony Napja)
  Location: Hungary
  Date: August 15

  BkFest-1937, 172

Assumption, Feast of the
  Location: Pilgrimage to Cataldo Mission in Idaho
  Ethnic or religious group: Coeur d'Alene Indians
  Date: August 15

  AmerBkDays-1978, 756

Assumption, Feast of the
  Location: Iowa
  Ethnic or religious group: Czech-Americans
  Date: August 15

  FolkAmerHol-1987, 258

Assumption, Feast of the (Bowing Procession)
  Location: Italy
  Date: August 15

  AmerBkDays-1978, 756
  BkFestHolWrld-1970, 109
  DaysCustFaith-1957, 207

Assumption, Feast of the
 Location: Minnesota
 Ethnic or religious group: Czech-Americans
 Date: August 15

 FolkAmerHol-1987, 258

Assumption, Feast of the
 Location: New Mexico pueblos
 Date: August 15

 AmerBkDays-1978, 756
 IndianAmer-1989, 288, 321

Assumption, Feast of the (Harvest Festival for Our Lady of Flowers)
 Location: Orange County, New York
 Ethnic or religious group: Polish-Americans
 Established: 1939
 Date: August 15

 FolkAmerHol-1987, 257
 HolFestCelWrld-1994, 88

Assumption, Feast of the
 Location: Peru: Pacarigtambo
 Date: August 15

 FolkWrldHol-1992, 270

Assumption, Feast of the (Dia da Nussa Senhora da Assumçao, Day of Our Lady of the Angels)
 Location: Portugal
 Date: August 15

 BkFest-1937, 270
 DictFolkMyth-1984, 886
 FestWestEur-1958, 184

Assumption, Feast of the (Uspeniye Presvyato or Bogoroditzy)
 Location: Russia
 Date: August 15, Gregorian calendar (N.S.); August 28, Julian calendar (O.S.)

 BkFest-1937, 294

Assumption, Feast of the (Bowing Procession)
 Location: Sicily
 Date: August 15

 AmerBkDays-1978, 756
 FestSaintDays-1915, 173
 FolkWrldHol-1992, 419

Assumption, Feast of the
 Location: Sicily: Messina

 Date: Two weeks, including August 15

 FolkWrldHol-1992, 419
 HolFestCelWrld-1994, 17

Assumption, Feast of the
 Location: Spain
 Date: August 15

 BkFestHolWrld-1970, 109
 DaysCustFaith-1957, 207
 DictFolkMyth-1984, 1065
 FestSaintDays-1915, 171
 FestWestEur-1958, 203
 FolkWrldHol-1992, 420
 HolFestCelWrld-1994, 17
 IntlThFolk-1979, 335

Assumption, Feast of the (El Misterio de Elche, Mystery Play of Elche)
 Location: Spain: Elche, Valencia
 Established: 13th century
 Date: August 14-15

 FestSaintDays-1915, 171
 FestWestEur-1958, 203
 FolkWrldHol-1992, 420
 HolFestCelWrld-1994, 17
 IntlThFolk-1979, 335

Assumption, Feast of the ('Id Rakad-ai-Sayyidah)
 Location: Syria: Monastery of the Virgin at Saidnaya near Damascus
 Ethnic or religious group: Christian and Muslim
 Date: August 15, Gregorian calendar (N.S.); August 28, Julian calendar (O.S.)

 BkFest-1937, 331
 BkFestHolWrld-1970, 110
 DaysCustFaith-1957, 208

Assumption, Feast of the
 Location: United States
 Ethnic or religious group: Italian-Americans
 Date: August 15

 DaysCustFaith-1957, 207

Aston Magna Festival
 Location: Great Barrington, Massachusetts
 Date: Three consecutive Saturday evenings in early July

 MusFestAmer-1990, 73

Asturias Day
 Location: Spain: Gijon, Oviedo
 Date: First Sunday in August

 IntlThFolk-1979, 336

Athens Festival
Location: Greece: Athens
Established: 1955
Date: June through last week in September

GdWrldFest-1985, 101
IntlThFolk-1979, 192
MusFestEurBrit-1980, 107
MusFestWrld-1963, 231

Ati-Atihan Festival
Location: Philippines: Kalibo, Akland, Panay Island
Ethnic or religious group: Negrito and Malay peoples
Established: Commemorates 13th-century peace agreement
Date: Three days in January, including feast day of Santo Nino (Holy Child Jesus) and ending on a Sunday

Chases-1993, 65
GdWrldFest-1985, 152
HolFestCelWrld-1994, 17
IntlThFolk-1979, 288

Atomic Bomb, First Use of the
See **Peace Festival**

Atonement, Day of
See **Yom Kippur**

Auckland Festival
Location: New Zealand: Auckland
Established: 1949
Date: Even-numbered years during March-April

GdWrldFest-1985, 143
IntlThFolk-1979, 284

Audry, St.
See **St. Etheldreda's Day**

Audubon Day
Named for: John James Audubon (1785-1851)
Location: United States
Date: April 26

AmerBkDays-1978, 380
AnnivHol-1983, 57
BkFestHolWrld-1970, 93
Chases-1993, 181

Austin Day
See **Father of Texas Day**

Australia Day
Named for: January 26, 1788, landing by Arthur Phillip (1738-1814)

Location: Australia
Date: January 26 or following Monday

AnnivHol-1983, 14
Chases-1993, 74, 81
DictDays-1988, 7
HolFestCelWrld-1994, 18
IntlThFolk-1979, 11
NatlHolWrld-1968, 16

Australia Day
Location: Western Australia
Date: On or around June 1

DictDays-1988, 43

Australia Day at the Rocks
Named for: January 26, 1788, landing by Arthur Phillip (1738-1814)
Location: Australia: the Rocks, Sydney, New South Wales
Date: Late January

IntlThFolk-1979, 11

Australian Open Tennis
Location: Australia: Sydney and Melbourne
Established: Men's matches since 1905, women's matches since 1922, and public matches since 1969
Date: January

HolFestCelWrld-1994, 18

Austrian State Treaty Day
Named for: Signing of the Austrian State Treaty on May 15, 1955
Date: May 15

NatlHolWrld-1968, 49

Author's Day
Location: United States: reading clubs
Date: November 1

AnnivHol-1983, 140
Chases-1993, 428

Automobile Hall of Fame Week
See **Sebring 12 Hours (Sebring, Florida)**

Autumn, Styrian (Steirischer Herbst)
Location: Austria: Graz, Styria
Established: 1968
Date: Eight weeks in October-November

GdWrldFest-1985, 12
IntlThFolk-1979, 33
MusFestEurBrit-1980, 28

Autumn Festival (China), (Hong Kong), (Japan), (Macao), (Malaysia), (Singapore), (Taiwan), and (Vietnam)
  See **Mid-Autumn Festival (China), (Hong Kong), (Japan), (Macao), (Malaysia), (Singapore), (Taiwan), and (Vietnam)**

Autumn Festival, Paris (Festival d'Automne)
  Location: France: Paris
  Established: 1972
  Date: Mid-September through end of December

  IntlThFolk-1979, 117
  MusFestEurBrit-1980, 86

Autumnal Equinox
  Date: September 22-23

  AmerBkDays-1978, 859
  BkDays-1864, ii. 364
  Chases-1993, 381
  DictDays-1988, 37
  HolFestCelWrld-1994, 18

Autumnal Equinox (Jugowa)
  Location: Okinawa
  Date: On or around September 21-22; full moon day of the eighth lunar month

  FolkWrldHol-1992, 487

Autumnal Equinox Day (Higan Ritual)
  Location: Japan
  Ethnic or religious group: Buddhist
  Established: Official holiday, Subun No Hi, observed since 1946
  Date: September 23 or 24

  AnnivHol-1983, 121
  FolkWrldHol-1992, 486
  HolFestCelWrld-1994, 18, 137

Autumn of Culture
  Location: Yugoslavia: Backi Petrovac, Vojvodina
  Date: Second half of October

  IntlThFolk-1979, 379

Avak Shapat
  See **Holy Saturday (Armenia)**

Avani Avittan
  See **Sacred Thread Festival (southern India)**

Avani Mulam
  Location: India: Madura
  Ethnic or religious group: Hindu

  Date: August or September

  BkFestHolWrld-1970, 107

Avignon Festival (Festival d'Avignon)
  Location: France: Avignon
  Established: 1947
  Date: Three and one-half weeks in July-August

  HolFestCelWrld-1994, 89
  IntlThFolk-1979, 99
  MusFestEurBrit-1980, 74

Awakeners, Day of the (Den na Buditelite)
  Location: Bulgaria
  Date: November 1

  BkFest-1937, 72
  HolFestCelWrld-1994, 80

Awa Odori
  See **Fools' Dance (Japan)**

Awe, Days of
  See **New Year, Jewish (Rosh Hashanah)**

Awoojoh
  See **Thanksgiving (Yoruba, Christian Creoles, and Muslim Aku people in Sierra Leone)**

Awuru Odo Festival
  See **Dead, Return of the (Odo Festival)**

Awwal Muharram
  See **New Year (Muslim)**

Ayyam-i-Ha
  Ethnic or religious group: Bahá'í
  Date: February 26-March 1

  AnnivHol-1983, 29
  HolFestCelWrld-1994, 19
  RelHolCal-1993, 60

Azincourt, Battle of
  See **St. Crispin's Day**

Azumi
  See **Ramadan (Hausa people in Katsina, Nigeria)**

Bä alä mäsällät (Feast of the Tabernacles)
  See **Sukkot (Ethiopia)**

Baalbek Festival
  Location: Lebanon: Baalbek
  Established: 1955-56
  Date: Mid-July to mid-August

  IntlThFolk-1979, 262
  MusFestWrld-1963, 225

Báb, Birth of the
Named for: Mirza Ali Mohammad (1819-1850)
Ethnic or religious group: Bahá'í
Date: October 20

AnnivHol-1983, 134
Chases-1993, 415
DictWrldRel-1989, 86, 87
HolFestCelWrld-1994, 21
RelHolCal-1993, 62

Báb, Declaration of the
Named for: Mirza Ali Mohammad (1819-1850)
Ethnic or religious group: Bahá'í
Established: May 23, 1844
Date: May 23

AnnivHol-1983, 60
Chases-1993, 218
DictWrldRel-1989, 86, 87
HolFestCelWrld-1994, 21
RelHolCal-1993, 71

Báb, Martyrdom of the
Named for: Mirza Ali Mohammad (1819-1850)
Ethnic or religious group: Bahá'í
Date: July 9

AnnivHol-1983, 91
Chases-1993, 285
DictWrldRel-1989, 86, 87
HolFestCelWrld-1994, 21
RelHolCal-1993, 93

Babin Den
See **Grandmother's Day (Bulgaria)**

Baby Parade
Location: Ocean City, New Jersey
Established: 1901
Date: Second Thursday in August

Chases-1993, 325
GdUSFest-1984, 118
HolFestCelWrld-1994, 21

Bacchanalia
Location: Rome
Date: Spring

DictMyth-1962, i.170
See also **Dionysus**

Bachelors' Day
See **Leap Year Day**

Bach Festival (Bachwoche Ansbach)
Named for: Johann Sebastian Bach (1685-1750)
Location: Federal Republic of Germany: Ansbach
Established: 1947
Date: Ten days in late July during odd-numbered years

MusFestEurBrit-1980, 95

Bach Festival, Baldwin-Wallace
Named for: Johann Sebastian Bach (1685-1750)
Location: Berea, Ohio
Established: 1932
Date: Two days in mid-May

MusFestAmer-1990, 121

Bach Festival, Carmel
Named for: Johann Sebastian Bach (1685-1750)
Location: Carmel, California
Established: 1935
Date: Mid-July to early August

MusFestAmer-1990, 26

Bach Festival, English
Named for: Johann Sebastian Bach (1685-1750)
Location: England: Oxford and London
Established: 1963
Date: April and May

MusFestEurBrit-1980, 53

Bach Festival, International
Named for: Johann Sebastian Bach (1685-1750)
Location: Portugal: Funchal, Madeira Island
Established: 1979
Date: June

GdWrldFest-1985, 155
HolFestCelWrld-1994, 22

Bach Festival, Oregon
Named for: Johann Sebastian Bach (1685-1750)
Location: Eugene, Oregon
Established: 1970
Date: Late June to second week in July

Chases-1993, 265
MusFestAmer-1990, 129

Bach Festival of Winter Park
Named for: Johann Sebastian Bach (1685-1750)
Location: Winter Park, Florida
Established: 1937
Date: Three days in late February or early March

MusFestAmer-1990, 51

Bach Music Festival
   Named for: Johann Sebastian Bach (1685-1750)
   Location: Bethlehem, Pennsylvania
   Established: 1900
   Date: Two weekends in May

   GdUSFest-1984, 155
   MusFestAmer-1990, 130

Bachok Festival of Culture
   Location: Malaysia: Bachok, Kelantan
   Date: Two weeks in May

   GdWrldFest-1985, 131
   IntlThFolk-1979, 266

Bachwoche Ansbach
   See **Bach Festival (Federal Republic of Germany: Ansbach)**

Back Badge Day
   Named for: Battle of Alexandria in 1801
   Location: England: Gloucestershire Regiment of the British Army
   Date: March 21

   DictDays-1988, 8

Bad Hersfeld in the Monastery Ruins, Festival of
   Location: Federal Republic of Germany: Bad Hersfeld, Hesse
   Date: July-August

   IntlThFolk-1979, 141

Badnyi Dan
   See **Christmas Eve (Yugoslavia)**

Bahá'u'lláh, Ascension of
   Named for: Death of Mirza Husayn Ali (1817-1892)
   Ethnic or religious group: Bahá'í
   Date: May 29

   AnnivHol-1983, 72
   Chases-1993, 224
   HolFestCelWrld-1994, 22
   RelHolCal-1993, 58

Bahá'u'lláh, Birth of the
   Named for: Mirza Husayn Ali (1817-1892)
   Ethnic or religious group: Bahá'í
   Date: November 12

   AnnivHol-1983, 146
   Chases-1993, 439
   DictWrldRel-1989, 87, 89
   HolFestCelWrld-1994, 22
   RelHolCal-1993, 62

Bahá'u'lláh, Declaration of (Feast of Ridvan)
   Named for: 1863 declaration of Mirza Husayn Ali (1817-1892) near Baghdad
   Ethnic or religious group: Bahá'í
   Date: April 21-May 2

   AnnivHol-1983, 54
   Chases-1993, 174
   DictWrldRel-1989, 87, 89
   HolFestCelWrld-1994, 273
   RelHolCal-1993, 109

Baika-sai
   See **Plum Blossom Festival (Japan)**

Baisakh
   See **New Year (Vaisakha) (Hindu)**

Bakrid
   See **Sacrifice, Feast of (India) and (Pakistan)**

Balfour Declaration Day
   Named for: Arthur J. Balfour (1848-1930), British secretary of state who represented England in favor of a Jewish homeland in Palestine on November 2, 1917
   Location: Israel
   Ethnic or religious group: Jewish
   Date: November 2

   AnnivHol-1983, 141
   DaysCustFaith-1957, 282-283
   DictWrldRel-1989, 89
   HolFestCelWrld-1994, 23

Ballet, International Festival of (Festival Internacional de Ballet de La Habana)
   Location: Cuba: Havana
   Established: 1960
   Date: Even-numbered years in autumn

   IntlThFolk-1979, 80

Ballet, International Festival of
   Location: Italy: Nervi, Liguria
   Established: 1963
   Date: Even-numbered years during July

   IntlThFolk-1979, 244

Ballet and Music Festival, Copenhagen Royal Danish
   Location: Denmark: Copenhagen
   Date: Last two weeks in May

   MusFestWrld-1963, 182

Ballet Biennial
Location: Yugoslavia: Ljubljana, Slovenia
Established: 1971
Date: Odd-numbered years in June-July

IntlThFolk-1979, 393

Ballet Biennial, International
Location: Poland: Lodz
Established: 1966
Date: Even-numbered years in May

IntlThFolk-1979, 293

Ballet Days, Hamburg
Location: Federal Republic of Germany: Hamburg
Date: July

IntlThFolk-1979, 140

Ballet Festival, Bharatiya Kala Kendra
Location: India: New Delhi
Established: Early 1950s
Date: September-October, three weeks during Durga Puja, Festival of the Mother Goddess

IntlThFolk-1979, 204
See also **Mother Goddess, Festival of the**

Ballet Festival, Javanese
Location: Indonesia: Pandaan, East Java
Date: Two nights each month during full moon from June to November

IntlThFolk-1979, 223

Ballet Festival, Kathak Kendra
Location: India: New Delhi
Date: Annual; date varies

IntlThFolk-1979, 204

Ballet Festival, Monte Carlo Winter
Location: Monaco: Monte Carlo
Date: 10 days in late December-early January

MusFestWrld-1963, 122

Ballet Festival, National
Location: Philippines: Manila, Quezon, Luzon Island
Date: May

IntlThFolk-1979, 290

Ballet Festival, Ramayana
Location: Indonesia: Prambanan near Jogjakarta, Java
Established: Dance reenactment of Rama and the epic story, Ramayana, since 1970s

Date: May-October, four consecutive nights during each full moon

GdWrldFest-1985, 113
HolFestCelWrld-1994, 268
IntlThFolk-1979, 225

Ballet Festival, Triveni Kala Sangam
Location: India: New Delhi
Date: Annual; date varies

IntlThFolk-1979, 206

Ballet Festival Week
Location: Federal Republic of Germany: Munich, Bavaria
Date: March or May

IntlThFolk-1979, 144

Balloon Fiesta, Albuquerque International
Location: Albuquerque, New Mexico
Date: Nine days in early October

HolFestCelWrld-1994, 5

Bambuco, Festival of
Location: Colombia: Neiva, Huila
Date: June

GdWrldFest-1985, 64
IntlThFolk-1979, 79

Banana Festival, International
Location: Fulton, Kentucky, and South Fulton, Tennessee
Established: 1963
Date: Mid-September

HolFestCelWrld-1994, 23

Banderesi, Festival of the
Location: Italy: Bucchianico, Abruzzi
Established: Commemorates battle between Bucchianico and Chieti in May, 1370
Date: Six days in May

IntlThFolk-1979, 240

Bank Holiday
Location: England
Date: New Year's Day, Good Friday, Easter Monday, Christmas Day, and Boxing Day

HolFestCelWrld-1994, 24

Bank Holiday
Location: England, Ireland, and Wales
Date: Last Monday of August

AnnivHol-1983, 112

Bank Holiday *(cont.)*
  Chases-1993, 347
  DictDays-1988, 6, 8
  HolFestCelWrld-1994, 24

Bank Holiday
  Location: England, Ireland, Scotland, and Wales
  Date: First Monday in May

  Chases-1993, 194
  DictDays-1988, 8, 35

Bank Holiday
  See also **Whit Monday (England)**

Bankside Globe Festival
  Location: England: London Borough of Southwark
  Date: July-August

  IntlThFolk-1979, 167

Bannock, Bannocky, or Brose and Bannock Day
  See **Mardi Gras (Scotland)**

Bannockburn Day
  Location: Scotland
  Established: Commemorates June 24, 1314, independence
    from England
  Date: June 24

  AnnivHol-1983, 84

Baptism of the Lord, Feast of the
  Ethnic or religious group: Christian
  Date: Sunday following Epiphany, January 6

  AmerBkDays-1978, 65
  AnnivHol-1983, 7
  HolFestCelWrld-1994, 24
  RelHolCal-1993, 60

Baptism of the Lord, Feast of the
  Ethnic or religious group: Eastern Orthodox
  Established: End of second century
  Date: Sunday following Epiphany, January 6

  AmerBkDays-1978, 65
  HolFestCelWrld-1994, 24
  RelHolCal-1993, 60

Baptism of the Lord, Feast of the
  Ethnic or religious group: Roman Catholic
  Established: 1961
  Date: Sunday following Epiphany, January 6

  AmerBkDays-1978, 65
  HolFestCelWrld-1994, 24

Bara Wafat
  See **Muhammad's Birthday (India)**

Bar-B-Q Festival, International
  Location: Owensboro, Kentucky
  Established: Beginning of the 20th century
  Date: Mid-May

  HolFestCelWrld-1994, 24

Barnaby Bright or St. Barnaby's Day
  See **St. Barnabas's Day**

Barnum Festival
  Named for: P.T. (Phineas Taylor) Barnum (1810-1891)
  Location: Bridgeport, Connecticut
  Established: 1949
  Date: 17 days from late June to July 4

  AmerBkDays-1978, 624, 631
  GdUSFest-1984, 28
  HolFestCelWrld-1994, 25

Baron Bliss Day
  Named for: Henry Edward Ernest Victor Bliss (1869-1926)
  Location: Belize
  Date: March 9

  AnnivHol-1983, 35
  Chases-1993, 124

Bartholomew Day
  See **Bartholomew Fair**

Bartholomew Fair
  Named for: St. Bartholomew (d. 44)
  Location: England: Smithfield, London
  Established: 1133-1855
  Date: August 24

  BkDays-1864, ii. 263
  DaysCustFaith-1957, 217
  DictDays-1988, 9
  DictMyth-1962, i.183
  FestSaintDays-1915, 176
  HolFestCelWrld-1994, 25

Basant Panchami
  See **Spring Festival (Hindu)** and **(Hindu people in Bengal, India)**

Basque Festival, National
  Location: Elko, Nevada
  Ethnic or religious group: Basque-Americans
  Established: 1962
  Date: First or second weekend in July

  GdUSFest-1984, 112
  HolFestCelWrld-1994, 26

Bastille, Festival de la
    Location: Augusta, Maine
    Ethnic or religious group: Acadian French
    Date: Weekend closest to July 14

    HolFestCelWrld-1994, 26

Bastille Day
    Named for: Citizens' storming of the Bastille prison on
        July 14, 1789
    Location: France
    Date: July 14

    AmerBkDays-1978, 659
    AnnivHol-1983, 93
    BkDays-1864, ii. 59
    BkHolWrld-1986, July 14
    Chases-1993, 291
    DictDays-1988, 9
    FolkWrldHol-1992, 372
    HolFestCelWrld-1994, 26
    NatlHolWrld-1968, 113

Bastille Day
    Location: Kaplan and other cities in Louisiana
    Established: Since 1906 in Kaplan
    Date: July 14

    AmerBkDays-1978, 659

Bastille Day
    Location: Boston, Massachusetts
    Date: July 14

    Chases-1993, 291

Bastille Day
    Location: New York, New York
    Ethnic or religious group: French Protestant and Roman
        Catholic people
    Established: 1950s
    Date: July 14

    AmerBkDays-1978, 659

Bastille Day
    Location: New Caledonia
    Date: July 14

    FolkWrldHol-1992, 373

Bastille Day (Tiurai)
    Location: Tahiti
    Established: 1881
    Date: July 14

    FolkWrldHol-1992, 373
    HolFestCelWrld-1994, 26

Bataan Day (Araw ng Kagitingan)
    Named for: Battle of Bataan in 1942
    Location: Philippines
    Date: April 9

    HolFestCelWrld-1994, 26

Bat Flight Breakfast
    Location: Carlsbad Caverns, New Mexico
    Established: Late 1950s
    Date: Second Thursday in August

    HolFestCelWrld-1994, 27

Bath Festival
    Location: England: Bath, Avon
    Established: 1947
    Date: May or June

    Chases-1993, 215
    GdWrldFest-1985, 89
    MusFestEurBrit-1980, 43
    MusFestWrld-1963, 24

Bathing Festival (Snan Yatra)
    Location: India: Orissa
    Date: May-June, full moon day of Hindu month of Jyeshta

    RelHolCal-1993, 115
    See also **Juggernaut**

Baths of Caracalla (Terme di Caracalla)
    Location: Italy: Rome
    Established: 1937
    Date: First week in July to second week in August

    MusFestEurBrit-1980, 113

Bathurst Carillon City Tourist Festival
    Location: Australia: Bathurst, New South Wales
    Date: September-October

    IntlThFolk-1979, 8

Battleford Chautauqua
    Location: Canada: Battleford, Saskatchewan
    Established: 1974
    Date: July

    IntlThFolk-1979, 76

Battle of Britain Day
    Named for: German bombing of Britain on September
        15, 1940
    Location: England
    Date: September 15

    AnnivHol-1983, 119
    Chases-1993, 370
    HolFestCelWrld-1994, 27

Battle of Flowers
  Location: Great Britain: St. Helier, Jersey, Channel Islands
  Established: 1902
  Date: Second Thursday in August

  AnnivHol-1983, 173
  Chases-1993, 326
  GdWrldFest-1985, 98

Battle of Flowers (Spain: Valencia)
  See **Valencia Fair Days (Spain: Valencia)**

Battle of Flowers, Vienna
  Location: Austria: Vienna
  Date: Summer

  HolFestCelWrld-1994, 27

Battle of Germantown, Reenactment of
  Named for: 1777 battle; reenacted since early 1970s
  Location: Germantown, Pennsylvania
  Date: First Saturday in October

  HolFestCelWrld-1994, 27

Battle of Iquique or Navy Day
  Named for: Chilean victory on May 21, 1879
  Location: Chile
  Date: May 21

  AnnivHol-1983, 68

Battle of Las Piedras Day
  Named for: End of war between Uruguay and Brazil on May 17, 1828
  Location: Uruguay
  Date: May 17

  AnnivHol-1983, 67

Battle of New Orleans Day
  Named for: British attack on New Orleans on January 8, 1815
  Location: Massachusetts
  Date: January 8

  AmerBkDays-1978, 51

Battle of New Orleans or Hickory's Day
  Named for: British attack on New Orleans on January 8, 1815
  Location: Louisiana
  Date: January 8

  AmerBkDays-1978, 49
  AnnivHol-1983, 6
  Chases-1993, 58
  DictDays-1988, 9, 61, 84

  FolkAmerHol-1987, 37
  HolFestCelWrld-1994, 28

Battle of the Moors and Christians
  Named for: Reenactment of the Moorish siege of 1276 since the 15th century
  Location: Spain: Alcoy and Petrel, Alicante
  Date: April 22-24, held over St. George's Day

  FolkWrldHol-1992, 249
  HolFestCelWrld-1994, 211
  IntlThFolk-1979, 332

Battle of the Moors and Christians
  Named for: Reenactment of conflicts between the two groups since the 15th century
  Location: Spain: Caudete, Albacete, and Villena, Alicante
  Date: September

  IntlThFolk-1979, 332

Battle of the Moors and Christians
  Named for: Reenactment of conflicts between the two groups since the 15th century
  Location: Spain: Villajoyosa, Alicante
  Date: July

  IntlThFolk-1979, 332

Battle of the Moors and Christians
  Named for: Reenactment of conflicts between the two groups since the 15th century
  Location: Spain: Penalsordo, Badajoz
  Date: June

  IntlThFolk-1979, 332

Battle of the Moors and Christians
  Named for: Reenactment of conflicts between the two groups since the 15th century
  Location: Spain: Bocairente, Valencia
  Date: February

  IntlThFolk-1979, 332

Battle of the Moors and Christians
  Named for: Reenactment of conflicts between the two groups since the 15th century
  Location: Spain: Onteniente, Valencia
  Date: August

  IntlThFolk-1979, 332

Battleship Day
  See **Maine Memorial Day**

Battles of Lexington and Concord Day
 See **Patriot's Day**

Battles of the Flowers (France: Nice)
 See **Mardi Gras (France: Nice)**

Bawming the Thorn Day
 Location: England: Appleton, Cheshire
 Established: 12th century
 Date: Late June or early July

AnnivHol-1983, 92
BkHolWrld-1986, June 29, 176
HolFestCelWrld-1994, 28

Bay Chamber Concerts
 Location: Rockport, Maine
 Established: 1961
 Date: Nine Thursday evenings in July and August

MusFestAmer-1990, 65

Baydar, Festival of the
 See **Boat or Baydar, Festival of the**

Bayreuth Festival (Bayreuther Festspiele and Richard Wagner Festival)
 Named for: Richard Wagner (1813-1883) and the city
 Location: Federal Republic of Germany: Bayreuth, Bavaria
 Established: August 1876
 Date: Five weeks in late July and August

Chases-1993, 306
GdWrldFest-1985, 83
HolFestCelWrld-1994, 28
MusFestEurBrit-1980, 97
MusFestWrld-1963, 47

Beach Day
 See **Blessing of the Waters Day (Uruguay)**

Bealtaine
 See **Beltane**

Bean Calends
 Location: Ancient Rome
 Date: June 1

DictFolkMyth-1984, 123

Beanfest or Beano
 See **Waygoose Feast (printers in England)**

Bean-Throwing Festival (Setsubun)
 Location: Japan
 Date: Early February, last day of winter in lunar calendar

AnnivHol-1983, 18

BkFest-1937, 196
BkHolWrld-1986, February 3
Chases-1993, 85
DictFolkMyth-1984, 541
FolkWrldHol-1992, 91
HolFestCelWrld-1994, 312

Bear Festival
 Location: Japan
 Ethnic or religious group: Ainu people
 Date: Early December

FolkWrldHol-1992, 574
HolFestCelWrld-1994, 28

Beating the Bounds
 See **Ascension Day (England)** and **Rogation Days (England)**

Beethoven Concerts, Martonvásár
 Named for: Ludwig van Beethoven (1770-1827)
 Location: Hungary: Martonvásár
 Date: Summer

MusFestWrld-1963, 158

Beethoven Festival
 Named for: Ludwig van Beethoven (1770-1827)
 Location: San Francisco, California
 Established: 1979
 Date: Three weeks beginning mid-June

MusFestAmer-1990, 24

Beethoven Festival
 Named for: Ludwig van Beethoven (1770-1827)
 Location: Federal Republic of Germany: Bonn
 Date: September-October

MusFestWrld-1963, 75

Befana Festival
 Location: Italy and Sicily
 Ethnic or religious group: Christian
 Date: January 5-6

AmerBkDays-1978, 30
AnnivHol-1983, 4
BkFest-1937, 178
BkHolWrld-1986, January 5
Chases-1993, 57
DictFolkMyth-1984, 131
FestSaintDays-1915, 16
FestWestEur-1958, 87
FolkWrldHol-1992, 14
HolFestCelWrld-1994, 28
RelHolCal-1993, 67

Bega Ceremonies
    Location: Upper Volta: Yatenga Region
    Ethnic or religious group: Mossi people
    Date: One week opening the planting season

    FolkWrldHol-1992, 228

Beggar's Day
    See **St. Martin's Day (Netherlands)**

Beggars' Night
    See **Halloween**

Beginning of Work Day (Shigoto Hajime)
    Location: Japan
    Date: January 2

    AnnivHol-1983, 3
    FolkWrldHol-1992, 46

Begonia Festival
    Location: Belgium: Lochristi
    Established: 19th century
    Date: Three days in August

    GdWrldFest-1985, 21
    HolFestCelWrld-1994, 183

Begonia Festival, Ballarat
    Location: Australia: Ballarat, Victoria
    Date: March

    IntlThFolk-1979, 26

Beheading, Feast of the
    See **St. John the Baptist, Martyrdom of**

Beiramun 'Id al Milad
    See **Christmas Eve (Syria)**

Bĕla Kampong
    Location: Malaysia: Endau
    Ethnic or religious group: Malay people
    Date: Annual; date uncertain

    DictFolkMyth-1984, 132

Belfast Festival
    Location: Northern Ireland: Belfast
    Established: 1963
    Date: Two and one half weeks in November

    Chases-1993, 435
    IntlThFolk-1979, 182

Belgian-American Days
    Location: Ghent, Minnesota
    Ethnic or religious group: Belgian-Americans
    Date: Four days in August

    HolFestCelWrld-1994, 29

Bellac Festival
    Location: France: Bellac, Haute-Vienne
    Established: 1953
    Date: June-July

    IntlThFolk-1979, 100

Belmont Stakes
    Location: Long Island, New York
    Established: 1867
    Date: June, fifth Saturday after the Kentucky Derby

    HolFestCelWrld-1994, 29

Beltane
    Ethnic or religious group: Celtic people
    Date: April 30

    AmerBkDays-1978, 407
    AnnivHol-1983, 59
    BkDays-1864, i. 571
    Chases-1993, 185
    DictDays-1988, 10
    DictFolkMyth-1984, 135, 181, 203, 304, 789
    FestSaintDays-1915, 104
    FolkAmerHol-1987, 163
    HolFestCelWrld-1994, 29
    RelHolCal-1993, 60
    See also **May Day**

Beltane
    Location: Brittany
    Date: April 30

    DictFolkMyth-1984, 135
    HolFestCelWrld-1994, 29

Beltane
    Location: Ireland
    Date: April 30

    AmerBkDays-1978, 408
    AnnivHol-1983, 59
    BkDays-1864, i.571
    DictFolkMyth-1984, 135
    FestSaintDays-1915, 104
    HolFestCelWrld-1994, 29

Beltane
    Location: Isle of Man
    Date: April 30

    BkDays-1864, i.571
    DictFolkMyth-1984, 135, 203
    HolFestCelWrld-1994, 29

Beltane
Location: Scotland
Date: April 30

AmerBkDays-1978, 408
BkDays-1864, i.571
DictFolkMyth-1984, 135
FestSaintDays-1915, 104
FolkAmerHol-1987, 163
HolFestCelWrld-1994, 29

Beltane
Location: United States
Ethnic or religious group: Gardnerian Witches
Date: April 30

RelHolCal-1993, 60

Beltane
Location: Wales
Date: April 30

DictFolkMyth-1984, 135
HolFestCelWrld-1994, 29

Beltein, Festival of
See **Beltane**

Benihana Grand Prix Power Boat Regatta
See **Regatta, New Jersey Offshore Grand Prix**

Bennington Battle Day
Named for: Battle on August 16, 1777
Location: Bennington, Vermont
Date: August 16

AmerBkDays-1978, 758
AnnivHol-1983, 108
Chases-1993, 332
DictDays-1988, 11
HolFestCelWrld-1994, 30

Berat Kandili
See **Night of Forgiveness (Turkey)**

Berchtold's Day (Berchtoldstag)
Named for: Berchtold (late 12th-early 13th century)
Location: Switzerland
Date: January 2

AnnivHol-1983, 3
BkFest-1937, 316
FestWestEur-1958, 225
HolFestCelWrld-1994, 30

Bergen International Festival (Festspillene i Bergen)
Location: Norway: Bergen
Established: 1953
Date: 15 days beginning last week in May

Chases-1993, 231
GdWrldFest-1985, 144
HolFestCelWrld-1994, 30
IntlThFolk-1979, 286
MusFestEurBrit-1980, 126
MusFestWrld-1963, 186

Berlin Festival Weeks (Berliner Festwochen)
Location: Federal Republic of Germany: Berlin
Established: 1951
Date: Four weeks beginning first week in September

Chases-1993, 348
GdWrldFest-1985, 84
IntlThFolk-1979, 131
MusFestEurBrit-1980, 99
MusFestWrld-1963, 67

Berlioz International Festival (Internationales Festival Hector Berlioz)
Named for: Hector Berlioz (1803-1869)
Location: France: Lyon and La Côte-Saint-André
Established: 1979
Date: One week in mid-September

MusFestEurBrit-1980, 75

Bermuda College Weeks
Location: Bermuda: Hamilton
Established: 1936; official, 1948
Date: Four to five weeks in March-April

GdWrldFest-1985, 22
HolFestCelWrld-1994, 30

Bermuda Festival
Location: Bermuda: Hamilton
Established: 1976
Date: January-February

GdWrldFest-1985, 22
HolFestCelWrld-1994, 31
IntlThFolk-1979, 50
MusFestAmer-1990, 157

Bernadette, Visions of St.
See **Our Lady of Lourdes, Feast of**

Besançon International Festival (Festival International de Besançon)
Location: France: Besançon, Doubs
Established: 1947
Date: Two weeks beginning September 1

GdWrldFest-1985, 79
IntlThFolk-1979, 101
MusFestEurBrit-1980, 77
MusFestWrld-1963, 137

Bettara-Ichi
See **Pickle-Market (Japan: near Ebisu Shrine, Tokyo)**

Bhagavatha Mela Festival
Location: India: Melattur, Tamil Nadu
Established: 1940
Date: One week in May

IntlThFolk-1979, 215

Bhai-Dooj or Bhaiya Duj
See **Brother and Sister Day (Hindu)**

Bhairava Ashtami
Ethnic or religious group: Hindu
Date: November-December, eighth day of waning half of Hindu month of Margashirsha

RelHolCal-1993, 61

Bharatiya Lok Kala Festival
Location: India: Udaipur, Rajasthan
Date: Annual; date varies

IntlThFolk-1979, 214

Bhima or Bhima-sena, Festival of
Location: India: central provinces
Ethnic or religious group: Hindu Gond people
Date: Near time of monsoon

DictFolkMyth-1984, 139

Bhishma Ashtami
Location: India
Ethnic or religious group: Hindu
Date: Eighth day of waxing half of Magha (January-February), or during Karthika (October-November) or Margashirsha (November-December)

DictFolkMyth-1984, 139
RelHolCal-1993, 61

Bhogali Bihu, Festival of Feasts
See **Harvest Festival (India: Assam)**

Bhratri Dwitya
See **Brother and Sister Day (Hindu people in India)**

Bhutan Paro Festival
See **Paro Tshechu**

Bianou
Location: Niger: Agadés
Date: First new moon in February

HolFestCelWrld-1994, 31

Bible Sunday
Location: United States
Ethnic or religious group: Protestant
Date: Last Sunday in November or Sunday before Thanksgiving

Chases-1993, 449
RelHolCal-1993, 62

Bible Week, National
Location: United States
Ethnic or religious group: National Laymen's Committee
Date: Third week in October

DaysCustFaith-1957, 275

Bicycle Ride Across Iowa (Ragbrai)
Location: Iowa
Established: 1973
Date: Midsummer

AnnivHol-1983, 181
Chases-1993, 306
HolFestCelWrld-1994, 267

Big House Ceremony
Location: United States
Ethnic or religious group: Delaware Indians
Date: Annual twelve-night ceremony

DictFolkMyth-1984, 140, 710

Big Sea Day
Location: New Jersey
Date: Second Saturday in August

DictFolkMyth-1984, 140

Big Thursday
See **Holy Thursday**

Bílí Sobota, White Saturday
See **Holy Saturday (Czechoslovakia)**

Bill of Rights Day
Named for: Ratification of the Bill of Rights, the first ten amendments to the United States constitution in 1787

Bill of Rights Day *(cont.)*
Location: United States
Date: December 15

DaysCustFaith-1957, 314
HolFestCelWrld-1994, 31

Billy Bowlegs Festival
Named for: William Augustus Bowles (d. 1803)
Location: Fort Walton Beach, Florida
Established: 1954
Date: First full weekend in June

HolFestCelWrld-1994, 32

Binding Monday or Tuesday
See **Easter Monday (England)**

Binding of Wreaths or Feast of July (Vainikinas)
Location: Lithuania
Date: July

BkFest-1937, 221

Binghamton Festival
Location: Binghamton, New York
Established: 1986
Date: July and August

MusFestAmer-1990, 98

Birchat Hahamah
See **Blessing the Sun (Jewish people in Israel and the United States)**

Bird and Arbor Day
Location: California
Date: March 7

DictDays-1988, 5
See also **Arbor Day (United States)**

Bird Week
Location: Japan
Date: Begins May 10

BkFestHolWrld-1970, 94

Birkebeiner, American (The Birkie)
Location: Cable, Wisconsin
Date: Three days in late February

Chases-1993, 110
GdUSFest-1984, 210
HolFestCelWrld-1994, 8

Birth of Mary, Feast of the
See **Nativity of the Virgin, Feast of the**

Birth of the Prophet
See **Muhammad's Birthday**

Bitowa Outdoor Festival
Location: Canada: Tracadie, New Brunswick
Established: 1974
Date: Third full weekend in June

GdWrldFest-1985, 40

Bix Beiderbecke Memorial Jazz Festival
See **Jazz Festival, Bix Beiderbecke Memorial**

Black Christ, Festival of the
Named for: Jesus (c. 6 B.C.-c. 30 A.D.)
Location: Guatemala: Esquipulas
Date: January 15

AnnivHol-1983, 9

Black Christ, Festival of the
Named for: Jesus (c. 6 B.C.-c. 30 A.D.)
Location: Panama: Porotobelo
Ethnic or religious group: Roman Catholic
Established: About 17th century
Date: October 21, day of town's patron saint, El Jesus Nazarene

GdWrldFest-1985, 148
HolFestCelWrld-1994, 33

Black History Month
Location: United States
Established: Negro History Week was established in 1926; Black History Month observed since 1976; it is held during February to commemorate the birthdays of Frederick Douglass (1817-1895) and Abraham Lincoln (1809-1865)
Date: February

HolFestCelWrld-1994, 34

Black Nazarene Fiesta
Named for: Jesus (c. 6 B.C.-c. 30 A.D.)
Location: Philippines: Manila and Quezon, Luzon Island
Date: January 1-9

AnnivHol-1983, 173
Chases-1993, 51
GdWrldFest-1985, 153
HolFestCelWrld-1994, 35

Black Ship Day
Named for: Arrival of Matthew Perry (1794-1858) in Japan in 1853
Location: Japan: Yokosuka, Shimoda, and other port cities, and Newport, Rhode Island

Black Ship Day *(cont.)*
Established: Since 1934 in Japan; since 1984 in Newport, Rhode Island
Date: May 16 and 17 in Japan; last weekend in July in Rhode Island

AnnivHol-1983, 93
HolFestCelWrld-1994, 35

Black Spirit Festival (Genji Bi Hori)
Location: Niger
Ethnic or religious group: Songhay people
Date: April

FolkWrldHol-1992, 226
HolFestCelWrld-1994, 229

Blajini or the Meek, Feast of the (Sarbatoarea Blajinilor)
Location: Romania
Date: April, second Monday after Easter

BkFest-1937, 277
FolkWrldHol-1992, 207
HolFestCelWrld-1994, 35

Blavatsky, Death of Helena
Named for: Helena Petrovna Blavatsky (1831-1891)
Ethnic or religious group: Theosophical Society
Date: May 9

DictWrldRel-1989, 757
RelHolCal-1993, 70

Bled Evenings (Bled na Gorenjskem)
Location: Yugoslavia: Slovenia
Date: July-August

IntlThFolk-1979, 385

Blessed Sacrament, Feast of
Location: New Bedford, Massachusetts
Ethnic or religious group: Christian Madeiran-Americans
Established: 1914 in the United States
Date: Four days beginning last Thursday in August

GdUSFest-1984, 87
HolFestCelWrld-1994, 36

Blessing of Seeds and Tools
Location: Mozambique: Kambine
Ethnic or religious group: Christian
Date: Annual; at the beginning of the planting season

FolkWrldHol-1992, 226

Blessing of the Animals
See **Holy Saturday (Mexican-Americans in Los Angeles, California); St. Anthony the Abbot of Egypt, Feast of (Christian)**

Blessing of the Fields with Corn or Flag Dance
Location: Tesuque Pueblo, New Mexico
Date: May, date varies

IndianAmer-1989, 286, 319

Blessing of the Fishing Fleet and Biloxi Shrimp Festival and Fais Do Do
Location: Biloxi, Alabama
Established: 1924
Date: First weekend in June

GdUSFest-1984, 100
HolFestCelWrld-1994, 36

Blessing of the Fleet (Louisiana Shrimp and Petroleum Festival)
Location: Morgan City, Louisiana
Established: Blessing of the Fleet since 1937
Date: September, Labor Day weekend

HolFestCelWrld-1994, 185

Blessing of the Shrimp Fleet
Location: Bayou La Batre, Alabama
Ethnic or religious group: Roman Catholic
Established: Late 1940s
Date: Last weekend in June

HolFestCelWrld-1994, 36
RelHolCal-1993, 64

Blessing of the Waters
See **Epiphany (Eastern Orthodox)**

Blessing of the Waters (Family Day)
Location: Uruguay
Date: December 8

AnnivHol-1983, 158

Blessing of Wheat
See **St. Mark's Day (Calvinists in Hungary)**

Blessing the Fields
See **Rogation Days (Austria) and St. Mark, Feast of (Austria)**

Blessing the Sun (Birchat Hahamah)
Location: Israel and the United States
Ethnic or religious group: Jewish
Date: Every 28 years on the first Wednesday of Jewish month of Nisan

FolkAmerHol-1987, 157
HolFestCelWrld-1994, 37

44

Blood, Day of
Location: Ancient Rome
Ethnic or religious group: Galli, priests of Attis
Established: About 204 B.C.
Date: March 24, climax of six-day festival

DictFolkMyth-1984, 90, 352

Bloomsday
Named for: The day, June 16, 1904, described in the novel,
  Ulysses, 1922, by James Joyce (1882-1941)
Location: Ireland: Dublin
Date: June 16

AnnivHol-1983, 80
Chases-1993, 250
DictDays-1988, 13

Blowing the Shofar, Day of
See **New Year, Jewish (Rosh Hashanah)**

Blueberry Festival, Alabama
Named for: Commemorates Dr. W.T. Brightell (b. 1916) and
  his improvements on the Rabbiteye blueberry
Location: Brewton, Alabama
Date: Third Saturday in June

HolFestCelWrld-1994, 4

Bluegrass and Country Music Festival, Telluride
Location: Telluride, Colorado
Established: 1974
Date: Three days in late June

Chases-1993, 252
MusFestAmer-1990, 240

Bluegrass and Old-Time Music Festival, Grant's Annual
Location: Hugo, Oklahoma
Established: 1969
Date: Five days in early August

HolFestCelWrld-1994, 123
MusFestAmer-1990, 248

Bluegrass Fan Fest
Named for: Commemorates the "father of bluegrass music,"
  Bill Monroe (b. 1912)
Location: Owensboro, Kentucky
Date: Third weekend in September

HolFestCelWrld-1994, 37

Bluegrass Festival, Bean Blossom
Location: Bean Blossom, Indiana

Date: Five days in spring

MusFestAmer-1990, 243

Bluegrass Festival, Winterhawk
Location: Hillsdale, New York
Date: Three days during third week in July

MusFestAmer-1990, 245

Blue Gum Festival of Tasmania
Location: Australia: Tasmania
Date: March

IntlThFolk-1979, 25

Boat or Baydar, Festival of the
Location: Russia: Siberia
Ethnic or religious group: Chukchi people
Date: Early spring

FolkWrldHol-1992, 227

Boat Race Day
Location: England: Oxford and Cambridge universities,
  Putney to Martlake
Date: March-April

DictDays-1988, 14
HolFestCelWrld-1994, 37

Boat Race Day (Gods of the Sea Festival in Minatogawa)
Location: Okinawa: Minatogawa and Taira
Date: May, 14th day of fifth lunar month

FolkWrldHol-1992, 316
HolFestCelWrld-1994, 37

Boat Rendezvous, Antique and Classic
Location: Mystic Seaport Museum, Mystic, Connecticut
Established: 1975
Date: Last weekend in July

HolFestCelWrld-1994, 11

Bob Apple Night
See **Halloween (England)**

Bobby Ack Day
See **Shick-Shack Day**

Bobo Masquerade
Location: Burkina Faso
Date: April or May, before the first rain

BkHolWrld-1986, March 29, 176

Bodrum Festival
Location: Turkey: Bodrum
Date: September

IntlThFolk-1979, 367

Boetprocessie van Veurne
See **Penitents, Procession of the (Belgium: Furnes, West Flanders)**

Boganda Day
Named for: Barthélémy Boganda (1910-1959)
Location: Central African Republic
Date: March 29

AnnivHol-1983, 43

Bogoroditza
See **Assumption, Feast of the (Bulgaria)**

Bogoroditzy
See **Assumption, Feast of the (Russia)**

Bogoyavleniye
See **Epiphany (Bulgaria)**

Bogoyavleniye and Blessing of the Waters
See **Epiphany (Russia) and (Eastern Orthodox people in Yugoslavia)**

Bohag Bihu
See **New Year (India: Assam)** and **Vernal Equinox (India: Assam)**

Bok Kai Festival
Location: Marysville, California
Ethnic or religious group: Chinese-Americans
Established: 1880s
Date: March or April, second day of second Chinese month

HolFestCelWrld-1994, 38

Bolívar Day
Named for: Simon Bolívar (1783-1830)
Location: Venezuela
Date: July 24

AnnivHol-1983, 96
Chases-1993, 304

Bolshevik Revolution Day
See **October Socialist Revolution Day**

Bona Dea (Great Mother Festival)
Location: Ancient Rome
Date: May 1

AmerBkDays-1978, 406

FestSaintDays-1915, 110
DictFolkMyth-1984, 867

Bon Festival
See **Dead, Festival of the (Buddhist)**

Bonfim Festival
Location: Brazil: Salvador, Bahia
Established: 1875
Date: Ten days beginning second Thursday in January

BkHolWrld-1986, January 23, 177
Chases-1993, 69
FolkWrldHol-1992, 27
HolFestCelWrld-1994, 38

Bonfire Night
Location: Canada: Newfoundland
Date: November 5

FolkWrldHol-1992, 550

Bonfire Night
Location: Scotland
Date: Monday nearest May 24

DictDays-1988, 14
HolFestCelWrld-1994, 39

Bonfire Night
See **St. Catherine's Day**

Bonfires of St. Joseph
See **St. Joseph's Day (Spain: Valencia)**

Bonneville Speed Week
Location: Bonneville Salt Flats, Utah
Established: 1949
Date: Third week in August

HolFestCelWrld-1994, 39

Bon Odori
See **Dead, Festival of the (Buddhist people in China, especially at the monastery of Ch'ing Liang Shan), (Buddhist people in Japan), and (Buddhist Japanese-Americans in the United States)**

Bonten Festival
Location: Japan: Akita
Date: February

BkHolWrld-1986, Feb 17

Book Reading Week
Location: Japan
Date: Begins October 27

BkFestHolWrld-1970, 115

Boomerang Festival
   Location: Hampton, Virginia
   Established: 1985
   Date: Usually October

   HolFestCelWrld-1994, 39

Boone Festival, Daniel
   Named for: Daniel Boone (c. 1734-1820)
   Location: Barbourville, Kentucky
   Established: October 6, 1948
   Date: First through second Saturdays in October

   AmerBkDays-1978, 901
   HolFestCelWrld-1994, 78

Booths, Feast of
   See **Sukkot (Jewish) and (United States)**

Borglum Day, Gutzon
   Named for: John Gutzon de la Mothe Borglum (1867-1941),
      carver of presidents' faces on Mount Rushmore
   Location: Mount Rushmore, South Dakota
   Date: August 10

   HolFestCelWrld-1994, 128

Boston Marathon
   Location: Boston, Massachusetts
   Established: 1896
   Date: April 19, Patriot's Day, or nearest Monday

   AmerBkDays-1978, 362
   AnnivHol-1983, 53
   Chases-1993, 172
   HolFestCelWrld-1994, 39

Boston Massacre Day
   Named for: March 5, 1770, battle between patriots and
      British soldiers
   Location: Boston, Massachusetts
   Date: March 5

   AmerBkDays-1978, 235
   AnnivHol-1983, 33
   Chases-1993, 119
   HolFestCelWrld-1994, 40

Boston Massacre Day (Crispus Attucks Day)
   Named for: March 5, 1770, battle between patriots and
      British soldiers, and Crispus Attucks (1723-1770), who
      led the patriots' fight
   Location: New Jersey

Date: March 5

   AmerBkDays-1978, 236
   AnnivHol-1983, 33
   Chases-1993, 119
   HolFestCelWrld-1994, 40

Boston Pops
   Location: Boston, Massachusetts
   Established: 1885
   Date: First week in May to middle of July

   MusFestAmer-1990, 209

Boston's Fourth of July
   See **Bunker Hill Day**

Botev Day
   Named for: Khristo Botev (1848-1876)
   Location: Bulgaria
   Date: May 20

   AnnivHol-1983, 68

Bottle Kicking and Hare Pie Scramble, Annual
   Location: England: Hallaton, Leicestershire
   Established: Seven hundred years ago
   Date: March-April, Easter Monday

   HolFestCelWrld-1994, 40

Boun Bang Fai or Fay (Festival of Rockets)
   See **Buddha's Birthday, Enlightenment, and
      Salvation (Laos)**

Boundary Walk (Grenzumgang)
   Location: Germany: Springe Deister, Lower Saxony
   Established: Middle Ages
   Date: Every ten years (1951, 1961 . . .)

   FestWestEur-1958, 73

Bounds Thursday
   See **Holy Thursday (Church of England)**

Boun Phan Vet
   Named for: Honors Prince Vessantara, earlier incarnation
      of the Buddha
   Location: Laos: Vientiane
   Ethnic or religious group: Buddhist
   Date: November, twelfth lunar month

   FolkWrldHol-1992, 567
   HolFestCelWrld-1994, 40

Boun Pimay
See **New Year's Day (Laos)**

Box Day
See **Boxing Day (England)**

Boxing Day
Date: December 26, St. Stephen's Day

AnnivHol-1983, 164
BkDays-1864, ii. 764
BkHolWrld-1986, December 26
Chases-1993, 483
DaysCustFaith-1957, 322
DictDays-1988, 15
FolkAmerHol-1987, 405
FolkWrldHol-1992, 639
HolFestCelWrld-1994, 41
NatlHolWrld-1968, 79

Boxing Day
Location: Australia
Date: December 26, St. Stephen's Day

DictDays-1988, 15

Boxing Day (Bahama Islands)
See **Junkanoo Festival**

Boxing Day
Location: Canada
Date: December 26, St. Stephen's Day

Chases-1993, 483
DictDays-1988, 15

Boxing Day
Location: England
Date: December 26, St. Stephen's Day

BkDays-1864, ii.764
BkHolWrld-1986, December 26
Chases-1993, 483
DaysCustFaith-1957, 322
DictDays-1988, 15
FolkAmerHol-1987, 405
NatlHolWrld-1968, 79

Boxing Day
Location: Ireland
Date: December 26, St. Stephen's Day

FolkWrldHol-1992, 639

Boxing Day
Location: South Africa

Date: December 26, St. Stephen's Day

DictDays-1988, 28

Boxing Day
Location: Sweden
Date: December 26, St. Stephen's Day

FolkWrldHol-1992, 639

Boy Scouts Day
Named for: February 8, 1910, incorporation of the Boy
  Scouts of America
Location: Boy Scouts in the United States
Date: February 8

AnnivHol-1983, 21
Chases-1993, 91
HolFestCelWrld-1994, 41

Boys' Day
Location: USSR
Date: February 22, Army Day

FolkWrldHol-1992, 137

Boys' Festival, Tango No Sekku
See **Children's Day (Japan)**

Boys' Rifle Match (Knabenschiessen)
Location: Switzerland: Zurich
Established: 17th century
Date: Second weekend in September

HolFestCelWrld-1994, 172

Boże Narodzenie
See **Christmas (Poland)**

Božic
See **Christmas (Yugoslavia)**

Braaiveleis
See **Covenant, Day of the (Afrikaaner people in
  South Africa)**

Brady Day, Captain
Named for: Captain Samuel Brady (1758-1795)
Location: Brady Lake, Ohio
Established: 1973
Date: July-August

FolkAmerHol-1987, 249-50
HolFestCelWrld-1994, 50

Braggot Sunday
See **Mid-Lent Sunday (England)**

Brass Band Festival, Great American
  Location: Centre College, Danville, Kentucky
  Date: Mid-June

  HolFestCelWrld-1994, 124

Brauteln
  See **Wooing a Bride (Germany: Sigmaringen,
    Baden-Württemberg)**

Bregenz Festival (Bregenzer Festspiele)
  Location: Austria: Bregenz, Vorarlberg
  Established: 1946
  Date: Four weeks in July-August

  GdWrldFest-1985, 11
  HolFestCelWrld-1994, 42
  IntlThFolk-1979, 31
  MusFestEurBrit-1980, 17

Brent Festival
  Location: England: London Borough of Brent, Middlesex
  Established: 1950
  Date: January-February

  IntlThFolk-1979, 165

Bretzelsonndeg, Pretzel Sunday
  See **Mid-Lent Sunday (Luxembourg)**

Bridge Day
  Location: New River Gorge Bridge, Fayetteville, West Virginia
  Established: 1980
  Date: Third Saturday in October

  HolFestCelWrld-1994, 42

**Bridge Fair and International Equestrian Festival,
Hortobágy**
  Location: Hungary: Hortobágy
  Date: July

  HolFestCelWrld-1994, 145

Bright Day
  See **Easter (Greece)**

Brighton Festival
  Location: England: Brighton, Sussex
  Established: 1967
  Date: April-May

  Chases-1993, 198
  IntlThFolk-1979, 156
  MusFestEurBrit-1980, 45

Brighton Field Day and Rodeo
  Location: Okeechobee, Florida
  Ethnic or religious group: Seminole Indians
  Date: Third weekend in February

  Chases-1993, 104

Brigit's Day
  See **Imbolc**

British Open Golf Tournament
  Location: England and Scotland
  Established: 1860
  Date: Summer

  HolFestCelWrld-1994, 42

Britt Festival
  Named for: Peter Britt (1819-1905)
  Location: Jacksonville, Oregon
  Established: 1963
  Date: June-September

  GdUSFest-1984, 150
  MusFestAmer-1990, 126

Broadstairs Dickens Festival
  Named for: Charles Dickens (1812-1870)
  Location: England: Broadstairs, Kent
  Established: 1936
  Date: Eight days in June

  Chases-1993, 255
  GdWrldFest-1985, 90
  IntlThFolk-1979, 157

**Broken Needles Festival (Hari-Kuyo; Festival or Mass of the
Broken Needles; or Needle Day)**
  Location: Japan
  Established: Since at least the fourth century
  Date: December 8 in Kyoto; February 8 in Tokyo

  AnnivHol-1983, 174
  Chases-1993, 91
  FolkWrldHol-1992, 586
  HolFestCelWrld-1994, 135

Brose Day or Brose and Bannock Day
  See **Mardi Gras (Scotland)**

**Brother and Sister Day (Bhai-Dooj, Bhaiya Duj, Bhratri
Dwitya, or Yama Dvitiya)**
  Location: India
  Ethnic or religious group: Hindu

Brother and Sister Day *(cont.)*
Date: October-November, second day of waxing half of Hindu month of Karthika

BkFest-1937, 162
BkHolWrld-1986, November 3
RelHolCal-1993, 61

Brotherhood Sunday
Date: Sunday nearest February 22, George Washington's birthday

DictDays-1988, 15
HolFestCelWrld-1994, 43

Brotherhood Week
Location: United States
Ethnic or religious group: National Conference of Christians and Jews
Established: 1934
Date: Week which contains February 22, George Washington's birthday

AmerBkDays-1978, 200
Chases-1993, 98
DaysCustFaith-1957, 60
HolFestCelWrld-1994, 43

Brothers, Festival of
See **Brother and Sister Day**

Brown Day, John
Named for: John Brown (1800-1859)
Ethnic or religious group: Civil rights groups
Date: May 9

AnnivHol-1983, 64
Chases-1993, 201

Bruckner Festival, International (Internationales Brucknerfest)
Named for: Anton Bruckner (1824-1896)
Location: Austria: Linz
Established: 1974
Date: Four weeks in September

MusFestEurBrit-1980, 21

Bruegel Feesten
Named for: Pieter Bruegel (c. 1525 or 1530-1569)
Location: Belgium: Wigene
Date: Second Sunday in September every other year

BkHolWrld-1986, September 13, 176

Brussels International Fair
Location: Belgium: Brussels
Established: 1927
Date: April-May

GdWrldFest-1985, 20

B'Shevat
See **New Year of Trees (Jewish people in Israel)**

Buart or Buat Nark
See **Buddhist Priesthood, Admission to the**

Buccaneer Days
Named for: Commemorates finding of Corpus Christi Bay by Alonzo Alvarez Pineda in 1519
Location: Corpus Christi, Texas
Established: 1940
Date: Last weekend in April through first weekend in May

HolFestCelWrld-1994, 43

Bud Billiken Day
Named for: Character created by Robert S. Abbott (1868-1940) in 1923
Location: Chicago, Illinois
Date: August 14; observed second Saturday in August

AnnivHol-1983, 107
Chases-1993, 328
HolFestCelWrld-1994, 43

Buddha Jayanti
See **Buddha's Birthday, Enlightenment, and Salvation (Buddhist people in India)**

Buddha's Birthday, Enlightenment, and Salvation
Named for: Siddhartha Gautama (c. 563 B.C.- c. 483 B.C.)
Ethnic or religious group: Buddhist
Date: April-May, eighth day of fourth Buddhist month, Vaisakha or Vesak; observed April 8 in Japan

AnnivHol-1983, 183
BkFestHolWrld-1970, 76, 78
BkHolWrld-1986, May 26, 170
Chases-1993, 158, 234
DictWrldRel-1989, 121, 135
FolkAmerHol-1987, 155
FolkWrldHol-1992, 141, 253, 257, 308
HolFestCelWrld-1994, 166, 356
IntlThFolk-1979, 345
RelHolCal-1993, 64, 121

Buddha's Birthday, Enlightenment, and Salvation (Kason Festival of Watering the Banyon Tree or Full Moon of Waso)
    Named for: Siddhartha Gautama (c. 563 B.C.- c. 483 B.C.)
    Location: Burma; now Myanmar
    Ethnic or religious group: Buddhist
    Date: April-May, eighth day of fourth Buddhist
      month

    AnnivHol-1983, 183
    FolkWrldHol-1992, 308
    HolFestCelWrld-1994, 166
    See also **Buddha's Birthday, Enlightenment, and Salvation**
    (Myanmar)

Buddha's Birthday, Enlightenment, and Salvation
    Named for: Siddhartha Gautama (c. 563 B.C.- c. 483 B.C.)
    Location: California
    Ethnic or religious group: Buddhist
    Date: April-May, eighth day of fourth Buddhist
      month

    FolkAmerHol-1987, 155

Buddha's Birthday, Enlightenment, and Salvation
    Named for: Siddhartha Gautama (c. 563 B.C.- c. 483 B.C.)
    Location: China
    Ethnic or religious group: Buddhist
    Date: April-May, eighth day of fourth Buddhist
      month

    BkFestHolWrld-1970, 78
    DictWrldRel-1989, 135
    FolkWrldHol-1992, 253
    HolFestCelWrld-1994, 319, 320

Buddha's Birthday, Enlightenment, and Salvation
    Named for: Siddhartha Gautama (c. 563 B.C.- c. 483 B.C.)
    Location: China: Xinan
    Ethnic or religious group: Buddhist Dai people
    Date: April-May, eighth day of fourth Buddhist
      month

    HolFestCelWrld-1994, 319, 320
    See also **New Year (China)**

Buddha's Birthday, Enlightenment, and Salvation
    Named for: Siddhartha Gautama (c. 563 B.C.- c. 483 B.C.)
    Location: Hong Kong
    Ethnic or religious group: Buddhist
    Date: April-May, eighth day of fourth Buddhist
      month

    Chases-1993, 223

Buddha's Birthday, Enlightenment, and Salvation (Buddha Jayanti)
    Named for: Siddhartha Gautama (c. 563 B.C.- c. 483 B.C.)
    Location: India
    Ethnic or religious group: Buddhist
    Date: April-May, full moon day of Hindu month of Vaisakha

    DictWrldRel-1989, 135
    FolkWrldHol-1992, 257
    RelHolCal-1993, 64

Buddha's Birthday, Enlightenment, and Salvation (Buddha Jayanti)
    Named for: Siddhartha Gautama (c. 563 B.C.- c. 483 B.C.)
    Location: India: Bodh Gaya
    Ethnic or religious group: Buddhist
    Date: April-May, full moon day of Hindu month of Vaisakha

    FolkWrldHol-1992, 257
    HolFestCelWrld-1994, 356
    RelHolCal-1993, 64

Buddha's Birthday, Enlightenment, and Salvation (Buddha Jayanti)
    Named for: Siddhartha Gautama (c. 563 B.C.- c. 483 B.C.)
    Location: India: Kusinagar near Gorakhpur
    Ethnic or religious group: Buddhist
    Date: April-May, full moon day of Hindu month of Vaisakha

    FolkWrldHol-1992, 257
    RelHolCal-1993, 64

Buddha's Birthday, Enlightenment, and Salvation (Buddha Jayanti)
    Named for: Siddhartha Gautama (c. 563 B.C.- c. 483 B.C.)
    Location: India: Sarnath at Deer Park near Varanasi
    Ethnic or religious group: Buddhist
    Date: April-May, full moon day of Hindu month of Vaisakha

    FolkWrldHol-1992, 257
    HolFestCelWrld-1994, 356
    RelHolCal-1993, 64

Buddha's Birthday, Enlightenment, and Salvation (Buddha Jayanti)
    Named for: Siddhartha Gautama (c. 563 B.C.- c. 483 B.C.)
    Location: India: Sanchi near Vidisha
    Ethnic or religious group: Buddhist
    Date: April-May, full moon day of Hindu month of Vaisakha

    FolkWrldHol-1992, 257
    RelHolCal-1993, 64

Buddha's Birthday, Enlightenment, and Salvation (Hana Matsuri, Flower Festival)
   Named for: Siddhartha Gautama (c. 563 B.C.- c. 483 B.C.)
   Location: Japan
   Ethnic or religious group: Buddhist
   Date: April 8

   BkFestHolWrld-1970, 76
   Chases-1993, 159
   HolFestCelWrld-1994, 132, 356

Buddha's Birthday, Enlightenment, and Salvation
   Named for: Siddhartha Gautama (c. 563 B.C.- c. 483 B.C.)
   Location: Korea
   Ethnic or religious group: Buddhist
   Date: April-May, eighth day of fourth Buddhist month

   FolkWrldHol-1992, 253

Buddha's Birthday, Enlightenment, and Salvation (Vixakha Bouxa or Boun Bang Fay, Festival of Rockets)
   Named for: Siddhartha Gautama (c. 563 B.C.- c. 483 B.C.)
   Location: Laos
   Ethnic or religious group: Buddhist
   Date: April-May, full moon day of Hindu month of Vaisakha

   BkHolWrld-1986, May 26, 170
   FolkWrldHol-1992, 308
   HolFestCelWrld-1994, 44

Buddha's Birthday, Enlightenment, and Salvation (Kason Festival of Watering the Banyon Tree)
   Named for: Siddhartha Gautama (c. 563 B.C.- c. 483 B.C.)
   Location: Myanmar; formerly Burma
   Ethnic or religious group: Buddhist
   Date: February-March, full moon day

   FolkWrldHol-1992, 141
   See also **Buddha's Birthday, Enlightenment, and Salvation (Burma; now Myanmar)**

Buddha's Birthday, Enlightenment, and Salvation (Vesak)
   Named for: Siddhartha Gautama (c. 563 B.C.- c. 483 B.C.)
   Location: Nepal
   Ethnic or religious group: Buddhist
   Date: April-May, full moon day of Hindu month of Vaisakha

   HolFestCelWrld-1994, 356

Buddha's Birthday, Enlightenment, and Salvation (Wesak)
   Named for: Siddhartha Gautama (c. 563 B.C.- c. 483 B.C.)
   Location: Sri Lanka

   Ethnic or religious group: Buddhist
   Date: April-May, eighth day of fourth Hindu month, Vaisakha

   FolkWrldHol-1992, 309
   IntlThFolk-1979, 345

Buddha's Birthday, Enlightenment, and Salvation (Visakha)
   Named for: Siddhartha Gautama (c. 563 B.C.- c. 483 B.C.)
   Location: Thailand
   Ethnic or religious group: Buddhist
   Date: April-May, eighth day of fourth Buddhist month

   FolkWrldHol-1992, 309
   HolFestCelWrld-1994, 44

Buddha's Birthday, Enlightenment, and Salvation
   Named for: Siddhartha Gautama (c. 563 B.C.- c. 483 B.C.)
   Location: Vietnam
   Ethnic or religious group: Buddhist
   Date: April-May, eighth day of fourth Buddhist month

   FolkAmerHol-1987, 155

Buddhist Priesthood, Admission to the (Buart Nark)
   Location: Thailand
   Ethnic or religious group: Buddhist
   Date: April-May

   AnnivHol-1983, 174

Budget Day
   Location: Britain
   Date: April 9

   AnnivHol-1983, 49
   DictDays-1988, 16

Budnivecher
   See **Christmas Eve (Bulgaria)**

Buffalo Days
   Location: Canada: Regina, Saskatchewan
   Established: 1884
   Date: Six days in July-August

   GdWrldFest-1985, 59

Buhé
   See **Transfiguration, Feast of the (Ethiopian Church in Ethiopia)**

Bullfinch Exchange Festival (Usokae)
   Location: Japan: Dazaifu, Fukuoka
   Date: January 7

   Chases-1993, 58

Bumba-meu-Boi Folk Drama
See **Juninas, Festas (Brazil)**

Bumbershoot
Location: Seattle, Washington
Established: 1971
Date: September, four days during Labor Day weekend

HolFestCelWrld-1994, 44

Bun Day
See **Mardi Gras (Iceland)**

Bun Festival
Named for: Honors legendary ruler Pak Tai
Location: Hong Kong: Cheung Chau Island
Ethnic or religious group: Chinese Taoist
Date: Four to five days in May

BkHolWrld-1986, May 25, 176
GdWrldFest-1985, 105
HolFestCelWrld-1994, 58
IntlThFolk-1979, 197

Bungan
See **Harvest Festival (Berawan people in Sarawak, Malaysia)**

Bunker Hill Day
Named for: June 17, 1775, battle
Location: Boston and Suffolk County, Massachusetts
Date: June 17

AmerBkDays-1978, 563
AnnivHol-1983, 80
BkDays-1864, i. 790
Chases-1993, 251
DictDays-1988, 16
HolFestCelWrld-1994, 44

Burbank Day
Named for: Luther Burbank (1849-1926)
Location: California
Date: March 7

AnnivHol-1983, 34
Chases-1993, 122

Burgoyne's Surrender Day
Named for: John Burgoyne (1722-1792) and surrender at
  Saratoga on October 17, 1777
Location: New York
Date: October 17

AnnivHol-1983, 134

Burgsonndeg
Location: Luxembourg
Date: February or March

AnnivHol-1983, 36
Chases-1993, 96
HolFestCelWrld-1994, 45

Burial of the Sardine (Entierro de la Sardina)
Location: Spain
Date: Four to five days beginning Easter Monday

BkFest-1937, 299
FestSaintDays-1915, 49
FestWestEur-1958, 194
See also **Ash Wednesday (Panama) and (Spain)**

Burning of the Three Firs
Location: France: Thann
Date: June 30

BkHolWrld-1986, June 30

Burning of the Witches
See **May Day Eve (Czechoslovakia)**

Burning the Devil (La Quema del Diablo)
Location: Guatemala: San Cristóbal Totonicapán and
  Guatemala City
Date: December 7

FolkWrldHol-1992, 583
HolFestCelWrld-1994, 45

**Burning the Moon House (Dal-jip-tae-u-gee or Viewing
the First Full Moon, Dal-ma-ji)**
Location: Korea: Kyungsang Province
Date: February, 15th day of first lunar month

FolkWrldHol-1992, 72
HolFestCelWrld-1994, 45

Burns Night
Named for: Robert Burns (1759-1796)
Location: Canada: Newfoundland
Date: January 25

AnnivHol-1983, 13
Chases-1993, 74
HolFestCelWrld-1994, 45

Burns Night
Named for: Robert Burns (1759-1796)
Location: England

Burns Night *(cont.)*
   Date: January 25

   AnnivHol-1983, 13
   Chases-1993, 74

Burns Night
   Named for: Robert Burns (1759-1796)
   Location: Scotland
   Date: January 25

   AnnivHol-1983, 13
   BkHolWrld-1986, January 25
   Chases-1993, 74
   DictDays-1988, 16
   FolkWrldHol-1992, 38
   HolFestCelWrld-1994, 45

Burns Night
   Named for: Robert Burns (1759-1796)
   Location: United States
   Ethnic or religious group: Scottish-Americans
   Date: January 25

   AmerBkDays-1978, 109

Burro Races, Triple Crown Pack
   Location: Fairplay, Leadville, and Buena Vista, Colorado
   Established: Since 1949 in Fairplay and Leadville; since 1979 in Buena Vista
   Date: Last weekend in July through August

   HolFestCelWrld-1994, 345

Burry Man's Walk
   Location: Scotland: South Queensferry
   Date: Second week of August

   BkHolWrld-1986, August 12, 176

Bursa Festival
   Location: Turkey: Bursa
   Date: July

   IntlThFolk-1979, 367

Bursing Day
   See **Mardi Gras (Iceland)**

Buss and Bettag Day
   See **Penance Day (Federal Republic of Germany)**

Butler Days, Jim
   Named for: Jim Butler (1855-1923)
   Location: Tonopah, Nevada
   Established: 1970

   Date: Memorial Day weekend in May

   GdUSFest-1984, 116

Butter Sculpture Festival (Mönlam or Prayer Festival)
   Location: Tibet: Lhasa
   Ethnic or religious group: Buddhist
   Established: 15th century
   Date: Usually February; two to three weeks during first month of Tibetan calendar

   BkHolWrld-1986, March 9, 176
   FolkWrldHol-1992, 64, 68
   HolFestCelWrld-1994, 46, 210
   RelHolCal-1993, 96

Butter Week
   See **Mardi Gras (Russia)**

Buxton Festival
   Location: England: Buxton
   Established: July 1979
   Date: Three and one-half weeks in July

   MusFestEurBrit-1980, 47

"Buy from Me" Fair (Aymara Indians in Bolivia)
   See **Alasita Fair (Aymara Indians in Bolivia)**

Buza-Szentelo, Blessing of Wheat
   See **St. Mark's Day (Calvinist people in Hungary)**

Buzzard Day
   Location: Hinckley Ridge near Hinckley, Ohio
   Established: 1957
   Date: First Sunday after March 15

   AnnivHol-1983, 37
   Chases-1993, 130
   FolkAmerHol-1987, 107
   HolFestCelWrld-1994, 46

Byblos Festival
   Location: Lebanon: Byblos
   Established: Late 1960s
   Date: May-September

   IntlThFolk-1979, 264

Cabrillo Day
   Named for: Juan Rodríguez Cabrillo (d. 1543), who landed in California on September 28, 1542
   Location: San Diego area, California
   Date: Six days in September

   AmerBkDays-1978, 873

Cabrillo Day *(cont.)*
AnnivHol-1983, 124
Chases-1993, 385, 388
HolFestCelWrld-1994, 47

Cactus Jack Festival
Named for: John Nance Garner (1868-1967), vice president
of the United States
Location: Uvalde, Texas
Date: Second weekend in October

HolFestCelWrld-1994, 47

Cajun and Bluegrass Festival
Location: Escoheag, Rhode Island
Established: 1980
Date: First weekend in September, including Labor Day

Chases-1993, 352
MusFestAmer-1990, 249

Cake Day
See **New Year's Eve (Scotland)**

Calan Gaeaf
See **Samhain**

Calaveras County Fair and Frog Jumping Jubilee
Named for: Based on a story by Mark Twain (pseud. for
Samuel Langhorne Clemens, 1835-1910) written in 1865
Location: Calaveras Fairgrounds, Angels Camp, California
Established: 1928
Date: May 13-16

AmerBkDays-1978, 1065
AnnivHol-1983, 69
BkHolWrld-1986, May 22, 178
Chases-1993, 205
HolFestCelWrld-1994, 47

Calderon Festival in the Old Courtyard
Named for: Calderon de la Barca (1600-1681)
Location: Federal Republic of Germany: Bamberg, Bavaria
Established: 1973
Date: June-July

IntlThFolk-1979, 131

Calendimaggio
See **May Day (Italy)** and **May Day Eve (Italy)**

Calends or Kalends
See **Ides**

Calgary Exhibition and Stampede
Location: Canada: Calgary, Alberta
Established: 1912

Date: July

GdWrldFest-1985, 28
HolFestCelWrld-1994, 48

Calico Pitchin', Cookin', and Spittin' Hullabaloo
Location: Calico, California
Established: 1977
Date: March-April, Palm Sunday weekend

HolFestCelWrld-1994, 48

California Gold Rush Day
Named for: January 24, 1848, discovery of gold
Location: Marshall Gold Discovery State Historical Park,
Coloma, California
Date: Weekend nearest January 24

AmerBkDays-1978, 109
AnnivHol-1983, 13
Chases-1993, 73

Caluser or Caluseri
See **Dance of Transylvania, Men's (Romania: Deva,
Hunedoara)**

Cambridge Festival
Location: England: Cambridge
Established: 1964
Date: Last two weeks in July

IntlThFolk-1979, 157

Camden Festival
Location: England: London
Established: 1954
Date: Two weeks in March

MusFestEurBrit-1980, 48

Camel Market
Location: Morocco: Guelmime
Date: Usually in July

HolFestCelWrld-1994, 48

Camel Races, International
Location: Virginia City, Nevada
Established: 1954
Date: September, weekend after Labor Day

HolFestCelWrld-1994, 49

Camões Memorial Day
See **National Day (Portugal)**

Camp Fire Founders' Day
  Named for: Camp Fire Girls founding on March 17, 1910
  Location: Camp Fire Girls and Boys groups
  Date: March 17

  HolFestCelWrld-1994, 49

Canada Day
  Named for: Uniting of Canada on July 1, 1867
  Location: Canada
  Date: July 1-2

  AnnivHol-1983, 87
  BkHolWrld-1986, July 1, 176
  Chases-1993, 271
  DictDays-1988, 18, 32
  FolkWrldHol-1992, 362
  HolFestCelWrld-1994, 49
  NatlHolWrld-1968, 98

Canadian National Exhibition
  Location: Canada: Toronto, Ontario
  Established: 1879
  Date: Three weeks in August and September

  GdWrldFest-1985, 53
  HolFestCelWrld-1994, 49

Canberra Week
  Named for: Founding of the city of Canberra on
    March 12, 1913
  Location: Australia: Canberra, Australian Capital Territory
  Date: Ten days in March, including Canberra Day, third
    Monday in March

  AnnivHol-1983, 37
  Chases-1993, 133
  HolFestCelWrld-1994, 50
  IntlThFolk-1979, 8

La Candelora
  See **Candlemas (Italy)**

Candlemas
  Named for: Prophesy that Jesus would be ''a light to lighten
    the Gentiles''
  Ethnic or religious group: Christian
  Established: Seventh century, Rome; late fourth century,
    Eastern Church
  Date: February 2

  AmerBkDays-1978, 135
  AnnivHol-1983, 17, 18
  BkDays-1864, i. 212

  BkFest-1937, 226
  BkFestHolWrld-1970, 28
  BkHolWrld-1986, February 2
  Chases-1993, 83
  DaysCustFaith-1957, 45
  DictDays-1988, 18, 90, 92
  DictFolkMyth-1984, 181, 186, 787
  DictWrldRel-1989, 156, 569
  FestSaintDays-1915, 27
  FestWestEur-1958, 105
  FolkAmerHol-1987, 57
  FolkWrldHol-1992, 92
  HolFestCelWrld-1994, 50
  RelHolCal-1993, 104
  SaintFestCh-1904, 90

Candlemas
  Ethnic or religious group: Church of England
  Date: February 2

  BkDays-1864, i. 213
  SaintFestCh-1904, 90

Candlemas
  Ethnic or religious group: Eastern Orthodox
  Date: February 2

  AmerBkDays-1978, 135
  AnnivHol-1983, 17
  BkFestHolWrld-1970, 28
  Chases-1993, 83
  DictFolkMyth-1984, 186
  RelHolCal-1993, 104

Candlemas
  Ethnic or religious group: Episcopalian
  Date: February 2

  AmerBkDays-1978, 135

Candlemas
  Ethnic or religious group: Lutheran
  Date: February 2

  AmerBkDays-1978, 135

Candlemas
  Ethnic or religious group: Protestant
  Date: February 2

  AmerBkDays-1978, 135
  AnnivHol-1983, 17
  SaintFestCh-1904, 90

Candlemas
  Ethnic or religious group: Roman Catholic
  Date: February 2

  AmerBkDays-1978, 135
  AnnivHol-1983, 17
  BkDays-1864, i.213
  Chases-1993, 83
  DictDays-1988, 18
  DictWrldRel-1989, 156
  RelHolCal-1993, 104
  SaintFestCh-1904, 90

Candlemas (Dyarntarach)
  Location: Armenia
  Ethnic or religious group: Armenian Church
  Date: February 14

  BkFest-1937, 21, 23
  DictFolkMyth-1984, 186
  DictWrldRel-1989, 156

Candlemas
  Location: Austria
  Date: February 2

  FolkWrldHol-1992, 92

Candlemas
  Location: Brazil: Porto Alegere
  Date: February 2

  AnnivHol-1983, 18

Candlemas
  Location: Canada: Newfoundland and Maritime Provinces
  Date: February 2

  FolkWrldHol-1992, 92

Candlemas (Virgin de la Candelaria)
  Location: Colombia: Cartegna
  Date: February 2

  FolkWrldHol-1992, 92

Candlemas
  Location: England
  Date: February 2

  BkDays-1864, i.213
  FestSaintDays-1915, 28
  FolkWrldHol-1992, 93
  SaintFestCh-1904, 90

Candlemas (La Chandeleur)
  Location: France
  Date: February 2

  DictFolkMyth-1984, 181
  FolkWrldHol-1992, 93

Candlemas
  Location: Germany
  Date: February 2

  BkDays-1864, i. 214
  FolkWrldHol-1992, 93

Candlemas (Tees Ypapantees)
  Location: Greece
  Date: February 2

  BkFest-1937, 145
  FolkWrldHol-1992, 94

Candlemas
  Location: Guatemala
  Date: February 2

  FolkWrldHol-1992, 94

Candlemas (Gyertyaszentel Boldog Asszony)
  Location: Hungary
  Date: February 2

  BkFest-1937, 166

Candlemas (La Candelora)
  Location: Italy
  Date: February 2

  BkFest-1937, 180

Candlemas
  Location: Liechtenstein
  Date: February 2

  AnnivHol-1983, 18

Candlemas (Lîchtmesdâg)
  Location: Luxembourg
  Date: February 2

  FestWestEur-1958, 105

Candlemas (Día de la Candelaria)
  Location: Mexico
  Date: February 2, Aztec New Year

  BkFest-1937, 226
  BkFestHolWrld-1970, 29

Candlemas (Día de la Candelaria) *(cont.)*
　DictFolkMyth-1984, 186, 787, 981
　DictWrldRel-1989, 569
　FolkAmerHol-1987, 57

Candlemas
　Location: Mexico: Michoacán
　Date: February 2

　DictFolkMyth-1984, 981

Candlemas
　Location: Mexico: San Juan de los Lagos, Jalisco
　Date: February 2

　DictFolkMyth-1984, 186
　DictWrldRel-1989, 569

Candlemas
　Location: San Felipe Pueblo, New Mexico
　Date: February 2

　IndianAmer-1989, 285, 309

Candlemas
　Location: New Mexico pueblos
　Date: February 2

　AmerBkDays-1978, 136
　IndianAmer-1989, 285, 309

Candlemas (Świeto Matki Boskiej Gromnicznej)
　Location: Poland
　Date: February 2

　BkFest-1937, 258

Candlemas (Virgin de la Candelaria)
　Location: Puerto Rico
　Date: February 2

　AmerBkDays-1978, 136

Candlemas
　Location: Rome
　Date: February 2

　AmerBkDays-1978, 135
　BkDays-1864, i. 213
　DictWrldRel-1989, 156
　FestSaintDays-1915, 27

Candlemas
　Location: Scotland
　Date: February 2

　BkFest-1937, 53
　BkDays-1864, i. 214

　DictDays-1988, 18, 93
　FestSaintDays-1915, 29

Candlemas
　Location: Spain
　Date: February 2

　FolkWrldHol-1992, 94

Candlemas (Dukkul al-Sayyid ila-l-Haykal)
　Location: Syria
　Date: February 2

　BkFest-1937, 327

Candlewalk, The
　Location: England and the United States
　Date: December 31

　FolkAmerHol-1987, 409

Candy Festival
　See **Fast, Feast of Breaking the (Turkey)**

Canicular Days
　See **Dog Days**

Cantate Sunday
　See **Rogation Days**

Capac Raimi
　Location: Peru: Huanacaurí
　Ethnic or religious group: Inca people
　Date: December, at the summer solstice

　DictFolkMyth-1984, 190, 1032

Capital Expo
　Location: Frankfort, Kentucky
　Established: 1974
　Date: Two days in early June

　GdUSFest-1984, 62

Capo d'Anno
　See **New Year's Day (Italy)**

Carabao
　See **Water Buffalo Festival (Philippines: Pulilan, San Isidro, Angono, Sariaya, and Lucban, Quezon Province)**

Caramoor Festival
　Location: Katonah, New York
　Established: 1946
　Date: Nine weeks from mid-June to mid-August

　MusFestAmer-1990, 99

Carberry Day
  Location: Brown University, Providence, Rhode Island
  Established: 1929
  Date: Every Friday the 13th

  FolkAmerHol-1987, 39
  HolFestCelWrld-1994, 51

Carcassone, Festival of
  Location: France: Carcassone, Aude
  Established: 1974
  Date: Two weeks in July

  IntlThFolk-1979, 103

Care Sunday
  See **Carling Sunday**

Caribana
  Location: Canada: Toronto, Ontario
  Ethnic or religious group: West Indian people
  Established: 1967; based on Carnival in Trinidad and Tobago
  Date: One week ending the first Monday in August,
  Toronto's Civic Holiday

  GdWrldFest-1985, 54

Caribou Carnival and Championship Dog Derby
  Location: Canada: Yellowknife, Northwest Territories
  Established: 1967
  Date: One week in March

  GdWrldFest-1985, 43

Caricom Day
  Named for: July 4, 1973, establishment of Caribbean
  Community
  Location: Antigua and Barbuda
  Date: First Saturday in June

  HolFestCelWrld-1994, 51

Caricom Day
  Named for: July 4, 1973, establishment of Caribbean
  Community
  Location: Barbados, Guyana, and St. Vincent
  Date: On or near July 4

  AnnivHol-1983, 88
  Chases-1993, 281
  HolFestCelWrld-1994, 51

Carillon Festival, International
  Location: Springfield, Illinois
  Established: 1962

  Date: One week in mid-June

  MusFestAmer-1990, 55

Carinthischer Sommer
  See **Summer Festival, Carinthian (Austria: Ossiach
  and Villach)**

Carle Sunday
  See **Carling Sunday**

Carling Sunday
  Location: Czechoslovakia
  Date: March-April, fifth Sunday in Lent

  DictFolkMyth-1984, 181

Carling Sunday
  Location: Germany
  Date: March-April, fifth Sunday in Lent

  FestSaintDays-1915, 53

Carling Sunday
  Location: Great Britain
  Date: March-April, fifth Sunday in Lent

  BkDays-1864, i.336
  BkFest-1937, 56
  DictDays-1988, 19
  FestSaintDays-1915, 53
  FolkWrldHol-1992, 128
  HolFestCelWrld-1994, 51

Carnaval
  See **Mardi Gras (Canada: Quebec City, Quebec), (Mexico),
  (Portugal), and (Spain)**

Carnaval, Fiesta of Games
  See **Mardi Gras (Mexico: Zinacantun)**

Carnaval, Quebec
  Location: Canada: Quebec City, Quebec
  Established: 1955
  Date: Ten days in February

  Chases-1993, 85
  FolkWrldHol-1992, 109
  GdWrldFest-1985, 56
  HolFestCelWrld-1994, 51, 263

Carnaval Miami
  Location: Miami, Florida
  Ethnic or religious group: Hispanic-Americans
  Established: 1938
  Date: First two full weeks in March

  HolFestCelWrld-1994, 52

Carnea
Named for: Honored Apollo
Location: Greece: Cyrene, Magna Græcia, Peloponnesus, and Sparta
Established: 676 B.C.
Date: August, ancient Greek month of Carneus

DictFolkMyth-1984, 67, 192
HolFestCelWrld-1994, 52
RelHolCal-1993, 65

Carnevale
See **Mardi Gras (Italy)**

Carnival
See **Mardi Gras (Aruba: Oranjestad), (Bohemia), (Brazil), (Brazil: Rio de Janeiro), (Colombia: Barranquilla, Atlántico), (Cyprus: Limassol), (France: Paris), (France: Saint-Lô, Burgendy), (Grenada: Carriacou), (Malta), (Martinique and Guadeloupe), (St. Vincent), (Switzerland: Basel), (Thrace), (Trinidad and Tobago), and (Virgin Islands)**

Carnival and Burial of the Sardine on Ash Wednesday
See **Mardi Gras (Panama)**

Carnival of Flowers
Location: Australia: Toowoomba, Queensland
Established: 1950
Date: End of September-early October

GdWrldFest-1985, 7
IntlThFolk-1979, 18

Carnival of Mamoiada
Location: Italy: Mamoiada, Sardinia
Date: February-March, Sunday and Tuesday preceding Ash Wednesday

IntlThFolk-1979, 245

Carnival of the Clowns, Carnival of the Gilles
See **Mardi Gras (Belgium: Binche)**

Carnival Thursday
See **Mardi Gras (Syria)**

Carnival Week
See **Mardi Gras (Bolivia)**

Carnuntum Festival
Location: Austria: Deutsch-Altenburg, Lower Austria
Established: 1967
Date: July-August

IntlThFolk-1979, 31

Carp-Flying Day
See **Children's Day (Japan)**

Carthage, International Festival of
Location: Tunisia: Carthage, North Tunis Region
Established: 1963-64
Date: July and August

GdWrldFest-1985, 178
IntlThFolk-1979, 358

Caruaru Roundup
Location: Brazil: Pernambuco
Date: Three days in September

HolFestCelWrld-1994, 54

Casals Festival
Named for: Pablo Casals (1876-1973)
Location: Puerto Rico: San Juan
Established: 1957
Date: 16 days in June

GdUSFest-1984, 220
HolFestCelWrld-1994, 54
MusFestAmer-1990, 156

Castelo de Vide, National Festival of
Location: Portugal: Castelo de Vide, Portalegre
Established: 1976
Date: August

IntlThFolk-1979, 304

Castle Festival, Moyang
Named for: Commemorates castle's completion in 1453
Location: Republic of Korea: Gochang
Date: Mid-October, ninth day of the ninth lunar month

GdWrldFest-1985, 127

Castle Festival at Jagsthausen
Location: Federal Republic of Germany: Jagsthausen, Baden-Wurttemberg
Date: June-August

IntlThFolk-1979, 141

Castle Gottorf, Festival at
Location: Federal Republic of Germany: Schleswig, Schleswig-Holstein
Established: 1954
Date: July-August

IntlThFolk-1979, 149

Castle Hill Festival
  Location: Ipswich, Massachusetts
  Established: 1972
  Date: Weekends from early July to mid-August

  MusFestAmer-1990, 75

Castle Kobersdorf Festival
  Location: Austria: Kobersdorf, Burgenland
  Established: 1972
  Date: July

  IntlThFolk-1979, 35

Castle Neulengbach Festival (Schloss Neulengbach)
  Location: Austria: Neulengbach, Lower Austria
  Established: 1975
  Date: July

  IntlThFolk-1979, 37

Castle Play Festival, Moers
  Location: Federal Republic of Germany: Moers, North
    Rhine-Westphalia
  Established: 1970
  Date: Five weeks in summer

  IntlThFolk-1979, 143

Castle Plays Festival
  Location: Austria: Forchtenstein, Burgenland
  Established: 1959; features plays by Franz Grillparzer
    (1791-1872)
  Date: June-July

  IntlThFolk-1979, 32

Castle Theatre Hohenlimburg
  Location: Federal Republic of Germany: Hagen and
    Hohenlimburg, North Rhine-Westphalia
  Established: 1953
  Date: June-July

  IntlThFolk-1979, 139

Castor and Pollux, Festival of
  Named for: The twins identified with the stars in the
    constellation Gemini
  Location: Ancient Rome
  Date: July 8

  AmerBkDays-1978, 608

Cataclysmos (Cyprus)
  See **Kataklysmos Festival (Flood Festival) (Cyprus: Larnaca,
    Limassol, Paphos, and other seaside towns)**

Cat Festival (Kattestoet)
  Named for: Commemorates the occasion on which
    Baudoin III, Count of Flanders (fl. tenth century),
    threw cats from his tower
  Location: Belgium: Ypres
  Established: 962; civic festival since 1938; Cat Parade
    since 1955
  Date: Second Sunday in May every three years

  BkHolWrld-1986, May 12
  GdWrldFest-1985, 21
  HolFestCelWrld-1994, 167

Cathern Day
  See **St. Catherine's Day**

Catoctin Colorfest
  Location: Thurmont, Maryland
  Established: 1963
  Date: Two days in early October

  Chases-1993, 403
  GdUSFest-1984, 84

Caudillo, Day of the
  Location: Spain
  Established: October 1, 1936, formation of the nation by
    Francisco Franco (1892-1975)
  Date: October 1

  AnnivHol-1983, 127

Cavalcata Sarda
  See **Sardinian Cavalcade (Italy: Sassari, Sardinia)**

Cenacula
  See **Passion Play (Philippines)**

Cerealia
  Named for: Roman goddess Ceres
  Location: Ancient Rome
  Date: Beginning of April

  AmerBkDays-1978, 314, 1053
  DictFolkMyth-1984, 207

Ceremonial Day
  Location: Between Perry and Eastport, Maine
  Ethnic or religious group: Passamaquoddy Indians
  Date: Usually August 1

  IndianAmer-1989, 165

Ceres, Festival
  Location: Tunisia: Pont du Fahs, Zaghouan Region
  Date: May

  IntlThFolk-1979, 363

Cervantes Festival, International
Named for: Miguel de Cervantes (1547-1616)
Location: Mexico: Guanajuato
Established: 1973
Date: Three weeks in April-May, sometimes
    October-November

GdWrldFest-1985, 134
IntlThFolk-1979, 269

Chaitra Parb
Location: India: Orissa
Ethnic or religious group: Hindu
Date: March-April, eight days prior to full moon day of
    Hindu month of Chaitra

RelHolCal-1993, 65

Chaitra Purnima
See **Marriage of Meenakshi and Shiva, Festival of the**
    (Hindu people at the Meenakshi Temple, Madurai, India)

Chakkirako Festival
Location: Japan: Kainan Temple, Miura, Kanagawa
Date: Mid-January

IntlThFolk-1979, 256

Chakkri Day
Named for: Rama I, Chao Phraya Chakkri (1737-1809) and
    the late-18th-century founding of Chakkri dynasty
Location: Thailand
Date: April 6

AnnivHol-1983, 48
Chases-1993, 157
HolFestCelWrld-1994, 55

Chalanda Marz
See **First of March (Switzerland: Engadine, Grisons)**

Chalk Sunday
Location: Ireland
Date: February, first Sunday in Lent

FolkWrldHol-1992, 126
HolFestCelWrld-1994, 55

Chandan Yatra
Location: India: Puri, Orissa, Bhubaneshwar, Baripada,
    and Balanga
Ethnic or religious group: Hindu
Date: April-May, 21 days beginning third day of waxing
    half of Hindu month of Vaisakha

RelHolCal-1993, 66

La Chandeleur
See **Candlemas (France)**

Change of Season
See **Bean-Throwing Festival (Japan)**

Chanukah
See **Hanukkah**

Chaomos
Location: Pakistan: near Chitral
Ethnic or religious group: Kafir Kalash people
Date: December 21, winter solstice

HolFestCelWrld-1994, 56

Charfreudeg
See **Good Friday (Luxembourg)**

Chariot Festival of Macchendranath (Festival of the
God of Rain)
Location: Nepal: Patan and Kathmandu
Ethnic or religious group: Buddhist Newar and Hindu
    people
Established: Thousands of years ago
Date: April-May, begins first day of waning half of Hindu
    month of Vaisakha and lasts two months; every few years,
    festival is extended through August

GdWrldFest-1985, 138
HolFestCelWrld-1994, 269

Charlottetown Festival
Location: Canada: Charlottetown, Prince Edward Island
Established: 1965
Date: June-September

GdWrldFest-1985, 55
IntlThFolk-1979, 75

Charro Days Fiesta
Location: Brownsville, Texas, and Matamoros, Mexico
Ethnic or religious group: Spanish and Mexican
Established: 1938
Date: February-March, four days beginning Thursday of
    the weekend before Lent

AmerBkDays-1978, 141
AnnivHol-1983, 174
Chases-1993, 110
HolFestCelWrld-1994, 56

Charsamsdeg
See **Holy Saturday (Luxembourg)**

Charter Day
  Named for: March 4, 1681, charter by Charles II (1630-1685) to William Penn (1644-1718) to found the state
  Location: Pennsylvania
  Date: March 4

  AnnivHol-1983, 33
  Chases-1993, 118

Chateauvallon Festival
  Location: France: Toulon/Ollioules, Var
  Established: 1970
  Date: July-August

  IntlThFolk-1979, 125

La Chaux-de-Fonds, Biennial of
  Location: Switzerland: La Chaux-de-Fonds, Neuchatel
  Established: 1972
  Date: Even-numbered years usually in May-June, sometimes autumn

  IntlThFolk-1979, 352

Chaw-Se Big Time Celebration
  Location: Indian Grinding Rock State Park near Pine Grove, California
  Ethnic or religious group: Pomo Indians and Maidu Indians
  Date: Usually last weekend in September

  IndianAmer-1989, 340, 346

Cheesefare Sunday
  See **Mardi Gras (Macedonia)**

Cherokee Days of Recognition
  Location: Cleveland, Tennessee
  Ethnic or religious group: Cherokee Indians
  Date: First weekend in August

  Chases-1993, 320

Cherokee National Holiday
  Location: Tahlequah, Oklahoma
  Ethnic or religious group: Cherokee Indians
  Date: September, Thursday-Sunday of Labor Day weekend

  Chases-1993, 351
  IndianAmer-1989, 65

Cherokee of Hoke Intertribal Festival
  Location: Rockfish, North Carolina
  Ethnic or religious group: Cherokee and Tuscarora Indians
  Date: Fourth Saturday in July

  Chases-1993, 304

Cherokee Strip Day
  Location: Ponca City, Enid, and Perry, Oklahoma
  Established: 1893
  Date: September 16

  AmerBkDays-1978, 844
  AnnivHol-1983, 119
  Chases-1993, 371
  HolFestCelWrld-1994, 56

Cherry Blossom Festival
  Location: Japantown, San Francisco, California
  Established: 1968
  Date: One week in April

  Chases-1993, 168
  GdUSFest-1984, 22

Cherry Blossom Festival
  Location: Honolulu, Oahu Island, Hawaii
  Established: 1953
  Date: Mid-February through April

  GdUSFest-1984, 43
  HolFestCelWrld-1994, 57

Cherry Blossom Festival (Hanami)
  Location: Japan
  Date: Two weeks in April or May

  AnnivHol-1983, 174
  BkFestHolWrld-1970, 89
  FolkWrldHol-1992, 220
  HolFestCelWrld-1994, 133

Cherry Blossom Festival
  Location: Washington, D.C.
  Established: Commemorates 1912 planting of the Japanese trees; festival since 1948
  Date: Six days in late March-April

  AmerBkDays-1978, 330
  AnnivHol-1983, 174
  Chases-1993, 155
  GdUSFest-1984, 203
  HolFestCelWrld-1994, 57

Cherry Blossom Festival, Chinhae
  Named for: Honors Yi Sun-shin (fl. 16th century)
  Location: Korea: Chinhae
  Date: Early April

  HolFestCelWrld-1994, 60

Cherry Blossom Festival, Macon
  Location: Macon, Georgia
  Established: 1982
  Date: Ten days in mid-March

  HolFestCelWrld-1994, 191

Cherry Festival, National
  Location: Traverse City, Michigan
  Established: 1926
  Date: First full week after July 4

  AmerBkDays-1978, 635
  Chases-1993, 277
  GdUSFest-1984, 94
  HolFestCelWrld-1994, 57

Chesapeake Appreciation Days
  Location: Annapolis, Maryland
  Established: 1964
  Date: Last weekend in October

  GdUSFest-1984, 79
  HolFestCelWrld-1994, 57

Chester Festival
  Location: England: Chester
  Date: June-July

  IntlThFolk-1979, 158

Cheyenne Frontier Days
  Location: Cheyenne, Wyoming
  Established: September 23, 1897
  Date: Last full week in July

  AmerBkDays-1978, 682
  AnnivHol-1983, 121, 175
  BkHolWrld-1986, July 28, 176
  Chases-1993, 303
  DictDays-1988, 45
  GdUSFest-1984, 215
  HolFestCelWrld-1994, 58

**Chhit Sek, Seventh Evening and Birthday of the
Chhit-niu-ma, or Seven Old Maids**
  See **Double Seventh (Taiwan)**

Chiang Kai-shek Day
  Named for: Chiang Kai-shek (1887-1975), president of the
    Republic of China
  Location: Taiwan

  Date: October 31 or November 1

  AnnivHol-1983, 140
  Chases-1993, 426

Chiapa de Corzo, Fiesta of
  Location: Mexico: Chiapas
  Date: January 20

  DictFolkMyth-1984, 844

Chichester '900' Festivities
  Location: England: Chichester, West Sussex
  Established: 1975
  Date: Two weeks beginning second week in July

  MusFestEurBrit-1980, 51

Chichibu Yamaburi
  Location: Japan: Chichibu Shrine, Chichibu City, Saitama
  Date: Three days in early December

  IntlThFolk-1979, 252

Chickaban (Feast of the Storm God Kukulcan)
  Location: Mexico: Mani, Yucatan
  Ethnic or religious group: Mayan people
  Date: End of October, Mayan month of Xul

  DictFolkMyth-1984, 594

Chickahominy Fall Festival
  Location: Near Roxbury, Virginia
  Ethnic or religious group: Chickahominy Indians
  Date: Usually weekend over fourth Saturday in September

  Chases-1993, 383
  IndianAmer-1989, 175

Chickasaw Nation Annual Day
  Location: Byng School near Ada, Oklahoma
  Date: First Saturday in October

  IndianAmer-1989, 68

Chicomecoatl
  Ethnic or religious group: Aztec
  Date: April, Aztec month of Huey Tozoztli

  DictFolkMyth-1984, 251
  See also **Easter (Mexico)**

Chicoutimi Olden-Days Carnival
  Location: Canada: Chicoutimi, Quebec
  Date: Ten days in February

  AnnivHol-1983, 174
  Chases-1993, 93

Chief Crazy Horse Pageant
   See **Custer's Last Stand (Hot Springs, South Dakota)**

Chieh Tsu
   See **Hungry Ghosts, Festival of (China)**

Chi Hsi, Festival of the Milky Way
   See **Double Seventh (China)**

Child, Yugoslav Festival of the
   Location: Yugoslavia: Sibenik, Croatia
   Established: 1958
   Date: June-July

   IntlThFolk-1979, 403

Childermas
   See **Holy Innocents' Day (England)**

Children's Book Day, International
   Date: April 2, birthday of Hans Christian Andersen
   (1805-1875)

   AnnivHol-1983, 47
   BkHolWrld-1986, April 2
   Chases-1993, 151
   HolFestCelWrld-1994, 59

Children's Day
   Location: Cape Verde
   Date: June 1

   AnnivHol-1983, 74

Children's Day
   Location: People's Republic of the Congo
   Date: December 25

   AnnivHol-1983, 164

Children's Day
   Location: Iceland
   Date: April 24

   AnnivHol-1983, 56

Children's Day
   Location: India
   Date: November 14

   Chases-1993, 441

Children's Day (Kodomo-no-hi; formerly Tango No Sekku, Boys' Festival)
   Location: Japan
   Date: May 5

   AnnivHol-1983, 61
   BkFest-1937, 199
   BkFestHolWrld-1970, 93

   BkHolWrld-1986, May 5
   Chases-1993, 195
   DictFolkMyth-1984, 540
   DictMyth-1962, i.239
   FolkAmerHol-1987, 173
   FolkWrldHol-1992, 274
   HolFestCelWrld-1994, 172

Children's Day (Kodomo-no-hi; formerly Tango No Sekku, Boys' Festival)
   Location: Hamamatsu, Japan
   Date: May 1-5 kite-flying contest

   BkFestHolWrld-1970, 93

Children's Day
   Location: Korea
   Established: 1975
   Date: May 5

   Chases-1993, 196

Children's Day (Urini Nal)
   Location: Republic of Korea
   Established: 1975
   Date: May 5

   AnnivHol-1983, 61
   HolFestCelWrld-1994, 352

Children's Day
   Location: Nigeria
   Date: May 27

   AnnivHol-1983, 72

Children's Day
   Location: Turkey
   Established: April 23, 1923
   Date: April 23

   AnnivHol-1983, 56
   BkFestHolWrld-1970, 80
   BkHolWrld-1986, April 23
   Chases-1993, 178
   HolFestCelWrld-1994, 59

Children's Day (Kodomo-no-hi; formerly Tango No Sekku, Boys' Festival; also known as Festival of Flags or Banners)
   Location: United States
   Ethnic or religious group: Japanese-Americans
   Date: May 5

   FolkAmerHol-1987, 173

Children's Day
  Location: United States
  Ethnic or religious group: National Council of Churches
  Established: June 1856, by Universalist Church, Chelsea,
    Massachusetts
  Date: Second Sunday in June

  AmerBkDays-1978, 555
  AnnivHol-1983, 79
  Chases-1993, 246
  DaysCustFaith-1957, 157
  HolFestCelWrld-1994, 59
  RelHolCal-1993, 66

Children's Day
  Location: Uruguay
  Date: January 6

  AnnivHol-1983, 5

Children's Day (Dechiyi Dan)
  Location: Yugoslavia
  Date: December, a Sunday before Christmas

  BkFest-1937, 344
  HolFestCelWrld-1994, 59

Children's Day, National
  Location: Indonesia
  Date: June 17

  AnnivHol-1983, 81

Children's Poetry Day
  Location: International
  Date: March 21

  AnnivHol-1983, 40

Children's Protection Day
  Location: Japan
  Date: April 17

  AnnivHol-1983, 52

Children's Reckoning (Kinderzeche)
  Location: Federal Republic of Germany: Dinkelsbühl,
    Bavaria
  Established: 1632
  Date: Saturday before the third Monday of June

  BkHolWrld-1986, July 16, 178
  HolFestCelWrld-1994, 170
  IntlThFolk-1979, 137

Chili Cookoff, Terlingua
  Location: Terlingua, Texas
  Established: 1967
  Date: First full weekend in November

  HolFestCelWrld-1994, 334

Chilympiad, Republic of Texas Chili Cookoff
  Location: San Marcos, Texas
  Date: Third weekend in September

  HolFestCelWrld-1994, 60

Ching Che
  See **Excited Insects, Feast of (People's Republic of China)**

Ching Ming Festival
  See **Grave-Sweeping and Cold Food Festival**

Chitlin' Strut
  Location: Salley, South Carolina
  Established: 1966
  Date: Saturday or Sunday after fourth Thursday in
    November, Thanksgiving

  GdUSFest-1984, 171
  HolFestCelWrld-1994, 60

Chitra Gupta
  Location: India: Kanchipuram near Madras
  Ethnic or religious group: Hindu
  Date: March-April, full moon day of Hindu month of Chaitra

  RelHolCal-1993, 66

Chogna Choeba
  See **Butter Sculpture Festival**

Chong Jiu Festival
  Location: China
  Date: October 15

  BkHolWrld-1986, October 15

Choosuk
  See **Mid-Autumn Festival (Korea)**

Chorégies d'Orange
  See **Orange Festival (France: Orange)**

Choyo
  See **Chrysanthemum Festival (Japan), (Korea),
  and (Okinawa)**

Chreestoogenna
  See **Christmas (Greece)**

Chreshdagôvend
See **Christmas Eve (Luxembourg)**

Christfest
See **Christmas (Austria)**

Christkindlesmarkt (Kriss Kringle's Fair)
Location: Germany: Nuremberg, Bavaria
Established: At least since 1697
Date: Early December until Christmas, December 25

AnnivHol-1983, 178
BkFestHolWrld-1970, 129
BkHolWrld-1986, December 4
FestWestEur-1958, 80
HolFestCelWrld-1994, 61

Christmas
Named for: Birth of Jesus (c. 6 B.C. - c. 30 A.D.)
Ethnic or religious group: Christian
Established: About 200 A.D. by early Egyptian Christians; since 343 in Rome
Date: December 25

AmerBkDays-1978, 43, 1128, 1141
AnnivHol-1983, 164
BkDays-1864, ii. 733, 744
BkFest-1937, 10, 11, 20, 35, 49, 62, 73, 93, 99, 108, 117, 130,
    140, 150, 155, 175, 192, 216, 223, 234, 247, 254, 256, 272,
    281, 287, 296, 305, 314, 323, 333, 345
BkFestHolWrld-1970, 135
BkHolWrld-1986, December 25
Chases-1993, 482
DaysCustFaith-1957, 319, 351
DictDays-1988, 20, 131, 135
DictFolkMyth-1984, 182, 193, 229, 501, 554, 571, 591, 628,
    689, 761, 779, 854, 1063, 1065, 1133
DictWrldRel-1989, 154, 175, 182, 380
FestSaintDays-1915, 231
FestWestEur-1958, 20, 30, 53, 83, 104, 148, 158, 186, 208,
    222, 241
FolkAmerHol-1987, 371
FolkWrldHol-1992, 602
HolFestCelWrld-1994, 61, 279, 367
RelHolCal-1993, 66
SaintFestCh-1904, 37

Christmas
Ethnic or religious group: Anglican
Date: December 25

RelHolCal-1993, 67

Christmas
Ethnic or religious group: Eastern Orthodox

Date: January 6

AmerBkDays-1978, 43, 1141
BkFest-1937, 287
HolFestCelWrld-1994, 61
RelHolCal-1993, 66

Christmas
Ethnic or religious group: Protestant
Date: December 25

AmerBkDays-1978, 1141
BkDays-1864, ii.746
RelHolCal-1993, 67

Christmas
Ethnic or religious group: Roman Catholic
Date: December 25

AmerBkDays-1978, 1141
AnnivHol-1983, 164
BkDays-1864, ii.746
DictFolkMyth-1984, 229
DictWrldRel-1989, 182
HolFestCelWrld-1994, 61
RelHolCal-1993, 66

Christmas
Location: Alaska
Ethnic or religious group: Eskimos
Date: December 25

AmerBkDays-1978, 1148
BkFestHolWrld-1970, 143

Christmas (Krishtlindjet)
Location: Albania
Date: December 25

BkFest-1937, 10
FolkWrldHol-1992, 602

Christmas
Location: Argentina
Date: December 25

DictFolkMyth-1984, 779
FolkWrldHol-1992, 602

Christmas (Dznoont)
Location: Armenia
Date: January 6

BkFest-1937, 22
BkFestHolWrld-1970, 150
DictWrldRel-1989, 182
FolkWrldHol-1992, 602

Christmas
Location: Australia
Date: December 25

BkFestHolWrld-1970, 154
FolkWrldHol-1992, 603

Christmas
Location: Australia
Ethnic or religious group: Aboriginal people
Date: December 25

FolkWrldHol-1992, 603

Christmas (Christfest)
Location: Austria
Date: December 25

BkFest-1937, 35
HolFestCelWrld-1994, 63

Christmas
Location: Azerbaijan
Date: December 25

FolkWrldHol-1992, 618

Christmas (Kerstdag)
Location: Belgium
Date: December 25

BkFest-1937, 49
BkFestHolWrld-1970, 141
FestWestEur-1958, 20
FolkWrldHol-1992, 604
HolFestCelWrld-1994, 62

Christmas
Location: Belize
Date: December 25

FolkWrldHol-1992, 604

Christmas
Location: Bohemia
Date: December 25

DictFolkMyth-1984, 230
FolkWrldHol-1992, 608

Christmas
Location: Brazil
Date: December 25

BkFestHolWrld-1970, 156
FolkWrldHol-1992, 604

Christmas
Location: British West Indies
Ethnic or religious group: African people
Date: December 25

DictFolkMyth-1984, 554

Christmas (Koleda, Rozhdestvo Khristovo)
Location: Bulgaria
Date: December 25

BkFest-1937, 73
FolkWrldHol-1992, 604
HolFestCelWrld-1994, 172

Christmas
Location: Burkina Faso; formerly Upper Volta
Date: December 25

HolFestCelWrld-1994, 62

Christmas
Location: Canada: Newfoundland
Date: December 25

FolkWrldHol-1992, 605

Christmas
Location: Canada: Northwest Territories
Date: December 25

FolkWrldHol-1992, 605

Christmas
Location: Canada: Nova Scotia
Date: December 25

FolkWrldHol-1992, 606

Christmas
Location: Chile
Date: December 25

FolkWrldHol-1992, 607
HolFestCelWrld-1994, 62

Christmas
Location: Colombia
Date: December 25

BkFestHolWrld-1970, 157

Christmas
Location: People's Republic of the Congo
Date: December 25

BkFestHolWrld-1970, 151

Christmas (Vánoce)
Location: Czechoslovakia
Date: December 25

BkFest-1937, 93
FolkWrldHol-1992, 607

Christmas (Juledag)
Location: Denmark
Date: December 25-26

BkFest-1937, 99
BkFestHolWrld-1970, 141
FestWestEur-1958, 30
FolkWrldHol-1992, 608

Christmas
Location: England
Date: December 25

AmerBkDays-1978, 1144
BkDays-1864, ii.746
BkFest-1937, 62
DictDays-1988, 20
DictFolkMyth-1984, 76, 182, 230
FestSaintDays-1915, 238
FolkAmerHol-1987, 371
FolkWrldHol-1992, 615

Christmas (Jõulud)
Location: Estonia
Date: December 25

BkFest-1937, 108
DictFolkMyth-1984, 182
FolkWrldHol-1992, 610

Christmas (Ganna or Genna; officially called Leddat)
Location: Ethiopia
Ethnic or religious group: Coptic Church
Date: January 7

AnnivHol-1983, 6
BkFestHolWrld-1970, 151
BkHolWrld-1986, January 7
FolkWrldHol-1992, 22
GdWrldFest-1985, 74
HolFestCelWrld-1994, 114

Christmas (Joulupäivä)
Location: Finland
Date: December 25

BkFest-1937, 117
FolkWrldHol-1992, 610

Christmas (Noël)
Location: France
Date: December 25

BkFest-1937, 130
BkFestHolWrld-1970, 143, 145
DictFolkMyth-1984, 182, 230
FestSaintDays-1915, 246
FestWestEur-1958, 53
FolkWrldHol-1992, 611

Christmas
Location: Gambia
Date: December 25

FolkWrldHol-1992, 612

Christmas (Weihnachten)
Location: Germany
Date: December 25-26

AmerBkDays-1978, 1145
BkFest-1937, 140
BkFestHolWrld-1970, 141
DictFolkMyth-1984, 230, 501, 591
FestWestEur-1958, 83
FolkWrldHol-1992, 612
See also **Knocking Nights**

Christmas (Abron)
Location: Ghana
Date: December 25

FolkWrldHol-1992, 614

Christmas (Chreestoogenna)
Location: Greece
Date: December 25

BkFest-1937, 155
BkFestHolWrld-1970, 146
FolkWrldHol-1992, 615

Christmas (Karácsony)
Location: Hungary
Date: December 25

BkFest-1937, 175
FolkWrldHol-1992, 616

Christmas
Location: Iceland
Date: December 25

FolkWrldHol-1992, 616

Christmas
  Location: India
  Date: December 25

  BkFestHolWrld-1970, 151

Christmas
  Location: Iran; formerly Persia
  Date: December 25

  FolkWrldHol-1992, 618

Christmas
  Location: Iraq
  Ethnic or religious group: Coptic Church
  Date: December 25

  BkFestHolWrld-1970, 150
  FolkWrldHol-1992, 618

Christmas
  Location: Isle of Man
  Date: December 25

  FestSaintDays-1915, 243

Christmas (Il Natale)
  Location: Italy
  Date: December 25

  AmerBkDays-1978, 1144
  BkFest-1937, 192
  BkFestHolWrld-1970, 143, 146
  FestSaintDays-1915, 247
  FestWestEur-1958, 104
  FolkWrldHol-1992, 619
  HolFestCelWrld-1994, 62
  RelHolCal-1993, 67
  See also **Befana Festival**

Christmas
  Location: Jamaica
  Date: December 25

  FolkWrldHol-1992, 620

Christmas
  Location: Japan
  Date: December 25

  BkFestHolWrld-1970, 153
  FolkWrldHol-1992, 621
  HolFestCelWrld-1994, 62

Christmas
  Location: Jordan: Bethlehem

  Date: December 25

  BkFestHolWrld-1970, 149

Christmas
  Location: Lappland
  Date: December 25

  FolkWrldHol-1992, 622

Christmas (Ziemas Svētku Diena)
  Location: Latvia
  Date: December 25-26

  BkFest-1937, 216

Christmas (Kalēdos)
  Location: Lithuania
  Date: December 25

  BkFest-1937, 223
  DictFolkMyth-1984, 628
  FolkWrldHol-1992, 622

Christmas
  Location: Louisiana
  Date: December 25

  AmerBkDays-1978, 1146
  DictFolkMyth-1984, 501

Christmas
  Location: Malawi; formerly Nyasaland
  Date: December 25

  FolkWrldHol-1992, 626

Christmas
  Location: Malaysia
  Ethnic or religious group: Sarawak people
  Date: December 25

  FolkWrldHol-1992, 622

Christmas
  Location: Malta
  Date: December 25

  FolkWrldHol-1992, 623

Christmas
  Location: Marshall Islands
  Date: December 25

  BkFestHolWrld-1970, 154
  FolkWrldHol-1992, 623

Christmas (Navidad)
  Location: Mexico

Christmas (Navidad) *(cont.)*
  Date: December 25

  BkFest-1937, 234
  FolkWrldHol-1992, 623
  HolFestCelWrld-1994, 64, 257
  See also **Christmas Festival (Posadas, Feast of the Lodgings)**

Christmas (Eerste and Tweede Kerstdag)
  Location: Netherlands/Holland
  Date: December 25-26

  BkFest-1937, 247
  BkFestHolWrld-1970, 141
  FestWestEur-1958, 148
  FolkWrldHol-1992, 624

Christmas
  Location: New Mexico pueblos
  Date: December 25

  AmerBkDays-1978, 1148
  DictFolkMyth-1984, 571, 689, 1133

Christmas
  Location: Nicaragua
  Date: December 25

  BkFestHolWrld-1970, 156

Christmas
  Location: Nigeria
  Date: December 25

  FolkWrldHol-1992, 624

Christmas (Juledag)
  Location: Norway
  Date: December 25

  BkFest-1937, 254
  BkFestHolWrld-1970, 140
  FestWestEur-1958, 158
  FolkWrldHol-1992, 624

Christmas
  Location: Peru
  Date: December 25

  FolkWrldHol-1992, 626

Christmas (Boże Narodzenie; Wigilia)
  Location: Poland
  Date: December 24-January 6

  BkFest-1937, 256
  BkFestHolWrld-1970, 142

  FolkWrldHol-1992, 627
  HolFestCelWrld-1994, 62, 367

Christmas (Día de Natal or Día da Familia, Day of the Family)
  Location: Portugal
  Date: December 25

  BkFest-1937, 272
  BkFestHolWrld-1970, 143
  DictFolkMyth-1984, 761
  FestWestEur-1958, 186
  FolkWrldHol-1992, 629

Christmas
  Location: Puerto Rico
  Date: December 25

  AmerBkDays-1978, 1149
  FolkAmerHol-1987, 380
  FolkWrldHol-1992, 629

Christmas (Crăciun)
  Location: Romania
  Date: December 25

  BkFest-1937, 281
  BkFestHolWrld-1970, 142
  FolkWrldHol-1992, 629

Christmas (Rozhdestvo Khristovo)
  Location: Russia
  Date: December 25; January 7 in Russian Orthodox
    Church

  BkFest-1937, 296
  BkFestHolWrld-1970, 142
  DictFolkMyth-1984, 230
  FolkWrldHol-1992, 636
  HolFestCelWrld-1994, 279

Christmas
  Location: St. Kitts and Nevis
  Date: December 25

  FolkWrldHol-1992, 630

Christmas
  Location: Scandinavia
  Date: December 25

  BkFestHolWrld-1970, 136, 138

Christmas (Yule Day)
  Location: Scotland
  Date: December 25

  BkDays-1864, ii.746
  BkFest-1937, 62
  DictDays-1988, 135

Christmas
Location: Senegal
Date: December 25

FolkWrldHol-1992, 612

Christmas
Location: Serbia
Date: December 25

DictFolkMyth-1984, 182
FestSaintDays-1915, 248

Christmas (Boys' Alikali Devils in Bo)
Location: Sierra Leone
Date: December 25

FolkWrldHol-1992, 630

Christmas
Location: Silesia
Date: December 25

DictFolkMyth-1984, 182

Christmas
Location: South Africa
Ethnic or religious group: Afrikaaner people
Date: December 25

BkFestHolWrld-1970, 152
FolkWrldHol-1992, 631

Christmas
Location: South Africa
Ethnic or religious group: native South African people
Date: December 25

BkFestHolWrld-1970, 152

Christmas (Navidad)
Location: Spain
Date: December 25

BkFest-1937, 305
BkFestHolWrld-1970, 143, 145
DictFolkMyth-1984, 779, 1063, 1065
FestWestEur-1958, 208
FolkWrldHol-1992, 631

Christmas
Location: Surinam
Date: December 25, two-day holiday

FolkWrldHol-1992, 632

Christmas (Juldagen)
Location: Sweden
Date: December 25

BkFest-1937, 314
BkFestHolWrld-1970, 140
DictFolkMyth-1984, 230
FestWestEur-1958, 222
FolkWrldHol-1992, 632

Christmas (Weihnachten)
Location: Switzerland
Date: December 25

BkFest-1937, 323
BkFestHolWrld-1970, 142
FestWestEur-1958, 241

Christmas ('Id al Milad)
Location: Syria
Date: December 25

BkFest-1937, 333
BkFestHolWrld-1970, 150
FolkWrldHol-1992, 635

Christmas
Location: Thailand
Date: December 25

BkFestHolWrld-1970, 152

Christmas
Location: Thrace
Date: December 25

DictFolkMyth-1984, 761

Christmas (Mukutanik)
Location: Uganda
Ethnic or religious group: Sebei people
Date: December 25

FolkWrldHol-1992, 635

Christmas
Location: United States
Date: December 25

AmerBkDays-1978, 1145
BkFest-1937, 11, 20
BkFestHolWrld-1970, 137
DictFolkMyth-1984, 571, 689, 854, 1133
FolkAmerHol-1987, 371
RelHolCal-1993, 67

Christmas
Location: United States
Ethnic or religious group: Moravian Czech-Americans
Date: December 25

AmerBkDays-1978, 1147
FolkAmerHol-1987, 371

Christmas
Location: United States
Ethnic or religious group: Pennsylvania-Dutch people
Date: December 25

DictFolkMyth-1984, 854
FolkAmerHol-1987, 375

Christmas
Location: United States
Ethnic or religious group: Russian-Americans
Date: December 25

BkFest-1937, 287

Christmas
Location: Upper Volta; now Burkina Faso
Date: December 25

FolkWrldHol-1992, 635

Christmas
Location: Uruguay
Date: December 25

FolkWrldHol-1992, 636

Christmas
Location: Venezuela
Date: December 25

FolkWrldHol-1992, 636

Christmas (Virgin Islands)
See **Christmas Festival, Caribbean**

Christmas
Location: Wales
Date: December 25

DictFolkMyth-1984, 501
FolkWrldHol-1992, 636

Christmas (Božic)
Location: Yugoslavia
Date: December 25

BkFest-1937, 345

Christmas
Location: Zaire
Date: December 25

FolkWrldHol-1992, 637

Christmas
Location: Zimbabwe
Date: December 25

FolkWrldHol-1992, 637

Christmas
Location: Zululand
Date: December 25

FolkWrldHol-1992, 637

Christmas, Nine Days Before
Ethnic or religious group: Roman Catholic
Date: December 16

AnnivHol-1983, 161

Christmas, Twelve Days of
Location: Europe, Latin America, and Mexico
Date: December 25-January 6

FolkAmerHol-1987, 401
RelHolCal-1993, 68

Christmas, Twelve Days of
Location: United States
Date: December 25-January 6

FolkAmerHol-1987, 401

Christmas Around the World
Location: Chicago, Illinois
Established: 1941
Date: Late November through early January

AmerBkDays-1978, 1147
GdUSFest-1984, 46

Christmas Boat Parade, Newport Harbor
Location: Newport Beach, California
Established: 1908
Date: December 17-23

HolFestCelWrld-1994, 224

Christmas Carol Mass (Misa de Aguinaldo)
Location: Venezuela: Caracas
Date: December 16-24

BkHolWrld-1986, December 18, 179
HolFestCelWrld-1994, 63

Christmas Dances
Location: Wyoming
Ethnic or religious group: Shoshone Indians
Date: December

IndianAmer-1989, 115

Christmas Eve
Ethnic or religious group: Christian
Date: December 24

AmerBkDays-1978, 1135
AnnivHol-1983, 163
BkDays-1864, ii.733
BkFest-1937, 9, 20, 22, 35, 48, 62, 73, 92, 98, 107, 116,
  129, 139, 154, 175, 191, 215, 222, 234, 252, 272, 280, 287,
  296, 304, 313, 322, 333, 344
BkHolWrld-1986, December 24
Chases-1993, 481
DaysCustFaith-1957, 350
DictDays-1988, 20, 135
DictFolkMyth-1984, 549, 591, 1063
FestSaintDays-1915, 8, 228
FestWestEur-1958, 27, 28, 50, 82, 83, 102, 120, 156, 206,
  219, 239
HolFestCelWrld-1994, 63, 341
RelHolCal-1993, 67

Christmas Eve
Ethnic or religious group: Breton people
Date: December 24

DictFolkMyth-1984, 549

Christmas Eve
Ethnic or religious group: Eastern Orthodox
Date: December 24

AmerBkDays-1978, 1135
BkFest-1937, 287
RelHolCal-1993, 68

Christmas Eve
Ethnic or religious group: Episcopalian
Date: December 24

AmerBkDays-1978, 1135

Christmas Eve
Ethnic or religious group: Protestant
Date: December 24

AmerBkDays-1978, 1135

Christmas Eve
Ethnic or religious group: Roman Catholic
Date: December 24

AmerBkDays-1978, 1135
BkDays-1864, ii.736

Christmas Eve
Ethnic or religious group: Slavic people
Date: December 24

RelHolCal-1993, 68

Christmas Eve
Ethnic or religious group: Welsh people
Date: December 24

FestSaintDays-1915, 229

Christmas Eve (Duke Gdhirë Krishtlindjet)
Location: Albania
Date: December 24

BkFest-1937, 9

Christmas Eve
Location: Hot Springs National Park, Hot Springs,
  Arkansas
Established: Pageant since 1931
Date: December 24

AmerBkDays-1978, 1138

Christmas Eve
Location: Armenia
Date: January 5

BkFest-1937, 22
DaysCustFaith-1957, 351

Christmas Eve (Heiliger Abend)
Location: Austria
Date: December 24

BkFest-1937, 35

Christmas Eve (Kerstavond)
Location: Belgium
Date: December 24

AmerBkDays-1978, 1139
BkFest-1937, 48

Christmas Eve (Budnivecher)
Location: Bulgaria
Date: December 24

BkFest-1937, 73

Christmas Eve
Location: Olvera Street, Los Angeles, California
Date: December 24

AmerBkDays-1978, 1136

Christmas Eve
Location: Canada: Newfoundland and Nova Scotia
Date: December 24

HolFestCelWrld-1994, 63

Christmas Eve (Štědrý Večer)
Location: Czechoslovakia
Date: December 24

BkFest-1937, 92

Christmas Eve (Juleaftgen)
Location: Denmark
Date: Begins December 23

AmerBkDays-1978, 1135
BkFest-1937, 98
FestWestEur-1958, 27

Christmas Eve
Location: England
Date: December 24

AmerBkDays-1978, 1139
BkDays-1864, ii.733, ii.738
BkFest-1937, 62
FestSaintDays-1915, 229
HolFestCelWrld-1994, 341

Christmas Eve (Tolling the Devil's Knell)
Location: England: Dewsbury, Yorkshire
Date: December 24

HolFestCelWrld-1994, 341

Christmas Eve
Location: England: medieval Cambridge and London
Date: December 24

BkDays-1864, ii.741

Christmas Eve (Jõulu Laupäev)
Location: Estonia
Date: December 24

BkFest-1937, 107

Christmas Eve (Jouluaatto)
Location: Finland
Date: December 24

BkFest-1937, 116

Christmas Eve (Veille de Noël)
Location: France
Date: December 24

AmerBkDays-1978, 1136, 1139
BkFest-1937, 129
BkHolWrld-1986, December 24
DaysCustFaith-1957, 351
FestSaintDays-1915, 229
FestWestEur-1958, 50

Christmas Eve (Heiligabend and Christmas Shooting)
Location: Germany
Date: December 24

AmerBkDays-1978, 1139
BkDays-1864, ii.737
BkFest-1937, 139
DictFolkMyth-1984, 591
FestWestEur-1958, 82
HolFestCelWrld-1994, 64

Christmas Eve (Christmas Shooting)
Location: Germany: Berchtesgaden
Date: December 24

HolFestCelWrld-1994, 64

Christmas Eve (Paramonee ton Chreestoogennon)
Location: Greece
Date: December 24

BkFest-1937, 154
FestSaintDays-1915, 230

Christmas Eve (Karácsony Vigiliája; also known as Adam and Eve Day)
Location: Hungary
Date: December 24

BkFest-1937, 175

Christmas Eve (La Vigilia)
Location: Italy
Date: December 24

AmerBkDays-1978, 1136, 1139
BkFest-1937, 191
FestSaintDays-1915, 229
FestWestEur-1958, 102

Christmas Eve
Location: Japan
Ethnic or religious group: Buddhist
Date: December 24

HolFestCelWrld-1994, 63

Christmas Eve
Location: Jordan: Bethlehem
Date: December 24

AmerBkDays-1978, 1135

Christmas Eve (Ziemas Svētku Vakars)
Location: Latvia
Date: December 24

BkFest-1937, 215

Christmas Eve (Kūčios)
Location: Lithuania
Date: December 24

BkFest-1937, 222

Christmas Eve
Location: Louisiana
Date: December 24

AmerBkDays-1978, 1136

Christmas Eve (Chreshdagôvend)
Location: Luxembourg
Date: December 24

AmerBkDays-1978, 1139
FestWestEur-1958, 120

Christmas Eve (Noche Buena)
Location: Mexico
Date: December 24; part of Posadas season

BkFest-1937, 232, 234
See also **Christmas Festival (Posadas, Feast of the Lodgings)**

Christmas Eve
Location: Netherlands
Date: December 24

AmerBkDays-1978, 139

Christmas Eve
Location: New Mexico
Date: December 24

HolFestCelWrld-1994, 63

Christmas Eve
Location: New Mexico pueblos
Date: December 24

AmerBkDays-1978, 1136
HolFestCelWrld-1994, 304

Christmas Eve
Location: Taos Pueblo, New Mexico
Date: December 24

AmerBkDays-1978, 1136
HolFestCelWrld-1994, 304

Christmas Eve
Location: North Carolina
Ethnic or religious group: Moravian people
Date: December 24

AmerBkDays-1978, 1137

Christmas Eve (Julaften)
Location: Norway
Date: December 24

BkFest-1937, 252
FestWestEur-1958, 156

Christmas Eve
Location: Pennsylvania
Ethnic or religious group: German-Americans
Date: December 24

BkDays-1864, ii.737

Christmas Eve
Location: Pennsylvania
Ethnic or religious group: Moravians
Date: December 24

AmerBkDays-1978, 1137

Christmas Eve (Vespera de Natal)
Location: Portugal
Date: December 24

BkFest-1937, 272

Christmas Eve (Noaptea de Crăciun, Ajunul Crăciunului)
Location: Romania
Date: December 24

BkFest-1937, 280
DaysCustFaith-1957, 351

Christmas Eve (Sochelnik)
Location: Russia
Date: December 24

BkFest-1937, 287, 296

Christmas Eve
Location: Scandinavia
Date: December 24

AmerBkDays-1978, 1139
DictFolkMyth-1984, 591

Christmas Eve
Location: Scotland
Date: December 24

BkDays-1864, ii.739
DictDays-1988, 135

Christmas Eve (Noche Buena)
Location: Spain
Date: December 24

BkFest-1937, 304
DictFolkMyth-1984, 1063
FestWestEur-1958, 206

Christmas Eve
Location: Spain
Ethnic or religious group: Basque people
Date: December 24

DictFolkMyth-1984, 1063

Christmas Eve (Julafton)
Location: Sweden
Date: December 24

BkFest-1937, 313
BkHolWrld-1986, December 24
FestWestEur-1958, 219

Christmas Eve (Heiliger Abend)
Location: Switzerland
Date: December 24

AmerBkDays-1978, 1139
BkFest-1937, 322
FestWestEur-1958, 239

Christmas Eve (Beiramun 'Id al Milad)
Location: Syria
Date: December 24

BkFest-1937, 333

Christmas Eve
Location: Thurgovia: Huttweilen
Date: December 24

FestSaintDays-1915, 8

Christmas Eve
Location: United States
Date: December 24

AmerBkDays-1978, 1136
BkDays-1864, ii.737

BkFest-1937, 20
FolkAmerHol-1987, 371
HolFestCelWrld-1994, 63
RelHolCal-1993, 67

Christmas Eve
Location: Venezuela
Date: December 24

HolFestCelWrld-1994, 63

Christmas Eve
Location: Wales: Tenby
Date: December 24; three-week Mumming Drama during Christmas season

BkDays-1864, ii.740

Christmas Eve (Badnyi Dan)
Location: Yugoslavia
Date: December 24

BkFest-1937, 344

Christmas Festival (Posadas, Feast of the Lodgings)
Ethnic or religious group: Hispanic-Americans
Date: December 16-24 or 25

AnnivHol-1983, 161
BkFestHolWrld-1970, 137
FolkAmerHol-1987, 369
HolFestCelWrld-1994, 64, 257
RelHolCal-1993, 89

Christmas Festival (Posadas, Feast of the Lodgings)
Location: Mexico
Date: December 16-24 or 25

AnnivHol-1983, 161
BkFest-1937, 232
BkFestHolWrld-1970, 155
BkHolWrld-1986, December 16
Chases-1993, 475
FolkWrldHol-1992, 623
HolFestCelWrld-1994, 64, 257

Christmas Festival (Night of the Radishes and Nativity Festival)
Location: Mexico: Oaxaca
Date: December 23-24

BkHolWrld-1986, December 23
Chases-1993, 481
HolFestCelWrld-1994, 227
IntlThFolk-1979, 274

Christmas Festival, Caribbean
   Location: Virgin Islands: Christiansted, St. Croix
   Date: Two weeks beginning December 23

   AmerBkDays-1978, 1149
   AnnivHol-1983, 174

Christmas in Newport
   Location: Newport, Rhode Island
   Established: 1971
   Date: Month of December

   GdUSFest-1984, 166

Christmas Novena
   Location: South America
   Date: Nine days beginning December 16

   AnnivHol-1983, 175

Christmas Season (Hodening)
   Location: England: Kent

   DictFolkMyth-1984, 499

Christmas Season (Festival of Lights)
   Location: Niagara Falls, New York
   Date: Late November through early January

   HolFestCelWrld-1994, 181

Christmas Season (Giant Lantern Festival)
   Location: Philippines: San Fernando, Pampanga
   Date: December 24-25

   HolFestCelWrld-1994, 118

Christmas Season (Mari Lwyd)
   Location: South Wales

   DictFolkMyth-1984, 203, 678

Christmas Season and Cock's Mass (Misa de Gallo)
   Location: Philippines
   Date: December 16-January 6

   AnnivHol-1983, 161
   BkFestHolWrld-1970, 144, 154
   Chases-1993, 476
   FolkWrldHol-1992, 593, 627
   GdWrldFest-1985, 151
   HolFestCelWrld-1994, 207
   IntlThFolk-1979, 289

Christmas Torchlight Parade and Muster, Old Saybrook
   Location: Old Saybrook, Connecticut
   Established: Revived in 1970

   Date: Second Saturday night in December

   HolFestCelWrld-1994, 234

Christmas Tree, Lighting of the National
   Location: White House lawn, Washington, D.C.
   Established: 1923
   Date: Mid-December through January 1

   GdUSFest-1984, 205
   HolFestCelWrld-1994, 181

Christ of Esquipulas, Feast of
   See **Black Christ, Festival of the (Guatemala: Esquipulas)**

Christ the King, Feast of
   Named for: Jesus (c. 6 B.C.-c. 30 A.D.)
   Ethnic or religious group: Protestant
   Established: 1937
   Date: Last Sunday in August

   AnnivHol-1983, 169
   DaysCustFaith-1957, 276
   HolFestCelWrld-1994, 64
   RelHolCal-1993, 66

Christ the King, Feast of
   Named for: Jesus (c. 6 B.C.-c. 30 A.D.)
   Ethnic or religious group: Roman Catholic
   Established: 1925
   Date: Last Sunday in October

   AnnivHol-1983, 169
   DaysCustFaith-1957, 276
   HolFestCelWrld-1994, 64
   RelHolCal-1993, 66

Christ the King, Feast of
   Named for: Jesus (c. 6 B.C.-c. 30 A.D.)
   Location: Guam/Northern Marianas
   Ethnic or religious group: Chamorros people
   Date: Mid-November

   FolkWrldHol-1992, 267

Chrysanthemum Festival (Choyo)
   Location: Japan
   Established: Ancient times
   Date: September-October, ninth day of ninth lunar month

   DictFolkMyth-1984, 540
   FolkWrldHol-1992, 495
   HolFestCelWrld-1994, 64

Chrysanthemum Festival (Choyo)
　Location: Korea
　Established: Ancient times
　Date: September-October, ninth day of ninth lunar month

　FolkWrldHol-1992, 496
　HolFestCelWrld-1994, 64

Chrysanthemum Festival (Choyo)
　Location: Okinawa
　Established: Ancient times
　Date: September-October, ninth day of ninth lunar month

　FolkWrldHol-1992, 496
　HolFestCelWrld-1994, 64

Chugiak-Eagle River Bear Paw Festival
　Location: Chugiak and Eagle River, Alaska
　Date: Mid-July

　HolFestCelWrld-1994, 64

Ch'u Hsi
　See **Thirtieth, Night of the (China)**

Chulalongkorn Day
　Named for: Rama V of Siam, Chulalongkorn (1853-1910)
　Location: Thailand
　Date: October 23

　AnnivHol-1983, 136
　Chases-1993, 419
　HolFestCelWrld-1994, 64
　See also **Coronation Day (Thailand)**

Chung Ch'iu
　See **Mid-Autumn Festival (China) and (Hong Kong)**

Chung Yeung
　See **Double Ninth**

Chunhyang Festival
　Location: Republic of Korea: Namwon, North Jeolla
　Date: Early May; three days from eighth day of the fourth lunar month, to coincide with Buddha's birthday

　GdWrldFest-1985, 128
　HolFestCelWrld-1994, 65

Chusok
　See **Mid-Autumn Festival (Korea)**

Cincinnati May Festival
　Location: Cincinnati, Ohio
　Established: 1873

Date: Friday and Saturday evenings for two weeks in mid-May

　MusFestAmer-1990, 124

Cinco de Mayo
　Named for: May 5, 1862, Battle of Puebla
　Location: Calexico, Los Angeles, and San Diego, California
　Date: May 5

　AnnivHol-1983, 61

Cinco de Mayo
　Named for: May 5, 1862, Battle of Puebla
　Location: Los Angeles, California
　Date: May 5

　AmerBkDays-1978, 421
　AnnivHol-1983, 61
　HolFestCelWrld-1994, 65

Cinco de Mayo
　Named for: May 5, 1862, Battle of Puebla
　Location: Nogales, Arizona, and Nogales, Sonora, Mexico
　Date: May 5

　AmerBkDays-1978, 421

Cinco de Mayo
　Named for: May 5, 1862, Battle of Puebla
　Location: Mexico: especially Puebla
　Date: May 5

　AmerBkDays-1978, 421
　Chases-1993, 196
　DictFolkMyth-1984, 1065
　FolkWrldHol-1992, 273
　HolFestCelWrld-1994, 65

Cinco de Mayo
　Named for: May 5, 1862, Battle of Puebla
　Location: Goliad and San Antonio, Texas
　Date: May 5

　AmerBkDays-1978, 421
　HolFestCelWrld-1994, 65

Cinteotl, Festival for
　Ethnic or religious group: Aztec
　Date: April, Aztec month of Huey Tozoztli

　DictFolkMyth-1984, 251
　See also **Easter (Mexico)**

Circumcision, Feast of the
  Named for: Circumcision of Jesus (c. 6 B.C.-c. 30 A.D.)
  Ethnic or religious group: Christian
  Established: About sixth century, Rome
  Date: January 1, Gregorian calendar (N.S.); January 14, Julian calendar (O.S.)

  AmerBkDays-1978, 8
  BkFest-1937, 326
  Chases-1993, 49
  DaysCustFaith-1957, 17
  DictDays-1988, 21
  FolkWrldHol-1992, 9
  HolFestCelWrld-1994, 66
  RelHolCal-1993, 68
  SaintFestCh-1904, 50

Circumcision, Feast of the
  Ethnic or religious group: Anglican
  Established: 1549
  Date: January 1

  HolFestCelWrld-1994, 66

Circumcision, Feast of the
  Ethnic or religious group: Eastern Orthodox
  Date: January 1, Gregorian calendar (N.S.); January 14, Julian calendar (O.S.)

  AmerBkDays-1978, 9
  HolFestCelWrld-1994, 66
  RelHolCal-1993, 68

Circumcision, Feast of the (Feast of the Holy Name of Our Lord Jesus Christ)
  Ethnic or religious group: Episcopalian
  Date: January 1

  AmerBkDays-1978, 9
  HolFestCelWrld-1994, 66
  RelHolCal-1993, 68

Circumcision, Feast of the (Feast of the Circumcision and the Name of Jesus)
  Ethnic or religious group: Lutheran
  Date: January 1

  AmerBkDays-1978, 9
  HolFestCelWrld-1994, 66
  RelHolCal-1993, 68

Circumcision, Feast of the (Solemnity of Mary, the Mother of God)
  Ethnic or religious group: Roman Catholic

  Established: About sixth century, Rome
  Date: January 1

  AmerBkDays-1978, 9
  HolFestCelWrld-1994, 66
  RelHolCal-1993, 68

Circumcision, Feast of the
  Location: Costa Rica
  Date: January 1

  FolkWrldHol-1992, 9

Circumcision, Feast of the
  Location: England
  Date: January 1

  AmerBkDays-1978, 8

Circumcision, Feast of the ('Id al-Khitan)
  Location: Syria
  Date: January 1, Gregorian calendar (N.S.); January 14, Julian calendar (O.S.)

  BkFest-1937, 326
  FolkWrldHol-1992, 9

Circumcision, Feast of the
  Location: United States
  Date: January 1

  AmerBkDays-1978, 8

Circus Festival, International
  Location: Monaco: Monte Carlo
  Established: 1974
  Date: Five days in December

  GdWrldFest-1985, 136

Circus Festival and Parade, Sarasota
  Location: Sarasota, Florida
  Date: First week in January

  HolFestCelWrld-1994, 307

Círio de Nazaré
  Location: Brazil
  Date: Second Sunday in October

  HolFestCelWrld-1994, 66

Citadel Festival
  Location: Romania: Cetatea Ica, Cernat, Covasna
  Date: Second Sunday in June

  IntlThFolk-1979, 320

Citizenship Day
  Location: United States
  Established: 1952
  Date: September 17

  AmerBkDays-1978, 850
  AnnivHol-1983, 120
  Chases-1993, 373
  DictDays-1988, 21
  HolFestCelWrld-1994, 66

Civil Defense Day
  See **Pearl Harbor Day**

Clean Tent Ceremony
  Location: USSR: Siberia
  Ethnic or religious group: Nganasan people
  Date: February

  FolkWrldHol-1992, 86

Climbing the Hills, Têng Kao
  See **Double Ninth (China)**

Clipping the Church Day
  Location: England: Guiseley, Yorkshire
  Date: August 5, St. Oswald's Day

  AnnivHol-1983, 103

Cloister Festival
  Location: Federal Republic of Germany: Feuchtwangen,
  Bavaria
  Established: 1949
  Date: June-August

  IntlThFolk-1979, 138

Close Sunday
  See **Low Sunday**

Clown Festival, Emmett Kelly
  Named for: Emmett Kelly (1898-1979)
  Location: Houston, Missouri
  Established: 1988
  Date: Early May

  HolFestCelWrld-1994, 98

Coca Cola 600
  Location: Charlotte Motor Speedway, Charlotte, North
  Carolina
  Date: May, Memorial Day weekend

  HolFestCelWrld-1994, 67

Cock Festival (Fiesta del Gallo)
  Location: Spain
  Date: Usually on February 2, Candlemas

  DictFolkMyth-1984, 1062

Cock's Mass, Misa de Gallo
  See **Christmas Season and Cock's Mass, Misa de Gallo
  (Philippines)**

Coconut Day
  Location: India: Nariyal

  DictFolkMyth-1984, 240

Cocopah Festivities Day
  Location: Somerton, Arizona
  Ethnic or religious group: Cocopah Indians
  Date: March or April

  IndianAmer-1989, 259

Coffee Fair and Flower Festival
  Location: Panama: Boquete
  Established: 1966
  Date: Four days in late April

  GdWrldFest-1985, 145

Colete Encarnado, Festa do
  See **Red Waistcoat Festival (Portugal: Vila Franca de Xira,
  Lisboa District, Ribatejo)**

Collop Monday
  See **Mardi Gras (England)**

Colorado Day (Colorado)
  See **Admission Day (Colorado)**

Columbus Day
  Named for: Christopher Columbus (1451-1506)
  Date: October 12

  AmerBkDays-1978, 918
  AnnivHol-1983, 132
  BkDays-1864, ii. 437
  BkFest-1937, 18
  BkHolWrld-1986, October 12
  Chases-1993, 406, 407
  DaysCustFaith-1957, 255
  DictDays-1988, 22, 31
  FolkAmerHol-1987, 301
  HolFestCelWrld-1994, 67, 85

Columbus Day (Discovery Day)
  Named for: Christopher Columbus (1451-1506)
  Location: Bahama Islands
  Date: October 12

  AnnivHol-1983, 132

Columbus Day (Discovery Day)
  Named for: Christopher Columbus (1451-1506)
  Location: Cayman Islands
  Date: May 17

  AnnivHol-1983, 67

Columbus Day (Day of the Race)
  Named for: Christopher Columbus (1451-1506)
  Location: Chile
  Date: October 12

  AnnivHol-1983, 132
  BkHolWrld-1986, October 12

Columbus Day (Day of the Race)
  Named for: Christopher Columbus (1451-1506)
  Location: Colombia
  Date: October 12

  AnnivHol-1983, 132
  BkHolWrld-1986, October 12

Columbus Day (Day of the Race)
  Named for: Christopher Columbus (1451-1506)
  Location: Costa Rica
  Date: October 12

  AnnivHol-1983, 132
  BkHolWrld-1986, October 12

Columbus Day (Discovery Day)
  Named for: Christopher Columbus (1451-1506)
  Location: Haiti
  Date: December 5

  AnnivHol-1983, 156
  Chases-1993, 466
  HolFestCelWrld-1994, 85

Columbus Day (Discoverers' Day)
  Named for: Christopher Columbus (1451-1506)
  Location: Hawaii
  Date: Second Monday in October

  AnnivHol-1983, 132
  Chases-1993, 406
  DictDays-1988, 31
  HolFestCelWrld-1994, 67

Columbus Day (America's Discovery Day)
  Named for: Christopher Columbus (1451-1506)
  Location: Honduras
  Date: October 12

  AnnivHol-1983, 132

Columbus Day (Dia de la Hispanidad)
  Named for: Christopher Columbus (1451-1506)
  Location: Panama
  Date: October 12

  AnnivHol-1983, 132

Columbus Day (Day of the Race)
  Named for: Christopher Columbus (1451-1506)
  Location: Paraguay
  Date: October 12

  AnnivHol-1983, 132
  BkHolWrld-1986, October 12

Columbus Day (Discovery Day)
  Named for: Christopher Columbus (1451-1506)
  Location: Puerto Rico
  Date: October 12; also commemorates Columbus's sighting
    of Puerto Rico on November 19, 1493

  AnnivHol-1983, 149
  BkHolWrld-1986, 176
  Chases-1993, 446
  HolFestCelWrld-1994, 85

Columbus Day (Discovery Day)
  Named for: Christopher Columbus (1451-1506) and his 1498
    sighting of St. Vincent
  Location: St. Vincent
  Date: January 22

  AnnivHol-1983, 12

Columbus Day (Hispanity Day or Day of Spanish Consciousness)
  Named for: Christopher Columbus (1451-1506)
  Location: Spain
  Date: October 12

  AnnivHol-1983, 132
  Chases-1993, 407

Columbus Day (Discovery Day) (Trinidad and Tobago)
  See **Emancipation Day (Trinidad and Tobago)**

Columbus Day
  Named for: Christopher Columbus (1451-1506)
  Location: United States

Columbus Day *(cont.)*
Date: Second Monday in October

AmerBkDays-1978, 918
DaysCustFaith-1957, 255
DictDays-1988, 22
HolFestCelWrld-1994, 67

Columbus Day
Named for: Christopher Columbus (1451-1506)
Location: United States
Ethnic or religious group: Italian-Americans
Date: Second Monday in October

DaysCustFaith-1957, 255

Comedy, Week of
Location: Romania: Galati, Moldavia
Established: 1974
Date: Autumn

IntlThFolk-1979, 324

Comedy Festival, Days of
Location: Yugoslavia: Svetozarevo, Serbia
Date: March

IntlThFolk-1979, 407

Comedy Festival at Porcia Castle
Location: Austria: Spittal an der Drau, Carinthia
Date: July-August

IntlThFolk-1979, 40

Coming of the Rivermen
See **Santa Cruz Days (Cochiti and Taos pueblos, New Mexico)**

Commemoration Day
See **Encaenia Day (England: Oxford University)**

Common Prayer Day (Store Bededag)
Location: Denmark
Established: 18th century
Date: April-May, fourth Friday after Easter

AnnivHol-1983, 175
Chases-1993, 198
FestWestEur-1958, 25
HolFestCelWrld-1994, 67

Common Ridings Day
Location: Scotland
Date: June-July

AnnivHol-1983, 175
HolFestCelWrld-1994, 67

Common Ridings Day
Named for: Also commemorates death of King James IV (1473-1513) in Battle of Flodden of 1513
Location: Scotland: Selkirk and Haywick
Date: June

HolFestCelWrld-1994, 67

Common Sense Day
See **Paine Day, Thomas (Hugenot-Thomas Paine Historical Society)**

Commonwealth Day
Location: Canada
Date: Second Monday in March

Chases-1993, 123
HolFestCelWrld-1994, 68
See also **Victoria Day**

Commonwealth Day (formerly Empire Day)
Location: Great Britain and Commonwealth countries
Date: Second Monday in March

Chases-1993, 123
DictDays-1988, 23, 36
HolFestCelWrld-1994, 68
See also **Victoria Day**

Commonwealth Day (Puerto Rico)
See **Constitution Day (Puerto Rico)**

Compitalia
Named for: Honored lares, spirits of the household
Location: Ancient Rome

DictFolkMyth-1984, 604
FestSaintDays-1915, 19

Concepción, Fiesta of
See **Immaculate Conception, Feast of the (Bolivia: Sopocachi Alto barrio of La Paz)**

Concordia Day
Named for: November 11, 1648, territorial agreement between the Dutch and the French
Location: St. Maarten
Date: November 11

AnnivHol-1983, 146
HolFestCelWrld-1994, 68

Confederate Heroes Day
See **Confederate Memorial Day**

Confederate Memorial Day
Location: Alabama
Date: Last Monday in April

AmerBkDays-1978, 383
AnnivHol-1983, 57
Chases-1993, 181
HolFestCelWrld-1994, 203

Confederate Memorial Day
Location: Florida
Date: April 26

AmerBkDays-1978, 383
Chases-1993, 181

Confederate Memorial Day
Location: Georgia
Date: April 26

AmerBkDays-1978, 383
AnnivHol-1983, 57
Chases-1993, 181

Confederate Memorial Day
Location: Kentucky
Date: June 3

AmerBkDays-1978, 383
HolFestCelWrld-1994, 160

Confederate Memorial Day
Location: Louisiana
Date: June 3

AmerBkDays-1978, 383
AnnivHol-1983, 75
HolFestCelWrld-1994, 160

Confederate Memorial Day
Location: Mississippi
Date: Fourth Monday in April

AmerBkDays-1978, 383
AnnivHol-1983, 57
Chases-1993, 181

Confederate Memorial Day
Location: North and South Carolina
Date: May 10

AmerBkDays-1978, 383
AnnivHol-1983, 64
Chases-1993, 203

Confederate Memorial Day
Location: Texas
Date: January 19

AnnivHol-1983, 11
Chases-1993, 68
DictDays-1988, 23
HolFestCelWrld-1994, 68, 203

Confederate Memorial Day
Location: Virginia
Date: Last Monday in May

AmerBkDays-1978, 384
AnnivHol-1983, 71
Chases-1993, 227
HolFestCelWrld-1994, 160

Confederation Day
Named for: August 1, 1291, founding of Swiss Confederation
Location: Switzerland
Date: August 1

AnnivHol-1983, 101
Chases-1993, 313
FestWestEur-1958, 224
HolFestCelWrld-1994, 328
NatlHolWrld-1968, 132

Confolens Festival
Location: France: Confolens, Charente
Established: 1957
Date: One week in August

IntlThFolk-1979, 104

Confucius's Birthday
Named for: Confucius (551 B.C.-479 B.C.)
Location: China
Date: September-October, 27th day of eighth lunar month

AnnivHol-1983, 175
BkFest-1937, 76
DictWrldRel-1989, 191
HolFestCelWrld-1994, 68

Confucius's Birthday
Named for: Confucius (551 B.C.-479 B.C.)
Location: Hong Kong
Date: September-October, 27th day of eighth lunar month

BkFest-1937, 76
Chases-1993, 407
DictWrldRel-1989, 191
HolFestCelWrld-1994, 68

Confucius's Birthday (Teachers' Day)
  Named for: Confucius (551 B.C.-479 B.C.)
  Location: Taiwan
  Date: September-October, 27th day of eighth lunar month

  AnnivHol-1983, 175
  BkFest-1937, 76
  Chases-1993, 388
  DictWrldRel-1989, 191
  HolFestCelWrld-1994, 68

Congreso Centroamericano de Folclorologia
  See **Folklore, Central American Congress of (Costa Rica: Nicoya)**

Constitution and Flag Day
  Named for: Commemorates ascension of Gustav I (1496?-1560) in 1523 and 1809 Constitution
  Location: Sweden
  Date: June 6

  AnnivHol-1983, 76
  Chases-1993, 239
  HolFestCelWrld-1994, 107

Constitution and National Day
  Named for: June 1, 1959, constitution
  Location: Tunisia
  Date: Two-day holiday, including June 1

  AnnivHol-1983, 74
  Chases-1993, 230
  NatlHolWrld-1968, 76

Constitution Day
  Named for: September 29, 1959, constitution
  Location: Brunei
  Date: September 29

  AnnivHol-1983, 124

Constitution Day
  Named for: May 20, 1972, constitution
  Location: Cameroon
  Date: May 20

  AnnivHol-1983, 68
  Chases-1993, 215

Constitution Day
  Named for: June 5, 1953, constitution
  Location: Denmark
  Date: June 5

  AnnivHol-1983, 76
  Chases-1993, 235
  NatlHolWrld-1968, 33

Constitution Day
  Named for: August 20, 1949, constitution
  Location: Hungary
  Date: August 20

  AnnivHol-1983, 108

Constitution Day
  Named for: December 6, 1922, constitution
  Location: Republic of Ireland
  Date: December 6

  AnnivHol-1983, 156

Constitution Day (Italy)
  See **Republic Day (Constitution Day) (Italy)**

Constitution Day
  Named for: May 3, 1947, formation of democratic government
  Location: Japan
  Date: May 3

  AnnivHol-1983, 60
  Chases-1993, 193

Constitution Day
  Named for: July 17, 1963, constitution
  Location: Republic of Korea
  Date: July 17

  AnnivHol-1983, 94
  Chases-1993, 296

Constitution Day
  Named for: May 11, 1947, constitution
  Location: Laos
  Date: May 11

  NatlHolWrld-1968, 61

Constitution Day
  Location: Mongolia
  Date: June 30

  NatlHolWrld-1968, 90

Constitution Day
  Named for: May 17, 1968, constitution
  Location: Nauru
  Date: May 17

  AnnivHol-1983, 67

Constitution Day
  Named for: December 16, 1962, constitution
  Location: Nepal
  Date: December 16

  AnnivHol-1983, 160

Constitution Day
  Named for: May 17, 1814, independence from Sweden;
    observed since 1820s
  Location: Norway
  Date: May 17

  AnnivHol-1983, 67
  BkHolWrld-1986, May 17
  Chases-1993, 212
  HolFestCelWrld-1994, 69
  NatlHolWrld-1968, 64

Constitution Day
  Named for: August 25, 1967, revision of the
    constitution
  Location: Paraguay
  Date: August 25

  AnnivHol-1983, 110

Constitution Day
  Named for: May 14, 1935, ratification of the
    constitution
  Location: Philippines
  Date: May 14

  AnnivHol-1983, 66

Constitution Day (Swieto Trzeciego Majo)
  Named for: May 3, 1794, constitution
  Location: Poland
  Date: May 3

  AnnivHol-1983, 60
  Chases-1993, 194
  HolFestCelWrld-1994, 256

Constitution Day (Commonwealth Day)
  Named for: July 25, 1952, constitution
  Location: Puerto Rico
  Date: July 25

  AmerBkDays-1978, 694
  AnnivHol-1983, 97
  Chases-1993, 306

Constitution Day
  Named for: December 25, 1946, constitution
  Location: Taiwan

  Date: December 25

  AnnivHol-1983, 164

Constitution Day
  Named for: December 10, 1932, constitution
  Location: Thailand
  Date: December 10

  AnnivHol-1983, 158
  Chases-1993, 471

Constitution Day (United States)
  See **Citizenship Day (United States)**

Constitution Day
  Named for: 1951 constitution
  Location: Uruguay
  Date: July 18

  AnnivHol-1983, 94

Constitution Day, Norway (Syttende Mai Fest)
  Location: Spring Grove, Minnesota
  Date: May 17

  HolFestCelWrld-1994, 328

Constitution Day, Norway
  Location: Brooklyn, New York
  Date: May 17

  NatlHolWrld-1968, 64

Constitution Day, Norway
  Location: United States
  Date: May 17

  AnnivHol-1983, 67
  Chases-1993, 212
  HolFestCelWrld-1994, 328
  NatlHolWrld-1968, 64

Constitution Day, Norway
  Location: Seattle, Washington
  Date: May 17

  Chases-1993, 212

Constitution Day, Norway (Syttende Mai Fest)
  Location: Stoughton, Wisconsin
  Date: Weekend nearest May 17

  HolFestCelWrld-1994, 328, 329

Consualia
  Location: Ancient Rome
  Date: August 21 and December 15

  AmerBkDays-1978, 713
  DictFolkMyth-1984, 248

Continental Army, Departure of
Named for: Camp set up here December 19, 1777, by George
  Washington (1732-1799) and his men
Location: Valley Forge National Historical Park,
  Pennsylvania
Date: Sunday nearest June 19

  HolFestCelWrld-1994, 82

Cooks' Festival (Fête de Cuisinieres)
Location: Guadeloupe: Pointe-a-Pitre
Ethnic or religious group: Roman Catholic
Date: Saturday nearest August 10, Feast of St. Lawrence

  GdWrldFest-1985, 104
  HolFestCelWrld-1994, 74

Coolidge, Birthday Celebration of Calvin
Named for: Calvin Coolidge (1872-1933)
Location: Plymouth Notch, Vermont
Date: July 4

  AmerBkDays-1978, 628
  HolFestCelWrld-1994, 48

Coon Carnival
Location: South Africa: Cape Town
Date: January 1

  AnnivHol-1983, 2

Corn Palace Festival
Location: Mitchell, South Dakota
Established: 1892
Date: Four days in September

  Chases-1993, 371
  GdUSFest-1984, 173
  HolFestCelWrld-1994, 69

Cornwall, Festival of
Location: France: Quimper, Finistere
Ethnic or religious group: Breton people
Established: 1928
Date: One week in July

  IntlThFolk-1979, 120

Coronado Day
Named for: Francisco Vásquez de Coronado (c. 1510-1554)
Location: North American southwest
Date: February 25

  AnnivHol-1983, 29

Coronation Day (Chulalongkorn's Day)
Named for: May 5, 1950, coronation of King Bhumibol
  Adulyadej (b. 1927)
Location: Thailand
Date: May 5

  AnnivHol-1983, 62
  Chases-1993, 196

Corpus Christi
Named for: The Eucharistic sacrament which observes the
  Last Supper of Jesus (c. 6 B.C.- c. 30 A.D.)
Ethnic or religious group: Christian
Established: 1246, Liège, France
Date: May-June, the Sunday following Trinity Sunday
  (Roman Catholic and in the United States); the Thursday
  following Trinity Sunday (other Christian)

  AnnivHol-1983, 169
  BkDays-1864, i. 686
  BkFest-1937, 124, 186, 303
  BkFestHolWrld-1970, 67
  BkHolWrld-1986, June 11
  Chases-1993, 241, 246
  DaysCustFaith-1957, 156
  DictDays-1988, 24
  DictFolkMyth-1984, 253, 747, 749, 754, 787, 980, 1065
  DictWrldRel-1989, 195
  FestSaintDays-1915, 131
  FestWestEur-1958, 67, 98, 165, 198, 234
  FolkAmerHol-1987, 201
  FolkWrldHol-1992, 288
  HolFestCelWrld-1994, 70
  IntlThFolk-1979, 275, 276
  RelHolCal-1993, 69
  SaintFestCh-1904, 263

Corpus Christi
Ethnic or religious group: Roman Catholic
Date: May-June, the Sunday following Trinity Sunday (first
  Sunday after Pentecost)

  BkDays-1864, i.686
  BkHolWrld-1986, June 11
  Chases-1993, 241, 246
  DaysCustFaith-1957, 156
  DictDays-1988, 24
  DictFolkMyth-1984, 253, 747
  DictWrldRel-1989, 195
  FestWestEur-1958, 67
  FolkAmerHol-1987, 201
  HolFestCelWrld-1994, 70
  RelHolCal-1993, 69
  SaintFestCh-1904, 263

Corpus Christi
Location: Austria
Date: May-June

BkFestHolWrld-1970, 69

Corpus Christi
Location: Belgium
Date: May-June

BkFest-1937, 44

Corpus Christi
Location: England
Date: May-June

BkFestHolWrld-1970, 69
FestSaintDays-1915, 133

Corpus Christi (Fête Dieu)
Location: France
Date: May-June

BkFest-1937, 124
DictFolkMyth-1984, 253
FestSaintDays-1915, 133
FestWestEur-1958, 42
FolkWrldHol-1992, 288
HolFestCelWrld-1994, 70

Corpus Christi (Fron Leichnam)
Location: Germany
Date: May-June

FestSaintDays-1915, 137
FestWestEur-1958, 67
FolkWrldHol-1992, 288

Corpus Christi (Corpus Domini)
Location: Italy
Date: May-June

BkFest-1937, 186
BkFestHolWrld-1970, 69
FestSaintDays-1915, 135
FestWestEur-1958, 98
HolFestCelWrld-1994, 81

Corpus Christi (Procession of the Decorated Horse)
Location: Italy: Brindisi
Date: May-June

BkFest-1937, 186
FestWestEur-1958, 98
HolFestCelWrld-1994, 81

Corpus Christi
Location: Mexico
Date: May-June

BkFestHolWrld-1970, 70
DictFolkMyth-1984, 253, 749, 787
FolkWrldHol-1992, 253, 288
IntlThFolk-1979, 275, 276
See also **Battle of the Moors and Christians**

Corpus Christi (Dia de Corpo de Deus)
Location: Portugal
Date: May-June

FestWestEur-1958, 165
DictFolkMyth-1984, 253, 754
HolFestCelWrld-1994, 70

Corpus Christi (Corpus Crist́i)
Location: Spain
Date: May-June

BkFest-1937, 303
BkFestHolWrld-1970, 68
DictFolkMyth-1984, 253, 980, 1065
FestSaintDays-1915, 135, 136
FestWestEur-1958, 198
HolFestCelWrld-1994, 70
See also **Battle of the Moors and Christians**

Corpus Christi (Fronleichnamsfest)
Location: Switzerland
Date: May-June

FestWestEur-1958, 234

Corpus Christi
Location: United States
Date: May-June, the Sunday following Trinity Sunday (first Sunday after Pentecost)

BkFestHolWrld-1970, 68
Chases-1993, 246
RelHolCal-1993, 69

Corpus Crist́i
See **Corpus Christi (Spain)**

Corpus Domini
See **Corpus Christi (Italy)**

Corroboree
Location: Australia: Arnhem Land

DictFolkMyth-1984, 1128

Cotton Bowl Classic
  Location: Dallas, Texas
  Date: January 1

  Chases-1993, 49
  HolFestCelWrld-1994, 70

Cotton Carnival and Musicfest
  Location: Memphis, Tennessee
  Established: 1931
  Date: May-June

  AmerBkDays-1978, 434
  AnnivHol-1983, 31
  GdUSFest-1984, 175
  HolFestCelWrld-1994, 70

Counting of the Omer
  See **Lag b'Omer**

Country Fair
  Location: Panama: Ocu
  Established: 1966
  Date: During January, including Feast of San Sebastian, January 20

  GdWrldFest-1985, 147

Country Music and Bluegrass Festival
  Location: Payson, Arizona
  Date: Third weekend in June

  Chases-1993, 263
  MusFestAmer-1990, 238

Country Music Contest and Festival, National Old-Time
  Location: Avoca, Iowa
  Established: 1976
  Date: September, Labor Day weekend

  HolFestCelWrld-1994, 235

Country Music Fan Fair, International
  Location: Nashville, Tennessee
  Established: 1970-72
  Date: One week in early June

  Chases-1993, 239
  GdUSFest-1984, 178
  HolFestCelWrld-1994, 71
  MusFestAmer-1990, 251

Covenant, Day of the
  Ethnic or religious group: Bahá'í

Date: November 26 or 27

  AnnivHol-1983, 151
  HolFestCelWrld-1994, 80
  RelHolCal-1993, 70

Covenant, Day of the (Braaiveleis)
  Named for: December 16, 1838, defeat of Zulu King Dingaan (d. 1840)
  Location: South Africa
  Ethnic or religious group: Afrikaaner people
  Date: December 16

  AnnivHol-1983, 161
  DictDays-1988, 28
  FolkWrldHol-1992, 592
  HolFestCelWrld-1994, 80

Cow, Festival of the (Fiesta de la Vaca)
  Location: Spain: San Pablo de los Montes, Toledo
  Date: January 25

  DictFolkMyth-1984, 1063

Cowboy Parade, Black
  Location: Oakland, California
  Established: 1975
  Date: First Saturday in October

  HolFestCelWrld-1994, 33

Cow Fights (Kuhkämpfe)
  Location: Switzerland: Valais
  Date: April

  FestWestEur-1958, 228
  HolFestCelWrld-1994, 71

Cow Holiday (Gopastami)
  Location: India
  Ethnic or religious group: Hindu

  DictWrldRel-1989, 198

Cows, Procession of Sacred (Gai Jatra)
  Location: Nepal
  Ethnic or religious group: Hindu
  Date: July-August, first day of waning half of Hindu month of Sravana

  BkHolWrld-1986, October 8, 177
  FolkWrldHol-1992, 395
  HolFestCelWrld-1994, 113

Crab Apple Night
  See **Halloween (England)**

Crab Derby, National Hard
  Location: Crisfield, Maryland
  Established: 1947
  Date: September, Labor Day weekend

  HolFestCelWrld-1994, 134

Crab Races, World Championship
  Location: Crescent City, California
  Established: 1976
  Date: Sunday before third Monday in February

  HolFestCelWrld-1994, 370

Crăciun
  See **Christmas (Romania)**

Crack-Nut Night
  See **Halloween; Michaelmas**

Craft's Fair
  Named for: Honors Luis Munoz Rivera (1859-1916)
  Location: Puerto Rico: Barranquitas
  Established: 1961
  Date: Three days in July, including Munoz Rivera's
    birthday, July 17

  GdUSFest-1984, 218
  See also **Munoz Rivera Day**

Craftsmen's Fair
  Location: Mount Sunapee State Park, Newbury,
    New Hampshire
  Established: 1934
  Date: Six days beginning first Tuesday in August

  GdUSFest-1984, 117
  HolFestCelWrld-1994, 72

Craigmillar Festival
  Location: Scotland: Craigmillar, Edinburgh
  Established: 1962
  Date: June or August

  IntlThFolk-1979, 184

Cranberry Harvest Festival
  Location: South Carver, Massachusetts
  Established: 1949
  Date: Two days in late September or early October

  HolFestCelWrld-1994, 72

Crandall Day, Prudence
  Named for: Prudence Crandall (1803-1890)
  Location: Canterbury, Connecticut

  Established: 1987
  Date: September, Saturday of Labor Day weekend

  HolFestCelWrld-1994, 261

Crane Watch (Wings over the Platte)
  Location: Kearney and Grand Island, Nebraska
  Date: March-April

  HolFestCelWrld-1994, 72

Crawfish Festival
  Location: Breaux Bridge, Louisiana
  Date: First weekend in May

  Chases-1993, 187
  GdUSFest-1984, 66
  HolFestCelWrld-1994, 72

Creole Week (Semana Criolla)
  Location: Uruguay
  Date: March-April, Holy Week

  FolkWrldHol-1992, 203

Cricket Festival
  See **Ascension Day (Italy: Florence, Tuscany)**

Crispus Attucks Day
  See **Boston Massacre Day (New Jersey)**

Cromm Dub's Sunday
  Location: Ireland: Mount Callen, County Clare
  Date: First Sunday in August

  DictFolkMyth-1984, 201, 263
  HolFestCelWrld-1994, 73

Cromwell Day
  Named for: Oliver Cromwell (1599-1658)
  Location: England
  Date: September 3

  BkDays-1864, ii.308
  DictDays-1988, 24
  HolFestCelWrld-1994, 73

Cronia
  Named for: Cronus, youngest of the Titans
  Location: Greece: Athens, Rhodes, and Thebes
  Established: Ancient times

  DictFolkMyth-1984, 263

Crop Over
  Location: Barbados: especially Bridgetown
  Established: 17th-century slave festival; current civic festival
    since 1973

Crop Over *(cont.)*
  Date: Last three weeks in June through first week in July

  FolkWrldHol-1992, 444
  GdWrldFest-1985, 17
  HolFestCelWrld-1994, 73

Cross, Exaltation of the Holy
  See **Exaltation of the Cross**

Cross, Invention of
  See **Exaltation of the Cross**

Cross Day
  See **Exaltation of the Cross; Holy Innocents' Day (Ireland)**

Cross Days
  See **Rogation Days**

Crouchmas Day
  See **Exaltation of the Cross**

Crow Fair
  Location: Crow Agency near Hardin, Montana
  Ethnic or religious group: Crow Indians, northwest
    Canadian Indians, and Plains States Indians, Peruvian
    Inca people, and Alaskan Eskimos
  Established: 1904
  Date: At least six days in mid-August

  GdUSFest-1984, 107
  HolFestCelWrld-1994, 74
  IndianAmer-1989, 33

Crucifixion Friday
  See **Good Friday**

Cruft's Dog Show
  Location: England
  Established: 1886
  Date: Three days in January or February

  Chases-1993, 63
  GdWrldFest-1985, 94

Cruz, Fiesta de la
  Location: Southern Arizona and Mexico
  Ethnic or religious group: Yaqui and Mayo Indians

  DictFolkMyth-1984, 258

La Cruz de Mayo
  See **Exaltation of the Cross (Chile)**

Cruz Velakuy
  See **Exaltation of the Cross (Peru: Pacarigtambo)**

Crystal Night
  See **Kristallnacht**

Cuauhtemoc, Homage to (Homenaje a Cuauhtemoc)
  Named for: Cuauhtemoc (c. 1495-1522)
  Location: Mexico: Mexico City
  Date: August 21

  IntlThFolk-1979, 273

Cuci Baileo Ceremony
  See **Panas Pela (Indonesia: Pelau versi Ulilima,**
    Maluku, Moluccas)

Cuenca Encounter
  Location: Spain: Cuenca
  Date: March

  IntlThFolk-1979, 335

Cultural Days
  Location: Tunisia: El Alaa, Kairouan Region
  Date: March

  IntlThFolk-1979, 359

Cultural Festival of Oum Ezzine
  Location: Tunisia: Jamel, Monastir Region
  Date: End of September

  IntlThFolk-1979, 361

Culture Day (Bunka-no-hi)
  Location: Japan
  Date: November 3

  AnnivHol-1983, 141
  Chases-1993, 430
  HolFestCelWrld-1994, 44

Cumbia Festival
  Location: Colombia: El Banco, Magdalena
  Date: June

  IntlThFolk-1979, 78

Cup Final Day
  Location: Britain
  Date: May

  DictDays-1988, 24

Cure Salée
  See **Salted Cure (Niger)**

Curium Festival
  Location: Cyprus: Curium near Limassol
  Established: 1961; amphitheater dates from 50-175 A.D.
  Date: June-July

  GdWrldFest-1985, 66
  IntlThFolk-1979, 81

Cussing Day
See **Ash Wednesday**

Custer's Last Stand
Named for: George Armstrong Custer (1839-1876)
Location: Crow Reservation in Montana
Ethnic or religious group: Crow Indians
Established: June 25, 1876, Battle of Little Big Horn
Date: Observed with a pageant in late June

AmerBkDays-1978, 591, 593
Chases-1993, 263
HolFestCelWrld-1994, 182

Custer's Last Stand
Named for: George Armstrong Custer (1839-1876)
Location: Custer, South Dakota
Established: July 27, 1874, discovery of gold near Custer, South Dakota
Date: Observed in late July during Gold Discovery Days

AmerBkDays-1978, 594
Chases-1993, 303
HolFestCelWrld-1994, 120

Custer's Last Stand and Chief Crazy Horse Pageant
Named for: George Armstrong (1839-1876) and Oglala Sioux Chief Crazy Horse (1842?-1877)
Location: Hot Springs, South Dakota
Established: June 25, 1876
Date: Mid-June to late August

AmerBkDays-1978, 594

Cveti, Day of Flowers
See **Palm Sunday (Yugoslavia)**

Cyprus International Fair
Location: Cyprus: Nicosia
Established: 1976
Date: Two weeks in May-June

IntlThFolk-1979, 83

Czech Festival
Location: Wilber, Nebraska
Ethnic or religious group: Czech-Americans
Established: 1962
Date: First weekend in August

Chases-1993, 319
GdUSFest-1984, 112
HolFestCelWrld-1994, 75

Daddy Frost Day
See **Granddad Frost Day**

Dædala
Location: ancient Boeothia
Date: Spring, about every six years Little Dædala was held; Great Dædala was held every sixty years

DictFolkMyth-1984, 273
HolFestCelWrld-1994, 77

Dalai Lama, Birthday of
Named for: The current Dalai Lama
Location: India
Ethnic or religious group: Tibetan exiles
Established: The line of Dalai Lamas began in the 14th century
Date: July 6

HolFestCelWrld-1994, 78

Dal-jip-tae-u-gee, Viewing the First Full Moon, or Dal-ma-ji
See **Burning the Moon House (Korea: Kyungsang Province)**

Damba Festival
See **Muhammad's Birthday (Mande-Dyula people in Dagomba, Upper Volta)**

Dance, Basket
Location: San Juan Pueblo, New Mexico
Date: January 27

IndianAmer-1989, 285, 312

Dance, Bear
Location: Janesville and Greenville, California
Ethnic or religious group: Maidu Indians
Date: Varies

IndianAmer-1989, 340

Dance, Buffalo
Location: Rio Grande pueblos
Date: November to January

DictFolkMyth-1984, 168

Dance, Calinda
Location: New Orleans, Louisiana
Ethnic or religious group: African and Creole peoples
Established: 1820s, when Sanité Dédé (n.d.) initiated annual ceremony
Date: June 23, St. John's Eve

FolkAmerHol-1987, 215

Dance, Corn
Location: Cochiti Pueblo, New Mexico
Date: May 13

IndianAmer-1989, 286, 296

Dance, Deer; Lenten Ceremonies (Yaqui Indians in Arizona)
See **Holy Week (Yaqui Indians in Arizona)**

Dance, Deer
Location: Japan: Hananomaki, Iwate
Date: March

IntlThFolk-1979, 253

Dance, Deer
Location: San Juan Pueblo, New Mexico
Date: February, date varies

IndianAmer-1989, 285, 312

Dance, Deer
Location: Taos, New Mexico

DictFolkMyth-1984, 571

Dance, Deer and Buffalo
Location: Santa Clara Pueblo, New Mexico
Date: February, date varies

IndianAmer-1989, 285, 315

Dance, Eagle
Location: Tesuque, Jemez, and other New Mexico pueblos
Date: Early spring

DictFolkMyth-1984, 333

Dance, Evergreen
Location: Isleta Pueblo, New Mexico
Date: February, date varies

IndianAmer-1989, 285, 296

Dance, Fools' (Awa Odori)
Location: Japan
Date: August 15-18

AnnivHol-1983, 173
IntlThFolk-1979, 259

Dance, Green Corn
Ethnic or religious group: Alabama Indians

DictFolkMyth-1984, 918
FolkAmerHol-1987, 185

Dance, Green Corn
Ethnic or religious group: Cherokee Indians

FolkAmerHol-1987, 185
DictFolkMyth-1984, 701

Dance, Green Corn
Ethnic or religious group: Iroquois Indians
Date: September, on or near Labor Day, first Monday in September

DictFolkMyth-1984, 483, 792, 835, 1121

Dance, Green Corn
Ethnic or religious group: Menominee Indians

DictFolkMyth-1984, 918

Dance, Green Corn
Ethnic or religious group: Natchez Indians

FolkAmerHol-1987, 185

Dance, Green Corn
Ethnic or religious group: Seneca Indians

DictFolkMyth-1984, 348
IndianAmer-1989, 97

Dance, Green Corn
Ethnic or religious group: Timuquan Indians

FolkAmerHol-1987, 185

Dance, Green Corn
Ethnic or religious group: Yuchi Indians

DictFolkMyth-1984, 918, 1133

Dance, Green Corn
Location: Florida
Ethnic or religious group: Seminole Indians
Date: Spring or summer

BkHolWrld-1986, July 3, 178
DictFolkMyth-1984, 918
FolkAmerHol-1987, 185
IndianAmer-1989, 239

Dance, Green Corn
Location: Near Horton, Kansas
Ethnic or religious group: Kickapoo Indians
Date: About the third weekend in July

IndianAmer-1989, 18

Dance, Green Corn
Location: San Felipe, Santo Domingo, and other pueblos in New Mexico

DictFolkMyth-1984, 252

Dance, Green Corn
  Location: North America
  Ethnic or religious group: Native Americans
  Date: Varies

BkHolWrld-1986, July 3, 178
DictFolkMyth-1984, 175, 252, 348, 483, 701, 792, 835,
  918, 1121
FolkAmerHol-1987, 185
IndianAmer-1989, 18, 74, 97, 239

Dance, Green Corn
  Location: Miami, Oklahoma
  Ethnic or religious group: Cayuga Indians
  Date: July or August

IndianAmer-1989, 97

Dance, Green Corn
  Location: Okmulgee, Oklahoma
  Ethnic or religious group: Muskogee-Creek Indians
  Date: Late summer

HolFestCelWrld-1994, 72

Dance, Green Corn
  Location: Southeastern United States
  Ethnic or religious group: Creek Indians
  Date: Weekend ceremonies in May-September lead up
   to festival

AnnivHol-1983, 185
DictFolkMyth-1984, 175, 918
IndianAmer-1989, 74

Dance, Hopi Niman
  Location: United States
  Ethnic or religious group: Hopi Indians
  Date: Third or fourth Saturday in July

BkHolWrld-1986, July 26, 178
DictFolkMyth-1984, 566, 793
HolFestCelWrld-1994, 227

Dance, Hopi Snake
  Location: Arizona
  Ethnic or religious group: Hopi Indians
  Date: August-September every other year

BkHolWrld-1986, August 22, 178
HolFestCelWrld-1994, 144

Dance, Hopi Snake-Antelope
  Location: Had been in Arizona at Walpi, Mishongnovi,
   Chimopovi one year; at Shipaulovi and Hotevilla the next

  Date: Held in alternate years in Oraibi until 1912

DictFolkMyth-1984, 1030

Dance, Horn
  Location: England: Abbots Bromley, Staffordshire
  Date: Monday after September 4

DictFolkMyth-1984, 3, 947
HolFestCelWrld-1994, 145

Dance, Hupa Autumn (Tunchitdilya)
  Location: Northern California
  Ethnic or religious group: Hupa Indians
  Date: October

DictFolkMyth-1984, 562

Dance, Hupa Winter (Haichitdilya)
  Location: Northern California
  Ethnic or religious group: Hupa Indians
  Date: Twenty days during winter

DictFolkMyth-1984, 562

Dance, International Summer Academy of
  See **Summer Academy of Dance, International (Federal**
   Republic of Germany: Cologne, North Rhine-Westphalia)

Dance, Klo
  Location: Ivory Coast
  Ethnic or religious group: Baoulé people
  Date: Harvest season

FolkWrldHol-1992, 453
HolFestCelWrld-1994, 171

Dance, Longevity (Ennen-no-mai)
  Location: Japan: Nikko, Tochigi
  Established: 12th century
  Date: June

IntlThFolk-1979, 258

Dance, Los Comanches
  Location: Taos Pueblo, New Mexico
  Date: February 4-5

IndianAmer-1989, 285, 319

Dance, Matchina
  Location: San Juan Pueblo, New Mexico
  Date: December 24-25

IndianAmer-1989, 290, 312

Dance, Matchina or Deer
  Location: Tesuque Pueblo, New Mexico
  Date: December 25

  IndianAmer-1989, 291, 319

Dance, Peyote (Híkuli)
  Location: Journey to eastern Chihuahua, Mexico
  Ethnic or religious group: Tarahumara and Huichol
  Indians
  Date: October and November

  DictFolkMyth-1984, 861

Dance, Red Paint Kachina
  Location: Zuñi Pueblo, New Mexico
  Date: September 12

  DictFolkMyth-1984, 589

Dance, Southern Ute Sun
  Location: Ignacio, Colorado
  Ethnic or religious group: Ute Indians
  Date: First weekend after July 4

  HolFestCelWrld-1994, 320
  IndianAmer-1989, 121, 360

Dance, Sun
  Ethnic or religious group: Blackfeet Indians
  Date: Usually during summer solstice

  DictFolkMyth-1984, 1088

Dance, Sun
  Ethnic or religious group: Great Plains Indians, including
  Ponca, Kiowa, Bûngi, Mandan, Hidatsa, Arapahoe,
  Cheyenne, Crow, Shoshone, Ute, Comanche and others
  Date: Usually during summer solstice

  DictFolkMyth-1984, 1088
  IndianAmer-1989, 68, 360

Dance, Sun
  Ethnic or religious group: Sioux Indians
  Established: Unknown, but the Teton Sioux people last
  observed the Sun Dance in 1881
  Date: One to four days at end of June, during summer
  solstice

  DictFolkMyth-1984, 1032, 1088
  IndianAmer-1989, 104, 360

Dance, Sun
  Location: Oklahoma

  Ethnic or religious group: Southern Cheyenne Indians

  IndianAmer-1989, 68, 360

Dance, Sun
  Location: Utah
  Ethnic or religious group: Northern Ute Indians
  Date: July and August

  IndianAmer-1989, 139, 360

Dance, Sun
  Location: Wyoming
  Ethnic or religious group: Shoshone Indians
  Date: July or August

  IndianAmer-1989, 115, 360

Dance, Sunrise
  Location: Arizona
  Ethnic or religious group: White Mountain Apache Indians
  Date: September, four days including Labor Day, first
  Monday in September

  BkHolWrld-1986, September 4, 181

Dance, Turtle
  Location: San Juan Pueblo, New Mexico
  Date: December 26

  IndianAmer-1989, 291, 312

Dance, Ute Bear
  Location: Ignacio, Colorado
  Ethnic or religious group: Ute Indians
  Date: May, Memorial Day weekend

  HolFestCelWrld-1994, 352
  IndianAmer-1989, 121

Dance, Ute Bear (Ma'makoni-ni'tkap)
  Location: Ouray, Randlett, Whiterocks, Utah
  Ethnic or religious group: Ute Indians
  Date: Three to five days in April

  DictFolkMyth-1984, 668
  GdUSFest-1984, 190
  IndianAmer-1989, 139

Dance, Waraku
  Location: Japan: near Waraku Pond, Nikko, Tochigi
  Date: August

  IntlThFolk-1979, 258

Dance and Drama, Festival of
  Location: India: Hyderabad, Andhra Pradesh
  Date: Five days in November

  IntlThFolk-1979, 202

Dance and Ethete Celebration, Sun
  Location: Ethete, Wyoming
  Ethnic or religious group: Arapaho Indians
  Date: July

  IndianAmer-1989, 110, 360

Dance and Folk Festival, Asheville Mountain
  Location: Asheville, North Carolina
  Established: Late 1920s
  Date: First Thursday, Friday, and Saturday in August

  Chases-1993, 317
  HolFestCelWrld-1994, 15
  MusFestAmer-1990, 226

Dance and Music Festival, Kuopio
  Location: Finland: Kuopio
  Date: June

  Chases-1993, 239
  IntlThFolk-1979, 95

Dance Festival, Alberta
  Location: Canada: Edmonton, Alberta
  Date: May-June

  IntlThFolk-1979, 60

Dance Festival, Chhau Mask
  Location: India: Seraikalla, Bihar
  Date: April 11-13

  IntlThFolk-1979, 203

Dance Festival, Darpana
  Location: India: Ahmedabad, Gujarat
  Date: Five days during first week in October

  IntlThFolk-1979, 207

Dance Festival, Hora at Prislop (Prislop Round)
  Location: Romania: Mount Prislop, Borsa, Maramures
  County
  Established: 19th century
  Date: Second Sunday in August

  GdWrldFest-1985, 157
  HolFestCelWrld-1994, 144
  IntlThFolk-1979, 317

Dance Festival, Jacob's Pillow
  Location: Becket, Massachusetts
  Established: 1932
  Date: Eight weeks from June to September

  GdUSFest-1984, 85
  HolFestCelWrld-1994, 159

Dance Festival, Kala Vikash Kendra
  Location: India: Cuttack, Orissa
  Date: Twice yearly: three days in October-November and
  on August 10, anniversary of Academy's founding

  IntlThFolk-1979, 213

Dance Festival, Kerala Kalamandalam
  Location: India: Cheruthuruthy, Kerala
  Date: March

  IntlThFolk-1979, 208

Dance Festival, Krishnattam
  Location: India: Guruvayur, Kerala
  Date: September-October

  IntlThFolk-1979, 209
  See also **Mother Goddess, Festival of Durga, the**

Dance Festival, Kuchipudi
  Location: India: Kuchipudi, Andhra Pradesh
  Date: Three days in August-September

  IntlThFolk-1979, 202

**Dance Festival, Mayurbhanj Chhau (Spring Festival,
Chaitra Parva)**
  Location: India: Mayurbhanj, Orissa
  Date: April 11-13

  IntlThFolk-1979, 213

Dance Festival, Ras
  Location: India: Manipur
  Date: Three times yearly: full moon of March-April, known
  as Basant Ras; September-October, during Dasahara,
  Festival of Durga, the Mother Goddess (Kunj Ras); and
  full moon night of December, known as Maha Ras

  IntlThFolk-1979, 212

Dance Festival of Paris, International
  Location: France: Paris
  Established: 1963
  Date: October-December

  IntlThFolk-1979, 116

Dance Festivals, Kathakali
  Location: India: Trivandrum, Kerala
  Date: March-April and October-November

  IntlThFolk-1979, 209

Dance of the Stilts
  See **St. Mary Magdalene, Feast of (Spain: Anguiano, Logrono)**

Dance of Thanksgiving (Whe'wahchee)
  Location: Omaha Reservation in Nebraska
  Ethnic or religious group: Omaha Indians
  Established: At least since 1803
  Date: First full moon in August

  HolFestCelWrld-1994, 78, 366

Dance of Transylvania, Men's (Caluser or Caluseri)
  Location: Romania: Deva, Hunedoara
  Date: Third week in January

  DictFolkMyth-1984, 947
  IntlThFolk-1979, 322

Dances, Basket
  Location: Northeastern Arizona
  Ethnic or religious group: Hopi Indians
  Date: Late October through November

  HolFestCelWrld-1994, 26
  IndianAmer-1989, 266

Dances, Little Pony Society
  Location: Apache Park, Apache, Oklahoma
  Ethnic or religious group: Comanche Indians
  Date: April

  IndianAmer-1989, 71

Dances, Matchina
  Location: Picuris Pueblo, New Mexico
  Date: December 24-25

  IndianAmer-1989, 290, 303

Dances, Matchina
  Location: San Ildefonso Pueblo, New Mexico
  Date: December 25

  IndianAmer-1989, 290, 309

Dances, Matchina
  Location: Santa Clara Pueblo, New Mexico
  Date: December 25

  IndianAmer-1989, 290, 315

Dances, Old Pecos Bull and Corn
  Location: Jemez Pueblo, New Mexico
  Date: August 2

  AmerBkDays-1978, 718
  IndianAmer-1989, 287, 300

Dances, Osage Tribal Ceremonial
  Location: Greyhorse, Homin, and Pawhuska, Oklahoma
  Date: June

  IndianAmer-1989, 56, 85

Dances and Songs of Crnorecje
  Location: Yugoslavia: Boljevac, Serbia
  Date: May

  IntlThFolk-1979, 385

Dances of Obando
  Named for: Honors San Pascual Baylon, Santa Clara, and the Virgen de Salambao
  Location: Philippines: Obando, Bulacan, Luzon Island
  Date: Three days in mid-May

  IntlThFolk-1979, 289

Dance Workshop, Bonn International
  Location: Federal Republic of Germany: Bonn, North Rhine-Westphalia
  Date: July

  IntlThFolk-1979, 135

Dancing Procession (Sprangprozessio'n)
  Location: Luxembourg: Echternach
  Established: Seventh century in honor of St. Willibrod (Wilfred, 658?-739)
  Date: May-June, Tuesday after Pentecost, about 50 days after Easter

  BkHolWrld-1986, June 3
  FestWestEur-1958, 112
  GdWrldFest-1985, 128
  HolFestCelWrld-1994, 78

Danger Night
  See **Mischief Night**

Danish Ethnic Festival
  See **Nebraska Danish Days (Danish-Americans in Minden, Nebraska)**

Danzantes y Pecados Festival
  Location: Spain: Camunas, Toledo
  Established: Middle Ages
  Date: June

  IntlThFolk-1979, 334

Darwin Show Day
    Location: Australia
    Date: July

    DictDays-1988, 56

Darwin Youth Festival
    Location: Australia: Darwin, Northern Territory
    Date: August, during school holidays

    IntlThFolk-1979, 16

Dasain or Dasara
    See **Mother Goddess, Festival of Durga, the (Nepal)**

Data Ganj Baksh Death Festival
    Named for: Data Ganj Baksh, He Who Gives Generously
      (Syed Ali Abdul Hasan Bin Usman Hajweri, d. 1072)
    Location: Pakistan: Mausoleum of Data Ganj Baksh, Lahore
    Date: Safar 18-19

    HolFestCelWrld-1994, 79

Dattatreya's Birthday (Dattatreya Jayanti)
    Named for: Hindu god Dattatreya
    Location: India: Maharashtra
    Ethnic or religious group: Hindu
    Date: November-December, full moon day of Hindu month
      of Margashirsha

    RelHolCal-1993, 70

Dauwtrappen
    See **Dew Treading (Netherlands)**

Davis Cup
    Named for: Dwight F. Davis (1879-1945), who began
      the international tennis competition
    Location: United States
    Established: 1900
    Date: November-December

    HolFestCelWrld-1994, 79

Davis's Birthday, Jefferson
    Named for: Jefferson Davis (1808-1889)
    Location: Alabama, Florida, Georgia, Kentucky,
      Mississippi, South Carolina, Tennessee, and Texas
    Date: June 3

    AmerBkDays-1978, 519
    AnnivHol-1983, 75
    Chases-1993, 231
    DictDays-1988, 61
    HolFestCelWrld-1994, 160
    See also **Confederate Memorial Day**

Dayak Festival Day (Gawai Dayak)
    Location: Malaysia: Sarawak
    Ethnic or religious group: Dayak people
    Established: Centuries old
    Date: June 1-2

    BkHolWrld-1986, June 2, 177
    FolkWrldHol-1992, 323, 465
    GdWrldFest-1985, 132
    HolFestCelWrld-1994, 115

Day of Sweet Soup
    See **New Year (Turkey)**

Day of the Dead
    See **Memorial Day (Romania)**

Day of the Race (Chile), (Colombia), (Costa Rica),
and (Paraguay)
    See **Columbus Day (Chile), (Colombia), (Costa Rica),**
      and (Paraguay)

Daytona 500
    Location: Daytona International Speedway, Daytona
      Beach, Florida
    Date: February

    HolFestCelWrld-1994, 80

A Day to Remember
    Named for: Commemorates 19th-century settlement of
      Wales, Ontario
    Location: Canada: Morrisburg, Ontario
    Date: July-August

    IntlThFolk-1979, 71

D-Day (Allied Landing Observances Day)
    Named for: June 6, 1944, Allied invasion of Normandy
    Location: France: Normandy
    Date: June 6

    AmerBkDays-1978, 527
    AnnivHol-1983, 76
    Chases-1993, 238
    DictDays-1988, 29
    HolFestCelWrld-1994, 81

Dead, Day of the (Mexico) and (Portugal)
    See **All Souls' Day (Mexico) and (Portugal)**

Dead, Feast for the (Ohgiwe)
    Ethnic or religious group: Iroquois Indian women
    Date: During Iroquois White Dog Feast, in autumn,
      spring, or occasional

    DictFolkMyth-1984, 816, 963
    See also **Iroquois White Dog Feast**

Dead, Feast of the (Celtic)
  See **Samhain**

Dead, Feast of the (Pitra Pasksha or Pitra Visarjana and Amavasya)
  Ethnic or religious group: Hindu
  Date: September-October, waning half of Hindu month of Asvina

BkFest-1937, 160
FolkWrldHol-1992, 503
HolFestCelWrld-1994, 254
RelHolCal-1993, 103

Dead, Feast of the (Pitra Pasksha or Pitra Visarjana and Amavasya)
  Location: India
  Ethnic or religious group: Hindu
  Date: September-October, waning half of Hindu month of Asvina

BkFest-1937, 160
FolkWrldHol-1992, 503
HolFestCelWrld-1994, 254

Dead, Feast of the (Pitra Pasksha or Pitra Visarjana and Amavasya)
  Location: India: Gaya
  Ethnic or religious group: Hindu
  Date: September-October, waning half of Hindu month of Asvina

BkFest-1937, 160

Dead, Feast of the (Ho Khao Padap Dinh)
  Location: Laos
  Date: August-September, ninth lunar month

FolkWrldHol-1992, 427

Dead, Festival of the (Bon or Obon Matsuri)
  Ethnic or religious group: Buddhist
  Established: 538 A.D. in China and c. 552 A.D. in Japan
  Date: 15th day of seventh lunar month

AmerBkDays-1978, 501
AnnivHol-1983, 174, 181
BkFest-1937, 80, 200
BkHolWrld-1986, July 13
Chases-1993, 290
DictFolkMyth-1984, 154, 155, 541, 542, 730, 812, 1051
DictWrldRel-1989, 31, 135, 374
FolkAmerHol-1987, 229
FolkWrldHol-1992, 389
HolFestCelWrld-1994, 108, 231

IntlThFolk-1979, 261
RelHolCal-1993, 99

Dead, Festival of the (Bon Odori or Obon)
  Location: China: especially at the monastery of Ch'ing Liang Shan
  Ethnic or religious group: Buddhist
  Established: 538 A.D.
  Date: 15th day of seventh lunar month

BkFest-1937, 80

Dead, Festival of the (Toro Nagashi, Floating Lantern Ceremony)
  Location: Honolulu, Hawaii
  Established: Also commemorates end of World War Two
  Ethnic or religious group: Buddhist
  Date: August 15

Chases-1993, 331
FolkAmerHol-1987, 229
HolFestCelWrld-1994, 108
RelHolCal-1993, 77

Dead, Festival of the (Bon Odori, Obon Matsuri, or Rokusai Nembutsu)
  Location: Japan
  Ethnic or religious group: Buddhist
  Established: About 552 A.D.
  Date: 15th day of seventh lunar month; observed July 13-15

AmerBkDays-1978, 501
AnnivHol-1983, 181
BkFest-1937, 200
BkHolWrld-1986, July 13
Chases-1993, 290
DictFolkMyth-1984, 154, 155, 541, 542, 730, 812, 1051
DictWrldRel-1989, 31, 135, 374
FolkAmerHol-1987, 229
FolkWrldHol-1992, 389
HolFestCelWrld-1994, 231
IntlThFolk-1979, 261
RelHolCal-1993, 99

Dead, Festival of the (Bon Odori or Obon Matsuri)
  Location: United States
  Ethnic or religious group: Buddhist Japanese-Americans
  Date: 15th day of seventh lunar month; observed July 12-16

Chases-1993, 286
FolkAmerHol-1987, 229
HolFestCelWrld-1994, 231
RelHolCal-1993, 99

Dead, Observance for the (Keruk)
  Location: California and Arizona
  Ethnic or religious group: Diegueño and Yuma Indians
    in California and Yuma Indians in Arizona
  Date: Seven nights annually

  DictFolkMyth-1984, 574

Dead, Return of the (Odo Festival)
  Location: Nigeria: Nsukka
  Ethnic or religious group: Igbo people
  Date: Every other year in April (Awuru Odo celebration
    for departure of the dead) and sometime between September
    and November (arrival of the dead)

  FolkWrldHol-1992, 218, 575
  HolFestCelWrld-1994, 19, 232

Dead, Time of the (Velu Laiks)
  Location: Latvia
  Date: Autumn

  DictFolkMyth-1984, 608

Dead Remembrance Thursday (Khamis al-Amwat)
  Location: Jordan
  Date: March-April, Thursday following Easter

  FolkWrldHol-1992, 197
  HolFestCelWrld-1994, 169

Death of the Ground
  See **Summer, First Day of (Morocco)**

Decoration Day (Psychosavato)
  Location: Greece
  Date: The Saturday preceding the Saturday before Mardi Gras
    (nine days before Mardi Gras)

  BkFest-1937, 146

Decoration Day (United States)
  See **Memorial Day (United States)**

Dedication, Feast of (Jewish)
  See **Hanukkah**

Dedication, Feast of the (Christian)
  See **Exaltation of the Cross**

Deepavali
  See **Lights, Festival of (Malaya)**

Deer-Hunting Festival (Aboakyer)
  Location: Ghana
  Ethnic or religious group: Effutu people
  Date: April-May

  FolkWrldHol-1992, 226
  HolFestCelWrld-1994, 1

Defenders' Day
  Named for: September 12, 1814, Battle of North Point
  Location: Baltimore, Maryland
  Date: September 12

  AmerBkDays-1978, 833
  AnnivHol-1983, 117
  Chases-1993, 368
  DictDays-1988, 30
  HolFestCelWrld-1994, 82

Déjeuner Matrimonial, Matrimonial Tea
  See **Whit Monday (Belgium)**

Delaware Swedish Colonial Day
  Named for: March 29, 1638, settlement of colony
  Location: Delaware Swedish Colonial Society and others
    in Delaware
  Date: March 29

  AnnivHol-1983, 43

Deliverance, Day of (Hagodol or Great Sabbath)
  Ethnic or religious group: Jewish
  Date: April, prior to Passover

  DaysCustFaith-1957, 111

Del Mundo Festival
  See **Transfiguration, Feast of the (El Salvador)**

Democracy Day
  Location: Rwanda
  Date: January 28

  AnnivHol-1983, 15

Demon-God Festival
  Location: Japan: Rakuhoji Temple, Yamatomura, Ibaraki
  Date: One day in April

  IntlThFolk-1979, 261

Den na Buditelite
  See **Awakeners, Day of the (Bulgaria)**

Den Svatých Tří Králů
  See **Epiphany (Czechoslovakia)**

Departure of the Swallows
  See **Swallows of San Juan Capistrano**

Derby Day
  Location: England
  Date: Late May or early June

  Chases-1993, 230
  DictDays-1988, 30
  HolFestCelWrld-1994, 82

De Soto Celebration
See **Soto Celebration**

Devali
See **Lights, Festival of (Dewali) (Hindu)**

Devathani Ekadashi
See **Vishnu's Awakening (Hindu)**

Devil's Night
Location: Detroit, Michigan
Date: October 30

DictDays-1988, 30

Devil's Night
Location: United States
Date: October 30

Chases-1993, 425
DictDays-1988, 30

Devil's Promenade
Ethnic or religious group: Comanche, Kiowa, and
  Creek Indians
Date: July 3-6

DictFolkMyth-1984, 311

Dewali
See **Lights, Festival of (Hindu), (India), (India: Bengal),**
  (India: Gujarat), (India: Maharashtra), (Jaina people in
  India), (Sikh people in India), (Punjab), and (Hindu
  people in the United States)

The Dew Grows Cold
See **Han Lu (China)**

Dew Treading (Dauwtrappen)
Location: Netherlands
Date: April-June, Ascension Day

FestWestEur-1958, 133
HolFestCelWrld-1994, 83

Dhan Teras or Dhanvantri Trayodashi
Ethnic or religious group: Hindu
Date: October-November, 13th day of waning half of Hindu
  month of Karthika, two days prior to Dewali, Hindu
  New Year

RelHolCal-1993, 72
See also **Lights, Festival of (Hindu)**

Día da Familia, Day of the Family
See **Christmas (Portugal)**

**Dia da Nussa Senhora da Assumçao, Day of Our Lady of
the Angels**
See **Assumption, Feast of the (Portugal)**

Dia de Corpo de Deus
See **Corpus Christi (Portugal)**

Día de Finados, Day of the Dead
See **All Souls' Day (Catholic people in Portugal)**

Día de la Candelaria
See **Candlemas (Mexico)**

Día de la Hispanidad
See **Columbus Day (Panama)**

Día de la Santa Cruz
See **Exaltation of the Cross (Roman Catholic Latin**
  America) and (Mexico)

Día del Indio
See **Indian, Day of the (Peru and other Latin American**
  countries)

Día Del Maestro
See **Teachers' Day (Venezuela)**

Día de los Angelitos
See **All Souls' Day (Colombia)**

Día de los Inocentes
See **Holy Innocents' Day (Mexico)**

Día de los Reyes Magos
See **Epiphany (Mexico) and (Spain)**

Día de los Santos, El
See **All Saints' Day (Mexico: Santa Cruz)**

Dia de Muertos, Day of the Dead or Festival of Hungry Ghosts
See **All Souls' Day (Catholic people in Mexico)**

Día de Natal
See **Christmas (Portugal)**

Día de San Giuseppe
See **St. Joseph's Day (Italy)**

Dia de San Juan
See **Midsummer (Mexico)**

Día de San Lorenzo
See **St. Lawrence of Rome, Feast Day of (Mexico)**

Día de San Sebastián
See **St. Sebastian's Day (Mexico)**

Dia dos Reis, Day of the Kings
See **Epiphany (Portugal)** and **(Roman Catholic people in Moguerinha, Portugal)**

Diamond Day
Location: England: Ascot
Date: July, day of the King George VI (1895-1952) and Queen Elizabeth (b. 1900) Diamond Stakes race

DictDays-1988, 30

Diana Jana, Festival of
See **Nemoralia (Nemi; now a village in Italy)**

Dicing for the Maid's Money Day
Named for: Annual fulfillment of terms of 17th-century will
Location: England: Guildford, Surrey
Date: Late January

AnnivHol-1983, 16
HolFestCelWrld-1994, 84

Dieu, the Fête
See **Corpus Christi (France)**

Dijon Festival
Location: France: Dijon, Cote-d'Or
Established: 1946
Date: September

IntlThFolk-1979, 105

Dinagyang
Location: Philippines: Iloilo City, Panay
Date: Last weekend in January

HolFestCelWrld-1994, 84

Dingaan's Day
See **Covenant, Day of the (South Africa)**

Dinkelsbühl Festival Week
See **Children's Reckoning**

Dinner of the Milpa (u hanli col)
Location: Mexico: Chan Kom, Yucatan
Ethnic or religious group: Mayan people
Date: Every four years when corn ripens

FolkWrldHol-1992, 454

Dinosaur Days
Location: Dinosaur National Monument near Grand Junction, Colorado
Established: 1986
Date: Last week in July

HolFestCelWrld-1994, 84

Dionysiad
Location: Romania: Husi, Vaslui
Date: First Sunday in October

GdWrldFest-1985, 157
IntlThFolk-1979, 325

Dionysus
Location: Greece: Athens
Date: Spring and winter

DictMyth-1962, i.447
DictFolkMyth-1984, 830, 867
HolFestCelWrld-1994, 84
See also **Bacchanalia**

Dipping or Dippy Day
Location: England: Cornwall
Date: May 1

DictDays-1988, 31

Dipri Festival
Location: Ivory Coast: Gomon
Ethnic or religious group: Abidji people
Date: March-April

HolFestCelWrld-1994, 85

Discoverers' Day
See **Columbus Day (Hawaii)**

Discovery Day (Bahama Islands), (Cayman Islands), (Haiti), (Hawaii), (Puerto Rico), (St. Vincent), and (Trinidad and Tobago)
See **Columbus Day (Bahama Islands), (Cayman Islands), (Haiti), (Hawaii), (Puerto Rico), (St. Vincent), and (Trinidad and Tobago)**

Discovery Day
Named for: June 24, 1497, landfall by John Cabot (c. 1450-c. 1499)
Location: Canada: Newfoundland
Date: On or near June 24

AnnivHol-1983, 83
Chases-1993, 261
DictDays-1988, 31

Discovery Day (Guam)
See **Magellan Day (Guam)**

Discovery Days
Named for: Discovery of gold on August 17, 1896
Location: Canada: Dawson City, Yukon
Date: August

BkHolWrld-1986, August 17, 182
Chases-1993, 326

Distaff Day
  Location: England
  Date: January 7

  AnnivHol-1983, 6
  BkDays-1864, i. 68
  DaysCustFaith-1957, 22
  DictDays-1988, 32, 96
  FolkWrldHol-1992, 21
  HolFestCelWrld-1994, 85
  SaintFestCh-1904, 57

Divali
  See **Lights, Festival of (Mauritius)**

Dividing of the Cheese (Käseteilet)
  Location: Switzerland: Justis Valley area
  Date: September

  BkHolWrld-1986, September 10, 178

Divine Mother, Festival of the
  See **Mother Goddess, Festival of Durga, the**

Divino, Festo do
  Location: Brazil: Alcântara and Paraty
  Date: May-June, Saturday before Pentecost

  HolFestCelWrld-1994, 85

Diwali
  See **Lights, Festival of (Nepal)**

Djakovo Embroidery
  Location: Yugoslavia: Djakovo, Croatia
  Date: Two days in early July

  IntlThFolk-1979, 387

Djem Festival, El
  See **El Djem Festival**

Djerakoloytz, Day of Illumination
  See **Holy Saturday (Armenia)**

Doctors' Day
  Location: United States
  Established: 1933
  Date: March 30

  AnnivHol-1983, 44
  Chases-1993, 146

Dodge City Days
  Location: Dodge City, Kansas
  Established: 1960

  Date: Six days in late July

  Chases-1993, 309
  GdUSFest-1984, 60
  HolFestCelWrld-1994, 86

Dodonea Festival
  Location: Greece: Ioannina
  Established: 1960
  Date: A weekend in August

  IntlThFolk-1979, 194

Dog Days
  Location: Ancient Rome
  Date: Early July-early August

  BkDays-1864, ii. 5
  Chases-1993, 276
  DictDays-1988, 32
  DictFolkMyth-1984, 918
  HolFestCelWrld-1994, 86

Doggett's Coat and Badge Race
  Named for: Thomas Doggett (c. 1670-1721), actor
  Location: England: Thames River
  Established: 1716
  Date: August 1

  AnnivHol-1983, 176
  HolFestCelWrld-1994, 86

Dogwood Festival
  Location: Atlanta, Georgia
  Established: 1936
  Date: April

  HolFestCelWrld-1994, 86

Doleing Day (Gooding Day)
  Location: England: Sussex and elsewhere
  Date: December 21, St. Thomas's Day

  BkDays-1864, ii. 724
  DictDays-1988, 32,49, 78
  HolFestCelWrld-1994, 86

Dol-Jatra, Swing Festival
  See **Fire Festival (Bangladesh)**

Dollard des Ormeaux, Fête de
  Location: Canada: Quebec
  Date: May 24

  FolkWrldHol-1992, 301
  See also **Victoria Day**

Doll Festival, Hina Matsuri or Hina-No-Sekku
See **Girls' Doll Festival (Japan)**

Dol Purnima
See **Fire Festival (India: Bengal)**

Domenica delle Palme
See **Palm Sunday (Italy)**

Domenica delle Passione
See **Passion Sunday (Italy)**

Dom Fair
  Location: Germany: Hamburg
  Ethnic or religious group: Christian
  Date: November through Christmas, December 25

FestWestEur-1958, 79
HolFestCelWrld-1994, 87

Domingo de Palmas
See **Palm Sunday (Mexico)**

Domingo de Ramos
See **Palm Sunday (Portugal) and (Spain)**

Domingo de Resurrección
See **Easter (Mexico) and (Spain)**

Dominican Restoration Day
See **Political Restitution Day (Dominican Republic)**

Dominion Day
See **Canada Day**

Dookie Apple Night
See **Halloween (England)**

Dormition of the Mother of God
See **Assumption, Feast of the**

Dosmoche Festival
See **New Year (Tibet: Leh and Lhasa)**

Double Fifth (Tuan Yang, Dragon Boat Festival, and Festival of the Five Poisonous Creatures)
  Location: China
  Established: Third century; Dragon Boat Festival commemorates death of Ch'ü Yüan (328-298 B.C.)
  Date: May-June, fifth day of fifth lunar month

BkFest-1937, 79
BkFestHolWrld-1970, 103
BkHolWrld-1986, June 18
Chases-1993, 261
DictFolkMyth-1984, 206, 225, 1130, 1185
FolkAmerHol-1987, 175
FolkWrldHol-1992, 310
HolFestCelWrld-1994, 88

Double Fifth (Dragon Boat Festival and Festival of the Five Poisonous Creatures)
  Location: Hong Kong
  Established: Third century; Dragon Boat Festival commemorates death of Ch'ü Yüan (328-298 B.C.)
  Date: May-June, fifth day of fifth lunar month

Chases-1993, 276
FolkWrldHol-1992, 312
GdWrldFest-1985, 106
HolFestCelWrld-1994, 88
IntlThFolk-1979, 197

Double Fifth (Dragon Boat Festival and Festival of the Five Poisonous Creatures)
  Location: Macao
  Established: Third century; Dragon Boat Festival commemorates death of Ch'ü Yüan (328-298 B.C.)
  Date: May-June, fifth day of fifth lunar month

AnnivHol-1983, 176

Double Fifth (Tuan Wu, Dragon Boat Festival ,and Festival of the Five Poisonous Creatures)
  Location: Taiwan
  Established: Third century; Dragon Boat Festival commemorates death of Ch'ü Yüan (328-298 B.C.)
  Date: May-June, fifth day of fifth lunar month

AnnivHol-1983, 176
FolkWrldHol-1992, 313

Double Fifth (Dragon Boat Festival and Festival of the Five Poisonous Creatures)
  Location: United States
  Ethnic or religious group: Chinese-Americans
  Established: Dragon Boat Festival commemorates death of Ch'ü Yüan (328-298 B.C.)
  Date: May-June, fifth day of fifth lunar month

FolkAmerHol-1987, 175
HolFestCelWrld-1994, 88

Double Ninth Day (Ch'ung Yang or Têng Kao, Climbing the Hills)
  Location: China
  Date: September-October, ninth day of ninth lunar month

AnnivHol-1983, 175
BkFest-1937, 81
BkFestHolWrld-1970, 117
DictFolkMyth-1984, 225, 1106
FolkAmerHol-1987, 281
FolkWrldHol-1992, 493
HolFestCelWrld-1994, 65

Double Ninth Day
   Location: Hong Kong
   Date: September-October, ninth day of ninth lunar month

   AnnivHol-1983, 175
   Chases-1993, 419
   FolkWrldHol-1992, 493
   HolFestCelWrld-1994, 65

Double Ninth Day
   Location: Macao
   Date: September-October, ninth day of ninth lunar month

   AnnivHol-1983, 175
   HolFestCelWrld-1994, 65

Double Ninth Day (Tiong-iong Choeh or Double Yang)
   Location: Taiwan
   Date: September-October, ninth day of ninth lunar month

   FolkWrldHol-1992, 494

Double Seventh (Festival of the Weaving Maid and the Herd Boy or Chi Hsi, Festival of the Milky Way)
   Named for: Legendary characters based on the annual celestial positions of Altair, in the Aquila constellation, and Vegas, in the Lyra constellation
   Location: China
   Date: Seventh day of seventh lunar month

   BkFest-1937, 79
   BkHolWrld-1986, August 10
   DictFolkMyth-1984, 216
   FolkWrldHol-1992, 385
   HolFestCelWrld-1994, 312

Double Seventh (Festival of the Weaving Maid and the Herd Boy)
   Named for: Legendary characters based on the annual celestial positions of Altair, in the Aquila constellation, and Vegas, in the Lyra constellation
   Location: Hong Kong
   Date: Seventh day of seventh lunar month

   FolkWrldHol-1992, 385
   HolFestCelWrld-1994, 312

Double Seventh (Festival of the Weaving Maid and the Herd Boy or Tanabata Matsuri, the Weaver Princess Festival; also known as Star Festival)
   Named for: Legendary characters based on the annual celestial positions of Altair, in the Aquila constellation, and Vegas, in the Lyra constellation
   Location: Japan
   Established: 755 A.D.
   Date: July 7

   AnnivHol-1983, 90
   BkFest-1937, 199
   Chases-1993, 283
   DictFolkMyth-1984, 540
   FolkWrldHol-1992, 387
   HolFestCelWrld-1994, 332

Double Seventh (Festival of the Weaving Maid and the Herd Boy or Tanabata Matsuri, the Weaver Princess Festival; also known as Star Festival)
   Named for: Legendary characters based on the annual celestial positions of Altair, in the Aquila constellation, and Vegas, in the Lyra constellation
   Location: Japan: Sendai
   Established: 755 A.D.
   Date: August 6-8

   HolFestCelWrld-1994, 332

Double Seventh (Festival of the Weaving Maid and the Herd Boy, Gyunoo and Jingny O)
   Named for: Legendary characters based on the annual celestial positions of Altair, in the Aquila constellation, and Vegas, in the Lyra constellation
   Location: Korea
   Date: Seventh day of seventh lunar month

   FolkWrldHol-1992, 385
   HolFestCelWrld-1994, 312

Double Seventh (Festival of the Seven Sisters)
   Named for: Legendary characters based on the annual celestial positions of Altair, in the Aquila constellation, and Vegas, in the Lyra constellation
   Location: Malaysia
   Date: Seventh day of seventh lunar month

   BkHolWrld-1986, August 10

Double Seventh (Festival of the Weaving Maid and the Herd Boy or Chhit Sek, Seventh Evening and Birthday of the Chhit-niu-ma, or Seven Old Maids)
   Named for: Legendary characters based on the annual celestial positions of Altair, in the Aquila constellation, and Vegas, in the Lyra constellation
   Location: Taiwan
   Date: Seventh day of seventh lunar month

   FolkWrldHol-1992, 384, 386
   HolFestCelWrld-1994, 312

Double Sixth Day
  See **Airing the Classics (Buddhist people in China)**

Double Tenth Day
  Named for: October 10, 1911, proclamation of the Republic
    of Sun Yat-sen (1866-1925)
  Location: Taiwan
  Date: October 10

  AnnivHol-1983, 131
  Chases-1993, 405
  HolFestCelWrld-1994, 87
  NatlHolWrld-1968, 189
  See also **Sun Yat-sen Day**

Double Yang
  See **Double Ninth Day (Taiwan)**

Dougga, Festival of
  Location: Tunisia: Dougga, Beja Region
  Date: July

  IntlThFolk-1979, 359

Doughnut Day
  See **Mardi Gras (England)**

Dozynki Festival
  See **Harvest Festival (Poland)**

Dragacevo Assembly of Village Trumpeters
  Location: Yugoslavia: Guca, Serbia
  Established: 1961
  Date: End of August

  IntlThFolk-1979, 388

Dragon, Spearing the (Drachenstich)
  Location: Germany: Fürth
  Established: About 500 years ago
  Date: Mid-August

  HolFestCelWrld-1994, 88

**Dragon Boat Festival and Festival of the Five
Poisonous Creatures**
  See **Double Fifth (China), (Hong Kong), (Macao),
    (Taiwan), and (Chinese-Americans in the United States)**

Drama, Cycle of Classical
  Location: Italy: Siracusa, Sicily
  Date: Even-numbered years in May-June

  IntlThFolk-1979, 248

Drama, Festival of Ancient
  See **Theater Festival, Epidauros**

Drama, Festival of Ancient
  Location: Greece: Philippi
  Established: 1961
  Date: July-August

  IntlThFolk-1979, 195

Drama, Festival of Ancient
  Location: Greece: Thasos
  Date: July-August

  IntlThFolk-1979, 196

Drama, National Review of Modern Bulgarian
  Location: Bulgaria: Sofia
  Date: Every five years in June

  IntlThFolk-1979, 55

Drama, Paphos Festival of Ancient
  Location: Cyprus: Paphos
  Date: June-July

  IntlThFolk-1979, 85

Drama, Review of Classical
  Location: Bulgaria: Vidin
  Date: Every five years; date varies

  IntlThFolk-1979, 58

Drama, Review of Historical
  Location: Bulgaria: Veliko Turnovo
  Date: Every three years; date varies

  IntlThFolk-1979, 58

Drama Amateurs, Yugoslav
  Location: Yugoslavia: Trebinje, Bosnia and Herzegovina
  Date: End of June-beginning of July

  IntlThFolk-1979, 407

Drama Amateurs of Croatia, Festival of
  Location: Yugoslavia: Murter by Sibenik, Croatia
  Established: 1960
  Date: May

  IntlThFolk-1979, 395

Drama Amateurs of Montenegro, Festival of
  Location: Yugoslavia: Bijelo Polje, Montenegro
  Established: 1972
  Date: June

  IntlThFolk-1979, 384

Drama Festival, All-Ireland Amateur
  Location: Ireland: Athlone, County Westmeath
  Date: April-May

  IntlThFolk-1979, 231

Drama Festival, Bombay
  Location: India: Bombay, Maharashtra
  Established: 1953
  Date: January

  IntlThFolk-1979, 210

Drama Festival, Burnie Youth
  Location: Australia: Burnie, Tasmania
  Established: 1964
  Date: Last week in July

  IntlThFolk-1979, 23

Drama Festival, Catholic School
  Location: Australia: Melbourne, Victoria
  Established: 1964
  Date: June

  IntlThFolk-1979, 26

Drama Festival, Deloraine Youth
  Location: Australia: Deloraine, Tasmania
  Established: 1954
  Date: One week in July

  IntlThFolk-1979, 23

Drama Festival, Goa Academy
  Location: India: Goa, Daman, and Diu Union Territory,
  Panjim
  Date: Five to ten days in November-December or
  February-March

  IntlThFolk-1979, 206

Drama Festival, Gujarat Academy
  Location: India: Ahmedabad, Gujarat
  Date: Five days during second week in February

  IntlThFolk-1979, 208

Drama Festival, Kalidasa
  Named for: Kalidasa (fl. fifth century), poet and playwright
  Location: India: Bhopal, Madhya Pradesh
  Established: 1960
  Date: First week in November

  IntlThFolk-1979, 210

Drama Festival, Manipur Academy
  Location: India: Imphal, Manipur
  Date: Five days in February-March

  IntlThFolk-1979, 211

Drama Festival, Marathi
  Location: India: Goa, Daman, and Diu Union Territory,
  Panjim
  Established: 1930
  Date: February-March

  IntlThFolk-1979, 207

Drama Festival, National School of
  Location: India: New Delhi
  Date: February-March

  IntlThFolk-1979, 205

Drama Festival, National Student
  Location: England: location varies
  Established: 1955
  Date: March-April, usually week before or after Easter Week

  IntlThFolk-1979, 182

Drama Festival, Newfoundland
  Location: Canada: Newfoundland, location varies annually
  Established: 1950
  Date: April-May, six days during Easter holidays

  GdWrldFest-1985, 40

Drama Festival, New South Wales
  Location: Australia: New South Wales
  Date: August-October

  IntlThFolk-1979, 15

Drama Festival, New South Wales High Schools
  Location: Australia: New South Wales
  Date: May-August

  IntlThFolk-1979, 15

Drama Festival, Okanagan Zone
  Location: Canada: Vernon, British Columbia
  Date: May

  IntlThFolk-1979, 61

Drama Festival, Orissa Academy
  Location: India: Bhubaneswar, Orissa
  Date: Five days in March-April

  IntlThFolk-1979, 213

Drama Festival, Rajasthan Academy
  Location: India: Jaipur, Udaipur, Jodhpur, and elsewhere
  in Rajasthan
  Date: Usually February or March

  IntlThFolk-1979, 214

107

Drama Festival, Sri Ram Center
  Location: India: New Delhi
  Established: 1977
  Date: 15 days beginning second week in February

  IntlThFolk-1979, 206

Drama Festival, Warana (Blue Skies)
  Location: Australia: Brisbane, Queensland
  Established: 1963
  Date: Two weeks in September-October, coincides with
    Warana Spring Festival

  IntlThFolk-1979, 17

Drama Memorial, Riznic-Djadja
  Named for: Petar Riznic-Djadja (n.d.)
  Location: Yugoslavia: Ruski Krstur, Vojvodina
  Date: April

  IntlThFolk-1979, 400

Drama Festivals, Academy
  Location: India: Jammu and Srinigar, Jammu and Kashmir
  Date: February in Jammu; August in Srinagar

  IntlThFolk-1979, 208

Drama of the Passion, Sacred (Spain: Ulldecona, Tarragona)
  See **Passion, Sacred Drama of the**

Dramatic Groups, "Istvan Horvath Cadet" Festival of
  Location: Hungary: Kazincbarcika
  Date: Even-numbered years in July

  IntlThFolk-1979, 200

Dreikoningenavond, Three Kings' Eve
  See **Twelfth Night (Netherlands)**

Dreikönigsfest, Festival of the Three Kings
  See **Epiphany (Germany)**

Dreikoningendag, Day of the Kings
  See **Epiphany (Belgium)**

Drugie Świeto Wielkanocne
  See **Easter Monday (Poland)**

Drums Festival, Hundred (Wangala)
  Location: India: Garo Hills, Meghalaya
  Date: Several days during late autumn, after harvest

  HolFestCelWrld-1994, 361

Drymiais
  See **First of March**

Duarte Day
  Named for: Juan Pablo Duarte (1813-1876)

  Location: Dominican Republic
  Date: January 26

  AnnivHol-1983, 14
  Chases-1993, 74

Dubrovnik Festival (Dubrovacke Ljetne Igre)
  Location: Yugoslavia: Dubrovnik, Croatia
  Established: 1950
  Date: Seven weeks from second week in July to third week
    in August

  GdWrldFest-1985, 185
  IntlThFolk-1979, 387
  MusFestEurBrit-1980, 152
  MusFestWrld-1963, 219

Duck Apple Night
  See **Halloween (England)**

**Duck Calling Contest and Wings Over the Prairie Festival,
World's Championship**
  Location: Stuttgart, Arkansas
  Established: 1937
  Date: November, Tuesday through Saturday of
    Thanksgiving week

  HolFestCelWrld-1994, 371

Duck Race, Great American
  Location: Deming, New Mexico
  Established: 1979
  Date: Fourth weekend in August

  HolFestCelWrld-1994, 124

Duisburg Trends
  Location: Federal Republic of Germany: Duisburg, North
    Rhine-Westphalia
  Established: 1977
  Date: Odd-numbered years in May

  IntlThFolk-1979, 138

Duke Gdhirë Krishtlindjet
  See **Christmas Eve (Albania)**

Dukkul al-Sayyid ila-l-Haykal
  See **Candlemas (Syria)**

Dulcimer and Harp Convention
  Location: Cosby, Tennessee
  Established: 1962
  Date: Second weekend in June

  MusFestAmer-1990, 228

Dulcimer Days
Location: Coshocton, Ohio
Date: Third weekend in May

HolFestCelWrld-1994, 89

Dullin Prize Competition
Named for: Charles Dullin (1885-1949)
Location: France: Aix-les-Bains, Savoie
Established: 1962
Date: Thursday to Sunday evening of Ascension Day
during even-numbered years

IntlThFolk-1979, 97

Duminica Pastilor
See **Easter (Romania)**

Dump Week, National
Location: Kennebunkport, Maine
Established: 1965
Date: Thursday after the Fourth of July through Labor Day

GdUSFest-1984, 76
HolFestCelWrld-1994, 89

Durga Puja
See **Mother Goddess, Festival of Durga, the (India: Bengal)**

Dussehra or Dasahara
See **Mother Goddess, Festival of Durga, the (northern India) and (India: Mysore)**

Dyarntarach
See **Candlemas (Armenian Church in Armenia)**

Dynasty Day (Fête de la Dynastie)
Location: Belgium
Date: November 15

AnnivHol-1983, 147
Chases-1993, 442

Dysmas Day
See **St. Dismas's Day**

Dyzemas Day
See **Holy Innocents' Day; St. Dismas's Day**

Dzam Ling Chi Sang
See **Prayer Day, Universal (Buddhist people in Tibet)**

Dznoont
See **Christmas (Armenia)**

Earls Court Day
Location: Iowa, Kansas, Minnesota, Virginia, and Wyoming
Date: May 9

DictDays-1988, 35

Earth Day
Location: International
Established: 1970
Date: April 22

AnnivHol-1983, 55
Chases-1993, 176
HolFestCelWrld-1994, 93

Earth Day (Vernal Equinox)
Location: Areas of North America; Western Europe
Date: March 20

AnnivHol-1983, 40
Chases-1993, 135, 136
DictDays-1988, 35

Easter
Ethnic or religious group: Christian
Date: March-April, first Sunday after first full moon after
the vernal equinox

AmerBkDays-1978, 299
AnnivHol-1983, 169
BkDays-1864, i. 423
BkFest-1937, 6, 16, 24, 30, 42, 57, 70, 87, 96, 113, 121,
133, 148, 168, 185, 211, 219, 228, 241, 249, 260, 268, 276,
287, 292, 301, 309, 317, 330, 339
BkFestHolWrld-1970, 56
BkHolWrld-1986, April 12
Chases-1993, 163
DaysCustFaith-1957, 108, 353
DictDays-1988, 35, 62, 86
DictFolkMyth-1984, 129, 181, 212, 334, 561, 628, 687, 789,
854, 947
DictWrldRel-1989, 175
FestSaintDays-1915, 73
FestWestEur-1958, 9, 24, 35, 61, 95, 108, 126, 130, 152,
164, 213, 231
FolkAmerHol-1987, 129
FolkWrldHol-1992, 189
GdUSFest-1984, 144
HolFestCelWrld-1994, 93
IndianAmer-1989, 274, 277
RelHolCal-1993, 73
SaintFestCh-1904, 162

Easter
Ethnic or religious group: Congregationalists
Date: March-April, first Sunday after first full moon after
the vernal equinox

AmerBkDays-1978, 300

Easter
Ethnic or religious group: Eastern Orthodox
Date: April-May, first Sunday after first full moon after the vernal equinox (using the Julian calendar)

AmerBkDays-1978, 300
BkDays-1864, i.423
BkFest-1937, 287, 330, 339
BkFestHolWrld-1970, 56
DaysCustFaith-1957, 110
FolkWrldHol-1992, 189
HolFestCelWrld-1994, 93

Easter
Ethnic or religious group: Episcopalian
Date: March-April, first Sunday after first full moon after the vernal equinox

AmerBkDays-1978, 300

Easter
Ethnic or religious group: Greek Orthodox
Date: April-May, first Sunday after first full moon after the vernal equinox (using the Julian calendar)

AmerBkDays-1978, 300
BkDays-1864, i.423
BkFestHolWrld-1970, 56
BkHolWrld-1986, April 26, 178

Easter
Ethnic or religious group: Lutheran
Date: March-April, first Sunday after first full moon after the vernal equinox

AmerBkDays-1978, 300

Easter
Ethnic or religious group: Missouri Synod Lutheran
Date: March-April, first Sunday after first full moon after the vernal equinox

AmerBkDays-1978, 300

Easter
Ethnic or religious group: Protestant
Date: March-April, first Sunday after first full moon after the vernal equinox

AmerBkDays-1978, 300
BkFestHolWrld-1970, 57

Easter
Ethnic or religious group: Roman Catholic
Date: March-April, first Sunday after first full moon after the vernal equinox

AmerBkDays-1978, 300
BkDays-1864, i.426
RelHolCal-1993, 74

Easter (Pashkët)
Location: Albania
Date: March-April, first Sunday after first full moon after the vernal equinox

BkFest-1937, 6
FolkWrldHol-1992, 189

Easter
Location: Mission San Xavier del Bac, Arizona
Ethnic or religious group: Papago Indians
Date: March-April, first Sunday after first full moon after the vernal equinox; ceremony observed Friday after Easter Sunday

IndianAmer-1989, 277

Easter
Location: Near Tucson, Arizona
Ethnic or religious group: Yaqui Indians
Date: March-April, first Sunday after first full moon after the vernal equinox

AmerBkDays-1978, 304
DictFolkMyth-1984, 212
IndianAmer-1989, 274

Easter
Location: Hot Springs National Park, Hot Springs, Arkansas
Established: Sunrise service since 1935
Date: March-April, first Sunday after first full moon after the vernal equinox

AmerBkDays-1978, 303

Easter (Zadig)
Location: Armenia
Date: March-April, first Sunday after first full moon after the vernal equinox

BkFest-1937, 24
FolkWrldHol-1992, 189

Easter (Ostern)
Location: Austria
Date: March-April, first Sunday after first full moon after the vernal equinox

BkFest-1937, 30
FolkWrldHol-1992, 189

Easter
  Location: Austria: Vorarlberg in the Tirol
  Date: March-April, first Sunday after first full moon
    after the vernal equinox

  BkDays-1864, i.431

Easter
  Location: Azerbaijan
  Date: March-April, first Sunday after first full moon
    after the vernal equinox

  FolkWrldHol-1992, 197

Easter (Paschen)
  Location: Belgium
  Date: March-April, first Sunday after first full moon
    after the vernal equinox

  BkFest-1937, 42
  FestWestEur-1958, 9
  FolkWrldHol-1992, 190
  HolFestCelWrld-1994, 94

Easter
  Location: Bermuda
  Date: March-April, first Sunday after first full moon
    after the vernal equinox

  FolkWrldHol-1992, 191

Easter
  Location: Bohemia
  Date: March-April, first Sunday after first full moon
    after the vernal equinox

  FolkWrldHol-1992, 191

**Easter (Velikdien, the Great Day, or Vuzkresenie,
Resurrection Day)**
  Location: Bulgaria
  Date: March-April, first Sunday after first full moon
    after the vernal equinox

  BkFest-1937, 70
  FestSaintDays-1915, 82

Easter
  Location: Hollywood Bowl, California
  Established: Hollywood Bowl Sunrise Service since 1921
  Date: March-April, first Sunday after first full moon
    after the vernal equinox

  BkFestHolWrld-1970, 59

Easter
  Location: Mount Rubidoux Memorial Park, Riverside,
  California

  Established: Sunrise service since 1909
  Date: March-April, first Sunday after first full moon
    after the vernal equinox

  AmerBkDays-1978, 303
  BkFest-1937, 16

Easter
  Location: Corfu
  Date: March-April, first Sunday after first full moon
    after the vernal equinox

  DictFolkMyth-1984, 561

Easter
  Location: Costa Rica
  Date: March-April, first Sunday after first full moon
    after the vernal equinox

  FolkWrldHol-1992, 192

Easter
  Location: Cyprus
  Date: April-May, first Sunday after first full moon
    after the vernal equinox (using Julian calendar)

  HolFestCelWrld-1994, 93

Easter (Velikonoce)
  Location: Czechoslovakia
  Date: March-April, first Sunday after first full moon
    after the vernal equinox

  BkFest-1937, 87
  FolkWrldHol-1992, 192

Easter (Paaske)
  Location: Denmark
  Date: March-April, first Sunday after first full moon
    after the vernal equinox

  BkFest-1937, 96
  FestWestEur-1958, 24

Easter (Pasch Day in northern England)
  Location: England
  Date: March-April, first Sunday after first full moon
    after the vernal equinox

  BkDays-1864, i.425
  BkFest-1937, 57
  DaysCustFaith-1957, 353
  DictDays-1988, 87
  DictFolkMyth-1984, 335
  FestSaintDays-1915, 75, 80, 85
  FolkWrldHol-1992, 194

Easter (Ülestôusmise Pühad)
Location: Estonia
Date: March-April, first Sunday, Monday, and Tuesday
after first full moon after the vernal equinox

BkFest-1937, 103
FolkWrldHol-1992, 192

Easter (Fasika)
Location: Ethiopia
Date: March-April, first Sunday after first full moon
after the vernal equinox

FolkWrldHol-1992, 193
HolFestCelWrld-1994, 94

Easter (Pääsiäissunnuntai)
Location: Finland
Date: March-April, first Sunday after first full moon
after the vernal equinox

BkFest-1937, 113

Easter (Pâques)
Location: France
Date: March-April, first Sunday after first full moon
after the vernal equinox

BkFest-1937, 121
FestWestEur-1958, 35
FolkWrldHol-1992, 193

Easter (Ostern)
Location: Germany
Date: March-April, first Sunday after first full moon
after the vernal equinox

BkFest-1937, 133
BkFestHolWrld-1970, 60
DictFolkMyth-1984, 335, 561
FestWestEur-1958, 61
FolkWrldHol-1992, 194
RelHolCal-1993, 74

Easter (To Ayeeon Pascha or Lambri, Bright Day)
Location: Greece
Date: March-April, first Sunday after first full moon
after the vernal equinox

BkFest-1937, 148
BkHolWrld-1986, April 26, 178
FestSaintDays-1915, 79, 82
FolkWrldHol-1992, 196

Easter (Husvét)
Location: Hungary
Date: March-April, first Sunday after first full moon
after the vernal equinox

BkFest-1937, 168

Easter
Location: Ireland
Date: March-April, first Sunday after first full moon
after the vernal equinox

FolkWrldHol-1992, 197

Easter
Location: Israel: Jerusalem
Date: March-April, first Sunday after first full moon
after the vernal equinox

FestSaintDays-1915, 73

Easter (La Pasqua)
Location: Italy
Date: March-April, first Sunday after first full moon
after the vernal equinox

BkDays-1864, i.426
BkFest-1937, 185
FestSaintDays-1915, 75
FestWestEur-1958, 95

Easter (Scoppio del Carro, Ceremony of the Car)
Location: Italy: Florence
Date: March-April, first Sunday after first full moon
after the vernal equinox

FestSaintDays-1915, 75

Easter
Location: Latin America
Date: March-April, first Sunday after first full moon
after the vernal equinox

DictFolkMyth-1984, 561

Easter (Lieldienas Svetdiena)
Location: Latvia
Date: March-April, first Sunday after first full moon
after the vernal equinox

BkFest-1937, 211

Easter (Velykos)
Location: Lithuania
Date: March-April, first Sunday after first full moon
after the vernal equinox

BkFest-1937, 219
DictFolkMyth-1984, 628

Easter (O'schtersonndeg)
  Location: Luxembourg
  Date: March-April, first Sunday after first full moon
    after the vernal equinox

  FestWestEur-1958, 108

Easter
  Location: Macedonia
  Date: March-April, first Sunday after first full moon
    after the vernal equinox

  FolkWrldHol-1992, 197

Easter
  Location: Malta
  Date: March-April, first Sunday after first full moon
    after the vernal equinox

  FolkWrldHol-1992, 198

Easter (Domingo de Resurrección)
  Location: Mexico
  Date: March-April, first Sunday after first full moon
    after the vernal equinox

  BkFest-1937, 288
  DictFolkMyth-1984, 212, 335, 561
  FolkWrldHol-1992, 199

Easter
  Location: Mexico: Sonora
  Ethnic or religious group: Mayo and Yaqui Indians
  Date: March-April, first Sunday after first full moon
    after the vernal equinox

  DictFolkMyth-1984, 212

Easter
  Location: Moravia
  Date: March-April, first Sunday after first full moon
    after the vernal equinox

  FolkWrldHol-1992, 200

Easter (Paschen or Paasch Zonday)
  Location: Netherlands
  Date: March-April, first Sunday after first full moon
    after the vernal equinox

  BkFest-1937, 241
  FestWestEur-1958, 126, 130
  FolkWrldHol-1992, 201

Easter
  Location: New Mexico pueblos

  Date: March-April, first Sunday after first full moon
    after the vernal equinox

  AmerBkDays-1978, 304

Easter
  Location: Nigeria: Calabar
  Date: March-April, first Sunday after first full moon
    after the vernal equinox

  FolkWrldHol-1992, 201

Easter (Paske)
  Location: Norway
  Date: March-April, first Sunday after first full moon
    after the vernal equinox

  BkFest-1937, 249
  FestWestEur-1958, 152
  FolkWrldHol-1992, 201

Easter
  Location: Wichita Mountains Wildlife Refuge in Lawton,
    Oklahoma
  Established: Oberammergau sunrise service since 1926
  Date: March-April, first Sunday after first full moon
    after the vernal equinox

  AmerBkDays-1978, 303
  GdUSFest-1984, 144

Easter (Wielkanoc)
  Location: Poland
  Date: March-April, first Sunday after first full moon
    after the vernal equinox

  BkFest-1937, 260
  FolkWrldHol-1992, 202

Easter (Paschoa)
  Location: Portugal
  Date: March-April, first Sunday after first full moon
    after the vernal equinox

  BkFest-1937, 268
  DictFolkMyth-1984, 561
  FestWestEur-1958, 164

Easter
  Location: Rhodesia
  Date: March-April, first Sunday after first full moon
    after the vernal equinox

  BkFestHolWrld-1970, 62

Easter (Duminica Pastilor)
Location: Romania
Date: March-April, first Sunday after first full moon
after the vernal equinox

BkFest-1937, 276
DictFolkMyth-1984, 181

Easter (Paskha)
Location: Russia
Date: March-April, first Sunday after first full moon
after the vernal equinox

BkFest-1937, 287, 292
FestSaintDays-1915, 80, 88

Easter (Pace or Pasch Day)
Location: Scotland
Date: March-April, first Sunday after first full moon
after the vernal equinox

BkDays-1864, i.425
DictDays-1988, 86, 87
FolkWrldHol-1992, 194, 202

Easter
Location: Sicily
Date: March-April, first Sunday after first full moon
after the vernal equinox

FolkWrldHol-1992, 202

Easter (Domingo de Resurreccion)
Location: Spain
Date: March-April, first Sunday after first full moon
after the vernal equinox

BkFest-1937, 301
DictFolkMyth-1984, 561
FestSaintDays-1915, 84, 87
FolkWrldHol-1992, 202

Easter
Location: Spain
Ethnic or religious group: Catalan people
Date: March-April, first Sunday after first full moon
after the vernal equinox

FolkWrldHol-1992, 203

Easter (Paskdagen)
Location: Sweden
Date: March-April, first Sunday after first full moon
after the vernal equinox

BkFest-1937, 309
FestWestEur-1958, 213
FolkWrldHol-1992, 203

Easter (Ostern)
Location: Switzerland
Date: March-April, first Sunday after first full moon
after the vernal equinox

BkFest-1937, 317
FestWestEur-1958, 231

Easter (Al-'Id al-Kabir)
Location: Syria
Ethnic or religious group: Eastern Orthodox
Date: March-April, first Sunday after first full moon
after the vernal equinox

BkFest-1937, 330

Easter
Location: Ukraine
Date: March-April, first Sunday after first full moon
after the vernal equinox

FolkWrldHol-1992, 203

Easter
Location: United States
Date: March-April, first Sunday after first full moon
after the vernal equinox

AmerBkDays-1978, 302
BkFest-1937, 16
BkFestHolWrld-1970, 59
DaysCustFaith-1957, 109
DictFolkMyth-1984, 212, 335, 687, 854
FolkAmerHol-1987, 137
GdUSFest-1984, 144
HolFestCelWrld-1994, 94
IndianAmer-1989, 274, 277

Easter
Location: United States
Ethnic or religious group: African-Americans
Date: March-April, first Sunday after first full moon
after the vernal equinox

DictFolkMyth-1984, 335

Easter
Location: United States
Ethnic or religious group: Armenian-Americans
Date: March-April, first Sunday after first full moon
after the vernal equinox

FolkAmerHol-1987, 137

Easter
  Location: United States
  Ethnic or religious group: Moravian people
  Established: Sunrise service since 1743
  Date: March-April, first Sunday after first full moon
    after the vernal equinox

AmerBkDays-1978, 303
FolkAmerHol-1987, 138

Easter
  Location: United States
  Ethnic or religious group: Pennsylvania-Dutch people
  Date: March-April, first Sunday after first full moon
    after the vernal equinox

DictFolkMyth-1984, 854

Easter
  Location: United States
  Ethnic or religious group: Ukrainian-Americans
  Date: March-April, first Sunday after first full moon
    after the vernal equinox

FolkAmerHol-1987, 138

Easter (Burning of Judas)
  Location: Venezuela
  Date: March-April, first Sunday after first full moon
    after the vernal equinox

FolkWrldHol-1992, 204
HolFestCelWrld-1994, 45

Easter (Uskrs)
  Location: Yugoslavia
  Ethnic or religious group: Eastern Orthodox
  Date: March-April, first Sunday after first full moon
    after the vernal equinox

BkFest-1937, 339

Easter Eve or Even
  See **Easter**

Easter Festival (Osterfestspiele)
  Location: Austria: Salzburg
  Established: 1967
  Date: March-April, from Palm Sunday to Easter Monday

MusFestEurBrit-1980, 20

Easter Festival of Sacred Music
  Location: France: Lourdes, Hautes-Pyrénées
  Ethnic or religious group: Roman Catholic
  Established: 1968
  Date: March-April, 10 days beginning Good Friday

GdWrldFest-1985, 79
See also **Our Lady of Lourdes, Feast of**

Easter Fires Pageant
  See **Holy Saturday (Fredericksburg, Texas)**

Easter Monday
  Ethnic or religious group: Slavic people
  Date: March-April, Monday after Easter

DictFolkMyth-1984, 335

Easter Monday
  Location: Armenia
  Date: March-April, Monday after Easter

FolkWrldHol-1992, 189

Easter Monday
  Location: Austria
  Date: March-April, Monday after Easter

DictFolkMyth-1984, 335
FolkWrldHol-1992, 189

Easter Monday
  Location: Bohemia
  Date: March-April, Monday after Easter

DictFolkMyth-1984, 335

Easter Monday
  Location: Canada
  Date: March-April, Monday after Easter

Chases-1993, 164

Easter Monday (Velikonoční Pondělí)
  Location: Czechoslovakia
  Date: March-April, Monday after Easter

BkFest-1937, 87

Easter Monday (Anden Paaskedag)
  Location: Denmark
  Date: March-April, Monday after Easter

BkFest-1937, 96
FestWestEur-1958, 25

Easter Monday (Hocktide, Hock Monday, Hock Tuesday or Tutti Day)
  Location: England
  Date: March-April, Monday and Tuesday after Easter

AmerBkDays-1978, 309
BkFest-1937, 16, 57
Chases-1993, 164
DictDays-1988, 8, 11, 35, 55, 56, 122
FestSaintDays-1915, 91
FolkWrldHol-1992, 194, 208
HolFestCelWrld-1994, 94, 139

Easter Monday
Location: Estonia
Date: March-April, Monday and Tuesday after Easter

BkFest-1937, 103

Easter Monday (Toinen Pääsiäispäivä)
Location: Finland
Date: March-April, Monday after Easter

BkFest-1937, 113
FolkWrldHol-1992, 193

Easter Monday (Lundi de Pâques)
Location: France
Date: March-April, Monday after Easter

AmerBkDays-1978, 309
BkFest-1937, 122

Easter Monday
Location: Germany
Date: March-April, Monday after Easter

DictFolkMyth-1984, 335
FestWestEur-1958, 62

Easter Monday (Thefteratoo Pascha)
Location: Greece
Date: March-April, Monday after Easter

BkFest-1937, 148

Easter Monday (Husvét Hétfoje or Ducking Monday)
Location: Hungary
Date: March-April, Monday after Easter

BkFest-1937, 168

Easter Monday
Location: South Bend, Indiana
Ethnic or religious group: Polish-Americans
Established: Paas Festival since 19th century
Date: March-April, Monday after Easter

AmerBkDays-1978, 309

Easter Monday (Lieldienas Otrie Svētki)
Location: Latvia
Date: March-April, Monday after Easter

BkFest-1937, 212

Easter Monday (Velyku Antra Diena)
Location: Lithuania
Date: March-April, Monday after Easter

BkFest-1937, 220

Easter Monday
Location: Luxembourg
Date: March-April, Monday after Easter

AmerBkDays-1978, 309

Easter Monday (Paasch Maandag)
Location: Netherlands
Date: March-April, Monday after Easter

BkFest-1937, 242
FestWestEur-1958, 130, 131

Easter Monday (Vlöggelen, Winging Ceremony)
Location: Netherlands: Ootmarsum
Date: March-April, Easter Sunday and Monday

FestWestEur-1958, 130
HolFestCelWrld-1994, 359

Easter Monday
Location: North Carolina
Date: March-April, Monday after Easter

Chases-1993, 164
DictDays-1988, 35

Easter Monday
Location: Northern Ireland
Date: March-April, Monday after Easter

Chases-1993, 164

Easter Monday (Drugie Świeto Wielkanocne)
Location: Poland
Date: March-April, Monday after Easter

BkFest-1937, 261
FolkWrldHol-1992, 202
HolFestCelWrld-1994, 94

Easter Monday (Lunia Paştilor)
Location: Romania
Date: March-April, Monday after Easter

BkFest-1937, 276

Easter Monday
Location: Russia
Date: March-April, Monday after Easter

BkFest-1937, 292

Easter Monday
Location: Scotland
Date: March-April, Monday after Easter

DictDays-1988, 86

Easter Monday
   Location: South Africa
   Date: March-April, Monday after Easter begins Family Week

   DictDays-1988, 38
   RelHolCal-1993, 76

Easter Monday (Annandag Påsk)
   Location: Sweden
   Date: March-April, Monday after Easter

   BkFest-1937, 309

Easter Monday
   Location: Switzerland
   Date: March-April, Monday after Easter

   AmerBkDays-1978, 309

Easter Monday
   Location: Wales
   Date: March-April, Monday after Easter

   Chases-1993, 164

Easter Monday
   Location: White House lawn, Washington, D.C.
   Established: Easter Egg Roll since 1810s
   Date: March-April, Monday after Easter

   AmerBkDays-1978, 308
   BkFest-1937, 16
   Chases-1993, 165
   HolFestCelWrld-1994, 94

Easter Play of Muri
   Location: Switzerland: Muri, Aargau
   Established: 1971; play is based on mid-13th-century
     manuscript
   Date: Every five or six years in June

   IntlThFolk-1979, 354

Easter Saturday
   See **Easter; Holy Saturday**

Easter Show, Royal
   Location: Australia: Moore Park Showground, Sydney,
     New South Wales
   Established: 1882
   Date: March-April, during the Easter holidays

   GdWrldFest-1985, 6
   HolFestCelWrld-1994, 278

East Var, Festival of
   Location: France: Montauroux and surrounding towns in Var

   Date: Six weeks in July-August

   IntlThFolk-1979, 113

Eating the New Millet Ceremony
   Location: Niger
   Ethnic or religious group: Songhay people
   Date: After harvest

   FolkWrldHol-1992, 454

Eddy, Birthday of Mary Baker
   Named for: Mary Baker Eddy (1821-1910)
   Ethnic or religious group: Christian Science
   Date: July 16

   AnnivHol-1983, 94
   Chases-1993, 293
   DaysCustFaith-1957, 183
   DictWrldRel-1989, 168
   RelHolCal-1993, 63

Edinburgh Fringe Festival
   Location: Scotland: Edinburgh
   Established: 1947
   Date: August-September; coincides with Edinburgh
     International Festival

   Chases-1993, 331
   IntlThFolk-1979, 185

Edinburgh International Festival
   Location: Scotland: Edinburgh
   Established: 1947
   Date: Three weeks beginning third week in August

   Chases-1993, 331
   GdWrldFest-1985, 99
   HolFestCelWrld-1994, 95
   IntlThFolk-1979, 184
   MusFestEurBrit-1980, 132
   MusFestWrld-1963, 8

Edison Pageant of Light
   Named for: Thomas Alva Edison (1847-1931)
   Location: Fort Myers, Florida
   Established: 1938
   Date: Second Wednesday through third Saturday in February,
     including February 11

   AmerBkDays-1978, 164
   Chases-1993, 86
   GdUSFest-1984, 35
   HolFestCelWrld-1994, 95

Edison's Birthday, Thomas
Named for: Thomas Alva Edison (1847-1931)
Location: United States
Date: February 11

AmerBkDays-1978, 163
HolFestCelWrld-1994, 338

Eed-al-Fittur
See **Fast, Feast of Breaking the (Iraq)**

Eed el Fitur
See **Fast, Feast of Breaking the (Bahrain)**

Eerste and Tweede Kerstdag
See **Christmas (Netherlands/Holland)**

Ee Ypsosis too Timjou Stavrou
See **Exaltation of the Cross (Greece)**

Egbodo Oba Ooni
See **New Yam Festival (Yoruba people in Oyo, Nigeria)**

Egg Feast
See **Egg Saturday**

Egg Festival, Central Maine
Location: Pittsfield, Maine
Established: 1972
Date: Fourth Saturday in July

Chases-1993, 300
GdUSFest-1984, 77

Egg Saturday
Location: England: Oxfordshire
Date: February, Saturday before Ash Wednesday

DictDays-1988, 36

Egungun Festival
Location: Nigeria: Ede
Ethnic or religious group: Yoruba people
Date: June

FolkWrldHol-1992, 322, 459
HolFestCelWrld-1994, 95

Eid
See **Fast, Feast of Breaking the (Pakistan)**

Eid al Fitr
See **Fast, Feast of Breaking the (Libya)**

Eid il-Fitr
See **Fast, Feast of Breaking the (Egypt)**

Eid Saghir
See **Fast, Feast of Breaking the (Sudan)**

Eight Hour Day
Location: South Australia
Date: October 11

AnnivHol-1983, 131
HolFestCelWrld-1994, 95, 175

Eight Hour Day or Labour Day
Location: Western Australia and Tasmania
Established: 1890
Date: March 5

AnnivHol-1983, 31
BkHolWrld-1986, March 5, 177
Chases-1993, 119
DictDays-1988, 36, 65
HolFestCelWrld-1994, 95, 175

Eisheiligan
See **Frost, or Ice, Saints Day (Roman Catholics in France and Germany)**

Eisteddfod, Cynonfardd
Location: Pennsylvania
Ethnic or religious group: Welsh-Americans
Established: 1889
Date: Last Saturday in April

HolFestCelWrld-1994, 74

Eisteddfod, Eastern Shore
Location: Australia: Hobart, Tasmania
Established: 1968
Date: October

DictFolkMyth-1984, 342
IntlThFolk-1979, 24

Eisteddfod, Hobart
Location: Australia: Hobart, Tasmania
Established: 1951
Date: June

DictFolkMyth-1984, 342
IntlThFolk-1979, 25

Eisteddfod, International Musical (Gerddorol Gydwladol Llangollen)
Location: Wales: Llangollen, Denbighshire
Established: 1947
Date: Six days during first week in July

Chases-1993, 282
DictFolkMyth-1984, 342
GdWrldFest-1985, 101
IntlThFolk-1979, 189
MusFestEurBrit-1980, 149
MusFestWrld-1963, 37

Eisteddfod Festival of Traditional Music and Crafts
  Location: Southeastern Massachusetts University, North
    Dartmouth, Massachusetts
  Established: 1971
  Date: Three days over third weekend in September

MusFestAmer-1990, 222

**Eisteddfod of Wales, Royal National (Eisteddfod Genedlaethol
Frenhinol Cymru)**
  Location: Alternates between northern and southern Wales
    each year
  Established: Fourth century
  Date: First full week in August

AnnivHol-1983, 176
BkFest-1937, 60
BkHolWrld-1986, August 3, 177
Chases-1993, 311
DictFolkMyth-1984, 342
GdWrldFest-1985, 100
HolFestCelWrld-1994, 96
IntlThFolk-1979, 191
MusFestEurBrit-1980, 150

Eisteddfod Society Festival
  Location: Australia: Devonport, Tasmania
  Established: 1920
  Date: August-September

DictFolkMyth-1984, 342
IntlThFolk-1979, 24

Eka Dasa Rudra
  Location: Indonesia: Pura Besakih temple, Bali
  Ethnic or religious group: Balinese religion
  Date: Once every hundred years

HolFestCelWrld-1994, 96

Ekadashi
  See **Eleventh**

Ekako, Ekeko or Eq'eq'o
  See **Alasita Fair**

El-Bugat
  Ethnic or religious group: Arabic people
  Established: Ancient ceremony in honor of Adonis

DictMyth-1962, i.498

El Djem Festival
  Location: Tunisia: El Djem [formerly, Thysdrus],
    Mahdia Region

Date: June

IntlThFolk-1979, 360

Election Day
  Location: United States
  Established: 1845
  Date: The Tuesday after the first Monday in November

AmerBkDays-1978, 991
AnnivHol-1983, 142
Chases-1993, 429
DictDays-1988, 36
HolFestCelWrld-1994, 96

Elephant God, Festival of the (Ganesha Chaturthi)
  Ethnic or religious group: Hindu
  Date: August-September, fourth day of Hindu month
    of Bhadrapada

AnnivHol-1983, 177
BkFest-1937, 162
BkHolWrld-1986, September 5, 177
DictFolkMyth-1984, 440
DictWrldRel-1989, 273
FolkWrldHol-1992, 434
HolFestCelWrld-1994, 114
RelHolCal-1993, 77

Elephant God, Festival of the (Ganesha Chaturthi)
  Location: India
  Ethnic or religious group: Hindu
  Date: August-September, fourth day of Hindu month
    of Bhadrapada

AnnivHol-1983, 177
Chases-1993, 378
DictFolkMyth-1984, 440
FolkWrldHol-1992, 434
HolFestCelWrld-1994, 114
RelHolCal-1993, 77

Elephant God, Festival of the (Ganesha Chaturthi)
  Location: India: the Deccan
  Ethnic or religious group: Hindu
  Date: August-September, fourth day of Hindu month
    of Bhadrapada

DictFolkMyth-1984, 440

Elephant God, Festival of the (Ganesha Chaturthi)
  Location: India: Maharashtra
  Ethnic or religious group: Hindu

Elephant God, Festival of the (Ganesha Chaturthi) *(cont.)*
Date: August-September, fourth day of Hindu month
of Bhadrapada

FolkWrldHol-1992, 434
RelHolCal-1993, 77

Elephant God, Festival of the (Ganesha Chaturthi)
Location: India: Bombay, Maharashtra
Ethnic or religious group: Hindu
Date: August-September, one week including fourth day of
Hindu month of Bhadrapada

AnnivHol-1983, 177
FolkWrldHol-1992, 434
HolFestCelWrld-1994, 114
RelHolCal-1993, 77

Elephant God, Festival of the (Ganesha Chaturthi)
Location: India: Poona, Maharashtra
Ethnic or religious group: Hindu
Date: August-September, fourth day of Hindu month
of Bhadrapada

FolkWrldHol-1992, 435

Elephant God, Festival of the (Ganesha Chaturthi)
Location: Nepal
Ethnic or religious group: Hindu
Date: August-September, fourth day of Hindu month
of Bhadrapada

FolkWrldHol-1992, 434

Elephant Round-Up
Location: Thailand: Surin
Established: 1961
Date: Third week of November

BkHolWrld-1986, November 16, 177
Chases-1993, 448
GdWrldFest-1985, 175
HolFestCelWrld-1994, 97

Eleusinia
Location: Ancient Greece: Eleusis and Athens
Date: Every five years: the Lesser Eleusinia, early
spring; the Greater Eleusinia, between harvest and
seed time

DictFolkMyth-1984, 512
DictMyth-1962, i.502

Elevation of the Cross
See **Exaltation of the Cross**

Eleven Cities Race (Elfstedentocht)
Location: Netherlands: Friesland Province
Established: 18th century
Date: January 22

BkHolWrld-1986, January 22
HolFestCelWrld-1994, 97

Eleventh (Ekadashi)
Ethnic or religious group: Hindu
Date: 11th day of each waxing and waning moon
(24 times yearly)

RelHolCal-1993, 74
See also **Amalaka Ekadashi; Hari-Shayani Ekadashi;
Nirjala Ekadashi; Putrada Ekadashi; Vaikuntha
Ekadashi; Vishnu's Awakening (Devathani Ekadashi);
and Wish-Fulfilling Eleventh (Kamada Ekadashi)**

Elfreth's Alley Fete Days
Location: Philadelphia, Pennsylvania
Established: 1934
Date: Two days in early June

GdUSFest-1984, 160
HolFestCelWrld-1994, 97

Elfstedentocht
See **Eleven Cities Race**

Elijah Day
Named for: Elijah, who lived about 1000 years before
Christian era began
Ethnic or religious group: Roman Catholic and
Greek churches
Date: July 20

DaysCustFaith-1957, 187

El Karraka International Festival
Location: Tunisia: La Goulette, North Tunis Region
Date: July-August

IntlThFolk-1979, 362

Elvis International Tribute Week
Named for: Elvis Presley (1935-1977)
Location: Graceland, Memphis, Tennessee
Date: Week including August 16

AnnivHol-1983, 108
Chases-1993, 332
HolFestCelWrld-1994, 97

Emancipation Day
  Named for: Emancipation of British slaves in 1838
  Location: Bahama Islands
  Date: First Monday of August

  AnnivHol-1983, 101
  Chases-1993, 314

Emancipation Day
  Named for: June 4, 1970, independence of Tonga
  Location: Kingdom of Tonga
  Date: June 4

  AnnivHol-1983, 75
  Chases-1993, 235

Emancipation Day
  Location: Trinidad and Tobago
  Established: 1985, when it replaced Columbus Day
  (Discovery Day)
  Date: August 1

  AnnivHol-1983, 102
  Chases-1993, 311
  HolFestCelWrld-1994, 85, 98

Emancipation Day (African-Americans in Texas and other southern United States)
  See **Juneteenth**

Emancipation of the Slaves Day
  Named for: March 22, 1873, abolishment of slavery
  Location: Puerto Rico
  Date: March 22

  AnnivHol-1983, 41

Emancipation Proclamation Day
  Named for: January 1, 1863, emancipation of African
  American slaves
  Location: United States
  Date: January 1

  AmerBkDays-1978, 9
  AnnivHol-1983, 2
  Chases-1993, 50
  FolkAmerHol-1987, 21
  HolFestCelWrld-1994, 98

Ember Days
  Ethnic or religious group: Anglican
  Date: Wednesday, Friday and Saturday of the weeks
  following 1) first Sunday in Lent; 2) Pentecost;

3) September 14, Holy Cross Day; and 4) December 13,
St. Lucy's Day

  DictMyth-1962, i.507
  DictWrldRel-1989, 237
  HolFestCelWrld-1994, 98
  RelHolCal-1993, 74

Ember Days
  Ethnic or religious group: Church of England
  Date: Wednesday, Friday and Saturday of the weeks
  following 1) first Sunday in Lent; 2) Pentecost;
  3) September 14, Holy Cross Day; and 4) December 13,
  St. Lucy's Day

  BkDays-1864, ii.687
  DictDays-1988, 48
  HolFestCelWrld-1994, 98

Ember Days
  Ethnic or religious group: Roman Catholic
  Established: instituted by Pope Calixtus I in third century
  Date: Wednesday, Friday and Saturday of the weeks
  following 1) first Sunday in Lent; 2) Pentecost;
  3) September 14, Holy Cross Day; and 4) December 13,
  St. Lucy's Day

  DaysCustFaith-1957, 163
  DictDays-1988, 48
  DictMyth-1962, 507
  DictWrldRel-1989, 237
  HolFestCelWrld-1994, 98
  RelHolCal-1993, 74
  SaintFestCh-1904, 253

Empire Day
  See **Commonwealth Day (Great Britain)** and **Victoria
  Day (Canada), (England and British Commonwealth
  countries), and (New Zealand)**

Emume Ala
  Location: Nigeria
  Ethnic or religious group: Igbo people
  Date: On or near March 20

  FolkWrldHol-1992, 182

Emume Ibo Uzo
  See **Road Building Festival**

Encaenia Day
  Location: England: Oxford University
  Date: June

  DictDays-1988, 23, 36
  HolFestCelWrld-1994, 98

Enchilada Fiesta, Whole
Location: Las Cruces, New Mexico
Date: First full weekend in October

HolFestCelWrld-1994, 367

Encounter with History
Location: Romania: Costesti, Orastioara de Sus
  Commune, Hunedoara
Date: First Sunday in May

IntlThFolk-1979, 322

Endiablada Festival
Location: Spain: Almonacid del Marquesado, Cuenca
Date: Early February

IntlThFolk-1979, 332

Enkutatash
See **New Year (Ethiopia)**

Ennen-no-mai
See **Dance, Longevity (Japan: Nikko, Tochigi)**

Entierro de la Sardina
See **Burial of the Sardine (Spain)**

Entrance of the Lord into Jerusalem
See **Palm Sunday**

EOKA (Greek National Union of Cypriot Fighters Day)
Named for: Cypriots who fought against British control
  in 1955
Location: Cyprus
Date: April 1

AnnivHol-1983, 46

Ephesus, Festival of
Location: Turkey: Selcuk
Date: May

IntlThFolk-1979, 372

Epidauros Festival
See **Theater Festival, Epidauros**

Epifania
See **Epiphany (Italy)**

Epiphany
Ethnic or religious group: Christian
Established: End of second century
Date: January 6, Gregorian calendar (N.S.); January 19,
  Julian calendar (O.S.)

AmerBkDays-1978, 34, 89
AnnivHol-1983, 5, 11

BkDays-1864, i. 53, i. 61-64
BkFest-1937, 3, 22, 37, 66, 84, 94, 101, 110, 119, 131, 144,
  165, 179, 210, 218, 225, 256, 266, 289, 297, 307, 325, 335
BkFestHolWrld-1970, 19
BkHolWrld-1986, January 6
Chases-1993, 57
DaysCustFaith-1957, 20
DictDays-1988, 37, 70, 83, 120
DictFolkMyth-1984, 346
DictMyth-1962, i.516
DictWrldRel-1989, 154, 237
FestSaintDays-1915, 9, 17
FestWestEur-1958, 4, 22, 54, 89, 150
FolkAmerHol-1987, 25
FolkWrldHol-1992, 12, 23
HolFestCelWrld-1994, 83, 99, 234, 239, 339, 340
RelHolCal-1993, 75, 100
SaintFestCh-1904, 54

Epiphany
Ethnic or religious group: Anglican
Date: January 6

RelHolCal-1993, 75

Epiphany
Ethnic or religious group: Eastern Orthodox
Date: January 6, Gregorian calendar (N.S.); January 19,
  Julian calendar (O.S.)

AmerBkDays-1978, 34, 37, 38, 89
AnnivHol-1983, 5, 11
BkFest-1937, 3, 144, 289, 335
BkFestHolWrld-1970, 19, 22
Chases-1993, 57
DictWrldRel-1989, 237
FestSaintDays-1915, 17
FolkAmerHol-1987, 31
FolkWrldHol-1992, 13, 14, 23
HolFestCelWrld-1994, 99, 239
RelHolCal-1993, 75

Epiphany
Ethnic or religious group: Greek Orthodox
Date: January 6, Gregorian calendar (N.S.); January 19,
  Julian calendar (O.S.)

AmerBkDays-1978, 38, 89
AnnivHol-1983, 5, 11
BkFest-1937, 144
BkFestHolWrld-1970, 22
FestSaintDays-1915, 17
FolkAmerHol-1987, 32
HolFestCelWrld-1994, 239

Epiphany
    Ethnic or religious group: Lutheran
    Date: January 6

    RelHolCal-1993, 75

Epiphany
    Ethnic or religious group: Protestant
    Date: January 6

    AmerBkDays-1978, 34
    DaysCustFaith-1957, 20
    HolFestCelWrld-1994, 99
    RelHolCal-1993, 75

Epiphany
    Ethnic or religious group: Roman Catholic
    Date: January 6

    AmerBkDays-1978, 34
    BkFestHolWrld-1970, 20
    DaysCustFaith-1957, 20
    HolFestCelWrld-1994, 99
    RelHolCal-1993, 75

Epiphany (Ujët e Bekuar and Blessing of the Waters)
    Location: Albania
    Date: January 6

    BkFest-1937, 3

Epiphany (Lailat-al-Quade, Night of Destiny)
    Location: Arab countries
    Ethnic or religious group: Christian
    Date: January 5, Epiphany Eve

    BkFestHolWrld-1970, 23

Epiphany (Asdvadzahaïdnootyoon)
    Location: Armenia
    Date: January 6

    BkFest-1937, 22
    DictWrldRel-1989, 237

Epiphany
    Location: Austria
    Date: January 6

    BkFestHolWrld-1970, 21
    DictFolkMyth-1984, 346
    FolkWrldHol-1992, 12

Epiphany (Dreikoningendag, Day of the Kings)
    Location: Belgium

    Date: January 5-6

    BkFest-1937, 37
    FestWestEur-1958, 4
    FolkWrldHol-1992, 16

Epiphany (Bogoyavleniye, Blessing of the Waters)
    Location: Bulgaria
    Date: January 6, Gregorian calendar (N.S.); January 19,
    Julian calendar (O.S.)

    BkFest-1937, 66

Epiphany (Old Christmas)
    Location: Canada
    Ethnic or religious group: Ukrainian-Canadians
    Date: January 7

    FolkWrldHol-1992, 23

Epiphany
    Location: Canada: Makkovik, Labrador, Newfoundland
    Date: January 6

    FolkWrldHol-1992, 12

Epiphany
    Location: Cyprus
    Date: January 6, Gregorian calendar (N.S.); January 19,
    Julian calendar (O.S.)

    FolkWrldHol-1992, 13
    HolFestCelWrld-1994, 239, 240

Epiphany (Den Svatých Tří Králu)
    Location: Czechoslovakia
    Date: January 6

    BkFest-1937, 84

Epiphany (Helligtrekongersdag, Day of the Three Holy Kings)
    Location: Denmark
    Date: January 6

    BkFest-1937, 94
    FestWestEur-1958, 22

Epiphany
    Location: England
    Date: January 6

    DictDays-1988, 83
    DictFolkMyth-1984, 346
    FestSaintDays-1915, 10
    FolkWrldHol-1992, 23
    See also **Twelfth Night**

Epiphany (Kolme Kuninga Päev)
  Location: Estonia
  Date: January 6

  BkFest-1937, 101

Epiphany (Timqat or Timkat)
  Location: Ethiopia: Amhara
  Date: January 19

  BkFestHolWrld-1970, 23
  FolkWrldHol-1992, 32
  HolFestCelWrld-1994, 340

Epiphany (Loppiainen)
  Location: Finland
  Date: January 6

  BkFest-1937, 110

Epiphany
  Location: Tarpon Springs, Florida
  Ethnic or religious group: Greek Orthodox Greek-Americans
  Date: January 6

  AmerBkDays-1978, 37, 38
  AnnivHol-1983, 5
  BkFest-1937, 144
  FolkAmerHol-1987, 31, 284
  HolFestCelWrld-1994, 239

Epiphany (Le Jour des Rois)
  Location: France
  Date: January 6

  BkDays-1864, i.62
  BkFest-1937, 119
  FestSaintDays-1915, 15
  FestWestEur-1958, 33
  FolkWrldHol-1992, 13
  HolFestCelWrld-1994, 99

Epiphany (Dreikönigsfest, Festival of the Three Kings)
  Location: Germany
  Date: January 6

  AmerBkDays-1978, 38
  BkFest-1937, 131
  BkFestHolWrld-1970, 21
  DictFolkMyth-1984, 346
  FestSaintDays-1915, 9
  FestWestEur-1958, 54
  FolkWrldHol-1992, 13

Epiphany (Old Christmas)
  Location: Great Britain
  Date: January 6

  FolkWrldHol-1992, 23

Epiphany
  Location: Greece
  Date: January 19

  AmerBkDays-1978, 89
  BkFest-1937, 144
  BkFestHolWrld-1970, 22
  BkHolWrld-1986, January 6
  FolkAmerHol-1987, 89
  FolkWrldHol-1992, 14

Epiphany (Vizkereszt, Blessing of the Waters)
  Location: Hungary
  Date: January 6

  BkFest-1937, 165

Epiphany
  Location: Ireland
  Date: January 6

  FolkWrldHol-1992, 14

Epiphany (Epifania)
  Location: Italy
  Date: January 6

  AmerBkDays-1978, 37
  BkFest-1937, 179
  FestSaintDays-1915, 13
  FestWestEur-1958, 89
  FolkWrldHol-1992, 14
  See also **Befana Festival**

Epiphany (Zvaigznes Diena)
  Location: Latvia
  Date: January 6

  BkFest-1937, 210

Epiphany (Triju Karaliu Švente)
  Location: Lithuania
  Date: January 6

  BkFest-1937, 218

Epiphany (King's Day)
  Location: New Orleans, Louisiana
  Date: January 6

  FolkAmerHol-1987, 27

Epiphany (Día de los Reyes Magos)
  Location: Mexico
  Date: January 5-6

  BkFest-1937, 225
  DictFolkMyth-1984, 346
  FolkWrldHol-1992, 16
  HolFestCelWrld-1994, 83
  See also **Pilgrimage to Chalma**

Epiphany (King's Day with Deer, Buffalo, Eagle, Elk Dances)
  Location: New Mexico pueblos
  Date: January 6

  AmerBkDays-1978, 38
  DictFolkMyth-1984, 346, 571
  DictMyth-1962, i.516
  FolkAmerHol-1987, 27
  HolFestCelWrld-1994, 339
  IndianAmer-1989, 285, 306

Epiphany (Fiesta of the Three Kings)
  Location: Paraguay: Tobatí
  Date: January 5-6

  FolkWrldHol-1992, 16

Epiphany
  Location: Poland
  Date: January 6; Three Kings' Day ends Christmas Time
    (Boże Narodzenie)

  BkFest-1937, 256
  FestSaintDays-1915, 14

Epiphany (Dia dos Reis, Day of the Kings)
  Location: Portugal
  Date: January 6

  BkFest-1937, 266
  DictFolkMyth-1984, 346, 1082
  FestWestEur-1958, 160

Epiphany (Dia dos Reis, Day of the Kings)
  Location: Portugal: Moguerinha
  Ethnic or religious group: Roman Catholic
  Date: January 6

  DictFolkMyth-1984, 848

Epiphany
  Location: Puerto Rico
  Date: January 6

  AmerBkDays-1978, 38
  FolkAmerHol-1987, 29

Epiphany (Bogoyavleniye and Blessing of the Waters)
  Location: Russia
  Date: January 6, Gregorian calendar (N.S.); January 19,
    Julian calendar (O.S.)

  AmerBkDays-1978, 37
  BkFest-1937, 289
  HolFestCelWrld-1994, 239

Epiphany
  Location: Scotland
  Date: January 6

  DictDays-1988, 83

Epiphany (Día de los Reyes Magos)
  Location: Spain
  Date: January 5-6

  AmerBkDays-1978, 38
  BkFest-1937, 297
  BkFestHolWrld-1970, 21
  BkHolWrld-1986, January 6
  DictFolkMyth-1984, 1063
  FestSaintDays-1915, 17
  FestWestEur-1958, 188
  FolkWrldHol-1992, 17

Epiphany (Trettondag Jul)
  Location: Sweden
  Date: January 6

  BkFest-1937, 307
  BkFestHolWrld-1970, 21
  FestWestEur-1958, 210
  FolkWrldHol-1992, 15

Epiphany
  Location: Switzerland
  Date: January 6

  BkFestHolWrld-1970, 21

Epiphany ('Īd al-Ghitās and Epiphany Eve, Lailat al-Qadr)
  Location: Syria
  Date: January 5-6

  BkFest-1937, 325, 326
  FolkWrldHol-1992, 15

Epiphany
  Location: Turkey: on the shores of the Bosporus
  Ethnic or religious group: Eastern Orthodox
  Date: January 6

  AnnivHol-1983, 5

Epiphany
Location: United States
Date: January 6, Gregorian calendar (N.S.); January 19, Julian calendar (O.S.)

AmerBkDays-1978, 36, 89
AnnivHol-1983, 5
BkFest-1937, 144, 289
BkFestHolWrld-1970, 20
DictFolkMyth-1984, 346
FolkAmerHol-1987, 25
RelHolCal-1993, 75

Epiphany
Location: United States
Ethnic or religious group: Armenian-Americans
Date: Sunday following January 6 if it doesn't fall on a Sunday

BkFest-1937, 22

Epiphany (Día de los Tres Reyes)
Location: Venezuela
Date: January 6

HolFestCelWrld-1994, 83

Epiphany
Location: Virgin Islands: St. Croix
Date: January 6; Christmas Festival ends January 6

AmerBkDays-1978, 38
See also **Christmas Festival, Caribbean**

Epiphany (Bogoyavlyeniye, Blessing of the Waters)
Location: Yugoslavia
Ethnic or religious group: Eastern Orthodox
Date: January 6, Gregorian calendar (N.S.); January 19, Julian calendar (O.S.)

BkFest-1937, 335

Epiphany Eve
See **Epiphany; Twelfth Night**

E Prëmte e Zezë, Black Friday
See **Good Friday (Albania)**

Equal Opportunity Day
Named for: November 19, 1863, Gettysburg Address by Abraham Lincoln (1809-1865)
Location: National Cemetery, Washington, D.C.
Date: November 19

AnnivHol-1983, 149
HolFestCelWrld-1994, 100

Equestrian Tournament of the Quintain
Location: Italy: Ascoli Piceno, Marches
Date: First Sunday in August

IntlThFolk-1979, 240

Equinox
See **Autumnal Equinox; Vernal Equinox**

Esala Perahera (Mahanuwara Esala Dalada Perahera)
Location: Sri Lanka: Kandy
Ethnic or religious group: Buddhist and Hindu
Established: Since about 1 A.D.; since third century honors Sacred Tooth Relic of Buddha; since 1775 festival has incorporated Hindu beliefs
Date: July-August, nine nights during annual festival, including full moon day of eighth Buddhist month of Esala

AnnivHol-1983, 176
BkHolWrld-1986, August 20, 177
DictWrldRel-1989, 135
FolkWrldHol-1992, 400
GdWrldFest-1985, 165
HolFestCelWrld-1994, 100
IntlThFolk-1979, 344

Escalade
Named for: Successful defense against invading French soldiers on December 11 and 12, 1602
Location: Switzerland: Geneva
Date: December 11

AnnivHol-1983, 159
HolFestCelWrld-1994, 100

Esplanade Concerts
Location: Boston, Massachusetts
Established: July 4, 1929
Date: Early July

MusFestAmer-1990, 211

Esther, Fast of
See **Ta'anit Esther (Jewish)**

Eternal Heroes, Festival of
Location: Romania: Mosna, Jassy
Date: Second weekend in July

IntlThFolk-1979, 327

Ether Day
Named for: First use of ether as surgical anesthetic on October 15, 1846
Location: Massachusetts General Hospital in Boston
Date: October 15

AnnivHol-1983, 133

European Festival Weeks
  Location: Federal Republic of Germany: Passau, Bavaria
  Established: 1952
  Date: June-July

  IntlThFolk-1979, 147

Evacuation Day
  Named for: Evacuation of British troops
  Location: Egypt
  Established: June 18, 1956
  Date: June 18

  AnnivHol-1983, 81
  Chases-1993, 253

Evacuation Day
  Named for: Evacuation of French troops
  Location: Syria
  Date: April 17

  AnnivHol-1983, 52
  Chases-1993, 170
  NatlHolWrld-1968, 48

Evacuation Day
  Named for: Evacuation of French troops on October 15, 1962
  Location: Tunisia
  Date: October 15

  AnnivHol-1983, 133

Evacuation Day, American Bases
  Named for: June 11, 1970, closing of American Air Force base
  Location: Libya
  Date: June 11

  AnnivHol-1983, 78

Evamelunga, the Taking Away of Burden and Sin
  See **Thanksgiving (Cameroon)**

"Evenings of Fraternity"
  See **Theatre Amateurs, Encounter of Yugoslav**

Evil Days
  See **St. Dismas's Day**

Exaltation of the Cross
  Ethnic or religious group: Christian
  Established: 326 recovery of the cross by St. Helena
    (c. 250-c. 330) observed since 335 in Jerusalem
  Date: September 14; formerly May 3 in Roman Catholic
    Church

  AnnivHol-1983, 61, 118, 181
  BkDays-1864, i. 586, ii. 340

  BkFest-1937, 27, 152, 228, 295, 332
  BkFestHolWrld-1970, 93, 113
  BkHolWrld-1986, May 3
  Chases-1993, 193
  DaysCustFaith-1957, 118, 234
  DictDays-1988, 37, 57, 97
  FestSaintDays-1915, 110, 177
  FolkAmerHol-1987, 171, 283
  FolkWrldHol-1992, 269, 479
  HolFestCelWrld-1994, 101
  RelHolCal-1993, 118
  SaintFestCh-1904, 224, 404

Exaltation of the Cross (Invention of the Cross)
  Ethnic or religious group: Eastern Orthodox
  Date: September 14

  BkDays-1864, ii.340
  BkFest-1937, 152, 295
  BkFestHolWrld-1970, 113
  FolkAmerHol-1987, 283
  HolFestCelWrld-1994, 101
  RelHolCal-1993, 118

Exaltation of the Cross
  Ethnic or religious group: Greek Orthodox
  Date: September 14

  BkDays-1864, ii.340
  BkFest-1937, 152
  FolkAmerHol-1987, 283

Exaltation of the Cross (Holyrood Day)
  Ethnic or religious group: Roman Catholic
  Date: September 14; formerly May 3

  BkDays-1864, i.586, ii.340
  HolFestCelWrld-1994, 101

Exaltation of the Cross
  Location: Argentina: La Rioja and Santiago del Estero
    provinces
  Date: May 3

  FolkWrldHol-1992, 269

Exaltation of the Cross (Kud Khach)
  Location: Armenia
  Date: Sunday nearest September 15

  BkFest-1937, 27

Exaltation of the Cross (Santacruzan)
  Location: California
  Ethnic or religious group: Filipino-Americans
  Date: May 3

  FolkAmerHol-1987, 171

Exaltation of the Cross (La Cruz de Mayo)
  Location: Chile
  Date: May 3

  FolkWrldHol-1992, 269

Exaltation of the Cross
  Location: Dominican Republic
  Established: 1606
  Date: May 2-3

  FolkWrldHol-1992, 269

Exaltation of the Cross
  Location: El Salvador
  Date: May 3

  BkHolWrld-1986, May 3

Exaltation of the Cross (Holyrood Day)
  Location: England
  Date: September 14

  BkDays-1864, ii.340
  FestSaintDays-1915, 112, 177, 179
  SaintFestCh-1904, 407

Exaltation of the Cross (Meskel, Finding of the True Cross)
  Location: Ethiopia
  Ethnic or religious group: Coptic and Ethiopian churches
  Established: More than 1,600 years old
  Date: September 27; end of the rainy season

  AnnivHol-1983, 124
  BkHolWrld-1986, September 27
  FolkWrldHol-1992, 490
  GdWrldFest-1985, 75
  HolFestCelWrld-1994, 199

Exaltation of the Cross (Ee Ypsosis too Timjou Stavrou)
  Location: Greece
  Date: September 14

  BkFest-1937, 152
  BkFestHolWrld-1970, 113

Exaltation of the Cross
  Location: Israel: Jerusalem
  Established: 335 A.D.
  Date: September 14

  DaysCustFaith-1957, 234
  FestSaintDays-1915, 177
  RelHolCal-1993, 118
  SaintFestCh-1904, 404

Exaltation of the Cross (Dia de la Santa Cruz)
  Location: Mexico
  Date: May 3

  AnnivHol-1983, 61
  BkFest-1937, 228
  BkFestHolWrld-1970, 93
  BkHolWrld-1986, May 3
  Chases-1993, 193
  HolFestCelWrld-1994, 83

Exaltation of the Cross (La Adoracion de la Cruz)
  Location: Paraguay
  Date: May 2-3

  FolkWrldHol-1992, 269

Exaltation of the Cross
  Location: Peru
  Date: May 3

  BkHolWrld-1986, May 3
  FolkWrldHol-1992, 270

Exaltation of the Cross (Cruz Velakuy)
  Location: Peru: Pacarigtambo
  Date: May 3; alternate years

  FolkWrldHol-1992, 270

Exaltation of the Cross (Santacruzan Festival)
  Location: Philippines
  Ethnic or religious group: Christian
  Date: Nine days in May

  AnnivHol-1983, 181
  FolkWrldHol-1992, 270
  HolFestCelWrld-1994, 101

Exaltation of the Cross (Vozdvizheniye)
  Location: Russia
  Date: September 14

  BkFest-1937, 295
  HolFestCelWrld-1994, 239

Exaltation of the Cross (Holyrood or Rude Day)
  Location: Scotland
  Date: September 14

  BkDays-1864, ii.340
  SaintFestCh-1904, 407

Exaltation of the Cross
  Location: Sicily
  Date: September 14

  FestSaintDays-1915, 178

Exaltation of the Cross
    Location: Spain: western Andalusia
    Date: May 3

    FolkWrldHol-1992, 270

Exaltation of the Cross ('Id Raf'al-Salīb)
    Location: Syria
    Date: September 14, Gregorian calendar (N.S.); September 27, Julian calendar (O.S.)

    BkFest-1937, 332
    FestSaintDays-1915, 178
    FolkWrldHol-1992, 479

Exaltation of the Cross (Holy Cross Day)
    Location: United States
    Ethnic or religious group: Armenian-Americans
    Date: May 3

    FolkAmerHol-1987, 171

Exaltation of the Cross (Recovery of the True Cross)
    Location: United States
    Ethnic or religious group: Greek-Americans
    Date: September 14

    FolkAmerHol-1987, 283

Exaltation of the Cross
    Location: Venezuela
    Date: May 3

    BkHolWrld-1986, May 3

Exaltation of the Shellfish
    Location: Spain: grove in Pontevedra Province
    Date: Fourth Sunday in October

    BkHolWrld-1986, October 26, 177

Excited Insects, Feast of (Ching Che)
    Location: People's Republic of China
    Date: On or near March 5

    FolkWrldHol-1992, 159
    HolFestCelWrld-1994, 102

Excited Insects, Feast of (Kyongchip)
    Location: Korea
    Date: On or near March 5

    FolkWrldHol-1992, 159
    HolFestCelWrld-1994, 102

Exhibition Day
    See **Regatta Day, Hobart**

Eyo Masquerade
    Location: Nigeria: Lagos
    Date: August

    BkHolWrld-1986, August 31, 177

Ezzahra, Festival
    Location: Tunisia: Ezzahra, North Tunis Region
    Date: July-August

    IntlThFolk-1979, 361

Fairhope Jubilee
    Location: Fairhope, Alabama
    Date: Summer

    HolFestCelWrld-1994, 103

Faka Me
    See **Sunday School Day (Methodist people in Tonga)**

Falkland Islands Day
    See **Queen Elizabeth II, Birthday of (Falkland Islands)**

Fallas de San José
    See **St. Joseph's Day (Spain: Valencia)**

Fall Festival
    Location: Jay, Oklahoma
    Ethnic or religious group: Cherokee Indians
    Date: October

    IndianAmer-1989, 65

Fall Festival, Fairmount Park
    Location: Philadelphia, Pennsylvania
    Established: 1974
    Date: 22 days in September-October

    GdUSFest-1984, 161

Fall Harvest Day
    Location: Westminster, Maryland
    Date: Second Saturday in October

    DictDays-1988, 38

Fall Pilgrimage
    See **Spring, Natchez (Natchez, Mississippi)**

Famalicao, International Festival of
    Location: Portugal: Famalicao, Porto
    Established: 1978
    Date: August

    IntlThFolk-1979, 305

Family Day
    Location: Angola
    Date: December 25

    AnnivHol-1983, 164
    RelHolCal-1993, 76

Family Day
Location: Lesotho
Date: First Monday in July

AnnivHol-1983, 89

Family Day
Location: Namibia
Date: December 26

AnnivHol-1983, 164
RelHolCal-1993, 76

Family Day
Location: Sao Tomé and Principe
Date: December 25

AnnivHol-1983, 164

Family Day (South Africa)
See **Easter Monday (South Africa)**

Family Day (Uruguay)
See **Blessing of the Waters Day (Uruguay)**

Family Week, National
Location: United States
Ethnic or religious group: Jewish, Protestant, and Roman
  Catholic
Date: Begins first Sunday in May, Mother's Day

Chases-1993, 192
DaysCustFaith-1957, 133
HolFestCelWrld-1994, 103
RelHolCal-1993, 76

Fandroana
Location: Madagascar
Established: 16th century
Date: June 30

FolkWrldHol-1992, 347

Fantasia (Horse Festival)
Location: Morocco: Fez
Date: October

GdWrldFest-1985, 137

Fantasia (Horse Festival)
Location: Morocco: Meknes
Date: October

BkHolWrld-1986, October 7, 177

Farmer's Day
Location: Korea
Date: June 15

AnnivHol-1983, 80

Farmer's Day (Saba Saba Day)
Location: Tanzania
Established: July 7, 1954, founding of TANU political party
Date: July 7

AnnivHol-1983, 90
Chases-1993, 283
HolFestCelWrld-1994, 281

Farmers' Day
Location: Zambia
Date: August 2

AnnivHol-1983, 102

Farmers' Wash Day
See **Big Sea Day (New Jersey)**

Farsang
See **Mardi Gras (Hungary)**

Fasching, Fasenacht, Fastnacht, or Fasnet
See **Mardi Gras (Austria), (Bavaria), and (Germany)**

Fasching Carnival
See **Mardi Gras (Germany: Munich)**

Fasika
See **Easter (Ethiopia)**

Fasinada
Location: Gospa od Skrpjela, Montenegro; formerly
  Yugoslavia
Date: July 22

HolFestCelWrld-1994, 104

Fasnacht
See **Mardi Gras (Pennsylvania Dutch people in the
  United States)**

Fasslrutschen
See **St. Leopold, Feast Day of (Austria)**

**Fast, Feast of Breaking the ('Id al-Fitr or 'Id as-saghîr,
Little Festival)**
Ethnic or religious group: Muslim
Date: First day of Shawwal, the tenth Islamic month; ends
  month-long fast during Ramadan, the ninth month

AnnivHol-1983, 171
BkFest-1937, 238
BkFestHolWrld-1970, 80, 113
BkHolWrld-1986, June 27
Chases-1993, 140
DictWrldRel-1989, 597
FolkWrldHol-1992, 162, 173
HolFestCelWrld-1994, 150
RelHolCal-1993, 85
See also **Ramadan**

Fast, Feast of Breaking the (Eed el Fitur)
  Location: Bahrain
  Ethnic or religious group: Muslim
  Date: First day of Shawwal, the tenth Islamic month;
    ends month-long fast during Ramadan, the ninth month

  FolkWrldHol-1992, 162
  See also **Ramadan**

Fast, Feast of Breaking the (Eid il-Fitr or Kafr el-Elow)
  Location: Egypt
  Ethnic or religious group: Muslim
  Date: First day of Shawwal, the Islamic tenth month;
    ends month-long fast during Ramadan, the ninth month

  FolkWrldHol-1992, 173
  See also **Ramadan**

Fast, Feast of Breaking the
  Location: Western Guinea
  Ethnic or religious group: Muslim
  Date: First day of Shawwal, the tenth Islamic month;
    ends month-long fast during Ramadan, the ninth month

  HolFestCelWrld-1994, 150
  See also **Ramadan**

Fast, Feast of Breaking the
  Location: India
  Ethnic or religious group: Muslim
  Date: First day of Shawwal, the tenth Islamic month;
    ends month-long fast during Ramadan, the ninth month

  RelHolCal-1993, 85
  See also **Ramadan**

Fast, Feast of Breaking the (Lebaran or Hari Raya or Pasa or Puasa)
  Location: Indonesia
  Ethnic or religious group: Muslim
  Date: First day of Shawwal, the tenth Islamic month;
    ends month-long fast during Ramadan, the ninth month

  FolkWrldHol-1992, 163, 173
  HolFestCelWrld-1994, 150
  See also **Ramadan**

Fast, Feast of Breaking the (Eed-al-Fittur)
  Location: Iraq
  Ethnic or religious group: Muslim
  Date: First day of Shawwal, the tenth Islamic month;
    ends month-long fast during Ramadan, the ninth month

  FolkWrldHol-1992, 173
  See also **Ramadan**

Fast, Feast of Breaking the (Id-el-Fitr or al-zid al-Saghir)
  Location: Jordan
  Ethnic or religious group: Muslim
  Date: First day of Shawwal, the tenth Islamic month;
    ends month-long fast during Ramadan, the ninth month

  FolkWrldHol-1992, 166, 174
  See also **Ramadan**

Fast, Feast of Breaking the (Eid al Fitr)
  Location: Libya
  Ethnic or religious group: Muslim
  Date: First day of Shawwal, the tenth Islamic month;
    ends month-long fast during Ramadan, the ninth month

  FolkWrldHol-1992, 174
  See also **Ramadan**

Fast, Feast of Breaking the (Hari Raya)
  Location: Malaya
  Ethnic or religious group: Muslim
  Date: First day of Shawwal, the tenth Islamic month;
    ends month-long fast during Ramadan, the ninth month

  HolFestCelWrld-1994, 150
  See also **Ramadan**

Fast, Feast of Breaking the (Lebaran or Hari Raya)
  Location: Malaysia
  Ethnic or religious group: Muslim
  Date: First day of Shawwal, the tenth Islamic month;
    ends month-long fast during Ramadan, the ninth month

  HolFestCelWrld-1994, 150
  See also **Ramadan**

Fast, Feast of Breaking the (Iid el Sageer)
  Location: Morocco: Marrakech
  Ethnic or religious group: Muslim
  Date: First day of Shawwal, the tenth Islamic month;
    ends month-long fast during Ramadan, the ninth month

  FolkWrldHol-1992, 167
  See also **Ramadan**

Fast, Feast of Breaking the
  Location: Morocco: Salé
  Ethnic or religious group: Muslim
  Date: First day of Shawwal, the tenth Islamic month;
    ends month-long fast during Ramadan, the ninth month

  FolkWrldHol-1992, 174
  See also **Ramadan**

Fast, Feast of Breaking the (Salla)
Location: Niger and Nigeria
Ethnic or religious group: Hausa Muslim people
Date: First day of Shawwal, the tenth Islamic month;
　ends month-long fast during Ramadan, the ninth month

FolkWrldHol-1992, 173
See also **Ramadan**

Fast, Feast of Breaking the (Id-ul-Fitr or Eid)
Location: Pakistan
Ethnic or religious group: Muslim
Date: First day of Shawwal, the tenth Islamic month;
　ends month-long fast during Ramadan, the ninth month

BkHolWrld-1986, June 27
FolkWrldHol-1992, 174
HolFestCelWrld-1994, 150
RelHolCal-1993, 85
See also **Ramadan**

Fast, Feast of Breaking the (Hari-Raya Poasa)
Location: Philippines
Ethnic or religious group: Muslim
Date: First day of Shawwal, the tenth Islamic month;
　ends month-long fast during Ramadan, the ninth month

FolkWrldHol-1992, 175
See also **Ramadan**

Fast, Feast of Breaking the (Korité Feast)
Location: Senegal
Ethnic or religious group: Muslim
Date: First day of Shawwal, the tenth Islamic month;
　ends month-long fast during Ramadan, the ninth month

FolkWrldHol-1992, 169
See also **Ramadan**

Fast, Feast of Breaking the (Lebaran)
Location: South Africa: Cape Malay
Ethnic or religious group: Muslim
Date: First day of Shawwal, the tenth Islamic month;
　ends month-long fast during Ramadan, the ninth month

FolkWrldHol-1992, 175
See also **Ramadan**

Fast, Feast of Breaking the (Eid Saghir)
Location: Sudan
Ethnic or religious group: Muslim
Date: First day of Shawwal, the tenth Islamic month;
　ends month-long fast during Ramadan, the ninth month

BkHolWrld-1986, June 27
FolkWrldHol-1992, 175
See also **Ramadan**

Fast, Feast of Breaking the (Urou Raja Puasa or Idulfitri)
Location: Sumatra
Ethnic or religious group: Muslim
Date: First day of Shawwal, the tenth Islamic month;
　ends month-long fast during Ramadan, the ninth month

FolkWrldHol-1992, 164
See also **Ramadan**

Fast, Feast of Breaking the (Idul Fitre)
Location: Surinam
Ethnic or religious group: Muslim
Date: First day of Shawwal, the tenth Islamic month;
　ends month-long fast during Ramadan, the ninth month

FolkWrldHol-1992, 175
See also **Ramadan**

Fast, Feast of Breaking the (Hari Raya Puasa)
Location: Thailand
Ethnic or religious group: Muslim
Date: First day of Shawwal, the tenth Islamic month;
　ends month-long fast during Ramadan, the ninth month

FolkWrldHol-1992, 170, 176
HolFestCelWrld-1994, 150
See also **Ramadan**

Fast, Feast of Breaking the (Seker Bayram, Sugar Feast)
Location: Turkey
Ethnic or religious group: Muslim
Date: Three-day festival including first day of Shawwal,
　the tenth Islamic month; ends month-long fast during
　Ramadan, the ninth month

AnnivHol-1983, 174
BkFest-1937, 238
BkHolWrld-1986, June 27
FolkWrldHol-1992, 170, 176
HolFestCelWrld-1994, 150
See also **Ramadan**

Fast, Feast of Breaking the (Salla or 'Id-al-Fitr)
Location: West Africa
Ethnic or religious group: Muslim
Date: First day of Shawwal, the tenth Islamic month;
　ends month-long fast during Ramadan, the ninth month

FolkWrldHol-1992, 176
HolFestCelWrld-1994, 150
See also **Ramadan**

Fast and Prayer Day
Location: Liberia
Date: April 9

AnnivHol-1983, 49

Fast Day
Location: New Hampshire
Established: 1679
Date: Fourth Monday in April

AnnivHol-1983, 57
Chases-1993, 181
DictDays-1988, 39
HolFestCelWrld-1994, 104

Fastelavn or Fastelavan
See **Mardi Gras (Denmark) and (Norway)**

Fastens Tuesday or Fastens-een
See **Mardi Gras (Scotland and northern England)**

Fastern's E'en
See **Mardi Gras (Scotland)**

Fast Evening
See **Mardi Gras**

Fastgong, Fastingong Eve, or Fastingong Tuesday
See **Mardi Gras**

Fastlagen
See **Lent (Sweden)**

Fastlagsafton
See **Mardi Gras (Sweden)**

Fastnacht
See **Mardi Gras (Switzerland)**

Fastnacht and Rosemontag, Rose Monday
See **Mardi Gras (Germany)**

Fastnachtsbär, Fastnacht Bear or Shrovetide Bear
See **Mardi Gras (Bohemia), (Germany), and (Moravia)**

Fastnachtsschmaus
See **Waygoose Feast (printers in England, Germany, and the United States)**

Father of Texas Day
Named for: Stephen Fuller Austin (1793-1836)
Location: Austin, Texas
Date: November 3

AnnivHol-1983, 141
Chases-1993, 430

Father's Day
Location: Canada
Date: Third Sunday in June

BkHolWrld-1986, June 2

Father's Day (Gokarna Aunsi)
Location: Nepal
Date: August-September, last day of waning half of Hindu month of Bhadrapada

FolkWrldHol-1992, 436

Father's Day
Location: United States
Established: 1910
Date: Third Sunday in June

AmerBkDays-1978, 574
AnnivHol-1983, 82
BkHolWrld-1986, June 21
Chases-1993, 257
DaysCustFaith-1957, 158
DictDays-1988, 39
HolFestCelWrld-1994, 105

Father's Day (Ochichi, or Očevi)
Location: Yugoslavia
Date: Third Sunday in December

BkFest-1937, 344
FolkWrldHol-1992, 594
HolFestCelWrld-1994, 59

Fat Tuesday
See **Mardi Gras**

Faunalia
Named for: Faunus, woodland deity
Location: Ancient Rome
Date: February 13 and December 15

DictFolkMyth-1984, 372

Fawkes Day, Guy
Named for: Guy Fawkes (1750-1606), a participant in the November 5, 1605, Gunpowder plot to blow up Parliament
Location: England
Established: January 1606
Date: November 5

AnnivHol-1983, 143
BkDays-1864, ii. 546
BkFest-1937, 61
BkFestHolWrld-1970, 120
BkHolWrld-1986, November 5
Chases-1993, 432
DaysCustFaith-1957, 284

Fawkes Day, Guy *(cont.)*
DictDays-1988, 51, 90, 96
FestSaintDays-1915, 199
FolkAmerHol-1987, 317
FolkWrldHol-1992, 518, 551
HolFestCelWrld-1994, 128

Fawkes Day, Guy
Named for: Guy Fawkes (1750-1606), a participant in the
November 5, 1605, Gunpowder plot to blow up Parliament
Location: Formerly in Boston and Newburyport, Massa-
chusetts; New Castle and Portsmouth, New Hampshire;
and Charleston, South Carolina
Date: November 5

FolkAmerHol-1987, 317

Fawkes Day, Guy
Named for: Guy Fawkes (1750-1606), a participant in the
November 5, 1605, Gunpowder plot to blow up Parliament
Location: New Zealand: Christchurch and Wellington
Date: November 5

FolkWrldHol-1992, 551

Febrero, Fiesta de
See **Mardi Gras (Mexico: Tzintzuntzan)**

Feis Ceoil
Location: Ireland: Dublin, County Dublin
Established: 1897
Date: Week of second Monday in May

AnnivHol-1983, 67

Feralia
Location: Ancient Rome
Date: February 21

DictFolkMyth-1984, 673
FestSaintDays-1915, 191

Festa del Grillo
See **Ascension Day (Italy: Florence, Tuscany)**

Festa Season
Location: Gozo and Malta
Date: May to October, peaking in July

FolkWrldHol-1992, 354

Festidanza
Location: Peru: Arequipa
Established: 1971
Date: August

IntlThFolk-1979, 288

Festival d'Automne
See **Autumn Festival, Paris (France: Paris)**

Festival-Institute at Round Top
Location: Round Top, Texas
Established: 1971
Date: Late May to mid-July

GdUSFest-1984, 185
MusFestAmer-1990, 139

Festival Internacional de Ballet de La Habana
See **Ballet, International Festival of (Cuba: Havana)**

**Festival International d'Art Lyrique et de Musique
d'Aix-en-Provence**
See **Opera and Music, Aix-en-Provence International
Festival of**

Festspillene i Bergen
See **Bergen International Festival (Norway: Bergen)**

Fête de Cuisinieres
See **Cooks' Festival (Roman Catholic people in
Pointe-a-Pitre, Guadeloupe)**

Fête de la Dynastie
See **Dynasty Day (Belgium)**

Fête des Marins, Sailors' Festival
See **Pentecost (France)**

La Fête des Saintes Maries
See **Holy Maries, Feast of (Romanies and others'
pilgrimage to Les Saintes-Maries-de-la-Mer, Provence,
France)**

Fête Dieu
See **Corpus Christi (France)**

Fête Nationale (France)
See **Bastille Day**

Fête Nationale
Location: Monaco
Date: November 19

Chases-1993, 446
NatlHolWrld-1968, 208

Fetten Donneschdeg
See **Mardi Gras (Luxembourg)**

Ffair Ffyliaid
See **Fool's Fair (Wales: Llanerfyl)**

Fiddler's and Bluegrass Festival, Old Time
Location: Union Grove, North Carolina
Established: 1970
Date: Three days over Memorial Day weekend, last weekend in May

HolFestCelWrld-1994, 235
MusFestAmer-1990, 246

Fiddlers' Contest, National Old-Time
Location: Weiser, Idaho
Established: 1914; revived 1953
Date: Third full week in June

Chases-1993, 258
GdUSFest-1984, 45
HolFestCelWrld-1994, 235
MusFestAmer-1990, 241

Fiddler's Contest and Festival, Old Time
Location: Payson, Arizona
Established: 1970
Date: Two days over last weekend in September

Chases-1993, 386
MusFestAmer-1990, 238

Fiddler's Convention, Old
Location: Galax, Virginia
Established: 1935
Date: Four days during second week in August

Chases-1993, 325
HolFestCelWrld-1994, 234
MusFestAmer-1990, 252

Fiddlers Jamboree and Crafts Festival, Old Time
Location: Smithville, Tennessee
Date: Weekend nearest July 4

Chases-1993, 274
GdUSFest-1984, 179

Fiddling Contest, Maritime Old Time
Location: Canada: Dartmouth, Nova Scotia
Established: 1952
Date: Two days in July

GdWrldFest-1985, 45

Fields, Blessing the
See **Rogation Days (Austria); St. Mark, Feast of (Austria)**

Fields, Going to the (Veldgang)
Location: Netherlands: Mekkelhorst, Overijssel

Date: Monday preceding Ascension Thursday

FestWestEur-1958, 132

Fifteenth of Av (Hamishah Asar be-Av)
Ethnic or religious group: Jewish
Date: July-August, 15th day of Jewish month of Av

HolFestCelWrld-1994, 105

Fifth Month Festival (Gogatsu Matsuri)
Location: Okinawa
Date: 15th day of fifth lunar month

FolkWrldHol-1992, 317

Fifth of November
See **Guy Fawkes Day**

Fighter's or Warrior's Day
Location: Yugoslavia
Date: July 5

AnnivHol-1983, 90

Fig Pudding Day
See **Palm Sunday**

Fig Sunday
See **Palm Sunday**

Fiji Day
Named for: October 10, 1970, establishment of British Commonwealth status
Location: Fiji
Date: On or near October 10

AnnivHol-1983, 130
Chases-1993, 405

Filipina, Fiesta
Location: Hawaii
Date: May 2-June 27

AmerBkDays-1978, 549

Film and Song Festival, International Trade Fair
Location: Greece: Thessaloniki
Established: 1935
Date: September-October

GdWrldFest-1985, 103

Film Festival, Cannes
Location: France: Cannes
Established: 1947
Date: May

HolFestCelWrld-1994, 50

Film Festival, International
Location: Telluride, Colorado
Established: 1974
Date: First weekend in September, including Labor Day

Chases-1993, 354
GdUSFest-1984, 28
HolFestCelWrld-1994, 334

Fire Festival (Holi)
Named for: Celebrates Krishna and, in some places,
 birthday of Gauranga (Chaitanya Mahaprabhu,
 1485-1533)
Ethnic or religious group: Hindu
Date: February-March, begins 14th day of Hindu month
 of Phalguna or Dol; length varies

AmerBkDays-1978, 315
AnnivHol-1983, 178
BkDays-1864, i.462
BkFest-1937, 163
BkFestHolWrld-1970, 8
BkHolWrld-1986, March 27
Chases-1993, 123
DictFolkMyth-1984, 500, 591, 941
FolkWrldHol-1992, 144, 145
HolFestCelWrld-1994, 87, 140
RelHolCal-1993, 57, 72, 83

Fire Festival (Holi and Dol-Jatra, Swing Festival)
Location: Bangladesh
Date: February-March, begins 14th day of Hindu month
 of Phalguna or Dol; length varies

FolkWrldHol-1992, 145
HolFestCelWrld-1994, 140

Fire Festival (Holi)
Location: India
Date: February-March, begins 14th day of Hindu month
 of Phalguna; length varies

AnnivHol-1983, 178
BkFest-1937, 163
BkFestHolWrld-1970, 8
BkHolWrld-1986, March 27
DictFolkMyth-1984, 500, 941
FolkWrldHol-1992, 144, 145
HolFestCelWrld-1994, 87, 140, 251
RelHolCal-1993, 72, 83

Fire Festival (Holi)
Location: India: Barsnar
Date: February-March, begins 14th day of Hindu month
 of Phalguna or Dol; length varies

HolFestCelWrld-1994, 140

Fire Festival (Dol Purnima)
Named for: Celebrates Krishna and birthday of Gauranga
 (Chaitanya Mahaprabhu, 1485-1533)
Location: India: Bengal
Date: February-March, begins 14th day of Hindu month
 of Phalguna or Dol; length varies

BkFest-1937, 163
HolFestCelWrld-1994, 87
RelHolCal-1993, 72

Fire Festival (Holi)
Location: India: Mathura
Date: February-March, begins 14th day of Hindu month
 of Phalguna and lasts 16 days

HolFestCelWrld-1994, 140

Fire Festival (Holi)
Location: India: Nandgaon
Date: February-March, begins 14th day of Hindu month
 of Phalguna and lasts 16 days

HolFestCelWrld-1994, 140

Fire Festival (Holi)
Location: India
Ethnic or religious group: North Dravidian people
Date: February-March, begins 14th day of Hindu month
 of Phalguna or Dol; length varies

DictFolkMyth-1984, 941

Fire Festival
Location: Japan: Kumano Nachi Shrine, Nachi No
 Falls, Wakayama
Date: July 13

IntlThFolk-1979, 257

Fire Festival (Holi)
Location: Mauritius
Date: February-March, begins 14th day of Hindu month
 of Phalguna or Dol; length varies

FolkWrldHol-1992, 146

Fire Festival (Holi or Rung Khelna, Playing with Color)
Location: Nepal
Date: February-March, begins 14th day of Hindu month
 of Phalguna or Dol; length varies

FolkWrldHol-1992, 146
HolFestCelWrld-1994, 140

Fire Festival (Holi)
Location: Pakistan
Date: February-March, begins 14th day of Hindu month
 of Phalguna or Dol; length varies

FolkWrldHol-1992, 146

Fire Festival (Holi Phagwa)
  Location: Surinam
  Date: February-March, begins 14th day of Hindu month
    of Phalguna or Dol; length varies

  FolkWrldHol-1992, 146
  HolFestCelWrld-1994, 140, 141

Fire Festival (Phagwa)
  Location: Trinidad and Tobago
  Ethnic or religious group: Hindu
  Date: Full moon day in March

  HolFestCelWrld-1994, 251

Fire Prevention Week
  Location: United States
  Established: In commemoration of the Chicago fire on
    October 8, 1871
  Date: Week including October 8

  AnnivHol-1983, 130
  Chases-1993, 397

Fireworks Day
  See **Fawkes Day, Guy**

First-Born, Fast of the
  Ethnic or religious group: Jewish
  Date: March-April, 14th of Jewish month of Nisan, the
    day before Passover

  HolFestCelWrld-1994, 106
  RelHolCal-1993, 76

First-Foot Day
  See **New Year's Day (England; parts of United States)**

First Fruits Festival (Celtic)
  See **Lúgnasad (Celtic people on hilltops in Ireland), (Celtic
    people in Teltown on River Boyne in Meath, Ireland), and
    (Gardnerian Witches and other Neo-pagans in the
    United States)**

First Fruits Festival
  Location: South Africa
  Ethnic or religious group: Zulu people

  FolkWrldHol-1992, 466

First Fruits Festival (Swaziland)
  See **New Year (Newala Ceremonies) (Swaziland:
    Lozithehlezi to Gunundvwini, and Lobamba)**

First Fruits Festival
  Location: Tanzania: Zinza
  Date: March

  FolkWrldHol-1992, 469

First Fruits of the Alps Sunday (Les Prémices des Alpes)
  Location: Switzerland: Vissoie, Val d'Anniviers, Valais
  Date: Fourth Sunday in August

  BkFestHolWrld-1970, 105
  FestWestEur-1958, 236

First Night
  See **New Year's Eve (Huntington, West Virginia; Boston,
    Massachusetts; Hartford, Connecticut; and Waynesboro,
    Virginia)**

**First of March (Drymiais in Macedonia; Martenitza in
Bulgaria, Albania, Greece, and Cyprus)**
  Location: Albania, Bulgaria, Cyprus, Greece,
    and Macedonia
  Ethnic or religious group: Macedonian- and
    Bulgarian-Canadians
  Date: March 1

  FolkWrldHol-1992, 151
  HolFestCelWrld-1994, 89, 196

First of March (Marzas)
  Location: Spain
  Date: Last night of February and first of March

  DictFolkMyth-1984, 1063

First of March (Chalanda Marz)
  Location: Switzerland: Engadine, Grisons
  Date: March 1

  AnnivHol-1983, 32
  Chases-1993, 116
  FestWestEur-1958, 226

First of May
  See **May Day, Premier Mai (France)**

First of May Is Our Day
  Location: Yugoslavia: Belgrade, Serbia
  Date: May 1-2

  IntlThFolk-1979, 383

First Writing of the Year (Kakizome)
  Location: Japan
  Date: January 2, second day of the New Year

  BkHolWrld-1986, January 2
  Chases-1993, 54

Fish Carnival (Groppenfasnacht)
  Location: Switzerland: Ermatingen
  Date: Third Sunday before Easter, every three years
    (1988, 1991 . . .)

  HolFestCelWrld-1994, 127

Fisherman's Day (Iceland)
See **Seaman's Day (Iceland)**

Fisherman's Day
Location: Zaire
Date: June 24

AnnivHol-1983, 83

Fish Fry, World's Biggest
Location: Paris, Tennessee
Established: 1954
Date: Usually last full week in April

GdUSFest-1984, 178
HolFestCelWrld-1994, 371

Fishing Rodeo, Deep Sea
Location: Gulfport, Mississippi
Established: 1949
Date: July 4th weekend

HolFestCelWrld-1994, 81

Fjortende Februar
See **Fourteenth of February (Denmark)**

Flag Day
Named for: July 4, 1959, addition to the flag of the
49th star
Location: Alaska
Date: July 4

AnnivHol-1983, 88

Flag Day
Named for: Commemorates April 17, 1900, cession to the
United States
Location: American Samoa: Pago Pago
Date: April 17

AnnivHol-1983, 52
Chases-1993, 169
GdUSFest-1984, 218

Flag Day
Named for: Commemorates King Valdemar II (1170-1241)
Location: Denmark
Date: June 15

HolFestCelWrld-1994, 107

Flag Day
Location: Hawaii
Date: July 4

AnnivHol-1983, 89

Flag Day
Location: Liberia
Date: August 24

AnnivHol-1983, 109

Flag Day
Location: Panama
Date: November 4

AnnivHol-1983, 142
Chases-1993, 431

Flag Day (Paraguay)
See **Independence and Flag Day (Paraguay)**

Flag Day (Sweden)
See **Constitution and Flag Day (Sweden)**

Flag Day
Location: United States
Established: 1949
Date: June 14

AmerBkDays-1978, 551
AnnivHol-1983, 79
BkHolWrld-1986, June 14
Chases-1993, 248
DictDays-1988, 42
HolFestCelWrld-1994, 107

Flag Day, National
Location: Swaziland
Date: April 25

AnnivHol-1983, 56

Flag Day of the Army
Location: Finland
Date: May 19

AnnivHol-1983, 67

Flanders, Festival of (Festival van Vlaanderen)
Location: Belgium: Antwerp, Bruges, Brussels, Ghent,
Kortrijk, Leuven, Limburg, and Mechelen
Established: 1958-59
Date: April to October

GdWrldFest-1985, 18
IntlThFolk-1979, 43
MusFestEurBrit-1980, 30

Fleadh Nua
Location: Ireland: Ennis, County Clare
Date: May-June

IntlThFolk-1979, 234

Flemington Fair
   Location: Flemington, New Jersey
   Established: 1856
   Date: One week from late August through Labor Day

   Chases-1993, 348
   GdUSFest-1984, 117
   HolFestCelWrld-1994, 108

Flitting Day
   Location: Scotland
   Date: May 25

   BkDays-1864, i. 679
   DictDays-1988, 42
   FolkWrldHol-1992, 265
   HolFestCelWrld-1994, 214

Floating Festival
   Named for: Commemorates birth of Tirumala Nayak
      (fl. 17th century)
   Location: India: from the Meenakshi Temple in Madurai,
      Tamil Nadu, to Marriamman Teppakulam, Sarovar
   Ethnic or religious group: Hindu
   Date: January-February, full moon day of Hindu month
      of Magha

   Chases-1993, 88
   HolFestCelWrld-1994, 108
   RelHolCal-1993, 95
   See also **Marriage of Meenakshi and Shiva, Festival of**

Floating Lantern Ceremony, Toro Nagashi
   See **Dead, Festival of the (Buddhist people in Hawaii)**

Floating Leaf Cups
   See **Lights, Festival of (Loy Krathong)**

Flood Festival
   See **Kataklysmos Festival (Cyprus: Larnaca, Limassol,
      Paphos, and other towns)**

Floral Carnival, National
   Location: Hungary: Debrecen
   Established: 1968
   Date: August 20, St. Stephen's Day and Constitution Day

   GdWrldFest-1985, 108

Floralia
   Named for: Flora, goddess of flowers
   Location: Ancient Rome
   Established: 238 B.C.
   Date: April 28-May 3

   AmerBkDays-1978, 314, 407

Flores de Mayo
   Location: El Salvador: San Vicente
   Date: Month of May

   FolkWrldHol-1992, 258

Flores de Mayo
   Location: Philippines
   Date: Month of May

   FolkWrldHol-1992, 306
   HolFestCelWrld-1994, 108

Floriade
   Location: Netherlands: Amsterdam
   Date: Once every ten years in April-October

   HolFestCelWrld-1994, 108

Florida Seminole Green Corn Dance
   See **Dance, Green Corn**

Flower Festival (Ghent Floralies)
   Location: Belgium: Ghent
   Established: 1809
   Date: April or May; every five years

   HolFestCelWrld-1994, 118

Flower Festival, Bikfaya
   Location: Lebanon: Bikfaya
   Established: 1945
   Date: One day in mid-August

   IntlThFolk-1979, 263

Flower Festival, Broom (Genzefest)
   Location: Luxembourg: Wiltz
   Date: May-June, Whit Monday, Monday after Pentecost

   GdWrldFest-1985, 130

Flower Festival, Hana Matsuri
   See **Buddha's Birthday, Enlightenment, and Salvation
      (Japan)**

Flowers, Battle of
   See **Valencia Fair Days (Spain: Valencia)**

Flowers, Day of
   See **Anthesteria (Greece)**

Flower Show, Chelsea
   Location: England: London
   Established: 1888
   Date: Last full week in May

   Chases-1993, 221
   GdWrldFest-1985, 95

Flower Show, Keukenhof
  Location: Netherlands: Lisse, South Holland
  Established: 1949
  Date: March-May

  GdWrldFest-1985, 142
  HolFestCelWrld-1994, 169

Flower Sunday or Flowers, Day of
  See **Palm Sunday**

Fluitjes Maken
  See **Whistle Making (Netherlands: Ootmarsum, Overijssel)**

Flutes, Day of the (Pffiferdaj)
  Location: France: Ribeauvillé
  Date: First Sunday in September

  BkHolWrld-1986, September 9, 180
  HolFestCelWrld-1994, 251

Flyttedag
  See **Moving Day (Norway: Bergen and other large towns)**

Focus '78, '80, etc.
  See **Arts, Festival of the (Australia: Adelaide, South Australia)**

Foire de la Saint Martin
  See **Martinmas (France)**

Folk Art, National Festival of
  Location: Bulgaria: Koprivshtitsa
  Established: 1961
  Date: Every five years during the summer

  IntlThFolk-1979, 53

Folk-Art Festival
  Location: Bulgaria: Bourgas
  Established: 1965
  Date: Late summer

  IntlThFolk-1979, 52

Folk Art Festival: Pampaphia
  Location: Cyprus: Paphos
  Established: 1970
  Date: Four days in early August

  IntlThFolk-1979, 85

Folk Arts Festival
  Location: Canada: St. Catharines, Ontario
  Date: May-June

  IntlThFolk-1979, 73

Folk Dance, International Festival of
  Location: Hungary: Szeged
  Date: Odd-numbered years in July

  IntlThFolk-1979, 200

Folk Dances, Greek
  Location: Greece: Philopappou Hill, Athens
  Established: 1965
  Date: May-September

  IntlThFolk-1979, 193

Folk Dance and Music, International Festival of (Rattviksdansen)
  Location: Sweden: Rattvik
  Established: 1974
  Date: One week in July-August

  IntlThFolk-1979, 346

Folk Dance and Music Festival, Silifke
  Location: Turkey: Silifke
  Date: May

  IntlThFolk-1979, 372

Folk Dance Festival, Cork International Choral and
  Location: Ireland: Cork, County Cork
  Date: April

  IntlThFolk-1979, 232

Folk-Dance Festival, International (International Volksdansfestival)
  Location: Belgium: Schoten
  Established: 1959
  Date: One week beginning first weekend after first Sunday in July

  IntlThFolk-1979, 49

Folk-Dance Festival, Republic Day
  Location: India: New Delhi
  Established: 1953
  Date: January 27-28

  IntlThFolk-1979, 205

Folk Dance Festival of Ireland, International
  Location: Ireland: Cobh, County Cork
  Date: One week beginning first Sunday in July

  IntlThFolk-1979, 231

Folk Dance Theatre of Rhodes
  Location: Greece: Rhodes
  Established: 1971
  Date: June-October

  IntlThFolk-1979, 195

Folk Dancing at Corfu, Greek
Location: Greece: Kerkyra, Corfu
Date: Mid-May to September

IntlThFolk-1979, 195

Folk Drama, Bumba-meu-Boi
See **Juninas, Festas (Brazil)**

Folk Fair, Holiday
Location: Milwaukee, Wisconsin
Established: 1944
Date: Three days in November

Chases-1993, 445
GdUSFest-1984, 212

Folk Festival
Location: Peru: Arequipa
Date: August

GdWrldFest-1985, 149

Folk Festival, Arkansas
Location: Mountain View, Arkansas
Established: 1962
Date: Third weekend in April

Chases-1993, 168
GdUSFest-1984, 14

Folk Festival, Florida
Location: White Springs, Florida
Established: 1953
Date: Two to three days in late May

Chases-1993, 222
MusFestAmer-1990, 220

Folk Festival, Goschenhoppen Historians'
Location: Goschenhoppen Park, East Greenville,
Pennsylvania
Ethnic or religious group: Pennsylvania Dutch people
Established: 1967
Date: Second Friday and Saturday in August

HolFestCelWrld-1994, 122

Folk Festival, Letterkenny International
Location: Ireland: Letterkenny, County Donegal
Established: 1969
Date: Five days in late August

IntlThFolk-1979, 235

Folk Festival, Newcastle
Location: Australia: Newcastle, New South Wales

Established: 1972
Date: Mid-June

IntlThFolk-1979, 10

Folk Festival, Newcastle
Location: England: Newcastle upon Tyne, Northumberland
Date: June-July

IntlThFolk-1979, 170

Folk Festival, New England
Location: Natick, Massachusetts
Established: 1944
Date: Third weekend in April

MusFestAmer-1990, 224

Folk Festival, Numeralla
Location: Australia: Numeralla, New South Wales
Established: 1975
Date: End of January, including Australia Day, January 26

IntlThFolk-1979, 10

Folk Festival, Ozark
Location: Eureka Springs, Arkansas
Established: 1948
Date: Two to three days in early November

HolFestCelWrld-1994, 242
MusFestAmer-1990, 218

Folk Festival, Pennsylvania Dutch
Location: Kutztown, Pennsylvania
Ethnic or religious group: Pennsylvania Dutch, Amish,
Dunkard, and Mennonite peoples
Established: 1950
Date: Nine days in July, including July 4

AmerBkDays-1978, 600
AnnivHol-1983, 178
Chases-1993, 266
GdUSFest-1984, 158
HolFestCelWrld-1994, 174

Folk Festival, Philadelphia
Location: Philadelphia/Schwenksville, Pennsylvania
Established: 1962
Date: Three days over last weekend in August

MusFestAmer-1990, 227

Folk Festival, Pittsburgh
Location: David L. Lawrence Convention Center,
Pittsburgh, Pennsylvania
Established: 1950s
Date: First weekend in June

GdUSFest-1984, 163

Folk Festival, Top Half
  Location: Australia: location varies—Alice Springs,
    Darwin, or Mount Isa, Northern Territory
  Date: Weekend in June, coincides with Queen Elizabeth
    II's Birthday

  IntlThFolk-1979, 16

Folk Festival, Wagga
  Location: Australia: Wagga Wagga, New South Wales
  Established: 1973
  Date: Three days in October

  IntlThFolk-1979, 14

Folk Festival, Winnipeg
  Location: Canada: Winnipeg, Manitoba
  Established: 1974
  Date: Three or four days during second weekend in July

  GdWrldFest-1985, 36
  IntlThFolk-1979, 65
  MusFestAmer-1990, 234

Folk Festival Day (Mnarja) (Malta: Buskett Gardens)
  See **Harvest Festival (Imnarja or Mnarja) (Malta:**
    Buskett Gardens)

Folklife, Festival of American
  Location: Washington, D.C.
  Established: 1967
  Date: Two weeks in late June and early July

  HolFestCelWrld-1994, 8
  MusFestAmer-1990, 219

Folklife Festival, Northwest
  Location: Seattle, Washington
  Established: 1972
  Date: Four days over Memorial Day weekend, last weekend
    in May

  Chases-1993, 223
  HolFestCelWrld-1994, 229
  MusFestAmer-1990, 230

Folklife Festival, Texas
  Location: HemisFair grounds of the Institute of Texan
    Cultures, San Antonio, Texas
  Established: 1972
  Date: Four days during first week in August

  Chases-1993, 317
  GdUSFest-1984, 187
  MusFestAmer-1990, 229

Folklorama
  Location: Canada: Winnipeg, Manitoba
  Date: One week in mid-August

  Chases-1993, 312
  GdWrldFest-1985, 37
  IntlThFolk-1979, 63

**Folklore, Central American Congress of (Congreso
Centroamericano de Folclorologia)**
  Location: Costa Rica: Nicoya
  Date: One week in August

  IntlThFolk-1979, 80

Folklore, Danube Festival of
  Location: Hungary: Kalocsa, Baja, and Szekszard
  Date: Every three years in July

  IntlThFolk-1979, 200

Folklore, Festival of
  Location: Morocco: grounds of Ksar El Badi Palace,
    Marrakesh
  Date: Ten days in May

  GdWrldFest-1985, 138
  IntlThFolk-1979, 281

Folklore, Gouveia International Festival of
  Location: Portugal: Gouveia, Viseu
  Established: 1975
  Date: August

  IntlThFolk-1979, 307

Folklore, National Festival of
  Location: Uruguay: Durazno
  Established: 1970
  Date: Three days in January

  GdWrldFest-1985, 183
  IntlThFolk-1979, 375

**Folklore, Prime Minister's Best Village Trophy Competition
and Festival of**
  Location: Trinidad and Tobago: Port of Spain
  Established: 1963
  Date: Three weeks beginning first Saturday in November

  IntlThFolk-1979, 357

Folklore, Sydney Festival of
  Location: Australia: Sydney, New South Wales
  Established: 1978
  Date: Two weeks in January, coincides with Festival of Sydney

  IntlThFolk-1979, 13

Folklore, World Festival of
  Location: France: Gannat, Allier
  Established: 1974
  Date: One week in July

  IntlThFolk-1979, 106

Folklore and Amateur Work in Culture and Arts
  Location: Yugoslavia: Bihac, Bosnia and Herzegovina
  Date: Autumn

  IntlThFolk-1979, 384

Folklore Festival, Arad
  Location: Romania: Moneasa, Arad
  Date: August 24

  IntlThFolk-1979, 326

Folklore Festival, Billingham International
  Location: England: Billingham, Cleveland
  Established: 1965
  Date: Eight days in August

  IntlThFolk-1979, 155

Folklore Festival, Briteiros
  Location: Portugal: Briteiros, Braga
  Established: 1977
  Date: August

  IntlThFolk-1979, 303

Folklore Festival, Canajacua
  Location: Panama: Macaracas
  Ethnic or religious group: Christian and secular
  Established: 1972
  Date: Four days including Epiphany, January 6

  GdWrldFest-1985, 146

Folklore Festival, "Hercules"
  Location: Romania: Baile Herculane, Caras Severin
  Date: First week in August

  IntlThFolk-1979, 317

Folklore Festival, International
  Location: Belgium: Mechelen
  Established: 1973
  Date: Four days in August

  IntlThFolk-1979, 48

Folklore Festival, International
  Location: France: Oloron-Sainte-Marie, Lot-et-Garonne
  Established: 1962

  Date: About one week in August

  IntlThFolk-1979, 115

Folklore Festival, International
  Location: Italy: Agrigento, Sicily
  Established: 1954
  Date: February

  IntlThFolk-1979, 239

Folklore Festival, Maramuresean
  Location: Romania: Sighetu Marmatiei, Maramures
  Date: Last weekend in December

  IntlThFolk-1979, 330

Folklore Festival, National
  Location: Romania: Mamaia, Efore, and Sinala, Constanta
  County and the Black Sea Coast
  Date: Month of August

  GdWrldFest-1985, 157

Folklore Festival, Sao Torcato International
  Location: Portugal: Sao Torcato, Braga
  Established: 1972
  Date: July

  IntlThFolk-1979, 312

Folklore Festival of St. Martha of Portozelo, International
  Location: Portugal: Portozelo, Viana do Castelo
  Established: 1956
  Date: August

  IntlThFolk-1979, 311

Folklore Festival of Straznice
  Location: Czechoslovakia: Straznice, Moravia
  Established: 1940s
  Date: Three days in June

  GdWrldFest-1985, 69
  IntlThFolk-1979, 90

Folklore Festival of the Socialist Republic of Serbia
  Location: Yugoslavia: Leskovac, Serbia
  Date: June

  IntlThFolk-1979, 393

Folklore Groups of Vojvodina, Encounter of Hungarian
  Location: Yugoslavia: location varies within Vojvodina
  Established: 1964
  Date: June

  IntlThFolk-1979, 413

Folklore in Vojvodina, Slovakian
Location: Yugoslavia: Kovacica, Vojvodina
Date: May

IntlThFolk-1979, 391

Folklore Review, International
Location: Yugoslavia: Zagreb, Croatia
Established: 1966
Date: July

GdWrldFest-1985, 187
IntlThFolk-1979, 409

Folkloric Festival of Rouergue, International
Location: France: Rouergue, Aveyron
Established: 1955
Date: One week in August

IntlThFolk-1979, 122

Folk Music Festival Kaustinen
Location: Finland: Kaustinen
Established: 1968
Date: Third week in July

Chases-1993, 296
GdWrldFest-1985, 77
IntlThFolk-1979, 95

Folk Pilgrimage to Our Lady of Nazo
See **Pilgrimage to Our Lady of Nazo (Portugal: Povoa, Braganca)**

Folk Song Festival, Miramichi
Location: Canada: Newcastle, New Brunswick
Established: 1957
Date: Three days in late June

GdWrldFest-1985, 38
IntlThFolk-1979, 65

Folk Songs and Dances, Balkan Festival of
Location: Yugoslavia: Ohrid, Macedonia
Date: July 3-8

IntlThFolk-1979, 397

Fond Pleeaf, Fond Plough, or Fool Plough
See **Plough Monday**

Fontalia (Festival of Fountains)
Location: Ancient Rome
Date: October 13

AmerBkDays-1978, 884

Fooling the April Fish Day
See **April Fools' Day**

Fools, Feast of
Location: Medieval Europe
Date: Between Christmas and January 1

DictFolkMyth-1984, 374, 947
DictMyth-1962, i.555
FestSaintDays-1915, 253, 255

Fools, Festival of
Location: Netherlands: Amsterdam
Established: 1975
Date: Three weeks in June

IntlThFolk-1979, 282

Fool's Fair (Ffair Ffyliaid)
Location: Wales: Llanerfyl
Date: First Tuesday in May

FolkWrldHol-1992, 260

Football Day
See **Mardi Gras (England) and (Scotland)**

Footwashing Day
Location: Kentucky
Ethnic or religious group: Protestant
Date: A Sunday in early summer or Holy Thursday

FolkAmerHol-1987, 221
HolFestCelWrld-1994, 108
RelHolCal-1993, 77

Forefathers' Day
Named for: 1620 landing at Plymouth Rock
Location: Plymouth, Massachusetts
Date: December 21

AmerBkDays-1978, 1121
AnnivHol-1983, 163
Chases-1993, 479
DictDays-1988, 43
HolFestCelWrld-1994, 109

Forgiveness, Feast of
See **St. Francis of Assisi (Arroyo Hondo, New Mexico; southern Colorado)**

Fornacalia (Fornax or Feast of Ovens)
Location: Ancient Rome
Date: One week beginning about February 17; date varied

FestSaintDays-1915, 43

Första Maj
  See **May Day (Sweden)**

Fortune, Festival of, Vičak or Vijag
  See **Ascension Day (Armenia)**

Forum des Arts et de la Musique
  See **Arts and Music, Frejus Forum of (France: Frejus, Var)**

Foster Memorial Day
  Named for: Stephen Foster (1826-1864)
  Location: Stephen Foster Memorial Association and
    musical societies; White Springs, Florida
  Date: January 13

  AnnivHol-1983, 8
  Chases-1993, 63
  HolFestCelWrld-1994, 322

Foundation Day (Australia)
  See **Australia Day**

Foundation Day
  Named for: French settlement in 1555
  Location: Brazil: Rio de Janeiro
  Date: January 20

  AnnivHol-1983, 11

Foundation Day (German Democratic Republic)
  See **Republic Day (German Democratic Republic)**

Foundation Day (Tangun Day)
  Named for: Mythical founding in 2333 B.C.
  Location: Republic of Korea
  Date: October 3

  AnnivHol-1983, 127
  Chases-1993, 398
  HolFestCelWrld-1994, 219

Foundation Day, Japanese National (Kigensetsu)
  Location: Japan
  Established: Observed since 1966 on the anniversary of the
    February 11, 660 B.C., ascension of Emperor Jimmu
    Tenno (fl. seventh century B.C.)
  Date: February 11

  AnnivHol-1983, 22
  BkFest-1937, 196
  Chases-1993, 94
  DictWrldRel-1989, 382

Foundation Day, State
  Location: Western Australia
  Date: June 1

  DictDays-1988, 113

Foundation Days
  Location: Taiwan
  Date: January 1-2

  AnnivHol-1983, 2

Foundation of Panama
  Named for: August 15, 1518, settlement
  Location: Panama: Panama City
  Date: August 15

  AnnivHol-1983, 107
  Chases-1993, 331

Foundation Week Celebrations
  Location: Australia: Parramatta, New South Wales
  Date: Two weeks in October-November

  IntlThFolk-1979, 11

Founder's Day
  Named for: Jan Van Riebeek (1619-1677)
  Location: South Africa
  Date: April 6

  AnnivHol-1983, 48
  Chases-1993, 157
  HolFestCelWrld-1994, 110

Founders Day and Youth Day
  Location: Zaire
  Date: October 14

  AnnivHol-1983, 132

Founding Day
  See **Independence Day (Korea, Democratic People's
    Republic of)**

**Founding of the Church of Jesus Christ of the Latter
Day Saints**
  Ethnic or religious group: Church of Jesus Christ of the
    Latter Day Saints
  Established: April 6, 1830, Fayette, New York
  Date: April 6

  Chases-1993, 157
  DaysCustFaith-1957, 94
  DictWrldRel-1989, 423
  FolkAmerHol-1978, 151
  HolFestCelWrld-1994, 178
  RelHolCal-1993, 77

Founding of the Church of Jesus Christ of the Latter Day Saints
  Location: Jackson County, Missouri
  Ethnic or religious group: Church of Jesus Christ of the Latter Day Saints
  Date: April 6

  FolkAmerHol-1987, 151
  HolFestCelWrld-1994, 178

Founding of the Church of Jesus Christ of the Latter Day Saints
  Ethnic or religious group: Reorganized Church of Jesus Christ of the Latter Day Saints
  Date: April 6

  DictWrldRel-1989, 423
  RelHolCal-1993, 77

Founding of the Republic
  Named for: 1911 revolution that led to forming of the republic
  Location: China
  Date: October 10

  BkFest-1937, 76
  See also **Double Tenth Day**

Four an' Twenty Day
  See **Twelfth Day (Scotland)**

Four Miracles Assembly (Magha Puja)
  Ethnic or religious group: Buddhist
  Date: February-March, full moon day of third lunar month

  BkHolWrld-1986, March 6
  FolkWrldHol-1992, 142
  HolFestCelWrld-1994, 191

Four Miracles Assembly (Magha Puja)
  Location: India
  Ethnic or religious group: Buddhist
  Date: February-March, full moon day of third lunar month

  HolFestCelWrld-1994, 191

Four Miracles Assembly (Makha Bouxa)
  Location: Laos
  Ethnic or religious group: Buddhist
  Date: February-March, full moon day of third lunar month

  FolkWrldHol-1992, 142
  HolFestCelWrld-1994, 191

Four Miracles Assembly (Magha Puja)
  Location: Thailand
  Ethnic or religious group: Buddhist
  Date: February-March, full moon day of third lunar month

  FolkWrldHol-1992, 142
  HolFestCelWrld-1994, 191

Fourteenth Day of Bhadra, Eternal Anniversary of (Anant Chaturdashi)
  Ethnic or religious group: Hindu
  Date: August-September, 14th day of waxing half of Hindu month of Bhadrapada

  BkFest-1937, 160
  RelHolCal-1993, 57

Fourteenth of February (Fjortende Februar)
  Location: Denmark
  Date: February 14

  AnnivHol-1983, 24
  FestWestEur-1958, 22

Fourth of July
  See **Independence Day (United States)**

Fourth of June
  Named for: Birthday of George III (1738-1820)
  Location: England
  Date: On or near June 4

  Chases-1993, 233
  DictDays-1988, 44

Fox, Death of George
  Named for: George Fox (1624-1691), founder of the Religious Society of Friends
  Ethnic or religious group: Quaker (Religious Society of Friends)
  Date: January 13

  RelHolCal-1993, 70

Fox Hill Day
  Location: Bahama Islands: Nassau, New Providence Island
  Established: 19th century; commemorates abolishment of slavery
  Date: Second Tuesday in August

  Chases-1993, 324
  GdWrldFest-1985, 16
  HolFestCelWrld-1994, 110

Franconian Festival Week
  Location: Federal Republic of Germany: Bayreuth, Bavaria
  Date: June

  MusFestWrld-1963, 54

Frankenmuth Bavarian Festival
  Location: Frankenmuth, Michigan
  Ethnic or religious group: German-American
  Date: Second weekend and third week in June

  HolFestCelWrld-1994, 110

Franklin's Birthday, Benjamin
  Named for: Benjamin Franklin (1706-1790)
  Location: Philadelphia, Pennsylvania
  Date: January 17

  AmerBkDays-1978, 85
  AnnivHol-1983, 10
  Chases-1993, 66
  DictDays-1988, 44
  HolFestCelWrld-1994, 29

Fraternal Day
  Location: Alabama
  Date: Second Tuesday in October

  DictDays-1988, 44

Fravashi Festivals
  Location: Armenia
  Date: Saturdays and before major festivals

  DictFolkMyth-1984, 415

Fravashi Festivals
  Ethnic or religious group: Zoroastrian
  Date: 19th of each month and during last ten days of the year

  DictFolkMyth-1984, 415

Freedom, Day of
  Named for: 1863 abolishment of slavery
  Location: Surinam
  Date: July 1

  AnnivHol-1983, 87

Freedom Day
  Named for: Emancipation from slavery under the British in 1837
  Location: Guyana
  Date: August 2

  AnnivHol-1983, 102

Freedom Festival, International
  Location: Canada: Windsor, Ontario, and Detroit, Michigan
  Established: 1959
  Date: Mid-June to July 4

  Chases-1993, 260
  GdWrldFest-1985, 55
  HolFestCelWrld-1994, 49

Free Entertainment in the Parks
  Location: Australia: Melbourne, Victoria
  Established: 1972
  Date: Year-round

  IntlThFolk-1979, 27

Freeing the Insects Festival
  Location: Japan
  Established: Since feudal times
  Date: August-September

  FolkWrldHol-1992, 472
  HolFestCelWrld-1994, 111

Fremantle Week
  Location: Australia: Fremantle, Western Australia
  Established: 1972
  Date: Late October-early November

  IntlThFolk-1979, 28

French Festival (French Day)
  Location: Cape Vincent, New York
  Ethnic or religious group: French-Americans
  Established: 1968
  Date: Saturday before Bastille Day, July 14

  GdUSFest-1984, 123
  HolFestCelWrld-1994, 50
  See also **Night Watch**

French Open Tennis Championships
  Location: France: Auteil
  Established: 1891; open internationally since 1925
  Date: May-June

  HolFestCelWrld-1994, 111

Friday in Lide
  Location: England: Cornwall
  Date: First Friday in March

  DictDays-1988, 45

Frisbee Festival, National
  Location: The Mall near the National Air and Space Museum, Washington, D.C.
  Date: First weekend in September

  HolFestCelWrld-1994, 111

Fritter Thursday
  See **Mardi Gras (England)**

Fron Leichnam
  See **Corpus Christi (Germany)**

Fronleichnamsfest
  See **Corpus Christi (Switzerland)**

Frontier Day (Cheyenne, Wyoming)
  See **Cheyenne Frontier Days**

Frost, or Ice, Saints Day (Eisheiligan)
  Named for: Sts. Boniface (d. May 14, 307), Mammertus
  (461-475; d. May 11), Pancras (d. May 12, 304), and
  Servatus (d. May 13, 384)
  Location: France and Germany
  Ethnic or religious group: Roman Catholic
  Date: May 11-14

  DaysCustFaith-1957, 122
  FolkWrldHol-1992, 295
  HolFestCelWrld-1994, 112

Frost, or Ice, Saints Day
  Named for: Sts. Boniface (d. May 14, 307), Pancras
  (d. May 12, 304), and Ignatius (fl. first century)
  Location: Ellis County, Kansas
  Ethnic or religious group: Roman Catholic German-
  Russians
  Date: May 12-14

  FolkAmerHol-1987, 181

Full Moon of Waso
  See **Buddha's Birthday, Enlightenment, and Salvation**

Furrinalia
  Named for: Roman goddess Furrina or Furina
  Location: Ancient Rome
  Date: July 25

  DictFolkMyth-1984, 428

Furry Day
  Location: England: Helston, Cornwall
  Ethnic or religious group: Celtic origins; Roman
  Catholic
  Established: 492 A.D.
  Date: May 8

  AnnivHol-1983, 63
  BkFest-1937, 58
  BkHolWrld-1986, May 8
  Chases-1993, 200
  DaysCustFaith-1957, 120
  DictDays-1988, 45
  DictFolkMyth-1984, 204
  DictMyth-1962, i.618
  HolFestCelWrld-1994, 112

Fur Trade Days
  Location: Chadron, Nebraska
  Date: July

  HolFestCelWrld-1994, 112

Fyr-Bål Fest
  Location: Ephraim, Wisconsin
  Ethnic or religious group: Norwegian- and Swedish-
  Americans
  Date: Two days on weekend nearest June 24

  AmerBkDays-1978, 584, 587
  See also **Midsummer Day**

Gable Birthday Celebration, Clark
  Named for: Clark Gable (1901-1960)
  Location: Cadiz, Ohio
  Established: 1987
  Date: Saturday nearest February 1

  HolFestCelWrld-1994, 66

Gaelic Mod
  Location: Canada: St. Ann's, Cape Breton, Nova Scotia
  Ethnic or religious group: Scottish-Canadians
  Established: 1939
  Date: First full week in August

  GdWrldFest-1985, 46
  IntlThFolk-1979, 67
  See also **Gaelic Mod (Scotland)**

Gaelic Mod
  Location: Scotland
  Established: 1892 in northern Scotland
  Date: Two weeks in September-October

  AnnivHol-1983, 177
  IntlThFolk-1979, 67

Gaense Tag, Goose Day
  See **St. Leopold, Feast Day of (Austria)**

Gagaku Festival
  Location: Japan: Kasuga Shrine, Nara
  Date: Early November

  IntlThFolk-1979, 257

Gaghant, Nor Dary
  See **New Year's Day (Armenia)**

Gai Jatra
  See **Cows, Procession of Sacred (Hindu people in Nepal)**

Gala of One-Man Shows
  Location: Romania: Bacau, West Moldavia
  Established: 1972
  Date: 10-12 days in October or November

  IntlThFolk-1979, 316

Galicnik Wedding
    Location: Yugoslavia: Galicnik, Macedonia
    Date: July 12

    HolFestCelWrld-1994, 364
    IntlThFolk-1979, 388

Gallo, Fiesta del
    See **Cock Festival (Spain)**

Galungan
    See **New Year (Indonesia: Bali)**

Game Festival
    See **Muhammad's Birthday (West Africa: Hausaland, Nupe, and Borgu)**

Game of St. Evermaire (Spel van Sint Evermarus)
    Named for: St. Evermaire who, with his companions, was murdered on May 1, 699, while on pilgrimage to Jerusalem
    Location: Belgium: Rutten, Limburg
    Established: Ninth century
    Date: May 1

    FestWestEur-1958, 9
    HolFestCelWrld-1994, 288

Games of May
    Location: Yugoslavia: Becej, Vojvodina
    Established: 1957
    Date: May

    IntlThFolk-1979, 380

Gandhi's Birthday (Gandhi Jayanti)
    Named for: Mohandas Karamchand Gandhi (1869-1948)
    Location: India
    Date: October 2

    AnnivHol-1983, 127
    BkHolWrld-1986, October 2
    Chases-1993, 395
    DictWrldRel-1989, 271
    HolFestCelWrld-1994, 114

Ganeo'o
    See **Iroquois White Dog Feast**

Ganesh Chaturthi or Ganesh's Fourth
    See **Elephant God, Festival of the (Hindu), (Hindu people in India), (Hindu people in the Deccan, India), (Hindu people in Maharashtra, India), (Hindu people in Bombay, Maharashtra, India), (Hindu people in Poona, Maharashtra, India), and (Hindu people in Nepal)**

Gang or Gange Days
    See **Rogation Days**

Ganga Dussehra
    See **Ganges River Festival (Hindu) and (Hindu people along the Ganges River, India)**

Gangaur or Gauri (Parvati Tritiya)
    Location: India: Rajasthan and elsewhere in northern India
    Ethnic or religious group: Hindu
    Date: March-April, 18-day festival held two weeks after Holi during Hindu month of Chaitra

    Chases-1993, 141
    HolFestCelWrld-1994, 333
    RelHolCal-1993, 78

Ganges River Festival (Ganga Dussehra)
    Ethnic or religious group: Hindu
    Date: May-June, tenth day of waxing half of Hindu month of Jyeshta

    DictFolkMyth-1984, 671
    FolkWrldHol-1992, 318
    HolFestCelWrld-1994, 114
    RelHolCal-1993, 78

Ganges River Festival (Ganga Dussehra)
    Location: India: along the Ganges River
    Ethnic or religious group: Hindu
    Date: May-June, tenth day of waxing half of Hindu month of Jyeshta

    FolkWrldHol-1992, 318
    HolFestCelWrld-1994, 114
    RelHolCal-1993, 73

Ganjitsu
    See **New Year's Day (Japan)**

Ganna
    See **Christmas (Coptic Church in Ethiopia)**

Gansabhauet
    Location: Switzerland: Sursee
    Established: 1821
    Date: November 11

    HolFestCelWrld-1994, 115

Garbanzo, Fiesta Sopa de
    Location: Ybor City, Florida
    Ethnic or religious group: Spanish-, Cuban-, and Italian-Americans
    Date: Begins Sunday nearest February 9 and ends Saturday

    AmerBkDays-1978, 155
    See also **Gasparilla Pirate Festival and Invasion**

Garland Day
  Location: England: Abbotsbury, Dorsetshire
  Date: May 12 or 13

  AnnivHol-1983, 65
  DictDays-1988, 46
  HolFestCelWrld-1994, 115
  RelHolCal-1993, 55

Gasparilla Pirate Festival and Invasion
  Named for: José Gasparilla (d. 1820s)
  Location: Tampa, Florida
  Established: 1904
  Date: Six days beginning the Monday after the first
    Tuesday in February

  AmerBkDays-1978, 154
  AnnivHol-1983, 23
  BkHolWrld-1986, February 7, 177
  Chases-1993, 88
  FolkAmerHol-1987, 65
  GdUSFest-1984, 37
  HolFestCelWrld-1994, 115
  See also **Garbanzo, Fiesta Sopa de**

Gaspee Days
  Named for: British ship, *HMS Gaspee,* which burned on
    June 9, 1772
  Location: Cranston, Warwick, Rhode Island
  Established: 1966
  Date: 16 days in May-June

  AmerBkDays-1978, 624
  GdUSFest-1984, 166

Gathering of the Clans
  Location: Canada: Pugwash, Nova Scotia
  Ethnic or religious group: Scottish-Canadians
  Date: July 1

  IntlThFolk-1979, 66

Gathering of the Fruits
  Location: Albania
  Date: September

  AnnivHol-1983, 177

Gaukler Festival
  See **Pantomime Festival (Federal Republic of Germany:
    Cologne, North Rhine-Westphalia)**

Gawai Dayak
  See **Dayak Festival Day (Dayak people in Sarawak, Malaysia)**

Gedaliah, Fast of
  Named for: Gedaliah ben Ahikam (fl. 586 B.C.)
  Ethnic or religious group: Jewish
  Date: September-October, the day following Rosh
    Hashanah (Jewish New Year)

  Chases-1993, 378
  DaysCustFaith-1957, 245
  HolFestCelWrld-1994, 115
  RelHolCal-1993, 76
  See also **New Year, Jewish (Rosh Hashanah)**

Geerewol Celebrations
  Location: Niger
  Ethnic or religious group: Wodaabe people
  Date: June-September, one week during the rainy season

  HolFestCelWrld-1994, 116

Gelede
  Location: Nigeria
  Ethnic or religious group: Yoruba people
  Date: Occasional: end of dry seasons (March-May);
    August; and during emergencies and funerals

  BkHolWrld-1986, August 29, 177

Genji Bi Hori
  See **Black Spirit Festival (Songhay people in Niger)**

Genna
  See **Christmas (Coptic Church in Ethiopia)**

Genshi-Sai
  Location: Japan
  Date: January 3

  BkFest-1937, 195

Genzefest
  See **Flower Festival, Broom (Luxembourg: Wiltz)**

Georgemas
  See **St. George's Day**

Georgia Week Celebrations
  Location: Savannah, Georgia
  Established: Commemorates founding of colony February
    12, 1733, by James Edward Oglethorpe (1696-1785);
    observance began in 1933
  Date: One week in February, including February 12,
    Oglethorpe Day

  AmerBkDays-1978, 174
  AnnivHol-1983, 23
  Chases-1993, 96
  GdUSFest-1984, 39
  HolFestCelWrld-1994, 117

Georgiritt Parade
See **St. George's Day (Germany: Traunstein, Upper Bavaria)**

Geranium Day
Location: England
Established: 1920s
Date: Early April

DictDays-1988, 47
HolFestCelWrld-1994, 117

Gerddorol Gydwladol Llangollen
See **Eisteddfod, International Musical (Wales: Llangollen, Denbighshire)**

German Alps Festival
Location: Hunter Mountain Ski Bowl, Hunter, New York
Established: 1973
Date: 18 days in July

GdUSFest-1984, 124

German Day
Location: United States
Ethnic or religious group: German-American communities
Date: October 6

Chases-1993, 400
DictDays-1988, 47

German Pioneer or Settlement Day
See **German Day**

Gettysburg Civil War Heritage Days
Location: Gettysburg, Pennsylvania
Established: 1983
Date: Last weekend in June and first week in July

HolFestCelWrld-1994, 118

Gettysburg Day
Named for: July 1, 1863, battle of Gettysburg
Location: Gettysburg, Pennsylvania
Date: July 1

AnnivHol-1983, 87
Chases-1993, 271

Ghanta Karna
Location: Nepal
Ethnic or religious group: Buddhist
Date: July-August, 14th day of waning half of Hindu month of Sravana

BkHolWrld-1986, August 23, 178
FolkWrldHol-1992, 396
HolFestCelWrld-1994, 118

Giants, Festival of the (Fête des Géants)
Location: France: Douai
Date: Three days beginning Sunday after July 5

HolFestCelWrld-1994, 119

Giants of Belgium and France, Procession of
See **Whit Monday (France: Lille)**

Gift of the Waters Pageant
Location: Thermopolis, Wyoming
Established: 1925
Date: First weekend in August

GdUSFest-1984, 217

Giglio, Festa del
See **Lily Festival**

Gila River Festival
Location: Sacaton, Arizona
Ethnic or religious group: Pima and Maricopa Indians
Date: Second weekend in March

IndianAmer-1989, 261

Ginem
Location: Philippines
Ethnic or religious group: Bagobo people
Date: At least one day in December

DictFolkMyth-1984, 454

Gion Matsuri
Named for: Honors Emperor Seiwa (850-880)
Location: Japan: Kyoto
Established: 869 A.D.
Date: July

AnnivHol-1983, 177
BkHolWrld-1986, July 17
HolFestCelWrld-1994, 119

Giovedì Santo
See **Holy Thursday (Italy) and (Sicily)**

Girl Guides Thinking Day
Location: England and British Commonwealth countries
Established: Birthday of Boy Scouts founder Robert Baden-Powell (1857-1941)
Date: February 22

AnnivHol-1983, 27

Girl Scout Day
Named for: March 12, 1912, founding of the Girl Scouts in Savannah, Georgia
Location: United States

Girl Scout Day *(cont.)*
  Date: March 12

  AmerBkDays-1978, 245
  AnnivHol-1983, 36
  Chases-1993, 127
  DictDays-1988, 47
  HolFestCelWrld-1994, 120

Girls' Doll Festival (Hina Matsuri or Hina-No-Sekku, Peach Blossom Festival)
  Location: Japan and United States
  Ethnic or religious group: Japanese-Americans
  Established: 18th century
  Date: March 3

  AnnivHol-1983, 33
  BkFest-1937, 196
  BkFestHolWrld-1970, 72
  BkHolWrld-1986, March 3
  Chases-1993, 117
  DictFolkMyth-1984, 540
  FolkAmerHol-1987, 105
  FolkWrldHol-1992, 156
  HolFestCelWrld-1994, 138

Girls' Festival
  See **St. Agatha Festival (France)**

Gita Jayanti
  Named for: The *Bhagavad Gita*
  Ethnic or religious group: Hindu
  Date: November-December, 11th day of waxing half of Hindu month of Margashirsha

  RelHolCal-1993, 79

Glarus Festival
  Location: Switzerland
  Established: Commemorates residents' defeat of Austrian troops on April 9, 1388
  Date: First Thursday in April

  AnnivHol-1983, 49

Glorious Fourth
  See **Independence Day (United States)**

Glorious Twelfth (Northern Ireland)
  See **Orange Day**

Glorious Twelfth
  Location: Scotland and Scots elsewhere

  Date: August 12, open of grouse hunting season

  AnnivHol-1983, 106
  DictDays-1988, 48, 51, 103, 122
  HolFestCelWrld-1994, 120

Glory Thursday
  See **Holy Thursday**

God, Day of
  See **Corpus Christi**

Goddess of Fortune, Festival of the (Lukshmi or Laksmi Puja)
  Ethnic or religious group: Hindu
  Date: September-October, Hindu month of Asvina

  BkFest-1937, 161
  DictWrldRel-1989, 280

Goddess of Fortune, Festival of the (Lukshmi or Laksmi Puja)
  Location: India: Bengal
  Ethnic or religious group: Hindu
  Date: September-October, Hindu month of Asvina

  BkFest-1937, 161

Goddess of Mercy, Kuan Yin, Birthday of the
  Location: China, Japan, Korea, Malaysia, Tibet
  Ethnic or religious group: Buddhist
  Date: March-April, 19th day of third lunar month

  HolFestCelWrld-1994, 120

Goddess of Mercy, Kuan Yin, Birthday of the
  Location: Hong Kong
  Ethnic or religious group: Buddhist
  Date: October-November, 19th day of tenth lunar month

  HolFestCelWrld-1994, 120

God of Rain, Festival of the
  See **Chariot Festival of Macchendranath (Buddhist Newar and Hindu peoples in Patan and Kathmandu, Nepal)**

Gods of the Sea Festival (Okinawa)
  See **Boat Race Day in Okinawa**

God's Sunday
  See **Easter**

Goede Vrydag
  See **Good Friday (Belgium)**

Gogatsu Matsuri
  See **Fifth Month Festival (Okinawa)**

Gokarna Aunsi
  See **Father's Day (Nepal)**

Gold Cup Day
  Named for: Ascot Gold Cup race held since 1807
  Location: England
  Date: Last day of four-day race in June

  DictDays-1988, 48

Gold Discovery Days
  See **Custer's Last Stand (Custer, South Dakota)**

Golden Chariot and Battle of the Lumecon, Procession of the
  Location: Belgium: Mons
  Established: Commemorates end of the plague in the
    town in 1349
  Date: May-June, Trinity Sunday

  HolFestCelWrld-1994, 120

Golden Days
  Named for: Discovery of gold on July 22, 1902
  Location: Fairbanks, Alaska
  Date: Third week in July

  HolFestCelWrld-1994, 121

Golden Dolphin
  Location: Bulgaria: Varna
  Date: Every three years in October

  IntlThFolk-1979, 57

Golden Friday
  See **Ember Days**

Golden Orange Festival
  Location: Turkey: Antalya
  Date: August-September

  IntlThFolk-1979, 366

Golden Orpheus
  Location: Bulgaria: Slunchev Bryag
  Established: 1960s
  Date: Ten days in June

  GdWrldFest-1985, 27

Golden Spike Day
  Named for: May 10, 1869, completion of transcontinental
    railroad
  Location: Golden Spike Historical Monument at
    Corrine, Utah
  Established: Reenactment held since 1952
  Date: May 10

  AnnivHol-1983, 64
  Chases-1993, 203
  HolFestCelWrld-1994, 121

Gold Rush Days
  Location: Wickenburg, Arizona
  Date: Second weekend in February

  AmerBkDays-1978, 180
  Chases-1993, 95

Gold Rush Days, Dahlonega
  Named for: Gold rush days of 1820s and 1830s
  Location: Dahlonega, Georgia
  Date: October

  HolFestCelWrld-1994, 77

Gold Star Mothers Day
  Named for: Mothers of deceased servicepeople
  Location: United States
  Date: Last Sunday of September

  AnnivHol-1983, 125
  Chases-1993, 387

Gondomar, International Festival of
  Location: Portugal: Gondomar, Porto
  Established: 1973
  Date: August

  IntlThFolk-1979, 306

Good Friday
  Ethnic or religious group: Christian
  Date: March-April, Friday preceding Easter Sunday

  AmerBkDays-1978, 294
  AnnivHol-1983, 169
  BkFest-1937, 6, 16, 30, 41, 56, 70, 86, 96, 103, 112, 121,
    147, 167, 184, 211, 227, 249, 259, 275, 291, 300, 309,
    330, 338
  BkFestHolWrld-1970, 53
  BkHolWrld-1986, April 10
  Chases-1993, 159
  DaysCustFaith-1957, 107
  DictDays-1988, 48, 69
  DictFolkMyth-1984, 181, 961, 1072
  DictWrldRel-1989, 175, 283
  FestSaintDays-1915, 62
  FestWestEur-1958, 8, 93, 107, 152, 212
  FolkAmerHol-1987, 130
  FolkWrldHol-1992, 191
  HolFestCelWrld-1994, 122, 255
  RelHolCal-1993, 79
  SaintFestCh-1904, 160

Good Friday
Ethnic or religious group: Eastern Orthodox
Date: March-April, Friday preceding Easter Sunday

AmerBkDays-1978, 296
BkFest-1937, 291, 330
HolFestCelWrld-1994, 122

Good Friday
Ethnic or religious group: Episcopalian
Date: March-April, Friday preceding Easter Sunday

AmerBkDays-1978, 295

Good Friday
Ethnic or religious group: Greek Orthodox
Date: March-April, Friday preceding Easter Sunday

AmerBkDays-1978, 296
BkFest-1937, 330

Good Friday
Ethnic or religious group: Lutheran
Date: March-April, Friday preceding Easter Sunday

AmerBkDays-1978, 295

Good Friday
Ethnic or religious group: Protestant
Date: March-April, Friday preceding Easter Sunday

AmerBkDays-1978, 295
BkFestHolWrld-1970, 54
DaysCustFaith-1957, 107
RelHolCal-1993, 79

Good Friday
Ethnic or religious group: Roman Catholic
Date: March-April, Friday preceding Easter Sunday

AmerBkDays-1978, 295
BkFestHolWrld-1970, 53, 54
FolkAmerHol-1987, 130, 143
RelHolCal-1993, 79
SaintFestCh-1904, 160

Good Friday (E Prëmte e Zezë, Black Friday)
Location: Albania
Date: March-April, Friday preceding Easter Sunday

BkFest-1937, 6

Good Friday (Kar Freitag)
Location: Austria
Date: March-April, Friday preceding Easter Sunday

BkFest-1937, 30
FestSaintDays-1915, 65

Good Friday (Kar Freitag)
Location: Austria: Riva
Date: March-April, Friday preceding Easter Sunday

FestSaintDays-1915, 65

Good Friday (Goede Vrydag)
Location: Belgium
Date: March-April, Friday preceding Easter Sunday

BkFest-1937, 41
BkFestHolWrld-1970, 54
FestWestEur-1958, 8

Good Friday
Location: Bermuda
Date: March-April, Friday preceding Easter Sunday

BkHolWrld-1986, April 10
FolkWrldHol-1992, 191

Good Friday (Raspeti Petuk, Crucifixion Friday)
Location: Bulgaria
Date: March-April, Friday preceding Easter Sunday

BkFest-1937, 70

Good Friday (Velký Pátek, Great Friday)
Location: Czechoslovakia
Date: March-April, Friday preceding Easter Sunday

BkFest-1937, 86

Good Friday (Langfredag, Long Friday)
Location: Denmark
Date: March-April, Friday preceding Easter Sunday

BkFest-1937, 96

Good Friday (Long Rope Day in Sussex and other parts of England)
Location: England
Date: March-April, Friday preceding Easter Sunday

BkFest-1937, 56
DictDays-1988, 69
FestSaintDays-1915, 63
FolkWrldHol-1992, 194

Good Friday (Suur Reede)
Location: Estonia
Date: March-April, Friday preceding Easter Sunday

BkFest-1937, 103

Good Friday (Pitkäperjantai, Long Friday)
Location: Finland
Date: March-April, Friday preceding Easter Sunday

BkFest-1937, 112
HolFestCelWrld-1994, 122

Good Friday (Vendredi-Saint)
Location: France
Date: March-April, Friday preceding Easter Sunday

BkFest-1937, 121
FolkWrldHol-1992, 193

Good Friday
Location: Germany
Date: March-April, Friday preceding Easter Sunday

FolkWrldHol-1992, 194

Good Friday (Meghalee Paraskevee, Holy Friday)
Location: Greece
Date: March-April, Friday preceding Easter Sunday

BkFest-1937, 147

Good Friday (Nagypéntek)
Location: Hungary
Date: March-April, Friday preceding Easter Sunday

BkFest-1937, 167

Good Friday (Venerdì Santo)
Location: Italy
Date: March-April, Friday preceding Easter Sunday

BkFest-1937, 184
FestSaintDays-1915, 64
FestWestEur-1958, 93

Good Friday (Lielā Lūdzamā Diena, Great Friday)
Location: Latvia
Date: March-April, Friday preceding Easter Sunday

BkFest-1937, 211

Good Friday (Charfreudeg)
Location: Luxembourg
Date: March-April, Friday preceding Easter Sunday

FestWestEur-1958, 107

Good Friday
Location: Macedonia
Date: March-April, Friday preceding Easter Sunday

FolkWrldHol-1992, 197

Good Friday
Location: Malta
Date: March-April, Friday preceding Easter Sunday

FolkWrldHol-1992, 198

Good Friday (Viernes Santo)
Location: Mexico

Date: March-April, Friday preceding Easter Sunday

AmerBkDays-1978, 297
BkFest-1937, 227
DictFolkMyth-1984, 1072
FolkWrldHol-1992, 199

Good Friday
Location: New Mexico
Ethnic or religious group: Penitentes
Date: March-April, Friday preceding Easter Sunday

DictFolkMyth-1984, 1072
FolkAmerHol-1987, 143

Good Friday (Langfredag, Long Friday)
Location: Norway
Date: March-April, Friday preceding Easter Sunday

BkFest-1937, 249
FestWestEur-1958, 152
HolFestCelWrld-1994, 122

Good Friday (Wielki Piatek, Great Friday)
Location: Poland
Date: March-April, Friday preceding Easter Sunday

BkFest-1937, 259

Good Friday (Vinerea Mare)
Location: Romania
Date: March-April, Friday preceding Easter Sunday

BkFest-1937, 275

Good Friday (Velikaya Pyatnitza, Great Friday)
Location: Russia
Ethnic or religious group: Eastern Orthodox
Date: March-April, Friday preceding Easter Sunday

BkFest-1937, 291

Good Friday (Viernes Santo)
Location: Spain: Seville
Established: Procession since the Middle Ages
Date: March-April, Friday preceding Easter Sunday

AmerBkDays-1978, 297
BkFest-1937, 300
BkFestHolWrld-1970, 54

Good Friday (Langfredagen, Long Friday)
Location: Sweden
Date: March-April, Friday preceding Easter Sunday

BkFest-1937, 309
FestWestEur-1958, 212

Good Friday (Ceremony of Pleureuses)
  Location: Switzerland: Church of Romont
  Established: 15th century
  Date: March-April, Friday before Easter

  HolFestCelWrld-1994, 255

Good Friday (Al-Jum'ah al-Hazinah, Sorrowful Friday)
  Location: Syria
  Ethnic or religious group: Eastern Orthodox
  Date: March-April, Friday preceding Easter Sunday

  BkFest-1937, 330

Good Friday
  Location: United States
  Date: March-April, Friday preceding Easter Sunday

  AmerBkDays-1978, 295
  BkFest-1937, 16
  BkFestHolWrld-1970, 54
  DaysCustFaith-1957, 107
  DictFolkMyth-1984, 1072
  FolkAmerHol-1987, 130, 143

Good Friday
  Location: United States
  Ethnic or religious group: Greek-Americans
  Date: March-April, Friday preceding Easter Sunday

  BkFest-1937, 147

Good Friday
  Location: United States
  Ethnic or religious group: Roman Catholic Italian-Americans
  Date: March-April, Friday preceding Easter Sunday

  FolkAmerHol-1987, 130

Good Friday (Veliki Petak)
  Location: Yugoslavia
  Ethnic or religious group: Serbian people
  Date: March-April, Friday preceding Easter Sunday

  BkFest-1937, 338
  FolkWrldHol-1992, 205

Gooding Day
  See **Doleing Day**

Good Neighbours Festival
  Location: Scotland: Dumfries
  Date: One week in late June

  AnnivHol-1983, 177

Good Road Days
  See **Proclamation Days**

Good Thief Sunday
  See **St. Dismas's Day**

Good Will, Day of
  See **Boxing Day (South Africa)**

Goombay Festival
  Location: Bahama Islands: Freeport, Grand Bahama Island, and Nassau, New Providence Island
  Established: 1971
  Date: July and August

  GdWrldFest-1985, 15

Goose and River Festival, Palio of the
  Location: Italy: Pavia
  Established: Since medieval times
  Date: June 28-29

  HolFestCelWrld-1994, 243

Gopastami
  See **Cow Holiday (Hindu people in India)**

Govardhan Puja and Annakut
  Location: India: Mount Govardhan and elsewhere in northern India
  Ethnic or religious group: Hindu
  Date: October-November, first day of waxing half of Hindu month of Karthika, the day after Dewali festivities

  RelHolCal-1993, 80
  See also **Lights, Festival of (Dewali)**

Governor's Feast
  Location: Acoma Pueblo, New Mexico
  Date: First week in February

  IndianAmer-1989, 285, 294

Gowkie or Gowkin' Day
  See **April Fools' Day (Scotland)**

Grain, Festival of Ears of (Schrulblha)
  Location: Tibet
  Date: Early July

  FolkWrldHol-1992, 361

Granddad Frost Day
  Location: USSR
  Date: January 1

  AnnivHol-1983, 2
  Chases-1993, 52

Grand Duke, or National, Day
   Location: Luxembourg
   Date: June 23

   AnnivHol-1983, 83
   Chases-1993, 261
   NatlHolWrld-1968, 88

Grande Parade du Jazz
   See **Jazz, Nice Grand Parade of (France: Nice)**

Grandmother's Day (Babin Den)
   Location: Bulgaria
   Date: January 20

   AnnivHol-1983, 12
   BkFest-1937, 66
   BkHolWrld-1986, January 20
   Chases-1993, 71
   HolFestCelWrld-1994, 21

Grand National Day
   Location: England: Aintree, Liverpool
   Established: Race since 1839
   Date: March-April

   Chases-1993, 148
   DictDays-1988, 50
   HolFestCelWrld-1994, 122

Grandparents' Day
   Established: September 6, 1979
   Date: First Sunday after Labor Day in September

   AnnivHol-1983, 115
   Chases-1993, 368
   DictDays-1988, 50
   HolFestCelWrld-1994, 123

Grant Park Concerts
   Location: Chicago, Illinois
   Established: 1934
   Date: Ten weeks from last week in June to last week in August

   MusFestAmer-1990, 208

Grape and Wine Festival, Niagara
   Location: Canada: St. Catharines, Ontario
   Established: 1952
   Date: Ten days in late September

   GdWrldFest-1985, 51

Grape Festival (Wedding of the Wine and Cheese Pageant)
   Location: Nauvoo, Illinois

Established: Since 1940s
Date: September, Labor Day weekend

   GdUSFest-1984, 49
   HolFestCelWrld-1994, 123

Grape Harvest, National Festival of the
   Location: Argentina: Mendoza
   Established: 1936
   Date: First week in March

   GdWrldFest-1985, 4

Grasmere Sports
   Location: England: Lake District
   Established: 19th century
   Date: Third Thursday in August

   HolFestCelWrld-1994, 124

Grave-Sweeping and Cold Food Festival (Qing Ming, Clear and Bright Festival)
   Location: China
   Established: 206 B.C.-221 C.E., Han Dynasty
   Date: Fourth or fifth day of third lunar month, 105 or 106 days after the winter solstice

   AmerBkDays-1978, 501
   BkFestHolWrld-1970, 87
   BkHolWrld-1986, April 6
   Chases-1993, 156
   DictFolkMyth-1984, 225, 228, 478, 789
   FolkWrldHol-1992, 233
   HolFestCelWrld-1994, 263
   RelHolCal-1993, 105

Grave-Sweeping and Cold Food Festival (Qing Ming, Clear and Bright Festival)
   Location: Hong Kong
   Date: Fourth or fifth day of third lunar month, 105 or 106 days after the winter solstice

   BkHolWrld-1986, April 6
   FolkWrldHol-1992, 232

Grave-Sweeping and Cold Food Festival (Han Sik-il, Cold Food Day)
   Location: Korea
   Date: Fourth or fifth day of third lunar month, 105 or 106 days after the winter solstice

   FolkWrldHol-1992, 232
   HolFestCelWrld-1994, 263

Grave-Sweeping and Cold Food Festival (Han Shih, Cold Food Feast)
  Location: Taiwan
  Date: Fourth or fifth day of third lunar month, 105 or 106
    days after the winter solstice

  AnnivHol-1983, 48
  Chases-1993, 156
  FolkWrldHol-1992, 233
  HolFestCelWrld-1994, 263

Grave-Sweeping and Cold Food Festival (Thanh-Minh, Pure and Bright Festival)
  Location: Vietnam
  Date: Fifth day of third lunar month

  FolkWrldHol-1992, 211
  HolFestCelWrld-1994, 337

Graveyard Cleaning and Decoration Day
  Location: Kentucky, Tennessee, and Texas
  Date: July

  FolkAmerHol-1987, 251

Great American Smokeout
  Date: Third Thursday in November

  Chases-1993, 444
  HolFestCelWrld-1994, 124

Great Festival (Muslim)
  See **Sacrifice, Feast of**

Great Fifteenth
  Location: Korea
  Date: 15th day of first lunar month

  FolkWrldHol-1992, 70
  HolFestCelWrld-1994, 124

Great Friday
  See **Good Friday**

Great Lakes Festival
  Location: Notre Dame, Indiana
  Date: Three weekends in mid-June

  MusFestAmer-1990, 58

Great Sabbath
  See **Hagodol (Jewish)**

Great Saturday
  See **Holy Saturday**

Great Sunday
  See **Palm Sunday**

Great Thursday
  See **Holy Thursday**

Greek Cross Day
  See **Epiphany (Greece)**

Greek National Union of Cypriot Fighters Day
  See **EOKA (Cyprus)**

Green Bean Festival
  Ethnic or religious group: Iroquois Indians
  Date: One day in August

  DictFolkMyth-1984, 123, 440

Green Corn Ceremony or Dance
  See **Dance, Green Corn**

Green George Festival
  Named for: St. George (d. c. 303)
  Ethnic or religious group: Romanian and Transylvanian
    Romanies and Slavic people
  Date: April 24, St. George's Day

  DictFolkMyth-1984, 534, 954

Green Ribbon Day
  See **St. Patrick's Day**

Green River Rendezvous
  Location: Pinedale, Wyoming
  Established: 1936
  Date: Second Sunday in July

  GdUSFest-1984, 216
  HolFestCelWrld-1994, 126

Green Squash Festival (Wima'kwari)
  Location: Mexico: Huichol
  Date: October

  AnnivHol-1983, 177

Green Thursday
  See **Holy Thursday (Germany)**

Greenwich Festival
  Location: England: London Borough of Greenwich
  Established: 1972
  Date: Last two weeks in June

  IntlThFolk-1979, 166

Greenwood Day, Chester
  Named for: Chester Greenwood (1858-1937), inventor of
    ear muffs
  Location: Farmington, Maine
  Date: First Saturday in December

  HolFestCelWrld-1994, 57

Grenzumgang
 See **Boundary Walk (Germany: Springe Deister, Lower Saxony)**

Grey Cup Day
 Location: Canada
 Date: Mid-November

 DictDays-1988, 50
 HolFestCelWrld-1994, 126

Grillo, Festa del
 See **Ascension Day (Italy: Florence, Tuscany)**

Groppenfasnacht
 See **Fish Carnival (Switzerland: Ermatingen)**

Grotto Day
 Location: England: London
 Date: August 5, St. James's Day

 DictDays-1988, 50, 85
 HolFestCelWrld-1994, 127

Ground, Death of the
 See **Summer, First Day of (Morocco)**

Groundhog Day
 Location: England
 Date: February 2

 AmerBkDays-1978, 138
 BkFestHolWrld-1970, 29
 HolFestCelWrld-1994, 127

Groundhog Day
 Location: Germany
 Date: February 2

 AmerBkDays-1978, 138
 BkFestHolWrld-1970, 29
 HolFestCelWrld-1994, 127

Groundhog Day
 Location: New York
 Date: February 2

 FolkAmerHol-1987, 58

Groundhog Day
 Location: Punxsutawney, Pennsylvania
 Date: February 2

 AmerBkDays-1978, 138
 Chases-1993, 84
 DictDays-1988, 51
 FolkAmerHol-1987, 57
 HolFestCelWrld-1994, 127

Groundhog Day
 Location: United States
 Date: February 2

 AmerBkDays-1978, 138
 BkFestHolWrld-1970, 29
 Chases-1993, 83, 84
 DictDays-1988, 51
 FolkAmerHol-1987, 57

Groundhog Day
 Location: United States
 Ethnic or religious group: English and German immigrants
 Date: February 2

 AmerBkDays-1978, 138
 BkFestHolWrld-1970, 29

Groundhog Day
 Location: United States
 Ethnic or religious group: Pennsylvania Dutch people
 Date: February 2

 AmerBkDays-1978, 138
 DaysCustFaith-1957, 45
 FolkAmerHol-1987, 57
 HolFestCelWrld-1994, 127

Groundhog Day
 Location: Sun Prairie, Wisconsin
 Date: February 2

 AmerBkDays-1978, 138
 Chases-1993, 83, 84

Grouse Day
 See **Glorious Twelfth**

Gründonnerstag, Green Thursday
 See **Holy Thursday (Germany)**

Gualterianas, Festas
 See **St. Walter, Festivals of (Portugal: Guimarães, Minho)**

Guanacaste Day
 Location: Costa Rica
 Date: July 25

 AnnivHol-1983, 97

Guarda, National Festival of
 Location: Portugal: Guarda
 Established: 1974
 Date: Summer

 IntlThFolk-1979, 307

Guardian Angel, Festival of the (Schutzengelfest)
  Location: Switzerland: Appenzell
  Established: 1679
  Date: Second Sunday in July

  HolFestCelWrld-1994, 309

Guardian Angels, Festival of
  Ethnic or religious group: Roman Catholic
  Established: 16th century, Spain
  Date: October 2

  DaysCustFaith-1957, 249
  RelHolCal-1993, 80

Guavaween
  Location: Ybor City, Florida
  Ethnic or religious group: Cuban-Americans
  Date: Last Saturday in October

  HolFestCelWrld-1994, 128

Gudi Parva
  See **New Year (Hindu people in Maharashtra, India)**

Guelaguetza
  See **Monday on the Hill (Lunes del Cerro)**

Gula, Feast of
  Named for: Gula, goddess of healing
  Location: Babylonia
  Date: Late April

  DictFolkMyth-1984, 469

Gules of August
  See **Lammas (Great Britain)**

Gulpilhares, International Festival of
  Location: Portugal: Gulpilhares, Porto
  Established: 1964
  Date: July

  IntlThFolk-1979, 308

Gum Tree Festival
  Location: Tupelo, Mississippi
  Established: 1972
  Date: Usually second weekend in May or sometime in June

  Chases-1993, 200
  GdUSFest-1984, 103

Gunpowder Plot or Gunpowder Treason Day
  See **Fawkes Day, Guy**

Gunpunhi
  See **Sacred Thread Festival (Buddhist and Hindu people in Nepal)**

Guru Purnima (also known as Ashadha Purnima and Guru Vyas Purnima)
  Location: India
  Ethnic or religious group: Hindu
  Date: June-July, full moon day of Hindu month of Ashadha

  RelHolCal-1993, 81

Gustafus Adolphus Day
  Named for: Gustafus Adolphus II (1594-1632)
  Location: Sweden
  Date: November 6

  BkFest-1937, 312
  Chases-1993, 433
  HolFestCelWrld-1994, 128

Guy Fawkes Day
  See **Fawkes Day, Guy**

Gyertyaszentel Boldog Asszony
  See **Candlemas (Hungary)**

Gynaecocratia
  Location: Greece: Komotini, Xanthi, Kilkis, and Serres
  Date: January 8

  HolFestCelWrld-1994, 129

Gyunoo and Jingny O, Herdboy and Weaving Maid
  See **Double Seventh (Korea)**

Habye Festival
  Location: Togo
  Ethnic or religious group: Habye people
  Date: Small festival every third year, larger festival every fifth year in November

  BkHolWrld-1986, November 23, 178

Hadaga
  See **Agricultural Festival (Hadaga) (India: Maharashtra)**

Haghoghy Ortnovtyoon or Navasard Armenian Grape Festival, Blessing of the Grapes
  See **Assumption, Feast of the (Armenia)**

Hagodol (Great Sabbath)
  Ethnic or religious group: Jewish
  Date: March-April, festival preceding Passover

  DaysCustFaith-1957, 111
  HolFestCelWrld-1994, 131

Haichitdilya
  See **Dance, Hupa Winter (Hupa Indians in northern California)**

Hajj
See **Mecca, Pilgrimage to**

Hakata Dontaku
  Location: Japan: Fukuoka City
  Date: May 3-4

  HolFestCelWrld-1994, 131

Halashasti or Balarama Shashti
  Location: Northern India
  Ethnic or religious group: Hindu
  Date: August-September, sixth day of waning half of Hindu
    month of Bhadrapada

  FolkWrldHol-1992, 437
  RelHolCal-1993, 81

Halcyon Days
  Date: Seven days preceding and after the winter solstice,
    December 14-28

  BkDays-1864, ii. 726
  Chases-1993, 474
  DictFolkMyth-1984, 475

Half-Vasten
See **Mid-Lent Sunday (Belgium)**

Half-Year Day
  Location: Hong Kong
  Date: July 1

  AnnivHol-1983, 87

Halifax Day
  Named for: April 12, 1776, Halifax Resolves of Independence
  Location: North Carolina
  Date: On or near April 12

  AnnivHol-1983, 50
  Chases-1993, 164
  DictDays-1988, 54
  HolFestCelWrld-1994, 132

Halloween
  Date: October 31

  AmerBkDays-1978, 968
  AnnivHol-1983, 138
  BkDays-1864, ii. 519
  BkFest-1937, 60
  BkFestHolWrld-1970, 119
  BkHolWrld-1986, October 31

  Chases-1993, 426
  DaysCustFaith-1957, 280
  DictDays-1988, 33, 82, 120, 122
  DictFolkMyth-1984, 181, 869, 961
  FestSaintDays-1915, 191
  FolkAmerHol-1987, 309
  FolkWrldHol-1992, 518
  HolFestCelWrld-1994, 132
  RelHolCal-1993, 81
  SaintFestCh-1904, 468

Halloween
  Location: Anaheim, California
  Established: Halloween parade since 1923
  Date: Saturday before October 31

  AmerBkDays-1978, 971

Halloween
  Location: Canada
  Date: October 31

  BkFestHolWrld-1970, 119
  BkHolWrld-1986, October 31
  DictDays-1988, 122

**Halloween (Nut Crack Night; also known in parts of
England as Crab Apple Night, Dookie Apple Night, and
Duck Apple Night)**
  Location: England
  Date: October 31

  AmerBkDays-1978, 969
  BkDays-1864, ii.519
  BkFest-1937, 60
  DictDays-1988, 33, 82, 120, 122
  FolkWrldHol-1992, 518
  HolFestCelWrld-1994, 132

Halloween
  Location: Ireland
  Date: October 31

  AmerBkDays-1978, 969
  BkDays-1864, ii.519
  BkHolWrld-1986, October 31
  FestSaintDays-1915, 194
  FolkWrldHol-1992, 520

Halloween (Thump-the-Door Night or Hollantide)
  Location: Isle of Man
  Date: October 31

  DictDays-1988, 120
  FestSaintDays-1915, 196

Halloween
   Location: New Orleans, Louisiana
   Date: October 31

   HolFestCelWrld-1994, 132

Halloween
   Location: Allentown, Pennsylvania
   Established: Halloween parade since 1930s
   Date: October 31

   AmerBkDays-1978, 971

Halloween
   Location: Philippines
   Date: October 31

   FolkWrldHol-1992, 521

Halloween
   Location: Scotland
   Date: October 31

   AmerBkDays-1978, 969
   BkDays-1864, ii.520
   FestSaintDays-1915, 193
   FolkWrldHol-1992, 522

Halloween
   Location: Spain
   Date: October 31

   FestSaintDays-1915, 196

Halloween
   Location: United States
   Date: October 31

   AmerBkDays-1978, 968, 971
   AnnivHol-1983, 138
   BkFest-1937, 19
   BkFestHolWrld-1970, 119
   BkHolWrld-1986, October 31
   DictDays-1988, 122
   FolkAmerHol-1987, 309
   HolFestCelWrld-1994, 132
   RelHolCal-1993, 81

Halloween (Apple and Candle Night)
   Location: Wales
   Date: October 31

   AmerBkDays-1978, 969
   DictDays-1988, 4
   DictFolkMyth-1984, 869

FestSaintDays-1915, 192
FolkWrldHol-1992, 523
HolFestCelWrld-1994, 12

Hallowmas
   See **All Saints' Day; Samhain**

Haloa, Festival of
   Location: Ancient Greece
   Ethnic or religious group: Greek women
   Date: Autumn

   DictFolkMyth-1984, 867

Hambletonian Harness Racing Classic
   Location: East Rutherford, New Jersey
   Established: 1926
   Date: First Saturday in August

   HolFestCelWrld-1994, 132

Hamburger Don
   See **Dom's Fair**

Hammamet, International Festival of
   Location: Tunisia: Hammamet, Nabeul Region
   Established: 1963
   Date: July-August

   GdWrldFest-1985, 179
   IntlThFolk-1979, 361

Hana Matsuri, Flower Festival
   See **Buddha's Birthday, Enlightenment, and Salvation (Buddhist people in Japan)**

Hanami
   See **Cherry Blossom Festival (Japan)**

Handel Festival
   Named for: Georg Friedrich Handel (1685-1759)
   Location: German Democratic Republic: Halle
   Date: Six days in summer

   MusFestWrld-1963, 78

Handsel Monday
   Location: Scotland
   Date: January, first Monday of the year

   BkDays-1864, i. 52
   DictDays-1988, 54
   DictFolkMyth-1984, 478
   HolFestCelWrld-1994, 133

Hangawi, Moon Festival
   See **Mid-Autumn Festival (Korea)**

Hang Gliding Festival, Telluride
  Location: Telluride, Colorado
  Date: Second week in September

  HolFestCelWrld-1994, 334

Han-gul or Hangul Nal
  See **Alphabet Day**

Han Lu (The Dew Grows Cold)
  Location: China
  Date: October

  AnnivHol-1983, 177

Hanukkah (Feast of Dedication; Jewish Festival of Lights)
  Ethnic or religious group: Jewish
  Established: Commemorates victory of Judas Maccabee
    over the Syrians in 164 B.C.
  Date: November-December, eight days beginning 25th day
    of Jewish month of Kislev

  AmerBkDays-1978, 1131
  AnnivHol-1983, 172
  BkFest-1937, 205
  BkFestHolWrld-1970, 134
  BkHolWrld-1986, December 10
  Chases-1993, 469
  DaysCustFaith-1957, 326
  DictFolkMyth-1984, 479
  DictWrldRel-1989, 155, 293
  FolkAmerHol-1987, 355
  FolkWrldHol-1992, 577
  HolFestCelWrld-1994, 134
  RelHolCal-1993, 82

Hanukkah
  Location: Iran; formerly Persia
  Ethnic or religious group: Jewish
  Established: Commemorates victory of Judas Maccabee
    over the Syrians in 164 B.C.
  Date: November-December, eight days beginning 25th day
    of Jewish month of Kislev

  FolkWrldHol-1992, 577

Hanukkah
  Location: Israel
  Ethnic or religious group: Jewish
  Established: Commemorates victory of Judas Maccabee
    over the Syrians in 164 B.C.
  Date: November-December, eight days beginning 25th day
    of Jewish month of Kislev

  FolkWrldHol-1992, 577

Hanukkah
  Location: Tunisia
  Ethnic or religious group: Jewish
  Established: Commemorates victory of Judas Maccabee
    over the Syrians in 164 B.C.
  Date: November-December, eight days beginning 25th day
    of Jewish month of Kislev

  FolkWrldHol-1992, 577

Hanukkah
  Location: United States
  Ethnic or religious group: Jewish
  Established: Commemorates victory of Judas Maccabee
    over the Syrians in 164 B.C.
  Date: November-December, eight days beginning 25th day
    of Jewish month of Kislev

  AmerBkDays-1978, 1131
  DaysCustFaith-1957, 326
  FolkAmerHol-1987, 355

Han Shih, Cold Food Feast
  See **Grave-Sweeping and Cold Food Festival (Taiwan)**

Han Sik-il, Cold Food Day
  See **Grave-Sweeping and Cold Food Festival (Korea)**

Hanuman Jayanti
  See **Monkey God Festival (Hindu), (India), and (Vaishnavite)**

Happy Hunting Party, Festival of the Forest (Kiamichi Owa Chito)
  Location: Beavers Bend State Park, Broken Bow, Oklahoma
  Ethnic or religious group: Choctaw Indians
  Established: 1973; revival of Forest Festival of the 1950s
  Date: Late June

  Chases-1993, 251
  GdUSFest-1984, 144
  HolFestCelWrld-1994, 169

Harbor Festival
  Location: New York, New York
  Established: Since bicentennial celebration in 1976
  Date: Late June to July 4

  GdUSFest-1984, 127
  HolFestCelWrld-1994, 134

Harborfest Norfolk
  Location: Norfolk, Virginia
  Established: 1976; began as part of New York City's
    Harbor Festival
  Date: Four days in June

  GdUSFest-1984, 200

Hari-Kuyo
See **Broken Needles Festival (Japan)**

Hari Raya (Indonesia)
See **Fast, Feast of Breaking the (Indonesia)**

Hari Raya (Malaya)
See **Ramadan (Malaya)**

Hari-Raya Poasa
See **Fast, Feast of Breaking the (Philippines)**

Hari Raya Puasa
See **Fast, Feast of Breaking the (Thailand)**

Hari-Shayani Ekadashi
Ethnic or religious group: Hindu
Date: October-November, 11th day of Hindu month of Karthika

RelHolCal-1993, 82

Haritlika Teej
See **Teej (Hindu women)**

Hariyali Teej
See **Teej, Hariyali (Hindu women in Uttar Pradesh, India)**

Harrogate International Festival
Location: England: Harrogate
Established: 1966
Date: First two weeks in August

MusFestEurBrit-1980, 56

Harvest (Mandela Ceremony)
Location: India: Ladakh
Ethnic or religious group: Buddhist
Date: Harvest season

FolkWrldHol-1992, 453

Harvest, Feast of the (Jewish)
See **Shavuot**

Harvest, Wheat
Location: Romania: Transylvania
Date: Late summer

HolFestCelWrld-1994, 365

Harvest Celebration (Obzinky-secular name; Posviceni-religious name)
Location: Czechoslovakia
Date: Late August or early September

FolkWrldHol-1992, 447
HolFestCelWrld-1994, 232

Harvest Celebration, Grain (Nubaigai)
Location: Lithuania

Date: End of harvest

FolkWrldHol-1992, 453
HolFestCelWrld-1994, 232

Harvest Dance
Location: San Juan Pueblo, New Mexico
Date: Last week in September

IndianAmer-1989, 289, 312

Harvest Dance (Kyaiya)
Location: Gran Chaco, South America
Ethnic or religious group: Lengua Indians
Date: Spring, summer, and autumn

DictFolkMyth-1984, 597

Harvest Feast
Location: Cambodia: Phum Thuy

FolkWrldHol-1992, 445

Harvest Festival (Canada) and (England)
See **Lammas**

Harvest Festival (China)
See **Mid-Autumn Festival**

Harvest Festival (Kojagara)
Named for: Honors goddess Lakshmi
Location: India
Ethnic or religious group: Hindu
Date: September-October, full moon of Hindu month of Asvina

RelHolCal-1993, 88

Harvest Festival (Makara Sankranti in northern India, Pongal in southern India)
Location: India
Ethnic or religious group: Hindu
Date: Mid-January, three days during Hindu month of Pausha: first day is Bhogi or Bogi Pongal, Day of Joy; second day is Pongal (literally, "it boils"); and third day is Mattu Pongal, Festival of the Cows

AnnivHol-1983, 179
BkHolWrld-1986, January 14
Chases-1993, 62
FolkWrldHol-1992, 80
HolFestCelWrld-1994, 256
RelHolCal-1993, 93, 103

Harvest Festival (Magha Bihu or Bhogali Bihu, Festival of Feasts)
Location: India: Assam
Date: Mid-January, three days during Hindu month of Pausha: first day is Bhogi or Bogi Pongal, Day of Joy; second day is Pongal (literally, "it boils"); and third day is Mattu Pongal, Festival of the Cows

RelHolCal-1993, 93

Harvest Festival
Location: India: Ganga Sagar
Date: Mid-January, three days during Hindu month of Pausha: first day is Bhogi or Bogi Pongal, Day of Joy; second day is Pongal (literally, "it boils"); and third day is Mattu Pongal, Festival of the Cows

RelHolCal-1993, 93

Harvest Festival (Sankranti)
Location: India: Karnaraka
Date: Mid-January, three days during Hindu month of Pausha: first day is Bhogi or Bogi Pongal, Day of Joy; second day is Pongal (literally, "it boils"); and third day is Mattu Pongal, Festival of the Cows

FolkWrldHol-1992, 80

Harvest Festival (Onam)
Location: India: Kerala
Date: August-September, four to ten days in Malyalam month of Chingam

AnnivHol-1983, 180
BkHolWrld-1986, September 15, 180
Chases-1993, 346
GdWrldFest-1985, 111
HolFestCelWrld-1994, 238
RelHolCal-1993, 100

Harvest Festival (Jellikattu Festival)
Location: India: Madurai, Tiruchirapalli, and Tanjore
Date: Mid-January, three days during Hindu month of Pausha: first day is Bhogi or Bogi Pongal, Day of Joy; second day is Pongal (literally, "it boils"); and third day is Mattu Pongal, Festival of the Cows

FolkWrldHol-1992, 80
HolFestCelWrld-1994, 256

Harvest Festival (Lohri)
Location: India: Punjab
Date: Mid-January, three days during Hindu month of Pausha: first day is Bhogi or Bogi Pongal, Day of Joy;

second day is Pongal (literally, "it boils"); and third day is Mattu Pongal, Festival of the Cows

RelHolCal-1993, 93

Harvest Festival (Pongal)
Location: India: Tamil Nadu
Date: Mid-January, three days during Hindu month of Pausha: first day is Bhogi or Bogi Pongal, Day of Joy; second day is Pongal (literally, "it boils"); and third day is Mattu Pongal, Festival of the Cows

FolkWrldHol-1992, 80
HolFestCelWrld-1994, 256

Harvest Festival
Location: Ireland: County Offaly and other northern areas
Established: Centuries-old

FolkWrldHol-1992, 452

Harvest Festival (Pongal)
Location: Malaya
Ethnic or religious group: Tamil people
Date: Mid-January, three days during Hindu month of Pausha: first day is Bhogi or Bogi Pongal, Day of Joy; second day is Pongal (literally, "it boils"); and third day is Mattu Pongal, Festival of the Cows

FolkWrldHol-1992, 81

Harvest Festival, Padi
Location: Malaysia: Sabah
Ethnic or religious group: Kadazan or Dusun people
Date: May 30-31

HolFestCelWrld-1994, 243

Harvest Festival (Bungan)
Location: Malaysia: Sarawak
Ethnic or religious group: Berawan people
Date: February

FolkWrldHol-1992, 464

Harvest Festival (Imnarja or Mnarja)
Location: Malta: Buskett Gardens
Date: Last week in June, including June 29, Sts. Peter and Paul Day

AnnivHol-1983, 85
Chases-1993, 259
FolkWrldHol-1992, 345
HolFestCelWrld-1994, 209, 299

Harvest Festival (Makara or Magh Sankranti)
Location: Nepal
Date: Mid-January, three days during Hindu month of
    Pausha: first day is Bhogi or Bogi Pongal, Day of Joy;
    second day is Pongal (literally, "it boils"); and third
    day is Mattu Pongal, Festival of the Cows

FolkWrldHol-1992, 79
HolFestCelWrld-1994, 192

Harvest Festival (Nigeria)
See **New Yam Festival (Nigeria)**

**Harvest Festival (Pod Debami or Dozynki Festival; also
known as Okrezne)**
Location: Poland
Date: August 15

FolkWrldHol-1992, 462
HolFestCelWrld-1994, 88

Harvest Festival
Location: Yugoslavia: Daruvar, Croatia
Date: Second half of August

IntlThFolk-1979, 387

Harvest Festival in Provins, France, Wheat
Location: France: Provins
Established: Ancient times
Date: Last weekend in August

HolFestCelWrld-1994, 366

Harvest Festival for Our Lady of Flowers
See **Assumption, Feast of the (Polish-Americans in Orange
County, New York)**

Harvest Festivities, Duzijanca
Location: Yugoslavia: Subotica, Serbia
Date: July

IntlThFolk-1979, 406

Harvest Home Festival (Ingathering or Inning)
Location: England
Ethnic or religious group: Church of England
Date: September 24

AmerBkDays-1978, 1053
AnnivHol-1983, 122
BkDays-1864, ii. 376
DictFolkMyth-1984, 484
HolFestCelWrld-1994, 135
SaintFestCh-1904, 424

Harvest Home Festival (Mell Supper)
Location: Northern England
Date: September 24

BkDays-1864, ii.376

Harvest Home Festival (Kern or Kirn Supper)
Location: Scotland
Date: September 24

AmerBkDays-1978, 1053
BkDays-1864, ii.376
DictFolkMyth-1984, 484
HolFestCelWrld-1994, 135
SaintFestCh-1904, 424

Harvest of Grapes (Szüret)
Location: Hungary
Date: Late October

FolkWrldHol-1992, 451
HolFestCelWrld-1994, 329

Harvest Season (Lara)
Location: Uganda
Ethnic or religious group: Dodoth people

FolkWrldHol-1992, 469

Hauts-de-Saone Festival
Location: France: Luxeuil-les-Bains, Haute-Saône
Established: 1969
Date: Last weekend in June and first weekend in July

IntlThFolk-1979, 110

Haxey Hood Game
Location: England: Haxey
Established: Over six hundred years ago
Date: January 6

HolFestCelWrld-1994, 135

Haydn Memorial Concerts
Named for: Franz Joseph Haydn (1732-1809)
Location: Hungary: Eszterháza Palace, Fertöd
Date: Summer

MusFestWrld-1963, 157

Headdresses, Festival of the
See **Tabuleiros Festival (Christians in Tomar, Ribatejo,
Portugal)**

Heaving Day
See **Easter Monday (England)**

Heb-sed
Location: Ancient Egypt
Ethnic or religious group: Pharaohs

DictFolkMyth-1984, 487

Hede Festival
Location: France: Hede, Ille-et-Vilaine
Established: 1974
Date: About one week in August

IntlThFolk-1979, 108

Heiligabend
See **Christmas Eve (Germany)**

Heiliger Abend
See **Christmas Eve (Austria) and (Switzerland)**

Hellbrunn Festival (Fest in Hellbrunn)
Location: Austria: Salzburg
Established: 1970
Date: First two weekends in August

IntlThFolk-1979, 38

Helligtrekongersdag, Day of the Three Holy Kings
See **Epiphany (Denmark)**

Helsinki Day
Named for: June 12, 1550, founding of the city
Location: Finland
Established: 1959
Date: June 12

AnnivHol-1983, 78

Helsinki Festival (Helsingin Juhlaviikot)
Location: Finland: Helsinki
Established: 1967, when combined with Festival for Jean Sibelius (1865-1957)
Date: 18 days beginning August 24

Chases-1993, 341
GdWrldFest-1985, 75
IntlThFolk-1979, 94
MusFestEurBrit-1980, 66
MusFestWrld-1963, 188

Helston Furry Dance
See **Furry Day**

Hemingway Days
Named for: Ernest Hemingway (1899-1961)
Location: Key West, Florida
Established: 1980

Date: Week including July 21

HolFestCelWrld-1994, 136

Hemis Festival
Named for: Commemorates birthday of Guru Padmasambhava, Tantric Buddhist mystic who lived during the eighth century
Location: India: Hemis Gompa monastery, Ladakh
Ethnic or religious group: Buddhist
Date: Three days in June or July

HolFestCelWrld-1994, 136
RelHolCal-1993, 83

Herb Evening
See **Midsummer Eve**

Heritage Holidays
Named for: Commemorates John Wisdom (1820-1909), "Paul Revere of the South," who rode from Alabama to Rome to warn of a Union attack during the Civil War
Location: Rome, Georgia
Date: Mid-October

HolFestCelWrld-1994, 137

Heritage Month
Location: Rhode Island
Date: May

AmerBkDays-1978, 419
GdUSFest-1984, 164
See also **Independence Day (Rhode Island)**

Hermit, Feast of the
Named for: Juan Maria de Castellano (fl. late 19th-early 20th century)
Location: Hot Springs, New Mexico
Ethnic or religious group: Roman Catholic Hispanic-Americans
Date: September 1

FolkAmerHol-1987, 269

Hero, Day of the National
Location: Angola
Date: September 17

AnnivHol-1983, 120

Heroes Day
Location: Cape Verde
Date: January 20

AnnivHol-1983, 11

Heroes Day
Named for: April 11, 1856, Battle of Rivas
Location: Costa Rica
Date: April 11

AnnivHol-1983, 50

Heroes Day
Location: Jamaica
Date: October 18

AnnivHol-1983, 134
Chases-1993, 414

Heroes Day
Named for: May 22, 1971, rebellion
Location: Sri Lanka
Date: May 22

AnnivHol-1983, 69

Heroes' Day
Location: Zambia
Date: First Monday in July

AnnivHol-1983, 89
Chases-1993, 281

Heroes Days
Location: Zimbabwe
Date: Two-day holiday, including August 11

AnnivHol-1983, 105

Heshwash Ceremony
Ethnic or religious group: California Yokuts Indians
Date: Uncertain; two nights

DictFolkMyth-1984, 494

Hesi Ceremony
Location: Central California
Ethnic or religious group: Kuksu secret society of North
  American Indians

DictFolkMyth-1984, 494

Hexham Abbey Festival
Location: England: Hexham, Northumberland
Established: 1964
Date: Last two weeks in October

IntlThFolk-1979, 161

Hickory's Day
See **Battle of New Orleans Day**

Higan Ritual
See **Autumnal Equinox Day (Buddhist people in Japan)**

High Holiday or High Holy Days
See **New Year, Jewish (Rosh Hashanah); Yom Kippur**

Highland Festival and Games
Location: Alma, Michigan
Ethnic or religious group: Scottish-Americans
Established: May 1968
Date: Last weekend in May

Chases-1993, 222
GdUSFest-1984, 91
HolFestCelWrld-1994, 7

Highland Games
Location: Scotland
Date: Around August 1 into September

AnnivHol-1983, 177
Chases-1993, 356
HolFestCelWrld-1994, 137

Highland Games, Brantford
Location: Canada: Brantford, Ontario
Ethnic or religious group: Scottish-Canadians
Established: 1964
Date: Second Saturday in July

IntlThFolk-1979, 68

Highland Games, Fergus
Location: Canada: Fergus, Ontario
Date: Second Saturday in August

IntlThFolk-1979, 69

Highland Games, Glengarry
Location: Canada: Maxville, Ontario
Established: 1948
Date: Saturday before the first Monday in August

IntlThFolk-1979, 70

**Highland Games and Gathering of Scottish Clans,
Grandfather Mountain**
Location: Grandfather Mountain near Linville,
  North Carolina
Ethnic or religious group: Scottish-Americans
Established: 1956
Date: Second full weekend in July

AmerBkDays-1978, 653
HolFestCelWrld-1994, 122

Highland Gathering, Braemar
  Location: Scotland: Braemar
  Established: 11th century
  Date: First Saturday in September

  AnnivHol-1983, 174
  BkHolWrld-1986, September 6, 176
  Chases-1993, 356
  HolFestCelWrld-1994, 41

High Places, Festival of
  See **Double Ninth (China)**

Híkuli
  See **Dance, Peyote (Tarahumara and Huichol Indians'
   journey to eastern Chihuahua, Mexico)**

Hilaria
  Named for: Honored Cybele
  Location: Ancient Rome
  Date: March 15

  DaysCustFaith-1957, 89
  FestSaintDays-1915, 50
  HolFestCelWrld-1994, 138

Hill Cumorah Pageant
  Location: Cumorah Hill, near Palmyra, New York
  Ethnic or religious group: Mormon (Church of Jesus Christ
   of the Latter Day Saints)
  Date: Nine days (excluding Sunday and Monday) beginning
   third weekend in July

  GdUSFest-1984, 129
  HolFestCelWrld-1994, 138
  RelHolCal-1993, 83

Hill of Doves
  See **Majuba Day (Boer people in South Africa)**

Himmelfahrstag
  See **Ascension Day (Germany)**

Hina Matsuri
  See **Girls' Doll Festival (Japan)**

Hippokrateia
  Named for: Hippocrates (c. 460 B.C.-c. 377 B.C.)
  Location: Greece: Kos
  Date: August

  HolFestCelWrld-1994, 138

Hirohito's Birthday (Tencho Setsu)
  Named for: Hirohito (1901-1989)
  Location: Japan

  Date: April 29

  AnnivHol-1983, 58
  BkFest-1937, 198
  Chases-1993, 184
  NatlHolWrld-1968, 52

Hiroshima Day
  Named for: August 6, 1945, U.S. atomic bombing of
   Hiroshima
  Date: August 6

  AnnivHol-1983, 104
  Chases-1993, 318
  DictDays-1988, 56
  See also **Peace Festival**

Hispanity Day
  See **Columbus Day (Spain)**

Hobart Cup Day
  Location: Australia: southern Tasmania
  Date: On or near January 23

  DictDays-1988, 75
  HolFestCelWrld-1994, 139

Hobo Convention
  Location: Britt, Iowa
  Established: 1900
  Date: Three days in August

  HolFestCelWrld-1994, 139

Hock Day, Hock Monday, Hock Tuesday, or Hocktide
  See **Easter Monday (England)**

Hodening
  See **Christmas Season (England: Kent)**

Hogmanay
  See **New Year's Eve (northern England and Scotland)**

Hoi Lim Festival
  Location: Vietnam: Ha Bac Province
  Date: Usually February, 13th day of first lunar month

  HolFestCelWrld-1994, 140

Hoke Day
  See **Easter Monday (England)**

Ho Khao Padap Dinh
  See **Dead, Feast of the (Laos)**

Ho Khao Slak
  See **Lenten Season (Buddhist people in Laos)**

Hola Mohalla
Location: India: Anandpur Sahib
Ethnic or religious group: Sikh people
Date: March 8

Chases-1993, 123
HolFestCelWrld-1994, 140

Holi
See **Fire Festival (Bangladesh), (Hindu), (India), (North Dravidian people in India), (Mauritius), (Nepal), and (Pakistan)**

Holi Phagwa
See **Fire Festival (Surinam)**

Holland Festival
Location: Netherlands: Amsterdam, Rotterdam, Scheveningen, The Hague, and other cities
Established: 1947
Date: 23 days in June

GdWrldFest-1985, 141
HolFestCelWrld-1994, 141
IntlThFolk-1979, 283
MusFestEurBrit-1980, 124
MusFestWrld-1963, 193

Hollerin' Contest, National
Location: Spivey's Corner, North Carolina
Established: 1969
Date: Third Saturday in June

Chases-1993, 256
GdUSFest-1984, 133

Hollybush Festival
Location: Glassboro, New Jersey
Established: 1983
Date: May and June

MusFestAmer-1990, 92

Hollyhock Festival (Aoi Matsuri)
Location: Japan: Kyoto
Established: Sixth century
Date: May 15

Chases-1993, 209
GdWrldFest-1985, 122
HolFestCelWrld-1994, 12

Holocaust Day (Yom Hashoah)
Ethnic or religious group: Jewish
Date: March-April, 27th of Jewish month of Nisan

AnnivHol-1983, 172

Chases-1993, 172
DictWrldRel-1989, 325, 392
HolFestCelWrld-1994, 141
RelHolCal-1993, 122

Holy Blood, Procession of the (Processie van het Heilig Bloed)
Location: Belgium: Bruges, West Flanders
Ethnic or religious group: Roman Catholic
Established: April 7, 1150, return to Bruges of Count Thierry of Alsace (1100-1168) with the relic of the Holy Blood; legal holiday since 1820
Date: First Monday after May 2

AnnivHol-1983, 63
BkFest-1937, 42
BkHolWrld-1986, May 21
Chases-1993, 215
FestWestEur-1958, 11
GdWrldFest-1985, 19
HolFestCelWrld-1994, 141

Holy Cross Day
See **Exaltation of the Cross (Armenian-Americans in the United States)**

Holy Day of Letters
Named for: Sts. Cyril (c. 827-869) and Methodius (c. 825-884) of Thessalonica
Location: Bulgaria
Date: May 24, Gregorian calendar (N.S.); May 11, Julian calendar (O.S.)

BkFest-1937, 71
BkHolWrld-1986, May 24
HolFestCelWrld-1994, 142

Holy Day of Letters
Named for: Sts. Cyril (c. 827-869) and Methodius (c. 825-884) of Thessalonica
Location: Yugoslavia
Date: May 24, Gregorian calendar (N.S.); May 11, Julian calendar (O.S.)

BkFest-1937, 341

Holy Family, Feast of the
Ethnic or religious group: Roman Catholic
Established: 17th century; official church day since 1921
Date: January, Sunday after Epiphany

DaysCustFaith-1957, 37
HolFestCelWrld-1994, 142
RelHolCal-1993, 84

Holy Friday
See **Good Friday**

Holy Ghost, Feast of the (Altura Do Espírito Santo)
Location: Portugal: Ponta Delgada, Sao Miguel Island,
  Azores
Ethnic or religious group: Roman Catholic
Established: Since 14th or late 15th century
Date: March-August

FolkWrldHol-1992, 276
GdUSFest-1984, 156
HolFestCelWrld-1994, 142
IntlThFolk-1979, 311

Holy Ghost, Festival of the
Location: Plymouth, Massachusetts
Ethnic or religious group: Roman Catholic Portuguese-
  Americans
Established: 1910
Date: Three days in mid-July

GdUSFest-1984, 88

Holy Innocents' Day
Named for: All the male children under two years old
  killed by King Herod in his attempt to kill Jesus
  (c. 6 B.C.- c. 30 A.D.)
Ethnic or religious group: Christian
Established: Beginning of first century a.d.; Church holy
  day since end of fifth century
Date: December 28

AmerBkDays-1978, 1155
AnnivHol-1983, 165
BkDays-1864, ii. 776, 777
BkFest-1937, 49, 63, 175, 223, 234, 347
BkHolWrld-1986, December 28
Chases-1993, 484
DaysCustFaith-1957, 324
DictDays-1988, 20, 57, 59
DictFolkMyth-1984, 218, 525, 950, 951, 1018
FestSaintDays-1915, 252, 255
FestWestEur-1958, 20, 84
FolkAmerHol-1987, 407
FolkWrldHol-1992, 645
HolFestCelWrld-1994, 142
IndianAmer-1989, 291, 315
RelHolCal-1993, 84
SaintFestCh-1904, 44

Holy Innocents' Day
Ethnic or religious group: Anglican
Date: December 28

DictFolkMyth-1984, 1018

Holy Innocents' Day
Ethnic or religious group: Church of England
Date: December 28

BkDays-1864, ii.776

Holy Innocents' Day
Ethnic or religious group: Eastern Orthodox
Date: December 29

AmerBkDays-1978, 1156
AnnivHol-1983, 165

Holy Innocents' Day
Ethnic or religious group: Episcopalian
Date: December 28

AmerBkDays-1978, 1155

Holy Innocents' Day
Ethnic or religious group: Greek Orthodox
Date: December 28

AmerBkDays-1978, 1156

Holy Innocents' Day
Ethnic or religious group: Lutheran
Date: December 28

AmerBkDays-1978, 1155

Holy Innocents' Day
Ethnic or religious group: Protestant
Date: December 28

AmerBkDays-1978, 1155

Holy Innocents' Day
Ethnic or religious group: Roman Catholic
Date: December 28

AmerBkDays-1978, 1155
BkHolWrld-1986, December 28
DictFolkMyth-1984, 1018
SaintFestCh-1904, 44

Holy Innocents' Day
Location: Austria
Date: December 28

FolkWrldHol-1992, 645

Holy Innocents' Day (Le Jour des Innocents)
Location: Belgium
Date: December 28

AmerBkDays-1978, 1156
AnnivHol-1983, 165
BkFest-1937, 49
FestWestEur-1958, 20

Holy Innocents' Day
  Location: Bohemia
  Date: December 28

  DictFolkMyth-1984, 950

Holy Innocents' Day
  Location: Colombia
  Date: December 28

  AnnivHol-1983, 165

Holy Innocents' Day (Childermas)
  Location: England
  Date: December 28

  AmerBkDays-1978, 1157
  BkDays-1864, ii.776
  BkFest-1937, 63
  DictFolkMyth-1984, 218, 525
  FestSaintDays-1915, 255
  FolkWrldHol-1992, 645
  SaintFestCh-1904, 44

Holy Innocents' Day
  Location: France
  Date: December 28

  AmerBkDays-1978, 1157
  DictFolkMyth-1984, 525

Holy Innocents' Day (Allerkinder Tag)
  Location: Germany: Thüringia
  Date: December 28

  AmerBkDays-1978, 1156
  BkFest-1937, 141
  DictFolkMyth-1984, 951
  FestWestEur-1958, 84

Holy Innocents' Day (Cross Day)
  Location: Ireland
  Date: December 28

  AnnivHol-1983, 165
  BkFest-1937, 63
  DictFolkMyth-1984, 218, 525

Holy Innocents' Day (Nekaltuju Šventė)
  Location: Lithuania
  Date: December 28

  BkFest-1937, 223

Holy Innocents' Day
  Location: Maryland

  Ethnic or religious group: African-Americans
  Date: December 28

  FolkAmerHol-1987, 407

Holy Innocents' Day (Día de los Inocentes)
  Location: Mexico
  Date: December 28

  AmerBkDays-1978, 1156
  AnnivHol-1983, 165
  BkFest-1937, 234
  FolkAmerHol-1987, 407
  FolkWrldHol-1992, 645
  HolFestCelWrld-1994, 142

Holy Innocents' Day
  Location: Santa Clara Pueblo, New Mexico
  Date: December 28

  IndianAmer-1989, 291, 315

Holy Innocents' Day
  Location: Spain
  Ethnic or religious group: Catalan people
  Date: December 28

  FolkWrldHol-1992, 645

Holy Innocents' Day (Mladenci)
  Location: Yugoslavia
  Ethnic or religious group: Croatian people
  Date: December 28

  BkFest-1937, 347

Holy Kings' Day
  See **Epiphany**

Holy Maries, Feast of (La Fête des Saintes Maries)
  Location: France: pilgrimage to Les Saintes-Maries-de-la-Mer, Provence
  Ethnic or religious group: Romany people
  Date: May 24-25

  AnnivHol-1983, 70
  BkFest-1937, 123
  DictFolkMyth-1984, 954
  FestWestEur-1958, 38
  FolkWrldHol-1992, 302
  HolFestCelWrld-1994, 288

Holy Queen, Festival of the (Festa da Rainha Santa Isabel)
  Location: Portugal: Coimbra, Beira Litoral
  Named for: St. Isabel (c. 1271-1336)
  Date: First two weeks in July during even-numbered years

  FestWestEur-1958, 170

Holyrood Day
See **Exaltation of the Cross (England), (Roman Catholic),
and (Scotland)**

Holy Saturday (Easter Even)
Ethnic or religious group: Christian
Date: March-April, Saturday before Easter Sunday

AmerBkDays-1978, 297
AnnivHol-1983, 169
BkDays-1864, i.421
BkFest-1937, 24, 41, 70, 87, 96, 148, 168, 184, 211,
  227, 260, 275, 292, 301, 339
BkFestHolWrld-1970, 55
BkHolWrld-1986, April 11
Chases-1993, 161
DaysCustFaith-1957, 108
DictFolkMyth-1984, 258
FestSaintDays-1915, 74
FestWestEur-1958, 9, 60, 94, 108
FolkWrldHol-1992, 190, 197, 199, 202
HolFestCelWrld-1994, 142
IndianAmer-1989, 274
RelHolCal-1993, 64
SaintFestCh-1904, 161

Holy Saturday
Ethnic or religious group: Anglican
Date: March-April, Saturday before Easter Sunday

HolFestCelWrld-1994, 143

Holy Saturday
Ethnic or religious group: Eastern Orthodox
Date: March-April, Saturday before Easter Sunday

AmerBkDays-1978, 298
BkFest-1937, 292
HolFestCelWrld-1994, 143

Holy Saturday
Ethnic or religious group: Episcopalian
Date: March-April, Saturday before Easter Sunday

AmerBkDays-1978, 297
DaysCustFaith-1957, 108

Holy Saturday
Ethnic or religious group: Lutheran
Date: March-April, Saturday before Easter Sunday

AmerBkDays-1978, 297

Holy Saturday
Ethnic or religious group: Roman Catholic

Date: March-April, Saturday before Easter Sunday

AmerBkDays-1978, 297
BkDays-1864, i.421
BkFest-1937, 339
BkFestHolWrld-1970, 55
FolkAmerHol-1987, 134
SaintFestCh-1904, 161

Holy Saturday
Location: Arizona
Ethnic or religious group: Yaqui Indians
Date: March-April, Saturday before Easter Sunday

DictFolkMyth-1984, 258
IndianAmer-1989, 273

Holy Saturday
Location: Southern Arizona and Mexico
Ethnic or religious group: Yaqui and Mayo Indians
Date: March-April, Saturday before Easter Sunday

DictFolkMyth-1984, 258

**Holy Saturday (Avak Shapat; Djerakoloytz, Day of
Illumination)**
Location: Armenia
Date: March-April, Saturday before Easter Sunday

BkFest-1937, 24

Holy Saturday (Zaterdag voor Paschen)
Location: Belgium
Date: March-April, Saturday before Easter Sunday

BkFest-1937, 41
FestWestEur-1958, 9
FolkWrldHol-1992, 190

Holy Saturday (Strastna Subota, Passion Saturday)
Location: Bulgaria
Date: March-April, Saturday before Easter Sunday

BkFest-1937, 70
See also **Lazarus Day**

Holy Saturday (Blessing of the Animals)
Location: Los Angeles, California
Ethnic or religious group: Mexican-Americans
Date: March-April, Saturday before Easter Sunday

AmerBkDays-1978, 299
FolkAmerHol-1987, 134
HolFestCelWrld-1994, 143

Holy Saturday (Bílí Sobota, White Saturday)
Location: Czechoslovakia
Date: March-April, Saturday before Easter Sunday

BkFest-1937, 87

Holy Saturday (Paaskeaften)
Location: Denmark
Date: March-April, Saturday before Easter Sunday

BkFest-1937, 96

Holy Saturday (Pääsiäisaatto, Easter Eve)
Location: Finland
Date: March-April, Saturday before Easter Sunday

BkFest-1937, 112

Holy Saturday (Karsamstag)
Location: Germany
Date: March-April, Saturday before Easter Sunday

FestWestEur-1958, 60

Holy Saturday
Location: Great Britain
Date: March-April, Saturday before Easter Sunday

RelHolCal-1993, 64

Holy Saturday (Meghalo Savato)
Location: Greece
Date: March-April, Saturday before Easter Sunday

BkFest-1937, 148

Holy Saturday (Nagyszombat)
Location: Hungary
Date: March-April, Saturday before Easter Sunday

BkFest-1937, 168

Holy Saturday (Sabato Santo)
Location: Italy
Date: March-April, Saturday before Easter Sunday

BkDays-1864, i.421
BkFest-1937, 184
FestSaintDays-1915, 74
FestWestEur-1958, 94

Holy Saturday (Scoppia del Carro, Explosion of the Car)
Location: Italy: Florence, Tuscany
Date: March-April, Saturday before Easter Sunday

FestWestEur-1958, 94

Holy Saturday (Klusā Sestdiena, Quiet Saturday)
Location: Latvia
Date: March-April, Saturday before Easter Sunday

BkFest-1937, 211

Holy Saturday (Charsamsdeg)
Location: Luxembourg
Date: March-April, Saturday before Easter Sunday

FestWestEur-1958, 108

Holy Saturday
Location: Macedonia
Date: March-April, Saturday before Easter Sunday

FolkWrldHol-1992, 197

Holy Saturday (Sábato de Gloria, Saturday of Glory)
Location: Mexico
Date: March-April, Saturday before Easter Sunday

BkFest-1937, 227
BkHolWrld-1986, April 11
DictFolkMyth-1984, 258
FolkWrldHol-1992, 199

Holy Saturday
Location: New York Mills, New York
Ethnic or religious group: Polish-Americans
Date: March-April, Saturday before Easter Sunday

FolkAmerHol-1987, 133

Holy Saturday (Wielka Sobota, Great Saturday)
Location: Poland
Date: March-April, Saturday before Easter Sunday

BkFest-1937, 260
FolkWrldHol-1992, 202

Holy Saturday (Sâmbăta Mare)
Location: Romania
Date: March-April, Saturday before Easter Sunday

BkFest-1937, 275

Holy Saturday (Velikaya Subbota, Great Saturday)
Location: Russia
Date: March-April, Saturday before Easter Sunday

BkFest-1937, 292

Holy Saturday (Sabado de Gloria)
Location: Spain
Date: March-April, Saturday before Easter Sunday

BkFest-1937, 301

Holy Saturday
  Location: Sweden
  Date: March-April, Saturday before Easter Sunday

  FolkWrldHol-1992, 203

Holy Saturday (Easter Fires Pageant)
  Location: Fredericksburg, Texas
  Established: 1846
  Date: March-April, Saturday before Easter Sunday

  AmerBkDays-1978, 299
  HolFestCelWrld-1994, 94

Holy Saturday
  Location: United States
  Ethnic or religious group: Eastern Orthodox
  Date: March-April, Saturday before Easter Sunday

  AmerBkDays-1978, 299

Holy Saturday
  Location: United States
  Ethnic or religious group: Neo-pagans
  Date: March-April, Saturday before Easter Sunday

  RelHolCal-1993, 64

Holy Saturday (Velika Subota)
  Location: Yugoslavia
  Ethnic or religious group: Roman Catholic
  Date: March-April, Saturday before Easter Sunday

  BkFest-1937, 339

Holy Spirit, Festival of the Divine
  Location: Brazil: Diamantina and other cities
  Established: 16th century
  Date: One week in May

  HolFestCelWrld-1994, 85

Holy Thursday
  Ethnic or religious group: Christian
  Date: March-April, Thursday preceding Easter

  AmerBkDays-1978, 291
  AnnivHol-1983, 169, 181
  BkDays-1864, i.411
  BkFest-1937, 56, 183, 227, 329
  BkFestHolWrld-1970, 61
  Chases-1993, 159
  DaysCustFaith-1957, 106
  DictDays-1988, 58, 74, 110, 112
  DictFolkMyth-1984, 694, 1163

  DictWrldRel-1989, 261, 468
  FestSaintDays-1915, 61
  FestWestEur-1958, 8, 60, 93, 212
  FolkAmerHol-1987, 129
  FolkWrldHol-1992, 190, 193, 197, 199, 203
  HolFestCelWrld-1994, 200
  SaintFestCh-1904, 158

Holy Thursday
  Ethnic or religious group: Anglican
  Date: March-April, Thursday before Easter

  HolFestCelWrld-1994, 200

Holy Thursday
  Ethnic or religious group: Eastern Orthodox
  Date: March-April, Thursday preceding Easter

  AmerBkDays-1978, 291
  DictFolkMyth-1984, 694
  DictWrldRel-1989, 261, 468

Holy Thursday
  Ethnic or religious group: Greek Orthodox
  Date: March-April, Thursday preceding Easter

  BkFestHolWrld-1970, 53

Holy Thursday
  Ethnic or religious group: Protestant
  Date: March-April, Thursday preceding Easter

  AmerBkDays-1978, 291

Holy Thursday
  Ethnic or religious group: Roman Catholic
  Date: March-April, Thursday preceding Easter

  AmerBkDays-1978, 291
  BkDays-1864, i.411
  BkFestHolWrld-1970, 53
  DaysCustFaith-1957, 106
  DictDays-1988, 74
  DictFolkMyth-1984, 694
  DictWrldRel-1989, 261, 468
  HolFestCelWrld-1994, 200

Holy Thursday
  Location: Austria
  Date: March-April, Thursday preceding Easter

  BkDays-1864, i.411

Holy Thursday (Witte Donderdag)
  Location: Belgium
  Date: March-April, Thursday preceding Easter

  FestWestEur-1958, 8
  FolkWrldHol-1992, 190

Holy Thursday
   Location: England
   Ethnic or religious group: Church of England
   Date: May, Ascension Day, fortieth day after Easter Sunday

   BkDays-1864, i. 595
   DaysCustFaith-1957, 135
   DictDays-1988, 6, 58
   DictWrldRel-1989, 261, 468
   HolFestCelWrld-1994, 143
   RelHolCal-1993, 58
   SaintFestCh-1904, 231

Holy Thursday
   Location: France
   Date: March-April, Thursday preceding Easter

   FolkWrldHol-1992, 193

Holy Thursday (Gründonnerstag, Green Thursday)
   Location: Germany
   Date: March-April, Thursday preceding Easter

   FestSaintDays-1915, 62
   FestWestEur-1958, 60
   HolFestCelWrld-1994, 200

Holy Thursday (Maundy Thursday)
   Location: Great Britain
   Date: March-April, Thursday preceding Easter

   AnnivHol-1983, 181
   BkDays-1864, i.411
   BkFest-1937, 56
   DaysCustFaith-1957, 106
   DictDays-1988, 58, 74, 110, 112
   DictFolkMyth-1984, 694
   FestSaintDays-1915, 61
   SaintFestCh-1904, 158

Holy Thursday (Giovedì Santo)
   Location: Italy
   Date: March-April, Thursday preceding Easter

   BkDays-1864, i.412
   BkFest-1937, 183
   FestSaintDays-1915, 61
   FestWestEur-1958, 93

Holy Thursday (Khamis al-Jasad)
   Location: Jerusalem
   Date: March-April, Thursday preceding Easter

   BkFest-1937, 329

Holy Thursday
   Location: Macedonia
   Date: March-April, Thursday preceding Easter

   FolkWrldHol-1992, 197

Holy Thursday (Jueves Santo)
   Location: Mexico
   Date: March-April, Thursday preceding Easter

   BkFest-1937, 227
   FolkWrldHol-1992, 199

Holy Thursday
   Location: Rome
   Date: March-April, Thursday preceding Easter

   BkDays-1864, i.411
   DictWrldRel-1989, 261
   FestSaintDays-1915, 61
   SaintFestCh-1904, 158

Holy Thursday (Votjak or Udmurt)
   Location: Russia: Kazan, Vjatka, and Perm
   Ethnic or religious group: Finno-Ugric people
   Date: March-April, Thursday preceding Easter

   DictFolkMyth-1984, 1163

Holy Thursday (Giovedì Santo)
   Location: Sicily
   Date: March-April, Thursday preceding Easter

   FestWestEur-1958, 93

Holy Thursday (Skärtorsdag)
   Location: Sweden
   Date: March-April, Thursday preceding Easter

   FestWestEur-1958, 193
   FolkWrldHol-1992, 203

Holy Thursday (Khamis al-Jasad)
   Location: Syria
   Date: March-April, Thursday preceding Easter

   BkFest-1937, 329

Holy Thursday
   Location: Turkey: Istanbul
   Date: March-April, Thursday preceding Easter

   AmerBkDays-1978, 291

Holy Thursday
   Location: United States
   Date: March-April, Thursday preceding Easter

   AmerBkDays-1978, 292
   FolkAmerHol-1987, 129

Holy Thursday
  Location: United States
  Ethnic or religious group: Italian-Americans
  Date: March-April, Thursday preceding Easter

  FestWestEur-1958, 93

Holy Week
  Ethnic or religious group: Christian
  Date: March-April, week preceding Easter

  BkFest-1937, 69, 274
  BkFestHolWrld-1970, 51, 53, 54
  Chases-1993, 154
  DaysCustFaith-1957, 103, 106
  DictDays-1988, 111, 113
  DictFolkMyth-1984, 1063, 1171
  DictWrldRel-1989, 326
  FestSaintDays-1915, 67
  FestWestEur-1958, 164, 192
  FolkWrldHol-1992, 196
  GdWrldFest-1985, 65
  HolFestCelWrld-1994, 143, 317
  IntlThFolk-1979, 276

Holy Week
  Ethnic or religious group: Greek Orthodox
  Date: March-April, week preceding Easter

  BkFestHolWrld-1970, 51, 53

Holy Week
  Ethnic or religious group: Protestant
  Date: March-April, week preceding Easter

  DaysCustFaith-1957, 103

Holy Week
  Ethnic or religious group: Roman Catholic
  Date: March-April, week preceding Easter

  BkFestHolWrld-1970, 51
  DaysCustFaith-1957, 103
  HolFestCelWrld-1994, 143

Holy Week (Deer Dance and Lenten Ceremonies)
  Location: Arizona
  Ethnic or religious group: Yaqui Indians
  Date: March-April, week preceding Easter

  IndianAmer-1989, 273
  See also **Lent (Yaqui Indians in Arizona)**

Holy Week (Strastna Nedelya)
  Location: Bulgaria
  Date: March-April, week preceding Easter

  BkFest-1937, 69

Holy Week
  Location: Colombia: Popayan
  Established: Observances and processions since mid-16th century
  Date: March-April, week preceding Easter

  GdWrldFest-1985, 65

Holy Week
  Location: France
  Date: March-April, week preceding Easter

  DictFolkMyth-1984, 1171

Holy Week (Still or Silent Week)
  Location: Germany
  Date: March-April, week preceding Easter

  DaysCustFaith-1957, 103

Holy Week (Semana Santa)
  Location: Guatemala
  Date: March-April, week preceding Easter

  FolkWrldHol-1992, 196
  HolFestCelWrld-1994, 311

Holy Week (Semana Santa)
  Location: Guatemala: Antigua
  Date: March-April, week preceding Easter

  HolFestCelWrld-1994, 311

Holy Week
  Location: Guatemala: Cantel
  Date: March-April, week preceding Easter

  FolkWrldHol-1992, 196

Holy Week
  Location: Italy: Tuscany
  Date: March-April, week preceding Easter

  FolkWrldHol-1992, 197

Holy Week
  Location: Macedonia
  Date: March-April, week preceding Easter

  FolkWrldHol-1992, 197

Holy Week
  Location: Mexico
  Date: March-April, week preceding Easter

  FolkWrldHol-1992, 199
  IntlThFolk-1979, 276

Holy Week
Location: Mexico: Potam, Sonora
Ethnic or religious group: Yaqui Indians
Date: March-April, week preceding Easter; ceremonies include Deer Dance

IntlThFolk-1979, 276

Holy Week
Location: Palestine
Date: March-April, week preceding Easter

FolkWrldHol-1992, 201

Holy Week (Semana Santo)
Location: Portugal
Date: March-April, week preceding Easter; processions in Covilha and Vila do Conde

FestWestEur-1958, 164

Holy Week (Saptamînapatimilor)
Location: Romania
Date: March-April, week preceding Easter

BkFest-1937, 274

Holy Week
Location: Rome
Date: March-April, week preceding Easter

BkDays-1864, i.407

Holy Week
Location: Sicily
Date: March-April, week preceding Easter

FolkWrldHol-1992, 202

Holy Week (Semana Santa)
Location: Spain
Date: March-April, week preceding Easter; processions in Seville and Murcia

BkFestHolWrld-1970, 54
DictFolkMyth-1984, 1063
FestSaintDays-1915, 67
FestWestEur-1958, 192
FolkWrldHol-1992, 202

Holy Week
Location: United States
Date: March-April, week preceding Easter

DaysCustFaith-1957, 103
FolkAmerHol-1987, 129

Holy Years
Ethnic or religious group: Roman Catholic
Established: 1300, Rome
Date: Every 25 years

DictWrldRel-1989, 326

Homenaje a Cuauhtemoc
See **Cuauhtemoc, Homage to (Mexico: Mexico City)**

Homolje Motifs
Location: Yugoslavia: Kucevo, Serbia
Date: May

IntlThFolk-1979, 391

Homowo
See **Hooting at Hunger**

Homstrom
Location: Switzerland and United States
Ethnic or religious group: Swiss-Americans
Date: First Sunday in February

AnnivHol-1983, 18
Chases-1993, 90
RelHolCal-1993, 84

Honey Day
Location: Russia
Ethnic or religious group: Christian
Date: August 1

FolkWrldHol-1992, 411

Hong Kong, Festival of
Location: Hong Kong
Date: Ten days in November-December during odd-numbered years

IntlThFolk-1979, 197

Hooting at Hunger (Homowo)
Location: Ghana
Ethnic or religious group: Ga people
Date: August

BkHolWrld-1986, August 1
FolkWrldHol-1992, 450
HolFestCelWrld-1994, 143

Horaiji Temple Dengaku Festival
Location: Japan: Horai, Aichi
Date: Early February

IntlThFolk-1979, 253

Horizon '79, '81, etc.
Location: Federal Republic of Germany: West Berlin
Established: 1979
Date: Three to four weeks in June-July during odd-
numbered years

IntlThFolk-1979, 132

Horns, Festival of (Kil'vey)
Location: Russia
Ethnic or religious group: Koryak people
Date: Spring

FolkWrldHol-1992, 227

Horse, Festival of the
Location: Oklahoma City, Oklahoma
Date: Nine days in October

HolFestCelWrld-1994, 145

Horse Fair
Location: Spain: Jerez de la Frontera, Cádiz
Established: 1284
Date: May

IntlThFolk-1979, 338

Horse Festival
See **Fantasia (Morocco: Fez) and (Morocco: Meknes)**

Horse Festival (Lejkonik)
Location: Poland: Kraków
Date: Second Thursday after Corpus Christi

BkFest-1937, 262

Horse Festival, Wild (Nomaoi Matsuri)
Location: Japan: Honshu
Date: Three days in July or August

AnnivHol-1983, 183
Chases-1993, 303

Horse Meet Show and Races, National
Location: Iceland: Skagafjordur
Date: Four days in July every four years

GdWrldFest-1985, 109

Horse Sacrifice, October
Location: Ancient Rome
Date: October 15

DictFolkMyth-1984, 811

Horses, Blessing of
See **Nativity of the Virgin, Feast of the (Germany:
St. Märgen, Black Forest)**

Horse Show, Dublin
Location: Ireland: Dublin
Date: Six days in August

GdWrldFest-1985, 113

Horse Show and Country Fair, Devon
Location: Devon, Pennsylvania
Established: 1896
Date: Nine days in May

GdUSFest-1984, 157

Hosay Festival
See **Husayn Day (Jamaica), (Trinidad), and (Afro- and
Indo-Guyanese people in Guyana)**

Hoshana Rabbah (Great Salvation)
Ethnic or religious group: Jewish
Date: September-October, seventh day of Sukkot on 21st
of Jewish month of Tishri

DaysCustFaith-1957, 272
HolFestCelWrld-1994, 146

Hospital Day or Hospital Saturday (Great Britain)
See **Alexandra Rose Day**

Hospital Day and Week, National
Named for: Commemorated during week including
May 12, birthday of Florence Nightingale (1820-1910)
Location: Hospitals and hospital associations in the
United States
Established: 1921
Date: Week including May 12

AnnivHol-1983, 65
Chases-1993, 202
DictDays-1988, 58
HolFestCelWrld-1994, 146

Hostos, Birthday of (Hostos Day)
Named for: Eugenio Maria de Hostos (1839-1903)
Location: Puerto Rico and the United States
Date: January 11

AnnivHol-1983, 7
BkHolWrld-1986, January 11
Chases-1993, 61

Hot Air Balloon Championships, United States National
Location: Indianola, Iowa
Established: 1970
Date: Ten days in late July or early August

Chases-1993, 310
GdUSFest-1984, 58
HolFestCelWrld-1994, 146

Houses and Gardens, Festival of
  Location: Charleston, South Carolina
  Established: 1947
  Date: 26 days in March-April

  GdUSFest-1984, 168
  HolFestCelWrld-1994, 146

Humane Sunday
  Location: American Humane Society-sponsored;
   United States
  Date: First Sunday in May

  AnnivHol-1983, 61

Human Rights Day and Week
  Location: United Nations-sponsored; observed in
   Equatorial Guinea and the United States
  Established: 1948
  Date: December 10; Human Rights Week, December 10-17

  AmerBkDays-1978, 1089, 1106
  AnnivHol-1983, 158
  HolFestCelWrld-1994, 31

Human Towers of Valls (Xiquets de Valls)
  Location: Spain: Valls, Catalonia
  Date: June 24, St. John's or Midsummer Day

  AnnivHol-1983, 183
  FestWestEur-1958, 200
  HolFestCelWrld-1994, 147

Humor and Satire Festival, National
  Location: Bulgaria: Gabrovo
  Established: 1967
  Date: Late May

  GdWrldFest-1985, 26
  HolFestCelWrld-1994, 147

Hungry Ghosts, Festival of (Ullambana)
  Ethnic or religious group: Buddhist
  Established: Probably since sixth century
  Date: July-August, 15th day of seventh lunar month

  AnnivHol-1983, 177
  BkHolWrld-1986, August 18
  DictFolkMyth-1984, 225, 1051
  DictWrldRel-1989, 135, 581
  FolkWrldHol-1992, 393
  HolFestCelWrld-1994, 147
  RelHolCal-1993, 84

Hungry Ghosts, Festival of
  Ethnic or religious group: Taoist
  Date: July-August, 15th day of seventh lunar month

  HolFestCelWrld-1994, 147

Hungry Ghosts, Festival of (Yü-Lan Hui or Chieh Tsu)
  Location: China
  Date: July-August, 15th day of seventh lunar month

  AnnivHol-1983, 177
  BkHolWrld-1986, August 18
  Chases-1993, 334
  DictFolkMyth-1984, 225, 1051
  DictWrldRel-1989, 135, 581
  FolkWrldHol-1992, 393
  HolFestCelWrld-1994, 147

Hungry Ghosts, Festival of
  Location: Japan
  Date: July-August, 15th day of seventh lunar month

  DictWrldRel-1989, 135
  See also **Dead, Festival of the (Buddhist)**

Hungry Ghosts, Festival of
  Location: Korea
  Date: July-August, 15th day of seventh lunar month

  DictWrldRel-1989, 135

Hungry Ghosts, Festival of
  Location: Taiwan
  Date: July-August, 15th day of seventh lunar month

  FolkWrldHol-1992, 393
  HolFestCelWrld-1994, 147

**Hungry Ghosts, Festival of (Trung Nguyen, Wandering
Souls' Day)**
  Location: Vietnam
  Date: July-August, 15th day of seventh lunar month

  FolkWrldHol-1992, 394
  HolFestCelWrld-1994, 148

Hunters' Moon, Feast of the
  Location: Lafayette, Indiana
  Established: 1968; commemorates 18th-century gathering
   of French settlers and Indians at Fort Ouiatenon
  Date: October

  Chases-1993, 404
  GdUSFest-1984, 53
  HolFestCelWrld-1994, 148

Huntigowk Day
See **April Fools' Day (Scotland)**

Hunting and Fishing Day
  Location: United States
  Date: Fourth Saturday in September

  AnnivHol-1983, 122
  Chases-1993, 386

Hunting the Wren
  See **St. Stephen's Day (England), (Ireland), (Isle of Man), and (Wales)**

Hurricane Supplication Day
  Named for: Since 1726 when Rev. Philip Adams Dietrichs gave Thanksgiving service at the end of hurricane season at St. Thomas, Virgin Islands
  Location: Virgin Islands
  Date: Fourth Monday in July (near beginning of hurricane season) and second or third Monday in October

  AnnivHol-1983, 95, 134
  BkFestHolWrld-1970, 125
  BkHolWrld-1986, October 18, 178
  Chases-1993, 307
  FolkAmerHol-1987, 245
  HolFestCelWrld-1994, 148

Husayn or Husain Day
  Named for: Commemorates death of Imam Husayn (624-680) on October 9
  Ethnic or religious group: Shiite Muslims
  Date: Observed during 10th day of Muharram, the first Islamic month, following the New Year; often celebrated in conjunction with the New Year during the first ten days of Muharram

  AnnivHol-1983, 130
  BkFest-1937, 237
  BkHolWrld-1986, October 6
  DictWrldRel-1989, 331
  FolkWrldHol-1992, 365
  HolFestCelWrld-1994, 15
  RelHolCal-1993, 59, 96

Husayn or Husain Day
  Named for: Commemorates death of Imam Husayn (624-680) on October 9
  Location: Egypt
  Date: Observed during 10th day of Muharram, the first Islamic month, following the New Year; often celebrated in conjunction with the New Year during the first ten days of Muharram

  FolkWrldHol-1992, 367

Husayn or Husain Day
  Named for: Commemorates death of Imam Husayn (624-680) on October 9
  Location: Guinea
  Date: Observed during 10th day of Muharram, the first Islamic month, following the New Year; often celebrated in conjunction with the New Year during the first ten days of Muharram

  HolFestCelWrld-1994, 15

Husayn or Husain Day (Hosay and Tadja)
  Named for: Commemorates death of Imam Husayn (624-680) on October 9
  Location: Guyana
  Ethnic or religious group: Afro- and Indo-Guyanese Muslims
  Date: Observed during 10th day of Muharram, the first Islamic month, following the New Year; often celebrated in conjunction with the New Year during the first ten days of Muharram

  FolkWrldHol-1992, 367
  HolFestCelWrld-1994, 15

Husayn or Husain Day
  Named for: Commemorates death of Imam Husayn (624-680) on October 9
  Location: India
  Date: Observed during 10th day of Muharram, the first Islamic month, following the New Year; often celebrated in conjunction with the New Year during the first ten days of Muharram

  FolkWrldHol-1992, 366, 367
  HolFestCelWrld-1994, 15

Husayn or Husain Day
  Named for: Commemorates death of Imam Husayn (624-680) on October 9
  Location: Southern India
  Date: Observed during 10th day of Muharram, the first Islamic month, following the New Year; often celebrated in conjunction with the New Year during the first ten days of Muharram

  FolkWrldHol-1992, 366, 367

Husayn or Husain Day
  Named for: Commemorates death of Imam Husayn (624-680) on October 9
  Location: Iran; formerly Persia
  Date: Observed during 10th day of Muharram, the first Islamic month, following the New Year; often celebrated in conjunction with the New Year during the first ten days of Muharram

  BkFest-1937, 237
  BkHolWrld-1986, October 6
  FolkWrldHol-1992, 366, 368
  RelHolCal-1993, 59

Husayn or Husain Day
  Named for: Commemorates death of Imam Husayn (624-680) on October 9
  Location: Iraq
  Date: Observed during 10th day of Muharram, the first Islamic month, following the New Year; often celebrated in conjunction with the New Year during the first ten days of Muharram

  FolkWrldHol-1992, 366, 368
  HolFestCelWrld-1994, 15

Husayn or Husain Day (Hosay)
  Named for: Commemorates death of Imam Husayn (624-680) on October 9
  Location: Jamaica
  Date: Observed during 10th day of Muharram, the first Islamic month, following the New Year; often celebrated in conjunction with the New Year during the first ten days of Muharram

  FolkWrldHol-1992, 367, 368
  HolFestCelWrld-1994, 15

Husayn or Husain Day
  Named for: Commemorates death of Imam Husayn (624-680) on October 9
  Location: Lebanon
  Date: Observed during 10th day of Muharram, the first Islamic month, following the New Year; often celebrated in conjunction with the New Year during the first ten days of Muharram

  FolkWrldHol-1992, 366

Husayn or Husain Day
  Named for: Commemorates death of Imam Husayn (624-680) on October 9
  Location: Pakistan
  Date: Observed during 10th day of Muharram, the first Islamic month, following the New Year; often celebrated

in conjunction with the New Year during the first ten days of Muharram

  FolkWrldHol-1992, 369

Husayn or Husain Day
  Named for: Commemorates death of Imam Husayn (624-680) on October 9
  Location: Senegal
  Date: Observed during 10th day of Muharram, the first Islamic month, following the New Year; often celebrated in conjunction with the New Year during the first ten days of Muharram

  HolFestCelWrld-1994, 15

Husayn or Husain Day
  Named for: Commemorates death of Imam Husayn (624-680) on October 9
  Location: Sierra Leone
  Date: Observed during 10th day of Muharram, the first Islamic month, following the New Year; often celebrated in conjunction with the New Year during the first ten days of Muharram

  HolFestCelWrld-1994, 15

Husayn or Husain Day (Hosay)
  Named for: Commemorates death of Imam Husayn (624-680) on October 9
  Location: Trinidad
  Established: 1884
  Date: February-March

  FolkWrldHol-1992, 367, 370
  HolFestCelWrld-1994, 15, 145

Husayn or Husain Day
  Named for: Commemorates death of Imam Husayn (624-680) on October 9
  Location: Turkey
  Date: Observed during 10th day of Muharram, the first Islamic month, following the New Year; often celebrated in conjunction with the New Year during the first ten days of Muharram

  FolkWrldHol-1992, 366, 370

Husayn or Husain Day
  Named for: Commemorates death of Imam Husayn (624-680) on October 9
  Location: Turkey: Eastern Anatolia
  Date: Observed during 10th day of Muharram, the first Islamic month, following the New Year; often celebrated in conjunction with the New Year during the first ten days of Muharram

  FolkWrldHol-1992, 366

Hussein Day
   Named for: King Hussein (b. 1935)
   Location: Jordan
   Date: November 14

   AnnivHol-1983, 147
   Chases-1993, 441

Husvét
   See **Easter (Hungary)**

Husvét Hétfoje or Ducking Monday
   See **Easter Monday (Hungary)**

Hyacinthia
   Location: Ancient Sparta
   Date: July

   DictFolkMyth-1984, 67

Ibnou Abi Dhiaf Festival
   Location: Tunisia: Siliana, Siliana Region
   Date: July

   IntlThFolk-1979, 364

Ibu Afo Festival
   See **New Year (Ibo people in Nigeria)**

Ice and Snow Festival, Harbin
   Location: China: Harbin
   Date: January 5-February 5

   HolFestCelWrld-1994, 134

Ice Classic, Nenana
   Location: Nenana, Alaska
   Established: 1906
   Date: Late February and early spring

   HolFestCelWrld-1994, 222

Ice Golf Classic, Bering Sea
   Location: Nome, Alaska
   Date: Mid-March

   HolFestCelWrld-1994, 30

Icelandic Festival (Islendingadagurinn)
   Location: Canada: Gimli, Manitoba
   Ethnic or religious group: Icelandic-Canadians
   Established: 1890
   Date: Last week in July or first week in August

   GdWrldFest-1985, 33
   HolFestCelWrld-1994, 149
   IntlThFolk-1979, 63

Icemänner Days
   See **Frost, or Ice, Saints Day**

Ice Worm Festival
   Location: Cordova, Alaska
   Established: 1961
   Date: First week or weekend in February

   BkFestHolWrld-1970, 31
   Chases-1993, 86
   GdUSFest-1984, 8
   HolFestCelWrld-1994, 149

'Id al-Adha
   See **Sacrifice, Feast of (Muslim), (Egypt), (Iraq),
   and (Kuwait)**

'Id al-Arba'in Shahid
   See **Martyrs' Day, Forty (Christians in Syria)**

'Id al-Fitr
   See **Fast, Feast of Breaking the (Muslim) and (West Africa)**

'Id al-Ghitās
   See **Epiphany (Syria)**

Al-'Id al-Kabir
   See **Easter (Eastern Orthodox Church in Syria)**

'Id al-Kabir
   See **Sacrifice, Feast of (Muslim), (Morocco: Salé),
   and (West Africa)**

'Id al-Khitan
   See **Circumcision, Feast of the (Syria)**

'Id al Milad
   See **Christmas (Syria)**

'Id al-Tajalli
   See **Transfiguration, Feast of the (Syria)**

Id-el-Fitr
   See **Fast, Feast of Breaking the (Jordan)**

Ides
   Date: First day of any month in the Roman calendar

   AnnivHol-1983, 37
   Chases-1993, 130
   DictDays-1988, 18
   HolFestCelWrld-1994, 150

Iditarod Trail Sled Dog Race
   Location: Anchorage, Alaska
   Date: 11-32 day-long race begins first Saturday in March

   Chases-1993, 121
   HolFestCelWrld-1994, 151

'Id Marjurjus
  See St. George's Day (Syria: monastery at Humeira)

'Id Raf'al-Salib
  See Exaltation of the Cross (Syria)

'Id Rakad-ai-Sayyidah
  See Assumption, Feast of the (Christians and Muslims
  at the Monastery of the Virgin at Saidnaya near
  Damascus, Syria)

'Id Ras al-Sanah
  See New Year's Day (Syria)

Id-ul-Bakr, Sacrifice of the Ram
  See Sacrifice, Feast of (Pakistan)

Id-ul-Fitr
  See Fast, Feast of Breaking the (Pakistan)

Idul Fitre
  See Fast, Feast of Breaking the (Surinam)

Idulfitri
  See Fast, Feast of Breaking the (Sumatra)

Iemanjá Festival (Brazil: Rio Vermelho)
  Date: February

  HolFestCelWrld-1994, 151

Igbi
  See Midwinter Festival (Tsezy people in Shaitli,
  Dagestan, USSR)

Igun Efon Festival
  See New Yam Festival (Yoruba people in Oyo, Nigeria)

Igun Ekun Ajinida Festival
  See New Yam Festival (Yoruba people in Oyo, Nigeria)

Igun Luwo Festival
  See New Yam Festival (Yoruba people in Oyo, Nigeria)

Iid el Sageer
  See Fast, Feast of Breaking the (Morocco: Marrakech)

Ilaja Isu Titun
  See New Yam Festival (Yoruba people in Oyo, Nigeria)

Il Giorno Dei Morti
  See All Souls' Day (Italy) and (Sicily)

Ilinden Days Festival
  Location: Yugoslavia: Bitola, Macedonia
  Established: 1971
  Date: July-August

  IntlThFolk-1979, 385

Ille Festival
  Location: France: Betton, Ille-et-Vilaine
  Established: 1976
  Date: One week in May or June

  IntlThFolk-1979, 101

Illumination, Day of
  See Holy Saturday

Illuminations, Festival of
  See Lights, Festival of (Hindu)

Il Natale
  See Christmas (Italy)

Imaculada Conceição, Festa da
  See Immaculate Conception, Feast of the (Portugal)

Imbolc (Brigit's Day)
  Ethnic or religious group: Wiccan
  Date: February 2

  Chases-1993, 84
  HolFestCelWrld-1994, 152

Imechi Festival
  Location: Nigeria
  Ethnic or religious group: Igbo people
  Date: July-August

  FolkWrldHol-1992, 407

La Immaculada Concepción
  See Immaculate Conception, Feast of the (Honduras:
  Juticalpa)

Immaculate Conception, Feast of the
  Named for: The believed impregnation of Mary, mother
  of Jesus (c. 6 B.C.-c. 30 A.D.), by the Holy Spirit
  Ethnic or religious group: Christian
  Established: 14th or 15th century, Western church; c.
  eighth century, Eastern church
  Date: December 8

  AmerBkDays-1978, 1084
  AnnivHol-1983, 157
  BkFest-1937, 190, 271
  BkFestHolWrld-1970, 131
  BkHolWrld-1986, December 8
  DaysCustFaith-1957, 308
  DictWrldRel-1989, 338
  FolkWrldHol-1992, 585
  HolFestCelWrld-1994, 152
  RelHolCal-1993, 85
  SaintFestCh-1904, 14

Immaculate Conception, Feast of the
  Ethnic or religious group: Anglican
  Date: December 8

  DaysCustFaith-1957, 308
  HolFestCelWrld-1994, 152

Immaculate Conception, Feast of the
  Ethnic or religious group: Church of England
  Date: December 8

  SaintFestCh-1904, 14

Immaculate Conception, Feast of the
  Ethnic or religious group: Eastern Orthodox
  Date: December 9

  AmerBkDays-1978, 1085
  DaysCustFaith-1957, 308
  RelHolCal-1993, 85

Immaculate Conception, Feast of the
  Ethnic or religious group: Roman Catholic
  Date: December 8

  AmerBkDays-1978, 1084
  AnnivHol-1983, 157
  BkHolWrld-1986, December 8
  Chases-1993, 469
  DaysCustFaith-1957, 308
  DictWrldRel-1989, 339
  HolFestCelWrld-1994, 152
  RelHolCal-1993, 85
  SaintFestCh-1904, 14

Immaculate Conception, Feast of the (Virgen de Valle)
  Location: Argentina: Catamarca
  Date: December 8

  FolkWrldHol-1992, 585

Immaculate Conception, Feast of the (Fiesta of Concepción)
  Location: Bolivia: Sopocachi Alto barrio of La Paz
  Date: December 8

  FolkWrldHol-1992, 585

Immaculate Conception, Feast of the
  Location: England
  Date: December 8

  DaysCustFaith-1957, 309

Immaculate Conception, Feast of the
  Location: France
  Date: December 8

  DaysCustFaith-1957, 309

Immaculate Conception, Feast of the (La Immaculada Concepción)
  Location: Honduras: Juticalpa
  Date: Begins several days before December 8

  FolkWrldHol-1992, 585

Immaculate Conception, Feast of the
  Location: Ireland
  Date: December 8

  RelHolCal-1993, 85

Immaculate Conception, Feast of the (L'Immacolata)
  Location: Italy
  Date: December 8

  BkFest-1937, 190

Immaculate Conception, Feast of the
  Location: Philippines
  Date: December 8

  BkFestHolWrld-1970, 131

Immaculate Conception, Feast of the (Festa da Imaculada Conceição)
  Location: Portugal
  Date: December 8

  BkFest-1937, 271

Immaculate Conception, Feast of the (Fiesta de la Inmaculada Concepción de María)
  Location: Puerto Rico
  Date: December 8

  AmerBkDays-1978, 1085

Immaculate Conception, Feast of the
  Location: Spain
  Date: December 8

  BkHolWrld-1986, December 8

Immaculate Heart of Mary, Feast of the
  Ethnic or religious group: Roman Catholic
  Established: 17th century; authorized in 1799
  Date: Saturday following the second Sunday after Pentecost

  RelHolCal-1993, 85

Imnarja
  See **Harvest Festival (Malta: Buskett Gardens)**

Impruneta, Festa del
  Location: Italy: Florence, Tuscany
  Established: Three centuries old
  Date: Late October

  HolFestCelWrld-1994, 152

Inauguration Day
   Location: United States
   Established: 1933; formerly March 4
   Date: January 20

   AmerBkDays-1978, 96
   AnnivHol-1983, 11
   Chases-1993, 69
   DictDays-1988, 59
   HolFestCelWrld-1994, 152

Inconfidencia Week
   See **Tiradentes (Tooth Puller) (Brazil)**

Incwala
   Location: Swaziland
   Date: Three week- to one month-long ceremony: Little
   Incwala lasts two days beginning at the summer solstice
   and new moon; the Big Incwala takes place for six days
   after the full moon

   BkHolWrld-1986, December 22, 178
   FolkWrldHol-1992, 467
   HolFestCelWrld-1994, 153

Independence, Festival of Mexico (Mexican Declaration of Independence Day)
   Named for: Independence of Mexico in 1810
   Location: Mexico: procession from the Zocolo to the
   Independence Monument on Paseo de la Reforma in
   Mexico City
   Date: September 15-16

   AnnivHol-1983, 119
   BkFest-1937, 229
   Chases-1993, 372
   GdWrldFest-1985, 135
   HolFestCelWrld-1994, 154
   NatlHolWrld-1968, 172

Independence and Flag Day
   Named for: Independence from Spain in 1811
   Location: Paraguay
   Date: Observed May 14-15

   AnnivHol-1983, 65
   Chases-1993, 207
   NatlHolWrld-1968, 62

Independence and Republic Day
   Named for: Independence from Britain in 1961
   Location: Tanzania
   Date: December 9

   AnnivHol-1983, 158

   Chases-1993, 470
   HolFestCelWrld-1994, 154
   NatlHolWrld-1968, 222

Independence and Thanksgiving Day
   Named for: Independence from Britain on October 27, 1979
   Location: St. Vincent
   Date: October 27

   AnnivHol-1983, 137
   Chases-1993, 422

Independence Day (Jeshn)
   Named for: Independence from Britain on August 8,
   1919; achieved full independence on May 27, 1921
   Location: Afghanistan
   Date: Observed in late August

   HolFestCelWrld-1994, 160
   NatlHolWrld-1968, 71

Independence Day
   Named for: Independence from Turkish rule on
   November 28, 1912
   Location: Albania
   Date: Observed November 28-29

   AnnivHol-1983, 152
   Chases-1993, 458
   NatlHolWrld-1968, 210

Independence Day
   Named for: Independence from French rule on
   July 3, 1962
   Location: Algeria
   Date: July 3

   AnnivHol-1983, 88

Independence Day
   Named for: November 11, 1975, independence
   Location: Angola
   Date: November 11

   AnnivHol-1983, 145
   Chases-1993, 437

Independence Day
   Named for: November 1, 1981, independence
   Location: Antigua
   Date: November 1

   AnnivHol-1983, 138
   Chases-1993, 428

Independence Day
  Named for: Independence from Spanish rule: May 25, 1810, revolution and July 9, 1816, proclamation
  Location: Argentina: Buenos Aires
  Date: May 25 and July 9

  AnnivHol-1983, 91
  Chases-1993, 219
  HolFestCelWrld-1994, 13

Independence Day
  Named for: July 10, 1973, independence
  Location: Bahama Islands
  Date: July 10

  AnnivHol-1983, 91
  Chases-1993, 286

Independence Day
  Named for: Independence from Portugal in 1823
  Location: Bahia
  Date: July 2

  HolFestCelWrld-1994, 22

Independence Day
  Location: Bahrain
  Date: December 16

  Chases-1993, 475

Independence Day
  Named for: Forming of the state on March 26, 1971
  Location: Bangladesh
  Date: March 26

  AnnivHol-1983, 42
  Chases-1993, 141

Independence Day
  Named for: November 30, 1966, British Commonwealth status
  Location: Barbados
  Date: November 30

  AnnivHol-1983, 153
  Chases-1993, 458
  NatlHolWrld-1968, 215

Independence Day
  Named for: Commemorates the accession of Leopold I (1790-1865) on July 21, 1831, and separation from the Netherlands
  Location: Belgium

  Date: July 21

  AnnivHol-1983, 95
  Chases-1993, 300
  NatlHolWrld-1968, 119

Independence Day
  Named for: Independence from Britain on September 21, 1981
  Location: Belize
  Date: September 21

  AnnivHol-1983, 121
  Chases-1993, 380

Independence Day
  Named for: August 1, 1960, independence
  Location: Benin
  Date: August 1

  AnnivHol-1983, 101
  NatlHolWrld-1968, 130

Independence Day
  Named for: Independence from Spanish rule on August 6, 1825
  Location: Bolivia
  Date: Two days including August 6

  Chases-1993, 318
  NatlHolWrld-1968, 134

Independence Day
  Named for: Independence from South Africa on December 6, 1977
  Location: Bophuthatswana
  Date: December 6

  AnnivHol-1983, 156

Independence Day
  Named for: September 30, 1966, independence
  Location: Botswana
  Date: September 30

  AnnivHol-1983, 125
  Chases-1993, 389
  NatlHolWrld-1968, 179

Independence Day
  Named for: Independence from Portugal on September 7, 1822
  Location: Brazil
  Date: September 7

  AnnivHol-1983, 115
  Chases-1993, 360
  NatlHolWrld-1968, 158

Independence Day
  Named for: January 4, 1948, independence
  Location: Burma; now Myanmar
  Date: January 4

  AnnivHol-1983, 4
  Chases-1993, 55
  NatlHolWrld-1968, 12

Independence Day
  Named for: July 1, 1962, independence
  Location: Burundi
  Date: July 1

  AnnivHol-1983, 87
  Chases-1993, 271
  NatlHolWrld-1968, 97

Independence Day
  Named for: Independence from France on November 9, 1955
  Location: Cambodia
  Date: November 9

  Chases-1993, 436
  NatlHolWrld-1968, 204

Independence Day
  Location: Federal Republic of Cameroon: Yaounde
  Date: January 1

  NatlHolWrld-1968, 4

Independence Day
  Named for: Independence from Portugal on July 5, 1975
  Location: Cape Verde
  Date: July 5

  AnnivHol-1983, 89
  Chases-1993, 367

Independence Day
  Named for: August 13, 1960, independence
  Location: Central African Republic
  Date: Observed on December 1, commemorating
    proclamation of the republic in 1958

  AnnivHol-1983, 106, 154
  Chases-1993, 327
  NatlHolWrld-1968, 218

Independence Day
  Named for: August 11, 1960, independence
  Location: Chad
  Date: Observed on January 11

  AnnivHol-1983, 105
  Chases-1993, 324
  NatlHolWrld-1968, 15

Independence Day
  Named for: Independence from Spain on September 18, 1818
  Location: Chile
  Date: September 18

  AnnivHol-1983, 120
  Chases-1993, 375
  NatlHolWrld-1968, 174

Independence Day
  Named for: July 20, 1810, independence
  Location: Colombia
  Date: July 20

  AnnivHol-1983, 95
  Chases-1993, 300
  NatlHolWrld-1968, 117

Independence Day
  Named for: July 6, 1975, independence
  Location: Comoros
  Date: July 6

  Chases-1993, 282

Independence Day
  Named for: August 15, 1960, independence from France
  Location: People's Republic of the Congo; formerly part
    of French Equatorial Africa
  Date: August 15

  AnnivHol-1983, 107
  Chases-1993, 330
  NatlHolWrld-1968, 142
  See also **Three Glorious Days**

Independence Day
  Named for: June 30, 1960, independence from Belgium
  Location: Democratic Republic of Congo; formerly Belgian
    Congo; now Zaire
  Date: June 30

  AnnivHol-1983, 86
  Chases-1993, 270
  NatlHolWrld-1968, 92

Independence Day
  Named for: Independence from Spanish rule on September
    15, 1821
  Location: Costa Rica
  Date: September 15

  AnnivHol-1983, 118
  Chases-1993, 370
  NatlHolWrld-1968, 163

Independence Day
Named for: May 20, 1902, independence from Spain
Location: Cuba
Date: May 20

NatlHolWrld-1968, 65

Independence Day
Named for: Independence from the Ottoman Empire on
March 25, 1821
Location: Cyprus
Date: March 25

AnnivHol-1983, 42

Independence Day
Named for: Independence from Britain on August 16, 1960
Location: Cyprus
Date: October 1

AnnivHol-1983, 107
Chases-1993, 392
NatlHolWrld-1968, 145

Independence Day
Named for: October 28, 1918, independence from Austro-
Hungary
Location: Czechoslovakia
Date: October 28

AmerBkDays-1978, 963
AnnivHol-1983, 137
Chases-1993, 422
HolFestCelWrld-1994, 75

Independence Day
Named for: November 3, 1978, independence
Location: Dominica
Date: Two days including November 3

AnnivHol-1983, 141
Chases-1993, 430

Independence Day
Named for: Withdrawal of Haitian forces on February
27, 1844
Location: Dominican Republic
Date: February 27

AnnivHol-1983, 29
Chases-1993, 112
HolFestCelWrld-1994, 87
NatlHolWrld-1968, 27

Independence Day
Named for: Independence from Spain on August 10, 1809
Location: Ecuador
Date: August 10

AnnivHol-1983, 105
Chases-1993, 324
NatlHolWrld-1968, 140

Independence Day
Named for: Independence from Spain on September 15, 1821
Location: El Salvador
Date: September 15

AnnivHol-1983, 118
Chases-1993, 370
NatlHolWrld-1968, 165

Independence Day
Named for: Independence from Spain on October 12, 1968
Location: Equatorial Guinea
Date: October 12

AnnivHol-1983, 132
Chases-1993, 407

Independence Day
Named for: February 24, 1920, peace treaty confirming
independence
Location: Estonia
Date: February 24

AnnivHol-1983, 28
Chases-1993, 109

Independence Day
Named for: Independence from Russian rule on December
6, 1917
Location: Finland
Date: December 6

AnnivHol-1983, 156
Chases-1993, 467
HolFestCelWrld-1994, 153
NatlHolWrld-1968, 221

Independence Day
Named for: Independence from France on August 17, 1960
Location: Gabon
Date: August 17

AnnivHol-1983, 108
Chases-1993, 333
NatlHolWrld-1968, 146

Independence Day
    Named for: Independence from Britain on February 18, 1965
    Location: Gambia
    Date: February 18

    Chases-1993, 102
    NatlHolWrld-1968, 25

Independence Day
    Named for: Independence from Britain on March 6, 1957
    Location: Ghana
    Date: March 6

    AnnivHol-1983, 34
    Chases-1993, 121
    NatlHolWrld-1968, 100

Independence Day
    Named for: End of Turkish occupation on March 25, 1821
    Location: Greece
    Date: March 25

    AmerBkDays-1978, 285
    AnnivHol-1983, 42
    Chases-1993, 140
    DictDays-1988, 50
    HolFestCelWrld-1994, 126
    NatlHolWrld-1968, 39

Independence Day
    Named for: February 7, 1974, independence
    Location: Grenada
    Date: February 7

    AnnivHol-1983, 20
    Chases-1993, 90

Inependence Day
    Named for: Independence from Spain on September 15, 1821
    Location: Guatemala
    Date: September 15

    AnnivHol-1983, 118
    Chases-1993, 370
    NatlHolWrld-1968, 167

Independence Day
    Named for: October 2, 1958, independence from France
    Location: Guinea
    Date: October 2

    AnnivHol-1983, 127
    Chases-1993, 395
    NatlHolWrld-1968, 185

Independence Day
    Named for: Independence from Portuguese rule on
        September 8, 1974
    Location: Guinea-Bissau
    Date: Observed on September 24, date of proclamation

    AnnivHol-1983, 116
    Chases-1993, 384

Independence Day
    Named for: Independence from Britain on May 26, 1966
    Location: Guyana
    Date: May 26

    AnnivHol-1983, 71
    NatlHolWrld-1968, 70

Independence Day
    Named for: Honors first head of the republic, Jean-Jacques
        Dessalines (1758?-1806); founded on January 1, 1804
    Location: Haiti: Port-au-Prince
    Date: January 1

    AnnivHol-1983, 1
    Chases-1993, 50
    NatlHolWrld-1968, 6

Independence Day
    Named for: Independence from Spain on September 15, 1821
    Location: Honduras
    Date: September 15

    AnnivHol-1983, 119
    Chases-1993, 370
    NatlHolWrld-1968, 169

Independence Day
    Named for: Observed on the birthday of Jón Sigurdsson
        (1811-1879)
    Location: Iceland
    Established: June 17, 1944
    Date: June 17

    AnnivHol-1983, 80
    Chases-1993, 251
    HolFestCelWrld-1994, 149
    NatlHolWrld-1968, 85

Independence Day
    Named for: Independence from British rule on August
        15, 1947
    Location: India
    Date: August 15

    AnnivHol-1983, 107
    Chases-1993, 331

Independence Day
  Named for: August 17, 1945, proclamation; full
    independence from the Netherlands achieved on
    December 27, 1949
  Location: Indonesia
  Date: Observed August 17

  AnnivHol-1983, 108
  Chases-1993, 333
  IntlThFolk-1979, 227
  NatlHolWrld-1968, 147

Independence Day (Yom Ha'atzma'ut)
  Named for: May 15, 1948, provisional government in Israel
  Location: Israel
  Date: Observed April-May, 5th of Jewish month of Iyar

  AnnivHol-1983, 66
  Chases-1993, 181
  HolFestCelWrld-1994, 157
  NatlHolWrld-1968, 60

Independence Day
  Named for: Independence from France on August 7, 1960
  Location: Ivory Coast
  Date: Observed December 7

  AnnivHol-1983, 157
  Chases-1993, 468
  NatlHolWrld-1968, 139

Independence Day
  Named for: August 2, 1962, membership in the British
    Commonwealth
  Location: Jamaica
  Date: Observed first Monday in August

  AnnivHol-1983, 102
  Chases-1993, 314
  HolFestCelWrld-1994, 153
  NatlHolWrld-1968, 136

Independence Day
  Named for: May 25, 1946, establishment of the monarchy
  Location: Jordan
  Date: May 25

  AnnivHol-1983, 71
  Chases-1993, 220
  NatlHolWrld-1968, 69

Independence Day (Jamhuri Day)
  Named for: December 12, 1963, independence from Britain
  Location: Kenya
  Date: December 12

  AnnivHol-1983, 159

Chases-1993, 473
HolFestCelWrld-1994, 159
NatlHolWrld-1968, 226

Independence Day
  Named for: July 12, 1979, independence
  Location: Kiribati
  Date: July 12

  AnnivHol-1983, 92
  Chases-1993, 290

Independence Day (National Day)
  Named for: September 9, 1948, founding of the republic
  Location: Democratic People's Republic of Korea
  Date: September 9

  AnnivHol-1983, 116
  Chases-1993, 362
  NatlHolWrld-1968, 161

Independence Day (Republic Day)
  Named for: June 19, 1961, independence from Britain
  Location: Kuwait
  Date: June 19

  AnnivHol-1983, 81
  NatlHolWrld-1968, 87

Independence Day
  Named for: Treaty on June 19, 1949; full independence
    from France achieved December 24, 1954
  Location: Laos
  Date: June 19

  AnnivHol-1983, 81

Independence Day
  Location: Latvia
  Date: November 18

  Chases-1993, 444

Independence Day
  Named for: Independence from France on November
    22, 1943
  Location: Lebanon
  Date: November 22

  AnnivHol-1983, 150
  Chases-1993, 450
  NatlHolWrld-1968, 209

Independence Day
  Named for: October 4, 1966, independence from Britain
  Location: Lesotho
  Date: October 4

  AnnivHol-1983, 128
  NatlHolWrld-1968, 186

Independence Day
 Named for: July 26, 1847, independence
 Location: Liberia
 Date: July 26

AnnivHol-1983, 97
Chases-1993, 307
HolFestCelWrld-1994, 153
NatlHolWrld-1968, 124

Independence Day
 Named for: December 24, 1951, independence
 Location: Libya
 Date: December 24

NatlHolWrld-1968, 229

Independence Day
 Named for: Independence from the Soviet Union on
   March 11, 1990
 Location: Lithuania
 Date: March 11

Chases-1993, 101

Independence Day
 Named for: June 26, 1960, independence from France
 Location: Madagascar
 Date: June 26

AnnivHol-1983, 84
Chases-1993, 265
NatlHolWrld-1968, 89

Independence Day
 Named for: Independence from Britain on July 6, 1964
 Location: Malawi
 Date: July 6

AnnivHol-1983, 90
Chases-1993, 282
NatlHolWrld-1968, 111

Independence Day
 Named for: September 16, 1963, independence from Britain
 Location: Malaysia
 Date: September 16

NatlHolWrld-1968, 171

Independence Day (Merdeka)
 Named for: Independence from Britain on August 31, 1957
 Location: Malaysia: Kuala Lumpur, Selangor

 Date: August 31

AnnivHol-1983, 112
GdWrldFest-1985, 131
HolFestCelWrld-1994, 203
IntlThFolk-1979, 267

Independence Day
 Named for: Independence from Britain on July 26, 1965
 Location: Maldive Islands
 Date: July 26

AnnivHol-1983, 97
Chases-1993, 307
NatlHolWrld-1968, 126

Independence Day
 Named for: September 22, 1960, independence from France
 Location: Mali
 Date: September 22

AnnivHol-1983, 121
Chases-1993, 381
NatlHolWrld-1968, 177

Independence Day
 Named for: September 21, 1964, independence from Britain
 Location: Malta
 Date: September 21

AnnivHol-1983, 121
Chases-1993, 380
HolFestCelWrld-1994, 154
NatlHolWrld-1968, 176

Independence Day
 Named for: Independence from France on November
   28, 1960
 Location: Mauritania
 Date: November 28

AnnivHol-1983, 152
Chases-1993, 457
NatlHolWrld-1968, 211

Independence Day
 Named for: Independence from Britain on March 12, 1968
 Location: Mauritius
 Date: March 12

AnnivHol-1983, 36
Chases-1993, 127

Independence Day (National Day)
Named for: March 2, 1956, independence from France and Spain
Location: Morocco
Date: March 2

AnnivHol-1983, 32
NatlHolWrld-1968, 30

Independence Day
Named for: Independence from Portuguese rule on June 25, 1975
Location: Mozambique
Date: June 25

AnnivHol-1983, 84
Chases-1993, 264

Independence Day
Named for: January 31, 1968, independence from Australia
Location: Nauru
Date: January 31

AnnivHol-1983, 16
Chases-1993, 80
NatlHolWrld-1968, 19

Independence Day
Named for: Independence from Britain on December 21, 1923
Location: Nepal
Date: December 21

AnnivHol-1983, 163

Independence Day
Location: Netherlands
Date: July 25

AnnivHol-1983, 97

Independence Day
Named for: September 15, 1821, independence from Spain
Location: Nicaragua
Date: September 15

AnnivHol-1983, 119
Chases-1993, 370
NatlHolWrld-1968, 170

Independence Day
Named for: Independence from France on August 3, 1960
Location: Niger
Date: August 3

AnnivHol-1983, 102

Independence Day
Named for: October 1, 1960, independence from Britain
Location: Nigeria
Date: October 1

Chases-1993, 393
NatlHolWrld-1968, 183

Independence Day
Named for: Independence from British rule and formation of Pakistan as a nation on August 14, 1946
Location: Pakistan
Date: August 14

AnnivHol-1983, 106
NatlHolWrld-1968, 37

Independence Day
Named for: Independence from Colombia on November 3, 1903
Location: Panama
Date: November 3

AnnivHol-1983, 142
Chases-1993, 430
NatlHolWrld-1968, 200

Independence Day
Named for: Independence from Spain on November 28, 1821
Location: Panama
Date: November 28

AnnivHol-1983, 152
Chases-1993, 457

Independence Day
Named for: Declaration of independence from Spain on July 28, 1821; full independence achieved 1824
Location: Peru
Date: July 28

AnnivHol-1983, 98
Chases-1993, 308
NatlHolWrld-1968, 127

Independence Day
Named for: Independence from Spain on June 12, 1898
Location: Philippines
Date: June 12

AmerBkDays-1978, 547
AnnivHol-1983, 78
Chases-1993, 246
NatlHolWrld-1968, 83
See also **Filipina, Fiesta**

Independence Day
  Named for: Independence from Austrian, Prussian, and
    Russian partitions on November 11, 1918
  Location: Poland
  Date: November 11

  AnnivHol-1983, 145

Independence Day
  Location: Portugal
  Date: December 1

  Chases-1993, 461

Independence Day
  Named for: Independence from Britain on September 3, 1971
  Location: Qatar
  Date: September 3

  AnnivHol-1983, 114
  Chases-1993, 353

Independence Day
  Named for: May 4, 1776, declaration of independence
    from Britain
  Location: Anthony, Newport, and Providence, Rhode Island
  Date: May 4

  AmerBkDays-1978, 419
  AnnivHol-1983, 61
  Chases-1993, 195
  HolFestCelWrld-1994, 273

Independence Day
  Named for: November 11, 1965, independence from
    Britain; not recognized by the United Nations because
    of government's white-supremacist policies
  Location: Rhodesia
  Date: November 11

  NatlHolWrld-1968, 205

Independence Day
  Named for: Independence from Belgium on July 1, 1962
  Location: Rwanda
  Date: July 1

  AnnivHol-1983, 87
  NatlHolWrld-1968, 102

Independence Day
  Named for: Independence from Britain on February 22, 1979
  Location: St. Lucia
  Date: February 22

  AnnivHol-1983, 27
  Chases-1993, 107

Independence Day
  Named for: Independence from France on April 4, 1960
  Location: Senegal
  Date: April 4

  AnnivHol-1983, 47
  Chases-1993, 155
  NatlHolWrld-1968, 46

Independence Day
  Named for: April 27, 1961, independence from Britain
  Location: Sierra Leone
  Date: April 27

  Chases-1993, 183
  NatlHolWrld-1968, 50

Independence Day
  Named for: August 9, 1965, independence
  Location: Singapore
  Date: August 9

  AnnivHol-1983, 104
  Chases-1993, 323

Independence Day
  Named for: July 7, 1978, independence
  Location: Solomon Islands
  Date: July 7

  AnnivHol-1983, 90
  Chases-1993, 283

Independence Day
  Named for: Independence on June 26, 1960, from Britain
    and on July 1, 1960, from Italy
  Location: Somalia
  Date: June 26 and July 1

  AnnivHol-1983, 84, 87
  NatlHolWrld-1968, 103

Independence Day
  Named for: November 29, 1967, independence from Britain
  Location: Southern Yemen; now People's Democratic
    Republic of Yemen
  Date: November 29

  NatlHolWrld-1968, 212

Independence Day
  Named for: Independence from Britain on February 4, 1948
  Location: Sri Lanka
  Date: February 4

  AnnivHol-1983, 19
  Chases-1993, 86
  IntlThFolk-1979, 345
  NatlHolWrld-1968, 22

Independence Day
Named for: January 1, 1956, independence from Anglo-Egyptian rule
Location: Sudan
Date: January 1

AnnivHol-1983, 2
Chases-1993, 52
NatlHolWrld-1968, 10

Independence Day
Named for: November 25, 1975, independence
Location: Surinam
Date: November 25

AnnivHol-1983, 151
Chases-1993, 453

Independence Day (Somhlolo Day)
Named for: Somhlolo or Subhuza (fl. 19th century) and independence achieved on September 6, 1968
Location: Swaziland
Date: September 6

AnnivHol-1983, 115
Chases-1993, 359

Independence Day
Named for: Sam Houston (1793-1863) and independence from Mexico on March 2, 1836
Location: Texas
Date: March 2

AmerBkDays-1978, 227
AnnivHol-1983, 32
Chases-1993, 117
DictDays-1988, 118
HolFestCelWrld-1994, 335

Independence Day
Named for: April 27, 1960, independence from France
Location: Togo
Date: April 27

AnnivHol-1983, 57
Chases-1993, 183
NatlHolWrld-1968, 51

Independence Day
Named for: August 31, 1962, independence from Britain
Location: Trinidad and Tobago
Date: August 31

AnnivHol-1983, 112

Chases-1993, 348
NatlHolWrld-1968, 152

Independence Day
Named for: Independence from France on March 20, 1956
Location: Tunisia
Date: March 20

AnnivHol-1983, 40
Chases-1993, 136

Independence Day
Named for: Independence from British rule on October 9, 1962
Location: Uganda
Date: October 9

AnnivHol-1983, 130
Chases-1993, 404
NatlHolWrld-1968, 187

Independence Day (Fourth of July)
Named for: Independence from Britain on July 4, 1776
Location: United States
Date: July 4

AmerBkDays-1978, 619
AnnivHol-1983, 89
BkFest-1937, 18
BkHolWrld-1986, July 4
Chases-1993, 279
DaysCustFaith-1957, 169
DictDays-1988, 44, 59
FolkAmerHol-1987, 223
GdUSFest-1984, 165, 201, 220
HolFestCelWrld-1994, 110, 153
IntlThFolk-1979, 90
NatlHolWrld-1968, 105

Independence Day (Rebild Festival)
Location: United States and Denmark: Aalborg, Rebild, North Jutland
Established: 1912
Date: July 4

Chases-1993, 272
GdWrldFest-1985, 70
HolFestCelWrld-1994, 110

Independence Day
Named for: August 5, 1960, independence
Location: Upper Volta; now Burkina Faso
Date: August 5

AnnivHol-1983, 103

Independence Day
Named for: Independence from Brazil on August 25, 1825
Location: Uruguay
Date: August 25

AnnivHol-1983, 110
Chases-1993, 341
NatlHolWrld-1968, 150

Independence Day
Named for: July 30, 1980, independence
Location: Vanuatu; formerly New Hebrides
Date: July 30

AnnivHol-1983, 99
Chases-1993, 310

Independence Day
Named for: Independence from Spain on July 5, 1811
Location: Venezuela
Date: July 5

AnnivHol-1983, 89
Chases-1993, 281
NatlHolWrld-1968, 109

Independence Day
Named for: Proclamation on September 2, 1945; official independence on March 8, 1949
Location: Democratic Republic of Vietnam
Date: September 2

AnnivHol-1983, 113
Chases-1993, 352
NatlHolWrld-1968, 156

Independence Day
Named for: Independence from New Zealand on January 1, 1962
Location: Western Samoa
Date: Observed first three days in June

AnnivHol-1983, 2, 74
Chases-1993, 230
NatlHolWrld-1968, 9

Independence Day
Named for: November 30, 1967, independence
Location: People's Democratic Republic of Yemen
Date: November 30

AnnivHol-1983, 153

Independence Day (Zaire)
See **Independence Day (Democratic Republic of the Congo)**

Independence Day
Named for: October 24, 1964, independence from Britain
Location: Zambia; formerly Northern Rhodesia
Date: Two days including October 24

AnnivHol-1983, 136
Chases-1993, 420
GdWrldFest-1985, 188
NatlHolWrld-1968, 190

Independence Day
Named for: April 18, 1980, independence from Britain
Location: Zimbabwe; formerly Southern Rhodesia
Date: April 18

AnnivHol-1983, 52
Chases-1993, 172
HolFestCelWrld-1994, 154

Independence Day, Czechoslovakia
Location: United States and elsewhere outside Czechoslovakia
Ethnic or religious group: Czech and Slovak peoples
Date: October 28

AmerBkDays-1978, 963
AnnivHol-1983, 137

Independence Day, First Call for
Named for: First rebellion against Spain on November 5, 1811
Location: El Salvador
Date: November 5

AnnivHol-1983, 142

Independence Day, Greek
Named for: End of Turkish occupation in Greece on March 25, 1821
Location: New York, New York
Date: Sunday nearest March 25

AmerBkDays-1978, 285, 286
AnnivHol-1983, 42
HolFestCelWrld-1994, 126

Independence Day, Greek
Named for: End of Turkish occupation in Greece on March 25, 1821
Location: United States
Ethnic or religious group: Greek-Americans
Date: March 25

AmerBkDays-1978, 285
AnnivHol-1983, 42
DictDays-1988, 50
HolFestCelWrld-1994, 126

Independence Day, Hungary
  Named for: Hungarian independence from Soviet rule
  on October 23, 1989
  Location: Hungary and United States
  Ethnic or religious group: Hungarian-Americans
  Date: October 23

  Chases-1993, 419

Independence Day, Lithuania
  Named for: Lithuania's statehood as a Soviet republic on
  February 16, 1918
  Location: United States
  Ethnic or religious group: Lithuanian-American
  communities
  Date: February 16

  AnnivHol-1983, 25
  Chases-1993, 101

Independence Movement Day (Samiljol)
  Named for: March 1, 1919, protests against Japanese
  occupation
  Location: Republic of Korea
  Date: March 1

  AnnivHol-1983, 31
  Chases-1993, 114
  HolFestCelWrld-1994, 302

Indianapolis 500
  Location: Indianapolis, Indiana
  Established: 1930s
  Date: Month-long event, ending with race on Memorial
  Day, last Monday in May

  Chases-1993, 227
  GdUSFest-1984, 52
  HolFestCelWrld-1994, 154

Indian, Day of the (Día del Indio)
  Location: Peru and other Latin American countries
  Date: June 24

  AnnivHol-1983, 84

Indian Acorn Festival, Mi-Wuk
  Location: Tuolumne Indian Rancheria near Tuolumne,
  California
  Date: Annual

  IndianAmer-1989, 341

Indian Celebration, American
  Named for: Celebrates Feast of Kateri Tekakwitha
  (1656-1680)

  Location: Belleville, Illinois
  Date: July 17

  Chases-1993, 295

Indian Celebration, Badlands
  Location: Brockton, Montana
  Date: Fourth weekend in June

  Chases-1993, 265

Indian Celebration, O'Odham Tash
  Location: Casa Grande, Arizona
  Ethnic or religious group: Papago Indians
  Date: February

  IndianAmer-1989, 277

Indian Celebration, Red Bottom
  Location: Frazer, Montana
  Date: Third weekend in June

  Chases-1993, 254

Indian Celebration, Tygh Valley
  Location: North of Warm Springs, Oregon
  Date: May

  IndianAmer-1989, 198, 349

Indian Ceremonial, Intertribal
  Location: Gallup, New Mexico
  Established: 1922
  Date: Mid-August

  HolFestCelWrld-1994, 113
  IndianAmer-1989, 288

Indian Ceremonial Dancing, American
  Location: Taos, New Mexico
  Date: September 29-30, including San Geronimo Day

  Chases-1993, 389

Indian Chief, Day of the
  See **Juárez Day (Mexico)**

Indian Dances, Traditional
  Location: Gallup, New Mexico
  Date: Memorial Day through Labor Day

  Chases-1993, 228

Indian Day
  Location: Cotati, California
  Ethnic or religious group: Pomo Indians
  Date: August

  IndianAmer-1989, 346

Indian Day (Native American Day)
  Location: Oklahoma
  Date: First Saturday after full moon in September

  AmerBkDays-1978, 863
  Chases-1993, 355

Indian Day, American
  Location: United States
  Established: 1916
  Date: Varies

  HolFestCelWrld-1994, 8

Indian Day, American (Native Americans' Day)
  Location: South Dakota
  Established: 1916
  Date: Second Monday in October

  HolFestCelWrld-1994, 8

Indian Days
  Location: Fort Washakie, Wyoming
  Ethnic or religious group: Shoshone Indians
  Date: Late June

  IndianAmer-1989, 115

Indian Days, All American
  Location: Sheridan, Wyoming
  Established: 1953
  Date: Last weekend in July or first in August

  AmerBkDays-1978, 707
  HolFestCelWrld-1994, 5

Indian Days, Fort Hall
  Location: Fort Hall, Idaho
  Ethnic or religious group: Bannock Shoshone Indians
  Date: August

  IndianAmer-1989, 123

Indian Days, North American
  Location: Blackfeet Reservation at Browning, Montana
  Ethnic or religious group: Indians from Canada and the
    United States
  Date: Second week in July

  HolFestCelWrld-1994, 229
  IndianAmer-1989, 23

Indian Days, Rocky Boy
  Location: Box Elder, Montana
  Ethnic or religious group: Chippewa and Cree Indians

  Date: Usually first weekend in August

  IndianAmer-1989, 31

Indian Exposition, American
  Location: Anadarko, Oklahoma
  Ethnic or religious group: Southern Cheyenne and
    other Indians
  Date: Six days beginning second Monday of August

  AnnivHol-1983, 173
  IndianAmer-1989, 58, 68

Indian Fair
  Location: Wyoming
  Ethnic or religious group: Shoshone Indians
  Date: August

  IndianAmer-1989, 115

Indian Fair, Choctaw
  Location: Pearl River Indian Community near
    Philadelphia, Mississippi
  Ethnic or religious group: Choctaw Indians
  Established: July 1949; formerly Green Corn Ceremony
  Date: Four days in July beginning the Wednesday after
    July 4

  Chases-1993, 291
  GdUSFest-1984, 102
  HolFestCelWrld-1994, 61
  IndianAmer-1989, 242

Indian Fair, Heard Museum Guild
  Location: Heard Museum, Phoenix, Arizona
  Ethnic or religious group: Hopi, Navajo, Apache, Plains,
    Pima, and Mohave Indians
  Established: 1950s
  Date: Two days in late February

  GdUSFest-1984, 12

Indian Festival, Iroquois
  Location: State University of New York in Cobleskill
  Ethnic or religious group: Iroquois Indians
  Date: First weekend in September, including Labor Day

  Chases-1993, 355
  IndianAmer-1989, 171

Indian Festival, Katari
  Location: Fonda, New York
  Ethnic or religious group: Iroquois Indians

  IndianAmer-1989, 171

Indian Festival, Mountain Eagle
  Location: Hunter, New York
  Ethnic or religious group: Iroquois Indians

  IndianAmer-1989, 171

Indian Heritage Days Celebration, Oklahoma
  Location: Oklahoma
  Ethnic or religious group: Miami and Peoria Indians
  Date: Late May

  IndianAmer-1989, 84, 90

Indian Market
  Location: Santa Fe Plaza, Santa Fe, New Mexico
  Ethnic or religious group: Southwestern Indians, including
    Hopi, Navajo, and Zuni
  Established: 1922
  Date: Third weekend in August

  GdUSFest-1984, 119
  HolFestCelWrld-1994, 155

Indian Memorial Stampede Rodeo
  Location: Stroud, Oklahoma
  Ethnic or religious group: Sac and Fox Indians
  Date: Summer

  IndianAmer-1989, 93

Indian Pueblos Arts and Crafts Show, Annual Eight Northern
  See **Arts and Crafts Show, Annual Eight Northern**
    Indian Pueblos

Indian Pueblos Spring Arts and Crafts Show, Eight Northern
  See **Arts and Crafts Show, Eight Northern Indian**
    Pueblos Spring

Indian Rodeo and Stampede Days, All
  Established: Fallon, Nevada
  Ethnic or religious group: Nevada and other Indians from
    Canada and the United States
  Established: 1967
  Date: Third or fourth weekend in July

  GdUSFest-1984, 114

Indian Summer Festival
  Location: Milwaukee, Wisconsin
  Date: Second weekend in September

  Chases-1993, 363

Indra Jatra and Kumari Jatra, Festival of the Child Goddess
  Location: Nepal: Kathmandu
  Ethnic or religious group: Hindu

  Date: September, eight days during Hindu months of
    Bhadrapada-Asvina; 12th day of waxing moon is
    Kumari Jatra

  FolkWrldHol-1992, 438
  HolFestCelWrld-1994, 155

Industry Festival of Wetzlar
  Location: Federal Republic of Germany: Wetzlar, Hesse
  Established: 1952
  Date: Mid-June to mid-July

  IntlThFolk-1979, 151

Ingathering, Feast of (England and Scotland)
  See **Harvest Home Festival (Church of England in**
    England), (England), and (Scotland)

Ingathering, Feast of (Jewish)
  See **Sukkot (Jewish)**

Inmaculada Concepción de María, Fiesta de la
  See **Immaculate Conception, Feast of the (Puerto Rico)**

Innocent Martyr Saints Day
  See **Holy Innocents' Day**

Innocento' or Innocents' Day
  See **Holy Innocents' Day**

Interlake Festival
  Location: Canada: Winnipeg, Manitoba
  Date: June-August

  IntlThFolk-1979, 64

Interlaken Festival
  Location: Switzerland: Interlaken, Bern
  Established: 1961
  Date: June-August

  IntlThFolk-1979, 351

Internationales Brucknerfest
  See **Bruckner Festival, International (Austria: Linz)**

Internationales Festival Hector Berlioz
  See **Berlioz International Festival (France: Lyon and**
    La Côte-Saint-André)

International Festival
  Location: Toledo, Ohio
  Established: 1958
  Date: Third weekend in May

  GdUSFest-1984, 142

In the Sunlit Plain
Named for: Honors Tudor Vladimirescu (c. 1780-1821), leader of 1821 revolution in Wallachia
Location: Romania: Pades, Gorj
Date: First week in June

IntlThFolk-1979, 328

Inti Raymi or Raimi Fiesta
See **Sun Festival (Inca people in Cuzco, Peru)**

Intruz, Carnival
See **Mardi Gras (India: Goa)**

Invention or Finding of the Cross
See **Exaltation of the Cross**

Inventors Day
Location: National Inventors Hall of Fame, United States
Date: February 8

AnnivHol-1983, 21

Iowa State Fair
Location: Des Moines, Iowa
Established: 1854
Date: 11 days through last Sunday in August

HolFestCelWrld-1994, 156

Iri ji Ohuru
See **New Yam Festival (Igbo people in Nigeria)**

Iris Day
See **Children's Day (Japan)**

Irish Houses Festival, Great
Location: Ireland: County Wicklow
Established: 1970
Date: First two weeks in June

MusFestEurBrit-1980, 110

Iro Festivals
Ethnic or religious group: Yoruba people
Date: Five festivals annually

DictFolkMyth-1984, 528

Ironman Triathlon Championships
Location: Kailua-Kona, Hawaii
Established: 1978
Date: Saturday nearest full moon in October

HolFestCelWrld-1994, 156

Iroquois White Dog Feast (New Year or Midwinter Festival)
Location: Canada and the United States

Ethnic or religious group: Senaca, Cayuga, and other Iroquois Indians
Date: Several days, including first quarter moon in January

BkHolWrld-1986, January 10, 178
DictFolkMyth-1984, 303, 348, 430, 440, 835, 1166
FolkAmerHol-1987, 41

Irrigation Festival
Location: Sequim, Washington
Established: 1896; formerly May Days
Date: First full weekend in May

HolFestCelWrld-1994, 156

Islendingadagurinn
See **Icelandic Festival (Icelandic-Canadians in Gimli, Manitoba, Canada)**

Israel Festival
Location: Israel: Caesarea, Haifa, Jerusalem, and Tel Aviv
Established: 1961
Date: Varies; some time between May and September

GdWrldFest-1985, 115
IntlThFolk-1979, 238
MusFestWrld-1963, 259
See also **Music Festival, En Gev**

Is'ru Chag
See **Simhat Torah**

Issa Aka
See **Washing the Hands (Ibo people in Nigeria)**

Istanbul Festival, International
Location: Turkey: Istanbul
Established: 1973
Date: June-July

GdWrldFest-1985, 180
IntlThFolk-1979, 369

Isthmian Games
Location: Ancient Greece: Corinth
Established: 581 B.C.
Date: First month of spring every second year

HolFestCelWrld-1994, 157

Italian Festival
Location: McAlester, Oklahoma
Ethnic or religious group: Italian-American
Date: Late May

HolFestCelWrld-1994, 157

Italian Heritage Festival, West Virginia
Location: Clarksburg, West Virginia
Established: 1979
Date: September, Labor Day weekend

HolFestCelWrld-1994, 365

Itensi Festival
See **Okpesi (Igbo people in Nigeria)**

Itul
Location: Congo: Mushenge
Ethnic or religious group: Kuba people
Date: Around December 7-8, but date varies and festival
occurs according to king's authorization

FolkWrldHol-1992, 584
HolFestCelWrld-1994, 157

Ivy Day
Named for: Honors Charles Stewart Parnell (1846-1891)
Date: October 6

HolFestCelWrld-1994, 157

Izmir International Fair
Location: Turkey: Izmir
Date: August-September

GdWrldFest-1985, 181
IntlThFolk-1979, 370

Jackalope Days
Location: Douglas, Wyoming
Date: Late June

HolFestCelWrld-1994, 159

Jack Frost Day
See **Granddad Frost Day**

Jackson Day
See **Battle of New Orleans Day**

Jackson's Birthday, Andrew
Named for: Andrew Jackson (1767-1845)
Location: Tennessee
Date: March 15

AmerBkDays-1978, 252
Chases-1993, 130
HolFestCelWrld-1994, 10

Jade or Pearly Emperor
See **Yü Huang Shang Ti (Taoist people in Chinese)**

Jaganna—tha
See **Juggernaut**

Jamaica Festival
Location: Jamaica: especially Kingston, Montego Bay
Established: 1963
Date: Five days in late July ending first Monday in August,
Jamaican Independence Day

GdWrldFest-1985, 121

Jamestown Day
Named for: May 13, 1607, landing of first English
colonizers and establishment of Jamestown, Virginia
Location: United States
Ethnic or religious group: Christian
Date: Sunday nearest May 13

AmerBkDays-1978, 447
AnnivHol-1983, 65
Chases-1993, 207
DaysCustFaith-1957, 123

Jamhuri Day
See **Independence Day (Kenya)**

Jamshed Navaroz
See **New Year (Parsis and other Zoroastrians) and (Parsis
and other Zoroastrians in the United States)**

Janai Purnima
See **Sacred Thread Festival (Buddhist and Hindu people
in Nepal)**

Janaki Navami
Ethnic or religious group: Hindu
Date: April-May, ninth day of waxing half of Hindu
month of Vaisakha

RelHolCal-1993, 86

Janmashtami
See **Krishna's Birthday (Hindu)**

Janus, Feast of (Ancient Rome)
See **Agonalia (Ancient Rome)**

Jatra Festival
Location: India: Imphal, Manipur
Date: Two weeks in December-January

IntlThFolk-1979, 211

Jatra Festivals of Calcutta
Location: India: Calcutta, West Bengal
Date: 10-15 days in winter

IntlThFolk-1979, 217

Jauna Gada Diena
See **New Year's Day (Latvia)**

Jayuya Festival of Indian Lore (Jayuya Indian Festival)
  Location: Puerto Rico: Jayuya
  Established: 1969; commemorates Columbus's arrival on
    November 19, 1493
  Date: Mid-November

  GdUSFest-1984, 219
  See also **Columbus Day**

Jazz, Nice Grand Parade of (Grande Parade du Jazz)
  Location: France: Nice
  Established: 1974
  Date: 11 days beginning first week in July

  Chases-1993, 223
  MusFestEurBrit-1980, 83

Jazz and Heritage Festival, New Orleans
  Location: New Orleans, Louisiana
  Established: 1970
  Date: Ten days in mid-April to early May

  GdUSFest-1984, 71
  HolFestCelWrld-1994, 223
  MusFestAmer-1990, 194

Jazz Festival, Annual National Ragtime and Traditional (Saint Louis, Missouri)
  See **Ragtime and Traditional Jazz Festival, Annual National**

Jazz Festival, Barbados/Caribbean
  Location: Barbados
  Established: 1985
  Date: A Thursday through Sunday in late May

  HolFestCelWrld-1994, 24

Jazz Festival, Bix Beiderbecke Memorial
  Named for: Bix Beiderbecke (1903-1931)
  Location: Davenport, Iowa
  Established: 1972
  Date: Three days during last weekend in July

  HolFestCelWrld-1994, 33
  MusFestAmer-1990, 192

Jazz Festival, *Boston Globe*
  Location: Boston, Massachusetts
  Established: 1966
  Date: One week in March

  MusFestAmer-1990, 196

Jazz Festival, Chicago
  Location: Chicago, Illinois
  Established: 1979

  Date: Five days in late August or early September

  Chases-1993, 352
  HolFestCelWrld-1994, 58
  MusFestAmer-1990, 191

Jazz Festival, Concord
  Location: Concord, California
  Established: 1969
  Date: One weekend in August

  MusFestAmer-1990, 182

Jazz Festival, JVC
  Location: Newport, Rhode Island
  Established: 1954
  Date: Three days in mid-August

  MusFestAmer-1990, 200

Jazz Festival, Mellon
  Location: Philadelphia, Pennsylvania
  Date: Ten days in mid-June

  MusFestAmer-1990, 199

Jazz Festival, Molde International (Jazzfestpillene i Molde)
  Location: Norway: Molde
  Established: 1961
  Date: One week in late July

  Chases-1993, 299
  MusFestEurBrit-1980, 128

Jazz Festival, Monterey
  Location: Monterey, California
  Established: 1958
  Date: Third weekend in September

  Chases-1993, 374
  GdUSFest-1984, 21
  HolFestCelWrld-1994, 210
  MusFestAmer-1990, 184

Jazz Festival, Montreal
  Location: Canada: Montreal
  Established: 1980
  Date: June-July

  HolFestCelWrld-1994, 210

Jazz Festival, Montreux International (Montreux Festival Internacional de Jazz)
  Location: Switzerland: Montreux, Vaud
  Established: 1966
  Date: Two weeks beginning first week in July

  GdWrldFest-1985, 170
  MusFestEurBrit-1980, 145

Jazz Festival, Playboy
  Location: Hollywood, California
  Established: 1979
  Date: Third weekend in June

  MusFestAmer-1990, 186

Jazz Festival, Pori International
  Location: Finland: Pori
  Established: 1965-66
  Date: Four days in mid-July

  Chases-1993, 287
  GdWrldFest-1985, 77
  MusFestEurBrit-1980, 69

Jazz Festival, Summer
  Location: Oakville, California
  Established: 1969
  Date: Five weekend concerts over July and August

  MusFestAmer-1990, 189

Jazz Festival, Telluride
  Location: Telluride, Colorado
  Established: 1977
  Date: Three days in mid-August

  HolFestCelWrld-1994, 334
  MusFestAmer-1990, 190

Jazzfestpillene i Molde
  See **Jazz Festival, Molde International (Norway: Molde)**

Jazz Jubilee, Sacramento Dixieland
  Location: Sacramento, California
  Established: 1974
  Date: Four days over Memorial Day weekend, last weekend in May

  MusFestAmer-1990, 187

Jefferson's Birthday, Thomas
  Named for: Thomas Jefferson (1743-1826)
  Location: United States
  Date: April 13

  HolFestCelWrld-1994, 338

Jellikattu Festival
  See **Harvest Festival (India: Madurai, Tiruchirapalli, and Tanjore)**

Jerash Festival
  Location: Jordan: Jerash
  Established: 1981

  Date: Nine days in August

  GdWrldFest-1985, 125

Jerusalem Day (Yom Yerushalayim)
  Named for: Capture of Jerusalem on June 7, 1967
  Location: Israel
  Ethnic or religious group: Jewish
  Date: May-June, 28th of Jewish month of Iyar

  HolFestCelWrld-1994, 376

Jesus dos Navegantes, Bom
  Location: Brazil: Salvador
  Date: January 1

  HolFestCelWrld-1994, 38

Jhulan Latra
  Location: India: Jagannath Temple at Puri, Orissa
  Ethnic or religious group: Hindu
  Date: July-August, full moon day of Hindu month of Sravana

  RelHolCal-1993, 87
  See also **Juggernaut**

Jicarilla Apache Fair
  Location: San Ildefonso Pueblo, New Mexico
  Date: September 14-15

  IndianAmer-1989, 289, 309

Jidai Matsuri (Japan: Kyoto)
  See **Ages, Festival of the (Japan: Kyoto)**

Jinnah Day
  Named for: Muhammed Ali Jinnah (1876-1948)
  Location: Pakistan
  Date: September 11

  AnnivHol-1983, 117

Jizo-Ennichi or Jiso Kshitigarba
  Location: China and Japan
  Ethnic or religious group: Buddhist
  Date: 24th of each lunar month

  DictWrldRel-1989, 418

Job's Birthday
  Location: Maryland
  Ethnic or religious group: African-Americans
  Date: February 30

  FolkAmerHol-1987, 75

Jodlerfests
  See **Yodeling Festivals (Switzerland)**

John Canoe Days
See **Junkanoo Festival**

Johnny Appleseed, Birthday of
Named for: John Chapman (1774-1845)
Location: United States
Date: September 26

AmerBkDays-1978, 868
BkHolWrld-1986, September 26
Chases-1993, 387

Johnny Appleseed Day
Named for: John Chapman (1774-1845)
Location: United States
Date: March 11

AnnivHol-1983, 36
Chases-1993, 126
DaysCustFaith-1957, 76

Johnny Appleseed Festival
Named for: John Chapman (1774-1845)
Location: Fort Wayne, Indiana
Date: Third week in September

HolFestCelWrld-1994, 162

Johnny Appleseed Week
Named for: John Chapman (1774-1845)
Location: Ohio
Established: 1941
Date: Last week in September

AmerBkDays-1978, 868
DictFolkMyth-1984, 555

Johnson's Birthday, Lyndon B.
Named for: Lyndon Baines Johnson (1908-1973)
Location: Texas
Date: August 27

AmerBkDays-1978, 783
Chases-1993, 343
DictDays-1988, 71

Jonquil Festival
Location: Washington, Arkansas
Date: Third weekend in March

HolFestCelWrld-1994, 163

Jonsok
See **Midsummer (Norway)**

Jordbruksdagarna
See **Agricultural Days (Swedish Americans in Bishop Hill, Illinois)**

Joropo Festival, International
Location: Colombia: Villavicencio, Meta
Date: December

IntlThFolk-1979, 79

Jouluaatto
See **Christmas Eve (Finland)**

Jõulud
See **Christmas (Estonia)**

Jõulu Laupäev
See **Christmas Eve (Estonia)**

Joulupäivä
See **Christmas (Finland)**

Jour de Fête a Sainte Genevieve Days of Celebration
Location: Ste. Genevieve, Missouri
Ethnic or religious group: French-, German-, and Spanish-Americans
Established: 1965
Date: Second weekend in August

Chases-1993, 328
GdUSFest-1984, 106
HolFestCelWrld-1994, 289

Le Jour de l'An or Le Jour des Étrennes
See **New Year's Day (France)**

Le Jour de Morts
See **All Souls' Day (Brittany)**

Le Jour des Innocents
See **Holy Innocents' Day (Belgium)**

Le Jour des Rois
See **Epiphany (France)**

Jousting the Bear (La Giostra dell'Orso)
Location: Italy: Pistoia
Date: March 10

HolFestCelWrld-1994, 163

Jousting Tournament
Location: Mount Solon, Virginia
Established: 1821-23
Date: Third Saturday in June and second Sunday in October

AmerBkDays-1978, 756
HolFestCelWrld-1994, 163

Joust of the Quintain
Location: Italy: Foligno, Umbria
Established: 17th century; current version since 1946
Date: Second weekend in September

IntlThFolk-1979, 243

Jovanovic, Festivities in Honor of
  Named for: Ljubisa Jovanovic (b. 1936)
  Location: Yugoslavia: Sabac, Serbia
  Established: 1972
  Date: October

  IntlThFolk-1979, 401

Joy of Living
  Location: Australia: Toowoomba, Queensland
  Date: One week in September-early October

  GdWrldFest-1985, 7
  IntlThFolk-1979, 18
  See also **Flowers, Carnival of**

Juárez Day (Day of the Indian Chief)
  Named for: Benito Palbo Juárez (1806-1872)
  Location: Mexico
  Date: March 21

  AnnivHol-1983, 40
  Chases-1993, 137

Jubilate Sunday
  Ethnic or religious group: Roman Catholic
  Date: Third Sunday after Easter

  DictDays-1988, 61

Judgment, Day of (Jewish)
  See **New Year, Jewish (Rosh Hashanah)**

Judgement Day (Christian)
  See **Easter**

Judica Sunday
  See **Palm Sunday**

Jueves Santo
  See **Holy Thursday (Mexico)**

Juggernaut (Rath Yatra, Festival of Jagannatha)
  Location: India: Jagannatha temple at Puri, Orissa
  Ethnic or religious group: Hindu
  Date: June-July, second day of waxing half of Hindu
    month of Ashadha

  BkHolWrld-1986, July 12, 173
  Chases-1993, 258
  DictFolkMyth-1984, 537
  DictWrldRel-1989, 304, 368
  HolFestCelWrld-1994, 269
  RelHolCal-1993, 108
  See also **Bathing Festival (Snan Yatra)**

Jugowa
  See **Autumnal Equinox (Okinawa)**

Juhannus Day
  See **Midsummer (Finland)** and **St. John the Baptist's Day**
    (Finland)

Julaften
  See **Christmas Eve (Norway)**

Julafton
  See **Christmas Eve (Sweden)**

Juldagen
  See **Christmas (Sweden)**

Juleaftgen
  See **Christmas Eve (Denmark)**

Juledag
  See **Christmas (Denmark)** and **(Norway)**

July, Feast of
  See **Binding of Wreaths (Lithuania)**

Al-Jum'ah al-Hazinah, Sorrowful Friday
  See **Good Friday (Greek Orthodox Church in Syria)**

Jumping Frog Jubilee Day
  See **Calaveras County Fair and Frog Jumping Jubilee**

June Festival, International
  Location: Switzerland: Zurich
  Established: 1909
  Date: May-early June

  GdWrldFest-1985, 172
  IntlThFolk-1979, 356
  MusFestEurBrit-1980, 148
  MusFestWrld-1963, 210

Juneteenth (Emancipation Day)
  Named for: Date news of abolishment of slavery arrived
    in parts of southern U.S., June 19, 1865
  Location: Texas and other southern United States
  Ethnic or religious group: African-Americans
  Date: June 19

  AnnivHol-1983, 81
  BkHolWrld-1986, June 19
  Chases-1993, 255
  DictDays-1988, 36
  FolkAmerHol-1987, 213
  HolFestCelWrld-1994, 164

Juninas, Festas (Bumba-meu-Boi Folk Drama)
   Location: Brazil
   Date: June 13-29

   FolkWrldHol-1992, 326
   HolFestCelWrld-1994, 44

Junkanoo Festival
   Location: Bahama Islands: Nassau
   Date: December 26-January 1

   Chases-1993, 484
   DictFolkMyth-1984, 554
   FolkWrldHol-1992, 639
   GdWrldFest-1985, 16
   HolFestCelWrld-1994, 162

Junkanoo Festival
   Location: Belize

   HolFestCelWrld-1994, 162

Junkanoo Festival
   Location: Guatemala

   HolFestCelWrld-1994, 162

Junkanoo Festival
   Location: Jamaica
   Date: December 23-January 23

   AnnivHol-1983, 178
   HolFestCelWrld-1994, 162

Juno Caprotina
   Location: Ancient Rome
   Date: July 7

   AmerBkDays-1978, 608

Jurokunichi
   Location: Okinawa: Hanashiro
   Date: 16th day of first lunar month

   FolkWrldHol-1992, 77

Juturnalia
   Named for: The nymph Juturna or Diuturna, personi-
      fication of healing springs and wells
   Location: Ancient Rome
   Date: January 11

   DictFolkMyth-1984, 564

Juul, Feast of
   Location: Ancient Scandinavia
   Date: December, winter solstice festival

   DaysCustFaith-1957, 352

Juvenalia
   Location: Poland: Kraków
   Date: Late May or early June

   BkHolWrld-1986, June 4, 178
   HolFestCelWrld-1994, 164

Juwo
   See **Pig Festival (Kapauka Papuan people in Papua
   New Guinea)**

Jyeshta Ashtami
   Location: Kashmir: Khir Bhawani
   Ethnic or religious group: Hindu
   Date: May-June, eighth day of waxing half of Hindu month
      of Jyeshta

   RelHolCal-1993, 87

Kachina Come, the
   See **Shalako Ceremonial (Zuñi Pueblo, New Mexico)**

Kafr el-Elow
   See **Fast, Feast of Breaking the (Egypt)**

Kakizome
   See **First Writing of the Year (Japan)**

Kalēdos
   See **Christmas (Lithuania)**

Kalends
   See **Ides**

Kalevala Päivä Day
   Named for: The publication of *Kalevala* in 1835 by Elias
      Lönnrot (1802-1884)
   Location: Finland
   Date: February 28

   AnnivHol-1983, 29
   BkFest-1937, 111
   BkHolWrld-1986, February 28

Kali Festival
   See **Lights, Festival of (India: Bengal)**

Kallemooi
   Location: Netherlands: Schiermonnikoog, North
      Coast Islands
   Date: Saturday preceding Pentecost

   FestWestEur-1958, 134

**Kalojan or Caloian Ceremony (Kalos Johannes or
Kalos Adonis)**
   Location: Romania
   Date: Monday preceding Assumption, August 25

   DictFolkMyth-1984, 569

Kalpa Vruksha
See **New Year (Hindu people in rural India)**

Kamada Ekadashi
See **Wish-Fulfilling Eleventh (Hindu)**

Kamakura Matsuri
See **Snowhut Festival (northern Japan)**

Kamarampaka Day
Named for: September 25, 1961, abolishment of
 monarchical rule
Location: Rwanda
Date: September 25

AnnivHol-1983, 122

Kamehameha Day
Named for: Kamehameha I (1758?-1819)
Location: Iolani Palace, Honolulu, Oahu Island, Hawaii
Established: 1872
Date: June 11

AmerBkDays-1978, 545
AnnivHol-1983, 78
Chases-1993, 243
DictDays-1988, 63
GdUSFest-1984, 44
HolFestCelWrld-1994, 170

Kandy Esala Perahera
See **Esala Perahera**

Kannon Festival
Location: Japan: Asakusa Kannon Temple
Date: Two days in mid-March

AnnivHol-1983, 178

Kapesi
See **Planting-Time Festival (Angola)**

Karácsony
See **Christmas (Hungary)**

Karácsony Vigiliája
See **Christmas Eve (Hungary)**

Kar Freitag
See **Good Friday (Austria) and (Austria: Riva)**

Karraka International Festival, El
See **El Karraka International Festival**

Karsamstag
See **Holy Saturday (Germany)**

Karthika Purnima
Ethnic or religious group: Hindu
Date: October-November, full moon day of Hindu
 month of Karthika

RelHolCal-1993, 87

Karthika Snan
Location: India: along the Ganges and Yamuna rivers
Ethnic or religious group: Hindu
Date: October-November, Hindu month of Karthika

RelHolCal-1993, 88

Kartini Day
Named for: Raden Adjeng Kartini (1879-1904)
Location: Indonesia
Date: April 21

BkHolWrld-1986, April 21
Chases-1993, 174
HolFestCelWrld-1994, 166

Karwachoth or Karwa Chauth
Location: India
Ethnic or religious group: Married Hindu women
Date: October-November, fourth day of waning half
 of Hindu month of Karthika

FolkWrldHol-1992, 533
HolFestCelWrld-1994, 166
RelHolCal-1993, 88

Käseteilet
See **Dividing of the Cheese (Switzerland: Justis Valley area)**

Kashihara Shinto Festival
Location: Japan: Kashihara Shrine, Kashihara, Nara
Date: April 3

IntlThFolk-1979, 254

Kason Festival of Watering the Banyan Tree
See **Buddha's Birthday, Enlightenment, and Salvation
 (Buddhist people in Burma) and (Buddhist people in
 Myanmar)**

Kassada
Location: Indonesia: Mount Bromo, Tengger Mountains,
 East Java
Ethnic or religious group: Tenggerese Buddha Dharma
 religion
Date: January, 14th of Kassada, 12th month of
 Tenggerese year

BkHolWrld-1986, January 8, 178

Kataklysmos Festival (Flood Festival)
   Location: Cyprus: Larnaca, Limassol, Paphos, and other
      seaside towns
   Established: Predates Christian era
   Date: May-June, three to five days including fiftieth day after
      Greek Orthodox Easter (Pentecost)

   BkHolWrld-1986, June 8, 176
   Chases-1993, 239
   FolkWrldHol-1992, 324
   HolFestCelWrld-1994, 166
   IntlThFolk-1979, 86

Kataragama Festival
   Location: Sri Lanka: Kataragama
   Ethnic or religious group: Buddhist and Hindu
   Established: 3000 years old
   Date: June-July

   DictWrldRel-1989, 569
   IntlThFolk-1979, 345

Katherine Show Day
   Location: Australia
   Date: July

   DictDays-1988, 56

Kathin Season
   See **Robe Offering Month (Buddhist people in Thailand)**

Kati Bihu
   Location: India: Assam
   Ethnic or religious group: Hindu
   Date: September 21, 22

   FolkWrldHol-1992, 486

Kawate Bunjiro, Festival of
   Location: Japan and Japanese elsewhere
   Ethnic or religious group: Konko-kyo religion
   Established: Commemorates founding of the Konko-kyo
      religion on October 21, 1859
   Date: Observed on or near October 25

   DictWrldRel-1989, 411

Kawsasqanchis, Our Living with the Dead
   See **All Saints' Day (Bolivia)**

Keaw Yed Wakes Festival
   Location: England: Westhoughton, Lancashire
   Established: Over four hundred years old
   Date: Sunday of or after August 24

   HolFestCelWrld-1994, 167

Keiro-no-ki
   See **Respect for the Aged Day (Japan)**

Kekri
   See **All Saints' Day (Finland); St. Michael's Day (Finland)**

Keller Festival, Helen
   Named for: Helen Keller (1880-1968)
   Location: Tuscumbia, Alabama
   Date: Last weekend in June

   AmerBkDays-1978, 598
   HolFestCelWrld-1994, 136

Kennedy Day, John F.
   Named for: John F. Kennedy (1917-1963)
   Location: Massachusetts
   Date: November 24; observed last Sunday in November

   AnnivHol-1983, 150
   Chases-1993, 457

Kent State Memorial Day
   Named for: Killing of four students and wounding of nine
      by National Guard soldiers during a campus protest
      against the Vietnam War on May 4, 1970
   Location: Kent State University, Ohio
   Date: May 3-4

   AnnivHol-1983, 61
   Chases-1993, 194
   HolFestCelWrld-1994, 167

Kentucky Derby Day
   Location: Churchill Downs, Louisville, Kentucky
   Established: 1875
   Date: 15-day festival precedes race, which occurs on
      the first Saturday in May

   AmerBkDays-1978, 414
   AnnivHol-1983, 60
   Chases-1993, 188
   FolkAmerHol-1987, 177-79
   GdUSFest-1984, 63
   HolFestCelWrld-1994, 168

Keretkun Festival
   See **Seal Festival (USSR: Chuckchi)**

Kern or Kirn Supper
   See **Harvest Home Festival (Scotland)**

Kerstavond
   See **Christmas Eve (Belgium)**

Kerstdag
   See **Christmas (Belgium)**

Keruk
See **Dead, Observance for the (Diegueño and Yuma Indians in California and Yuma Indians in Arizona)**

Kevad Püha
See **Spring, Bringing of the (Estonia)**

Kewpiesta
Named for: Kewpie doll created by Rose O'Neill (1874-1944), Ozark writer and artist
Location: Branson, Missouri
Established: 1967
Date: Third weekend in April

GdUSFest-1984, 104
HolFestCelWrld-1994, 169

Khamis al-Amwat
See **Dead Remembrance Thursday (Jordan)**

Khamis al-Jasad
See **Holy Thursday (Jerusalem) and (Syria)**

Khamis al-Marfa, Carnival Thursday
See **Mardi Gras (Syria)**

Khomeini Day
Named for: Ayatollah Khomeini (1901-1989)
Location: Iran
Established: February 1, 1979
Date: February 1

AnnivHol-1983, 17

Khordad Sal
Named for: Commemorates birth of the Prophet Spitaman Zarathustra or Zoroaster (c. 628-c. 551 B.C.)
Location: India and elsewhere
Ethnic or religious group: Parsis and other Zoroastrians
Date: March 21 by Fasli sect; July 13 by Kadmi sect; and August 15 by Shahenshai sect

AnnivHol-1983, 178
FolkWrldHol-1992, 441
HolFestCelWrld-1994, 169

Kiamichi Owa Chito
See **Happy Hunting Party, Festival of the Forest (Choctaw Indians at Beavers Bend State Park, Broken Bow, Oklahoma)**

Kiddies' Carnival
Location: Trinidad and Tobago

Date: February, week preceding Carnival

BkHolWrld-1986, February 19, 178
HolFestCelWrld-1994, 169
See also **Mardi Gras (Trinidad and Tobago)**

Kids' Day
Established: Sponsored by Kiwanis International
Date: Fourth Saturday in September

Chases-1993, 386
DictDays-1988, 63

Kiel Week
Location: Federal Republic of Germany: Kiel, Schleswig-Holstein
Established: 1882
Date: One week in June

HolFestCelWrld-1994, 170
IntlThFolk-1979, 142

Kigensetsu
See **Foundation Day, Japanese National (Japan)**

Killing the Pigs, Festival of (Seatapmise Päev)
Location: Estonia
Date: September

BkFest-1937, 106

Kil'vey
See **Horns, Festival of (Koryak people in Russia)**

Kinderzeche
See **Children's Reckoning (Federal Republic of Germany: Dinkelsbühl, Bavaria)**

King, Birthday of His Majesty the
Named for: King Birendra Bir Bikram Shah Dev (b. 1945)
Location: Nepal
Date: December 29

HolFestCelWrld-1994, 170

King, Jr.'s Birthday, Martin Luther
Named for: Martin Luther King, Jr. (1929-1968)
Location: United States
Date: January 15; observed third Monday in January

AmerBkDays-1978, 77
AnnivHol-1983, 9
BkHolWrld-1986, January 15
Chases-1993, 67
DictDays-1988, 73
DictWrldRel-1989, 407
HolFestCelWrld-1994, 197
RelHolCal-1993, 63

Kingdom Days
  Named for: Civil War treaty that named Callaway County
    a kingdom in 1861
  Location: Fulton, Missouri
  Date: Last weekend in June

  HolFestCelWrld-1994, 170

Kingdom or Statute Days
  Named for: December 15, 1954, statute which allowed
    autonomous rule
  Location: Netherlands Antilles
  Date: December 15

  AnnivHol-1983, 160

King's Birthday
  Named for: George V (1865-1936)
  Location: Most states in Australia
  Date: A Monday in early June

  DictDays-1988, 63

King's Birthday
  Named for: Jigme Singye Wangchuk (b. 1955)
  Location: Bhutan
  Date: November 11

  AnnivHol-1983, 145

King's Birthday
  Named for: Frederick IX (1899-1972)
  Location: Denmark
  Date: March 11

  NatlHolWrld-1968, 32

King's Birthday
  Named for: Subhuza II (1899-1982)
  Location: Swaziland
  Date: July 22

  AnnivHol-1983, 96

King's Birthday
  Named for: Gustav IV, Adolph (1778-1837)
  Location: Sweden
  Date: November 11; observed June 2

  NatlHolWrld-1968, 81

King's Coronation
  Location: Saudi Arabia
  Date: November 12

  NatlHolWrld-1968, 206

King's Day
  See **Epiphany (New Orleans, Louisiana) and (New
    Mexico pueblos)**

Kings, Day of the
  See **Epiphany (Le Jour des Rois) (France)**

King's Day with Deer, Buffalo, Eagle, Elk Dances
  See **Epiphany (New Mexico pueblos)**

Kipawo Showboat Company
  Location: Canada: Wolfville, Nova Scotia
  Date: July-August

  IntlThFolk-1979, 67

Kissing Day
  See **New Year's Day (Chippewa Indians in Minnesota)**

Kitchen God Celebration (Tsao Chün)
  Location: China
  Date: 23rd or 24th day of twelfth lunar month and
    New Year's Eve and Day

  AnnivHol-1983, 182
  BkFest-1937, 82
  BkHolWrld-1986, February 5
  DictFolkMyth-1984, 1129
  FolkWrldHol-1992, 656
  GdWrldFest-1985, 63
  See also **New Year's Day (China)**

Kite Battles
  Location: Japan: Shirone, Niigata
  Date: June 5-12

  HolFestCelWrld-1994, 331

Kite Battles of Hamamatsu
  Location: Japan: Hamamatsu, Shizuoka
  Established: 16th century or earlier
  Date: May 3-5, ending on Children's Day

  GdWrldFest-1985, 122
  HolFestCelWrld-1994, 331

Kite Festival, International
  Location: India: Ahmedabad, Gujarat
  Date: December-January, during Hindu month of Pausha

  HolFestCelWrld-1994, 257

Kite Festival, Maryland
  Location: Baltimore, Maryland
  Established: 1967
  Date: Last Saturday in April

  GdUSFest-1984, 80

Kite Festival, Singapore
Location: Singapore
Date: Three to four weekends in January

BkHolWrld-1986, January 19, 181

Kite Festival, Smithsonian
Location: The Mall, Washington, D.C.
Established: 1966
Date: Late March-early April

HolFestCelWrld-1994, 319

Kite Flying Competition
Location: Indonesia
Date: During weeks preceding the rainy season, which
begins in November

BkHolWrld-1986, September 20, 178

Kite-Flying Contest (Nagasaki Takoage)
Location: Japan: Nagasaki
Date: Late April

AnnivHol-1983, 179
HolFestCelWrld-1994, 331

Kite Flying Day
Location: Korea
Date: February 8

AnnivHol-1983, 21

Kite Flying Season
Location: Thailand: Sanam Luang in front of the Grand
Palace, Bangkok
Date: Three-month contest from February-April on
weekday afternoons

GdWrldFest-1985, 174

Kivi Day
Named for: Aleksis Kivi (pseud. for Aleksis Stenvall,
1834-1872)
Location: Finland
Date: October 10

AnnivHol-1983, 131

Klondike Days Exposition
Location: Canada: Edmonton, Alberta
Established: 1962; commemorates Gold Rush of 1898
Date: July

Chases-1993, 301
GdWrldFest-1985, 30

Klondike Gold Discovery Day
Named for: August 17, 1896, discovery of gold
Location: Yukon
Date: Observed the Monday nearest August 17

AnnivHol-1983, 108
Chases-1993, 332
HolFestCelWrld-1994, 171

Klöpfelnächte or Klöpfleinsnächte
See **Knocking Nights (Germany)**

Klusā Sestdiena, Quiet Saturday
See **Holy Saturday (Latvia)**

Knabenschiessen
See **Boys' Rifle Match (Switzerland: Zurich)**

Knecht Ruprecht
Location: Northern Germany
Date: December 5 or 6 or December 24

DictFolkMyth-1984, 584
See also **Kriss Kringle; St. Nicholas's Day**

Kneeling Sunday
See **Pentecost (Greece)**

Kneisel Hall
Location: Blue Hill, Maine
Established: 1900s
Date: Seven weeks from last week in June to mid-August

MusFestAmer-1990, 69

Knocking Nights (Klöpfelnächte or Klöpfleinsnächte)
Location: Germany
Date: December, the three Thursday evenings before
Christmas

BkHolWrld-1986, December 17

Kodomo-no-hi
See **Children's Day (Japan)**

Koimesis tees Theotokou
See **Assumption, Feast of the (Greece)**

Kojagara
See **Harvest Festival (Hindu people in India)**

Koko awia (the Kachina Come)
See **Shalako Ceremonial (Zuñi Pueblo, New Mexico)**

Kokochi
Location: Zuñi Pueblo, New Mexico
Date: Summer solstice

DictFolkMyth-1984, 566

Koleda, Rozhdestvo Khristovo
See **Christmas (Bulgaria)**

Kolme Kuninga Päev
See **Epiphany (Estonia)**

Komatsu Otabi Festival
Location: Japan: Uhashi and Hiyoshi shrines, Komatsu, Ishikawa
Date: Mid-May

IntlThFolk-1979, 255

Konigsfelden Festival
Location: Switzerland: Brugg/Windisch, Aargau
Established: 1973
Date: Even-numbered years during weekends in August-September

IntlThFolk-1979, 350

Kope Procession or Festival (Kopenfahrt)
See **Mardi Gras (Germany: Lüneburg, Lower Saxony)**

Korcula, Festival of (Moreska)
Location: Yugoslavia: Korcula, Croatia
Date: July 27, Croatia's Insurrection Day, and every Thursday from April-September

HolFestCelWrld-1994, 211
IntlThFolk-1979, 390

Korité Feast
See **Fast, Feast of Breaking the (Senegal)**

Kosciuszko Day
Named for: Tadeusz Kosciuszko (1746-1817)
Location: United States
Ethnic or religious group: Polish-American communities
Date: February 4

AnnivHol-1983, 19
Chases-1993, 95

Kosovo, Village Festivities of
Location: Yugoslavia: Klina by Pec, Kosovo
Established: 1970
Date: June

IntlThFolk-1979, 390

Kossuth Day
Named for: Lajos Kossuth (1802-1894)
Location: Hungary and Hungarians elsewhere
Date: March 20

AnnivHol-1983, 40

Kotohira Kompira Festival
Location: Japan: Kotohira, Kagawa
Ethnic or religious group: Shinto religion
Date: October

IntlThFolk-1979, 255

Kourban Bairam
See **Sacrifice, Feast of (Turkey)**

Krems Outdoor Festival (Sommerspiele Krems)
Location: Austria: Krems, Lower Austria
Established: 1974
Date: June-July

IntlThFolk-1979, 36

Krishna's Birthday (Janmashtami)
Named for: Sri Krishna, eighth avatar
Ethnic or religious group: Hindu
Date: August-September, eighth day of waning half of Hindu month of Bhadrapada

AnnivHol-1983, 178
BkFest-1937, 160
BkHolWrld-1986, August 26
Chases-1993, 324
DictFolkMyth-1984, 590, 924
DictWrldRel-1989, 304
FolkWrldHol-1992, 439
HolFestCelWrld-1994, 160
RelHolCal-1993, 86

Krishna's Birthday
Named for: Sri Krishna, eighth avatar
Location: India
Date: August-September, eighth day of waning half of Hindu month of Bhadrapada; twelve-day celebration in Manipur

AnnivHol-1983, 178
BkHolWrld-1986, August 26
DictFolkMyth-1984, 924
FolkWrldHol-1992, 439
HolFestCelWrld-1994, 160
RelHolCal-1993, 86

Krishna's Birthday (Krishna Jayanti)
Named for: Sri Krishna, eighth avatar
Location: Nepal
Date: August-September, eighth day of waning half of Hindu month of Bhadrapada

FolkWrldHol-1992, 440
HolFestCelWrld-1994, 160

Krishtlindjet
See **Christmas (Albania)**

Kriss Kringle Day
Location: Austria and Germany
Date: December 5 or December 24

DictFolkMyth-1984, 591
See also **Knecht Ruprecht; St. Nicholas's Day**

Kriss Kringle's Fair
See **Christkindlesmarkt (Germany: Nuremberg, Bavaria)**

Kristallnacht
Named for: Nazi attack on Jewish homes and businesses throughout Germany and Austria on November 9-10, 1938
Date: November 9-10

AnnivHol-1983, 144
Chases-1993, 436
DictWrldRel-1989, 202
HolFestCelWrld-1994, 172

Kristi Himmelsfärdsdag
See **Ascension Day (Sweden)**

Kruger Day
Named for: Stephanus Johannes Paulus Kruger (1825-1904)
Location: South Africa
Date: October 10

Chases-1993, 405
DictDays-1988, 64

'Ksan Celebrations
Location: Canada: Hazelton, British Columbia
Ethnic or religious group: 'Ksan Indians
Established: Since pre-history; revived in 1958
Date: Friday evenings in July and August

HolFestCelWrld-1994, 173

Kuan Ti, Festival of
Named for: Kuan Ti, Chinese god of war
Location: China
Date: May 13

DictFolkMyth-1984, 592

Kūčios
See **Christmas Eve (Lithuania)**

Kud Khach
See **Exaltation of the Cross (Armenia)**

Kuhio Kalanianaole Day
Named for: Prince Jonah Kuhio Kalanianaole (1871-1921)
Location: Kauai, Hawaii

Established: 1970
Date: One week in March, including March 26

AmerBkDays-1978, 293
AnnivHol-1983, 42
BkHolWrld-1986, March 26
Chases-1993, 141
HolFestCelWrld-1994, 260

Kuhkämpfe
See **Cow Fights (Switzerland: Valais)**

Kuhmon Kamarmusiikki
See **Music Festival, Kuhmo Chamber (Finland: Kuhmo)**

Kule Loklo Celebration
Location: Kule Loklo Miwok Indian Village, California
Ethnic or religious group: Pomo Indians
Date: July or August

IndianAmer-1989, 346

Kulig
See **Winter Sleigh Party (Poland)**

Kumar Sasthi
See **Sithinakha (Hindu people in Nepal)**

Kumbh Mela Festival
Location: India: Allahabad
Ethnic or religious group: Hindu
Date: Every twelfth year on a date determined by astronomers; every six years at Hardvar, Ujjain, and Nasik; Magh Mela held each spring

AnnivHol-1983, 179
DictWrldRel-1989, 305
HolFestCelWrld-1994, 173
RelHolCal-1993, 92

Kuningen
See **New Year's Celebration (Kuningen, Feast of All Souls) (Hindu people in Bali)**

Kuomboka
Location: Zambia: Lealul Knoll, Mongu, Western Province
Ethnic or religious group: Malozi people
Established: 19th century
Date: February-March, when Zambezi River rises

BkHolWrld-1986, February 18, 178
FolkWrldHol-1992, 149
GdWrldFest-1985, 188
HolFestCelWrld-1994, 173

Kurban Bayram
See **Sacrifice, Feast of (Turkey)**

Kurokowa Noh
Location: Japan: Kushiki-machi, Higishitagawa-gun,
Yamagata
Date: Early February

IntlThFolk-1979, 255

Kusadasi, Festival of
Location: Turkey: Kusadasi
Date: June-July

IntlThFolk-1979, 371

Kusiut
See **Midwinter Rites, Bella Coola (Bella Coola,
Kimsquit, and other Indians in coastal British Columbia,
Canada)**

Kutztown Fair
See **Folk Festival, Pennsylvania Dutch**

Kvetna Nedele
See **Palm Sunday (Czechoslovakia)**

Kwanzaa
Location: Canada
Ethnic or religious group: African-Canadians
Established: 1966 by Maulana Karenga (b. 1941), chairman,
Black Studies Department, California State University in
Long Beach
Date: December 26 through January 1

FolkWrldHol-1992, 641
HolFestCelWrld-1994, 174

Kwanzaa
Location: United States
Ethnic or religious group: African-Americans
Established: 1966 by Maulana Karenga (b. 1941), chairman,
Black Studies Department, California State University
in Long Beach
Date: December 26 through January 1

AnnivHol-1983, 164
Chases-1993, 483
HolFestCelWrld-1994, 174
RelHolCal-1993, 89

Kwatipuni
See **Sacred Thread Festival (Buddhist and Hindu people
in Nepal)**

Kyaiya
See **Harvest Dance (Lengua Indians in Gran Chaco,
South America)**

Kyongchip
See **Excited Insects, Feast of (Korea)**

Labor Day
Location: Canada
Date: First Monday in September

AnnivHol-1983, 114
Chases-1993, 359
DictDays-1988, 65
HolFestCelWrld-1994, 175

Labor Day
Location: Binger, Oklahoma
Ethnic or religious group: Caddo Indians
Date: Three days, including Labor Day, first Monday
in September

IndianAmer-1989, 62

Labor Day
Location: Bucks County, Pennsylvania
Date: First Monday in September

FolkAmerHol-1987, 271-73

Labor Day
Location: Rhode Island
Ethnic or religious group: Portuguese-Americans
Date: First Monday in September

FolkAmerHol-1987, 271-73

Labor Day
Location: United States
Established: 1882
Date: First Monday in September

AmerBkDays-1978, 817
AnnivHol-1983, 114
BkFest-1937, 18
BkHolWrld-1986, September 7, 178
Chases-1993, 359
DaysCustFaith-1957, 248
DictDays-1988, 65
HolFestCelWrld-1994, 175

Labor Day, International
Date: May 1

AnnivHol-1983, 59
Chases-1993, 189

Labor Day Celebration
Location: Wellpinit, Washington
Ethnic or religious group: Spokan Indians
Date: Labor Day, first Monday in September

IndianAmer-1989, 214

Labor Day Festivities, Choctaw Nation of Oklahoma
Location: Tuskahoma, Oklahoma
Date: Labor Day weekend, first weekend and Monday in September

IndianAmer-1989, 69

Labor Day Powwow
Location: Oklahoma
Ethnic or religious group: Southern Arapaho Indians
Date: Labor Day weekend, first weekend and Monday in September

IndianAmer-1989, 68

Labor Day Powwow
Location: Ethete, Wyoming
Ethnic or religious group: Arapaho Indians
Date: Labor Day, first Monday in September

IndianAmer-1989, 110

Labor Thanksgiving Day
Location: Japan
Date: November 23

AnnivHol-1983, 150
Chases-1993, 451

Labour Day
Location: Australia: Queensland
Date: May 3

AnnivHol-1983, 60
DictDays-1988, 65

Labour Day
Location: Australia: Victoria
Date: March 8

AnnivHol-1983, 34
DictDays-1988, 65

Labour Day (Australian Capital Territory; New South Wales; and South Australia)
See **Eight Hour Day (South Australia)**

Labour Day
Location: Bahama Islands
Date: June 4

AnnivHol-1983, 75
Chases-1993, 232

Labour Day
Location: England, Northern Ireland, Scotland, and Wales
Date: First Monday in May

AnnivHol-1983, 60
DictDays-1988, 65
HolFestCelWrld-1994, 175
See also **May Day (England)**

Labour Day
Location: Jamaica
Date: May 23

AnnivHol-1983, 70

Labour Day
Location: New Zealand
Date: Last Monday in October

AnnivHol-1983, 135

Labour Day (Tasmania and Western Australia)
See **Eight Hour Day**

Labour Day
Location: Trinidad and Tobago
Date: June 19

AnnivHol-1983, 81

Labour Day
Location: Zambia
Date: May 3; observed first Monday in May

AnnivHol-1983, 60
Chases-1993, 194

Ladouvane
See **Singing to Rings (Bulgaria)**

Lady Day (Quarter Day)
Location: England and Ireland
Date: March 25, Feast of the Annunciation

AnnivHol-1983, 42
DictDays-1988, 93
FolkWrldHol-1992, 188
HolFestCelWrld-1994, 175
RelHolCal-1993, 57, 105
See also **Quarter Days (England and Ireland)**

Lady Day
See **Annunciation, Feast of the (England) and (Finnish Lapland villages) and (Lutherans in Sweden)**

Lady of Neves, Festival of the
Location: Portugal: Neves, Viana do Castelo
Established: Middle Ages
Date: August

IntlThFolk-1979, 310

Laetare Sunday
See **Mid-Lent Sunday (Roman Catholic)**

Lag b'Omer
  Ethnic or religious group: Jewish
  Established: Commemorates Bar Kokhba rebellion against
    Rome c. 135 A.D.
  Date: April-May, 18th of Jewish month of Iyar, the 33rd
    day in the fifty-day period between Passover and Shavuot,
    in addition to the fifty-day period itself

  AnnivHol-1983, 172
  BkFest-1937, 207
  Chases-1993, 202
  DaysCustFaith-1957, 137
  DictWrldRel-1989, 155
  FolkWrldHol-1992, 268
  RelHolCal-1993, 69

Lag b'Omer
  Location: Persia; now Iran
  Established: Commemorates Bar Kokhba rebellion against
    Rome c. 135 A.D.
  Date: April-May, 18th of Jewish month of Iyar, the 33rd
    day in the fifty-day period between Passover and Shavuot,
    in addition to the fifty-day period itself

  FolkWrldHol-1992, 268

Lai Haroba Festival
  Location: India: Mairang Village, Manipur
  Date: April-May

  IntlThFolk-1979, 212

Lai-Lai-Tu-Gadri (Day of Light)
  See **Night of Power (Sierra Leone)**

Lailat al Mi'raj
  See **Night Journey of Muhammad (Muslim)**

Lailat al-Qadr
  See **Nights of Power (Muslim), (Lebanon), and (West Africa)**

Lailat al-Qadr (Syria)
  See **Epiphany Eve (Syria)**

Lailat-al-Quade (Night of Destiny)
  See **Epiphany (Christians in Arab countries)**

Lajkonik
  Location: Poland
  Established: Middle Ages
  Date: May-June, first Thursday after Corpus Christi,

second Sunday after Pentecost

  FolkWrldHol-1992, 293
  HolFestCelWrld-1994, 175

Lake Festival (Seespiele)
  Location: Austria: Morbisch am See, Burgenland
  Established: 1957
  Date: August

  IntlThFolk-1979, 37

Lamayote
  See **Mardi Gras (Haiti)**

Lambri
  See **Easter (Greek Orthodox)**

Lamego, Festival of (Portugal: Lamego, Viseu)
  See **Pilgrimage to the Sanctuary of Our Lady of the
    Remedies (Pardon of Nossa Senhora dos Remédios)
    (Portugal: Lamego, Viseu)**

Lammas
  Ethnic or religious group: Greek Orthodox
  Date: August 1

  FestSaintDays-1915, 169

Lammas
  Location: Canada
  Date: August 1

  AnnivHol-1983, 101
  DaysCustFaith-1957, 199
  RelHolCal-1993, 89

Lammas
  Location: England
  Date: August 1

  BkDays-1864, ii.154
  DaysCustFaith-1957, 199
  DictDays-1988, 66
  DictFolkMyth-1984, 601
  FestSaintDays-1915, 163, 167
  FolkWrldHol-1992, 412
  SaintFestCh-1904, 349

Lammas
  Location: France: Paris
  Established: Formerly a feast for the Society of the Trade
    of Cobblers
  Date: August 1

  FestSaintDays-1915, 168

Lammas (Gules of August)
  Location: Great Britain
  Date: August 1

  AnnivHol-1983, 101
  BkDays-1864, ii. 154
  DaysCustFaith-1957, 199
  DictDays-1988, 51, 66
  DictFolkMyth-1984, 601, 961
  FestSaintDays-1915, 163
  FolkWrldHol-1992, 412
  HolFestCelWrld-1994, 176
  RelHolCal-1993, 64, 89
  SaintFestCh-1904, 349

Lammas
  Location: Isle of Man
  Date: August 1

  FestSaintDays-1915, 165

Lammas
  Location: Scotland
  Date: August 1

  DictFolkMyth-1984, 601
  FestSaintDays-1915, 163
  HolFestCelWrld-1994, 176
  See also **Quarter Days (Scotland)**

Lammas
  Location: United States
  Ethnic or religious group: Neo-pagans
  Date: August 1

  DictFolkMyth-1984, 961
  RelHolCal-1993, 64, 89

Lammas Fair Day
  Location: Ireland: Ballycastle
  Date: Last Tuesday in August

  AnnivHol-1983, 112

Landimere's or Lanimer Day
  Location: England: Lanark
  Date: The Thursday which falls between June 6-12

  DictDays-1988, 66

Landing Day
  See **Columbus Day**

Landing of d'Iberville
  Named for: The landing of Pierre Le Moyne, sieur
    d'Iberville (1661-1706) at Biloxi Bay in 1699

  Location: Ocean Springs, Mississippi
  Established: Reenactment since 1939
  Date: Last weekend in April

  HolFestCelWrld-1994, 176

Landsgemeinden
  Location: Switzerland: Appenzell
  Date: Last Sunday in April

  HolFestCelWrld-1994, 176

Landshut Wedding
  Named for: 1475 wedding of Prince George (d. 1503)
    to Princess Hedwig (1457-1502)
  Location: Federal Republic of Germany: Landshut, Bavaria
  Date: Three weeks, including four Sundays in June-July,
    every third year (1989, 1992 . . .)

  GdWrldFest-1985, 85
  HolFestCelWrld-1994, 177

Langfredag, Long Friday
  See **Good Friday (Denmark) and (Norway)**

Langfredagen, Long Friday
  See **Good Friday (Sweden)**

Lanimer Day
  See **Landimere's Day**

Lantern Festival (Yaun Shaw)
  Location: China
  Date: February-March, 13th-15th days of first lunar month

  BkFestHolWrld-1970, 9
  BkHolWrld-1986, February 27
  Chases-1993, 88
  DictFolkMyth-1984, 603
  FolkWrldHol-1992, 73
  GdWrldFest-1985, 63
  HolFestCelWrld-1994, 177
  RelHolCal-1993, 89
  See also **New Year (China)**

Lantern Festival (Yaun Shaw)
  Location: Hong Kong
  Date: February-March, 13th-15th days of first lunar month

  FolkWrldHol-1992, 74
  HolFestCelWrld-1994, 177

Lantern Festival
  Location: Malaysia: Penang
  Date: February-March, 13th-15th days of first lunar month

  HolFestCelWrld-1994, 177

Lantern Festival (Yaun Shaw)
  Named for: Also celebrates Siong Goan, birthday of
    Thian-koan Tai-te, the Emperor of the Heavens
  Location: Taiwan
  Date: February-March, 13th-15th days of first lunar month

  BkHolWrld-1986, February 27
  Chases-1993, 89
  FolkWrldHol-1992, 74, 76
  GdWrldFest-1985, 63
  HolFestCelWrld-1994, 177

Lantern-Floating Festival
  Location: Rural Japan
  Date: July-August, after harvest

  AnnivHol-1983, 178

Lara
  See **Harvest Season (Dodoth people in Uganda)**

Larentalia
  Named for: Lares, spirits of the household
  Location: Ancient Rome

  DictFolkMyth-1984, 604

Laskiaispäivä
  See **Mardi Gras (Finland)**

L'Assomption
  See **Assumption, Feast of the (France)**

Last Night
  Location: England: Royal Albert Hall, London
  Date: A Saturday in mid-September

  DictDays-1988, 66

La Toussaint
  See **All Saints' Day (France)**

Latter-Day Saints, Founding of Church of Jesus Christ of the
  See **Founding of the Church of Jesus Christ of the
    Latter-Day Saints**

Laulipidu
  See **Singing Festival (Estonia: Tallinn)**

Launceston Cup Day
  Location: Australia: northern Tasmania
  Date: February

  DictDays-1988, 75
  HolFestCelWrld-1994, 139

Lausanne, Festival of the City of
  Location: Switzerland: Lausanne, Vaud

  Date: June

  IntlThFolk-1979, 353

**Lausanne International Festival (Festival International
de Lausanne)**
  Location: Switzerland: Lausanne, Vaud
  Established: 1955
  Date: Thirty concerts from May to first week in July

  GdWrldFest-1985, 169
  IntlThFolk-1979, 353
  MusFestEurBrit-1980, 140
  MusFestWrld-1963, 203

Law Day
  Location: American Bar Association; United States
  Established: 1958
  Date: May 1

  AmerBkDays-1978, 411
  AnnivHol-1983, 59
  Chases-1993, 188
  DictDays-1988, 67

Lawn Tennis Championships
  See **Wimbledon**

Laylat al-Bara'ah
  See **Night of Forgiveness (Azerbaijan) and (Muslim)**

Laylat al-Mi'raj
  See **Night Journey of Muhammad (Muslim)**

Laylat al-Qadr
  See **Night of Power or Destiny (Muslim)**

Laylat il-Qader
  See **Night of Power (Egypt)**

Lazarus Saturday
  See **St. Lazarus's Day (Eastern Orthodox), (Russian
    Orthodox), and (Yugoslavia)**

Lazybones Day
  See **Luilak**

Leap Day
  See **Leap Year Day**

Leap Year Day
  Date: February 29; occurs every four years (1988, 1992 . . .)

  AmerBkDays-1978, 217
  AnnivHol-1983, 30
  BkHolWrld-1986, February 29
  DaysCustFaith-1957, 59

Leap Year Day *(cont.)*
  DictDays-1988, 8, 67
  FolkAmerHol-1987, 73
  FolkWrldHol-1992, 140
  HolFestCelWrld-1994, 179
  RelHolCal-1993, 90

Leap Year Privilege (Bachelors' Day)
  Location: England, Ireland, and Scotland
  Date: February 29; occurs every four years (1988, 1992 . . .)

  DaysCustFaith-1957, 59
  HolFestCelWrld-1994, 179

Lebaran
  See **Fast, Feast of Breaking the (Indonesia) and (South Africa: Cape Malay) and Ramadan (Indonesia)**

Lee, Birthday of Ann
  Named for: Ann Lee (1736-1784), founder of Shakerism in the U.S.
  Location: United States
  Ethnic or religious group: Shakers (United Society of Believers in Christ's Second Appearing, the Millennial Church)
  Date: February 29

  AmerBkDays-1978, 218
  AnnivHol-1983, 30
  DictWrldRel-1989, 674

Lee Day, Robert E.
  Named for: Robert E. Lee (1807-1870)
  Location: Southern United States
  Date: January 19; may be observed third Monday in January

  AnnivHol-1983, 10, 11
  Chases-1993, 68
  DictDays-1988, 73, 96
  HolFestCelWrld-1994, 274

Lee-Jackson Day
  Named for: Robert E. Lee (1807-1870) and Thomas Jonathan "Stonewall" Jackson (1824-1863)
  Location: North Carolina and Virginia
  Date: January 18; observed third Monday in January

  AnnivHol-1983, 10
  Chases-1993, 67
  HolFestCelWrld-1994, 274

Lee-Jackson-King Day
  See **King Jr.'s Birthday, Martin Luther; Lee Day, Robert E.; and Lee-Jackson Day**

Lei Day
  Location: Hawaii
  Established: 1928
  Date: May 1

  AmerBkDays-1978, 412
  AnnivHol-1983, 59
  Chases-1993, 188
  DictDays-1988, 67
  HolFestCelWrld-1994, 179

Leiden Day (Leiden Ontzet)
  Named for: October 3, 1574, lifting of the Siege of Leiden
  Location: Leiden, Netherlands, and Holland Society of New York
  Date: October 3

  AnnivHol-1983, 128
  BkFest-1937, 244
  BkHolWrld-1986, October 3
  Chases-1993, 398
  FestWestEur-1958, 139
  HolFestCelWrld-1994, 180

Leif Eriksson Day
  Named for: Leif Eriksson (fl. 1000)
  Location: Iceland
  Date: October 9

  AnnivHol-1983, 130
  Chases-1993, 404
  HolFestCelWrld-1994, 179

Leif Eriksson Day
  Named for: Leif Eriksson (fl. 1000)
  Location: Norway
  Date: October 9

  AnnivHol-1983, 130
  HolFestCelWrld-1994, 179

Leif Eriksson Day
  Named for: Leif Eriksson (fl. 1000)
  Location: United States
  Ethnic or religious group: Norwegian- and other Scandinavian-Americans
  Established: 1964
  Date: October 9

  AmerBkDays-1978, 909
  AnnivHol-1983, 130
  Chases-1993, 404
  FolkAmerHol-1987, 299
  HolFestCelWrld-1994, 179

Lejkonik
See **Horse Festival (Poland: Kraków)**

Lélé-Bereat
See **Night of Forgiveness (Turkey)**

Lélé-I-Kadir
See **Night of Power or Destiny (Turkey)**

Lélé-I-Mirach
See **Night Journey of Muhammad (Turkey)**

Le Mans Grand Prix
Location: France: Le Mans, Sarthe
Established: 1923
Date: June

HolFestCelWrld-1994, 179

Lemoore Celebration
Location: Near Porterville, California
Ethnic or religious group: Tuchi Yokuts Indians
Date: Late August

IndianAmer-1989, 349

Lemuralia or Lemuria, Festival of the Dead
Location: Ancient Rome
Date: May 9, 11, and 15

AmerBkDays-1978, 406
DictFolkMyth-1984, 123, 613
FestSaintDays-1915, 110
HolFestCelWrld-1994, 180

Lenin, Anniversary of the Death of
Named for: Vladimir Ilich Lenin (1870-1924)
Location: Russia: Moscow
Date: January 21

AnnivHol-1983, 12
BkFest-1937, 284

Lennoxville, Festival
Location: Canada: Lennoxville, Quebec
Established: 1972
Date: July-August

IntlThFolk-1979, 76

Lent
Ethnic or religious group: Christian
Established: By Gregory the Great (590-604) in late sixth century

Date: February-March, forty-day season preceding Easter

BkFest-1937, 68, 308
BkFestHolWrld-1970, 45
Chases-1993, 109
DaysCustFaith-1957, 65
DictFolkMyth-1984, 181, 212, 851
DictWrldRel-1989, 154, 175, 425
FestWestEur-1958, 211
FolkWrldHol-1992, 122
HolFestCelWrld-1994, 180, 201
IndianAmer-1989, 273
RelHolCal-1993, 90
SaintFestCh-1904, 115
See also **Mardi Gras and Twelfth Night**

Lent (Meat Fare Sunday)
Ethnic or religious group: Eastern Orthodox
Date: February-March, forty-day season preceding Easter; Meat Fare Sunday is eight days before Lent begins

HolFestCelWrld-1994, 201

Lent
Ethnic or religious group: Greek Orthodox
Date: February-March, forty-day season preceding Easter

BkFestHolWrld-1970, 46

Lent
Ethnic or religious group: Protestant
Date: February-March, forty-day season preceding Easter

DaysCustFaith-1957, 65
DictWrldRel-1989, 175

Lent
Ethnic or religious group: Roman Catholic
Date: February-March, forty-day season preceding Easter

BkFestHolWrld-1970, 45
DaysCustFaith-1957, 65
DictWrldRel-1989, 175

Lent
Location: Arizona
Ethnic or religious group: Yaqui Indians
Date: February-March, forty-day season preceding Easter; observances every Friday from Ash Wednesday through Holy Week

DictFolkMyth-1984, 212
IndianAmer-1989, 273
See also **Holy Week (Deer Dance) (Yaqui Indians in Arizona)**

Lent
   Location: Bulgaria
   Date: February-March, forty-day season preceding Easter

   BkFest-1937, 68

Lent
   Location: Denmark
   Date: February-March, forty-day season preceding Easter

   FolkWrldHol-1992, 122

Lent
   Location: Great Britain
   Date: February-March, forty-day season preceding Easter

   FolkWrldHol-1992, 122

Lent (Megali Sarakosti)
   Location: Greece
   Date: February-March, forty-day season preceding Easter

   FolkWrldHol-1992, 103, 122

Lent
   Location: Hungary
   Date: February-March, forty-day season preceding Easter

   DictFolkMyth-1984, 181

Lent
   Location: Iceland
   Date: February-March, forty-day season preceding Easter

   FolkWrldHol-1992, 122

Lent
   Location: Italy
   Date: February-March, forty-day season preceding Easter

   FolkWrldHol-1992, 123

Lent
   Location: Lebanon
   Date: February-March, forty-day season preceding Easter

   FolkWrldHol-1992, 123

Lent
   Location: Sonora, Mexico
   Ethnic or religious group: Yaqui and Mayo Indians
   Date: February-March, forty-day season preceding Easter

   DictFolkMyth-1984, 212

Lent
   Location: New Mexico pueblos
   Date: February-March, forty-day season preceding Easter

   DictFolkMyth-1984, 851

Lent
   Location: Palestine
   Date: February-March, forty-day season preceding Easter

   FolkWrldHol-1992, 124

Lent
   Location: Russia: St. Petersburg
   Date: February-March, forty-day season preceding Easter

   FolkWrldHol-1992, 124

Lent (Fastlagen)
   Location: Sweden
   Date: February-March, forty-day season preceding Easter

   BkFest-1937, 308
   FestWestEur-1958, 211

Lenten Season (Vassa)
   Ethnic or religious group: Buddhist
   Date: July-October, begins during Wazo, fourth Buddhist month, and ends on the 15th or full moon day of Thadingyut, seventh month

   AnnivHol-1983, 180, 182, 183
   BkHolWrld-1986, July 23, October 20, October 27, 180
   FolkWrldHol-1992, 348, 525
   HolFestCelWrld-1994, 336, 362

Lenten Season (Paung-daw-U Pagoda Festival)
   Location: Burma; formerly Myanmar
   Ethnic or religious group: Buddhist
   Date: July-October, begins during Wazo, fourth Buddhist month, and ends on the 15th or full moon day of Thadingyut, seventh month

   AnnivHol-1983, 180, 182
   BkHolWrld-1986, October 20, October 27, 180
   FolkWrldHol-1992, 348, 526
   HolFestCelWrld-1994, 336, 362

Lenten Season (Vossa)
   Location: Cambodia
   Ethnic or religious group: Buddhist
   Date: July-October, begins during Wazo, fourth Buddhist month, and ends on the 15th or full moon day of Thadingyut, seventh month

   FolkWrldHol-1992, 348
   HolFestCelWrld-1994, 362

Lenten Season (Vassa)
Location: China
Ethnic or religious group: Buddhist
Date: July-October, begins during Wazo, fourth Buddhist month, and ends on the 15th or full moon day of Thadingyut, seventh month

HolFestCelWrld-1994, 362

Lenten Season (Vassa)
Location: India
Ethnic or religious group: Buddhist
Date: July-October, begins during Wazo, fourth Buddhist month, and ends on the 15th or full moon day of Thadingyut, seventh month

HolFestCelWrld-1994, 362

Lenten Season (Vassa)
Location: Japan
Ethnic or religious group: Buddhist
Date: July-October, begins during Wazo, fourth Buddhist month, and ends on the 15th or full moon day of Thadingyut, seventh month

HolFestCelWrld-1994, 362

Lenten Season (Vassa)
Location: Korea
Ethnic or religious group: Buddhist
Date: July-October, begins during Wazo, fourth Buddhist month, and ends on the 15th or full moon day of Thadingyut, seventh month

HolFestCelWrld-1994, 362

Lenten Season (Ho Khao Slak)
Location: Laos
Ethnic or religious group: Buddhist
Date: July-October, begins during Wazo, fourth Buddhist month, and ends on the 15th or full moon day of Thadingyut, seventh month; beginning of lent is called Khao Vatsa; end of lent, Boun Ok Vatsa, Festival of the Waters

BkHolWrld-1986, September 22, 178
FolkWrldHol-1992, 525, 527
HolFestCelWrld-1994, 336, 362

Lenten Season (Vassa)
Location: Thailand
Ethnic or religious group: Buddhist
Date: July-October, begins during Wazo, fourth Buddhist

month, and ends on the 15th or full moon day of Thadingyut, seventh month; first day of lent is called Khao Waso; last day, Ok-Barnsa

BkHolWrld-1986, October 29
FolkWrldHol-1992, 349, 527
HolFestCelWrld-1994, 336, 362

Leonard's Ride (Leonhardiritt)
See **St. Leonard's Day (Germany: Bad Tölz, Bavaria)**

Lexington Day
See **Patriots' Day**

Leyden Day
See **Leiden Day (Leiden Ontzet) (Netherlands)**

Liberalia
Named for: Liber and Libera, deities of the vine
Location: Ancient Rome
Date: March 17

DictFolkMyth-1984, 618

Liberation Anniversary, October War of
Named for: Arab-Israeli War begun October 6, 1973
Location: Syria
Date: October 6

HolFestCelWrld-1994, 232

Liberation Day
Named for: March 3, 1878, liberation from Ottoman rule
Location: Bulgaria
Date: March 3

AnnivHol-1983, 33
Chases-1993, 117

Liberation Day
Named for: End of Spanish rule on January 1, 1899
Location: Cuba
Date: January 1

AnnivHol-1983, 1
Chases-1993, 49

Liberation Day
Named for: Liberation from German occupation on May 9, 1945
Location: Czechoslovakia
Date: May 9

AnnivHol-1983, 64
NatlHolWrld-1968, 58

Liberation Day
  Named for: Liberation from German occupation on
    May 5, 1945
  Location: Denmark
  Date: May 5

  AnnivHol-1983, 61

Liberation Day
  Named for: Liberation from German occupation of Paris
    on August 25, 1944
  Location: France
  Date: August 25

  AnnivHol-1983, 110

Liberation Day
  Location: German Democratic Republic
  Established: May 8, 1945
  Date: May 8

  NatlHolWrld-1968, 77

Liberation Day
  Named for: Liberation from German occupation
  Location: Great Britain: Jersey, Channel Islands
  Date: May 9

  AnnivHol-1983, 64
  DictDays-1988, 68

Liberation Day
  Named for: Liberation from Japanese occupation on
    July 21, 1944
  Location: Guam
  Date: July 21

  AnnivHol-1983, 95
  Chases-1993, 301

Liberation Day
  Named for: Liberation from German occupation on
    April 4, 1945
  Location: Hungary
  Date: April 4

  AnnivHol-1983, 47
  NatlHolWrld-1968, 44

Liberation Day
  Location: Italy
  Date: April 25

  AnnivHol-1983, 56

Liberation Day
  Named for: Liberation from Japanese occupation on
    August 15, 1945, and 1948 proclamation of the republic
  Location: Republic of Korea
  Date: August 15

  Chases-1993, 331
  HolFestCelWrld-1994, 181
  NatlHolWrld-1968, 144

Liberation Day
  Named for: Liberation from German occupation on
    May 5, 1945
  Location: Netherlands
  Date: May 5

  AnnivHol-1983, 61
  Chases-1993, 196
  HolFestCelWrld-1994, 91

Liberation Day
  Named for: July 22, 1944, end of war and 1952 constitution
  Location: Poland
  Date: July 22; January 17 in Warsaw

  AnnivHol-1983, 95
  HolFestCelWrld-1994, 256
  NatlHolWrld-1968, 121

Liberation Day
  Named for: August 23, 1948, liberation from
    monarchical rule
  Location: Romania
  Date: August 23

  Chases-1993, 340
  NatlHolWrld-1968, 148

Liberation Day
  Location: Seychelles
  Date: June 5

  AnnivHol-1983, 76
  Chases-1993, 237

Liberation Day
  Named for: January 13, 1980, constitution
  Location: Togo
  Date: January 13

  AnnivHol-1983, 8
  Chases-1993, 63

Liberation Day
  Named for: Liberation from rule of Idi Amin (b. 1925)
    on April 11, 1979
  Location: Uganda
  Date: April 11

  AnnivHol-1983, 50
  Chases-1993, 164

Liberation Forces Day, Popular
  Location: Mozambique
  Date: September 25

  AnnivHol-1983, 122

Liberty Day
  Named for: April 25, 1974, coup removing Antonio de
    Oliveira (1889-1970) and Marcello Caetano (1906-1980)
    from power
  Location: Portugal
  Date: April 25

  AnnivHol-1983, 56
  Chases-1993, 180

Liberty Day
  Named for: November 4, 1915, establishment of the first press
  Location: Virgin Islands
  Date: Observed first Monday in November

  AnnivHol-1983, 142
  Chases-1993, 429

Liberty Tree Day
  Named for: August 14, 1765, rebellion of Americans
    against British
  Location: Massachusetts
  Date: August 14

  AnnivHol-1983, 106
  Chases-1993, 328

Lîchtmesdâg
  See **Candlemas (Luxembourg)**

Lichtschmaus
  See **Waygoose Feast (printers in Germany)**

Li Chun
  See **Spring Festival (China)**

Lielā Lūdzamā Diena, Great Friday
  See **Good Friday (Latvia)**

Lieldienas Otrie Svētki
  See **Easter Monday (Latvia)**

Lieldienas Svetdiena
  See **Easter (Latvia)**

Life-Bearing Spring (Zoodochos Pege)
  Named for: Spring discovered by Leo, Emperor of
    Constantinople
  Location: Greece
  Date: March-April, the Friday following Easter

  BkFest-1937, 149

Lifeboat Day
  Location: England: Manchester
  Date: March

  DictDays-1988, 68

Lifeboat Saturday
  See **Lifeboat Day**

Lights, Feast of (Jewish)
  See **Hanukkah**

Lights, Festival of (Dewali)
  Named for: Honors the goddess Lakshmi and, in
    Bengal, India, the goddess Kali
  Ethnic or religious group: Hindu
  Date: October-November, one week during waning half
    of Hindu month of Karthika, including 15th day

  AnnivHol-1983, 176
  BkFest-1937, 161
  BkHolWrld-1986, November 1
  Chases-1993, 440
  DictMyth-1962, i.437, i.563
  FolkAmerHol-1987, 307
  FolkWrldHol-1992, 530
  GdWrldFest-1985, 110
  HolFestCelWrld-1994, 82, 340
  RelHolCal-1993, 71

Lights, Festival of (Dewali)
  Named for: Honors the goddess Lakshmi and, in
    Bengal, India, the goddess Kali
  Location: India
  Ethnic or religious group: Hindu
  Date: October-November, one week during waning half
    of Hindu month of Karthika, including 15th day

  AnnivHol-1983, 176
  BkFest-1937, 161
  Chases-1993, 440
  FolkWrldHol-1992, 530
  GdWrldFest-1985, 110
  HolFestCelWrld-1994, 82
  RelHolCal-1993, 71

Lights, Festival of (Dewali)
Named for: Honors the goddess or Lakshmi, and death
of Lord Mahavira (Vardhamana, c. 599-527 B.C.)
Location: India
Ethnic or religious group: Jaina
Date: October-November, one week during waning half
of Hindu month of Karthika, including 15th day

FolkWrldHol-1992, 531
HolFestCelWrld-1994, 82
RelHolCal-1993, 72

Lights, Festival of (Dewali)
Location: India
Ethnic or religious group: Sikh people
Date: October-November, one week during waning half
of Hindu month of Karthika, including 15th day

FolkWrldHol-1992, 532

Lights, Festival of (Dewali and Kali Festival)
Named for: Honors the goddess Kali
Location: India: Bengal
Ethnic or religious group: Hindu
Date: October-November, one week during waning half
of Hindu month of Karthika, including 15th day

BkFest-1937, 161
FolkWrldHol-1992, 530
GdWrldFest-1985, 110
HolFestCelWrld-1994, 82
RelHolCal-1993, 72

Lights, Festival of (Dewali)
Named for: Honors the goddess Lakshmi
Location: India: Gujarat
Ethnic or religious group: Hindu
Date: October-November, one week during waning half
of Hindu month of Karthika, including 15th day

FolkWrldHol-1992, 530, 531
HolFestCelWrld-1994, 82
RelHolCal-1993, 72

Lights, Festival of (Dewali)
Named for: Honors the goddess Lakshmi
Location: India: Maharashtra
Ethnic or religious group: Hindu
Date: October-November, one week during waning half
of Hindu month of Karthika, including 15th day

FolkWrldHol-1992, 530
HolFestCelWrld-1994, 82

Lights, Festival of (Dewali)
Named for: Honors the goddess Lakshmi, and death
of Lord Mahavira (Vardhamana, c. 599-527 B.C.)
Location: India: Pava, Bihar
Ethnic or religious group: Jaina
Date: October-November, one week during waning half
of Hindu month of Karthika, including 15th day

FolkWrldHol-1992, 531
HolFestCelWrld-1994, 82
RelHolCal-1993, 72

Lights, Festival of (Deepavali)
Location: Malaya
Ethnic or religious group: Hindu
Date: October-November, one week during waning half
of Hindu month of Karthika, including 15th day

FolkWrldHol-1992, 531, 532

Lights, Festival of (Dewali)
Named for: Honors the goddess Lakshmi
Location: Malaysia
Ethnic or religious group: Hindu
Date: October-November, one week during waning half
of Hindu month of Karthika, including 15th day

HolFestCelWrld-1994, 82

Lights, Festival of (Divali)
Named for: Commemorates Rama's victory over Ravana
Location: Mauritius
Ethnic or religious group: Hindu
Date: October-November, one week during waning half
of Hindu month of Karthika, including 15th day

FolkWrldHol-1992, 532
HolFestCelWrld-1994, 82

Lights, Festival of (Diwali or Tihar)
Named for: Honors the goddess Lakshmi
Location: Nepal
Ethnic or religious group: Hindu
Date: October-November, one week during waning half
of Hindu month of Karthika, including 15th day

FolkWrldHol-1992, 532
HolFestCelWrld-1994, 82, 340

Lights, Festival of (Dewali and Tika Festival)
Named for: Commemorates coronation of Rama after
victory over Ravana
Location: Punjab

Lights, Festival of (Dewali and Tika Festival) *(cont.)*
  Ethnic or religious group: Hindu
  Date: October-November, one week during waning half
    of Hindu month of Karthika, including 15th day

  FolkWrldHol-1992, 530, 531
  HolFestCelWrld-1994, 82

Lights, Festival of (Dewali)
  Named for: Commemorates coronation of Rama after
    victory over Ravana
  Location: United States
  Ethnic or religious group: Hindu
  Date: October-November, one week during waning half
    of Hindu month of Karthika, including 15th day

  FolkAmerHol-1987, 307

Lights, Festival of (Loy Krathong)
  Location: Thailand
  Ethnic or religious group: Buddhist; formerly Brahman
  Established: Centuries-old observance
  Date: Usually mid-November, full moon day of twelfth
    lunar month

  AnnivHol-1983, 178
  BkHolWrld-1986, November 17, 179
  FolkWrldHol-1992, 568
  GdWrldFest-1985, 173
  HolFestCelWrld-1994, 183
  RelHolCal-1993, 90

Lights, Festival of (Sang-joe)
  Named for: Commemorates death of Lamaist reformer
    Je-Tsong-Kha-Pa (1357-1419)
  Location: Tibet: Lhasa
  Date: October-November, 25th day of tenth Tibetan month

  FolkWrldHol-1992, 529
  HolFestCelWrld-1994, 181

Lights, Winter Festival of
  Location: Wheeling, West Virginia
  Established: 1985
  Date: Early November through late January

  HolFestCelWrld-1994, 369

Ligo Festival
  See **Midsummer Day (Latvia)**

Lilies and Roses Day
  Named for: Commemorates death of Henry VI (1421-1471)
  Location: England: Tower of London, London

  Date: May 21

  AnnivHol-1983, 69

Lily Festival (Italy: Nola, Campania)
  See **St. Paulinus of Nola, Feast of (Italy: Nola, Campania)**

Lily Festival
  Location: Japan: Nara
  Ethnic or religious group: Shinto religion
  Date: June 17

  BkHolWrld-1986, June 17

Lime-Tree Day
  Location: Romania: Buciumeni, Galati
  Date: Last Sunday in June

  IntlThFolk-1979, 320

L'Immacolata
  See **Immaculate Conception, Feast of the (Italy)**

Lincoln Center Out-of-Doors Festival
  Location: New York, New York
  Established: 1971
  Date: Three weeks from mid-August into September

  GdUSFest-1984, 127

Lincoln's Birthday, Abraham
  Named for: Abraham Lincoln (1809-1865)
  Location: United States
  Established: 1887
  Date: February 12; observed first Monday in February

  AmerBkDays-1978, 168, 1073
  AnnivHol-1983, 23
  BkFest-1937, 15
  BkHolWrld-1986, February 12
  Chases-1993, 95
  DictDays-1988, 68
  HolFestCelWrld-1994, 182

Linden Tree Festival (Lindenfest)
  Location: Germany: Geisenheim, Rhineland
  Date: Second weekend in July

  FestWestEur-1958, 68
  HolFestCelWrld-1994, 182

Linus, Festival of
  Location: Greece: Argos

  DictFolkMyth-1984, 625

Literacy Day, International
   Established: Sponsored by the United Nations and UNESCO
   Date: September 8

   AnnivHol-1983, 116
   BkHolWrld-1986, September 8
   Chases-1993, 361
   HolFestCelWrld-1994, 182

Literature, Hay-on-Wye Festival of
   Location: Wales: Hay-on-Wye
   Established: 1988
   Date: Ten days in late May

   HolFestCelWrld-1994, 136

Literature Festival, Ilkley
   Location: England: Ilkley, West Yorkshire
   Date: Odd-numbered years in June

   IntlThFolk-1979, 161

Little Angels (Los Angelitos)
   Location: Mexico: Cancún
   Ethnic or religious group: Mayan people
   Date: October 30

   BkHolWrld-1986, October 30
   HolFestCelWrld-1994, 10
   See also **All Souls' Day (Mexico)**

Little Easter Sunday
   See **Low Sunday**

Little League World Series
   Location: Williamsport, Pennsylvania
   Date: Late August

   HolFestCelWrld-1994, 182

Little Saints Day
   See **Holy Innocents' Day**

Little Shell Celebration
   Location: New Town, North Dakota
   Date: Second weekend in August

   IndianAmer-1989, 52

Livestock, Horse Show, and Rodeo, American Royal
   Location: Kansas City, Missouri
   Established: 1899
   Date: Two weeks in November

   HolFestCelWrld-1994, 9

Livestock Show & Rodeo, Southwestern Exposition &
   Location: Fort Worth, Texas

   Established: 1896; rodeo since 1918
   Date: Last two weeks in January

   HolFestCelWrld-1994, 321

Living Chess Game (La Partita a Scácchi Viventi)
   Location: Italy: Marchóstica
   Established: Based on 1454 duel
   Date: Second weekend in September during even-
      numbered years

   HolFestCelWrld-1994, 183

Llama Ch'uyay
   Location: Bolivia: Sonqo
   Date: July 31-August 1

   FolkWrldHol-1992, 409
   HolFestCelWrld-1994, 183

Llamas, Fiesta of the
   See **St. James's Day (Quechua Indians in South America)**

Llangollen International Musical Eisteddfod
   See **Eisteddfod, International Musical**

Lobster Festival
   Location: Canada: Shediac, New Brunswick
   Established: 1952
   Date: Six days in July

   GdWrldFest-1985, 39

Locomotive Chase Festival, Great
   Named for: Confederate thwarting of attempted Union
      burglary of a Confederate locomotive on April 12, 1862
   Location: Adairsville, Georgia
   Date: First weekend in October

   HolFestCelWrld-1994, 125

Logging Days, Buena Vista
   Location: Bemidji, Minnesota
   Date: Last Saturday in February

   HolFestCelWrld-1994, 43

Lohri
   See **Harvest Festival (India: Punjab)**

London, Festival of the City of
   Location: England: London
   Established: 1963
   Date: Even-numbered years in July

   GdWrldFest-1985, 94
   IntlThFolk-1979, 163

London Bridge Days
  Location: Lake Havasu City, Arizona
  Established: 1971
  Date: First two weekends in October

  Chases-1993, 399
  GdUSFest-1984, 11
  HolFestCelWrld-1994, 184

Long Barnaby
  See **St. Barnabas's Day**

Long Day, Huey P.
  Named for: Huey P. Long (1893-1935)
  Location: Louisiana
  Established: 1937
  Date: August 30

  AmerBkDays-1978, 790
  AnnivHol-1983, 112
  Chases-1993, 347
  DictDays-1988, 58
  HolFestCelWrld-1994, 147

Longest Day
  See **Midsummer Day; Summer Solstice**

Long Friday
  See **Good Friday**

Long Rope Day
  See **Good Friday**

Loppiainen
  See **Epiphany (Finland)**

Lord Mayor's Show
  Location: England: procession through London to
    Westminster
  Date: November 9; observed second Saturday in November

  AnnivHol-1983, 144
  BkDays-1864, ii. 561
  BkHolWrld-1986, November 12, 179
  Chases-1993, 440
  DictDays-1988, 69
  HolFestCelWrld-1994, 184

Lord of Misrule
  Location: Medieval western Europe
  Date: Christmas through Epiphany (December 25-
    January 6) or Allhallows through Candlemas (October 31
    or November 1-February 2)

  DictFolkMyth-1984, 645

Lorient Festival
  Location: France: Lorient, Morbihan
  Ethnic or religious group: Gaelic
  Established: 1971
  Date: Ten days at beginning of August

  IntlThFolk-1979, 109

Los Angelitos
  See **All Souls' Day (Mexico); Little Angels (Mayan
    people in Cancún, Mexico)**

Losar
  See **New Year (Bhutan) and (Buddhist people in Tibet)**

Lost Day
  See **Epiphany**

Lost Sunday
  Ethnic or religious group: Christian
  Date: Third Sunday before Lent

  DictDays-1988, 70
  See also **Septuagesima Sunday**

Lots, Feast of
  See **Purim**

Lotu-A-Tamaiti
  See **White Sunday (Samoa)**

Lotus, Birthday of
  Location: China: Peking
  Ethnic or religious group: Buddhist
  Date: 24th day of sixth lunar month

  FolkWrldHol-1992, 353
  HolFestCelWrld-1994, 185

Lou Bunch Day
  Location: Central City, Colorado
  Date: Third Saturday in June

  Chases-1993, 255
  DictDays-1988, 70
  HolFestCelWrld-1994, 185

Low Easterday
  See **Low Sunday**

**Low Sunday (also known as Close Sunday, Low Easterday,
and Quasimodo Sunday)**
  Ethnic or religious group: Christian
  Date: March-April, Sunday following Easter

  DictDays-1988, 21, 70, 93
  FestSaintDays-1915, 92
  HolFestCelWrld-1994, 186
  RelHolCal-1993, 106

Low Sunday
   Location: Brazil
   Date: March-April, Sunday following Easter

   FestSaintDays-1915, 93

Low Sunday
   Location: Germany: Moravia
   Date: March-April, Sunday following Easter

   FestSaintDays-1915, 92

Loyalty Day
   Location: Cooch's Bridge, Delaware
   Date: May 1

   AmerBkDays-1978, 411
   AnnivHol-1983, 60
   HolFestCelWrld-1994, 186

Loyalty Day
   Location: U.S. Veterans of Foreign Wars; New York, New York
   Date: May 1 parade

   AmerBkDays-1978, 411
   HolFestCelWrld-1994, 186

Loyalty Day
   Location: United States
   Date: May 1

   AmerBkDays-1978, 411
   AnnivHol-1983, 60
   Chases-1993, 189
   HolFestCelWrld-1994, 186

Loy Krathong
   See **Lights, Festival of (Buddhist people in Thailand)**

Luciadagen
   See **St. Lucy's Day (Sweden)**

Ludi
   Location: Ancient Rome
   Established: Oldest games were the Ludi Romani, from 366 B.C.
   Date: Varied

   AmerBkDays-1978, 313, 794
   HolFestCelWrld-1994, 186

Lúgnasad (First Fruits Festival)
   Location: Hilltops in Ireland
   Ethnic or religious group: Celtic people

Established: Ancient festival; observed as late as the 19th century
   Date: August 1

   FolkWrldHol-1992, 413

Lúgnasad (First Fruits Festival)
   Location: Ireland: Teltown on River Boyne in Meath
   Ethnic or religious group: Celtic people
   Date: August 1

   DictFolkMyth-1984, 202, 652
   FestSaintDays-1915, 165
   FolkWrldHol-1992, 413

Lúgnasad (First Fruits Festival)
   Location: United States
   Ethnic or religious group: Gardnerian Witches and other Neo-pagans
   Date: August 1

   RelHolCal-1993, 91

Luilak (Lazybones Day or Sluggard's Feast)
   Location: Netherlands: Zaandam, Haarlem, Amsterdam, and other western towns
   Named for: Piet Lak (fl. 1672)
   Date: Saturday preceding Pentecost or Whit Sunday

   BkFest-1937, 243
   BkFestHolWrld-1970, 66
   FestWestEur-1958, 134
   FolkWrldHol-1992, 284
   HolFestCelWrld-1994, 187

Luisenburg Festival
   Location: Federal Republic of Germany: Wunsiedel, Bavaria
   Established: End of 19th century
   Date: June-August

   IntlThFolk-1979, 152

Lukesmas
   See **St. Luke's Day (Scotland)**

Lukshmi or Laksmi Puja
   See **Goddess of Fortune, Festival of the (Hindu) and (Hindu people in Bengal, India)**

Lumberjack Days, Clearwater County Fair and
   Location: Orofino, Idaho
   Established: Early 1940s
   Date: Third weekend in September

   HolFestCelWrld-1994, 66

Lumberjack World Championships
  Location: Hayward, Wisconsin
  Established: 1960
  Date: Three days in July

  GdUSFest-1984, 211
  HolFestCelWrld-1994, 187

Lundi de Pâques
  See **Easter Monday (France)**

Lunes del Cerro
  See **Monday on the Hill (Zapotec Indians in Oaxaca, Mexico)**

Lunia Paştilor
  See **Easter Monday (Romania)**

Lu Pan, Birthday of
  Named for: Lu Pan (b. 606 B.C.), carpenter
  Location: Hong Kong
  Date: July 18

  BkHolWrld-1986, July 18
  Chases-1993, 311
  HolFestCelWrld-1994, 189

Lupercalia
  Location: Ancient Rome
  Date: Mid-February

  AmerBkDays-1978, 132, 178
  BkHolWrld-1986, February 14
  Chases-1993, 100
  DaysCustFaith-1957, 54
  DictDays-1988, 70
  FestSaintDays-1915, 34
  HolFestCelWrld-1994, 189, 353

Luther, Birthday of
  See **Martinsfest (Protestants in Germany)**

Luther's Theses Day
  See **Reformation Day**

Lyon International Festival (Festival International de Lyon)
  Location: France: Lyon, Rhone
  Established: 1946
  Date: June-July

  GdWrldFest-1985, 80
  IntlThFolk-1979, 112
  MusFestEurBrit-1980, 79

Macao Grand Prix
  Location: Macao
  Established: 1953
  Date: Ten days in mid-November

  GdWrldFest-1985, 130

MacArthur Day, Douglas
  Named for: Douglas MacArthur (1880-1964)
  Location: Arkansas
  Date: January 26

  AnnivHol-1983, 14
  Chases-1993, 74

Madaraka Day (Responsibility Day; Self-Government Day)
  Location: Kenya
  Date: June 1

  AnnivHol-1983, 74
  Chases-1993, 229

Madeleine, Fête de la
  See **St. Mary Magdalene, Feast of (France: St. Baume, Provence)**

La Madonna del Carmine
  See **Our Lady of Carmel (Chamorros people in Guam/ Northern Marianas) and (Italy and Italian-Americans in the United States)**

Madonna del Voto Day
  Location: Italy: Siena
  Date: August 16

  AnnivHol-1983, 108
  See also **Palio, Festival of the**

Mad Sunday
  Location: Isle of Man
  Date: May, Sunday preceding the Tourist Trophy Motorcycle Races

  DictDays-1988, 72

Mad Thursday
  See **Mardi Gras (England)**

Magdalene Festival
  See **St. Mary Magdalene, Feast of (France: St. Baume, Provence)**

Magellan or Discovery Day
  Named for: Ferdinand Magellan (c. 1480-1521) and his March 6, 1521, landfall
  Location: Guam
  Date: March 6

  AnnivHol-1983, 31
  Chases-1993, 121
  HolFestCelWrld-1994, 191

Maggio Musicale Fiorentino
See **Musical May, Florence (Italy: Florence, Tuscany)**

Magha Bihu
See **Harvest Festival (India: Assam)**

Magha Puja
See **Four Miracles Assembly (Buddhist) and (Thailand)**

Magha Purnima
  Location: India
  Ethnic or religious group: Hindu
  Date: January-February, full moon day of Hindu month
    of Magha

  RelHolCal-1993, 91

Magh Mela Fair
See **Kumbh Mela Festival**

Magh Sankranti
See **Harvest Festival (Makara Sankranti) (Nepal)**

Magna Charta Day
  Named for: June 15, 1215, signing of the document
  Location: England
  Date: June 15

  AnnivHol-1983, 80
  Chases-1993, 249
  DaysCustFaith-1957, 148
  HolFestCelWrld-1994, 192
  RelHolCal-1993, 92

Magna Mater
  Location: Ancient Rome
  Date: April 4

  AmerBkDays-1978, 313
  DictFolkMyth-1984, 809

Mahanuwara Esala Dalada Perahera
See **Esala Perahera (Buddhist and Hindu people in Kandy, Sri Lanka)**

Maha Shivaratree
See **Shiva, Night of (Mauritius)**

Mahashivaratri
See **Shiva, Night of (Hindu), (India), and (Nepal)**

Mahavira's Birthday (Mahavira Jayanti)
  Named for: Mahavira, Lord Vardhamana (c. 599-527 B.C.), a founder of Jaina

  Location: India
  Ethnic or religious group: Jaina religion
  Date: March-April, 13th day of waxing half of Hindu
    month of Chaitra

  AnnivHol-1983, 179
  Chases-1993, 156
  DictWrldRel-1989, 451
  FolkWrldHol-1992, 215
  HolFestCelWrld-1994, 192
  RelHolCal-1993, 92
  See also **Pajjusana**

Mahdia, Festival of
  Location: Tunisia: Mahdia, Mahdia Region
  Date: July-August

  IntlThFolk-1979, 363

Mahrajan
See **Soul, Festival of the (Syria and Lebanese-Americans in Bridgeport, Connecticut)**

Maia-Hemelvaart Dat
See **Assumption, Feast of the (Belgium)**

Maidens' Fair on Mount Gaina (Tirgul de fete de pe muntele Gaina)
  Location: Romania: Mount Gaina, Transylvania
  Date: Third Sunday in July

  HolFestCelWrld-1994, 341

Maifest
See **Mayfest (German-Americans in Hermann, Missouri)**

Maimona or Maimonides
  Named for: Moses Ben Maimon (1135-1204)
  Ethnic or religious group: Jewish
  Date: Evening of last day of Passover and day after Passover

  DictWrldRel-1989, 494
  FolkWrldHol-1992, 238
  HolFestCelWrld-1994, 192

Maimona or Maimonides
  Named for: Moses Ben Maimon (1135-1204)
  Location: Libya
  Ethnic or religious group: Jewish
  Date: Evening of last day of Passover and day after Passover

  FolkWrldHol-1992, 238
  HolFestCelWrld-1994, 192

Maimona or Maimonides
  Named for: Moses Ben Maimon (1135-1204)
  Location: Morocco
  Ethnic or religious group: Jewish
  Date: Evening of last day of Passover and day after Passover

  FolkWrldHol-1992, 238
  HolFestCelWrld-1994, 192

Mai Musical International
  See **Musical, Bordeaux International May (France: Bordeaux, Gironde)**

Maine Lobster or Seafoods Festival
  Location: Rockland, Maine
  Established: 1949
  Date: Three days in late July-early August

  Chases-1993, 309
  GdUSFest-1984, 78
  HolFestCelWrld-1994, 193

Maine Memorial Day (Battleship Day; Remember the Maine Day; Spanish-American War Memorial Day)
  Named for: February 15, 1898, explosion aboard the American battleship, the *Maine,* which sparked off the Spanish-American War
  Location: Connecticut, Maine, and Massachusetts
  Date: February 15

  AmerBkDays-1978, 187
  AnnivHol-1983, 25
  Chases-1993, 100
  DictDays-1988, 10

Maiorga, International Festival of
  Location: Portugal: Figueira da Foz, Coimbra
  Established: 1974
  Date: September

  IntlThFolk-1979, 306

Maitag Vorabend
  See **May Day Eve (Switzerland)**

Majuba Day (Hill of Doves)
  Location: South Africa
  Ethnic or religious group: Boer people
  Date: February 27

  DictDays-1988, 72

Maka Buja
  See **Four Miracles Assembly (Buddhist)**

Makara Sankranti
  See **Harvest Festival (northern India) and (Nepal)**

Makha Bouxa
  See **Four Miracles Assembly (Laos)**

Making Happiness Festival (Tso-Fu)
  Location: Taiwan
  Date: Ninth day of first lunar month

  FolkWrldHol-1992, 67
  HolFestCelWrld-1994, 193

Malcolm X Day
  Named for: Malcolm X (Malcolm Little, 1925-1965)
  Location: Washington, D.C.
  Date: Third Sunday in May

  HolFestCelWrld-1994, 193

Malki Museum Fiesta
  Location: California
  Ethnic or religious group: Cahuilla Indians
  Date: Memorial Day weekend, last weekend in May

  IndianAmer-1989, 331

Mallard Ceremony
  Location: England: All Souls College, Oxford University
  Established: Commemorates founding of the college in 1437
  Date: Every hundred years

  HolFestCelWrld-1994, 193

Malvern Festival
  Location: England: Malvern, Worcestershire
  Established: 1929
  Date: May-June

  IntlThFolk-1979, 168

Ma'makoni-ni'tkap
  See **Dance, Ute Bear (Ute Indians in Ouray, Randlett, Whiterocks, Utah)**

Mambembao
  Location: Brazil: Brasilia, Rio de Janeiro, and Sao Paulo
  Established: 1978
  Date: January-March

  IntlThFolk-1979, 51

Mandaree Celebration
  Location: Mandaree, North Dakota
  Ethnic or religious group: Arikara, Hidatsa, and Mandan Indians
  Date: Third weekend in July

  IndianAmer-1989, 52

Mandela Ceremony
  See **Harvest (Buddhist people in Ladakh, India)**

Mandi Safar
  Location: Malaysia: Malacca
  Ethnic or religious group: Muslim
  Established: Commemorated the last time Muhammad (c. 570- 632) was thought to bathe in the sea before his death; currently a secular event
  Date: During Islamic month of Safar

  BkHolWrld-1986, August 7
  HolFestCelWrld-1994, 194

Mankind, Birthday of
  Location: China
  Date: Seventh day of first lunar month

  BkFest-1937, 78

Manomin
  See **Rice Celebration, Wild (Bad River Ojibwa Indians in Odanah, Wisconsin)**

Marais Festival
  Location: France: Paris
  Established: 1962
  Date: June-July

  IntlThFolk-1979, 116

Marathon, International Open
  Location: Greece: Marathon to Athens
  Date: Mid-October

  HolFestCelWrld-1994, 239

Marble and Sound
  Location: Yugoslavia: Arandjelovac, Serbia
  Date: July-September

  IntlThFolk-1979, 379

Mardi Gras
  Date: February-March, celebration of varying length before Lent begins on Ash Wednesday

  AmerBkDays-1978, 43, 156
  AnnivHol-1983, 179
  BkDays-1864, i.65, 236
  BkFest-1937, 4, 29, 38, 54, 67, 95, 102, 111, 120, 132, 146, 166, 179, 219, 241, 249, 259, 267, 289, 298, 316, 328
  BkFestHolWrld-1970, 32
  BkHolWrld-1986, February 9, February 12, February 20, February 21, February 24, February 25, March 4, April 9, 176, 177, 181

  Chases-1993, 95, 104, 105, 106, 108
  DaysCustFaith-1957, 63
  DictDays-1988, 9, 15, 22, 33, 38, 39, 42, 45, 72, 73, 82, 87, 110
  DictFolkMyth-1984, 105, 178, 181, 192, 193, 197, 220, 370, 397, 543, 568, 629, 747, 749, 757, 759, 787, 807, 842, 844, 947, 977, 980, 1082
  DictMyth-1962, i.549
  FestWestEur-1958, 6, 23, 34, 55, 56, 89, 124, 151, 163, 191, 211, 230
  FolkAmerHol-1987, 77
  FolkWrldHol-1992, 103, 104, 106
  GdUSFest-1984, 5, 68, 133
  GdWrldFest-1985, 4, 24, 64, 96, 133, 147, 175
  HolFestCelWrld-1994, 28, 52, 53, 54, 56, 67, 104, 105, 112, 165, 172, 194, 227, 244, 268, 276, 309, 317, 344, 358
  IntlThFolk-1979, 44, 82, 278
  RelHolCal-1993, 65, 76, 93

Mardi Gras
  Location: Mobile, Alabama
  Established: 1702
  Date: February-March, the two weeks before Ash Wednesday

  AmerBkDays-1978, 158
  Chases-1993, 108
  GdUSFest-1984, 5
  HolFestCelWrld-1994, 195

Mardi Gras (Të Lidhurat, Carnival Sunday)
  Location: Albania
  Date: February-March, Sunday before Ash Wednesday

  BkFest-1937, 4

Mardi Gras (Tincunaco Ceremony)
  Location: Argentina: Calchaqui Valley
  Date: February, Thursday before Ash Wednesday

  BkHolWrld-1986, February 21, 181

Mardi Gras (Pareegentahn)
  Location: Armenia
  Date: February-March

  FolkWrldHol-1992, 106

Mardi Gras (Carnival)
  Location: Aruba: Oranjestad
  Established: 1944
  Date: February-March, Sunday-Tuesday before Ash Wednesday

  FolkWrldHol-1992, 106
  GdWrldFest-1985, 4

Mardi Gras (Fasching, Carnival)
Location: Austria
Date: February-March, the week before Ash Wednesday

AmerBkDays-1978, 43
AnnivHol-1983, 176
BkFest-1937, 29
Chases-1993, 107
DictFolkMyth-1984, 370
DictMyth-1962, i.549
HolFestCelWrld-1994, 104, 309
RelHolCal-1993, 76

Mardi Gras (Schemenlauf, Running of the Spectres)
Location: Austria: Imst, Tirol
Established: Medieval times
Date: January-March, week before Ash Wednesday

HolFestCelWrld-1994, 309

Mardi Gras (Fasching)
Location: Bavaria
Date: February-March

DictMyth-1962, i.549
HolFestCelWrld-1994, 104
RelHolCal-1993, 76

Mardi Gras (Vastenavond)
Location: Belgium
Date: February-March

AmerBkDays-1978, 43
BkFest-1937, 38
BkFestHolWrld-1970, 34
FestWestEur-1958, 6
FolkWrldHol-1992, 106
HolFestCelWrld-1994, 53
IntlThFolk-1979, 44

Mardi Gras (Carnival of the Gilles, or Clowns)
Location: Belgium: Binche
Established: 1549
Date: February-March, Sunday-Tuesday before Ash
Wednesday

AmerBkDays-1978, 43
BkFest-1937, 38
BkFestHolWrld-1970, 34
FestWestEur-1958, 6
FolkWrldHol-1992, 106
HolFestCelWrld-1994, 53
IntlThFolk-1979, 44

Mardi Gras (Bal du Rat Mort, Dead Rat's Ball)
Location: Belgium: Ostend
Established: End of the 19th century
Date: January-March, usually the weekend before Lent

HolFestCelWrld-1994, 23

Mardi Gras (Carnival)
Location: Bohemia
Date: February-March

DictFolkMyth-1984, 370, 807

Mardi Gras (Carnival Week)
Location: Bolivia: Oruro
Date: February-March, week before Lent begins

FolkWrldHol-1992, 106
HolFestCelWrld-1994, 54

Mardi Gras (Carnival)
Location: Brazil
Date: February-March

AmerBkDays-1978, 43, 157
BkFestHolWrld-1970, 40
BkHolWrld-1986, February 25
Chases-1993, 104
DictFolkMyth-1984, 193
FolkWrldHol-1992, 108
GdWrldFest-1985, 24
HolFestCelWrld-1994, 52
RelHolCal-1993, 65

Mardi Gras (Carnival)
Location: Brazil: Rio de Janeiro
Established: Centuries old
Date: February-March, the four days before Ash
Wednesday

AmerBkDays-1978, 43, 157
BkFestHolWrld-1970, 40
Chases-1993, 104
DictFolkMyth-1984, 193
GdWrldFest-1985, 24
HolFestCelWrld-1994, 52
RelHolCal-1993, 65

Mardi Gras (Sirna Sedmitza, Cheese Week)
Location: Bulgaria
Date: February-March, the week before Ash
Wednesday

BkFest-1937, 67
FolkWrldHol-1992, 103

Mardi Gras (Carnaval)
  Location: Canada: Quebec City, Quebec
  Established: 1954
  Date: February-March

  FolkWrldHol-1992, 109

Mardi Gras (Carnival)
  Location: Colombia: Barranquilla, Atlántico
  Date: February-March, Friday-Tuesday before Ash
  Wednesday

  GdWrldFest-1985, 64

Mardi Gras (Carnival)
  Location: Cyprus: Limassol
  Established: Early 20th century
  Date: February-March, twelve days ending Ash
  Wednesday

  IntlThFolk-1979, 82

Mardi Gras (Fastelavn or Fastelavan)
  Location: Denmark
  Date: February-March, Monday before Ash Wednesday

  AnnivHol-1983, 177
  BkFest-1937, 95
  BkHolWrld-1986, February 24, 177
  FestWestEur-1958, 23
  HolFestCelWrld-1994, 104

**Mardi Gras (Collop Monday and Shrove or Pancake Tuesday;
Shrove Tuesday known as Nickanan Night in Cornwall)**
  Location: England
  Date: February-March, Monday and Tuesday before Ash
  Wednesday

  AmerBkDays-1978, 157
  AnnivHol-1983, 175, 180
  BkDays-1864, i.236
  BkFest-1937, 54
  BkHolWrld-1986, February 25
  DaysCustFaith-1957, 64
  DictDays-1988, 22, 33, 39, 42, 45, 72, 82, 87, 110
  DictFolkMyth-1984, 181, 842
  FestSaintDays-1915, 45
  FolkWrldHol-1992, 104
  GdWrldFest-1985, 96
  HolFestCelWrld-1994, 67, 105, 112, 244, 317

Mardi Gras (Pancake Day)
  Location: Olney, England, and Liberal, Kansas
  Established: Since 1445 in Olney; since 1950 in Kansas

  Date: February-March, Tuesday before Ash Wednesday

  AmerBkDays-1978, 158
  AnnivHol-1983, 180
  BkHolWrld-1986, February 25
  Chases-1993, 108
  DictDays-1988, 87
  DictFolkMyth-1984, 842
  GdWrldFest-1985, 96
  HolFestCelWrld-1994, 244

Mardi Gras (Vastla Päev)
  Location: Estonia
  Date: February-March, Tuesday before Ash Wednesday

  BkFest-1937, 102

Mardi Gras (Laskiaispäivä)
  Location: Finland
  Date: February-March, Tuesday before Ash Wednesday

  BkFest-1937, 111

Mardi Gras
  Location: Florida
  Date: February-March

  AmerBkDays-1978, 158
  Chases-1993, 108

Mardi Gras
  Location: France
  Date: February-March, Tuesday before Ash Wednesday

  AmerBkDays-1978, 43
  BkFest-1937, 120
  BkFestHolWrld-1970, 33
  BkHolWrld-1986, February 25
  DictFolkMyth-1984, 181
  FestWestEur-1958, 34
  FolkWrldHol-1992, 110

Mardi Gras (Carnival and Battle of the Flowers)
  Location: France: Nice
  Date: February-March, twelve days ending Ash Wednesday

  AmerBkDays-1978, 43
  BkFest-1937, 120
  BkFestHolWrld-1970, 33
  BkHolWrld-1986, February 20
  Chases-1993, 95
  DictFolkMyth-1984, 192
  FestWestEur-1958, 34
  HolFestCelWrld-1994, 28, 227

Mardi Gras (Carnival)
Location: France: Paris
Date: February-March

BkDays-1864, i.65
BkFest-1937, 120
FestWestEur-1958, 34

Mardi Gras (Carnival)
Location: France: Saint-Lô, Burgendy
Date: February-March

DictFolkMyth-1984, 757

Mardi Gras (Fastnacht and Rosemontag, Rose Monday)
Location: Germany
Date: February-March, Monday and Tuesday before
Ash Wednesday

AmerBkDays-1978, 43, 157
AnnivHol-1983, 176, 181
BkFest-1937, 132
BkHolWrld-1986, February 25
Chases-1993, 58, 107
DictDays-1988, 38
DictFolkMyth-1984, 192, 370, 977, 1082
DictMyth-1962, i.549
FestWestEur-1958, 55, 56
FolkWrldHol-1992, 110
HolFestCelWrld-1994, 104, 165, 172, 276
RelHolCal-1993, 65, 76, 110

Mardi Gras (Karneval)
Location: Germany: Cologne
Date: December 31 until Ash Wednesday

AmerBkDays-1978, 43
HolFestCelWrld-1994, 165

Mardi Gras (Kopenfahrt, Kope Procession or Festival)
Location: Germany: Lüneburg, Lower Saxony
Established: 15th century
Date: February-March, Tuesday before Ash Wednesday

FestWestEur-1958, 56
HolFestCelWrld-1994, 172

Mardi Gras (Fasching Carnival)
Location: Germany: Munich
Date: January 7-Tuesday before Ash Wednesday

AmerBkDays-1978, 43
BkFest-1937, 132
Chases-1993, 58

DictDays-1988, 38
DictFolkMyth-1984, 977
FestWestEur-1958, 55
HolFestCelWrld-1994, 276

Mardi Gras (Apokreos, Carnival)
Location: Greece
Date: February-March, three weeks before Ash Wednesday;
last week is called Cheese Week

BkFest-1937, 146
BkFestHolWrld-1970, 35
FolkWrldHol-1992, 111
HolFestCelWrld-1994, 56, 317

Mardi Gras (Carnival)
Location: Grenada: Carriacou
Date: February-March, Tuesday and Ash Wednesday

Chases-1993, 107

Mardi Gras (Rara and Bruler Carnival)
Location: Haiti
Date: February-March, before Lent through Easter Week

BkHolWrld-1986, February 9, April 9, 176
FolkWrldHol-1992, 111
HolFestCelWrld-1994, 53, 268
RelHolCal-1993, 65

Mardi Gras (Farsang)
Location: Hungary
Date: January 6-Ash Wednesday

BkFest-1937, 166
FolkWrldHol-1992, 112

Mardi Gras (Bursting Day and Bun Day)
Location: Iceland
Date: February-March, Monday and Tuesday before Ash
Wednesday

AnnivHol-1983, 174
Chases-1993, 108
FolkWrldHol-1992, 103
HolFestCelWrld-1994, 317

Mardi Gras (Intruz, Carnival)
Location: India: Goa
Date: February-March, Saturday-Ash Wednesday

FolkWrldHol-1992, 111

Mardi Gras (Shrove Tuesday)
  Location: Ireland
  Date: February-March, Tuesday before Ash Wednesday

  DictFolkMyth-1984, 842

Mardi Gras (Carnevale)
  Location: Italy
  Date: January 17-Ash Wednesday

  AmerBkDays-1978, 43
  BkDays-1864, i.65
  BkFest-1937, 179
  BkFestHolWrld-1970, 35
  Chases-1993, 106
  DictDays-1988, 38
  FestSaintDays-1915, 44, 46
  FestWestEur-1958, 89
  FolkWrldHol-1992, 112
  HolFestCelWrld-1994, 53

Mardi Gras (Carnevale)
  Location: Italy: Milan
  Date: February-March, one week

  Chases-1993, 106

Mardi Gras
  Location: Italy: Tuscany
  Date: February-March, Tuesday before Ash Wednesday

  FestSaintDays-1915, 46

Mardi Gras
  Location: Italy: Venice
  Date: February-March, ending Tuesday before Ash
  Wednesday

  HolFestCelWrld-1994, 53

Mardi Gras (Užgavenēs)
  Location: Lithuania
  Date: February-March, Tuesday before Ash Wednesday

  BkFest-1937, 219
  DictFolkMyth-1984, 629

Mardi Gras
  Location: Lafayette, Louisiana
  Date: February-March

  Chases-1993, 105

Mardi Gras
  Location: New Orleans, Louisiana
  Established: 1820s

  Date: Begins no later than January 6, Epiphany, and
  ends Fat Tuesday, the day before Ash Wednesday

  AmerBkDays-1978, 43, 157, 158
  AnnivHol-1983, 179
  BkFestHolWrld-1970, 32
  Chases-1993, 108
  DictFolkMyth-1984, 193
  FolkAmerHol-1987, 77
  HolFestCelWrld-1994, 194, 317
  RelHolCal-1993, 65, 93

Mardi Gras (Fetten Donneschdeg)
  Location: Luxembourg
  Date: Thursday before the beginning of Lent

  FestWestEur-1958, 106

Mardi Gras (Cheesefare Sunday)
  Location: Macedonia
  Date: February-March, Sunday before Lent begins

  BkFestHolWrld-1970, 36
  FolkWrldHol-1992, 102

Mardi Gras (Carnival)
  Location: Malta
  Established: 1500s
  Date: February-March, before Ash Wednesday

  FolkWrldHol-1992, 113
  HolFestCelWrld-1994, 53

Mardi Gras (Carnival)
  Location: Martinique and Guadeloupe
  Date: February-March, Sunday-Ash Wednesday

  FolkWrldHol-1992, 113
  GdWrldFest-1985, 133

Mardi Gras
  Location: Boston, Massachusetts
  Date: February-March

  Chases-1993, 108

Mardi Gras (Carnaval)
  Location: Mexico
  Date: February-March

  BkFestHolWrld-1970, 36
  DictFolkMyth-1984, 193, 197, 220, 543, 749, 759, 787, 844
  FolkWrldHol-1992, 104, 113, 115
  IntlThFolk-1979, 278

Mardi Gras (Tahimoltik, Festival of the Games)
  Location: Mexico: Chamula
  Ethnic or religious group: Chamula Mayan people
  Date: February-March, five days, coinciding with lost days of Mayan calendar

  DictFolkMyth-1984, 543
  FolkWrldHol-1992, 113

Mardi Gras
  Location: Mexico: Morelos
  Date: February-March

  DictFolkMyth-1984, 193, 220, 749

Mardi Gras
  Location: Mexico: Tlaxcala
  Date: February-March

  DictFolkMyth-1984, 193, 197, 749, 844
  IntlThFolk-1979, 278

Mardi Gras (Fiesta de Febrero)
  Location: Mexico: Tzintzuntzan
  Date: February-March, Tuesday before Ash Wednesday

  FolkWrldHol-1992, 104

Mardi Gras (Carnaval, Fiesta of Games)
  Location: Mexico: Zinacantun
  Date: February-March, one week ending Ash Wednesday

  FolkWrldHol-1992, 115

Mardi Gras (Vastenavond)
  Location: Netherlands
  Date: February-March, Tuesday before Ash Wednesday

  BkFest-1937, 241
  FestWestEur-1958, 124

Mardi Gras (Vastenavond)
  Location: New York
  Ethnic or religious group: Dutch-Americans
  Date: February-March, Tuesday before Ash Wednesday

  FolkAmerHol-1987, 89

Mardi Gras (Fastelavn)
  Location: Norway
  Date: February-March, Monday before Ash Wednesday

  BkFest-1937, 249
  FestWestEur-1958, 151

Mardi Gras (Carnival and Burial of the Sardine on Ash Wednesday)
  Location: Panama
  Established: Official celebration since 1910

  Date: February-March, Saturday-Ash Wednesday

  FolkWrldHol-1992, 115
  GdWrldFest-1985, 147

Mardi Gras
  Location: Peru
  Date: February-March

  BkFestHolWrld-1970, 37

Mardi Gras (Zapusty, Fat Thursday)
  Location: Poland
  Date: February-March, Thursday before Lent, which begins on Friday

  BkFest-1937, 259

Mardi Gras (Carnaval)
  Location: Portugal
  Date: February-March, Sunday-Tuesday before Ash Wednesday

  BkFest-1937, 267
  BkFestHolWrld-1970, 34
  DictFolkMyth-1984, 397
  FestWestEur-1958, 163

Mardi Gras
  Location: Puerto Rico: San Juan
  Date: February-March, before Ash Wednesday

  AmerBkDays-1978, 157

Mardi Gras
  Location: Rome
  Date: February-March, eight days

  BkDays-1864, i.65

Mardi Gras (Maslyanitza, Butter Week)
  Location: Russia
  Date: February-March, the week before Ash Wednesday

  BkFest-1937, 289

Mardi Gras (Carnival)
  Location: St. Vincent
  Date: February-March, before Ash Wednesday

  FolkWrldHol-1992, 115

Mardi Gras (Fastern's E'en)
  Location: Scotland
  Date: February-March, Tuesday before Ash Wednesday

  AmerBkDays-1978, 157
  BkDays-1864, i.236
  BkFest-1937, 54
  DictDays-1988, 9, 15, 39, 42
  HolFestCelWrld-1994, 105

Mardi Gras (Carnaval)
Location: Spain
Date: February-March, Sunday-Tuesday before Ash
  Wednesday

BkFest-1937, 298
BkFestHolWrld-1970, 34
DictFolkMyth-1984, 105, 178, 193, 747, 980
FestSaintDays-1915, 43
FestWestEur-1958, 191

Mardi Gras
Location: Spain: Catalonia
Date: February-March

DictFolkMyth-1984, 105, 178, 193

Mardi Gras (Fastlagsafton)
Location: Sweden
Date: February-March

FestWestEur-1958, 211
FolkWrldHol-1992, 105
HolFestCelWrld-1994, 317

Mardi Gras (Fastnacht)
Location: Switzerland
Date: February-March, sometimes celebrated before, and
  sometimes after, Ash Wednesday

BkFest-1937, 316
BkHolWrld-1986, March 4, 177
DictFolkMyth-1984, 193
FestWestEur-1958, 230
FolkWrldHol-1992, 116

Mardi Gras (Carnival)
Location: Switzerland: Basel
Date: February-March

BkFest-1937, 316
BkHolWrld-1986, March 4, 177
FestWestEur-1958, 230
FolkWrldHol-1992, 117

Mardi Gras (al-Marfa, Carnival, and Khamis al-Marfa,
Carnival Thursday)
Location: Syria
Date: February-March, the week before Lent, especially
  Thursday

BkFest-1937, 328

Mardi Gras
Location: Galveston, Texas
Established: 1860s

Date: February-March

FolkAmerHol-1987, 84
HolFestCelWrld-1994, 195

Mardi Gras (Carnival)
Location: Thrace
Date: February-March

DictFolkMyth-1984, 568, 947

Mardi Gras (Carnival)
Location: Trinidad and Tobago
Established: 17th century
Date: February-March, Monday and Tuesday before
  Ash Wednesday

FolkWrldHol-1992, 117
GdWrldFest-1985, 175
HolFestCelWrld-1994, 344

Mardi Gras (Rosemontag, Rose Monday)
Location: United States
Ethnic or religious group: German-Americans
Date: February-March, Monday preceding Lent

AnnivHol-1983, 181
RelHolCal-1993, 110

Mardi Gras (Fasnacht)
Location: United States
Ethnic or religious group: Pennsylvania Dutch people
Date: February-March, Tuesday before Ash Wednesday

FolkAmerHol-1987, 87

Mardi Gras
Location: Uruguay: Montevideo
Date: January-February, about one month before
  Ash Wednesday

AmerBkDays-1978, 43

Mardi Gras (Carnival)
Location: Virgin Islands
Established: February 14, 1912; current version since 1952
Date: After Easter, usually last two weeks in April

AmerBkDays-1978, 387
AnnivHol-1983, 183
BkFestHolWrld-1970, 36
GdUSFest-1984, 221
HolFestCelWrld-1994, 53, 358

Mardi Gras
Location: De Pere, Wisconsin
Date: February-March

Chases-1993, 104

Mardi Gras
   Location: Yucatan
   Date: February-March

   DictFolkMyth-1984, 105, 193

al-Marfa (Carnival)
   See **Mardi Gras (Syria)**

Marie Bebadelsedag
   See **Annunciation, Feast of the (Lutherans in Sweden)**

Mari Lwyd
   See **Christmas Season (South Wales)**

Marimo Festival
   Location: Japan: Akan Lake, Hokkaido
   Ethnic or religious group: Ainu people
   Date: Second weekend in October

   IntlThFolk-1979, 252

Marins, Fête des
   See **Pentecost (France)**

Marksmen's Festival (Schützenfeste)
   Location: Germany
   Established: 14th-15th century
   Date: July-August, date varies according to location

   AnnivHol-1983, 181
   FestWestEur-1958, 74
   HolFestCelWrld-1994, 309

Marmaris Festival
   Location: Turkey: Marmaris
   Date: May-June

   IntlThFolk-1979, 371

Maroon Festival
   Named for: Commemorates 18th-century Treaty of Cudjoe
   Location: Jamaica
   Date: January 6

   Chases-1993, 57
   HolFestCelWrld-1994, 196

Marriage Fair
   Location: Morocco: Imilchil
   Ethnic or religious group: Ait Hadiddou Berber people
   Date: September

   HolFestCelWrld-1994, 196

Marriage of Goliath (Les Vêpres de Gouyasse)
   Location: Belgium: Ath, Hainaut

   Established: 15th century
   Date: Fourth weekend in August

   Chases-1993, 339
   FestWestEur-1958, 16
   HolFestCelWrld-1994, 118, 196

Marriage of Meenakshi and Shiva, Festival of the (Chaitra Purnima or Meenakshi Kalyanam)
   Location: India: Meenakshi Temple, Madurai
   Ethnic or religious group: Hindu
   Date: March-April, ten days during Hindu months of Chaitra or Vaisakha

   BkHolWrld-1986, May 10
   Chases-1993, 193
   DictWrldRel-1989, 482, 570
   HolFestCelWrld-1994, 202
   RelHolCal-1993, 65

Marten Gas
   See **Martinmas (Sweden)**

Martenitza
   See **First of March**

Martinmas (Martin's Goose Day; Martin's Mass)
   Named for: St. Martin, Bishop of Tours, France (c. 316-c. 397)
   Established: Sixth century, Rome
   Date: November 11

   AmerBkDays-1978, 1013
   AnnivHol-1983, 146
   BkDays-1864, ii.567
   BkFest-1937, 107
   BkFestHolWrld-1970, 121
   BkHolWrld-1986, November 11
   Chases-1993, 438
   DaysCustFaith-1957, 286
   DictDays-1988, 73, 105
   DictFolkMyth-1984, 682
   FestSaintDays-1915, 204
   FestWestEur-1958, 18, 27, 48, 101, 140, 185, 216
   FolkWrldHol-1992, 556
   HolFestCelWrld-1994, 197
   SaintFestCh-1904, 481

Martinmas
   Named for: St. Martin, Bishop of Tours, France (c. 316-c. 397)
   Ethnic or religious group: Protestant
   Date: November 11

   AmerBkDays-1978, 1015
   SaintFestCh-1904, 481

Martinmas
  Named for: St. Martin, Bishop of Tours, France
    (c. 316-c. 397)
  Ethnic or religious group: Roman Catholic
  Date: November 11

  AmerBkDays-1978, 1013
  SaintFestCh-1904, 481

Martinmas (Wine Festival)
  Named for: St. Martin, Bishop of Tours, France
    (c. 316-c. 397)
  Location: Austria
  Date: November 11

  BkFestHolWrld-1970, 121

Martinmas
  Named for: St. Martin, Bishop of Tours, France
    (c. 316-c. 397)
  Location: Belgium
  Date: November 11

  FestWestEur-1958, 18
  HolFestCelWrld-1994, 197

Martinmas (Mortensaftenn)
  Named for: St. Martin, Bishop of Tours, France
    (c. 316-c. 397)
  Location: Denmark
  Date: November 11

  FestWestEur-1958, 27
  FolkWrldHol-1992, 556

Martinmas
  Named for: St. Martin, Bishop of Tours, France
    (c. 316-c. 397)
  Location: England
  Date: November 11

  BkDays-1864, ii.568
  BkHolWrld-1986, November 11
  DictFolkMyth-1984, 682
  FestSaintDays-1915, 206
  FolkWrldHol-1992, 557
  HolFestCelWrld-1994, 197
  SaintFestCh-1904, 481

Martinmas
  Named for: St. Martin, Bishop of Tours, France
    (c. 316-c. 397)
  Location: Estonia
  Date: November 29

  BkFest-1937, 107

Martinmas (Foire de la Saint Martin)
  Named for: St. Martin, Bishop of Tours, France
    (c. 316-c. 397)
  Location: France
  Date: November 11

  DictFolkMyth-1984, 682
  FestWestEur-1958, 48
  HolFestCelWrld-1994, 197

Martinmas (Martinstag)
  Named for: St. Martin, Bishop of Tours, France
    (c. 316-c. 397)
  Location: Germany
  Date: November 11

  AmerBkDays-1978, 1015
  DictFolkMyth-1984, 682
  FolkWrldHol-1992, 556
  HolFestCelWrld-1994, 197

Martinmas
  Named for: St. Martin, Bishop of Tours, France
    (c. 316-c. 397)
  Location: Ireland
  Date: November 11

  DaysCustFaith-1957, 287
  DictFolkMyth-1984, 682
  FestSaintDays-1915, 207
  FolkWrldHol-1992, 557

Martinmas (San Martino)
  Named for: St. Martin, Bishop of Tours, France
    (c. 316-c. 397)
  Location: Italy
  Date: November 11

  FestWestEur-1958, 101

Martinmas
  Named for: St. Martin, Bishop of Tours, France
    (c. 316-c. 397)
  Location: Netherlands
  Date: November 11; in Hoorn, observed fourth Monday
    in August

  FestWestEur-1958, 140
  FolkWrldHol-1992, 557
  HolFestCelWrld-1994, 197

Martinmas (Feast of São Martinho)
  Named for: St. Martin, Bishop of Tours, France
    (c. 316-c. 397)
  Location: Portugal
  Date: November 11

  FestWestEur-1958, 185
  FolkWrldHol-1992, 557

Martinmas
    Named for: St. Martin, Bishop of Tours, France
        (c. 316-c. 397)
    Location: Scotland
    Date: November 11

    BkDays-1864, ii.568
    DictFolkMyth-1984, 682
    FestSaintDays-1915, 207

Martinmas (Marten Gas)
    Named for: St. Martin, Bishop of Tours, France
        (c. 316-c. 397)
    Location: Sweden
    Date: November 11

    FestWestEur-1958, 216
    FolkWrldHol-1992, 557
    HolFestCelWrld-1994, 197

Martinmas
    Named for: St. Martin, Bishop of Tours, France
        (c. 316-c. 397)
    Location: United States
    Ethnic or religious group: European-Americans
    Date: November 11

    AmerBkDays-1978, 1015

Martinmas Sunday
    See **Martinmas**

Martinschmaus
    See **Waygoose Feast (printers in Germany)**

Martin's Day
    See **Martinmas; Martinsfest; St. Martin's Day**

Martinsfest
    Named for: St. Martin (c. 316-c. 397) and Martin Luther
        (1483-1546)
    Location: Germany: Erfurt and Thuringia
    Ethnic or religious group: Protestant
    Date: November 10-11

    AnnivHol-1983, 145
    BkFest-1937, 138
    BkFestHolWrld-1970, 122
    Chases-1993, 437
    DictWrldRel-1989, 440, 606
    FestWestEur-1958, 77
    HolFestCelWrld-1994, 197, 198
    RelHolCal-1993, 63

Martinsfest
    Named for: St. Martin (c. 316-c. 397) and Martin Luther
        (1483-1546)
    Location: Germany: Düsseldorf and Lower Rhine
    Ethnic or religious group: Roman Catholic
    Date: November 10-11

    BkFest-1937, 138
    BkFestHolWrld-1970, 122
    DictWrldRel-1989, 440, 606
    FestWestEur-1958, 77
    HolFestCelWrld-1994, 197, 198

Martin's Goose Day, Martin's Mass, or Martlemas
    See **Martinmas**

Martinstag
    See **Martinmas (Germany)**

Martyr Day
    Named for: Commemorates St. Peter Baptist and others
        killed by Emperor Tagosama (Go-Yozei, reigned
        1586-1611) in 1597
    Location: Japan
    Date: February 5

    AnnivHol-1983, 19
    DaysCustFaith-1957, 48

Martyrs' Day
    Ethnic or religious group: Armenians worldwide
    Established: April 24, 1915
    Date: April 24

    AnnivHol-1983, 56
    Chases-1993, 178
    HolFestCelWrld-1994, 14

Martyrs Day (Bangladesh)
    See **Shaheel Day (Bangladesh)**

Martyrs Day
    Named for: Assassination of General Aung San
        (1914-1947) on July 19
    Location: Burma; now Myanmar
    Date: July 19

    AnnivHol-1983, 94

Martyr's Day
    Location: Malawi
    Date: March 3

    AnnivHol-1983, 32
    Chases-1993, 117

Martyrs Day
Named for: February 3, 1953, Batepa Massacre
Location: Sao Tomé and Principe
Date: February 3

AnnivHol-1983, 18

Martyrs Day
Location: Syria
Date: April 6

AnnivHol-1983, 48

Martyrs' Day
Location: Zaire
Date: January 4

AnnivHol-1983, 4

Martyrs' Day, Canton
Named for: 72 martyrs at Yellow Flowers Hill at Canton in 1911
Location: China: especially in Kwantung Province
Date: March 29

BkFest-1937, 76

Martyrs' Day, Forty ('Id al-Arba'in Shahid)
Named for: March 9, 320, martyrdoms in Sevastia
Location: Syria
Ethnic or religious group: Christian
Date: March 9

BkFest-1937, 328
HolFestCelWrld-1994, 109

Martyrs' Day, Forty
Named for: March 9, 320, martyrdoms in Sevastia
Location: Greece
Date: March 9

FolkWrldHol-1992, 161
HolFestCelWrld-1994, 109

Martyrs' Day, Forty
Named for: March 9, 320, martyrdoms in Sevastia
Location: Romania
Date: March 9

FolkWrldHol-1992, 161
HolFestCelWrld-1994, 109

Martyrs of North America, Feast of
Location: Canada and the United States
Ethnic or religious group: Roman Catholic

Date: September 26

AnnivHol-1983, 123
DaysCustFaith-1957, 242
HolFestCelWrld-1994, 198

Mary, Month of (Mois de Marie)
Location: France
Date: May

BkFest-1937, 122

Marya
Location: Nepal: Patan
Date: July-August, third day of waning half of Hindu month of Sravana

FolkWrldHol-1992, 402
HolFestCelWrld-1994, 198

Maryland Day
Named for: March 25, 1634, landing of the colonists
Location: Maryland
Date: March 25

AmerBkDays-1978, 287
AnnivHol-1983, 42
Chases-1993, 140
DictDays-1988, 74
HolFestCelWrld-1994, 198

Maryland Hunt Club
Location: Glyndon, Maryland
Established: 1922
Date: Last Saturday in April

HolFestCelWrld-1994, 198

Marymass Fair
Location: Scotland: Irvine, Ayrshire
Established: twelfth century
Date: Third or fourth Monday in August

RelHolCal-1993, 94

Marzanna Day
Location: Poland: along the Vistula River
Date: March 21; observed Saturday or Sunday nearest March 21

AnnivHol-1983, 40
BkHolWrld-1986, March 23, 179
HolFestCelWrld-1994, 199

Marzas
See **First of March (Spain)**

Masi Magham
  Location: India: Kumbakonam
  Ethnic or religious group: Hindu
  Date: February-March, two-day festival during full moon
    of Masi; larger festival every twelve years

  BkFestHolWrld-1970, 91

Masi Magham
  Location: Malaya: Malacca
  Date: February-March, two-day festival during full moon
    of Masi

  FolkWrldHol-1992, 147

Maskal, Finding of the True Cross
  See **Exaltation of the Cross (Coptic and Ethiopian
    churches in Ethiopia)**

Maslyanitza, Butter Week
  See **Mardi Gras (Russia)**

Mass of the Broken Needles
  See **Broken Needles Festival (Japan)**

Master Draught Pageant (Meistertrunk Pageant)
  Location: Federal Republic of Germany: Rothernburg on
    the Tauber, Bavaria
  Established: Commemorates town's victory over invading
    troops in 1631, during Thirty Years' War
  Date: May-June, Pentecost (Whitsunday)

  FestWestEur-1958, 66
  GdWrldFest-1985, 87
  HolFestCelWrld-1994, 202

Master's Golf Tournament
  Location: Augusta National Golf Club, Georgia
  Established: 1934
  Date: First full week in April

  HolFestCelWrld-1994, 199

Matchina Dance
  See **Dance, Matchina**

Materice
  See **Mother's Day (Yugoslavia: Serbia)**

Matralia
  Location: Ancient Rome: Forum Boarium, the Temple
    of Hercules
  Date: June 11

  DictFolkMyth-1984, 693

Matrimonial Tea
  See **Whit Monday (Belgium)**

Matsu, Birthday of (Matsu Festival)
  Location: Taiwan
  Ethnic or religious group: Buddhist
  Date: 23rd day of third lunar month

  FolkWrldHol-1992, 212
  HolFestCelWrld-1994, 199, 200

Maulid
  See **Muhammad's Birthday (Sufis and other Muslims
    in Egypt)**

Maulid al-Nabi
  See **Muhammad's Birthday**

Ma'ulid Annabi
  See **Muhammad's Birthday (Libya)**

Maulidi
  See **Muhammad's Birthday (Kenya: Lamu)**

Maundy Thursday
  See **Holy Thursday (Maundy Thursday) (England)**

Mauni Amavasya
  Location: India: Prayag and along the Ganges River
  Ethnic or religious group: Hindu
  Date: January-February, 15th day of waning half of Hindu
    month of Magha

  RelHolCal-1993, 94

Maverick Sunday Concerts
  Location: Woodstock, New York
  Established: About 1916
  Date: Sunday afternoons from July to early September

  MusFestAmer-1990, 103

Mawlid al-Nabi
  See **Muhammad's Birthday (Muslim)**

May Day
  Date: May 1

  AmerBkDays-1978, 407
  AnnivHol-1983, 60
  BkDays-1864, i. 570
  BkFest-1937, 17, 58, 88, 113, 122, 186, 261, 278, 310
  BkFestHolWrld-1970, 84
  BkHolWrld-1986, May 1
  Chases-1993, 189
  DaysCustFaith-1957, 115
  DictDays-1988, 74
  DictFolkMyth-1984, 129, 202, 203, 534, 695, 750, 866,
    946, 1064
  FestSaintDays-1915, 102, 105, 109

May Day *(cont.)*
FestWestEur-1958, 37
FolkAmerHol-1987, 165
FolkWrldHol-1992, 262
HolFestCelWrld-1994, 201, 259, 354
RelHolCal-1993, 95
See also **Beltane; Walpurgis Night**

May Day
Location: Belgium
Date: May 1

BkFestHolWrld-1970, 85

May Day
Location: Canada
Date: May 1

DictFolkMyth-1984, 695
FolkWrldHol-1992, 262

May Day (Prvého Máje)
Location: Czechoslovakia
Date: May 1

BkFest-1937, 88

May Day
Location: England
Date: May 1

AnnivHol-1983, 60
BkDays-1864, i.571, 574
BkFest-1937, 58
BkFestHolWrld-1970, 85
BkHolWrld-1986, May 1
DaysCustFaith-1957, 115
DictDays-1988, 74
DictFolkMyth-1984, 129, 202, 695, 534, 866, 750
FestSaintDays-1915, 102, 105, 109
FolkWrldHol-1992, 263
See also **Labour Day (England)**

May Day (Vappu)
Location: Finland
Date: May 1

BkFest-1937, 113
HolFestCelWrld-1994, 354

May Day (Premier Mai)
Location: France

Date: May 1

BkDays-1864, i.579
BkFest-1937, 122
BkFestHolWrld-1970, 85
DictFolkMyth-1984, 696
FestWestEur-1958, 37
FolkWrldHol-1992, 262
HolFestCelWrld-1994, 259

May Day
Location: Germany
Date: May 1

BkDays-1864, i.577
FolkWrldHol-1992, 263

May Day
Location: Great Britain
Established: Ancient Celtic holiday
Date: May 1; observed first Monday in May in Great
    Britain and Northern Ireland

AmerBkDays-1978, 407
AnnivHol-1983, 60
BkDays-1864, i.571
BkFest-1937, 58
BkFestHolWrld-1970, 85
BkHolWrld-1986, May 1
DaysCustFaith-1957, 116
DictDays-1988, 74
DictFolkMyth-1984, 129, 202, 534, 695, 750, 866
FestSaintDays-1915, 102, 105, 109
FolkWrldHol-1992, 263
RelHolCal-1993, 95

May Day
Location: Holland
Date: May 1

BkFestHolWrld-1970, 85

May Day
Location: Ireland
Date: May 1

BkFest-1937, 58
DictFolkMyth-1984, 696
FolkWrldHol-1992, 263

May Day
Location: Isle of Man
Date: May 1

DictFolkMyth-1984, 203, 696

May Day (Calendimaggio)
  Location: Italy
  Date: May 1

  BkFest-1937, 186

May Day
  Location: Japan
  Date: May 1

  BkFestHolWrld-1970, 84

May Day
  Location: Macedonia
  Date: May 1

  FolkWrldHol-1992, 264

May Day
  Location: Norway
  Date: May 1

  FolkWrldHol-1992, 264

May Day
  Location: Philippines
  Date: May 1

  BkFestHolWrld-1970, 84

May Day (Świeto Pierwszego Maja)
  Location: Poland
  Date: May 1

  BkFest-1937, 261

May Day (Armindini)
  Location: Romania
  Date: May 1

  BkFest-1937, 278

May Day
  Location: Scandinavia
  Date: May 1

  DictFolkMyth-1984, 696
  FestSaintDays-1915, 108

May Day
  Location: Scotland
  Date: May 1

  BkDays-1864, i.574
  DaysCustFaith-1957, 115
  DictFolkMyth-1984, 203
  FolkWrldHol-1992, 265

May Day
  Location: Silesia
  Date: May 1

  FestSaintDays-1915, 108

May Day
  Location: Spain
  Date: May 1

  DictFolkMyth-1984, 1064
  FolkWrldHol-1992, 265

May Day (Första Maj)
  Location: Sweden
  Date: May 1

  BkFest-1937, 310
  DaysCustFaith-1957, 116
  FolkWrldHol-1992, 265
  See also **Walpurgis Night (Valborgsmässoafton)**

May Day
  Location: Switzerland
  Date: May 1

  BkFestHolWrld-1970, 85

May Day
  Location: Turkey
  Date: May 1

  AnnivHol-1983, 60

May Day
  Location: USSR
  Date: May 1

  BkFestHolWrld-1970, 84
  BkHolWrld-1986, May 1
  FolkWrldHol-1992, 266
  HolFestCelWrld-1994, 201

May Day
  Location: United States
  Established: 1628
  Date: May 1

  AmerBkDays-1978, 407
  AnnivHol-1983, 60
  BkFest-1937, 17
  BkFestHolWrld-1970, 85
  DictFolkMyth-1984, 695
  FolkAmerHol-1987, 165
  HolFestCelWrld-1994, 201

May Day
  Location: Yugoslavia
  Date: May 1

  FolkWrldHol-1992, 265

May Day Bank Holiday (Great Britain)
  See **Bank Holiday (England, Ireland, Scotland, and Wales)**

May Day Eve
  Date: April 30-May 1

  BkFest-1937, 88, 113, 149, 185, 318
  DictFolkMyth-1984, 202
  FestWestEur-1958, 232
  GdWrldFest-1985, 68

May Day Eve (Páleni Čarodějnic, Burning of the Witches)
  Location: Czechoslovakia
  Date: April 30

  BkFest-1937, 88
  GdWrldFest-1985, 68

May Day Eve (Vapun Aatto or Vappu)
  Location: Finland
  Date: April 30

  AnnivHol-1983, 58
  BkFest-1937, 113
  FolkWrldHol-1992, 262

May Day Eve (Proto Mayea)
  Location: Greece
  Date: April 30

  BkFest-1937, 149

May Day Eve
  Location: Ireland
  Ethnic or religious group: Celtic people
  Date: April 30

  DictFolkMyth-1984, 202
  FolkWrldHol-1992, 252

May Day Eve (Calendimaggio)
  Location: Italy
  Date: April 30

  BkFest-1937, 185

May Day Eve (Maitag Vorabend)
  Location: Switzerland
  Date: April 30

  BkFest-1937, 318

Mayfest (Maifest)
  Location: Hermann, Missouri
  Ethnic or religious group: German-Americans
  Established: 1952
  Date: Third weekend in May

  GdUSFest-1984, 105

Mayfest, International
  Location: Tulsa, Oklahoma
  Date: Five days in May

  HolFestCelWrld-1994, 201

May Festival
  Named for: Karl May (1842-1912)
  Location: Federal Republic of Germany: Bad Segeberg, Schleswig-Holstein
  Established: 1952
  Date: July-August

  IntlThFolk-1979, 150

May Festival, Wiesbaden International (Internationale Maifestspiele)
  Location: Federal Republic of Germany: Wiesbaden, Hesse
  Established: 1896
  Date: Month of May

  GdWrldFest-1985, 87
  IntlThFolk-1979, 151
  MusFestEurBrit-1980, 106
  MusFestWrld-1963, 71

May International Festival, Memphis in
  Location: Memphis, Tennessee
  Established: 1979
  Date: Month of May

  Chases-1993, 189
  GdUSFest-1984, 176

Mayoring Day
  Location: Great Britain
  Date: Late May

  AnnivHol-1983, 70
  DictDays-1988, 75
  HolFestCelWrld-1994, 201

Mayor's Sunday
  See **Mayoring Day**

Maytime Fairies
  Location: Ireland
  Date: First days of May

  BkHolWrld-1986, May 4, 179

Maytime Festival, International
  Location: Ireland: Dundalk, County Louth
  Established: Festival center since 12th century
  Date: Third week in May

  IntlThFolk-1979, 233

McClure Bean Soup Festival
  Location: McClure, Pennsylvania
  Established: October 20, 1883
  Date: Five days in September

  GdUSFest-1984, 159

McDonogh Day
  Named for: John McDonogh (1779-1850)
  Location: New Orleans, Louisiana
  Date: First Friday in May

  AnnivHol-1983, 61

Meadela, International Festival of
  Location: Portugal: Meadela, Viana do Castelo
  Established: Local since 1957; international since 1970
  Date: August

  IntlThFolk-1979, 308

Meat Fare Sunday
  See **Lent (Eastern Orthodox)**

Mecca, Pilgrimage to
  Location: Saudi Arabia: Mecca
  Ethnic or religious group: Muslim
  Established: Seventh century
  Date: Eighth through 13th days of Dhu'l-Hijjah, twelfth Islamic month

  AnnivHol-1983, 171
  BkHolWrld-1986, August 27, 174
  Chases-1993, 229
  DictMyth-1962, ii.1082
  DictWrldRel-1989, 290, 569
  FolkWrldHol-1992, 328, 332
  HolFestCelWrld-1994, 253, 301
  RelHolCal-1993, 81
  See also **Sallah**

Mecca, Pilgrimage to
  Location: Saudi Arabia: Mecca
  Ethnic or religious group: Muslims from Africa
  Date: Eighth through 13th days of Dhu'l-Hijjah, twelfth Islamic month

  FolkWrldHol-1992, 328

Mecca, Pilgrimage to
  Location: Saudi Arabia: Mecca
  Ethnic or religious group: Muslims from Cameroon
  Date: Eighth through 13th days of Dhu'l-Hijjah, twelfth Islamic month

  FolkWrldHol-1992, 328

Mecca, Pilgrimage to
  Location: Saudi Arabia: Mecca
  Ethnic or religious group: Muslims from Egypt
  Date: Eighth through 13th days of Dhu'l-Hijjah, twelfth Islamic month

  FolkWrldHol-1992, 329

Mecca, Pilgrimage to
  Location: Saudi Arabia: Mecca
  Ethnic or religious group: Muslims from Iraq
  Date: Eighth through 13th days of Dhu'l-Hijjah, twelfth Islamic month

  FolkWrldHol-1992, 330

Mecca, Pilgrimage to
  Location: Saudi Arabia: Mecca
  Ethnic or religious group: Muslims from Jordan
  Date: Eighth through 13th days of Dhu'l-Hijjah, twelfth Islamic month

  FolkWrldHol-1992, 330

Mecca, Pilgrimage to
  Location: Saudi Arabia: Mecca
  Ethnic or religious group: Muslims from Kuwait
  Date: Eighth through 13th days of Dhu'l-Hijjah, twelfth Islamic month

  FolkWrldHol-1992, 331

Mecca, Pilgrimage to
  Location: Saudi Arabia: Mecca
  Ethnic or religious group: Muslims from Pakistan
  Date: Eighth through 13th days of Dhu'l-Hijjah, twelfth Islamic month

  FolkWrldHol-1992, 332

Mecca, Pilgrimage to
  Location: Saudi Arabia: Mecca
  Ethnic or religious group: Muslims from Syria
  Date: Eighth through 13th days of Dhu'l-Hijjah, twelfth Islamic month

  FolkWrldHol-1992, 333

Mecca, Pilgrimage to
  Location: Saudi Arabia: Mecca
  Ethnic or religious group: Muslims from Turkey
  Date: Eighth through 13th days of Dhu'l-Hijjah,
    twelfth Islamic month

  FolkWrldHol-1992, 333

Mecklenburg Day
  Named for: May 20, 1775, adoption of Mecklenburg
    Declaration of Independence
  Location: North Carolina
  Date: May 20

  AnnivHol-1983, 68
  Chases-1993, 215
  DictDays-1988, 75
  HolFestCelWrld-1994, 201

Medan Anniversary
  Location: Indonesia: Medan, North Sumatra, Sumatra
  Date: April 1

  IntlThFolk-1979, 227

Mediterranean Festival
  Location: Turkey: Izmir
  Date: June

  IntlThFolk-1979, 370

Meenakshi Kalyanam
  See **Marriage of Meenakshi and Shiva, Festival of
    (Hindu people at Meenakshi Temple, Madurai, India)**

Megali Sarakosti
  See **Lent (Greece)**

Meghalee Paraskevee, Holy Friday
  See **Good Friday (Greece)**

Meghalo Savato
  See **Holy Saturday (Greece)**

Meiji Setsu
  Named for: Emperor Meiji Setsu, who ruled 1864-1911
  Location: Japan
  Date: November 3

  BkFest-1937, 200

Meistertrunk Pageant
  See **Master Draught Pageant (Federal Republic of
    Germany: Rothernburg on the Tauber, Bavaria)**

Meitlisunntig
  Location: Switzerland: Seetal district of Aargau
  Established: Reenactment of Villmergen War of 1712
  Date: Second Sunday in January

  AnnivHol-1983, 8
  Chases-1993, 60

Melbourne Cup Day
  Location: Australia: Melbourne, Victoria
  Established: 1867
  Date: First Tuesday in November

  AnnivHol-1983, 141
  DictDays-1988, 75
  HolFestCelWrld-1994, 202

Melk, Festival of (Melker Festspiele)
  Location: Austria: Melk, Lower Austria
  Established: 1961
  Date: July-August

  IntlThFolk-1979, 37

Mell Supper
  See **Harvest Home Festival (northern England)**

Memorial Day
  Location: Brazil
  Date: November 2

  AnnivHol-1983, 141
  See also **All Souls' Day (Brazil)**

Memorial Day
  Location: Japan: Nagasaki
  Date: August 9
  AnnivHol-1983, 105

Memorial Day
  Location: Republic of Korea
  Date: June 6

  AnnivHol-1983, 76

Memorial Day (Commemoration Day)
  Named for: March 29, 1947, rebellion against French rule
  Location: Madagascar
  Date: March 29

  AnnivHol-1983, 43
  Chases-1993, 146

Memorial Day (Day of the Dead)
  Location: Romania
  Date: May 31

  FolkWrldHol-1992, 307

Memorial Day
   Location: United States
   Established: 1865; formerly Decoration Day
   Date: May 30; observed last Monday in May

   AmerBkDays-1978, 501
   AnnivHol-1983, 73
   BkFest-1937, 18
   BkHolWrld-1986, May 30, 179
   Chases-1993, 227, 228
   DaysCustFaith-1957, 132
   DictDays-1988, 30
   FolkAmerHol-1987, 187-89
   HolFestCelWrld-1994, 202

Memorial Day, Camões
   See **National Day (Portugal)**

Memorial Day, World War II
   See **V-J Day (Arkansas)**

Memorial to Broken Dolls Day
   Location: Japan
   Ethnic or religious group: Buddhist
   Date: June 3

   AnnivHol-1983, 75

Menuhin Festival
   Named for: Yehudi Menuhin (b. 1916)
   Location: Switzerland: Gstaad-Saanen
   Established: 1956
   Date: Three weeks in August

   MusFestEurBrit-1980, 143

Merchant Marine Week
   See **National Maritime Day (United States)**

Merchants' Flower Market
   See **Pentecost (Netherlands: Haarlem)**

Merdeka Day
   See **Independence Day (Malaysia: Kuala Lumpur, Selangor)**

Merrie Monarch Festival
   Named for: King David Kalakaua (1836-1891)
   Location: Hilo, Hawaii
   Date: March-April, several days beginning Easter Sunday

   Chases-1993, 163
   HolFestCelWrld-1994, 203

Merton Festival
   Location: England: London Borough of Merton

   Established: 1972
   Date: May

   IntlThFolk-1979, 167

Mescalero Apache Gahan Ceremonial
   Location: Mescalero, New Mexico
   Ethnic or religious group: Mescalero Apache Indians
   Date: July 1-4

   IndianAmer-1989, 287, 301

Mesir Festival
   Location: Turkey: Mansia
   Established: 16th century
   Date: May

   IntlThFolk-1979, 371

Meskel, Finding of the True Cross
   See **Exaltation of the Cross (Coptic and Ethiopian churches in Ethiopia)**

Messiah Festival
   Location: Lindsborg, Kansas
   Established: 1882
   Date: March-April, eight days during Easter week

   Chases-1993, 154
   MusFestAmer-1990, 61

Metamusik Festival
   Location: Federal Republic of Germany: West Berlin
   Established: 1974
   Date: Even-numbered years in October

   IntlThFolk-1979, 132

La Meuse Festival
   Location: Belgium: Dinant
   Established: 1978
   Date: July-August

   IntlThFolk-1979, 46

Mevlana (Festival of Whirling Dervishes)
   Named for: 13th-century group founded by Persian poet-mystic Jalāl ad-Din Rūmi (c. 1207-1273); revived 1954
   Location: Turkey: Konya
   Ethnic or religious group: Mevlana Muslims
   Date: Nine days to two weeks in December

   DictWrldRel-1989, 632
   GdWrldFest-1985, 181
   IntlThFolk-1979, 370

Mezhdunarodnyi Zhenski Den'
See **Woman's Day, International (USSR)**

Mezza Quaresima
See **Mid-Lent Sunday (Spain)**

M'Hamed Ben Khelifa Festival
   Location: Tunisia: El Kaalaa El Khasba, Le Kef Region
   Date: October

   IntlThFolk-1979, 360

Mibu Dainembutsu Kyogen
   Location: Japan: Mibu Temple, Kyoto
   Ethnic or religious group: Buddhist
   Date: End of April

   IntlThFolk-1979, 256

Mi-Carême
See **Mid-Lent Sunday (France)**

Michael, the Archangel, St.
See **Michaelmas**

Michaelmas
   Ethnic or religious group: Christian
   Established: fifth century
   Date: Observed September 29, Western church;
   November 8, Eastern church

   AmerBkDays-1978, 876
   AnnivHol-1983, 125
   BkDays-1864, ii. 387
   BkFest-1937, 153
   Chases-1993, 389
   DaysCustFaith-1957, 242
   DictDays-1988, 75, 86, 105
   DictFolkMyth-1984, 504, 716
   FestSaintDays-1915, 180
   FestWestEur-1958, 155
   FolkWrldHol-1992, 492
   HolFestCelWrld-1994, 203
   RelHolCal-1993, 95
   SaintFestCh-1904, 428

Michaelmas
   Ethnic or religious group: Anglican
   Date: September 29

   AmerBkDays-1978, 876
   FestSaintDays-1915, 180
   HolFestCelWrld-1994, 203
   RelHolCal-1993, 95
   SaintFestCh-1904, 428

Michaelmas
   Ethnic or religious group: Church of England
   Date: September 29

   BkDays-1864, ii.387

Michaelmas
   Ethnic or religious group: Eastern Orthodox
   Date: November 8

   AmerBkDays-1978, 876
   BkFest-1937, 153
   DictFolkMyth-1984, 716
   HolFestCelWrld-1994, 203

Michaelmas (Feast of St. Michael and All Angels)
   Ethnic or religious group: Episcopalian
   Date: September 29

   AmerBkDays-1978, 876

Michaelmas (Feast of St. Michael and All Angels)
   Ethnic or religious group: Lutheran
   Date: September 29

   AmerBkDays-1978, 876
   RelHolCal-1993, 95

Michaelmas (Feast of SS. Michael, Gabriel, and Raphael, Archangels)
   Ethnic or religious group: Roman Catholic
   Date: September 29

   AmerBkDays-1978, 876
   BkDays-1864, ii.387
   Chases-1993, 389
   FestSaintDays-1915, 180
   HolFestCelWrld-1994, 203
   RelHolCal-1993, 95
   SaintFestCh-1904, 428

Michaelmas
   Location: Abyssinia
   Date: Observed twelfth of every month

   DictFolkMyth-1984, 716

Michaelmas
   Location: England
   Date: September 29

   AmerBkDays-1978, 878
   BkDays-1864, ii.387
   DictDays-1988, 75, 86
   DictFolkMyth-1984, 716
   FestSaintDays-1915, 180, 182
   FolkWrldHol-1992, 492
   RelHolCal-1993, 95
   SaintFestCh-1904, 428

Michaelmas
   Location: Ireland
   Date: September 29

   DictFolkMyth-1984, 716
   FestSaintDays-1915, 184
   FolkWrldHol-1992, 492
   HolFestCelWrld-1994, 203

Michaelmas
   Location: Isle of Iona
   Date: September 29

   DictFolkMyth-1984, 504

Michaelmas
   Location: Isle of Skye
   Date: September 29

   DictFolkMyth-1984, 716

Michaelmas
   Location: Normandy
   Date: September 29

   AmerBkDays-1978, 877
   FestSaintDays-1915, 181

Michaelmas (Mikkelsmesse)
   Location: Norway
   Date: September 29

   FestWestEur-1958, 155

Michaelmas
   Location: Scotland
   Date: September 29

   FestSaintDays-1915, 184

Michaelmas Eve
   See **Michaelmas**

Mid-Autumn Festival
   Location: Asia
   Date: September-October, 15th day of eighth lunar month

   AnnivHol-1983, 179
   BkFest-1937, 81
   BkFestHolWrld-1970, 115
   BkHolWrld-1986, September 16
   Chases-1993, 390
   DictFolkMyth-1984, 191, 225, 231
   DictWrldRel-1989, 412
   FolkWrldHol-1992, 428
   GdWrldFest-1985, 158
   HolFestCelWrld-1994, 204
   IntlThFolk-1979, 198

Mid-Autumn Festival (Chung Ch'iu)
   Location: China
   Date: 15th, or full moon, day of eighth lunar month

   AnnivHol-1983, 179
   BkFest-1937, 81
   BkFestHolWrld-1970, 115
   BkHolWrld-1986, September 16
   Chases-1993, 390
   DictFolkMyth-1984, 191, 225, 231
   FolkWrldHol-1992, 428
   HolFestCelWrld-1994, 204

Mid-Autumn Festival (Chung Ch'iu)
   Location: Hong Kong
   Date: 15th, or full moon, day of eighth lunar month

   AnnivHol-1983, 179
   Chases-1993, 390
   FolkWrldHol-1992, 429
   HolFestCelWrld-1994, 204
   IntlThFolk-1979, 198

Mid-Autumn Festival
   Location: Japan
   Date: 15th, or full moon, day of eighth lunar month

   HolFestCelWrld-1994, 204

Mid-Autumn Festival (Choosuk, Chusok, or Hangawi, Moon Festival)
   Location: Korea
   Date: 15th, or full moon, day of eighth lunar month

   AnnivHol-1983, 175
   Chases-1993, 390
   DictWrldRel-1989, 412
   FolkWrldHol-1992, 430
   HolFestCelWrld-1994, 204

Mid-Autumn Festival
   Location: Macao
   Date: 15th, or full moon, day of eighth lunar month

   AnnivHol-1983, 179

Mid-Autumn Festival
   Location: Malaysia
   Date: 15th, or full moon, day of eighth lunar month

   HolFestCelWrld-1994, 204

Mid-Autumn Festival
   Location: Singapore
   Date: 15th, or full moon, day of eighth lunar month

   Chases-1993, 390
   GdWrldFest-1985, 158

Mid-Autumn Festival
    Location: Taiwan
    Date: 15th, or full moon, day of eighth lunar month

    AnnivHol-1983, 179
    Chases-1993, 390
    FolkWrldHol-1992, 431
    HolFestCelWrld-1994, 204

Mid-Autumn Festival
    Location: Vietnam
    Date: 15th, or full moon, day of eighth lunar month

    HolFestCelWrld-1994, 204

Middfest International
    Location: Middletown, Ohio
    Established: 1981
    Date: Three days in late September-early October

    HolFestCelWrld-1994, 205

Midimu Ceremony
    Location: Tanzania: Newala, Mtwara, and Lindi;
    Mozambique: Tunduru; Malawi; Zambia; Zimbabwe
    Ethnic or religious group: Makonde people
    Date: June through October, begins night during the
    period when the moon moves from the quarter to its
    half phase for three days

    FolkWrldHol-1992, 469
    HolFestCelWrld-1994, 206

Mid-Lent Sunday
    Ethnic or religious group: Christian
    Date: March, fourth Sunday in Lent

    BkDays-1864, i. 335
    Chases-1993, 136
    DaysCustFaith-1957, 89
    DictDays-1988, 15, 76, 95, 112
    DictFolkMyth-1984, 871, 1013
    FestSaintDays-1915, 51
    FestWestEur-1958, 35, 92, 106
    HolFestCelWrld-1994, 203, 205, 212, 259
    SaintFestCh-1904, 143

Mid-Lent Sunday (Mothering Sunday)
    Ethnic or religious group: Anglican
    Date: March, fourth Sunday in Lent

    DaysCustFaith-1957, 89
    HolFestCelWrld-1994, 212

Mid-Lent Sunday (Laetare Sunday)
    Ethnic or religious group: Roman Catholic
    Date: March, fourth Sunday in Lent

    BkFestHolWrld-1970, 48
    DaysCustFaith-1957, 89
    DictDays-1988, 66
    HolFestCelWrld-1994, 212

Mid-Lent Sunday
    Ethnic or religious group: Slavic people
    Date: March, fourth Sunday in Lent

    FestSaintDays-1915, 52

Mid-Lent Sunday
    Location: Bavaria and Rhine countries
    Date: March, fourth Sunday in Lent

    FestSaintDays-1915, 51

Mid-Lent Sunday (Half-Vasten)
    Location: Belgium
    Date: March, fourth Sunday in Lent

    HolFestCelWrld-1994, 203

Mid-Lent Sunday (Mothering Sunday)
    Location: England
    Date: March, fourth Sunday in Lent

    BkDays-1864, i. 335
    BkFest-1937, 55
    BkFestHolWrld-1970, 47
    BkHolWrld-1986, March 22, 179
    Chases-1993, 136
    DaysCustFaith-1957, 89
    DictDays-1988, 15, 76, 78, 95, 112
    DictFolkMyth-1984, 752, 1013
    FestSaintDays-1915, 50
    FolkWrldHol-1992, 127
    HolFestCelWrld-1994, 212
    RelHolCal-1993, 96
    SaintFestCh-1904, 143

Mid-Lent Sunday (Mi-Carême)
    Location: France
    Date: March, fourth Sunday in Lent

    FestSaintDays-1915, 52
    FestWestEur-1958, 35
    HolFestCelWrld-1994, 203

Mid-Lent Sunday
  Location: Italy
  Date: March, fourth Sunday in Lent

  FestSaintDays-1915, 52
  FestWestEur-1958, 92
  HolFestCelWrld-1994, 205

Mid-Lent Sunday (Bretzelsonndeg, Pretzel Sunday)
  Location: Luxembourg
  Date: March, fourth Sunday in Lent

  FestWestEur-1958, 106
  HolFestCelWrld-1994, 259

Mid-Lent Sunday
  Location: Palatinate
  Date: March, fourth Sunday in Lent

  FestSaintDays-1915, 51

Mid-Lent Sunday
  Location: Silesia
  Date: March, fourth Sunday in Lent

  DictFolkMyth-1984, 871

Mid-Lent Sunday (Mezza Quaresima)
  Location: Spain
  Date: March, fourth Sunday in Lent

  FestSaintDays-1915, 52

Mid-Lent Sunday (Mothering Sunday)
  Location: United States
  Ethnic or religious group: Episcopalian
  Date: March, fourth Sunday in Lent

  DaysCustFaith-1957, 89

Mid-Lent Sunday (Mi-Carême)
  Location: West Indies
  Date: March, fourth Sunday in Lent

  HolFestCelWrld-1994, 203

Midsommar
  See **Midsummer Day (Sweden)**

Midsummer
  Date: June 23-24, St. John the Baptist's Day

  AmerBkDays-1978, 582
  AnnivHol-1983, 83
  BkDays-1864, i. 814
  BkFest-1937, 32, 59, 125, 136, 213, 220
  BkFestHolWrld-1970, 99

  Chases-1993, 261
  DaysCustFaith-1957, 151
  DictDays-1988, 76
  DictFolkMyth-1984, 105, 157, 168, 202, 203, 253, 486,
    606, 629, 723, 747, 754, 789, 866, 871, 930, 961, 966,
    1032, 1172
  FestSaintDays-1915, 142
  FestWestEur-1958, 13, 27, 43, 68, 153, 167, 199, 235
  FolkAmerHol-1987, 215
  FolkWrldHol-1992, 336
  HolFestCelWrld-1994, 164, 206, 290, 291, 292
  RelHolCal-1993, 64, 95
  SaintFestCh-1904, 301

Midsummer
  Location: Austria
  Date: June 23-24, St. John the Baptist's Day

  BkFest-1937, 32

Midsummer (Sint Jans Vorravond)
  Location: Belgium
  Date: June 23-24, St. John the Baptist's Day

  FestWestEur-1958, 13

Midsummer
  Location: Bohemia
  Date: June 23-24, St. John the Baptist's Day

  DictFolkMyth-1984, 871

Midsummer
  Location: Brazil
  Ethnic or religious group: Roman Catholic
  Date: June 23-24, St. John the Baptist's Day, until
    June 29, St. Peter's Day

  BkFestHolWrld-1970, 101

Midsummer
  Location: Canada
  Ethnic or religious group: French-Canadians
  Date: June 23-24, St. John the Baptist's Day

  BkFestHolWrld-1970, 100
  HolFestCelWrld-1994, 292

Midsummer (Sankt Hans Aften)
  Location: Denmark
  Date: June 23-24, St. John the Baptist's Day

  AmerBkDays-1978, 583, 586
  BkFestHolWrld-1970, 101
  FestWestEur-1958, 27

Midsummer
  Location: England
  Date: June 23-24, St. John the Baptist's Day

  BkDays-1864, i.815
  DictDays-1988, 76
  DictFolkMyth-1984, 723
  FestSaintDays-1915, 148
  RelHolCal-1993, 64, 95
  SaintFestCh-1904, 301

Midsummer (Juhannus Day, St. John the Baptist's Day)
  Location: Finland
  Date: June 24; observed Saturday closest to June 24

  AnnivHol-1983, 96
  FolkWrldHol-1992, 335
  HolFestCelWrld-1994, 164

Midsummer (La Veille de la Saint Jean)
  Location: France
  Date: June 23-24, St. John the Baptist's Day

  AmerBkDays-1978, 582
  BkFest-1937, 125
  FestSaintDays-1915, 148
  FestWestEur-1958, 43
  FolkWrldHol-1992, 336

Midsummer (Sommersonnonwende)
  Location: Germany
  Date: June 23-24, St. John the Baptist's Day

  BkFest-1937, 136
  DictFolkMyth-1984, 486, 723
  FestSaintDays-1915, 148
  FestWestEur-1958, 68
  FolkWrldHol-1992, 337

Midsummer
  Location: Greece
  Date: June 23-24, St. John the Baptist's Day

  BkFestHolWrld-1970, 99
  FestSaintDays-1915, 146

Midsummer
  Location: Ireland
  Date: June 23-24, St. John the Baptist's Day

  BkFest-1937, 59
  BkDays-1864, i.815
  DictFolkMyth-1984, 202, 723

  FestSaintDays-1915, 146, 148
  FolkWrldHol-1992, 337

Midsummer
  Location: Isle of Man
  Ethnic or religious group: Manx people
  Date: June 23-24, St. John the Baptist's Day

  DictFolkMyth-1984, 203

Midsummer
  Location: Italy
  Date: June 23-24, St. John the Baptist's Day

  FolkWrldHol-1992, 337, 340

Midsummer (Ligo Feast)
  Location: Latvia
  Date: Three days including June 23-24, St. John the
  Baptist's Day

  BkFest-1937, 213
  DictFolkMyth-1984, 606
  FolkWrldHol-1992, 337

Midsummer
  Location: Lithuania
  Date: June 23-24, St. John the Baptist's Day

  BkFest-1937, 220

Midsummer
  Location: Macedonia
  Date: June 23-24, St. John the Baptist's Day

  FolkWrldHol-1992, 338

Midsummer (Dia de San Juan)
  Location: Mexico
  Date: June 23-24, St. John the Baptist's Day

  AmerBkDays-1978, 582
  BkFestHolWrld-1970, 101
  FolkWrldHol-1992, 338
  HolFestCelWrld-1994, 292

Midsummer (Jonsok)
  Location: Norway
  Date: June 23-24, St. John the Baptist's Day

  AmerBkDays-1978, 583, 586
  FestWestEur-1958, 153
  FolkWrldHol-1992, 339
  HolFestCelWrld-1994, 290

Midsummer
  Location: Paraguay
  Date: June 23-24, St. John the Baptist's Day

  FolkWrldHol-1992, 339
  See also **Sts. John and Peter, Feast of (San Juan and San Pedro fiestas) (Paraguay)**

Midsummer (Véspera de São João)
  Location: Portugal
  Date: June 23-24, St. John the Baptist's Day

  DictFolkMyth-1984, 105, 168, 754, 930
  FestWestEur-1958, 167
  HolFestCelWrld-1994, 291

Midsummer
  Location: Puerto Rico
  Date: June 23-24, St. John the Baptist's Day

  AmerBkDays-1978, 582
  FolkAmerHol-1987, 218

Midsummer
  Location: Scandinavia
  Date: June 23-24, St. John the Baptist's Day

  BkFestHolWrld-1970, 99
  Chases-1993, 261
  DictFolkMyth-1984, 723

Midsummer
  Location: Scotland
  Date: June 23-24, St. John the Baptist's Day

  BkDays-1864, i.816

Midsummer (La Víspera de San Juan)
  Location: Spain
  Date: June 23-24, St. John the Baptist's Day

  DictFolkMyth-1984, 157, 253
  FestWestEur-1958, 199
  FolkWrldHol-1992, 336, 340

Midsummer (Midsommer Day)
  Location: Sweden
  Date: Begins Friday evening before June 24

  AmerBkDays-1978, 583, 586
  AnnivHol-1983, 83
  BkFest-1937, 311
  BkHolWrld-1986, June 20, 179
  FestWestEur-1958, 215
  FolkWrldHol-1992, 341
  HolFestCelWrld-1994, 206

Midsummer (Midsommer Day)
  Location: Sweden: Rättvik
  Date: Begins Friday evening before June 24

  BkFest-1937, 311
  FestWestEur-1958, 215
  HolFestCelWrld-1994, 206

Midsummer (Mitsommer Fest)
  Location: Switzerland
  Date: June 24

  BkFest-1937, 319
  Chases-1993, 261
  FestWestEur-1958, 235

Midsummer (Kupalo Festival)
  Location: Ukraine
  Date: June 24

  HolFestCelWrld-1994, 173

Midsummer
  Location: United States
  Date: June 23-24, St. John the Baptist's Day

  AmerBkDays-1978, 583, 586
  FolkAmerHol-1987, 215
  HolFestCelWrld-1994, 292
  RelHolCal-1993, 64, 95

Midsummer
  Location: United States
  Ethnic or religious group: Neo-pagans
  Date: June 23-24, St. John the Baptist's Day

  RelHolCal-1993, 64, 95

Midsummer (Kupalo Festival)
  Location: United States
  Ethnic or religious group: Ukrainian-Americans
  Date: June 24

  HolFestCelWrld-1994, 173

Midwife's Day
  See **St. Dominique's Day**

Midwinter Bear Ceremony
  Ethnic or religious group: Delaware Indians

  DictFolkMyth-1984, 625, 710, 792

Midwinter Bear Society Dance
  Ethnic or religious group: Seneca and Cayuga Iroquois Indians

  DictFolkMyth-1984, 724

Midwinter Festival (Iroquois Indians)
See **Iroquois White Dog Feast**

Midwinter Festival (Igbi)
  Location: USSR: Shaitli, Dagestan
  Ethnic or religious group: Tsezy people
  Date: Usually observed on Sunday nearest February 5

  FolkWrldHol-1992, 97
  HolFestCelWrld-1994, 151

Midwinter Horn, Blowing the (Midwinterhoorn Blazen)
  Location: Netherlands: Overijssel
  Date: December-January, from beginning of Advent to
    Sunday following Epiphany

  BkHolWrld-1986, December 15, 179
  Chases-1993, 457
  FestWestEur-1958, 143
  HolFestCelWrld-1994, 37

Midwinter Rites, Bella Coola (Kusiut)
  Location: Canada: coastal British Columbia
  Ethnic or religious group: Bella Coola, Kimsquit, and
    other Indians
  Date: November-February

  DictFolkMyth-1984, 596, 946, 963, 1186

Miedzynarodowy Festiwal Oratoryjno-Kantatowy
See **Wratislavia Cantans-International Oratorio
  Festival (Poland: Wroclaw)**

Mihr, Festival of
  Location: Armenia
  Established: Ancient spring festival; with advent of
    Christianity, became Dyarntarach, Presentation of
    Christ in the Temple
  Date: January, forty days after Christmas

  BkFest-1937, 23
  HolFestCelWrld-1994, 206
  See also **Candlemas (Armenia)**

Mihrajan
See **Mithra, Feast of (Persia; now Iran)**

Mikkelin Paiva
See **St. Michael's Day (Finland)**

Mikkelsmesse
See **Michaelmas (Norway)**

Milan Trade Fair
  Location: Italy: Milan, Lombardy

  Established: 1920
  Date: Ten days in April

  GdWrldFest-1985, 117

Milky Way, Festival of
See **Double Seventh (China)**

Mille Miglia
  Location: Race through Italy
  Established: 1927
  Date: Three days in early May

  HolFestCelWrld-1994, 206

Mime Festival
  Location: England: London
  Established: 1977
  Date: January-February

  IntlThFolk-1979, 163

Mimes, International Creative Workshop of
  Location: Poland
  Established: 1974
  Date: September-October

  IntlThFolk-1979, 302

Mimes, International Festival of Deaf
  Location: Czechoslovakia: Brno, Moravia
  Established: 1970
  Date: Odd-numbered years during second half of November

  IntlThFolk-1979, 88

Mind and Body, Festival of
  Location: England: London
  Date: March-April

  IntlThFolk-1979, 162

Minehead & Exmoor Festival
  Location: England: Minehead, Somerset
  Established: 1963
  Date: Last two weeks in July

  IntlThFolk-1979, 170

Minehead Hobby Horse Parade
  Location: England: Minehead, Somerset
  Established: 15th century
  Date: May

  BkHolWrld-1986, May 2
  HolFestCelWrld-1994, 207

Minstrels' Carnival, Annual (Second New Year)
  Location: South Africa: Cape Town
  Date: January 2

  FolkWrldHol-1992, 10
  HolFestCelWrld-1994, 207

Mint Julep Day
  Location: England: New College, Oxford
  Date: June 1

  AnnivHol-1983, 75

Miracles at Glastonbury
  Location: England: Glastonbury, Somerset
  Established: 14th century; current version since 1970
  Date: End of June through end of first week in August

  IntlThFolk-1979, 159

Misa de Aguinaldo
  See **Christmas Carol Mass (Venezuela: Caracas)**

Misa de Gallo
  See **Christmas Season and Cock's Mass (Philippines)**

Mischief Night
  Location: Australia and New Zealand
  Date: November 4

  Chases-1993, 431

Mischief Night
  Location: England
  Established: Mid-17th century
  Date: November 4

  AnnivHol-1983, 142
  BkHolWrld-1986, November 4
  Chases-1993, 431
  DictDays-1988, 26, 77
  HolFestCelWrld-1994, 208

Misisi Beer Feast
  Location: Uganda
  Ethnic or religious group: Sebei people
  Date: Around October and at Christmas; after millet harvest, during month of Twamo

  FolkWrldHol-1992, 470
  HolFestCelWrld-1994, 208

Miss America Pageant
  Location: Atlantic City, New Jersey

  Date: Third Saturday in September

  AmerBkDays-1978, 821
  Chases-1993, 376
  HolFestCelWrld-1994, 208

Missouri Day
  Location: Missouri
  Date: Third Wednesday in October

  AnnivHol-1983, 127
  Chases-1993, 415

El Misterio de Elche, Mystery Play of Elche
  See **Assumption, Feast of the (Spain: Elche, Valencia)**

Mithra, Feast of (Mihrajan)
  Location: Persia; now Iran
  Date: Six days beginning on or near September 7

  DictFolkMyth-1984, 732

Mitsommer Fest
  See **Midsummer (Switzerland)**

Mix Roundup, Tom
  Named for: Tom Mix (1880-1940)
  Location: Sinnemahoning, Driftwood, and Mix Run, Pennsylvania
  Established: 1986
  Date: Three days in July

  HolFestCelWrld-1994, 342

Mladenci
  See **Holy Innocents' Day (Croatian people in Yugoslavia)**

Mnarja Folk Festival Day
  See **Harvest Festival (Malta: Buskett Gardens)**

Mobog
  Location: Borneo
  Ethnic or religious group: Tuaran Dusun people
  Date: Annual

  DictFolkMyth-1984, 740

Mochi No Matsuri
  Location: Okinawa
  Date: December-January, eighth day of twelfth lunar month

  FolkWrldHol-1992, 654
  HolFestCelWrld-1994, 209

Mocidade Day
  Location: Portuguese Guinea
  Date: December 1

  AnnivHol-1983, 154

Mohawk Trail Concerts
  Location: Charlemont, Massachusetts
  Established: 1970
  Date: Weekends from mid-July to mid-August

  MusFestAmer-1990, 77

Mohegan Homecoming
  Location: Norwich, Connecticut
  Ethnic or religious group: Mohegan Indians
  Established: Green Corn Festival until 1941
  Date: Third Sunday in August

  HolFestCelWrld-1994, 209

Mois de Marie
  See **Mary, Month of (France)**

Mollyockett Day
  Named for: Mollyockett (fl. 18th century)
  Location: Bethel, Maine
  Established: 1950s
  Date: Third Saturday in July

  HolFestCelWrld-1994, 209

Moment of Silence
  See **Memorial Day (Japan: Nagasaki)**

Monaco Grand Prix
  Location: Monaco: Monte Carlo
  Established: 1929
  Date: Four days in late May-June

  GdWrldFest-1985, 137
  HolFestCelWrld-1994, 209

Monday on the Hill (Lunes del Cerro or Guelaguetza)
  Location: Mexico: Oaxaca
  Ethnic or religious group: Zapotec Indians
  Date: Third and fourth Mondays in July

  HolFestCelWrld-1994, 128
  IntlThFolk-1979, 274

Monkey God Festival (Hanuman Jayanti)
  Ethnic or religious group: Hindu
  Date: March-April, full moon day of Hindu month of Chaitra

  DictWrldRel-1989, 294
  FolkWrldHol-1992, 214
  HolFestCelWrld-1994, 134
  RelHolCal-1993, 82

Monkey God Festival (Hanuman Jayanti)
  Ethnic or religious group: Vaishnavite
  Date: March-April, full moon day of Hindu month of Chaitra

  RelHolCal-1993, 82

Monkey God Festival (Hanuman Jayanti)
  Location: India
  Date: March-April, full moon day of Hindu month of Chaitra

  FolkWrldHol-1992, 214
  HolFestCelWrld-1994, 134
  RelHolCal-1993, 82

Monkey's Festival (Birthday of Ts'oi, T'in Tai Seng Yeh)
  Location: Hong Kong
  Date: August-September, 16th day of eighth lunar month

  BkHolWrld-1986, September 17, 179

Monkey's Festival (Birthday of Ts'oi, T'in Tai Seng Yeh)
  Location: Singapore
  Date: August-September, 16th day of eighth lunar month

  Chases-1993, 394
  FolkWrldHol-1992, 433
  GdWrldFest-1985, 158
  HolFestCelWrld-1994, 210

Monklands Festival
  Location: Scotland: Airdrie and Coatbridge, Lanarkshire
  Established: 1975
  Date: June

  IntlThFolk-1979, 183

Mönlam Prayer Festival
  See **Butter Sculpture Festival**

Monodrama and Pantomime, Festival of
  Location: Yugoslavia: Zemun, Serbia
  Established: 1972
  Date: April

  IntlThFolk-1979, 411

Monsanto, National Festival of
  Location: Portugal: Monsanto, Castelo Branco
  Established: 1978
  Date: Every Sunday in September

  IntlThFolk-1979, 309

Montreux Festival Internacional de Jazz
See **Jazz Festival, Montreux International (Switzerland: Montreux, Vaud)**

Moomba ("let's get together and have fun") Festival
Location: Australia: Melbourne, Victoria
Established: 1954-55
Date: Ten days in March

GdWrldFest-1985, 10
IntlThFolk-1979, 28

Moon Festival (China)
See **Mid-Autumn Festival (Chung-Ch'iu)**

Moon Festival (Korea)
See **Mid-Autumn Festival (Choosuk)**

Moore Days, Billy
Named for: Billy Moore (1840-1934)
Location: Avondale, Goodyear, and Litchfield Park, Arizona
Established: 1954
Date: Second weekend in October

HolFestCelWrld-1994, 32

Moreska
See **Korcula, Festival of (Yugoslavia: Korcula, Croatia)**

Moriones Festival
Location: Philippines: Boac, Gasan, and Mogpog, Marinduque Island
Established: 19th century
Date: March-April, Good Friday to Easter Sunday

Chases-1993, 159
GdWrldFest-1985, 152
HolFestCelWrld-1994, 211
IntlThFolk-1979, 289

Moro-Moro Play
Location: Philippines: San Dionisio, Rizal, Luzon Island
Date: April or May

IntlThFolk-1979, 290

Mortensaftenn
See **Martinmas (Denmark)**

Moscow Stars Festival
Location: USSR: Moscow, Russia
Established: 1964
Date: Nine days in May

GdWrldFest-1985, 182
IntlThFolk-1979, 374

Moshoeshoe Day
Named for: Moshoeshoe (c. 1790-1870)
Location: Lesotho
Established: 19th century
Date: March 12

AnnivHol-1983, 36
BkHolWrld-1986, March 12
Chases-1993, 127
HolFestCelWrld-1994, 212

Mother Festival, Great
See **Bona Dea (ancient Rome)**

Mother Goddess, Festival of Durga, the
Ethnic or religious group: Hindu
Date: September-October, first ten days of waxing half of Hindu month of Asvina

AnnivHol-1983, 175, 176
BkFest-1937, 161
BkHolWrld-1986, October 13
Chases-1993, 416
DictMyth-1962, i.416
DictWrldRel-1989, 280
FolkWrldHol-1992, 500
GdWrldFest-1985, 110
HolFestCelWrld-1994, 90
RelHolCal-1993, 69, 72
See also **Ballet Festival, Bharatiya Kala Kendra**

Mother Goddess, Festival of Durga, the
Location: India
Date: September-October, first ten days of waxing half of Hindu month of Asvina

AnnivHol-1983, 176
BkFest-1937, 161
BkHolWrld-1986, October 13
Chases-1993, 416
DictMyth-1962, i.416
DictWrldRel-1989, 280
FolkWrldHol-1992, 500
GdWrldFest-1985, 110
HolFestCelWrld-1994, 90
RelHolCal-1993, 72

Mother Goddess, Festival of Durga, the (Dussehra or Dasahara)
Location: Northern India
Date: September-October, first ten days of waxing half of Hindu month of Asvina

BkFest-1937, 161
BkHolWrld-1986, October 13
FolkWrldHol-1992, 501
GdWrldFest-1985, 110
RelHolCal-1993, 73

Mother Goddess, Festival of Durga, the (Durga Puja)
Location: India: Bengal
Date: September-October, first ten days of waxing half
of Hindu month of Asvina

BkFest-1937, 161
DictWrldRel-1989, 280
FolkWrldHol-1992, 500, 501
GdWrldFest-1985, 110
HolFestCelWrld-1994, 90
RelHolCal-1993, 73

Mother Goddess, Festival of Durga, the
Location: India: Delhi
Date: September-October, first ten days of waxing half
of Hindu month of Asvina

FolkWrldHol-1992, 501
GdWrldFest-1985, 110
HolFestCelWrld-1994, 90

Mother Goddess, Festival of Durga, the
Location: India: Gujarat
Date: September-October, first ten days of waxing half
of Hindu month of Asvina

FolkWrldHol-1992, 500
HolFestCelWrld-1994, 90

Mother Goddess, Festival of Durga, the
Location: India: Kulu
Date: September-October, first ten days of waxing half
of Hindu month of Asvina

GdWrldFest-1985, 110
HolFestCelWrld-1994, 90

Mother Goddess, Festival of Durga, the (Dussehra)
Location: India: Mysore
Date: September-October, first ten days of waxing half
of Hindu month of Asvina

FolkWrldHol-1992, 501
GdWrldFest-1985, 110
HolFestCelWrld-1994, 90

Mother Goddess, Festival of Durga, the
Location: India: Tamil Nadu
Date: September-October, first ten days of waxing half
of Hindu month of Asvina

FolkWrldHol-1992, 500

Mother Goddess, Festival of Durga, the
Location: India: Uttar Pradesh
Date: September-October, first ten days of waxing half
of Hindu month of Asvina

FolkWrldHol-1992, 500

Mother Goddess, Festival of Durga, the (Dasain)
Location: Nepal
Date: September-October, first ten days of waxing half
of Hindu month of Asvina

AnnivHol-1983, 175
FolkWrldHol-1992, 502
HolFestCelWrld-1994, 90
RelHolCal-1993, 69

Mother Goddess, Festival of Durga, the (Navaratri)
Location: Punjab
Date: September-October, first ten days of waxing half
of Hindu month of Asvina

FolkWrldHol-1992, 500

Mothering Sunday
See **Mid-Lent Sunday (Anglican), (England), (Episcopalian
Church in the United States)**

Mother-in-law Day
Location: Amarillo, Texas
Established: March 5, 1934
Date: Fourth Sunday in October

AnnivHol-1983, 34
DictDays-1988, 78
HolFestCelWrld-1994, 212

Mother-in-law Day
Location: United States
Date: Fourth Sunday in October

Chases-1993, 420
HolFestCelWrld-1994, 212

Mother's Day
Location: Costa Rica
Date: August 15

AnnivHol-1983, 107

Mother's Day (England)
See **Mid-Lent Sunday (England)**

Mother's Day (Antrosht)
Location: Ethiopia: Gurage province
Date: Two to three days in October or November, after rainy season ends

FolkWrldHol-1992, 507
HolFestCelWrld-1994, 12

Mothers' Day
Location: Malawi
Date: Two days beginning October 17

AnnivHol-1983, 134

Mothers' Day
Location: Panama
Date: December 8

AnnivHol-1983, 157

Mother's Day
Location: Spain
Date: December 8

AnnivHol-1983, 158

Mother's Day
Location: United States
Established: 1911
Date: Second Sunday in May

AmerBkDays-1978, 439
AnnivHol-1983, 64
BkHolWrld-1986, May 14
Chases-1993, 202
DaysCustFaith-1957, 133
DictDays-1988, 78
FolkAmerHol-1987, 183
HolFestCelWrld-1994, 212

Mother's Day
Location: Yugoslavia
Date: A Sunday in December

AmerBkDays-1978, 439
BkFest-1937, 344
FolkWrldHol-1992, 587

Mother's Day (Materice)
Location: Yugoslavia: Serbia
Date: December, second Sunday before Christmas

FolkWrldHol-1992, 587
HolFestCelWrld-1994, 59

Mot'i Ri
See **New Year's Day (Albania)**

Motor Classic, Black Hills
Location: Sturgis, South Dakota
Established: 1938
Date: First Monday in August through following Sunday

HolFestCelWrld-1994, 34

Motorcycle Week
Location: Daytona Beach, Florida
Established: 1937
Date: First week in March

HolFestCelWrld-1994, 213

Moulidi-n-nabi
See **Muhammad's Birthday (South Africa: Cape Malay)**

Mountain Laurel Festival, Kentucky
Location: Pineville, Kentucky
Established: 1931
Date: Four days in May

GdUSFest-1984, 65

Mountain Man Rendezvous
Location: Fort Bridger, Wyoming
Established: 1973
Date: September, Labor Day weekend

HolFestCelWrld-1994, 213

Mountain Pasture, Return from (Almabtrieb)
Location: German Alps
Date: September

FestWestEur-1958, 70
HolFestCelWrld-1994, 7

Mountain State Forest Festival
Location: Elkins, West Virginia
Established: 1930
Date: First Wednesday through Sunday in October

AmerBkDays-1978, 881
Chases-1993, 396
GdUSFest-1984, 209
HolFestCelWrld-1994, 213

Mountains, Festival of the (Nedeia Muntilor)
Location: Romania: Fundata, Brasov
Established: 1972
Date: Last weekend in June

IntlThFolk-1979, 323

Mount Cameroon Race
Location: Cameroon: Mount Cameroon
Date: Last Sunday in January

HolFestCelWrld-1994, 214

Mount Ceahlau Feast
Location: Romania: Durau
Date: Second Sunday in August

HolFestCelWrld-1994, 213

Mount Fuji Climbing Season
Location: Japan: Yoshida
Date: July 1-August 26

BkFestHolWrld-1970, 110

Moving Day (Flyttedag)
Location: Norway: Bergen and other large towns
Date: During autumn and April 14

BkFest-1937, 252
FestWestEur-1958, 155
HolFestCelWrld-1994, 214

Moxie Festival
Location: Lisbon, Maine
Established: 1982
Date: Second Saturday in July

HolFestCelWrld-1994, 214

Mozart, Birthday of
Named for: Wolfgang Amadeus Mozart (1756-1791)
Location: Music societies worldwide
Date: January 27

AnnivHol-1983, 14
Chases-1993, 75

Mozart Festival (Mozartfest)
Named for: Wolfgang Amadeus Mozart (1756-1791)
Location: Germany: Würzburg
Established: 1922; interrupted in 1942 and resumed 1951
Date: Three weeks in June

MusFestEurBrit-1980, 102

Mozart Festival, German (Deutsches Mozartfest)
Named for: Wolfgang Amadeus Mozart (1756-1791)
Location: Federal Republic of Germany: location
   alternates between Augsburg and other German cities
Date: Eight days during second week in June

MusFestEurBrit-1980, 100

Mozart Festival, Mostly
Named for: Wolfgang Amadeus Mozart (1756-1791)
Location: New York, New York
Established: 1966
Date: Seven weeks from mid-July to last week in August

MusFestAmer-1990, 105

Mozart Festival, San Luis Obispo
Named for: Wolfgang Amadeus Mozart (1756-1791)
Location: San Luis Obispo, California
Established: 1971
Date: Six days in late July and early August

Chases-1993, 307
MusFestAmer-1990, 41

Mozart Festival, Vermont
Named for: Wolfgang Amadeus Mozart (1756-1791)
Location: Burlington, Vermont
Established: 1973
Date: Three weeks from mid-July to first week in August

MusFestAmer-1990, 144

Mozart Week (Mozartwoche)
Named for: Wolfgang Amadeus Mozart (1756-1791)
Location: Austria: Salzburg
Established: 1956
Date: Nine days at end of January

Chases-1993, 71
MusFestEurBrit-1980, 22

Muhammadan Lent
See **Ramadan**

Muhammad's Birthday (Mawlid al-Nabi)
Named for: Muhammad (c. 570-632), founder of Islam
Ethnic or religious group: Muslim
Established: 12th century
Date: Twelfth day of Rabi al-Awwal, third Islamic month

AnnivHol-1983, 170
BkFest-1937, 237
BkFestHolWrld-1970, 79
BkHolWrld-1986, December 3
Chases-1993, 346
DictWrldRel-1989, 365, 348, 468, 498
FolkWrldHol-1992, 482
HolFestCelWrld-1994, 200
RelHolCal-1993, 63, 94

Muhammad's Birthday (Maulid)
Named for: Muhammad (c. 570-632), founder of Islam
Location: Egypt
Ethnic or religious group: Sufis and other Muslims

Muhammad's Birthday (Maulid) *(cont.)*
Date: Twelfth day of Rabī al-Awwal, third Islamic month

BkFest-1937, 237
FolkWrldHol-1992, 482

Muhammad's Birthday (Bara Wafat)
Named for: Muhammad (c. 570-632), founder of Islam
Location: India
Date: Twelfth day of Rabī al-Awwal, third Islamic month

RelHolCal-1993, 63, 94

Muhammad's Birthday (Sekartan Festival)
Named for: Muhammad (c. 570-632), founder of Islam
Location: Indonesia: Jogjakarta
Date: Twelfth day of Rabī al-Awwal, third Islamic month

DictWrldRel-1989, 365
FolkWrldHol-1992, 482
HolFestCelWrld-1994, 200

Muhammad's Birthday
Named for: Muhammad (c. 570-632), founder of Islam
Location: Iran
Date: Twelfth day of Rabī al-Awwal, third Islamic month

FolkWrldHol-1992, 483

Muhammad's Birthday (Maulidi)
Named for: Muhammad (c. 570-632), founder of Islam
Location: Kenya: Lamu
Date: Twelfth day of Rabī al-Awwal, third Islamic month

FolkWrldHol-1992, 483

Muhammad's Birthday (Ma'ulid Annabi)
Named for: Muhammad (c. 570-632), founder of Islam
Location: Libya
Date: Twelfth day of Rabī al-Awwal, third Islamic month

FolkWrldHol-1992, 484
HolFestCelWrld-1994, 200

Muhammad's Birthday (Moulidi-n-nabi)
Named for: Muhammad (c. 570-632), founder of Islam
Location: South Africa: Cape Malay
Date: Twelfth day of Rabī al-Awwal, third Islamic month

FolkWrldHol-1992, 484

Muhammad's Birthday
Named for: Muhammad (c. 570-632), founder of Islam
Location: Turkey
Date: Twelfth day of Rabī al-Awwal, third Islamic month

FolkWrldHol-1992, 484

Muhammad's Birthday (Damba Festival)
Named for: Muhammad (c. 570-632), founder of Islam
Location: Upper Volta: Dagomba
Ethnic or religious group: Mande-Dyula people
Date: Twelfth day of Rabī al-Awwal, third Islamic month

FolkWrldHol-1992, 485
HolFestCelWrld-1994, 200

Muhammad's Birthday
Named for: Muhammad (c. 570-632), founder of Islam
Location: West Africa: Bornu, and at mosques throughout West Africa
Date: Twelfth day of Rabī al-Awwal, third Islamic month

FolkWrldHol-1992, 485

Muhammad's Birthday (Game Festival)
Named for: Muhammad (c. 570-632), founder of Islam
Location: West Africa: Hausaland, Nupe, and Borgu
Date: Twelfth day of Rabī al-Awwal, third Islamic month

FolkWrldHol-1992, 485

Muharram
See **New Year (Muslim), (Morocco: Marrakech), (Pakistan), (Muslims in South Carolina), (Hausa people in West Africa), (Songhay people in West Africa), and (Susu people in West Africa)**

Mukutanik
See **Christmas (Sebei people in Uganda)**

Mule Days
Location: Bishop, California
Established: 1970
Date: Last weekend in May, Memorial Day weekend

GdUSFest-1984, 15
HolFestCelWrld-1994, 214

Mummers' Parade
See **New Year's Day (Philadelphia, Pennsylvania)**

Mumping Day
See **Doleing Day**

Münchner Opernfestspiele
See **Opera Festival, Munich (Federal Republic of Germany: Munich, Bavaria)**

Munich Fasching Carnival
See **Mardi Gras (Germany: Munich)**

Munoz Rivera Day
  Named for: Luis Munoz Rivera (1859-1916)
  Location: Puerto Rico
  Date: July 17

  AnnivHol-1983, 94
  Chases-1993, 297
  See also **Craft's Fair (Puerto Rico)**

Muny, The
  Location: Saint Louis Municipal Opera; Saint Louis, Missouri
  Established: 1919
  Date: Mid-June to end of August

  MusFestAmer-1990, 212

Mushroom Festival
  Location: Richmond, Missouri
  Established: 1980
  Date: First weekend in May

  HolFestCelWrld-1994, 215

Mushroom Harvest
  Location: USSR: Byelorussia
  Date: Late September or early October

  BkHolWrld-1986, September 12, 179

Music, Anchorage Festival of
  Location: Anchorage, Alaska
  Established: 1956
  Date: 18 days in June

  HolFestCelWrld-1994, 5
  MusFestAmer-1990, 21
  MusFestWrld-1963, 285

Music, Barcelona International Festival of (Festival Internacional de Musica de Barcelona)
  Location: Spain: Barcelona
  Established: 1962-63
  Date: Month of October

  GdWrldFest-1985, 161
  HolFestCelWrld-1994, 25
  MusFestEurBrit-1980, 134

Music, Cheltenham International Festival of
  Location: England: Cheltenham Spa
  Established: 1945
  Date: Nine days beginning first week in July

  Chases-1993, 276
  MusFestEurBrit-1980, 50
  MusFestWrld-1963, 245

Music, Easter Festival of Sacred
  See **Easter Festival of Sacred Music (Roman Catholics in Lourdes, Hautes-Pyrénées, France)**

Music, Festival of Contemporary
  Location: Lenox, Massachusetts
  Date: August

  MusFestAmer-1990, 83

Music, Gamper Festival of Contemporary
  Location: Brunswick, Maine
  Date: One week in late July

  MusFestAmer-1990, 68

Music, International Society of Contemporary
  Location: England: based in London, festival location varies
  Established: 1920s

  MusFestWrld-1963, 256

Music, Louisiana State University Festival of Contemporary
  Location: Baton Rouge, Louisiana
  Established: 1944
  Date: One week in early spring

  MusFestAmer-1990, 62

Music, Lucerne International Festival of (Luzern Internationale Musikfestwochen)
  Location: Switzerland: Lucerne
  Established: 1938
  Date: Mid-August to mid-September

  GdWrldFest-1985, 169
  IntlThFolk-1979, 354
  MusFestEurBrit-1980, 141
  MusFestWrld-1963, 207

Music, Mariposa-the Festival of Roots
  Location: Canada: Toronto, Ontario
  Established: 1961
  Date: Last weekend in June

  IntlThFolk-1979, 74
  MusFestAmer-1990, 232

Music, Mount Desert Festival of Chamber
  Location: Northeast Harbor, Maine
  Established: 1963
  Date: Five Tuesday evenings from mid-July to August

  MusFestAmer-1990, 72

Music, Opera and Theatre, Durbuy Festival of
Location: Belgium: Durbuy
Established: 1971
Date: July-August

IntlThFolk-1979, 46

Music, Saintes Festival of Ancient (Saintes Festival de Musique Ancienne)
Location: France: Saintes
Established: 1971
Date: One week in early July

MusFestEurBrit-1980, 89

Music, Venice International Festival of Contemporary
Location: Italy: Venice, Veneto
Established: 1937
Date: Second and third weeks in April

MusFestWrld-1963, 245

Music Academy of the West Summer Festival
Location: Santa Barbara, California
Established: 1947
Date: Eight weeks from last week in June to third week in August

MusFestAmer-1990, 32

Musical, Bordeaux International May (Mai Musical International)
Location: France: Bordeaux, Gironde
Established: 1949-50
Date: 16 days beginning first week in May

GdWrldFest-1985, 79
IntlThFolk-1979, 102
MusFestEurBrit-1980, 78
MusFestWrld-1963, 131

Musical, Medora
Named for: Commemorates Theodore Roosevelt (1858-1919) and his "Rough Riders," the First Voluntary Cavalry
Location: Medora, North Dakota
Date: Mid-June to Labor Day

HolFestCelWrld-1994, 201

Musical Festival of La Sainte-Baume
Location: France: Sainte-Baume, Var
Date: Two weeks in July-August

IntlThFolk-1979, 124

Musical May, Florence (Maggio Musicale Fiorentino)
Location: Italy: Florence, Tuscany
Established: 1930s
Date: Eight weeks in May and June

GdWrldFest-1985, 117
IntlThFolk-1979, 242
MusFestEurBrit-1980, 114
MusFestWrld-1963, 100

Musical Theatre, Summer
Location: Canada: Winnipeg, Manitoba
Date: July-August

IntlThFolk-1979, 64

Musical Weeks, Stresa (Settimane Musicali di Stresa Festival Internazionale)
Location: Italy: Stresa
Established: 1962
Date: Late August to late September

Chases-1993, 340
MusFestEurBrit-1980, 119

Musical Weeks of Luberon (Semaines Musicales du Luberon)
Location: France: Luberon and surrounding towns, Vauclude
Established: 1972
Date: Two weeks in July-August

IntlThFolk-1979, 110

Musical Weeks of Orleans, International (Semaines Musicales Internationale d'Orleans)
Location: France: Orleans, Loiret
Established: 1968
Date: Two weeks in November-December

IntlThFolk-1979, 115

Music and Dance, Santander International Festival of (Festival Internacional de Musica y Danza de Santander)
Location: Spain: Santander
Established: 1951
Date: July-August

GdWrldFest-1985, 163
IntlThFolk-1979, 341
MusFestEurBrit-1980, 137
MusFestWrld-1963, 169

Music and Dance Festival, Granada International (Festival Internacional de Musica y Danza de Granada)
Location: Spain: Granada
Established: 1951

Music and Dance Festival, Granada International (Festival Internacional de Musica y Danza de Granada) *(cont.)*
Date: Three weeks beginning in mid-June

GdWrldFest-1985, 162
HolFestCelWrld-1994, 215
IntlThFolk-1979, 337
MusFestEurBrit-1980, 136
MusFestWrld-1963, 165

Music and Drama, Llantilio Crossenny Festival of
Location: Wales: Llantilio Crossenny
Established: 1963
Date: First weekend in May

IntlThFolk-1979, 189

Music and Folklore of Romanians Living in Vojvodina
Location: Yugoslavia: location varies within Vojvodina
Established: 1961
Date: May

IntlThFolk-1979, 414

Music and Popular Arts, Regional Festival of
Location: Tunisia: Sfax, Sfax Region
Date: June

IntlThFolk-1979, 364

Music and the Arts, Aldeburgh Festival of
Location: England: Aldeburgh, Suffolk
Established: 1947
Date: Ten to 17 days in June or July

GdWrldFest-1985, 89
IntlThFolk-1979, 155
MusFestEurBrit-1980, 42
MusFestWrld-1963, 21

Music and the Arts, King's Lynn Festival of
Location: England: King's Lynn, Norfolk
Established: 1951
Date: Nine days in July

GdWrldFest-1985, 93
IntlThFolk-1979, 162
MusFestEurBrit-1980, 60

Music and the Arts, Norfolk and Norwich Triennial Festival of
Location: England: Norwich, Norfolk
Established: 1824
Date: Every three years in October

IntlThFolk-1979, 171

Music and the Arts, Swansea Festival of
Location: Wales: Swansea
Established: 1947
Date: Three weeks in October

IntlThFolk-1979, 190

Music and Theatre in Herrenhausen
Location: Federal Republic of Germany: Hannover, Lower Saxony
Established: 1954
Date: June-August

IntlThFolk-1979, 140

Music at Gretna
Location: Mount Gretna, Pennsylvania
Established: 1976
Date: Mid-June to early September

MusFestAmer-1990, 132

Music at La Defense
Location: France: La Defense, Paris
Established: 1975
Date: Month of June

IntlThFolk-1979, 118

Music Camp, National
Location: Interlochen, Michigan
Established: 1928
Date: Eight weeks from last week in June to mid-August

MusFestAmer-1990, 88

Music Center, Blossom
Location: Cuyahoga Falls, Ohio
Established: 1968
Date: First week in June to second week in September

MusFestAmer-1990, 122

Music Center, Brevard
Location: Brevard, North Carolina
Established: late 1940s
Date: Seven weeks from late June to mid-August

MusFestAmer-1990, 115

Music Center, Mann
Location: Philadelphia, Pennsylvania
Established: 1930
Date: Mid-June to first week in August

MusFestAmer-1990, 131

Music Center, Sewanee Summer
  Location: Sewanee, Tennessee
  Established: 1950s
  Date: Last week in June to last week in July

  Chases-1993, 266
  MusFestAmer-1990, 138

Music Competition, Queen Elisabeth International (Concours Musical International Reine Elisabeth)
  Location: Belgium: Brussels
  Established: 1937
  Date: May

  MusFestEurBrit-1980, 33

Music Festival, American
  Location: Washington, D.C.
  Established: 1943
  Date: Sunday evenings in April and May

  MusFestAmer-1990, 50

Music Festival, Aspen
  Location: Aspen, Colorado
  Established: 1949
  Date: Nine weeks from last week in June to last week in August

  Chases-1993, 263
  GdUSFest-1984, 23
  HolFestCelWrld-1994, 16
  MusFestAmer-1990, 42
  MusFestWrld-1963, 277

Music Festival, Bar Harbor
  Location: Bar Harbor, Maine
  Established: 1967
  Date: Mid-July to mid-August

  MusFestAmer-1990, 64

Music Festival, Berkshire
  Location: Tanglewood, Lenox, Massachusetts
  Established: 1934
  Date: July-September

  GdUSFest-1984, 86
  HolFestCelWrld-1994, 30
  MusFestAmer-1990, 81
  MusFestWrld-1963, 280

Music Festival, Bowdoin Summer
  Location: Brunswick, Maine

  Established: 1964
  Date: Last week in June to first week in August

  MusFestAmer-1990, 67

Music Festival, Bratislava
  Location: Czechoslovakia: Bratislava, Slovakia
  Established: 1965
  Date: October 1-15

  GdWrldFest-1985, 67
  IntlThFolk-1979, 87

Music Festival, Brno International
  Location: Czechoslovakia: Brno, Moravia
  Established: 1966
  Date: October

  IntlThFolk-1979, 87

Music Festival, Cabrillo
  Location: Aptos, California
  Established: 1963
  Date: Ten days in late July

  MusFestAmer-1990, 25

Music Festival, Cape and Islands Chamber
  Location: Yarmouth Port, Massachusetts
  Established: 1980
  Date: Three weeks from end of July to mid-August

  MusFestAmer-1990, 74

Music Festival, Carcoar Folk and Traditional Bush
  Location: Australia: Carcoar, New South Wales
  Established: 1978
  Date: A weekend in April

  IntlThFolk-1979, 9

Music Festival, Colorado
  Location: Boulder, Colorado
  Established: 1976
  Date: Mid-June to early August

  MusFestAmer-1990, 44

Music Festival, Connecticut Early
  Location: New London, Connecticut
  Established: 1983
  Date: First three weeks in June

  MusFestAmer-1990, 46

Music Festival, Cornell College Spring
  Location: Mount Vernon, Iowa
  Established: 1898
  Date: Three days in late April or early May

  MusFestAmer-1990, 59

Music Festival, Eastern
  Location: Greensboro, North Carolina
  Established: 1960s
  Date: Six weeks from late June to early August

  Chases-1993, 255
  MusFestAmer-1990, 117

Music Festival, En Gev
  Location: Israel: En Gev
  Established: 1943
  Date: April

  IntlThFolk-1979, 237
  See also **Israel Festival**

Music Festival, Golden Isles Chamber
  Location: Sea Islands, Georgia
  Established: 1988
  Date: Nine days in early May

  MusFestAmer-1990, 54

Music Festival, Grand Teton
  Location: Teton Village, Wyoming
  Established: 1962
  Date: Early July to last week in August

  Chases-1993, 233
  MusFestAmer-1990, 154

Music Festival, Idyllwild
  Location: Idyllwild, California
  Established: 1956
  Date: Last two weeks in August

  MusFestAmer-1990, 29

Music Festival, International
  Location: France: Gourdon-en-Quercy, Lot
  Established: 1972
  Date: July-August

  IntlThFolk-1979, 107

Music Festival, International Classical
  Location: Luxembourg: Echternach
  Date: Mid-June to mid-July

  IntlThFolk-1979, 265

Music Festival, Kuhmo Chamber (Kuhmon Kamarmusiikki)
  Location: Finland: Kuhmo
  Established: 1970
  Date: Ten days in late July or early August

  MusFestEurBrit-1980, 67

Music Festival, Marblehead Summer
  Location: Marblehead, Massachusetts
  Established: 1977
  Date: Five or six Sunday concerts beginning mid-July

  MusFestAmer-1990, 76

Music Festival, Marlboro
  Location: Marlboro, Vermont
  Established: 1950
  Date: Twelve weekend concerts from mid-July to mid-August

  HolFestCelWrld-1994, 195
  MusFestAmer-1990, 142

Music Festival, McCall Summer
  Location: McCall, Idaho
  Established: 1979
  Date: Third weekend in July

  MusFestAmer-1990, 221

Music Festival, Meadowbrook
  Location: Rochester, Michigan
  Established: 1964
  Date: Twelve weeks from mid-June to last week in August

  MusFestAmer-1990, 87

Music Festival, Mendocino
  Location: Mendocino, California
  Established: 1987
  Date: Two weeks in mid-July

  MusFestAmer-1990, 30

Music Festival, Menton (Festival de Musique de Menton)
  Location: France: Menton
  Established: 1950
  Date: Month of August

  MusFestEurBrit-1980, 80

Music Festival, Metz International Contemporary (Rencontres Internationales de Musique Contemporaine)
  Location: France: Metz
  Established: 1972
  Date: Five days in mid-November

  MusFestEurBrit-1980, 82

Music Festival, Monadnock
   Location: Peterborough, New Hampshire
   Established: 1966
   Date: Seven weeks from mid-July to end of August

   MusFestAmer-1990, 90

Music Festival, Monte Carlo
   Location: Monaco: Monte Carlo
   Date: July-August

   MusFestWrld-1963, 122, 125

Music Festival, Montreux-Vevey (Festival de Musique Montreux-Vevey)
   Location: Switzerland: Montreux and Vevey, Vaud
   Established: 1945-46
   Date: Six weeks beginning in late August

   GdWrldFest-1985, 171
   MusFestEurBrit-1980, 147
   MusFestWrld-1963, 205

Music Festival, New Hampshire
   Location: Center Harbor, New Hampshire
   Established: 1940s
   Date: Six weeks from early June to late August

   MusFestAmer-1990, 91

Music Festival, Newport
   Location: Newport, Rhode Island
   Established: 1968
   Date: Two weeks in July

   Chases-1993, 289
   GdUSFest-1984, 167
   HolFestCelWrld-1994, 224
   MusFestAmer-1990, 134

Music Festival, Norfolk Chamber
   Location: Norfolk, Connecticut
   Established: 1900s
   Date: Late June to mid-August on weekends

   MusFestAmer-1990, 48

Music Festival, Orford International
   Location: Canada: Magog, Quebec
   Established: 1951
   Date: Eight weeks in July and August

   MusFestAmer-1990, 160

Music Festival, Peninsula
   Location: Fish Creek, Wisconsin
   Established: 1953
   Date: Two weeks in mid-August

   GdUSFest-1984, 211
   MusFestAmer-1990, 152

Music Festival, Ravello (Festival Musicale di Ravello)
   Location: Italy: Ravello
   Established: 1953
   Date: Four to five days during first week in July

   MusFestEurBrit-1980, 116

Music Festival, Redlands Bowl Summer
   Location: Redlands, California
   Established: 1924
   Date: Tuesday and Friday evenings from late June to late August

   MusFestAmer-1990, 40

Music Festival, Ronne
   Location: Denmark: Ronne, Bornholm
   Established: 1963
   Date: Wednesdays and Fridays in July and August

   MusFestEurBrit-1980, 39

Music Festival, Santa Fe Chamber
   Location: Santa Fe, New Mexico
   Established: 1973
   Date: Seven weeks in July and August

   Chases-1993, 297
   GdUSFest-1984, 121
   HolFestCelWrld-1994, 306
   MusFestAmer-1990, 95

Music Festival, Sea
   Location: Mystic Seaport Museum, Mystic, Connecticut
   Established: 1980
   Date: First weekend in June

   HolFestCelWrld-1994, 310

Music Festival, Seoul International
   Location: Korea: Seoul
   Established: 1962
   Date: First two weeks in May

   MusFestWrld-1963, 262

Music Festival, Sevenars
Location: Worthington, Massachusetts
Established: 1968
Date: Five Sundays from mid-July to mid-August

MusFestAmer-1990, 78

Music Festival, Shenandoah Valley
Location: Orkney Springs, Virginia
Established: 1963
Date: Four weekends from mid-July to early September

MusFestAmer-1990, 147

Music Festival, Sitka Summer
Location: Sitka, Alaska
Established: 1972
Date: Three consecutive Tuesdays, Fridays, and Saturdays
 in early June

Chases-1993, 234
HolFestCelWrld-1994, 319
MusFestAmer-1990, 22

Music Festival, Spring
Location: Potsdam, New York
Established: 1930s
Date: Two days during last week in April

MusFestAmer-1990, 112

Music Festival, Stern Grove Midsummer
Location: San Francisco, California
Established: 1938
Date: Mid-June to mid-August for ten Sundays

MusFestAmer-1990, 205

Music Festival, Stockholm
Location: Sweden: Stockholm
Date: Six weeks in June-July

MusFestWrld-1963, 177
See also **Theatre, Drottningholm Court**

**Music Festival, Strasbourg International (Festival International
de Musique de Strasbourg)**
Location: France: Strasbourg, Alsace, Bas-Rhin
Established: 1932
Date: 16 days beginning first week in June

GdWrldFest-1985, 83
MusFestEurBrit-1980, 91
MusFestWrld-1963, 134

Music Festival, Telluride Chamber
Location: Telluride, Colorado
Date: Two weekends in mid-August

MusFestAmer-1990, 45

Music Festival, Toulon (Festival de Musique de Toulon)
Location: France: Toulon, Var
Established: 1951; formerly, Festival of the Royal Tower
Date: June-July

IntlThFolk-1979, 125
MusFestEurBrit-1980, 92

Music Festival, Touraine (Fêtes Musicales en Touraine)
Location: France: Tours
Established: 1963
Date: One week in late June or early July

MusFestEurBrit-1980, 94

Music Festival, Umbria Sacred (Sagra Musicale Umbra)
Location: Italy: Perugia
Established: 1947
Date: Two weeks in mid-September

MusFestEurBrit-1980, 121

Music Festival, Waterloo Summer
Location: Stanhope, New Jersey
Established: 1968
Date: Six weeks from late June through July

MusFestAmer-1990, 93

Music Festival, W.C. Handy
Named for: William Christopher Handy (1873-1958)
Location: Muscle Shoals area, Alabama
Date: First full week in August

HolFestCelWrld-1994, 364

Music Festival, Wolf Trap Farm Park Summer
Location: Vienna, Virginia
Established: 1971
Date: 13 weeks from June to first week in September

HolFestCelWrld-1994, 370
MusFestAmer-1990, 149

Music Festival, Worcester
Location: Worcester, Massachusetts
Established: 1858
Date: October and November

MusFestAmer-1990, 84

Music Festival, Yellow Barn
Location: Putney, Vermont
Established: Early 1970s
Date: Five weeks in July and August

MusFestAmer-1990, 146

Music Festival and Seminar, Moravian
Location: Winston-Salem, North Carolina
Established: 1950
Date: One week in mid-June every two or three years; location alternates

MusFestAmer-1990, 119

Music Festival of Florida
Location: Sarasota, Florida
Established: 1965
Date: Three weekends in June

MusFestAmer-1990, 52

Music Festival of Saint-Denis
Location: France: Saint-Denis, Seine
Date: May-June

IntlThFolk-1979, 123

Music from Bear Valley
Location: Bear Valley, California
Established: 1969
Date: Last week in July to second week in August

MusFestAmer-1990, 33

Music in the Mountains
Location: Nevada City, California
Established: 1982
Date: Two weeks in mid-June

MusFestAmer-1990, 34

Music Mountain
Location: Falls Village, Connecticut
Established: 1929
Date: Saturday evenings and Sunday afternoons from mid-June to early September

MusFestAmer-1990, 47

Music Northwest, Chamber
Location: Portland, Oregon
Established: 1970
Date: Mid-June to late July

MusFestAmer-1990, 128

Music of Warsaw, International Festival of Contemporary and Warsaw Autumn Festival (Warszawka Jesien)
Location: Poland: Warsaw
Established: 1956
Date: Nine days in mid-September

GdWrldFest-1985, 154
IntlThFolk-1979, 298
MusFestEurBrit-1980, 130
MusFestWrld-1963, 254

Music Program, Chautauqua Summer
Location: Chautauqua, New York
Established: 1929
Date: Late June to late August

MusFestAmer-1990, 101

Music Series, Contemporary
Location: Hungary
Date: One week in October

MusFestEurBrit-1980, 109

Music Series, Silvermine Chamber
Location: New Canaan, Connecticut
Established: 1959
Date: Four Sunday evening concerts from mid-June to mid-August

MusFestAmer-1990, 49

Music under the Stars
Location: Milwaukee, Wisconsin
Established: 1938
Date: Eight weeks from early July to mid-August

MusFestAmer-1990, 151

Music Weeks, Budapest
Location: Hungary: Budapest
Established: 1959
Date: September-October

IntlThFolk-1979, 199
MusFestEurBrit-1980, 109
MusFestWrld-1963, 145
See also **Artistic Weeks, Budapest**

Music Weeks in Drome, Contemporary
Location: France: Romans, Drome
Established: 1976
Date: Two weeks in June-July

IntlThFolk-1979, 121

Muster Day
Location: New Hampshire
Date: Sometime in June

DictDays-1988, 79

Mut l-ard, the Death of the Ground
See **Summer, First Day of (Morocco)**

Muttergottesprozessión Op d'Bildchen
See **Our Lady of Bildchen, Procession to (Luxembourg: Vianden)**

Mystery of San Guillen and Santa Felicia
Location: Spain: Obanos, Navarra
Established: 1965
Date: August

IntlThFolk-1979, 340

Mystery of the Passion
Location: Spain: Moncada, Valencia
Date: March-April, Easter Week

IntlThFolk-1979, 340
See also **Easter (Spain); Holy Week (Spain)**

Mystery Play of Elche, El Misterio de Elche
See **Assumption, Feast of the (Spain: Elche, Valencia)**

Mystery Play of Tibet
Location: Tibet
Ethnic or religious group: Buddhist
Date: Last day of the year

DictFolkMyth-1984, 777

Mystery Plays, York Festival and
Location: England: York, Yorkshire
Established: 1350; current version since 1951
Date: Every three years in June

GdWrldFest-1985, 97
HolFestCelWrld-1994, 376
IntlThFolk-1979, 181
MusFestEurBrit-1980, 64

Naag Panchami
See **Snake Festival (Hindu), (India: Bengal), and (Nepal)**

Nadam
See **Revolution Day (Mongolia)**

Nagahama Yamakyogen
Location: Japan: Hachiman Shrine, Nagahama, Shiga
Date: Two days in mid-April

IntlThFolk-1979, 257

Nagarapanchami
See **Snake Festival (southern India)**

Nagasaki Takoage
See **Kite-Flying Contest (Japan: Nagasaki)**

Nagoya City Festival
Location: Japan: Nagoya
Date: October 10-20

HolFestCelWrld-1994, 217

Nagyboldog Asszony Napja
See **Assumption, Feast of the (Hungary)**

Nagypéntek
See **Good Friday (Hungary)**

Nagyszombat
See **Holy Saturday (Hungary)**

Nairobi Show
Location: Kenya
Date: One week during September or October

BkHolWrld-1986, October 5, 179

Naltësimi i Virgjereshës
See **Assumption, Feast of the (Albania)**

Nambe Falls Ceremonial
Location: Nambe Pueblo, New Mexico
Date: July 4

IndianAmer-1989, 287, 302

Nanak's Day (Nanak Parab)
Named for: Guru Nanak (1469-1539), founder of Sikhism
Ethnic or religious group: Sikh
Date: October-November, full moon day of Hindu month of Karthika

Chases-1993, 458
RelHolCal-1993, 80

Nanakusa Matsuri
See **Seven Herbs Festival (Japan)**

Nanda Deven
Location: India: Kumaon region
Ethnic or religious group: Hindu
Date: August-September

AnnivHol-1983, 179

Napoleon's Day
Named for: Napoleon Bonaparte (1761-1821)
Location: France: the Invalides in Paris
Date: May 5

Napoleon's Day *(cont.)*

AnnivHol-1983, 62
HolFestCelWrld-1994, 218

Narak Chaturdashi
　Ethnic or religious group: Hindu
　Date: October-November, 14th day of waning half of Hindu
　month of Karthika

RelHolCal-1993, 97

Narcissus Festival
　See **New Year (Honolulu, Oahu Island, Hawaii)**

Narieli Purnima
　Location: Southern India
　Ethnic or religious group: Hindu
　Date: July-August, full moon day of Hindu month of Sravana

RelHolCal-1993, 97

Narsimha Jayanti
　Ethnic or religious group: Hindu and Vaishnavite
　Date: April-May, 14th day of waxing half of Hindu month
　of Vaisakha

RelHolCal-1993, 98

Nasreddin Hoca Festival
　Named for: Nasreddin Hoca (fl. 13th century)
　Location: Turkey: Aksehir
　Date: July

IntlThFolk-1979, 366

Natchez Spring (Fall Pilgrimage)
　Location: Natchez, Mississippi
　Established: 1932
　Date: Month-long program from early March to early April
　and for 15 days in October

Chases-1993, 120, 396
GdUSFest-1984, 101
HolFestCelWrld-1994, 218

National Agriculture Day
　Location: Farm bureaus, marketing associations, and Future
　Farmers of America in Maryland and elsewhere
　Date: First day of spring, March 21

AnnivHol-1983, 39
Chases-1993, 136

National Anthem Day
　Named for: September 14, 1814, composition by Francis Scott
　Key (1779-1843), "The Star-Spangled Banner"
　Location: Maryland
　Date: September 14

AnnivHol-1983, 118
Chases-1993, 369

National Anti-Drugs Day
　Location: England: King's College, London
　Established: 1987
　Date: March 11

DictDays-1988, 80

National Aviation Day
　Location: United States
　Established: 1939; honors Orville (1871-1948) and Wilbur
　(1867-1912) Wright
　Date: August 19

AmerBkDays-1978, 766
AnnivHol-1983, 108
Chases-1993, 335
HolFestCelWrld-1994, 18

National Boss Day
　Location: United States
　Date: October 16

AnnivHol-1983, 133
Chases-1993, 412

National Day
　Named for: November 1, 1954, revolution against French
　occupation
　Location: Algeria
　Date: November 1

Chases-1993, 428
NatlHolWrld-1968, 198

National Day
　Named for: May 25, 1810, revolution against Spain
　Location: Argentina
　Date: May 25

AnnivHol-1983, 70
Chases-1993, 219
NatlHolWrld-1968, 67

National Day
Named for: Commemorates 1798 Battle of St. George's Cay
Location: Belize
Date: September 10

AnnivHol-1983, 117

National Day
Named for: September 9, 1944, expulsion of German troops
Location: Bulgaria
Date: September 9

AnnivHol-1983, 116
NatlHolWrld-1968, 162

National Day
Location: Burma; now Myanmar
Date: December 10

AnnivHol-1983, 158

National Day
Named for: April 13, 1975, assassination of President Nagarta Francois Tombalbaye (1918-1975)
Location: Chad
Date: April 13

AnnivHol-1983, 51

National Day
Named for: June 27, 1977, independence from France
Location: Djibouti
Date: June 27

AnnivHol-1983, 85
Chases-1993, 267

National Day
Named for: July 23, 1952, end of royal rule
Location: Egypt
Date: July 23

AnnivHol-1983, 96
Chases-1993, 303
NatlHolWrld-1968, 122

National Day
Named for: September 12, 1974, end of rule of Haile Selassie (Ras Tafari, 1892-1975)
Location: Ethiopia
Date: September 12

AnnivHol-1983, 117
Chases-1993, 367

National Day
Named for: March 13, 1979, revolution
Location: Grenada
Date: March 13

AnnivHol-1983, 36
Chases-1993, 128

National Day
Named for: Commemorates birth of Shah Mohammed Riza Pahlevi (1919-1980)
Location: Iran
Date: October 26

NatlHolWrld-1968, 192

National Day (Israel)
See **Independence Day (Israel)**

National Day
Named for: Celebrated accession of Shaykh Sir 'Abdallah Al-Salim al-Sabah (1895-1965)
Location: Kuwait
Date: February 25

AnnivHol-1983, 28
Chases-1993, 110

National Day
Named for: September 1, 1969, end of royal rule
Location: Libya
Date: September 1

AnnivHol-1983, 113

National Day (Tribhuvan Jayanti)
Named for: February 18, 1951, proclamation of constitutional monarchy
Location: Nepal: Kathmandu
Date: February 18

AnnivHol-1983, 26
NatlHolWrld-1968, 26

National Day (Camões Memorial Day)
Named for: Death of Luiz Vaz de Camões (1524?-1580)
Location: Portugal
Date: June 10

AnnivHol-1983, 77
Chases-1993, 242
NatlHolWrld-1968, 83

National Day
   Named for: Union of Romania and Transylvania in 1918; observed since 1990 fall of Romanian Communist Party
   Location: Romania
   Date: December 1

   HolFestCelWrld-1994, 218

National Day
   Named for: July 12, 1975, independence from Portugal
   Location: São Tomé and Principe
   Date: July 12

   AnnivHol-1983, 92
   Chases-1993, 290

National Day
   Location: Saudi Arabia
   Date: September 12

   AnnivHol-1983, 117

National Day
   Location: Singapore
   Date: August 9

   AnnivHol-1983, 104
   Chases-1993, 323
   GdWrldFest-1985, 159
   HolFestCelWrld-1994, 218

National Day
   Named for: July 18, 1936, beginning of the Spanish Civil War
   Location: Spain
   Date: July 18

   NatlHolWrld-1968, 116

National Day
   Named for: Birth of King Bhumibol Adulyadej in 1927
   Location: Thailand
   Date: December 5

   Chases-1993, 466
   HolFestCelWrld-1994, 171
   NatlHolWrld-1968, 219

National Day
   Named for: December 2, 1971, independence
   Location: United Arab Emirates
   Date: December 2

   AnnivHol-1983, 155

National Day
   Named for: September 26, 1962, revolution against monarchical rule
   Location: People's Democratic Republic of Yemen
   Date: September 26

   AnnivHol-1983, 123

National Day
   Named for: 1962 rebellion
   Location: People's Democratic Republic of Yemen
   Date: October 14

   AnnivHol-1983, 132
   Chases-1993, 408

National Day
   Named for: September 26, 1962, overthrow of government
   Location: Yemen Arab Republic
   Date: September 26

   AnnivHol-1983, 123
   Chases-1993, 387
   NatlHolWrld-1968, 178

National Days
   Named for: October 1, 1949, founding of the republic
   Location: People's Republic of China
   Date: Two days including October 1

   AnnivHol-1983, 126
   Chases-1993, 393
   NatlHolWrld-1968, 182

National Eisteddfod
   See **Eisteddfod**

National Freedom Day
   Location: United States
   Established: 1949; commemorates February 1, 1865, signing of 13th Amendment
   Date: February 1

   AmerBkDays-1978, 134
   AnnivHol-1983, 17
   Chases-1993, 82

National Grandparents Day
   Location: United States
   Established: 1979
   Date: September, first Sunday after Labor Day

   Chases-1993, 368
   DictDays-1988, 50

National Magic Day
Named for: Commemorates death of Harry Houdini
  (1874-1926)
Location: United States
Date: October 31

AnnivHol-1983, 139
Chases-1993, 427

National Maritime Day and Merchant Marine Week
Location: United States
Established: Commemorates first transatlantic voyage by
  steam-powered vessel in 1819; proclaimed official day
  in 1933
Date: May 22

AmerBkDays-1978, 475
AnnivHol-1983, 69
Chases-1993, 217
HolFestCelWrld-1994, 195

National No Smoking Day
Location: Britain
Date: March 11

DictDays-1988, 80

National Unity Day (Prithvi Jayanti)
Named for: Commemorates founding of kingdom in 1769
  by King Prithvinarayan Shah (1730-1775)
Location: Nepal
Date: January 11

AnnivHol-1983, 7
Chases-1993, 61

Nation of Heroes
Named for: Commemorates 1475 battles led by Stephen
  the Great, Prince of Moldavia (1435-1504)
Location: Romania: Munteni de Jos, Vaslui
Date: First Sunday in July

IntlThFolk-1979, 327
See also **Razboieni, Festival of**

Nations, Festival of
Location: St. Paul, Minnesota
Established: 1932
Date: Last weekend in April

Chases-1993, 184
GdUSFest-1984, 97
HolFestCelWrld-1994, 220

Nations, Festival of
Location: Red Lodge, Montana
Established: 1951
Date: Nine days in early August

Chases-1993, 320
GdUSFest-1984, 108
HolFestCelWrld-1994, 220

Native American Cultural Festival, Red Earth
Location: Oklahoma City, Oklahoma
Date: First or second weekend in June

Chases-1993, 243
HolFestCelWrld-1994, 270

Native American Day
Location: Arizona, California, Connecticut, and Illinois
Date: Fourth Friday in September

AmerBkDays-1978, 863

Native American Day
Location: Penobscot Reservation near Old Town, Maine
Date: Late July

AmerBkDays-1978, 863

Native American Day
Location: Massachusetts
Established: 1935
Date: August 12

AmerBkDays-1978, 863

Native American Day
Location: New York
Date: September

AmerBkDays-1978, 863

Native American Day (Oklahoma)
See **Indian Day (Native American Day) (Oklahoma)**

Native American Day
Location: United States
Established: 1912
Date: Varies according to state; usually fourth Friday of
  September

AmerBkDays-1978, 863
AnnivHol-1983, 122
BkHolWrld-1986, September 23, 179

Nativity
See **Christmas Day**

Nativity of Our Lord, Feast of the
See **Christmas**

Nativity of the Sun
Location: Northern Europe
Date: December 21-25

DictFolkMyth-1984, 785

Nativity of the Sun (Mithraic Festival)
Location: Persia; now Iran
Date: December 25

DictFolkMyth-1984, 785

Nativity of the Virgin, Feast of the
Ethnic or religious group: Christian
Established: Fifth century in Jerusalem; established in
  Roman Catholic church by late seventh century
Date: September 8

AmerBkDays-1978, 822
DaysCustFaith-1957, 232
FestWestEur-1958, 70
FolkWrldHol-1992, 475
HolFestCelWrld-1994, 220
IndianAmer-1989, 289, 301
RelHolCal-1993, 98
SaintFestCh-1904, 400

**Nativity of the Virgin, Feast of the (Nativity of Our Most
Holy Lady, the Theotokas or Nativity of the Theotokas)**
Ethnic or religious group: Eastern Orthodox
Date: September 8; some churches observe on September 21

AmerBkDays-1978, 822
SaintFestCh-1904, 400

Nativity of the Virgin, Feast of the
Ethnic or religious group: Protestant
Date: September 8

SaintFestCh-1904, 400

Nativity of the Virgin, Feast of the
Ethnic or religious group: Roman Catholic
Established: Late seventh century
Date: September 8

AmerBkDays-1978, 822
SaintFestCh-1904, 400

Nativity of the Virgin, Feast of the
Location: England
Date: September 8

SaintFestCh-1904, 400

**Nativity of the Virgin, Feast of the (Pferdeweihe, Blessing
of Horses)**
Location: Germany: St. Märgen, Black Forest
Date: September 8

FestWestEur-1958, 70

Nativity of the Virgin, Feast of the
Location: Italy: Florence
Date: September 8

FolkWrldHol-1992, 475

Nativity of the Virgin, Feast of the (Virgin of the Remedies)
Location: Mexico
Date: One week beginning September 8

DaysCustFaith-1957, 232

Nativity of the Virgin, Feast of the
Location: Laguna and other pueblos in New Mexico
Date: September 8; observed with harvest, social, and
  corn dances

AmerBkDays-1978, 823
IndianAmer-1989, 289, 301

Nativity Plays
Location: Mexico: Celaya and Yuriria, Guanajuato
Date: Mid-December to January

IntlThFolk-1979, 268

Naumburg Orchestral Concerts
Location: New York, New York
Established: 1905
Date: Four concerts between Memorial Day, last Monday
  in May, and Labor Day, first Monday in September

MusFestAmer-1990, 107

Nauroz
See **New Year's Day (Afghanistan)**

Navajo Nation Fair
Location: Window Rock, Arizona
Established: 1908
Date: Second week in September, usually Wednesday
  or Thursday through Sunday

AmerBkDays-1978, 832
AnnivHol-1983, 179
HolFestCelWrld-1994, 220
IndianAmer-1989, 289

Navajo Nation Festival, Shiprock (Northern Navajo Fair)
Location: Shiprock, New Mexico
Ethnic or religious group: Navajo Indians
Established: 1924
Date: Usually first weekend in October

HolFestCelWrld-1994, 316
IndianAmer-1989, 269, 289
RelHolCal-1993, 115

Navajo Nightway and Mountain Topway Ceremonials
Location: Window Rock, Arizona
Ethnic or religious group: Navajo Indians
Date: December (date varies)

IndianAmer-1989, 290

Navajo Trails Fiesta
Location: Durango, Colorado
Established: 1965
Date: First weekend in August

GdUSFest-1984, 27

Navaratri
See **Mother Goddess, Festival of Durga, the (Punjab)**

Navasard Armenian Grape Festival
See **Assumption, Feast of the (Armenia)**

Navidad
See **Christmas (Mexico) and (Spain)**

Nauju Metu Diena
See **New Year's Day (Lithuania)**

Nav Roz
See **New Year's Day (Kashmir)**

Navy Day (Chile)
See **Battle of Iquique Day**

Navy Day (Romania)
See **Sea Celebrations (Romania)**

Naw Roz
See **New Year's Day (Iran)**

Nawruz
See **New Year (Bahá'í)**

Nazareth Baptist Church Festival
See **Zulu/Shembe Festival**

Ndok Ceremony
Location: Nigeria
Date: Every other year in November-December

FolkWrldHol-1992, 650

Nebuta Matsuri
Location: Japan: Aomori
Established: According to legend, when Sakanoue-no-Tamuramaro (758-811) stopped a rebellion
Date: August 2-7

HolFestCelWrld-1994, 222

Nebi Mousa, Feast of
Location: Israel: Jerusalem
Ethnic or religious group: Muslim
Date: March-April, Saturday before Easter

HolFestCelWrld-1994, 169

Nebraska Danish Days (Danish Ethnic Festival)
Location: Minden, Nebraska
Ethnic or religious group: Danish-Americans
Established: June 1973
Date: May-June

GdUSFest-1984, 109

NEBRASKAland DAYS
Location: North Platte, Nebraska
Established: 1965
Date: Third week in June

HolFestCelWrld-1994, 221

Nedeia Muntilor
See **Mountains, Festival of the (Romania: Fundata, Brasov)**

Needle Mass
See **Broken Needles Festival**

Neitjorsdâg
See **New Year's Day (Luxembourg)**

Nekaltuju Šventē
See **Holy Innocents' Day (Lithuania)**

Nelson Day
See **Trafalgar Day (Great Britain)**

Nembutsu Kyogen
Location: Japan: Mushio Village, Hikari-machi, Sosa-gun, Chiba
Date: Mid-July

IntlThFolk-1979, 256

Nemean Games
  Location: Ancient Greece: valley of Nemea
  Date: Probably August

  HolFestCelWrld-1994, 222

Nemoralia (Festival of Diana Jana)
  Location: Nemi; now a village in Italy
  Date: August 13

  FestSaintDays-1915, 173

Neri-Kuyo
  Location: Japan: Joshinji Temple, Tokyo
  Ethnic or religious group: Buddhist
  Date: August 16 every three years (1990...)

  HolFestCelWrld-1994, 222

Nestroy Festival (Nestroy-Spiele)
  Named for: Johann Nestroy (1801-1862)
  Location: Austria: Schwechat, Lower Austria
  Established: 1973
  Date: July

  IntlThFolk-1979, 39

Netherlands University Festival
  Location: Netherlands: Amsterdam
  Established: 1975
  Date: Every four years in December

  IntlThFolk-1979, 284

Nettle Day
  See **Shick-Shack Day**

Neujahr
  See **New Year's Day (Germany)**

Neujahrstag
  See **New Year's Day (Austria) and (Switzerland)**

Nevis Tea Meeting
  Location: Nevis
  Date: A full moon night in summer

  FolkWrldHol-1992, 408
  HolFestCelWrld-1994, 223

Newala Ceremonies
  See **New Year (Newala Ceremonies, First Fruits Festival) (Swaziland: Lozithehlezi to Gunundvwini, and Lobamba)**

New Church Day
  Named for: June 19, 1770, founding of church by Emmanuel Swedenborg (1688-1772) in Philadelphia, Pennsylvania

Ethnic or religious group: Swedenborgians, or Church of the New Jerusalem
  Date: June 19

  DaysCustFaith-1957, 148
  DictWrldRel-1989, 728
  HolFestCelWrld-1994, 223
  RelHolCal-1993, 98

New Fire Ceremony
  Location: Valley of Mexico
  Ethnic or religious group: Aztec people
  Date: Every 52 years

  DictFolkMyth-1984, 713

New Moon, Feast of (Jewish)
  See **Rosh Chodesh**

Newport Day, Matilda
  Named for: Matilda Newport (fl. 1822)
  Location: Liberia
  Date: December 1

  AnnivHol-1983, 154
  NatlHolWrld-1968, 125

Newport to Bermuda Race
  Location: From Newport, Rhode Island, to Bermuda
  Established: 1904, from New York; since 1936, from Newport
  Date: June during even-numbered years

  HolFestCelWrld-1994, 224

New Yam Festival (Odwira)
  Location: Ghana
  Ethnic or religious group: Abron, Aburi, Akan, and Asante peoples
  Date: September-October, varies in length from several days to forty days

  FolkWrldHol-1992, 448
  HolFestCelWrld-1994, 232

New Yam Festival (Odwira)
  Location: Ghana
  Ethnic or religious group: Ewe people
  Date: September

  BkHolWrld-1986, September 19, 182
  FolkWrldHol-1992, 449

New Yam Festival (Odwira)
  Location: Ivory Coast
  Ethnic or religious group: Dan, Wobe, Senoufo, Baoule, Bete, and Lobi peoples
  Date: October

  FolkWrldHol-1992, 452

New Yam Festival
  Location: Nigeria
  Date: Around the end of June

  FolkWrldHol-1992, 455

New Yam Festival
  Location: Nigeria
  Date: October 12

  AnnivHol-1983, 132

New Yam Festival (Onwasato)
  Location: Nigeria
  Ethnic or religious group: Ibo people
  Date: Around August

  FolkWrldHol-1992, 456
  HolFestCelWrld-1994, 238

New Yam Festival (Iri ji Ohuru)
  Location: Nigeria
  Ethnic or religious group: Igbo people
  Date: August-September

  FolkWrldHol-1992, 456

New Yam Festival (Eje)
  Location: Nigeria
  Ethnic or religious group: Yoruba people
  Date: Two-day festival

  FolkWrldHol-1992, 457

New Yam Festival
  Location: Nigeria: Ondo's shrine in Pobe, Benin
  Ethnic or religious group: Yoruba people
  Date: Two days in August

  FolkWrldHol-1992, 458

New Yam Festival (Egbodo Oba Ooni)
  Location: Nigeria: Oyo
  Ethnic or religious group: Yoruba people
  Date: Late June

  FolkWrldHol-1992, 459

New Yam Festival (Igun Efon Festival)
  Location: Nigeria: Oyo
  Ethnic or religious group: Yoruba people

  FolkWrldHol-1992, 460

New Yam Festival (Igun Ekun Ajinida Festival)
  Location: Nigeria: Oyo
  Ethnic or religious group: Yoruba people
  Date: Annual

  FolkWrldHol-1992, 460

New Yam Festival (Igun Luwo Festival)
  Location: Nigeria: Oyo
  Ethnic or religious group: Yoruba people

  FolkWrldHol-1992, 460

New Yam Festival (Ilaja Isu Titun)
  Location: Nigeria: Oyo
  Ethnic or religious group: Yoruba people

  FolkWrldHol-1992, 460

New Yam Festival (Ogijan Festival)
  Location: Nigeria: Oyo
  Ethnic or religious group: Yoruba people
  Date: Annual

  FolkWrldHol-1992, 460

New Year
  Ethnic or religious group: Coptic Orthodox Church
  Date: September 11

  FolkWrldHol-1992, 477
  HolFestCelWrld-1994, 69

New Year (Vaisakhi)
  Ethnic or religious group: Hindu
  Date: April-May, first day of Hindu month of Vaisakha

  AnnivHol-1983, 173, 178
  BkFest-1937, 157
  Chases-1993, 165
  DictFolkMyth-1984, 790
  FolkWrldHol-1992, 254, 255
  HolFestCelWrld-1994, 353
  RelHolCal-1993, 60, 80, 87

New Year (Muharram Celebrations)
  Ethnic or religious group: Muslim
  Date: New Year's Day is the first day of Muharram, first
    Islamic month, but celebrations may extend to the 10th
    of Muharram

  AnnivHol-1983, 170
  BkFest-1937, 236
  BkFestHolWrld-1970, 9
  BkHolWrld-1986, September 24
  Chases-1993, 258
  FolkAmerHol-1987, 19
  FolkWrldHol-1992, 365, 369
  RelHolCal-1993, 59, 96

New Year (Jamshed Navaroz or Patati, Day of Repentance)
  Ethnic or religious group: Parsis and other Zoroastrians
  Date: March 21

  FolkWrldHol-1992, 186
  HolFestCelWrld-1994, 160, 221
  RelHolCal-1993, 85

New Year (Vaisakhi)
  Ethnic or religious group: Sikh
  Date: April-May, first day of Hindu month of Vaisakha

  Chases-1993, 165
  FolkWrldHol-1992, 254
  HolFestCelWrld-1994, 353

New Year (Wüwüchim)
  Location: Northeastern Arizona
  Ethnic or religious group: Hopi and Pueblo Indians
  Date: Four days, including eve of new moon in November

  DictMyth-1962, ii.1694
  DictFolkMyth-1984, 1185
  HolFestCelWrld-1994, 373
  IndianAmer-1989, 265
  RelHolCal-1993, 122

New Year (Vaisakhi)
  Location: Bangladesh
  Date: April-May, first day of Hindu month of Vaisakha

  HolFestCelWrld-1994, 353

New Year (Losar)
  Location: Bhutan
  Date: Beginning or end of February

  FolkWrldHol-1992, 61

New Year (Thingyan Pwe, Water Festival)
  Location: Burma; now Myanmar

  Date: Mid-April, when Sun is in Aries, first-fourth days of
    Burmese month of Tagu

  AnnivHol-1983, 182
  BkHolWrld-1986, April 13
  DictMyth-1962, ii.1556
  DictFolkMyth-1984, 913, 1108
  FolkWrldHol-1992, 41, 239
  HolFestCelWrld-1994, 338
  RelHolCal-1993, 117

New Year
  Location: Cambodia; formerly Kampuchea and Khmer
    Republic
  Date: Mid-April, when Sun is in Aries

  FolkWrldHol-1992, 240

New Year
  Location: Canada
  Ethnic or religious group: Coptic Orthodox Church,
    Egyptian-Canadians
  Date: September 11

  FolkWrldHol-1992, 477
  HolFestCelWrld-1994, 69

New Year (Vaisakhi)
  Location: Ceylon; now Sri Lanka
  Ethnic or religious group: Vedda people
  Date: April-May, first day of Hindu month of Vaisakha

  DictFolkMyth-1984, 790

New Year
  Location: China
  Date: January-February, ten-day to two-week long
    celebration at the first new moon after sun enters
    Aquarius; 1-15 days of first lunar month

  AmerBkDays-1978, 146, 148
  AnnivHol-1983, 175
  BkFest-1937, 75, 77
  BkFestHolWrld-1970, 1, 9
  BkHolWrld-1986, February 13, 171
  Chases-1993, 71
  DictMyth-1962, i.555
  DictFolkMyth-1984, 224, 626, 706, 790
  FolkWrldHol-1992, 43, 56
  HolFestCelWrld-1994, 187, 188

New Year
  Location: Egypt
  Ethnic or religious group: Coptic Orthodox Church
  Date: September 11

  HolFestCelWrld-1994, 69

New Year (Enkutatash)
  Location: Ethiopia
  Date: September 11

  AnnivHol-1983, 117
  FolkWrldHol-1992, 478
  HolFestCelWrld-1994, 99

New Year (Narcissus Festival)
  Location: Honolulu, Oahu Island, Hawaii
  Established: 1950
  Date: Early January to early February

  BkFestHolWrld-1970, 26
  GdUSFest-1984, 42
  HolFestCelWrld-1994, 218

New Year (Vaisakhi)
  Location: Himalayas: pilgrimage to Shrine of Badrinath
  Date: April-May, first day of Hindu month of Vaisakha

  RelHolCal-1993, 60

New Year
  Location: Hong Kong
  Date: January-February, ten-day to two-week long
    celebration at the first new moon after sun enters
    Aquarius; 1-15 days of first lunar month

  AnnivHol-1983, 175
  FolkWrldHol-1992, 44
  HolFestCelWrld-1994, 187, 188
  IntlThFolk-1979, 197

New Year (Vaisakhi)
  Location: India
  Date: April-May, first day of Hindu month of Vaisakha

  AnnivHol-1983, 173, 178
  BkFest-1937, 157
  DictFolkMyth-1984, 790
  FolkWrldHol-1992, 254, 255
  HolFestCelWrld-1994, 353
  RelHolCal-1993, 60, 80, 87

New Year (Kalpa Vruksha)
  Location: Rural India
  Ethnic or religious group: Hindu
  Date: April

  AnnivHol-1983, 178
  RelHolCal-1993, 87

New Year (Losar)
  Location: India
  Ethnic or religious group: Buddhist Tibetan exiles

  Date: Three days, usually in February; date annually
    determined by Tibetan astrologers in Dharmsala, India

  FolkWrldHol-1992, 62
  HolFestCelWrld-1994, 185

New Year (Ugadi Parva)
  Location: India: Andhra
  Ethnic or religious group: Hindu
  Date: March-April, first day of Hindu month of Chaitra

  RelHolCal-1993, 119

New Year (Bohag Bihu)
  Location: India: Assam
  Date: April-May, first day of Hindu month of Vaisakha

  Chases-1993, 165
  HolFestCelWrld-1994, 353

New Year (Vaisakhi)
  Location: India: Bengal
  Date: April-May, first day of Hindu month of Vaisakha

  DictFolkMyth-1984, 790
  FolkWrldHol-1992, 255

New Year (Vishu)
  Location: India: Kerala
  Date: April-May, first day of Hindu month of Vaisakha

  Chases-1993, 165
  HolFestCelWrld-1994, 353

New Year (Gudi Parva)
  Location: India: Maharashtra
  Ethnic or religious group: Hindu
  Date: March-April, first day of Hindu month of Chaitra

  RelHolCal-1993, 80

New Year (Baisakh)
  Location: India: Punjab
  Date: April-May, first day of Hindu month of Vaisakha

  HolFestCelWrld-1994, 353

New Year (Galungan)
  Location: Indonesia: Bali
  Date: Ten-day celebration according to Wauku calendar
    of 210 days per year

  AnnivHol-1983, 177
  GdWrldFest-1985, 112
  HolFestCelWrld-1994, 113
  IntlThFolk-1979, 218

New Year (Sol)
Location: Korea
Date: January-February, ten-day to two-week long celebration at the first new moon after sun enters Aquarius; 1-15 days of first lunar month

FolkWrldHol-1992, 52
HolFestCelWrld-1994, 187, 189, 319

New Year (Boun Pimay)
Location: Laos
Date: Mid-April, when Sun is in Aries

AnnivHol-1983, 174
FolkWrldHol-1992, 241

New Year
Location: Malaya
Ethnic or religious group: Hindu
Date: Mid-April, when Sun is in Aries

FolkWrldHol-1992, 243

New Year (Vaisakhi)
Location: Malaya
Ethnic or religious group: Sikh
Date: April-May, first day of Hindu month of Vaisakha

FolkWrldHol-1992, 254

New Year (Vaisakhi)
Location: Malaysia
Date: April-May, first day of Hindu month of Vaisakha

HolFestCelWrld-1994, 353

New Year
Location: Mauritius
Date: January-February, ten-day to two-week long celebration at the first new moon after sun enters Aquarius; 1-15 days of first lunar month

AnnivHol-1983, 175
FolkWrldHol-1992, 55

New Year
Location: Micronesia: Satawal
Date: April, month of Ceuta

FolkWrldHol-1992, 222

New Year (Tsagan Sara, White Moon celebration)
Location: Mongolia
Date: Around February

FolkWrldHol-1992, 87

New Year (Muharram Celebrations)
Location: Morocco: Marrakech
Date: New Year's Day is the first day of Muharram, first Islamic month, but celebrations may extend to the 10th of Muharram

FolkWrldHol-1992, 369

New Year (Losar)
Location: Nepal: Bodhnath
Ethnic or religious group: Buddhist Tibetan exiles
Date: Three days, usually in February; date annually determined by Tibetan astrologers in Dharmsala, India

HolFestCelWrld-1994, 185

New Year (Bisket Jatra)
Location: Nepal: Bhaktapur
Date: Mid-April, first day of Hindu month of Vaisakha

HolFestCelWrld-1994, 33

New Year (Tet Nguyenden)
Location: New York
Ethnic or religious group: Vietnamese-Americans
Date: January-February, several days beginning first day of first lunar month

FolkAmerHol-1987, 55

New Year (Ibu Afo Festival)
Location: Nigeria
Ethnic or religious group: Ibo people
Date: March, first day of first month, Onwa Izizi, of the Ibu calendar, or determined by council of elders

BkHolWrld-1986, March 18, 178
FolkWrldHol-1992, 181
HolFestCelWrld-1994, 149

New Year (Shogatsu)
Location: Okinawa
Date: January-February, ten-day to two-week long celebration at the first new moon after sun enters Aquarius; 1-15 days of first lunar month

FolkWrldHol-1992, 55
HolFestCelWrld-1994, 187, 189

New Year (Muharram Celebrations)
Location: Pakistan
Date: New Year's Day is the first day of Muharram, first Islamic month, but celebrations may extend to the 10th of Muharram

FolkWrldHol-1992, 369

New Year (Vaisakhi)
  Location: Punjab
  Date: April-May, first day of Hindu month of Vaisakha

  RelHolCal-1993, 60

New Year (Tabaski)
  Location: Senegal, Guinée, and Sierra Leone
  Date: New Year's Day is the first day of Muharram, first Islamic month, but celebrations may extend to the 10th of Muharram

  FolkWrldHol-1992, 370

New Year
  Location: Sierra Leone
  Ethnic or religious group: Mandigo people
  Date: One and one-half days in late April or early May

  BkFestHolWrld-1970, 15

New Year (Muharram Celebrations)
  Location: South Carolina
  Ethnic or religious group: Muslim
  Date: New Year's Day is the first day of Muharram, first Islamic month, but celebrations may extend to the 10th of Muharram

  FolkAmerHol-1987, 19

New Year (Sinhala Avurudu)
  Location: Sri Lanka
  Ethnic or religious group: Buddhist and Hindu Sinhalese and Tamil peoples
  Date: Two days in April, first of Sinhala month of Bak and Tamil month of Chittrai

  AnnivHol-1983, 181
  GdWrldFest-1985, 165
  HolFestCelWrld-1994, 318
  IntlThFolk-1979, 345

New Year (Newala Ceremonies, First Fruits Festival)
  Location: Swaziland: Lozithehlezi to Gunundvwini, and Lobamba
  Date: Six days in December-January

  FolkWrldHol-1992, 467
  HolFestCelWrld-1994, 223

New Year
  Location: Taiwan
  Date: January-February, ten-day to two-week long

celebration at the first new moon after sun enters Aquarius; 1-15 days of first lunar month

  AmerBkDays-1978, 146, 148
  AnnivHol-1983, 175
  FolkWrldHol-1992, 58
  GdWrldFest-1985, 62
  HolFestCelWrld-1994, 187, 188

New Year (Songkran; Solar New Year)
  Location: Thailand
  Ethnic or religious group: Buddhist
  Date: Mid-April, when Sun is in Aries; observed April 13-15

  AnnivHol-1983, 182
  BkFestHolWrld-1970, 11
  BkHolWrld-1986, April 13
  DictMyth-1962, ii.1475
  FolkWrldHol-1992, 6, 244
  GdWrldFest-1985, 174
  HolFestCelWrld-1994, 319
  RelHolCal-1993, 116

New Year (Losar)
  Location: Tibet
  Ethnic or religious group: Buddhist
  Date: Three days, usually in February; date annually determined by Tibetan astrologers in Dharmsala, India

  BkHolWrld-1986, February 23, 179
  FolkWrldHol-1992, 62
  HolFestCelWrld-1994, 185
  RelHolCal-1993, 90

New Year (Dosmoche Festival)
  Location: Tibet: Leh and Lhasa
  Date: December-January, 28th day of twelfth lunar month; five-day festival

  FolkWrldHol-1992, 150, 658
  HolFestCelWrld-1994, 87
  See also **Storlog**

New Year (Yevmi Ashurer, Day of Sweet Soup)
  Location: Turkey
  Date: New Year's Day is the first day of Muharram, first Islamic month, but celebrations may extend to the 10th of Muharram

  FolkWrldHol-1992, 370

New Year
  Location: United States
  Ethnic or religious group: Chinese-American communities

New Year *(cont.)*
Date: January-February, ten-day to two-week long
celebration at the first new moon after sun enters
Aquarius; 1-15 days of first lunar month

AmerBkDays-1978, 146
DictFolkMyth-1984, 626
FolkAmerHol-1987, 43
HolFestCelWrld-1994, 187, 188

New Year (Jamshed Navaroz or Patati, Day of Repentance)
Location: United States
Ethnic or religious group: Parsis and other Zoroastrians
Date: March

RelHolCal-1993, 86

New Year (Tet Nguyenden)
Location: Vietnam
Date: January-February, several days beginning first
day of first lunar month

AnnivHol-1983, 182
FolkAmerHol-1987, 55
FolkWrldHol-1992, 59
HolFestCelWrld-1994, 187, 188, 335
RelHolCal-1993, 117

New Year (Tabaski or Ashura)
Location: West Africa
Date: New Year's Day is the first day of Muharram, first
Islamic month, but celebrations may extend to the 10th
of Muharram

FolkWrldHol-1992, 370

New Year (Muharram Celebrations)
Location: West Africa
Ethnic or religious group: Hausa people
Date: New Year's Day is the first day of Muharram, first
Islamic month, but celebrations may extend to the 10th
of Muharram

FolkWrldHol-1992, 370

New Year (Muharram Celebrations)
Location: West Africa
Ethnic or religious group: Songhay people
Date: New Year's Day is the first day of Muharram, first
Islamic month, but celebrations may extend to the 10th
of Muharram

FolkWrldHol-1992, 370

New Year (Muharram Celebrations)
Location: West Africa
Ethnic or religious group: Susu people
Date: New Year's Day is the first day of Muharram, first
Islamic month, but celebrations may extend to the 10th
of Muharram

FolkWrldHol-1992, 370

New Year (Midwinter Festival)
See **Iroquois White Dog Feast (Senaca, Cayuga, and other
Iroquois Indians in Canada and the United States)**

New Year, Jewish (Rosh Hashanah; Day of Blowing the Shofar)
Ethnic or religious group: Jewish
Date: September-October, first day of Jewish month of Tishri

AmerBkDays-1978, 884
AnnivHol-1983, 171
BkFest-1937, 203
BkFestHolWrld-1970, 1, 5
BkHolWrld-1986, September 18, 175
Chases-1993, 372
DaysCustFaith-1957, 244, 331, 337
DictDays-1988, 27, 56, 97, 134
DictFolkMyth-1984, 1009
DictWrldRel-1989, 155, 390, 630
FolkAmerHol-1987, 287
FolkWrldHol-1992, 476
HolFestCelWrld-1994, 277
RelHolCal-1993, 110

New Year, Jewish (Rosh Hashanah)
Location: Libya
Date: September-October, first day of Jewish month of Tishri

FolkWrldHol-1992, 476

New Year, Jewish (Rosh Hashanah)
Location: Persia; now Iran
Date: September-October, first day of Jewish month of Tishri

FolkWrldHol-1992, 476

New Year, Jewish (Rosh Hashanah)
Location: United States
Date: September-October, first day of Jewish month of Tishri

FolkAmerHol-1987, 287

New Year Harvest Festivals
Location: West Africa

DictWrldRel-1989, 9

New Year of Trees (B'Shevat or Hamishah Assar Bi-Shebat)
  Location: Israel
  Ethnic or religious group: Jewish
  Date: January-February, 15th of Jewish month of Shevat

  AnnivHol-1983, 172
  BkFest-1937, 206
  BkFestHolWrld-1970, 18
  BkHolWrld-1986, January 29, 175
  Chases-1993, 89
  DaysCustFaith-1957, 40
  FolkWrldHol-1992, 40
  HolFestCelWrld-1994, 32
  RelHolCal-1993, 63

New Year Purification before Planting
  Location: Volta: Dudulsi, a Gurunsi village in Lela
  Date: April, just before planting

  FolkWrldHol-1992, 229

New Year's Celebration (Kuningen, Feast of All Souls)
  Location: Indonesia: Bali
  Ethnic or religious group: Hindu
  Date: Final day of ten-day New Year's celebration, Galungan; every 210 days

  IntlThFolk-1979, 219
  See also **New Year (Galungan) (Indonesia: Bali)**

New Year's Day
  Date: January 1

  AmerBkDays-1978, 2
  AnnivHol-1983, 2
  BkDays-1864, i. 27
  BkFest-1937, 3, 14, 22, 29, 37, 51, 65, 77, 84, 94, 101, 110, 118, 131, 143, 157, 165, 178, 194, 203, 210, 218, 236, 240, 248, 266, 273, 288, 297, 307, 316, 326, 335
  BkFestHolWrld-1970, 2
  BkHolWrld-1986, January 1
  Chases-1993, 51
  DaysCustFaith-1957, 17, 355
  DictDays-1988, 81, 134
  DictFolkMyth-1984, 181, 790, 791, 950, 1063
  FestSaintDays-1915, 1, 2, 4, 7
  FestWestEur-1958, 3, 22, 32, 54, 87, 105, 121, 150, 160, 188, 210, 225
  FolkAmerHol-1987, 1
  FolkWrldHol-1992, 1, 225
  HolFestCelWrld-1994, 106, 171, 221, 225, 332

New Year's Day
  Ethnic or religious group: Aztec people
  Date: February 2

  DictFolkMyth-1984, 791

New Year's Day (Nawruz)
  Ethnic or religious group: Bahá'í
  Date: March 21, vernal equinox

  AnnivHol-1983, 40
  Chases-1993, 137
  RelHolCal-1993, 98

New Year's Day
  Ethnic or religious group: Eskimos
  Date: Autumn

  DictFolkMyth-1984, 791

New Year's Day
  Ethnic or religious group: Hopi Indians
  Date: November

  DictFolkMyth-1984, 791

New Year's Day
  Ethnic or religious group: Seneca Iroquois Indians
  Date: February

  DictFolkMyth-1984, 791

New Year's Day (Nauroz)
  Location: Afghanistan
  Date: March 21, vernal equinox

  FolkWrldHol-1992, 186
  HolFestCelWrld-1994, 221

New Year's Day
  Location: Sitka, Alaska
  Ethnic or religious group: Eskimos
  Date: January 1

  AmerBkDays-1978, 8

New Year's Day (Mot'i Ri)
  Location: Albania
  Date: January 1

  BkFest-1937, 3

New Year's Day (Gaghant, Nor Dary)
  Location: Armenia
  Date: January 1

  BkFest-1937, 22

New Year's Day (Neujahrstag)
  Location: Austria
  Date: January 1

  BkFest-1937, 29
  FolkWrldHol-1992, 1

New Year's Day
Location: Babylon

DictFolkMyth-1984, 676

New Year's Day (Nieuwjaarsdag)
Location: Belgium
Date: January 1

BkFest-1937, 37
FestWestEur-1958, 3
FolkWrldHol-1992, 1

New Year's Day
Location: Bohemia
Date: January 1

DictFolkMyth-1984, 950

New Year's Day
Location: Eastern Bolivia
Ethnic or religious group: Mojo Indians
Date: When the Pleiades appear

DictFolkMyth-1984, 875

New Year's Day
Location: Brazil
Date: January 1

BkFestHolWrld-1970, 17

New Year's Day (Nova Godina)
Location: Bulgaria
Date: January 1

BkFest-1937, 65

New Year's Day
Location: Northwest California
Ethnic or religious group: Northwest California Indians
Date: Late July

DictFolkMyth-1984, 791

New Year's Day (Nový Rok)
Location: Czechoslovakia
Date: January 1

BkFest-1937, 84

New Year's Day (Nytaarsdag)
Location: Denmark
Date: January 1

BkFest-1937, 94
BkFestHolWrld-1970, 2
FestWestEur-1958, 22

New Year's Day
Location: Ecuador
Date: January 1

BkFestHolWrld-1970, 16

New Year's Day (First-Foot Day)
Location: England
Date: January 1

AmerBkDays-1978, 5
AnnivHol-1983, 2
BkDays-1864, i.27
DaysCustFaith-1957, 18
DictDays-1988, 81
FestSaintDays-1915, 2
FolkWrldHol-1992, 3
HolFestCelWrld-1994, 106

New Year's Day (Uus Aasta)
Location: Estonia
Date: January 1

BkFest-1937, 101
DictFolkMyth-1984, 791

New Year's Day (Uudenvuoden Päivä)
Location: Finland
Date: January 1

BkFest-1937, 110

New Year's Day (Le Jour de l'An or Le Jour des Étrennes)
Location: France
Date: January 1

AmerBkDays-1978, 6
BkDays-1864, i.33
BkFest-1937, 118
DictFolkMyth-1984, 181, 791
FestWestEur-1958, 32
FolkWrldHol-1992, 2

New Year's Day (Neujahr)
Location: Germany
Date: January 1

BkFest-1937, 131
BkFestHolWrld-1970, 3
FestWestEur-1958, 54

New Year's Day (Protochroneea)
Location: Greece
Date: January 1

BkFest-1937, 143
BkFestHolWrld-1970, 4
BkHolWrld-1986, January 1

New Year's Day
  Location: Haiti
  Date: January 1

  FolkWrldHol-1992, 4

New Year's Day (Ujév Napja)
  Location: Hungary
  Date: January 1

  BkFest-1937, 165

New Year's Day (No Ruz or Naw Roz)
  Location: Iran
  Date: March 21, vernal equinox

  BkFestHolWrld-1970, 7
  BkHolWrld-1986, March 21
  Chases-1993, 137
  FolkWrldHol-1992, 186
  HolFestCelWrld-1994, 221

New Year's Day (Capo d'Anno)
  Location: Italy
  Date: January 1

  BkFest-1937, 178
  FestWestEur-1958, 87

New Year's Day (Sacred Mysteries Performance)
  Location: Italy: Como
  Date: January 1

  BkFest-1937, 178

New Year's Day (Oshagatsu)
  Location: Japan
  Date: January 1

  BkFest-1937, 194
  BkFestHolWrld-1970, 2, 14
  Chases-1993, 50
  DictMyth-1962, i.555
  DictFolkMyth-1984, 181, 540, 730, 790, 871
  DictWrldRel-1989, 374
  FolkWrldHol-1992, 45, 50
  HolFestCelWrld-1994, 240
  RelHolCal-1993, 79

New Year's Day (Nav Roz)
  Location: Kashmir
  Date: March-May; Water Festival from Hindu months of Chaitra to Vaisakha

  FolkWrldHol-1992, 187

New Year's Day (Jauna Gada Diena)
  Location: Latvia
  Date: January 1

  BkFest-1937, 210

New Year's Day (Nauju Metu Diena)
  Location: Lithuania
  Date: January 1

  BkFest-1937, 218

New Year's Day (Neitjorsdâg)
  Location: Luxembourg
  Date: January 1

  FestWestEur-1958, 105

New Year's Day
  Location: Mexico
  Date: January 1

  BkFestHolWrld-1970, 17

New Year's Day (Kissing Day)
  Location: Minnesota
  Ethnic or religious group: Chippewa Indians
  Date: January 1

  FolkAmerHol-1987, 8
  HolFestCelWrld-1994, 171

New Year's Day
  Location: Montana
  Ethnic or religious group: Crow Indians
  Date: January 1

  AmerBkDays-1978, 8

New Year's Day (Nieuwjaarsdag)
  Location: Netherlands
  Date: January 1

  BkFest-1937, 240
  FestWestEur-1958, 121

New Year's Day
  Location: Taos, Sandia, and other New Mexico pueblos
  Date: January 1

  AmerBkDays-1978, 8
  DictFolkMyth-1984, 791

New Year's Day
  Location: Nigeria
  Ethnic or religious group: Ibibio people
  Date: End of Ndok season

  FolkWrldHol-1992, 4

New Year's Day (Nyttårsdag)
  Location: Norway
  Date: January 1

  BkFest-1937, 248
  FestWestEur-1958, 150

New Year's Day
  Location: Paraguay
  Date: January 1

  FolkWrldHol-1992, 4

New Year's Day (Mummers Parade)
  Location: Philadelphia, Pennsylvania
  Established: 1876
  Date: January 1

  AmerBkDays-1978, 14
  AnnivHol-1983, 2
  FolkAmerHol-1987, 3
  HolFestCelWrld-1994, 225

New Year's Day
  Location: Poland
  Date: January 1

  FolkWrldHol-1992, 4

New Year's Day
  Location: Polynesia
  Date: When the Pleiades appear

  DictFolkMyth-1984, 875

New Year's Day (Anno Novo)
  Location: Portugal
  Date: January 1

  BkFest-1937, 266
  BkFestHolWrld-1970, 3, 5
  FestWestEur-1958, 160

New Year's Day (Anul Nou)
  Location: Romania
  Date: January 1

  BkFest-1937, 273

New Year's Day (Novyi God)
  Location: Russia
  Date: January 1

  BkFest-1937, 288
  FolkWrldHol-1992, 7
  HolFestCelWrld-1994, 225

New Year's Day
  Location: Scotland
  Date: January 1

  AmerBkDays-1978, 5
  BkDays-1864, i.28
  BkFest-1937, 51
  DictDays-1988, 81
  FestSaintDays-1915, 1, 4
  FolkWrldHol-1992, 3
  HolFestCelWrld-1994, 106

New Year's Day
  Location: Sicily
  Date: January 1

  FolkWrldHol-1992, 6

New Year's Day
  Location: South Africa
  Ethnic or religious group: Kaffir people
  Date: When Pleiades appear

  DictFolkMyth-1984, 875

New Year's Day (Año Nuevo)
  Location: Spain
  Date: January 1

  BkFest-1937, 297
  BkFestHolWrld-1970, 5
  DictFolkMyth-1984, 1063
  FestWestEur-1958, 188
  FolkWrldHol-1992, 6

New Year's Day
  Location: Surinam
  Date: January 1

  FolkWrldHol-1992, 6

New Year's Day (Nyårsdagen)
  Location: Sweden
  Date: January 1

  BkFest-1937, 307
  DictFolkMyth-1984, 791
  FestWestEur-1958, 210

New Year's Day (Neujahrstag)
  Location: Switzerland
  Date: January 1

  BkFest-1937, 316
  FestWestEur-1958, 225

New Year's Day ('Id Ras al-Sanah)
  Location: Syria
  Date: January 1

  BkFest-1937, 326

New Year's Day (Ta'u Fo'ou)
  Location: Tonga
  Date: January 1

  FolkWrldHol-1992, 7
  HolFestCelWrld-1994, 332

New Year's Day
  Location: Trinidad
  Date: January 1

  FolkWrldHol-1992, 7

New Year's Day (First-Foot Day in parts of the U.S.)
  Location: United States
  Date: January 1

  AmerBkDays-1978, 6, 8
  AnnivHol-1983, 2
  BkFest-1937, 14
  BkFestHolWrld-1970, 2
  DictFolkMyth-1984, 791
  FolkAmerHol-1987, 1
  HolFestCelWrld-1994, 106, 225

New Year's Day
  Location: United States
  Ethnic or religious group: Greek-Americans
  Date: January 1

  BkFest-1937, 143

New Year's Day
  Location: Wales
  Date: January 1

  FolkWrldHol-1992, 3

New Year's Day (Nova Godina)
  Location: Yugoslavia
  Date: January 1

  BkFest-1937, 335
  FolkWrldHol-1992, 8

New Year's Eve
  Date: December 31

  AmerBkDays-1978, 1166
  AnnivHol-1983, 166, 167
  BkDays-1864, ii. 787

  BkFest-1937, 63, 99, 117, 306, 335
  BkHolWrld-1986, December 31
  Chases-1993, 487
  DaysCustFaith-1957, 325
  DictDays-1988, 81, 84, 129
  DictFolkMyth-1984, 123, 842, 1100
  FestSaintDays-1915, 256
  FestWestEur-1958, 21, 30, 84, 149, 159, 187, 209, 242
  FolkWrldHol-1992, 647
  GdWrldFest-1985, 168
  HolFestCelWrld-1994, 107, 225, 300

New Year's Eve
  Location: Armenia
  Date: December 31

  FolkWrldHol-1992, 647
  HolFestCelWrld-1994, 226

New Year's Eve
  Location: Austria
  Date: December 31

  AmerBkDays-1978, 1166

New Year's Eve
  Location: Belgium
  Date: December 31

  FestWestEur-1958, 21
  See also **St. Sylvester's Day**

New Year's Eve
  Location: Bolivia
  Date: December 31

  FolkWrldHol-1992, 647

New Year's Eve
  Location: Brazil
  Ethnic or religious group: Umbanda religion
  Date: January 31

  HolFestCelWrld-1994, 226

New Year's Eve (Nytårsaften)
  Location: Denmark
  Date: December 31

  FestWestEur-1958, 30
  HolFestCelWrld-1994, 225

New Year's Eve
  Location: Ecuador
  Date: December 31

  BkHolWrld-1986, December 31

New Year's Eve
  Location: England
  Date: December 31

  AmerBkDays-1978, 1166
  BkDays-1864, ii.787
  DictDays-1988, 81, 84
  FolkWrldHol-1992, 648
  HolFestCelWrld-1994, 225

New Year's Eve (Hogmanay)
  Location: Northern England and Scotland
  Date: December 31

  AnnivHol-1983, 167
  BkDays-1864, ii. 788
  BkFest-1937, 63
  BkHolWrld-1986, December 31
  Chases-1993, 487
  DictDays-1988, 56, 81, 84
  DictFolkMyth-1984, 181, 499, 791
  FolkWrldHol-1992, 651
  HolFestCelWrld-1994, 140, 225

New Year's Eve (Uudenvuoden)
  Location: Finland
  Date: December 31

  BkFest-1937, 117

New Year's Eve
  Location: Germany
  Date: December 31

  AmerBkDays-1978, 1166
  FestWestEur-1958, 84
  FolkWrldHol-1992, 648
  See also **Silvesterabend**

New Year's Eve
  Location: Iceland
  Date: December 31

  FolkWrldHol-1992, 648
  HolFestCelWrld-1994, 225

New Year's Eve
  Location: Ireland
  Date: December 31

  FolkWrldHol-1992, 649

New Year's Eve
  Location: Italy
  Date: December 31

  FolkWrldHol-1992, 649

New Year's Eve
  Location: Italy
  Ethnic or religious group: Neapolitan people
  Date: December 31

  HolFestCelWrld-1994, 226

New Year's Eve (Omisoka)
  Location: Japan
  Date: December 31

  AnnivHol-1983, 166
  BkFest-1937, 201
  Chases-1993, 486
  DictFolkMyth-1984, 123, 1100
  FolkWrldHol-1992, 42, 649
  HolFestCelWrld-1994, 226, 237

New Year's Eve
  Location: Macedonia
  Date: December 31

  DictFolkMyth-1984, 842

New Year's Eve
  Location: Mexico
  Date: December 31

  FolkWrldHol-1992, 649

New Year's Eve (Noche de Pedimento, Wishing Night)
  Location: Mexico: Mitla, Oaxaca
  Ethnic or religious group: Indians
  Date: December 31

  AnnivHol-1983, 167

New Year's Eve (Oudejaars Avond)
  Location: Netherlands
  Date: December 31

  FestWestEur-1958, 149
  FolkWrldHol-1992, 650

New Year's Eve
  Location: Nigeria
  Date: December 31

  FolkWrldHol-1992, 650
  See also **Ndok Ceremony**

New Year's Eve (Nytaarsaften)
  Location: Norway
  Date: December 31

  BkFest-1937, 99
  BkHolWrld-1986, December 31
  FestWestEur-1958, 159
  FolkWrldHol-1992, 647

New Year's Eve (Véspera de Ano Novo)
  Location: Portugal
  Date: December 31

  FestWestEur-1958, 187

New Year's Eve
  Location: Romania
  Date: December 31

  FolkWrldHol-1992, 650
  HolFestCelWrld-1994, 226

New Year's Eve
  Location: Russia
  Date: December 31

  FolkWrldHol-1992, 651

New Year's Eve
  Location: Scandinavia
  Date: December 31

  AmerBkDays-1978, 1167

New Year's Eve
  Location: Serbia
  Date: December 31

  BkFest-1937, 335

New Year's Eve (Noche Vieja)
  Location: Spain
  Date: December 31

  BkFest-1937, 306
  BkHolWrld-1986, December 31
  FestWestEur-1958, 209

New Year's Eve (Silversterabend)
  Location: Switzerland
  Ethnic or religious group: Protestant
  Established: 1582
  Date: December 31

  FestWestEur-1958, 242
  GdWrldFest-1985, 168
  HolFestCelWrld-1994, 300

New Year's Eve
  Location: United States
  Date: December 31

  AmerBkDays-1978, 1166
  DaysCustFaith-1957, 325
  HolFestCelWrld-1994, 107, 225

New Year's Eve (Watch Night Service)
  Location: United States
  Ethnic or religious group: Methodist, Baptist, and
    Presbyterian churches
  Established: 1770
  Date: December 31

  AnnivHol-1983, 167
  DaysCustFaith-1957, 325
  DictDays-1988, 129

New Year's Eve (First Night)
  Location: Huntington, West Virginia, Boston,
    Massachusetts, Hartford, Connecticut, and Waynesboro,
    Virginia
  Date: December 31

  Chases-1993, 486
  HolFestCelWrld-1994, 107

New York City Marathon
  Location: New York, New York
  Established: 1970
  Date: First Sunday in November

  Chases-1993, 434
  HolFestCelWrld-1994, 226

New York Philharmonic Free Outdoor Park Concerts
  Location: New York, New York
  Established: 1918
  Date: Three weeks in August

  MusFestAmer-1990, 108

New Zealand Day (Waitangi)
  Named for: February 6, 1840, treaty signed between
    Maoris and Europeans
  Location: New Zealand
  Date: February 6

  AnnivHol-1983, 20
  Chases-1993, 88
  DictDays-1988, 127
  HolFestCelWrld-1994, 361
  NatlHolWrld-1968, 24

Nganja, Feast of
  Location: Angola
  Date: April

  FolkWrldHol-1992, 444
  HolFestCelWrld-1994, 227

Nickanan Night
  See **Mardi Gras (England)**

Nicosia Festival
   Location: Cyprus: Nicosia
   Established: 1976
   Date: Two to four weeks in May or June

   IntlThFolk-1979, 83

Nieuwjaarsdag
   See **New Year's Day (Belgium) and (Netherlands)**

Night Journey of Muhammad (Laylat al-Mi'raj)
   Named for: Ascension of Muhammad (c. 570-632)
      into heaven
   Ethnic or religious group: Muslim
   Date: 27th of Rajab, seventh Islamic month

   AnnivHol-1983, 170
   BkHolWrld-1986, April 29
   Chases-1993, 69
   FolkWrldHol-1992, 101
   HolFestCelWrld-1994, 178
   RelHolCal-1993, 89

Night Journey of Muhammad (Lélé-I-Mirach)
   Named for: Ascension of Muhammad (c. 570-632)
      into heaven
   Location: Turkey
   Date: 27th of Rajab, seventh Islamic month

   FolkWrldHol-1992, 101

Night of Forgiveness (Laylat al-Bara'ah)
   Ethnic or religious group: Muslim
   Date: 15th of Shaban, eighth Islamic month

   BkHolWrld-1986, May 13
   FolkWrldHol-1992, 154
   HolFestCelWrld-1994, 313
   RelHolCal-1993, 113

Night of Forgiveness (Laylat al-Bara'ah)
   Location: Azerbaijan
   Date: 15th of Shaban, eighth Islamic month

   FolkWrldHol-1992, 154

Night of Forgiveness (Shaaban or Shab-i-Barat)
   Location: India
   Date: 15th of Shaban, eighth Islamic month

   BkHolWrld-1986, May 13
   FolkWrldHol-1992, 154
   HolFestCelWrld-1994, 313
   RelHolCal-1993, 113

Night of Forgiveness (Shab-i-Barat or Shaban)
   Location: Iran
   Date: 15th of Shaban, eighth Islamic month

   FolkWrldHol-1992, 154

Night of Forgiveness (Shab-i-Barat)
   Location: Pakistan
   Date: 15th of Shaban, eighth Islamic month

   BkHolWrld-1986, May 13
   FolkWrldHol-1992, 155
   HolFestCelWrld-1994, 313
   RelHolCal-1993, 113

Night of Forgiveness (Berat Kandili or Lélé-Bereat)
   Location: Turkey
   Date: 15th of Shaban, eighth Islamic month

   FolkWrldHol-1992, 155

Night of Power or Destiny (Laylat al-Qadr)
   Named for: Commemorates revelation of the Koran to
      Muhammad (c. 570-632) in 610
   Ethnic or religious group: Muslim
   Date: One of the last ten days of Ramadan, ninth Islamic
      month; usually observed on the 27th

   AnnivHol-1983, 171
   BkHolWrld-1986, June 23
   Chases-1993, 135
   DictWrldRel-1989, 661
   FolkWrldHol-1992, 163, 167, 169, 171, 172
   HolFestCelWrld-1994, 178

Night of Power (Laylat il-Qader)
   Named for: Commemorates revelation of the Koran to
      Muhammad (c. 570-632) in 610
   Location: Egypt
   Date: One of the last ten days of Ramadan, ninth Islamic
      month; usually observed on the 27th

   FolkWrldHol-1992, 163

Night of Power (Lailat alqadr)
   Named for: Commemorates revelation of the Koran to
      Muhammad (c. 570-632) in 610
   Location: Lebanon
   Date: One of the last ten days of Ramadan, ninth Islamic
      month; usually observed on the 27th

   FolkWrldHol-1992, 167

Night of Power (Lai-Lai-Tu-Gadri, Day of Light)
Named for: Commemorates revelation of the Koran to
Muhammad (c. 570-632) in 610
Location: Sierra Leone
Established: Lanterns Festival since 1930s
Date: Observed 30th of Ramadan

FolkWrldHol-1992, 169
HolFestCelWrld-1994, 178

Night of Power or Destiny (Lélé-I-Kadir)
Named for: Commemorates revelation of the Koran to
Muhammad (c. 570-632) in 610
Location: Turkey
Date: Observed 27th of Ramadan

FolkWrldHol-1992, 171

Night of Power or Destiny (Lailat al-Qadr)
Named for: Commemorates revelation of the Koran to
Muhammad (c. 570-632) in 610
Location: West Africa
Date: One of the last ten days of Ramadan, ninth Islamic
month; usually observed on the 27th

FolkWrldHol-1992, 172

Night of the Candle Ceremony
See **All Souls' Day (Pala and Ricon Indian reservations
near Oceanside, California)**

Night of the Radishes and Nativity Festival
See **Christmas Festival (Oaxaca, Mexico)**

Night of the Shooting Stars (The Perseids Meteor Shower)
Location: Observers everywhere but at the South Pole
Established: 830 A.D.
Date: August 11

BkHolWrld-1986, August 11
Chases-1993, 303
HolFestCelWrld-1994, 227

**Nights of Bourgogne, Festival of the (Festival des Nuits
de Bourgogne)**
Location: France: Dijon, Cote-d'Or
Established: 1958
Date: Odd-numbered years in June-July

IntlThFolk-1979, 105

Nights of the Enclave (Nuits de l'Enclave des Papes)
Location: France: Valreas, Vaucluse
Established: 1964

Date: July-August

IntlThFolk-1979, 127

Night Watch (La Retraite aux Flambeaux)
Location: France
Date: July 13, eve of Bastille Day

AnnivHol-1983, 93
BkFest-1937, 125
Chases-1993, 290
HolFestCelWrld-1994, 227
See also **Bastille Day**

Niiname-Sai, Festival of
Location: Japan
Date: November 23

BkFest-1937, 201

Nile, Festival of the
Location: Egypt: Luxor
Established: 1979
Date: Spring

IntlThFolk-1979, 93

Ni-Mi-Win Celebration
Location: Duluth, Minnesota
Ethnic or religious group: Ojibwa Indians
Date: Third weekend in August

IndianAmer-1989, 152

Nine Imperial Gods, Festival of
Location: Singapore
Date: September-October, ninth day of ninth lunar month

Chases-1993, 419
FolkWrldHol-1992, 497
HolFestCelWrld-1994, 228

Nineteen-Day Feast
Ethnic or religious group: Bahá'í
Date: First day of each of 19 months in Bahá'í calendar

RelHolCal-1993, 99

Nippy Lug Day
Location: Northern England and Scotland: Westmorland
and other areas
Date: February-March, Friday after Ash Wednesday

DictDays-1988, 82
HolFestCelWrld-1994, 228

Nirjala Ekadashi
Ethnic or religious group: Hindu
Date: May-June, eleventh day of waxing half of Hindu
  month of Jyeshta

RelHolCal-1993, 99

Nisei Week
Location: Little Tokyo, Los Angeles, California
Ethnic or religious group: Japanese-Americans
Established: 1940s
Date: August

HolFestCelWrld-1994, 228

Nja Festival
Location: Cameroon
Ethnic or religious group: Bamum people
Date: During the dry season, December or early January

FolkWrldHol-1992, 446

Noaptea de Crăciun, Ajunul Crăciunului
See **Christmas Eve (Romania)**

Noche Buena
See **Christmas Eve (Mexico) and (Spain)**

Noche de Pedimento
See **New Year's Eve (Wishing Night) (Mexico: Mitla, Oaxaca)**

Noche Vieja
See **New Year's Eve (Spain)**

Noël
See **Christmas (France)**

Nomaoi Matsuri
See **Horse Festival, Wild (Japan: Honshu)**

Nones
See **Ides**

Nordic Fest
Location: Decorah, Iowa
Established: 1967
Date: Last full weekend in July

GdUSFest-1984, 55

Norsk Høstfest
Location: Minot, North Dakota
Ethnic or religious group: Scandinavian-Americans
Established: 1978
Date: Five days in October

HolFestCelWrld-1994, 228

Northern Games
Location: Canada: Inuvik area, Northwest Territories
Ethnic or religious group: Inuit people and Indians of Alaska,
  Yukon, Labrador and the Northwest territories
Established: 1970
Date: Four days in mid-July

GdWrldFest-1985, 42
HolFestCelWrld-1994, 229

Northern Navajo Fair
See **Navajo Nation Festival, Shiprock (Navajo Indians
  in Shiprock, New Mexico)**

Noruz
See **New Year's Day (Iran)**

Norway, Festival of Northern
Location: Norway: Harstad
Established: 1965
Date: June

IntlThFolk-1979, 287

Nossa Senhora dos Milagres or Festa de Serreta
See **Our Lady of Miracles (Roman Catholic Azorean
  Portuguese people in Gustine, California) and (Portugal:
  Azores)**

Nossa Senhora dos Navegantes
See **Assumption, Feast of the (Brazil: São Paulo)**

Nossa Senhora dos Remédios, Pardon of
See **Pilgrimage to the Sanctuary of Our Lady of the
  Remedies (Portugal: Lamego, Viseu)**

Notre Dame de la Prospérité
See **Annunciation, Feast of the (Belgium)**

Notre Dame de Mars
See **Annunciation, Feast of the (France)**

Nottingham Festival
Location: England: Nottingham, Nottinghamshire
Established: 1974
Date: June

IntlThFolk-1979, 171

Nova Godina
See **New Year's Day (Bulgaria) and (Yugoslavia)**

November Eve
See **Samhain**

Novyi God
See **New Year's Day (Russia)**

Nový Rok
See **New Year's Day (Czechoslovakia)**

Nubaigai
See **Harvest Celebration, Grain (Lithuania)**

Nuestra Señora de los Angeles
See **Our Lady of the Angels**

Nuestra Senora de Peñafrancia, Feast of
See **Our Lady of Peñafrancia, Feast of (Philippines: Naga City)**

Nuits de Bourgogne, Festival des
See **Nights of Bourgogne, Festival of the (France: Dijon, Cote-d'Or)**

Nuits de l'Enclave des Papes
See **Nights of the Enclave (France: Valreas, Vaucluse)**

Nuremberg Christmas Fair
See **Christkindlesmarkt (Germany)**

Nurses' Week
Named for: Observed during week including birthday of Florence Nightingale (1820-1910)
Location: International
Date: First or second week of May; usually includes Nurses' Day, May 12

AnnivHol-1983, 65
Chases-1993, 194
See also **National Hospital Day**

Nutcrack Night
See **Halloween (England)**

Nut Monday
Location: Great Britain
Date: First Monday in August

DictDays-1988, 82

Nutting Day
See **Nut Monday**

NVB Festival (Nykterhetsrorelsens Bildningsversamhet)
Location: Sweden: Molnlycke
Date: Two weeks in June

IntlThFolk-1979, 346

Nyambinyambi
See **Rain-Calling Ceremony (Kwangali people in Namibia)**

Nyårsdagen
See **New Year's Day (Sweden)**

Nyepi
See **Vernal Equinox (Bali)**

Nytaarsaften
See **New Year's Eve (Norway)**

Nytaarsdag
See **New Year's Day (Denmark)**

Nytårsaften
See **New Year's Eve (Denmark)**

Nyttårsdag
See **New Year's Day (Norway)**

Oak Apple or Oak Ball Day
See **Shick-Shack Day**

Oakley Festival, Annie
Named for: Annie Oakley (Phoebe Ann Moses, 1860-1926)
Location: Greenville, Ohio
Date: Last full week in July

HolFestCelWrld-1994, 11

Oaqöl
Ethnic or religious group: Hopi Indian women
Date: Formerly in autumn; now held irregularly

DictFolkMyth-1984, 807

Oath Monday
Location: Germany: Ulm
Established: 1397
Date: July

HolFestCelWrld-1994, 231

Obando, Dances of
See **Dances of Obando**

Oberammergau Passion Play
See **Passion Play, Oberammergau**

Obon Festival
See **Dead, Festival of the (Buddhist) and (Buddhist in China, especially at the monastery of Ch'ing Liang Shan)**

Obon Matsuri
See **Dead, Festival of the (Buddhist), (Buddhist in Japan), and (Buddhist Japanese-Americans in the United States)**

Obzinky, Posviceni
See **Harvest Celebration (Czechoslovakia)**

Occitanie Festival
Location: France: Montauban, Tarn-et-Garonne
Established: 1957
Date: One week from late June to early July

IntlThFolk-1979, 113

Ochichi, or Očevi
See **Father's Day (Yugoslavia)**

October Days of Culture
Location: Yugoslavia: Sarajevo, Bosnia and Herzegovina
Established: 1968
Date: October

IntlThFolk-1979, 402

October Fair (Fiestas de Octubre)
Location: Mexico: Guadalajara
Date: Month-long, October-November

GdWrldFest-1985, 133

October Fair
Location: Portugal: Castro Verde-Beja
Ethnic or religious group: People from Alentejo and
  Algarve regions
Established: 1636
Date: Nine days in October

GdWrldFest-1985, 155

October Festival
See **Oktoberfest**

October Socialist Revolution Day
Named for: November 7, 1917, Bolshevik revolution
Location: USSR
Date: Observed November 7-8 in Moscow

AnnivHol-1983, 143
BkFest-1937, 286
Chases-1993, 434
FolkWrldHol-1992, 554
HolFestCelWrld-1994, 273
NatlHolWrld-1968, 202

Octubre, Fiestas de
See **October Fair (Mexico: Guadalajara)**

Odo Festival
See **Dead, Return of the (Igbo people in Nsukka, Nigeria)**

Odwira
See **New Yam Festival (Abron, Aburi, Akan, and Asante peoples in Ghana), (Ewe people in Ghana), and (Dan, Wobe, Senoufo, Baoule, Bete, and Lobi peoples in Ivory Coast)**

Offering Ceremony
Location: Indonesia: Pelabuhan Ratu, Java
Date: April

IntlThFolk-1979, 223

Offering Ceremony
Location: Indonesia: Tasikmalaya and Pantai Charita, Java
Date: July

IntlThFolk-1979, 223

Offering Ceremony
Location: Indonesia: Tegal, Central Java, Java
Date: August

IntlThFolk-1979, 223

Offering Ceremony
Location: Indonesia: Ambar Ketawang, Jogjakarta, Java
Date: January

IntlThFolk-1979, 225

Offering Ceremony
Location: Indonesia: Parang Kusuma, Jogjakarta, Java
Date: April

IntlThFolk-1979, 223

Offering Ceremony
Location: Indonesia: Pangandaran, West Java, Java
Date: January

IntlThFolk-1979, 223

Offering Day
Location: International
Ethnic or religious group: Western churches
Date: Date determined by the Church

DictDays-1988, 83

Ogijan Festival
See **New Yam Festival (Yoruba people in Oyo, Nigeria)**

Oglethorpe Day
See **Georgia Day**

Ogun Festival
See **Olojo (Ife and Yoruba peoples in Oyo, Nigeria)**

Ogwugwu Festival (Igbo people in Nigeria)
See **New Yam Festival (Ibgo people in Nigeria)**

Ohgíwe
See **Dead, Feast for the (Iroquois Indian women)**

Oimelc
See **Imbolc**

Ojai Festival
Location: Ojai, California
Established: 1947
Date: Three days in late May

MusFestAmer-1990, 36

Okambondondo, Feast of
Location: Angola
Date: February, March, and April

FolkWrldHol-1992, 444
HolFestCelWrld-1994, 227

Okere Juju
Location: Nigeria
Ethnic or religious group: Itsekiri people
Date: Five weeks from May to July (height of rainy season)

FolkWrldHol-1992, 261

Oklahoma Day
Named for: April 22, 1889, settlement
Location: Guthrie, Lexington, Midwest City, and Norman, Oklahoma; U.S. Naval Station, Adak, Alaska
Date: April 22 in Oklahoma; observed early autumn in Alaska

AmerBkDays-1978, 369
Chases-1993, 176
HolFestCelWrld-1994, 233

Oklahoma Historical Day
Named for: Held on birthday of Jean Pierre Chouteau (1758-1849), founder of Salina settlement in 1796
Location: Salina, Oklahoma
Date: October 10

AnnivHol-1983, 131
Chases-1993, 406
HolFestCelWrld-1994, 233

Okpesi or Itensi Festival
Location: Nigeria
Ethnic or religious group: Igbo people

Date: Around September

FolkWrldHol-1992, 473
HolFestCelWrld-1994, 234

Oktoberfest
Location: Canada: Kitchener, Waterloo, Ontario
Ethnic or religious group: German-Canadian
Established: 1969
Date: Nine days in early October, beginning the Friday before Thanksgiving Monday

GdWrldFest-1985, 48

Oktoberfest
Location: Germany: Munich, Bavaria
Established: 1810, when wedding took place between King Ludwig I of Bavaria (1786-1868) and Princess Therese of Saxony-Hildburghausen (1792-1854)
Date: 16 days, usually beginning first Sunday in October

AnnivHol-1983, 180
BkFest-1937, 137
BkHolWrld-1986, September 21, 180
FestWestEur-1958, 72
GdWrldFest-1985, 86
HolFestCelWrld-1994, 234

Olavsoka
See **Olsok**

Old Candlemas
See **Epiphany**

Old Christmas
See **Epiphany (Ukrainian-Canadians in Canada) and (Great Britain)**

Old Hickory's Day
See **Battle of New Orleans Day**

Old Island Days
Location: Key West, Florida
Established: 1961
Date: Seven weeks from early February to late March

GdUSFest-1984, 36

Old Lady Day
See **Annunciation; Lady Day**

Old Man's Day
Location: England: Braughing, Hertfordshire
Date: October 2

DictDays-1988, 84

Old Midsummer Day
See **Epiphany; Old Midsummer Eve**

Old Midsummer Eve
   Location: England
   Date: July 4

   DictDays-1988, 84

Old New Year's Day
   Location: Wales
   Date: January 12 or 13

   AnnivHol-1983, 8
   FolkWrldHol-1992, 26

Old Silvester
See **St. Sylvester's Day (Switzerland)**

Old Spanish Days
   Location: Santa Barbara, California
   Established: 1924
   Date: Five days during full moon in August

   AmerBkDays-1978, 750

Old Twelfth Day
See **Twelfth Day (Scotland)**

Old Year's Day
See **New Year's Eve**

Olojo (Ogun Festival)
   Named for: The god Ogun and birth of King Oranmiyan, who lived sometime between the late 12th and 15th centuries
   Location: Nigeria: Oyo
   Ethnic or religious group: Ife and Yoruba peoples
   Date: Around July

   FolkWrldHol-1992, 359

Olsok
   Named for: July 29, 1030, death of St. Olaf Haraldson the Fat (995-1030)
   Location: Faroe Islands
   Date: July 29-30

   FolkWrldHol-1992, 383
   HolFestCelWrld-1994, 296

Olsok
   Named for: July 29, 1030, death of St. Olaf Haraldson the Fat (995-1030)
   Location: Norway

   Date: Observed last week in July

   AnnivHol-1983, 99
   BkHolWrld-1986, July 29
   Chases-1993, 309
   FestWestEur-1958, 154
   HolFestCelWrld-1994, 296
   RelHolCal-1993, 100

Olsok
   Named for: July 29, 1030, death of St. Olaf Haraldson the Fat (995-1030)
   Location: United States
   Ethnic or religious group: Norwegian-Americans
   Date: Observed last week in July

   AnnivHol-1983, 99
   RelHolCal-1993, 100

Oltenian Ballad
   Location: Romania: Corabia, Olt
   Date: First weekend in October

   IntlThFolk-1979, 322

Olympic Games
   Location: Varies
   Established: 776 B.C. in Greece; international since 1896
   Date: Summer games: early April-late July; winter games: late January-mid February

   BkHolWrld-1986, August 5, 180
   HolFestCelWrld-1994, 235

Olympics, World Eskimo Indian
   Location: Fairbanks, Alaska
   Established: 1961
   Date: Three days in late July or early August

   Chases-1993, 301
   GdUSFest-1984, 9
   HolFestCelWrld-1994, 371

Olympus Festival
   Location: Greece: Katerini
   Established: 1970
   Date: July-August

   IntlThFolk-1979, 194

Omer, Counting of the
See **Lag B'Omer**

Omisoka
See **New Year's Eve (Japan)**

Omizutori Matsuri
  See **Water Drawing Festival (Buddhist and Shinto people at Todaiji Temple in Nara, Japan)**

Ommegang Pageant
  Location: Belgium: Brussels
  Established: Reenactment of 1549 pageant; festival since 1930
  Date: First Thursday in July

  BkHolWrld-1986, July 2, 180
  Chases-1993, 271
  HolFestCelWrld-1994, 238

Onam
  See **Harvest Festival (India: Kerala)**

One-Man Shows, National Festival of
  Location: Poland: Torun
  Established: 1966
  Date: November

  IntlThFolk-1979, 298

Onion Market (Zibelemarit or Zybelemärit)
  Location: Switzerland: Bern
  Date: Fourth Monday in November

  AnnivHol-1983, 151
  Chases-1993, 450
  FestWestEur-1958, 238
  HolFestCelWrld-1994, 379

Onwasato Festival
  See **New Yam Festival (Ibo people in Nigeria)**

Opalia
  Named for: Ops, fertility goddess
  Location: Ancient Rome
  Date: December 19

  DictFolkMyth-1984, 825
  See also **Opiconsivia**

Opera, Ballet and Music Festival, Vichy
  Location: France: Vichy
  Date: June-September

  MusFestWrld-1963, 139

Opera, Des Moines Metro Summer Festival of
  Location: Indianola, Iowa
  Established: 1973
  Date: Three weeks from late June to early July

  MusFestAmer-1990, 170

Opera, Glimmerglass
  Location: Cooperstown, New York
  Established: 1975
  Date: Late June to Labor Day, first Monday in September

  MusFestAmer-1990, 174

Opera, Glyndebourne Festival
  Location: England: Glyndebourne, East Sussex
  Established: 1934
  Date: Ten to eleven weeks from late May to early August

  GdWrldFest-1985, 92
  MusFestEurBrit-1980, 54
  MusFestWrld-1963, 1

Opera, International Festival of Light
  Location: Ireland: Waterford, County Waterford
  Established: Late 1950s
  Date: September

  IntlThFolk-1979, 236

Opera, Naples Open-Air Festival of Summer
  Location: Italy: Naples
  Date: July-August

  MusFestWrld-1963, 113

Opera, Rome Open-Air Festival of Summer
  Location: Italy: Rome
  Date: July-August

  MusFestWrld-1963, 115

Opera, Wexford Festival
  Location: Ireland: Wexford, County Wexford
  Established: 1951
  Date: Two weeks in late October

  GdWrldFest-1985, 115
  IntlThFolk-1979, 236
  MusFestEurBrit-1980, 111
  MusFestWrld-1963, 42

Opera and Ballet, Annual Festival of Chamber
  Location: Yugoslavia: Osijek, Croatia
  Date: May-June

  IntlThFolk-1979, 399

Opera and Ballet, Budapest Concerts and Open-Air
  Location: Hungary: Budapest
  Date: Late June to late August

  MusFestWrld-1963, 159

Opera and Ballet Festival
Location: Italy: Verona, Veneto
Established: 1922
Date: July-September

IntlThFolk-1979, 251

Opera and Music, Aix-en-Provence International Festival of (Festival International d'Art Lyrique et de Musique d'Aix-en-Provence)
Location: France: Aix-en-Provence
Established: 1947-48
Date: Three and one-half weeks in July

MusFestEurBrit-1980, 72
MusFestWrld-1963, 117

Opera Festival, Cincinnati Summer
Location: Cincinnati, Ohio
Established: 1920
Date: Mid-June to mid-July

MusFestAmer-1990, 176
MusFestWrld-1963, 282

Opera Festival, Colorado
Location: Colorado Springs, Colorado
Established: 1970
Date: One week in July

MusFestAmer-1990, 169

Opera Festival, Italian
Location: Switzerland: Théâtre de Beaulieu, Lausanne
Established: 1950s
Date: October

MusFestWrld-1963, 205

Opera Festival, Lake George
Location: Glen Falls, New York
Established: 1962
Date: Six weeks from mid-July to last week in August

MusFestAmer-1990, 175

Opera Festival, Munich (Münchner Opernfestspiele)
Location: Federal Republic of Germany: Munich, Bavaria
Established: 1901
Date: 25 days in July-August

GdWrldFest-1985, 85
MusFestEurBrit-1980, 103
MusFestWrld-1963, 55

Opera Festival, Santa Fe
Location: Santa Fe, New Mexico
Established: 1957
Date: Eight weeks in July and August or September

GdUSFest-1984, 121
HolFestCelWrld-1994, 307
MusFestAmer-1990, 172
MusFestWrld-1963, 273

Opera Festival, Savonlinna (Savonlinnan Oopperajuhlat)
Location: Finland: Savonlinna
Established: 1967
Date: First three weeks in July

Chases-1993, 270
GdWrldFest-1985, 78
HolFestCelWrld-1994, 308
MusFestEurBrit-1980, 70

Opera Festival, Spring
Location: Houston, Texas
Established: 1972
Date: May

MusFestAmer-1990, 177

Opera Festival, Verona (Arena di Verona)
Location: Italy: Verona, Veneto
Established: 1913
Date: Second week in July to first week in September

MusFestEurBrit-1980, 122
MusFestWrld-1963, 114

Opera Plus, Festival Ottawa
Location: Canada: Ottawa, Ontario
Established: 1971
Date: Three weeks in July

GdWrldFest-1985, 51

Opera Theatre of Saint Louis
Location: Saint Louis, Missouri
Established: 1976
Date: Late May to end of June

MusFestAmer-1990, 171

Operatic Society Festival, Haddo House Choral and
Location: Scotland: Aberdeen
Date: Late summer

IntlThFolk-1979, 183

Operetta Weeks (Operettenwochen)
Location: Austria: Bad Ischl, Upper Austria
Established: 1961
Date: Eight weeks from early July to first week in September

IntlThFolk-1979, 35
MusFestEurBrit-1980, 24

Opiconsivia
Named for: Ops, fertility goddess
Location: Ancient Rome
Date: August 25

DictFolkMyth-1984, 825
See also **Opalia**

Oral Interpretation, Competition in
Location: Bulgaria: Stara Zagora
Date: Even-numbered years, date varies

IntlThFolk-1979, 56

Orange Bowl Football Classic
Location: Miami, Florida
Date: January 1

Chases-1993, 51
HolFestCelWrld-1994, 239

Orange Day
Named for: Commemorates 1690 Battle of the Boyne
Location: Northern Ireland
Ethnic or religious group: Protestant
Date: July 12

AnnivHol-1983, 92
Chases-1993, 290
DaysCustFaith-1957, 178
DictDays-1988, 84
HolFestCelWrld-1994, 239

Orange Festival (Chorégies d'Orange)
Location: France: Orange
Established: 1971
Date: Four productions in late July to early August

MusFestEurBrit-1980, 85

Orangemen's Day
See **Orange Day**

Oranges and Lemons Day
Location: England: London
Ethnic or religious group: Christian
Date: March 31

AnnivHol-1983, 45

Organization of African Unity Day (OAU Day)
Named for: May 25, 1963, founding of the organization
Location: Equatorial Guinea
Date: May 25

AnnivHol-1983, 71

Osaka International Festival
Location: Japan: Osaka
Established: 1958
Date: 18 days in April-May

GdWrldFest-1985, 124
IntlThFolk-1979, 258
MusFestWrld-1963, 264

O'schtersonndeg
See **Easter (Luxembourg)**

Oshagatsu
See **New Year's Day (Japan)**

Osterfestspiele
See **Easter Festival (Austria: Salzburg)**

Ostern
See **Easter (Austria), (Germany), and (Switzerland)**

Oudejaars Avond
See **New Year's Eve (Netherlands)**

Our Lady, Consoler of the Afflicted, Octave of
Location: Luxembourg: Luxembourg-Ville
Established: 15th century
Date: Eight to 15 days beginning fifth Sunday after Easter

FestWestEur-1958, 109

Our Lady Aparecida, Festival of
Location: Brazil: Aparecida
Date: May 11

HolFestCelWrld-1994, 240

Our Lady Day
See **Lady Day**

Our Lady of Agony, Festival of
Location: Portugal: Viana do Castelo
Date: Three days in August

Chases-1993, 337
HolFestCelWrld-1994, 242
IntlThFolk-1979, 314

Our Lady of Bildchen, Procession to (Muttergottesprozessio'n Op d'Bildchen)
  Location: Luxembourg: Vianden
  Date: Sunday following August 15, Assumption

  FestWestEur-1958, 116

Our Lady of Carmel (La Madonna del Carmine)
  Location: Guam/Northern Marianas
  Ethnic or religious group: Chamorros people
  Date: Mid-July

  FolkWrldHol-1992, 267

Our Lady of Carmel (La Madonna del Carmine)
  Location: Italy and United States
  Ethnic or religious group: Italian-Americans
  Date: July 16

  BkFest-1937, 188
  HolFestCelWrld-1994, 240

Our Lady of Czestochowa, Feast of (Feast of the Black Madonna of Jasna Gora)
  Location: Poland: Jasna Gora monastery, Czestochowa
  Date: August 15

  HolFestCelWrld-1994, 34

Our Lady of Czestochowa, Feast of
  Location: Poland: Polish National Shrine of Czestochowa
  Date: May 3

  AnnivHol-1983, 60

Our Lady of Fátima Day
  Named for: Several sightings of the Virgin Mary which occurred between May 13 and October 13, 1917, in Fátima, Portugal
  Location: Portugal: Fátima, Estremadura
  Ethnic or religious group: Roman Catholic
  Date: July 13, official holy day

  AnnivHol-1983, 92
  Chases-1993, 205, 407
  DaysCustFaith-1957, 179
  DictWrldRel-1989, 254
  FestWestEur-1958, 161
  HolFestCelWrld-1994, 241

Our Lady of Flowers, Harvest Festival for
  See **Assumption, Feast of the (Polish-Americans in Orange County, New York)**

Our Lady of Guadalupe
  Ethnic or religious group: Roman Catholic
  Date: December 12

  AmerBkDays-1978, 1097
  AnnivHol-1983, 159
  BkFest-1937, 232
  BkHolWrld-1986, December 12
  Chases-1993, 472
  DaysCustFaith-1957, 311
  DictFolkMyth-1984, 258
  DictWrldRel-1989, 569
  FolkAmerHol-1987, 363
  FolkWrldHol-1992, 588
  IndianAmer-1989, 290, 300, 303
  IntlThFolk-1979, 272

Our Lady of Guadalupe
  Location: Southern Arizona
  Ethnic or religious group: Yaqui and Mayo Indians
  Date: December 12

  DictFolkMyth-1984, 258

Our Lady of Guadalupe
  Location: Tucson, Arizona
  Date: December 12

  FolkAmerHol-1987, 363

Our Lady of Guadalupe
  Location: Olvera Street, Los Angeles, California
  Date: December 12

  AnnivHol-1983, 159

Our Lady of Guadalupe
  Location: Our Lady of Guadalupe Church, San Diego, California
  Date: December 12

  AmerBkDays-1978, 1097

Our Lady of Guadalupe (Día del Indio, Day of the Indian)
  Location: El Salvador
  Date: December 12

  FolkWrldHol-1992, 588

Our Lady of Guadalupe
  Location: Mexico
  Ethnic or religious group: Yaqui and Mayo Indians
  Date: December 12

  DictFolkMyth-1984, 258

Our Lady of Guadalupe (Nuestra Señora de Guadalupe)
Location: Mexico: Basilica of Our Lady of Guadalupe,
  Mexico City
Established: 1531
Date: December 12

AmerBkDays-1978, 1097
AnnivHol-1983, 159
BkFest-1937, 232
BkHolWrld-1986, December 12
Chases-1993, 472
DaysCustFaith-1957, 311
DictWrldRel-1989, 569
FolkAmerHol-1987, 363
FolkWrldHol-1992, 588
HolFestCelWrld-1994, 241
IntlThFolk-1979, 272

Our Lady of Guadalupe
Location: Taos, Jemez, and other pueblos in New Mexico
Ethnic or religious group: Tortugas Indians and
  Pueblo Indians
Date: December 12; observed with Matachine Dances

AmerBkDays-1978, 1097
FolkAmerHol-1987, 364
IndianAmer-1989, 290, 300, 303

Our Lady of Guadalupe
Location: Ponce, Puerto Rico
Date: December 12

AmerBkDays-1978, 1097

Our Lady of Guadalupe (Festival Guadalupaño)
Location: Our Lady of Guadalupe Church, and throughout
  San Antonio, Texas
Date: Sunday nearest December 12

AmerBkDays-1978, 1097

Our Lady of Lourdes, Feast of
Named for: Commemorates 18 appearances of the
  Virgin Mary to St. Bernadette Soubirous (1844-1879)
  between February 11 and July 16, 1858
Location: France: Lourdes
Ethnic or religious group: Roman Catholic
Date: February 11, official holy day; festival between
  February 11-18

AnnivHol-1983, 25, 52
BkHolWrld-1986, February 11
DaysCustFaith-1957, 50, 96
DictWrldRel-1989, 439, 569

Our Lady of Lourdes, Feast of
Named for: Commemorates 18 appearances of the Virgin
  Mary to St. Bernadette Soubirous (1844-1879)
  between February 11 and July 16, 1858
Location: Guam/Northern Marianas
Ethnic or religious group: Chamorros people
Date: February 11, official holy day; festival between
  February 11-18

FolkWrldHol-1992, 267

Our Lady of Mercy, Festival of
Location: Spain: Barcelona
Established: 1868
Date: September

IntlThFolk-1979, 333

**Our Lady of Miracles (Nossa Senhora dos Milagres or
Festa de Serreta)**
Location: Gustine, California
Ethnic or religious group: Roman Catholic Azorean
  Portuguese people
Established: 1932
Date: September 8-15

FolkAmerHol-1987, 277
HolFestCelWrld-1994, 311
RelHolCal-1993, 76

**Our Lady of Miracles (Nossa Senhora dos Milagres or
Festa de Serreta)**
Location: Portugal: Azores
Established: 1842
Date: September 8-15

HolFestCelWrld-1994, 311
RelHolCal-1993, 76

Our Lady of Mount Carmel (Senhora do Monte do Carmo)
Location: Portugal: Moura, Beja
Established: 14th century
Date: October

IntlThFolk-1979, 309

Our Lady of Nazaré Festival
Named for: Miracle which saved the life of Fuas Roupinho,
  on September 8, 1182
Location: Portugal: Nazaré, Estremadura
Date: September 8-18

Chases-1993, 361
FestWestEur-1958, 184
HolFestCelWrld-1994, 241

Our Lady of Peñafrancia, Feast of (Feast of Nuestra Senora de Peñafrancia)
Location: Philippines: Naga City
Date: Third week in September

HolFestCelWrld-1994, 229

Our Lady of Sorrows, Festival of Mary,
Ethnic or religious group: Roman Catholic
Established: 17th century; authorized 1817 by Pope Pius VII
Date: September 15

RelHolCal-1993, 94

Our Lady of the Angels
Location: Costa Rica: pilgrimage to basilica in Cartago
Date: August

AnnivHol-1983, 102
BkHolWrld-1986, August 2

Our Lady of the Angels, Day of
See **Assumption (Portugal)**

Our Lady of the Happy Ending
Location: Brazil
Date: January

AnnivHol-1983, 180
BkHolWrld-1986, January 23
Chases-1993, 69
FolkWrldHol-1992, 27

Our Lady of the Remedies
See **Pilgrimage to the Sanctuary of Our Lady of the Remedies (Portugal: Lamego, Viseu)**

Our Lady of Victories Day
See **Victory Day (Malta)**

Our Lord of Passos, Procession of
Location: Macao
Ethnic or religious group: Christian
Date: February-March

GdWrldFest-1985, 130

Outback Festival
Location: Australia: Winton, Queensland
Established: Commemorates Winton's settlement in 1875 and founding in 1878
Date: Ten days in August during odd-numbered years

IntlThFolk-1979, 19

Ovens, Feast of
See **Fornacalia or Fornax (ancient Rome)**

Oxen's Feast
See **St. Modesto's Day (Greece)**

Oxford Festival
Location: England: Oxford
Date: July-August

IntlThFolk-1979, 1972

Oxi Day
Named for: Greeks' response to attempted invasion by Benito Mussolini in 1940 (oxi means "no" in Greek)
Location: Greece
Date: October 28

HolFestCelWrld-1994, 242

Oyster Day
See **Grotto Day**

Oyster Festival
Location: Norwalk, Connecticut
Established: 1977
Date: September, the weekend after Labor Day

GdUSFest-1984, 31

Oyster Festival, Galway
Location: Ireland: Galway, County Connemara
Established: 1954
Date: Four days in mid-September

GdWrldFest-1985, 114
HolFestCelWrld-1994, 113

Oyster Festival, St. Mary's County Maryland
Location: Leonardtown, Maryland
Established: 1967
Date: Second weekend in October

Chases-1993, 412
GdUSFest-1984, 83
HolFestCelWrld-1994, 295

Paasch Maandag
See **Easter Monday (Netherlands)**

Paasch Zonday
See **Easter (Netherlands)**

Pääsiäisaatto, Easter Eve
See **Holy Saturday (Finland)**

Pääsiäissunnuntai
See **Easter (Finland)**

Paaske
See **Easter (Denmark)**

Paaskeaften
See **Holy Saturday (Denmark)**

Pace Day, Pace-Egg Day, or Pace Monday
See **Easter (Scotland); Easter Monday (Scotland)**

Pacific Northwest Festival
Location: Seattle, Washington
Established: 1975
Date: Last week in July and first week in August

GdUSFest-1984, 207
MusFestAmer-1990, 178

Pack Rag Day
See **Michaelmas**

Pageant of Peace
See **Christmas Tree, Lighting of the National**

Pages of History
Location: Romania: Brebu, Prahova
Date: Last weekend in July

IntlThFolk-1979, 319

Paine Day, Thomas (Common Sense Day)
Named for: Thomas Paine (1737-1809)
Location: Hugenot-Thomas Paine Historical Society
Date: Sunday nearest January 29

AmerBkDays-1978, 121
AnnivHol-1983, 15
BkDays-1864, i.755
Chases-1993, 77

Pajjusana
Named for: Commemorates birth of Mahavira, Lord
   Vardhamana (c. 599-527 B.C.)
Ethnic or religious group: Jaina religion
Date: Eight-day penance in August

AnnivHol-1983, 180
RelHolCal-1993, 100
See also **Mahavira's Birthday**

Pakistan Day
Named for: March 23, 1956, proclamation of the republic
Location: Pakistan: Rawalpindi
Date: March 23

AnnivHol-1983, 41
Chases-1993, 139
NatlHolWrld-1968, 37

Páleni Čarodějnic, Burning of the Witches
See **May Day Eve (Czechoslovakia)**

Palermo Festival
Location: Italy: Palermo, Sicily
Established: 1959
Date: First week in October

MusFestWrld-1963, 250

Palio, Festival of the (Festa del Palio, Corso del Palio, or Palio of the Contrade)
Location: Italy: Siena, Tuscany
Established: 13th century
Date: Held twice during the summer: July 2 and August 16,
   Madonna del Voto Day

AnnivHol-1983, 88, 108
BkFest-1937, 187
BkHolWrld-1986, August 16
FestWestEur-1958, 98
GdWrldFest-1985, 119
HolFestCelWrld-1994, 243

Palm Beach Festival
Location: Palm Beach, Florida
Established: 1978
Date: Two weeks in December

MusFestAmer-1990, 207

Palmsonntag
See **Palm Sunday (Germany)**

Palm Sunday
Named for: The palm branches people in Jerusalem spread
   in the streets when Jesus (c. 6 B.C.-c. 30 A.D.) returned to the
   city during Passover
Ethnic or religious group: Christian
Established: Predates ninth century, Rome
Date: March-April, the Sunday preceding Easter

AmerBkDays-1978, 278
AnnivHol-1983, 169
BkDays-1864, i. 395
BkFest-1937, 183, 300, 337
BkFestHolWrld-1970, 49
BkHolWrld-1986, April 5
Chases-1993, 155
DaysCustFaith-1957, 104
DictDays-1988, 41, 86
DictFolkMyth-1984, 181, 841, 954, 1171
DictWrldRel-1989, 558
FestSaintDays-1915, 54
FestWestEur-1958, 59, 92, 107, 125, 163, 192

Palm Sunday *(cont.)*
FolkAmerHol-1987, 129
FolkWrldHol-1992, 131, 193
HolFestCelWrld-1994, 106, 243
IndianAmer-1989, 274
RelHolCal-1993, 101
SaintFestCh-1904, 157

Palm Sunday
Ethnic or religious group: Eastern Orthodox
Date: March-April, the Sunday preceding Easter

AmerBkDays-1978, 280
SaintFestCh-1904, 157

Palm Sunday
Ethnic or religious group: Episcopalian
Date: March-April, the Sunday preceding Easter

AmerBkDays-1978, 279

Palm Sunday
Ethnic or religious group: Lutheran
Date: March-April, the Sunday preceding Easter

AmerBkDays-1978, 279

Palm Sunday
Ethnic or religious group: Protestant
Date: March-April, the Sunday preceding Easter

AmerBkDays-1978, 279
BkFestHolWrld-1970, 49

Palm Sunday
Ethnic or religious group: Roman Catholic
Date: March-April, the Sunday preceding Easter

AmerBkDays-1978, 279
BkFestHolWrld-1970, 49
FestSaintDays-1915, 55

Palm Sunday
Location: Arizona
Ethnic or religious group: Yaqui Indians
Date: March-April, the Sunday preceding Easter

IndianAmer-1989, 274

Palm Sunday
Location: Austria
Date: March-April, the Sunday preceding Easter

AmerBkDays-1978, 280
BkHolWrld-1986, April 5

Palm Sunday
Location: Bavaria
Date: March-April, the Sunday preceding Easter

AmerBkDays-1978, 280
FestWestEur-1958, 59

Palm Sunday
Location: Bulgaria
Date: March-April, the Sunday preceding Easter

DictFolkMyth-1984, 181

Palm Sunday (Kvetna Nedele)
Location: Czechoslovakia
Date: March-April, the Sunday preceding Easter

BkFestHolWrld-1970, 49

Palm Sunday
Location: England
Date: March-April, the Sunday preceding Easter

BkDays-1864, i.396
DaysCustFaith-1957, 105
DictDays-1988, 41, 86
FestSaintDays-1915, 55
HolFestCelWrld-1994, 106
SaintFestCh-1904, 157

Palm Sunday
Location: Southern Europe
Ethnic or religious group: Romany people
Date: March-April, the Sunday preceding Easter

DictFolkMyth-1984, 954

Palm Sunday
Location: Finland
Date: March-April, the Sunday preceding Easter

FolkWrldHol-1992, 193

Palm Sunday (Rameaux)
Location: France
Date: March-April, the Sunday preceding Easter

FolkWrldHol-1992, 131

Palm Sunday (Palmsonntag)
Location: Germany
Date: March-April, the Sunday preceding Easter

FestWestEur-1958, 59

Palm Sunday
Location: Greece
Date: March-April, the Sunday preceding Easter

BkFestHolWrld-1970, 50
FestSaintDays-1915, 54

Palm Sunday
Location: Ireland
Date: March-April, the Sunday preceding Easter

DictFolkMyth-1984, 841

Palm Sunday (Domenica delle Palme)
Location: Italy
Date: March-April, the Sunday preceding Easter

AmerBkDays-1978, 280
BkDays-1864, i.397
BkFest-1937, 183
BkFestHolWrld-1970, 50
DaysCustFaith-1957, 104
FestSaintDays-1915, 55
FestWestEur-1958, 92
FolkWrldHol-1992, 131

Palm Sunday (Pellemsonndeg)
Location: Luxembourg
Date: March-April, the Sunday preceding Easter

FestWestEur-1958, 107

Palm Sunday (Domingo de Palmas)
Location: Mexico
Date: March-April, the Sunday preceding Easter

BkFestHolWrld-1970, 49

Palm Sunday (Palm Zondag)
Location: Netherlands
Date: March-April, the Sunday preceding Easter

FestWestEur-1958, 125
FolkWrldHol-1992, 131

Palm Sunday (La Fiesta de Ramos)
Location: Peru: Moche
Date: March-April, the Sunday preceding Easter

FolkWrldHol-1992, 131

Palm Sunday (Domingo de Ramos)
Location: Portugal
Date: March-April, the Sunday preceding Easter

FestWestEur-1958, 163

Palm Sunday
Location: Rome
Date: March-April, the Sunday preceding Easter

BkDays-1864, i.397
DaysCustFaith-1957, 104

Palm Sunday (Domingo de Ramos)
Location: Spain
Date: March-April, the Sunday preceding Easter

BkFest-1937, 300
FestWestEur-1958, 192
FolkWrldHol-1992, 132

Palm Sunday
Location: United States
Date: March-April, the Sunday preceding Easter

AmerBkDays-1978, 280
DaysCustFaith-1957, 104
FolkAmerHol-1987, 129

Palm Sunday (Cveti, Day of Flowers)
Location: Yugoslavia
Date: March-April, the Sunday preceding Easter

BkFest-1937, 337

Palmsun or Palmsun Even
See **Palm Sunday**

Palm Tree Sunday
See **Palm Sunday**

Palm Zondag
See **Palm Sunday (Netherlands)**

Pamukkale, Festival of
Location: Turkey: Denizli
Date: May

IntlThFolk-1979, 368

Pan, Feast of
See **Imbolc**

Pan American Day
Location: Central, North, and South America
Established: 1931
Date: April 14

AmerBkDays-1978, 353
AnnivHol-1983, 51
BkHolWrld-1986, April 14
Chases-1993, 166
DictDays-1988, 87
HolFestCelWrld-1994, 244

Pan American Festival Week
Location: Lakewood, California
Established: 1946
Date: Two days in late April or early May

GdUSFest-1984, 20

Panas Pela (Cuci Baileo Ceremony)
   Location: Indonesia: Pelau versi Ulilima, Maluku, Moluccas
   Date: Every three years in May

   IntlThFolk-1979, 226

Panathenaea
   Named for: Athena, Greek goddess
   Location: Greece: Athens
   Date: Midsummer

   DictMyth-1962, ii.1231
   HolFestCelWrld-1994, 244

Pancake Day
   See **Mardi Gras (England)** and **(Olney, England, and Liberal, Kansas)**

Panchadaan
   Location: Nepal
   Ethnic or religious group: Buddhist
   Date: August, third day of waning half of Hindu month of Bhadrapada in Kathmandu and Bhadgaon, and eighth day waxing half of Hindu month of Sravana in Patan and the rest of Nepal

   FolkWrldHol-1992, 442
   HolFestCelWrld-1994, 244

Panguni Uttiram
   Location: Malaya
   Ethnic or religious group: Hindu
   Date: March-April, ten days, including the full moon day of Hindu month of Chaitra

   FolkWrldHol-1992, 216

Panguni Uttiram
   Location: Malaysia
   Ethnic or religious group: Hindu
   Date: March-April, ten days, including the full moon day of Hindu month of Chaitra

   FolkWrldHol-1992, 216
   HolFestCelWrld-1994, 202

Panguni Uttiram
   Location: Malaysia: Sri Mariamman Temple at Bukit Mertajam
   Ethnic or religious group: Hindu
   Date: March-April, ten days, including the full moon day of Hindu month of Chaitra

   FolkWrldHol-1992, 216

Panguni Uttiram
   Location: Singapore: Sri Veeramakaliamman Temple
   Ethnic or religious group: Hindu
   Date: March-April, two days, including the full moon day of Hindu month of Chaitra

   FolkWrldHol-1992, 216
   HolFestCelWrld-1994, 202

Pantomime Festival (Gaukler Festival)
   Location: Federal Republic of Germany: Cologne, North Rhine-Westphalia
   Established: 1976
   Date: October

   IntlThFolk-1979, 136

Pantomime-Music-Dance-Theatre
   Location: Federal Republic of Germany: West Berlin
   Date: April-June

   IntlThFolk-1979, 133

Panunuluyan
   Location: Philippines: Lubang, Mindoro, Luzon Island, and Manila
   Date: December 24

   IntlThFolk-1979, 290

Pâques
   See **Easter (France)**

Parade of Dragons
   See **New Year (China)**

Parade of the Months (Italy)
   See **Mardi Gras (Italy)**

Paramonee ton Chreestoogennon
   See **Christmas Eve (Greece)**

Pardon of Nossa Senhora dos Remédios
   See **Pilgrimage to the Sanctuary of Our Lady of the Remedies (Portugal: Lamego, Viseu)**

Pareegentahn
   See **Mardi Gras (Armenia)**

Parentalia
   Location: Ancient Rome
   Date: February 13-21

   DaysCustFaith-1957, 53
   DictFolkMyth-1984, 673
   FestSaintDays-1915, 31
   HolFestCelWrld-1994, 245

Parents' Day
 Location: Zaire
 Date: July 31, two-day holiday

 AnnivHol-1983, 99

Parilia or Palilia (Festival of Pales)
 Named for: Pales, protector of shepherds and flocks;
  commemorates founding of Rome in 753 B.C.
 Location: Ancient Rome
 Date: April 21

 AmerBkDays-1978, 313
 Chases-1993, 174
 DictFolkMyth-1984, 845

Paris Air and Space Show
 Location: France: Paris
 Established: 1908
 Date: 11 days in June during odd-numbered years

 GdWrldFest-1985, 81
 HolFestCelWrld-1994, 245

Paris Festival Estival (Festival Estival de Paris)
 Location: France: Paris
 Established: 1967
 Date: Mid-July to mid-September

 GdWrldFest-1985, 82
 IntlThFolk-1979, 118
 MusFestEurBrit-1980, 87

Paris Marathon
 Location: France: Paris
 Established: 1975
 Date: Third Saturday in May

 GdWrldFest-1985, 81

Parliament Day
 Location: England: London
 Date: Early November

 AnnivHol-1983, 180
 HolFestCelWrld-1994, 322

Paro Tshechu
 Named for: Honors Padmasambhava (Guru Rinpoche,
  eighth century)
 Location: Bhutan: Paro
 Ethnic or religious group: Buddhist
 Date: 10th-15th days of second lunar month or date in
  early spring determined by lamas

 BkHolWrld-1986, April 20, 180
 HolFestCelWrld-1994, 245

Parshurama Jayanti
 Named for: Parshurama, sixth incarnation of Vishnu
 Ethnic or religious group: Hindu

 Date: April-May, third day of waxing half of Hindu month
  of Vaisakha

 RelHolCal-1993, 101

Partridge Day
 Location: England
 Date: September 1, opening of partridge season

 DictDays-1988, 87
 HolFestCelWrld-1994, 246

Paryushana or Partyshana Parva
 Ethnic or religious group: Digambar Jaina religion
 Date: August-September, Hindu month of Bhadrapada

 FolkWrldHol-1992, 443
 HolFestCelWrld-1994, 246
 RelHolCal-1993, 101

Paryushana or Partyshana Parva
 Location: India
 Ethnic or religious group: Jaina religion
 Date: August-September, Hindu month of Bhadrapada

 FolkWrldHol-1992, 443
 HolFestCelWrld-1994, 246
 RelHolCal-1993, 101

Paryushana or Partyshana Parva
 Ethnic or religious group: Svetambar Jaina religion
 Date: August-September, Hindu month of Bhadrapada

 FolkWrldHol-1992, 443
 HolFestCelWrld-1994, 246
 RelHolCal-1993, 101

Pasa
 See **Fast, Feast of Breaking the (Indonesia); Ramadan
  (Indonesia: Java)**

Pasch Day
 See **Easter (northern England and Scotland)**

Paschen
 See **Easter (Belgium) and (Netherlands)**

Paschoa
 See **Easter (Portugal)**

Pascua Florida Day
 Location: Florida
 Established: Observed since 1953; since 1973, Pascua Florida
  Week is March 27-April 2; commemorates 1513 landing on
  Florida by Ponce de León (1460-1521)
 Date: April 2

 AmerBkDays-1978, 316
 AnnivHol-1983, 47
 DictDays-1988, 87
 HolFestCelWrld-1994, 246

Pashkët
See **Easter (Albania)**

Paskdagen
See **Easter (Sweden)**

Paske
See **Easter (Norway)**

Paskha
See **Easter (Russia)**

La Pasqua
See **Easter (Italy)**

La Passio Festival
Location: Spain: Esparraguera, Barcelona
Established: About 16th century
Date: February-March, during Lent, the forty days preceding Easter

IntlThFolk-1979, 336

Passion, Sacred Drama of the
Location: Spain: Ulldecona, Tarragona
Date: Sundays during Lent until month after Easter

IntlThFolk-1979, 342

Passion Play
Location: Austria: St. Margarethen, Burgenland
Established: 1926; every five years since 1946
Date: May-September

IntlThFolk-1979, 38

Passion Play
Location: Austria: Erl, Tirol
Established: 1613; current version, 1959
Date: Every six years from June to September

IntlThFolk-1979, 32

Passion Play
Location: Austria: Thiersee, Tirol
Established: 1779
Date: June-September

IntlThFolk-1979, 41

Passion Play
Location: Mexico: Ixtapalapa, Federal District
Date: March-April, Good Friday, Friday before Easter

IntlThFolk-1979, 270

Passion Play
Location: Mexico: Malinalco
Date: March-April, Holy Week, week before Easter

IntlThFolk-1979, 271

Passion Play
Location: Mexico: Tzintzuntzan, Michoacán
Date: March-April, Holy Week, week before Easter

DictFolkMyth-1984, 851
IntlThFolk-1979, 277

Passion Play, Black Hills
Location: Spearfish, South Dakota
Established: 1939
Date: June-August

HolFestCelWrld-1994, 34

Passion Play, Cenaculo
Location: Philippines: Cainta, Malabon, and Navota, Rizal, Luzon Island
Date: March-April, Holy Week, week before Easter

Chases-1993, 155
IntlThFolk-1979, 290

Passion Play, Cenaculo
Location: Philippines: Samal, Bataan, Luzon Island
Date: March-April, Holy Week, week before Easter

Chases-1993, 155
IntlThFolk-1979, 288

Passion Play, Oberammergau
Location: Federal Republic of Germany: Oberammergau, Bavaria
Established: 1634
Date: Every ten years, in decades ending with zero, from May to September

GdWrldFest-1985, 86
HolFestCelWrld-1994, 231
IntlThFolk-1979, 146

Passion Plays
Location: Philippines

DictFolkMyth-1984, 1072

Passion Plays
Location: Spain

DictFolkMyth-1984, 1072

Passion Saturday
See **Holy Saturday**

Passion Sunday
Ethnic or religious group: Christian
Date: March, Sunday preceding Palm Sunday, fifth Sunday in Lent

BkFest-1937, 183
DaysCustFaith-1957, 90
DictDays-1988, 87

Passion Sunday
  Location: England
  Date: March, Sunday preceding Palm Sunday, fifth Sunday in Lent

  DictDays-1988, 87

Passion Sunday (Domenica delle Passione)
  Location: Italy
  Date: March, Sunday preceding Palm Sunday, fifth Sunday in Lent

  BkFest-1937, 183

Passion Thursday
  See **Holy Thursday**

Passiontide
  Ethnic or religious group: Christian
  Date: March, last two weeks of Lent

  Chases-1993, 144

Passion Week
  See **Holy Week**

Passover (Pesach)
  Ethnic or religious group: Jewish
  Established: Observed for more than 3000 years
  Date: March-April, seven or eight days beginning 15th of Jewish month of Nisan

  AmerBkDays-1978, 362
  AnnivHol-1983, 172
  BkFest-1937, 207
  BkFestHolWrld-1970, 52, 63
  BkHolWrld-1986, April 4, 175
  Chases-1993, 157
  DaysCustFaith-1957, 112
  DictMyth-1962, i.555, ii.1242
  DictWrldRel-1989, 155, 390, 560, 668
  FolkAmerHol-1987, 123
  FolkWrldHol-1992, 235
  HolFestCelWrld-1994, 246, 253
  RelHolCal-1993, 102

Passover
  Ethnic or religious group: Conservative Jews
  Date: March-April, eight days beginning 15th of Jewish month of Nisan

  AmerBkDays-1978, 362
  DictWrldRel-1989, 561
  RelHolCal-1993, 102

Passover (Pesach)
  Ethnic or religious group: Orthodox Jews
  Date: March-April, eight days beginning 15th of Jewish month of Nisan

  AmerBkDays-1978, 362
  BkFest-1937, 207
  DictWrldRel-1989, 561
  RelHolCal-1993, 102

Passover (Pesach)
  Ethnic or religious group: Reform Jews
  Date: March-April, seven days beginning 15th of Jewish month of Nisan

  AmerBkDays-1978, 362
  DictWrldRel-1989, 561
  HolFestCelWrld-1994, 246
  RelHolCal-1993, 102

Passover
  Location: Bukhara
  Date: March-April, eight days beginning 15th of Jewish month of Nisan

  FolkWrldHol-1992, 235

Passover (Pesach)
  Location: Israel
  Date: March-April, seven days beginning 15th of Jewish month of Nisan

  AmerBkDays-1978, 362
  DaysCustFaith-1957, 114
  DictWrldRel-1989, 561
  FolkWrldHol-1992, 235
  HolFestCelWrld-1994, 246

Passover
  Location: Libya
  Date: March-April, eight days beginning 15th of Jewish month of Nisan

  FolkWrldHol-1992, 236

Passover
  Location: Morocco
  Date: March-April, eight days beginning 15th of Jewish month of Nisan

  FolkWrldHol-1992, 236

Passover (Pesach)
  Location: Palestine
  Date: March-April, eight days beginning 15th of Jewish month of Nisan

  BkFest-1937, 207

Passover
Location: Tunis
Date: March-April, eight days beginning 15th of Jewish
month of Nisan

FolkWrldHol-1992, 237

Passover
Location: United States
Date: March-April, eight days beginning 15th of Jewish
month of Nisan

FolkAmerHol-1987, 123

Passover
Location: Yemen
Date: March-April, eight days beginning 15th of Jewish
month of Nisan

FolkWrldHol-1992, 237

Pastoral Album
Location: Romania: Rasinari, Sibiu
Date: Third Sunday in April

IntlThFolk-1979, 329

Patati, Day of Repentance
See **New Year (Parsis and other Zoroastrians) and (Parsis
and other Zoroastrians in the United States)**

Path Clearing Festival (Akwambo)
Location: Ghana
Date: September 3

BkHolWrld-1986, 176

Patient Sunday
See **Passion Sunday**

Patios Festival
Location: Spain: Cordoba
Date: May

IntlThFolk-1979, 334

Patrickmas Day
See **St. Patrick's Day**

Patriots' Day
Named for: April 19, 1775, Battle of Lexington and Concord
Location: Connecticut, Maine, and Massachusetts
Date: Observed third Monday in April

AmerBkDays-1978, 359
AnnivHol-1983, 53
Chases-1993, 173
DictDays-1988, 68, 88
HolFestCelWrld-1994, 247

Patriots' Weekend, Annual
Location: Bethel/Redding area of Connecticut
Established: 1975
Date: Last weekend in September

HolFestCelWrld-1994, 11

Patron Crosses, Fiesta of the
Location: Mexico: Quintana Roo
Ethnic or religious group: Roman Catholic Mayan people
Date: Late April

DictFolkMyth-1984, 817

La Patum Festival
Location: Spain: Berga, Barcelona
Date: During Corpus Christi week

IntlThFolk-1979, 334

Pau Festival
Location: France: Pau, Basses-Pyrenees
Date: One week in June

IntlThFolk-1979, 119

Paul Bunyan Show
Location: Nelsonville, Ohio
Established: 1952
Date: First full weekend in October

HolFestCelWrld-1994, 247

Paul Pitcher Day
Location: England: Cornwall
Date: January 24, eve of St. Paul's Day

DictDays-1988, 88

Paung-daw-U Pagoda Festival
See **Lenten Season (Buddhists in Myanmar; formerly
Burma) and (Myanmar; formerly Burma)**

Pavasario Svente
See **Spring, Feast of (Ancient Lithuania)**

Payment of Quit Rent
Location: England: London
Established: 1235
Date: September 29

HolFestCelWrld-1994, 247

Peace, International Day of
Location: Sponsored by the United Nations; observed in the
United States
Established: 1982
Date: Third Tuesday in September

HolFestCelWrld-1994, 79

Peace and National Unity Day
  Location: Rwanda
  Date: July 5

  AnnivHol-1983, 89

Peace Festival
  Named for: Marks United States's use of the atomic bomb
    on Japan in 1945
  Location: Japan: Peace Memorial Park in Hiroshima
  Established: 1947
  Date: August 6

  AmerBkDays-1978, 722
  HolFestCelWrld-1994, 138

Peaceful Revolution Day
  See **Revolution Day, July (Iraq)**

Peace Sunday
  See **Easter**

Peace with Bolivia Day
  Named for: June 12, 1938, ending of war with Bolivia
  Location: Paraguay
  Date: June 12

  AnnivHol-1983, 78

Peach Festival
  Location: Supai, Arizona
  Ethnic or religious group: Havasupai Indians
  Date: August

  IndianAmer-1989, 262

Peach Festival, South Carolina
  Location: Gaffney, South Carolina
  Date: Ten days in mid-July

  HolFestCelWrld-1994, 320

Pearl Harbor Day
  Named for: Japanese bombing of Pearl Harbor on
    December 7, 1941
  Location: United States
  Date: December 7

  AmerBkDays-1978, 1082
  AnnivHol-1983, 157
  Chases-1993, 468
  HolFestCelWrld-1994, 248

Pearly Emperor
  See **Yü Huang Shang Ti (Chinese Taoist)**

Peasants' Day
  Location: Burma
  Date: One week, including March 2

  AnnivHol-1983, 32

Peer Gynt Festival Days
  Named for: Character created by dramatist Henrik Ibsen
    (1828-1906)
  Location: Norway
  Date: Begins August 4

  AnnivHol-1983, 103

Peko, Feast of
  Named for: Peko, fertility god
  Location: Estonia: Setumaa
  Date: October 1

  DictFolkMyth-1984, 850

Pellemsonndeg
  See **Palm Sunday (Luxembourg)**

Penance Day (Buss and Bettag Day)
  Location: Federal Republic of Germany
  Date: November 17

  AnnivHol-1983, 148
  Chases-1993, 443

Pendleton Round-Up
  Location: Pendleton, Oregon
  Established: 1910
  Date: Second full week in September

  AmerBkDays-1978, 846
  Chases-1993, 370
  HolFestCelWrld-1994, 249

Penguin Plunge
  Location: Mackeral Cove, Jamestown, Rhode Island
  Date: January 1

  Chases-1993, 51

Penitents, Procession of the (Boetprocessie van Veurne)
  Location: Belgium: Furnes, West Flanders
  Established: Observed since 1644; commemorates crusader
    Count Robert II of Flanders return in 1099 with fragment
    of the Cross
  Date: Last Sunday in July

  BkHolWrld-1986, July 27
  FestWestEur-1958, 14
  HolFestCelWrld-1994, 249

Penitents, Procession of the (La Procesion De La Penitencia)
  Location: Spain: Roncesvalles, Navarre
  Date: Week preceding Pentecost

  FestSaintDays-1915, 112
  FestWestEur-1958, 196

Pennsylvania Day
  Named for: Founder William Penn (1644-1718)
  Location: Pennsylvania
  Established: 1932
  Date: October 24

  AmerBkDays-1978, 951
  BkDays-1864, ii.60
  DictWrldRel-1989, 564
  HolFestCelWrld-1994, 249

Pennsylvania Dutch Days
  Location: Hershey, Pennsylvania
  Established: 1948
  Date: August

  AmerBkDays-1978, 776

Pennsylvania Relay Carnival, University of
  Location: University of Pennsylvania, Philadelphia, Pennsylvania
  Established: 1895
  Date: One week beginning Sunday before last weekend in April

  HolFestCelWrld-1994, 351

Pentecost
  Ethnic or religious group: Christian
  Established: Third century
  Date: May-June, the Sunday fifty days after Easter, the seventh Sunday after Easter Sunday

  AmerBkDays-1978, 461, 464
  AnnivHol-1983, 169
  BkDays-1864, i. 629
  BkFest-1937, 97, 135, 244, 268
  BkFestHolWrld-1970, 64
  BkHolWrld-1986, May 31
  Chases-1993, 227
  DaysCustFaith-1957, 161, 354
  DictDays-1988, 89, 131
  DictMyth-1962, i.555, ii.1253, 1678
  DictFolkMyth-1984, 629, 750, 1127, 1175, 1176
  DictWrldRel-1989, 154, 175, 564
  FestSaintDays-1915, 118
  FestWestEur-1958, 26, 42, 65, 153, 165, 215, 233
  FolkAmerHol-1987, 197
  FolkWrldHol-1992, 282
  HolFestCelWrld-1994, 250, 254
  RelHolCal-1993, 102, 121
  SaintFestCh-1904, 245

Pentecost (Whitsunday or White Sunday)
  Ethnic or religious group: Anglican; Church of England
  Date: May-June, the Sunday fifty days after Easter, the seventh Sunday after Easter Sunday

  BkDays-1864, i.629
  DaysCustFaith-1957, 161
  SaintFestCh-1904, 245

Pentecost
  Ethnic or religious group: Eastern Orthodox
  Date: May-June, the Sunday fifty days after Easter, the seventh Sunday after Easter Sunday

  AmerBkDays-1978, 461

Pentecost (Whitsunday)
  Ethnic or religious group: Episcopalian
  Date: May-June, the Sunday fifty days after Easter, the seventh Sunday after Easter Sunday

  DaysCustFaith-1957, 161

Pentecost
  Ethnic or religious group: Lutheran
  Date: May-June, the Sunday fifty days after Easter, the seventh Sunday after Easter Sunday

  AmerBkDays-1978, 461

Pentecost
  Ethnic or religious group: Protestant
  Date: May-June, the Sunday fifty days after Easter, the seventh Sunday after Easter Sunday

  AmerBkDays-1978, 461

Pentecost
  Ethnic or religious group: Roman Catholic
  Date: May-June, the Sunday fifty days after Easter, the seventh Sunday after Easter Sunday

  AmerBkDays-1978, 461
  DaysCustFaith-1957, 354

Pentecost
  Location: Austria: Carinthia
  Date: May-June, the Sunday fifty days after Easter, the seventh Sunday after Easter Sunday

  DictFolkMyth-1984, 1176

Pentecost
  Location: Belgium
  Date: May-June, the Sunday fifty days after Easter, the seventh Sunday after Easter Sunday

  BkFestHolWrld-1970, 66

Pentecost
  Location: Bohemia
  Date: May-June, the Sunday fifty days after Easter, the seventh Sunday after Easter Sunday

  DictFolkMyth-1984, 1127, 1176

Pentecost
  Location: Brazil
  Date: May-June, the Sunday fifty days after Easter, the seventh Sunday after Easter Sunday

  FolkWrldHol-1992, 282

Pentecost
  Location: Point Loma, California
  Ethnic or religious group: Portuguese-Americans
  Date: May-June, the Sunday fifty days after Easter, the seventh Sunday after Easter Sunday

  AmerBkDays-1978, 463

Pentecost
  Location: Czechoslovakia
  Date: May-June, the Sunday fifty days after Easter, the seventh Sunday after Easter Sunday

  BkHolWrld-1986, May 31

Pentecost (Pintse)
  Location: Denmark
  Date: May-June, the Sunday fifty days after Easter, the seventh Sunday after Easter Sunday

  BkFest-1937, 97
  FestWestEur-1958, 26

Pentecost (Whitsunday or White Sunday)
  Location: England
  Date: May-June, the Sunday fifty days after Easter, the seventh Sunday after Easter Sunday

  AmerBkDays-1978, 463
  BkDays-1864, i.629
  BkFestHolWrld-1970, 66, 67
  BkHolWrld-1986, May 31
  DaysCustFaith-1957, 161, 354
  DictFolkMyth-1984, 750
  FestSaintDays-1915, 124
  FolkWrldHol-1992, 283
  HolFestCelWrld-1994, 250
  RelHolCal-1993, 121
  SaintFestCh-1904, 245

Pentecost
  Location: Medieval England, France, Germany, and Italy
  Date: May-June, the Sunday fifty days after Easter, the seventh Sunday after Easter Sunday

  AmerBkDays-1978, 463
  BkDays-1864, i.630
  DaysCustFaith-1957, 354

Pentecost
  Location: Estonia

  Date: May-June, the Sunday fifty days after Easter, the seventh Sunday after Easter Sunday

  FolkWrldHol-1992, 283
  HolFestCelWrld-1994, 250

Pentecost
  Location: Finland
  Date: May-June, the Sunday fifty days after Easter, the seventh Sunday after Easter Sunday

  HolFestCelWrld-1994, 250

Pentecost (La Pentecôte and Fête des Marins, Sailors' Festival in Honfleur)
  Location: France
  Established: 11th century
  Date: May-June, the Sunday fifty days Easter, the seventh Sunday and Monday after Easter Sunday

  BkHolWrld-1986, June 1, 177
  DictFolkMyth-1984, 1175
  FestWestEur-1958, 42

Pentecost (Pfingsten)
  Location: Germany
  Date: May-June, the Sunday fifty days after Easter, the seventh Sunday after Easter Sunday

  BkFest-1937, 135
  DaysCustFaith-1957, 162
  DictFolkMyth-1984, 1176
  DictMyth-1962, ii.1260
  FestWestEur-1958, 65
  FolkWrldHol-1992, 283
  HolFestCelWrld-1994, 250

Pentecost (Kneeling Sunday)
  Location: Greece
  Date: May-June, the Sunday fifty days after Easter, the seventh Sunday after Easter Sunday

  BkFestHolWrld-1970, 66

Pentecost
  Location: Iceland
  Date: May-June, the Sunday fifty days after Easter, the seventh Sunday after Easter Sunday

  FolkWrldHol-1992, 284

Pentecost
  Location: Ireland
  Date: May-June, the Sunday fifty days after Easter, the seventh Sunday after Easter Sunday

  DictFolkMyth-1984, 1176

Pentecost
   Location: Lithuania
   Date: May-June, the Sunday fifty days after Easter, the seventh Sunday after Easter Sunday

   DictFolkMyth-1984, 629

Pentecost
   Location: Luxembourg: Echternach
   Date: May-June, the Sunday fifty days after Easter, the seventh Sunday after Easter Sunday

   FestSaintDays-1915, 127

Pentecost
   Location: Italy: Messina, Sicily
   Date: May-June, the Sunday fifty days after Easter, the seventh Sunday after Easter Sunday

   FestSaintDays-1915, 123

Pentecost
   Location: Netherlands
   Date: May-June, the Sunday fifty days after Easter, the seventh Sunday after Easter Sunday

   BkFest-1937, 244
   BkFestHolWrld-1970, 65, 66
   BkHolWrld-1986, May 31
   FestWestEur-1958, 136
   FolkWrldHol-1992, 284
   See also **Luilak (Lazybones Day or Sluggard's Feast)**

Pentecost (Merchants' Flower Market)
   Location: Netherlands: Haarlem
   Date: May-June, the Sunday fifty days after Easter, the seventh Sunday after Easter Sunday

   BkFestHolWrld-1970, 65

Pentecost (Pinkster Day)
   Location: New York
   Ethnic or religious group: Dutch-Americans
   Established: 1800s
   Date: May-June, the Sunday fifty days after Easter, the seventh Sunday after Easter Sunday

   BkFest-1937, 244
   DaysCustFaith-1957, 162
   DictDays-1988, 89
   FolkAmerHol-1987, 197
   HolFestCelWrld-1994, 254

Pentecost (Pinse)
   Location: Norway

Date: May-June, the Sunday fifty days after Easter, the seventh Sunday after Easter Sunday

   FestWestEur-1958, 153
   FolkWrldHol-1992, 282

Pentecost (Pingsht-Moondawg, Whitmonday)
   Location: Pennsylvania
   Ethnic or religious group: Pennsylvania Dutch people
   Established: 1811
   Date: May-June, the Sunday fifty days after Easter, the seventh Sunday after Easter Sunday

   FolkAmerHol-1987, 197

Pentecost (Pentecoste)
   Location: Portugal
   Date: May-June, the Sunday fifty days after Easter, the seventh Sunday after Easter Sunday

   AmerBkDays-1978, 464
   BkFest-1937, 268
   FestWestEur-1958, 165

Pentecost (Rusalii)
   Location: Romania
   Date: May-June, the Sunday fifty days after Easter, the seventh Sunday after Easter Sunday; one week beginning Pentecost Eve

   DictFolkMyth-1984, 1176
   FolkWrldHol-1992, 285
   See also **Trinity Sunday (Romania)**

Pentecost
   Location: Romania: Transylvania
   Date: May-June, the Sunday fifty days after Easter, the seventh Sunday after Easter Sunday

   DictFolkMyth-1984, 1176

Pentecost
   Location: Russia
   Date: May-June, the Sunday fifty days after Easter, the seventh Sunday after Easter Sunday

   DaysCustFaith-1957, 354
   DictFolkMyth-1984, 1176

Pentecost
   Location: Scotland
   Date: May-June, the Sunday fifty days after Easter, the seventh Sunday after Easter Sunday

   DictDays-1988, 131
   DictMyth-1962, ii.1678
   HolFestCelWrld-1994, 250

Pentecost (Pingst)
    Location: Sweden
    Date: May-June, the Sunday fifty days after Easter, the
        seventh Sunday after Easter Sunday; two-day festival

    FestWestEur-1958, 215

Pentecost (Pfingsten)
    Location: Switzerland
    Date: May-June, the Sunday fifty days after Easter, the
        seventh Sunday after Easter Sunday

    DictFolkMyth-1984, 1176
    FestWestEur-1958, 233

Pentecost (Pfingsten)
    Location: Switzerland: Lucerne
    Date: May-June, the Sunday fifty days after Easter, the
        seventh Sunday after Easter Sunday

    FestWestEur-1958, 233

Pentecost
    Location: United States
    Date: May-June, the Sunday fifty days after Easter, the
        seventh Sunday after Easter Sunday

    AmerBkDays-1978, 463
    DaysCustFaith-1957, 162
    FolkAmerHol-1987, 197

Pentecost, Feast of (Jewish)
    See **Shavuot**

Pentecost and Whit Monday
    Location: Hungary: Ozora
    Date: May-June, the Sunday fifty days after Easter, the
        seventh Sunday after Easter Sunday and the following
        Monday

    FolkWrldHol-1992, 283

Peony Day
    Location: Romania: Baneasa, Galati
    Date: Second Sunday in May

    IntlThFolk-1979, 317

People Power Anniversary
    Named for: Commemorates ousting of Ferdinand Marcos
        (1917- 1989) by people of the Philippines on February 22-25,
        1986
    Location: Philippines: Quezon City, Manila
    Date: February 25

    HolFestCelWrld-1994, 105

Peppercorn Day
    Location: Bermuda
    Established: 1816
    Date: On or near April 23, St. George's Day

    AnnivHol-1983, 56
    Chases-1993, 176
    HolFestCelWrld-1994, 250

Perchtenlauf
    Location: Austria: Imst and Thaur in Tirol
    Date: Usually January 6

    HolFestCelWrld-1994, 250

La Percingula
    See **St. Francis of Assisi (Arroyo Hondo, New Mexico;
        southern Colorado)**

Performance Season, Canadian Experimental
    Location: Canada: Niagara-on-the-Lake, Ontario
    Established: 1977
    Date: Month of July

    IntlThFolk-1979, 71

Performance '78 ('79, '80 . . .)
    Location: Canada: location varies within British Columbia
    Date: June

    IntlThFolk-1979, 61

Performing Arts for Young People, Come Out-Festival of
    Location: Australia: Adelaide, South Australia
    Established: 1974
    Date: Odd-numbered years during first two weeks in May

    IntlThFolk-1979, 21

Performing Arts for Young People, The Leap-Festival of
    Location: Australia: Sydney, New South Wales
    Date: Last week in February

    IntlThFolk-1979, 13

Pergamum, Festival of
    Location: Turkey: Bergama
    Date: May

    IntlThFolk-1979, 367

Perseids Meteor Shower
    See **Night of the Shooting Stars**

Pershore Festival
    Location: England: Pershore, Worcestershire
    Established: 1960
    Date: Last two weeks in June

    IntlThFolk-1979, 172

Perth, Festival of
  Location: Australia: Perth, Western Australia
  Established: 1953
  Date: February-March

  GdWrldFest-1985, 10
  IntlThFolk-1979, 29

Pesach
  See **Passover (Israel) and (Jewish)**

Pferdeweihe, Blessing of Horses
  See **Nativity of the Virgin, Feast of the (Germany: St.
  Märgen, Black Forest)**

Pffiferdaj
  See **Flutes, Day of the (France: Ribeauvillé)**

Pfingsten
  See **Pentecost (Germany), (Switzerland), and (Lucerne,
  Switzerland)**

Philippine-American Friendship Day
  Location: Philippines
  Date: July 4

  AnnivHol-1983, 89
  Chases-1993, 280

Phra Buddha Bat Fair
  Location: Thailand: Phra Buddha Bat temple near Saraburi
  Date: March

  HolFestCelWrld-1994, 251

Physical Education or Sports Day
  Location: Japan
  Established: Commemorates 1964 Tokyo Olympics
  Date: October 10

  AnnivHol-1983, 130
  Chases-1993, 405

Pickle-Market or Sticky-Sticky Fair (Bettara-Ichi)
  Location: Japan: near Ebisu Shrine, Tokyo
  Date: October 19

  BkFestHolWrld-1970, 114
  BkHolWrld-1986, October 19

Picnic Day
  Location: Australia: Northern Territory
  Date: First Monday in August

  AnnivHol-1983, 102
  Chases-1993, 314
  DictDays-1988, 89

Pied Piper of Hamelin Festival
  Named for: Man who allegedly rid the town of rats on
  July 22, 1376
  Location: Federal Republic of Germany: Hamelin
  Date: Every Sunday at noon during the summer

  BkHolWrld-1986, July 22
  HolFestCelWrld-1994, 251

Pig Face Sunday
  Location: England: Avening, Gloucestershire
  Date: The Sunday following September 14

  DictDays-1988, 89
  HolFestCelWrld-1994, 252

Pig Festival
  Location: Papua New Guinea
  Ethnic or religious group: Bundi people

  FolkWrldHol-1992, 461
  HolFestCelWrld-1994, 252

Pig Festival (Juwo)
  Location: Papua New Guinea
  Ethnic or religious group: Kapauka Papuan people

  FolkWrldHol-1992, 462

Pike Festival, National
  Location: Along Route 40 through Pennsylvania, Maryland,
  West Virginia, and Ohio
  Established: 1974
  Date: May-June

  HolFestCelWrld-1994, 219

Pike Festival, Northern
  Location: Canada: Nipawin, Saskatchewan
  Established: 1969
  Date: June to August

  GdWrldFest-1985, 59

Pilar Festival
  See **Virgin of the Pillar, Feast of**

Pilgrimage, Lough Derg
  Location: Ireland: pilgrimage of St. Patrick's Purgatory
  Date: June 1 through August 15

  AnnivHol-1983, 178

Pilgrimage at Cercio to Santa Barbara
  Location: Portugal: Cercio to Santa Barbara
  Ethnic or religious group: Roman Catholic
  Date: Last Sunday in August

  DictFolkMyth-1984, 848

Pilgrimage of Castelejo
  Named for: Honors St. Lucia and St. Euphemia
  Location: Portugal: Castelejo, Castelo Branco
  Ethnic or religious group: Christian
  Date: September

  IntlThFolk-1979, 304

Pilgrimage of La Dandelada (Romería of La Dandelada)
  Location: Spain: Ávila
  Date: Second Sunday in September

  FolkWrldHol-1992, 511

Pilgrimage of Our Lady of the Cabeza (Romería of the Virgen de la Cabeza)
  Location: Spain: Andujar, Jaen, Andalucia
  Established: Middle Ages
  Date: End of April

  FolkWrldHol-1992, 511
  IntlThFolk-1979, 333

Pilgrimage of Our Lady of Valme (Romarío of Our Lady of Valme)
  Location: Spain: Dos Hermanas, near Sevilla
  Date: October 17

  FolkWrldHol-1992, 511
  HolFestCelWrld-1994, 275

Pilgrimage of Pedro Bervardo (Romería of Pedro Bervardo)
  Location: Spain: Ávila
  Date: September 5-17

  FolkWrldHol-1992, 511

Pilgrimage of the Black Madonna
  Named for: Commemorates September 14, 948, church consecration
  Location: Switzerland: Einseideln
  Date: September 14

  AnnivHol-1983, 118

Pilgrimage of the Dew (Romería Del Rocío)
  Location: Spain: Almonte, Huelva, Andalusia
  Ethnic or religious group: Christian
  Date: Thursday or Friday before Pentecost Sunday through Monday or Tuesday after Pentecost

  FestWestEur-1958, 196
  FolkWrldHol-1992, 511
  HolFestCelWrld-1994, 252

Pilgrimage of the Virgen de la Pena (Romería of the Virgen de la Pena)
  Location: Spain: Puebla de Guaman, Huelva, Andalusia
  Date: Last Sunday in April

  FolkWrldHol-1992, 511

Pilgrimage to Chalma
  Location: Mexico: Chalma
  Ethnic or religious group: Christian
  Date: First week of January; also held in February, August, September, and during Holy Week

  AnnivHol-1983, 174
  DictFolkMyth-1984, 346
  IntlThFolk-1979, 269
  See also **Epiphany (Mexico)**

Pilgrimage to Fátima
  See **Our Lady of Fátima**

Pilgrimage to Moulay Idriss
  Named for: Moulay Idriss I (fl. eighth century)
  Location: Morocco: Moulay Idriss
  Ethnic or religious group: Muslim
  Date: Late August or September

  HolFestCelWrld-1994, 253

Pilgrimage to Nossa Senhora dos Altos Ceus
  Location: Portugal: Lousa, Beira Baixa

  DictFolkMyth-1984, 276

Pilgrimage to Our Lady of Nazo
  Location: Portugal: Povoa, Braganca
  Date: September

  IntlThFolk-1979, 311

Pilgrimage to St. Anne d'Auray
  Named for: St. Anne d'Auray (fl. first century)
  Location: Canada: Beaupré, Quebec
  Date: July 26, official holy day

  AmerBkDays-1978, 695
  AnnivHol-1983, 96
  DaysCustFaith-1957, 192
  HolFestCelWrld-1994, 282

Pilgrimage to St. Anne d'Auray
  Named for: St. Anne d'Auray (fl. first century)
  Location: France: Auray, Brittany
  Established: 17th century

Pilgrimage to St. Anne d'Auray *(cont.)*
Date: July 26, official holy day; last weekend in July

AmerBkDays-1978, 695
BkFest-1937, 126
BkHolWrld-1986, July 25, 180
FestWestEur-1958, 46
FolkWrldHol-1992, 382
HolFestCelWrld-1994, 245

Pilgrimage to Saut d'Eau
Location: Haiti: Ville-Bonheur
Date: Early July-July 16

BkHolWrld-1986, July 10

Pilgrimage to Shrine of Father Laval
Named for: Père Jacques Désiré Laval (1803-1884)
Location: Mauritius: Port Louis
Ethnic or religious group: Roman Catholic
Date: September 8

HolFestCelWrld-1994, 253

Pilgrimage to Shrines of Tsai Shên
Location: China
Date: Second day of first lunar month and 15th day of ninth lunar month

DictFolkMyth-1984, 1129

Pilgrimage to the Sanctuary of Our Lady of the Remedies (Pardon of Nossa Senhora dos Remédios and Festival of Lamego)
Location: Portugal: Lamego, Viseu
Date: Early September

HolFestCelWrld-1994, 245
IntlThFolk-1979, 308

Pilgrim Progress Pageant
Location: Up Leyden Street to the Fort-Meetinghouse, now the church of the Pilgrimage on Main Street on Burial Hill in Plymouth, Massachusetts
Established: 1921
Date: Every Friday in August

GdUSFest-1984, 88

Pinenut Festival
Location: Schurz, Nevada
Ethnic or religious group: Walker River Paiute Indians
Date: October

IndianAmer-1989, 135

Pingsht-Moondawg, Whitmonday
See **Pentecost (Pennsylvania Dutch people in Pennsylvania)**

Pingst
See **Pentecost (Sweden)**

Pinkster Bruid or Pinksterbloem (Whitsun Bride or Whitsun Flower Festival)
Location: Netherlands: Overijssel
Date: Whit Tuesday, the Tuesday after Pentecost Sunday

FestWestEur-1958, 138

Pinkster Day
See **Pentecost (Dutch-Americans in New York)**

Pinse
See **Pentecost (Norway)**

Pintea the Brave Day
Named for: Pintea the Brave (fl. 18th century) and commemorates battle of 1703-1711
Location: Romania: Magoaja, Commune of Chiuesti, Cluj
Date: First Sunday in September

IntlThFolk-1979, 325

Pintse
See **Pentecost (Denmark)**

Pioneer Day
Ethnic or religious group: Mormon (Church of Jesus Christ of the Latter Day Saints)
Named for: July 24, 1847, Mormon settlement in the Salt Lake Valley, Utah
Date: July 24

AmerBkDays-1978, 686
AnnivHol-1983, 96
Chases-1993, 272, 305
DictDays-1988, 89
FolkAmerHol-1987, 235
HolFestCelWrld-1994, 211
RelHolCal-1993, 103

Pioneer Day
Location: Bloomington, Idaho
Ethnic or religious group: Mormon (Church of Jesus Christ of the Latter Day Saints)
Date: July 24

FolkAmerHol-1987, 235

Pioneer Day
  Named for: June 15, 1860, settlement
  Location: Franklin, Idaho
  Established: 1910s
  Date: June 15

  AnnivHol-1983, 80
  DictDays-1988, 89

Pioneer Day
  Location: Salt Lake City, Utah
  Ethnic or religious group: Mormon (Church of Jesus
    Christ of the Latter Day Saints)
  Date: July 24

  AmerBkDays-1978, 686
  AnnivHol-1983, 96
  Chases-1993, 272
  DictDays-1988, 89
  FolkAmerHol-1987, 235
  HolFestCelWrld-1994, 211

Pioneer Days
  Location: Canada: Saskatoon, Saskatchewan
  Established: 1905; current version since 1974
  Date: July

  GdWrldFest-1985, 60

Pioneers' Day
  Location: Liberia
  Date: January 7

  AnnivHol-1983, 6
  NatlHolWrld-1968, 125

Pioneers Day
  Location: South Dakota
  Date: October

  DictDays-1988, 89

Pirate Week Festival
  Location: Cayman Islands: George Town, Grand Cayman
  Established: 1977
  Date: Third week in October

  GdWrldFest-1985, 61
  HolFestCelWrld-1994, 254

Pispalan Sottiisi
  Location: Finland: Tampere
  Date: Even-numbered years in June

  IntlThFolk-1979, 96

Pitkäperjantai, Long Friday
  See **Good Friday (Finland)**

Pitlochry Festival
  Location: Scotland: Pitlochry, Perthshire
  Established: 1951
  Date: April-October

  IntlThFolk-1979, 187

Pitra Paksha or Pitra Visarjana Amavasya
  See **Dead, Feast of the (Hindu people in India)**

Pjodhatid
  Location: Iceland: Vestmannaeyjar
  Established: Commemorates constitution of July 1, 1874
  Date: Three days in early August

  HolFestCelWrld-1994, 254

Plague Sunday
  Named for: Plague of 1665
  Location: England: Eyam, Derbyshire
  Date: Last Sunday in August

  DictDays-1988, 89
  HolFestCelWrld-1994, 255

Planting Ceremony
  Location: Togo: Agome-yo village
  Ethnic or religious group: Ewé people

  FolkWrldHol-1992, 227

Planting-Time Festival (Kapesi)
  Location: Angola

  FolkWrldHol-1992, 225

Play, Spiez Castle
  Location: Switzerland: Spiez, Bern
  Established: 1959
  Date: Three times per week in August

  IntlThFolk-1979, 355

Play at Altdorf, Tell
  Location: Switzerland: Altdorf, Uri
  Established: 1899
  Date: Even-numbered years on weekends in August-
    September

  IntlThFolk-1979, 348

Play at Interlaken, Tell Pastoral
  Location: Switzerland: Interlaken, Bern
  Established: 1912
  Date: July-August

  IntlThFolk-1979, 352

Play Festival, Act Five
  Location: Australia: Canberra, Australian Capital Territory
  Established: 1971
  Date: One week in August

  IntlThFolk-1979, 7

Play of Muri, Easter
  See **Easter Play of Muri (Switzerland: Muri, Aargau)**

Plays, Festival of Contemporary Polish
  Location: Poland: Wroclaw
  Established: 1960
  Date: May

  IntlThFolk-1979, 299

Plays, Festival of Russian and Soviet
  Location: Poland: Katowice
  Established: 1969
  Date: November

  IntlThFolk-1979, 293

Plays, Festival of Short
  Location: Romania: Oradea, Transylvania
  Established: 1975
  Date: One week in February

  IntlThFolk-1979, 328

Plays, Holidays of the Soviet
  Location: Bulgaria: Pazardzik and Pleven
  Date: Every five years, date varies

  IntlThFolk-1979, 53

Plays, Oni-Mai
  Location: Japan: Sosa, Chiba
  Date: Mid-August

  IntlThFolk-1979, 259

Plays, Wagga Wagga School of Arts Annual Festival of
  Location: Australia: Wagga Wagga, New South Wales
  Established: 1954
  Date: Two consecutive weekends in August-September

  IntlThFolk-1979, 14

Plays Festival, Gandersheim Cathedral
  Location: Federal Republic of Germany: Bad Gandersheim, Lower Saxony
  Established: 1958
  Date: May-June

  IntlThFolk-1979, 139

Plays from Iranian Provinces
  Location: Iran: Tehran
  Established: 1976
  Date: Ten days in April

  IntlThFolk-1979, 229

Plays in the Town Hall
  Location: Federal Republic of Germany: Osnabruck, Lower Saxony
  Date: May-June to September for two consecutive years followed by two-year interim

  IntlThFolk-1979, 147

Plays '78 ('79, '80 . . .)
  Location: Federal Republic of Germany: Mulheim, North Rhine-Westphalia
  Established: 1976
  Date: One week in May

  IntlThFolk-1979, 144

Pleureuses, Ceremony of
  See **Good Friday (Switzerland: Church of Romont)**

Plot Night
  See **Fawkes Day, Guy**

Ploughing Ceremony
  Location: Thailand
  Ethnic or religious group: Brahman
  Date: April-May

  AnnivHol-1983, 180
  HolFestCelWrld-1994, 278

Plough Monday
  Ethnic or religious group: Roman Catholic
  Date: First Monday after Epiphany or Twelfth Day, January 6

  SaintFestCh-1904, 63

Plough Monday
  Location: Bulgaria
  Date: First Monday after Epiphany or Twelfth Day, January 6

  DictFolkMyth-1984, 181

Plough Monday
    Location: England
    Established: Since medieval times
    Date: First Monday after Epiphany or Twelfth Day,
        January 6

    AnnivHol-1983, 6
    BkDays-1864, i. 94
    Chases-1993, 61
    DaysCustFaith-1957, 38
    DictDays-1988, 90
    DictFolkMyth-1984, 138, 410
    FestSaintDays-1915, 19
    FolkWrldHol-1992, 20
    HolFestCelWrld-1994, 255
    RelHolCal-1993, 103
    SaintFestCh-1904, 63

Plough Monday
    Location: Great Britain
    Date: First Monday after Epiphany or Twelfth Day,
        January 6

    AnnivHol-1983, 6
    BkDays-1864, i. 94
    Chases-1993, 61
    DaysCustFaith-1957, 38
    DictDays-1988, 90
    DictFolkMyth-1984, 138, 410
    FestSaintDays-1915, 19
    FolkWrldHol-1992, 20
    RelHolCal-1993, 103
    SaintFestCh-1904, 63

Plough Monday
    Location: Scotland
    Date: First Monday after Epiphany or Twelfth Day,
        January 6

    DaysCustFaith-1957, 38

Plough Sunday
    See **Plough Monday**

Plow, Festival of the (Saban Tuy)
    Named for: Originally a farming festival; now
        commemorates the founding of the Tatar Republic
        on June 25, 1920
    Location: USSR: Kazan, Tatar Republic, Russia
    Date: June 25

    BkHolWrld-1986, June 25
    FolkWrldHol-1992, 344
    HolFestCelWrld-1994, 255

Plum Blossom Festival (Baika-sai)
    Location: Japan
    Date: February

    AnnivHol-1983, 173

Poetry Day, Black
    Location: New York and Oregon
    Established: 1970s
    Date: October 17

    HolFestCelWrld-1994, 35

Poetry Festival
    Location: Bisbee, Arizona
    Date: Two days in mid-August
    Established: 1979

    GdUSFest-1984, 10

Poetry Festival, Geraldine R. Dodge
    Named for: Geraldine R. Dodge (1882-1973)
    Location: Waterloo, New Jersey
    Established: 1986
    Date: Three days in September

    HolFestCelWrld-1994, 117

Poetry Festival, Palamas
    Named for: Costis Palamas (1859-1943)
    Location: Cyprus: Paphos
    Established: 1950
    Date: Early March

    IntlThFolk-1979, 84

Poetry Gathering, Cowboy
    Location: Elko, Nevada
    Established: 1985
    Date: Six days in January

    HolFestCelWrld-1994, 71

Poetry Gathering, Dakota Cowboy
    Location: Medora, North Dakota
    Established: 1987
    Date: May, Memorial Day weekend

    HolFestCelWrld-1994, 77

Poetry of Friendship
    Location: Bulgaria: Shumen
    Date: Even-numbered years in March

    IntlThFolk-1979, 54

Poisson d'Avril
    See **April Fools' Day (France)**

Pola Festival
See **Agricultural Festival (India: Maharashtra)**

Polar Bear Swim Day
Location: Canada: English Bay, Vancouver, British Columbia
Date: January 1

AnnivHol-1983, 2
HolFestCelWrld-1994, 255

Polar Bear Swim Day
Location: Northside Beach, Sheboygan, Wisconsin
Date: January 1

AnnivHol-1983, 2
Chases-1993, 51
HolFestCelWrld-1994, 255, 256

Police Memorial Day
Location: United States
Date: May 15

AnnivHol-1983, 66
Chases-1993, 210

Police Week Festival
Location: Antigua: St. John's
Established: 1969
Date: August-September

GdWrldFest-1985, 3

Polish Festival
Location: National Shrine of Our Lady of Czestochowa, Doylestown, Pennsylvania
Ethnic or religious group: Polish-Americans
Established: 1966
Date: September, Labor Day weekend

GdUSFest-1984, 157

Polish Solidarity Day
Named for: November 10, 1980, founding of the Polish labor party
Location: United States
Ethnic or religious group: Polish-Americans
Date: August 31

AnnivHol-1983, 145
HolFestCelWrld-1994, 256

Political Restitution Day
Named for: August 16, 1963, reestablishment of independence
Location: Dominican Republic

Date: August 16

AnnivHol-1983, 108
Chases-1993, 332

Polka Festival, International
Location: Hunter Mountain, Hunter, New York
Established: 1977
Date: Three to four days in early August

Chases-1993, 309
GdUSFest-1984, 125

Ponape Feast
Location: Eastern Caroline Islands: Ponape Island
Date: Winter months

FolkWrldHol-1992, 463

Pongal
See **Harvest Festival (Hindu people in India), (India: Tamil Nadu), and (Tamil people in Malaya)**

Pony Express Ride
Named for: Riders in late-18th-century Pennsylvania
Location: Pennsylvania
Established: Reenactment since 1989
Date: Two days in August

HolFestCelWrld-1994, 257

Pony Penning on Chincoteague Island
Location: Chincoteague Island, Virginia
Established: 1924
Date: Late July

AmerBkDays-1978, 703
AnnivHol-1983, 183
Chases-1993, 308
GdUSFest-1984, 199
HolFestCelWrld-1994, 60

Pooram
Location: India: Trichur
Ethnic or religious group: Hindu
Date: April-May, Hindu month of Vaisakha

Chases-1993, 188
HolFestCelWrld-1994, 257
RelHolCal-1993, 104

Pope Day
See **Fawkes Day, Guy**

Pope Foot Race, Annual
Location: San Juan Pueblo, New Mexico
Date: July 20

IndianAmer-1989, 287, 312

Poppy Day
Location: Great Britain
Date: November 11, Remembrance Day; observed second
Sunday in November

DictDays-1988, 90
HolFestCelWrld-1994, 357

Populaire de Martigues, Festival
See **People's Festival of Martigues**

Popular Festival of Sidi-Ali-El Hattab
Location: Tunisia: Sidi-Ali-El Hattab, Zaghouan Region
Date: April

IntlThFolk-1979, 364

Popular Traditions, Festival of
Location: Iran: Isfahan
Established: 1977
Date: October

IntlThFolk-1979, 228

Porcingula, Feast of
See **Dances, Old Pecos Bull and Corn**

Portsmouth Festival
Location: England: Portsmouth, Hampshire
Date: Mid-May

IntlThFolk-1979, 174

Posadas, Feast of the Lodgings
See **Christmas Festival (Hispanic-Americans) and (Mexico)**

Poson or Dhamma Vijaya, Full Moon Day
Location: Sri Lanka: especially Anuradhapura and Mihintale
Ethnic or religious group: Buddhist
Date: May-June, full moon day of Hindu month of Jyeshta

HolFestCelWrld-1994, 258

Posviceni
See **Harvest Celebration (Czechoslovakia)**

Potato Blossom Festival
Location: Canada: O'Leary, Prince Edward Island
Established: 1950
Date: Last week in July

GdWrldFest-1985, 56

Potato Days (Potetserie)
Location: Norway
Date: October

BkHolWrld-1986, October 28, 180
FolkWrldHol-1992, 461
HolFestCelWrld-1994, 258

Pottery Festival
Location: Luxembourg: Luxembourg City
Established: Several hundred years ago
Date: Easter Monday

GdWrldFest-1985, 129

Pottery Festival
Location: Crooksville and Roseville, Ohio
Established: 1966
Date: Three days during weekend nearest July 20

GdUSFest-1984, 140

Powamû
See **Sky-God Festival (Hopi Indians at Walpi
Pueblo, Arizona)**

Powwow, American Indian
Location: Bedford, Pennsylvania
Date: Second Saturday and Sunday in July

Chases-1993, 286

Powwow, Arapaho Community
Location: Arapahoe, Wyoming
Ethnic or religious group: Arapaho Indians
Date: June

IndianAmer-1989, 110

Powwow, Arlee Fourth of July Celebration
Location: Arlee, Vermont
Ethnic or religious group: Salish Indians
Date: First weekend in July

Chases-1993, 274

Powwow, Bear River
Location: Lac du Flambeau, Wisconsin
Ethnic or religious group: Ojibwa Indians
Date: July

IndianAmer-1989, 178

Powwow, Citizen Band of Potawatomi Indians of Oklahoma
Location: Shawnee, Oklahoma
Date: Last weekend in June

IndianAmer-1989, 70

Powwow, Comanche Annual
Location: Sultan Park, Walters, Oklahoma
Date: July

IndianAmer-1989, 71

Powwow, Connecticut River
Location: Farmington, Connecticut
Ethnic or religious group: Schaghiticoke, Paucatuck
Pequot, Mashantucket Pequot, Mohegan, and Golden
Hill Paugussett Indians
Established: 1985
Date: August, weekend before Labor Day

HolFestCelWrld-1994, 68

Powwow, Epethes
Location: Lapwai, Idaho
Ethnic or religious group: Nez Perce Indians
Date: First weekend in March

HolFestCelWrld-1994, 184
IndianAmer-1989, 126

Powwow, Fond du Lac
Location: Cloquet, Minnesota
Ethnic or religious group: Ojibwa Indians
Date: July

IndianAmer-1989, 148

Powwow, Four Nations
Location: Lapwai, Idaho
Ethnic or religious group: Nez Perce Indians
Date: October

HolFestCelWrld-1994, 184
IndianAmer-1989, 126

Powwow, Honor the Earth
Location: Hayward, Wisconsin
Ethnic or religious group: Lac Courte Oreilles Ojibwa Indians
Date: July

IndianAmer-1989, 177

Powwow, Kihekah Steh Club Annual
Location: Skiatook, Oklahoma
Date: August

IndianAmer-1989, 58, 85

Powwow, La Ka Le'l Ba
Location: Carson City, Nevada
Ethnic or religious group: Washo Indians
Date: Annual

IndianAmer-1989, 137

Powwow, Land of the Menominee
Location: Woodland Bowl, Keshena, Wisconsin
Ethnic or religious group: Menominee Indians
Date: First weekend in August

IndianAmer-1989, 178

Powwow, Lenape Delaware
Location: Near Copan, Oklahoma
Ethnic or religious group: Lenape Delaware Indians
Date: Late May or early June

IndianAmer-1989, 77

Powwow, Little Beaver Rodeo and
Location: Dulce, New Mexico
Ethnic or religious group: Jicarilla Apache Indians
Date: Late July

IndianAmer-1989, 300

Powwow, Looking Glass
Named for: Chief Looking Glass (d. 1877)
Location: Kamiah, Idaho
Ethnic or religious group: Nez Perce Indians
Date: August

HolFestCelWrld-1994, 184
IndianAmer-1989, 126

Powwow, Mesquakie Celebration
Location: Tama, Iowa
Ethnic or religious group: Mesquakie Algonquian Indians
Date: Second weekend in August, Thursday-Sunday

IndianAmer-1989, 17

Powwow, Mid-America All-American Indian Center
Location: Wichita, Kansas
Date: Last full weekend in July

Chases-1993, 305

Powwow, Nanticoke Indian
Location: Millsboro, Delaware
Date: Second weekend in September

Chases-1993, 366

Powwow, Narragansett
Location: Charlestown, Rhode Island
Ethnic or religious group: Narragansett Indians
Date: August

IndianAmer-1989, 175

Powwow, Nesika Illahee
Location: Siletz, Oregon
Ethnic or religious group: Siletz Indian tribes
Date: Second weekend in August

IndianAmer-1989, 195

Powwow, Northern Arapaho
Location: Arapaho, Wyoming
Date: August

IndianAmer-1989, 110

Powwow, Northern Cheyenne
Location: Lame Deer, Montana
Date: July

IndianAmer-1989, 40

Powwow, Ojibwa
Location: Nett Lake Reservation, Minnesota
Ethnic or religious group: Ojibwa Indians
Date: First weekend in June

IndianAmer-1989, 152

Powwow, Ojibwa
Location: Mille Lacs Reservation, Onamia, Minnesota
Ethnic or religious group: Ojibwa Indians
Date: Mid-August

IndianAmer-1989, 150

Powwow, Ojibwa
Location: Red Cliff Indian Reservation near Bayfield, Wisconsin
Ethnic or religious group: Ojibwa Indians
Date: August or September

IndianAmer-1989, 183

Powwow, Oneida
Location: Oneida, Wisconsin
Ethnic or religious group: Oneida Indians
Date: Weekend nearest July 4

IndianAmer-1989, 182

Powwow, Otoe-Missouri
Location: Red Rock, Oklahoma
Date: July

IndianAmer-1989, 57, 87

Powwow, Ottawa
Location: Quapaw, Oklahoma

Date: One in August and one in September

IndianAmer-1989, 58, 59, 84, 88

Powwow, Pawnee Fourth of July
Location: Pawnee, Oklahoma
Date: Weekend nearest July 4

IndianAmer-1989, 88

Powwow, Poarch Creek Indian Thanksgiving Day
Location: Atmore, Alabama
Ethnic or religious group: Poarch Creek Indians
Date: Last Thursday in November, Thanksgiving Day

Chases-1993, 453

Powwow, Potawatomi Indians of Oklahoma
Location: Shawnee, Oklahoma
Date: Last weekend in June

IndianAmer-1989, 70

Powwow, Quapaw
Location: Quapaw, Oklahoma
Ethnic or religious group: Shawnee, Miami, and Quapaw Indians
Date: Second weekend in July

IndianAmer-1989, 57, 60, 84, 92

Powwow, Sac and Fox
Location: Stroud, Oklahoma
Date: Second weekend in July

IndianAmer-1989, 57, 92

Powwow, Santee Sioux
Location: Flandreau, South Dakota
Date: July

IndianAmer-1989, 103

Powwow, Schonchin Days
Named for: Chief Schonchin (c. 1790s-1892)
Location: Klamath Falls, Oregon
Ethnic or religious group: Klamath Indians
Date: Memorial Day weekend, last weekend in May

IndianAmer-1989, 196

Powwow, Seminole
Location: Seminole Reservation near Hollywood, Florida
Ethnic or religious group: Seminole Indians
Date: February

IndianAmer-1989, 239

Powwow, Shinnecock
Location: Southampton, New York
Ethnic or religious group: Shinnecock Indians
Date: Labor Day weekend, first weekend in September

IndianAmer-1989, 173

Powwow, Sioux
Location: South Dakota
Ethnic or religious group: Sioux Indians
Date: Usually in August

IndianAmer-1989, 103

Powwow, Sioux
Location: Little Eagle, South Dakota
Ethnic or religious group: Sioux Indians
Date: Usually in July

IndianAmer-1989, 50

Powwow, Sioux
Location: Sioux-Lake Village, Sisseton, South Dakota
Ethnic or religious group: Sioux Indians
Date: July

IndianAmer-1989, 106

Powwow, Spotted Tail
See **Rosebud Tribal Fair**

Powwow, Standing Arrow
Location: Elmo, Montana
Ethnic or religious group: Kootenai Indians
Date: Third weekend in July

Chases-1993, 294

Powwow, Toppenish
See **White Swan Celebrations**

Powwow, Warm Springs
Location: Warm Springs, Oregon
Ethnic or religious group: Shahaptian and Chinookan
 Indians
Date: June

IndianAmer-1989, 198

Powwow, Warriors Memorial
Named for: Chief Joseph, In-mut-too-yah-lat-lat
 (c. 1840-1904) and his men
Location: Lapwai, Idaho
Ethnic or religious group: Nez Perce Indians
Date: Third weekend in June

HolFestCelWrld-1994, 184
IndianAmer-1989, 126

Powwow, White Earth Chippewa
Location: White Earth, Minnesota
Date: Weekend of or before June 14

IndianAmer-1989, 155

Powwow, Winnebago
Location: Winnebago, Nebraska
Ethnic or religious group: Winnebago Indians
Date: Usually late July

IndianAmer-1989, 49

Powwow, Wyoming Indian High School
Location: Ethete, Wyoming
Ethnic or religious group: Arapaho Indians
Date: May

IndianAmer-1989, 110

Powwow, Yakima
Location: Yakima Reservation, Washington
Ethnic or religious group: Yakima Indians
Date: September

IndianAmer-1989, 223

Powwow, Yellow Calf Memorial
Location: Ethete, Wyoming
Ethnic or religious group: Arapaho Indians
Date: May

IndianAmer-1989, 110

Powwow and Expo, Black Hills and Northern Plains Indian
Location: Rapid City, South Dakota
Date: July 10-11

Chases-1993, 286

Powwow and Root Feast, Mat-Al-YM'A
Location: Kamiah, Idaho
Ethnic or religious group: Nez Perce Indians
Date: Third weekend in May

IndianAmer-1989, 126

Powwow Days, Rosebud
Location: Rosebud, South Dakota
Ethnic or religious group: Sioux Indians
Date: August

IndianAmer-1989, 104

Powwows, Ojibwa
  Location: Leech Lake Reservation, Cass Lake, Minnesota
  Ethnic or religious group: Ojibwa Indians
  Date: Labor Day, Memorial Day, and in winter, spring, and midsummer

  IndianAmer-1989, 150

Prachum Ben
  Location: Cambodia
  Date: August-September, 12th day of waning half of Cambodian month of Photrobot

  FolkWrldHol-1992, 426
  HolFestCelWrld-1994, 165

Prayer Day, Universal (Dzam Ling Chi Sang)
  Location: Tibet
  Ethnic or religious group: Buddhist
  Date: Usually June or July, 14th-16th days of fifth Tibetan lunar month

  HolFestCelWrld-1994, 351

Preakness Stakes
  Location: Baltimore, Maryland
  Established: 1837
  Date: Nine days in May; race is second Saturday in May

  Chases-1993, 210
  GdUSFest-1984, 81
  HolFestCelWrld-1994, 259

Precious Blood, Feast of the Most
  Ethnic or religious group: Roman Catholic
  Established: Pope Pius IX's authorization in 1849; suppressed in 1969
  Date: July 1

  DaysCustFaith-1957, 166
  HolFestCelWrld-1994, 212
  RelHolCal-1993, 96

Les Prémices des Alpes
  See **First Fruits of the Alps Sunday (Switzerland: Vissoie, Val d'Anniviers, Valais)**

Premier Mai
  See **May Day (France)**

Presentation of Blessed Virgin Mary, Feast of the
  Ethnic or religious group: Greek Orthodox
  Established: Eighth century

  Date: November 21

  HolFestCelWrld-1994, 259
  RelHolCal-1993, 104
  SaintFestCh-1904, 493

Presentation of Blessed Virgin Mary, Feast of the
  Ethnic or religious group: Roman Catholic
  Established: Middle Ages
  Date: November 21

  HolFestCelWrld-1994, 259
  RelHolCal-1993, 104
  SaintFestCh-1904, 493

Presentation of Blessed Virgin Mary, Feast of the
  Location: Greece
  Established: Greek Orthodox since eighth century
  Date: November 21

  FolkWrldHol-1992, 564

Presentation of Christ in the Temple
  See **Candlemas**

Presidential Inauguration Day
  See **Inauguration Day**

Presidents Day
  Location: United States
  Date: Third Monday in February

  AnnivHol-1983, 25
  Chases-1993, 100
  DictDays-1988, 91
  HolFestCelWrld-1994, 259
  See also **Lincoln's Birthday; Washington's Birthday**

Pretzel Sunday
  See **Mid-Lent Sunday (Luxembourg)**

Primavera, Fiesta de la
  Location: San Diego, California
  Established: 1969
  Date: Three days in May

  GdUSFest-1984, 22

Primrose Day
  Named for: Honors Benjamin Disraeli, Earl of Beaconsfield (1804-1881)
  Location: England
  Date: April 19

  DictDays-1988, 91
  HolFestCelWrld-1994, 260

Prince, Birthday of the Third
Location: Singapore
Ethnic or religious group: Chinese Taoist
Date: Eighth and ninth days of fourth lunar month

HolFestCelWrld-1994, 338

Prince's Birthday
Named for: Prince Franz Joseph II (b. 1905)
Location: Liechtenstein
Date: August 15

HolFestCelWrld-1994, 260

Prinsjesdag
Location: Netherlands: The Hague
Date: Third Tuesday in September

HolFestCelWrld-1994, 260

Printing Week
See **Franklin's Birthday, Benjamin**

Prislop Round
See **Dance Festival, Hora at Prislop (Romania: Mount Prislop, Borsa, Maramures County)**

Prithvi Jayanti
See **National Unity Day (Nepal)**

La Procesion De La Penitencia
See **Penitents, Procession of the (Spain: Roncesvalles, Navarre)**

Processie van het Heilig Bloed
See **Holy Blood, Procession of the (Roman Catholics in Bruges, West Flanders, Belgium)**

Procession of Giants of Belgium and France
See **Whit Monday (France: Lille)**

Procession of the Penitents
See **Penitents, Procession of the**

Proclamation Day
Location: South Australia
Date: December 28; observed on December 28 or nearest Monday

DictDays-1988, 91
See also **State Foundation Day (Western Australia)**

Progress of the Precious and Vivifying Cross, Feast of the
Location: Macedonia
Date: August 1

FolkWrldHol-1992, 410

Proms, the
See **Wood Promenade Concerts, Henry**

Protection, Festival to Pledge (Rakhi)
Location: India
Ethnic or religious group: Hindu
Date: July-August, Hindu month of Sravana

BkFest-1937, 159

Protochroneea
See **New Year's Day (Greece)**

Proto Mayea
See **May Day Eve (Greece)**

Provincial Anniversary
Location: New Zealand: Auckland
Date: January 28

DictDays-1988, 91

Provincial Anniversary
Location: New Zealand: Chatham and Westland
Date: December 1

DictDays-1988, 91

Provincial Anniversary
Location: New Zealand: Marlborough
Date: November 4

DictDays-1988, 91

Provincial Anniversary
Location: New Zealand: Nelson
Date: February 4

DictDays-1988, 91

Provincial Anniversary
Location: New Zealand: Otago and Southland
Date: March 23

Chases-1993, 139

Provincial Anniversary
Location: New Zealand: Taranaki
Date: March 11

DictDays-1988, 91

Provincial Anniversary
Location: New Zealand: Wellington
Date: January 21

DictDays-1988, 91

Prvého Máje
See **May Day (Czechoslovakia)**

Psychosavato
See **Decoration Day (Greece)**

Puasa
See **Fast, Feast of Breaking the (Indonesia)**

Puck's Fair (Gathering Day; Scattering Day)
Location: Ireland: Killorglin, County Kerry
Established: Hundreds of years old
Date: August 10-12

FolkWrldHol-1992, 418
HolFestCelWrld-1994, 261

Puja Ketek Celebrations
Location: Malaysia: Bachok, Kelantan
Date: October

IntlThFolk-1979, 266

Pulaski Day
Named for: Count Casimir Pulaski (c. 1748-1779)
Location: United States
Established: About 1915
Date: October 11; first Monday in March in Illinois

AmerBkDays-1978, 913
AnnivHol-1983, 131
Chases-1993, 406
HolFestCelWrld-1994, 261

Pulver Wednesday
See **Ash Wednesday**

Punky Night
Location: England: Lopen and Hinton St. George, Somerset
Date: October 28 or 29 or last Thursday in October

AnnivHol-1983, 138
DictDays-1988, 92
FolkWrldHol-1992, 517
HolFestCelWrld-1994, 261

Puno, Día del
Location: Peru: Puno
Ethnic or religious group: Andean, Quechua, and Aymara Indians
Date: November 5

HolFestCelWrld-1994, 83

Puppeteers, National and International Festivals of Amateur
Location: Czechoslovakia: Chrudim, East Bohemia
Established: 1951
Date: National festival, June-July; International festival, every five years

IntlThFolk-1979, 88

Puppet Festival, International
Location: Yugoslavia: Zagreb, Croatia
Established: 1968
Date: September-October

IntlThFolk-1979, 410

Puppet Festival, UNIMA (Union Internationale de la Marionnette) Congress and
Location: Varies
Established: 1961
Date: Every four years

IntlThFolk-1979, 5

Puppet Festival of Venezuela, National
Location: Venezuela
Established: 1969
Date: One week usually between August and November

IntlThFolk-1979, 378

Puppet Play Encounter
Location: Federal Republic of Germany: Ostfildern, Baden-Wurttemberg
Date: Three days in October during odd-numbered years

IntlThFolk-1979, 147

Puppet Play Week, International
Location: Federal Republic of Germany: Braunschweig, Lower Saxony
Date: One week in March during odd-numbered years

IntlThFolk-1979, 135

Puppets, International Festival of
Location: Spain: Barcelona
Established: 1973
Date: April or May

IntlThFolk-1979, 333

Puppet Theatre, International Festival of
Location: Poland: Bielsko-Biala
Date: Even-numbered years in May-June

IntlThFolk-1979, 291

Puppet Theatre Festival, International
Location: Poland: Bialystok
Established: 1972
Date: Odd-numbered years in March

IntlThFolk-1979, 291

Puppet Theatre of the Nations, International Festival Week
Location: Federal Republic of Germany: Bochum, North Rhine-Westphalia
Established: 1956
Date: One week in May or June

IntlThFolk-1979, 134

Puppet Theatres, All-Poland Festival of
Location: Poland: Opole
Established: 1963
Date: Odd-numbered years in November

IntlThFolk-1979, 295

Puppet Theatres, Holidays of Amateur
Location: Bulgaria: Haskovo
Established: 1976
Date: Even-numbered years in April

IntlThFolk-1979, 52

Puppet Theatres, National Review of Professional
Location: Bulgaria: Sofia
Date: Every five years in October

IntlThFolk-1979, 56

Puppet Theatres, Skupa Festival of Professional
Location: Czechoslovakia: Plzen, West Bohemia
Established: 1967
Date: May

IntlThFolk-1979, 89

Puppet Theatres of Bosnia and Herzegovina, Meeting of
Location: Yugoslavia: location varies within Bosnia and Herzegovina
Established: 1971
Date: May

IntlThFolk-1979, 411

Puppet Theatres of Serbia
Location: Yugoslavia: location varies within Serbia
Date: September-October

IntlThFolk-1979, 412

Puppet Theaters of Slovenia, Encounter of
Location: Yugoslavia: Slovenska Gorica, Slovenia
Established: 1971
Date: February

IntlThFolk-1979, 404

Puppet Theatre Week 1978 (1979, 1980, . . .)
Location: Federal Republic of Germany: location varies
Date: One week in January

IntlThFolk-1979, 154

Purification of the Blessed Virgin Mary
See **Candlemas**

Purilia Chhau Festival
Location: India: Bagmundi Village, Purilia District, West Bengal
Date: April 11-13

IntlThFolk-1979, 217

Purim
Ethnic or religious group: Jewish
Date: February-March, 14th of Jewish month of Adar

AmerBkDays-1978, 281
AnnivHol-1983, 172
BkFest-1937, 206
BkFestHolWrld-1970, 42
BkHolWrld-1986, March 16, 175
Chases-1993, 122
DaysCustFaith-1957, 68
DictDays-1988, 92
DictFolkMyth-1984, 477
DictMyth-1962, i.555, ii.1303
DictWrldRel-1989, 155, 588
FolkAmerHol-1987, 95
FolkWrldHol-1992, 139
HolFestCelWrld-1994, 262
RelHolCal-1993, 105

Purim
Location: Iran; formerly Persia
Date: February-March, 14th of Jewish month of Adar

FolkWrldHol-1992, 139

Purim
Location: Italy: Padua
Date: May-June, 11th of Jewish month of Sivan

RelHolCal-1993, 105

Purim
Location: Morocco: Casablanca
Date: November-December, 2nd of Jewish month of Kislev

RelHolCal-1993, 105

Purim
Location: United States
Date: February-March, 14th of Jewish month of Adar

FolkAmerHol-1987, 95

Purim
    Location: Yemen
    Date: February-March, 14th of Jewish month of Adar

    FolkWrldHol-1992, 139

La Purissima
    Location: Spain

    DictFolkMyth-1984, 980

Purple Spring
    Named for: Honors Señor de los Milagrous (fl. before 1655)
    Location: Peru
    Date: Month of October

    BkFestHolWrld-1970, 95

Puruli
    Ethnic or religious group: Ancient Semite people
    Date: Seasonal festival

    DictFolkMyth-1984, 990

Pushkar Fair
    Location: India: Pushkar Lake, Pushkar, Rajasthan
    Ethnic or religious group: Hindu
    Date: October-November, begins night before full moon
    of Hindu month of Karthika

    BkHolWrld-1986, October 21, 180
    Chases-1993, 454
    GdWrldFest-1985, 112
    HolFestCelWrld-1994, 262

Putrada Ekadashi
    Ethnic or religious group: Hindu
    Date: July-August, 11th day of waxing half of Hindu
    month of Sravana

    RelHolCal-1993, 105

Puye Cliff Ceremonial
    Location: Santa Ana Pueblo, New Mexico
    Date: Last weekend in July

    IndianAmer-1989, 287, 315

Pythian Games
    Location: Ancient Greece
    Established: 586 B.C.
    Date: Every fourth summer

    DictFolkMyth-1984, 67
    HolFestCelWrld-1994, 262

Qing Ming
    See **Grave-Sweeping and Cold Food Festival (China)**
    and (Hong Kong)

Quadragesima Sunday (Firebrand Sunday)
    Ethnic or religious group: Christian
    Date: February, first Sunday in Lent

    DictDays-1988, 93
    DictMyth-1962, i.249
    FestWestEur-1958, 8
    HolFestCelWrld-1994, 263
    RelHolCal-1993, 64, 105
    SaintFestCh-1904, 97

Quadragesima Sunday
    Location: Belgium
    Date: February, first Sunday in Lent

    FestWestEur-1958, 8

Quadragesima Sunday
    Location: Britain
    Date: February, first Sunday in Lent

    DictMyth-1962, i.249
    RelHolCal-1993, 64

Quadragesima Sunday
    Location: United States
    Ethnic or religious group: Neo-pagans
    Date: February, first Sunday in Lent

    DictMyth-1962, i.249
    RelHolCal-1993, 64

Quadrilles of San Martin
    See **St. Martin's Day (Colombia: San Martin, Meta)**

Quarter Days
    Location: England and Ireland
    Date: March 25, June 24, September 29, and December 25

    AnnivHol-1983, 42
    DictDays-1988, 75, 93
    DictMyth-1962, ii.1098, 1100, 1310
    FolkWrldHol-1992, 188, 492
    HolFestCelWrld-1994, 263
    RelHolCal-1993, 95, 105

Quarter Days
    Location: Scotland
    Date: February 2, May 15, August 1, and November 11

    DictDays-1988, 18, 66, 73, 93, 131
    DictFolkMyth-1984, 601
    DictMyth-1962, ii.968, 1310, 1678
    FestSaintDays-1915, 163, 166, 204
    FolkWrldHol-1992, 557
    HolFestCelWrld-1994, 263
    RelHolCal-1993, 105

Quasimodo Sunday
See **Low Sunday**

Quecholli, Feast of Mixcoatl
Ethnic or religious group: Aztec people
Date: 280th day of the Aztec year (14th day, counting by twenties, from February)

DictFolkMyth-1984, 734

Queen Elizabeth II, Birthday of (Falkland Islands Day)
Named for: Elizabeth II (b. 1926)
Location: Falkland Islands
Date: April 21

AnnivHol-1983, 54

Queen Elizabeth II, Official Birthday of
Named for: Elizabeth II (b. 1926)
Location: London, England and throughout Great Britain
Date: June 12 or second Saturday in June

AnnivHol-1983, 78
BkHolWrld-1986, June 13, 181
Chases-1993, 244
DictDays-1988, 112
HolFestCelWrld-1994, 264
NatlHolWrld-1968, 78

Queen Elizabeth's Day
Named for: Elizabeth II (b. 1926)
Location: Australia and Fiji
Date: Monday nearest to official date proclaimed in England

AnnivHol-1983, 79
HolFestCelWrld-1994, 264

Queen Isabella Day
Named for: Isabella (1451-1504)
Location: Spain and parts of the United States
Date: April 22

AnnivHol-1983, 55

Queen Juliana's Birthday
Named for: Juliana (b. 1909)
Location: Netherlands: Amsterdam and The Hague
Date: April 30

AnnivHol-1983, 58
Chases-1993, 186
HolFestCelWrld-1994, 264
NatlHolWrld-1968, 54

Queen Margrethe's Birthday
Named for: Margrethe II (b. 1940)

Location: Denmark: Copenhagen
Date: April 16

BkHolWrld-1986, April 16
Chases-1993, 168

Queen's Birthday
Location: Nepal
Date: November 8

AnnivHol-1983, 143

Queen's Birthday
Named for: Sirikit (b. 1932)
Location: Thailand
Date: August 12

AnnivHol-1983, 105
Chases-1993, 326
HolFestCelWrld-1994, 264

Queen's Day
Named for: Elizabeth I (1533-1603)
Location: Britain
Date: November 17

Chases-1993, 443
DictDays-1988, 93
HolFestCelWrld-1994, 264

Queenship of Mary
Ethnic or religious group: Roman Catholic
Date: August 22

RelHolCal-1993, 106

La Quema del Diablo
See **Burning the Devil (Guatemala: San Cristóbal Totonicapán and Guatemala City)**

Quiet Saturday
See **Holy Saturday**

Quinquagesima Sunday
Ethnic or religious group: Christian
Date: February, Sunday before Lent

DaysCustFaith-1957, 63
DictDays-1988, 93
SaintFestCh-1904, 97

La Quintane
Named for: Honors St. Leonard (n.d.)
Location: France: St.-Léonard-de-Noblat
Date: Second Sunday in November

BkHolWrld-1986, November 8, 180
HolFestCelWrld-1994, 265

Quirinalia
  Named for: Quirinus, god of agriculture and war
  Location: Ancient Rome
  Date: February 17

  AmerBkDays-1978, 223
  DictFolkMyth-1984, 916
  DictMyth-1962, ii.1314
  HolFestCelWrld-1994, 265

Race, Day of the
  See **Columbus Day (Chile, Columbia, Costa Rica, and Paraguay)**

Race for the Palio
  See **Palio, Festival of the**

Race Relations Sunday
  Location: United States
  Ethnic or religious group: Protestant
  Date: February, Sunday nearest Lincoln's Birthday, February 12

  Chases-1993, 98
  DaysCustFaith-1957, 60
  HolFestCelWrld-1994, 267

Race Unity Day
  Ethnic or religious group: Bahá'í
  Established: 1957
  Date: June 13, observed second Sunday in June

  AnnivHol-1983, 79
  Chases-1993, 247
  HolFestCelWrld-1994, 267
  RelHolCal-1993, 106

Radha Ashtami
  Ethnic or religious group: Hindu
  Date: August-September, eighth day of waning half of Hindu month of Bhadrapada

  RelHolCal-1993, 106

Ragbrai
  See **Bicycle Ride across Iowa (Iowa)**

Ragtime and Traditional Jazz Festival, Annual National
  Location: Saint Louis, Missouri
  Established: 1965
  Date: Five days in mid-June

  MusFestAmer-1990, 197

Rain-Bringing Ceremony (Yenaandi)
  Location: Niger

  Ethnic or religious group: Songhay people
  Date: End of the hot-dry season, usually on a Thursday

  FolkWrldHol-1992, 226
  HolFestCelWrld-1994, 229

Rain-Calling Ceremony (Nyambinyambi)
  Location: Namibia
  Ethnic or religious group: Kwangali people
  Date: Spring

  FolkWrldHol-1992, 226
  HolFestCelWrld-1994, 229

Rainha Santa Isabel, Festa da
  See **Holy Queen, Festival of the (Portugal: Coimbra, Beira Litoral)**

Rainmaking Ceremony
  Location: South Africa
  Ethnic or religious group: Lovedu people
  Date: Prior to rainy season

  BkHolWrld-1986, October 22, 180

Raisin Monday
  Location: Scotland: St. Andrew's University
  Date: November

  DictDays-1988, 94

Rakhi
  See **Protection, Festival to Pledge (Hindu people in India)**

Raksha Bandhan
  See **Sacred Thread Festival (Hindu), (India), (India: Bombay)**

Rama, Festival of (Rama-Navami)
  Named for: Sri Rama
  Location: India
  Ethnic or religious group: Hindu and Vaishnavite religions
  Date: March-April, ninth day of waning half of Hindu month of Chaitra

  BkFest-1937, 164
  BkHolWrld-1986, April 18
  Chases-1993, 148
  DictFolkMyth-1984, 923
  DictWrldRel-1989, 304, 597
  FolkWrldHol-1992, 217
  HolFestCelWrld-1994, 268
  RelHolCal-1993, 107

Rama, Festival of (Rama-Navami)
　Named for: Sri Rama
　Location: India: Ayodhya
　Date: March-April, ninth day of waning half of Hindu
　　month of Chaitra

　RelHolCal-1993, 107

Ramadan
　Ethnic or religious group: Muslim
　Date: Ninth month of Islamic year, month of fasting

　AnnivHol-1983, 170
　BkFest-1937, 238
　BkFestHolWrld-1970, 80, 112
　BkHolWrld-1986, May 29
　Chases-1993, 107
　DictDays-1988, 94
　DictWrldRel-1989, 65, 365, 597, 661
　FolkWrldHol-1992, 162
　HolFestCelWrld-1994, 268
　RelHolCal-1993, 107

Ramadan
　Ethnic or religious group: Bedouin people
　Date: Ninth month of Islamic year, month of fasting

　FolkWrldHol-1992, 162

Ramadan
　Location: Southeast Asia
　Date: Ninth month of Islamic year, month of fasting

　DictWrldRel-1989, 365

Ramadan
　Location: Bahrain
　Date: Ninth month of Islamic year, month of fasting

　BkHolWrld-1986, May 29
　FolkWrldHol-1992, 162

Ramadan
　Location: Egypt
　Date: Ninth month of Islamic year, month of fasting

　FolkWrldHol-1992, 163

Ramadan (Lebaran)
　Location: Indonesia
　Date: Ninth month of Islamic year, month of fasting

　FolkWrldHol-1992, 163

Ramadan (Pasa)
　Location: Indonesia: Java

　Date: Ninth month of Islamic year, month of fasting

　FolkWrldHol-1992, 164

Ramadan (Ramazan)
　Location: Iran
　Date: Ninth month of Islamic year, month of fasting

　FolkWrldHol-1992, 165

Ramadan
　Location: Iraq
　Date: Ninth month of Islamic year, month of fasting

　FolkWrldHol-1992, 166

Ramadan
　Location: Jordan
　Date: Ninth month of Islamic year, month of fasting

　FolkWrldHol-1992, 166

Ramadan
　Location: Lebanon
　Date: Ninth month of Islamic year, month of fasting

　FolkWrldHol-1992, 167

Ramadan (Hari Raya)
　Location: Malaya
　Date: Ninth month of Islamic year, month of fasting

　FolkWrldHol-1992, 167

Ramadan
　Location: Morocco
　Date: Ninth month of Islamic year, month of fasting

　FolkWrldHol-1992, 167

Ramadan (Azumi)
　Location: Nigeria: Katsina
　Ethnic or religious group: Hausa people
　Date: Ninth month of Islamic year, month of fasting

　FolkWrldHol-1992, 168

Ramadan (Ramazan)
　Location: Pakistan
　Date: Ninth month of Islamic year, month of fasting

　FolkWrldHol-1992, 168

Ramadan
　Location: Saudi Arabia: Mecca
　Date: Ninth month of Islamic year, month of fasting

　FolkWrldHol-1992, 168

Ramadan
Location: Senegal: Dakar
Date: Ninth month of Islamic year, month of fasting

FolkWrldHol-1992, 169

Ramadan
Location: Sierra Leone: Freetown
Date: Ninth month of Islamic year, month of fasting

FolkWrldHol-1992, 169

Ramadan
Location: Syria: Tell Toqaan
Date: Ninth month of Islamic year, month of fasting

FolkWrldHol-1992, 170

Ramadan
Location: Thailand
Ethnic or religious group: Malay people
Date: Ninth month of Islamic year, month of fasting

FolkWrldHol-1992, 170

Ramadan (Ramazan)
Location: Turkey
Date: Ninth month of Islamic year, month of fasting

FolkWrldHol-1992, 170

Ramadan
Location: United Arab Emirates: Dubai
Date: Ninth month of Islamic year, month of fasting

BkHolWrld-1986, May 29

Ramadan (Boys' Dodo Masquerade)
Location: Upper Volta; now Burkina Faso
Established: Boys' Dodo Masquerade since mid-nineteenth century
Date: Full moon day during ninth month of Islamic year, month of fasting

FolkWrldHol-1992, 171
HolFestCelWrld-1994, 41

Ramadan
Location: West Africa
Date: Ninth month of Islamic year, month of fasting

FolkWrldHol-1992, 172
HolFestCelWrld-1994, 268

Rama Leela Festival
Named for: Commemorates victory of Rama over Ravana
Location: India: Rama Nagar, Uttar Pradesh

Date: Between seven and 31 days in September-October

IntlThFolk-1979, 216

Rama-Navami
See **Rama, Festival of (Hindu and Vaishnavite religions in India) and (India: Ayodhya)**

Ramazan
See **Ramadan (Iran), (Pakistan), and (Turkey)**

Rameaux
See **Palm Sunday (France)**

Ramos, La Fiesta de
See **Palm Sunday (Peru: Moche)**

Ramp Festival, Cosby
Location: Kineauvista Hill near Cosby, Tennessee
Established: 1951
Date: First Sunday in May

HolFestCelWrld-1994, 70

Rand Show
Location: South Africa: Milner Park, Johannesburg
Established: 1895
Date: April-May

GdWrldFest-1985, 160

Rara and Bruler Carnival
See **Mardi Gras (Haiti)**

Rasa Leela Festival
Location: India: Manipur and Uttar Pradesh
Date: One month during August-September, during Janmashtami, Krishna's birthday celebration

DictFolkMyth-1984, 924
IntlThFolk-1979, 216
See also **Janmashtami**

Raspeti Petuk, Crucifixion Friday
See **Good Friday (Bulgaria)**

Rath Yatra, Festival of Jagannatha
See **Juggernaut (Hindu people at Jagannatha temple in Puri, Orissa, India)**

Ratification Day
Named for: January 14, 1784, end of Revolutionary War and Treaty of Paris that ratified the United States; observed since 1962
Location: State House, Annapolis, Maryland

Ratification Day *(cont.)*
Date: January 14

AmerBkDays-1978, 76
AnnivHol-1983, 9
Chases-1993, 63
HolFestCelWrld-1994, 269

Rat's Wedding Day
Location: China
Date: 19th day of first lunar month

FolkWrldHol-1992, 78
HolFestCelWrld-1994, 270

Rattlesnake Roundup, Morris
Location: Morris, Pennsylvania
Established: 1956
Date: Second weekend in June

HolFestCelWrld-1994, 211

Rattlesnake Roundup, Sweetwater
Location: Sweetwater, Texas
Established: 1958
Date: Second weekend in March

FolkAmerHol-1987, 100
HolFestCelWrld-1994, 328

Rattviksdansen
See **Folk Dance and Music, International Festival of (Sweden: Rattvik)**

Ravinia Festival
Location: Chicago or Highland Park, Illinois
Established: 1904
Date: Last week in June to second week in September

GdUSFest-1984, 48
HolFestCelWrld-1994, 270
MusFestAmer-1990, 56
MusFestWrld-1963, 292

Razboieni, Festival of
Named for: Commemorates 1476 battle between the Ottoman army and the Moldavians led by Stephen the Great, Prince of Moldavia (1435-1504)
Location: Romania: Razboieni, Neamt
Date: Last Sunday in July

IntlThFolk-1979, 329
See also **Nation of Heroes**

Rebenlichter
See **Turnip Lantern Festival (Switzerland: Richterswil, Winterthur, and Zurich)**

Rebild Festival
See **Independence Day (United States and Aalborg, Rebild, North Jutland, Denmark)**

Recontres Internationales d'Art Contemporain
See **Arts, Festival of International Contemporary (France: La Rochelle)**

Recovery of the Cross
See **Exaltation of the Cross**

Recovery of the True Cross
See **Exaltation of the Cross (Greek-Americans in the United States)**

Recreation Day
Location: Australia: northern Tasmania
Date: First Monday in November

AnnivHol-1983, 140
Chases-1993, 428
DictDays-1988, 95

Red Bird Smith Ceremony
Named for: Red Bird Smith (1850-1918)
Location: Red Bird Smith Ceremonial Grounds near Vian, Oklahoma
Date: August 17

IndianAmer-1989, 65

Rededication
See **Hanukkah**

Redeemer, Feast of the (Festa del Redentore)
Location: Italy: Nuoro, Sardinia
Established: 1900
Date: Last Sunday in August

IntlThFolk-1979, 245

Redeemer, Feast of the (Festa del Redentore)
Location: Italy: Giudecca Island and Venice, Veneto
Established: 1576, end of the plague
Date: Third Sunday in July

BkHolWrld-1986, July 19, 177
Chases-1993, 298
GdWrldFest-1985, 120
HolFestCelWrld-1994, 270

Redentore, Festa del
See **Redeemer, Feast of the (Italy: Nuoro, Sardinia) and (Italy: Giudecca Island and Venice, Veneto)**

Red Inn Festival
Location: Romania: Gura Vitioarei, Prahova
Date: Last Sunday in June

IntlThFolk-1979, 324

"Red Rose" Festival of Culture
Location: Yugoslavia: Ruski Krstur, Vojvodina
Established: 1960
Date: June-July

IntlThFolk-1979, 401

Red Waistcoat Festival (Festival of the Colete Encarnado)
Location: Portugal: Vila Franca de Xira, Lisboa District,
Ribatejo
Date: July

Chases-1993, 275
FestWestEur-1958, 180
GdWrldFest-1985, 156
HolFestCelWrld-1994, 270
IntlThFolk-1979, 314

Reed Dance (Umhlanga)
Location: Swaziland
Date: One week in late August-early September

AnnivHol-1983, 93
BkHolWrld-1986, August 21, 181
FolkWrldHol-1992, 425
HolFestCelWrld-1994, 270

Reek Sunday
Location: Ireland: pilgrimage to Croagh Patrick Mountain
in County Mayo
Ethnic or religious group: Roman Catholic
Date: Last Sunday in July

AnnivHol-1983, 97
FolkWrldHol-1992, 413
RelHolCal-1993, 108
See also **Lúgnasad**

Refection Sunday
See **Mid-Lent Sunday**

Reformation Day
Named for: Reform of the Roman church led by Martin
Luther (1483-1546) on October 31, 1517
Ethnic or religious group: Lutheran
Date: Observed Sunday preceding October 31

AmerBkDays-1978, 974
AnnivHol-1983, 139
HolFestCelWrld-1994, 271
RelHolCal-1993, 109

Reformation Day
Named for: Reform of the Roman church led by Martin
Luther (1483-1546) on October 31, 1517
Ethnic or religious group: Protestant
Date: Observed Sunday preceding October 31

AmerBkDays-1978, 974
AnnivHol-1983, 139
BkFest-1937, 106
Chases-1993, 427
DaysCustFaith-1957, 277
DictWrldRel-1989, 606
HolFestCelWrld-1994, 271
RelHolCal-1993, 109

Reformation Day
Named for: Reform of the Roman church led by Martin
Luther (1483-1546) on October 31, 1517
Ethnic or religious group: Roman Catholic
Date: Observed Sunday preceding October 31

AmerBkDays-1978, 974

Reformation Day (Usupuhastus Püha)
Named for: Reform of the Roman church led by Martin
Luther (1483-1546) on October 31, 1517
Location: Estonia
Date: Observed Sunday preceding October 31

BkFest-1937, 106

Reformation Day
Named for: Reform of the Roman church led by Martin
Luther (1483-1546) on October 31, 1517
Location: United States
Date: Observed Sunday preceding October 31

AmerBkDays-1978, 974

Reformation Sunday
See **Reformation Day**

Reform Movement Day
Named for: Governmental reforms in 1974
Location: Yemen Arab Republic
Date: June 13

AnnivHol-1983, 79

Refreshment Sunday
See **Mid-Lent Sunday**

Regatta, Charleston Sternwheel
Location: Charleston, West Virginia
Established: 1971
Date: September, ten days ending Labor Day

HolFestCelWrld-1994, 56

Regatta, General Clinton Canoe
  Named for: General George Clinton (1739-1812)
  Location: Cooperstown to Bainbridge, New York
  Established: 1962
  Date: Memorial Day weekend in May

  GdUSFest-1984, 122
  HolFestCelWrld-1994, 116

Regatta, Idaho
  Location: Burley, Idaho
  Date: Last weekend in June

  HolFestCelWrld-1994, 149

Regatta, International
  Location: Netherlands Antilles: Kralendijk, Bonaire
  Established: 1968
  Date: Four days in October

  GdWrldFest-1985, 23

Regatta, New Jersey Offshore Grand Prix (Benihana Grand Prix Power Boat)
  Location: Point Pleasant Beach, New Jersey
  Established: 1964
  Date: Four days in mid-July

  GdUSFest-1984, 119
  HolFestCelWrld-1994, 223

Regatta, Yale-Harvard
  Location: New London, Connecticut
  Established: 1865
  Date: Usually first Sunday in June

  GdUSFest-1984, 30
  HolFestCelWrld-1994, 375

Regatta Day
  Named for: Commemorates 1565 Turkish siege and 1943 German siege
  Location: Malta
  Date: Observed on or near September 5

  AnnivHol-1983, 115
  Chases-1993, 361

Regatta Day, Hobart
  Location: Australia: southern Tasmania
  Date: February 9-10

  AnnivHol-1983, 22
  DictDays-1988, 56, 95
  HolFestCelWrld-1994, 139

Regatta of the Great Maritime Republics
  Location: Italy: Pisa
  Established: 13th century
  Date: First Sunday in June

  HolFestCelWrld-1994, 271

Regatta Week
  Location: Great Britain: Crowes, Isle of Wight
  Established: 1812
  Date: July-August

  GdWrldFest-1985, 98

Reggae Sunsplash
  Named for: Commemorates Bob Marley (1945-1981), popularizer of reggae music
  Location: Jamaica: Montego Bay
  Date: Four nights in August

  HolFestCelWrld-1994, 271

Reindeer Driving Competition
  Location: Finland: Inari
  Ethnic or religious group: Lapp people
  Date: Third week in March

  BkHolWrld-1986, March 15
  HolFestCelWrld-1994, 271

Reindeer Slaughtering
  Location: USSR: Chukchi
  Date: Autumn

  FolkWrldHol-1992, 470

Rejoicing in the Law
  See **Simhat Torah (Israel) and (Jewish)**

Relic Sunday
  Ethnic or religious group: Christian
  Established: 16th century
  Date: Third Sunday after Midsummer Day, June 24

  DictDays-1988, 95

Remedies, Virgin of the
  See **Nativity of the Virgin, Feast of the (Mexico)**

Remembrance, Day of
  See **Yom Ha-Zikkaron**

Remembrance Day
  Location: Bermuda
  Date: November 11

  AnnivHol-1983, 145

Remembrance Day
  Location: Canada
  Date: November 11

  AnnivHol-1983, 145
  Chases-1993, 438

Remembrance Day
  Location: England; formerly Armistice Day
  Date: November 11; observed second Sunday in November

  BkHolWrld-1986, November 11
  DaysCustFaith-1957, 287
  DictDays-1988, 95

Remembrance Day
  Named for: Commemorates liberation by George Patton
    (1885-1945) and troops in 1945
  Location: Luxembourg
  Date: July 6

  AnnivHol-1983, 90

Remembrance of the Departed Days
  Ethnic or religious group: Parsi
  Date: March, last ten days of the Parsi year, the ten days
    preceding the vernal equinox; observed in March by Fasli
    sect; July by Kadmi sect; and August by Shahenshai sect

  AnnivHol-1983, 180
  HolFestCelWrld-1994, 103
  RelHolCal-1993, 101

Remembrance Sunday
  See **Remembrance Day**

Renaissance Festival, Michigan
  Location: Holly, Michigan
  Established: 1980
  Date: August-September

  HolFestCelWrld-1994, 204

Rencontres Internationales de Musique Contemporaine
  See **Music Festival, Metz International Contemporary**
  (France: Metz)

Rendezvous Days
  Location: Grand Portage, Minnesota
  Ethnic or religious group: Ojibwa Indians
  Date: Second weekend in August

  IndianAmer-1989, 149

Republic Day
  Named for: January 11, 1946, founding of the republic

  Location: Albania
  Date: January 11

  AnnivHol-1983, 7

Republic Day
  Named for: November 12, 1918, founding of the republic
  Location: Austria
  Date: November 12

  AnnivHol-1983, 146

Republic Day
  Location: Chad
  Date: November 28

  AnnivHol-1983, 152

Republic Day
  Location: People's Republic of the Congo
  Date: December 31

  AnnivHol-1983, 166

Republic Day (Foundation Day)
  Named for: October 7, 1949, constitution
  Location: German Democratic Republic
  Date: October 7

  AnnivHol-1983, 129
  NatlHolWrld-1968, 77

Republic Day
  Location: Federal Republic of Germany
  Date: June 2

  NatlHolWrld-1968, 77

Republic Day
  Named for: July 1, 1960, republic status within British
    Commonwealth
  Location: Ghana
  Date: July 1

  AnnivHol-1983, 87
  Chases-1993, 272
  NatlHolWrld-1968, 100

Republic Day
  Named for: February 23, 1970, independence within the
    British Commonwealth
  Location: Guyana
  Date: February 23

  AnnivHol-1983, 28
  Chases-1993, 107

Republic Day
   Named for: January 26, 1950, full independence from Britain
   Location: India: New Delhi
   Date: January 26

   AnnivHol-1983, 14, 173
   Chases-1993, 74
   GdWrldFest-1985, 111
   HolFestCelWrld-1994, 271
   IntlThFolk-1979, 205
   NatlHolWrld-1968, 18
   See also **Folk-Dance Festival, Republic Day**

Republic Day (Iraq)
   See **Revolution Day (Iraq)**

Republic Day (Constitution Day)
   Named for: June 2, 1946, founding of the republic
   Location: Italy
   Date: June 2

   AnnivHol-1983, 75
   Chases-1993, 230
   NatlHolWrld-1968, 80

Republic Day
   Location: Republic of Korea
   Date: August 15

   AnnivHol-1983, 107
   Chases-1993, 331

Republic Day
   Named for: December 2, 1975, founding of the republic
   Location: Laos
   Date: December 2

   AnnivHol-1983, 155
   Chases-1993, 462

Republic Day
   Named for: December 30, 1975, founding of the republic
   Location: Madagascar
   Date: December 30

   AnnivHol-1983, 166

Republic Day
   Location: Maldives
   Date: November 11; observed November 11-12

   AnnivHol-1983, 145

Republic Day
   Named for: December 13, 1974, republic within the British
   Commonwealth

Location: Malta
Date: December 13

   AnnivHol-1983, 159
   Chases-1993, 473

Republic Day
   Named for: December 18, 1958, vote for autonomy
   Location: Niger
   Date: December 18

   AnnivHol-1983, 162
   Chases-1993, 477
   NatlHolWrld-1968, 228

Republic Day
   Named for: December 30, 1947, founding of the republic
   Location: Romania
   Date: December 30

   AnnivHol-1983, 166

Republic Day
   Location: Seychelles
   Date: June 29

   AnnivHol-1983, 85

Republic Day
   Named for: April 19, 1971, founding of the republic
   Location: Sierra Leone
   Date: April 19

   AnnivHol-1983, 53
   Chases-1993, 173

Republic Day (Union Day)
   Named for: 1910 union of South Africa, and founding of
   the republic on May 31, 1961
   Location: South Africa: Capetown, Pretoria, and
   Bloemfontein
   Date: May 31

   AnnivHol-1983, 73
   Chases-1993, 228
   DictDays-1988, 95, 124
   HolFestCelWrld-1994, 272
   NatlHolWrld-1968, 72

Republic Day
   Named for: July 25, 1957, founding of republic after end
   of monarchical rule
   Location: Tunisia
   Date: July 25

   AnnivHol-1983, 97

Republic Day
  Named for: October 29, 1923, founding of the republic by
    Mustafa Kemal Atatürk (1881-1938)
  Location: Turkey
  Date: Two days, including October 29

  AnnivHol-1983, 138
  Chases-1993, 424
  HolFestCelWrld-1994, 272
  IntlThFolk-1979, 373
  NatlHolWrld-1968, 194

Republic Day
  Named for: January 22, 1918, proclamation of the republic
  Location: Ukrainian Republic
  Date: January 22

  AnnivHol-1983, 12

Republic Day
  Named for: December 11, 1958, vote for autonomy
  Location: Upper Volta; now Burkina Faso
  Date: December 11

  AnnivHol-1983, 159
  NatlHolWrld-1968, 224

Republic Day
  Location: Republic of Vietnam
  Date: October 26

  NatlHolWrld-1968, 193

Republic Day
  Named for: Founding of the republic in 1945
  Location: Yugoslavia
  Date: November 29-30

  AnnivHol-1983, 152
  NatlHolWrld-1968, 213

Republic Day, Islamic
  Named for: April 1, 1979, founding of the republic
  Location: Iran
  Date: April 1

  AnnivHol-1983, 46

Republic Day, Second
  Named for: April 27, 1945, founding of the second republic
  Location: Austria
  Date: April 27

  AnnivHol-1983, 57
  NatlHolWrld-1968, 49

Republics Day, United Arab
  Named for: September 1, 1971, confederation of Arab
    Republics
  Location: Syria
  Date: September 1

  AnnivHol-1983, 113

Repudiation Day
  Named for: November 23, 1765, resistance to Stamp Act
  Location: Frederick County, Maryland
  Date: November 23

  AnnivHol-1983, 152
  DictDays-1988, 95
  HolFestCelWrld-1994, 272

Resistance Day
  Named for: Resistance against invasion during World War II
  Location: Burma
  Date: March 27

  AnnivHol-1983, 43

Respect for the Aged Day (Keiro-no-ki)
  Location: Japan
  Date: September 15

  AnnivHol-1983, 119
  Chases-1993, 470
  FolkWrldHol-1992, 480
  HolFestCelWrld-1994, 167

Responsibility Day (Kenya)
  See **Madaraka Day**

Restoration Day (northern England)
  See **Shick-Shack Day**

Restoration Day
  Location: Siletz, Oregon
  Ethnic or religious group: Siletz Indian tribes
  Date: November 18 or following Saturday

  IndianAmer-1989, 195

Resurrection Day
  See **Easter**

La Retraite aux Flambeaux
  See **Night Watch (France)**

Return Day
  Location: Delaware, especially Sussex County
  Established: 1828

Return Day *(cont.)*
   Date: Thursday after Presidential Election Day, every leap
      year

   Chases-1993, 431
   FolkAmerHol-1987, 321
   HolFestCelWrld-1994, 272

Revelation of the Koran, Day of the
   See **Night of Power or Destiny**

Revolution Day
   Named for: July 14, 1958, military overthrow of Hashemite
      rule
   Location: Iraq
   Date: July 14

   AnnivHol-1983, 93
   NatlHolWrld-1968, 115

Revolution Day (Nadam)
   Named for: 1921 revolution
   Location: Mongolia
   Date: July 11

   AnnivHol-1983, 92
   Chases-1993, 289
   FolkWrldHol-1992, 364
   HolFestCelWrld-1994, 217

Revolution Day
   Named for: May 25, 1969, revolution
   Location: Sudan
   Date: May 25

   AnnivHol-1983, 71

Revolution Day
   Named for: March 8, 1963, revolution
   Location: Syria
   Date: March 8

   AnnivHol-1983, 35
   Chases-1993, 123

Revolution Day
   Location: Tunisia
   Date: January 18

   AnnivHol-1983, 10
   Chases-1993, 68

Revolution Day (USSR)
   See **October Socialist Revolution Day**

Revolution Day, July (Peaceful Revolution Day)
   Named for: July 17, 1968, government overthrow
   Location: Iraq
   Date: July 17

   AnnivHol-1983, 94
   Chases-1993, 296

Revolution Day, Sandinista
   Named for: Sandinista overthrow of Anastasio Somoza
      (1925-1980) on July 19, 1979
   Location: Nicaragua
   Date: July 19

   AnnivHol-1983, 94
   Chases-1993, 299

Revolution Day, Saur
   Named for: April 27, 1978, Great Saur revolution
   Location: Afghanistan
   Date: April 27

   AnnivHol-1983, 57
   Chases-1993, 182

Revolution Day, Zanzibar
   Named for: January 12, 1963, overthrow of monarchical rule
   Location: Tanzania
   Date: January 12

   AnnivHol-1983, 8
   Chases-1993, 62

Rice Celebration, Wild (Manomin)
   Location: Odanah, Wisconsin
   Ethnic or religious group: Bad River Ojibwa Indians
   Date: August, usually weekend before Labor Day

   IndianAmer-1989, 176

Rice Festival
   Location: Japan
   Date: June-July, date varies

   BkHolWrld-1986, June 7, 180

Richmondshire Festival
   Location: England: Richmond, North Yorkshire
   Established: 1965
   Date: Odd-numbered years in May-June

   IntlThFolk-1979, 174

Ridvan, Feast of
   See **Bahá'u'lláh, Declaration of (Bahá'í)**

Riel, Trial of
Named for: November 16, 1885, execution of Louis Riel (1844-1885)
Location: Canada: Regina, Saskatchewan
Date: Tuesdays, Wednesdays and Fridays in June-August

Chases-1993, 443
IntlThFolk-1979, 77

Rijeka Summer
Location: Yugoslavia: Rijeka, Croatia
Date: July-August

IntlThFolk-1979, 400

Rikugun-Kinenbi
See **Army Commemoration Day (Japan)**

Riley Festival, James Whitcomb
Named for: James Whitcomb Riley (1849-1916)
Location: Greenfield, Indiana
Established: 1911
Date: Three days, including October 7

Chases-1993, 403
GdUSFest-1984, 51
HolFestCelWrld-1994, 159

Ringing Day
Location: England
Date: November 5

DictDays-1988, 96
See also **Fawkes Day, Guy**

Rishi Panchami
Ethnic or religious group: Hindu
Date: August-September, fifth day of waxing half of Hindu month of Bhadrapada

RelHolCal-1993, 109

Rishi-tarpani
See **Sacred Thread Festival (Buddhist and Hindu peoples in Nepal)**

Rithma
See **Theatrical, Musical and Artistic Encounters of Grasse, International (France: Grasse, Alpes-Maritimes)**

River Kwai Bridge Week
Location: Thailand: River Kwai Bridge, Kanchanaburi
Established: Commemorates construction of bridge by Allied prisoners of war and Asian impressed laborers between 1942 and 1945
Date: Last week in November; services at Kanchanaburi War Cemetery on April 25

HolFestCelWrld-1994, 274

Rivermen, Coming of the
See **Santa Cruz Days (Cochiti and Taos pueblos, New Mexico)**

Rizal Day
Named for: José Protasio Rizal (1861-1896)
Location: Philippines
Date: December 30

AnnivHol-1983, 166
Chases-1993, 486
HolFestCelWrld-1994, 274

Road Building Festival (Emume Ibo Uzo)
Location: Nigeria: Mbaise area
Ethnic or religious group: Igbo people
Date: Around April

FolkWrldHol-1992, 221
HolFestCelWrld-1994, 274

Robe Offering Month (Kathin Season or Tod Kathin)
Location: Thailand
Ethnic or religious group: Buddhist
Date: October-December, full moon day of eleventh lunar month to full moon day of twelfth lunar month

BkHolWrld-1986, October 29, 170
DictWrldRel-1989, 135
FolkWrldHol-1992, 527

Robigalia
Named for: Robigus, Roman god
Location: Rome
Date: April 25

AmerBkDays-1978, 313
DictFolkMyth-1984, 916
DictMyth-1962, ii.1343
HolFestCelWrld-1994, 274

Roche-Jagu, Festival of
Location: France: Ploezal-Runan, Cotes-du-Nord
Established: 1977
Date: June-September

IntlThFolk-1979, 119

Rock Day
See **Distaff's Day**

Rockets, Festival of, Boun Bang Fay
See **Buddha's Birthday, Enlightenment, and Salvation (Laos)**

Rodeo, Ellensburg
Location: Ellensburg, Washington
Date: September, Labor Day weekend

HolFestCelWrld-1994, 97

Rodeo, National Circuit Finals
  Location: Pocatello, Idaho
  Established: 1986
  Date: Four days ending third Saturday in March

  HolFestCelWrld-1994, 65

Rodeo, National Finals
  Location: United States: location varies
  Established: 1959
  Date: Nine days in early December

  Chases-1993, 463
  GdUSFest-1984, 146
  HolFestCelWrld-1994, 219

Rodeo, Payson
  Location: Payson, Arizona
  Established: 1885
  Date: Three days in mid-August

  HolFestCelWrld-1994, 248

Rodgers Festival, Jimmie
  Named for: Jimmie Rodgers (1897-1933), country music
  singer
  Location: Meridian, Mississippi
  Date: Last full week in May

  HolFestCelWrld-1994, 161

Rogation Days
  Ethnic or religious group: Christian
  Established: Fifth century; established observance in 511 by
  Council of Orleans
  Date: May, fifth Sunday through Wednesday after Easter

  BkDays-1864, i. 582
  Chases-1993, 211
  DaysCustFaith-1957, 135
  DictDays-1988, 19, 46, 96
  FestSaintDays-1915, 99
  FolkWrldHol-1992, 279
  HolFestCelWrld-1994, 275
  RelHolCal-1993, 109
  SaintFestCh-1904, 227

Rogation Days
  Ethnic or religious group: Church of England
  Date: May, fifth Sunday through Wednesday after Easter

  BkDays-1864, i. 582

Rogation Days
  Ethnic or religious group: Protestant
  Date: May, fifth Sunday through Wednesday after Easter

  HolFestCelWrld-1994, 275
  SaintFestCh-1904, 227

Rogation Days
  Ethnic or religious group: Roman Catholic
  Date: May, fifth Sunday through Wednesday after Easter

  BkDays-1864, i. 582
  DictDays-1988, 19,46,96
  HolFestCelWrld-1994, 275
  SaintFestCh-1904, 227

Rogation Days (Blessing the Fields)
  Location: Austria
  Date: May, fifth Sunday through Wednesday after Easter

  FolkWrldHol-1992, 279
  See also **St. Mark's Day**

Rogation Days (Beating the Bounds)
  Location: England
  Date: May, fifth Sunday through Wednesday after Easter

  FestSaintDays-1915, 102
  HolFestCelWrld-1994, 275
  RelHolCal-1993, 109
  SaintFestCh-1904, 227

Rogation Days
  Location: France
  Date: May, fifth Sunday through Wednesday after Easter

  FolkWrldHol-1992, 279

Rogation Days
  See **Rural Life Sunday (United States)**

Rogers Day, Will
  Named for: William Penn Adair Rogers (1879-1935)
  Location: Oklahoma
  Established: 1947
  Date: November 4

  AmerBkDays-1978, 994
  Chases-1993, 431
  HolFestCelWrld-1994, 368

Rokusai Nembutsu
  See **Dead, Festival of the (Buddhist in Japan)**

Romanian "Calus"
  Location: Romania: Slatina, Olt
  Date: Last weekend in August

  IntlThFolk-1979, 330

Romantic Festival
  Location: Clowes Memorial Hall, Butler University,
    Indianapolis, Indiana
  Established: 1968
  Date: Last two weekends in April

  GdUSFest-1984, 52

Romario
  See **Pilgrimage**

Romario Del Rocio
  See **Pilgrimage of the Dew (Spain: Almonte, Andalusia)**

Rood Day or Roodmas
  See **Exaltation of the Cross**

Roosevelt Day, Franklin D.
  Named for: Franklin D. Roosevelt (1882-1945)
  Location: Kentucky
  Date: January 30

  AmerBkDays-1978, 122
  AnnivHol-1983, 16
  DictDays-1988, 44

Roosevelt Day, Franklin D.
  Named for: Franklin D. Roosevelt (1882-1945)
  Location: Virgin Islands
  Date: January 30

  AmerBkDays-1978, 122

Root Festival
  Location: Warm Springs, Oregon
  Ethnic or religious group: Shahaptian and Chinookan
    Indians
  Date: Mid-April

  IndianAmer-1989, 198

Ropotine
  Location: Romania
  Date: April-May, 28th day after Easter

  FolkWrldHol-1992, 210
  HolFestCelWrld-1994, 275

Rosary, Festival of the
  Ethnic or religious group: Roman Catholic
  Established: October 7, 1571, victory over Muslims prompted
    holy day proclaimed in 1573

Date: First Sunday in October

  BkDays-1864, ii. 402
  DictWrldRel-1989, 630
  HolFestCelWrld-1994, 276
  RelHolCal-1993, 94

Rose Bowl Game
  Location: Pasadena, California
  Established: 1902; Tournament of Roses Parade since 1890
  Date: January 1

  AmerBkDays-1978, 16
  BkFestHolWrld-1970, 3
  BkHolWrld-1986, January 1
  Chases-1993, 51
  DictDays-1988, 97
  FolkAmerHol-1987, 7
  HolFestCelWrld-1994, 276
  See also **Tournament of Roses Parade**

Rosebud Tribal Fair
  Location: Rosebud, South Dakota
  Ethnic or religious group: Sioux Indians
  Date: August

  IndianAmer-1989, 104

Rose Day
  See **Alexandra Rose Day**

Rose Day
  Location: Manheim, Pennsylvania
  Ethnic or religious group: Lutheran
  Date: June 10; observed second Sunday in June

  AnnivHol-1983, 78
  Chases-1993, 247

Rose Festival
  Location: Bulgaria: Kazanluk
  Date: Ten days from late May to early June

  GdWrldFest-1985, 27

Rose Festival
  Location: Thomasville, Georgia
  Established: 1922
  Date: One week in late April

  GdUSFest-1984, 41

Rose Festival, Portland
  Location: Portland, Oregon
  Established: 1889; current version since 1907
  Date: Ten days in early June, beginning the Friday before
    schools close for the summer

Rose Festival, Portland *(cont.)*
AmerBkDays-1978, 525
Chases-1993, 232
GdUSFest-1984, 151
HolFestCelWrld-1994, 257

Rose Festival, Saffron
Location: Spain. Consuegra
Date: Last Sunday in October

HolFestCelWrld-1994, 281

Rose Festival, Texas
Location: Tyler, Texas
Date: Five days in October

HolFestCelWrld-1994, 336

Rose Monday, Rosemontag
See **Mardi Gras (Germany and German-Americans)**

Rose of Tralee International Festival
Location: Ireland: Tralee, County Kerry
Established: 1959
Date: Six days in August-September

GdWrldFest-1985, 114
HolFestCelWrld-1994, 276
IntlThFolk-1979, 236

Rose Sunday (Protestant)
See **Children's Day (National Council of Churches)**

Rose Sunday
Ethnic or religious group: Roman Catholic
Date: Fourth Sunday in Lent

DaysCustFaith-1957, 90
DictDays-1988, 97

Rosh Chodesh
Ethnic or religious group: Jewish
Date: First day of every Jewish month; day of new moon
and last day of each month with 30 days

DictMyth-1962, i.555, 1350

Rosh Hashanah
See **New Year, Jewish**

Round Up—Festival of Performing Arts for Young People
See **Arts for Young People, Festival of Performing
(Australia: Perth, Western Australia)**

Rousa, Feast of
Location: Greece
Date: March-April, 25th day after Easter

FolkWrldHol-1992, 209
HolFestCelWrld-1994, 277

Rovinj Festival
Location: Yugoslavia: Rovinj, Croatia
Date: End of August

IntlThFolk-1979, 400

Royal Maundy
See **Holy Thursday (Great Britain)**

Royal Oak Day
See **Shick-Shack Day**

Royal Tournament
Location: England: London
Date: July

AnnivHol-1983, 181

Rozhdestvo Khristovo
See **Christmas (Russia)**

Rude Day
See **Exaltation of the Cross (Scotland)**

Ruhr Festival
Location: Federal Republic of Germany: Recklinghausen,
North Rhine-Westphalia
Established: 1946
Date: May-June

IntlThFolk-1979, 148

Rukmani Ashtami
Ethnic or religious group: Vaishnavite Hindus
Date: December-January, eighth day of waning half of
Hindu month of Pausha

RelHolCal-1993, 110

Runeberg, Birthday of Johan Ludvig
Named for: Johan Ludvig Runeberg (1804-1877),
Finnish poet
Location: Finland: Helsinki
Date: February 5

BkFest-1937, 110

Rung Khelna, Playing with Color
See **Fire Festival (Nepal)**

Running of the Bulls
Location: Mexico: Huamantla
Ethnic or religious group: Aztec and Christian
Established: Since time Spanish conquistadors brought
cattle; faded around 1700; revived 1920s
Date: Sunday following August 15, Feast of the Assumption

GdWrldFest-1985, 135
HolFestCelWrld-1994, 279

Running of the Bulls (San Fermín Festival)
  Location: Spain: Pamplona, Navarre
  Established: 1591
  Date: July 6-20

  AnnivHol-1983, 90
  BkHolWrld-1986, July 7
  FestWestEur-1958, 201
  GdWrldFest-1985, 163
  HolFestCelWrld-1994, 303

Rural Life Sunday (Soil Stewardship Sunday)
  Location: United States
  Established: 1929
  Date: May, fifth Sunday after Easter

  AmerBkDays-1978, 417
  AnnivHol-1983, 182
  Chases-1993, 211
  DaysCustFaith-1957, 134
  HolFestCelWrld-1994, 275
  RelHolCal-1993, 109

Rusalii
  See **Pentecost (Romania); Trinity Sunday (Romania)**

Rush-Bearing Day
  Location: England: Grasmere
  Established: Over a thousand years ago
  Date: Observed the Saturday nearest St. Oswald's Day, August 5

  AnnivHol-1983, 103
  HolFestCelWrld-1994, 279

Rye Festival
  Location: England: Rye, Sussex
  Established: 1970
  Date: First week in September

  IntlThFolk-1979, 175

Saban Tuy
  See **Plow, Festival of the (USSR: Tatar Republic)**

Saba Saba Day
  See **Farmer's Day (Tanzania)**

Sábato de Gloria, Saturday of Glory
  See **Holy Saturday (Mexico) and (Spain)**

Sabato Santo
  See **Holy Saturday (Italy)**

Sacaea
  Location: Babylonia
  Date: Five-day New Year feast

  DictMyth-1962, ii.1357

Sacred Heart of Jesus, Feast of the
  Ethnic or religious group: Roman Catholic
  Established: 16th-17th century; official since 1865
  Date: May-June, the Friday following Corpus Christi

  AnnivHol-1983, 181
  DictWrldRel-1989, 637
  HolFestCelWrld-1994, 281
  RelHolCal-1993, 111
  SaintFestCh-1904, 273

Sacred Mysteries Performance
  See **New Year's Day (Italy: Como)**

Sacred Thread Festival (Raksha Bandhan)
  Ethnic or religious group: Hindu
  Date: July-August, full moon day of Hindu month of Sravana

  Chases-1993, 314
  FolkWrldHol-1992, 398, 399
  HolFestCelWrld-1994, 268
  RelHolCal-1993, 106

Sacred Thread Festival (Raksha Bandhan)
  Location: India
  Date: July-August, full moon day of Hindu month of Sravana

  AnnivHol-1983, 181
  Chases-1993, 314
  FolkWrldHol-1992, 398
  HolFestCelWrld-1994, 268
  RelHolCal-1993, 106

Sacred Thread Festival (Raksha Bandhan)
  Location: India: Bombay
  Date: July-August, full moon day of Hindu month of Sravana

  RelHolCal-1993, 107

Sacred Thread Festival (Raksha Bandhan)
  Location: Northern India
  Date: July-August, full moon day of Hindu month of Sravana

  Chases-1993, 314
  FolkWrldHol-1992, 398
  HolFestCelWrld-1994, 268

Sacred Thread Festival (Avani Avittam)
    Location: Southern India
    Date: July-August, full moon day of Hindu month of Sravana

    RelHolCal-1993, 107

Sacred Thread Festival (Janai Purnima or Gunpunhi or Kwatipuni or Rishi-tarpani)
    Location: Nepal
    Ethnic or religious group: Buddhist and Hindu
    Date: July-August, full moon day of Hindu month of Sravana

    FolkWrldHol-1992, 399
    HolFestCelWrld-1994, 268

Sacrifice, Day of the Supreme
    Named for: Assassination of President Marien Ngouabi
        (1938-1977) on March 18
    Location: People's Republic of Congo
    Date: March 18

    AnnivHol-1983, 39

Sacrifice, Feast of ('Id al-Adha)
    Ethnic or religious group: Muslim
    Date: Tenth-twelfth days of Dhu'l-Hijjah, twelfth Islamic
        month

    AnnivHol-1983, 171
    BkFest-1937, 238
    BkFestHolWrld-1970, 80
    BkHolWrld-1986, August 28
    DictWrldRel-1989, 290, 569
    FolkWrldHol-1992, 328
    HolFestCelWrld-1994, 150
    RelHolCal-1993, 84

Sacrifice, Feast of (Tabaski)
    Location: Cameroon
    Date: Tenth-twelfth days of Dhu'l-Hijjah, twelfth Islamic
        month

    FolkWrldHol-1992, 328
    HolFestCelWrld-1994, 150

Sacrifice, Feast of (Tabaski)
    Location: Chad
    Date: Tenth-twelfth days of Dhu'l-Hijjah, twelfth Islamic
        month

    FolkWrldHol-1992, 328
    HolFestCelWrld-1994, 150

Sacrifice, Feast of ('Id al-Adha)
    Location: Egypt
    Date: Tenth-twelfth days of Dhu'l-Hijjah, twelfth Islamic
        month

    FolkWrldHol-1992, 329

Sacrifice, Feast of (Bakrid)
    Location: India
    Date: Tenth-twelfth days of Dhu'l-Hijjah, twelfth Islamic
        month

    RelHolCal-1993, 84

Sacrifice, Feast of (Arafa)
    Location: Iran
    Date: Tenth-twelfth days of Dhu'l-Hijjah, twelfth Islamic
        month

    FolkWrldHol-1992, 330

Sacrifice, Feast of ('Id al-Adha)
    Location: Iraq
    Date: Tenth-twelfth days of Dhu'l-Hijjah, twelfth Islamic
        month

    FolkWrldHol-1992, 330

Sacrifice, Feast of (al-Adha al-zid al-kabir)
    Location: Jordan
    Date: Tenth-twelfth days of Dhu'l-Hijjah, twelfth Islamic
        month

    FolkWrldHol-1992, 331

Sacrifice, Feast of ('Id al-Adha)
    Location: Kuwait
    Date: Tenth-twelfth days of Dhu'l-Hijjah, twelfth Islamic
        month

    FolkWrldHol-1992, 331

Sacrifice, Feast of ('Id al-Kabir)
    Location: Morocco: Salé
    Date: Tenth-twelfth days of Dhu'l-Hijjah, twelfth Islamic
        month

    FolkWrldHol-1992, 331

Sacrifice, Feast of (Bakrid or Id-ul-Bakr, Sacrifice of the Ram)
    Location: Pakistan
    Date: Tenth-twelfth days of Dhu'l-Hijjah, twelfth Islamic
        month

    FolkWrldHol-1992, 332
    RelHolCal-1993, 84

Sacrifice, Feast of (Tabaski)
  Location: Senegal
  Date: Tenth-twelfth days of Dhu'l-Hijjah, twelfth Islamic
    month

  FolkWrldHol-1992, 332

Sacrifice, Feast of (Kurban Bayram or Kourban Bairam)
  Location: Turkey
  Date: Tenth-twelfth days of Dhu'l-Hijjah, twelfth Islamic
    month

  BkFest-1937, 238
  FolkWrldHol-1992, 333
  HolFestCelWrld-1994, 150

Sacrifice, Feast of (al-'id al-kabir)
  Location: West Africa
  Date: Tenth-twelfth days of Dhu'l-Hijjah, twelfth Islamic
    month

  FolkWrldHol-1992, 334

Sadie Hawkins Day
  Named for: A character in a Li'l Abner comic strip drawn
    by Al Capp (pseud. for Alfred Gerald Caplin, 1909-1979)
  Established: November 9, 1928
  Date: First Saturday in November

  AnnivHol-1983, 144
  Chases-1993, 433
  DictDays-1988, 100
  HolFestCelWrld-1994, 281

Safari Rally
  Location: Kenya: Nairobi
  Established: 1960
  Date: March-April, Easter weekend

  GdWrldFest-1985, 126
  HolFestCelWrld-1994, 281

Sahara National Festival
  Location: Tunisia: Douz, South Sahara Region
  Established: centuries old
  Date: One week in November-December, depending on the
    weather and the harvest

  GdWrldFest-1985, 178

Sailors' Festival, Fête des Marins
  See **Pentecost (France)**

St. Agatha Festival (Girls' Festival)
  Named for: St. Agatha (d. 251)
  Location: France
  Date: February 5

  FolkWrldHol-1992, 96

St. Agatha Festival
  Named for: St. Agatha (d. 251)
  Location: San Marino
  Date: February 5

  AnnivHol-1983, 19
  NatlHolWrld-1968, 157

St. Agatha Festival
  Named for: St. Agatha (d. 251)
  Location: Sicily: Catania
  Date: February 5; observed February 3-5

  DictMyth-1962, ii.1362
  FestSaintDays-1915, 32
  FestWestEur-1958, 90
  HolFestCelWrld-1994, 282

St. Agnes Eve
  Named for: St. Agnes (d. 304?)
  Ethnic or religious group: Christian
  Date: January 20

  AmerBkDays-1978, 97
  AnnivHol-1983, 12
  BkDays-1864, i. 136, 140
  BkFest-1937, 180
  BkHolWrld-1986, January 21
  DaysCustFaith-1957, 28
  DictDays-1988, 100
  DictFolkMyth-1984, 28
  DictMyth-1962, ii.1362
  FestSaintDays-1915, 20
  HolFestCelWrld-1994, 282
  SaintFestCh-1904, 75

St. Agnes Eve
  Named for: St. Agnes (d. 304?)
  Ethnic or religious group: Anglican
  Date: January 20

  BkHolWrld-1986, January 21

St. Agnes Eve
  Named for: St. Agnes (d. 304?)
  Ethnic or religious group: Eastern Orthodox
  Date: January 20

  AmerBkDays-1978, 97

St. Agnes Eve
Named for: St. Agnes (d. 304?)
Ethnic or religious group: Episcopalian
Date: January 20

AmerBkDays-1978, 97

St. Agnes Eve
Named for: St. Agnes (d. 304?)
Ethnic or religious group: Roman Catholic
Date: January 20

AmerBkDays-1978, 97
AnnivHol-1983, 12
BkDays-1864, i. 140, 141
BkHolWrld-1986, January 21
SaintFestCh-1904, 75

St. Agnes Eve
Named for: St. Agnes (d. 304?)
Location: England
Date: January 20

AmerBkDays-1978, 97
BkHolWrld-1986, January 21
DictFolkMyth-1984, 28
SaintFestCh-1904, 75

St. Agnes Eve
Named for: St. Agnes (d. 304?)
Location: Rome
Date: January 20

AmerBkDays-1978, 97
BkDays-1864, i. 136, 140
DaysCustFaith-1957, 28
FestSaintDays-1915, 22

St. Agnes Eve
Named for: St. Agnes (d. 304?)
Location: Scotland
Date: January 20

AmerBkDays-1978, 97
DictFolkMyth-1984, 28

St. Agnes Eve
Named for: St. Agnes (d. 304?)
Location: Sicily: Catania
Date: January 20; five-day festival in February

BkFest-1937, 180

St. Agnes of Assisi, Feast of
Named for: St. Agnes of Assisi (1196-1253)
Ethnic or religious group: Christian
Date: November 16

DaysCustFaith-1957, 290

St. Alban's Day
Named for: St. Alban (d. c. 304)
Ethnic or religious group: Christian
Date: June 22

BkDays-1864, i.808
DaysCustFaith-1957, 149
DictMyth-1962, ii.1362

St. All-Fools Morn
See **April Fools' Day**

St. Andrew Corsini, Feast Day of
Named for: St. Andrew Corsini (1302-1373)
Ethnic or religious group: Christian
Date: February 4

AnnivHol-1983, 19

St. Andrew-Mass
See **St. Andrew's Day**

St. Andrew's Day
Named for: St. Andrew (d. c. 60-70)
Ethnic or religious group: Christian
Date: November 30

AmerBkDays-1978, 1063
BkDays-1864, ii.635
BkFest-1937, 62, 174
Chases-1993, 459
DaysCustFaith-1957, 296-297
DictDays-1988, 100
DictFolkMyth-1984, 55
DictMyth-1962, ii.1362
FestSaintDays-1915, 216
FolkWrldHol-1992, 566
HolFestCelWrld-1994, 282

St. Andrew's Day
Named for: St. Andrew (d. c. 60-70)
Ethnic or religious group: Eastern Orthodox
Date: November 30

AmerBkDays-1978, 1063

St. Andrew's Day
  Named for: St. Andrew (d. c. 60-70)
  Ethnic or religious group: Episcopalian
  Date: November 30

  AmerBkDays-1978, 1064

St. Andrew's Day
  Named for: St. Andrew (d. c. 60-70)
  Ethnic or religious group: Lapp people
  Date: November 30

  FolkWrldHol-1992, 566
  HolFestCelWrld-1994, 282

St. Andrew's Day
  Named for: St. Andrew (d. c. 60-70)
  Ethnic or religious group: Lutheran
  Date: November 30

  AmerBkDays-1978, 1064

St. Andrew's Day
  Named for: St. Andrew (d. c. 60-70)
  Ethnic or religious group: Roman Catholic
  Date: November 30

  AmerBkDays-1978, 1063

St. Andrew's Day
  Named for: St. Andrew (d. c. 60-70)
  Location: Austria
  Date: November 30

  FestSaintDays-1915, 219
  FolkWrldHol-1992, 566
  HolFestCelWrld-1994, 282

St. Andrew's Day
  Named for: St. Andrew (d. c. 60-70)
  Location: England
  Date: November 30

  BkFest-1937, 62
  FestSaintDays-1915, 217
  DictFolkMyth-1984, 55

St. Andrew's Day
  Named for: St. Andrew (d. c. 60-70)
  Location: Germany
  Date: November 30

  DictFolkMyth-1984, 55

St. Andrew's Day
  Named for: St. Andrew (d. c. 60-70)
  Location: Greece
  Date: November 30

  FestSaintDays-1915, 219

St. Andrew's Day (Szent András Napja)
  Named for: St. Andrew (d. c. 60-70)
  Location: Hungary
  Date: November 30

  BkFest-1937, 174

St. Andrew's Day (Día de San Andrés)
  Named for: St. Andrew (d. c. 60-70)
  Location: Peru: Pacariqtambo
  Date: November 30

  FolkWrldHol-1992, 566

St. Andrew's Day
  Named for: St. Andrew (d. c. 60-70)
  Location: Poland: Sieradz
  Date: November 30

  FestSaintDays-1915, 219

St. Andrew's Day
  Named for: St. Andrew (d. c. 60-70)
  Location: Russia: Moscow
  Date: November 30

  FestSaintDays-1915, 218

St. Andrew's Day
  Named for: St. Andrew (d. c. 60-70)
  Location: Scotland
  Date: November 30

  AmerBkDays-1978, 1065
  BkDays-1864, ii.636
  BkFest-1937, 62
  DictDays-1988, 100
  DictFolkMyth-1984, 55
  FestSaintDays-1915, 217
  FolkWrldHol-1992, 566
  HolFestCelWrld-1994, 282

St. Andrew's Day
  Named for: St. Andrew (d. c. 60-70)
  Location: United States and elsewhere
  Ethnic or religious group: Scottish people and St. Andrew's societies

St. Andrew's Day *(cont.)*
Date: November 30

AmerBkDays-1978, 1065
BkDays-1864, ii.636
DictFolkMyth-1984, 55

St. Andrew's Eve (Andrzejki)
Location: Ohio
Ethnic or religious group: Polish-Americans
Date: November 29-30

FolkAmerHol-1987, 329
HolFestCelWrld-1994, 282

St. Andrew's Eve (Andrzejki)
Location: Poland
Date: November 29

AnnivHol-1983, 152
HolFestCelWrld-1994, 282

St. Andrew's Festival
Location: Scotland: St. Andrews, Fife
Established: 1971
Date: Ten days in February during odd-numbered years

IntlThFolk-1979, 188

St. Anne's Day
Named for: St. Anne d'Auray (fl. first century)
Ethnic or religious group: Christian
Date: July 26

AmerBkDays-1978, 695
AnnivHol-1983, 97
BkFest-1937, 171
DaysCustFaith-1957, 192
DictDays-1988, 100
DictMyth-1962, ii.1362
FestSaintDays-1915, 159, 160
FolkWrldHol-1992, 381
IndianAmer-1989, 287, 312
SaintFestCh-1904, 341, 400
See also **Pilgrimage to St. Anne d'Auray (Canada: Beaupré, Quebec)**

St. Anne's Day
Named for: St. Anne d'Auray (fl. first century)
Location: Canada: Quebec
Date: July 26

AmerBkDays-1978, 695
AnnivHol-1983, 97

DaysCustFaith-1957, 192
FolkWrldHol-1992, 381
HolFestCelWrld-1994, 282
See also **Pilgrimage to St. Anne d'Auray (Canada: Beaupré, Quebec)**

St. Anne's Day
Named for: St. Anne d'Auray (fl. first century)
Location: England
Date: July 26

FestSaintDays-1915, 159

St. Anne's Day (Anna Napja)
Named for: St. Anne d'Auray (fl. first century)
Location: Hungary
Date: July 26

BkFest-1937, 171

St. Anne's Day
Named for: St. Anne d'Auray (fl. first century)
Location: Acoma Pueblo, New Mexico
Date: July 26

AmerBkDays-1978, 696

St. Anne's Day
Named for: St. Anne d'Auray (fl. first century)
Location: Santa Ana Pueblo, New Mexico
Date: July 26

AmerBkDays-1978, 696
IndianAmer-1989, 287, 312

St. Anne's Day
Named for: St. Anne d'Auray (fl. first century)
Location: Taos Pueblo, New Mexico
Date: July 26

AmerBkDays-1978, 696

St. Anne's Day
Named for: St. Anne d'Auray (fl. first century)
Location: Shrine of St. Anne at church of St. Jean Baptiste, New York, New York
Date: July 26

AmerBkDays-1978, 696

St. Anne's Day
Named for: St. Anne d'Auray (fl. first century)
Location: United States
Date: July 26

AmerBkDays-1978, 696
IndianAmer-1989, 287, 312

St. Anthony of Padua, Feast of
  Named for: St. Anthony of Padua (1195-1231)
  Ethnic or religious group: Christian
  Date: June 13

  AmerBkDays-1978, 549
  AnnivHol-1983, 79
  BkFest-1937, 187
  Chases-1993, 246
  DaysCustFaith-1957, 144
  DictMyth-1962, ii.1363
  DictWrldRel-1989, 42
  FestWestEur-1958, 166
  FolkAmerHol-1987, 205
  FolkWrldHol-1992, 267, 325
  HolFestCelWrld-1994, 283
  IndianAmer-1989, 286, 288, 301, 303, 306, 309, 312, 315, 319

St. Anthony of Padua, Feast of
  Named for: St. Anthony of Padua (1195-1231)
  Ethnic or religious group: Roman Catholic
  Date: June 13

  AmerBkDays-1978, 549
  BkFest-1937, 187
  DaysCustFaith-1957, 144
  FestWestEur-1958, 166
  FolkWrldHol-1992, 325
  HolFestCelWrld-1994, 283

St. Anthony of Padua, Feast of (Día de San Antonio)
  Named for: St. Anthony of Padua (1195-1231)
  Location: Chile
  Date: June 13

  FolkWrldHol-1992, 325

St. Anthony of Padua, Feast of
  Named for: St. Anthony of Padua (1195-1231)
  Location: Italy: Rome, Padua
  Date: June 13

  BkFest-1937, 187
  DaysCustFaith-1957, 145
  FolkAmerHol-1987, 205
  FolkWrldHol-1992, 325

St. Anthony of Padua, Feast of
  Named for: St. Anthony of Padua (1195-1231)
  Location: San Antonio and Hot Springs, New Mexico
  Date: June 13

  FolkAmerHol-1987, 206

St. Anthony of Padua, Feast of
  Named for: St. Anthony of Padua (1195-1231)
  Location: New Mexico pueblos
  Date: June 13; observed August 15 at Laguna Pueblo

  AmerBkDays-1978, 551
  IndianAmer-1989, 286, 288, 301, 303, 306, 309, 312, 315, 319

St. Anthony of Padua, Feast of
  Named for: St. Anthony of Padua (1195-1231)
  Location: Shrine Church of St. Anthony of Padua, New York, New York
  Date: June 13

  AmerBkDays-1978, 550
  FolkAmerHol-1987, 205
  HolFestCelWrld-1994, 283

St. Anthony of Padua, Feast of
  Named for: St. Anthony of Padua (1195-1231)
  Location: Portugal: Lisbon
  Date: June 13

  AnnivHol-1983, 79
  Chases-1993, 246
  FestWestEur-1958, 166
  FolkAmerHol-1987, 205
  FolkWrldHol-1992, 325
  HolFestCelWrld-1994, 283

St. Anthony of Padua, Feast of
  Named for: St. Anthony of Padua (1195-1231)
  Location: Puerto Rico
  Date: June 13

  AmerBkDays-1978, 551
  HolFestCelWrld-1994, 283

St. Anthony of Padua, Feast of (Fiesta of San Antonio de Padua)
  Named for: St. Anthony of Padua (1195-1231)
  Location: Spain; Giants and Big Head (Cabezudos) parade in El Pinar village
  Date: June 13

  FolkWrldHol-1992, 325
  HolFestCelWrld-1994, 283

St. Anthony the Abbot of Egypt, Feast of (Blessing of the Animals)
  Named for: St. Anthony the Abbot of Egypt (c. 251-356)
  Ethnic or religious group: Christian
  Established: Fifth century, Jerusalem

St. Anthony the Abbot of Egypt, Feast of (Blessing of the Animals) *(cont.)*
Date: January 17; observed Sunday nearest January 17

AmerBkDays-1978, 84
BkFest-1937, 225, 298
Chases-1993, 67
DictMyth-1962, ii. 1362
FestWestEur-1958, 189, 226
HolFestCelWrld-1994, 283
RelHolCal-1993, 64

St. Anthony the Abbot of Egypt, Feast of (Blessing of the Animals)
Named for: St. Anthony the Abbot of Egypt (c. 251-356)
Ethnic or religious group: Eastern Orthodox
Date: January 17

AmerBkDays-1978, 84

St. Anthony the Abbot of Egypt, Feast of (Blessing of the Animals)
Named for: St. Anthony the Abbot of Egypt (c. 251-356)
Ethnic or religious group: Roman Catholic
Date: January 17

AmerBkDays-1978, 84
RelHolCal-1993, 64

St. Anthony the Abbot of Egypt, Feast of (Blessing of the Animals)
Named for: St. Anthony the Abbot of Egypt (c. 251-356)
Location: Los Angeles, California
Date: January 17

HolFestCelWrld-1994, 283

St. Anthony the Abbot of Egypt, Feast of (Blessing of the Animals)
Named for: St. Anthony the Abbot of Egypt (c. 251-356)
Location: Mexico
Date: January 17

HolFestCelWrld-1994, 283

St. Anthony the Abbot of Egypt, Feast of (Día de San Antón)
Named for: St. Anthony the Abbot of Egypt (c. 251-356)
Location: Spain
Date: January 17

BkFest-1937, 298
FestWestEur-1958, 189
IntlThFolk-1979, 338

St. Anthony the Abbot of Egypt, Feast of
Named for: St. Anthony the Abbot of Egypt (c. 251-356)
Location: Spain: La Puebla, Majorca

Established: 1365
Date: January

IntlThFolk-1979, 338

St. Anthony the Abbot of Egypt, Feast of (Festa di Sant' Antonio)
Named for: St. Anthony the Abbot of Egypt (c. 251-356)
Location: Switzerland: Ticino
Date: January 17

FestWestEur-1958, 226

St. Anthony the Abbot of Egypt, Feast of (Festa di Sant' Antonio)
Named for: St. Anthony the Abbot of Egypt (c. 251-356)
Location: United States
Ethnic or religious group: Hispanic-Americans
Date: January 17

HolFestCelWrld-1994, 283

St. Anthony's Day (San Antonio Abad)
Location: Mexico: Zacatecas and elsewhere
Date: January 17

BkFest-1937, 225
BkHolWrld-1986, January 17

St. Apollonia's Day
Named for: St. Apollonia (d. 250)
Date: February 9

DaysCustFaith-1957, 48
DictMyth-1962, ii.1363
SaintFestCh-1904, 99

St. Augustine, Feast of and Harvest Dance
Location: Isleta Pueblo, New Mexico
Date: September 4

IndianAmer-1989, 288, 296

St. Augustine of Canterbury, Feast of
Named for: St. Augustine of Canterbury (d. c. 605)
Ethnic or religious group: Christian
Date: May 26, Anglican and Episcopalian; May 27, Roman Catholic

AnnivHol-1983, 71
DaysCustFaith-1957, 128
DictMyth-1962, ii.1364

St. Augustine of Hippo, Feast Day of
Named for: St. Augustine of Hippo (354-430)
Ethnic or religious group: Christian
Established: 1565
Date: August 28

AnnivHol-1983, 111
BkDays-1864, ii.277

St. Augustine of Hippo, Feast Day of *(cont.)*
Chases-1993, 244
DaysCustFaith-1957, 221
DictMyth-1962, ii.1364
DictWrldRel-1989, 77
SaintFestCh-1904, 384

St. Barbara's Day
Named for: St. Barbara (fl. third century)
Ethnic or religious group: Christian
Date: December 4

AnnivHol-1983, 155
BkFest-1937, 128
Chases-1993, 465
DaysCustFaith-1957, 305
DictMyth-1962, ii.1364
DictFolkMyth-1984, 950
FestWestEur-1958, 49
FolkAmerHol-1987, 359
FolkWrldHol-1992, 578
HolFestCelWrld-1994, 284

St. Barbara's Day
Named for: St. Barbara (fl. third century)
Location: Bohemia
Date: December 4

DictFolkMyth-1984, 950

St. Barbara's Day
Named for: St. Barbara (fl. third century)
Location: France
Date: December 4

BkFest-1937, 128
DaysCustFaith-1957, 306
FestWestEur-1958, 49
FolkAmerHol-1987, 359
HolFestCelWrld-1994, 284

St. Barbara's Day
Named for: St. Barbara (fl. third century)
Location: Germany
Date: December 4

DaysCustFaith-1957, 306
FolkWrldHol-1992, 578
HolFestCelWrld-1994, 284

St. Barbara's Day
Named for: St. Barbara (fl. third century)
Location: Minnesota and Iowa

Ethnic or religious group: Czech-Americans
Date: December 4

FolkAmerHol-1987, 359

St. Barbara's Day
Named for: St. Barbara (fl. third century)
Location: Poland
Date: December 4

HolFestCelWrld-1994, 284

St. Barbara's Day
Named for: St. Barbara (fl. third century)
Location: Syria
Date: December 4

DaysCustFaith-1957, 306
FolkWrldHol-1992, 578
HolFestCelWrld-1994, 284

St. Barbara's Festival
Location: Portugal: Miranda do Douro, Braganca
Date: August

IntlThFolk-1979, 309

St. Barnabas's Day
Named for: St. Barnabas the Apostle (fl. first century)
Location: England
Ethnic or religious group: Christian
Date: June 11

BkDays-1864, i. 769
DaysCustFaith-1957, 143
DictDays-1988, 9, 69, 100
DictMyth-1962, ii.1364
HolFestCelWrld-1994, 284

St. Bartholomew's Day
Ethnic or religious group: Christian
Date: August 24

AmerBkDays-1978, 774
Chases-1993, 340
DaysCustFaith-1957, 217
DictMyth-1962, ii.1364
FestSaintDays-1915, 173
FestWestEur-1958, 69
FolkAmerHol-1987, 261
See also **Bartholomew Fair**

St. Bartholomew's Day
Location: Armenia
Date: August 24; observed December 8

FestSaintDays-1915, 175

St. Bartholomew's Day
Location: Belgium
Date: August 24

FestSaintDays-1915, 175

St. Bartholomew's Day
Location: Brittany
Date: August 24

FestSaintDays-1915, 175

St. Bartholomew's Day
Location: England
Date: August 24

FestSaintDays-1915, 175
See also **Bartholomew Fair**

St. Bartholomew's Day
Location: Germany: Markgrönigen, Swabia
Date: August 24

FestWestEur-1958, 69

St. Bartholomew's Day
Location: United States
Date: August 24

AmerBkDays-1978, 774
FolkAmerHol-1987, 261

St. Bartholomew's Festival
Location: Portugal: Oporto, Porto
Date: August

IntlThFolk-1979, 310

St. Basil's Day
Named for: St. Basil, Bishop of Caesarea (329-379)
Ethnic or religious group: Christian
Date: January 1, Gregorian calendar (N.S.); January 14, Julian calendar (O.S.)

BkFest-1937, 3, 143, 273, 288
BkFestHolWrld-1970, 4
Chases-1993, 52
DictMyth-1962, ii.1364
DictWrldRel-1989, 93
FolkWrldHol-1992, 11
HolFestCelWrld-1994, 284

St. Basil's Day
Named for: St. Basil, Bishop of Caesarea (329-379)
Ethnic or religious group: Eastern Orthodox

Date: January 1, Gregorian calendar (N.S.); January 14, Julian calendar (O.S.)

Chases-1993, 52
HolFestCelWrld-1994, 284

St. Basil's Day
Named for: St. Basil, Bishop of Caesarea (329-379)
Ethnic or religious group: Greek Orthodox
Date: January 1, Gregorian calendar (N.S.); January 14, Julian calendar (O.S.)

BkFestHolWrld-1970, 4

St. Basil's Day (Shën Vasili)
Named for: St. Basil, Bishop of Caesarea (329-379)
Location: Albania
Ethnic or religious group: Christian and Muslim
Date: January 1

BkFest-1937, 3

St. Basil's Day (Too Ayeeoo Vasilee oo)
Named for: St. Basil, Bishop of Caesarea (329-379)
Location: Greece
Date: January 1, Gregorian calendar (N.S.); January 14, Julian calendar (O.S.)

BkFest-1937, 143
BkFestHolWrld-1970, 4
FolkWrldHol-1992, 11
HolFestCelWrld-1994, 284

St. Basil's Day (Sfântul Vasile)
Named for: St. Basil, Bishop of Caesarea (329-379)
Location: Romania
Date: January 1, Gregorian calendar (N.S.); January 14, Julian calendar (O.S.)

BkFest-1937, 273

St. Basil's Day (Den' Svyatovo Vasil'ya)
Named for: St. Basil, Bishop of Caesarea (329-379)
Location: Russia
Date: January 1, Gregorian calendar (N.S.); January 14, Julian calendar (O.S.)

BkFest-1937, 288

St. Bede the Venerable, Feast of
Named for: St. Bede the Venerable (673-735)
Ethnic or religious group: Roman Catholic
Date: May 25

AmerBkDays-1978, 480
DaysCustFaith-1957, 129
DictMyth-1962, ii.1364

St. Benedict's Day
Named for: St. Benedict of Nursia (480-543)
Location: United States
Ethnic or religious group: Christian Pennsylvania-Dutch people
Date: March 21

DictMyth-1962, ii.1364
FolkAmerHol-1987, 121

St. Bernadette Soubirous at Lourdes
See **Our Lady of Lourdes, Feast of**

St. Bernard of Montjoux
Named for: St. Bernard of Montjoux (923-1008)
Location: French Alps
Ethnic or religious group: Christian
Date: May 28

BkHolWrld-1986, May 28
Chases-1993, 223
DictMyth-1962, ii.1365

St. Blaise's Day
Named for: St. Blaise or Blasius, Bishop of Sebaste (d. 316)
Ethnic or religious group: Christian
Date: February 3

AnnivHol-1983, 18
BkDays-1864, i. 219
DaysCustFaith-1957, 46
DictDays-1988, 100
DictMyth-1962, ii.1365
FestSaintDays-1915, 31
FolkAmerHol-1987, 61
FolkWrldHol-1992, 96
HolFestCelWrld-1994, 284

St. Blaise's Day
Named for: St. Blaise or Blasius, Bishop of Sebaste (d. 316)
Ethnic or religious group: Roman Catholic
Date: February 3

DaysCustFaith-1957, 46
FolkAmerHol-1987, 61
HolFestCelWrld-1994, 284

St. Blaise's Day
Named for: St. Blaise or Blasius, Bishop of Sebaste (d. 316)
Location: England
Date: February 3

BkDays-1864, i.219
HolFestCelWrld-1994, 284

St. Blaise's Day
Named for: St. Blaise or Blasius, Bishop of Sebaste (d. 316)
Location: France
Date: February 3

FolkWrldHol-1992, 96

St. Blaise's Day
Named for: St. Blaise or Blasius, Bishop of Sebaste (d. 316)
Location: New York and Pennsylvania
Ethnic or religious group: Roman Catholic
Date: February 3

FolkAmerHol-1987, 61

St. Blaise's Day (St. Blas's Day)
Named for: St. Blaise or Blasius, Bishop of Sebaste (d. 316)
Location: Paraguay
Date: February 3

AnnivHol-1983, 18
HolFestCelWrld-1994, 284

St. Blaise's Day
Named for: St. Blaise or Blasius, Bishop of Sebaste (d. 316)
Location: Spain
Date: February 3

FolkWrldHol-1992, 96
HolFestCelWrld-1994, 284

St. Bonaventura, Feast of
Named for: St. Bonaventura (1221-1274)
Ethnic or religious group: Christian
Date: July 14

DictMyth-1962, ii.1365

St. Bonaventura, Feast of and Corn Dance
Named for: St. Bonaventura (1221-1274)
Location: Cochiti Pueblo, New Mexico
Date: July 14

IndianAmer-1989, 287, 296

St. Boniface, Feast Day of
Named for: St. Boniface (c. 675-c. 754)
Ethnic or religious group: Anglican and Roman Catholic
Date: June 5

AnnivHol-1983, 75
DictMyth-1962, ii.1365

St. Brendan's Day
  Named for: St. Brendan (c. 484-578)
  Location: Ireland
  Ethnic or religious group: Christian
  Date: May 16

  AnnivHol-1983, 66
  BkHolWrld-1986, May 16
  DaysCustFaith-1957, 124
  DictMyth-1962, ii.1365

St. Brictiva's Day
  Location: Norway
  Ethnic or religious group: Christian
  Date: January 11

  FolkWrldHol-1992, 25

St. Bridget's Day
  Named for: St. Bridget (c. 453-c. 523)
  Ethnic or religious group: Christian
  Date: February 1

  BkDays-1864, i.206
  BkFest-1937, 53
  BkHolWrld-1986, February 1
  DaysCustFaith-1957, 43
  DictFolkMyth-1984, 165, 966
  DictMyth-1962, i.249, ii.1366
  FestSaintDays-1915, 24
  FolkWrldHol-1992, 89
  HolFestCelWrld-1994, 285
  RelHolCal-1993, 64

St. Bridget's Day
  Named for: St. Bridget (c. 453-c. 523)
  Location: Great Britain
  Date: February 1

  BkDays-1864, i.206
  BkFest-1937, 53
  DictFolkMyth-1984, 966
  FestSaintDays-1915, 24

St. Bridget's Day
  Named for: St. Bridget (c. 453-c. 523)
  Location: Ireland
  Ethnic or religious group: Roman Catholic
  Date: February 1

  BkHolWrld-1986, February 1
  DictFolkMyth-1984, 966

  DictMyth-1962, ii.1366
  FolkWrldHol-1992, 89
  HolFestCelWrld-1994, 285

St. Bridget's Day
  Named for: St. Bridget (c. 453-c. 523)
  Location: Scotland
  Date: February 1

  BkDays-1864, i.206
  DictFolkMyth-1984, 966

St. Bridget's Day
  Named for: St. Bridget (c. 453-c. 523)
  Location: United States
  Ethnic or religious group: Neo-pagans
  Date: February 1

  RelHolCal-1993, 64

St. Catherine's Day
  Named for: St. Catherine of Alexandria (supposedly fl.
    fourth century)
  Ethnic or religious group: Christian
  Date: November 25

  BkFest-1937, 128
  BkHolWrld-1986, November 25
  Chases-1993, 453
  DaysCustFaith-1957, 295
  DictDays-1988, 19, 101
  DictFolkMyth-1984, 197, 1168
  DictMyth-1962, ii.1366
  FestSaintDays-1915, 213, 215
  FestWestEur-1958, 48
  FolkWrldHol-1992, 565
  HolFestCelWrld-1994, 285

St. Catherine's Day (La Tire Sainte-Catherine)
  Named for: St. Catherine of Alexandria (supposedly fl.
    fourth century)
  Location: Canada
  Date: November 25

  BkHolWrld-1986, November 25
  FolkWrldHol-1992, 565

St. Catherine's Day
  Named for: St. Catherine of Alexandria (supposedly fl.
    fourth century)
  Location: Carpathian Mountains
  Date: November 25

  DictFolkMyth-1984, 1168

St. Catherine's Day (El Catarina)
  Named for: St. Catherine of Alexandria (supposedly fl. fourth century)
  Location: El Salvador: Apopa
  Date: November 25

  FolkWrldHol-1992, 565

St. Catherine's Day
  Named for: St. Catherine of Alexandria (supposedly fl. fourth century)
  Location: England
  Date: November 25

  DictDays-1988, 19
  DictFolkMyth-1984, 197
  HolFestCelWrld-1994, 285

St. Catherine's Day
  Named for: St. Catherine of Alexandria (supposedly fl. fourth century)
  Location: France
  Date: November 25

  BkFest-1937, 128
  BkHolWrld-1986, November 25
  DictFolkMyth-1984, 197
  FestWestEur-1958, 48
  FolkWrldHol-1992, 565
  HolFestCelWrld-1994, 285

St. Catherine's Day
  Named for: St. Catherine of Alexandria (supposedly fl. fourth century)
  Location: Ireland
  Date: November 25

  FestSaintDays-1915, 215

St. Catherine's Day
  Named for: St. Catherine of Alexandria (supposedly fl. fourth century)
  Location: Spain
  Date: November 25

  DictFolkMyth-1984, 197

St. Cecilia's Day
  Named for: St. Cecilia of Rome (d. 230)
  Ethnic or religious group: Christian
  Date: November 22

  AnnivHol-1983, 150
  BkDays-1864, ii. 604

  Chases-1993, 450
  DaysCustFaith-1957, 293
  DictDays-1988, 101
  FolkAmerHol-1987, 327
  HolFestCelWrld-1994, 285
  SaintFestCh-1904, 494

St. Cecilia's Day
  Named for: St. Cecilia of Rome (d. 230)
  Location: England
  Date: November 22

  BkDays-1864, ii. 604
  DaysCustFaith-1957, 293
  HolFestCelWrld-1994, 285

St. Cecilia's Day
  Named for: St. Cecilia of Rome (d. 230)
  Location: Italy: Rome
  Date: November 22

  AnnivHol-1983, 150

St. Cecilia's Day
  Named for: St. Cecilia of Rome (d. 230)
  Location: Charleston, South Carolina
  Date: November 22

  FolkAmerHol-1987, 327

St. Charlemagne's Day
  Named for: Charlemagne (742-814; not officially canonized)
  Location: France
  Date: January 28

  AnnivHol-1983, 15
  DaysCustFaith-1957, 34
  DictMyth-1962, i.314

St. Charles's Day
  Named for: Charles I (1600-1649)
  Location: England
  Ethnic or religious group: Anglican
  Date: January 30; observed on or near February 2 at Trafalgar Square, London

  AnnivHol-1983, 15
  BkDays-1864, i.189
  Chases-1993, 78
  DaysCustFaith-1957, 35
  DictDays-1988, 19
  HolFestCelWrld-1994, 285
  SaintFestCh-1904, 87

St. Charles's Day
Named for: Charles I (1600-1649)
Location: United States
Ethnic or religious group: Episcopalian
Date: January 30

DaysCustFaith-1957, 35

St. Christina's Day (Festival of Santa Cristina)
Location: Spain: Lloret de Mar, Gerona
Ethnic or religious group: Christian
Date: July 24, feast day; festival held in July

IntlThFolk-1979, 339

St. Christopher's Day
Named for: St. Christopher (fl. c. third century)
Ethnic or religious group: Christian
Date: July 25

AmerBkDays-1978, 692
AnnivHol-1983, 96
BkDays-1864, ii.122
DaysCustFaith-1957, 190
DictMyth-1962, ii.1367
FestSaintDays-1915, 156
FolkAmerHol-1987, 243
HolFestCelWrld-1994, 286

St. Christopher's Day
Named for: St. Christopher (fl. c. third century)
Ethnic or religious group: Eastern Orthodox
Date: July 25

AmerBkDays-1978, 693

St. Christopher's Day
Named for: St. Christopher (fl. c. third century)
Ethnic or religious group: Roman Catholic
Date: July 25

AmerBkDays-1978, 692
DaysCustFaith-1957, 190
FolkAmerHol-1987, 243
HolFestCelWrld-1994, 286

St. Christopher's Day
Named for: St. Christopher (fl. c. third century)
Location: Nesquehaning, Pennsylvania
Ethnic or religious group: Roman Catholic
Date: July 25

FolkAmerHol-1987, 243
HolFestCelWrld-1994, 286

St. Clare of Assisi, Feast of
Named for: St. Clare of Assisi (c. 1194-1253)
Ethnic or religious group: Christian
Date: August 11

AmerBkDays-1978, 747
AnnivHol-1983, 105
Chases-1993, 325
DaysCustFaith-1957, 205
IndianAmer-1989, 288, 315

St. Clare of Assisi, Feast of
Named for: St. Clare of Assisi (c. 1194-1253)
Ethnic or religious group: Episcopalian
Date: August 11

AmerBkDays-1978, 747

St. Clare of Assisi, Feast of
Named for: St. Clare of Assisi (c. 1194-1253)
Ethnic or religious group: Roman Catholic
Date: August 11

AmerBkDays-1978, 747

St. Clare of Assisi, Feast of
Named for: St. Clare of Assisi (c. 1194-1253)
Location: Santa Clara Pueblo, New Mexico
Date: August 11; observed August 12 with Corn, Harvest, Comanche or Buffalo dances

IndianAmer-1989, 288, 315

St. Clement's Day
Named for: St. Clement (d. c. 100)
Location: England
Ethnic or religious group: Christian
Date: November 23

DaysCustFaith-1957, 293
DictDays-1988, 101
DictMyth-1962, ii.1367
FestSaintDays-1915, 210

St. Columba's Day
Named for: Columcille (c. 521-597)
Ethnic or religious group: Roman Catholic
Date: June 9

AnnivHol-1983, 77
DaysCustFaith-1957, 142
DictMyth-1962, ii.1367
HolFestCelWrld-1994, 286

St. Crispin's Day
 Named for: Crispin and Crispinian (both d. c. 287)
 Ethnic or religious group: Christian
 Date: October 25

BkDays-1864, ii. 492
BkHolWrld-1986, October 25
DaysCustFaith-1957, 267
DictDays-1988, 101
DictFolkMyth-1984, 261
DictMyth-1962, ii.1367
FestSaintDays-1915, 188
FolkWrldHol-1992, 514
HolFestCelWrld-1994, 286

St. Crispin's Day
 Named for: Crispin and Crispinian (both d. c. 287)
 Location: England
 Date: October 25

BkHolWrld-1986, October 25
DictDays-1988, 101
DictFolkMyth-1984, 261
FestSaintDays-1915, 188
FolkWrldHol-1992, 514

St. Crispin's Day
 Named for: Crispin and Crispinian (both d. c. 287)
 Location: France
 Date: October 25

BkHolWrld-1986, October 25
DictFolkMyth-1984, 261

St. Crispin's Day
 Named for: Crispin and Crispinian (both d. c. 287)
 Location: Germany: Westphalia
 Date: Observed June 20

DictFolkMyth-1984, 261

St. Crispin's Day
 Named for: Crispin and Crispinian (both d. c. 287)
 Location: Ireland
 Date: October 25

FestSaintDays-1915, 189

St. Crispin's Day
 Named for: Crispin and Crispinian (both d. c. 287)
 Location: Scotland
 Date: October 25

FestSaintDays-1915, 190

St. Crispin's Day
 Named for: Crispin and Crispinian (both d. c. 287)
 Location: Wales: Tenby
 Date: October 25

BkDays-1864, ii.492
DictFolkMyth-1984, 261

St. Daniel's Day
 Named for: St. Daniel the Stylite (409-493)
 Ethnic or religious group: Christian
 Date: December 11

DaysCustFaith-1957, 310
SaintFestCh-1904, 18

St. David's Day
 Named for: St. David, Archbishop of Caerleon
  (fl. sixth century)
 Ethnic or religious group: Christian
 Date: March 1

AmerBkDays-1978, 223
AnnivHol-1983, 31, 32
BkDays-1864, i. 315
BkFest-1937, 55
BkHolWrld-1986, March 1
Chases-1993, 116
DaysCustFaith-1957, 70
DictDays-1988, 102, 107
DictFolkMyth-1984, 612
DictMyth-1962, ii.1367
FestSaintDays-1915, 37
FolkAmerHol-1987, 103
FolkWrldHol-1992, 153
HolFestCelWrld-1994, 286

St. David's Day
 Named for: St. David, Archbishop of Caerleon
  (fl. sixth century)
 Location: England
 Date: March 1

BkDays-1864, i. 315
BkFest-1937, 55

St. David's Day
 Named for: St. David, Archbishop of Caerleon
  (fl. sixth century)
 Location: United States
 Ethnic or religious group: Welsh-Americans
 Date: March 1

AmerBkDays-1978, 223
FolkAmerHol-1987, 103
HolFestCelWrld-1994, 286

St. David's Day
Named for: St. David, Archbishop of Caerleon
(fl. sixth century)
Location: Wales
Date: March 1

AmerBkDays-1978, 223
AnnivHol-1983, 32
BkHolWrld-1986, March 1
Chases-1993, 116
DictDays-1988, 102, 107
DictFolkMyth-1984, 612
FestSaintDays-1915, 37
FolkWrldHol-1992, 153
HolFestCelWrld-1994, 286

St. Demetrius, Festival of
Named for: St. Demetrius (d. 306); formerly ancient
Greek festival of Demeter
Ethnic or religious group: Christian
Date: October 26

DictFolkMyth-1984, 867
FolkWrldHol-1992, 515
GdWrldFest-1985, 103
HolFestCelWrld-1994, 287
IntlThFolk-1979, 196

St. Demetrius, Festival of
Named for: St. Demetrius (d. 306); formerly ancient
Greek festival of Demeter
Location: Greece: Thessaloniki
Established: 1966, a revival of 12th-century version
Date: October, including October 26

GdWrldFest-1985, 103
HolFestCelWrld-1994, 287
IntlThFolk-1979, 196

St. Demetrius, Festival of
Named for: St. Demetrius (d. 306); formerly ancient
Greek festival of Demeter
Location: Greece: Thrace
Date: October 26

FolkWrldHol-1992, 515

St. Denis's Day
Named for: St. Denis (d. c. 250)
Ethnic or religious group: Christian
Date: October 9

DaysCustFaith-1957, 253
DictMyth-1962, ii.1367
SaintFestCh-1904, 443

St. Devota's Day
Named for: St. Devota (d. c. 303)
Location: Monaco
Ethnic or religious group: Christian
Date: January 27

AnnivHol-1983, 14

St. Dismas's Day
Named for: St. Dismas (d. c. 30)
Ethnic or religious group: Christian
Date: March 25

DaysCustFaith-1957, 88
DictDays-1988, 33
DictMyth-1962, ii.1368
HolFestCelWrld-1994, 287
RelHolCal-1993, 57

St. Dismas's Day
Named for: St. Dismas (d. c. 30)
Location: Prisons in the United States
Ethnic or religious group: National Catholic Prison
Chaplains Association
Date: Second Sunday in October

DictDays-1988, 49
HolFestCelWrld-1994, 287

St. Distaff's Day
See **Distaff's Day**

St. Dominic, Feast of
Named for: St. Dominic (d. 1221)
Ethnic or religious group: Christian
Date: August 4

DictMyth-1962, ii.1368

St. Dominic, Feast of, and Corn Dance
Named for: St. Dominic (d. 1221)
Location: Jemez and Santo Domingo pueblos, New Mexico
Date: August 4

IndianAmer-1989, 288, 300, 315

St. Dominique's Day (Midwife's Day)
Named for: St. Dominique (c. 1170-1221)
Location: Greece and Macedonia
Ethnic or religious group: Greeks, Macedonians, and Greek
refugees from Bulgaria
Date: January 22

Chases-1993, 59
FolkWrldHol-1992, 35
HolFestCelWrld-1994, 287

St. Dorothy, Feast of
  Named for: St. Dorothy (d. c. 303-313)
  Ethnic or religious group: Christian
  Date: February 6

  AnnivHol-1983, 20
  DictMyth-1962, ii.1368

St. Dunstan's Day
  Named for: St. Dunstan, Archbishop of Canterbury
  (c. 908-988)
  Ethnic or religious group: Christian
  Date: May 19

  BkDays-1864, i. 653
  DaysCustFaith-1957, 126
  DictMyth-1962, ii.1368

St. Dymphna's Day
  Named for: St. Dymphna (fl. seventh century)
  Location: Belgium: Geel, Antwerp
  Ethnic or religious group: Christian
  Established: 13th century
  Date: May 15

  AnnivHol-1983, 66
  BkFest-1937, 42
  DaysCustFaith-1957, 123
  DictMyth-1962, ii.1368
  FestWestEur-1958, 11
  HolFestCelWrld-1994, 287

St. Edmund Campion, Feast Day of
  Named for: St. Edmund Campion (1540-1581)
  Ethnic or religious group: Christian
  Date: December 1

  AnnivHol-1983, 154

St. Edward the Confessor's Day
  Named for: St. Edward (c. 1003-1066)
  Ethnic or religious group: Christian
  Date: October 13

  AnnivHol-1983, 132
  DaysCustFaith-1957, 256

St. Efisio, Festival of
  Location: Italy: Cagliari, Sardinia
  Established: 1657
  Date: May 1-4

  Chases-1993, 188
  HolFestCelWrld-1994, 307
  IntlThFolk-1979, 241

St. Elias Day
  Location: Macedonia
  Ethnic or religious group: Christian
  Date: August 2, also National Day

  AnnivHol-1983, 102
  Chases-1993, 315

St. Elizabeth, Feast of
  Named for: St. Elizabeth of Hungary (fl. 1207-1231)
  Ethnic or religious group: Christian
  Date: November 19

  DaysCustFaith-1957, 291
  DictMyth-1962, ii.1369

St. Elizabeth, Feast of
  Location: Paguate Village, Laguna Pueblo,
  New Mexico
  Date: September 25

  IndianAmer-1989, 289, 301

St. Elizabeth, Feast of
  Named for: St. Elizabeth of Hungary (fl. 1207-1231)
  Location: Peru
  Date: November 19

  DaysCustFaith-1957, 291
  HolFestCelWrld-1994, 288

St. Elizabeth, Feast of
  Named for: St. Elizabeth, mother of John the Baptist
  (fl. first century)
  Location: Peru: Huyalas
  Ethnic or religious group: Christian
  Date: July 8

  FolkWrldHol-1992, 363
  HolFestCelWrld-1994, 288

St. Elizabeth Ann Seton, Feast of
  Named for: St. Elizabeth Ann Seton (1774-1821)
  Location: United States
  Ethnic or religious group: Roman Catholic
  Date: January 4; observed as Mother Seton Day, December
  1 by the Sisters of Charity of St. Vincent De Paul

  AmerBkDays-1978, 23
  AnnivHol-1983, 4
  Chases-1993, 56
  HolFestCelWrld-1994, 287
  RelHolCal-1993, 96

St. Elmo's Day
  Named for: St. Erasmus (d. c. 303)
  Ethnic or religious group: Christian
  Date: June 2

  AnnivHol-1983, 75
  DaysCustFaith-1957, 140-141
  DictMyth-1962, ii.1369

St. Eric's Day
  Named for: St. Eric (d. 1160)
  Location: Sweden and United States
  Ethnic or religious group: Swedish-American
    Christians
  Date: May 18

  DaysCustFaith-1957, 125

St. Etheldreda's Day
  Named for: St. Etheldreda or Audry, abbess of Ely (d. 679)
  Ethnic or religious group: Roman Catholic
  Date: June 23

  BkDays-1864, ii. 459
  DictMyth-1962, ii.1363

St. Etheldreda's Day
  Named for: St. Etheldreda or Audry, abbess of Ely (d. 679)
  Location: England: Ely
  Ethnic or religious group: Church of England
  Date: October 17

  BkDays-1864, ii. 459

St. Fiacre's Day
  Named for: St. Fiacre (fl. seventh century)
  Ethnic or religious group: Roman Catholic
  Date: August 30

  AnnivHol-1983, 113
  DaysCustFaith-1957, 224
  DictMyth-1962, ii.1369

St. Frances Cabrini, Feast of
  Named for: St. Francesca Xaviera Cabrini
    (1850-1917)
  Location: United States
  Ethnic or religious group: Roman Catholic
  Date: November 13

  AmerBkDays-1978, 1019
  Chases-1993, 292
  HolFestCelWrld-1994, 288

St. Frances of Rome, Feast Day of
  Named for: St. Frances of Rome (1384-1440)
  Location: Italy: Rome
  Ethnic or religious group: Christian
  Date: March 9

  AnnivHol-1983, 35
  Chases-1993, 124
  HolFestCelWrld-1994, 289

St. Francis of Assisi, Feast of
  Named for: Francesco di Pietro di Bernardone (1182?-1226)
  Ethnic or religious group: Christian
  Date: October 4

  AmerBkDays-1978, 892
  BkFestHolWrld-1970, 111
  BkHolWrld-1986, October 4
  Chases-1993, 399
  DaysCustFaith-1957, 251
  DictMyth-1962, ii.1369
  DictWrldRel-1989, 266
  FolkAmerHol-1987, 295
  HolFestCelWrld-1994, 109, 289
  IndianAmer-1989, 257, 289, 302

St. Francis of Assisi, Feast of
  Named for: Francesco di Pietro di Bernardone (1182?-1226)
  Ethnic or religious group: Episcopalian
  Date: October 4

  AmerBkDays-1978, 892

St. Francis of Assisi, Feast of
  Named for: Francesco di Pietro di Bernardone (1182?-1226)
  Ethnic or religious group: Roman Catholic
  Date: October 4

  AmerBkDays-1978, 892
  DaysCustFaith-1957, 251

St. Francis of Assisi, Feast of
  Named for: Francesco di Pietro di Bernardone (1182?-1226)
  Location: Maricopa, Arizona
  Ethnic or religious group: Pima and Maricopa Indians
  Date: October 4

  IndianAmer-1989, 257

St. Francis of Assisi, Feast of
  Named for: Francesco di Pietro di Bernardone (1182?-1226)
  Location: Sells, Arizona
  Ethnic or religious group: Papago Indians
  Date: October 4

  AmerBkDays-1978, 895

St. Francis of Assisi, Feast of
Named for: Francesco di Pietro di Bernardone (1182?-1226)
Location: Mission of San Antonio de Pala, San Diego County, California
Ethnic or religious group: Native Americans
Date: October 4

AmerBkDays-1978, 894

St. Francis of Assisi, Feast of
Named for: Francesco di Pietro di Bernardone (1182?-1226)
Location: Italy: Assisi
Date: August 1-2

HolFestCelWrld-1994, 109, 289

St. Francis of Assisi, Festival of
Named for: Francesco di Pietro di Bernardone (1182?-1226)
Location: Mexico: Cuetzalan, Puebla
Date: Early October

IntlThFolk-1979, 276

St. Francis of Assisi (La Percíngula)
Named for: Francesco di Pietro di Bernardone (1182?-1226)
Location: Arroyo Hondo, New Mexico; southern Colorado
Established: 13th century
Date: August 2

FolkAmerHol-1987, 255
HolFestCelWrld-1994, 109

St. Francis of Assisi, Feast of
Named for: Francesco di Pietro di Bernardone (1182?-1226)
Location: Nambe Pueblo, New Mexico
Date: October 4

AmerBkDays-1978, 895
IndianAmer-1989, 289, 302

St. Francis of Assisi, Feast of
Named for: Francesco di Pietro di Bernardone (1182?-1226)
Location: Santa Fe, New Mexico
Date: October 4

AmerBkDays-1978, 895

St. Francis of Assisi, Feast of
Named for: Francesco di Pietro di Bernardone (1182?-1226)
Location: Taos Pueblo, New Mexico
Date: October 4

AmerBkDays-1978, 895

St. Francis of Assisi, Feast of (San Francisco's Day)
Named for: Francesco di Pietro di Bernardone (1182?-1226)
Location: Peru: Lima
Date: October 4

BkFestHolWrld-1970, 111

St. Francis of Assisi, Feast of
Named for: Francesco di Pietro di Bernardone (1182?-1226)
Location: United States
Date: October 4

HolFestCelWrld-1994, 289

St. Francis de Sales, Feast of
Named for: St. Francis de Sales, Bishop of Genova (1567-1622)
Ethnic or religious group: Christian
Date: January 24

AnnivHol-1983, 13
DictWrldRel-1989, 266

St. Francis Xavier, Feast Day of
Named for: St. Francis Xavier (1506-1552)
Ethnic or religious group: Christian
Date: December 3

AnnivHol-1983, 155
DictWrldRel-1989, 266

St. Gall, Feast of
Named for: St. Gall (d. 646)
Ethnic or religious group: Christian
Date: October 16

AnnivHol-1983, 133

St. Geneviève's Day
Named for: St. Geneviève (c. 422-512)
Ethnic or religious group: Roman Catholic
Date: January 3

BkDays-1864, i. 42
DictMyth-1962, ii.1370

St. Gennaro
See **St. Januarius's Feast Day**

St. Gens, Festival of (La Fête de St. Gens)
Location: France: Monteux, Provence
Date: Twice yearly: Sunday following May 15 at Monteux and first weekend in September at Beaucet

FestWestEur-1958, 37

St. George's Day
 Named for: St. George (d. c. 303)
 Ethnic or religious group: Christian
 Established: 1222
 Date: April 23

 AmerBkDays-1978, 373
 AnnivHol-1983, 55
 BkDays-1864, i. 539
 BkFest-1937, 58, 104, 169, 330
 BkFestHolWrld-1970, 81
 BkHolWrld-1986, April 23
 Chases-1993, 177
 DaysCustFaith-1957, 98, 287
 DictDays-1988, 46, 102
 DictMyth-1962, ii.1370
 FestSaintDays-1915, 93
 FestWestEur-1958, 63, 231
 FolkWrldHol-1992, 247
 HolFestCelWrld-1994, 289

St. George's Day
 Named for: St. George (d. c. 303)
 Ethnic or religious group: Eastern Orthodox
 Date: April 23, Gregorian calendar (N.S.); May 6, Julian calendar (O.S.)

 AmerBkDays-1978, 373

St. George's Day
 Named for: St. George (d. c. 303)
 Ethnic or religious group: Protestant
 Date: April 23

 AmerBkDays-1978, 373

St. George's Day
 Named for: St. George (d. c. 303)
 Ethnic or religious group: Roman Catholic
 Date: April 23

 AmerBkDays-1978, 373

St. George's Day
 Named for: St. George (d. c. 303)
 Location: Bulgaria
 Date: April 23

 HolFestCelWrld-1994, 290

St. George's Day
 Named for: St. George (d. c. 303)
 Location: England
 Date: April 23

 AmerBkDays-1978, 374

 BkFest-1937, 58
 BkFestHolWrld-1970, 81
 BkHolWrld-1986, April 23
 DictDays-1988, 102
 FestSaintDays-1915, 93
 FolkWrldHol-1992, 247

St. George's Day (Jüri Päev)
 Named for: St. George (d. c. 303)
 Location: Estonia
 Date: April 23

 BkFest-1937, 104

St. George's Day (Georgiritt Parade)
 Named for: St. George (d. c. 303)
 Location: Germany: Traunstein, Upper Bavaria
 Date: April 23

 FestWestEur-1958, 63

St. George's Day
 Named for: St. George (d. c. 303)
 Location: Greece
 Date: April 23

 BkFestHolWrld-1970, 81

St. George's Day (Szent György Napja)
 Named for: St. George (d. c. 303)
 Location: Hungary
 Date: April 23

 BkFest-1937, 169

St. George's Day
 Named for: St. George (d. c. 303)
 Location: Macedonia
 Date: April 23

 FolkWrldHol-1992, 247

St. George's Day
 Named for: St. George (d. c. 303)
 Location: Newfoundland
 Date: April 23

 AnnivHol-1983, 55
 DictDays-1988, 103

St. George's Day
 Named for: St. George (d. c. 303)
 Location: Romania
 Date: April 23

 FolkWrldHol-1992, 247

St. George's Day (Jerjew Den)
Named for: St. George (d. c. 303)
Location: Russia
Date: April 23 and November 26

AmerBkDays-1978, 373
BkFestHolWrld-1970, 81
FolkWrldHol-1992, 248

St. George's Day
Named for: St. George (d. c. 303)
Location: Spain: Alicante
Date: April 22-23 festival commemorating 1276
  Moorish siege

FolkWrldHol-1992, 249

St. George's Day
Named for: St. George (d. c. 303)
Location: Spain: Barcelona
Date: April 23

AnnivHol-1983, 55

St. George's Day
Named for: St. George (d. c. 303)
Location: Switzerland: Turtmann, Valais
Date: April 23

FestWestEur-1958, 231

St. George's Day ('Id Marjurjus)
Named for: St. George (d. c. 303)
Location: Syria: monastery at Humeira
Date: April 23

BkFest-1937, 330
BkFestHolWrld-1970, 81

St. George's Day
Named for: St. George (d. c. 303)
Location: USSR: Mtskheta, Georgian Republic
Date: Observed February 25, National Day

DictMyth-1962, ii.1370
FolkWrldHol-1992, 138
HolFestCelWrld-1994, 289

St. George's Day
Named for: St. George (d. c. 303)
Location: United States
Date: April 23

AmerBkDays-1978, 374
BkFestHolWrld-1970, 81
HolFestCelWrld-1994, 289

St. George's Day
Named for: St. George (d. c. 303)
Location: Yugoslavia: Orasac
Date: April 23

FolkWrldHol-1992, 249

St. Giles's Day
Named for: St. Giles (d. eighth century)
Ethnic or religious group: Christian
Date: September 1

DaysCustFaith-1957, 229
DictMyth-1962, ii.1371

St. Gregory I the Great, Feast of
Named for: St. Gregory I the Great (c. 540-604)
Ethnic or religious group: Roman Catholic
Date: September 3

AnnivHol-1983, 114
DictWrldRel-1989, 285

St. Gregory's Day
Named for: St. Gregory I the Great (c. 540-604)
Ethnic or religious group: Christian
Date: March 12

DaysCustFaith-1957, 77
DictMyth-1962, ii.1371

St. Gregory's Day
Named for: St. Gregory I the Great (c. 540-604)
Location: Belgium
Date: March 12

FestWestEur-1958, 5

St. Grouse's Day
See **Glorious Twelfth (Scotland)**

St. Gudula's Day
Named for: St. Gudula (c. 650-712)
Location: Belgium
Ethnic or religious group: Roman Catholic
Date: January 8

BkDays-1864, i. 73
BkFest-1937, 38
Chases-1993, 59
DictMyth-1962, ii.1371
FestWestEur-1958, 4
HolFestCelWrld-1994, 290

St. Helena's Day
Named for: St. Helena (c. 250-c. 330)
Ethnic or religious group: Christian

St. Helena's Day *(cont.)*
  Date: August 18

  AnnivHol-1983, 108
  DaysCustFaith-1957, 210

St. Hilary's Day
  Named for: St. Hilary, Bishop of Poitiers (c. 315-c. 367)
  Ethnic or religious group: Anglican
  Date: January 13

  AnnivHol-1983, 8
  DictDays-1988, 103

St. Hilary's Day
  Named for: St. Hilary, Bishop of Poitiers (c. 315-c. 367)
  Ethnic or religious group: Roman Catholic
  Date: January 14

  DictDays-1988, 103

St. Honoratus's Day
  Named for: St. Honoratus (c. 350-429)
  Location: France
  Ethnic or religious group: Christian
  Date: January 16

  FolkWrldHol-1992, 31

St. Hubert, Feast Day of
  Named for: St. Hubert, Bishop of Liége (d. 727)
  Ethnic or religious group: Christian
  Date: November 3

  AnnivHol-1983, 141
  BkFest-1937, 46
  DaysCustFaith-1957, 283
  DictMyth-1962, ii.1371
  FestWestEur-1958, 17, 118
  FolkWrldHol-1992, 549
  HolFestCelWrld-1994, 290

St. Hubert, Feast Day of
  Named for: St. Hubert, Bishop of Liége (d. 727)
  Location: Belgium
  Date: November 3

  AnnivHol-1983, 141
  BkFest-1937, 46
  FestWestEur-1958, 17
  FolkWrldHol-1992, 549

St. Hubert, Feast Day of
  Named for: St. Hubert, Bishop of Liége (d. 727)
  Location: Luxembourg

  Date: November 3

  AnnivHol-1983, 141
  FestWestEur-1958, 118
  HolFestCelWrld-1994, 290

St. Ignatius Loyola, Feast of
  Named for: St. Inigo de Onaz y Loyola (1491-1556)
  Ethnic or religious group: Roman Catholic
  Established: 1623
  Date: July 31

  AmerBkDays-1978, 709
  BkDays-1864, ii.148
  BkHolWrld-1986, July 31
  Chases-1993, 311
  DictMyth-1962, ii.1371
  DictWrldRel-1989, 336
  HolFestCelWrld-1994, 290

St. Ignatius Loyola, Feast of
  Named for: St. Inigo de Onaz y Loyola (1491-1556)
  Location: Boise, Idaho
  Ethnic or religious group: Basque-Americans
  Date: July 31

  AmerBkDays-1978, 709
  HolFestCelWrld-1994, 290

St. Ignatius Loyola, Feast of
  Named for: St. Inigo de Onaz y Loyola (1491-1556)
  Location: Spain
  Ethnic or religious group: Basque people
  Established: 1623
  Date: July 31

  BkHolWrld-1986, July 31
  HolFestCelWrld-1994, 290

St. Ildephonsus, Feast Day of
  Named for: St. Ildephonsus (c. 606-667)
  Location: San Ildefonso Pueblo, New Mexico
  Ethnic or religious group: Roman Catholic
  Date: January 23; observed with Buffalo and Deer dances

  AnnivHol-1983, 13
  IndianAmer-1989, 285, 309

St. Iria Fair
  Location: Portugal: Faro
  Date: October

  IntlThFolk-1979, 305

St. Isidore, Festival of
Location: Mexico: Metepec
Date: Mid-May

IntlThFolk-1979, 272

St. Isidore, Festival of
Location: Mexico: Acapantzingo, Morelos
Date: May

IntlThFolk-1979, 272

St. Isidore, Festival of
Location: Mexico: Matamoros, Tamaulipas
Date: Mid-May

IntlThFolk-1979, 272

St. Isidore of Seville, Feast of (San Isidro)
Named for: St. Isidore of Seville (c. 560-636)
Location: Colombia: Río Frío
Ethnic or religious group: Christian
Date: April 4

FolkWrldHol-1992, 231
HolFestCelWrld-1994, 304

St. Isidore the Husbandman or Farmer, Feast of
Named for: San Isidro Labrador (1070-1130)
Ethnic or religious group: Christian
Date: May 15

AnnivHol-1983, 66
BkFest-1937, 302
Chases-1993, 209
FestWestEur-1958, 195
FolkWrldHol-1992, 298
HolFestCelWrld-1994, 304
IntlThFolk-1979, 272

St. Isidore the Husbandman or Farmer, Feast of
Named for: San Isidro Labrador (1070-1130)
Location: Marianas: Saipan
Ethnic or religious group: Roman Catholic Carolinians
Date: May 15

FolkWrldHol-1992, 298
HolFestCelWrld-1994, 303

St. Isidore the Husbandman or Farmer, Feast of (Philippines)
See **Water Buffalo Festival (Carabao)**

St. Isidore the Husbandman or Farmer, Feast of
Named for: San Isidro Labrador (1070-1130)
Location: Spain: Madrid
Established: 12th century

Date: May 10-17

AnnivHol-1983, 66
BkFest-1937, 302
FestWestEur-1958, 195
FolkWrldHol-1992, 299
HolFestCelWrld-1994, 303

St. Ivo, Pardon of
Named for: St. Ivo (1253-1303)
Location: Pilgrimage in France
Ethnic or religious group: Christian
Date: May 19

AnnivHol-1983, 67

St. James the Greater's Day
Named for: St. James the Greater (d. 44)
Ethnic or religious group: Christian
Date: July 25

AmerBkDays-1978, 69
DaysCustFaith-1957, 189
DictDays-1988, 103
DictMyth-1962, ii.1372
DictFolkMyth-1984, 963, 971, 1063, 1111
FestSaintDays-1915, 152
FestWestEur-1958, 202
FolkAmerHol-1987, 237
FolkWrldHol-1992, 380
HolFestCelWrld-1994, 291
IndianAmer-1989, 287, 309, 319

St. James the Greater's Day
Named for: St. James the Greater (d. 44)
Ethnic or religious group: Eastern Orthodox
Date: April 30

AmerBkDays-1978, 693
HolFestCelWrld-1994, 291

St. James the Greater's Day
Named for: St. James the Greater (d. 44)
Ethnic or religious group: Episcopalian
Date: July 25

AmerBkDays-1978, 693

St. James the Greater's Day
Named for: St. James the Greater (d. 44)
Ethnic or religious group: Roman Catholic
Date: July 25

AmerBkDays-1978, 693
FestWestEur-1958, 202
FolkAmerHol-1987, 237

St. James the Greater's Day
  Named for: St. James the Greater (d. 44)
  Location: Bolivia
  Date: July 25

  DictFolkMyth-1984, 1111
  HolFestCelWrld-1994, 183

St. James the Greater's Day
  Named for: St. James the Greater (d. 44)
  Location: Great Britain
  Date: July 25

  FolkWrldHol-1992, 380

St. James the Greater's Day
  Named for: St. James the Greater (d. 44)
  Location: Acoma, Santa Ana, and other pueblos in
   New Mexico
  Date: July 25

  AmerBkDays-1978, 694, 696
  DictFolkMyth-1984, 963
  IndianAmer-1989, 287, 309, 319

St. James the Greater's Day (Fiestas de Santiago y Santa Ana)
  Named for: St. James the Greater (d. 44)
  Location: Taos Pueblo, New Mexico
  Date: July 25-26 or nearest weekend

  AmerBkDays-1978, 694, 696
  IndianAmer-1989, 287, 319

St. James the Greater's Day
  Named for: St. James the Greater (d. 44)
  Location: Peru
  Date: July 25

  DictFolkMyth-1984, 1111

St. James the Greater's Day (Fiesta of Santiago)
  Named for: St. James the Greater (d. 44)
  Location: Puerto Rico: Loíza
  Date: July 25

  FolkAmerHol-1987, 237
  FolkWrldHol-1992, 380
  HolFestCelWrld-1994, 291

St. James's the Greater's Day (Fiesta of the Llamas)
  Named for: St. James the Greater (d. 44)
  Location: South America
  Ethnic or religious group: Quechua Indians
  Date: July 25

  DictFolkMyth-1984, 971

St. James the Greater's Day (El Día de Santiago)
  Named for: St. James the Greater (d. 44)
  Location: Spain
  Date: July 25

  AmerBkDays-1978, 694
  DaysCustFaith-1957, 190
  DictFolkMyth-1984, 1063
  FestWestEur-1958, 202
  HolFestCelWrld-1994, 291

St. James the Greater's Day (Fiesta de Santiago Appostol)
  Named for: St. James the Greater (d. 44)
  Location: Spain: Santiago de Compostela, Galicia
  Date: July 25, during holy years, when St. James's Day
   falls on a Sunday

  AmerBkDays-1978, 694
  DaysCustFaith-1957, 190
  FestWestEur-1958, 202
  HolFestCelWrld-1994, 291

St. Januarius's Feast Day
  Named for: St. Januarius, Bishop of Benevento (272?-305?)
  Ethnic or religious group: Christian
  Date: September 19

  AnnivHol-1983, 120
  Chases-1993, 379
  DaysCustFaith-1957, 238
  DictMyth-1962, ii.1372
  FolkAmerHol-1987, 285
  GdUSFest-1984, 125
  HolFestCelWrld-1994, 303

St. Januarius's Feast Day
  Named for: St. Januarius, Bishop of Benevento (272?-305?)
  Location: Italy: shrine at Naples
  Date: September 19

  DaysCustFaith-1957, 239
  HolFestCelWrld-1994, 303

St. Januarius's Feast Day
  Named for: St. Januarius, Bishop of Benevento
   (272?-305?)
  Location: Little Italy, New York
  Ethnic or religious group: Roman Catholic Italian-
   Americans
  Established: 1925
  Date: Two weeks, including September 19

  FolkAmerHol-1987, 285
  GdUSFest-1984, 125
  HolFestCelWrld-1994, 303

St. Jean Baptise Day
See **Midsummer Day (French-Canadians in Canada)**

St. Jerome's Day
Named for: St. Jerome (c. 341-420)
Ethnic or religious group: Christian
Date: September 30

Chases-1993, 390
DaysCustFaith-1957, 243
DictMyth-1962, ii.1372
DictWrldRel-1989, 378
HolFestCelWrld-1994, 303
IndianAmer-1989, 289, 319

St. Jerome's Day
Named for: St. Jerome (c. 341-420)
Ethnic or religious group: Roman Catholic
Date: September 30

DaysCustFaith-1957, 243

St. Jerome's Day
Named for: St. Jerome (c. 341-420)
Location: Taos Pueblo, New Mexico
Date: Observed September 29-30

HolFestCelWrld-1994, 303
IndianAmer-1989, 289, 319

St. Joan of Arc, Feast of
Named for: St. Joan of Arc (Jeanne la Pucelle, c. 1412-1431)
Ethnic or religious group: Christian
Date: May 31

AnnivHol-1983, 73
BkFest-1937, 123
BkHolWrld-1986, May 11, 180
Chases-1993, 227
DaysCustFaith-1957, 130
DictMyth-1962, ii.881
DictWrldRel-1989, 383
HolFestCelWrld-1994, 161

St. Joan of Arc, Feast of (Fête de Jeanne d'Arc)
Named for: St. Joan of Arc (Jeanne la Pucelle, c. 1412-1431)
Location: France: Rouen and Orleans
Date: Second Sunday in May

BkFest-1937, 123
BkHolWrld-1986, May 11, 180
HolFestCelWrld-1994, 161

St. Joan of Arc, Feast of
Named for: St. Joan of Arc (Jeanne la Pucelle, c. 1412-1431)
Location: New Orleans, Louisiana
Date: May 9

DaysCustFaith-1957, 130
HolFestCelWrld-1994, 161

St. John Damascene, Feast of
Named for: St. John Damascene (c. 676-749)
Ethnic or religious group: Christian
Date: December 4

AnnivHol-1983, 155

St. John Lateran's Dedication
Location: Italy: Roman Catholic Church of St. John the Baptist, Rome
Ethnic or religious group: Roman Catholic
Established: November 9, 324
Date: November 9

AnnivHol-1983, 144
DaysCustFaith-1957, 285
RelHolCal-1993, 71

St. John Nepomucene Neumann, Feast of
Named for: St. John Nepomucene Neumann (1811-1860)
Ethnic or religious group: Roman Catholic
Date: January 5

AmerBkDays-1978, 33
AnnivHol-1983, 4
Chases-1993, 145

St. John, Apostle and Evangelist, Feast of
Named for: St. John (c. 6-100)
Ethnic or religious group: Christian
Date: December 27

AmerBkDays-1978, 1154
AnnivHol-1983, 165
BkDays-1864, ii. 771
Chases-1993, 484
DaysCustFaith-1957, 323
DictMyth-1962, ii.1373
FolkWrldHol-1992, 644
HolFestCelWrld-1994, 292

St. John, Apostle and Evangelist, Feast of
Named for: St. John (c. 6-100)
Ethnic or religious group: Eastern Orthodox
Date: May 8

AmerBkDays-1978, 1154
AnnivHol-1983, 165
Chases-1993, 484

St. John, Apostle and Evangelist, Feast of
Named for: St. John (c. 6-100)
Ethnic or religious group: Protestant
Date: December 27

AmerBkDays-1978, 1154

St. John, Apostle and Evangelist, Feast of
Named for: St. John (c. 6-100)
Ethnic or religious group: Roman Catholic
Date: December 27; May 6, festival in Rome

AmerBkDays-1978, 1154
BkDays-1864, ii. 771
DaysCustFaith-1957, 323

St. John, Apostle and Evangelist, Feast of
Named for: St. John (c. 6-100)
Location: Austria
Date: December 27

FolkWrldHol-1992, 644

St. John, Apostle and Evangelist, Feast of (San Juan's Day)
Named for: St. John (c. 6-100)
Location: Bolivia
Date: December 27

FolkWrldHol-1992, 644

St. John the Baptist's Day
Named for: St. John the Baptist (d. c. 29)
Ethnic or religious group: Christian
Date: June 24

AmerBkDays-1978, 587
BkDays-1864, i. 814
BkFest-1937, 229
BkFestHolWrld-1970, 98
BkHolWrld-1986, June 24
Chases-1993, 262
DaysCustFaith-1957, 151, 222
DictDays-1988, 103
DictFolkMyth-1984, 1063, 1082
DictMyth-1962, ii.1372
DictWrldRel-1989, 384
FestSaintDays-1915, 140
HolFestCelWrld-1994, 292, 306
IndianAmer-1989, 287, 296, 312, 319
See also **Midsummer Day**

St. John the Baptist's Day
Named for: St. John the Baptist (d. c. 29)
Ethnic or religious group: Anglican
Date: June 24

HolFestCelWrld-1994, 292

St. John the Baptist's Day
Named for: St. John the Baptist (d. c. 29)
Ethnic or religious group: Eastern Orthodox
Date: June 24 and August 29, the martyrdom of St. John

AmerBkDays-1978, 588
AnnivHol-1983, 111
DaysCustFaith-1957, 152
HolFestCelWrld-1994, 291, 292

St. John the Baptist's Day
Named for: St. John the Baptist (d. c. 29)
Ethnic or religious group: Episcopalian
Date: June 24

AmerBkDays-1978, 588

St. John the Baptist's Day
Named for: St. John the Baptist (d. c. 29)
Ethnic or religious group: Lutheran
Date: June 24

AmerBkDays-1978, 588
HolFestCelWrld-1994, 292

St. John the Baptist's Day
Named for: St. John the Baptist (d. c. 29)
Ethnic or religious group: Roman Catholic
Date: June 24 and August 29, the martyrdom of St. John

AmerBkDays-1978, 588
AnnivHol-1983, 111
HolFestCelWrld-1994, 292

St. John the Baptist's Day (Fiesta de San Juan Bautista)
Named for: St. John the Baptist (d. c. 29)
Location: San Juan Bautista, California
Date: June 24

AmerBkDays-1978, 590

St. John the Baptist's Day
Named for: St. John the Baptist (d. c. 29)
Location: Canada: Montreal, Quebec, and other parts of French Canada
Date: June 24

AmerBkDays-1978, 589
BkHolWrld-1986, June 24
HolFestCelWrld-1994, 292

St. John the Baptist's Day
Named for: St. John the Baptist (d. c. 29)
Location: Greece
Date: January 7

FolkWrldHol-1992, 24

St. John the Baptist's Day
  Named for: St. John the Baptist (d. c. 29)
  Location: Italy
  Date: June 24

  FolkAmerHol-1987, 220

St. John the Baptist's Day
  Named for: St. John the Baptist (d. c. 29)
  Location: Mexico
  Date: June 24

  BkFest-1937, 229
  HolFestCelWrld-1994, 292

St. John the Baptist's Day
  Named for: St. John the Baptist (d. c. 29)
  Location: Moravia
  Date: June 24

  BkHolWrld-1986, June 24

St. John the Baptist's Day
  Named for: St. John the Baptist (d. c. 29)
  Location: New Mexico pueblos
  Date: June 24

  AmerBkDays-1978, 590
  FolkAmerHol-1987, 219
  HolFestCelWrld-1994, 306
  IndianAmer-1989, 286, 287, 296, 312, 319

St. John the Baptist's Day
  Named for: St. John the Baptist (d. c. 29)
  Location: Cochiti Pueblo, New Mexico
  Date: June 24

  AmerBkDays-1978, 590
  FolkAmerHol-1987, 219
  IndianAmer-1989, 287, 296

St. John the Baptist's Day (San Juan Pueblo Feast Day)
  Named for: St. John the Baptist (d. c. 29)
  Location: San Juan Pueblo, New Mexico
  Date: June 24

  HolFestCelWrld-1994, 306

St. John the Baptist's Day (San Juan Fiesta)
  Named for: St. John the Baptist (d. c. 29)
  Location: New York, New York
  Established: 1953
  Date: Sunday nearest June 24

  AmerBkDays-1978, 589
  AnnivHol-1983, 83
  HolFestCelWrld-1994, 292, 306

St. John the Baptist's Day (Fiesta de San Juan)
  Named for: St. John the Baptist (d. c. 29)
  Location: Paraguay
  Date: June 24

  FolkWrldHol-1992, 339
  HolFestCelWrld-1994, 305

St. John the Baptist's Day (San Juan Day)
  Named for: St. John the Baptist (d. c. 29)
  Location: Peru: Pacarigtambo
  Date: June 24

  FolkWrldHol-1992, 270

St. John the Baptist's Day
  Named for: St. John the Baptist (d. c. 29)
  Location: Portugal
  Date: June 24

  DictFolkMyth-1984, 1082
  HolFestCelWrld-1994, 291

St. John the Baptist's Day (San Juan Bautista)
  Named for: St. John the Baptist (d. c. 29)
  Location: Puerto Rico
  Date: One week, including June 24

  AmerBkDays-1978, 590
  AnnivHol-1983, 83
  FolkAmerHol-1987, 218
  HolFestCelWrld-1994, 306

St. John the Baptist's Day
  Named for: St. John the Baptist (d. c. 29)
  Location: Spain
  Date: June 24

  BkHolWrld-1986, June 24
  DictFolkMyth-1984, 1063

St. John's Day or Eve
  See **Midsummer Day**

St. Joseph of Arimathea, Feast Day of
  Named for: St. Joseph of Arimathea (fl. first century)
  Ethnic or religious group: Christian
  Date: March 19; formerly observed March 17

  AnnivHol-1983, 38, 39
  BkFest-1937, 181, 299
  Chases-1993, 134
  DaysCustFaith-1957, 82
  DictMyth-1962, ii.1373
  FestWestEur-1958, 90
  FolkAmerHol-1987, 113
  FolkWrldHol-1992, 180
  GdUSFest-1984, 72
  HolFestCelWrld-1994, 292
  NatlHolWrld-1968, 36

St. Joseph of Arimathea, Feast Day of
   Named for: St. Joseph of Arimathea (fl. first century)
   Ethnic or religious group: Roman Catholic
   Date: March 19; formerly observed March 17

   AnnivHol-1983, 39
   BkHolWrld-1986, March 19
   Chases-1993, 134
   FolkAmerHol-1987, 113

St. Joseph of Arimathea, Feast Day of
   Named for: St. Joseph of Arimathea (fl. first century)
   Location: Liechtenstein
   Date: March 19; formerly observed March 17

   NatlHolWrld-1968, 36

St. Joseph of Arimathea, Feast Day of
   Named for: St. Joseph of Arimathea (fl. first century)
   Location: Sicily
   Date: March 19; formerly observed March 17

   FestWestEur-1958, 90
   FolkWrldHol-1992, 180

St. Joseph of Arimathea, Feast Day of
   Named for: St. Joseph of Arimathea (fl. first century)
   Location: Southern California; Detroit, Michigan; Buffalo, New York; and elsewhere in the United States
   Ethnic or religious group: Sicilian- and Italian-Americans
   Date: March 19; formerly observed March 17

   BkFest-1937, 181
   FolkAmerHol-1987, 113
   GdUSFest-1984, 72
   HolFestCelWrld-1994, 292

St. Joseph's Day
   Location: Guam/Northern Marianas
   Ethnic or religious group: Chamorros people
   Date: May 1

   FolkWrldHol-1992, 267

St. Joseph the Worker, Feast of
   Location: Malta
   Ethnic or religious group: Christian
   Date: May 1

   HolFestCelWrld-1994, 293

St. Joseph's Day (Dia de San Giuseppe)
   Location: Italy

Date: March 19

   BkFest-1937, 181
   BkHolWrld-1986, March 19
   FestWestEur-1958, 90
   HolFestCelWrld-1994, 292

St. Joseph's Day (International Fair of San José)
   Location: Panama: David
   Ethnic or religious group: Roman Catholic
   Established: 1950
   Date: Ten days, including March 19, St. Joseph's Day

   GdWrldFest-1985, 146

St. Joseph's Day Bonfires (Fallas de San José)
   Location: Spain: Valencia
   Established: 16th century
   Date: March 12-19

   AnnivHol-1983, 39, 176
   BkFest-1937, 299
   BkHolWrld-1986, March 14
   FestWestEur-1958, 190
   FolkWrldHol-1992, 180
   GdWrldFest-1985, 164
   HolFestCelWrld-1994, 292

St. Juan Capistrano's Day (San Juan Capistrano Mission)
   See **Swallows of San Juan Capistrano**

St. Jude's Day
   Named for: St. Jude (fl. first century)
   Ethnic or religious group: Christian
   Date: October 28

   AnnivHol-1983, 137
   Chases-1993, 423
   DictMyth-1962, ii.1373
   FolkAmerHol-1987, 305

St. Jude's Day
   Named for: St. Jude (fl. first century)
   Location: Buffalo, New York
   Ethnic or religious group: Roman Catholic
   Date: October 28

   FolkAmerHol-1987, 305

St. Julian the Hospitaler, Feast of
   Named for: St. Julian (n.d.; probably mythical)
   Ethnic or religious group: Christian
   Date: January 9 or February 12

   AnnivHol-1983, 23
   DaysCustFaith-1957, 22
   DictMyth-1962, ii.1373

St. Knut's Day (Tjugondag Knut)
  Named for: Canute the Great (c. 995-1035)
  Location: Sweden
  Date: January 13

  AnnivHol-1983, 8
  BkFest-1937, 308
  BkHolWrld-1986, January 13
  FestWestEur-1958, 211
  FolkWrldHol-1992, 28
  HolFestCelWrld-1994, 293

St. Lambert's Day
  Named for: St. Lambert, Bishop of Maestricht (c. 635-c. 705)
  Ethnic or religious group: Christian
  Date: September 17

  DictDays-1988, 104

St. Lawrence of Rome, Feast Day of
  Named for: St. Lawrence (d. 258)
  Ethnic or religious group: Christian
  Date: August 10

  AnnivHol-1983, 105
  DaysCustFaith-1957, 204
  DictMyth-1962, ii.1374
  HolFestCelWrld-1994, 84
  IndianAmer-1989, 288, 294, 296, 301, 303

St. Lawrence of Rome, Feast Day of (Día de San Lorenzo)
  Named for: St. Lawrence (d. 258)
  Location: Mexico: Zinacantan
  Date: August 10

  FolkWrldHol-1992, 417
  HolFestCelWrld-1994, 84

St. Lawrence of Rome, Feast Day of
  Named for: St. Lawrence (d. 258)
  Location: New Mexico pueblos
  Date: August 10

  IndianAmer-1989, 288, 294, 296, 301, 303

St. Lawrence of Rome, Feast of (Festival of San Lorenzo)
  Named for: St. Lawrence (d. 258)
  Location: Spain: Foz, Lugo
  Date: August

  IntlThFolk-1979, 336

St. Lawrence of Rome, Feast Day of
  Named for: St. Lawrence (d. 258)
  Location: Spain: the Escorial, Madrid

  Date: August 10

  AnnivHol-1983, 105

St. Lazarus's Day
  Named for: St. Lazarus (fl. first century)
  Ethnic or religious group: Christian
  Date: March-April, Saturday preceding Palm Sunday

  AnnivHol-1983, 178
  BkFest-1937, 290, 337
  DictMyth-1962, ii.978
  FolkWrldHol-1992, 129, 130
  HolFestCelWrld-1994, 178, 293

St. Lazarus's Day
  Named for: St. Lazarus (fl. first century)
  Ethnic or religious group: Eastern Orthodox
  Date: March-April, Saturday preceding Palm Sunday

  HolFestCelWrld-1994, 178

St. Lazarus's Day
  Named for: St. Lazarus (fl. first century)
  Ethnic or religious group: Russian Orthodox
  Date: March-April, Saturday preceding Palm Sunday

  HolFestCelWrld-1994, 178

St. Lazarus's Day
  Named for: St. Lazarus (fl. first century)
  Location: Bulgaria
  Ethnic or religious group: Slavic people
  Date: March-April, Saturday preceding Palm or
    Easter Sunday

  AnnivHol-1983, 178
  FolkWrldHol-1992, 129
  HolFestCelWrld-1994, 179, 293

St. Lazarus's Day
  Named for: St. Lazarus (fl. first century)
  Location: Greece
  Date: March-April, Saturday preceding Palm Sunday

  FolkWrldHol-1992, 130
  HolFestCelWrld-1994, 179

St. Lazarus's Day
  Named for: St. Lazarus (fl. first century)
  Location: Romania
  Date: March-April, Saturday preceding Palm Sunday

  FolkWrldHol-1992, 130
  HolFestCelWrld-1994, 179

St. Lazarus's Day
  Named for: St. Lazarus (fl. first century)
  Location: Russia
  Date: March-April, Saturday preceding Palm Sunday

  BkFest-1937, 290, 337

St. Lazarus's Day
  Named for: St. Lazarus (fl. first century)
  Location: Yugoslavia
  Date: March-April, Saturday before Palm Sunday

  HolFestCelWrld-1994, 179

St. Leo III, Feast of
  Named for: St. Leo III (d. 816)
  Ethnic or religious group: Christian
  Date: June 12

  AnnivHol-1983, 78

St. Leonard's Day
  Named for: St. Leonard (d. c. 559)
  Ethnic or religious group: Christian
  Date: November 6

  BkFest-1937, 138
  BkHolWrld-1986, November 6
  DictMyth-1962, ii.1374
  FestWestEur-1958, 75
  HolFestCelWrld-1994, 180
  SaintFestCh-1904, 476

St. Leonard's Day
  Named for: St. Leonard (d. c. 559)
  Location: Austria
  Date: November 6

  FestWestEur-1958, 75

St. Leonard's Day
  Named for: St. Leonard (d. c. 559)
  Location: Germany
  Date: November 6

  BkFest-1937, 138
  BkHolWrld-1986, November 6
  FestWestEur-1958, 75
  HolFestCelWrld-1994, 180

St. Leonard's Ride (Leonhardiritt)
  Named for: St. Leonard (d. c. 559)
  Location: Germany: Bad Tölz, Bavaria

  Date: November 6

  BkFest-1937, 138
  BkHolWrld-1986, November 6
  FestWestEur-1958, 75

St. Leopold, Feast Day of (Fasslrutschen or Gaense Tag, Goose Day)
  Named for: St. Leopold (1073-1136)
  Location: Austria
  Ethnic or religious group: Christian
  Date: November 15

  AnnivHol-1983, 147
  BkFest-1937, 33
  HolFestCelWrld-1994, 293

St. Lubbock's Day
  Named for: Sir John Lubbock (1834-1913)
  Location: England
  Date: First Monday in August, August Bank Holiday

  DictDays-1988, 104

St. Lucia Day
  See **St. Lucy's Day**

St. Lucy's Day
  Named for: St. Lucy (c. 283-304)
  Ethnic or religious group: Christian
  Established: Sixth century, Rome
  Date: December 13

  AmerBkDays-1978, 1000
  AnnivHol-1983, 159
  BkDays-1864, ii. 687
  BkFest-1937, 191, 312
  BkFestHolWrld-1970, 132, 133
  Chases-1993, 473
  DaysCustFaith-1957, 313
  DictDays-1988, 104
  DictMyth-1962, ii.1374
  FestWestEur-1958, 101, 217
  FolkAmerHol-1987, 367
  FolkWrldHol-1992, 589, 590
  GdWrldFest-1985, 166
  HolFestCelWrld-1994, 294
  RelHolCal-1993, 91
  SaintFestCh-1904, 20

St. Lucy's Day
  Named for: St. Lucy (c. 283-304)
  Ethnic or religious group: Lutheran
  Date: December 13

  FolkAmerHol-1987, 367

St. Lucy's Day
  Named for: St. Lucy (c. 283-304)
  Ethnic or religious group: Roman Catholic
  Date: December 13

  AmerBkDays-1978, 1100
  BkDays-1864, ii.687

St. Lucy's Day
  Named for: St. Lucy (c. 283-304)
  Location: Finland
  Date: December 13

  FolkWrldHol-1992, 589
  HolFestCelWrld-1994, 294

St. Lucy's Day
  Named for: St. Lucy (c. 283-304)
  Location: Hungary
  Date: December 13

  FolkWrldHol-1992, 589

St. Lucy's Day
  Named for: St. Lucy (c. 283-304)
  Location: Italy
  Date: December 13

  AmerBkDays-1978, 1100
  FestWestEur-1958, 101

St. Lucy's Day
  Named for: St. Lucy (c. 283-304)
  Location: Norway
  Date: December 13

  AmerBkDays-1978, 1100
  HolFestCelWrld-1994, 294

St. Lucy's Day
  Named for: St. Lucy (c. 283-304)
  Location: Sicily: Syracuse
  Date: December 13

  AmerBkDays-1978, 1100
  BkFest-1937, 191
  BkFestHolWrld-1970, 133
  FestWestEur-1958, 101
  FolkWrldHol-1992, 589

St. Lucy's Day (Luciadagen)
  Named for: St. Lucy (c. 283-304)
  Location: Sweden
  Date: December 13

  AmerBkDays-1978, 1101
  AnnivHol-1983, 159

  BkFest-1937, 312
  Chases-1993, 473
  DictDays-1988, 104
  FestWestEur-1958, 217
  FolkWrldHol-1992, 590
  GdWrldFest-1985, 166
  HolFestCelWrld-1994, 294

St. Lucy's Day
  Named for: St. Lucy (c. 283-304)
  Location: United States
  Ethnic or religious group: Swedish- and other
    Scandinavian-Americans
  Date: December 13

  AmerBkDays-1978, 1101
  AnnivHol-1983, 159
  DictDays-1988, 104
  FolkAmerHol-1987, 367
  HolFestCelWrld-1994, 294
  RelHolCal-1993, 91

St. Luke, Feast Day of
  Named for: St. Luke (d. c. 68)
  Ethnic or religious group: Christian
  Date: October 18

  AnnivHol-1983, 134
  BkDays-1864, i.645, ii.464
  Chases-1993, 414
  DaysCustFaith-1957, 262
  DictDays-1988, 104
  DictMyth-1962, ii.1374
  FestSaintDays-1915, 186
  FolkWrldHol-1992, 513
  SaintFestCh-1904, 455

St. Luke, Feast Day of
  Named for: St. Luke (d. c. 68)
  Location: England
  Date: October 18

  BkDays-1864, i.645
  FestSaintDays-1915, 186
  FolkWrldHol-1992, 513

St. Luke's Day (Lukesmas)
  Named for: St. Luke (d. c. 68)
  Location: Scotland
  Date: October 18

  DictDays-1988, 70

St. Magnus Festival
  Location: Scotland: Kirkwall, Orkney Islands
  Established: 1977

St. Magnus Festival *(cont.)*
Date: Five days over third weekend in June

IntlThFolk-1979, 186

St. Mammertus
See **Frost, or Ice, Saints Day**

St. Marinus's Day
Named for: St. Marinus (fl. fourth century)
Location: San Marino
Date: September 3

AnnivHol-1983, 114
HolFestCelWrld-1994, 294

St. Mark, Fair of (Feria de San Marcos)
Named for: St. Mark (d. c. 74)
Location: Mexico: Aguascalientes
Established: Early 17th century
Date: Ten days beginning April 25

IntlThFolk-1979, 267

St. Mark, Feast of
Named for: St. Mark (d. c. 74)
Ethnic or religious group: Christian
Date: April 25

AmerBkDays-1978, 379
AnnivHol-1983, 56
BkDays-1864, i.549
DaysCustFaith-1957, 101
DictDays-1988, 104
DictFolkMyth-1984, 1062
DictMyth-1962, ii.1375
FestSaintDays-1915, 97
FolkWrldHol-1992, 250, 279
HolFestCelWrld-1994, 295
IntlThFolk-1979, 267
SaintFestCh-1904, 212

St. Mark, Feast of
Named for: St. Mark (d. c. 74)
Ethnic or religious group: Greek Orthodox
Date: April 25

AmerBkDays-1978, 379

St. Mark, Feast of
Named for: St. Mark (d. c. 74)
Ethnic or religious group: Roman Catholic
Date: April 25

AmerBkDays-1978, 379

St. Mark, Feast of (Blessing the Fields)
Named for: St. Mark (d. c. 74)
Location: Austria
Date: April 25

FolkWrldHol-1992, 279
See also **Rogation Days (Austria)**

St. Mark, Feast of
Named for: St. Mark (d. c. 74)
Location: England
Date: April 25

BkDays-1864, i.549
DaysCustFaith-1957, 101
DictDays-1988, 104
FestSaintDays-1915, 98

St. Mark's Day (Szent Márk Napja and Buza-Szentelo, Blessing of Wheat)
Named for: St. Mark (d. c. 74)
Location: Hungary
Ethnic or religious group: Calvinist
Date: April 25

BkFest-1937, 169
FolkWrldHol-1992, 250
HolFestCelWrld-1994, 295

St. Mark, Feast of (Toro de san Marcos, Bull of St. Mark)
Named for: St. Mark (d. c. 74)
Location: Spain
Established: 16th-19th centuries
Date: April 24-25

DictFolkMyth-1984, 1062

St. Mark's Eve
See **St. Mark's Day**

St. Maron's Day
Named for: St. Maron (d. c. 433)
Location: Lebanon and in North and South America
Ethnic or religious group: Maronite Christians
Date: February 9

AnnivHol-1983, 22

St. Martha, Feast of
Named for: St. Martha (fl. first century)
Ethnic or religious group: Christian
Date: July 29

AnnivHol-1983, 98
DaysCustFaith-1957, 194
DictMyth-1962, ii.1375
FestWestEur-1958, 44
SaintFestCh-1904, 345

St. Martha, Feast of (Fête de la Tarasque)
Named for: St. Martha (fl. first century)
Location: France: Tarascon, Provence
Established: 1469
Date: Last Sunday in June and July 29

AnnivHol-1983, 98
Chases-1993, 269
FestWestEur-1958, 44

St. Martin's Day
Named for: St. Martin (c. 316-397)
Ethnic or religious group: Christian
Date: November 11

AnnivHol-1983, 145
BkFest-1937, 190, 215
Chases-1993, 438
DictMyth-1962, ii.1375
FolkWrldHol-1992, 557
GdWrldFest-1985, 65
See also **Martinmas; Martinsfest**

St. Martin's Day (Quadrilles of San Martin)
Named for: St. Martin (c. 316-397)
Location: Colombia: San Martin, Meta
Established: 18th century
Date: November 11

GdWrldFest-1985, 65

St. Martin's Day
Named for: St. Martin (c. 316-397)
Location: Italy
Date: November 11

AnnivHol-1983, 145
BkFest-1937, 190, 215

St. Martin's Day
Named for: St. Martin (c. 316-397)
Location: Netherlands
Date: November 11

AnnivHol-1983, 145
FolkWrldHol-1992, 557

St. Martin's Day
Named for: St. Martin (c. 316-397)
Location: Sweden
Date: November 11

Chases-1993, 438

St. Mary Magdalene, Feast of
Named for: St. Mary Magdalene (fl. first century)
Ethnic or religious group: Christian
Date: July 22

AmerBkDays-1978, 684
AnnivHol-1983, 95, 179
BkDays-1864, ii.101
DaysCustFaith-1957, 188
DictMyth-1962, ii.1376
FestWestEur-1958, 45
HolFestCelWrld-1994, 191
IntlThFolk-1979, 333
SaintFestCh-1904, 337

St. Mary Magdalene, Feast of
Named for: St. Mary Magdalene (fl. first century)
Location: France: pilgrimage to holy cave in Sainte
  Baume, Provence
Established: 13th century
Date: July 22

AnnivHol-1983, 95, 179
FestWestEur-1958, 45
HolFestCelWrld-1994, 191

**St. Mary Magdalene, Feast of (Dance of the Stilts,
part of Procession of St. Mary Magdalene)**
Named for: St. Mary Magdalene (fl. first century)
Location: Spain: Anguiano, Logrono
Date: July

IntlThFolk-1979, 333

St. Mary Margaret, Feast of
Location: Paraje Village, Laguna Pueblo, New Mexico
Date: October 17

IndianAmer-1989, 289, 301

St. Mary the Virgin, Feast of
See **Assumption, Feast of the**

St. Matthew's Day
Named for: St. Matthew (fl. first century)
Ethnic or religious group: Christian
Date: September 21

AmerBkDays-1978, 858
AnnivHol-1983, 121
DaysCustFaith-1957, 239
DictFolkMyth-1984, 1168
DictMyth-1962, ii.1377
SaintFestCh-1904, 417

St. Matthew's Day
  Named for: St. Matthew (fl. first century)
  Ethnic or religious group: Eastern Orthodox
  Date: November 16

  AmerBkDays-1978, 858

St. Matthew's Day
  Named for: St. Matthew (fl. first century)
  Location: Carpathian Mountains
  Date: September 21

  DictFolkMyth-1984, 1168

St. Matthias, Feast of
  Named for: St. Matthias (fl. first century)
  Ethnic or religious group: Eastern Orthodox
  Date: August 9

  AmerBkDays-1978, 739
  AnnivHol-1983, 28

St. Matthias, Feast of
  Named for: St. Matthias (fl. first century)
  Ethnic or religious group: Episcopalian and Lutheran
  Date: February 24

  AmerBkDays-1978, 208
  AnnivHol-1983, 28
  DaysCustFaith-1957, 58
  DictMyth-1962, ii.1377
  SaintFestCh-1904, 114

St. Matthias, Feast of
  Named for: St. Matthias (fl. first century)
  Ethnic or religious group: Roman Catholic
  Date: May 14; formerly February 24

  AmerBkDays-1978, 452

St. Médardus or Médard's Day
  Named for: St. Médardus or Médard, Bishop of Vermand
    (c. 470-560)
  Ethnic or religious group: Christian
  Date: June 8

  BkFest-1937, 43
  DictMyth-1962, ii.1377
  FestWestEur-1958, 13
  FolkAmerHol-1987, 203
  HolFestCelWrld-1994, 295

St. Médardus or Médard's Day
  Named for: St. Médardus or Médard, Bishop of Vermand
    (c. 470-560)
  Location: Belgium

  Date: June 8

  BkFest-1937, 43
  FestWestEur-1958, 13
  HolFestCelWrld-1994, 295

St. Médardus's Day
  Named for: St. Médardus or Médard, Bishop of Vermand
    (c. 470-560)
  Location: Louisiana
  Ethnic or religious group: French-Americans
  Date: June 8

  FolkAmerHol-1987, 203

St. Mennas's Day
  Named for: Two Sts. Mennas: an Egyptian (d. c. 300) and
    a Greek hermit (d. sixth century)
  Location: Greece
  Ethnic or religious group: Christian
  Date: November 11

  BkFestHolWrld-1970, 124
  FolkWrldHol-1992, 559

St. Michael and All Angels' Day
  See **Michaelmas**

St. Michael, Festival of
  Location: Mexico: Jesus Maria, Nayarit
  Date: September 28-29

  IntlThFolk-1979, 271

St. Michael's Day
  Ethnic or religious group: Christian
  Date: November 8, Eastern Church; September 29,
    Western Church

  AmerBkDays-1978, 876
  BkHolWrld-1986, September 29
  Chases-1993, 389
  DaysCustFaith-1957, 242
  DictFolkMyth-1984, 203, 504, 716
  DictMyth-1962, ii.1377
  FestWestEur-1958, 71
  FolkAmerHol-1987, 325
  FolkWrldHol-1992, 32, 491, 555
  HolFestCelWrld-1994, 295
  See also **Michaelmas**

St. Michael's Day
  Ethnic or religious group: Eastern Orthodox
  Date: November 8

  AmerBkDays-1978, 876
  BkHolWrld-1986, September 29
  FolkAmerHol-1987, 325

St. Michael's Day
  Ethnic or religious group: Roman Catholic
  Date: September 29

  AmerBkDays-1978, 876
  BkHolWrld-1986, September 29
  Chases-1993, 389
  DictFolkMyth-1984, 716

St. Michael's Day (Fiesta de San Miguel)
  Location: Bolivia: Taypi
  Date: September 29

  FolkWrldHol-1992, 491

St. Michael's Day (England)
  See **Furry Day**

St. Michael's Day (Mihkli Paev)
  Location: Estonia
  Date: September 29

  FolkWrldHol-1992, 492

St. Michael's Day
  Location: Ethiopia
  Date: November 8

  HolFestCelWrld-1994, 295

St. Michael's Day
  Location: Finland
  Date: First Sunday in October

  FolkWrldHol-1992, 504
  HolFestCelWrld-1994, 295

St. Michael's Day
  Location: Tarpon Springs, Florida
  Ethnic or religious group: Greek-Americans
  Date: November 8

  FolkAmerHol-1987, 325

St. Michael's Day (Tura Michele Markt or Fair)
  Location: Germany: Augsburg, Bavaria
  Date: September 29

  FestWestEur-1958, 71

St. Michael's Day
  Location: Hungary
  Date: September 29

  FolkWrldHol-1992, 492

St. Michael's Day
  Location: Puerto Rico
  Date: End of September

  AmerBkDays-1978, 878

St. Michael's Eve
  Location: Scotland: Hebrides, including Isle of Iona

  DictFolkMyth-1984, 203, 504

St. Michael's Feast
  Location: Ethiopia: Amhara
  Date: Monthly

  FolkWrldHol-1992, 32, 555

St. Modesto's Day (Oxen's Feast)
  Named for: Modestus, patriarch of Jerusalem from 631-34
  Location: Greece
  Ethnic or religious group: Eastern Orthodox
  Date: December 18

  FolkWrldHol-1992, 595
  HolFestCelWrld-1994, 295

St. Nicholas's Day
  Named for: St. Nicholas, Archbishop of Myra
    (fl. fourth century)
  Ethnic or religious group: Christian
  Date: December 6, Gregorian calendar (N.S.); December 19,
    Julian calendar (O.S.)

  AmerBkDays-1978, 1079
  AnnivHol-1983, 156, 157
  BkDays-1864, ii.661
  BkFest-1937, 34, 48, 129, 190, 245
  BkFestHolWrld-1970, 129
  BkHolWrld-1986, December 6
  Chases-1993, 467
  DaysCustFaith-1957, 306
  DictDays-1988, 105
  DictFolkMyth-1984, 591
  DictMyth-1962, ii.1378, ii.1397
  FestSaintDays-1915, 219
  FestWestEur-1958, 19, 49, 81, 118, 144
  FolkAmerHol-1987, 361
  FolkWrldHol-1992, 579
  HolFestCelWrld-1994, 295
  RelHolCal-1993, 67
  SaintFestCh-1904, 11

St. Nicholas's Day
  Named for: St. Nicholas, Archbishop of Myra
    (fl. fourth century)
  Ethnic or religious group: Eastern Orthodox

St. Nicholas's Day *(cont.)*
Date: December 6, Gregorian calendar (N.S.); December 19, Julian calendar (O.S.)

AmerBkDays-1978, 1079
AnnivHol-1983, 156

St. Nicholas's Day
Named for: St. Nicholas, Archbishop of Myra
(fl. fourth century)
Ethnic or religious group: Protestant
Date: December 6

AmerBkDays-1978, 1079

St. Nicholas's Day
Named for: St. Nicholas, Archbishop of Myra
(fl. fourth century)
Ethnic or religious group: Roman Catholic
Date: December 6

AmerBkDays-1978, 1079
BkDays-1864, ii.663
DictFolkMyth-1984, 591

St. Nicholas's Day (Nikolaustag)
Named for: St. Nicholas, Archbishop of Myra
(fl. fourth century)
Location: Austria
Date: December 6

BkFest-1937, 34
DictFolkMyth-1984, 591
FolkWrldHol-1992, 579

St. Nicholas's Day
Named for: St. Nicholas, Archbishop of Myra
(fl. fourth century)
Location: Belgium
Date: December 6

BkFest-1937, 48
FestWestEur-1958, 19
FolkWrldHol-1992, 580

St. Nicholas's Day
Named for: St. Nicholas, Archbishop of Myra
(fl. fourth century)
Location: Wilton, Connecticut
Date: December 6

AmerBkDays-1978, 1080

St. Nicholas's Day
Named for: St. Nicholas, Archbishop of Myra
(fl. fourth century)

Location: Czechoslovakia: Bohemia
Date: December 6

FolkWrldHol-1992, 580

St. Nicholas's Day
Named for: St. Nicholas, Archbishop of Myra
(fl. fourth century)
Location: England
Date: December 6

DaysCustFaith-1957, 308

St. Nicholas's Day
Named for: St. Nicholas, Archbishop of Myra
(fl. fourth century)
Location: Tarpon Springs, Florida
Ethnic or religious group: Greek-Americans
Date: December 6

FolkAmerHol-1987, 362

St. Nicholas's Day
Named for: St. Nicholas, Archbishop of Myra
(fl. fourth century)
Location: France
Date: December 6

BkFest-1937, 129
BkHolWrld-1986, December 6
FestWestEur-1958, 49

St. Nicholas's Day (Nikolaustag or Knecht Ruprecht)
Named for: St. Nicholas, Archbishop of Myra
(fl. fourth century)
Location: Germany
Date: December 6

AmerBkDays-1978, 1079
AnnivHol-1983, 156
BkHolWrld-1986, December 6
DictDays-1988, 105
DictFolkMyth-1984, 591
FestSaintDays-1915, 222
FestWestEur-1958, 81
FolkWrldHol-1992, 580
HolFestCelWrld-1994, 295

St. Nicholas's Day
Named for: St. Nicholas, Archbishop of Myra
(fl. fourth century)
Location: Greece
Date: December 6

BkFestHolWrld-1970, 130

St. Nicholas's Day (Sinterklass)
Named for: St. Nicholas, Archbishop of Myra
  (fl. fourth century)
Location: Holland/Netherlands
Date: December 6

AmerBkDays-1978, 1079
AnnivHol-1983, 156
BkFest-1937, 245
BkHolWrld-1986, December 6
FestSaintDays-1915, 222
FestWestEur-1958, 144
FolkWrldHol-1992, 581
HolFestCelWrld-1994, 295

St. Nicholas's Day
Location: Italy: Bari, Apulia
Date: May 7-8

BkDays-1864, ii.663
BkFest-1937, 190
FestSaintDays-1915, 224
FestWestEur-1958, 96
HolFestCelWrld-1994, 296

St. Nicholas's Day
Named for: St. Nicholas, Archbishop of Myra
  (fl. fourth century)
Location: Ellis County, Kansas
Ethnic or religious group: German- and Russian-Americans
Date: December 6

FolkAmerHol-1987, 361

St. Nicholas's Day (Neklosdag)
Named for: St. Nicholas, Archbishop of Myra
  (fl. fourth century)
Location: Luxembourg
Date: December 6

FestWestEur-1958, 118

St. Nicholas's Day
Named for: St. Nicholas, Archbishop of Myra
  (fl. fourth century)
Location: Russia
Date: December 6

FestSaintDays-1915, 222

St. Nicholas's Day
Named for: St. Nicholas, Archbishop of Myra
  (fl. fourth century)
Location: Spain

Ethnic or religious group: Basque people
Date: December 6

FolkWrldHol-1992, 582

St. Nicholas's Day (Samichlaus Abend, Santa Claus Night)
Named for: St. Nicholas, Archbishop of Myra
  (fl. fourth century)
Location: Switzerland
Date: December 6

AmerBkDays-1978, 1079
AnnivHol-1983, 156
BkHolWrld-1986, December 6
FestWestEur-1958, 238
HolFestCelWrld-1994, 295

St. Nicholas's Day (St. Nicholas Thaumaturgus, the Wonder-Worker)
Named for: St. Nicholas, Archbishop of Myra
  (fl. fourth century)
Location: Syria
Date: December 6

FolkWrldHol-1992, 582

St. Nicholas's Day
Named for: St. Nicholas, Archbishop of Myra
  (fl. fourth century)
Location: United States
Ethnic or religious group: Dutch-Americans
Date: December 6

AmerBkDays-1978, 1079
AnnivHol-1983, 157
FolkAmerHol-1987, 362

St. Nicholas's Eve
See **St. Nicholas's Day**

St. Nikephoros's Day
Named for: St. Nikephoros (c. 758-829)
Location: Greece
Ethnic or religious group: Greek Orthodox
Date: March 13

BkHolWrld-1986, March 13
SaintFestCh-1904, 133

St. Olav's Day
See **Olsok**

St. Oswald's Day
  Named for: St. Oswald, Archbishop of York (925-992)
  Ethnic or religious group: Christian
  Date: February 28

  BkDays-1864, i.309
  Chases-1993, 113
  FolkWrldHol-1992, 140

St. Partridge's Day
  See **Partridge Day**

St. Patrick's Day
  Named for: St. Patrick (c. 389-461)
  Ethnic or religious group: Christian
  Date: March 17

  AmerBkDays-1978, 262
  AnnivHol-1983, 38
  BkDays-1864, i.382
  BkFest-1937, 15, 55
  BkFestHolWrld-1970, 73
  BkHolWrld-1986, March 17
  Chases-1993, 132
  DaysCustFaith-1957, 78
  DictDays-1988, 50, 88, 105, 109
  DictMyth-1962, ii.1378
  DictWrldRel-1989, 563
  FestSaintDays-1915, 38
  FolkAmerHol-1987, 109
  FolkWrldHol-1992, 178
  HolFestCelWrld-1994, 296
  NatlHolWrld-1968, 34
  RelHolCal-1993, 111

St. Patrick's Day
  Named for: St. Patrick (c. 389-461)
  Ethnic or religious group: Anglican
  Date: March 17

  RelHolCal-1993, 111

St. Patrick's Day
  Named for: St. Patrick (c. 389-461)
  Ethnic or religious group: Episcopalian
  Date: March 17

  AmerBkDays-1978, 262

St. Patrick's Day
  Named for: St. Patrick (c. 389-461)
  Ethnic or religious group: Lutheran
  Date: March 17

  RelHolCal-1993, 111

St. Patrick's Day
  Named for: St. Patrick (c. 389-461)
  Ethnic or religious group: Roman Catholic
  Date: March 17

  AmerBkDays-1978, 262
  Chases-1993, 132
  RelHolCal-1993, 111

St. Patrick's Day
  Named for: St. Patrick (c. 389-461)
  Location: Canada
  Date: March 17

  FolkWrldHol-1992, 178

St. Patrick's Day
  Named for: St. Patrick (c. 389-461)
  Location: Parade in Savannah, Georgia
  Date: March 17

  HolFestCelWrld-1994, 297

St. Patrick's Day
  Named for: St. Patrick (c. 389-461)
  Location: Ireland
  Date: March 17

  AnnivHol-1983, 38
  BkFest-1937, 55
  BkFestHolWrld-1970, 74
  BkHolWrld-1986, March 17
  Chases-1993, 132
  DaysCustFaith-1957, 81
  FolkAmerHol-1987, 109
  FolkWrldHol-1992, 178
  HolFestCelWrld-1994, 296
  NatlHolWrld-1968, 34

St. Patrick's Day
  Named for: St. Patrick (c. 389-461)
  Location: New York, New York, and elsewhere in the
    United States
  Ethnic or religious group: Irish-Americans
  Established: Parade in New York since 1762
  Date: March 17

  AmerBkDays-1978, 263
  BkFest-1937, 15
  BkFestHolWrld-1970, 73
  Chases-1993, 132
  DaysCustFaith-1957, 80
  FolkAmerHol-1987, 109
  NatlHolWrld-1968, 34
  RelHolCal-1993, 111

St. Patrick's Day Encampment
  Location: Morristown, New Jersey
  Established: Reenactment of 1780 camp of George Washington (1732-1799) and his men, during which he allowed them to celebrate St. Patrick's Day
  Date: March 17

  HolFestCelWrld-1994, 297

St. Paul, Feast of the Conversion of
  Named for: St. Paul the Apostle (d. c. 67)
  Ethnic or religious group: Christian
  Established: Eighth century
  Date: January 25

  AmerBkDays-1978, 110
  AnnivHol-1983, 13
  BkDays-1864, i. 157
  BkFest-1937, 52
  DaysCustFaith-1957, 30, 155
  DictDays-1988, 105
  DictMyth-1962, ii.1379
  DictWrldRel-1989, 563
  FestSaintDays-1915, 22
  HolFestCelWrld-1994, 69
  SaintFestCh-1904, 80
  See also **Cow, Festival of the (Spain: San Pablo de los Montes, Toledo)**

St. Paul, Feast of the Conversion of
  Named for: St. Paul the Apostle (d. c. 67)
  Ethnic or religious group: Anglican
  Date: January 25

  DaysCustFaith-1957, 155

St. Paul, Feast of the Conversion of
  Named for: St. Paul the Apostle (d. c. 67)
  Ethnic or religious group: Eastern Orthodox
  Date: January 25

  AmerBkDays-1978, 110

St. Paul, Feast of the Conversion of
  Named for: St. Paul the Apostle (d. c. 67)
  Ethnic or religious group: Lutheran
  Date: January 25

  AmerBkDays-1978, 110

St. Paul, Feast of the Conversion of
  Named for: St. Paul the Apostle (d. c. 67)
  Location: England

  Date: January 25

  BkDays-1864, i.157
  BkFest-1937, 52
  FestSaintDays-1915, 22

St. Paul, Feast of the Conversion of
  Named for: St. Paul the Apostle (d. c. 67)
  Location: New York, New York
  Date: January 25

  HolFestCelWrld-1994, 69

St. Paulinus of Nola, Feast of
  Named for: St. Paulinus of Nola (c. 353-431)
  Ethnic or religious group: Christian
  Date: June 22

  AnnivHol-1983, 82
  DaysCustFaith-1957, 150
  GdWrldFest-1985, 118
  HolFestCelWrld-1994, 181

St. Paulinus of Nola, Feast of (Lily Festival)
  Named for: St. Paulinus of Nola (c. 353-431)
  Location: Italy: Nola, Campania
  Date: Fourth Sunday in June or Sunday following June 22

  AnnivHol-1983, 82
  BkHolWrld-1986, June 28, 177
  DaysCustFaith-1957, 150
  GdWrldFest-1985, 118
  HolFestCelWrld-1994, 181

St. Paul's Shipwreck, Feast of
  Named for: St. Paul's shipwreck there in 60
  Location: Malta
  Date: February 10

  Chases-1993, 92
  FolkWrldHol-1992, 99
  HolFestCelWrld-1994, 297

St. Peter's Chains, Feast of
  Ethnic or religious group: Roman Catholic
  Date: August 1

  DaysCustFaith-1957, 198
  SaintFestCh-1904, 351

St. Peter's Chair, Festival of
  Location: Rome
  Ethnic or religious group: Roman Catholic
  Date: January 18

  BkDays-1864, i. 130
  DaysCustFaith-1957, 24
  SaintFestCh-1904, 71

St. Peter's Day
Named for: St. Peter (d. c. 64)
Ethnic or religious group: Christian
Date: June 29

AmerBkDays-1978, 603
BkFest-1937, 44, 270
BkFestHolWrld-1970, 101
DictFolkMyth-1984, 176
DictMyth-1962, ii.1379
DictWrldRel-1989, 566
FestWestEur-1958, 14, 169
FolkWrldHol-1992, 270, 346
HolFestCelWrld-1994, 298
IndianAmer-1989, 287, 312, 315

St. Peter's Day
Named for: St. Peter (d. c. 64)
Ethnic or religious group: Episcopalian
Date: June 29

AmerBkDays-1978, 603

St. Peter's Day
Named for: St. Peter (d. c. 64)
Ethnic or religious group: Roman Catholic
Date: June 29

AmerBkDays-1978, 603
BkFestHolWrld-1970, 102
HolFestCelWrld-1994, 298

St. Peter's Day
Named for: St. Peter (d. c. 64)
Location: Belgium
Date: June 29

BkFest-1937, 44
BkFestHolWrld-1970, 102
FestWestEur-1958, 14

St. Peter's Day
Named for: St. Peter (d. c. 64)
Location: Finland
Date: June 29

BkFestHolWrld-1970, 102

St. Peter's Day
Named for: St. Peter (d. c. 64)
Location: Germany: Westphalia
Date: February 22

DictFolkMyth-1984, 176

St. Peter's Day
Named for: St. Peter (d. c. 64)
Location: Italy
Date: June 29

BkFestHolWrld-1970, 102

St. Peter's Day
Named for: St. Peter (d. c. 64)
Location: Gloucester, Massachusetts
Ethnic or religious group: Roman Catholic Italian-Americans
Date: June 29

AmerBkDays-1978, 603
BkFestHolWrld-1970, 102
HolFestCelWrld-1994, 298

St. Peter's Day
Named for: St. Peter (d. c. 64)
Location: New Mexico pueblos
Date: June 29; observed with various dances at Santa Ana and Santo Domingo pueblos; with rooster pulls at Acoma and San Felipe pueblos

AmerBkDays-1978, 603
IndianAmer-1989, 287, 294, 312, 315

St. Peter's Day (San Pedro)
Named for: St. Peter (d. c. 64)
Location: Peru: Pacarigtambo
Date: June 29

FolkWrldHol-1992, 270

St. Peter's Day
Named for: St. Peter (d. c. 64)
Location: Portugal
Date: June 29

BkFest-1937, 270
BkFestHolWrld-1970, 102
FestWestEur-1958, 169

St. Philibert's Day
Named for: St. Philibert (c. 608-c. 685)
Date: August 20

DictDays-1988, 105

St. Philip, Feast of and Green Corn Dance
Named for: St. Philip (fl. first century)
Location: San Felipe Pueblo, New Mexico
Date: May 1

IndianAmer-1989, 286, 309

St. Philip of Moscow's Day
  Named for: St. Philip of Moscow (1507-1569)
  Ethnic or religious group: Russian Orthodox
  Date: January 9

  BkHolWrld-1986, January 9

St. Piran's Day
  Named for: St. Piran (d. c. 480)
  Location: England: Cornwall
  Ethnic or religious group: Christian
  Date: March 5

  DictDays-1988, 105
  SaintFestCh-1904, 124

St. Placidus Festival
  Named for: St. Placidus (fl. 614)
  Location: Switzerland: Disentis, Grisons
  Ethnic or religious group: Christian
  Date: July 11

  BkFest-1937, 320
  FestWestEur-1958, 236

St. Plato the Martyr, Feast of
  Named for: St. Plato or Plane-tree (d. c. 306)
  Location: Macedonia
  Ethnic or religious group: Christian
  Date: November 18

  FolkWrldHol-1992, 563

St. Polycarp's Day
  Named for: St. Polycarp, Bishop of Smyrna (c. 69-c. 155)
  Ethnic or religious group: Christian
  Date: January 26

  AnnivHol-1983, 27
  BkDays-1864, i.165
  DaysCustFaith-1957, 33
  DictWrldRel-1989, 463
  SaintFestCh-1904, 81

St. Roch's Day
  Named for: St. Roch (c. 1350-c. 1380)
  Ethnic or religious group: Christian
  Date: August 16

  BkDays-1864, ii.226
  BkFest-1937, 188
  DaysCustFaith-1957, 209
  DictDays-1988, 106
  DictMyth-1962, ii.1380

St. Roch's Day (San Rocco)
  Named for: St. Roch (c. 1350-c. 1380)
  Location: Italy: Florence and Realmonte
  Date: August 16

  BkFest-1937, 188

St. Roch's Day (San Roque Festival)
  Named for: St. Roch (c. 1350-c. 1380)
  Location: Spain: Betanzos, La Coruna
  Established: 15th century
  Date: August

  IntlThFolk-1979, 334

St. Roch's Day (San Roque Festival)
  Named for: St. Roch (c. 1350-c. 1380)
  Location: Spain: Llanes, Oviedo
  Date: August

  IntlThFolk-1979, 339

St. Rose of Lima, Feast of
  Named for: Isabel de Flores (1586-1617)
  Ethnic or religious group: Christian
  Date: August 23

  AnnivHol-1983, 109
  BkHolWrld-1986, August 30
  Chases-1993, 347
  HolFestCelWrld-1994, 298
  SaintFestCh-1904, 388

St. Rose of Lima Day
  Named for: Isabel de Flores (1586-1617)
  Location: Peru
  Date: August 23; observed August 30

  AnnivHol-1983, 112
  BkHolWrld-1986, August 30
  Chases-1993, 347
  HolFestCelWrld-1994, 298
  SaintFestCh-1904, 388

St. Sarkis's Day
  Location: Armenia
  Ethnic or religious group: Christian
  Date: January 21

  FolkWrldHol-1992, 34
  HolFestCelWrld-1994, 298

St. Sava's Day
  Named for: St. Sava (c. 1174-1235)
  Location: Yugoslavia
  Ethnic or religious group: Serbian Christians
  Date: January 14

  AnnivHol-1983, 9
  BkFest-1937, 336
  HolFestCelWrld-1994, 298

St. Sebastian, Festival of (Fiesta de San Sebastian)
  Location: Mexico: Tenosique, Tabasco
  Date: January 20

  IntlThFolk-1979, 277

St. Sebastian's Day
  Named for: St. Sebastian (d. c. 288)
  Ethnic or religious group: Christian
  Date: January 20

  AnnivHol-1983, 11
  Chases-1993, 69
  DaysCustFaith-1957, 27
  DictMyth-1962, ii.1381
  FolkWrldHol-1992, 33
  SaintFestCh-1904, 75

St. Sebastian's Day
  Named for: St. Sebastian (d. c. 288)
  Location: Brazil: Rio de Janeiro
  Date: January 20

  AnnivHol-1983, 11
  Chases-1993, 69

St. Sebastian's Day (Día de San Sebastián)
  Named for: St. Sebastian (d. c. 288)
  Location: Mexico: Zinacantan
  Date: January 20; observed for nine days, from January 17-25

  FolkWrldHol-1992, 33

St. Sergius of Radonezh
  Named for: Bartholomew Kirillovich (1314-1392)
  Ethnic or religious group: Russian Orthodox
  Date: September 25

  BkHolWrld-1986, September 25

St. Servatus
  See **Frost, or Ice, Saints Day**

St. Simon Stylites's Day
  Named for: St. Simon Stylites (c. 390-459)

Ethnic or religious group: Christian
  Date: January 5

  BkDays-1864, i.53
  DaysCustFaith-1957, 19-20
  DictMyth-1962, ii.1381, ii.1502
  DictWrldRel-1989, 693
  SaintFestCh-1904, 53

St. Sofia's Day
  Location: Czechoslovakia
  Ethnic or religious group: Christian
  Date: May 15, following Frost Saints's Day

  FolkWrldHol-1992, 297

St. Spyridon, Feast Day of
  Named for: St. Spyridon, Bishop of Tremithus (d. c. 348)
  Location: Greece: Corfu
  Ethnic or religious group: Christian
  Date: December 14

  AnnivHol-1983, 160
  BkFest-1937, 154
  FolkWrldHol-1992, 591
  HolFestCelWrld-1994, 299

St. Stanislaus, Feast of
  Named for: St. Stanislaus of Kracow (1030-1079)
  Ethnic or religious group: Christian
  Date: April 11

  AnnivHol-1983, 50

St. Stephen, Feast of
  Named for: St. Stephen (d. c. 35)
  Ethnic or religious group: Christian
  Date: December 26

  AmerBkDays-1978, 1151
  AnnivHol-1983, 164
  BkDays-1864, ii. 763
  BkFest-1937, 35
  BkHolWrld-1986, December 26
  Chases-1993, 483
  DaysCustFaith-1957, 321
  DictDays-1988, 106
  DictFolkMyth-1984, 950
  DictMyth-1962, ii.1381
  FestSaintDays-1915, 249
  FestWestEur-1958, 104
  FolkAmerHol-1987, 405
  FolkWrldHol-1992, 642
  HolFestCelWrld-1994, 299
  SaintFestCh-1904, 40

St. Stephen, Feast of
Named for: St. Stephen (d. c. 35)
Ethnic or religious group: Anglican
Date: December 26

BkDays-1864, ii.763

St. Stephen, Feast of
Named for: St. Stephen (d. c. 35)
Ethnic or religious group: Eastern Orthodox
Date: December 27

AmerBkDays-1978, 1151
BkHolWrld-1986, December 26

St. Stephen, Feast of
Named for: St. Stephen (d. c. 35)
Ethnic or religious group: Episcopalian
Date: December 26

AmerBkDays-1978, 1151

St. Stephen, Feast of
Named for: St. Stephen (d. c. 35)
Ethnic or religious group: Lutheran
Date: December 26

AmerBkDays-1978, 1151

St. Stephen, Feast of
Named for: St. Stephen (d. c. 35)
Ethnic or religious group: Protestant
Date: December 26

AmerBkDays-1978, 1151
BkHolWrld-1986, December 26

St. Stephen, Feast of
Named for: St. Stephen (d. c. 35)
Ethnic or religious group: Roman Catholic
Date: December 26

AmerBkDays-1978, 1151
BkHolWrld-1986, December 26

St. Stephen, Feast of (Stefanstag)
Named for: St. Stephen (d. c. 35)
Location: Austria
Date: December 26

BkFest-1937, 35
Chases-1993, 483
HolFestCelWrld-1994, 299

St. Stephen, Feast of
Named for: St. Stephen (d. c. 35)
Location: Bohemia
Date: December 26

DictFolkMyth-1984, 950

St. Stephen, Feast of (Hunting the Wren)
Named for: St. Stephen (d. c. 35)
Location: England
Date: December 26

BkDays-1864, ii.763
DaysCustFaith-1957, 322
DictDays-1988, 106
FestSaintDays-1915, 251
HolFestCelWrld-1994, 299
See also **Boxing Day (England)**

St. Stephen, Feast of
Named for: St. Stephen (d. c. 35)
Location: France
Date: December 26

FestSaintDays-1915, 251

St. Stephen, Feast of (Hunting the Wren)
Named for: St. Stephen (d. c. 35)
Location: Ireland
Date: December 26

AmerBkDays-1978, 1152
AnnivHol-1983, 164
Chases-1993, 483
DaysCustFaith-1957, 322
DictDays-1988, 16
FolkWrldHol-1992, 642
HolFestCelWrld-1994, 299

St. Stephen, Feast of (Hunting the Wren)
Named for: St. Stephen (d. c. 35)
Location: Isle of Man
Date: December 26

AnnivHol-1983, 164
AmerBkDays-1978, 1152
DaysCustFaith-1957, 322
DictDays-1988, 106

St. Stephen, Feast of
Named for: St. Stephen (d. c. 35)
Location: Italy
Date: December 26

FestWestEur-1958, 104

St. Stephen, Feast of
Named for: St. Stephen (d. c. 35)
Location: Poland
Date: December 26

FolkWrldHol-1992, 643
HolFestCelWrld-1994, 299

St. Stephen, Feast of
Named for: St. Stephen (d. c. 35)
Location: Sweden
Date: December 26

FolkWrldHol-1992, 643

St. Stephen, Feast of (Hunting the Wren)
Named for: St. Stephen (d. c. 35)
Location: Wales
Date: December 26

DictDays-1988, 106

St. Stephen, Feast of and Harvest Dance (Feast of San Estevan)
Location: Acoma Pueblo, New Mexico
Date: September 2

HolFestCelWrld-1994, 303
IndianAmer-1989, 288, 294
RelHolCal-1993, 113

St. Stephen Day, Crown of
Date: January 6

AnnivHol-1983, 5

St. Stephen's Day
Named for: St. Stephen, King of Hungary (c. 975-1038)
Location: Hungary
Ethnic or religious group: Christian
Date: August 20

BkFest-1937, 172
FolkWrldHol-1992, 422

St. Stephen's Day
Named for: St. Stephen, King of Hungary (c. 975-1038)
Location: United States
Date: August 20

BkFest-1937, 172

St. Swithin's Day
Named for: St. Swithin, Bishop of Winchester (c. 800-862)
Ethnic or religious group: Christian

Date: July 15

AmerBkDays-1978, 665
AnnivHol-1983, 93
BkDays-1864, ii. 61
BkFest-1937, 60
BkHolWrld-1986, July 15
Chases-1993, 292
DaysCustFaith-1957, 181
DictDays-1988, 106
DictMyth-1962, ii.1382
FestSaintDays-1915, 150
FolkAmerHol-1987, 231
FolkWrldHol-1992, 375
HolFestCelWrld-1994, 299
SaintFestCh-1904, 328

St. Swithin's Day
Named for: St. Swithin, Bishop of Winchester (c. 800-862)
Ethnic or religious group: Anglican
Date: July 15

AmerBkDays-1978, 665

St. Swithin's Day
Named for: St. Swithin, Bishop of Winchester (c. 800-862)
Location: England
Date: July 15

AmerBkDays-1978, 665
AnnivHol-1983, 93
BkDays-1864, ii. 61
BkFest-1937, 60
BkHolWrld-1986, July 15
Chases-1993, 292
DaysCustFaith-1957, 181
DictMyth-1962, ii.1382
FestSaintDays-1915, 150
FolkWrldHol-1992, 375

St. Swithin's Day
Named for: St. Swithin, Bishop of Winchester (c. 800-862)
Location: Great Britain
Date: July 15

AmerBkDays-1978, 665
AnnivHol-1983, 93
BkDays-1864, ii. 61
BkFest-1937, 60
BkHolWrld-1986, July 15
Chases-1993, 292
DaysCustFaith-1957, 181
DictMyth-1962, ii.1382
FestSaintDays-1915, 150
FolkWrldHol-1992, 375

St. Swithin's Day
  Named for: St. Swithin, Bishop of Winchester (c. 800-862)
  Location: Pennsylvania
  Date: July 15

  FolkAmerHol-1987, 231

St. Sylvester's Day
  Named for: St. Sylvester (314-335)
  Ethnic or religious group: Christian
  Date: December 31

  AmerBkDays-1978, 1167
  AnnivHol-1983, 166
  BkFest-1937, 36, 49, 141, 176, 323, 347
  BkHolWrld-1986, January 13
  Chases-1993, 487
  DaysCustFaith-1957, 325
  FestWestEur-1958, 21, 84, 242
  FolkWrldHol-1992, 653
  HolFestCelWrld-1994, 235, 300
  SaintFestCh-1904, 48

St. Sylvester's Day (Sylvesterabend)
  Named for: St. Sylvester (314-335)
  Location: Austria
  Date: December 31

  BkFest-1937, 36
  FolkWrldHol-1992, 653
  HolFestCelWrld-1994, 300

St. Sylvester's Day
  Named for: St. Sylvester (314-335)
  Location: Belgium
  Date: December 31

  AmerBkDays-1978, 1167
  BkFest-1937, 49
  FestWestEur-1958, 21
  See also **New Year's Eve (Belgium)**

St. Sylvester's Day
  Named for: St. Sylvester (314-335)
  Location: France
  Date: December 31

  AmerBkDays-1978, 1167

St. Sylvester's Day (Sylvesterabend)
  Named for: St. Sylvester (314-335)
  Location: Germany

Date: December 31

  AmerBkDays-1978, 1167
  BkFest-1937, 141
  FestWestEur-1958, 84
  HolFestCelWrld-1994, 300

St. Sylvester's Day (Svilveszter Este)
  Named for: St. Sylvester (314-335)
  Location: Hungary
  Date: December 31

  BkFest-1937, 176
  HolFestCelWrld-1994, 300

St. Sylvester's Day
  Named for: St. Sylvester (314-335)
  Location: Portugal: Funchal, Madeira Island
  Date: December 31

  AmerBkDays-1978, 1167
  Chases-1993, 487

St. Sylvester's Day (Silvesterklause)
  Named for: St. Sylvester (314-335)
  Location: Switzerland
  Date: December 31

  AmerBkDays-1978, 1167
  AnnivHol-1983, 166
  BkFest-1937, 323
  BkHolWrld-1986, January 13
  FestWestEur-1958, 242
  FolkWrldHol-1992, 29, 653
  HolFestCelWrld-1994, 235, 300

St. Sylvester's Day (Silvestestrovo Veche)
  Named for: St. Sylvester (314-335)
  Location: Yugoslavia
  Date: December 31

  BkFest-1937, 347

St. Tammany's Day
  Named for: Delaware Indian Chief Tamanend (fl. 1685)
  Location: United States
  Date: May 1

  AnnivHol-1983, 60
  Chases-1993, 190
  DaysCustFaith-1957, 122
  DictMyth-1962, ii.1530
  FolkAmerHol-1987, 170
  HolFestCelWrld-1994, 300

St. Tavy's Day
  See **St. David's Day**

St. Teresa of Avila, Feast of
  Named for: St. Teresa of Avila (1515-1582)
  Ethnic or religious group: Christian
  Date: October 15

  AmerBkDays-1978, 929
  AnnivHol-1983, 133
  DaysCustFaith-1957, 259
  DictMyth-1962, ii.1382
  DictWrldRel-1989, 753
  SaintFestCh-1904, 450

St. Therese of Lisieux, Feast of
  Named for: St. Therese of Lisieux (1873-1897)
  Ethnic or religious group: Christian
  Date: October 1

  AnnivHol-1983, 126
  DaysCustFaith-1957, 250

St. Thomas Aquinas, Feast of
  Named for: St. Thomas Aquinas (c. 1225-1274)
  Ethnic or religious group: Christian
  Date: January 28; formerly March 7

  AnnivHol-1983, 15
  DaysCustFaith-1957, 74
  DictMyth-1962, ii.1382
  DictWrldRel-1989, 758

St. Thomas More, Feast Day of
  Named for: St. Thomas More (1478-1535)
  Ethnic or religious group: Christian
  Date: June 22; formerly July 9

  AnnivHol-1983, 83
  BkDays-1864, ii.25
  Chases-1993, 90
  DaysCustFaith-1957, 175

St. Thomas of Canterbury, Feast of
  Named for: St. Thomas á Becket of Canterbury
   (c. 1118-1170)
  Ethnic or religious group: Christian
  Date: December 29

  AnnivHol-1983, 165
  BkDays-1864, ii.782
  Chases-1993, 485
  DictDays-1988, 10
  DictMyth-1962, ii.1382
  DictWrldRel-1989, 94

St. Thomas's Day
  Location: Greece and Macedonia
  Date: March-April, first Sunday after Easter

  FolkWrldHol-1992, 206

St. Thomas the Apostle, Feast of
  Named for: St. Thomas the Apostle (d. 53)
  Ethnic or religious group: Christian
  Established: Twelfth century
  Date: December 21

  AmerBkDays-1978, 1123
  AnnivHol-1983, 162
  BkDays-1864, ii. 723
  BkFest-1937, 246
  BkHolWrld-1986, December 21
  DaysCustFaith-1957, 317
  DictDays-1988, 107, 111
  DictMyth-1962, ii.1382
  FestSaintDays-1915, 224
  FolkWrldHol-1992, 597
  HolFestCelWrld-1994, 300

St. Thomas the Apostle, Feast of
  Named for: St. Thomas the Apostle (d. 53)
  Ethnic or religious group: Eastern Orthodox
  Date: October 6

  AmerBkDays-1978, 1123
  AnnivHol-1983, 162
  HolFestCelWrld-1994, 300

St. Thomas the Apostle, Feast of
  Named for: St. Thomas the Apostle (d. 53)
  Ethnic or religious group: Episcopalian
  Date: December 21

  AmerBkDays-1978, 1123
  AnnivHol-1983, 162

St. Thomas the Apostle, Feast of
  Named for: St. Thomas the Apostle (d. 53)
  Ethnic or religious group: Lutheran
  Date: December 21

  AmerBkDays-1978, 1123
  AnnivHol-1983, 162

St. Thomas the Apostle, Feast of
  Named for: St. Thomas the Apostle (d. 53)
  Ethnic or religious group: Roman Catholic
  Date: July 3

  AmerBkDays-1978, 1123
  AnnivHol-1983, 162
  HolFestCelWrld-1994, 300

St. Thomas the Apostle, Feast of
Named for: St. Thomas the Apostle (d. 53)
Location: Austria
Date: December 21

FolkWrldHol-1992, 597

St. Thomas the Apostle, Feast of
Named for: St. Thomas the Apostle (d. 53)
Location: Belgium
Date: December 21

FestSaintDays-1915, 226
FolkWrldHol-1992, 597

St. Thomas the Apostle, Feast of (Doleing or Gooding Day)
Named for: St. Thomas the Apostle (d. 53)
Location: England
Date: December 21

BkDays-1864, ii.724
DictMyth-1962, ii.1382
FestSaintDays-1915, 226

St. Thomas the Apostle, Feast of
Named for: St. Thomas the Apostle (d. 53)
Location: Germany
Date: December 21

FolkWrldHol-1992, 597

St. Thomas the Apostle, Feast of
Named for: St. Thomas the Apostle (d. 53)
Location: Guatemala: Chichicastenago
Date: December 21

BkHolWrld-1986, December 21
HolFestCelWrld-1994, 300

St. Thomas the Apostle, Feast of
Named for: St. Thomas the Apostle (d. 53)
Location: India: Kerala
Ethnic or religious group: Malabar Christians
Date: December 21

HolFestCelWrld-1994, 300

St. Thomas the Apostle, Feast of
Named for: St. Thomas the Apostle (d. 53)
Location: Netherlands
Date: December 21

BkFest-1937, 246

St. Thomas the Apostle, Feast of
Named for: St. Thomas the Apostle (d. 53)
Location: Norway
Date: December 21

FolkWrldHol-1992, 597

St. Thorlak's Day
Named for: St. Thorlak Thorhalli, Bishop of Skalholt (1133-1193; canonized by Icelandic parliament)
Location: Iceland
Ethnic or religious group: Christian
Date: December 23

FolkWrldHol-1992, 601
HolFestCelWrld-1994, 300

St. Urban's Day
Named for: Pope Urban I (d. 230)
Location: Germany
Ethnic or religious group: Christian
Date: May 25

FolkWrldHol-1992, 304

St. Urho's Day
Location: United States
Ethnic or religious group: Finnish-Americans
Date: March 16

AnnivHol-1983, 38
Chases-1993, 131
HolFestCelWrld-1994, 301

St. Ursula's Day
Named for: St. Ursula (fl. fourth century)
Ethnic or religious group: Christian
Date: October 21

AnnivHol-1983, 135
DaysCustFaith-1957, 263
DictMyth-1962, ii.1383
SaintFestCh-1904, 458

St. Ursula's Day
Named for: St. Ursula (fl. fourth century)
Location: British Virgin Islands
Date: October 21

AnnivHol-1983, 135

St. Ursula's Day
Named for: St. Ursula (fl. fourth century)
Location: New Orleans, Louisiana
Date: October 21

DaysCustFaith-1957, 263

St. Valentine's Day
　See **Valentine's Day**

St. Veronica, Feast of
　Location: France: Valenciennes
　Ethnic or religious group: Christian
　Date: July 12; observed the following Monday

　DictFolkMyth-1984, 1171

St. Vicente, Feast Day of (São Vicente)
　Named for: St. Vicente (d. 1173)
　Location: Portugal
　Ethnic or religious group: Christian
　Date: January 22

　FestWestEur-1958, 161
　HolFestCelWrld-1994, 301

St. Vincent de Paul, Feast of
　Named for: St. Vincent de Paul (1581-1660)
　Ethnic or religious group: Christian
　Date: September 27; formerly July 19

　AnnivHol-1983, 123
　Chases-1993, 299, 388
　DaysCustFaith-1957, 184
　DictWrldRel-1989, 796
　SaintFestCh-1904, 333

St. Vincent of Sargossa, Feast Day of
　Named for: St. Vincent of Sargossa (d. 304)
　Ethnic or religious group: Christian
　Date: January 22

　AnnivHol-1983, 12
　BkDays-1864, i. 144
　Chases-1993, 71
　DictMyth-1962, ii.1383
　FolkWrldHol-1992, 36
　SaintFestCh-1904, 77

St. Vincent of Sargossa, Feast Day of
　Named for: St. Vincent of Sargossa (d. 304)
　Location: France
　Date: January 22

　BkDays-1864, i. 144
　FolkWrldHol-1992, 36

St. Vitus's Day
　Named for: St. Vitus (d. c. 303)
　Ethnic or religious group: Christian

　Date: June 15

　AnnivHol-1983, 80
　BkDays-1864, i.781
　DaysCustFaith-1957, 145
　DictMyth-1962, ii.1383
　SaintFestCh-1904, 290

St. Vlasios's Day
　Location: Greece
　Ethnic or religious group: Christian
　Date: February 11

　FolkWrldHol-1992, 100

St. Walpurga's Day
　See **Walpurgisnacht**

St. Walter, Festivals of (Festas Gualterianas)
　Location: Portugal: Guimarães, Minho
　Established: 1452
　Date: Four days beginning first Sunday in August

　Chases-1993, 319
　FestWestEur-1958, 181
　HolFestCelWrld-1994, 127

St. Wenceslaus's Day
　Named for: St. Wenceslaus, Duke of Bohemia (c. 907-929)
　Ethnic or religious group: Christian
　Date: September 28

　AnnivHol-1983, 123
　BkFest-1937, 90
　DictWrldRel-1989, 803
　FolkAmerHol-1987, 333
　HolFestCelWrld-1994, 301

St. Wenceslaus's Day
　Named for: St. Wenceslaus, Duke of Bohemia (c. 907-929)
　Location: Czechoslovakia
　Date: September 28

　BkFest-1937, 90
　HolFestCelWrld-1994, 301

St. Wenceslaus's Day
　Named for: St. Wenceslaus, Duke of Bohemia (c. 907-929)
　Location: Iowa and Minnesota
　Ethnic or religious group: Czech-Americans
　Date: September 28

　FolkAmerHol-1987, 333

Saintes Maries, La Fête des
See **Holy Maries, Festival of**

Sts. Cosmas and Damian Day
    Named for: Sts. Cosmas and Damian (both fl. fifth century or earlier)
    Ethnic or religious group: Christian
    Date: September 27

    BkFest-1937, 151
    BkHolWrld-1986, September 27
    DictMyth-1962, ii.1367

Sts. Cosmas and Damian Day (Cosme e Damião)
    Named for: Sts. Cosmas and Damian (both fl. fifth century or earlier)
    Location: Brazil
    Date: September 27

    BkHolWrld-1986, September 27

Sts. Cosmas and Damian Day
    Named for: Sts. Cosmas and Damian (both fl. fifth century or earlier)
    Location: Greece
    Date: September 27

    BkFest-1937, 151

Sts. Joachim and Anne, Feast of
    Named for: Sts. Joachim and Anne (both fl. first century)
    Ethnic or religious group: Christian
    Established: Eighth century in Western churches; sixth century in Eastern churches
    Date: July 26

    AmerBkDays-1978, 695
    AnnivHol-1983, 97
    DaysCustFaith-1957, 84, 192
    DictMyth-1962, ii.1362, ii.1372
    FestSaintDays-1915, 163
    SaintFestCh-1904, 341, 400
    See also **St. Anne's Day**

Sts. Peter and John Festival (San Pedro and San Juan)
    Location: Paraguay
    Ethnic or religious group: Christian
    Date: June 24-29

    FolkWrldHol-1992, 339, 345
    HolFestCelWrld-1994, 305

Sts. Peter and Paul Day
    Named for: Sts. Peter (d. c. 64) and Paul (d. c. 64)
    Ethnic or religious group: Christian
    Date: June 29

    AmerBkDays-1978, 603
    AnnivHol-1983, 85
    BkFest-1937, 7, 151, 171, 294, 331
    Chases-1993, 269
    DaysCustFaith-1957, 155
    DictWrldRel-1989, 563, 566
    FestWestEur-1958, 14
    FolkWrldHol-1992, 345, 346
    HolFestCelWrld-1994, 299
    SaintFestCh-1904, 308
    See also **St. Peter's Day**

Sts. Peter and Paul Day
    Named for: Sts. Peter (d. c. 64) and Paul (d. c. 64)
    Location: Albania
    Date: June 29

    BkFest-1937, 7

Sts. Peter and Paul Day
    Named for: Sts. Peter (d. c. 64) and Paul (d. c. 64)
    Location: Belgium
    Date: Ceremony of Blessing of the Sea at Ostend, Blankenberge, and other seaport towns on Sunday following June 29

    FestWestEur-1958, 14

Sts. Peter and Paul Day
    Named for: Sts. Peter (d. c. 64) and Paul (d. c. 64)
    Location: Chile: Valparaiso
    Established: 1682
    Date: June 29

    FolkWrldHol-1992, 345
    HolFestCelWrld-1994, 299

Sts. Peter and Paul Day
    Named for: Sts. Peter (d. c. 64) and Paul (d. c. 64)
    Location: Greece
    Date: June 29

    BkFest-1937, 151

Sts. Peter and Paul Day
    Named for: Sts. Peter (d. c. 64) and Paul (d. c. 64)
    Location: Hungary
    Date: June 29

    BkFest-1937, 171

Sts. Peter and Paul Day (Mnarja) (Malta)
  See **Harvest Festival (Imnarja or Mnarja) (Malta: Buskett Gardens)**

Sts. Peter and Paul Day (Día de San Pedro y San Pablo)
  Named for: Sts. Peter (d. c. 64) and Paul (d. c. 64)
  Location: Peru: Callao
  Date: June 29

  FolkWrldHol-1992, 346
  HolFestCelWrld-1994, 299

Sts. Peter and Paul Day
  Named for: Sts. Peter (d. c. 64) and Paul (d. c. 64)
  Location: Russia
  Date: June 29

  BkFest-1937, 294

Sts. Peter and Paul Day
  Named for: Sts. Peter (d. c. 64) and Paul (d. c. 64)
  Location: Syria
  Date: June 29

  BkFest-1937, 331

Sts. Peter and Paul Day
  Named for: Sts. Peter (d. c. 64) and Paul (d. c. 64)
  Location: Trinidad
  Date: June 29

  FolkWrldHol-1992, 346
  HolFestCelWrld-1994, 299

Sts. Philip and James, Feast of
  Named for: Sts. Philip and James the Less (both fl. first century)
  Ethnic or religious group: Anglican, Episcopalian, and Roman Catholic
  Date: May 3 (Roman Catholic); May 1 (Anglican and Episcopalian)

  AmerBkDays-1978, 414
  DaysCustFaith-1957, 116
  FestSaintDays-1915, 103
  SaintFestCh-1904, 220

Sts. Vartan and Ghevont Day
  Named for: Sts. Vartan and Ghevont (both d. 451)
  Location: Armenia
  Ethnic or religious group: Christian
  Date: February, Thursday before Lent

  BkFest-1937, 23

Saints, Doctors, Missionaries, and Martyrs Day
  Location: England
  Ethnic or religious group: Anglican; Church of England
  Established: 1928
  Date: November 8

  AnnivHol-1983, 143
  DaysCustFaith-1957, 284
  HolFestCelWrld-1994, 298
  RelHolCal-1993, 112

Sakata Chauth
  Named for: Honors Ganesh, the Elephant God
  Ethnic or religious group: Hindu
  Date: January-February, fourth day of waning half of Hindu month of Magha

  RelHolCal-1993, 112
  See also **Elephant God, Festival of the**

Salla
  See **Fast, Feast of Breaking the (Hausa people)**

Salla or 'Id-al-Fitr
  See **Fast, Feast of Breaking the (West Africa)**

Sallah
  Location: Nigeria: Katsina
  Ethnic or religious group: Hausa people
  Date: 10th of Dhu'l-Hijjah, twelfth Islamic month

  FolkWrldHol-1992, 332
  HolFestCelWrld-1994, 301
  See also **Mecca, Pilgrimage to (Hausa people in Nigeria)**

Salone
  See **Sacred Thread Festival**

Salted Cure (Cure Salée)
  Location: Niger: Ingal
  Ethnic or religious group: Taureg people
  Date: September or October

  BkHolWrld-1986, September 11, 177
  HolFestCelWrld-1994, 74

Salt Water Day
  Location: New Jersey
  Established: 19th century

  BkHolWrld-1986, August 7
  See also **Immaculate Conception, Feast of (Uruguay); Mandi Safar; St. John the Baptist's Day (Puerto Rico)**

Salvation Army Founder's Day
  Named for: William Booth (1829-1912)
  Date: April 10

  AmerBkDays-1978, 337
  AnnivHol-1983, 50
  Chases-1993, 161
  DictWrldRel-1989, 116, 646
  RelHolCal-1993, 112

Salzburg Festival (Salzburger Festspiele)
  Location: Austria: Salzburg
  Established: 1920
  Date: Five weeks in July and August

  AnnivHol-1983, 181
  GdWrldFest-1985, 13
  HolFestCelWrld-1994, 301
  IntlThFolk-1979, 39
  MusFestEurBrit-1980, 25
  MusFestWrld-1963, 79
  See also **Mozart Festival (Austria: Salzburg)**

Sâmbăta Mare
  See **Holy Saturday (Romania)**

Samhain (Summer's End)
  Ethnic or religious group: Ancient Celtic people
  Date: October 31

  AmerBkDays-1978, 968
  BkHolWrld-1986, October 31, November 1
  Chases-1993, 427
  DictFolkMyth-1984, 202, 968
  DictMyth-1962, ii.1393
  FestSaintDays-1915, 191
  FolkWrldHol-1992, 524
  HolFestCelWrld-1994, 302
  RelHolCal-1993, 64, 112
  See also **All Saints' Day; Halloween**

Samhain (Summer's End)
  Location: Ireland
  Date: October 31

  BkHolWrld-1986, October 31, November 1
  DictFolkMyth-1984, 202, 968
  FolkWrldHol-1992, 524

Samhain (Sauin, Summer's End)
  Location: Isle of Man
  Date: October 31

  DictMyth-1962, ii.1393

Samhain (Summer's End)
  Location: Scotland
  Ethnic or religious group: Gaelic people
  Date: October 31

  DictFolkMyth-1984, 968

Samhain (Summer's End)
  Location: United States
  Ethnic or religious group: Neo-pagans
  Date: October 31

  RelHolCal-1993, 64, 112

Samichlaus Abend
  See **St. Nicholas's Day (Switzerland)**

Samiljol
  See **Independence Day (Republic of Korea)**

San Antonio, Fiesta
  Location: San Antonio, Texas
  Established: 19th century; recalls Battle of San Jacinto, April 21, 1836
  Date: Ten days in April, including April 21

  AmerBkDays-1978, 365
  GdUSFest-1984, 186
  HolFestCelWrld-1994, 302
  See also **San Jacinto Day**

San Antonio Abad
  See **St. Anthony the Abbot, Feast of Day (Mexico: Zacatecas)**

San Benitino de Lerez Festival
  Location: Spain: Pontevedra
  Date: July; coincides with Galician Song and Dance Festival

  IntlThFolk-1979, 340

Sandcastle Days
  Location: Imperial Beach, California
  Established: 1981
  Date: Usually July

  HolFestCelWrld-1994, 302

San Diego, Feast of and Corn Dance
  Location: Jemez and Tesuque pueblos, New Mexico
  Date: November 12

  IndianAmer-1989, 290, 300, 319

San Ermengol Retaule Festival
  Location: Spain: Seo de Urgel, Lerida
  Date: August

  IntlThFolk-1979, 342

San Estevan, Feast of
   Location: Acoma Pueblo, New Mexico
   Date: September 2

   HolFestCelWrld-1994, 303
   IndianAmer-1989, 288, 294
   RelHolCal-1993, 113

San Felix Martyr, Feast of
   Location: Spain: Villafranca del Panades, Barcelona
   Established: Guild festival held since the Middle Ages
   Date: August

   IntlThFolk-1979, 343

San Fermín Festival
   See **Running of the Bulls (Spain: Pamplona, Navarre)**

San Francisco's Day
   See **St. Francis of Assisi, Feast of (Peru: Lima)**

Sangamitta Day
   Named for: Sangamitta (fl. 288 B.C.), princess of India;
      also honors King Devanamipiya of Ceylon (fl. second
      half of third century B.C.)
   Location: Sri Lanka
   Ethnic or religious group: Buddhist
   Established: 288 B.C.
   Date: December, full moon day of the first month or
      May-June, full moon day of Hindu month of Jyeshta

   BkHolWrld-1986, December 2, 180
   HolFestCelWrld-1994, 304

San Gennaro
   See **St. Januarius, Feast of**

Sango Festival
   Named for: Sango, third Alafin of Oyo, possible historical
      figure who lived during the 15th century
   Location: Nigeria: Ede
   Ethnic or religious group: Oyo and Yoruba peoples
   Date: Early November, seven days near end of rainy season

   FolkWrldHol-1992, 534
   HolFestCelWrld-1994, 304

Sang-joe
   See **Lights, Festival of (Tibet: Lhasa)**

San Isidro
   See **St. Isidore of Seville, Feast of (Colombia: Río Frío)**

San Jacinto Day
   Named for: Defeat of General Antonio López de Santa
      Anna (1795?-1876) at San Jacinto by General Sam
      Houston (1793-1863) and his soldiers in 1836

   Location: San Antonio and San Jacinto, Texas
   Date: April 21

   AmerBkDays-1978, 364
   AnnivHol-1983, 54
   Chases-1993, 175
   DaysCustFaith-1957, 97
   DictDays-1988, 108
   HolFestCelWrld-1994, 305

Sanja Matsuri
   See **Shrines Festival, Three (Japan: Asakusa Temple, Tokyo)**

San José, International Fair of
   See **St. Joseph's Day (Roman Catholic people in David, Panama)**

San Juan Capistrano
   See **Swallows of San Juan Capistrano**

San Juan Day
   See **Midsummer Day (Puerto Rico)**

San Juan Fiesta
   See **St. John the Baptist's Day (New York, New York)**

Sankranti
   See **Harvest Festival (India) and (India: Karnaraka)**

Sankt Hans Aften
   See **Midsummer (Denmark)**

San Lorenzo, Festival of
   See **St. Lawrence, Feast of (Spain: Foz, Lugo)**

San Macario, Festival of
   Location: Spain: Malda, Lérida
   Date: January 2

   DictFolkMyth-1984, 367

San Marcos, Toro de
   See **St. Mark, Feast of (Spain)**

San Marino, Founding of
   Named for: Founding of San Marinus by St. Marinus in the
      fourth century
   Location: San Marino
   Date: September 3

   NatlHolWrld-1968, 157

San Martin, Quadrilles of
   See **St. Martin's Day (Colombia: San Martin, Meta)**

San Martín Day
Named for: José Francisco de San Martín (1778-1850)
Location: Argentina
Date: August 17

AnnivHol-1983, 108

San Martino
See Martinmas (Italy)

San Pedro Rooster Pulls
See St. Peter's Day (New Mexico pueblos)

San Roque Festival (Spain: Betanzos, La Coruna) and (Spain: Llanes, Oviedo)
See St. Roch's Day (Spain: Betanzos, La Coruna) and (Spain: Llanes, Oviedo)

Santa Claus Night
See St. Nicholas's Day (Switzerland)

Santa Cristina, Festival of
See St. Christina's Day (Spain: Lloret de Mar, Gerona)

Santacruzan Festival
See Exaltation of the Cross (Filipino-Americans in California) and (Christians in Philippines)

Santa Cruz Days (Coming of the Rivermen)
Location: Cochiti and Taos pueblos, New Mexico
Date: May 3; observed with Green Corn dances

IndianAmer-1989, 286, 296, 319

Santa Cruz de Mayo or Santacruzan Festival
See Exaltation of the Cross (Philippines)

Santa Fe Fiesta
Location: Santa Fe, New Mexico
Established: 1712
Date: Three to four days over second weekend in September

AmerBkDays-1978, 800
HolFestCelWrld-1994, 307
RelHolCal-1993, 113

Santa Isabel, Fiesta de
See St. Elizabeth, Feast of

Santa Lucia, Feast of
See St. Lucy's Day

Santarém, International Festival of
Location: Portugal: Santarém
Established: 1957
Date: Second week in June

HolFestCelWrld-1994, 3
IntlThFolk-1979, 312

Santa Rosa de Lima
See St. Rose of Lima Day

Santiago
See St. James's Day (Quechua Indians in South America)

Santiago Fair and Festival of Setubal
Location: Portugal: Setubal
Date: July-August

IntlThFolk-1979, 313

Santo Cristo and San Vicente Ferrer, Festival of
Named for: Santo Cristo (c. third century) and San Vicente Ferrer (c. 1350-1419)
Location: Spain: Graus, Huesca
Date: September

IntlThFolk-1979, 337

Santo Domingo Promenade
Location: Peru: Lima
Date: August 4

BkFestHolWrld-1970, 111

Santo Isobel, Fiesta of
Location: Southern Arizona and Mexico
Ethnic or religious group: Yaqui Indians
Date: July 4

DictFolkMyth-1984, 258

Santon Fair
Location: France: Marseille
Date: December

BkFestHolWrld-1970, 128

San Xavier Pageant and Fiesta
Location: Tucson, Arizona
Ethnic or religious group: Tohono O'Odham and Yaqui Indians
Date: April

Chases-1993, 169

São Martinho, Feast of
See Martinmas (Portugal)

Saptamînapatimilor
  See **Holy Week (Romania)**

Saratoga Festival (Saratoga Performing Arts Center)
  Location: Saratoga Springs, New York
  Established: 1966
  Date: Early June to early September

  GdUSFest-1984, 130
  HolFestCelWrld-1994, 308
  MusFestAmer-1990, 110

Sarbatoarea Blajinilor
  See **Blajini (Meek), Feast of the (Romania)**

Sardinian Cavalcade (Cavalcata Sarda)
  Location: Italy: Sassari, Sardinia
  Established: Since about 1000
  Date: Last Sunday in May or on Ascension Day

  BkHolWrld-1986, May 23, 176
  GdWrldFest-1985, 118
  HolFestCelWrld-1994, 54

Saturday before Easter
  See **Holy Saturday**

Saturday of Glory
  See **Holy Saturday**

Saturnalia
  Location: Ancient Rome
  Date: December 17-23

  AmerBkDays-1978, 1069, 1128, 1143
  BkDays-1864, ii.745
  Chases-1993, 476
  DaysCustFaith-1957, 315
  DictDays-1988, 108
  DictFolkMyth-1984, 941, 974
  DictMyth-1962, ii.1403
  DictWrldRel-1989, 182
  FestSaintDays-1915, 232
  HolFestCelWrld-1994, 308
  RelHolCal-1993, 113
  SaintFestCh-1904, 36

Saturnalia
  Location: United States
  Ethnic or religious group: Neo-pagans

  RelHolCal-1993, 113

Sauin, Summer's End
  See **Samhain (Isle of Man)**

Sausage Fair (Bad Durkheim Wurstmarkt)
  Location: Germany: Bad Durkheim
  Established: 1417
  Date: Saturday-Tuesday during second weekend in
    September; Friday-Monday during third weekend
    in September

  HolFestCelWrld-1994, 22

Sausage Festival (Wurstfest)
  Location: New Braunfels, Texas
  Ethnic or religious group: German-Americans
  Date: End of October through first week in November

  HolFestCelWrld-1994, 373

Savaria Festival
  Location: Hungary: Szombathely
  Date: August

  IntlThFolk-1979, 201

Savitri-Vrata or Vow
  See **Vata Savitri (married Hindu women)**

Savonlinnan Oopperajuhlat
  See **Opera Festival, Savonlinna (Finland: Savonlinna)**

Sawm
  See **Ramadan**

Scaling Day
  See **Escalade**

Schäferlauf
  See **Shepherds' Race (Germany: Markgrönigen, Swabia)**

Schäfer Sonntag
  See **Shepherd Sunday (Switzerland: Belalp, Valais)**

Schäfflertanz or Böttchertanz
  See **Mardi Gras (Germany: Munich)**

Schiller Days
  Named for: Friedrich von Schiller (1759-1805)
  Location: Federal Republic of Germany: Mannheim,
    Baden-Wurttemberg
  Established: 1978
  Date: May

  IntlThFolk-1979, 143

Schloss Neulengbach
  See **Castle Neulengbach Festival (Austria: Neulengbach,
    Lower Austria)**

School Reunion Day
    Location: Spain
    Date: December 8

    AnnivHol-1983, 158

Schooner Days
    Location: Rockland and Thomaston, Maine
    Established: 1977
    Date: Weekend after July 4

    HolFestCelWrld-1994, 125

Schrulblha
    See **Grain, Festival of Ears of (Tibet)**

Schubertiade Hohenems
    Named for: Franz Schubert (1797-1828)
    Location: Austria: Hohenems
    Established: 1976
    Date: 16 days in June

    MusFestEurBrit-1980, 27

Schueberfo'er
    See **Shepherd's Fair (Luxembourg)**

Schützenfeste
    See **Marksmen's Festival (Germany)**

Schutzengelfest
    See **Guardian Angel, Festival of the (Switzerland: Appenzell)**

Schwetzingen Festival
    Location: Federal Republic of Germany: Schwetzingen,
       Baden-Wurttemberg
    Established: 1951
    Date: April-May

    IntlThFolk-1979, 150

Scoppio del Carro, Ceremony of the Car
    See **Easter (Italy: Florence)**

Scottish Games, Virginia
    Location: Alexandria, Virginia
    Ethnic or religious group: Scottish-Americans
    Date: Fourth weekend in July

    HolFestCelWrld-1994, 358

Sea Celebrations
    Location: Romania: Constanta and resorts on the
       seashore
    Date: One week ending first Sunday in August, Navy Day

    IntlThFolk-1979, 321

Seafair
    Location: Seattle, Washington
    Established: 1950
    Date: 16 days in July-August

    Chases-1993, 285
    GdUSFest-1984, 208

Seal Festival (Keretkun Festival)
    Location: USSR: Siberia
    Ethnic or religious group: Chukchi people
    Date: Two to three days in late autumn

    FolkWrldHol-1992, 540
    HolFestCelWrld-1994, 168

Seal Festival
    Location: USSR
    Ethnic or religious group: Koryak people
    Date: November, end of seal-hunting season

    FolkWrldHol-1992, 536
    HolFestCelWrld-1994, 168

Sealing the Frost
    Location: Guatemala: Santa Eulalia
    Ethnic or religious group: Cuchumatan Indians
    Date: April-early May

    BkHolWrld-1986, April 8, 180
    HolFestCelWrld-1994, 310

Seaman's Day
    Location: Iceland
    Date: June 2 or first Sunday in June

    AnnivHol-1983, 75
    HolFestCelWrld-1994, 310, 319

Seatapmise Päev
    See **Killing the Pigs, Festival of (Estonia)**

Seattle Days
    Named for: Chief Seatlh (1786?-1866)
    Location: Suquamish, Washington
    Ethnic or religious group: Suquamish Indians
    Date: August 18-20 or third weekend in August

    HolFestCelWrld-1994, 59
    IndianAmer-1989, 215

Sebring 12 Hours (Automobile Hall of Fame Week)
    Location: Sebring, Florida
    Established: 1950
    Date: Third week in March

    GdUSFest-1984, 36

Sechselauten
See Six O'Clock Ringing Festival (Switzerland: Zurich)

Second Easter Day
See Easter Monday

Second New Year
See Minstrels' Carnival, Annual (South Africa: Cape Town)

Secretaries' Day and Week
Location: United States
Established: 1952
Date: Last full week in April; Wednesday of Secretaries'
Week is Secretaries' Day

AnnivHol-1983, 55
Chases-1993, 175
DictDays-1988, 109
HolFestCelWrld-1994, 260

Seder
See Passover

Sedna, Feast of
Ethnic or religious group: Central Eskimos
Date: Autumn

DictFolkMyth-1984, 56, 979

Seespiele
See Lake Festival (Austria: Morbisch am See, Burgenland)

Seged
Location: Ethiopia
Ethnic or religious group: Falasha Jews
Date: November; 29th day of eighth Jewish month

FolkWrldHol-1992, 537
HolFestCelWrld-1994, 310

Seijin-No-Hi
See Adults Day (Japan)

Sekartan Festival
See Muhammad's Birthday (Indonesia: Jogjakarta)

Seker Bayrami
See Fast, Breaking of the (Turkey)

Selassie's Birthday, Haile
Named for: Haile Selassie (Ras Tafari, 1892-1975),
emperor of Ethiopia
Location: Ethiopia: Addis Ababa
Date: July 23

DictWrldRel-1989, 601
NatlHolWrld-1968, 123

Selassie's Coronation Day, Haile
Named for: Haile Selassie (Ras Tafari, 1892-1975),
emperor of Ethiopia
Location: Jamaica
Ethnic or religious group: Ras Tafarians
Established: November 2, 1930
Date: On or near November 15

DictWrldRel-1989, 601
FolkWrldHol-1992, 562
HolFestCelWrld-1994, 131

Self-Government Day
See Madaraka Day

Semaines Musicales du Luberon
See Musical Weeks of Luberon (France: Luberon and
surrounding towns, Vauclude)

Semaines Musicales Internationale d'Orleans
See Musical Weeks of Orleans, International (France:
Orleans, Loiret)

Semana Criolla
See Creole Week (Uruguay)

Semana Santa
See Holy Week (Guatemala: Antigua) and (Spain)

Semana Santo
See Holy Week (Portugal)

Semik
Location: Prerevolutionary Russia
Date: May-June, seventh Thursday after Easter

FolkWrldHol-1992, 291
HolFestCelWrld-1994, 311

Seminole Fair
Location: Seminole Reservation, Florida
Ethnic or religious group: Seminole Indians
Date: Fourth weekend in December

IndianAmer-1989, 239

Seminole Nation Days
Location: Seminole, Oklahoma
Ethnic or religious group: Seminole Indians
Date: September

IndianAmer-1989, 97

Sending the Winter Dress
See Winter Dress, Sending the

Senhora do Monte do Carmo
See Our Lady of Mount Carmel (Portugal: Moura, Beja)

Senior Citizens Day
Location: Massachusetts and other United States
Date: May 1

AnnivHol-1983, 60

Senior Citizens Day
Location: Oklahoma
Date: June 9

AnnivHol-1983, 77
Chases-1993, 241

September in the Town
Location: Italy: Casertavecchia, Caserta, Compania
Established: 1971
Date: End of August-beginning of September

IntlThFolk-1979, 241

Septuagesima Sunday
Ethnic or religious group: Christian
Date: Third Sunday before Lent

DaysCustFaith-1957, 63
DictDays-1988, 109
HolFestCelWrld-1994, 263
SaintFestCh-1904, 97

Serreta, Festa Da
See **Our Lady of Miracles (Portugal)**

Servatus, St.
See **Frost, or Ice, Saints Day**

Setsubun
See **Bean-Throwing Festival (Japan)**

Settimane Musicali di Stresa Festival Internazionale
See **Musical Weeks, Stresa (Italy: Stresa)**

Seven-Five-Three Festival Day (Shichi-Go-San)
Location: Japan
Date: November 15

AnnivHol-1983, 148
BkHolWrld-1986, November 15
Chases-1993, 442
FolkWrldHol-1992, 560
HolFestCelWrld-1994, 315

Seven Herbs Festival (Nanakusa Matsuri)
Location: Japan
Established: Seventh century

Date: Seventh day of first lunar month; observed January 7

Chases-1993, 58
DictFolkMyth-1984, 540
FolkWrldHol-1992, 65
HolFestCelWrld-1994, 217

Seven Old Maids or Seven Sisters Festival
See **Double Seventh**

Seven Sisters, Festival of the
See **Double Seventh (Malaysia)**

Seventeenth of Ireland
See **St. Patrick's Day**

Seventy-Six, Days of
Named for: Commemorates Wild Bill Hickok (1837-1876) and Calamity Jane (Cannary) Burk (1852?-1903)
Location: Deadwood, South Dakota
Established: 1924
Date: First full weekend in August

AnnivHol-1983, 176
GdUSFest-1984, 172
HolFestCelWrld-1994, 80

Seville Fair (April Fair)
Location: Spain: Seville
Date: One week in March or April, usually following Easter

FestWestEur-1958, 194
GdWrldFest-1985, 163
HolFestCelWrld-1994, 312
IntlThFolk-1979, 342

Seward's Day
Named for: William Henry Seward (1801-1872) and the United States' March 30, 1867, purchase of Alaska from Russia
Location: Alaska
Date: Observed last Monday in March

AmerBkDays-1978, 309
AnnivHol-1983, 44
BkHolWrld-1986, March 30, 180
Chases-1993, 146
DictDays-1988, 109
HolFestCelWrld-1994, 312

Sexagesima Sunday
Date: Second Sunday before Lent

DaysCustFaith-1957, 63
DictDays-1988, 109
HolFestCelWrld-1994, 263
SaintFestCh-1904, 97

Shaaban
See **Night of Forgiveness (India)**

Shab-Barat or Shaban
See **Night of Forgiveness (Iran)**

Shab-i-Barat
See **Night of Forgiveness (India) and (Pakistan)**

Shabuoth
See **Shavuot**

Shah Abdul Latif Death Festival
  Named for: Shah Abdul Latif (1689-1752), Sufi poet
  Location: Pakistan: Bhit Shah, Sind
  Date: 14-16 days of the Islamic month of Safar

  HolFestCelWrld-1994, 313

Shaheel or Shaheed Day or Martyrs Day
  Location: Bangladesh
  Date: February 21

  AnnivHol-1983, 26
  Chases-1993, 106

Shaker Festival
  Location: Auburn, Kentucky
  Ethnic or religious group: United Society of Believers in
    Christ's Second Appearing, the Millennial Church (Shakers)
  Date: Mid-July

  AmerBkDays-1978, 218

Shaker Festival
  Location: South Union, Kentucky
  Ethnic or religious group: United Society of Believers in
    Christ's Second Appearing, the Millennial Church (Shakers)
  Established: 1962
  Date: Ten days beginning second Thursday in July

  GdUSFest-1984, 65
  HolFestCelWrld-1994, 313

Shaker Festival
  Location: Old Chatham, New York
  Ethnic or religious group: United Society of Believers in
    Christ's Second Appearing, the Millennial Church (Shakers)
  Date: August

  AmerBkDays-1978, 218

Shakespeare Company Festival, Royal
  Named for: William Shakespeare (1564-1616)

  Location: England: Stratford-upon-Avon, Warwickshire
  Established: 1879
  Date: April-December

  Chases-1993, 148
  GdWrldFest-1985, 97
  HolFestCelWrld-1994, 313
  IntlThFolk-1979, 177

Shakespeare Days
  Named for: William Shakespeare (1564-1616)
  Location: German Democratic Republic: Weimar
  Date: April

  IntlThFolk-1979, 130

Shakespeare Festival
  Named for: William Shakespeare (1564-1616)
  Location: Italy: Verona, Veneto
  Established: 1948
  Date: June-September

  IntlThFolk-1979, 252

Shakespeare Festival, American
  Named for: William Shakespeare (1564-1616)
  Location: Stratford, Connecticut

  AmerBkDays-1978, 376

Shakespeare Festival, New York
  Named for: William Shakespeare (1564-1616)
  Location: Central Park, New York, New York
  Established: 1954
  Date: Summer

  AmerBkDays-1978, 376

Shakespeare Festival, Oregon
  Named for: William Shakespeare (1564-1616)
  Location: Ashland, Oregon
  Established: 1935
  Date: February through October

  AmerBkDays-1978, 376
  GdUSFest-1984, 150

Shakespeare Festival, San Diego National
  Named for: William Shakespeare (1564-1616)
  Location: San Diego, California
  Established: 1949
  Date: Early June through mid-September

  AmerBkDays-1978, 376

Shakespeare's Birthday
 Named for: William Shakespeare (1564-1616)
 Date: April 23

AmerBkDays-1978, 375
BkDays-1864, i.542
Chases-1993, 177
DictDays-1988, 109
HolFestCelWrld-1994, 313

Shakespeare's Birthday
 Named for: William Shakespeare (1564-1616)
 Location: England: Stratford-upon-Avon, Warwickshire
 Date: April 23

AmerBkDays-1978, 375
DictDays-1988, 109
HolFestCelWrld-1994, 313

Shakespeare's Birthday
 Named for: William Shakespeare (1564-1616)
 Location: Philadelphia, Pennsylvania
 Established: 1870s
 Date: April 23

AmerBkDays-1978, 375

Shalako Ceremonial (Koko Awia, the Kachina Come)
 Location: Zuñi Pueblo, New Mexico
 Date: Late November or early December

DictFolkMyth-1984, 566, 589, 1001
HolFestCelWrld-1994, 314
IndianAmer-1989, 290, 321
RelHolCal-1993, 113

Sham al-Neseem
 See **Spring Day, Smell the (Egypt)**

Shampoo Day (Yoodoonal)
 Location: Korea
 Date: 15th day of sixth lunar month

FolkWrldHol-1992, 352
HolFestCelWrld-1994, 314

Shankarachaya Jayanti or Birthday
 Named for: Adi Shankarachaya (788-820)
 Location: India
 Ethnic or religious group: Hindu
 Date: April-May, fifth day (southern India) or tenth day (northern India) of waxing half of Hindu month of Vaisakha

RelHolCal-1993, 114

Sharad Purnima
 Ethnic or religious group: Hindu
 Date: September-October, full moon day of Hindu month of Asvina

RelHolCal-1993, 114

Shark Angling Competition, International
 Location: Gibraltar: waters off City Wharf
 Established: 1967
 Date: One day in late April or early May

GdWrldFest-1985, 88

Sharp Tuesday
 See **Mardi Gras (England)**

Shasti, Festival of (Aranya Shasti)
 Location: India: Bengal
 Ethnic or religious group: Hindu Rajputanan women

BkFest-1937, 158

Shavuot, the Feast of Weeks (Jewish Feast of Pentecost)
 Ethnic or religious group: Jewish
 Date: May-June, sixth of Jewish month of Sivan

AmerBkDays-1978, 462, 544
AnnivHol-1983, 172
BkDays-1864, i.629
BkFest-1937, 208
BkFestHolWrld-1970, 70
BkHolWrld-1986, May 25, 175
Chases-1993, 221
DaysCustFaith-1957, 137, 159, 161
DictMyth-1962, ii.1253, ii.1428
DictWrldRel-1989, 155, 390, 564, 678
FestSaintDays-1915, 119
FolkAmerHol-1987, 195
FolkWrldHol-1992, 321
HolFestCelWrld-1994, 253, 314
RelHolCal-1993, 102, 114

Shavuot, the Feast of Weeks (Jewish Feast of Pentecost)
 Location: Israel
 Date: May-June, sixth of Jewish month of Sivan

AmerBkDays-1978, 462, 544
DaysCustFaith-1957, 137, 159, 161
DictWrldRel-1989, 155, 390, 564, 678
HolFestCelWrld-1994, 314
RelHolCal-1993, 102

Shavuot, the Feast of Weeks
  Location: Kurdistan
  Date: May-June, sixth of Jewish month of Sivan

  FolkWrldHol-1992, 321

Shavuot, the Feast of Weeks
  Location: Libya
  Date: May-June, sixth of Jewish month of Sivan

  FolkWrldHol-1992, 321

Shavuot, the Feast of Weeks
  Location: Persia; now Iran
  Date: May-June, sixth of Jewish month of Sivan

  FolkWrldHol-1992, 321

Shavuot, the Feast of Weeks
  Location: United States
  Date: May-June, sixth of Jewish month of Sivan

  FolkAmerHol-1987, 195

Shavuot, the Feast of Weeks
  Location: Yemen
  Date: May-June, sixth of Jewish month of Sivan

  FolkWrldHol-1992, 321

Shaw Festival
  Named for: George Bernard Shaw (1856-1950)
  Location: Canada: Niagara-on-the-Lake, Ontario
  Established: 1962
  Date: 22 weeks from May to October

  Chases-1993, 175
  GdWrldFest-1985, 49
  IntlThFolk-1979, 72

Sheelah's Day
  Location: Ireland
  Date: March 18

  AnnivHol-1983, 39
  DaysCustFaith-1957, 81-82
  DictDays-1988, 110
  HolFestCelWrld-1994, 314
  RelHolCal-1993, 114

Sheer Thursday
  See **Holy Thursday (England)**

Shellfish Gathering (Shiohi-gari)
  Location: Japan
  Date: April 4

  BkFestHolWrld-1970, 76

Shembe Festival
  See **Zulu/Shembe Festival**

Shemini Atzeret
  Ethnic or religious group: Jewish
  Date: September-October, eighth day of the Festival of Sukkot; observed on 22nd of Jewish month of Tishri

  AmerBkDays-1978, 928
  AnnivHol-1983, 172
  Chases-1993, 401
  HolFestCelWrld-1994, 315

Shepherd's Fair (Schueberfo'er)
  Location: Luxembourg
  Established: 1340
  Date: Two weeks beginning last Sunday in August

  Chases-1993, 339
  GdWrldFest-1985, 129

Shepherds' Race (Schäferlauf)
  Location: Germany: Markgrönigen, Swabia
  Date: August 23-25

  BkHolWrld-1986, August 24
  FestWestEur-1958, 69
  HolFestCelWrld-1994, 309
  See also **St. Bartolomew's Day**

Shepherd Sunday (Schäfer Sonntag)
  Location: Switzerland: Belalp, Valais
  Date: Second Sunday in September

  FestWestEur-1958, 237

Shichi-Go-San
  See **Seven-Five-Three Festival**

Shick-Shack Day
  Named for: Observed on the birthday of Charles II (1630-1685)
  Location: Northern England
  Date: May 29

  AnnivHol-1983, 72
  BkDays-1864, i. 696
  Chases-1993, 224
  DictDays-1988, 14, 81, 83, 96, 98, 110, 134
  FolkWrldHol-1992, 305
  HolFestCelWrld-1994, 115, 315

Shicsack Day
  See **Shick-Shack Day**

Shigoto Hajime
  See **Beginning of Work Day (Japan)**

Shig-Shag Day, Shik-Shak Day
See **Shick-Shack Day**

Shilla Cultural Festival
Location: Korea: Kyongju
Date: Three days in October during even-numbered years

HolFestCelWrld-1994, 316

Shimmeisha Oni Festival
Location: Japan: Shimmeisha Shrine, Toyohashi, Aichi
Date: Mid-February

IntlThFolk-1979, 261

Shinbyu
Location: Burma; now Myanmar
Ethnic or religious group: Buddhist
Date: Summer

BkHolWrld-1986, September 2, 180

Shiohi-gari
See **Shellfish Gathering (Japan)**

Ship's Island, Festival of
Location: Sweden: Stockholm
Established: 1977
Date: July

IntlThFolk-1979, 347

Shitala Ashtami
Ethnic or religious group: Hindu
Date: March-April, eighth day of waxing half of Hindu month of Chaitra

RelHolCal-1993, 114

Shiva, Gajan of
Location: India: Bengal
Ethnic or religious group: Hindu
Date: March-April, Hindu month of Chaitra

FolkWrldHol-1992, 213

Shiva, Night of (Mahashivaratri)
Ethnic or religious group: Hindu
Date: February-March, 13th night and 14th day of waning half of Hindu month of Phalguna

AnnivHol-1983, 179
BkHolWrld-1986, March 10
Chases-1993, 103
FolkWrldHol-1992, 148
HolFestCelWrld-1994, 316
RelHolCal-1993, 92

Shiva, Night of (Mahashivaratri)
Location: India
Date: February-March, 13th night and 14th day of waning half of Hindu month of Phalguna

AnnivHol-1983, 179
Chases-1993, 103
FolkWrldHol-1992, 148
HolFestCelWrld-1994, 316
RelHolCal-1993, 92

Shiva, Night of (Maha Shivaratree)
Location: Mauritius
Date: February-March, 13th night and 14th day of waning half of Hindu month of Phalguna

FolkWrldHol-1992, 148
HolFestCelWrld-1994, 316

Shiva, Night of (Mahashivaratri)
Location: Nepal
Date: February-March, 13th night and 14th day of waning half of Hindu month of Phalguna

FolkWrldHol-1992, 148
HolFestCelWrld-1994, 316
RelHolCal-1993, 92

Shogatsu
See **New Year (Okinawa)**

Shortest Day
See **St. Thomas's Day; Winter Solstice**

Showcase of Rivadavia
Location: Spain: Rivadavia, Orense
Date: May

IntlThFolk-1979, 341

Shrimp Festival
Location: Belgium: Oostduinkerke
Date: Early July

BkFestHolWrld-1970, 105

Shrimp Festival, National
Location: Gulf Shores, Alabama
Established: 1971
Date: Four days in early October

HolFestCelWrld-1994, 317

Shrine Festival, Chusonji
Location: Japan: Chusonji, Iwate
Date: May

IntlThFolk-1979, 253

Shrine Festival, Gokoku
  Location: Japan: Hikone City, Shiga
  Date: October-November

  IntlThFolk-1979, 253

Shrine Festival, Itsukushima
  Location: Japan: Itsukushima Island, Hiroshima
  Date: Two days in mid-April

  IntlThFolk-1979, 254

Shrine Festival, Kanda Myojin
  Location: Japan: Tokyo
  Date: Two days in mid-May

  IntlThFolk-1979, 260

Shrine Festival, Kasuga Wakamiya
  Location: Japan: Nara
  Date: December 13-18

  IntlThFolk-1979, 257

Shrine Festival, Kuromori Hie
  Location: Japan: Kuromori Village, Sakata City, Yamagata
  Date: Mid-February

  IntlThFolk-1979, 255

Shrine Festival, Yushima
  Location: Japan: Tokyo
  Date: Two days in late May

  IntlThFolk-1979, 261

Shrine Kagura Festival, Ise
  Location: Japan: Ise, Mie
  Date: April and September

  IntlThFolk-1979, 253

Shrine Rice Festival, Katori
  Location: Japan: Katori, Chiba
  Date: April

  IntlThFolk-1979, 260

Shrine Rice Festival, Sumiyashi
  Location: Japan: Osaka
  Date: June 14

  Chases-1993, 248

Shrine Rice Festival, Suwa
  Location: Japan: Tokyo
  Date: January

  IntlThFolk-1979, 260

Shrine Rite, Royal (Chongmyo Taeje)
  Location: Korea: Seoul
  Ethnic or religious group: Confucian
  Date: First Sunday in May

  HolFestCelWrld-1994, 61

Shrines Festival, Three (Sanja Matsuri)
  Location: Japan: Asakusa Temple, Tokyo
  Established: Late 1800s
  Date: Second weekend in May

  HolFestCelWrld-1994, 305

Shrove Monday (Iceland)
  See **Mardi Gras (Iceland)**

Shrove Sunday
  See **Quinquagesima Sunday; Mardi Gras**

Shrove Tuesday
  See **Mardi Gras (Ireland)**

Shunki Korei-Sai
  See **Vernal Equinox, Festival of (Japan)**

Shuttlecock Day
  See **Mardi Gras (England)**

Shvod
  Location: Armenia
  Date: Last day of February

  DictFolkMyth-1984, 1010

Sidi-Bou-Makhlouf, Festival
  Location: Tunisia: Le Kef, Le Kef Region
  Date: July

  IntlThFolk-1979, 362

Sigma Festival
  Location: France: Bordeaux, Gironde
  Established: 1965
  Date: One week in November

  IntlThFolk-1979, 103

Silent Days
  See **Holy Week**

"Silent Night, Holy Night" Celebration
Named for: Commemorates December 24, 1818, debut
of the Christmas carol written by Franz Xaver Gruber
(1787-1863) and Father Josef Mohr (1792-1848)
Location: Austria: Hallein, Oberndorf, Wagrain, all
of Salzburg
Date: December 24

Chases-1993, 481
GdWrldFest-1985, 12

Silvas Festival
Location: Romania: Hateg, Silvasul de Jos Commune,
Hunedoara
Date: Second Sunday in June

IntlThFolk-1979, 324

Silver Ball, Hurling the
Location: England: St. Ives, Cornwall
Date: Sunday nearest or Monday after February 3

HolFestCelWrld-1994, 148

Silversterabend
See **New Year's Eve (Protestants in Switzerland)**

Silvesterklause
See **St. Sylvester's Day (Switzerland)**

Simbang Gabi
See **Christmas Season (Misa de Gallo) (Philippines)**

Simhat bet Ha-sho'evah
See **Water-Drawing Festival (Jewish people in Israel)**

Simhat Torah (Rejoicing in the Law)
Ethnic or religious group: Jewish
Date: September-October, 22nd or 23rd of Jewish month
of Tishri, second day of Shemini Atzeret

AmerBkDays-1978, 928, 950
AnnivHol-1983, 172
BkHolWrld-1986, October 11, 175
BkFest-1937, 204
Chases-1993, 403
DictWrldRel-1989, 155, 693
FolkAmerHol-1987, 293
FolkWrldHol-1992, 508
HolFestCelWrld-1994, 317

Simhat Torah (Rejoicing in the Law)
Ethnic or religious group: Conservative Jews

Date: September-October, 23rd of Jewish month of
Tishri, second day of Shemini Atzeret

AmerBkDays-1978, 928, 950

Simhat Torah (Rejoicing in the Law)
Ethnic or religious group: Orthodox Jews
Date: September-October, 23rd of Jewish month of
Tishri, second day of Shemini Atzeret

AmerBkDays-1978, 928, 950

Simhat Torah (Rejoicing in the Law)
Ethnic or religious group: Reform Jews
Date: September-October, 22rd of Jewish month of
Tishri (in Israel)

AmerBkDays-1978, 928, 950
DictWrldRel-1989, 693
HolFestCelWrld-1994, 317

Simhat Torah (Rejoicing in the Law)
Location: Afghanistan
Date: September-October, 23rd of Jewish month of
Tishri, second day of Shemini Atzeret

HolFestCelWrld-1994, 317

Simhat Torah (Rejoicing in the Law)
Location: China: Cochin
Date: September-October, 23rd of Jewish month of
Tishri, second day of Shemini Atzeret

HolFestCelWrld-1994, 317

Simhat Torah (Rejoicing in the Law)
Location: France
Date: September-October, 23rd of Jewish month of
Tishri, second day of Shemini Atzeret

HolFestCelWrld-1994, 317

Simhat Torah (Rejoicing in the Law)
Location: Holland
Date: September-October, 23rd of Jewish month of
Tishri, second day of Shemini Atzeret

HolFestCelWrld-1994, 317

Simhat Torah (Rejoicing in the Law)
Location: India: Calcutta
Date: September-October, 23rd of Jewish month of
Tishri, second day of Shemini Atzeret

HolFestCelWrld-1994, 317

Simhat Torah (Rejoicing in the Law)
Location: Israel
Date: September-October, 22nd or 23rd of Jewish month of Tishri

DictWrldRel-1989, 155, 693
FolkWrldHol-1992, 508
HolFestCelWrld-1994, 317

Simhat Torah
Location: Kurdistan
Date: September-October, 23rd of Jewish month of Tishri, second day of Shemini Atzeret

FolkWrldHol-1992, 508

Simhat Torah (Rejoicing in the Law)
Location: Brooklyn, New York
Date: September-October, 24th of Jewish month of Tishri

FolkAmerHol-1987, 293

Simhat Torah (Rejoicing in the Law)
Location: Medieval Spain
Date: September-October, 23rd of Jewish month of Tishri, second day of Shemini Atzeret

HolFestCelWrld-1994, 317

Simhat Torah
Location: USSR
Date: September-October, 23rd of Jewish month of Tishri, second day of Shemini Atzeret

FolkWrldHol-1992, 508

Simhat Torah (Rejoicing in the Law)
Location: Yemen
Date: September-October, 23rd of Jewish month of Tishri, second day of Shemini Atzeret

HolFestCelWrld-1994, 317

Simnel Sunday
See **Mid-Lent Sunday (England)**

Singing Festival (Laulipidu)
Location: Estonia: Tallinn
Established: 1869
Date: Every fifth year on June 25

BkFest-1937, 105
BkFestHolWrld-1970, 99
HolFestCelWrld-1994, 23

Singing on the Mountain
Location: Linville, North Carolina
Established: 1925
Date: Fourth Sunday in June

Chases-1993, 268
GdUSFest-1984, 132

Singing to Rings (Ladouvane)
Location: Bulgaria
Date: January 1 in western Bulgaria; June 24 in the rest of the country

HolFestCelWrld-1994, 175

Sinhala Avurudu
See **New Year (Buddhist and Hindu Sinhalese and Tamil peoples in Sri Lanka)**

Sinj Iron-Ring Chivalric Tournament
Named for: Commemorates 1715 victory over Turks
Location: Yugoslavia: Sinj, Croatia
Date: First Sunday in August

HolFestCelWrld-1994, 318
IntlThFolk-1979, 403

Sinterklaas
See **St. Nicholas's Day (Netherlands)**

Sint Jans Vorravond
See **Midsummer (Belgium)**

Sinulog Festival
Location: Philippines: Cebu
Date: Third weekend in January

HolFestCelWrld-1994, 318

Sirna Sedmitza, Cheese Week
See **Mardi Gras (Bulgaria)**

Sithinakha (Kumar Sasthi)
Location: Nepal
Ethnic or religious group: Hindu
Date: May, sixth day of waxing half of Hindu month of Jyeshta

FolkWrldHol-1992, 319
HolFestCelWrld-1994, 318

Situa
Location: Peru
Ethnic or religious group: Inca people
Date: September

DictFolkMyth-1984, 1015

Six O'Clock Ringing Festival (Sechselauten)
  Location: Switzerland: Zurich
  Established: 14th century
  Date: Third Sunday and Monday in April

  AnnivHol-1983, 53
  BkFest-1937, 317
  BkHolWrld-1986, April 19, 180
  FestWestEur-1958, 227
  HolFestCelWrld-1994, 310

Sizdar-Bedah
  See **Thirteenth Day Out (Iran)**

Skanda Shashti
  Location: Southern India
  Ethnic or religious group: Hindu Tamil people
  Date: October-November, Tamil month of Tulam

  RelHolCal-1993, 115

Skärtorsdag
  See **Holy Thursday (Sweden)**

Ski Festival, Holmenkollen
  Location: Norway: Holmenkollen Hill
  Established: 1892
  Date: One week in March; second Sunday in March

  AnnivHol-1983, 37
  Chases-1993, 133
  HolFestCelWrld-1994, 141

Skipjack Races, Labor Day
  Location: Deal Island, Maryland
  Established: 1925
  Date: Labor Day, first Monday in September

  GdUSFest-1984, 82

Skire Thursday
  See **Holy Thursday (England)**

Skulls, Ceremony for the
  Ethnic or religious group: Aymara Indians
  Date: October

  DictFolkMyth-1984, 1056

Sky-God Festival (Powamû Festival)
  Location: Walpi Pueblo, Arizona
  Ethnic or religious group: Hopi Indians
  Date: February, nine-day kachina ceremony

  DictFolkMyth-1984, 123, 566, 883

FolkAmerHol-1987, 63
HolFestCelWrld-1994, 259

Slavic Script and Bulgarian Culture Day
  See **Holy Day of Letters**

Sled Dog Races, All American Championships
  Location: Ely, Minnesota
  Established: January 1969
  Date: Third weekend in January

  GdUSFest-1984, 95
  HolFestCelWrld-1994, 5

Sled Race, Tok Race of Champions Dog
  Location: Tok, Alaska
  Established: 1954
  Date: Late March

  HolFestCelWrld-1994, 341

Sliding Festival, Finnish
  Location: Aurora, Minnesota
  Established: At least since 1940s
  Date: Two days in February

  HolFestCelWrld-1994, 106

Sluggards' Feast
  See **Luilak**

Smith, Birthday of Joseph
  Named for: Joseph Smith (1805-1844)
  Ethnic or religious group: Mormon (Church of Jesus
   Christ of the Latter Day Saints)
  Date: April 24

  DictWrldRel-1989, 423, 696
  RelHolCal-1993, 62

Smith, Martyrdom of Joseph and Hyrum
  Named for: Joseph (1805-1844) and Hyrum (1800-1844)
   Smith and their deaths on June 27
  Ethnic or religious group: Church of Jesus Christ of
   the Latter Day Saints and smaller Mormon churches
  Date: June 27

  DaysCustFaith-1957, 154
  DictWrldRel-1989, 424
  RelHolCal-1993, 93

Snake Festival (Naag Panchami)
  Ethnic or religious group: Hindu

Snake Festival (Naag Panchami) *(cont.)*
Date: July-August, fifth day of waxing half of Hindu
   month of Sravana

BkFest-1937, 159
BkHolWrld-1986, August 8
DictFolkMyth-1984, 671, 921
DictWrldRel-1989, 431
FolkWrldHol-1992, 403
HolFestCelWrld-1994, 217
RelHolCal-1993, 97

**Snake Festival (Naagpanchami in northern India;
Nagarapanchami in southern India)**
Location: India
Date: July-August, fifth day of waxing half of Hindu
   month of Sravana

BkHolWrld-1986, August 8
Chases-1993, 284
DictFolkMyth-1984, 671, 921
FolkWrldHol-1992, 403
HolFestCelWrld-1994, 217
RelHolCal-1993, 97

Snake Festival (Naag Panchami)
Location: India: Bengal
Date: July-August, fifth day of waxing half of Hindu
   month of Sravana

BkFest-1937, 159

Snake Festival (Naag Panchami)
Location: Nepal
Date: July-August, fifth day of waxing half of Hindu
   month of Sravana

FolkWrldHol-1992, 403
HolFestCelWrld-1994, 217

Snan Yatra
   See **Bathing Festival (India: Orissa)**

Snow Festival (Yuki Matsuri)
Location: Japan: Odori Park, Sapporo, Hokkaido
Established: 1949
Date: February 8-12

AnnivHol-1983, 182
BkHolWrld-1986, February 6, 180
Chases-1993, 91
HolFestCelWrld-1994, 307

Snowgolf Championship
Location: Canada: Prince George, British Columbia

Established: 1970
Date: Three days in February

GdWrldFest-1985, 32

Snowhut or Snowcave Festival (Kamakura Matsuri)
Location: Northern Japan
Date: February 15-17

BkHolWrld-1986, February 15
FolkWrldHol-1992, 136
HolFestCelWrld-1994, 165

Soap Box Derby, All American
Location: Akron, Ohio
Established: 1934
Date: Six days in August

Chases-1993, 323
GdUSFest-1984, 137
HolFestCelWrld-1994, 6

Sochelnik
   See **Christmas Eve (Russia)**

Soil Stewardship Sunday
   See **Rural Life Sunday (United States)**

Sol
   See **New Year (Korea)**

Soldag
   See **Sun Pageant Day**

Solemnity of Mary, Mother of God
   See **Circumcision, Feast of the (Roman Catholic)**

Somhlolo Day
   See **Independence Day (Swaziland)**

Sommersonnonwende
   See **Midsummer (Germany)**

Sommerspiele Grein
   See **Summer Festival, Grein (Austria: Grein im
      Strudengau, Upper Austria)**

Sommerspiele Krems
   See **Krems Outdoor Festival (Austria: Krems, Lower Austria)**

Song Festival
Location: Latvia
Established: 1873
Date: Every five years in summer

HolFestCelWrld-1994, 23

Song Festival
  Location: Lithuania
  Date: Every five years in summer

  HolFestCelWrld-1994, 23

Song Festival (Skamba Kankliai)
  Location: Lithuania: Vilnius
  Date: May

  HolFestCelWrld-1994, 23

Songkran
  See **New Year (Buddhist people in Thailand)**

Song of Hiawatha Pageant
  Named for: Hiawatha, a character in the poem by Henry
    Wadsworth Longfellow (1807-1882)
  Location: Pipestone, Minnesota
  Ethnic or religious group: Dakota Indians
  Established: 1949
  Date: Last two weeks in July and first week in August

  AmerBkDays-1978, 215
  HolFestCelWrld-1994, 320

Song to Romania
  Location: Romania: Bucharest
  Established: 1976-77
  Date: Odd-numbered years in June; coincides with
    Independence Day

  IntlThFolk-1979, 319

Sorrowful Friday
  See **Good Friday**

(De) Soto Celebration
  Named for: Hernando De Soto (c. 1500-1542)
  Location: Bradenton, Florida
  Established: 1939; commemorates 1539 landing
  Date: One week in March or early April

  AmerBkDays-1978, 251
  GdUSFest-1984, 33
  HolFestCelWrld-1994, 82

Soul, Festival of the (Mahrajan)
  Location: Syria and Bridgeport, Connecticut
  Ethnic or religious group: Lebanese-Americans
  Established: Since 1930s has celebrated independence of
    Lebanon under French mandate in 1920
  Date: September 1

  BkFest-1937, 332

Souls, Feast of
  See **Samhain**

South, Festival of the
  Location: Yugoslavia: Budva, Kotor, Tivat, and
    Hercegnovi, Montenegro
  Date: July-August

  IntlThFolk-1979, 386

Southern 500 Stock Car Race
  Location: Darlington, South Carolina
  Established: 1950
  Date: Labor Day, first Monday in September

  FolkAmerHol-1987, 275
  HolFestCelWrld-1994, 320

South Mountain Concerts
  Location: Pittsfield, Massachusetts
  Established: 1918
  Date: Some Saturday and Sunday concerts in August
    and September

  MusFestAmer-1990, 79

Sovereignty and Thanksgiving Day
  Location: Haiti
  Date: May 22

  AnnivHol-1983, 69

Soyal or Soyala
  Ethnic or religious group: Hopi Indians
  Date: Nine-day winter solstice ceremony

  DictFolkMyth-1984, 1032, 1058

Spa, Festival of
  Location: Belgium: Spa
  Established: 1959
  Date: August

  IntlThFolk-1979, 49

Spanish-American War Memorial Day
  See **Maine Memorial Day**

Spanish and Indian Fiestas
  Location: Isleta Pueblo, New Mexico
  Date: August 28

  IndianAmer-1989, 288, 296

Spanish Consciousness, Day of
  See **Columbus Day (Spain)**

Spartakiade
  Location: Czechoslovakia: Prague, Bohemia
  Established: 1955
  Date: Eight days in June every five years

  GdWrldFest-1985, 69
  HolFestCelWrld-1994, 321

Spoleto Festival of Two Worlds (Festival dei Due Mondi)
  Location: Italy: Spoleto, Umbria
  Established: 1958
  Date: Late June to mid-July

  GdUSFest-1984, 169
  GdWrldFest-1985, 120
  IntlThFolk-1979, 248
  MusFestEurBrit-1980, 117
  MusFestWrld-1963, 106

Spoleto Festival of Two Worlds/U.S.A.
  Location: Charleston, South Carolina
  Established: 1977
  Date: Two weeks from last week in May to early June

  Chases-1993, 216
  GdUSFest-1984, 169
  GdWrldFest-1985, 120
  HolFestCelWrld-1994, 321
  IntlThFolk-1979, 248
  MusFestAmer-1990, 136

Sprangprozessio'n
  See **Dancing Procession (Luxembourg: Echternach)**

Spring, Bringing of the (Kevad Püha)
  Location: Estonia
  Date: May 1

  BkFest-1937, 104

Spring, Feast of
  Location: Latvia
  Date: On or near April 23, St. George's Day

  DictFolkMyth-1984, 608

Spring, Feast of (Pavasario Svente)
  Location: Ancient Lithuania
  Date: March 16

  BkFest-1937, 219

Spring, Festival of
  Location: Canada: Ottawa, Ontario
  Established: 1949

  Date: Nine days in mid-May

  GdWrldFest-1985, 50

Spring, Harghita
  Location: Romania: Miercurea Ciuc, Baile Jigodin Commune, Harghita
  Date: Third Sunday in May

  IntlThFolk-1979, 326

Spring, Kiev
  Location: USSR: Kiev, Ukraine
  Established: 1973
  Date: Second half of May

  IntlThFolk-1979, 373

Spring Bank Holiday
  See **Whit Monday (England)**

Spring Day, Smell the (Sham al-Neseem)
  Location: Egypt
  Date: Monday following Coptic Easter

  BkFestHolWrld-1970, 74
  BkHolWrld-1986, April 28, 180
  Chases-1993, 172
  FolkWrldHol-1992, 184
  HolFestCelWrld-1994, 314

Spring Festival (Li Chun, Spring Is Here)
  Location: China
  Date: February

  AnnivHol-1983, 178
  BkFestHolWrld-1970, 91
  DictFolkMyth-1984, 618

Spring Festival (Vasant or Basant Panchami)
  Named for: Honors goddess of literature and art, Sarasvati
  Ethnic or religious group: Hindu
  Date: January-February, fifth day of waxing half of Hindu month of Magha

  AnnivHol-1983, 173
  BkHolWrld-1986, February 16
  HolFestCelWrld-1994, 354
  RelHolCal-1993, 120

Spring Festival (Vasant or Basant Panchami)
  Named for: Honors goddess of literature and art, Sarasvati
  Location: India: Bengal

Spring Festival (Vasant or Basant Panchami) *(cont.)*
Ethnic or religious group: Hindu
Date: January-February, fifth day of waxing half of Hindu month of Magha

Chases-1993, 76
HolFestCelWrld-1994, 354
RelHolCal-1993, 120

Spring Festival
Location: Japan: Ube Shrine, Iwami, Tottori
Date: One day in mid-April

IntlThFolk-1979, 254

Spring Festival, Chaitra Parva
See **Dance Festival, Mayurbhanj Chhau (India: Mayurbhanj, Orissa)**

Spring Festival, Guelph
Location: Canada: Guelph, Ontario
Established: 1968
Date: Two to three weeks in April-May

Chases-1993, 198
GdWrldFest-1985, 47
IntlThFolk-1979, 69
MusFestAmer-1990, 159

Spring Festival, Prague
Location: Czechoslovakia: Prague
Established: 1945
Date: May 12-June 4

GdWrldFest-1985, 68
IntlThFolk-1979, 89
MusFestEurBrit-1980, 35
MusFestWrld-1963, 198

Spring Festival, Upper Mattaponi
Location: Near Walkerton, Virginia
Ethnic or religious group: Upper Mattaponi Indians
Date: Fourth Saturday in May

Chases-1993, 217

Spring Festival, Warana (Blue Skies)
Location: Australia: Brisbane, Queensland
Established: 1962
Date: September-October

IntlThFolk-1979, 17

Spring Festival of the Toshogu Shrine, Great (Toshogu Haru-No-Taisai)
Location: Japan: Nikko, Tochigi
Established: Commemorates 1617 burial of Tokugawa Ieyasu (1543-1616)
Date: May 17-18

GdWrldFest-1985, 123
HolFestCelWrld-1994, 343

Spring in Jerusalem Festival
Location: Israel: Jerusalem
Established: 1975
Date: Month-long in April-May, including May 12, Jerusalem Reunification Day

GdWrldFest-1985, 116
IntlThFolk-1979, 239

Spring Pageant
Location: Romania: Resita, Caras-Severin
Date: First weekend in April

IntlThFolk-1979, 330

Springtime Festival
Location: Bekáa Valley, throughout Syria, Lebanon and former Palestine
Date: March-April, four successive Thursdays before Orthodox Easter

HolFestCelWrld-1994, 321

Spruce Ceremony
Location: Isleta Pueblo, New Mexico

DictFolkMyth-1984, 566, 571, 1133

Spy Wednesday
Date: March-April, Wednesday before Easter

DictDays-1988, 113
HolFestCelWrld-1994, 322

Sravani Mela
Location: India: Deogarh, Bihar
Ethnic or religious group: Hindu
Date: July-August, Hindu month of Sravana

RelHolCal-1993, 115

Stage, Classics on the Yugoslav
Location: Yugoslavia: Leskovac, Serbia
Established: 1971
Date: October

IntlThFolk-1979, 392

Stampede Days
  Location: Omak, Washington
  Ethnic or religious group: Colville Indians
  Date: Second week in August

  HolFestCelWrld-1994, 237
  IndianAmer-1989, 203

Stanton Day, Elizabeth Cady
  Named for: Elizabeth Cady Stanton (1815-1902)
  Location: Observed by women's organizations
  Date: November 12

  AmerBkDays-1978, 1016
  AnnivHol-1983, 146
  Chases-1993, 439

Star Festival
  Location: China
  Date: 18th day of first lunar month

  BkFestHolWrld-1970, 25

Star Festival (Japan)
  See **Double Seventh (Japan)**

State Fair of Texas
  Location: Dallas, Texas
  Established: 1885-87
  Date: 17 days in October

  Chases-1993, 394
  GdUSFest-1984, 181
  HolFestCelWrld-1994, 322

Statehood Day
  Named for: February 27, 1967, autonomy from Britain
  Location: St. Kitts-Nevis
  Date: February 27

  AnnivHol-1983, 29

Statute Day
  See **Kingdom Days**

Štědrý Večer
  See **Christmas Eve (Czechoslovakia)**

Steirischer Herbst
  See **Autumn, Styrian (Austria: Graz)**

Sterija, Days of
  Location: Yugoslavia: Vrsac, Vojvodina
  Established: 1976
  Date: October

  IntlThFolk-1979, 408

Sternwheel Festival, Ohio River
  Location: Marietta, Ohio
  Date: September, weekend after Labor Day

  HolFestCelWrld-1994, 233

Stewardship Sunday
  Location: Canada and the United States
  Ethnic or religious group: Council of Churches
  Date: Second Sunday in November

  DaysCustFaith-1957, 300
  HolFestCelWrld-1994, 323

Stickdance
  Location: Kaltag and Nulato, Alaska
  Ethnic or religious group: Athapaskan Indians
  Established: Ancient ceremony
  Date: One week in spring

  HolFestCelWrld-1994, 323

Sticky-Sticky Fair, Bettara-Ichi
  See **Pickle-Market Fair (Japan: near Ebisu Shrine, Tokyo)**

Stiftungsfest
  Location: Young America, Minnesota
  Ethnic or religious group: German-Americans
  Established: 1861
  Date: Last weekend in August

  HolFestCelWrld-1994, 323

Still Days
  See **Holy Week**

Still or Silent Week
  See **Holy Week (Germany)**

Stilts, Dance of the
  See **St. Mary Magdalene, Feast of (Spain: Anguiano, Logrono)**

Stirling District Festival
  Location: Scotland: Stirling, Stirlingshire
  Date: May-June

  IntlThFolk-1979, 188

Stir-Up Sunday
  Location: England
  Ethnic or religious group: Anglican
  Date: Late November, Sunday preceding Advent Sunday

  BkHolWrld-1986, November 22
  DictDays-1988, 114
  FolkWrldHol-1992, 572
  HolFestCelWrld-1994, 323

Stockerau Outdoor Festival (Stockerau Festspiele)
  Location: Austria: Stockerau, Lower Austria
  Established: 1964
  Date: July-August

  IntlThFolk-1979, 40

Stommish
  See **Warrior Festival**

Stone Day, Lucy
  Named for: Lucy Stone (1818-1893)
  Location: Observed by many organizations, including the
  Lucy Stone League in New York
  Date: August 13

  AmerBkDays-1978, 752
  AnnivHol-1983, 106
  Chases-1993, 327
  HolFestCelWrld-1994, 186

Store Bededag
  See **Common Prayer Day (Denmark)**

Stork Day
  Location: Denmark: Ribe
  Date: May 8

  AnnivHol-1983, 63

Storlog
  Location: Tibet
  Date: Mid-March, one and one-half months after
  Dosmoche Festival

  FolkWrldHol-1992, 150
  See also **New Year (Dosmoche Festival) (Tibet: Leh
  and Lhasa)**

Storm God Kukulcan, Feast of the
  See **Chickaban (Mayan people in Mani, Yucatan, Mexico)**

Storytelling Festival, National
  Location: Jonesboro, Tennessee
  Established: 1973
  Date: Three days in October

  Chases-1993, 393
  GdUSFest-1984, 174
  HolFestCelWrld-1994, 324

Strassentheater
  See **Theatre Festival, Street (Austria: Salzburg)**

Strassentheaterfestspiele, Internationales
  See **Theatre Festival, International Street (Austria: Vienna)**

Strastna Nedelya
  See **Holy Week (Bulgaria)**

Strastna Subota, Passion Saturday
  See **Holy Saturday (Bulgaria)**

Straw Bear Day
  Location: England: Whittlesey, Cambridgeshire
  Date: Saturday preceding Plough Monday

  DictDays-1988, 114

Strawberry Festival
  Location: Kule Loklo Miwok Indian Village, California
  Ethnic or religious group: Pomo Indians
  Date: Spring

  IndianAmer-1989, 346

Strawberry Festival
  Named for: Commemorates teachings of Handsome
  Lake (fl. 1799)
  Location: Tonawanda, New York
  Ethnic or religious group: Iroquois Indians
  Date: Usually June

  HolFestCelWrld-1994, 324

Street Painting Festival, I Madonnari Italian
  Location: Santa Barbara, California
  Established: 1987
  Date: May, Memorial Day weekend

  HolFestCelWrld-1994, 151

Stroud Festival
  Location: England: Stroud, Gloucestershire
  Date: Second and third weeks in October

  IntlThFolk-1979, 178

Student Government Day
  Location: Massachusetts
  Date: First Friday in April

  AnnivHol-1983, 48
  Chases-1993, 152

Succoth
  See **Sukkot**

Sugar Ball Show
   Location: China: Haiyun Buddhist Convent, Qingdao, Shandong
   Established: 17th century
   Date: 16th day of first lunar month

   HolFestCelWrld-1994, 324

Sugar Bowl Classic
   Location: New Orleans, Louisiana
   Established: 1935
   Date: January 1 (January 2, if New Year's Day falls on a Sunday)

   BkFestHolWrld-1970, 3
   Chases-1993, 53
   GdUSFest-1984, 73
   HolFestCelWrld-1994, 325

Sukkot (Feast of Booths or Feast of the Tabernacles)
   Ethnic or religious group: Jewish
   Date: September-October, 15th-21st or 22nd of Jewish month of Tishri

   AmerBkDays-1978, 928, 1053
   AnnivHol-1983, 172
   BkFest-1937, 204
   BkFestHolWrld-1970, 118, 123
   BkHolWrld-1986, October 1, 175
   Chases-1993, 390
   DaysCustFaith-1957, 270
   DictWrldRel-1989, 155, 390, 723
   FolkAmerHol-1987, 291
   FolkWrldHol-1992, 488
   HolFestCelWrld-1994, 253, 325
   RelHolCal-1993, 102, 116

Sukkot (Feast of Booths or Feast of the Tabernacles)
   Ethnic or religious group: Orthodox and Reform Jews
   Date: September-October, 15th-21st or 22nd of Jewish month of Tishri

   HolFestCelWrld-1994, 325
   RelHolCal-1993, 116

Sukkot
   Location: Bukhara
   Date: September-October, 15th-21st or 22nd of Jewish month of Tishri

   FolkWrldHol-1992, 488

Sukkot (ba alä mäsällät, Feast of the Tabernacles)
   Location: Ethiopia

   Date: September-October, 15th-21st or 22nd of Jewish month of Tishri

   FolkWrldHol-1992, 488

Sukkot
   Location: Iran; formerly Persia
   Date: September-October, 15th-21st or 22nd of Jewish month of Tishri

   FolkWrldHol-1992, 488

Sukkot
   Location: Israel
   Date: September-October, 15th-21st or 22nd of Jewish month of Tishri

   DaysCustFaith-1957, 270
   FolkWrldHol-1992, 488
   RelHolCal-1993, 102, 116

Sukkot (Feast of Booths or Feast of the Tabernacles)
   Location: United States
   Date: September-October, 15th-21st or 22nd of Jewish month of Tishri

   AmerBkDays-1978, 928
   DaysCustFaith-1957, 270
   FolkAmerHol-1987, 291

Sukkot
   Location: Yemen
   Date: September-October, 15th-21st or 22nd of Jewish month of Tishri

   FolkWrldHol-1992, 489

Sultan's Birthday Celebration
   Location: Malaysia: Kota Bharu, Kelantan
   Date: July

   IntlThFolk-1979, 267

Sultan's Coronation
   Location: Indonesia: Surakarta, Central Java, Java
   Date: May

   IntlThFolk-1979, 222

Sumamao, Fiesta de
   Location: Argentina: an arroyo of the Rio Dulce
   Ethnic or religious group: Roman Catholic
   Date: December 26, San Estaban's Day

   DictFolkMyth-1984, 1086

Summer, First Day of
Location: Iceland
Date: Thursday between April 19 and 25

BkHolWrld-1986, April 22, 177
FolkWrldHol-1992, 246
HolFestCelWrld-1994, 106

Summer, First Day of (Mut l-ard, the Death of the Ground)
Location: Morocco
Date: May 17

FolkWrldHol-1992, 300
HolFestCelWrld-1994, 215

Summer Academy of Dance, International
Location: Federal Republic of Germany: Cologne, North Rhine-Westphalia
Established: 1956
Date: Two weeks in June-July

IntlThFolk-1979, 136

Summer Bank Holiday
See **Bank Holiday**

Summer Carnival, Whycocomagh
Location: Canada: Whycocomagh, Nova Scotia
Date: July

IntlThFolk-1979, 67

Summer Concerts, Lake Balaton
Location: Hungary: Lake Balaton area
Date: Summer

MusFestWrld-1963, 158, 159

Summerfest
Location: Milwaukee, Wisconsin
Established: 1968
Date: 11 days, including July 4

Chases-1993, 262
GdUSFest-1984, 213

Summer Festival
Location: Canada: Quebec City, Quebec
Established: 1967
Date: Ten days in July

Chases-1993, 283
GdWrldFest-1985, 57

Summer Festival
Location: Owensboro, Kentucky
Date: July 4

HolFestCelWrld-1994, 325

Summer Festival
Location: Tunisia: Kairouan, Kairouan Region
Established: 1974
Date: July-August

IntlThFolk-1979, 362

Summer Festival, Bavarian
Location: Barnesville, Pennsylvania
Ethnic or religious group: German-Americans
Established: 1969
Date: 11 days in July

GdUSFest-1984, 154

Summer Festival, Blyth
Location: Canada: Blyth, Ontario
Established: 1975
Date: July-August

IntlThFolk-1979, 68

Summer Festival, Carinthian (Carinthischer Sommer)
Location: Austria: Ossiach and Villach
Established: 1969
Date: Eight weeks from late June to late August

GdWrldFest-1985, 13
MusFestEurBrit-1980, 18

Summer Festival, Central City
Location: Central City, Colorado
Established: 1932
Date: Five weeks from first week in July to mid-August

GdUSFest-1984, 25
HolFestCelWrld-1994, 55
MusFestAmer-1990, 167

Summer Festival, Copenhagen
Location: Denmark: Copenhagen
Established: 1969
Date: Seven weeks beginning July 1

MusFestEurBrit-1980, 38

Summer Festival, Friesach
Location: Austria: Friesach, Carinthia
Established: 1975
Date: July-August

IntlThFolk-1979, 33

Summer Festival, Grein (Sommerspiele Grein)
  Location: Austria: Grein im Strudengau, Upper Austria
  Established: 1964
  Date: July-August

  IntlThFolk-1979, 34

Summer Festival, International
  Location: Belgium: Ostend
  Established: 1953
  Date: July-August

  IntlThFolk-1979, 48

Summer Festival, Ljubljana International (Festivala Ljubljana)
  Location: Yugoslavia: Ljubljana
  Established: early 1950s
  Date: 11 weeks from mid-June to end of August

  GdWrldFest-1985, 186
  IntlThFolk-1979, 393
  MusFestEurBrit-1980, 154

Summer Festival, Ludlow
  Location: England: Ludlow, Shropshire
  Date: Last week in June and first week in July

  IntlThFolk-1979, 168

Summer Festival, Ohrid
  Location: Yugoslavia: Ohrid, Macedonia
  Date: July-August

  IntlThFolk-1979, 398

Summer Festival, Opatija
  Location: Yugoslavia: Opatija, Croatia
  Established: 1960
  Date: June-September

  IntlThFolk-1979, 398

Summer Festival, Split
  Location: Yugoslavia: Split, Croatia
  Established: 1954
  Date: July-August

  GdWrldFest-1985, 186
  IntlThFolk-1979, 405
  MusFestWrld-1963, 219, 224

Summer Festival, Szeged
  Location: Hungary: Szeged
  Established: 1931

  Date: Third week in July to third week in August

  IntlThFolk-1979, 201
  MusFestWrld-1963, 160

Summer Festival for Children
  Location: Iran: Tehran
  Date: Mid-June to mid-August

  IntlThFolk-1979, 230

Summer Festival of Paris
  See **Paris Festival Estival**

Summer Festival of the Lake of Rodo Park
  Location: Uruguay: Montevideo
  Established: 1976
  Date: Three months, January-March

  GdWrldFest-1985, 184
  IntlThFolk-1979, 376

Summergarden
  Location: New York, New York
  Established: 1971
  Date: July and August

  MusFestAmer-1990, 113

Summer Meetings, International
  Location: France: Villeneuve-lez-Avignon, Gard
  Established: 1974
  Date: Month-long, July-August

  IntlThFolk-1979, 129
  See also **Avignon Festival**

Summer-Nights Festival, Basel
  Location: Switzerland: Basel
  Date: June

  IntlThFolk-1979, 349

Summer Season, Geneva
  Location: Switzerland: Geneva
  Date: June-August

  IntlThFolk-1979, 351

Summer's End
  See **Samhain (Ancient Celtic)**

Summer Series, Hollywood Bowl
  Location: Hollywood, California
  Date: 11 weeks from first week in July to late September

  MusFestAmer-1990, 27

Summer Series, Paul Masson
   Location: Saratoga, California
   Established: 1958
   Date: First weekend in June to last weekend in September

   MusFestAmer-1990, 38

Summer Solstice
   Date: June 21-22 in Northern Hemisphere; December 21-22
      in Southern Hemisphere

   BkFest-1937, 136
   Chases-1993, 259
   DictDays-1988, 69, 114
   DictFolkMyth-1984, 1032
   DictMyth-1962, ii.1506
   FestSaintDays-1915, 4
   FestWestEur-1958, 68
   HolFestCelWrld-1994, 86, 325
   See also **Midsummer Day**

Summer Solstice
   Location: Germany
   Date: June 21

   BkFest-1937, 136
   FestSaintDays-1915, 4
   FestWestEur-1958, 68

Summer Solstice
   Location: United States
   Date: June 21-22

   HolFestCelWrld-1994, 325

Summer Solstice Day (Doan Ngu)
   Location: Vietnam
   Date: June, fifth day of fifth lunar month

   HolFestCelWrld-1994, 86

Sun Celebration, Midnight (Ysyakh)
   Location: USSR: Yakutsk
   Date: Around December 21

   FolkWrldHol-1992, 596
   HolFestCelWrld-1994, 376

Sun Days, Midnight
   Location: Norway: North Cape
   Date: Mid-May through July

   AnnivHol-1983, 179

Sunday School Day (Faka Me)
   Location: Tonga
   Ethnic or religious group: Methodist
   Date: First Sunday in May

   FolkWrldHol-1992, 259
   HolFestCelWrld-1994, 325

**Sundown Torchlight Procession of the Virgin with Deer
or Matchina Dance**
   Location: Taos Pueblo, New Mexico
   Date: December 24-25

   IndianAmer-1989, 290, 319

Sun Festival (Suryapuja)
   Location: Bangladesh: Sylhet
   Ethnic or religious group: Hindu
   Date: Spring

   DictFolkMyth-1984, 1090

Sun Festival (Inti Raymi or Raimi Fiesta)
   Location: Peru: Cuzco
   Ethnic or religious group: Inca people
   Established: Ancient Incan
   Date: About one week, including June 24, the
      winter solstice

   AnnivHol-1983, 84
   DictFolkMyth-1984, 526, 1032, 1055
   FolkWrldHol-1992, 339
   GdWrldFest-1985, 149
   HolFestCelWrld-1994, 155

Sun Festivals, Midnight
   Location: Alaska, especially Nome
   Date: June 21

   AmerBkDays-1978, 587
   HolFestCelWrld-1994, 205

Sunflower Festival
   Location: Canada: Manitoba
   Ethnic or religious group: Mennonites
   Established: 1965
   Date: Last weekend in July

   AnnivHol-1983, 182
   HolFestCelWrld-1994, 194

Sun Fun Festival
   Location: Myrtle Beach, South Carolina
   Established: 1950

Sun Fun Festival *(cont.)*
Date: Four days in June

Chases-1993, 232
GdUSFest-1984, 171
HolFestCelWrld-1994, 326

Sun Pageant Day
Location: Norway: Rjukan
Date: End of January-beginning of February

BkHolWrld-1986, January 31, 181
HolFestCelWrld-1994, 326

Sun Pageant Day, Narvik
Location: Norway: Narvik
Date: February 8

AnnivHol-1983, 21

Sunrise Festival
Location: Romania: Timisoara, Timis
Date: Last Sunday in April during even-numbered years

IntlThFolk-1979, 331

Sun Yat-sen Day
Named for: Sun Yat-sen (1866-1925)
Location: Taiwan
Date: November 12

AnnivHol-1983, 146
Chases-1993, 439
HolFestCelWrld-1994, 326
See also **Double Tenth Day**

Super Bowl Sunday
Location: United States
Date: Last Sunday in January

Chases-1993, 80
HolFestCelWrld-1994, 326

Surfing Classic, Buffalo's Big Board
Named for: ''Buffalo'' Keaulana (n.d.)
Location: Makaha Beach, Oahu, Hawaii
Date: Two days in February

HolFestCelWrld-1994, 44

Sur-Kharban
See **Archery Festival (Buryat people in Siberia)**

Suryapuja
See **Sun Festival (Hindu people in Sylhet, Bangladesh)**

Surya Shashti
Ethnic or religious group: Married Hindu women
with children
Date: October-November, sixth day of waxing half
of Hindu month of Karthika

RelHolCal-1993, 116

Suur Reede
See **Good Friday (Estonia)**

Svenskarnas Dag
See **Swedes' Day**

Swallows of San Juan Capistrano
Location: San Juan Capistrano Mission, San Juan
Capistrano, California
Established: Mission founded in 1776
Date: Swallows arrive March 19 and depart October 23

AnnivHol-1983, 39, 136
BkHolWrld-1986, October 23
Chases-1993, 134, 419, 428
DictDays-1988, 116
FolkAmerHol-1987, 116
HolFestCelWrld-1994, 327

Swallow Songs
Location: Greece
Established: For over 2000 years
Date: Return of the swallows in March

BkFestHolWrld-1970, 71
DictFolkMyth-1984, 1091

Swan Upping
Location: England: Thames River, from Blackfriars
to London
Established: 1363
Date: Monday through Thursday during third full week
in July

BkHolWrld-1986, July 21, 181
GdWrldFest-1985, 95
HolFestCelWrld-1994, 327

Swarupa Dwadashi
Ethnic or religious group: Hindu women
Date: December-January, 12th day of waning half of
Hindu month of Pausha

RelHolCal-1993, 116

Swedes' Day (Svenskarnas Dag)
  Location: Chicago, Illinois
  Ethnic or religious group: Swedish-Americans
  Established: 1911
  Date: June 24

  AmerBkDays-1978, 586

Swedes' Day (Svenskarnas Dag)
  Location: Minnesota
  Ethnic or religious group: Swedish-Americans
  Established: Early 1900s; since 1934 in Minneapolis
  Date: Fourth Sunday in June

  AmerBkDays-1978, 586
  GdUSFest-1984, 97
  HolFestCelWrld-1994, 327

Swedish Festival, Kingsburg
  Location: Kingsburg, California
  Ethnic or religious group: Swedish-Americans
  Established: 1924
  Date: Third weekend in May

  HolFestCelWrld-1994, 171

Swedish Homage Festival
  Location: Lindsborg, Kansas
  Ethnic or religious group: Swedish-Americans
  Established: 1941
  Date: Three days during second week in October during odd-numbered years

  GdUSFest-1984, 61
  HolFestCelWrld-1994, 327

Sweeping Floors, Day for
  Location: Hong Kong
  Date: December-January, 20th day of twelfth lunar month

  FolkWrldHol-1992, 655

Sweetest Day
  Location: United States
  Date: Third Saturday in October

  AnnivHol-1983, 134
  Chases-1993, 412
  HolFestCelWrld-1994, 328

Święto Matki Boskiej Gromnicznej
  See **Candlemas (Poland)**

Święto Pierwszego Maja
  See **May Day (Poland)**

Święto Trzeciego Majo
  See **Constitution Day (Poland)**

Swing Festival (Tano)
  Location: Korea
  Date: May-June, fifth day of fifth lunar month

  BkHolWrld-1986, June 16, 181
  Chases-1993, 262
  FolkWrldHol-1992, 315
  HolFestCelWrld-1994, 332

Sydney, Festival of
  Location: Australia: Sydney, New South Wales
  Established: 1977-78
  Date: December 31 through January

  GdWrldFest-1985, 5
  IntlThFolk-1979, 12

Sydney to Hobart Yacht Race
  Location: Australia
  Date: Several days beginning December 26

  AnnivHol-1983, 164

Symbolic Relay Run
  Location: New Mexico pueblos
  Date: August 5-10

  IndianAmer-1989, 288

Symphony Concerts, Monteux Conducting School
  Location: Hancock, Maine
  Date: Late June to late July

  MusFestAmer-1990, 71

Symphony Pops, San Francisco
  Location: San Francisco, California
  Established: Early 1950s
  Date: Three weeks beginning mid-July

  MusFestAmer-1990, 204

Szüret
  See **Harvest of Grapes (Hungary)**

Ta'anit Esther
  Ethnic or religious group: Jewish
  Date: February-March, 13th of Jewish month of Adar

  AnnivHol-1983, 172
  Chases-1993, 118
  HolFestCelWrld-1994, 331

Tabarka, Festival of
Location: Tunisia: Tabarka, Jendouba Region
Date: July-August

IntlThFolk-1979, 365

Tabaski
See **New Year (Senegal, Guinée, and Sierra Leone) and (West Africa)**

Tabaski
See **Sacrifice, Feast of (Cameroon), (Chad), (Senegal)**

Tabernacles, Feast of
See **Sukkot (Jewish) and (United States)**

Tabuleiros Festival (Festa dos Tabuleiros, Festival of the Headdresses; Feast of the Holy Ghost)
Location: Portugal: Tomar, Ribatejo
Ethnic or religious group: Christian
Established: For over 600 years
Date: Three or four days in mid-July every third year during odd-numbered years

AnnivHol-1983, 182
BkHolWrld-1986, July 8
FestWestEur-1958, 171
HolFestCelWrld-1994, 331
IntlThFolk-1979, 313

Ta Chiu
Location: Hong Kong
Ethnic or religious group: Taoist
Date: Several days during 11th and 12th months of Chinese lunar calendar at 3-, 5-, 10-year, or longer, intervals

BkHolWrld-1986, December 27, 181

Tadja
See **Husayn Day (Afro- and Indo-Guyanese people in Guyana)**

Tag Day
See **Lifeboat Day**

Tagore, Birthday of Rabindranath
Named for: Rabindranath Tagore (1861-1941)
Location: India: Calcutta
Date: May 7

AnnivHol-1983, 63
Chases-1993, 197
HolFestCelWrld-1994, 267

Taholah Days
Named for: Chief Taholah (fl. late 18th century-early 19th century)
Location: Quinault Nation, Taholah, Washington
Ethnic or religious group: Hoh, Quinault, and Quileute Indians
Date: July 4th weekend

IndianAmer-1989, 200, 211, 212

Takigi Noh
Location: Japan: Hachiman Shrine, Kamakura City, Kanagawa
Date: Summer

IntlThFolk-1979, 254

Takigi Noh
Location: Japan: Heian Shrine, Kyoto
Date: Two days in early June

IntlThFolk-1979, 256

Takigi Noh
Location: Japan: Kofukuji Temple, Nara
Date: Mid-May

IntlThFolk-1979, 258

Takigi Noh
Location: Japan: Hie Shrine, Tokyo
Date: Summer

IntlThFolk-1979, 260

Tamasha Festival
Location: India: location rotates between Aurangabad, Bombay, Poona, and Sangli, Maharashtra
Date: November-December

IntlThFolk-1979, 210

Tam Kung Festival
Location: Hong Kong Island: Tam Kung Temple, Shau Kei Wan
Date: May, eighth day of fourth lunar month

HolFestCelWrld-1994, 331

Tammuz, Fast of the 17th of
Ethnic or religious group: Jewish
Established: 70 A.D., Jerusalem
Date: June-July, 17th of Jewish month of Tammuz

Chases-1993, 282
DaysCustFaith-1957, 159
DictWrldRel-1989, 155
HolFestCelWrld-1994, 332

Ta Mo's Day
 Named for: Bodhidharma, sixth century Indian monk
 who founded Ch'an school of Buddhism; known as
 Ta Mo in China and Daruma in Japan
 Location: China and Japan
 Date: Fifth day of tenth lunar month

 DictFolkMyth-1984, 1102

Tanabata Matsuri, the Weaver Princess Festival
 See **Double Seventh (Japan)**

Tang choeh i
 See **Winter Solstice (Taiwan)**

Tanglewood Music Festival
 See **Music Festival, Berkshire**

Tangun Day
 See **Foundation Day (Republic of Korea)**

Tano
 See **Swing Festival (Korea)**

Tarasque, Fête de la
 See **St. Martha, Feast of (France: Tarascon, Provence)**

Tartans, Festival of the
 Location: Canada: New Glasgow, Nova Scotia
 Date: August

 IntlThFolk-1979, 66

Ta'u Fo'ou
 See **New Year's Day (Tonga)**

Tawadeintha
 See **Tazaungdaing**

Tazaungdaing
 Location: Myanmar; formerly Burma
 Ethnic or religious group: Buddhist
 Date: October-November, full moon day of Burmese
 month of Tazauungmon

 BkHolWrld-1986, November 19, 181
 FolkWrldHol-1992, 570
 HolFestCelWrld-1994, 333

Teacher's Day
 Named for: Honors Jan Amos Komensky (1592-1670)
 Location: Czechoslovakia
 Date: March 28

 BkHolWrld-1986, March 28
 Chases-1993, 144

Teachers' Day (Taiwan)
 See **Confucius's Birthday (Taiwan)**

Teachers' Day (Dia Del Maestro)
 Location: Venezuela
 Date: January 15

 AnnivHol-1983, 9

Tea Meeting
 See **Nevis Tea Meeting**

Tea Party Festival, Chestertown
 Named for: Rebellion in May, 1774
 Location: Chestertown, Maryland
 Date: Third weekend in May

 HolFestCelWrld-1994, 58

Teatro, Festival Nacional del Nuevo
 See **Theatre, National Festival of New (Colombia: Bogota,
 Cundinamarca)**

Teatro Custombrista, Regional and National Festivals of
 Location: Colombia: Medellin, Antioquia
 Established: Regional festivals since 1972; national
 since 1976
 Date: September; regional and national festivals alternate

 IntlThFolk-1979, 78

Teej (Haritlika Teej)
 Named for: Honors Parvati and Shiva
 Ethnic or religious group: Hindu women
 Date: August-September, third day of waxing half of
 Hindu month of Bhadrapada

 RelHolCal-1993, 82

Teej
 Named for: Honors Parvati, Shiva's wife
 Location: India
 Ethnic or religious group: Hindu women
 Date: July-August, third day of waxing half of Hindu
 month of Sravana

 AnnivHol-1983, 182
 BkHolWrld-1986, August 6, 173
 FolkWrldHol-1992, 405
 HolFestCelWrld-1994, 333
 RelHolCal-1993, 83, 117

Teej
  Named for: Honors Parvati, Shiva's wife
  Location: India: Rajasthan
  Ethnic or religious group: Hindu women
  Date: July-August, third day of waxing half of Hindu
    month of Sravana

  BkHolWrld-1986, August 6
  Chases-1993, 302
  FolkWrldHol-1992, 405
  HolFestCelWrld-1994, 333

Teej (Hariyali Teej or Hari Tritiya)
  Named for: Honors Parvati, Shiva's wife
  Location: India: Uttar Pradesh
  Ethnic or religious group: Hindu women
  Date: July-August, third day of waxing half of Hindu
    month of Sravana

  RelHolCal-1993, 83

Teej
  Location: Nepal: Kathmandu
  Date: July-August, third day of waxing half of Hindu
    month of Sravana

  HolFestCelWrld-1994, 333

Tees Ypapantees
  See **Candlemas (Greece)**

Të Lidhurat, Carnival Sunday
  See **Mardi Gras (Albania)**

Tellabration
  Location: Bermuda, Canada, and the United States
  Established: Since 1988 in Connecticut by storyteller
    J.G. ("Paw Paw") Pinkerton (b. 1926)
  Date: November, Friday before Thanksgiving

  HolFestCelWrld-1994, 333

Temple Festivals
  Location: Indonesia: temples throughout Bali
  Date: Annual festivals marking temples' consecration

  IntlThFolk-1979, 220

Tenchi Kane no Kami, Festival of
  Location: Japan
  Ethnic or religious group: Konko-Kyo religion
  Established: 19th century
  Date: On or near April 25

  DictWrldRel-1989, 411, 750

Tencho Setsu
  See **Hirohito's Birthday (Japan)**

Têng Kao
  See **Double Ninth (China)**

Tennant Creek Show Day
  Location: Australia
  Date: July

  DictDays-1988, 56

Tennessee Walking Horse National Celebration
  Location: Shelbyville, Tennessee
  Established: 1939
  Date: Ten days in August

  Chases-1993, 342
  GdUSFest-1984, 179
  HolFestCelWrld-1994, 334

Ten Nhat
  See **New Year (Tet) (Vietnam)**

Terme di Caracalla
  See **Baths of Caracalla (Italy: Rome)**

Terminalia
  Location: Ancient Rome, along road to Laurentum
  Date: February 23

  DictFolkMyth-1984, 129, 493, 1106
  HolFestCelWrld-1994, 335

Tet Nguyenden
  See **New Year (Vietnam) and (Vietnamese-Americans in
    New York)**

Thadingyut
  See **Lenten Season (Buddhist)**

Thaipusam
  Named for: Celebrates birth of Hindu god, Lord
    Subramaniam
  Ethnic or religious group: Hindu
  Date: One day in January-February

  AnnivHol-1983, 182
  FolkWrldHol-1992, 82
  GdWrldFest-1985, 132
  HolFestCelWrld-1994, 336

Thaipusam
  Named for: Celebrates birth of Hindu god, Lord
    Subramaniam
  Location: Southern India
  Ethnic or religious group: Hindu Tamil people

Thaipusam *(cont.)*
Date: One day in January-February, during Tamil month of Tai

FolkWrldHol-1992, 82
HolFestCelWrld-1994, 336

Thaipusam
Named for: Celebrates birth of Hindu god, Lord Subramaniam
Location: Malaysia
Ethnic or religious group: Hindu
Date: One day in January-February

AnnivHol-1983, 182
FolkWrldHol-1992, 82
GdWrldFest-1985, 132
HolFestCelWrld-1994, 336

Thaipusam
Named for: Celebrates birth of Hindu god, Lord Subramaniam
Location: Malaysia: Kuala Lumpur to Cave Temple at Batu Caves
Ethnic or religious group: Hindu
Date: One day in January-February

FolkWrldHol-1992, 82
GdWrldFest-1985, 132
HolFestCelWrld-1994, 336

Thaipusam
Named for: Celebrates birth of Hindu god, Lord Subramaniam
Location: Malaysia: Gaja Berang, Malacca
Ethnic or religious group: Hindu
Date: One day in January-February

GdWrldFest-1985, 132

Thaipusam
Named for: Celebrates birth of Hindu god, Lord Subramaniam
Location: Malaysia: Waterfall Temple, Penang
Ethnic or religious group: Hindu
Date: One day in January-February

GdWrldFest-1985, 132

Thaipusam
Named for: Celebrates birth of Hindu god, Lord Subramaniam
Location: Mauritius

Ethnic or religious group: Hindu
Date: One day in January-February

FolkWrldHol-1992, 83
HolFestCelWrld-1994, 336

Thaipusam
Named for: Celebrates birth of Hindu god, Lord Subramaniam
Location: Singapore
Ethnic or religious group: Hindu
Date: One day in January-February

Chases-1993, 89
FolkWrldHol-1992, 83

Thaipusam
Named for: Celebrates birth of Hindu god, Lord Subramaniam
Location: South Africa
Ethnic or religious group: Hindu
Date: One day in January-February

FolkWrldHol-1992, 83
HolFestCelWrld-1994, 336

Thamesday
Location: England: London
Date: Early September

DictDays-1988, 118

Thanh Minh
See **Grave-Sweeping and Cold Food Festival (Vietnam)**

Thanksgiving (Evamelunga, the Taking Away of Burden and Sin)
Location: Cameroon
Date: September 8

FolkWrldHol-1992, 445
HolFestCelWrld-1994, 101

Thanksgiving
Location: Canada
Established: 1879
Date: Second Monday in October

AnnivHol-1983, 131
BkHolWrld-1986, October 11, 181
Chases-1993, 406
DictDays-1988, 118
HolFestCelWrld-1994, 337
RelHolCal-1993, 117

Thanksgiving
Location: Czechoslovakia
Date: October 28

FolkWrldHol-1992, 516
See also **Independence Day (Czechoslovakia)**

Thanksgiving
Location: Liberia
Date: First Thursday in November

AnnivHol-1983, 142

Thanksgiving
Location: Plymouth, Massachusetts
Established: 1621, Plymouth Colony; legal holiday since 1863
Date: Fourth Thursday in November

AmerBkDays-1978, 1053
GdUSFest-1984, 89
HolFestCelWrld-1994, 254

Thanksgiving (Waratambar)
Location: Papua New Guinea
Ethnic or religious group: Christian
Date: August, dates vary according to province

FolkWrldHol-1992, 424
HolFestCelWrld-1994, 361

Thanksgiving (Awoojoh)
Location: Sierra Leone
Ethnic or religious group: Yoruba, Christian Creole, and Muslim Aku peoples
Date: May occur on special occasions and during such holidays as Christmas, Easter, Good Friday, and New Year's Day

FolkWrldHol-1992, 466
HolFestCelWrld-1994, 18

Thanksgiving
Location: United States
Established: 1621 at Plymouth Colony, attended by Squanto (d. 1622) and Massasoit (d. 1661); legal holiday since 1863
Date: Fourth Thursday in November

AmerBkDays-1978, 1053
AnnivHol-1983, 151
BkDays-1864, ii.614
BkFest-1937, 13, 19
BkFestHolWrld-1970, 118, 124
BkHolWrld-1986, November 27, 181
Chases-1993, 453

DaysCustFaith-1957, 300
DictDays-1988, 118
FolkAmerHol-1987, 331
GdUSFest-1984, 89
HolFestCelWrld-1994, 309, 337
RelHolCal-1993, 117

Thanksgiving, Schwenkfelder
Named for: Kaspar Schwenkfeld (1490-1561)
Location: United States
Ethnic or religious group: Pennsylvania Dutch
Established: 1734
Date: September 24

DaysCustFaith-1957, 241
HolFestCelWrld-1994, 309

Thanksgobble Day
See **Thanksgiving Day (United States)**

Thargelia
Named for: Honored Greek god Apollo
Location: Ancient Greece
Date: May; early summer

DictFolkMyth-1984, 67
DictMyth-1962, ii.1552
HolFestCelWrld-1994, 337

Theatre, Biennial of International
Location: France: Vichy, Allier
Established: 1966
Date: Friday to Monday evening of Pentecost during odd-numbered years

IntlThFolk-1979, 127

Theatre, Chichester Festival
Location: England: Chichester, West Sussex
Established: 1962
Date: May-September

GdWrldFest-1985, 91
IntlThFolk-1979, 158

Theatre, Days of Young
Location: Yugoslavia: Zagreb, Croatia
Date: December

IntlThFolk-1979, 408

Theatre, Drottningholm Court
Location: Sweden: Stockholm
Date: June to August-September

GdWrldFest-1985, 167
MusFestEurBrit-1980, 139
MusFestWrld-1963, 179

Theater, Eastern Festival of
Location: Venezuela: Barcelona, Estado Anzoategui
Established: 1976
Date: Ten days annually, date varies

GdWrldFest-1985, 184
IntlThFolk-1979, 376

Theatre, Festival of Cafe
Location: France: Rennes, Ille-et-Vilaine
Established: 1974
Date: November

IntlThFolk-1979, 120

Theatre, Festival of Contemporary
Location: Romania: Brasov, Transylvania
Established: 1977
Date: One week in January

IntlThFolk-1979, 318

Theatre, Festival of Plays for the
Location: France: Sarlat, Dordogne
Established: 1952
Date: July-August

IntlThFolk-1979, 124

Theatre, Festival of Popular
Location: Venezuela: Guayana City, Bolivar
Established: 1976
Date: Annual, date varies

IntlThFolk-1979, 377

Theatre, Festival of Youth
Location: Romania: Piatra-Neamt, North Moldavia
Established: 1968
Date: Odd-numbered years in autumn

IntlThFolk-1979, 329

Theatre, Great World
Location: Switzerland: Einsiedeln, Schwyz
Date: Every five years in June-September

IntlThFolk-1979, 350

Theatre, Holidays of Amateur
Location: Bulgaria: Sliven
Established: 1970
Date: Even-numbered years in April

IntlThFolk-1979, 54

Theatre, International Festival of
Location: Portugal: Santarem
Established: 1978
Date: June-August

IntlThFolk-1979, 312

Theatre, International Festival of Children's and Youth's
Location: Bulgaria: Sofia
Established: 1968
Date: Every four years, date varies

IntlThFolk-1979, 55

Theatre, International Festival of Free
Location: Federal Republic of Germany: Munich, Bavaria
Established: 1977
Date: April-May

IntlThFolk-1979, 145

Theatre, International Festival of Open
Location: Poland: Wroclaw
Established: 1967
Date: Even-numbered years in September-October

IntlThFolk-1979, 300

Theatre, International Festival of University
Location: Italy: Parma, Emilia-Romagna
Established: 1953
Date: October

IntlThFolk-1979, 247

Theatre, Liège Festival of Young (Le Festival du Jeune Theatre de Liège)
Location: Belgium: Liège
Established: 1958
Date: October

IntlThFolk-1979, 47

Theatre, National Festival of New (Festival Nacional del Nuevo Teatro)
Location: Colombia: Bogota, Cundinamarca
Established: 1975
Date: November-December

IntlThFolk-1979, 77

Theatre, National Review of Children's and Youth's
Location: Bulgaria: Turgovishte
Date: Every three years, date varies

IntlThFolk-1979, 57

Theatre, National Review of Pocket
  Location: Bulgaria: Vratsa
  Established: 1977
  Date: Every five years, date varies

  IntlThFolk-1979, 59

Theatre, Polesden Lacey Open Air
  Location: England: Great Bookham, Surrey
  Established: 1951
  Date: End of June to beginning of July

  IntlThFolk-1979, 160

Theatre, Regional Festival of
  Location: Tunisia: Monastir, Monastir Region
  Date: June

  IntlThFolk-1979, 363

Theatre, St. George's Elizabethan
  Location: England: London Borough of Islington
  Date: Summer through autumn

  IntlThFolk-1979, 166

Theatre, Summer Festival at the Bergwald
  Location: Federal Republic of Germany: Weissenburg, Bavaria
  Established: 1929
  Date: Weekends in June-July

  IntlThFolk-1979, 151

Theatre, Summer Season at the Fort-Antoine
  Location: Monaco: Monte Carlo
  Date: June-August

  IntlThFolk-1979, 280

Theatre, World Festival of
  Location: France: Nancy, Meurthe-et-Moselle
  Established: 1963
  Date: Two weeks in April-May during odd-numbered years

  IntlThFolk-1979, 114

Theatre, World Festival of Amateur
  Location: Monaco: Monte Carlo
  Established: 1957
  Date: Every four years in August-September

  IntlThFolk-1979, 280

Theatre Amateurs, Encounter of Yugoslav
  Location: Yugoslavia: Prizren, Serbia
  Date: October

  IntlThFolk-1979, 399

Theatre Amateurs of the Villages of Serbia
  Location: Yugoslavia: Malo Crnice, Serbia
  Established: 1972
  Date: October

  IntlThFolk-1979, 394

Theatre and Music, Berlin Festival Days of
  Location: German Democratic Republic: East Berlin
  Established: 1957
  Date: October

  IntlThFolk-1979, 129

Theatre and Music Festival, International
  Location: Luxembourg: Wiltz
  Established: 1951
  Date: July-August

  IntlThFolk-1979, 265

Theater auf dem Bauernof
  See **Theatre Festival, Farmstead (Austria: Meggenhofen, Upper Austria)**

Theatre Community Festival
  Location: Yugoslavia: Belgrade, Serbia
  Date: Early September

  IntlThFolk-1979, 383

Theatre Competition of Figueira da Foz, Amateur
  Location: Portugal: Figueira da Foz, Coimbra
  Established: 1976
  Date: February-April

  IntlThFolk-1979, 306

Theatre Confrontations, Young
  Location: Poland: Lublin
  Established: 1976
  Date: November

  IntlThFolk-1979, 294

Theatre Days, Summer
  Location: Bulgaria: Vidin
  Established: 1963
  Date: Every three years in June-July

  IntlThFolk-1979, 58

Theatre Days Named after Drumev
  Named for: Vasil Drumev (c. 1840-1901)
  Location: Bulgaria: Shumen
  Date: During even-numbered years, date varies

  IntlThFolk-1979, 54

Theatre Days of Romanians in Vojvodina
  Location: Yugoslavia: Alibunar, Vojvodina
  Established: 1970
  Date: April

  IntlThFolk-1979, 379

Theatre Debuts, Start: National Festival of Student
  Location: Poland
  Established: 1971
  Date: February or March

  IntlThFolk-1979, 303

Theatre de Liège, Le Festival du Jeune
  See **Theatre, Liège Festival of Young (Belgium: Liège)**

Theatre de Stavelot, Les Vacances-
  See **Theatre Festival of Stavelot, Vacation (Belgium: Stavelot)**

Theatre du Silence, Carte Blanche au
  See **Theatre of Silence, Carte Blanche at the (France: La Rochelle, Charente-Maritime)**

Theatre Encounter, Jelenia Gora
  Location: Poland: Jelenia, Gora
  Established: 1970
  Date: September

  IntlThFolk-1979, 292

Theatre Encounters, Lodz
  Location: Poland: Lodz
  Date: Spring

  IntlThFolk-1979, 294

Theatre Encounters, Opole
  Location: Poland: Opole
  Established: 1975
  Date: March-April

  IntlThFolk-1979, 295

Theatre Federation One-Act Play Festival, New Zealand
  Location: New Zealand: location varies
  Established: 1932
  Date: July-September

  IntlThFolk-1979, 286

Theatre Festival
  Location: Italy: Taormina, Sicily
  Established: 1976
  Date: July-September

  IntlThFolk-1979, 250

Theatre Festival, Belgrade Amateur
  Location: Yugoslavia: Belgrade, Serbia
  Date: April

  IntlThFolk-1979, 381

Theatre Festival, Belgrade International
  Location: Yugoslavia: Belgrade, Serbia
  Established: 1967
  Date: September

  IntlThFolk-1979, 381

Theatre Festival, Brownsea Open Air
  Location: England: Poole, Dorset
  Established: 1964
  Date: Last week in July and first week in August

  IntlThFolk-1979, 173

Theatre Festival, Children's
  Location: Denmark: Copenhagen
  Date: Early November

  IntlThFolk-1979, 91

Theatre Festival, Dinkelsbühl Open-Air
  Location: Federal Republic of Germany: Dinkelsbühl, Bavaria
  Date: June-August

  IntlThFolk-1979, 137

Theatre Festival, Dublin
  Location: Ireland: Dublin
  Established: 1957
  Date: October

  IntlThFolk-1979, 233

Theater Festival, Epidauros
　Location: Greece: Epidauros, Peloponnese
　Established: Open-air theater built in the third century
　　B.C.; current version since 1954
　Date: June through August

GdWrldFest-1985, 102
HolFestCelWrld-1994, 99
IntlThFolk-1979, 193
MusFestEurBrit-1980, 108

Theatre Festival, Farmstead (Theater auf dem Bauernof)
　Location: Austria: Meggenhofen, Upper Austria
　Established: 1969
　Date: June-August

IntlThFolk-1979, 36

Theater Festival, International
　Location: Venezuela: Caracas
　Established: 1973
　Date: Varies during even-numbered years

GdWrldFest-1985, 185
IntlThFolk-1979, 377

Theatre Festival, International Arena
　Location: Federal Republic of Germany: Munster, North
　　Rhine-Westphalia
　Established: 1978
　Date: Even-numbered years in May

IntlThFolk-1979, 145

Theatre Festival, International Street (Internationales Strassentheaterfestspiele)
　Location: Austria: Vienna
　Date: Annual, dates vary

IntlThFolk-1979, 41

Theatre Festival, Medieval
　Location: Spain: Hita, Guadalajara
　Date: End of June

IntlThFolk-1979, 338

Theatre Festival, Minack
　Location: England: Porthcurno, Penzance, Cornwall
　Established: 1932
　Date: End of June to mid-September

IntlThFolk-1979, 173

Theatre Festival, Ontario
　Location: Canada: locations vary within Ontario
　Date: May

IntlThFolk-1979, 75

Theatre Festival, Open-Air
　Location: Federal Republic of Germany: Xanten/Birten,
　　North Rhine-Westphalia
　Established: 1924
　Date: Saturdays in July and August

IntlThFolk-1979, 152

Theatre Festival, Stratford
　Location: Canada: Stratford, Ontario
　Established: 1953
　Date: May-June to October

GdWrldFest-1985, 52
HolFestCelWrld-1994, 324
IntlThFolk-1979, 73
MusFestAmer-1990, 161

Theatre Festival, Street (Strassentheater)
　Location: Austria: Salzburg
　Established: 1970
　Date: July-August

IntlThFolk-1979, 39

Theatre Festival, "Vojdan Cernodrinski"
　Location: Yugoslavia: Prilep, Macedonia
　Date: Early June

IntlThFolk-1979, 399

Theatre Festival in Schwabisch-Hall, Open-Air
　Location: Federal Republic of Germany: Baden-
　　Wurttemberg
　Date: June-August

IntlThFolk-1979, 149

Theatre Festival in the Square
　Location: Italy: Sant'Arcangelo di Romagna, Emilia-
　　Romagna
　Established: 1971
　Date: July-August

IntlThFolk-1979, 247

Theatre Festival of Bosnia and Herzegovina
  Location: Yugoslavia: Jajce, Bosnia and Herzegovina
  Established: 1971
  Date: June

  IntlThFolk-1979, 389

Theatre Festival of Stavelot, Vacation (Les Vacances-Theatre de Stavelot)
  Location: Belgium: Stavelot
  Established: 1966
  Date: July

  IntlThFolk-1979, 49

Theatre Festivals, Children's Little
  Location: India: Calcutta, West Bengal
  Date: Second week in May and three weeks in December

  IntlThFolk-1979, 218

Theatre for Children and Young People, International Encounter of
  Location: France: Lyon, Rhone
  Established: 1977
  Date: First two weeks in June during odd-numbered years

  IntlThFolk-1979, 111

Theatre for Children and Young People Congress and Festival, International Association of (ASSITEJ—Association Internationale du Theatre pour l'Enfance et la Jeunesse)
  Location: Varies
  Established: 1965
  Date: Every three years

  IntlThFolk-1979, 3

Theatre Games, Yugoslav (Yugoslav Theatre Festival)
  Location: Yugoslavia: Novi Sad, Vojvodina
  Date: Second half of April

  IntlThFolk-1979, 396

Theatre Groups, Encounter of Andalucian
  Location: Spain: Granada
  Established: 1977
  Date: February

  IntlThFolk-1979, 337

Theatre Groups, Provincial Festival of Kosovo Amateur
  Location: Yugoslavia: Urosevac, Kosovo
  Established: 1957
  Date: June

  IntlThFolk-1979, 407

Theatre Groups, Regional Review of Kosovo Amateur
  Location: Yugoslavia: Kosovska Mitrovica, Gnjilane and Pec, Kosovo
  Date: April

  IntlThFolk-1979, 391

Theatre Groups of Slovenia, Encounter of
  Location: Yugoslavia: location varies within Slovenia
  Established: 1958
  Date: May-June

  IntlThFolk-1979, 413

Theatre Meeting, Viseu Amateur
  Location: Portugal: Viseu
  Established: 1977
  Date: One week in December

  IntlThFolk-1979, 315

Theatre Meetings, Kalisz
  Location: Poland: Kalisz
  Date: May

  IntlThFolk-1979, 292

Theatre Meetings, Rzeszow
  Location: Poland: Rzeszow
  Established: 1962
  Date: April

  IntlThFolk-1979, 296

Theatre Meetings, Warsaw
  Location: Poland: Warsaw
  Established: 1964
  Date: December

  IntlThFolk-1979, 299

Theatre Nettelstedt, Open-Air
  Location: Federal Republic of Germany: Lubbecke, North Rhine-Westphalia
  Established: 1923
  Date: Saturdays and Sundays from May to September

  IntlThFolk-1979, 142

Theatre of Hvar, Days of the
  Location: Yugoslavia: Hvar, Croatia
  Date: Four days in May

  IntlThFolk-1979, 389

Theatre of Nations
   Location: Varies
   Established: 1957
   Date: Summer

   IntlThFolk-1979, 4

Theatre of Silence, Carte Blanche at the (Carte Blanche au Theatre du Silence)
   Location: France: La Rochelle, Charente-Maritime
   Date: May-June

   IntlThFolk-1979, 108

Theatre on Margaret Island, Open-Air
   Location: Hungary: Budapest
   Date: July-August

   IntlThFolk-1979, 199

Theatre Rally
   Location: Federal Republic of Germany: West Berlin
   Established: 1964
   Date: May

   Chases-1993, 188
   IntlThFolk-1979, 133

Theatre Rally, North Germany
   Location: Federal Republic of Germany: location varies
   Established: 1970
   Date: One week in mid-May

   IntlThFolk-1979, 153

Theatre Review, International
   Location: Italy: Florence, Tuscany
   Established: 1965
   Date: April-May

   IntlThFolk-1979, 242

Theatre Review, Summer
   Location: Italy: Padova, Veneto
   Date: July-August

   IntlThFolk-1979, 246

Theatres, Algarve Meeting of Amateur
   Location: Portugal: Faro
   Date: Summer

   IntlThFolk-1979, 305

Theatres, Bern International Festival of Small
   Location: Switzerland: Bern
   Established: 1972
   Date: Three weeks in June

   IntlThFolk-1979, 349

Theatres, Biennial of Amateur
   Location: Poland
   Established: 1976
   Date: Even-numbered years in September

   IntlThFolk-1979, 301

Theatres, Borstnik Encounter of Slovenian
   Named for: Ignjat Borstnik (1859-1919)
   Location: Yugoslavia: Maribor, Slovenia
   Date: October

   IntlThFolk-1979, 395

Theatres, Encounter of Slovak Amateur Children's
   Location: Yugoslavia: Backi Petrovac, Vojvodina
   Date: April-May

   IntlThFolk-1979, 380

Theatres, Festival of National
   Location: Romania: Cluj-Napoca, Transylvania
   Established: 1973
   Date: One week in September or October

   IntlThFolk-1979, 321

Theatres, International Meeting of Experimental
   Location: Italy: Palermo, Sicily
   Established: 1970
   Date: April

   IntlThFolk-1979, 246

Theatres, National Festival of Youth
   Location: England: location varies
   Established: 1977
   Date: One week in September

   IntlThFolk-1979, 181

Theatres, Nova Gorica Meeting of Small
   Location: Yugoslavia: Nova Gorica, Slovenia
   Established: 1972
   Date: January

   IntlThFolk-1979, 396

Theatres, Regional Festival of Serbian Amateur
Location: Yugoslavia: Smederevska Palanka, Serbia
Date: May-June

IntlThFolk-1979, 405

Theatres, Showcase of Independent
Location: Spain: Las Palmas, Canary Islands
Date: Annual, date varies

IntlThFolk-1979, 339

Theatre Season, Open-Air
Location: England: London
Date: May-August

IntlThFolk-1979, 164

Theatres for Children and Youth, Encounter of Professional
Location: Yugoslavia: Zagreb, Croatia
Date: May

IntlThFolk-1979, 409

Theatres for Yugoslav Children and Youth, Festival of Professional
Location: Yugoslavia: Skopje, Macedonia
Date: Second half of November

IntlThFolk-1979, 404

Theatres of Bosnia and Herzegovina, Encounter of Professional
Location: Yugoslavia: Brcko, Bosnia and Herzegovina
Date: October

IntlThFolk-1979, 386

Theatres of Croatia, Encounter of Professional
Location: Yugoslavia: Slavonski Brod, Croatia
Date: October

IntlThFolk-1979, 404

Theatres of Iberian Expression, International Festival of
Location: Portugal: Oporto, Porto
Established: 1978
Date: November

IntlThFolk-1979, 310

Theatres of Northern Poland, Festival of
Location: Poland: Torun
Date: June

IntlThFolk-1979, 297

Theatres of Serbia, Festival of Amateur
Location: Yugoslavia: Kula, Serbia
Date: First half of June

IntlThFolk-1979, 392

Theatres of Serbia, Vujic Encounter of Professional
Named for: Joakim Vujic (1772-1847)
Location: Yugoslavia: location varies within Serbia
Date: May-June

IntlThFolk-1979, 412

Theatres of Vojvodina, Encounter of
Location: Yugoslavia: Novi Sad, Vojvodina
Date: May

IntlThFolk-1979, 396

Theatres of Vojvodina, Encounter of Amateur
Location: Yugoslavia: Kikinda, Vojvodina
Established: 1960
Date: May

IntlThFolk-1979, 389

Theatres of Vojvodina, Encounter of Slovak Amateur
Location: Yugoslavia: Stara Pazova, Vojvodina
Established: 1970
Date: February

IntlThFolk-1979, 406

Theatres of Yugoslavia, Festival of Small and Experimental
Location: Yugoslavia: Sarajevo, Bosnia and Herzegovina
Established: 1960
Date: March 27-April 6

IntlThFolk-1979, 402

Theatre Spring, Silesian
Location: Poland: Katowice
Established: 1953
Date: May

IntlThFolk-1979, 193

Theatre Summer, Amateur
Location: Finland: Seinajoki
Established: 1974
Date: Four days in August

IntlThFolk-1979, 96

Theatre Summer, Tampere
Location: Finland: Tampere
Established: 1968
Date: August

Chases-1993, 324
IntlThFolk-1979, 97

Theatre Weeks, International and English Amateur-
Location: England: London Borough of Ealing
Established: 1967
Date: Alternate years in April

IntlThFolk-1979, 165

Theatrical, Musical and Artistic Encounters of Grasse, International (Rithma)
Location: France: Grasse, Alpes-Maritimes
Established: 1972
Date: July

IntlThFolk-1979, 107

Theatrical Forms, Festival of Small
Location: Poland: Szczecin
Established: 1965
Date: March

IntlThFolk-1979, 297

Thefteratoo Pascha
See **Easter Monday (Greece)**

Their Grandfathers Arrive from the West, or from the Dead, Feast
See **All Souls' Day (Cochiti Pueblo, New Mexico)**

Theotokas, Nativity of the
See **Nativity of the Virgin, Feast of the (Eastern Orthodox)**

Thesmophoria
Location: Ancient Greece
Date: October 24-26

DictFolkMyth-1984, 867, 870, 1108
HolFestCelWrld-1994, 337

Thingyan Pwe
See **New Year (Burma; now Myanmar)**

Thinking Day
Named for: Observed on the birthday of Robert Baden-Powell (1857-1941)
Location: England
Date: February 22

DictDays-1988, 119

Thirteenth Day Out (Sizdar-Bedah)
Location: Iran
Date: 13th day after Noruz, New Year

BkHolWrld-1986, April 3
FolkWrldHol-1992, 230
See also **New Year (Iran)**

Thirtieth, Night of the (Ch'u Hsi)
Location: China
Date: 29th day of twelfth lunar month

BkFest-1937, 83

Thirtieth of January
See **St. Charles' Day (England)**

Thirty-third Day of the Counting of the Omar
See **Lag b'Omer**

Thomastide
See **St. Thomas's Day**

Thornton Festival
Named for: Birthplace of the Brontes—Charlotte (1816-1855), Emily (1818-1848), and Anne (1820-1849)—at Close Head Farm, Well Heads
Location: England: Thornton, Bradford, West Yorkshire
Established: 1965
Date: Last week in June

IntlThFolk-1979, 179

Three Choirs Festival
Location: England: Gloucester, Hereford, and Worcester
Established: Before 1719
Date: Seven to ten days in mid-August; location alternates annually

GdWrldFest-1985, 91
HolFestCelWrld-1994, 339
MusFestEurBrit-1980, 61
MusFestWrld-1963, 27

Three Glorious Days
Named for: August 15, 1960, independence
Location: People's Republic of the Congo
Date: Three days, including Congo Independence Day, August 15

AnnivHol-1983, 106
See also **Independence Day (Republic of Congo)**

Three Glorious Days (Les Trois Glorieuses)
Named for: Summer festival commemorates revolution
    that changed kings in 1830; fall festival celebrates grape
    harvest
Location: France: Nuits-St. Georges, Beaune, and
    Meursault, Cote-d'Or
Date: Twice annually: July 27-29 and third Saturday
    through Monday in November

AnnivHol-1983, 182
GdWrldFest-1985, 80
HolFestCelWrld-1994, 345

Three Hierarchs or Archbishops, Holiday of the
Named for: Basil the Great, Gregory the Theologian,
    and John Chrysostom, all fl. fourth century
Location: Greece
Established: 1081
Date: January 30

BkHolWrld-1986, January 30
HolFestCelWrld-1994, 80

Three Kings, Fiesta of the
    See **Epiphany (Tobatí, Paraguay)**

Three Kings Day
    See **Epiphany**

Three Weeks
Ethnic or religious group: Jewish
Date: June-July, 17th of Jewish month of Tammuz through
    9th of Jewish month of Av

HolFestCelWrld-1994, 339
See also **Asarah be-Tevet; Tisha B'Av**

Three Wise Men
    See **Epiphany**

Throats, Blessing of
    See **St. Blaises's Day**

Throne Day
Named for: Succession of King Hassan II (b. 1929)
    on March 3, 1961
Location: Morocco
Date: March 3

AnnivHol-1983, 32
Chases-1993, 117

Thump-the-Door Night
    See **Halloween (England and Isle of Man)**

Tichborne Dole
Location: England: Alresford, Hampshire
Established: 1150
Date: March 26

AnnivHol-1983, 43
HolFestCelWrld-1994, 340

Tihar
    See **Lights, Festival of (Nepal)**

Tij Day (Nepal)
    See **Woman's Day (Nepal)**

Tika Festival
    See **Lights, Festival of (Punjab)**

Tilting Tournament, Sonderborg
Location: Denmark: Sonderborg
Established: 1888
Date: Three days in July

GdWrldFest-1985, 73

Time Observance Day
Named for: Commemorates Emperor Tenchi (626-671)
Location: Japan
Date: June 10

BkFestHolWrld-1970, 97

Timkat or Timqat
    See **Epiphany (Ethiopia: Amhara)**

Tincunaco Ceremony
    See **Mardi Gras (Argentina: Calchaqui Valley)**

Tin Hau Festival
Location: Hong Kong
Date: 23rd day of third lunar month

HolFestCelWrld-1994, 341

Tinjaua
Location: Romania: Maramures
Date: Early May

BkHolWrld-1986, May 6, 181

Tiong-iong Choeh
    See **Double Ninth Day (Taiwan)**

Tiradentes (Tooth Puller; Inconfidência Week)
  Named for: Joaquim José da Silva Xavier (1748-1792)
  Location: Brazil
  Date: April

  AnnivHol-1983, 54
  Chases-1993, 117
  HolFestCelWrld-1994, 153
  NatlHolWrld-1968, 159

Tirgul de fete de pe muntele Gaina
  See **Maidens' Fair on Mount Gaina (Romania:
  Mount Gaina, Transylvania)**

Tirolese Summer
  Location: Austria: Innsbruck, Tirol
  Established: 1975
  Date: Mid-July to mid-August

  IntlThFolk-1979, 34

Tirupati Festival
  Location: India: shrine on Tirumala hills, Tirupati
  Ethnic or religious group: Hindu
  Date: August-September, ten days during Hindu month
  of Bhadrapada

  RelHolCal-1993, 117

Tisha B'Av
  Ethnic or religious group: Jewish
  Date: July-August, ninth day of Jewish month of Av

  AnnivHol-1983, 172
  BkFest-1937, 209
  BkHolWrld-1986, August 4, 175
  Chases-1993, 307
  DaysCustFaith-1957, 197
  FolkWrldHol-1992, 378
  HolFestCelWrld-1994, 341

Tisha B'Av
  Location: Iran
  Date: July-August, ninth day of Jewish month of Av

  FolkWrldHol-1992, 378

Tisha B'Av
  Location: Morocco
  Date: July-August, ninth day of Jewish month of Av

  FolkWrldHol-1992, 378

Tisha B'Av
  Location: Tunisia
  Date: July-August, ninth day of Jewish month of Av

  FolkWrldHol-1992, 378

Tisha B'Av
  Location: Yemen
  Date: July-August, ninth day of Jewish month of Av

  FolkWrldHol-1992, 378

Tismana Garden Festival
  Location: Romania: Tismana, Gorj
  Date: August 15

  IntlThFolk-1979, 331

Tito's Birthday
  See **Youth Day (Yugoslavia)**

Tiurai
  See **Bastille Day (Tahiti)**

Tivoli Concerts (Tivolis Koncertsal)
  Location: Denmark: Copenhagen
  Established: 1843
  Date: May 1 through mid-September

  Chases-1993, 187
  IntlThFolk-1979, 92
  MusFestEurBrit-1980, 41

To Ayeeon Pascha or Lambri, Bright Day
  See **Easter (Greece)**

Tod Kathin
  See **Robe Offering Month (Buddhist people in Thailand)**

Toinen Pääsiäispäivä
  See **Easter Monday (Finland)**

Toji
  See **Winter Solstice (Japan and Okinawa)**

Tolling the Devil's Knell
  See **Christmas Eve (England: Dewsbury, Yorkshire)**

Tom Sawyer Days, National
  Named for: Character created by Mark Twain (Samuel
  Langhorne Clemens, 1835-1910)
  Location: Hannibal, Missouri
  Established: 1956
  Date: Week of July 4

  AmerBkDays-1978, 624, 1065, 1067
  HolFestCelWrld-1994, 342

Tools, Festival of (Visvakarma Puja)
  Ethnic or religious group: Hindu
  Date: End of Bhadrapada, sixth Hindu month

  HolFestCelWrld-1994, 359

Toonik Time
  Location: Canada: Frobisher Bay, Northwest Territories
  Ethnic or religious group: Inuit people
  Date: One week from late April to early May

  GdWrldFest-1985, 41

Tooth Puller Day
  See **Tiradentes (Brazil)**

Top of the World Ski Meet
  Location: Canada: Inuvik, Northwest Territories
  Ethnic or religious group: Eskimos, Canadians, and
  Canadian-Indians
  Established: 1968
  Date: March-April, Easter weekend

  GdWrldFest-1985, 42

Top-Spinning Competitions
  Location: Malaysia
  Date: June-July, after harvest of rice

  BkHolWrld-1986, June 6, 181

Torches, Feast of
  See **Imbolc**

Torch Festival
  Location: China: Yunnan and Sichuan
  Date: 24th-26th days of sixth lunar month

  HolFestCelWrld-1994, 342

Tori-no-ichi
  Location: Japan
  Ethnic or religious group: Shinto religion
  Date: November

  FolkWrldHol-1992, 539
  HolFestCelWrld-1994, 342

Toro Nagashi, Floating Lantern Ceremony
  See **Dead, Festival of the (Buddhist people in
  Honolulu, Hawaii)**

Torredeita, International Festival of
  Location: Portugal: Torredeita, Viseu

Established: 1978
Date: One day in September

  IntlThFolk-1979, 313

Torta dei Fieschi
  Named for: Count Fieschi of Lavagna, whose 1240 wedding
  included a thirty-foot-high cake
  Location: Italy: Lavagna, Genoa
  Established: 1240
  Date: August 14

  BkHolWrld-1986, August 14
  HolFestCelWrld-1994, 343

Tortola Festival
  Location: British Virgin Islands: Tortola
  Established: Commemorates freeing of slaves in 1834
  Date: Begins first week in August

  GdWrldFest-1985, 25

Toshogu Haru-No-Taisai
  See **Spring Festival of the Toshogu Shrine, Great
  (Japan: Nikko, Tochigi)**

Tour de France
  Location: France
  Established: Instituted by Henri Desgranges (1865-1940)
  Date: Four weeks in July

  BkHolWrld-1986, July 5, 181
  HolFestCelWrld-1994, 343

Tournament of Roses
  Location: Pasadena, California
  Established: 1890
  Date: January 1

  AmerBkDays-1978, 17
  AnnivHol-1983, 3
  Chases-1993, 52
  FolkAmerHol-1987, 6
  HolFestCelWrld-1994, 343
  See also **Rose Bowl**

Town Meeting Day
  Location: Vermont
  Date: First Tuesday in March

  AnnivHol-1983, 32
  Chases-1993, 117
  DictDays-1988, 121
  HolFestCelWrld-1994, 344

Trafalgar Day (Nelson Day)
  Named for: Victory of Horatio Nelson (1758-1805) on
    October 21, 1805, during the Battle of Trafalgar
  Location: England: London
  Date: October 21

  AnnivHol-1983, 135
  Chases-1993, 416
  DictDays-1988, 81, 121

Transfer Day
  Named for: March 31, 1917, purchase by the United
    States from Denmark
  Location: Virgin Islands
  Date: Observed last Monday in March

  AmerBkDays-1978, 310
  AnnivHol-1983, 44
  Chases-1993, 147

Transfiguration, Feast of the
  Ethnic or religious group: Christian
  Established: Fourth century, Eastern church; 1457,
    Western church
  Date: August 6

  AmerBkDays-1978, 726
  AnnivHol-1983, 103
  DaysCustFaith-1957, 201
  DictDays-1988, 121
  FolkWrldHol-1992, 415
  HolFestCelWrld-1994, 344
  RelHolCal-1993, 118
  SaintFestCh-1904, 358

Transfiguration, Feast of the
  Ethnic or religious group: Anglican
  Date: August 6

  AmerBkDays-1978, 726
  DaysCustFaith-1957, 201
  HolFestCelWrld-1994, 344

Transfiguration, Feast of the
  Ethnic or religious group: Eastern Orthodox
  Established: Fourth century
  Date: August 6, Gregorian calendar (N.S.); August 19,
    Julian calendar (O.S.)

  AmerBkDays-1978, 726
  DaysCustFaith-1957, 202
  HolFestCelWrld-1994, 344
  SaintFestCh-1904, 358

Transfiguration, Feast of the
  Ethnic or religious group: Episcopalian
  Date: August 6

  AmerBkDays-1978, 726
  DaysCustFaith-1957, 201

Transfiguration, Feast of the
  Ethnic or religious group: Lutheran
  Date: August 6

  AmerBkDays-1978, 726
  DaysCustFaith-1957, 201
  HolFestCelWrld-1994, 344

Transfiguration, Feast of the
  Ethnic or religious group: Roman Catholic
  Date: August 6

  AmerBkDays-1978, 726
  DaysCustFaith-1957, 201
  HolFestCelWrld-1994, 344
  RelHolCal-1993, 118

Transfiguration, Feast of the
  Location: Armenia
  Date: Observed 99 days after Easter Sunday

  FolkWrldHol-1992, 415

**Transfiguration, Feast of the (Del Mundo Festival or
Fiesta Agostinas)**
  Location: El Salvador
  Date: August 5-6

  FolkWrldHol-1992, 415

Transfiguration, Feast of the (Buhé)
  Location: Ethiopia
  Ethnic or religious group: Ethiopian Church
  Date: August 19

  BkHolWrld-1986, August 19

Transfiguration, Feast of the
  Location: Greece
  Date: August 6

  FolkWrldHol-1992, 416

Transfiguration, Feast of the
  Location: Russia
  Date: August 6

  FolkWrldHol-1992, 416

Transfiguration, Feast of the ('Id al-Tajalli)
  Location: Syria
  Date: August 6

  FolkWrldHol-1992, 416

Transpac Race
  Location: Los Angeles, California, to Honolulu, Hawaii
  Established: 1906
  Date: July during odd-numbered years

  HolFestCelWrld-1994, 344

Trappers' Festival, Northern Manitoba
  Location: Canada: The Pas, Manitoba
  Established: 1916; current version since 1948
  Date: Nearly one week in mid-February

  GdWrldFest-1985, 35

Tree Festival Day (Tunisia)
  See **Arbor Day (Tunisia)**

Tree Planting Day
  Location: Lesotho
  Date: March 21 or 22

  AnnivHol-1983, 41
  Chases-1993, 137

Trettondag Jul
  See **Epiphany (Sweden)**

Tribal Day Celebration
  Location: Oakville, Washington
  Ethnic or religious group: Chehalis Salishan Indians
  Date: Late May

  IndianAmer-1989, 201

Tribhuvan Jayanti
  See **National Day (Nepal: Kathmandu)**

Trick or Treat Night
  See **Halloween**

Trifon Zarezan
  See **Vinegrower's Day (Bulgaria)**

Triju Karaliu Šventē
  See **Epiphany (Lithuania)**

Trinity Monday
  See **Trinity Sunday**

Trinity Sunday
  Ethnic or religious group: Christian
  Established: 10th century by the Western Church
  Date: May-June, observed first Sunday after Pentecost
    by Western Church; observed the Monday after
    Pentecost by Eastern Orthodox Church

  AnnivHol-1983, 169
  BkDays-1864, i.669
  Chases-1993, 239
  DaysCustFaith-1957, 164
  DictDays-1988, 122
  DictWrldRel-1989, 768
  FestSaintDays-1915, 128
  FolkWrldHol-1992, 286
  HolFestCelWrld-1994, 277, 345
  RelHolCal-1993, 118
  SaintFestCh-1904, 256

Trinity Sunday
  Location: Belgium
  Date: May-June, observed first Sunday after Pentecost
    by Western Church; observed the Monday after
    Pentecost by Eastern Orthodox Church

  DaysCustFaith-1957, 164

Trinity Sunday
  Location: England
  Established: Twelfth century
  Date: May-June, observed first Sunday after Pentecost

  BkDays-1864, i.669
  DaysCustFaith-1957, 164
  FestSaintDays-1915, 129
  HolFestCelWrld-1994, 345
  SaintFestCh-1904, 256

Trinity Sunday
  Location: France
  Date: May-June, observed first Sunday after Pentecost

  DictWrldRel-1989, 768

Trinity Sunday
  Location: Germany
  Date: May-June, observed first Sunday after Pentecost

  DaysCustFaith-1957, 164

Trinity Sunday (Rusalii)
　Location: Romania
　Date: May-June, observed first Sunday after Pentecost

　FolkWrldHol-1992, 286
　HolFestCelWrld-1994, 277
　See also **Pentecost (Romania)**

Trinity Sunday
　Location: Saxony
　Date: May-June, observed first Sunday after Pentecost

　FestSaintDays-1915, 130

Trinity Sunday
　Location: USSR: Russia
　Date: May-June, observed first Sunday after Pentecost
　by Western Church; observed the Monday after
　Pentecost by Eastern Orthodox Church

　FolkWrldHol-1992, 286

Triumph of the Cross, Feast of the
　See **Exaltation of the Cross**

Trois Glorieuses, Les
　See **Three Glorious Days (France: Nuits-St. Georges,
　Beaune, Meursault, Cote-d'Or)**

Trooping the Colour
　Location: Britain
　Established: 1805
　Date: Second Saturday in June

　BkHolWrld-1986, June 13, 181
　Chases-1993, 244

Troy at Hisarlik, Festival of
　Location: Turkey: Canakkale
　Date: August

　IntlThFolk-1979, 368

True Cross Day (Ethiopia)
　See **Exaltation of the Cross (Ethiopia)**

Truman's Birthday, Harry
　Named for: Harry S. Truman (1884-1972)
　Location: Missouri
　Date: May 8

　Chases-1993, 201
　DictDays-1988, 55

Trumpets, Feast of
　Ethnic or religious group: Post-Exilic Jews
　Date: First day of seventh Jewish month

　DictFolkMyth-1984, 1128

Trung Nguyen, Wandering Souls' Day
　See **Hungry Ghosts, Festival of (Vietnam)**

Trung-Thu
　Location: Vietnam
　Date: September-October, full moon after new moon in
　Virgo; 15th day of eighth lunar month

　AnnivHol-1983, 182
　RelHolCal-1993, 118

Tsagan Sara, White Moon celebration
　See **New Year (Mongolia)**

Tsao Chün
　See **Kitchen God Celebration (China)**

Tso-Fu
　See **Making Happiness Festival (Taiwan)**

Ts'oi, T'in Tai Seng Yeh, Birthday of
　See **Monkey's Festival (Hong Kong) and (Singapore)**

**Tuan Wu, Dragon Boat Festival and Festival of the Five
Poisonous Creatures**
　See **Double Fifth (Taiwan)**

**Tuan Yang, Dragon Boat Festival and Festival of the Five
Poisonous Creatures**
　See **Double Fifth (China)**

Tu Bishvat
　See **B'Shevat**

Tucson Festival
　Location: Tucson, Arizona
　Ethnic or religious group: Hispanic-Americans and Papago
　and Yaqui Indians
　Established: 1951
　Date: March-April, two weeks following Easter

　Chases-1993, 169
　GdUSFest-1984, 12

Tucson Meet Yourself Festival
　Location: Tucson, Arizona
　Ethnic or religious group: Czechoslovakian-, German-,
　Indian-, Italian-, and Mexican-Americans
　Established: 1974
　Date: Second weekend in October

　HolFestCelWrld-1994, 346

Tulip Festival
   Location: Netherlands: Hillegom, Lisse, and Sassenheim, South Holland
   Date: Last week in April and first week in May

   BkFestHolWrld-1970, 90

Tulip Time
   Location: Pella, Iowa
   Ethnic or religious group: Dutch-Americans
   Established: 1935
   Date: Second Thursday, Friday and Saturday in May

   Chases-1993, 197
   GdUSFest-1984, 59
   HolFestCelWrld-1994, 346

Tulip Time
   Location: Holland, Michigan
   Established: 1929
   Date: Four days beginning Wednesday nearest May 15

   AmerBkDays-1978, 449
   AnnivHol-1983, 65
   Chases-1993, 195
   GdUSFest-1984, 92

Tulsidas Jayanti
   Named for: Tulsidas (1543?-1623)
   Ethnic or religious group: Hindu
   Date: July-August, seventh day of waxing half of Hindu month of Sravana

   RelHolCal-1993, 118

Tunchitdilya
   See **Dance, Hupa Autumn (Hupa Indians in northern California)**

Tung Chih
   See **Winter Solstice (China)**

Tura Michele Markt or Fair
   See **St. Michael's Day (Germany: Augsburg, Bavaria)**

Turkey Day
   See **Thanksgiving Day (United States)**

Turnip Lantern Festival (Rebenlichter)
   Location: Switzerland: Richterswil, Winterthur, and Zurich
   Date: November 10-11

   BkHolWrld-1986, November 10

Turon
   Named for: Formerly a winter rite honoring winter god, Radegast
   Location: Poland
   Date: Currently observed the week after Christmas

   DictFolkMyth-1984, 1132
   DictMyth-1962, ii.1609
   HolFestCelWrld-1994, 346

Tus, Festival of
   Named for: Persian poet Ferdowsi of Tus (c. 935-c. 1020 or 1026)
   Location: Iran: Tus, Mashhad
   Established: 1975
   Date: July

   IntlThFolk-1979, 230

Tutti Day
   See **Easter Monday (England)**

Twelfth, The (England)
   See **Glorious Twelfth**

Twelfth, The (Northern Ireland)
   See **Orange Day**

Twelfth Day
   See **Epiphany**

Twelfth Night (Epiphany Eve)
   Date: January 5

   AmerBkDays-1978, 29, 34, 38, 43
   AnnivHol-1983, 5
   BkDays-1864, i. 55, i. 62
   BkFest-1937, 51, 119
   BkHolWrld-1986, January 5
   Chases-1993, 57
   DictDays-1988, 123
   DictFolkMyth-1984, 114, 137, 689, 856
   FestSaintDays-1915, 14
   FestWestEur-1958, 123
   FolkAmerHol-1987, 25
   FolkWrldHol-1992, 13, 18
   HolFestCelWrld-1994, 99, 110, 346
   RelHolCal-1993, 64, 75
   SaintFestCh-1904, 53

Twelfth Night (Epiphany Eve)
Location: Alsace
Date: January 5

DictFolkMyth-1984, 137

Twelfth Night (Epiphany Eve)
Location: Austria
Date: January 5

DictFolkMyth-1984, 137, 856

Twelfth Night (Epiphany Eve)
Location: Belgium
Date: January 5

AmerBkDays-1978, 30

Twelfth Night (Epiphany Eve)
Location: Denmark
Date: January 5

FolkWrldHol-1992, 18

Twelfth Night (Epiphany Eve; formerly known as Wassail Eve in northern England)
Location: England
Date: January 5

AmerBkDays-1978, 30
AnnivHol-1983, 5
BkDays-1864, i.55
BkFest-1937, 51
DictDays-1988, 123, 129
DictFolkMyth-1984, 581
FestSaintDays-1915, 14
FolkWrldHol-1992, 18
HolFestCelWrld-1994, 346
RelHolCal-1993, 64, 75
SaintFestCh-1904, 53

Twelfth Night (Epiphany Eve)
Location: France
Date: January 5

AmerBkDays-1978, 30
DictFolkMyth-1984, 182, 581
HolFestCelWrld-1994, 99

Twelfth Night (Epiphany Eve)
Location: Germany
Date: January 5

AmerBkDays-1978, 30
DictFolkMyth-1984, 137, 182, 581, 856

Twelfth Night (Epiphany Eve)
Location: Iceland
Date: January 5

FolkWrldHol-1992, 19

Twelfth Night (Epiphany Eve)
Location: Italy
Date: January 5

BkHolWrld-1986, January 5

Twelfth Night (Epiphany Eve)
Location: New Orleans, Louisiana
Date: January 5

AmerBkDays-1978, 31

Twelfth Night (Dreikoningenavond, Three Kings' Eve)
Location: Netherlands
Date: January 5

AmerBkDays-1978, 30
FestWestEur-1958, 123

Twelfth Night (Epiphany Eve)
Location: Portugal
Date: January 5

AmerBkDays-1978, 30

Twelfth Night (Epiphany Eve)
Location: Scandinavia
Date: January 5

DictFolkMyth-1984, 581

Twelfth Night (Epiphany Eve; also known as Four an' Twenty Day)
Location: Scotland
Date: January 5; formerly January 18

DictDays-1988, 43
HolFestCelWrld-1994, 110

Twelfth Night (Epiphany Eve)
Location: Switzerland
Date: January 5

DictFolkMyth-1984, 137

Twelfth Night (Epiphany Eve)
Location: United States
Ethnic or religious group: Neo-pagans
Date: January 5

RelHolCal-1993, 64

Twelve Days of Christmas
  See **Christmas, Twelve Days of**

Twentieth Day (Tyvendedagen)
  Location: Norway
  Date: January 13

  AnnivHol-1983, 8
  FestWestEur-1958, 151
  FolkWrldHol-1992, 28
  HolFestCelWrld-1994, 293
  See also **St. Knut's Day (Norway)**

Twin Buttes Celebration
  Location: Twin Buttes, North Dakota
  Date: Third weekend in August

  IndianAmer-1989, 52

Tying Iro
  See **Iro Festivals**

Tyi Wara
  Location: Mali
  Ethnic or religious group: Bambara people
  Date: Planting season in April, May, sometimes the
    entire summer

  BkHolWrld-1986, April 27, 181

Tynwald Day
  Location: Isle of Man
  Date: Varies

  DictDays-1988, 123

Tyvendedagen
  See **Twentieth Day (Norway)**

Udmurt
  See **Holy Thursday (Finno-Ugric people in Kazan,
    Vjatka, and Perm, Russia)**

Ugadi Parva
  See **New Year (Hindu people in Andhra, India)**

U hanli col
  See **Dinner of the Milpa (Mayan people in Chan Kom,
    Yucatan, Mexico)**

Uhola Festival
  Location: Nigeria
  Ethnic or religious group: Dakkarkari people
  Date: New moon in December-January

  FolkWrldHol-1992, 455
  HolFestCelWrld-1994, 349

Ujët e Bekuar and Blessing of the Waters
  See **Epiphany (Albania)**

Ujév Napja
  See **New Year's Day (Hungary)**

Ujung Pandang Anniversary
  Location: Indonesia: Ujung Pandang, South Sulawesi,
    Sulawesi, Celebes
  Date: April 1

  IntlThFolk-1979, 227

Ukrainian Festival, National
  Location: Canada: Dauphin, Manitoba
  Ethnic or religious group: Ukrainian-Canadians and
    Ukrainian-Americans
  Established: 1966
  Date: Four days in July or August

  GdWrldFest-1985, 33
  IntlThFolk-1979, 61

Ülestôusmise Pühad
  See **Easter (Estonia)**

Ullambana
  See **Hungry Ghosts, Festival of (Buddhist)**

Ullr Fest
  Location: Breckenridge, Colorado
  Ethnic or religious group: Norwegian-Americans
  Date: Third week in January

  HolFestCelWrld-1994, 349

Umhlanga
  See **Reed Dance (Swaziland)**

Undecaying Third (Akshya Tritiya)
  Named for: Festival and fast to worship Vishnu and Lakshmi
  Ethnic or religious group: Hindu
  Date: April-May, third day of waxing half of Hindu
    month of Vaisakha

  RelHolCal-1993, 56

Unification Day
Named for: October 1, 1961, union of East and
West Cameroon
Location: Cameroon
Date: October 1

AnnivHol-1983, 126

Union Day
Named for: Conference in 1947 that advanced the
union of Burma
Location: Burma; now Myanmar
Date: February 12

AnnivHol-1983, 23

Union Day
See **Republic Day (South Africa: Capetown, Pretoria,
and Bloemfontein)**

Union Day
Named for: April 26, 1964, union of Tanganyika, Zanzibar,
and Pemba
Location: Tanzania
Date: April 26

AnnivHol-1983, 57
Chases-1993, 182

Union Day, Miners'
Named for: June 13, 1878, founding of Local #1 of the
Western Federation of Miners
Location: Butte, Montana
Date: June 13

FolkAmerHol-1987, 211

United Nations Day
Named for: Founding of the United Nations on
October 24, 1945
Location: Member nations; a holiday in Haiti,
Mauritius, Nepal, and Swaziland
Date: October 24

AmerBkDays-1978, 953
AnnivHol-1983, 135
BkHolWrld-1986, October 24
Chases-1993, 420
DictDays-1988, 124
HolFestCelWrld-1994, 349

United Service Organizations (USO), Founding of
Named for: February 4, 1941, founding of the USO
Location: Service centers in the United States

Date: February 4

AnnivHol-1983, 19
Chases-1993, 86

United States Grand Prix
Location: United States
Established: 1959; not held since 1991
Date: First Sunday in October

HolFestCelWrld-1994, 350

United States Open Championships in Golf
Location: United States: location varies
Established: 1895
Date: Four days ending third Sunday in June

HolFestCelWrld-1994, 350

United States Open Tennis Championships
Location: Queens, New York
Established: Since 1915; an open since 1970
Date: September

HolFestCelWrld-1994, 350

Unity Day
Location: Sudan
Date: March 3

AnnivHol-1983, 33

Unity Day
Location: Zambia
Date: July 6; observed first Tuesday in July

AnnivHol-1983, 90
Chases-1993, 282

Universal Week of Prayer
Location: National Council of Churches, United States, and
World Evangelical Alliance, London, England
Established: 1846 World Evangelical Alliance, London,
England
Date: First through second Sunday in January

DaysCustFaith-1957, 36
RelHolCal-1993, 119

Unleavened Bread, Feast of
See **Passover**

Unto These Hills Festival
Location: Cherokee, North Carolina
Ethnic or religious group: Cherokee Indians

IndianAmer-1989, 247

Uphalie Day, Uphalimass, Uphalliday, Uphalli(Day) Even, Uphelya, Up-Helly-Day
  See **Up-Helly-Aa**

Up-Helly-Aa
  Location: Scotland: Lerwick, Shetland Islands
  Date: Last Tuesday in January

  AnnivHol-1983, 16
  BkHolWrld-1986, January 28, 181
  Chases-1993, 74
  DictDays-1988, 124
  FolkWrldHol-1992, 39
  HolFestCelWrld-1994, 351
  RelHolCal-1993, 119

Up-Helly-Aa
  Location: United States
  Ethnic or religious group: Neo-pagans
  Date: Last Tuesday in January

  RelHolCal-1993, 119

Urou Raja Puasa
  See **Fast, Feast of Breaking the (Sumatra)**

Uskrs
  See **Easter (Eastern Orthodox in Yugoslavia)**

Usokae
  See **Bullfinch Exchange Festival (Japan: Dazaifu, Fukuoka)**

Uspeniye Presvyato or Bogoroditzy
  See **Assumption, Feast of the (Russia)**

Usupuhastus Püha
  See **Reformation Day (Estonia)**

Ute Fair, Southern
  Location: Ignacio, Colorado
  Date: September

  IndianAmer-1989, 121

Uudenvuoden
  See **New Year's Eve (Finland)**

Uudenvuoden Päivä
  See **New Year's Day (Finland)**

Uus Aasta
  See **New Year's Day (Estonia)**

Užgavenēs
  See **Mardi Gras (Lithuania)**

Vaca, Fiesta de la
  See **Cow, Festival of the (Spain: San Pablo de los Montes, Toledo)**

Våffla, Waffle Day
  See **Annunciation, Feast of the (Lutherans in Sweden)**

Vaikunth Ekadashi
  Location: India: Tiruchirapalli, Madras
  Date: November-December, twenty-day pilgrimage over 11th days of waxing and waning halves of Hindu month of Margashirsha

  AnnivHol-1983, 183
  RelHolCal-1993, 119

Vainikinas
  See **Binding of Wreaths (Lithuania)**

Vaisakhi
  See **New Year (Vedda people in Ceylon), (pilgrimage to Shrine of Badrinath, Himalayas), (Hindu), (India), (India: Bengal), (Sikh people in Malaya), (Punjab), and (Sikh people)**

Vaison-la-Romaine and Carpentras, Festival of
  Location: France: Vaison-la-Romaine and Carpentras, Vauclude
  Established: At Vaison since 1952; at Carpentras since 1968
  Date: July-August

  IntlThFolk-1979, 126

Vaitarani
  Ethnic or religious group: Hindu
  Date: November-December, 11th day of waning half of Hindu month of Margashirsha

  RelHolCal-1993, 119

Valborg, Feast of
  See **Walpurgis Night**

Valborgsaften
  See **Walpurgis Night (Denmark)**

Valborgsmässoafton
  See **Walpurgis Night (Sweden: Lund, Stockholm, and Upsala)**

Valdemar's Day
Named for: Valdemar II (1170-1241) and his June 15, 1219, capture of Estonia
Location: Denmark
Date: June 15

AnnivHol-1983, 80
BkHolWrld-1986, June 15

Valencia Fair Days (Battle of Flowers)
Location: Spain: Valencia
Date: July 24

AnnivHol-1983, 96

Valentine's Day
Named for: Bishop of Terni (d. 270) and Valentine of Rome (fl. third century)
Date: February 14

AmerBkDays-1978, 177
AnnivHol-1983, 24
BkDays-1864, i. 255
BkFest-1937, 15
BkFestHolWrld-1970, 30
BkHolWrld-1986, February 14
Chases-1993, 99
DaysCustFaith-1957, 54
DictDays-1988, 107
DictFolkMyth-1984, 866
DictMyth-1962, ii.1383, ii.1636
FestSaintDays-1915, 34
FolkAmerHol-1987, 67
FolkWrldHol-1992, 133
HolFestCelWrld-1994, 353
RelHolCal-1993, 112
SaintFestCh-1904, 103
See also **Lupercalia**

Valentine's Day
Named for: Bishop of Terni (d. 270) and Valentine of Rome (fl. third century)
Location: Austria
Date: February 14

FolkWrldHol-1992, 133

Valentine's Day
Named for: Bishop of Terni (d. 270) and Valentine of Rome (fl. third century)
Location: Denmark
Date: February 14

FolkWrldHol-1992, 133

Valentine's Day
Named for: Bishop of Terni (d. 270) and Valentine of Rome (fl. third century)
Location: England
Established: 15th century
Date: February 14

AmerBkDays-1978, 178
AnnivHol-1983, 24
BkDays-1864, i.255
BkHolWrld-1986, February 14
DictFolkMyth-1984, 866
FolkWrldHol-1992, 133

Valentine's Day
Named for: Bishop of Terni (d. 270) and Valentine of Rome (fl. third century)
Location: France
Date: February 14

AnnivHol-1983, 24

Valentine's Day
Named for: Bishop of Terni (d. 270) and Valentine of Rome fl. third century)
Location: Germany
Date: February 14

FolkWrldHol-1992, 133

Valentine's Day
Named for: Bishop of Terni (d. 270) and Valentine of Rome (fl. third century)
Location: Italy
Date: February 14

FolkWrldHol-1992, 134

Valentine's Day
Named for: Bishop of Terni (d. 270) and Valentine of Rome (fl. third century)
Location: Japan
Date: February 14

FolkWrldHol-1992, 135

Valentine's Day
Named for: Bishop of Terni (d. 270) and Valentine of Rome (fl. third century)
Location: Scotland
Date: February 14

BkDays-1864, i.255

Valentine's Day
Named for: Bishop of Terni (d. 270) and Valentine of Rome
  (fl. third century)
Location: Spain
Date: February 14

FolkWrldHol-1992, 133

Valentine's Day
Named for: Bishop of Terni (d. 270) and Valentine of Rome
  (fl. third century)
Location: United States
Date: February 14

AmerBkDays-1978, 179
AnnivHol-1983, 24
BkFest-1937, 15
BkHolWrld-1986, February 14
FolkAmerHol-1987, 67

Valentine's Eve
See **Valentine's Day**

Valmiki's Jayanti or Birthday
Named for: Ai Kavi Valmiki, an author of the Sanskrit
  Ramayana, who lived sometime between 500-300 B.C.
Location: India
Date: September-October, full moon day of Hindu month
  of Asvina

RelHolCal-1993, 120

Vancouver Heritage Festival
Location: Canada: Vancouver, British Columbia
Date: May-June

IntlThFolk-1979, 60

Vancouver International Festival
Location: Canada: Vancouver, British Columbia
Established: 1958
Date: Late May to late June

MusFestWrld-1963, 288

Vandalia Gathering
Location: Charleston, West Virginia
Established: 1976
Date: May, Memorial Day weekend

HolFestCelWrld-1994, 354

Vánoce
See **Christmas (Czechoslovakia)**

Vappu
See **May Day (Finland)**

Vapun Aatto
See **May Day Eve (Finland)**

Vaqueiros de Alzada Festival
Location: Spain: Brana de Aristebano, Luarca, Oviedo
Date: July

IntlThFolk-1979, 339

Vaqueros, Fiesta de los
Location: Tucson, Arizona
Established: First parade held in 1925
Date: Four days beginning last Thursday in February

HolFestCelWrld-1994, 354

Varfrudagen
See **Annunciation, Feast of the (Lutherans in Sweden)**

Varsa
See **Lenten Season (Buddhist)**

Vartanantz Day
Ethnic or religious group: Armenians worldwide
Established: Commemorates over 1000 martyrs from 451
  war with Persia
Date: February, Thursday preceding Ash Wednesday

AnnivHol-1983, 183
RelHolCal-1993, 120

Varuna, Festival of
Location: India: eastern Bengal
Date: October-November, full moon day of Hindu month
  of Karthika

DictFolkMyth-1984, 1155

Vasaloppet
Named for: King Gustav I of Sweden (1496?-1560) and
  his leadership in revolt against the Danes in 1520
Location: Sweden
Established: National ski festival since 1922
Date: First Sunday in March

BkHolWrld-1986, March 7, 181
HolFestCelWrld-1994, 354

Vasant Panchami
See **Spring Festival (Hindu) and (Hindu people in
  Bengal, India)**

Vassa
See **Lenten Season (Buddhist) and (Thailand)**

Vastenavond
See **Mardi Gras (Belgium), (Netherlands), and (Dutch-Americans in New York)**

Vastla Päev
See **Mardi Gras (Estonia)**

Vata Savitri (Savitri Vrata or Vow)
Ethnic or religious group: Married Hindu women
Date: May-June, 13th day or full moon day of waning half of Hindu month of Jyeshta

BkFest-1937, 158
FolkWrldHol-1992, 320
HolFestCelWrld-1994, 308, 354
RelHolCal-1993, 120

V-E Day
Named for: May 8, 1945, end of World War Two in Europe
Date: May 8

AmerBkDays-1978, 423
AnnivHol-1983, 63
Chases-1993, 201
DictDays-1988, 125

Vegetarian Festival
Location: Thailand: Phuket
Date: September-October, first nine days of ninth lunar month

HolFestCelWrld-1994, 355

La Veille de la Saint Jean
See **Midsummer (France)**

Veille de Noël
See **Christmas Eve (France)**

Veldgang
See **Fields, Going to the (Netherlands: Mekkelhorst, Overijssel)**

Velika Subota
See **Holy Saturday (Roman Catholics in Yugoslavia)**

Velikaya Pyatnitza, Great Friday
See **Good Friday (Eastern Orthodox in Russia)**

Velikaya Subbota, Great Saturday
See **Holy Saturday (Russia)**

Velikdien, the Great Day
See **Easter (Bulgaria)**

Veliki Petak
See **Good Friday (Serbian people in Yugoslavia)**

Velikonoce
See **Easter (Czechoslovakia)**

Velikonočni Pondělí
See **Easter Monday (Czechoslovakia)**

Velký Pátek, Great Friday
See **Good Friday (Czechoslovakia)**

Velu Laiks
See **Dead, Time of the (Latvia)**

Velykos
See **Easter (Lithuania)**

Velyku Antra Diena
See **Easter Monday (Lithuania)**

Vendimia, Fiesta de la
See **Vintage Feast (Spain: Jerez de la Frontera, Cádiz)**

Vendredi-Saint
See **Good Friday (France)**

Venerdì Santo
See **Good Friday (Italy)**

Venice Biennial
Location: Italy: Venice, Veneto
Established: 1893
Date: Odd-numbered years in May-December

IntlThFolk-1979, 250

Les Vêpres de Gouyasse
See **Marriage of Goliath (Belgium: Ath, Hainaut)**

Verges Festival
Location: Spain: Verges, Gerona
Date: March-April, Holy Thursday

IntlThFolk-1979, 342

Vermont Maple Festival
Location: St. Albans, Vermont
Established: 1967
Date: Three days in April

Chases-1993, 168
GdUSFest-1984, 195
HolFestCelWrld-1994, 355

Vermont's World's Fair
 Location: Tunbridge, Vermont
 Established: 1861
 Date: Four days in mid-September

 Chases-1993, 372
 GdUSFest-1984, 196

Vernal Equinox
 Date: On or near March 21

 AmerBkDays-1978, 276
 AnnivHol-1983, 40
 BkDays-1864, ii.364
 Chases-1993, 136
 DictDays-1988, 37
 DictFolkMyth-1984, 1105
 DictMyth-1962, i.517, ii.1646
 FolkWrldHol-1992, 183
 HolFestCelWrld-1994, 315, 355
 See also **Earth Day (Vernal Equinox)**

Vernal Equinox
 Ethnic or religious group: Ancient Babylonian people
 Date: On or near March 21

 DictFolkMyth-1984, 1105

Vernal Equinox
 Ethnic or religious group: Ancient Sumerian people
 Date: On or near March 21

 DictFolkMyth-1984, 1105

Vernal Equinox (Shem al Nessim)
 Location: Egypt
 Date: On or near March 21

 HolFestCelWrld-1994, 315

Vernal Equinox (Bohag Bihu)
 Location: India: Assam
 Date: On or near March 21

 FolkWrldHol-1992, 183

Vernal Equinox (Nyepí)
 Location: Indonesia: Bali
 Date: On or near March 21

 FolkWrldHol-1992, 184
 HolFestCelWrld-1994, 230

Vernal Equinox
 Location: Okinawa
 Ethnic or religious group: Buddhist
 Date: On or near March 21

 FolkWrldHol-1992, 185

Vernal Equinox
 See **Earth Day (areas of North America; Western Europe)**

Vernal Equinox, Festival of (Shunki Korei-Sai)
 Location: Japan
 Date: Around March 21-22

 AnnivHol-1983, 40
 BkFest-1937, 197
 FolkWrldHol-1992, 185
 HolFestCelWrld-1994, 355

Vernal Fire Festival
 See **Fire Festival (Hindu)**

Verrazano Day
 Named for: April 17, 1524, landfall of Giovanni da Verrazano (1485?-1528?)
 Location: New York
 Date: April 17

 AnnivHol-1983, 52
 HolFestCelWrld-1994, 355

Verviers, Festival of
 Location: Belgium: Verviers
 Date: February

 IntlThFolk-1979, 50

Vesak
 See **Buddha's Birthday, Enlightenment, and Salvation**

Vesna Festival
 Location: Canada: Saskatoon, Saskatchewan
 Ethnic or religious group: Ukrainian-Canadians
 Established: 1973
 Date: Six days in May

 GdWrldFest-1985, 61

Véspera de Ano Novo
 See **New Year's Eve (Portugal)**

Vespera de Natal
 See **Christmas Eve (Portugal)**

Véspera de São João
See **Midsummer (Portugal)**

Vestalia
Named for: Vesta, goddess of the hearth
Location: Ancient Rome
Date: June 7-15

AmerBkDays-1978, 509

Veterans' Day
Location: United States
Established: 1918
Date: November 11

AmerBkDays-1978, 1011
AnnivHol-1983, 145
BkFest-1937, 19
BkHolWrld-1986, November 11
Chases-1993, 438
DaysCustFaith-1957, 287
DictDays-1988, 5, 125
DictFolkMyth-1984, 976
HolFestCelWrld-1994, 357

Veterans' Day
Location: United States
Ethnic or religious group: Sauk Indians
Date: November 11

DictFolkMyth-1984, 976

Vičak or Vijak, Festival of Fortune
See **Ascension Day (Armenia)**

Vic Festival
Location: England: Stoke-on-Trent, Staffordshire
Established: 1977
Date: Four weeks in May-June

IntlThFolk-1979, 175

Victoria Day (Empire Day)
Location: Canada
Date: Monday nearest May 24

AnnivHol-1983, 70
Chases-1993, 219
DictDays-1988, 125
FolkWrldHol-1992, 301
See also **Dollard des Ormeaux, Fête de**

Victoria Day (Empire Day)
Location: England and British Commonwealth countries
Date: Monday nearest May 24

AnnivHol-1983, 70
DictDays-1988, 125
FolkWrldHol-1992, 301

Victoria Day (Empire Day)
Location: New Zealand
Date: Monday nearest May 24

FolkWrldHol-1992, 301

Victoria International Festival
Location: Canada: Victoria, British Columbia
Established: 1971
Date: Six weeks beginning in early July

MusFestAmer-1990, 162

Victory Day
Named for: Victory over Pakistan on December 16, 1971
Location: Bangladesh
Date: December 16

AnnivHol-1983, 160
Chases-1993, 475

Victory Day (Our Lady of Victories Day)
Named for: Victory over the Turks in 1565 and over
 Germany and Italy in 1942
Location: Malta
Date: September 8

HolFestCelWrld-1994, 357

Victory Day
Named for: Announcement of Japan's surrender on
 August 14, 1945
Location: Rhode Island
Date: Second Monday in August

AmerBkDays-1978, 754
DictDays-1988, 125
HolFestCelWrld-1994, 359

Victory Day
Named for: Victory over Germany on May 7, 1945
Location: USSR
Date: Observed May 9

AnnivHol-1983, 64
Chases-1993, 202

Victory of Aduwa Day
  Named for: March 2, 1896, defeat of Italian troops
  Location: Ethiopia
  Date: March 2

  AnnivHol-1983, 32

Vienna Weeks (Wiener Festwochen)
  Location: Austria: Vienna
  Established: 1951
  Date: Six weeks from mid-May to June

  GdWrldFest-1985, 14
  HolFestCelWrld-1994, 358
  IntlThFolk-1979, 42
  MusFestEurBrit-1980, 29
  MusFestWrld-1963, 87

Vienne Festival
  Location: France: Vienne en Dauphine, Isere
  Established: 1972
  Date: June-August

  IntlThFolk-1979, 128

Viernes Santo
  See **Good Friday (Mexico) and (Spain: Seville)**

La Vigilia
  See **Christmas Eve (Italy)**

Vigil of Easter
  See **Holy Saturday**

Vignerons, Fête des
  See **Wine Growers' Festival (Switzerland: Vevey, Vaud)**

Vigo Days
  Location: Spain: Vigo, Pontevedra
  Date: October or November

  IntlThFolk-1979, 343

Vijag
  See **Ascension Day (Armenia)**

Viking Festival
  Location: Denmark: Frederikssund, Calf Island, Zealand
  Established: 1951-52
  Date: Three days to two weeks in June-July

  Chases-1993, 267
  GdWrldFest-1985, 72
  IntlThFolk-1979, 93

Vila Praia de Ancora, International Festival of
  Location: Portugal: Vila Praia de Ancora, Viana do Castelo
  Established: 1976
  Date: June or August

  IntlThFolk-1979, 315

Vincennes Day
  Named for: Victory of George Roger Clark (1752-1818)
    over the British in 1778
  Location: Indiana
  Date: February 24

  AnnivHol-1983, 28

Vinegrower's Day (Trifon Zarezan, Viticulturists' Day)
  Location: Bulgaria
  Date: February 14

  AnnivHol-1983, 24
  Chases-1993, 98
  HolFestCelWrld-1994, 358

Vinerea Mare
  See **Good Friday (Romania)**

Vintage Feast (Fiesta de la Vendimia)
  Location: Spain: Jerez de la Frontera, Cádiz
  Established: 1948
  Date: Mid-September

  AnnivHol-1983, 183
  DictFolkMyth-1984, 483
  FestWestEur-1958, 204
  GdWrldFest-1985, 161
  HolFestCelWrld-1994, 355

Vintage Festival
  Location: Yugoslavia: Subotica, Serbia
  Date: September

  IntlThFolk-1979, 406

Vintage Festival, Barossa Valley
  Location: Australia: Barossa Valley, Tanunda,
    South Australia
  Established: 1947
  Date: April, seven days beginning Easter Monday during
    odd-numbered years

  GdWrldFest-1985, 9
  IntlThFolk-1979, 22

Vintage Festival, Valley of the Moon
  Location: Sonoma, California
  Established: Late 1890s
  Date: Last full weekend in September

  HolFestCelWrld-1994, 353

Virga Jesse, Festival of
  See **Assumption, Feast of the (Belgium: Hasselt, Limburg)**

La Virgen de Guadalupe
  See **Our Lady of Guadalupe**

Virgen del Rosario, Fiesta for the
  Location: Mexico: Zinacantan
  Date: October 7

  FolkWrldHol-1992, 510

Virgen de Valle
  See **Immaculate Conception, Feast of the (Argentina: Catamarca)**

Virgen Festival, Bajada de la
  Location: Spain: El Hierro, Santa Cruz de Tenerife
  Established: 1740
  Date: Every four years in June

  IntlThFolk-1979, 335

Virgen Lustral Festival, Bajada de la
  Location: Spain: Santa Cruz de la Palma, Santa Cruz de Tenerife
  Established: 1676
  Date: Every five years in June

  IntlThFolk-1979, 341

Virgin de la Candelaria
  See **Candlemas (Colombia: Cartegna) and (Puerto Rico)**

Virgin Islands Donkey Races Day
  Location: Virgin Islands: Frederiksted and Christiansted
  Date: February 22

  AmerBkDays-1978, 200
  AnnivHol-1983, 27

Virgin of Carmen, Fiesta of
  Location: Mexico: Santa Cruz Etla
  Date: July 15

  FolkWrldHol-1992, 376

Virgin of Guadalupe
  See **Our Lady of Guadalupe**

Virgin of the Pillar, Feast of the (Virgen del Pilar)
  Location: Spain: Saragossa
  Date: Ten days in October

  AnnivHol-1983, 183
  DictWrldRel-1989, 569
  FestWestEur-1958, 205
  HolFestCelWrld-1994, 358
  IntlThFolk-1979, 344

Virgin of the Remedies
  See **Nativity of the Virgin (Mexico)**

Visakha
  See **Buddha's Birthday, Enlightenment, and Salvation (Buddhist people in Thailand)**

Visby Festival
  Location: Sweden: Visby, Gotland Island
  Established: 1929
  Date: July-August

  IntlThFolk-1979, 348

Vishnu's Awakening (Devathani Ekadashi)
  Ethnic or religious group: Hindu
  Date: October-November, 11th day of waxing half of Hindu month of Karthika

  RelHolCal-1993, 71

Vishu
  See **New Year (India: Kerala)**

Visitation of the Blessed Virgin Mary, Feast of the
  Ethnic or religious group: Christian
  Date: July 2, Anglican; May 31, Roman Catholic and Protestant

  AnnivHol-1983, 73
  BkDays-1864, ii.11
  BkFest-1937, 187
  DaysCustFaith-1957, 168
  HolFestCelWrld-1994, 359
  RelHolCal-1993, 121
  SaintFestCh-1904, 315

Visitation of the Blessed Virgin Mary, Feast of the
  Location: Italy
  Date: July 2

  BkFest-1937, 187

La Víspera de San Juan
  See **Midsummer (Spain)**

Visvakarma Puja
See **Tools, Festival of (Hindu)**

Viticulturists' Day
See **Vinegrower's Day (Bulgaria)**

Vitoria Encounter
Location: Spain: Vitoria, Alava
Date: October or December

IntlThFolk-1979, 343

Vittoriale, Festival of
Location: Italy: Gardone Riviera, Lombardy
Established: 1953
Date: July-August

IntlThFolk-1979, 244

Vixakha Bouxa
See **Buddha's Birthday, Enlightenment, and Salvation (Buddhist people in Laos)**

Vizela Festival
Location: Portugal: Caldas de Vizela, Braga
Date: One week in August

IntlThFolk-1979, 304

Vizkereszt, Blessing of the Waters
See **Epiphany (Hungary)**

V- J Day
Named for: August 14, 1945, announcement of Japan's surrender; September 2, 1945, signing of Japan's official surrender
Date: August 14

AmerBkDays-1978, 754, 794, 796
AnnivHol-1983, 107
Chases-1993, 330, 352
DictDays-1988, 126
HolFestCelWrld-1994, 359

V- J Day (World War II Memorial Day)
Named for: August 14, 1945, announcement of Japan's surrender
Location: Arkansas
Date: August 14

AmerBkDays-1978, 754

V- J Day (Rhode Island)
See **Victory Day (Rhode Island)**

Vlaanderen, Festival van
See **Flanders, Festival of (Belgium: Antwerp, Bruges, Brussels, Ghent, Kortrijk, Leuven, Limburg, and Mechelen)**

Vlaggetjesdag
Location: Netherlands: Ijmuiden, Katwijk, Scheveningen, and Vlaardingen
Established: Around 1813
Date: Anytime from middle to late May

BkHolWrld-1986, May 27, 181

Vlöggelen
See **Easter Monday (Netherlands: Ootmarsum)**

Volador Fiesta
Location: Guatemala and Mexico
Date: During Corpus Christi or Holy Week

DictFolkMyth-1984, 749, 787, 963, 1162

Volcanalia (Vulcanalia)
Named for: Volcanus or Vulcan, Juturna, and Ops
Location: Ancient Rome
Date: August 23

AmerBkDays-1978, 713
DictFolkMyth-1984, 564, 825, 1163

Volksdansfestival, International
See **Folk-Dance Festival, International (Belgium: Schoten)**

Volunteers of America, Founder of
Named for: Ballington Booth (1857-1940)
Location: Volunteers of America
Date: July 28

DaysCustFaith-1957, 194
RelHolCal-1993, 121

Von Steuben Day
Named for: Friedrich Wilhelm Ludolf Gerhard Augustus von Steuben (1730-1794)
Location: United States
Date: September 17; often observed fourth Sunday in September

HolFestCelWrld-1994, 360

Vossa
See **Lenten Season (Cambodia)**

Votjak
See Holy Thursday (Finno-Ugric people in Kazan, Vjatka, and Perm, Russia)

Vow, Day of the
See Covenant, Day of the (South Africa)

Voyageur, Festival du
Location: Canada: St. Boniface, Winnipeg, Manitoba
Established: Has commemorated 18th- and 19th-century fur traders since 1970
Date: About one week in February

AnnivHol-1983, 177
Chases-1993, 95
GdWrldFest-1985, 34

Vozdvizheniye
See Exaltation of the Cross (Russia)

Waitangi
See New Zealand Day

Walking Sunday
Location: Ireland
Date: Sunday before Donnybrook Fair begins at the end of August

DictDays-1988, 128
DictMyth-1962, i.462

Wallonia, Festival of (Festival de Wallonie)
Location: Belgium: Brabant Wallon, Brussels, Chimay, Hainaut, Huy, Liège, Luxembourg, Mons, Namur, Saint-Hubert, and Stavelot
Established: 1971
Date: June-September or October

IntlThFolk-1979, 44
MusFestEurBrit-1980, 34

Walpurgis Eve
See Walpurgis Night

Walpurgis Night (Feast of Valborg)
Named for: St. Walpurgis, Walpurga, or Walburga (c. 710-779)
Date: April 30

AmerBkDays-1978, 404
AnnivHol-1983, 58
BkFest-1937, 310
BkHolWrld-1986, April 30

Chases-1993, 186
DaysCustFaith-1957, 102
DictDays-1988, 128
DictFolkMyth-1984, 114, 425, 961, 1165
DictMyth-1962, ii.1664
FestWestEur-1958, 25, 214
FolkAmerHol-1987, 161
FolkWrldHol-1992, 251
HolFestCelWrld-1994, 361
RelHolCal-1993, 64

Walpurgis Night
Named for: St. Walpurgis, Walpurga, or Walburga (c. 710-779)
Location: Austria
Date: April 30

BkHolWrld-1986, April 30
HolFestCelWrld-1994, 361

Walpurgis Night
Named for: St. Walpurgis, Walpurga, or Walburga (c. 710-779)
Location: Britain
Date: April 30

RelHolCal-1993, 64

Walpurgis Night (Valborgsaften)
Named for: St. Walpurgis, Walpurga, or Walburga (c. 710-779)
Location: Denmark
Date: April 30

FestWestEur-1958, 25

Walpurgis Night
Named for: St. Walpurgis, Walpurga, or Walburga (c. 710-779)
Location: Finland
Date: April 30

AnnivHol-1983, 58
HolFestCelWrld-1994, 361

Walpurgis Night
Named for: St. Walpurgis, Walpurga, or Walburga (c. 710-779)
Location: Germany
Date: April 30

AnnivHol-1983, 58
DictDays-1988, 128
FolkWrldHol-1992, 251
HolFestCelWrld-1994, 361

Walpurgis Night (Valborgsmässoafton)
  Named for: St. Walpurgis, Walpurga, or Walburga
    (c. 710-779)
  Location: Sweden: Lund, Stockholm, and Upsala
  Date: April 30

  AmerBkDays-1978, 405
  BkFest-1937, 310
  BkHolWrld-1986, April 30
  Chases-1993, 186
  FestWestEur-1958, 214
  FolkWrldHol-1992, 251
  HolFestCelWrld-1994, 361

Walpurgis Night
  Named for: St. Walpurgis, Walpurga, or Walburga
    (c. 710-779)
  Location: United States
  Ethnic or religious group: Neo-pagans
  Date: April 30

  RelHolCal-1993, 64

Walpurgis Night
  Named for: St. Walpurgis, Walpurga, or Walburga
    (c. 710-779)
  Location: United States
  Ethnic or religious group: Scandinavian-Americans
  Date: April 30

  AmerBkDays-1978, 404
  FolkAmerHol-1987, 161

Wandering Souls' Day
  See **Hungry Ghosts, Festival of (Vietnam)**

Wangala
  See **Drums Festival, Hundred (India: Garo Hills, Meghalaya)**

Wangford Festival
  Location: England: Wangford, East Suffolk
  Established: 1966
  Date: Eight days in July

  IntlThFolk-1979, 179

Waqfat Arafat
  See **Mecca, Pilgrimage to**

Waratambar
  See **Thanksgiving (Christians in Papua New Guinea)**

Warrior or Veteran Festival, Stommish
  Location: Bellingham, Washington
  Ethnic or religious group: Lummi Indians
  Date: Month of June

  IndianAmer-1989, 206

Warszawka Jesien
  See **Music of Warsaw, International Festival of**
    Contemporary and Warsaw Autumn Festival
    (Poland: Warsaw)

Washing the Hands (Issa Aka)
  Location: Nigeria
  Ethnic or religious group: Ibo people
  Date: During yam festivals held in August, September,
    or October

  BkHolWrld-1986, September 30, 178

Washington's Birthday (Cherries Jubilee)
  Named for: George Washington (1732-1799)
  Location: Valley Forge State Park, Pennsylvania
  Date: Several days in February

  AmerBkDays-1978, 200

Washington's Birthday
  Named for: George Washington (1732-1799)
  Location: Laredo, Texas, and Nuevo Laredo, Mexico
  Established: 1898
  Date: Mid-February

  AmerBkDays-1978, 200
  HolFestCelWrld-1994, 361

Washington's Birthday
  Named for: George Washington (1732-1799)
  Location: United States
  Established: 1782 in Richmond, Virginia; congressional
    resolution in 1800
  Date: February 22; observed third Monday in February

  AmerBkDays-1978, 197
  AnnivHol-1983, 25, 27
  BkDays-1864, i.284
  BkHolWrld-1986, February 22
  Chases-1993, 101, 107
  DictDays-1988, 128
  DictMyth-1962, ii.1666
  GdUSFest-1984, 198
  HolFestCelWrld-1994, 361

Washington's Birthday
  Named for: George Washington (1732-1799)
  Location: Alexandria, Virginia
  Date: Third Monday in February and preceding weekend

  AmerBkDays-1978, 200
  HolFestCelWrld-1994, 116

Washington's Crossing of the Delaware
  Named for: George Washington (1732-1799) and the crossing he and his men made across the Delaware River before the Battle of Trenton in 1776
  Location: Washington Crossing, Pennsylvania and New Jersey
  Established: Reenactment since 1953
  Date: December 25

  HolFestCelWrld-1994, 74

Washington State Apple Blossom Festival
  See **Apple Blossom Festival, Washington State**

Waso
  See **Lenten Season (Buddhist)**

Wassail Eve
  See **Twelfth Night (England)**

Watch Night Service
  See **New Year's Eve (Methodist, Baptist, and Presbyterian churches in the United States)**

Water Buffalo Festival (Carabao)
  Named for: San Isidro Labrador (1070-1130)
  Location: Philippines: Pulilan, San Isidro, Angono, Sariaya, and Lucban, Quezon Province
  Established: One of oldest harvest festivals in the Philippines
  Date: May 14 or 15

  Chases-1993, 207
  FolkWrldHol-1992, 298
  GdWrldFest-1985, 153
  HolFestCelWrld-1994, 51, 305

Water-Drawing Festival (Simhat bet Ha-sho'evah)
  Location: Israel
  Ethnic or religious group: Jewish
  Date: September-October, night after first day of Sukkot and every night of Sukkot thereafter

  HolFestCelWrld-1994, 363

Water Drawing Festival (Omizutori Matsuri)
  Location: Japan: Todaiji Temple in Nara

  Ethnic or religious group: Buddhist and Shinto religions
  Established: 12th century
  Date: Two weeks in March

  AnnivHol-1983, 180
  Chases-1993, 114
  HolFestCelWrld-1994, 237
  RelHolCal-1993, 100

Water Festival
  Location: Cambodia: Phnom Penh
  Date: Late October or early November

  FolkWrldHol-1992, 553
  HolFestCelWrld-1994, 273

Water Festival at Menjer Lake
  Location: Indonesia: Garung Village, Central Java, Java
  Date: One week in September

  IntlThFolk-1979, 221

Watermelon Day
  Location: Iowa and Minnesota
  Date: Mid-July

  DictDays-1988, 129

Wat Simouang Festival
  Location: Laos: Vientiane
  Established: 1563
  Date: November, two days before full moon day of twelfth lunar month

  BkHolWrld-1986, November 28, 181

Wattle Day
  Location: Australia
  Date: August 1 or September 1

  DictDays-1988, 129

Wavendon Season
  Location: England: Milton Keynes, Buckinghamshire
  Established: 1969
  Date: May-July

  IntlThFolk-1979, 169

Wax Festival
  Named for: Muslim Saint Sidi Abdallah Ben Hassoun (n.d.)
  Location: Morocco: Salé
  Date: November

  BkHolWrld-1986, November 9, 181

Waxing Light, Feast of
See **Imbolc**

**Waygoose Feast, Beanfest, or Beano in England
(Fastnachtsschmaus, Lichtschmaus, or Martinschmaus
in Germany)**
   Location: Printers in England, Germany, and the
    United States
   Established: 17th century
   Date: Near St. Bartholomew's Day, August 24

   DictFolkMyth-1984, 1168
   DictMyth-1962, ii.1669

Weaving Maid and the Herd Boy, Festival of the
   See **Double Seventh (China), (Hong Kong), (Japan),
    (Korea), and (Taiwan)**

Wedding of the Wine and Cheese Pageant
   See **Grape Festival (Nauvoo, Illinois)**

Week of Sufferings
   See **Holy Week**

Weeks, Feast of
   See **Shavuot**

Weighing Festival
   Named for: Honors Nicolas Horia (or Horea, 17ᵃ5?-1785),
    leader of 1784 peasant uprising in Transylvania
   Location: Romania: Magura Priei, Commune of Cizer, Salaj
   Date: Second Sunday in May

   IntlThFolk-1979, 326

Weihnachten
   See **Christmas (Germany) and (Switzerland)**

Well Dressing
   Location: England
   Established: 17th century
   Date: Before Ascension Day

   BkHolWrld-1986, May 19, 181

Wellington Day
   Named for: January 18, 1840, establishment of city
   Location: New Zealand: Wellington
   Date: January 18

   AnnivHol-1983, 10

Wesak
   See **Buddha's Birthday, Enlightenment, and Salvation
   (Buddhist people in Sri Lanka)**

Western Festival
   Location: Canada: Saint-Tite, Quebec
   Established: 1968
   Date: September

   GdWrldFest-1985, 58

Western Stock Show, National
   Location: Denver, Colorado
   Established: 1906
   Date: Begins third Friday in January for 11 days

   Chases-1993, 62
   GdUSFest-1984, 26

Whale Festival
   Location: Mendocino, Fort Bragg, and Gualala, California
   Date: March

   HolFestCelWrld-1994, 365

Whe'wahchee
   See **Dance of Thanksgiving (Omaha Indians at the
   Omaha Reservation in Nebraska)**

Whipping of the Innocents
   See **Holy Innocents' Day**

Whirling Dervishes, Festival of
   See **Mevlana (Mevlana Muslims in Konya, Turkey)**

Whistle Making (Fluitjes Maken)
   Location: Netherlands: Ootmarsum, Overijssel
   Date: On or near May 1

   FestWestEur-1958, 131

Whistlers Convention, National
   Location: Louisburg, North Carolina
   Established: 1974
   Date: Second or third weekend in April

   HolFestCelWrld-1994, 366

White Dog Feast
   See **Iroquois White Dog Feast**

White Moon Celebration
   See **New Year (Mongolia)**

White Night Festival
   Location: USSR: Leningrad (now St. Petersburg), Russia
   Established: 1964
   Date: Nine days in June

   GdWrldFest-1985, 182
   HolFestCelWrld-1994, 366
   IntlThFolk-1979, 373

White Saturday
See **Holy Saturday**

White Shirt Day
Named for: February 11, 1937, sit-down strike at auto plants
Location: Flint, Michigan
Date: February 11

AnnivHol-1983, 23
Chases-1993, 94

White Sunday
Location: American Samoa
Date: Second Sunday in October

AnnivHol-1983, 130
Chases-1993, 405
FolkWrldHol-1992, 506
HolFestCelWrld-1994, 366

White Sunday
Location: Western Samoa
Date: Second Sunday in October

BkHolWrld-1986, October 14, 181
Chases-1993, 406
FolkWrldHol-1992, 506
HolFestCelWrld-1994, 366

White Swan Celebrations
Location: Yakima Reservation, Washington
Ethnic or religious group: Yakima Indians
Date: July 4th weekend

IndianAmer-1989, 223

Whitewater Wednesday
Location: New River Gorge National River, near Oakville, West Virginia
Date: Third Wednesday in June

HolFestCelWrld-1994, 366

Whit Monday
Date: May-June, Monday after Pentecost

AmerBkDays-1978, 463
AnnivHol-1983, 73
BkDays-1864, i.643
BkFest-1937, 98
BkFestHolWrld-1970, 65
Chases-1993, 228
DictDays-1988, 67, 131
FestWestEur-1958, 12, 26
FolkWrldHol-1992, 283
HolFestCelWrld-1994, 119, 367

Whit Monday (Déjeuner Matrimonial, Matrimonial Tea)
Location: Belgium
Date: May-June, Monday after Pentecost

FestWestEur-1958, 12

Whit Monday (Anden Pinsedag)
Location: Denmark
Date: May-June, Monday after Pentecost

BkFest-1937, 98
FestWestEur-1958, 26

Whit Monday
Location: England, Ireland, Scotland, and Wales
Date: May-June, Monday after Pentecost

AnnivHol-1983, 73
BkDays-1864, i.643
Chases-1993, 228
DictDays-1988, 67, 131

Whit Monday (Procession of Giants of Belgium and France)
Location: France: Lille
Date: May-June, Monday after Pentecost

BkFestHolWrld-1970, 65
HolFestCelWrld-1994, 119

Whit Monday
Location: Hungary
Date: May-June, Monday after Pentecost

FolkWrldHol-1992, 283

Whit Monday
Location: United States
Ethnic or religious group: Pennsylvania Dutch people
Date: May-June, Monday after Whit Sunday

HolFestCelWrld-1994, 367

Whitsun Bride, Whitsun Flower Festival
See **Pinkster Bruid (Netherlands: Overijssel)**

Whitsunday or White Sunday (Anglican and Episcopalian)
See **Pentecost (Anglican Church in England);
Pentecost (Episcopalian)**

Whit Sunday
Location: Scotland
Date: May 15

DictDays-1988, 93, 131
DictMyth-1962, ii.1678
FestSaintDays-1915, 166
See also **Quarter Days (Scotland)**

Whit Sunday or Whitsuntide
See **Pentecost (England)**

Whuppity Scoorie Day
  Location: Scotland: Lanark, Lanarkshire
  Date: March 1

  AnnivHol-1983, 32
  BkHolWrld-1986, March 1

Wielkanoc
  See **Easter (Poland)**

Wielka Sobota, Great Saturday
  See **Holy Saturday (Poland)**

Wielki Piatek, Great Friday
  See **Good Friday (Poland)**

Wiener Festwochen
  See **Vienna Weeks (Austria: Vienna)**

Wigilia
  See **Christmas (Poland)**

Wíikita Festivals
  Location: Southern Arizona and northern Sonora, Mexico
  Ethnic or religious group: Papago Indians
  Date: Winter festival at Archie, Arizona; summer
    festival at Quitovaca, Sonora, Mexico

  DictFolkMyth-1984, 1176

Wild Pony Round-Up
  See **Pony Penning on Chincoteague Island**

Williams Day, Roger
  Named for: The arrival of Roger Williams (c. 1603-1683)
    in Massachusetts on February 5, 1631
  Location: United States
  Ethnic or religious group: Baptist
  Date: February 5

  AmerBkDays-1978, 143
  AnnivHol-1983, 20
  DaysCustFaith-1957, 47
  DictWrldRel-1989, 91, 804
  HolFestCelWrld-1994, 275
  RelHolCal-1993, 58

William Tell Pageant
  Location: New Glarus, Wisconsin
  Ethnic or religious group: Swiss-Americans
  Established: 1938
  Date: September, Labor Day weekend

  HolFestCelWrld-1994, 368

Willow Sunday
  See **Palm Sunday**

Wima'kwari
  See **Green Squash Festival (Mexico: Huichol)**

Wimbledon, Lawn Tennis Championships at
  Location: England
  Established: 1877
  Date: June

  Chases-1993, 259
  HolFestCelWrld-1994, 368

Wind Festival
  Location: Korea
  Date: February-March, first day of second lunar month

  FolkWrldHol-1992, 143
  HolFestCelWrld-1994, 368

Windjammer Days
  Location: Boothbay Harbor, Maine
  Established: 1962
  Date: Three days in mid-July

  Chases-1993, 260
  GdUSFest-1984, 76
  HolFestCelWrld-1994, 368

Windmill Day
  Location: Netherlands
  Date: Second Saturday in May

  AnnivHol-1983, 63
  Chases-1993, 200

Windsor Festival
  Location: England: Windsor, Berkshire
  Established: 1969
  Date: Two weeks in mid-September

  IntlThFolk-1979, 180
  MusFestEurBrit-1980, 63

Wine Festival (Austria)
  See **Martinmas (Austria)**

Wine Festival
  Location: Greece: Rethymon, Crete
  Established: Ancient times
  Date: Two weeks in July

  GdWrldFest-1985, 103

Wine Festival, Jerez
Location: Spain: Jerez de la Frontera, Cádiz
Established: 1948
Date: September

IntlThFolk-1979, 338

Wine Festival, Limassol
Location: Cyprus: Limassol
Established: 1962
Date: September 15-30

GdWrldFest-1985, 67
HolFestCelWrld-1994, 181
IntlThFolk-1979, 82

Wine Festival, Stroumbi Village
Location: Cyprus: Stroumbi Village near Paphos
Established: 1976
Date: Several days in early September

IntlThFolk-1979, 86

Wine Festival, Zahle
Location: Lebanon: Zahle
Date: early September

IntlThFolk-1979, 264

Wine Growers' Festival (Fête des Vignerons)
Location: Switzerland: Vevey, Vaud
Established: 1797
Date: 16 days in August every 25 years

GdWrldFest-1985, 171
IntlThFolk-1979, 355

Wine Harvest, Festival of the
Location: Spain: Palma del Condado, Huelva, Andalusia
Date: September

IntlThFolk-1979, 340

Wings 'n Water Festival
Location: Southern New Jersey coast
Established: 1983
Date: Third weekend in September

HolFestCelWrld-1994, 369

Winston 500
Location: Talladega Speedway, Alabama
Date: First Sunday in May

HolFestCelWrld-1994, 369

Winter Carnival, Dartmouth
Location: Hanover, New Hampshire
Established: 1910
Date: A weekend in February

HolFestCelWrld-1994, 78

Winter Carnival, Fairbanks
Location: Fairbanks, Alaska
Date: Third week in March

HolFestCelWrld-1994, 103

Winter Carnival, North Pole
Location: North Pole, Alaska
Date: A weekend in early March

HolFestCelWrld-1994, 229

Winter Carnival, St. Paul
Location: St. Paul, Minnesota
Established: 1886
Date: Ten days including last week in January

Chases-1993, 75
GdUSFest-1984, 98
HolFestCelWrld-1994, 298

Winter Dress, Sending the
Location: China
Date: October-November, first day of tenth lunar month

FolkWrldHol-1992, 528
HolFestCelWrld-1994, 311

Winter Fair, Great Lapp
Location: Sweden: Jokkmokk, Lappland
Ethnic or religious group: Lapp people
Established: 19th century
Date: Four days in February

GdWrldFest-1985, 168
HolFestCelWrld-1994, 125

Winterfest
Location: Minot, North Dakota
Established: 1969
Date: Seven to ten days in February

GdUSFest-1984, 135

Winter Festival, Alpine
Location: Davis, West Virginia
Established: 1959
Date: Six days in early January

GdUSFest-1984, 208

Winter Festival, Russian
   Location: USSR: Moscow, Russia
   Established: 1964
   Date: Three weeks in December-January

   GdWrldFest-1985, 183
   IntlThFolk-1979, 375

Winter Games, Ounasvaara International
   Location: Finland: Rovaniemi
   Established: 1927
   Date: Two days in mid-March

   GdWrldFest-1985, 78

Winterlude
   Location: Canada: Ottawa, Ontario
   Date: Ten days in February

   Chases-1993, 86
   FolkWrldHol-1992, 88
   HolFestCelWrld-1994, 369

Winter Sleigh Party (Kulig)
   Location: Poland
   Date: During a heavy snowfall after Christmas and
     before Easter

   BkHolWrld-1986, December 29, 178

Winter Solstice
   Date: December 21-22 in Northern Hemisphere;
     June 21-22 in Southern Hemisphere

   AmerBkDays-1978, 1127
   BkFest-1937, 82
   Chases-1993, 480
   DictDays-1988, 110, 131
   FestSaintDays-1915, 4
   FolkWrldHol-1992, 599
   HolFestCelWrld-1994, 370
   RelHolCal-1993, 105
   SaintFestCh-1904, 32

Winter Solstice (Tung Chih)
   Location: China
   Date: During the eleventh lunar month

   BkFest-1937, 82

Winter Solstice
   Location: Germany
   Date: December 21

   FestSaintDays-1915, 4

Winter Solstice
   Location: Hong Kong
   Date: December 21

   FolkWrldHol-1992, 599

Winter Solstice
   Location: India: Assam
   Date: December 21

   FolkWrldHol-1992, 599
   See also **Harvest Festival (Magh Bihu)**

Winter Solstice (Toji)
   Location: Japan and Okinawa
   Date: December 21

   FolkWrldHol-1992, 600

Winter Solstice (Tang choeh î)
   Location: Taiwan
   Date: December 21

   FolkWrldHol-1992, 600

Winter Solstice Celebration
   Location: Northeastern Arizona
   Ethnic or religious group: Hopi Indians
   Date: December 21-22

   IndianAmer-1989, 266

Winter Solstice Festival
   Location: Egypt
   Established: Centuries old
   Date: January 6

   BkFestHolWrld-1970, 19

Winter Traditions, Festival of
   Location: Romania: Botosani
   Date: Last week in December

   IntlThFolk-1979, 318

Wisconsin Dells Stand Rock Ceremonials
   Location: Tomah, Wisconsin
   Ethnic or religious group: Winnebago Indians
   Date: Nightly from mid-June to Labor Day

   IndianAmer-1989, 186

Wise, Sabbath of
   Named for: Rabbi Isaac Mayer Wise (1819-1900)
   Ethnic or religious group: Reform Jews
   Date: Last Sabbath in March

   DaysCustFaith-1957, 91
   RelHolCal-1993, 110

Wise Men, Day of the
See **Epiphany**

Wish-Fulfilling Eleventh (Kamada Ekadashi)
Ethnic or religious group: Hindu
Date: 11th day of waning half of Hindu month of Sravana

RelHolCal-1993, 87
See also **Putrada Ekadashi**

Wishing Night
See **New Year's Eve (Indians at Mitla, Oaxaca, Mexico)**

Witches, Procession of the
Location: Belgium: Beselare
Established: Centuries-old festival; organized in 1958
Date: Last Sunday in July

GdWrldFest-1985, 19

Witte Donderdag
See **Holy Thursday (Belgium)**

Wolfe Festival, Thomas
Named for: Thomas Wolfe (1900-1938)
Location: Asheville, North Carolina
Date: October 3

HolFestCelWrld-1994, 339

Woman's Day (Tij Day)
Location: Nepal
Date: March 8

AnnivHol-1983, 35

Woman's Day, International (Mezhdunarodnyi Zhenski Den')
Location: USSR
Established: 1910
Date: March 8

AnnivHol-1983, 34
BkFest-1937, 284
BkFestHolWrld-1970, 73
Chases-1993, 123
FolkWrldHol-1992, 160
HolFestCelWrld-1994, 370

Woman's Equality Day
Location: United States
Established: 1920; designated holiday since 1970s
Date: August 26

AmerBkDays-1978, 779
AnnivHol-1983, 110

Chases-1993, 343
See also **Anthony Day, Susan B.**

Women's Day (Midwife's Day)
Location: Greece
Date: January 8

Chases-1993, 59

Women's Day
Location: Mauritania
Date: March 8

AnnivHol-1983, 35

Women's Day
Location: Tunisia
Date: August 13

AnnivHol-1983, 106
Chases-1993, 328

Women's Day, International
Location: Holiday in Afghanistan, Cape Verde, China, Guinea-Bissau, Mauritania, Nepal, and USSR
Date: March 8

AnnivHol-1983, 34
Chases-1993, 123
HolFestCelWrld-1994, 370

Women's Day, International
Location: Britain
Date: Usually a Sunday in early March

DictDays-1988, 60

Wood Promenade Concerts, Henry
Named for: Henry Wood (1869-1944)
Location: England: Royal Albert Hall, London
Established: 1895
Date: Nine weeks from mid-July to mid-September

MusFestEurBrit-1980, 58
MusFestWrld-1963, 32
See also **Last Night**

Wooing a Bride (Brauteln)
Location: Germany: Sigmaringen, Baden-Württemberg
Established: 1648
Date: February, Tuesday preceding Ash Wednesday

FestWestEur-1958, 57
HolFestCelWrld-1994, 41

World Community Day
   Ethnic or religious group: Church Women United
   Date: First Friday in November

   RelHolCal-1993, 122

World Cup Soccer
   Location: Varies
   Established: 1930
   Date: Host country schedules matches in May, June or July

   BkHolWrld-1986, July 30, 181
   HolFestCelWrld-1994, 370

World Day of Prayer
   Ethnic or religious group: Christian
   Date: First Friday in March

   AnnivHol-1983, 33
   BkFestHolWrld-1970, 47
   Chases-1993, 120
   DaysCustFaith-1957, 67
   RelHolCal-1993, 122

World Environment Day
   Location: United Nations member nations; holiday in
      Botswana and Czechoslovakia
   Ethnic or religious group: Oodi people in Botswana
   Established: 1972
   Date: June 5

   AnnivHol-1983, 76
   BkHolWrld-1986, June 5
   Chases-1993, 237

World Fellowship Day
   Location: YWCAs in 69 countries
   Date: November 18

   AnnivHol-1983, 149

World Food Day
   Location: Sponsored by the United Nations
   Established: 1945
   Date: October 16

   AnnivHol-1983, 133
   BkHolWrld-1986, October 16

World Food Day
   Location: Sponsored by the United Nations; holiday
      in Barbados
   Established: 1945
   Date: October 16

   BkHolWrld-1986, October 16

World Health Day
   Location: Sponsored by the United Nations
   Established: 1948
   Date: April 7

   BkHolWrld-1986, April 7
   Chases-1993, 158

World Peace Day
   Location: United States
   Ethnic or religious group: Bahá'í
   Date: September 19

   AnnivHol-1983, 121
   RelHolCal-1993, 122

World Religion Day
   Ethnic or religious group: Bahá'í
   Established: 1950
   Date: Third Sunday in January

   AnnivHol-1983, 10
   Chases-1993, 67
   HolFestCelWrld-1994, 371
   RelHolCal-1993, 122

World Renewal Ceremony
   Location: Northwestern California
   Ethnic or religious group: Yurok, Karok, Hupa, and
      Wiyot Indians
   Date: July and August

   DictFolkMyth-1984, 1184

World Series (Baseball)
   Location: Canada and the United States
   Established: 1903
   Date: Mid-October

   BkHolWrld-1986, October 17, 181
   HolFestCelWrld-1994, 372

World War II Memorial Day
   See **V-J Day (Arkansas)**

**Wratislavia Cantans-International Oratorio Festival
(Miedzynarodowy Festiwal Oratoryjno-Kantatowy)**
   Location: Poland: Wroclaw
   Established: 1966
   Date: Six days during first week in September

   MusFestEurBrit-1980, 131

Wreaths, Wianki Festival of
  Location: Poland and Washington, D.C.
  Ethnic or religious group: Poles and Polish-Americans
  Date: June 23

  HolFestCelWrld-1994, 367

Wrekin and Telford Festival
  Location: England: Telford, Shropshire
  Established: 1973
  Date: Five or six weeks in April-May

  IntlThFolk-1979, 178

Wren Day
  See **St. Stephen's Day (Ireland) and (Isle of Man)**

Wrestling Games of Kirkpinar
  Location: Turkey: Kirkpinar, Edirne
  Established: 14th century
  Date: One week in June

  GdWrldFest-1985, 179
  IntlThFolk-1979, 368

Wright Brothers Day
  Named for: Orville (1871-1948) and Wilbur
    (1867-1912) Wright
  Location: Kitty Hawk and Dayton, North Carolina
  Established: 1903 flight
  Date: December 17

  AmerBkDays-1978, 1111
  AnnivHol-1983, 162
  Chases-1993, 476
  HolFestCelWrld-1994, 373

Writers' Week Listowel
  Location: Ireland: Listowel, County Kerry
  Established: 1971
  Date: June

  IntlThFolk-1979, 235

Wu Kuan's Day
  Named for: Chinese king of fourth hell
  Location: China
  Date: 18th day of second lunar month

  DictFolkMyth-1984, 1185

Wurstfest
  See **Sausage Festival (New Braunfels, Texas)**

Wüwüchim
  See **New Year (Hopi and Pueblo Indians in
    northeastern Arizona)**

Wyoming Day
  Location: Wyoming
  Established: December 10, 1869, granting of the vote
    to women
  Date: December 10

  AmerBkDays-1978, 1093

Xilónen, Festival of
  Named for: Xilónen, Aztec goddess of young corn and beans
  Ethnic or religious group: Aztec people
  Date: June

  DictFolkMyth-1984, 483

Xipe, Festival of
  Ethnic or religious group: Aztec people
  Date: During Aztec month of Tlacaxipehualiztli
    (near Carnival time)

  DictFolkMyth-1984, 251
  See also **Mardi Gras (Mexico)**

Xiquets de Valls
  See **Human Towers of Valls (Spain: Valls, Catalonia)**

Xmas Day
  See **Christmas**

Yak Bob Day
  See **Shick-Shack Day**

Yakima Nation Summer Encampment
  See **White Swan Celebrations**

Yama Dvitiya
  See **Brother and Sister Day (Hindu people in India)**

Yasukini Matsuri
  Location: Japan: Yasukini Shrine, Tokyo
  Date: Four-day observance in April; also in summer,
    autumn, and winter

  AnnivHol-1983, 183
  IntlThFolk-1979, 260

Yaun Shaw
  See **Lantern Festival (China), (Hong Kong), and (Taiwan)**

Year or Year's Day
  See **New Year's Day**

Yellow Daisy Festival
  Location: Stone Mountain, Georgia
  Established: 1969
  Date: Second weekend in September

  Chases-1993, 365
  GdUSFest-1984, 40
  HolFestCelWrld-1994, 375

Yenaandi
  See **Rain-Bringing Ceremony (Songhay people in Niger)**

Yen Lo's Birthday
  Named for: Chinese king of fifth hell
  Location: China
  Ethnic or religious group: Buddhist
  Date: Eighth day of first lunar month

  DictFolkMyth-1984, 1190

Yevmi Ashurer, Day of Sweet Soup
  See **New Year (Turkey)**

Yodeling Festivals (Jodlerfests)
  Location: Switzerland
  Date: End of May through September during odd-
    numbered years

  HolFestCelWrld-1994, 162

Yom Ha'Atzma'Ut
  See **Independence Day (Israel)**

Yom Hashoah
  See **Holocaust Day (Jewish)**

Yom Ha-Zikkaron (Day of Remembrance)
  Location: Israel
  Ethnic or religious group: Jewish
  Date: April-May, fourth day of Jewish month of Iyar

  HolFestCelWrld-1994, 375

Yom Kippur (Day of Atonement; High Holiday)
  Ethnic or religious group: Jewish
  Established: 3000 years ago
  Date: September-October, 10th of Jewish month of Tishri

  AmerBkDays-1978, 910
  AnnivHol-1983, 172
  BkFest-1937, 203

  BkFestHolWrld-1970, 6
  BkHolWrld-1986, September 28, 175
  Chases-1993, 387
  DaysCustFaith-1957, 246
  DictDays-1988, 56, 134
  DictFolkMyth-1984, 1009
  DictWrldRel-1989, 65, 155, 390, 817
  FolkAmerHol-1987, 289
  FolkWrldHol-1992, 481
  HolFestCelWrld-1994, 375
  RelHolCal-1993, 123

Yom Kippur
  Location: Israel
  Date: September-October, 10th of Jewish month of
    Tishri

  FolkWrldHol-1992, 481

Yom Kippur
  Location: Persia; now Iran
  Date: September-October, 10th of Jewish month of
    Tishri

  FolkWrldHol-1992, 481

Yom Kippur
  Location: Tunisia
  Date: September-October, 10th of Jewish month of
    Tishri

  FolkWrldHol-1992, 481

Yom Kippur
  Location: United States
  Date: September-October, 10th of Jewish month of
    Tishri

  FolkAmerHol-1987, 289

Yom Kippur
  Location: Yemen
  Date: September-October, 10th of Jewish month of
    Tishri

  FolkWrldHol-1992, 481

Yom Teruah
  See **New Year, Jewish (Rosh Hashanah)**

Yom Yerushalayim
  See **Jerusalem Day (Jewish people in Israel)**

Yoodoonal
  See **Shampoo Day (Korea)**

Yorktown Day
  Named for: October 19, 1781, British surrender to
  George Washington's troops in Yorktown, Virginia;
  observed since 1881
  Location: Massachusetts and Yorktown, Virginia
  Date: October 19

  AmerBkDays-1978, 943
  AnnivHol-1983, 134
  Chases-1993, 415
  HolFestCelWrld-1994, 376

Yoruba Ibeji Ceremony
  Location: Nigeria
  Date: At least once monthly

  BkHolWrld-1986, May 18, 182

Young, Birthday of Brigham
  Named for: Brigham Young (1801-1877)
  Ethnic or religious group: Mormon (Church of Jesus
  Christ of the Latter Day Saints)
  Date: June 1

  Chases-1993, 230
  DictWrldRel-1989, 424
  RelHolCal-1993, 62

Young May
  Location: Yugoslavia: Zajecar, Serbia
  Date: April-May

  IntlThFolk-1979, 411

Young People's Festival
  Location: England: Plymouth, Devonshire
  Established: 1970
  Date: Easter season

  IntlThFolk-1979, 173

Young Writers' Festival
  Location: England: London
  Established: 1973
  Date: February-May

  IntlThFolk-1979, 164

Youth and Sports Day
  Location: Turkey
  Date: May 19

  AnnivHol-1983, 67
  Chases-1993, 214

Youth Culture Week
  Location: Yugoslavia: Ljubljana, Slovenia
  Date: May

  IntlThFolk-1979, 394

Youth Day
  Location: Cameroon
  Date: February 11

  AnnivHol-1983, 22

Youth Day
  Location: Taiwan
  Date: March 29

  AnnivHol-1983, 43
  Chases-1993, 146

Youth Day
  Location: Tunisia
  Date: June 2

  AnnivHol-1983, 75

Youth Day
  Location: Republic of Upper Volta
  Date: November 30

  AnnivHol-1983, 153

Youth Day (Marshall Tito's Birthday)
  Named for: Marshall Josip Broz Tito (1892-1980)
  Location: Yugoslavia
  Date: May 25

  AnnivHol-1983, 71
  BkFestHolWrld-1970, 75

Youth Day
  Location: Zambia
  Date: March 13 or first Monday in August

  AnnivHol-1983, 36
  Chases-1993, 315

**Youth Day, International (Internatzional'nyi Den'
Komsomola)**
  Location: USSR
  Established: 1921
  Date: First Sunday in September

  BkFest-1937, 286

Ysyakh
  See **Sun Celebration, Midnight (USSR: Yakutsk)**

Yü Huang Shang Ti, Jade or Pearly Emperor
  Ethnic or religious group: Chinese Taoist
  Date: Eighth day of first lunar month

  DictFolkMyth-1984, 537

Yuki Matsuri
  See **Snowhut Festival**

Yü-Lan Hui
  See **Hungry Ghosts, Festival of (China)**

Yule
  Date: December 22

  BkDays-1864, ii.735, ii.745
  Chases-1993, 480
  DaysCustFaith-1957, 352
  DictMyth-1962, ii.1712
  FestSaintDays-1915, 9, 232
  FolkAmerHol-1978, 397
  FolkWrldHol-1992, 625, 626, 632
  HolFestCelWrld-1994, 377
  RelHolCal-1993, 123
  SaintFestCh-1904, 40

Yule
  Ethnic or religious group: Ancient Saxon people
  Date: December 22

  BkDays-1864, ii.745
  RelHolCal-1993, 123
  SaintFestCh-1904, 40

Yule
  Location: England
  Date: December 22

  BkDays-1864, ii.735, ii.745
  FestSaintDays-1915, 233
  FolkAmerHol-1978, 397

Yule
  Location: Northern Germany
  Date: December 22

  FestSaintDays-1915, 233

Yule
  Location: Scandinavia

  Date: December 22

  DaysCustFaith-1957, 352
  FestSaintDays-1915, 232
  FolkWrldHol-1992, 624, 626

Yule
  Location: Spain
  Date: December 22

  FolkWrldHol-1992, 632

Yule
  Location: Romania: Transylvania
  Date: December 22

  FestSaintDays-1915, 234

Yule
  Location: United States
  Ethnic or religious group: Neo-pagans
  Date: December 22

  HolFestCelWrld-1994, 377
  RelHolCal-1993, 123

Yule Day
  See **Christmas (Scotland)**

Yule-Even
  See **Christmas Eve**

Yuletide Lads
  Location: Iceland
  Established: 1920s
  Date: Twelve days beginning December 12

  BkHolWrld-1986, December 14, 182
  FolkWrldHol-1992, 616

Zadig
  See **Easter (Armenia)**

Zagreb Evenings
  Location: Yugoslavia: Zagreb, Croatia
  Date: June-September

  IntlThFolk-1979, 410

Zapusty, Fat Thursday
  See **Mardi Gras (Poland)**

Zarthastno Diso
  Named for: Death of Zoroaster in 551 B.C.
  Ethnic or religious group: Parsis and other Zoroastrians
  Date: April 30 by Fasli sect; May 29 by Kadmi sect;
  and June 1 by Shahenshai sect

  HolFestCelWrld-1994, 379

Zaterdag voor Paschen
  See **Holy Saturday (Belgium)**

Zibelemarit or Zybelemärit
  See **Onion Market (Switzerland: Bern)**

al-zid al-Saghir
  See **Fast, Feast of Breaking the (Jordan)**

Ziemas Svētku Diena
  See **Christmas (Latvia)**

Ziemas Svētku Vakars
  See **Christmas Eve (Latvia)**

Znojmo Feast
  Named for: Battle of Znojmo, 1404, against King
  Sigismund of Hungary (1368-1437) and Duke Albrecht
  of Austria (1397-1439)
  Location: Czechoslovakia: Znojmo, Moravia
  Date: Every Friday and Saturday in June-September

  GdWrldFest-1985, 70

Zoodochos Pege
  See **Life-Bearing Spring (Greece)**

Zulu/Shembe Festival
  Named for: Isaiah Shembe (c. 1870-1935) founder of
  Nazareth Baptist Church
  Location: South Africa: Ekuphakemeni Shembe's Shrine,
  Inanda
  Ethnic or religious group: Nazareth Baptist Church
  Established: 1909
  Date: July 1 through last Sunday in July

  FolkWrldHol-1992, 357
  GdWrldFest-1985, 159
  HolFestCelWrld-1994, 379

Zvaigznes Diena
  See **Epiphany (Latvia)**

Special Indexes

Several different Special Indexes provide reference to entries (as appropriate) for each of the following categories.

Ethnic and Geographical Index

Lists all ethnic groups, nationalities, cities, counties, provinces, states, countries, and other places appearing within the entries.

Name Index

Lists all people associated with the events indexed.

Religion Index

Indexes events with a significant religious element by religious group and denomination.

Chronological Indexes

Gregorian Calendar Index —Indexes events that are celebrated on a specific date according to the Gregorian calendar.

Christian Movable Days Index—Indexes holy days and festivals whose dates depend on the date of Easter.

Jewish Calendar Index—Indexes Jewish holy days and holidays by the Jewish calendar.

Islamic Calendar Index—Indexes Islamic holy days and feasts by the Islamic calendar.

Chinese Calendar Index—Indexes holidays that are celebrated by the traditional Chinese calendar.

Hindu Calendar Index—Indexes Hindu and Buddhist festivals whose dates are determined by the Hindu calendar.

Other Movable Days Index—Indexes holidays observed annually or once during a given cycle of years, festivals celebrated according to seasonal or agricultural criteria, and events whose dates are variable or are determined by calendars other than those covered above.

Ethnic and Geographical Index

The Ethnic and Geographical Index lists all ethnic groups and geographic places appearing in the sources indexed.

Aalborg, Rebild, North Jutland, Denmark
Independence Day (Rebild Festival), July 4

Aargau, Switzerland
Easter Play of Muri, every five or six years in June
Konigsfelden Festival, weekends in August-September
  during even-numbered years
Meitlisunntig, second Sunday in January

Abbots Bromley, Staffordshire, England
Dance, Horn, Monday after September 4

Abbotsbury, Dorsetshire, England
Garland Day, May 12 or 13

Abbotsford, British Columbia, Canada
Air Show, International, three days in August

Aberdeen, Scotland
Operatic Society Festival, Haddo House Choral and,
  late summer

Abidji people in Ivory Coast: Gomon
Dipri Festival, March-April

Aboriginal people in Australia
Christmas, December 25

Abron people in Ghana
New Yam Festival (Odwira), September-October, up to
  forty days

Abruzzi, Italy
Banderesi, Festival of the, six days in May

Aburi people in Ghana
New Yam Festival (Odwira), September-October, up to
  forty days

Abu Simbel temple in Egypt
Abu Simbel Festival, February 22 and October 22

Abyssinia
Michaelmas, observed twelfth of every month

Acadian people
Acadian Festival, August 5-15
Acadian Festivals, July or August
Assumption, Feast of the, and Tintamarre celebration,
  August 15 and Sunday nearest August 15

Acadian people in Maine: Augusta
Bastille, Festival de la, weekend closest to July 14

Acapantzingo, Morelos, Mexico
St. Isidore, Festival of, May

Acoma Pueblo, New Mexico
All Souls' Day, November 2
Governor's Feast, first week in February
St. Anne's Day, July 26
St. James the Greater's Day, July 25
St. Peter's Day, June 29
St. Stephen, Feast of and Harvest Dance, September 2
San Estevan, Feast of, September 2

Ada, Oklahoma
Chickasaw Nation Annual Day, first Saturday in October

Adairsville, Georgia
Locomotive Chase Festival, Great, first weekend in October

Adak, Alaska
Oklahoma Day, April 22; observed early autumn

Addis Ababa, Ethiopia
Selassie's Birthday, Haile, July 23

Adelaide, South Australia, Australia
Arts, Festival of the, February-March during even-
  numbered years
Performing Arts for Young People, Come Out—Festival of,
  first two weeks in May during odd-numbered years

Afghanistan
Independence Day (Jeshn), May 27; observed in late August
New Year's Day (Nauroz), March 21
Revolution Day, Saur, April 27
Simhat Torah, 23rd day of Jewish month of Tishri
Women's Day, International, March 8

African-Americans
Easter, March-April, first Sunday after first full moon after
  the vernal equinox
Holy Innocents' Day, December 28
Job's Birthday, February 30
Juneteenth (Emancipation Day), June 19
Kwanzaa, December 26 through January 1

African-Canadians
Kwanzaa, December 26 through January 1

Africans in British West Indies
Christmas, December 25

Africans in Louisiana: New Orleans
Dance, Calinda, June 23

Afrikaaners
Christmas, December 25
Covenant, Day of the (Braaiveleis), December 16

Afro-Guyanese people in Guyana
Husayn or Husain Day (Hosay and Tadja), tenth day of
Islamic month of Muharram

Agadés, Niger
Bianou, first new moon in February

Agia Serres, Greece
Anastenaria, May 21-23

Agome-yo Village, Togo
Planting Ceremony

Agrigento, Sicily, Italy
Folklore Festival, International, February

Aguascalientes, Mexico
St. Mark, Fair of (Feria de San Marcos), ten days
beginning April 25

Ahmedabad, Gujarat, India
Dance Festival, Darpana, five days during first week in
October
Drama Festival, Gujarat Academy, five days during second
week in February
Kite Festival, International, during Hindu month of Pausha

Aichi, Japan
Horaiji Temple Dengaku Festival, early February
Shimmeisha Oni Festival, mid-February

Aintree, Liverpool, England
Grand National Day, March-April

Ainu people in Japan: Akan Lake, Hokkaido
Bear Festival, early December
Marimo Festival, second weekend in October

Airdrie, Lanarkshire, Scotland
Monklands Festival, June

Ait Hadiddou Berber people in Morocco: Imilchil
Marriage Fair, September

Aix-en-Provence, France
Opera and Music, Aix-en-Provence International Festival of
(Festival International d'Art Lyrique et de Musique d'Aix-
en-Provence), three and one-half weeks in July

Aix-les-Bains, Savoie, France
Dullin Prize Competition, May-June, Thursday to Sunday
evening of Ascension Day during even-numbered years

Akan Lake, Hokkaido, Japan
Marimo Festival, second weekend in October

Akan people in Ghana
Apo Festival
New Yam Festival (Odwira), September-October, up to
forty days

Akan people in Ghana: Tanosu
Apo Festival

Akita, Japan
Bonten Festival, February

Akland, Panay Island, Philippines
Ati-Atihan Festival, three days in January, including feast
day of Santo Nino (Holy Child Jesus) and ending on
a Sunday

Akron, Ohio
Soap Box Derby, All American, six days in August

**Ak-Sar-Ben Livestock Exposition and Rodeo, Omaha,
Nebraska**
Ak-Sar-Ben Livestock Exposition and Rodeo, nine days
from late September to early October

Aksehir, Turkey
Nasreddin Hoca Festival, July

Aku people in Sierra Leone
Thanksgiving (Awoojoh), may occur on special occasions
and during such holidays as Christmas, Easter, Good
Friday, and New Year's Day

Alabama
Admission Day, December 14
Arts, Birmingham Festival of the, two weeks in April-May
Blessing of the Fishing Fleet and Biloxi Shrimp Festival and
Fais Do Do, first weekend in June
Blessing of the Shrimp Fleet, last weekend in June
Blueberry Festival, Alabama, third Saturday in June
Confederate Memorial Day, last Monday in April
Davis's Birthday, Jefferson, June 3
Fairhope Jubilee, summer
Fraternal Day, second Tuesday in October
Keller Festival, Helen, last weekend in June
Mardi Gras, February-March, the two weeks before
Ash Wednesday
Music Festival, W.C. Handy, first full week in August
Powwow, Poarch Creek Indian Thanksgiving Day, last
Thursday in November
Shrimp Festival, National, four days in early October
Winston 500, first Sunday in May

Alabama Indians
Dance, Green Corn

Allentown, Pennsylvania
Halloween, October 31

Allier, France
Folklore, World Festival of, one week in July
Opera, Ballet and Music Festival, Vichy, June-September
Theatre, Biennial of International, May-June, Friday to
Monday evening of Pentecost during odd-numbered years

All Souls College, Oxford, England
Mallard Ceremony, once every hundred years

Alma, Michigan
Highland Festival and Games, last weekend in May

Almonacid del Marquesado, Cuenca, Spain
Endiablada Festival, early February

Almonte, Huelva, Andalusia, Spain
Pilgrimage of the Dew (Romería Del Rocío), May-June,
Thursday or Friday before Pentecost Sunday through
Monday or Tuesday after Pentecost

Alpes-Maritimes, France
Theatrical, Musical and Artistic Encounters of Grasse,
Rithma: International, July

Alps (French)
St. Bernard of Montjoux, May 28

Alps (German)
Mountain Pasture, Return from (Almabtrieb), September

Alresford, Hampshire, England
Tichborne Dole, March 26

Alsace (now part of France)
Twelfth Night (Epiphany Eve), January 5

Alsace, Bas-Rhin, France
Music Festival, Strasbourg International (Festival
International de Musique de Strasbourg), 16 days
beginning first week in June

Altdorf, Uri, Switzerland
Play at Altdorf, Wilhelm Tell, weekends in August-
September during even-numbered years

Amarillo, Texas
Mother-in-law Day, March 5

Ambar Ketawang, Jogjakarta, Java
Offering Ceremony, January

American Samoa
Flag Day, April 17
White Sunday, second Sunday in October

Amhara, Ethiopia
Epiphany (Timqat or Timkat), January 19
St. Michael's Feast, monthly

Amsterdam, Netherlands
Floriade, every ten years in April-October
Fools, Festival of, three weeks in June
Holland Festival, 23 days in June
Luilak (Lazybones Day or Sluggard's Feast), Saturday
preceding Pentecost or Whit Sunday
Netherlands University Festival, every four years in December
Queen Juliana's Birthday, April 30

Anadarko, Oklahoma
Indian Exposition, American, six days beginning second
Monday of August

Anaheim, California
Halloween, Saturday before October 31

Anamosa-Stone City, Iowa
Art Festival, Grant Wood, second Sunday in June

Anandpur Sahib, India
Hola Mohalla, March 8

Anchorage, Alaska
Anchorage Fur Rendezvous, ten days in February
Iditarod Trail Sled Dog Race, 11-32 day-long race begins
first Saturday in March
Music, Anchorage Festival of, 18 days in June

Andalusia, Spain
Pilgrimage of Our Lady of the Cabeza (Romería of
the Virgen de la Cabeza), end of April
Pilgrimage of the Dew (Romería Del Rocío), May-June,
Thursday or Friday before Pentecost Sunday through
Monday or Tuesday after Pentecost
Pilgrimage of the Virgen de la Pena (Romería of the
Virgen de la Pena), last Sunday in April
Wine Harvest, Festival of the, September

Andalusia (western), Spain
Exaltation of the Cross, May 3

Andean Indians in Peru: Puno
Puno, Día del, November 5

Andhra, India
New Year (Ugadi Parva), first day of Hindu month of
Chaitra

Appomattox, Virginia
Appomattox Day, April 9

Aptos, California
Music Festival, Cabrillo, ten days in late July

Apulia, Italy
St. Nicholas's Day, May 7-8

Arab countries
Epiphany (Lailat-al-Quade, Night of Destiny), January 5,
Epiphany Eve

Arabic people
El-Bugat

Arad, Romania
Folklore Festival, Arad, August 24

Arandjelovac, Serbia, Yugoslavia
Marble and Sound, July-September

Arapaho, Wyoming
Powwow, Arapaho Community, June
Powwow, Northern Arapaho, August

Arapaho Indians in the Great Plains of the United States
Dance, Sun, usually during summer solstice, June 21

Arapaho Indians in Wyoming: Arapaho
Powwow, Arapaho Community, June

Arapaho Indians in Wyoming: Ethete
Dance and Ethete Celebration, Sun, July
Labor Day Powwow, first Monday in September
Powwow, Wyoming Indian High School, May
Powwow, Yellow Calf Memorial, May

Archie, Arizona
Wiikita Festivals, winter festival at Archie, Arizona;
summer festival at Quitovaca, Sonora, Mexico

Arequipa, Peru
Festidanza, August
Folk Festival, August

Argentina
Christmas, December 25
Exaltation of the Cross, May 3
Grape Harvest, National Festival of the, first week in March
Immaculate Conception, Feast of the (Virgen de Valle),
December 8
Independence Day, May 25 and July 9
Mardi Gras (Tincunaco Ceremony), February-March,
Thursday before Ash Wednesday

National Day, May 25
San Martín Day, August 17
Sumamao, Fiesta de, December 26

Argos, Greece
Linus, Festival of

Argungu, Nigeria
Argungu Fishing Festival, February

Århus, Denmark
Århus Festival Week (Århus Festuge), nine days from
first Saturday through second Sunday in September

Arikara Indians in North Dakota: Mandaree
Mandaree Celebration, third weekend in July

Arizona
Admission Day, February 14
Apache Fair, weekend nearest Veterans Day, November 11
Apache Tribal Fair, first weekend in September, including
Labor Day
Arts, Flagstaff Festival of the, four weeks in July
Cinco de Mayo, May 5
Cocopah Festivities Day, March or April
Country Music and Bluegrass Festival, third weekend in June
Dance, Hopi Snake, August-September, every other year
Dance, Hopi Snake-Antelope
Dance, Sunrise, four days including Labor Day, first
Monday in September
Dances, Basket, late October through November
Dead, Observance for the (Keruk), seven nights annually
Easter, March-April, first Sunday after first full moon
after the vernal equinox
Fiddler's Contest and Festival, Old Time, two days over
last weekend in September
Gila River Festival, second weekend in March
Gold Rush Days, second weekend in February
Holy Saturday, March-April, Saturday before Easter Sunday
Holy Week (Deer Dance and Lenten Ceremonies), March-
April, week before Easter
Indian Celebration, O'Odham Tash, February
Indian Fair, Heard Museum Guild, two days in late February
Lent, February-March, forty-day season before Easter
London Bridge Days, first two weekends in October
Moore Days, Billy, second weekend in October
Native American Day, fourth Friday in September
Navajo Nation Fair, second week in September, usually
Wednesday or Thursday through Sunday
Navajo Nightway and Mountain Topway Ceremonials,
December (date varies)
New Year (Wüwüchim), four days, including eve of new
moon in November
Our Lady of Guadalupe, December 12
Palm Sunday, March-April, the Sunday preceding Easter

Ascoli Piceno, Marches, Italy
Equestrian Tournament of the Quintain, first Sunday
in August

Ascot, England
Diamond Day (Diamond Stakes race), July

Asheville, North Carolina
Dance and Folk Festival, Asheville Mountain, first
Thursday, Friday, and Saturday in August
Wolfe Festival, Thomas, October 3

Ashland, Oregon
Shakespeare Festival, Oregon, February through
October

Asia
Mid-Autumn Festival, 15th day of eighth lunar
month

Asia (southeast)
Ramadan, ninth Islamic month

Aspen, Colorado
Music Festival, Aspen, nine weeks from last week in June
to last week in August

Assam, India
Harvest Festival (Magha Bihu or Bhogali Bihu, Festival
of Feasts), three days during Hindu month of Pausha
Kati Bihu, September 21, 22
New Year (Bohag Bihu), first day of Hindu month
of Vaisakha
Vernal Equinox (Bohag Bihu), on or near March 21
Winter Solstice, December 21

Assisi, Italy
St. Francis of Assisi, Feast of, October 3-4

Ath, Hainaut, Belgium
Marriage of Goliath (Les Vêpres de Gouyasse), fourth
weekend in August

Athapaskan Indians in Alaska: Kaltag and Nulato
Stickdance, one week in spring

Athens, Greece
Anthesteria, February-March, 11th-13th day of Greek month
of Anthesterion
Athens Festival, June through last week in September
Cronia
Dionysus, spring and winter
Folk Dances, Greek, May-September
Marathon, International Open, mid-October
Panathenaea, midsummer

Athens, Greece (ancient)
Eleusinia, every five years: the Lesser Eleusinia, early
spring; the Greater Eleusinia, between harvest and
seed time

Athlone, County Westmeath, Ireland
Drama Festival, All-Ireland Amateur, April-May

Atlanta, Georgia
Arts Festival, nine days in May
Dogwood Festival, April

Atlantic City, New Jersey
Miss America Pageant, third Saturday in September

Atlántico, Colombia
Mardi Gras (Carnival), February-March, Friday-Tuesday
before Ash Wednesday

Atmore, Alabama
Powwow, Poarch Creek Indian Thanksgiving Day, last
Thursday in November

Auburn, Kentucky
Shaker Festival, mid-July

Auckland, New Zealand
Arts Festival, Maidment, April-May
Auckland Festival, March-April during even-numbered years
Provincial Anniversary, January 28

Aude, France
Carcassone, Festival of, two weeks in July

Augsburg, Bavaria, Germany
Mozart Festival, German (Deutsches Mozartfest), eight days
during second week in June; alternates with other
German cities
St. Michael's Day (Tura Michele Marky or Fair),
September 29

Augusta, Maine
Bastille, Festival de la, weekend closest to July 14

Augusta National Golf Club, Georgia
Master's Golf Tournament, first full week in April

Aurangabad, Maharashtra, India
Tamasha Festival, November-December (location rotates)

Auray, Brittany, France
Pilgrimage to St. Anne d'Auray, July 26; observed
last weekend in July

Aurora, Minnesota
Sliding Festival, Finnish, two days in February

Austin, Texas
  Father of Texas Day, November 3

Australia
  Anzac Day, April 25
  Arts, Big River Festival of, one week in May-June
  Arts, Festival of the, February-March during even-
    numbered years
  Arts, Northam Festival of the, June-July
  Arts, North Queensland Festival of, three weeks
    in December
  Arts, Orange Festival of the, one week in April during
    even-numbered years
  Arts for Young People, Festival of Performing—Round
    Up, five days in February
  Australia Day, January 26 or following Monday
  Australia Day at the Rocks, January 26; observed late
    January
  Australian Open Tennis, January
  Bathurst Carillon City Tourist Festival, September-October
  Begonia Festival, Ballarat, March
  Blue Gum Festival of Tasmania, March
  Boxing Day, December 26
  Canberra Week, ten days in March, including Canberra
    Day, third Monday in March
  Carnival of Flowers, end of September-early October
  Christmas, December 25
  Corroboree
  Darwin Show Day, July
  Darwin Youth Festival, August (during school holidays)
  Drama Festival, Burnie Youth, last week in July
  Drama Festival, Catholic School, June
  Drama Festival, Deloraine Youth, one week in July
  Drama Festival, New South Wales, August-October
  Drama Festival, New South Wales High Schools, May-August
  Drama Festival, Warana (Blue Skies), two weeks in
    September-October
  Easter Show, Royal, during the Easter holidays
  Eight Hour Day or Labour Day, March 5
  Eisteddfod, Eastern Shore, October
  Eisteddfod, Hobart, June
  Eisteddfod Society Festival, August-September
  Folk Festival, Newcastle, mid-June
  Folk Festival, Numeralla, end of January, including
    Australia Day, January 26
  Folk Festival, Top Half, weekend in June
  Folk Festival, Wagga, three days in October
  Folklore, Sydney Festival of, two weeks in January,
    coincides with Festival of Sydney
  Foundation Week Celebrations, two weeks in October-
    November
  Free Entertainment in the Parks, year-round
  Fremantle Week, late October-early November
  Hobart Cup Day, on or near January 23
  Joy of Living, one week in September-early October

  Katherine Show Day, July
  King's Birthday, a Monday in early June
  Labour Day, May 3
  Labour Day, March 8
  Launceston Cup Day, February
  Melbourne Cup Day, first Tuesday in November
  Mischief Night, November 4
  Moomba ("let's get together and have fun") Festival,
    ten days in March
  Music Festival, Carcoar Folk and Traditional Bush, a
    weekend in April
  Outback Festival, ten days in August during odd-numbered
    years
  Performing Arts for Young People, Come Out—Festival
    of, first two weeks in May during odd-numbered years
  Performing Arts for Young People, The Leap—Festival
    of, last week in February
  Perth, Festival of, February-March
  Picnic Day, first Monday in August
  Play Festival, Act Five, one week in August
  Plays, Wagga Wagga School of Arts Annual Festival of,
    two consecutive weekends in August-September
  Queen Elizabeth's Day, Monday nearest to official date
    proclaimed in England
  Recreation Day, first Monday in November
  Regatta Day, Hobart, February 9-10
  Spring Festival, Warana (Blue Skies), September-October
  Sydney, Festival of, December 31 through January
  Sydney to Hobart Yacht Race, several days beginning
    December 26
  Tennant Creek Show Day, July
  Vintage Festival, Barossa Valley, April, seven days
    beginning Easter Monday during odd-numbered years
  Wattle Day, August 1 or September 1

Australian Capital Territory, Australia
  Canberra Week, ten days in March, including Canberra
    Day, third Monday in March
  Play Festival, Act Five, one week in August

Austria
  Advent, four-week season beginning Sunday nearest
    November 30 and ending December 24
  All Saints' Day, November 1
  Ash Wednesday, February-March, fortieth day before
    Easter Sunday
  Austrian State Treaty Day, May 15
  Autumn, Styrian (Steirischer Herbst), eight weeks in
    October-November
  Battle of Flowers, Vienna, summer
  Bregenz Festival (Bregenzer Festspiele), four weeks in
    July-August
  Bruckner Festival, International (Internationales
    Brucknerfest), four weeks in September
  Candlemas, February 2

Austria *(cont.)*

Carnuntum Festival, July-August

Castle Kobersdorf Festival, July

Castle Neulengbach Festival (Schloss Neulengbach), July

Castle Plays Festival, June-July

Christmas (Christfest), December 25

Christmas Eve (Heiliger Abend), December 24

Comedy Festival at Porcia Castle, July-August

Corpus Christi, May-June

Easter (Ostern), March-April, first Sunday after first full moon after the vernal equinox

Easter Festival (Osterfestspiele), March-April, Palm Sunday to Easter Monday

Easter Monday, March-April, Monday after Easter

Epiphany, January 6

Good Friday (Kar Freitag), March-April, Friday preceding Easter Sunday

Hellbrunn Festival (Fest in Hellbrunn), first two weekends in August

Holy Innocents' Day, December 28

Holy Thursday, March-April, Thursday preceding Easter

Krems Outdoor Festival (Sommerspiele Krems), June-July

Kriss Kringle Day, December 5 or December 24

Lake Festival (Seespiele), August

Mardi Gras (Fasching, Carnival), February-March, the week before Ash Wednesday

Mardi Gras (Schemenlauf, Running of the Spectres), January-March, week before Ash Wednesday

Martinmas (Wine Festival), November 11

Melk, Festival of (Melker Festspiele), July-August

Midsummer, June 23-24

Mozart Week (Mozartwoche), nine days at end of January

Nestroy Festival (Nestroy-Spiele), July

New Year's Day (Neujahrstag), January 1

New Year's Eve, December 31

Operetta Weeks (Operettenwochen), eight weeks from early July to first week in September

Palm Sunday, March-April, the Sunday preceding Easter

Passion Play, every five years from May-September

Passion Play, June-September

Passion Play, every six years from June to September

Pentecost, May-June, the Sunday fifty days after Easter

Perchtenlauf, usually January 6

Republic Day, November 12

Republic Day, Second, April 27

Rogation Days (Blessing the Fields), May, fifth Sunday through Wednesday after Easter

St. Andrew's Day, November 30

St. John, Apostle and Evangelist, Feast of, December 27

St. Leonard's Day, November 6

St. Leopold, Feast Day of (Fasslrutschen or Gaense Tag, Goose Day), November 15

St. Mark, Feast of (Blessing the Fields), April 25

St. Nicholas's Day (Nikolaustag), December 6

St. Stephen, Feast of (Stefanstag), December 26

St. Sylvester's Day (Sylvesterabend), December 31

St. Thomas the Apostle, Feast of, December 21

Salzburg Festival (Salzburger Festspiele), five weeks in July and August

Schubertiade Hohenems, 16 days in June

"Silent Night, Holy Night" Celebration, December 24

Stockerau Outdoor Festival (Stockerau Festspiele), July-August

Summer Festival, Carinthian (Carinthischer Sommer), eight weeks from late June to late August

Summer Festival, Friesach, July-August

Summer Festival, Grein (Sommerspiele Grein), July-August

Theatre Festival, Farmstead (Theater auf dem Bauernof), June-August

Theatre Festival, International Street (Internationales Strassentheaterfestspiele), annual, dates vary

Theatre Festival, Street (Strassentheater), July-August

Tirolese Summer, mid-July to mid-August

Twelfth Night (Epiphany Eve), January 5

Valentine's Day, February 14

Vienna Weeks (Wiener Festwochen), six weeks from mid-May to June

Walpurgis Night, April 30

Auteil, France

French Open Tennis Championships, May-June

Avening, Gloucestershire, England

Pig Face Sunday, the Sunday following September 14

Aveyron, France

Folkloric Festival of Rouergue, International, one week in August

Avignon, France

Avignon Festival (Festival d'Avignon), three and one-half weeks in July-August

Ávila, Spain

Pilgrimage of La Dandelada (Romeria of La Dandelada), second Sunday in September

Pilgrimage of Pedro Bervardo (Romeria of Pedro Bervardo), September 5-17

Avoca, Iowa

Country Music Contest and Festival, National Old-Time, first weekend in September

Avon, England

Bath Festival, May or June

Avondale, Goodyear, and Litchfield Park, Arizona

Moore Days, Billy, second weekend in October

Aymara Indians
Alasita Fair ("Buy from Me" Fair), January 24
Skulls, Ceremony for the, October

Aymara Indians in Peru: Puno
Puno, Día del, November 5

Ayodhya, India
Rama, Festival of (Rama-Navami), ninth day of waning half of Hindu month of Chaitra

Ayrshire, Scotland
Marymass Fair, third or fourth Monday in August

Azerbaijan
Christmas, December 25
Easter, March-April, first Sunday after first full moon after the vernal equinox
Night of Forgiveness (Laylat al-Bar'ah), 15th of Islamic month of Shaban

Azorean Portuguese people in California: Gustine
Our Lady of Miracles (Nossa Senhora dos Milagres or Festa de Serreta), September 8-15

Azores, Portugal
Holy Ghost, Feast of the (Altura Do Espirito Santo), August
Our Lady of Miracles (Nossa Senhora dos Milagres or Festa de Serreta), September 8-15

Aztec people
Chicomecoatl, April, Aztec month of Huey Tozoztli
Cinteotl, Festival for, April, Aztec month of Huey Tozoztli
New Fire Ceremony, every 52 years
New Year's Day, February 2
Quecholli, Feast of Mixcoatl, 280th day of the year (14th day, counting by twenties, from February)
Running of the Bulls, Sunday following August 15
Xilónen, Festival of, June
Xipe, Festival of, near Carnival time, during Tlacaxipehualiztli

Baalbek, Lebanon
Baalbek Festival, mid-July to mid-August

Babylon, Babylonia
New Year's Day

Babylonia
Gula, Feast of, late April
Sacaea, five-day New Year feast, Anaitus

Babylonian people
Vernal Equinox, on or near March 21

Bacau, West Moldavia, Romania
Gala of One-Man Shows, ten to 12 days in October or November

Bachok, Kelantan, Malaysia
Bachok Festival of Culture, two weeks in May
Puja Ketek Celebrations, October

Backi Petrovac, Vojvodina, Yugoslavia
Autumn of Culture, second half of October
Theatres, Encounter of Slovak Amateur Children's, April-May

Badajoz, Spain
Battle of the Moors and Christians, June

Bad Durkheim, Germany
Sausage Fair (Bad Durkheim Wurstmarkt), Saturday-Tuesday during second weekend of September; Friday-Monday during third weekend of September

Baden-Wurttemberg, Federal Republic of Germany
Castle Festival at Jagsthausen, June-August
Puppet Play Encounter, three days in October during odd-numbered years
Schiller Days, May
Schwetzingen Festival, April-May
Theatre Festival in Schwabisch Hall, Open-Air, June-August
Wooing a Bride (Brauteln), February-March, Tuesday preceding Ash Wednesday

Bad Gandersheim, Lower Saxony, Federal Republic of Germany
Plays Festival, Gandersheim Cathedral, May-June

Bad Hersfeld, Hesse, Federal Republic of Germany
Bad Hersfeld in the Monastery Ruins, Festival of, July-August

Bad Ischl, Upper Austria, Austria
Operetta Weeks (Operettenwochen), eight weeks from early July to first week in September

Bad River Ojibwa Indians in Wisconsin: Odanah
Rice Celebration, Wild (Manomin), usually weekend before Labor Day, first Monday in September

Bad Segeberg, Schleswig-Holstein, Federal Republic of Germany
May Festival, July-August

Bad Tölz, Bavaria, Germany
St. Leonard's Ride (Leonhardiritt), November 6

Bagmundi Village, Purilia District, West Bengal, India
Purilia Chhau Festival, April 11-13

Bagobo people in the Philippines
Ginem, at least one day in December

Bahama Islands
Columbus Day (Discovery Day), October 12
Emancipation Day, first Monday of August
Fox Hill Day, second Tuesday in August
Goombay Festival, July and August
Independence Day, July 10
Junkanoo Festival, December 26-January 1
Labour Day, June 4

Bahia, Brazil
Bonfim Festival, ten days beginning second Thursday
in January

Bahrain
Fast, Feast of Breaking the (Eed el Fitur), first day
of Islamic month of Shawwal
Independence Day, December 16
Ramadan, ninth Islamic month

Baile Herculane, Caras Severin, Romania
Folklore Festival, "Hercules," first week in August

Baile Jigodin Commune, Harghita, Romania
Spring, Harghita, third Sunday in May

Bainbridge, New York
Regatta, General Clinton Canoe, last weekend in May

Baja, Hungary
Folklore, Danube Festival of, every three years in July

Balanga, India
Chandan Yatra, 21 days beginning third day of waxing
half of Hindu month of Vaisakha

Bali, Indonesia
Eka Dasa Rundra, once every hundred years
New Year (Galungan), ten-day celebration, according
to Wauku calendar on 210 days per year
New Year's Celebration (Kuningen, Feast of All Souls),
final day of ten-day New Year's celebration, Galungan;
every 210 days
Temple Festivals, annual (temples throughout Bali)
Vernal Equinox (Nyepi), on or near March 21

Ballarat, Victoria, Australia
Begonia Festival, Ballarat, March

Ballycastle, Ireland
Lammas Fair Day, last Tuesday in August

Baltimore, Maryland
Defenders' Day, September 12
Kite Festival, Maryland, last Saturday in April

Bambara people in Mali
Tyi Wara, planting season in April, May, sometimes
the entire summer

Bamberg, Bavaria, Federal Republic of Germany
Calderon Festival in the Old Courtyard, June-July

Bamum people in Cameroon
Nja Festival, during the dry season, December or early
January

Baneasa, Galati, Romania
Peony Day, second Sunday in May

Banff, Alberta, Canada
Arts, Banff Festival of the, early June to late August

Bangkok, Thailand
Kite Flying Season, February-April on weekday afternoons
Ploughing Ceremony, April-May

Bangladesh
Fire Festival (Holi and Dol-Jatra, Swing Festival), begins
14th day of Hindu month of Phalguna or Dol; length varies
Independence Day, March 26
New Year (Vaisakhi), first day of Hindu month of Vaisakha
Shaheel or Shaheed Day or Martyrs Day, February 21
Sun Festival (Suryapuja), spring
Victory Day, December 16

Bannock Shoshone Indians in Idaho: Fort Hall
Indian Days, Fort Hall, August

Baoulé people in Ivory Coast
Dance, Klo, harvest season
New Yam Festival (Odwira), October

Barbados
Caricom Day, observed on or near July 4
Crop Over, last three weeks in June through first week
in July
Independence Day, November 30
Jazz Festival, Barbados/Caribbean, a Thursday through
Sunday in late May
World Food Day, October 16

Barbourville, Kentucky
Boone Festival, Daniel, first through second Saturdays
in October

Barbuda
Caricom Day, first Saturday in June

Barcelona, Spain
Music, Barcelona International Festival of (Festival
Internacional de Musica de Barcelona), month of October
Our Lady of Mercy, Festival of, September
Passio Festival, La, February-March, during Lent, the
forty days preceding Easter
Patum Festival, La, May-June, during Corpus Christi week
Puppets, International Festival of, April or May
St. George's Day, April 23
San Felix Martyr, Feast of, August

Barcelona, Estado Anzoategui, Venezuela
Theater, Eastern Festival of, ten days annually, date varies

Bar Harbor, Maine
Music Festival, Bar Harbor, mid-July to mid-August

Bari, Apulia, Italy
St. Nicholas's Day, May 7-8

Baripada, India
Chandan Yatra, 21 days beginning third day of waxing half
of Hindu month of Vaisakha

Barnesville, Pennsylvania
Summer Festival, Bavarian, 11 days in July

Barossa Valley, Tanunda, South Australia, Australia
Vintage Festival, Barossa Valley, March-April, seven days
beginning Easter Monday during odd-numbered years

Barranquilla, Atlántico, Colombia
Mardi Gras (Carnival), February-March, Friday-Tuesday
before Ash Wednesday

Barranquitas, Puerto Rico
Craft's Fair, three days in July, including July 17

Barsnar, India
Fire Festival (Holi), begins 14th day of Hindu month of
Phalguna; length varies

Basel, Switzerland
Ascension Day (Banntag), May-June, fortieth day after
Easter
Mardi Gras (Carnival), February-March
Summer-Nights Festival, Basel, June

Basilica of Our Lady of Guadalupe, Mexico City, Mexico
Our Lady of Guadalupe (Nuestra Señora de Guadalupe),
December 12

Basque-Americans in Idaho: Boise
St. Ignatius Loyola, Feast of, July 31

Basque-Americans in Nevada: Elko
Basque Festival, National, first or second weekend in
July

Basque people in Spain
Christmas Eve, December 24
St. Ignatius Loyola, Feast of, July 31
St. Nicholas's Day, December 6

Bas-Rhin, France
Music Festival, Strasbourg International (Festival
International de Musique de Strasbourg), 16 days
beginning first week in June

Basses-Pyrenees, France
Pau Festival, one week in June

Bataan, Luzon Island, Philippines
Passion Play, Cenaculo, March-April, Holy Week

Bath, Avon, England
Bath Festival, May or June

Bathurst, New South Wales, Australia
Bathurst Carillon City Tourist Festival, September-
October

Baton Rouge, Louisiana
Music, Louisiana State University Festival of Contemporary,
one week in early spring

Battleford, Saskatchewan, Canada
Battleford Chautauqua, July

Batu Caves, Malaysia
Thaipusam, one day in January-February

Bavaria
All Souls' Day, November 2
Bayreuth Festival (Bayreuther Festspiele and Richard
Wagner Festival), five weeks in late July and August
Franconian Festival Week, June
Mardi Gras (Fasching), February-March
Mid-Lent Sunday, March, fourth Sunday in Lent
Palm Sunday, March-April, the Sunday preceding Easter

Bavaria, Federal Republic of Germany
Ballet Festival Week, March or May
Bayreuth Festival (Bayreuther Festspiele and Richard
Wagner Festival), five weeks in late July and August
Calderon Festival in the Old Courtyard, June-July
Children's Reckoning (Kinderzeche), Saturday before the
third Monday of June
Cloister Festival, June-August
European Festival Weeks, June-July

Bavaria, Federal Republic of Germany *(cont.)*
Franconian Festival Week, June
Landshut Wedding, three weeks, including four Sundays in June-July, every third year
Luisenburg Festival, June-August
Mardi Gras (Fasching Carnival), January 7-Tuesday before Ash Wednesday
Master Draught Pageant (Meistertrunk Pageant), May-June, Pentecost or Whitsunday
Oktoberfest, 16 days, usually beginning first Sunday in October
Opera Festival, Munich (Münchner Opernfestspiele), 25 days in July-August
Passion Play, Oberammergau, every ten years from May to September
Theatre, International Festival of Free, April-May
Theatre, Summer Festival at the Bergwald, weekends in June-July
Theatre Festival, Dinkelsbühl Open-Air, June-August

Bavaria, Germany
Christkindlesmarkt (Kriss Kringle's Fair), early December until Christmas, December 25
Mozart Festival, German (Deutsches Mozartfest), eight days during second week in June (alternates with other German cities)
St. Leonard's Ride (Leonhardiritt), November 6
St. Michael's Day (Tura Michele Marky or Fair), September 29

Bayfield, Wisconsin
Powwow, Ojibwa, August or September

Bayou La Batre, Alabama
Blessing of the Shrimp Fleet, last weekend in June

Bayreuth, Bavaria, Federal Republic of Germany
Bayreuth Festival (Bayreuther Festspiele and Richard Wagner Festival), five weeks in late July and August
Franconian Festival Week, June

Bean Blossom, Indiana
Bluegrass Festival, Bean Blossom, five days in spring

Bear Valley, California
Music from Bear Valley, last week in July to second week in August

Beaune, Meursault, and Nuit-St. Georges in Cote-d'Or, France
Three Glorious Days (Les Trois Glorieuses), twice annually: July 27-29 and third Saturday through Monday in November

Beaupré, Quebec, Canada
Pilgrimage to St. Anne d'Auray, July 26

Beavers Bend State Park, Broken Bow, Oklahoma
Happy Hunting Party, Festival of the Forest (Kiamichi Owa Chito), late June

Becej, Vojvodina, Yugoslavia
Games of May, May

Becket, Massachusetts
Dance Festival, Jacob's Pillow, eight weeks from June to September

Bedford, Pennsylvania
Powwow, American Indian, second Saturday and Sunday in July

Bedouin people
Ramadan, ninth Islamic month

Beira Baixa, Portugal
Pilgrimage to Nossa Senhora dos Altos Ceus

Beira Litoral, Portugal
Holy Queen, Festival of the (Festa da Rainha Santa Isabel), first two weeks in July during even-numbered years

Beja, Portugal
Our Lady of Mount Carmel (Senhora do Monte do Carmo), October

Beja Region, Tunisia
Dougga, Festival of, July

Bekáa Valley, throughout Syria, Lebanon, and former Palestine
Springtime Festival, March-April, four successive Thursdays before Orthodox Easter

Belalp, Valais, Switzerland
Shepherd Sunday (Schäfer Sonntag), second Sunday in September

Belfast, Northern Ireland
Belfast Festival, two and one-half weeks in November

Belgian-Americans in Minnesota: Ghent
Belgian-American Days, four days in August

Belgium
All Saints' Day (Aller Heiligen Dag), November 1
All Souls' Day, November 2
Annunciation, Feast of the (Notre Dame de la Prospérité), March 25
Armistice Day, November 11
Arts en Belgique, Europalia Festival des, every other autumn

Belgium *(cont.)*

Assumption, Feast of the (Festival of Virga Jesse), third and fourth Sundays in August every seven years

Assumption, Feast of the (Maia-Hemelvaart Dat), August 15

Begonia Festival, three days in August

Bruegel Feesten, second Sunday in September every other year

Brussels International Fair, April-May

Cat Festival (Kattestoet), second Sunday in May every three years

Christmas (Kerstdag), December 25

Christmas Eve (Kerstavond), December 24

Corpus Christi, May-June

Dynasty Day (Fête de la Dynastie), November 15

Easter (Paschen), March-April, first Sunday after first full moon after the vernal equinox

Epiphany (Dreikoningendag, Day of the Kings), January 5-6

Flanders, Festival of (Festival van Vlaanderen), April to October

Flower Festival (Ghent Floralies), April or May, every five years

Folk-Dance Festival, International (International Volksdansfestival), one week beginning first weekend after first Sunday in July

Folklore Festival, International, four days in August

Game of St. Evermaire (Spel van Sint Evermarus), May 1

Golden Chariot and Battle of the Lumecon, Procession of the, May-June, Trinity Sunday

Good Friday (Goede Vrydag), March-April, Friday preceding Easter Sunday

Holy Blood, Procession of the (Processie van het Heilig Bloed), observed first Monday after May 2

Holy Innocents' Day (Le Jour des Innocents), December 28

Holy Saturday (Zaterdag voor Paschen), March-April, Saturday before Easter Sunday

Holy Thursday (Witte Donderdag), March-April, Thursday preceding Easter

Independence Day, July 21

La Meuse Festival, July-August

Mardi Gras (Bal du Rat Mort, Dead Rat's Ball), January-March, usually the weekend before Lent

Mardi Gras (Carnival of the Gilles, or Clowns), February-March, Sunday-Tuesday before Ash Wednesday

Mardi Gras (Vastenavond), February-March

Marriage of Goliath (Les Vêpres de Gouyasse), fourth weekend in August

Martinmas, November 11

May Day, May 1

Midsummer (Sint Jans Vorravond), June 23-24

Music, Opera and Theatre, Durbuy Festival of, July-August

Music Competition, Queen Elisabeth International (Concours Musical International Reine Elisabeth), May

New Year's Day (Nieuwjaarsdag), January 1

New Year's Eve, December 31

Ommegang Pageant, first Thursday in July

Penitents, Procession of the (Boetprocessie van Veurne), last Sunday in July

Pentecost, May-June, the Sunday fifty days after Easter

Quadragesima Sunday, February-March, first Sunday in Lent

St. Bartholomew's Day, August 24

St. Dymphna's Day, May 15

St. Gregory's Day, March 12

St. Gudula's Day, January 8

St. Hubert, Feast Day of, November 3

St. Médardus or Médard's Day, June 8

St. Nicholas's Day, December 6

St. Peter's Day, June 29

St. Sylvester's Day, December 31

St. Thomas the Apostle, Feast of, December 21

Sts. Peter and Paul Day (Ceremony of Blessing of the Sea at Ostend, Blankenberge, and other seaport towns), Sunday following June 29

Shrimp Festival, early July

Spa, Festival of, August

Summer Festival, International, July-August

Theatre, Liège Festival of Young (Le Festival du Jeune Theatre de Liège), October

Theatre Festival of Stavelot, Vacation (Les Vacances-Theatre de Stavelot), July

Trinity Sunday, May-June; observed first Sunday after Pentecost

Twelfth Night (Epiphany Eve), January 5

Verviers, Festival of, February

Wallonia, Festival of (Festival de Wallonie), June-September or October

Whit Monday (Déjeuner Matrimonial, Matrimonial Tea), May-June, Monday after Pentecost

Witches, Procession of the, last Sunday in July

Belgrade, Serbia, Yugoslavia

Amateur Stages, Belgrade Review of Experimental, mid-May

Amateurs to Their City, October 20

First of May Is Our Day, May 1-2

Theatre Community Festival, early September

Theatre Festival, Belgrade Amateur, April

Theatre Festival, Belgrade International, September

Belize

Baron Bliss Day, March 9

Christmas, December 25

Independence Day, September 21

Junkanoo Festival

National Day, September 10

Bella Coola Indians in Canada: coastal British Columbia

Midwinter Rites, Bella Coola (Kusiut), November-February

Bellac, Haute-Vienne, France

Bellac Festival, June-July

Belleville, Illinois
Indian Celebration, American, July 17

Bellingham, Washington
Warrior or Veteran Festival, Stommish, month of June

Bemidji, Minnesota
Logging Days, Buena Vista, last Saturday in February

Bengal, India
Fire Festival (Dol Purnima), begins 14th day of Hindu
  month of Phalguna or Dol; length varies
Goddess of Fortune, Festival of the (Lukshmi or Laksmi
  Puja), during Hindu month of Asvina
Lights, Festival of (Dewali and Kali Festival), one week
  during waning half of Hindu month of Karthika, including
  15th day
Mother Goddess, Festival of Durga, the (Durga Puja), first
  ten days of waxing half of Hindu month of Asvina
New Year (Vaisakhi), first day of Hindu month of Vaisakha
Shasti, Festival of (Aranya Shasti)
Shiva, Gajan of, during Hindu month of Chaitra
Snake Festival (Naag Panchami), fifth day of waxing half
  of Hindu month of Sravana
Spring Festival (Vasant or Basant Panchami), fifth day
  of waxing half of Hindu month of Magha

Bengal (eastern), India
Varuna, Festival of, full moon day of Hindu month of
  Karthika

Benin
Independence Day, August 1

Benin, Nigeria
New Yam Festival, two-day festival in August

Bennington, Vermont
Bennington Battle Day, August 16

Berawan people in Malaysia: Sarawak
Harvest Festival (Bungan), February

Berea, Ohio
Bach Festival, Baldwin-Wallace, two days in mid-May

Berchtesgaden, Germany
Christmas Eve (Christmas Shooting), December 24

Berga, Barcelona, Spain
Patum Festival, La, May-June, during Corpus Christi
  week

Bergama, Turkey
Pergamum, Festival of, May

Bergen, Norway
Bergen International Festival (Festspillene i Bergen),
  15 days beginning last week in May
Moving Day (Flyttedag), autumn and April 14

Berkshire, England
Ascot, Royal, four days in mid-June
Windsor Festival, two weeks in mid-September

Berlin, Federal Republic of Germany
Berlin Festival Weeks (Berliner Festwochen), four weeks
  beginning first week in September

Bermuda
Bermuda College Weeks, four to five weeks in March-April
Bermuda Festival, January-February
Easter, March-April, first Sunday after first full moon
  after the vernal equinox
Good Friday, March-April, Friday preceding Easter Sunday
Newport to Bermuda Race, June during even-numbered years
Peppercorn Day, on or near April 23
Remembrance Day, November 11
Tellabration, November, the Friday before Thanksgiving

Bern, Switzerland
Interlaken Festival, June-August
Onion Market (Zibelemarit or Zybelemärit), fourth
  Monday in November
Play, Spiez Castle, three times per week in August
Plays at Interlaken, Wilhelm Tell Pastoral, July-August
Theatres, Bern International Festival of Small, three weeks
  in June

Besançon, Doubs, France
Besançon International Festival (Festival International
  de Besançon), two weeks beginning September 1

Beselare, Belgium
Witches, Procession of the, last Sunday in July

Betanzos, La Coruna, Spain
St. Roch's Day (San Roque Festival), August

Bete people in Ivory Coast
New Yam Festival (Odwira), October

Bethel, Maine
Mollyockett Day, third Saturday in July

Bethel/Redding area of Connecticut
Patriots' Weekend, Annual, last weekend in
  September

Bethlehem, Connecticut
Abbey Fair, two days in early August

Bethlehem, Jordan
Christmas, December 25
Christmas Eve, December 24

Bethlehem, Pennsylvania
Bach Music Festival, two weekends in May

Betton, Ille-et-Vilaine, France
Ille Festival, one week in May or June

Bhaktapur, Nepal
New Year (Bisket Jatra), first day of Hindu month of
Vaisakha

Bhit Shah, Sind, Pakistan
Shah Abdul Latif Death Festival, 14-16 days during
Islamic month of Safar

Bhopal, Madhya Pradesh, India
Drama Festival, Kalidasa, first week in November

Bhubaneswar, Orissa, India
Ashokashtami, eighth day of waxing half of Hindu
month of Chaitra
Chandan Yatra, 21 days beginning third day of waxing
half of Hindu month of Vaisakha
Drama Festival, Orissa Academy, five days in March-April

Bhutan
King's Birthday, November 11
New Year (Losar), beginning or end of February
Paro Tshechu, tenth to 15th days of second lunar month

Bialystok, Poland
Puppet Theatre Festival, International, March during
odd-numbered years

Bielsko-Biala, Poland
Puppet Theatre, International Festival of, May-June
during even-numbered years

Bihac, Bosnia and Herzegovina, Yugoslavia
Folklore and Amateur Work in Culture and Arts, autumn

Bihar, India
Dance Festival, Chhau Mask, Chaitra-Parva, April 11-13
Lights, Festival of (Dewali), one week during waning half
of Hindu month of Karthika, including 15th day
Sravani Mela, during Hindu month of Sravana

Bijelo Polje, Montenegro, Yugoslavia
Drama Amateurs of Montenegro, Festival of, June

Bikfaya, Lebanon
Flower Festival, Bikfaya, one day in mid-August

Billingham, Cleveland, England
Folklore Festival, Billingham International, eight days
in August

Biloxi, Alabama
Blessing of the Fishing Fleet and Biloxi Shrimp Festival
and Fais Do Do, first weekend in June

Binche, Belgium
Mardi Gras (Carnival of the Gilles, or Clowns), February-
March, Sunday-Tuesday before Ash Wednesday

Binger, Oklahoma
Labor Day, three days, including first Monday in
September

Binghamton, New York
Binghamton Festival, July and August

Birmingham, Alabama
Arts, Birmingham Festival of the, two weeks in April-May

Bisbee, Arizona
Poetry Festival, two days in mid-August

Bishop, California
Mule Days, last weekend in May

Bishop Hill, Illinois
Agricultural Days (Jordoruksdagarna), two days in late
September

Bitola, Macedonia, Yugoslavia
Ilinden Days Festival, July-August

Blackfeet Indians
Dance, Sun, usually during summer solstice, June 21

Blackfeet Reservation in Montana: Browning
Indian Days, North American, second week in July

Black Forest, Germany
Nativity of the Virgin, Feast of the (Pferdeweihe, Blessing
of Horses), September 8

Bloemfontein, South Africa
Republic Day (Union Day), May 31

Bloomington, Idaho
Pioneer Day, July 24

Blue Hill, Maine
Kneisel Hall, seven weeks from last week in June to
mid-August

Blyth, Ontario, Canada
Summer Festival, Blyth, July-August

Boac, Marinduque Island, Philippines
Moriones Festival, March-April, Good Friday to Easter Sunday

Bocairente, Valencia, Spain
Battle of the Moors and Christians, February

Bochum, North Rhine-Westphalia, Federal Republic of Germany
Puppet Theatre of the Nations, International Festival Week, one week in May or June

Bodh Gaya, India
Buddha's Birthday, Enlightenment, and Salvation (Buddha Jayanti), full moon day of Hindu month of Vaisakha

Bodrum, Turkey
Bodrum Festival, September

Boeothia (ancient)
Dædala, in spring about every six years (Little Dædala); every 60 years (Great Dædala)

Boer people in South Africa
Majuba Day (Hill of Doves), February 27

Bogota, Cundinamarca, Colombia
Theatre, National Festival of New (Festival Nacional del Nuevo Teatro), November-December

Bohemia (now part of Czechoslovakia)
Christmas, December 25
Easter, March-April, first Sunday after first full moon after the vernal equinox
Easter Monday, March-April, Monday after Easter
Holy Innocents' Day, December 28
Mardi Gras (Carnival), February-March
Midsummer, June 23-24
New Year's Day, January 1
Pentecost, May-June, the Sunday fifty days after Easter
St. Barbara's Day, December 4
St. Nicholas's Day, December 6
St. Stephen, Feast of, December 26

Boise, Idaho
St. Ignatius Loyola, Feast of, July 31

Bolivar, Venezuela
Theatre, Festival of Popular, annual, date varies

Bolivia
Alasita Fair ("Buy from Me" Fair), January 24

All Saints' Day (Kawsasqanchis, Our Living with the Dead), November 1
Immaculate Conception, Feast of the (Fiesta of Concepción), December 8
Independence Day, August 6, two-day festival
Llama Ch'uyay, July 31-August 1
Mardi Gras (Carnival Week), February-March, week before Lent begins
New Year's Eve, December 31
St. James the Greater's Day, July 25
St. John, Apostle and Evangelist, Feast of (San Juan's Day), December 27
St. Michael's Day (Fiesta de San Miguel), September 29

Bolivia (eastern)
New Year's Day, when the Pleiades appear

Boljevac, Serbia, Yugoslavia
Dances and Songs of Crnorecje, May

Bombay, Maharashtra, India
Drama Festival, Bombay, January
Elephant God, Festival of the (Ganesha Chaturthi), one-week festival, including fourth day of Hindu month of Bhadrapada
Sacred Thread Festival (Raksha Bandhan), full moon day of Hindu month of Sravana
Tamasha Festival, November-December (location rotates)

Bonaire, Netherlands Antilles
Regatta, International, four days in October

Bonn, North Rhine-Westphalia, Federal Republic of Germany
Beethoven Festival, September-October
Dance Workshop, Bonn International, July

Bonneville Salt Flats, Utah
Bonneville Speed Week, third week in August

Boothbay Harbor, Maine
Windjammer Days, three days in mid-July

Bophuthatswana
Independence Day, December 6

Boquete, Panama
Coffee Fair and Flower Festival, four days in late April

Bordeaux, Gironde, France
Musical, Bordeaux International May (Mai Musical International), 16 days beginning first week in May
Sigma Festival, one week in November

Borgu, West Africa
Muhammad's Birthday (Game Festival), twelfth day of Islamic month of Rabi al-Awwal

Borneo
Mobog, annual

Bornholm, Denmark
Music Festival, Ronne, Wednesdays and Fridays in July
and August

Bornu, West Africa
Muhammad's Birthday, twelfth day of Islamic month of
Rabi al-Awwal

Borsa, Maramures County, Romania
Dance Festival, Hora at Prislop (Prislop Round), second
Sunday in August

Bosnia and Herzegovina, Yugoslavia
Drama Amateurs, Yugoslav, end of June-beginning of July
Folklore and Amateur Work in Culture and Arts, autumn
October Days of Culture, October
Puppet Theatres of Bosnia and Herzegovina, Meeting
of, May
Theatre Festival of Bosnia and Herzegovina, June
Theatres of Bosnia and Herzegovina, Encounter of
Professional, October
Theatres of Yugoslavia, Festival of Small and
Experimental, March 27-April 6

Boston, Massachusetts
Bastille Day, July 14
Boston Marathon, April 19 or nearest Monday
Boston Massacre Day, March 5
Boston Pops, first week in May to middle of July
Bunker Hill Day, June 17
Esplanade Concerts, early July
Ether Day, October 15
Evacuation Day, March 17
Fawkes Day, Guy, November 5
Jazz Festival, *Boston Globe*, one week in March
Mardi Gras, February-March
New Year's Eve (First Night), December 31

Botosani, Romania
Winter Traditions, Festival of, last week in December

Botswana
Independence Day, September 30
World Environment Day, June 5

Bouches-du-Rhone, France
Arles Festival, July-August

Boulder, Colorado
Music Festival, Colorado, mid-June to early August

Bourgas, Bulgaria
Folk-Art Festival, late summer

Box Elder, Montana
Indian Days, Rocky Boy, usually first weekend in August

Brabant Wallon, Belgium
Wallonia, Festival of (Festival de Wallonie), June-September
or October

Bradenton, Florida
(De) Soto Celebration, one week in March or early April

Bradford, West Yorkshire, England
Thornton Festival, last week in June

Brady Lake, Ohio
Brady Day, Captain, July-August

Braemar, Scotland
Highland Gathering, Braemar, first Saturday in September

Braga, Portugal
Folklore Festival, Briteiros, August
Folklore Festival, Sao Torcato International, July
Vizela Festival, one week in August

Braganca, Portugal
Pilgrimage to Our Lady of Nazo, September
St. Barbara's Festival, August

Brahman caste in Thailand: Bangkok
Ploughing Ceremony, April-May

Braintree, Essex, England
Arts Festival, Braintree District, six weeks in April-May

Brana de Aristebano, Luarca, Oviedo, Spain
Vaqueiros de Alzada Festival, July

Branson, Missouri
Kewpiesta, third weekend in April

Brantford, Ontario, Canada
Highland Games, Brantford, second Saturday in July

Brasilia, Brazil
Mambembao, January-March

Brasov, Transylvania, Romania
Mountains, Festival of the (Nedeia Muntilor), last weekend
in June
Theatre, Festival of Contemporary, one week in January

Bratislava, Slovakia, Czechoslovakia
Music Festival, Bratislava, October 1-15

Braughing, Hertfordshire, England
Old Man's Day, October 2

Braunschweig, Lower Saxony, Federal Republic of Germany
Puppet Play Week, International, one week in March during odd-numbered years

Brazil
Assumption, Feast of the (Nossa Senhora dos Navegantes), August 15
Bonfim Festival, ten days beginning second Thursday in January
Candlemas, February 2
Caruaru Roundup, three days in September
Christmas, December 25
Círio de Nazaré, second Sunday in October
Divino, Festo do, May-June, Saturday before Pentecost
Foundation Day, January 20
Holy Spirit, Festival of the Divine, one week in May
Iemanjá Festival, February
Independence Day, September 7
Jesus dos Navegantes, Bom, January 1
Juninas, Festas (Bumba-meu-Boi folk drama), June 13-29
Low Sunday, March-April, Sunday following Easter
Mambembao, January-March
Mardi Gras (Carnival), February-March, the four days before Ash Wednesday
Memorial Day, November 2
Midsummer, June 23-24 until June 29
New Year's Day, January 1
New Year's Eve, January 31 (Umbanda religion)
Our Lady of Aparecida, May 11
Our Lady of the Happy Ending, January
Pentecost, May-June, the Sunday fifty days after Easter
St. Sebastian's Day, January 20
Sts. Cosmas and Damian Day (Cosme e Damião), September 27
Tiradentes (Tooth Puller Day; Inconfidência Week), April 21

Brcko, Bosnia and Herzegovina, Yugoslavia
Theatres of Bosnia and Herzegovina, Encounter of Professional, October

Breaux Bridge, Louisiana
Crawfish Festival, first weekend in May

Brebu, Prahova, Romania
Pages of History, last weekend in July

Breckenridge, Colorado
Ullr Fest, third week in January

Bregenz, Vorarlberg, Tirol, Austria
Bregenz Festival (Bregenzer Festspiele), four weeks in July-August

Breton people
Christmas Eve, December 24
Cornwall, Festival of, one week in July

Brevard, North Carolina
Music Center, Brevard, seven weeks from late June to mid-August

Brewton, Alabama
Blueberry Festival, Alabama, third Saturday in June

Bridgeport, Connecticut
Barnum Festival, P.T., 17 days from late June to July 4
Soul, Festival of the (Mahrajan), September 1

Bridgetown, Barbados
Crop Over, last three weeks in June through first week in July

Brighton, Sussex, England
Brighton Festival, April-May

Brindisi, Italy
Corpus Christi (Procession of the Decorated Horse), May-June

Brisbane, Queensland, Australia
Drama Festival, Warana (Blue Skies), two weeks in September-October
Spring Festival, Warana (Blue Skies), September-October

Britain
See **Great Britain**

Briteiros, Braga, Portugal
Folklore Festival, Briteiros, August

British Columbia, Canada
Air Show, International, three days in August
Drama Festival, Okanagan Zone, May
'Ksan Celebrations, Friday evenings in July and August
Performance '78,'79, etc., June
Polar Bear Swim Day, January 1
Snowgolf Championship, three days in February
Vancouver Heritage Festival, May-June
Vancouver International Festival, late May to late June
Victoria International Festival, six weeks beginning in early July

British Columbia (coastal), Canada
Midwinter Rites, Bella Coola (Kusiut), November-February

British Commonwealth countries
Commonwealth Day (formerly Empire Day), second Monday in March
Girl Guides Thinking Day, February 22
Victoria Day (Empire Day), Monday nearest May 24

British Isles
  See **Great Britain**

British Virgin Islands
  See **Virgin Islands**

British West Indies
  Christmas, December 25

Britt, Iowa
  Hobo Convention, three days in August

Brittany (now part of France)
  All Souls' Day (Le Jour de Morts), November 2
  Beltane, April 30
  St. Bartholomew's Day, August 24

Brittany, France
  Pilgrimage to St. Anne d'Auray, July 26; observed last
    weekend in July

Brno, Moravia, Czechoslovakia
  Mimes, International Festival of Deaf, odd-numbered
    years during second half of November
  Music Festival, Brno International, October

Broadstairs, Kent, England
  Broadstairs Dickens Festival, eight days in June

Brockton, Montana
  Indian Celebration, Badlands, fourth weekend
    in June

Broken Bow, Oklahoma
  Happy Hunting Party, Festival of the Forest (Kiamichi
    Owa Chito), late June

Bronx, New York
  Arts Series, Wave Hill Performing, September
    to May

Brooklyn, New York
  Constitution Day, Norway, May 17
  Simhat Torah (Rejoicing in the Law), 23rd of Jewish
    month of Tishri

Browning, Montana
  Indian Days, North American, second week in July

Brownsville, Texas
  Charro Days Fiesta, February-March, four days beginning
    Thursday of the weekend before Lent

Brown University, Providence, Rhode Island
  Carberry Day, every Friday the 13th

Bruges, West Flanders, Belgium
  Flanders, Festival of (Festival van Vlaanderen), April
    to October
  Holy Blood, Procession of the (Processie van het Heilig
    Bloed), observed first Monday after May 2

Brugg/Windisch, Aargau, Switzerland
  Konigsfelden Festival, weekends in August-September
    during even-numbered years

Brunei
  Constitution Day, September 29

Brunswick, Maine
  Music, Gamper Festival of Contemporary, one week
    in late July
  Music Festival, Bowdoin Summer, last week in June to
    first week in August

Brussels, Belgium
  Arts en Belgique, Europalia Festival des, every other autumn
  Brussels International Fair, April-May
  Flanders, Festival of (Festival van Vlaanderen), April
    to October
  Music Competition, Queen Elisabeth International
    (Concours Musical International Reine Elisabeth), May
  Ommegang Pageant, first Thursday in July
  Wallonia, Festival of (Festival de Wallonie), June-September
    or October

Bucchianico, Abruzzi, Italy
  Banderesi, Festival of the, six days in May

Bucharest, Romania
  Song to Romania, odd-numbered years in June

Buciumeni, Galati, Romania
  Lime-Tree Day, last Sunday in June

Buckinghamshire, England
  Wavendon Season, May-July

Bucks County, Pennsylvania
  Labor Day, first Monday in September

Budapest, Hungary
  Artistic Weeks, Budapest, September-October
  Music Weeks, Budapest, September-October
  Opera and Ballet, Budapest Concerts and Open-Air, late
    June to late August
  Theatre on Margaret Island, Open-Air, July-August

Budva, Montenegro, Yugoslavia
  South, Festival of the, July-August

Buena Vista, Fairplay and Leadville, Colorado
Burro Races, Triple Crown Pack, last weekend in July
through August

Buenos Aires, Argentina
Independence Day, May 25 and July 9

Buffalo, New York
St. Jude's Day, October 28

Bukhara
Passover (Pesach), March-April, eight days beginning
15th of Nisan
Sukkot (Feast of Booths or Feast of the Tabernacles),
15th-21st or 22nd of Jewish month of Tishri

Bukit Mertajam, Malaysia
Panguni Uttiram, ten days, including the full moon day
of Hindu month of Chaitra

Bulacan, Luzon Island, Philippines
Dances of Obando, three days in mid-May

Bulgaria
Assumption, Feast of the (Bogoroditza), August 15
Awakeners, Day of the (Den na Buditelite), November 1
Botev Day, May 20
Christmas (Koleda, Rozhdestvo Khristovo), December 25
Christmas Eve (Budnivecher), December 24
Drama, National Review of Modern Bulgarian, every five
years in June
Drama, Review of Classical, every five years, date varies
Drama, Review of Historical, every three years, date varies
Easter (Velikdien, the Great Day, or Vuzkresenie,
Resurrection Day), March-April, first Sunday after first
full moon after the vernal equinox
Epiphany (Bogoyavleniye, Blessing of the Waters),
January 6, Gregorian calendar (N.S.); January 19,
Julian calendar (O.S.)
First of March (Martenitza), March 1
Folk Art, National Festival of, every five years during
the summer
Folk-Art Festival, late summer
Golden Dolphin, every three years in October
Golden Orpheus, ten days in June
Good Friday (Raspeti Petuk, Crucifixion Friday), March-
April, Friday preceding Easter Sunday
Grandmother's Day (Babin Den), January 20
Holy Day of Letters (Sts. Cyril and Methodius of
Thessalonica), May 24, Gregorian calendar (N.S.);
May 11, Julian calendar (O.S.)
Holy Saturday (Strastna Subota, Passion Saturday),
March-April, Saturday before Easter Sunday
Holy Week (Strastna Nedelya), March-April, week
preceding Easter

Humor and Satire Festival, National, late May
Lent, February-March, forty-day season preceding Easter
Liberation Day, March 3
Mardi Gras (Sirna Sedmitza, Cheese Week), February-
March, the week before Ash Wednesday
National Day, September 9
New Year's Day (Nova Godina), January 1
Oral Interpretation, Competition in, even-numbered years,
date varies
Palm Sunday, March-April, the Sunday preceding Easter
Plays, Holidays of the Soviet, every five years, date varies
Plough Monday, first Monday after Epiphany or Twelfth
Day, January 6
Poetry of Friendship, even-numbered years in March
Puppet Theatres, Holidays of Amateur, even-numbered years
in April
Puppet Theatres, National Review of Professional, every five
years in October
Rose Festival, ten days from late May to early June
St. Lazarus's Day, March-April, Saturday before Palm
or Easter Sunday
Singing to Rings (Ladouvane), January 1 in western
Bulgaria; June 24 in the rest of the country
Theatre, Holidays of Amateur, April during even-
numbered years
Theatre, International Festival of Children's and Youth's,
every four years, date varies
Theatre, National Review of Children's and Youth's, every
three years, date varies
Theatre, National Review of Pocket, every five years, date
varies
Theatre Days, Summer, every three years in June-July
Theatre Days Named after Drumev, during even-numbered
years, date varies
Vinegrower's Day (Trifon Zarezan, Viticulturists' Day),
February 14

Bulgarian-Canadians
First of March, March 1

Bundi people in Papua New Guinea
Pig Festival

**Bûngi Indians in the Great Plains of the United
States**
Dance, Sun, usually during summer solstice, June 21

Burgundy, France
Mardi Gras (Carnival), February-March

Burgenland, Austria
Castle Kobersdorf Festival, July
Castle Plays Festival, June-July
Lake Festival (Seespiele), August
Passion Play, May-September; every five years

Burkina Faso (formerly Upper Volta)
Bobo Masquerade, April or May, before the first rain
See also **Upper Volta**

Burley, Idaho
Regatta, Idaho, last weekend in June

Burlington, Vermont
Mozart Festival, Vermont, three weeks from mid-July to
first week in August

Burma (now Myanmar)
Buddha's Birthday, Enlightenment, and Salvation (Kason
Festival of Watering the Banyon Tree or Full Moon
of Waso), eighth day of fourth lunar month
Independence Day, January 4
Lenten Season (Paung-daw-U Pagoda Festival), begins
during Wazo, fourth lunar month, and ends on the 15th
or full moon day of Thadingyut, seventh lunar month
Martyrs Day, July 19
National Day, December 10
New Year (Thingyan; Pwe), mid-April, when Sun is in
Aries, first through fourth days of Burmese month of Tagu
Peasants' Day, one week, including March 2
Resistance Day, March 27
Shinbyu, summer
Tazaungdaing, October-November, full moon day of
Burmese month of Tazauungmon
Union Day, February 12
See also **Myanmar**

Burnie, Tasmania, Australia
Drama Festival, Burnie Youth, last week in July

Bursa, Turkey
Bursa Festival, July

Burundi
Independence Day, July 1

Buryat people in Siberia
Archery Festival (Sur-Kharban), spring

Buskett Gardens, Malta
Harvest Festival (Imnarja or Mnarja), last week in June,
including June 29

Butler University, Indianapolis, Indiana
Romantic Festival, last two weekends in April

Butte, Montana
Union Day, Miners', June 13

Buxton, England
Buxton Festival, three and one-half weeks in July

Byblos, Lebanon
Byblos Festival, May-September

Byelorussia, USSR
Mushroom Harvest, late September or early October

Byng School near Ada, Oklahoma
Chickasaw Nation Annual Day, first Saturday in October

Cable, Wisconsin
Birkebeiner, American (the Birkie), three days in late
February

Caddo Indians in Oklahoma: Binger
Labor Day, three days, including first Monday in September

Cadiz, Ohio
Gable Birthday Celebration, Clark, Saturday nearest
February 1

Cádiz, Spain
Horse Fair, May
Vintage Feast (Fiesta de la Vendimia), mid-September
Wine Festival, Jerez, September

Caesarea, Israel
Israel Festival, dates vary, sometime between May and
September

Cagliari, Sardinia, Italy
St. Efisio, Festival of, May 1-4

Cahuilla Indians in California
Malki Museum Fiesta, last weekend in May

Cainta, Rizal, Luzon Island, Philippines
Passion Play, Cenaculo, March-April, Holy Week

Calabar, Nigeria
Easter, March-April, first Sunday after first full moon
after the vernal equinox

Calaveras Fairgrounds, Angels Camp, California
Calaveras County Fair and Frog Jumping Jubilee,
May 13-16

Calchaqui Valley, Argentina
Mardi Gras (Tincunaco Ceremony), February-March,
Thursday before Ash Wednesday

Calcutta, West Bengal, India
Jatra Festivals of Calcutta, ten to 15 days in winter
Simhat Torah, 23rd day of Jewish month of Tishri
Tagore, Birthday of Rabindranath, May 7
Theatre Festivals, Children's Little, second week in May
and three weeks in December

Caldas de Vizela, Braga, Portugal
Vizela Festival, one week in August

Calexico, California
Cinco de Mayo, May 5

Calf Island, Zealand, Denmark
Viking Festival, three days to two weeks in June-July

Calgary, Alberta, Canada
Calgary Exhibition and Stampede, July

Calico, California
Calico Pitchin', Cookin', and Spittin' Hullabaloo, March-April, Palm Sunday weekend

California
Acorn Festival, usually weekend after fourth Friday in September
Admission Day, September 9
All Souls' Day, November 2
All Souls' Day (Night of the Candle Ceremony), November 2
Arts and Pageant of the Masters, Festival of the, 45 days in July and August
Bach Festival, Carmel, mid-July to early August
Beethoven Festival, three weeks beginning mid-June
Bird and Arbor Day, March 7
Bok Kai Festival, March or April, second day of second lunar month
Buddha's Birthday, Enlightenment, and Salvation, eighth day of fourth lunar month
Burbank Day, March 7
Cabrillo Day, six days in September
Calaveras County Fair and Frog Jumping Jubilee, May 13-16
Calico Pitchin', Cookin', and Spittin' Hullabaloo, March-April, Palm Sunday weekend
California Gold Rush Day, observed weekend nearest January 24
Chaw-Se Big Time Celebration, usually last weekend in September
Cherry Blossom Festival, one week in April
Christmas Boat Parade, Newport Harbor, December 17-23
Christmas Eve, December 24
Cinco de Mayo, May 5
Cowboys Parade, Black, first Saturday in October
Crab Races, World Championship, Sunday before third Monday in February
Dance, Bear, dates vary
Dead, Observance for the (Keruk), seven nights annually
Easter (Hollywood Bowl Sunrise Service), March-April, first Sunday after first full moon after the vernal equinox
Easter (Sunrise Service), March-April, first Sunday after first full moon after the vernal equinox
Exaltation of the Cross (Santacruzan), May 3
Halloween, Saturday before October 31

Holy Saturday (Blessing of the Animals), March-April, Saturday before Easter Sunday
Indian Acorn Festival, Mi-Wuk, annual
Indian Day, August
Jazz Festival, Concord, one weekend in August
Jazz Festival, Monterey, third weekend in September
Jazz Festival, Playboy, third weekend in June
Jazz Festival, Summer, five weekend concerts over July and August
Jazz Jubilee, Sacramento Dixieland, four days over last weekend in May
Kule Loklo Celebration, July or August
Lemoore Celebration, late August
Malki Museum Fiesta, last weekend in May
Mozart Festival, San Luis Obispo, six days in late July and early August
Mule Days, last weekend in May
Music Academy of the West Summer Festival, eight weeks from last week in June to third week in August
Music Festival, Cabrillo, ten days in late July
Music Festival, Idyllwild, last two weeks in August
Music Festival, Mendocino, two weeks in mid-July
Music Festival, Redlands Bowl Summer, Tuesday and Friday evenings from late June to late August
Music Festival, Stern Grove Midsummer, mid-June to mid-August for ten Sundays
Music from Bear Valley, last week in July to second week in August
Music in the Mountains, two weeks in mid-June
Native American Day, fourth Friday in September
Nisei Week, August
Ojai Festival, three days in late May
Old Spanish Days, five days during full moon in August
Our Lady of Guadalupe, December 12
Our Lady of Miracles (Nossa Senhora dos Milagres or Festa de Serreta), September 8-15
Pan American Festival Week, two days in late April or early May
Pentecost, May-June, the Sunday fifty days after Easter
Primavera, Fiesta de la, three days in May
Rose Bowl Game, January 1
St. Anthony the Abbot of Egypt, Feast of (Blessing of the Animals), January 17
St. Francis of Assisi, Feast of, October 4
St. John the Baptist's Day (Fiesta de San Juan Bautista), June 24
Sandcastle Days, usually July
Shakespeare Festival, San Diego National, early June through mid-September
Strawberry Festival, spring
Street Painting Festival, I Madonnari Italian, last weekend in May
Summer Series, Hollywood Bowl, eleven weeks from first week in July to late September
Summer Series, Paul Masson, first weekend in June to last weekend in September

California *(cont.)*
Swallows of San Juan Capistrano, swallows arrive
March 19 and depart October 23
Swedish Festival, Kingsburg, third weekend in May
Symphony Pops, San Francisco, three weeks beginning
mid-July
Tournament of Roses, January 1
Transpac Race from Los Angeles to Honolulu, Hawaii,
July during odd-numbered years
Vintage Festival, Valley of the Moon, last full weekend
in September
Whale Festival, March

California (central)
Hesi Ceremony

California (northern)
Dance, Hupa Autumn (Tunchitdilya), October
Dance, Hupa Winter (Haichitdilya), twenty days during
winter

California (northwestern)
World Renewal Ceremony, July and August

California (southern)
St. Joseph of Arimathea, Feast Day of, March 19

California Indians (northwest)
New Year's Day, late July

California Yokuts Indians
Heshwash Ceremony, two nights

Callao, Peru
Sts. Peter and Paul Day (Día de San Pedro y San Pablo),
June 29

Cambodia
Harvest Feast
Independence Day, November 9
Lenten Season (Vossa), July-October, begins during Wazo,
fourth lunar month, and ends on the 15th or full moon
day of Thadingyut, seventh lunar month
New Year, mid-April, when Sun is in Aries
Prachum Ben, August-September, 12th day of waning
half of month of Photrobot
Water Festival, late October or early November

Cambridge, England
Cambridge Festival, last two weeks in July

Cambridge, England (medieval)
Christmas Eve, December 24

Cambridgeshire, England
Straw Bear Day, December-January, Saturday preceding
Plough Monday

Cambridge University, Putney to Martlake, England
Boat Race Day, March-April

Cameroon
Constitution Day, May 20
Independence Day, January 1
Mecca, Pilgrimage to, eighth through 13th days of Islamic
month of Dhu'l-Hijjah
Mount Cameroon Race, last Sunday in January
Nja Festival, during the dry season, December or early
January
Thanksgiving (Evamelunga, the Taking Away of Burden and
Sin), September 8
Unification Day, October 1
Youth Day, February 11

Campania, Italy
St. Paulinus of Nola, Feast of (Lily Festival), fourth
Sunday in June or Sunday following June 22
September in the Town, end of August-beginning of
September

Camunas, Toledo, Spain
Danzantes y Pecados Festival, June

Canada
Acadian Festival, August 5-15
Acadian Festivals, usually three to four days at the end
of June; sometimes in July or August
Air Force Day, September 10
Air Show, International, three days in August
Annapolis Valley Blossom Festival, last week in May
Apple Blossom Festival, five days in late May or early June
Arts, Banff Festival of the, early June to late August
Arts, Holiday Festival of the, July
Arts, International Festival of the, six weeks during June
and July
Arts, Summer Festival of the, month of July
Arts Festival, New Directions in the Performing, even-
numbered years in summer or autumn
Arts Week, Creative, last full week in August
Assumption, Feast of the, and Tintamarre celebration,
August 15 and Sunday nearest August 15
Battleford Chautauqua, July
Bitowa Outdoor Festival, third full weekend in June
Bonfire Night, November 5
Boxing Day, December 26
Buffalo Days, six days in July-August
Burns Night, January 25
Calgary Exhibition and Stampede, July
Canada Day, observed July 1-2
Canadian National Exhibition, three weeks in August
and September
Candlemas, February 2
Caribana, one week ending the first Monday in August

Canada *(cont.)*

Caribou Carnival and Championship Dog Derby, one week in March

Carnaval, Quebec, ten days in February

Charlottetown Festival, June-September

Chicoutimi Olden-Days Carnival, ten days in February

Christmas, December 25

Christmas Eve, December 24

Commonwealth Day, second Monday in March

Dance Festival, Alberta, May-June

A Day to Remember, July-August

Discovery Day, June 24; observed on or near June 24

Discovery Days, August

Dollard des Ormeaux, Fête de, May 24

Drama Festival, Newfoundland, April-May, six days during Easter holidays (location varies)

Drama Festival, Okanagan Zone, May

Easter Monday, March-April, Monday after Easter

Epiphany, January 6

Epiphany (Old Christmas), January 7

Father's Day, third Sunday in June

Fiddling Contest, Maritime Old Time, two days in July

First of March, March 1

Folk Arts Festival, May-June

Folk Festival, Winnipeg, three or four days during second weekend in July

Folklorama, one week in mid-August

Folk Song Festival, Miramichi, three days in late June

Freedom Festival, International, mid-June to July 4

Gaelic Mod, first full week in August

Gathering of the Clans, July 1

Grape and Wine Festival, Niagara, ten days in late September

Grey Cup Day, mid-November

Halloween, October 31

Highland Games, Brantford, second Saturday in July

Highland Games, Fergus, second Saturday in August

Highland Games, Glengarry, Saturday before the first Monday in August

Icelandic Festival (Islendingadagurinn), during last week in July or first week in August

Interlake Festival, June-August

Iroquois White Dog Feast (New Year or Midwinter Festival), several days, including first quarter moon in January

Jazz Festival, Montreal, June-July

Kipawo Showboat Company, July-August

Klondike Days Exposition, July

'Ksan Celebrations, Friday evenings in July and August

Kwanzaa, December 26 through January 1

Labor Day, first Monday in September

Lammas, August 1

Lennoxville, Festival, July-August

Lobster Festival, six days in July

Mardi Gras (Carnaval), February-March

Martyrs of North America, Feast of, September 26

May Day, May 1

Midsummer, June 23-24

Midwinter Rites, Bella Coola (Kusiut), November-February

Music, Mariposa-the Festival of Roots, last weekend in June

Pioneer Days, July

Musical Theatre, Summer, July-August

Music Festival, Orford International, eight weeks in July and August

New Year, September 11

Northern Games, four days in mid-July

Oktoberfest, nine days in early October, beginning the Friday before Thanksgiving Monday

Opera Plus, Festival Ottawa, three weeks in July

Performance Season, Canadian Experimental, month of July

Performance '78, '79, etc., June

Pike Festival, Northern, June to August

Pilgrimage to St. Anne d'Auray, July 26

Polar Bear Swim Day, January 1

Potato Blossom Festival, last week in July

Remembrance Day, November 11

Riel, Trial of, Tuesdays, Wednesdays and Fridays in June-August

St. Anne's Day, July 26

St. Catherine's Day (La Tire Sainte-Catherine), November 25

St. George's Day, April 23

St. John the Baptist's Day, June 24

St. Patrick's Day, March 17

Shaw Festival, 22 weeks from May to October

Snowgolf Championship, three days in February

Spring, Festival of, nine days in mid-May

Spring Festival, Guelph, two to three weeks in April-May

Stewardship Sunday, second Sunday in November

Summer Carnival, Whycocomagh, July

Summer Festival, ten days in July

Summer Festival, Blyth, July-August

Sunflower Festival, last weekend in July

Tartans, Festival of the, August

Tellabration, the Friday before Thanksgiving

Thanksgiving Day, second Monday in October

Theatre Festival, Ontario, May

Theatre Festival, Stratford, May-June to October

Toonik Time, one week from late April to early May

Top of the World Ski Meet, March-April, Easter weekend

Trappers' Festival, Northern Manitoba, nearly one week in mid-February

Ukrainian Festival, National, four days in July or August

Vancouver Heritage Festival, May-June

Vancouver International Festival, late May to late June

Vesna Festival, six days in May

Victoria Day (Empire Day), Monday nearest May 24

Victoria International Festival, six weeks beginning in early July

Voyageur, Festival du, about one week in February

Carson City, Nevada
Admission Day, October 31
Powwow, La Ka Le'l Ba, annual

Cartago, Costa Rica
Our Lady of the Angels, August (pilgrimage to basilica)

Cartegna, Colombia
Candlemas (Virgin de la Candelaria), February 2

Carthage, North Tunis Region, Tunisia
Art, International Festival of Popular, July-August during odd-numbered years
Carthage, International Festival of, July and August

Casablanca, Morocco
Purim, November-December, second day of Jewish month of Kislev

Casa Grande, Arizona
Indian Celebration, O'Odham Tash, February

Caserta, Campania, Italy
September in the Town, end of August-beginning of September

Casertavecchia, Caserta, Campania, Italy
September in the Town, end of August-beginning of September

Cass Lake, Minnesota
Powwows, Ojibwa, first Monday in September, last Monday in May, and in winter, spring, and midsummer

Castelejo, Castelo Branco, Portugal
Pilgrimage of Castelejo, September

Castelo Branco, Portugal
Monsanto, National Festival of, every Sunday in September
Pilgrimage of Castelejo, September

Castelo de Vide, Portalegre, Portugal
Castelo de Vide, National Festival of, August

Castro Verde-Beja, Portugal
October Fair, nine days in October

Catalan people in Spain
Easter, March-April, first Sunday after first full moon after the vernal equinox
Holy Innocents' Day, December 28
Mardi Gras, February-March

Catalonia, Spain
Human Towers of Valls (Xiquets de Valls), June 24

Catamarca, Argentina
Immaculate Conception, Feast of the (Virgen de Valle), December 8

Catania, Sicily
St. Agatha Festival, February 5; observed February 3-5
St. Agnes Eve, January 20; five-day festival in February

Caudete, Alicante, Spain
Battle of the Moors and Christians, September

Cayman Islands
Columbus Day (Discovery Day), May 17
Pirate Week Festival, third week in October

Cayuga Indians in Oklahoma: Miami
Dance, Green Corn, July or August

Cayuga Iroquois Indians
Midwinter Bear Society Dance

Cayuga Iroquois Indians in Canada and the United States
Iroquois White Dog Feast (New Year or Midwinter Festival), several days, including first quarter moon in January

Celaya, Guanajuato, Mexico
Nativity Plays, mid-December to January

Celebes (formerly Sulawesi), Indonesia
Ujung Pandang Anniversary, April 1

Celou, Philippines
Sinulog Festival, third weekend in January

Celtic people
Beltane, April 30
Furry Day, May 8
Lúgnasad (First Fruits Festival), August 1
May Day Eve, April 30
Samhain (Summer's End), October 31

Center Harbor, New Hampshire
Music Festival, New Hampshire, six weeks from early June to late August

Central African Republic
Boganda Day, March 29
Independence Day, August 13; observed on December 1

Central America
Pan American Day, April 14

Central City, Colorado
Lou Bunch Day, third Saturday in June

Central City, Colorado *(cont.)*
Summer Festival, Central City, five weeks from first
week in July to mid-August

Central Java, Java
Offering Ceremony, August
Sultan's Coronation, May
Water Festival at Menjer Lake, one week in
September

Central Park, New York, New York
Shakespeare Festival, New York, summer

Centre College, Danville, Kentucky
Brass Band Festival, Great American, mid-June

Cercio to Santa Barbara, Portugal
Pilgrimage at Cercio to Santa Barbara, last Sunday in
August

Cernat, Covasna, Romania
Citadel Festival, second Sunday in June

Cetatea Ica, Cernat, Covasna, Romania
Citadel Festival, second Sunday in June

Ceylon (now Sri Lanka)
New Year (Vaisakhi), first day of Hindu month of Vaisakha
See also **Sri Lanka**

Chad
Africa Day, May 25
Independence Day, August 11; observed on January 11
National Day, April 13
Republic Day, November 28

Chadron, Nebraska
Fur Trade Days, July

Chalma, Mexico
Pilgrimage to Chalma, first week of January; also held in
February, August, September, and during Holy Week

Chamorros people
All Souls' Day, November 2
Christ the King, Feast of, mid-November
Our Lady of Carmel (La Madonna del Carmine), mid-July
Our Lady of Lourdes, Feast of, February 11; festival
between February 11-18
St. Joseph's Day, May 1

Chamula Mayan people in Mexico
Mardi Gras (Tahimoltik, Festival of the Games), February-
March, five days, coinciding with lost days of Mayan
calendar

Chan Kom, Yucatan, Mexico
Dinner of the Milpa (u hanli col), every four years when
corn ripens

Channel Islands, Great Britain
Battle of Flowers, second Thursday in August
Liberation Day, May 9

Charente, France
Confolens Festival, one week in August

Charente-Maritime, France
Arts, Festival of International Contemporary (Recontres
Internationales d'Art Contemporain), two weeks in
June-July
Theatre of Silence, Carte Blanche at the (Carte Blanche
au Theatre du Silence), May-June

Charlemont, Massachusetts
Mohawk Trail Concerts, weekends from mid-July to
mid-August

Charleston, South Carolina
Fawkes Day, Guy, November 5
Houses and Gardens, Festival of, 26 days in March-April
St. Cecilia's Day, November 22
Spoleto Festival of Two Worlds/U.S.A., two weeks from
last week in May to early June

Charleston, West Virginia
Regatta, Charleston Sternwheel, August-September; ten days
ending first Monday in September
Vandalia Gathering, last weekend in May

Charlestown, Rhode Island
Powwow, Narragansett, August

Charlotte Motor Speedway, Charlotte, North Carolina
Coca Cola 600, last weekend in May

Charlottetown, Prince Edward Island, Canada
Charlottetown Festival, June-September

Chatham, New Zealand
Provincial Anniversary, December 1

Chautauqua, New York
Music Program, Chautauqua Summer, late June to late
August

Chehalis Salishan Indians in Washington: Oakville
Tribal Day Celebration, late May

Cheltenham Spa, England
Music, Cheltenham International Festival of, nine days
beginning first week in July

China *(cont.)*
Festival of the Five Poisonous Creatures), fifth day of fifth lunar month
Double Ninth Day (Ch'ung Yang or Tĕng Kao, Climbing the Hills), ninth day of ninth lunar month
Double Seventh (Festival of the Weaving Maid and the Herd Boy; Chi Hsi, Festival of the Milky Way), seventh day of seventh lunar month
Founding of the Republic, October 10
Goddess of Mercy, Birthday of, 19th day of third lunar month
Grave-Sweeping and Cold Food Festival (Qing Ming, Clear and Bright), fourth or fifth day of third month, 105 or 106 days after the winter solstice
Han Lu (the Dew Grows Cold), October
Hungry Ghosts, Festival of (Yü-Lan Hui or Chieh Tsu), 15th day of seventh lunar month
Ice and Snow Festival, Harbin, January 5-February 5
Jizo—Ennichi or Jiso Kshitigarba, 24th of each month
Kitchen God Celebration (Tsao Chün), 23rd or 24th day of twelfth lunar month and New Year's Eve and Day
Kuan Ti, Festival of, May 13
Lantern Festival (Yaun Shaw), 13th-15th days of first lunar month
Lotus, Birthday of, 24th day of sixth lunar month
Mankind, Birthday of, seventh day of first lunar month
Martyrs' Day, Canton, March 29
Mid-Autumn Festival (Chung Ch'iu), 15th, or full moon, day of eighth lunar month
New Year, ten-day to two-week long celebration at the first new moon after sun enters Aquarius; one to 15 days during first lunar month
Pilgrimage to Shrines of Tsai Shĕn, second day of first lunar month and 15th day of ninth lunar month
Rat's Wedding Day, 19th day of first lunar month
Simhat Torah, 23rd day of Jewish month of Tishri
Spring Festival (Li Chun, Spring Is Here), February
Star Festival, 18th day of first lunar month
Sugar Ball Show, 16th day of first lunar month
Ta Mo's Day, fifth day of tenth lunar month
Thirtieth, Night of the (Ch'u Hsi), 29th day of twelfth lunar month
Torch Festival, 24th-26th days of sixth lunar month
Winter Dress, Sending the, first day of tenth lunar month
Winter Solstice (Tung Chih), during the eleventh lunar month
Women's Day, International, March 8
Wu Kuan's Day, 18th day of second lunar month
Yen Lo's Birthday, eighth day of first lunar month

China, People's Republic of
Excited Insects, Feast of (Ching Che), on or around March 5
National Days, October 1, two-day holiday

Chincoteague Island, Virginia
Pony Penning on Chincoteague Island, late July

Chinese-Americans
Double Fifth (Dragon Boat Festival and Festival of the Five Poisonous Creatures), fifth day of fifth lunar month
New Year, ten-day to two-week long celebration at the first new moon after sun enters Aquarius; one to 15 days during first lunar month

Chinese-Americans in California: Marysville
Bok Kai Festival, March or April, second day of second lunar month

Chinese people
Yü Huang Shang Ti, Jade or Pearly Emperor, eighth day of first lunar month

Chinese Taoist people in Singapore
Prince, Birthday of the Third, eighth and ninth days of fourth lunar month

Ch'ing Liang Shan Monastery, China
Dead, Festival of the (Bon Odori or Obon), 15th day of seventh lunar month

Chinhae, Korea
Cherry Blossom Festival, Chinhae, early April

Chinju, Republic of Korea
Art Festival, National Foundation, November 1-5

Chinookan Indians in Oregon: Warm Springs
Powwow, Warm Springs, June
Root Festival, mid-April

Chippewa Indians in Minnesota
New Year's Day (Kissing Day), January 1

Chippewa Indians in Montana: Box Elder
Indian Days, Rocky Boy, usually first weekend in August

Chitral, Pakistan
Chaomos, December 21

Chiuesti Commune, Cluj, Romania
Pintea the Brave Day, first Sunday in September

Choctaw Indians in Mississippi: Pearl River Indian Community near Philadelphia
Indian Fair, Choctaw, four days in July beginning the Wednesday after July 4

Choctaw Indians in Oklahoma: Beavers Bend State Park, Broken Bow
Happy Hunting Party, Festival of the Forest (Kiamichi Owa Chito), late June

Christchurch, New Zealand
Arts Festival, Christchurch, March during even-numbered years
Fawkes Day, Guy, November 5

Christiansted, St. Croix, Virgin Islands
Christmas Festival, Caribbean, two weeks beginning December 23
Virgin Islands Donkey Races Day, February 22

Chrudim, East Bohemia, Czechoslovakia
Puppeteers, National and International Festivals of Amateur, national festival in June-July; international festival every five years

Chugiak, Alaska
Chugiak-Eagle River Bear Paw Festival, mid-July

Chukchi, USSR
Reindeer Slaughtering, autumn

Chukchi people in Russia: Siberia
Boat or Baydar, Festival of the, early spring

Chukchi people in USSR: Siberia
Seal Festival (Keretkun Festival), two to three days in late autumn

Churchill Downs, Louisville, Kentucky
Kentucky Derby Day, 15-day festival precedes race, which occurs on the first Saturday in May

Church of Romont, Switzerland
Good Friday (Ceremony of Pleureuses), March-April, Friday before Easter

Church of St. Jean Baptiste, New York, New York
St. Anne's Day, July 26

Chusonji, Iwate, Japan
Shrine Festival, Chusonji, May

Cincinnati, Ohio
Cincinnati May Festival, Friday and Saturday evenings for two weeks in mid-May
Opera Festival, Cincinnati Summer, mid-June to mid-July

City Wharf, Gibraltar
Shark Angling Competition, International, one day in late April or early May

Cizer Commune, Salaj, Romania
Weighing Festival, second Sunday in May

Clare (County), Ireland
Cromm Dub's Sunday, first Sunday in August
Fleadh Nua, May-June

Clarksburg, West Virginia
Italian Heritage Festival, West Virginia, first weekend in September

Cleveland, England
Folklore Festival, Billingham International, eight days in August

Cleveland, Tennessee
Cherokee Days of Recognition, first weekend in August

Cloquet, Minnesota
Powwow, Fond du Lac, July

Clowes Memorial Hall, Butler University, Indianapolis, Indiana
Romantic Festival, last two weekends in April

Cluj, Romania
Pintea the Brave Day, first Sunday in September

Cluj-Napoca, Transylvania, Romania
Theatres, Festival of National, one week in September or October

Coatbridge, Lanarkshire, Scotland
Monklands Festival, June

Cobh, County Cork, Ireland
Folk Dance Festival of Ireland, International, one week beginning first Sunday in July

Cobleskill, New York
Indian Festival, Iroquois, first weekend in September, including Labor Day

Cochin, China
Simhat Torah, 23rd day of Jewish month of Tishri

Cochiti Pueblo, New Mexico
All Souls' Day (Their Grandfathers Arrive from the West, or from the Dead, Feast), November 2
Dance, Corn, May 13
St. Bonaventura, Feast of and Corn Dance, July 14
St. John the Baptist's Day, June 24
Santa Cruz Days (Coming of the Rivermen), May 3

Cocopah Indians in Arizona: Somerton
Cocopah Festivities Day, March or April

Connecticut
Abbey Fair, two days in early August
Admission Day, January 9
Barnum Festival, P.T., 17 days from late June to July 4
Boat Rendezvous, Antique and Classic, last weekend in July
Christmas Torchlight Parade and Muster, Old Saybrook, second Saturday night in December
Crandall Day, Prudence, first Saturday in September
Maine Memorial Day, February 15
Mohegan Homecoming, third Sunday in August
Music Festival, Connecticut Early, first three weeks in June
Music Festival, Norfolk Chamber, late June to mid-August on weekends
Music Festival, Sea, first weekend in June
Music Mountain, Saturday evenings and Sunday afternoons from mid-June to early September
Music Series, Silvermine Chamber, four Sunday evening concerts from mid-June to mid-August
Native American Day, fourth Friday in September
New Year's Eve (First Night), December 31
Oyster Festival, second weekend in September
Patriots' Day, April 19; observed third Monday in April
Patriots' Weekend, Annual, last weekend in September
Powwow, Connecticut River, first weekend in September
Regatta, Yale-Harvard, usually first Sunday in June
St. Nicholas's Day, December 6
Shakespeare Festival, American
Soul, Festival of the (Mahrajan), September 1

Connemara (County), Ireland
Oyster Festival, Galway, four days in mid-September

Constanta, Romania
Sea Celebrations, one week ending first Sunday in August

Constanta County, Romania
Folklore Festival, National, month of August

Consuegra, Spain
Rose Festival, Saffron, last Sunday in October

Cooch's Bridge, Delaware
Loyalty Day, May 1

Cooperstown, New York
Opera, Glimmerglass, late June to Labor Day, first Monday in September

Cooperstown to Bainbridge, New York
Regatta, General Clinton Canoe, last weekend in May

Copan, Oklahoma
Powwow, Lenape Delaware, late May or early June

Copenhagen, Denmark
Ballet and Music Festival, Copenhagen Royal Danish, last two weeks in May
Queen Margrethe's Birthday, April 16
Summer Festival, Copenhagen, seven weeks beginning July 1
Theatre Festival, Children's, early November
Tivoli Concerts (Tivolis Koncertsal), May 1 through mid-September

Corabia, Olt, Romania
Oltenian Ballad, first weekend in October

Cordoba, Spain
Patios Festival, May

Cordova, Alaska
Ice Worm Festival, first week or weekend in February

Corfu, Greece
Easter, March-April, first Sunday after first full moon after the vernal equinox
Folk Dancing at Corfu, Greek, mid-May to September
St. Spyridon, Feast Day of, December 14

Corinth, Greece (ancient)
Isthmian Games, first month of spring every second year

Cork, County Cork, Ireland
Folk Dance Festival, Cork International Choral and, April

Cork (County), Ireland
Folk Dance Festival, Cork International Choral and, April
Folk Dance Festival of Ireland, International, one week beginning first Sunday in July

Cornwall, England
Dipping Day, May 1
Friday in Lide, first Friday in March
Furry Day, May 8
Paul Pitcher Day, January 24
St. Piran's Day, March 5
Silver Ball, Hurling the, Sunday nearest or Monday after February 3
Theatre Festival, Minack, end of June to mid-September

Corpus Christi, Texas
Buccaneer Days, last weekend in April through first weekend in May

Corrine, Utah
Golden Spike Day, May 10

Cosby, Tennessee
Dulcimer and Harp Convention, second weekend in June
Ramp Festival, Cosby, first Sunday in May

Coshocton, Ohio
Dulcimer Days, third weekend in May

Costa Rica
Circumcision, Feast of the, January 1
Columbus Day (Day of the Race), October 12
Easter, March-April, first Sunday after first full moon after the vernal equinox
Folklore, Central American Congress of (Congreso Centroamericano de Folclorologia Nicoya), one week in August
Guanacaste Day, July 25
Heroes Day, April 11
Independence Day, September 15
Mother's Day, August 15
Our Lady of the Angels, August (pilgrimage to basilica)

Costesti, Orastioara de Sus Commune, Hunedoara, Romania
Encounter with History, first Sunday in May

Cotati, California
Indian Day, August

Cote-d'Or, France
Dijon Festival, September
Nights of Bourgogne, Festival of the (Festival des Nuits de Bourgogne), June-July during odd-numbered years
Three Glorious Days (Les Trois Glorieuses), twice annually: July 27-29 and third Saturday through Monday in November

Cotes-du-Nord, France
Roche-Jagu, Festival of, June-September

Covasna, Romania
Citadel Festival, second Sunday in June

Craigmillar, Edinburgh, Scotland
Craigmillar Festival, June or August

Cranston, Warwick, Rhode Island
Gaspee Days, 16 days in May-June

Cree Indians in Montana: Box Elder
Indian Days, Rocky Boy, usually first weekend in August

Creek Indians
Devil's Promenade, July 3-6

Creek Indians in the southeastern United States
Dance, Green Corn, weekend ceremonies in May-September lead up to festival

Creole people in Louisiana: New Orleans
Dance, Calinda, June 23

Creole people in Sierra Leone
Thanksgiving (Awoojoh), may occur on special occasions and during such holidays as Christmas, Easter, Good Friday, and New Year's Day

Crescent City, California
Crab Races, World Championship, Sunday before third Monday in February

Crete, Greece
Wine Festival, two weeks in July

Crisfield, Maryland
Crab Derby, National Hard, first weekend in September

Croagh Patrick Mountain, County Mayo, Ireland
Reek Sunday, last Sunday in July (pilgrimage)

Croatia, Yugoslavia
Child, Yugoslav Festival of the, June-July
Djakovo Embroidery, two days in early July
Drama Amateurs of Croatia, Festival of, May
Dubrovnik Festival (Dubrovacke Ljetne Igre), seven weeks from second week in July to third week in August
Folklore Review, International, July
Harvest Festival, second half of August
Korcula, Festival of (Moreska), July 27 and every Thursday from April-September
Opera and Ballet, Annual Festival of Chamber, May-June
Puppet Festival, International, September-October
Rijeka Summer, July-August
Rovinj Festival, end of August
Sinj Iron-Ring Chivalric Tournament, first Sunday in August
Summer Festival, Opatija, June-September
Summer Festival, Split, July-August
Theatre, Days of Young, December
Theatre of Hvar, Days of the, four days in May
Theatres for Children and Youth, Encounter of Professional, May
Theatres of Croatia, Encounter of Professional, October
Zagreb Evenings, June-September

Croatian people in Yugoslavia
Holy Innocents' Day (Mladenci), December 28

Crooksville, Ohio
Pottery Festival, three days during weekend nearest July 20

Crow Agency near Hardin, Montana
Crow Fair, at least six days in mid-August

Crowes, Isle of Wight, Great Britain
Regatta Week, July-August

Crow Indians
Crow Fair, at least six days in mid-August
Custer's Last Stand, June 25; observed with a pageant
in late June
New Year's Day, January 1

Crow Indians in the Great Plains of the United States
Dance, Sun, usually during summer solstice, June 21

Crow Reservation, Montana
Custer's Last Stand, June 25; observed with a pageant
in late June

Cuba
Ballet, International Festival of (Festival Internacional
de Ballet de La Habana), autumn during even-
numbered years
Independence Day, May 20
Liberation Day, January 1

Cuban-Americans in Florida: Ybor City
Garbanzo, Fiesta Sopa de, begins Sunday nearest
February 9 and ends Saturday
Guavaween, last Saturday in October

Cuchumatan Indians in Guatemala: Santa Eulalia
Sealing the Frost, April-early May

Cuenca, Spain
Cuenca Encounter, March
Endiablada Festival, early February

Cuetzalan, Puebla, Mexico
St. Francis of Assisi, Festival of, early October

Cumorah Hill near Palmyra, New York
Hill Cumorah Pageant, nine days (excluding Sunday and
Monday) beginning third weekend in July

Cundinamarca, Colombia
Theatre, National Festival of New (Festival Nacional del
Nuevo Teatro), November-December

Curium near Limassol, Cyprus
Curium Festival, June-July

Custer, South Dakota
Custer's Last Stand, June 25; observed in late July

Cuttack, Orissa, India
Dance Festival, Kala Vikash Kendra, twice yearly: three
days in October-November and on August 10

Cuyahoga Falls, Ohio
Music Center, Blossom, first week in June to second week
in September

Cuzco, Peru
Sun Festival (Inti Raymi or Raimi Fiesta), about one week,
including June 24, the winter solstice

Cyprus
Anthestiria Flower Festival, early May
Art Festival, International, 10 days in July
Curium Festival, June-July
Cyprus International Fair, two weeks in May-June
Drama, Paphos Festival of Ancient, June-July
Easter, April-May, first Sunday after first full moon
after vernal equinox (using Julian calendar)
EOKA (Greek National Union of Cypriot Fighters Day),
April 1
Epiphany, January 6, Gregorian calendar (N.S.); January
19, Julian calendar (O.S.)
First of March (Martenitza), March 1
Folk Art Festival: Pampaphia, four days in early August
Independence Day, March 25
Independence Day, October 1
Kataklysmos (Flood Festival), May-June, three to five days
including fiftieth day after Greek Orthodox Easter
(Pentecost)
Mardi Gras (Carnival), February-March, twelve days
ending Ash Wednesday
Nicosia Festival, two to four weeks in May or June
Poetry Festival, Palamas, early March
Wine Festival, Limassol, September 15-30
Wine Festival, Stroumbi Village, several days in
early September

Cyrene, Greece
Carnea, August, Greek month of Carneus

Czech-Americans
Assumption, Feast of the, August 15
Czech Festival, first weekend in August
Independence Day, October 28
St. Barbara's Day, December 4
St. Wenceslaus's Day, September 28

Czech-Americans in Arizona: Tucson
Tucson Meet Yourself Festival, second weekend in October

Czechoslovakia
Carling Sunday, March-April, fifth Sunday in Lent
Christmas (Vánoce), December 25
Christmas Eve (Štědrý Večer), December 24
Easter (Velikonoce), March-April, first Sunday after first full
moon after the vernal equinox
Easter Monday (Velikonoční Pondělí), March-April,
Monday after Easter
Epiphany (Den Svatých Tří Králů), January 6
Folklore Festival of Straznice, three days in June
Good Friday (Velký Pátek, Great Friday), March-April,

Czechoslovakia *(cont.)*
Friday preceding Easter Sunday
Harvest Celebration (Obzinky or Posviceni), late August or early September
Holy Saturday (Bílí Sobota, White Saturday), March-April, Saturday before Easter Sunday
Independence Day, October 28
Liberation Day, May 9
May Day (Prvého Máje), May 1
May Day Eve (Páleni Carodějnic, Burning of the Witches), April 30
Mimes, International Festival of Deaf, second half of November during odd-numbered years
Music Festival, Bratislava, October 1-15
Music Festival, Brno International, October
New Year's Day (Nový Rok), January 1
Palm Sunday (Května Neděle), March-April, the Sunday preceding Easter
Pentecost, May-June, the Sunday fifty days after Easter
Puppeteers, National and International Festivals of Amateur, national festival in June-July; international festival every five years
Puppet Theatres, Skupa Festival of Professional, May
St. Sofia's Day, May 15
St. Wenceslaus's Day, September 28
Spartakiade, eight days in June every five years
Spring Festival, Prague, May 12-June 4
Teacher's Day, March 28
Thanksgiving, October 28
World Environment Day, June 5
Znojmo Feast, every Friday and Saturday in June-September

Czestochowa, Poland
Our Lady of Czestochowa, Feast of (Feast of the Black Madonna of Jasna Gora), August 15

Dagestan, USSR
Midwinter Festival (Igbi), usually observed on Sunday nearest February 5

Dagomba, Upper Volta
Muhammad's Birthday (Damba Festival), twelfth day of Islamic month of Rabi al-Awwal

Dahlonega, Georgia
Gold Rush Days, Dahlonega, October

Dai people in China: Xinan
Buddha's Birthday, Enlightenment, and Salvation, eighth day of fourth lunar month

Dakar, Senegal
Ramadan, ninth Islamic month

Dakkarkari people in Nigeria
Uhola Festival, new moon in December-January

Dakota Indians in Minnesota: Pipestone
Song of Hiawatha Pageant, last two weeks in July and first week in August

Dal-ma-ji Kyungsang Province, Korea
Burning the Moon House (Dal-jip-tae-u-gee or Viewing the First Full Moon), 15th day of first lunar month

Dallas, Texas
Cotton Bowl Classic, January 1
State Fair of Texas, 17 days in October

Daman and Diu Union Territory, Panjim, India
Drama Festival, Goa Academy, five to ten days in November-December or February-March
Drama Festival, Marathi, February-March

Damascus, Syria
Artistic Festival of the Damascus International Fair, 20 days in July
Assumption, Feast of the ('Id Rakad-ai-Sayyidah), August 15, Gregorian calendar (N.S.); August 28, Julian calendar (O.S.)

Danish-Americans in Nebraska: Minden
Nebraska Danish Days (Danish Ethnic Festival), May-June

Dan people in Ivory Coast
New Yam Festival (Odwira), October

Danville, Kentucky
Brass Band Festival, Great American, mid-June

Darlington, South Carolina
Southern 500 Stock Car Race, first Monday in September

Dartmouth, Nova Scotia, Canada
Fiddling Contest, Maritime Old Time, two days in July

Daruvar, Croatia, Yugoslavia
Harvest Festival, second half of August

Darwin, Northern Territory, Australia
Darwin Youth Festival, August, during school holidays
Folk Festival, Top Half, weekend in June

Dauphin, Manitoba, Canada
Ukrainian Festival, National, four days in July or August

Davenport, Iowa
Jazz Festival, Bix Beiderbecke Memorial, three days during last weekend in July

David, Panama
St. Joseph's Day (International Fair of San José), ten days,
including March 19

**David L. Lawrence Convention Center, Pittsburgh,
Pennsylvania**
Folk Festival, Pittsburgh, first weekend in June

Davis, West Virginia
Winter Festival, Alpine, six days in early January

Dawlish, Devonshire, England
Arts Festival, Dawlish, last two weeks in June

Dawson City, Yukon, Canada
Discovery Days, observed in August

Dayak people in Malaysia: Sarawak
Dayak Festival Day (Gawai Dayak), June 1-2

Dayton, North Carolina
Wright Brothers Day, December 17

Daytona Beach, Florida
Daytona 500, February
Motorcycle Week, first week in March

Daytona International Speedway, Daytona Beach, Florida
Daytona 500, February

Dazaifu, Fukuoka, Japan
Bullfinch Exchange Festival (Usokae), January 7

Deadwood, South Dakota
Seventy-Six, Days of, first full weekend in August

Deal Island, Maryland
Skipjack Races, Labor Day, first Monday in September

Debrecen, Hungary
Floral Carnival, National, August 20

The Deccan, India
Elephant God, Festival of the (Ganesha Chaturthi), fourth
day of Hindu month of Bhadrapada

Decorah, Iowa
Nordic Fest, last full weekend in July

Delaware
Admission Day, December 7
African Methodist Quarterly Meeting Day, last Saturday
in August
Delaware Swedish Colonial Day, March 29
Loyalty Day, May 1

Powwow, Nanticoke Indian, second weekend in September
Return Day, Thursday after Presidential Election Day,
every leap year

Delaware Indians
Big House Ceremony, annual twelve-night ceremony
Midwinter Bear Ceremony

Delft, Netherlands
Art and Antiques Fair, Old, October-November

Delhi, India
Mother Goddess, Festival of Durga, the, first ten days of
waxing half of Hindu month of Asvina

Deloraine, Tasmania, Australia
Drama Festival, Deloraine Youth, one week in July

Deming, New Mexico
Duck Race, Great American, fourth weekend in August

Denbighshire, Wales
Eisteddfod, International Musical (Gerddorol Gydwladol
Llangollen), six days during first week in July

Denizli, Turkey
Pamukkale, Festival of, May

Denmark
Andersen Festival, Hans Christian, month-long, July-August
Århus Festival Week (Århus Festuge), nine days from first
Saturday through second Sunday in September
Ascension Day, May-June, fortieth day after Easter Sunday
Ballet and Music Festival, Copenhagen Royal Danish, last
two weeks in May
Christmas (Juledag), December 25-26
Christmas Eve (Juleaftgen), begins December 23
Common Prayer Day (Store Bededag), April-May, fourth
Friday after Easter
Constitution Day, June 5
Easter (Paaske), March-April, first Sunday after first
full moon after the vernal equinox
Easter Monday (Anden Paaskedag), March-April, Monday
after Easter
Epiphany (Helligtrekongersdag, Day of the Three Holy
Kings), January 6
Fourteenth of February (Fjortende Februar), February 14
Good Friday (Langfredag, Long Friday), March-April,
Friday preceding Easter Sunday
Holy Saturday (Paaskeaften), March-April, Saturday
before Easter Sunday
Independence Day (Rebild Festival), July 4
King's Birthday, March 11
Lent, February-March, forty-day season preceding Easter
Liberation Day, May 5

Denmark *(cont.)*
  Mardi Gras (Fastelavn or Fastelavan), February-March,
    Monday before Ash Wednesday
  Martinmas (Mortensaftenn), November 11
  Midsummer (Sankt Hans Aften), June 23-24
  Music Festival, Ronne, Wednesdays and Fridays in July
    and August
  New Year's Day (Nytaarsdag), January 1
  New Year's Eve (Nytaarsaften), December 31
  Pentecost (Pintse), May-June, the Sunday fifty days
    after Easter
  Queen Margrethe's Birthday, April 16
  Stork Day, May 8
  Summer Festival, Copenhagen, seven weeks beginning
    July 1
  Theatre Festival, Children's, early November
  Tilting Tournament, Sonderborg, three days in July
  Tivoli Concerts (Tivolis Koncertsal), May 1 through
    mid-September
  Twelfth Night (Epiphany Eve), January 5
  Valdemar's Day, June 15
  Valentine's Day, February 14
  Viking Festival, three days to two weeks in June-July
  Walpurgis Night (Valborgsaften), April 30
  Whit Monday (Anden Pinsedag), May-June, Monday after
    Pentecost

Denver, Colorado
  Western Stock Show, National, begins third Friday in
    January for 11 days

Deogarh, Bihar, India
  Sravani Mela, during Hindu month of Sravana

De Pere, Wisconsin
  Mardi Gras, February-March

Derbyshire, England
  Plague Sunday, last Sunday in August

Des Moines, Iowa
  Iowa State Fair, 11 days through last Sunday in August

Detroit, Michigan
  Devil's Night, October 30
  Freedom Festival, International, mid-June to July 4
  St. Joseph of Arimathea, Feast Day of, March 19

Deutsch-Altenburg, Lower Austria, Austria
  Carnuntum Festival, July-August

Deva, Hunedoara, Romania
  Dance of Transylvania, Men's (Caluser or Caluseri),
    third week in January

DeVargas Mall, Santa Fe, New Mexico
  Arts and Crafts Show, Eight Northern Indian Pueblos
    Spring, April 19-20

Devon, Pennsylvania
  Horse Show and Country Fair, Devon, nine days in May

Devonport, Tasmania, Australia
  Eisteddfod Society Festival, August-September

Devonshire, England
  Arts Festival, Dawlish, last two weeks in June
  Young People's Festival, Easter season

Dewsbury, Yorkshire, England
  Christmas Eve (Tolling the Devil's Knell), December 24

Diamantina and other cities in Brazil
  Holy Spirit, Festival of the Divine, one week in May

Diegueño Indians in California
  Dead, Observance for the (Keruk), seven nights annually

Dijon, Cote-d'Or, France
  Dijon Festival, September
  Nights of Bourgogne, Festival of the (Festival des Nuits
    de Bourgogne), June-July during odd-numbered years

Dinant, Belgium
  La Meuse Festival, July-August

Dinkelsbühl, Bavaria, Federal Republic of Germany
  Children's Reckoning (Kinderzeche), Saturday before
    the third Monday of June
  Theatre Festival, Dinkelsbühl Open-Air, June-August

**Dinosaur National Monument near Grand Junction,
Colorado**
  Dinosaur Days, last week in July

Disentis, Grisons, Switzerland
  St. Placidus Festival, July 11

Djakovo, Croatia, Yugoslavia
  Djakovo Embroidery, two days in early July

Djibouti
  National Day, June 27

Dodge City, Kansas
  Dodge City Days, six days in late July

Dodoth people in Uganda
  Harvest Season (Lara)

Dominica
Independence Day, November 3, two-day celebration

Dominican Republic
Duarte Day, January 26
Exaltation of the Cross, May 2-3
Independence Day, February 27
Political Restitution Day, August 16

Donegal (County), Ireland
Folk Festival, Letterkenny International, five days in late August

Dordogne, France
Theatre, Festival of Plays for the, July-August

Dorset, England
Theatre Festival, Brownsea Open Air, last week in July and first week in August

Dorsetshire, England
Garland Day, May 12 or 13

Dos Hermanas near Seville, Spain
Pilgrimage of Our Lady of Valme (Romario of Our Lady of Valme), October 17

Douai, France
Giants, Festival of the (Fête des Géants), three days beginning Sunday after July 5

Doubs, France
Besançon International Festival (Festival International de Besançon), two weeks beginning September 1

Dougga, Beja Region, Tunisia
Dougga, Festival of, July

Douglas, Wyoming
Jackalope Days, late June

Douz, South Sahara Region, Tunisia
Sahara National Festival, one week in November-December, depending on the weather and the harvest

Doylestown, Pennsylvania
Polish Festival, first weekend in September

Driftwood, Sinnemahoning, and Mix Run, Pennsylvania
Mix Roundup, Tom, three days in July

Drome, France
Music Weeks in Drome, Contemporary, two weeks in June-July

Dubai, United Arab Emirates
Ramadan, ninth Islamic month

Dublin, County Dublin, Ireland
Arts Festival, Dublin, March
Bloomsday, June 16
Feis Ceoil, week of second Monday in May
Horse Show, Dublin, six days in August
Theatre Festival, Dublin, October

Dublin (County), Ireland
Arts Festival, Dublin, March
Bloomsday, June 16
Feis Ceoil, week of second Monday in May
Horse Show, Dublin, six days in August
Theatre Festival, Dublin, October

Dubrovnik, Croatia, Yugoslavia
Dubrovnik Festival (Dubrovacke Ljetne Igre), seven weeks from second week in July to third week in August

Dudulsi Village, Lela, Volta
New Year Purification before Planting, April, just before planting

Duisburg, North Rhine-Westphalia, Federal Republic of Germany
Duisburg Trends, May during odd-numbered years

Dulce, New Mexico
Powwow, Little Beaver Rodeo and, late July

Duluth, Minnesota
Ni-Mi-Win Celebration, third weekend in August

Dumfries, Scotland
Good Neighbours Festival, one week in late June

Dundalk, County Louth, Ireland
Maytime Festival, International, third week in May

Dunseith, North Dakota, and Manitoba, Canada
Arts, International Festival of the, six weeks during June and July

Durango, Colorado
Navajo Trails Fiesta, first weekend in August

Durau, Romania
Mount Ceahlau Feast, second Sunday in August

Durazno, Uruguay
Folklore, National Festival of, three days in January

Durbuy, Belgium
Music, Opera and Theatre, Durbuy Festival of, July-August

517

England *(cont.)*

Mardi Gras (Collop Monday and Shrove or Pancake Tuesday), February-March, Monday and Tuesday before Ash Wednesday

Mardi Gras (Pancake Day), February-March, Tuesday before Ash Wednesday

Martinmas, November 11

May Day, May 1

Merton Festival, May

Michaelmas, September 29

Mid-Lent Sunday (Mothering Sunday), March, fourth Sunday in Lent

Midsummer, June 23-24

Mime Festival, January-February

Mind and Body, Festival of, March-April

Minehead & Exmoor Festival, last two weeks in July

Minehead Hobby Horse Parade, May

Mint Julep Day, June 1

Miracles at Glastonbury, end of June through end of first week in August

Mischief Night, November 4

Music, Cheltenham International Festival of, nine days beginning first week in July

Music and the Arts, Aldeburgh Festival of, ten to 17 days in June or July

Music and the Arts, King's Lynn Festival of, nine days in July

Music and the Arts, Norfolk and Norwich Triennial Festival of, every three years in October

Mystery Plays, York Festival and, every three years in June

National Anti-Drugs Day, March 11

Nativity of the Virgin, Feast of the, September 8

New Year's Day (First-Foot Day), January 1

New Year's Eve, December 31

Nottingham Festival, June

Old Man's Day, October 2

Old Midsummer Eve, July 4

Opera, Glyndebourne Festival, ten to eleven weeks from late May to early August

Oranges and Lemons Day, March 31

Oxford Festival, July-August

Palm Sunday, March-April, the Sunday preceding Easter

Parliament Day, early November

Partridge Day, September 1

Passion Sunday, March, Sunday preceding Palm Sunday

Paul Pitcher Day, January 24

Payment of Quit Rent, September 29

Pentecost (Whitsunday or White Sunday), May-June, the Sunday fifty days after Easter

Pershore Festival, last two weeks in June

Pig Face Sunday, the Sunday following September 14

Plague Sunday, last Sunday in August

Plough Monday, first Monday after Epiphany or Twelfth Day, January 6

Portsmouth Festival, mid-May

Primrose Day, April 19

Punky Night, October 28 or 29 or last Thursday in October

Quarter Days, March 25, June 24, September 29, and December 25

Queen Elizabeth II, Official Birthday of, June 12 or second Saturday in June

Remembrance Day (formerly Armistice Day), November 11; observed second Sunday in November

Richmondshire Festival, May-June during odd-numbered years

Ringing Day, November 5

Rogation Days (Beating the Bounds), May, fifth Sunday through Wednesday after Easter

Royal Tournament, July

Rush-Bearing Day, observed the Saturday nearest August 5

Rye Festival, first week in September

St. Agnes Eve, January 20

St. Andrew's Day, November 30

St. Anne's Day, July 26

St. Barnabas's Day, June 11

St. Bartholomew's Day, August 24

St. Blaise's Day, February 3

St. Catherine's Day, November 25

St. Cecilia's Day, November 22

St. Charles's Day, January 30; observed on or near February 2 at Trafalgar Square, London

St. Clement's Day, November 23

St. Crispin's Day, October 25

St. David's Day, March 1

St. Etheldreda's Day, October 17

St. George's Day, April 23

St. Lubbock's Day, first Monday in August

St. Luke, Feast Day of, October 18

St. Mark, Feast of, April 25

St. Nicholas's Day, December 6

St. Paul, Feast of the Conversion of, January 25

St. Piran's Day, March 5

St. Stephen, Feast of (Hunting the Wren), December 26

St. Swithin's Day, July 15

St. Thomas the Apostle, Feast of (Doleing or Gooding Day), December 21

Saints, Doctors, Missionaries, and Martyrs Day, November 8

Shakespeare Company Festival, Royal, April-December

Shakespeare's Birthday, April 23

Silver Ball, Hurling the, Sunday nearest or Monday after February 3

Stir-Up Sunday, late November, Sunday preceding Advent Sunday

Straw Bear Day, December-January, Saturday preceding Plough Monday

Stroud Festival, second and third weeks in October

Summer Festival, Ludlow, last week in June and first week in July

England *(cont.)*
Swan Upping, Monday through Thursday during third full
  week in July
Thamesday, early September
Theatre, Chichester Festival, May-September
Theatre, Polesden Lacey Open Air, end of June to
  beginning of July
Theatre, St. George's Elizabethan, summer through autumn
Theatre Festival, Brownsea Open Air, last week in July
  and first week in August
Theatre Festival, Minack, end of June to mid-September
Theatre Season, Open-Air, May-August
Theatres, National Festival of Youth, one week in September
Theatre Weeks, International and English Amateur-,
  alternate years in April
Thinking Day, February 22
Thornton Festival, last week in June
Three Choirs Festival, seven to ten days in mid-August;
  location alternates annually
Tichborne Dole, March 26
Trafalgar Day (Horatio Nelson Day), October 21
Trinity Sunday, May-June, observed first Sunday after
  Pentecost
Twelfth Night (Epiphany Eve; formerly known as Wassail
  Eve in northern England), January 5
Universal Week of Prayer, first through second Sunday
  in January
Valentine's Day, February 14
Vic Festival, four weeks in May-June
Victoria Day (Empire Day), Monday nearest May 24
Wangford Festival, eight days in July
Wavendon Season, May-July
Well Dressing, before Ascension Day
Whit Monday, May-June, Monday after Pentecost
Wimbledon, Lawn Tennis Championships at, June
Windsor Festival, two weeks in mid-September
Wood Promenade Concerts, Henry, nine weeks from mid-
  July to mid-September
Wrekin and Telford Festival, five or six weeks in April-May
Young People's Festival, Easter season
Young Writers' Festival, February-May
Yule, December 22

England (medieval)
Christmas Eve, December 24

England (northern)
Harvest Home Festival (Mell Supper), September 24
New Year's Eve (Hogmanay), December 31
Nippy Lug Day, Friday after Ash Wednesday
Shick-Shack Day, May 29

England (printers in)
Waygoose Feast (Beanfest, or Beano in England;

Fastnachtsschmaus, Lichtschmaus, or Martinschmaus),
  near St. Bartholomew's Day, August 24

English Bay, Vancouver, British Columbia, Canada
Polar Bear Swim Day, January 1

English immigrants in the United States
Groundhog Day, February 2

Enid, Oklahoma
Cherokee Strip Day, September 16

Ennis, County Clare, Ireland
Fleadh Nua, May-June

Epidauros, Peloponnese, Greece
Theater Festival, Epidauros, June through August

Epsom Racecourse, Surrey, England
Derby Day, late May or early June

Equatorial Guinea
Human Rights Day, December 10
Independence Day, October 12
Organization of African Unity (OAU) Day, May 25

Erfurt, Germany
Martinsfest, November 10-11

Erl, Tirol, Austria
Passion Play, every six years from June to September

Ermatingen, Switzerland
Fish Carnival (Groppenfasnacht), March, third Sunday
  before Easter, every three years

Escoheag, Rhode Island
Cajun and Bluegrass Festival, first weekend in
  September, including Labor Day

The Escorial, Madrid, Spain
St. Lawrence of Rome, Feast Day of, August 10

Eskimo people
Asking Festival (Ai-yá-g'ûk)
Crow Fair, at least six days in mid-August
New Year's Day, January 1
New Year's Day, autumn
Top of the World Ski Meet, March-April, Easter weekend

Eskimo people, Central
Sedna, Feast of, autumn

Esparraguera, Barcelona, Spain
Passio Festival, La, February-March, during Lent, the forty
  days preceding Easter

Esquipulas, Guatemala
Black Christ, Festival of the, January 15

Essex, England
Arts Festival, Braintree District, six weeks in April-May

Estado Anzoategui, Venezuela
Theater, Eastern Festival of, ten days annually, date varies

Estonia
Christmas (Jõulud), December 25
Christmas Eve (Jõulu Laupäev), December 24
Easter (Ülestôusmise Pühad), March-April, first Sunday
  after first full moon after the vernal equinox; observed
  Sunday, Monday, and Tuesday
Easter Monday, March-April, Monday and Tuesday after
  Easter
Epiphany (Kolme Kuninga Päev), January 6
Good Friday (Suur Reede), March-April, Friday preceding
  Easter Sunday
Independence Day, February 24
Killing the Pigs, Festival of (Seatapmise Päev), September
Mardi Gras (Vastla Päev), February-March, Tuesday before
  Ash Wednesday
Martinmas, November 29
New Year's Day (Uus Aasta), January 1
Peko, Feast of, October 1
Pentecost, May-June, the Sunday fifty days after Easter
Reformation Day (Usupuhastus Püha), October 31;
  observed Sunday preceding October 31
St. George's Day (Jüri Päev), April 23
St. Michael's Day (Mihkli Paev), September 29
Singing Festival (Laulipidu), every fifth year on June 25
Spring, Bringing of the (Kevad Püha), May 1

Estremadura, Portugal
Our Lady of Fátima Day, July 13
Our Lady of Nazaré Festival, September 8-18

Eszterháza Palace, Fertöd, Hungary
Haydn Memorial Concerts, summer

Ethete, Wyoming
Dance and Ethete Celebration, Sun, July
Labor Day Powwow, first Monday in September
Powwow, Wyoming Indian High School, May
Powwow, Yellow Calf Memorial, May

Ethiopia
Assumption, Feast of the, 16-day fast in August
Christmas (Ganna, Genna, or Leddat), January 7
Easter (Fasika), March-April, first Sunday after first full
  moon after the vernal equinox
Epiphany (Timqat or Timkat), January 19
Exaltation of the Cross (Meskel, Finding of the True

Cross), September 27; end of the rainy season
Mother's Day (Antrosht), two to three days in October
  or November
National Day, September 12
New Year (Enkutatash), September 11
St. Michael's Day, November 8
St. Michael's Feast, monthly
Seged, November, 29th day of eighth month
Selassie's Birthday, Haile, July 23
Sukkot (bä alä mäsällät, Feast of the Tabernacles), 15th-
  21st or 22nd of Jewish month of Tishri
Transfiguration, Feast of the (Buhé), August 19
Victory of Aduwa Day, March 2

Eugene, Oregon
Bach Festival, Oregon, late June to second week in July

Eureka Springs, Arkansas
Arts Colony, Inspiration Point Fine, June to second week
  in July
Folk Festival, Ozark, two to three days in early November

Europe
Christmas, Twelve Days of, December 25-January 6

Europe (medieval)
Fools, Feast of, between Christmas and January 1
Lord of Misrule, Christmas through Epiphany (December
  25-January 6) or Allhallows through Candlemas (October
  31 or November 1-February 2)
Pentecost, May-June, the Sunday fifty days after Easter

Europe (northern)
Nativity of the Sun, December 21-25

European-Americans
Martinmas, November 11

Ewe people in Ghana
New Yam Festival (Odwira), September

Ewé people in Togo: Agome-yo Village
Planting Ceremony

Eyam, Derbyshire, England
Plague Sunday, last Sunday in August

Ezzahra, North Tunis Region, Tunisia
Ezzahra, Festival, July-August

Fairbanks, Alaska
Arts, Festival of Native, three days in late February
Golden Days, third week in July
Olympics, World Eskimo Indian, three days in late July
  or early August
Winter Carnival, Fairbanks, third week in March

Fairhope, Alabama
Fairhope Jubilee, summer

Fairplay, Buena Vista, and Leadville, Colorado
Burro Races, Triple Crown Pack, last weekend in July
through August

Falkland Islands
Queen Elizabeth II, Birthday of (Falkland Islands Day),
April 21

Fallon, Nevada
Indian Rodeo and Stampede Days, All, third or fourth
weekend in July

Falls Village, Connecticut
Music Mountain, Saturday evenings and Sunday afternoons from mid-June to early September

Famalicao, Porto, Portugal
Famalicao, International Festival of, August

Farmington, Connecticut
Powwow, Connecticut River, first weekend in September

Farmington, Maine
Greenwood Day, Chester, first Saturday in December

Faro, Portugal
Algarve, National Festival of the, two days in August
or September
St. Iria Fair, October
Theatres, Algarve Meeting of Amateur, summer

Faroe Islands
Olsok, July 29-30

Fátima, Estremadura, Portugal
Our Lady of Fátima Day, July 13

Fayetteville, West Virginia
Bridge Day, third Saturday in October

Federal District, Mexico
Passion Play, March-April, Good Friday

Fergus, Ontario, Canada
Highland Games, Fergus, second Saturday in August

Fertöd, Hungary
Haydn Memorial Concerts, summer

Feuchtwangen, Bavaria, Federal Republic of Germany
Cloister Festival, June-August

Fez, Morocco
Fantasia (Horse Festival), October

Fife, Scotland
St. Andrew's Festival, ten days in February during odd-
numbered years

Figueira da Foz, Coimbra, Portugal
Maiorga, International Festival of, September
Theatre Competition of Figueira da Foz, Amateur,
February-April

Fiji
Fiji Day, observed on or near October 10
Queen Elizabeth's Day, Monday nearest to official date
proclaimed in England

Filipino-Americans in California
Exaltation of the Cross (Santacruzan), May 3

Finistere, France
Cornwall, Festival of, one week in July

Finland
All Saints' Day (Kekri), November 1
Annunciation, Feast of the (Lady Day), March 25
Arts Festival, Jyvaskyla, several days in May-July
Christmas (Joulupäivä), December 25
Christmas Eve (Jouluaatto), December 24
Dance and Music Festival, Kuopio, June
Easter (Pääsiäissunnuntai), March-April, first Sunday
after first full moon after the vernal equinox
Easter Monday (Toinen Pääsiäispäivä), March-April,
Monday after Easter
Epiphany (Loppiainen), January 6
Flag Day of the Army, May 19
Folk Music Festival Kaustinen, third week in July
Good Friday (Pitkäperjantai, Long Friday), March-April,
Friday preceding Easter Sunday
Helsinki Day, June 12
Helsinki Festival (Helsingin Juhlaviikot), 18 days beginning
August 24
Holy Saturday (Pääsiäisaatto), Easter Eve, March-April,
Saturday before Easter Sunday
Independence Day, December 6
Jazz Festival, Pori International, four days in mid-July
Kalevala Päivä Day, February 28
Kivi Day, October 10
Mardi Gras (Laskiaispäivä), February-March, Tuesday
before Ash Wednesday
May Day (Vappu), May 1
May Day Eve (Vapun Aatto or Vappu), April 30
Midsummer (Juhannus Day), June 24; observed Saturday
closest to June 24
Music Festival, Kuhmo Chamber (Kuhmon Kamarmusiikki),

Finland *(cont.)*
ten days in late July or early August
New Year's Day (Uudenvuoden Päivä), January 1
New Year's Eve (Uudenvuoden), December 31
Opera Festival, Savonlinna (Savonlinnan Oopperajuhlat), first three weeks in July
Palm Sunday, March-April, the Sunday preceding Easter
Pentecost, May-June, the Sunday fifty days after Easter
Pispalan Sottiisi, June during even-numbered years
Reindeer Driving Competition, third week in March
Runeberg, Birthday of Johann Ludvig, February 5
St. Lucy's Day, December 13
St. Michael's Day, first Sunday in October
St. Peter's Day, June 29
Theatre Summer, Amateur, four days in August
Theatre Summer, Tampere, August
Walpurgis Night, April 30
Winter Games, Ounasvaara International, two days in mid-March

Finnish-Americans
St. Urho's Day, March 16

Finno-Ugric people in Russia: Kazan, Vjatka, and Perm
Holy Thursday (Votjak or Udmurt), March-April, Thursday preceding Easter

Fish Creek, Wisconsin
Music Festival, Peninsula, two weeks in mid-August

Flagstaff, Arizona
Arts, Flagstaff Festival of the, four weeks in July

Flandreau, South Dakota
Powwow, Santee Sioux, July

Flemington, New Jersey
Flemington Fair, one week from late August through Labor Day, first Monday in September

Flint, Michigan
White Shirt Day, February 11

Florence, Tuscany, Italy
Ascension Day (Cricket Festival, Festa del Grillo), May-June, fortieth day after Easter Sunday
Easter (Scoppio del Carro, Ceremony of the Car), March-April, first Sunday after first full moon after the vernal equinox
Holy Saturday (Scoppia del Carro, Explosion of the Car), March-April, Saturday before Easter Sunday
Impruneta, Festa del, late October
Musical May, Florence (Maggio Musicale Fiorentino), eight weeks in May and June
Nativity of the Virgin, Feast of the, September 8

St. Roch's Day (San Rocco), August 16
Theatre Review, International, April-May

Florida
Admission Day, March 3
Arts Festival, week after Christmas
Bach Festival of Winter Park, three days in late February or early March
Billy Bowlegs Festival, first full weekend in June
Brighton Field Day and Rodeo, third weekend in February
Carnaval Miami, first two full weeks in March
Circus Festival and Parade, Sarasota, first week in January
Confederate Memorial Day, April 26
Dance, Green Corn, spring or summer
Davis's Birthday, Jefferson, June 3
Daytona 500, February
Edison Pageant of Light, second Wednesday through third Saturday in February, including February 11
Epiphany, January 6
Folk Festival, Florida, two to three days in late May
Foster Memorial Day, January 13
Garbanzo, Fiesta Sopa de, begins Sunday nearest February 9 and ends Saturday
Gasparilla Pirate Festival and Invasion, six days beginning the Monday after the first Tuesday in February
Guavaween, last Saturday in October
Hemingway Days, week including July 21
Mardi Gras, February-March
Motorcycle Week, first week in March
Music Festival of Florida, three weekends in June
Old Island Days, seven weeks from early February to late March
Orange Bowl Football Classic, January 1
Palm Beach Festival, two weeks in December
Pascua Florida Day, April 2; Pascua Florida Week is March 27-April 2
Powwow, Seminole, February
St. Michael's Day, November 8
St. Nicholas's Day, December 6
Sebring 12 Hours (Automobile Hall of Fame Week), third week in March
Seminole Fair, fourth weekend in December
(De) Soto Celebration, one week in March or early April

Foligno, Umbria, Italy
Joust of the Quintain, second weekend in September

Fonda, New York
Indian Festival, Katari

Forchtenstein, Burgenland, Austria
Castle Plays Festival, June-July

Fort Bragg, Gualala, and Mendocino, California
Whale Festival, March

Fort Bridger, Wyoming
Mountain Man Rendezvous, first weekend in September

Fort Hall, Idaho
Indian Days, Fort Hall, August

Fort Myers, Florida
Edison Pageant of Light, second Wednesday through third Saturday in February, including February 11

Fort Walton Beach, Florida
Billy Bowlegs Festival, first full weekend in June

Fort Washakie, Wyoming
Indian Days, late June

Fort Wayne, Indiana
Johnny Appleseed Festival, third week in September

Fort Worth, Texas
Livestock Show and Rodeo, Southwestern Exposition and, last two weeks in January

Foz, Lugo, Spain
St. Lawrence of Rome, Feast of (Festival of San Lorenzo), August

France
All Saints' Day (La Toussaint), November 1
Anjou Festival, July-August
Annunciation, Feast of the (Notre Dame de Mars), March 25
April Fools' Day (Poisson d'Avril), April 1
Arles Festival, July-August
Armistice Day, November 11
Art and History in Saint-Aignan, Festival of, Sundays in July and August
Art and History in Valencay, Festival of, Thursdays, Saturdays, and Sundays in August
Arts, Festival of International Contemporary (Recontres Internationales d'Art Contemporain), two weeks in June-July
Arts, Festival of Traditional, March
Arts and Music, Frejus Forum of (Forum des Arts et de la Musique), July
Ash Wednesday, February-March, fortieth day before Easter Sunday
Assumption, Feast of the (L'Assomption), August 15
Autumn Festival, Paris (Festival d'Automne), mid-September through end of December
Avignon Festival (Festival d'Avignon), three and one-half weeks in July-August
Bastille Day (Fête Nationale), July 14
Bellac Festival, June-July
Berlioz International Festival (Internationales Festival Hector Berlioz), one week in mid-September

Besançon International Festival (Festival International de Besançon), two weeks beginning September 1
Burning of the Three Firs, June 30
Candlemas (La Chandeleur), February 2
Carcassone, Festival of, two weeks in July
Chateauvallon Festival, July-August
Christmas (Noël), December 25
Christmas Eve (Veille de Noël), December 24
Confolens Festival, one week in August
Cornwall, Festival of, one week in July
Corpus Christi (Fête Dieu), May-June
Dance Festival of Paris, International, October-December
D-Day (Allied Landing Observances Day), June 6
Dijon Festival, September
Dullin Prize Competition, May-June, Thursday to Sunday evening of Ascension Day during even-numbered years
Easter (Pâques), March-April, first Sunday after first full moon after the vernal equinox
Easter Festival of Sacred Music, March-April, ten days beginning Good Friday
Easter Monday (Lundi de Pâques), March-April, Monday after Easter
East Var, Festival of, six weeks in July-August
Epiphany (Le Jour des Rois), January 6
Film Festival, Cannes, May
Flutes, Day of the (Pffiferdaj), first Sunday of September
Folklore, World Festival of, one week in July
Folklore Festival, International, about one week in August
Folkloric Festival of Rouergue, International, one week in August
French Open Tennis Championships, May-June
Frost, or Ice, Saints Day (Eisheiligan), May 11-14
Giants, Festival of the (Fête des Géants), three days beginning Sunday after July 5
Good Friday (Vendredi-Saint), March-April, Friday preceding Easter Sunday
Harvest Festival of Provins, France, last weekend in August
Hauts-de-Saone Festival, last weekend in June and first weekend in July
Hede Festival, about one week in August
Holy Innocents' Day, December 28
Holy Maries, Feast of (La Fête des Saintes Maries), May 24-25
Lammas (formerly a feast for the Society of the Trade of Cobblers), August 1
Holy Thursday, March-April, Thursday preceding Easter
Holy Week, March-April, week preceding Easter
Ille Festival, one week in May or June
Immaculate Conception, Feast of the, December 8
Jazz, Nice Grand Parade of (Grande Parade du Jazz), eleven days beginning first week in July
Le Mans Grand Prix, June
Liberation Day, August 25
Lorient Festival, ten days at beginning of August

France *(cont.)*

Lyon International Festival (Festival International de Lyon), June-July

Marais Festival, June-July

Mardi Gras, February-March, Tuesday before Ash Wednesday

Mardi Gras (Carnival and Battle of the Flowers), February-March, twelve days ending Ash Wednesday

Martinmas (Foire de la Saint Martin), November 11

Mary, Month of (Mois de Marie), May

May Day (Premier Mai), May 1

Michaelmas, September 29

Mid-Lent Sunday (Mi-Carême), March, fourth Sunday in Lent

Midsummer (La Veille de la Saint Jean), June 23-24

Music, Saintes Festival of Ancient (Saintes Festival de Musique Ancienne), one week in early July

Musical, Bordeaux International May (Mai Musical International), 16 days beginning first week in May

Musical Festival of La Sainte-Baume, two weeks in July-August

Musical Weeks of Luberon (Semaines Musicales du Luberon), two weeks in July-August

Musical Weeks of Orleans, International (Semaines Musicales Internationale d'Orleans), two weeks in November-December

Music at La Defense, month of June

Music Festival, International, July-August

Music Festival, Menton (Festival de Musique de Menton), month of August

Music Festival, Metz International Contemporary (Rencontres Internationales de Musique Contemporaine), five days in mid-November

Music Festival, Strasbourg International (Festival International de Musique de Strasbourg), 16 days beginning first week in June

Music Festival, Toulon (Festival de Musique de Toulon), June-July

Music Festival, Touraine (Fêtes Musicales en Touraine), one week in late June or early July

Music Festival of Saint-Denis, May-June

Music Weeks in Drome, Contemporary, two weeks in June-July

Napoleon's Day, May 5

New Year's Day (Le Jour de l'An or Le Jour des Étrennes), January 1

Nights of Bourgogne, Festival of the (Festival des Nuits de Bourgogne), June-July during odd-numbered years

Nights of the Enclave (Nuits de l'Enclave des Papes), July-August

Night Watch (La Retraite aux Flambeaux), July 13

Occitanie Festival, one week from late June to early July

Opera, Ballet and Music Festival, Vichy, June-September

Opera and Music, Aix-en-Provence International Festival of (Festival International d'Art Lyrique et de Musique d'Aix-en-Provence), three and one-half weeks in July

Orange Festival (Chorégies d'Orange), four productions in late July to early August

Our Lady of Lourdes, Feast of, February 11; festival between February 11-18

Palm Sunday (Rameaux), March-April, the Sunday preceding Easter

Paris Air and Space Show, 11 days in June during odd-numbered years

Paris Festival Estival (Festival Estival de Paris), mid-July to mid-September

Paris Marathon, third Saturday in May

Pau Festival, one week in June

Pentecost (La Pentecôte or Fête des Marins, Sailors' Festival), May-June, the Sunday fifty days Easter; two-day holiday

Pilgrimage to St. Anne d'Auray, July 26; observed last weekend in July

Quintane, La, second Sunday of November

Roche-Jagu, Festival of, June-September

Rogation Days, May, fifth Sunday through Wednesday after Easter

St. Agatha Festival (Girls' Festival), February 5

St. Barbara's Day, December 4

St. Blaise's Day, February 3

St. Catherine's Day, November 25

St. Charlemagne's Day, January 28

St. Crispin's Day, October 25

St. Gens, Festival of (La Fête de St. Gens), twice yearly: Sunday following May 15 at Monteux and first weekend in September at Beaucet

St. Honoratus's Day, January 16

St. Ivo, Pardon of, May 19 (pilgrimage to)

St. Joan of Arc, Feast of (Fête de Jeanne d'Arc), second Sunday in May

St. Martha, Feast of (Fête de la Tarasque), last Sunday in June and July 29

St. Mary Magdalene, Feast of, July 22 (pilgrimage to holy cave)

St. Nicholas's Day, December 6

St. Stephen, Feast of, December 26

St. Sylvester's Day, December 31

St. Veronica, Feast of, July 12; observed the following Monday

St. Vincent of Sargossa, Feast Day of, January 22

Santon Fair, December

Sigma Festival, one week in November

Simhat Torah, 23rd day of Jewish month of Tishri

Summer Meetings, International, month-long, July-August

Theatre, Biennial of International, May-June, Friday to Monday evening of Pentecost during odd-numbered years

Theatre, Festival of Cafe, November

Theatre, Festival of Plays for the, July-August

Theatre, World Festival of, two weeks in April-May during odd-numbered years

France *(cont.)*
  Theatre for Children and Young People, International
    Encounter of, first two weeks in June during odd-numbered
    years
  Theatre of Silence, Carte Blanche at the (Carte Blanche au
    Theatre du Silence), May-June
  Theatrical, Musical and Artistic Encounters of Grasse,
    Rithma: International, July
  Three Glorious Days (Les Trois Glorieuses), twice annually:
    July 27-29 and third Saturday through Monday in
    November
  Tour de France, four weeks in July
  Trinity Sunday, May-June, observed first Sunday after
    Pentecost
  Twelfth Night (Epiphany Eve), January 5
  Vaison-la-Romaine and Carpentras, Festival of, July-August
  Valentine's Day, February 14
  Vienne Festival, June-August
  Whit Monday (Procession of Giants of Belgium and
    France), May-June, Monday after Pentecost

France (medieval)
  Ass, Feast of the, January 14

Frankenmuth, Michigan
  Frankenmuth Bavarian Festival, second weekend and third
    week in June

Frankfort, Kentucky
  Capital Expo, two days in early June

Franklin, Idaho
  Pioneer Day, June 15

Frazer, Montana
  Indian Celebration, Red Bottom, third weekend in June

Frederick County, Maryland
  Repudiation Day, November 23

Fredericksburg, Texas
  Holy Saturday (Easter Fires Pageant), March-April,
    Saturday before Easter Sunday

Frederikssund, Calf Island, Zealand, Denmark
  Viking Festival, three days to two weeks in June-July

Frederiksted, Virgin Islands
  Virgin Islands Donkey Races Day, February 22

Freeport, Grand Bahama Island, Bahama Islands
  Goombay Festival, July and August

Freetown, Sierra Leone
  Ramadan, ninth Islamic month

Frejus, Var, France
  Arts and Music, Frejus Forum of (Forum des Arts et de la
    Musique), July

Fremantle, Western Australia, Australia
  Fremantle Week, late October-early November

French Alps
  St. Bernard of Montjoux, May 28

French-Americans
  Bastille Day, July 14
  French Festival (French Day), Saturday before Bastille Day,
    July 14
  Jour de Fête a Sainte Genevieve Days of Celebration, second
    weekend in August
  St. Médardus's Day, June 8

French-Canadians
  Midsummer, June 23-24

French Guinea
  Armistice Day, November 11

French West Indies
  All Souls' Day, November 2

Friesach, Carinthia, Austria
  Summer Festival, Friesach, July-August

Friesland Province, Netherlands
  Eleven Cities Race (Elfstedentocht), January 22

Frobisher Bay, Northwest Territories, Canada
  Toonik Time, one week from late April to early May

Fukuoka, Japan
  Bullfinch Exchange Festival (Usokae), January 7

Fukuoka City, Japan
  Hakata Dontaku, May 3-4

Fulton, Kentucky
  Banana Festival, International, mid-September
  See also **South Fulton, Tennessee**

Fulton, Missouri
  Kingdom Days, last weekend in June

Funchal, Madeira Island, Portugal
  Bach Festival, International, June
  St. Sylvester's Day, December 31

Fundata, Brasov, Romania
  Mountains, Festival of the (Nedeia Muntilor), last weekend
    in June

Geisenheim, Rhineland, Germany
Linden Tree Festival (Lindenfest), second weekend in July

Geneva, Switzerland
Escalade, December 11
Summer Season, Geneva, June-August

Genoa, Italy
Torta dei Fieschi, August 14

George Town, Grand Cayman, Cayman Islands
Pirate Week Festival, third week in October

Georgia
Admission Day, January 2
Arts Festival, nine days in May
Cherry Blossom Festival, Macon, mid-March
Confederate Memorial Day, April 26
Davis's Birthday, Jefferson, June 3
Dogwood Festival, April
Georgia Week Celebrations, one week in February, including
    February 12
Gold Rush Days, Dahlonega, October
Heritage Holidays, mid-October
Locomotive Chase Festival, Great, first weekend in October
Master's Golf Tournament, first full week in April
Music Festival, Golden Isles Chamber, nine days in early May
Rose Festival, one week in late April
St. Patrick's Day, March 17
Yellow Daisy Festival, second weekend in September

Georgian Republic, USSR
St. George's Day, observed February 25

German Alps
Mountain Pasture, Return from (Almabtrieb), September

German-Americans
Ascension Day, May-June, fortieth day after Easter Sunday
Christmas Eve, December 24
German Day, October 6
Jour de Fête a Sainte Genevieve Days of Celebration, second
    weekend in August
Mardi Gras (Rosemontag, Rose Monday), February-March,
    Monday preceding Lent
Mayfest (Maifest), third weekend in May
St. Nicholas's Day, December 6
Summer Festival, Bavarian, 11 days in July

German-Americans in Arizona: Tucson
Tucson Meet Yourself Festival, second weekend in October

German-Americans in Michigan: Frankenmuth
Frankenmuth Bavarian Festival, second weekend and third
    week in June

German-Americans in Minnesota: Young America
Stiftungsfest, last weekend in August

German-Americans in Texas: New Braunfels
Sausage Festival (Wurstfest), end of October through first
    week in November

German- and Russian-Americans in Kansas: Ellis County
Frost, or Ice, Saints Day, May 12-14

German-Canadians in Canada: Kitchener, Waterloo, Ontario
Oktoberfest, nine days in early October, beginning the
    Friday before Thanksgiving Monday

German Democratic Republic
Handel Festival, six days in summer
Liberation Day, May 8
Republic Day (Foundation Day), October 7
Shakespeare Days, April
Theatre and Music, Berlin Festival Days of, October

German immigrants in the United States
Groundhog Day, February 2

Germantown, Pennsylvania
Battle of Germantown, Reenactment of, first Saturday in
    October

Germany
Advent, four-week season beginning Sunday nearest
    November 30 and ending December 24
All Saints' Day (Allerheiligen), November 1
Annunciation, Feast of the, March 25
April Fools' Day, observed April 1 and 30
Ascension Day (Himmelfahrstag), May-June, fortieth day
    after Easter Sunday
Ash Wednesday, February-March, fortieth day before Easter
    Sunday
Boundary Walk (Grenzumgang), every ten years (1951, 1961,
    etc.)
Candlemas, February 2
Carling Sunday, March-April, fifth Sunday in Lent
Christkindlesmarkt (Kriss Kringle's Fair), early December
    until Christmas, December 25
Christmas (Weihnachten), December 25-26
Christmas Eve (Heiligabend), December 24
Corpus Christi (Fron Leichnam), May-June
Dragon, Spearing the (Drachenstich), mid-August
Easter (Ostern), March-April, first Sunday after first full
    moon after the vernal equinox
Easter Monday, March-April, Monday after Easter
Epiphany (Dreikönigsfest, Festival of the Three Kings),
    January 6
Frost, or Ice, Saints Day (Eisheiligan), May 11-14
Good Friday, March-April, Friday preceding Easter Sunday

Germany *(cont.)*

Groundhog Day, February 2

Holy Innocents' Day (Allerkinder Tag), December 28

Holy Saturday (Karsamstag), March-April, Saturday before Easter Sunday

Holy Thursday (Gründonnerstag, Green Thursday), March-April, Thursday preceding Easter

Holy Week (Still or Silent Week), March-April, week preceding Easter

Knocking Nights (Klöpfelnächte or Klöpfleinsnächte), December, the three Thursday evenings before Christmas

Kriss Kringle Day, December 5 or December 24

Linden Tree Festival (Lindenfest), second weekend in July

Mardi Gras (Fastnacht and Rosemontag, Rose Monday), February-March, Monday and Tuesday before Ash Wednesday

Mardi Gras (Karneval), December 31 until Ash Wednesday

Mardi Gras (Kopenfahrt, Kope Procession or Festival), February-March, Tuesday before Ash Wednesday

Marksmen's Festival (Schützenfeste), July-August, date varies according to location

Martinmas (Martinstag), November 11

Martinsfest, November 10-11

May Day, May 1

Midsummer (Sommersonnonwende), June 23-24

Mozart Festival (Mozartfest), three weeks in June

Mozart Festival, German (Deutsches Mozartfest), eight days during second week in June (alternates with other German cities)

Nativity of the Virgin, Feast of the (Pferdeweihe, Blessing of Horses), September 8

New Year's Day (Neujahr), January 1

New Year's Eve, December 31

Palm Sunday (Palmsonntag), March-April, the Sunday preceding Easter

Pentecost (Pfingsten), May-June, the Sunday fifty days after Easter

St. Andrew's Day, November 30

St. Barbara's Day, December 4

St. Bartholomew's Day, August 24

St. Crispin's Day, observed June 20

St. George's Day (Georgiritt Parade), April 23

St. Leonard's Day, November 6

St. Leonard's Ride (Leonhardiritt), November 6

St. Michael's Day (Tura Michele Marky or Fair), September 29

St. Nicholas's Day (Nikolaustag or Knecht Ruprecht), December 6

St. Peter's Day, February 22

St. Sylvester's Day (Sylvesterabend), December 31

St. Thomas the Apostle, Feast of, December 21

St. Urban's Day, May 25

Sausage Fair (Bad Durkheim Wurstmarkt), Saturday-Tuesday during second weekend of September; Friday-Monday during third weekend of September

Shepherds' Race (Schäferlauf), August 23-25

Summer Solstice, June 21

Trinity Sunday, May-June, observed first Sunday after Pentecost

Twelfth Night (Epiphany Eve), January 5

Valentine's Day, February 14

Walpurgis Night, April 30

Waygoose Feast (Beanfest, or Beano in England; Fastnachtsschmaus, Lichtschmaus, or Martinschmaus), near St. Bartholomew's Day, August 24

Winter Solstice, December 21

Wooing a Bride (Brauteln), February-March, Tuesday preceding Ash Wednesday

Germany (northern)

Knecht Ruprecht, December 5 or 6 or December 24

Yule, December 22

Germany, Federal Republic of

Bach Festival (Bachwoche Ansbach), ten days in late July during odd-numbered years

Bad Hersfeld in the Monastery Ruins, Festival of, July-August

Ballet Days, Hamburg, July

Ballet Festival Week, March or May

Bayreuth Festival (Bayreuther Festspiele and Richard Wagner Festival), five weeks in late July and August

Beethoven Festival, September-October

Berlin Festival Weeks (Berliner Festwochen), four weeks beginning first week in September

Calderon Festival in the Old Courtyard, June-July

Castle Festival at Jagsthausen, June-August

Castle Gottorf, Festival at, July-August

Castle Play Festival, Moers, five weeks in summer

Castle Theatre Hohenlimburg, June-July

Children's Reckoning (Kinderzeche), Saturday before the third Monday of June

Cloister Festival, June-August

Dance Workshop, Bonn International, July

Dom Fair, November through Christmas, December 25

Duisburg Trends, May during odd-numbered years

European Festival Weeks, June-July

Franconian Festival Week, June

Horizon '79, '81, etc., three to four weeks in June-July during odd-numbered years

Industry Festival of Wetzlar, mid-June to mid-July

Kiel Week, one week in June

Landshut Wedding, three weeks, including four Sundays in June-July, every third year

Luisenburg Festival, June-August

Mardi Gras (Fasching Carnival), January 7-Tuesday before Ash Wednesday

Mardi Gras (Karneval), December 31 until Ash Wednesday

Master Draught Pageant (Meistertrunk Pageant), May-June, Pentecost (Whitsunday)

May Festival, July-August

Germany, Federal Republic of *(cont.)*
May Festival, Wiesbaden International (Internationale Maifestspiele), month of May
Metamusik Festival, October during even-numbered years
Mozart Festival, German (Deutsches Mozartfest), eight days during second week in June (alternates with other German cities)
Music and Theatre in Herrenhausen, June-August
Oktoberfest, 16 days, usually beginning first Sunday in October
Opera Festival, Munich (Münchner Opernfestspiele), 25 days in July-August
Pantomime Festival (Gaukler Festival), October
Pantomime-Music-Dance-Theatre, April-June
Passion Play, Oberammergau, every ten years from May to September
Penance Day, November 17
Pied Piper of Hamelin Festival, every Sunday at noon during the summer
Plays Festival, Gandersheim Cathedral, May-June
Plays in the Town Hall, May-June to September for two consecutive years followed by two-year interim
Plays '78, '79, etc., one week in May
Puppet Play Encounter, three days in October during odd-numbered years
Puppet Play Week, International, one week in March during odd-numbered years
Puppet Theatre of the Nations, International Festival Week, one week in May or June
Puppet Theatre Week 1978, 1979, etc., one week in January
Republic Day, June 2
Ruhr Festival, May-June
Schiller Days, May
Schwetzingen Festival, April-May
Summer Academy of Dance, International, two weeks in June-July
Theatre, International Festival of Free, April-May
Theatre, Summer Festival at the Bergwald, weekends in June-July
Theatre Festival, Dinkelsbühl Open-Air, June-August
Theatre Festival, International Arena, even-numbered years in May
Theatre Festival, Open-Air, Saturdays in July and August
Theatre Festival in Schwabisch-Hall, Open-Air, June-August
Theatre Nettelstedt, Open-Air, Saturdays and Sundays from May to September
Theatre Rally, May
Theatre Rally, North Germany, one week in mid-May

Gerona, Spain
St. Christina's Day (Festival of Santa Cristina), July 24; festival held in July
Verges Festival, March-April, Holy Thursday

Gettysburg, Pennsylvania
Gettysburg Civil War Heritage Days, last weekend in June

and first week in July
Gettysburg Day, July 1

Ghana
Apo Festival
Christmas (Abron), December 25
Deer-Hunting Festival, April-May
Hooting at Hunger (Homowo), August
Independence Day, March 6
New Yam Festival (Odwira), September
New Yam Festival (Odwira), September-October, up to forty days
Path Clearing Festival (Akwambo), September 3
Republic Day, July 1

Ghent, Belgium
Flanders, Festival of (Festival van Vlaanderen), April to October
Flower Festival (Ghent Floralies), April or May, every five years

Ghent, Minnesota
Belgian-American Days, four days in August

Gibraltar
Shark Angling Competition, International, one day in late April or early May

Gijon, Oviedo, Spain
Asturias Day, first Sunday in August

Gimli, Manitoba, Canada
Arts Week, Creative, last full week in August
Icelandic Festival (Islendingadagurinn), during last week in July or first week in August

Gironde, France
Musical, Bordeaux International May (Mai Musical International), 16 days beginning first week in May
Sigma Festival, one week in November

Giudecca Island, Italy
Redeemer, Feast of the (Festa del Redentore), third Sunday in July

Glassboro, New Jersey
Hollybush Festival, May and June

Glastonbury, Somerset, England
Miracles at Glastonbury, end of June through end of first week in August

Glen Falls, New York
Opera Festival, Lake George, six weeks from mid-July to last week in August

Gloucester, England
Three Choirs Festival, seven to ten days in mid-August; location alternates annually

Gloucester, Massachusetts
St. Peter's Day, June 29

Gloucestershire, England
Pig Face Sunday, the Sunday following September 14
Stroud Festival, second and third weeks in October

Gloucestershire Regiment of the British Army
Back Badge Day, March 21

Glyndebourne, East Sussex, England
Opera, Glyndebourne Festival, ten to eleven weeks from late May to early August

Glyndon, Maryland
Maryland Hunt Club, last Saturday in April

Gnjilane and Pec, Kosovo, Serbia, Yugoslavia
Theatre Groups, Regional Review of Kosovo Amateur, April

Goa, India
Drama Festival, Marathi, February-March
Drama Festival, Goa Academy, five to ten days in November-December or February-March
Mardi Gras (Intruz, Carnival), February-March, Saturday-Ash Wednesday

Gochang, Republic of Korea
Castle Festival, Moyang, mid-October, ninth day of ninth lunar month

Golden Hill Paugussett Indians in Connecticut: Farmington
Powwow, Connecticut River, first weekend in September

Golden Spike Historical Monument, Corrine, Utah
Golden Spike Day, May 10

Goliad, Texas
Cinco de Mayo, May 5

Gomon, Ivory Coast
Dipri Festival, March-April

Gondomar, Porto, Portugal
Gondomar, International Festival of, August

Gond people in central provinces of India
Bhima or Bhima-sena, Festival of, near time of monsoon

Goodyear, Avondale, and Litchfield Park, Arizona
Moore Days, Billy, second weekend in October

Gora, Poland
Theatre Encounter, Jelenia Gora, September

Gorey, County Wexford, Ireland
Arts Festival, Gorey, summer

Gorj, Romania
In the Sunlit Plain, first week in June
Tismana Garden Festival, August 15

Goschenhoppen Park, East Greenville, Pennsylvania
Folk Festival, Goschenhoppen Historians', second Friday and Saturday in August

Gospa od Skrpjelo, Montenegro (formerly in Yugoslavia)
Fasinada, July 22

Gotland Island, Sweden
Visby Festival, July-August

Gourdon-en-Quercy, Lot, France
Music Festival, International, July-August

Gouveia, Viseu, Portugal
Folklore, Gouveia International Festival of, August

Gozo (part of Malta)
Festa Season, May to October, peaking in July

Graceland, Memphis, Tennessee
Elvis International Tribute Week, week including August 16

Grafton, New South Wales, Australia
Arts, Big River Festival of, one week in May-June

Granada, Spain
Music and Dance Festival, Granada International (Festival Internacional de Musica y Danza de Granada), three weeks beginning in mid-June
Theatre Groups, Encounter of Andalucian, February

Gran Chaco, South America
Harvest Dance (Kyaiya), spring, summer, and autumn

Grand Bahama Island, Bahama Islands
Goombay Festival, July and August

Grand Cayman, Cayman Islands
Pirate Week Festival, third week in October

Grandfather Mountain near Linville, North Carolina
Highland Games and Gathering of Scottish Clans, Grandfather Mountain, second full weekend in July

Grand Island, Nebraska
Crane Watch (Wings over the Platte), March-April

Grand Junction, Colorado
Dinosaur Days, last week in July

Grand Portage, Minnesota
Rendezvous Days, second weekend in August

Grasmere, England
Rush-Bearing Day, observed the Saturday nearest August 5

Grasse, Alpes-Maritimes, France
Theatrical, Musical and Artistic Encounters of Grasse, Rithma: International, July

Graus, Huesca, Spain
Santo Cristo and San Vicente Ferrer, Festival of, September

Graz, Styria, Austria
Autumn, Styrian (Steirischer Herbst), eight weeks in October-November

Great Barrington, Massachusetts
Aston Magna Festival, three consecutive Saturday evenings in early July

Great Bookham, Surrey, England
Theatre, Polesden Lacey Open Air, end of June to beginning of July

Great Britain
Alexandra Rose Day, a Saturday in June
All Souls' Day, November 2
Battle of Flowers, second Thursday in August
Budget Day, April 9
Carling Sunday, March-April, fifth Sunday in Lent
Commonwealth Day (formerly Empire Day), second Monday in March
Cup Final Day, May
Derby Day, late May or early June
Epiphany (Old Christmas), January 6
Holy Saturday, March-April, Saturday before Easter Sunday
Holy Thursday (Maundy Thursday), March-April, Thursday before Easter
Lammas (Gules of August), August 1
Lent, February-March, forty-day season preceding Easter
May Day, May 1; observed first Monday in May
Mayoring Day, late May
National No Smoking Day, March 11
Nut Monday, first Monday in August
Plough Monday, first Monday after Epiphany or Twelfth Day, January 6
Poppy Day, November 11; observed second Sunday in November
Quadragesima Sunday, February-March, first Sunday in Lent
Queen Elizabeth II, Official Birthday of, June 12 or second Saturday in June

Queen's Day, November 17
Regatta Week, July-August
St. Bridget's Day, February 1
St. James the Greater's Day, July 25
St. Swithin's Day, July 15
Trooping the Colour, second Saturday in June
Walpurgis Night, April 30
Women's Day, International, usually a Sunday in early March

Great Plains Indians
Dance, Sun, usually during summer solstice, June 21

Great Plains states, United States
Dance, Sun, usually during summer solstice, June 21

Greece
All Souls' Day, November 2
Annunciation, Feast of the, March 25
Anastenaria, May 21-23
Anthesteria (Day of Flowers), May 1
Ash Wednesday, February-March, fortieth day before Easter Sunday
Assumption, Feast of the (Koimesis tees Theotokou), August 15
Athens Festival, June through last week in September
Candlemas (Tees Ypapantees), February 2
Carnea, August, Greek month of Carneus
Christmas (Chreestoogenna), December 25
Christmas Eve (Paramonee ton Chreestoogennon), December 24
Cronia
Decoration Day (Psychosavato), the Saturday preceding the Saturday before Mardi Gras
Dionysus, spring and winter
Dodonea Festival, a weekend in August
Easter (To Ayeeon Pascha or Lambri, Bright Day), March-April, first Sunday after first full moon after the vernal equinox
Easter Monday (Thefteratoo Pascha), March-April, Monday after Easter
Epiphany, January 19
Exaltation of the Cross (Ee Ypsosis too Timjou Stavrou), September 14
Film and Song Festival, International Trade Fair, September-October
First of March (Martenitza), March 1
Folk Dance Theatre of Rhodes, June-October
Folk Dances, Greek, May-September
Folk Dancing at Corfu, Greek, mid-May to September
Good Friday (Meghalee Paraskevee, Holy Friday), March-April, Friday preceding Easter Sunday
Gynaecocratia, January 8
Hippokrateia, August
Holy Saturday (Meghalo Savato), March-April, Saturday before Easter Sunday

Greece *(cont.)*
Independence Day, March 25
Lent (Megali Sarakosti), February-March, forty-day season
  preceding Easter
Life-Bearing Spring (Zoodochos Pege), March-April, the
  Friday following Easter
Linus, Festival of
Marathon, International Open, mid-October
Mardi Gras (Apokreos, Carnival), February, three weeks
  before Ash Wednesday
Martyrs' Day, Forty, March 9
May Day Eve (Proto Mayea), April 30
Midsummer, June 23-24
New Year's Day (Protochroneea), January 1
Olympus Festival, July-August
Palm Sunday, March-April, the Sunday preceding Easter
Panathenaea, midsummer
Pentecost (Kneeling Sunday), May-June, the Sunday fifty
  days after Easter
Presentation of Blessed Virgin Mary, Feast of the,
  November 21
Rousa, Feast of, 25th day after Easter
St. Andrew's Day, November 30
St. Basil's Day (Too Ayeeoo Vasilee oo), January 1, Gregorian
  calendar (N.S.); January 14, Julian calendar (O.S.)
St. Demetrius, Festival of, October, including October 26
St. Dominique's Day, January 22
St. George's Day, April 23
St. John the Baptist's Day, January 7
St. Lazarus's Day, March-April, Saturday before Palm
  Sunday
St. Mennas's Day, November 11
St. Modesto's Day (Oxen's Feast), December 18
St. Nicholas's Day, December 6
St. Nikephoros's Day, March 13
St. Spyridon, Feast Day of, December 14
St. Thomas's Day, first Sunday after Easter
St. Vlasios's Day, February 11
Sts. Cosmas and Damian Day, September 27
Sts. Peter and Paul Day, June 29
Swallow Songs, return of the swallows in March
Theater Festival, Epidauros, June through August
Three Hierarchs or Archbishops, Holiday of the, January 30
Transfiguration, Feast of the, August 6
Wine Festival, two weeks in July
Women's Day, January 8

Greece (ancient)
Anthesteria, February-March, 11th-13th day of Greek month
  of Anthesterion
Artemis Karyatis, Feast of, annual
Eleusinia, every five years: the Lesser Eleusinia, early spring;
  the Greater Eleusinia, between harvest and seed time
Haloa, Festival of, autumn
Isthmian Games, first month of spring every second year

Nemean Games, probably August
Pythian Games, every fourth summer
Thargelia, May; early summer
Thesmophoria, October 24-26

Greek-Americans
Epiphany, January 6
Exaltation of the Cross (Recovery of the True Cross),
  September 14
Good Friday, March-April, Friday preceding Easter Sunday
Independence Day, Greece, March 25
New Year's Day, January 1
St. Michael's Day, November 8
St. Nicholas's Day, December 6

Greek-Americans in Florida: Tarpon Springs
Epiphany, January 6
St. Michael's Day, November 8
St. Nicholas's Day, December 6

Greek refugees from Bulgaria
St. Dominique's Day, January 22

Greenfield, Indiana
Riley Festival, James Whitcomb, three days, including
  October 7

Greensboro, North Carolina
Music Festival, Eastern, six weeks from late June to early
  August

Greenville, California
Dance, Bear, dates vary

Greenville, Ohio
Oakley Festival, Annie, last full week in July

Grein im Strudengau, Upper Austria, Austria
Summer Festival, Grein (Sommerspiele Grein), July-August

Grenada
Independence Day, February 7
Mardi Gras (Carnival), February-March, Tuesday and Ash
  Wednesday
National Day, March 13

Greyhorse, Oklahoma
Dances, Osage Tribal Ceremonial, June

Grisons, Switzerland
First of March (Chalanda Marz), March 1
St. Placidus Festival, July 11

Gstaad-Saanen, Switzerland
Menuhin Festival, three weeks in August

Guadalajara, Mexico
October Fair (Fiestas de Octubre), month-long, October-November

Guadalajara, Spain
Theatre Festival, Medieval, end of June

Guadeloupe
Cooks' Festival (Fête de Cuisinieres), Saturday nearest August 10

Gualala, Mendocino, and Fort Bragg, California
Whale Festival, March

Guam/Northern Marianas
Christ the King, Feast of, mid-November
Liberation Day, July 21
Magellan or Discovery Day, March 6
Our Lady of Carmel (La Madonna del Carmine), mid-July
Our Lady of Lourdes, Feast of, February 11; festival between February 11-18
St. Joseph's Day, May 1

Guanajuato, Mexico
Cervantes Festival, International, three weeks in April-May, sometimes October-November
Nativity Plays, mid-December to January

Guarda, Portugal
Guarda, National Festival of, summer

Guatemala
Army Day (formerly Revolution Day), June 30
Black Christ, Festival of the, January 15
Burning the Devil (La Quema del Diablo), December 7
Candlemas, February 2
Holy Week, March-April, week preceding Easter
Independence Day, September 15
Junkanoo Festival
St. Thomas the Apostle, Feast of, December 21
Sealing the Frost, April-early May
Volador Fiesta, during Corpus Christi or Holy Week

Guatemala City, Guatemala
Burning the Devil (La Quema del Diablo), December 7

Guayana City, Bolivar, Venezuela
Theatre, Festival of Popular, annual, date varies

Guca, Serbia, Yugoslavia
Dragacevo Assembly of Village Trumpeters, end of August

Guelmime, Morocco
Camel Market, usually in July

Guelph, Ontario, Canada
Spring Festival, Guelph, two to three weeks in April-May

Guildford, Surrey, England
Dicing for the Maid's Money Day, January

Guimarães, Minho, Portugal
St. Walter, Festivals of (Festas Gualterianas), four days beginning first Sunday in August

Guinea
Ashura, first ten days of Islamic month of Muharram
Independence Day, October 2
New Year (Tabaski), first day of Islamic month of Muharram

Guinea (western)
Ramadan, ninth Islamic month

Guinea-Bissau (formerly Portuguese Guinea)
Independence Day, September 8; observed on September 24
Women's Day, International, March 8
See also **Portuguese Guinea**

Guiseley, Yorkshire, England
Clipping the Church Day, August 5

Gujarat, India
Dance Festival, Darpana, five days during first week in October
Drama Festival, Gujarat Academy, five days during second week in February
Kite Festival, International, during Hindu month of Pausha
Lights, Festival of (Dewali), one week during waning half of Hindu month of Karthika, including 15th day
Mother Goddess, Festival of Durga, the, first ten days of waxing half of Hindu month of Asvina

Gulfport, Mississippi
Fishing Rodeo, Deep Sea, July fourth weekend

Gulf Shores, Alabama
Shrimp Festival, National, four days in early October

Gulpilhares, Porto, Portugal
Gulpilhares, International Festival of, July

Gurage Province, Ethiopia
Mother's Day (Antrosht), two to three days in October or November

Gura Vitioarei, Prahova, Romania
Red Inn Festival, last Sunday in June

Gurunsi people in Volta: Dudulsi Village, Lela
New Year Purification before Planting, April, just before planting

Guruvayur, Kerala, India
Dance Festival, Krishnattam, September-October

Gustine, California
Our Lady of Miracles (Nossa Senhora dos Milagres or Festa de Serreta), September 8-15

Guthrie, Oklahoma
Oklahoma Day, April 22

Guyana
Caricom Day, observed on or near July 4
Freedom Day, August 2
Husayn or Husain Day (Hosay and Tadja), tenth day of Islamic month of Muharram
Independence Day, May 26
Republic Day, February 23

Haarlem, Netherlands
Luilak (Lazybones Day or Sluggard's Feast), May-June, Saturday preceding Pentecost or Whit Sunday
Pentecost (Merchants' Flower Market), May-June, the Sunday fifty days after Easter

Ha Bac Province, Vietnam
Hoi Lim Festival, usually February, 13th day of first lunar month

Habye people in Togo
Habye Festival, small festival every third year, larger festival every fifth year in November

Hachiman Shrine, Kamakura City, Kanagawa, Japan
Takigi Noh, summer

Hachiman Shrine, Nagahama, Shiga, Japan
Nagahama Yamakyogen, two days in mid-April

Hagen and Hohenlimburg, North Rhine-Westphalia, Federal Republic of Germany
Castle Theatre Hohenlimburg, June-July

The Hague, Netherlands
Holland Festival, 23 days in June
Prinsjesdag, third Tuesday in September
Queen Juliana's Birthday, April 30

Haifa, Israel
Israel Festival, dates vary, some time between May and September

Hainaut, Belgium
Marriage of Goliath (Les Vêpres de Gouyasse), fourth weekend in August
Wallonia, Festival of (Festival de Wallonie), June-September or October

Haiti
Ancestry Day, January 2
Columbus Day (Discovery Day), December 5
Independence Day, January 1
Mardi Gras (Rara and Bruler Carnival), February-March, before Lent through Easter Week
New Year's Day, January 1
Pilgrimage to Saut d'Eau, early July-July 16
Sovereignty and Thanksgiving Day, May 22
United Nations Day, October 24

Haiyun Buddhist Convent, Qingdao, Shandong, China
Sugar Ball Show, 16th day of first lunar month

Hallaton, Leicestershire, England
Bottle Kicking and Hare Pie Scramble, Annual, March-April, Easter Monday

Halle, German Democratic Republic
Handel Festival, six days in summer

Hallein, Salzburg, Austria
"Silent Night, Holy Night" Celebration, December 24

Hamamatsu, Shizuoka, Japan
Children's Day (Kodomo-no-hi; formerly Boys' Festival, Tango No Sekku), May 1-5
Kite Battles of Hamamatsu, May 3-5

Hamburg, Federal Republic of Germany
Ballet Days, Hamburg, July
Dom Fair, November through Christmas, December 25

Hamelin, Federal Republic of Germany
Pied Piper of Hamelin Festival, every Sunday at noon during the summer

Hamilton, Bermuda
Bermuda College Weeks, four to five weeks in March-April
Bermuda Festival, January-February

Hamilton, Ontario, Canada
Arts Festival, New Directions in the Performing, summer or autumn during even-numbered years

Hammamet, Nabeul Region, Tunisia
Hammamet, International Festival of, July-August

Hampshire, England
Arts, Winchester Festival of the, July
Portsmouth Festival, mid-May
Tichborne Dole, March 26

Hampton, Virginia
Boomerang Festival, usually October

Hananomaki, Iwate, Japan
Dance, Deer, March

Hanashiro, Okinawa
Jurokunichi, 16th day of first lunar month

Hancock, Maine
Symphony Concerts, Monteux Conducting School, late
  June to late July

Hannibal, Missouri
Tom Sawyer Days, National, week of July 4

Hannover, Lower Saxony, Federal Republic of Germany
Music and Theatre in Herrenhausen, June-August

Hanover, New Hampshire
Winter Carnival, Dartmouth, a weekend in February

Hanu-Conachi forest, Fundeni, Galati, Romania
Acacia Day, first Sunday in May

Harbin, China
Ice and Snow Festival, Harbin, January 5-February 5

Hardin, Montana
Crow Fair, at least six days in mid-August

Harghita, Romania
Spring, Harghita, third Sunday in May

Harrogate, England
Harrogate International Festival, first two weeks in August

Harstad, Norway
Norway, Festival of Northern, June

Hartford, Connecticut
New Year's Eve (First Night), December 31

Haskovo, Bulgaria
Puppet Theatres, Holidays of Amateur, April during even-
  numbered years

Hasselt, Limburg, Belgium
Assumption, Feast of the (Festival of Virga Jesse), third
  and fourth Sundays in August every seven years

Hateg, Silvasul de Jos Commune, Hunedoara, Romania
Silvas Festival, second Sunday in June

Hausaland, West Africa
Muhammad's Birthday (Game Festival), twelfth day of
  Islamic month of Rabi al-Awwal

Hausa people
Fast, Feast of Breaking the (Salla), first day of Islamic
  month of Shawwal
New Year (Muharram Celebrations), first day of Islamic
  month of Muharram
Ramadan (Azumi), ninth Islamic month
Sallah, tenth day of Islamic month of Dhu'l-Hijjah

Hausa people in West Africa
Ashura, first ten days of Islamic month of Muharram

Haute-Saone, France
Hauts-de-Saone Festival, last weekend in June and first
  weekend in July

Hautes-Pyrénées, France
Easter Festival of Sacred Music, March-April, ten days
  beginning Good Friday
Our Lady of Lourdes, Feast of, February 11; festival
  between February 11-18

Haute-Vienne, France
Bellac Festival, June-July

Havana, Cuba
Ballet, International Festival of (Festival Internacional
  de Ballet de La Habana), autumn during even-numbered
  years

Havasupai Indians in Arizona: Supai
Peach Festival, August

Hawaii
Admission Day, August 21; observed third Friday in August
Aloha Week, September-October
Cherry Blossom Festival, mid-February through April
Columbus Day (Discoverers' Day), October 12; observed
  second Monday in October
Dead, Festival of the (Toro Nagashi, Floating Lantern
  Ceremony), observed August 15
Filipina, Fiesta, May 2-June 27
Flag Day, July 4
Ironman Triathlon Championships, Saturday nearest full
  moon in October
Kamehameha Day, June 11
Kuhio Kalanianaole Day, one week in March, including
  March 26
Lei Day, May 1

Hawaii *(cont.)*
Merrie Monarch Festival, March-April, several days beginning Easter Sunday
New Year (Narcissus Festival), early January to early February
Surfing Classic, Buffalo's Big Board, two days in February
Transpac Race from Los Angeles to Honolulu, July during odd-numbered years

Haxey, England
Haxey Hood Game, January 6

Hay-on-Wye, Wales
Literature, Hay-on-Wye Festival of, ten days in late May

Hayward, Wisconsin
Lumberjack World Championships, three days in July
Powwow, Honor the Earth, July

Haywick, Scotland
Common Ridings Day, June

Hazelton, British Columbia, Canada
'Ksan Celebrations, Friday evenings in July and August

Heard Museum, Phoenix, Arizona
Indian Fair, Heard Museum Guild, two days in late February

Hebrides, including Isle of Iona, Scotland
St. Michael's Eve

Hede, Ille-et-Vilaine, France
Hede Festival, about one week in August

Heian Shrine, Kyoto, Japan
Takigi Noh, two days in early June

Helsinki, Finland
Helsinki Festival (Helsingin Juhlaviikot), 18 days beginning August 24
Runeberg, Birthday of Johann Ludvig, February 5

Helston, Cornwall, England
Furry Day, May 8

HemisFair grounds of the Institute of Texan Cultures, San Antonio, Texas
Folklife Festival, Texas, four days during first week in August

Hemis Gompa Monastery, Ladakh, India
Hemis Festival, three days in June or July

Hercegnovi, Montenegro, Yugoslavia
South, Festival of the, July-August

Hereford, England
Three Choirs Festival, seven to ten days in mid-August; location alternates annually

Hermann, Missouri
Mayfest (Maifest), third weekend in May

Hershey, Pennsylvania
Pennsylvania Dutch Days, August

Hertfordshire, England
Old Man's Day, October 2

Hesse, Federal Republic of Germany
Bad Hersfeld in the Monastery Ruins, Festival of, July-August
Industry Festival of Wetzlar, mid-June to mid-July
May Festival, Wiesbaden International (Internationale Maifestspiele), month of May

Hexham, Northumberland, England
Hexham Abbey Festival, last two weeks in October

Hidatsa Indians in North Dakota: Mandaree
Mandaree Celebration, third weekend in July

Hidatsa Indians in the Great Plains of the United States
Dance, Sun, usually during summer solstice, June 21

Hie Shrine, Tokyo, Japan
Takigi Noh, summer

Highland Park, Illinois
Ravinia Festival, last week in June to second week in September

Higishitagawa-gun, Yamagata, Japan
Kurokowa Noh, early February

Hikari-machi, Sosa-gun, Chiba, Japan
Nembutsu Kyogen, mid-July

Hikone City, Shiga, Japan
Shrine Festival, Gokoku, October-November

Hillegom, Holland
Tulip Festival, last week in April and first week in May

Hillsdale, New York
Bluegrass Festival, Winterhawk, three days during third week in July

Hilo, Hawaii
Merrie Monarch Festival, March-April, several days beginning Easter Sunday

Himalayas (pilgrimage to)
New Year (Vaisakhi), first day of Hindu month of Vaisakha

Hinckley Ridge near Hinckley, Ohio
Buzzard Day, first Sunday after March 15

Hiroshima, Japan
Peace Festival, August 6
Shrine Festival, Itsukushima, two days in mid-April

Hispanic-Americans
Carnaval Miami, first two full weeks in March
Christmas Festival (Posadas, Feast of the Lodgings),
  December 16-24 or 25
St. Anthony the Abbot of Egypt, Feast of (Blessing of
  the Animals), January 17
Tucson Festival, two weeks following Easter

Hispanic-Americans in Florida: Miami
Carnaval Miami, first two full weeks in March

Hispanic-Americans in New Mexico: Hot Springs
Hermit, Feast of the, September 1

Hita, Guadalajara, Spain
Theatre Festival, Medieval, end of June

Hiyoshi Shrine, Komatsu, Ishikawa, Japan
Komatsu Otabi Festival, mid-May

Hobart, Tasmania, Australia
Eisteddfod, Eastern Shore, October
Eisteddfod, Hobart, June

Hohenems, Austria
Schubertiade Hohenems, 16 days in June

**Hohenlimburg and Hagen, North Rhine-Westphalia, Federal
Republic of Germany**
Castle Theatre Hohenlimburg, June-July

Hoh Indians in Washington: Quinault Nation, Taholah
Taholah Days, July fourth weekend

Hokkaido, Japan
Marimo Festival, second weekend in October
Snow Festival (Yuki Matsuri), February 8-12

Holland, Michigan
Tulip Time, four days beginning Wednesday nearest May 15

Holland, Netherlands
May Day, May 1
St. Nicholas's Day (Sinterklass), December 6
Simhat Torah, 23rd day of Jewish month of Tishri
See also **South Holland, Netherlands**

Holly, Michigan
Renaissance Festival, Michigan, August-September

Hollywood, California
Easter (Hollywood Bowl Sunrise Service), March-April,
  first Sunday after first full moon after the vernal equinox
Jazz Festival, Playboy, third weekend in June
Summer Series, Hollywood Bowl, eleven weeks from first
  week in July to late September

Hollywood, Florida
Powwow, Seminole, February

Hollywood Bowl, California
Easter (Hollywood Bowl Sunrise Service), March-April,
  first Sunday after first full moon after the vernal equinox

Holmenkollen Hill, Norway
Ski Festival, Holmenkollen, one week in March; second
  Sunday in March

Homin, Oklahoma
Dances, Osage Tribal Ceremonial, June

Honduras
Columbus Day (America's Discovery Day), October 12
Immaculate Conception, Feast of the (La Immaculada
  Concepción), begins several days before December 8
Independence Day, September 15

Hong Kong
Arts, Festival of Asian, last two weeks in October
Arts Festival, Hong Kong, January-February
Buddha's Birthday, Enlightenment, and Salvation, eighth
  day of fourth lunar month
Bun Festival, four to five days in May
Confucius's Birthday, 27th day of eighth lunar month
Double Fifth (Dragon Boat Festival and Festival of the
  Five Poisonous Creatures), fifth day of fifth lunar month
Double Ninth Day, ninth day of ninth lunar month
Double Seventh (Festival of the Weaving Maid and the
  Herd Boy), seventh day of seventh lunar month
Goddess of Mercy, Birthday of, 19th day of tenth
  lunar month
Grave-Sweeping and Cold Food Festival (Qing Ming, Clear
  and Bright), fourth or fifth day of third lunar month,
  105 or 106 days after the winter solstice
Half-Year Day, July 1
Hong Kong, Festival of, ten days in November-December
  during odd-numbered years
Lantern Festival (Yaun Shaw), 13th-15th days of first lunar
  month
Lu Pan, Birthday of, July 18
Mid-Autumn Festival (Chung Ch'iu), 15th, or full moon,
  day of eighth lunar month

Hong Kong *(cont.)*
Monkey's Festival (Birthday of Ts'oi, T'in Tai Seng Yeh), 16th day of eighth lunar month
New Year, ten-day to two-week long celebration at the first new moon after sun enters Aquarius; one to 15 days of first month
Sweeping Floors, Day for, 20th day of twelfth lunar month
Ta Chiu, several days during eleventh and twelfth lunar months at three-, five-, ten-year, or longer, intervals
Tin Hau Festival, 23rd day of third lunar month
Winter Solstice, December 21

Hong Kong Island
Tam Kung Festival, May, eighth day of fourth lunar month

Honolulu, Oahu Island, Hawaii
Cherry Blossom Festival, mid-February through April
Dead, Festival of the (Toro Nagashi, Floating Lantern Ceremony), August 15
Kamehameha Day, June 11
New Year (Narcissus Festival), early January to early February
Transpac Race from Los Angeles to Honolulu, July during odd-numbered years

Honshu, Japan
Horse Festival, Wild (Nomaoi Matsuri), three days in July or August

Hopi Indians
Dance, Hopi Niman, third or fourth Saturday in July
Dance, Hopi Snake, August-September, every other year
Dances, Basket, late October through November
Indian Fair, Heard Museum Guild, two days in late February
New Year (Wüwüchim), four days, including eve of new moon in November
New Year's Day, November
Oaqöl, formerly in autumn; now held irregularly
Sky-God Festival (Powamû Festival), February, nine-day kachina ceremony
Soyal or Soyala, nine-day winter solstice ceremony
Winter Solstice Celebration, December 21-22

Hopi Indians in Arizona
Dance, Hopi Snake, August-September, every other year

Hopi Indians in New Mexico: Santa Fe Indian Market Plaza, Santa Fe
Indian Market, third weekend in August

Horai, Aichi, Japan
Horaiji Temple Dengaku Festival, early February

Hortobágy, Hungary
Bridge Fair and International Equestrian Festival, Hortobágy, July

Horton, Kansas
Dance, Green Corn, about the third weekend in July

Hot Springs, Arkansas
Christmas Eve, December 24
Easter (Sunrise Service), March-April, first Sunday after first full moon after the vernal equinox

Hot Springs, New Mexico
Hermit, Feast of the, September 1
St. Anthony of Padua, Feast of, June 13

Hot Springs, South Dakota
Custer's Last Stand (Chief Crazy Horse Pageant), mid-June to late August

Hot Springs National Park, Hot Springs, Arkansas
Christmas Eve, December 24
Easter (Sunrise Service), March-April, first Sunday after first full moon after the vernal equinox

Houston, Missouri
Clown Festival, Emmett Kelly, early May

Houston, Texas
Alamo Day, March 6
Opera Festival, Spring, May

Huamantla, Mexico
Running of the Bulls, Sunday following August 15

Huanacaurí, Peru
Capac Raimi, December, summer solstice

Huelva, Andalusia, Spain
Pilgrimage of the Dew (Romería Del Rocío), May-June, Thursday or Friday before Pentecost Sunday through Monday or Tuesday after Pentecost
Pilgrimage of the Virgen de la Pena (Romería of the Virgen de la Pena), last Sunday in April
Wine Harvest, Festival of the, September

Huesca, Spain
Santo Cristo and San Vicente Ferrer, Festival of, September

Hugenot-Thomas Paine Historical Society
Paine Day, Thomas (Common Sense Day), Sunday nearest January 29

Hugo, Oklahoma
Bluegrass and Old-Time Music Festival, Grant's Annual, five days in early August

Huichol, Mexico
Green Squash Festival (Wima'kwari), October

Huichol Indians in Mexico: eastern Chihuahua
Dance, Peyote (Híkuli), October and November

Huila, Colombia
Bambuco, Festival of, June

Humeira, Syria (monastery)
St. George's Day ('Id Marjurjus), April 23

Hunedoara, Romania
Dance of Transylvania, Men's (Caluser or Caluseri), third
week in January
Encounter with History, first Sunday in May
Silvas Festival, second Sunday in June

Hungarian-Americans
Independence Day, Hungary, October 23

Hungarian people
Kossuth Day, March 20

Hungary
Artistic Weeks, Budapest, September-October
Assumption, Feast of the (Nagyboldag Asszony Napja),
August 15
Beethoven Concerts, Martonvásár, summer
Bridge Fair and International Equestrian Festival,
Hortobágy, July
Candlemas (Gyertyaszentel Boldog Asszony), February 2
Christmas (Karácsony), December 25
Christmas Eve (Karácsony Vigiliája), December 24
Constitution Day, August 20
Dramatic Groups, "Istvan Horvath Cadet" Festival of,
July during even-numbered years
Easter (Husvét), March-April, first Sunday after first
full moon after the vernal equinox
Easter Monday (Husvét Hétfoje or Ducking Monday),
March-April, Monday after Easter
Epiphany (Vizkereszt, Blessing of the Waters), January 6
Floral Carnival, National, August 20
Folk Dance, International Festival of, July during odd-
numbered years
Folklore, Danube Festival of, every three years in July
Good Friday (Nagypéntek), March-April, Friday preceding
Easter Sunday
Harvest of Grapes (Szüret), late October
Haydn Memorial Concerts, summer
Holy Saturday (Nagyszombat), March-April, Saturday
before Easter Sunday
Kossuth Day, March 20
Lent, February-March, forty-day season preceding Easter
Liberation Day, April 4
Mardi Gras (Farsang), January 6-Ash Wednesday
Music Series, Contemporary, one week in October
Music Weeks, Budapest, September-October

New Years Day (Ujév Napja), January 1
Opera and Ballet, Budapest Concerts and Open-Air,
late June to late August
Pentecost and Whit Monday, May-June, the seventh
Sunday and Monday after Easter Sunday
St. Anne's Day (Anna Napja), July 26
St. Andrew's Day (Szent András Napja), November 30
St. George's Day (Szent György Napja), April 23
St. Lucy's Day, December 13
St. Mark's Day (Szent Márk Napja and Buza-Szentelo,
Blessing of Wheat), April 25
St. Michael's Day, September 29
St. Peter's Day, June 29
St. Stephen's Day, August 20
St. Sylvester's Day (Svilveszter Este), December 31
Savaria Festival, August
Summer Concerts, Lake Balaton, summer
Summer Festival, Szeged, third week in July to third week
in August
Theatre on Margaret Island, Open-Air, July-August
Whit Monday, May-June, Monday after Pentecost

Hunter, New York
German Alps Festival, 18 days in July
Indian Festival, Mountain Eagle
Polka Festival, International, three to four days in early
August

Hunter Mountain, Hunter, New York
Polka Festival, International, three to four days in early
August

Hunter Mountain Ski Bowl, Hunter, New York
German Alps Festival, 18 days in July

Huntington, New York
Arts Festival, Summerscape-Huntington Summer, late June
to late August

Huntington, West Virginia
New Year's Eve (First Night), December 31

Hupa Indians in northern California
Dance, Hupa Autumn (Tunchitdilya), October
Dance, Hupa Winter (Haichitdilya), twenty days during
winter

Hupa Indians in northwestern California
World Renewal Ceremony, July and August

Husi, Vaslui, Romania
Dionysiad, first Sunday in October

Huttweilen, Thurgovia
Christmas Eve, December 24

Huy, Belgium
Wallonia, Festival of (Festival de Wallonie), June-September or October

Huyalas, Peru
St. Elizabeth, Feast of, July 8

Hvar, Croatia, Yugoslavia
Theatre of Hvar, Days of the, four days in May

Hyderabad, Andhra Pradesh, India
Dance and Drama, Festival of, five days in November

Ibaraki, Japan
Demon-God Festival, one day in April

Ibibio people in Nigeria
New Year's Day, end of Ndok season

Ibo people in Nigeria
Agwunsi Festival, August-September
Emume Ala, on or near March 20
Imechi Festival, July-August
New Yam Festival (Iri ji Ohuru), August-September
New Yam Festival (Onwasato), around August
New Year (Ibu Afo Festival), March, first day of first month, Onwa Izizi, of the Ibu calendar, or determined by council of elders
Okpesi or Itensi Festival, around September
Washing the Hands (Issa Aka), during yam festivals held in August, September, or October

Ibo people in Nigeria: Mbaise area
Road Building Festival, around April

Ibo people in Nigeria: Nsukka
Dead, Return of the (Odo Festival), every other year in April (Awuru Odo celebration for departure of the dead) and sometime between September and November (arrival of the dead)

Iceland
Arts Festival, Reykjavik, 16 days in June during even-numbered years
Ash Wednesday, February-March, fortieth day before Easter Sunday
Children's Day, April 24
Christmas, December 25
Horse Meet Show and Races, National, four days in July every four years
Independence Day, June 17
Leif Eriksson Day, October 9
Lent, February-March, forty-day season preceding Easter
Mardi Gras (Bursting Day and Bun Day), February-March, Tuesday before Ash Wednesday; Monday also observed

New Year's Eve, December 31
Pentecost, May-June, the Sunday fifty days after Easter
Pjodhatid, three days in early August
St. Thorlak's Day, December 23
Seaman's Day, June 2 or first Sunday in June
Summer, First Day of, Thursday between April 19 and 25
Twelfth Night (Epiphany Eve), January 5
Yuletide Lads, twelve days beginning December 12

Icelandic-Canadians in Canada: Gimli, Manitoba
Icelandic Festival (Islendingadagurinn), during last week in July or first week in August

Idaho
Admission Day, July 3
Fiddlers' Contest, National Old-Time, third full week in June
Indian Days, Fort Hall, August
Lumberjack Days, Clearwater County Fair and, third weekend in September
Music Festival, McCall Summer, third weekend in July
Pioneer Day, June 15
Pioneer Day, July 24
Powwow, Chief Looking Glass, August
Powwow, Epethes, first weekend in March
Powwow, Four Nations, October
Powwow, Warriors Memorial, third weekend in June
Powwow and Root Feast, Mat-Al-YM'A, third weekend in May
Regatta, Idaho, last weekend in June
Rodeo, National Circuit Finals, four days ending third Saturday in March
St. Ignatius Loyola, Feast of, July 31

Idyllwild, California
Music Festival, Idyllwild, last two weeks in August

Ife people in Nigeria: Oyo
Olojo (Ogun Festival), around July

Igbo people in Nigeria
See **Ibo people in Nigeria**

Ignacio, Colorado
Dance, Southern Ute Sun, first weekend after July 4
Dance, Ute Bear, last weekend in May
Ute Fair, Southern, September

Ijmuiden, Netherlands
Vlaggetjesdag, anytime from middle to late May

Ilkley, West Yorkshire, England
Literature Festival, Ilkley, June during odd-numbered years

Ille-et-Vilaine, France

Arts, Festival of Traditional, March
Hede Festival, about one week in August
Ille Festival, one week in May or June
Theatre, Festival of Cafe, November

Illinois

Admission Day, December 3
Agricultural Days (Jordoruksdagarna), two days in late
September
Bud Billiken Day, second Saturday in August
Carillon Festival, International, one weeks in mid-June
Christmas Around the World, late November through
early January
Grant Park Concerts, ten weeks from last week in June
to last week in August
Grape Festival (Wedding of the Wine and Cheese Pageant),
first weekend in September
Indian Celebration, American, July 17
Jazz Festival, Chicago, five days in late August or early
September
Native American Day, fourth Friday in September
Pulaski Day, first Monday in March
Ravinia Festival, last week in June to second week in
September
Swedes' Day (Svenskarnas Dag), June 24

Iloilo City, Panay Island, Philippines

Dinagyand, last weekend in January

Imilchil, Morocco

Marriage Fair, September

Imperial Beach, California

Sandcastle Days, usually July

Imphal, Manipur, India

Drama Festival, Manipur Academy, five days in February-
March
Jatra Festival, two weeks in December-January

Imst, Tirol, Austria

Mardi Gras (Schemenlauf, Running of the Spectres),
January-March, week before Ash Wednesday
Perchtenlauf, usually January 6

Inanda, South Africa

Zulu/Shembe Festival, July 1 through last Sunday in July

Inari, Finland

Reindeer Driving Competition, third week in March

Inca people

All Saints' Day, November 1
Crow Fair, at least six days in mid-August

Inca people in Peru

Situa, September

Inca people in Peru: Cuzco

Sun Festival (Inti Raymi or Raimi Fiesta), about one week,
including June 24, the winter solstice

Inca people in Peru: Huanacauri

Capac Raimi, December, summer solstice

India

Agricultural Festival, during Hindu month of Ashadha
Agricultural Festival (Hadaga), during Hindu month
of Asvina
Agricultural Festival (Pola), during Hindu month of
Sravana
Agricultural Festival (Pola), during Hindu month of
Bhadrapada
Amarnath Yatra, full moon day during Hindu month
of Sravana
Arts Festival, Kalakshetra, December-January
Ashokashtami, eighth day of waxing half of Hindu month
of Chaitra
Ashura, first ten days of Islamic month of Muharram
Avani Mulam, August or September
Ballet Festival, Bharatiya Kala Kendra, September-October,
three weeks during Durga Puja, Festival of the Mother
Goddess
Ballet Festival, Kathak Kendra, annual, date varies
Ballet Festival, Triveni Kala Sangam, annual, date varies
Bathing Festival (Snan Yatra), full moon day of Hindu month
of Jyeshta
Bhagavatha Mela Festival, one week in May
Bharatiya Lok Kala Festival, annual, date varies
Bhishma Ashtami, eighth day of waxing half of Hindu month
of Magha or during Hindu month of Karthika
Brother and Sister Day (Bhai-Dooj, Bhaiya Duj, or Bhratri
Dwitya), second day of waxing half of Hindu month
of Karthika
Buddha's Birthday, Enlightenment, and Salvation (Buddha
Jayanti), full moon day of Hindu month of Vaisakha
Chaitra Parb, eight days prior to full moon day of Hindu
month of Chaitra
Chandan Yatra, 21 days beginning third day of waxing half
of Hindu month of Vaisakha
Children's Day, November 14
Chitra Gupta, full moon day of Hindu month of Chaitra
Christmas, December 25
Coconut Day
Cow Holiday (Gopastami)
Dalai Lama, Birthday of, July 6
Dance and Drama, Festival of, five days in November
Dance Festival, Chhau Mask, Chaitra-Parva, April 11-13
Dance Festival, Darpana, five days during first week in
October

India *(cont.)*

Mother Goddess, Festival of Durga, the (Dussehra), first ten days of waxing half of Hindu month of Asvina

Muhammad's Birthday (Bara Wafat), twelfth day of Islamic month of Rabi al-Awwal

Nanda Deven, August-September

New Year (Bohag Bihu), first day of Hindu month of Vaisakha

New Year (Gudi Parva), first day of Hindu month of Chaitra

New Year (Losar), three days, usually in February

New Year (Ugadi Parva), first day of Hindu month of Chaitra

New Year (Vaisakhi), first day of Hindu month of Vaisakha

New Year (Vishu), first day of Hindu month of Vaisakha

Night of Forgiveness (Shaaban or Shab-i-Barat), 15th of Islamic month of Shaban

Paryushana or Partyshana Parva, during Hindu month of Bhadrapada

Pooram, during Hindu month of Vaisakha

Protection, Festival to Pledge (Rakhi), during Hindu month of Sravana

Purilia Chhau Festival, April 11-13

Pushkar Fair, begins night before full moon of Hindu month of Karthika

Rama, Festival of (Rama-Navami), ninth day of waning half of Hindu month of Chaitra

Rama Leela Festival, between seven and 31 days in September-October

Rasa Leela Festival, one month during August-September

Republic Day, January 26

Sacred Thread Festival (Raksha Bandhan), full moon day of Hindu month of Sravana

Sacrifice, Feast of (Bakrid), tenth-twelfth days of Islamic month of Dhu'l-Hijjah

St. Thomas the Apostle, Feast of, December 21

Shankarachaya Jayanti or Birthday, fifth day (southern India) or tenth day (northern India) of waxing half of Hindu month of Vaisakha

Shasti, Festival of (Aranya Shasti)

Shiva, Gajan of, during Hindu month of Chaitra

Shiva, Night of (Mahashivaratri), 13th night and 14th day of waning half of Hindu month of Phalguna

Simhat Torah, 23rd day of Jewish month of Tishri

Snake Festival (Naagpanchami in northern India; Nagarapanchami in southern India), fifth day of waxing half of Hindu month of Sravana

Spring Festival (Vasant or Basant Panchami), fifth day of waxing half of Hindu month of Magha

Sravani Mela, during Hindu month of Sravana

Tagore, Birthday of Rabindranath, May 7

Tamasha Festival, November-December (location rotates)

Teej, third day of waxing half of Hindu month of Sravana

Teej (Hariyali Teej or Hari Tritiya), third day of waxing half of Hindu month of Sravana

Theatre Festivals, Children's Little, second week in May and three weeks in December

Tirupati Festival, ten days during Hindu month of Bhadrapada

Vaikunth Ekadashi, twenty-day pilgrimage over 11th days of waxing and waning halves of Hindu month of Margashirsha

Valmiki's Jayanti or Birthday, full moon day of Hindu month of Asvina

Varuna, Festival of, full moon day of Hindu month of Karthika

Vernal Equinox (Bohag Bihu), on or near March 21

Winter Solstice, December 21

India (central provinces)

Bhima or Bhima-sena, Festival of, near time of monsoon

India (northern)

Gangaur, Gauri, or Parvati Tritiya, 18-day festival during Hindu month of Chaitra

Govardhan Puja and Annakut, first day of waxing half of Hindu month of Karthika

Halashasti or Balarama Shashti, sixth day of waning half of Hindu month of Bhadrapada

Mother Goddess, Festival of Durga, the (Dussehra or Dasahara), first ten days of waxing half of Hindu month of Asvina

Sacred Thread Festival (Raksha Bandhan), full moon day of Hindu month of Sravana

India (rural)

New Year (Kalpa Vruksha), April

India (southern)

Husayn or Husain Day, tenth day of Islamic month of Muharram

Narieli Purnima, full moon day of Hindu month of Sravana

Sacred Thread Festival (Avani Avittam), full moon day of Hindu month of Sravana

Skanda Shashti, October-November, month of Tulam

Thaipusam, one day in January-February

Indiana

Admission Day, December 11

Bluegrass Festival, Bean Blossom, five days in spring

Easter Monday (Paas Festival), March-April, Monday after Easter

Great Lakes Festival, three weekends in mid-June

Hunters' Moon, Feast of the, October

Indianapolis 500, month-long event, ending with race on Memorial Day, last Monday in May

Johnny Appleseed Festival, third week in September

Riley Festival, James Whitcomb, three days, including October 7

Indiana *(cont.)*
Romantic Festival, last two weekends in April
Vincennes Day, February 24

Indian-Americans in Arizona: Tucson
Tucson Meet Yourself Festival, second weekend in October

Indianapolis, Indiana
Indianapolis 500, month-long event, ending with race on Memorial Day, last Monday in May
Romantic Festival, last two weekends in April

Indian Grinding Rock State Park near Pine Grove, California
Chaw-Se Big Time Celebration, usually last weekend in September

Indianola, Iowa
Hot Air Balloon Championships, United States National, ten days in late July or early August
Opera, Des Moines Metro Summer Festival of, three weeks from late June to early July

Indians (Native Americans in the United States)
See Alabama Indians; Alaskan Eskimos; Apache Indians; Arapaho Indians; Arikara Indians; Athapaskan Indians; Bad River Ojibwa Indians; Bannock Shoshone Indians; Blackfeet Indians; Bûngi Indians; Caddo Indians; Cahuilla Indians; California Indians; California Yokuts Indians; Cayuga Indians; Cayuga Iroquois Indians; Chehalis Salishan Indians; Cherokee Indians; Cheyenne Indians; Chickahominy Indians; Chinookan Indians; Chippewa Indians; Choctaw Indians; Cocopah Indians; Coeur d'Alene Indians; Colville Indians; Comanche Indians; Cree Indians; Creek Indians; Crow Indians; Dakota Indians; Delaware Indians; Diegueño Indians; Eskimo people; Great Plains Indians; Havasupai Indians; Hidatsa Indians; Hoh Indians; Hopi Indians; Hupa Indians; Iroquois Indians; Jicarilla Apache Indians; Karok Indians; Kickapoo Indians; Kiowa Indians; Klamath Indians; Kootenai Indians; Kuksu secret society of North American Indians; Lac Courte Oreilles Ojibwa Indians; Lenape Delaware Indians; Lummi Indians; Maidu Indians; Mandan Indians; Maricopa Indians; Mashantucket Indians; Mayo Indians; Menominee Indians; Mescalero Apache Indians; Mesquakie Algonquian Indians; Miami Indians; Miccosukee Indians; Mohave Indians; Mohegan Indians; Muskogee-Creek Indians; Narragansett Indians; Natchez Indians; Navajo Indians; Nevada Indians; New Mexico pueblos; Nez Perce Indians; Northern Ute Indians; Ojibwa Indians; Omaha Indians; Oneida Indians; Pala Indian Reservation; Papago Indians; Passamaquoddy Indians; Paucatuck Pequot Indians; Peoria Indians; Pequot Indians; Pima Indians; Plains Indians; Poarch Creek Indians; Pomo Indians; Ponca Indians; Pueblo Indians; Quapaw Indians; Quileute Indians; Quinault Indians; Sac and Fox Indians; Salish Indians; Sauk Indians; Schaghiticoke Indians; Seminole Indians; Seneca Iroquois Indians; Shahaptian Indians; Shawnee Indians; Shinnecock Indians; Shoshone Indians; Siletz Indians; Sioux Indians; Southern Arapaho Indians; Southern Cheyenne Indians; Spokan Indians; Suquamish Indians; Timuquan Indians; Tohono O'Odham Indians; Tortugas Indians; Tuchi Yokut Indians; Tuscarora Indians; Upper Mattaponi Indians; Ute Indians; Walker River Paiute Indians; Washo Indians; White Mountain Apache Indians; Winnebago Indians; Wiyot Indians; Yakima Indians; Yaqui Indians; Yuchi Indians; Yuma Indians; Yurok Indians; Zuni Indians

Indians, Native American, in California: Mission of San Antonio de Pala, San Diego County
St. Francis of Assisi, Feast of, October 4

Indians, North American
Dance, Green Corn, date varies

Indians, North American, in central California
Hesi Ceremony

Indians in Mexico: Mitla, Oaxaca
New Year's Eve (Noche de Pedimento, Wishing Night), December 31

Indians of Alaska, Yukon, Labrador and the Northwest territories in Canada: Inuvik area, Northwest Territories
Northern Games, four days in mid-July

Indo-Guyanese people in Guyana
Husayn or Husain Day (Hosay and Tadja), tenth day of Islamic month of Muharram

Indonesia
Ballet Festival, Javanese, two nights each month during full moon from June to November
Ballet Festival, Ramayana, May-October, four consecutive nights during each full moon
Children's Day, National, June 17
Eka Dasa Rundra, once every hundred years
Fast, Feast of Breaking the (Lebaran or Hari Raya or Pasa or Puasa), first day of Islamic month of Shawwal
Independence Day, August 17
Kartini Day, April 21
Kassada, January, 14th of Kassada, 12th month of Tenggerese year
Kite Flying Competition, during weeks preceding the rainy season, which begins in November
Medan Anniversary, April 1
Muhammad's Birthday (Sekartan Festival), twelfth day of Islamic month of Rabi al-Awwal
Panas Pela (Cuci Baileo Ceremony), every three years in May
Ramadan (Lebaran), ninth Islamic month

Indonesia *(cont.)*
Ramadan (Pasa), ninth Islamic month
Ujung Pandang Anniversary, April 1

Indre, France
Art and History, Festival of, Sundays in July and
August

Ingal, Niger
Salted Cure (Cure Salée), September or October

Innisfail, Queensland, Australia
Arts, North Queensland Festival of, three weeks in
December

Innsbruck, Tirol, Austria
Tirolese Summer, mid-July to mid-August

Institute of Texan Cultures, San Antonio, Texas
Folklife Festival, Texas, four days during first week in August

Interlaken, Bern, Switzerland
Interlaken Festival, June-August
Plays at Interlaken, Wilhelm Tell Pastoral, July-August

Interlochen, Michigan
Music Camp, National, eight weeks from last week in
June to mid-August

International
Arts and Culture, World Black and African Festival of,
held every four years, 1977, 1981, etc.
Children's Book Day, International, April 2
Children's Poetry Day, March 21
Earth Day, April 22
Labor Day, International, May 1
Music, International Society of Contemporary, annual
Nurses' Week, first or second week of May; usually
includes Nurses' Day, May 12
Olympic Games, summer games: early April-late
July; winter games: late January-mid February
Puppet Festival, UNIMA (Union Internationale de la
Marionnette) Congress and, every four years
Theatre for Children and Young People Congress and
Festival, International Association of (ASSITEJ—
Association Internationale du Theatre pour l'Enfance
et la Jeunesse), every three years
Theatre of Nations, summer
World Cup (soccer), four weeks of playoffs; host country
schedules matches in May, June or July
World Fellowship Day, November 18

International (observers everywhere but at the South Pole)
Night of the Shooting Stars (The Perseids Meteor
Shower), August 11

**International Peace Garden, Dunseith, North Dakota, and
Manitoba, Canada**
Arts, International Festival of the, six weeks during
June and July

Inuit people in Canada: Frobisher Bay, Northwest Territories
Toonik Time, one week from late April to early May

Inuit people in Canada: Inuvik area, Northwest Territories
Northern Games, four days in mid-July

Inuvik area, Northwest Territories, Canada
Northern Games, four days in mid-July
Top of the World Ski Meet, March-April, Easter weekend

The Invalides in Paris, France
Napoleon's Day, May 5

Ioannina, Greece
Dodonea Festival, a weekend in August

Iolani Palace, Honolulu, Oahu Island, Hawaii
Kamehameha Day, June 11

Iowa
Admission Day, December 28
Art Festival, Grant Wood, second Sunday in June
Assumption, Feast of the, August 15
Bicycle Ride Across Iowa (Ragbrai), midsummer
Country Music Contest and Festival, National Old-Time,
first weekend in September
Earls Court Day, May 9
Hobo Convention, three days in August
Hot Air Balloon Championships, United States National,
ten days in late July or early August
Iowa State Fair, 11 days through last Sunday in August
Jazz Festival, Bix Beiderbecke Memorial, three days during
last weekend in July
Music Festival, Cornell College Spring, three days in late
April or early May
Nordic Fest, last full weekend in July
Opera, Des Moines Metro Summer Festival of, three weeks
from late June to early July
Powwow, Mesquakie Celebration, second weekend in
August, Thursday-Sunday
St. Barbara's Day, December 4
St. Wenceslaus's Day, September 28
Tulip Time, second Thursday, Friday and Saturday in May
Watermelon Day, mid-July

Ipswich, Massachusetts
Castle Hill Festival, weekends from early July to mid-August

Iran (formerly Persia)
Arts, Shiraz Festival of, August-September

Iran (formerly Persia) *(cont.)*

Ashura, tenth day of Islamic month of Muharram

Christmas, December 25

Hanukkah, eight days beginning 25th day of Jewish month of Kislev

Husayn or Husain Day, tenth day of Islamic month of Muharram

Khomeini Day, February 1

Lag b'Omer, 18th of Jewish month of Iyar, the 33rd day in the fifty-day period between Passover and Shavuot, in addition to the fifty-day period itself

Mithra, Feast of (Mihrajan), six days beginning on or near September 7

Muhammad's Birthday, twelfth day of Islamic month of Rabi al-Awwal

National Day, October 26

Nativity of the Sun (Mithraic Festival), December 25

New Year, Jewish (Rosh Hashanah), first day of Jewish month of Tishri

New Year's Day (No Ruz or Naw Roz), March 21, vernal equinox

Night of Forgiveness (Shab-i-Barat or Shaban), 15th of Islamic month of Shaban

Plays from Iranian Provinces, ten days in April

Popular Traditions, Festival of, October

Purim, 14th of Jewish month of Adar

Ramadan (Ramazan), ninth Islamic month

Republic Day, Islamic, April 1

Sacrifice, Feast of (Arafa), tenth-twelfth days of Islamic month of Dhu'l-Hijjah

Shavuot, the Feast of Weeks, sixth day of Jewish month of Sivan

Sukkot (Feast of Booths or Feast of the Tabernacles), 15th-21st or 22nd of Jewish month of Tishri

Summer Festival for Children, mid-June to mid-August

Thirteenth Day Out (Sizdar-Bedah), 13th day after Noruz

Tisha B'Av, ninth day of Jewish month of Av

Tus, Festival of, July

Yom Kippur, tenth day of Jewish month of Tishri

Iraq

Army Day, January 6

Christmas, December 25

Fast, Feast of Breaking the (Eed-al-Fittur), first day of Islamic month of Shawwal

Husayn or Husain Day, tenth day of Islamic month of Muharram

Mecca, Pilgrimage to, eighth through 13th days of Islamic month of Dhu'l-Hijjah

Ramadan, ninth Islamic month

Revolution Day, July (Peaceful Revolution Day), July 17

Revolution Day, July 14

Sacrifice, Feast of ('Id al-Adha), tenth-twelfth days of Islamic month of Dhu'l-Hijjah

Ireland

Age of Goibniu, Feast of

All Saints' Day, November 1

AN tOIREACHTAS, October-November

Arts Festival, Dublin, March

Arts Festival, Gorey, summer

Bank Holiday, last Monday of August

Bank Holiday, first Monday in May

Beltane, April 30

Bloomsday, June 16

Boxing Day, December 26

Chalk Sunday, February-March, first Sunday in Lent

Cromm Dub's Sunday, first Sunday in August

Drama Festival, All-Ireland Amateur, April-May

Easter, March-April, first Sunday after first full moon after the vernal equinox

Epiphany, January 6

Feis Ceoil, week of second Monday in May

Fleadh Nua, May-June

Folk Dance Festival, Cork International Choral and, April

Folk Dance Festival of Ireland, International, one week beginning first Sunday in July

Folk Festival, Letterkenny International, five days in late August

Halloween, October 31

Holy Innocents' Day (Cross Day), December 28

Horse Show, Dublin, six days in August

Immaculate Conception, Feast of the, December 8

Irish Houses Festival, Great, first two weeks in June

Lammas Fair Day, last Tuesday in August

Leap Year Privilege (Bachelors' Day), February 29

Lúgnasad (First Fruits Festival), August 1

Mardi Gras (Shrove Tuesday), February-March, Tuesday before Ash Wednesday

Martinmas, November 11

May Day, May 1

May Day Eve, April 30

Maytime Fairies, first days of May

Maytime Festival, International, third week in May

Michaelmas, September 29

Midsummer, June 23-24

New Year's Eve, December 31

Opera, International Festival of Light, September

Opera, Wexford Festival, two weeks in late October

Oyster Festival, Galway, four days in mid-September

Palm Sunday, March-April, the Sunday preceding Easter

Pentecost, May-June, the Sunday fifty days after Easter

Pilgrimage, Lough Derg, June 1 through August 15

Puck's Fair, August 10-12

Quarter Days, March 25, June 24, September 29, and December 25

Reek Sunday, last Sunday in July (pilgrimage)

Rose of Tralee International Festival, six days in August-September

St. Brendan's Day, May 16

Ireland *(cont.)*
St. Bridget's Day, February 1
St. Catherine's Day, November 25
St. Crispin's Day, October 25
St. Patrick's Day, March 17
St. Stephen, Feast of (Hunting the Wren), December 26
Samhain (Summer's End), October 31
Sheelah's Day, March 18
Theatre Festival, Dublin, October
Walking Sunday, Sunday before Donnybrook Fair begins at
  the end of August
Whit Monday, May-June, Monday after Pentecost
Writers' Week Listowel, June

Ireland, Northern
See **Northern Ireland**

Ireland, Republic of
Constitution Day, December 6

Irish-Americans
St. Patrick's Day (Parade in New York, New York), March 17

Iroquois Indians
Dance, Green Corn, on or near Labor Day, first Monday
  in September
Dead, Feast for the (Ohgíwe), during Iroquois White Dog
  Feast, in autumn, spring, or occasional
Green Bean Festival, one day in August
Indian Festival, Iroquois, first weekend in September,
  including Labor Day
Indian Festival, Katari
Indian Festival, Mountain Eagle
Midwinter Bear Society Dance
New Year's Day, February

Iroquois Indians in Canada and the United States
Iroquois White Dog Feast (New Year or Midwinter Festival),
  several days, including first quarter moon in January

Iroquois Indians in New York: Tonawanda
Strawberry Festival, usually June

Iroquois women
Dead, Feast for the (Ohgíwe), during Iroquois White Dog
  Feast, in autumn, spring, or occasional

Irvine, Ayrshire, Scotland
Marymass Fair, third or fourth Monday in August

Ise, Mie, Japan
Shrine Kagura Festival, Ise, April and September

Isere, France
Vienne Festival, June-August

Isfahan, Iran
Popular Traditions, Festival of, October

Ishikawa, Japan
Komatsu Otabi Festival, mid-May

Isle of Iona, Scotland
Michaelmas, September 29
St. Michael's Eve

Isle of Man
Beltane, April 30
Christmas, December 25
Halloween (Thump-the-Door Night or Hollantide),
  October 31
Lammas, August 1
Mad Sunday, May, Sunday preceding the Tourist Trophy
  Motorcycle Races
May Day, May 1
Midsummer, June 23-24
Samhain (Sauin, Summer's End), October 31
St. Stephen, Feast of (Hunting the Wren), December 26
Tynwald Day, date varies

Isle of Skye
Michaelmas, September 29

Isle of Wight, Great Britain
Regatta Week, July-August

Isleta Pueblo, New Mexico
Dance, Evergreen, February, date varies
St. Augustine, Feast of and Harvest Dance, September 4
Spanish and Indian Fiestas, August 28
Spruce Ceremony

Israel
Balfour Declaration Day, November 2
Blessing the Sun (Birchat Hahamah), every 28 years on
  the first Wednesday of Jewish month of Nisan
Hanukkah, eight days beginning 25th day of Jewish month
  of Kislev
Independence Day (Yom Ha'atzma'ut), fifth day of Jewish
  month of Iyar
Israel Festival, dates vary, some time between May and
  September
Music Festival, En Gev, April
New Year of Trees (B'Shevat; Hamishah Assar), 15th of
  Jewish month of Shevat
Passover (Pesach), seven days beginning 15th of Jewish
  month of Nisan
Shavuot, the Feast of Weeks, sixth day of Jewish month
  of Sivan
Simhat Torah (Rejoicing in the Law), 22nd or 23rd of
  Jewish month of Tishri

Israel *(cont.)*

Sukkot (Feast of Booths or Feast of the Tabernacles), 15th-21st or 22nd of Jewish month of Tishri

Water-Drawing Festival (Simhat bet Ha-sho'evah), night after first day of Sukkot, and every night of Sukkot thereafter

Yom ha-Zikkaron (Day of Remembrance), fourth day of Jewish month of Iyar

Yom Kippur, tenth day of Jewish month of Tishri

Istanbul, Turkey

Holy Thursday, March-April, Thursday preceding Easter

Istanbul Festival, International, June-July

Italian-Americans

Assumption, Feast of the, August 15

Columbus Day, October 12, observed second Monday in October

Good Friday, March-April, Friday preceding Easter Sunday

Holy Thursday, March-April, Thursday preceding Easter

Our Lady of Carmel (La Madonna del Carmine), July 16

Italian-Americans in Arizona: Tucson

Tucson Meet Yourself Festival, second weekend in October

Italian-Americans in Florida: Ybor City

Garbanzo, Fiesta Sopa de, begins Sunday nearest February 9 and ends Saturday

Italian-Americans in Massachusetts: Gloucester

St. Peter's Day, June 29

Italian-Americans in New York: Little Italy

St. Januarius's Feast Day, two weeks, including September 19

Italian-Americans in Oklahoma: McAlester

Italian Festival, late May

Italian-Americans in southern California, Detroit, Michigan, Buffalo, New York, and elsewhere in the United States

St. Joseph of Arimathea, Feast Day of, March 19

Italy

All Saints' Day, November 1

All Souls' Day (Il Giorno Dei Morti), November 2

Annunciation, Feast of the, March 25

April Fools' Day, April 1

Ascension Day, May-June, fortieth day after Easter Sunday

Ascension Day (Cricket Festival, Festa del Grillo), May-June, fortieth day after Easter Sunday

Ash Wednesday, February-March, fortieth day before Easter Sunday

Assumption, Feast of the (Bowing Procession), August 15

Ballet, International Festival of, July during even-numbered years

Banderesi, Festival of the, six days in May

Baths of Caracalla (Terme di Caracalla), first week in July to second week in August

Befana Festival, January 5-6

Candlemas (La Candelora), February 2

Carnival of Mamoiada, Sunday and Tuesday preceding Ash Wednesday

Christmas (Il Natale), December 25

Christmas Eve (La Vigilia), December 24

Corpus Christi (Corpus Domini), May-June

Corpus Christi (Procession of the Decorated Horse in Brindisi), May-June

Drama, Cycle of Classical, May-June during even-numbered years

Easter (La Pasqua), March-April, first Sunday after first full moon after the vernal equinox

Easter (Scoppio del Carro, Ceremony of the Car), March-April, first Sunday after first full moon after the vernal equinox

Epiphany (Epifania), January 6

Equestrian Tournament of the Quintain, first Sunday in August

Folklore Festival, International, February

Good Friday (Venerdì Santo), March-April, Friday preceding Easter Sunday

Goose and River Festival, Palio of the, June 28-29

Holy Saturday (Sabato Santo), March-April, Saturday before Easter Sunday

Holy Saturday (Scoppia del Carro, Explosion of the Car), March-April, Saturday before Easter Sunday

Holy Thursday (Giovedì Santo), March-April, Thursday preceding Easter

Holy Week, March-April, week preceding Easter

Immaculate Conception, Feast of the (L'Immacolata), December 8

Impruneta, Festa del, late October

Jousting the Bear (La Giostra dell'Orso), March 10

Joust of the Quintain, second weekend in September

Lent, February-March, forty-day season preceding Easter

Liberation Day, April 25

Living Chess Game (La Partita a Scácchi Viventi), second weekend in September during even-numbered years

Madonna del Voto Day, August 16

Mardi Gras, February-March, eight days

Mardi Gras in Venice, February-March, ending Tuesday before Ash Wednesday

Mardi Gras, February-March, Tuesday before Ash Wednesday

Mardi Gras (Carnevale), January 17-Ash Wednesday

Mardi Gras (Carnevale), February-March, one week

Martinmas (San Martino), November 11

May Day (Calendimaggio), May 1

May Day Eve (Calendimaggio), April 30

Mid-Lent Sunday, March, fourth Sunday in Lent

Midsummer, June 23-24

Italy *(cont.)*

Milan Trade Fair, ten days in April

Mille Miglia, three-day race in early May

Music, Venice International Festival of Contemporary, second and third weeks in April

Musical May, Florence (Maggio Musicale Fiorentino), eight weeks in May and June

Musical Weeks, Stresa (Settimane Musicali di Stresa Festival Internazionale), late August to late September

Music Festival, Ravello (Festival Musicale di Ravello), four to five days during first week in July

Music Festival, Umbria Sacred (Sagra Musicale Umbra), two weeks in mid-September

Nativity of the Virgin, Feast of the, September 8

New Year's Day (Capo d'Anno), January 1

New Year's Day (Sacred Mysteries Performance), January 1

New Year's Eve, December 31

Opera, Naples Open-Air Festival of Summer, July-August

Opera, Rome Open-Air Festival of Summer, July-August

Opera and Ballet Festival, July-September

Opera Festival, Verona (Arena di Verona), second week in July to first week in September

Our Lady of Carmel (La Madonna del Carmine), July 16

Palermo Festival, first week in October

Palio, Festival of the (Festa del Palio or Corso del Palio, Palio of the Contrade), held twice during the summer: July 2 and August 16

Palm Sunday (Domenica delle Palme), March-April, the Sunday preceding Easter

Passion Sunday (Domenica delle Passione), March-April, Sunday preceding Palm Sunday

Pentecost, May-June, the Sunday fifty days after Easter

Purim, eleventh day of Jewish month of Sivan

Redeemer, Feast of the (Festa del Redentore), third Sunday in July

Redeemer, Feast of the (Festa del Redentore), last Sunday in August

Regatta of the Great Maritime Republics, first Sunday in June

Republic Day (Constitution Day), June 2

Robigalia, April 25

St. Agnes Eve, January 20

St. Anthony of Padua, Feast of, June 13

St. Cecilia's Day, November 22

St. Efisio, Festival of, May 1-4

St. Frances of Rome, Feast Day of, March 9

St. Francis of Assisi, Feast of, October 3-4

St. Januarius's Feast Day, September 19 (shrine at)

St. John Lateran's Dedication, November 9

St. John the Baptist's Day, June 24

St. Joseph's Day (Dia de San Giuseppe), March 19

St. Lucy's Day, December 13

St. Martin's Day, November 11

St. Nicholas's Day, May 7-8

St. Paulinus of Nola, Feast of (Lily Festival), fourth

Sunday in June or Sunday following June 22

St. Peter's Chair, Festival of, January 18

St. Peter's Day, June 29

St. Roch's Day (San Rocco), August 16

St. Stephen, Feast of, December 26

Sardinian Cavalcade (Cavalcata Sarda), last Sunday in May or on Ascension Day

September in the Town, end of August-beginning of September

Shakespeare Festival, June-September

Spoleto Festival of Two Worlds (Festival dei Due Mondi), late June to mid-July

Theatre, International Festival of University, October

Theatre Festival, July-September

Theatre Festival in the Square, July-August

Theatre Review, International, April-May

Theatre Review, Summer, July-August

Theatres, International Meeting of Experimental, April

Torta dei Fieschi, August 14

Twelfth Night (Epiphany Eve), January 5

Valentine's Day, February 14

Venice Biennial, odd-numbered years in May-December

Visitation of the Blessed Virgin Mary, Feast of the, July 2

Vittoriale, Festival of, July-August

Itsekiri people in Nigeria

Okere Juju, five weeks from May to July; height of rainy season

Itsukushima Island, Hiroshima, Japan

Shrine Festival, Itsukushima, two days in mid-April

Ivory Coast

Dance, Klo, harvest season

Dipri Festival, March-April

Independence Day, August 7; observed December 7

New Yam Festival (Odwira), October

Iwami, Tottori, Japan

Spring Festival, one day in mid-April

Iwate, Japan

Dance, Deer, March

Shrine Festival, Chusonji, May

Ixtapalapa, Federal District, Mexico

Passion Play, March-April, Good Friday

Izmir, Turkey

Izmir International Fair, August-September

Mediterranean Festival, June

Jackson County, Missouri

Founding of the Church of Jesus Christ of the Latter Day Saints, April 6

Jacksonville, Oregon
Britt Festival, Peter, June-September

Jaen, Andalusia, Spain
Pilgrimage of Our Lady of the Cabeza (Romería of the Virgen de la Cabeza), end of April

Jagannath Temple at Puri, Orissa, India
Jhulan Latra, full moon day of Hindu month of Sravana
Juggernaut (Rath Yatra, Festival of Jagannatha), second day of waxing half of Hindu month of Ashadha

Jagsthausen, Baden-Wurttemberg, Federal Republic of Germany
Castle Festival at Jagsthausen, June-August

Jaipur, Rajasthan, India
Drama Festival, Rajasthan Academy, usually February or March

Jajce, Bosnia and Herzegovina, Yugoslavia
Theatre Festival of Bosnia and Herzegovina, June

Jalisco, Mexico
Candlemas, February 2

Jamaica
Christmas, December 25
Heroes Day, October 18
Husayn or Husain Day (Hosay), tenth day of Islamic month of Muharram
Independence Day, August 2; observed first Monday in August
Jamaica Festival, five days in late July ending first Monday in August
Junkanoo Festival, December 23-January 23
Labour Day, May 23
Maroon Festival, January 6
Reggae Sunsplash, four nights in August
Selassie's Coronation Day, Haile, on or near November 15

Jamel, Monastir Region, Tunisia
Cultural Festival of Oum Ezzine, end of September

Jamestown, Rhode Island
Penguin Plunge, January 1

Jammu, Jammu and Kashmir, India
Drama Festivals, Academy, February in Jammu; August in Srinagar

Janesville, California
Dance, Bear, dates vary

Japan
Adults Day (Seijin-no-hi), January 15
Ages, Festival of the (Jidai Matsuri), October 22
Anjin Matsuri, April
Army Commemoration Day (Rikugun-Kinenbi), March 10
Autumnal Equinox Day (Higan Ritual), September 23 or 24
Bean-Throwing Festival (Setsubun), early February, last day of winter in lunar calendar
Bear Festival, early December
Beginning of Work Day (Shigoto Hajime), January 2
Bird Week, begins May 10
Black Ship Day, May-July, dates vary
Bonten Festival, February
Book Reading Week, begins October 27
Broken Needles Festival (Hari-Kuyo), December 8 in Kyoto; February 8 in Tokyo
Buddha's Birthday, Enlightenment, and Salvation (Hana Matsuri, Flower Festival), observed April 8
Bullfinch Exchange Festival (Usokae), January 7
Chakkirako Festival, mid-January
Cherry Blossom Festival, two weeks in April or May
Chichibu Yamaburi, three days in early December
Children's Day (Kodomo-no-hi; formerly Boys' Festival, Tango No Sekku), May 1-5
Children's Protection Day, April 17
Christmas, December 25
Christmas Eve, December 24
Chrysanthemum Festival (Choyo), ninth day of ninth lunar month
Constitution Day, May 3
Culture Day (Bunka-no-hi), November 3
Dance, Deer, March
Dance, Fools' (Awa Odori), August 15-18
Dance, Longevity (Ennen-no-mai), June
Dance, Waraku, August
Dead, Festival of the (Bon Odori, Obon Matsuri, or Rokusai), 15th day of seventh lunar month
Demon-God Festival, one day in April
Double Seventh (Festival of the Weaving Maid and the Herd Boy or Tanabata Matsuri, the Weaver Princess Festival; also known as Star Festival), observed July 7
Double Seventh in Sendai, August 6-8
Fire Festival, July 13
First Writing of the Year (Kakizome), January 2
Foundation Day, Japanese National (Kigensetsu), February 11
Freeing the Insects Festival, August-September
Gagaku Festival, early November
Genshi-Sai, January 3
Gion Matsuri, July
Girls' Doll Festival (Hina Matsuri; also known as Hina-No-Sekku, Peach Blossom Festival), observed March 3
Goddess of Mercy, Birthday of, 19th day of third lunar month
Hakata Dontaku, May 3-4

Jasna Gora Monastery, Czestochowa, Poland
Our Lady of Czestochowa, Feast of (Feast of the Black
Madonna of Jasna Gora), August 15

Jassy, Romania
Eternal Heroes, Festival of, second weekend in July

Java, Indonesia
Ballet Festival, Ramayana, May-October, four consecutive
nights during each full moon
Offering Ceremony, January
Offering Ceremony, April
Offering Ceremony, July
Offering Ceremony, August
Ramadan (Pasa), ninth Islamic month
Sultan's Coronation, May
Water Festival at Menjer Lake, one week in September

Jay, Oklahoma
Fall Festival, October

Jayuya, Puerto Rico
Jayuya Festival of Indian Lore (Jayuya Indian Festival),
mid-November

Jelenia, Gora, Poland
Theatre Encounter, Jelenia Gora, September

Jemez Pueblo, New Mexico
Dance, Eagle, early spring
Dances, Old Pecos Bull and Corn, August 2
Our Lady of Guadalupe, December 12
St. Dominic, Feast of, and Corn Dance, August 4
San Diego, Feast of and Corn Dance, November 12

Jendouba Region, Tunisia
Tabarka, Festival of, July-August

Jerash, Jordan
Jerash Festival, nine days in August

Jerez de la Frontera, Cádiz, Spain
Horse Fair, May
Vintage Feast (Fiesta de la Vendimia), mid-September
Wine Festival, Jerez, September

Jersey, Channel Islands, Great Britain
Battle of Flowers, second Thursday in August
Liberation Day, May 9

Jerusalem, Israel
Easter, March-April, first Sunday after first full moon
after the vernal equinox
Exaltation of the Cross, September 14
Holy Thursday (Khamis al-Jasad), March-April, Thursday
preceding Easter

Israel Festival, dates vary, some time between May and
September
Nebi Mousa, Feast of, March-April, Saturday before Easter
Spring in Jerusalem Festival, month-long in April-May,
including May 12

Jesien Warsaw, Poland
Music of Warsaw, International Festival of Contemporary
and Warsaw Autumn Festival (Warszawka), nine days in
mid-September

Jesus Maria, Nayarit, Mexico
St. Michael, Festival of, September 28-29

Jicarilla Apache Indians in New Mexico: Dulce
Powwow, Little Beaver Rodeo and, late July

Jodhpur, Rajasthan, India
Drama Festival, Rajasthan Academy, usually February
or March

Jogjakarta, Java, Indonesia
Ballet Festival, Ramayana, May-October, four consecutive
nights during each full moon
Muhammad's Birthday (Sekartan Festival), twelfth day
of Islamic month of Rabi al-Awwal
Offering Ceremony, January
Offering Ceremony, April

Johannesburg, South Africa
Rand Show, April-May

Jokkmokk, Lappland, Sweden
Winter Fair, Great Lapp, four days in February

Jonesboro, Tennessee
Storytelling Festival, National, three days in October

Jordan
Arab League Day, March 22
Christmas, December 25
Christmas Eve, December 24
Dead Remembrance Thursday (Khamis al-Amwat), March-
April, Thursday following Easter
Fast, Feast of Breaking the (Id-el-Fitr or al-zid al-Saghir),
first day of Islamic month of Shawwal
Hussein Day, November 14
Independence Day, May 25
Jerash Festival, nine days in August
Mecca, Pilgrimage to, eighth through 13th days of Islamic
month of Dhu'l-Hijjah
Ramadan, ninth Islamic month
Sacrifice, Feast of (al-Adha al-zid al-kabir), tenth-twelfth
days of Islamic month of Dhu'l-Hijjah

Joshinji Temple, Tokyo, Japan
Neri-Kuyo, August 16, every three years

Justis Valley area, Switzerland
Dividing of the Cheese (Käseteilet), September

Juticalpa, Honduras
Immaculate Conception, Feast of the (La Immaculada Concepción), begins several days before December 8

Jyvaskyla, Finland
Arts Festival, Jyvaskyla, several days in May-July

Kadazan people in Malaysia: Sabah
Harvest Festival, Padi, May 30-31

Kaffir people in South Africa
New Year's Day, when Pleiades appear

Kafir Kalash people in Pakistan: near Chitral
Chaomos, December 21, winter solstice

Kagawa, Japan
Kotohira Kompira Festival, October

Kailua-Kona, Hawaii
Ironman Triathlon Championships, Saturday nearest full moon in October

Kainan Temple, Miura, Kanagawa, Japan
Chakkirako Festival, mid-January

Kairouan, Kairouan Region, Tunisia
Summer Festival, July-August

Kairouan Region, Tunisia
Cultural Days, March
Summer Festival, July-August

Kalibo, Akland, Panay Island, Philippines
Ati-Atihan Festival, three days in January, including feast day of Santo Nino (Holy Child Jesus) and ending on a Sunday

Kalisz, Poland
Theatre Meetings, Kalisz, May

Kalocsa, Hungary
Folklore, Danube Festival of, every three years in July

Kaltag, Alaska
Stickdance, one week in spring

Kamakura City, Kanagawa, Japan
Takigi Noh, summer

Kambine, Mozambique
Blessing of Seeds and Tools, start of the planting season

Kamiah, Idaho
Powwow, Chief Looking Glass, August
Powwow and Root Feast, Mat-Al-YM'A, third weekend in May

Kampuchea
See **Cambodia**

Kanagawa, Japan
Chakkirako Festival, mid-January
Takigi Noh, summer

Kanchanaburi, Thailand
River Kwai Bridge Week, last week in November

Kanchipuram near Madras, India
Chitra Gupta, full moon day of Hindu month of Chaitra

Kandy, Sri Lanka
Esala Perahera (Mahanuwara Esala Dalada Perahera), July-August, nine nights during annual festival, full moon day of eighth month, Esala

Kansas
Admission Day, January 29
Dance, Green Corn, about the third weekend in July
Dodge City Days, six days in late July
Earls Court Day, May 9
Frost, or Ice, Saints Day, May 12-14
Mardi Gras (Pancake Day), February-March, Tuesday before Ash Wednesday
Messiah Festival, March-April, eight days during Easter week
Powwow, Mid-America All-American Indian Center, last full weekend in July
St. Nicholas's Day, December 6
Swedish Homage Festival, three days during second week in October every odd-numbered year

Kansas City, Missouri
Livestock, Horse Show, and Rodeo, American Royal, two weeks in November

Kapauka Papuan people in Papua New Guinea
Pig Festival (Juwo)

Kaplan, Louisiana
Bastille Day, July 14

Karnaraka, India
Harvest Festival (Sankranti), three days during Hindu month of Pausha

Karok Indians in northwestern California
World Renewal Ceremony, July and August

Karyai, Greece (ancient)
Artemis Karyatis, Feast of, annual

Kashihara Shrine, Kashihara, Nara, Japan
Kashihara Shinto Festival, April 3

Kashmir
Jyeshta Ashtami, eighth day of waxing half of Hindu
month of Jyeshta
New Year's Day (Nav Roz), Water Festival from Hindu
months of Chaitra to Vaisakha

Kashmir Himalayas (Amarnath cave in the), India
Amarnath Yatra, full moon day of Hindu month of
Sravana

Kasuga Shrine, Nara, Japan
Gagaku Festival, early November

Kataragama, Sri Lanka
Kataragama Festival, June-July

Katerini, Greece
Olympus Festival, July-August

Kathmandu, Nepal
Chariot Festival of Macchendranath (Festival of the
God of Rain), begins first day of waning half of Hindu
month of Vaisakha and lasts two months
Indra Jatra and Kumari Jatra, Festival of the Child
Goddess, eight days during Hindu months of
Bhadrapada-Asvina
National Day (Tribhuvan Jayanti), February 18
Teej, third day of waxing half of Hindu month of Sravana

Katonah, New York
Caramoor Festival, nine weeks from mid-June to mid-
August

Katori, Chiba, Japan
Shrine Rice Festival, Katori, April

Katowice, Poland
Plays, Festival of Russian and Soviet, November
Theatre Spring, Silesian, May

Katsina, Nigeria
Ramadan (Azumi), ninth Islamic month
Sallah, tenth day of Islamic month of Dhu'l-Hijjah

Katwijk, Netherlands
Vlaggetjesdag, anytime from middle to late May

Kauai, Hawaii
Kuhio Kalanianaole Day, one week in March, including
March 26

Kaustinen, Finland
Folk Music Festival Kaustinen, third week in July

Kazan, Russia
Holy Thursday (Votjak or Udmurt), March-April,
Thursday preceding Easter

Kazan, Tatar Republic, Russia, USSR
Plow, Festival of the (Saban Tuy), June 25

Kazanluk, Bulgaria
Rose Festival, ten days from late May to early June

Kazincbarcika, Hungary
Dramatic Groups, "Istvan Horvath Cadet" Festival of,
even-numbered years in July

Kearney, Nebraska
Crane Watch (Wings over the Platte), March-April

Kelantan, Malaysia
Bachok Festival of Culture, two weeks in May
Puja Ketek Celebrations, October
Sultan's Birthday Celebration, July

Kennebunkport, Maine
Dump Week, National, Thursday after the Fourth of July
through Labor Day, first Monday in September

Kent, England
Broadstairs Dickens Festival, eight days in June
Christmas Season (Hodening)

Kent State University, Kent, Ohio
Kent State Memorial Day, May 3-4

Kentucky
Admission Day, June 1
Banana Festival, International, mid-September
Bar-B-Q Festival, International, mid-May
Bluegrass Fan Fest, third weekend in September
Boone Festival, Daniel, first through second Saturdays
in October
Brass Band Festival, Great American, mid-June
Capital Expo, two days in early June
Confederate Memorial Day, June 3
Davis's Birthday, Jefferson, June 3
Footwashing Day, a Sunday in early summer or Holy
Thursday
Graveyard Cleaning and Decoration Day, July
Kentucky Derby Day, 15-day festival precedes race, which
occurs on the first Saturday in May

Kentucky *(cont.)*
Mountain Laurel Festival, Kentucky, four days in May
Roosevelt Day, Franklin D., January 30
Shaker Festival, ten days beginning second Thursday in July
Shaker Festival, mid-July
Summer Festival, July 4

Kenya
Independence Day (Jamhuri Day), December 12
Madaraka Day (Responsibility Day or Self-Government
    Day), June 1
Muhammad's Birthday (Maulidi), twelfth day of Islamic
    month of Rabi al-Awwal
Nairobi Show, one week during September or October
Safari Rally, March-April, Easter weekend

Kerala, India
Dance Festival, Kerala Kalamandalam, March
Dance Festival, Krishnattam, September-October
Dance Festivals, Kathakali, March-April and October-
    November
Harvest Festival (Onam), August-September, four to ten days
    in Malyalam month of Chingam
New Year (Vishu), first day of Hindu month of Vaisakha
St. Thomas the Apostle, Feast of, December 21

Kerkyra, Corfu, Greece
Folk Dancing at Corfu, Greek, mid-May to September

Kerry (County), Ireland
Puck's Fair, August 10-12
Rose of Tralee International Festival, six days in August-
    September
Writers' Week Listowel, June

Keshena, Wisconsin
Powwow, Land of the Menominee, first weekend in August

Key West, Florida
Hemingway Days, week including July 21
Old Island Days, seven weeks from early February to late
    March

Khir Bhawani, Kashmir
Jyeshta Ashtami, eighth day of waxing half of Hindu month
    of Jyeshta

Khmer Republic
See **Cambodia**

Kickapoo Indians in Kansas: near Horton
Dance, Green Corn, about the third weekend in July

Kiel, Schleswig-Holstein, Federal Republic of Germany
Kiel Week, one week in June

Kiev, Ukraine, USSR
Spring, Kiev, second half of May

Kikinda, Vojvodina, Yugoslavia
Theatres of Vojvodina, Encounter of Amateur, May

Kilkis, Greece
Gynaecocratia, January 8

Killorglin, County Kerry, Ireland
Puck's Fair, August 10-12

Kimsquit Indians in Canada: coastal British Columbia
Midwinter Rites, Bella Coola (Kusiut), November-February

Kineauvista Hill near Cosby, Tennessee
Ramp Festival, Cosby, first Sunday in May

Kingsburg, California
Swedish Festival, Kingsburg, third weekend in May

King's College, London, England
National Anti-Drugs Day, March 11

King's Lynn, Norfolk, England
Music and the Arts, King's Lynn Festival of, nine days
    in July

Kiowa Indians
Devil's Promenade, July 3-6

Kiowa Indians in the Great Plains of the United States
Dance, Sun, usually during summer solstice, June 21

Kiribati
Independence Day, July 12

Kirkpinar, Edirne, Turkey
Wrestling Games of Kirkpinar, one week in June

Kirkwall, Orkney Islands, Scotland
St. Magnus Festival, five days over third weekend in June

Kitchener, Waterloo, Ontario, Canada
Oktoberfest, nine days in early October, beginning the
    Friday before Thanksgiving Monday

Kitty Hawk, North Carolina
Wright Brothers Day, December 17

Klamath Falls, Oregon
Powwow, Chief Schonchin Days, last weekend in May

Klamath Indians in Oregon: Klamath Falls
Powwow, Chief Schonchin Days, last weekend in May

Klina by Pec, Kosovo, Yugoslavia
Kosovo, Village Festivities of, June

Knoxville, Tennessee
Arts Festival, Dogwood, 17 days in April

Kobersdorf, Burgenland, Austria
Castle Kobersdorf Festival, July

Kofukuji Temple, Nara, Japan
Takigi Noh, mid-May

Komatsu, Ishikawa, Japan
Komatsu Otabi Festival, mid-May

Komotini, Greece
Gynaecocratia, January 8

Konya, Turkey
Mevlana (Whirling Dervishes), Festival of, nine days to two weeks in December

Kootenai Indians in Montana: Elmo
Powwow, Standing Arrow, third weekend in July

Koprivshtitsa, Bulgaria
Folk Art, National Festival of, every five years during the summer

Korcula, Croatia, Yugoslavia
Korcula, Festival of (Moreska), July 27 and every Thursday from April-September

Korea
Alphabet Day (Han-gul), early October
Buddha's Birthday, Enlightenment, and Salvation, eighth day of fourth lunar month
Burning the Moon House (Dal-jip-tae-u-gee or Viewing the First Full Moon), 15th day of first lunar month
Cherry Blossom Festival, Chinhae, early April
Children's Day, May 5
Chrysanthemum Festival (Choyo), ninth day of ninth lunar month
Double Seventh (Festival of the Weaving Maid and the Herd Boy, Gyunoo and Jingny O), seventh day of seventh lunar month
Excited Insects, Feast of (Kyongchip), on or near March 5
Farmer's Day, June 15
Goddess of Mercy, Birthday of, 19th day of third lunar month
Grave-Sweeping and Cold Food Festival (Han Sik-il, Cold Food Day), fourth or fifth day of third lunar month, 105 or 106 days after the winter solstice
Great Fifteenth, 15th day of first lunar month
Hungry Ghosts, Festival of, 15th day of seventh lunar month

Kite Flying Day, February 8
Mid-Autumn Festival (Choosuk, Chusok, or Hangawi, Moon Festival), 15th, or full moon, day of eighth lunar month
Music Festival, Seoul International, first two weeks in May
New Year (Sol), ten-day to two-week long celebration at the first new moon after sun enters Aquarius; one to 15 days of first lunar month
Shampoo Day (Yoodoonal), 15th day of sixth lunar month
Shilla Cultural Festival, three days in October during even-numbered years
Shrine Rite, Royal (Chongmyo Taeje), first Sunday in May
Swing Festival (Tano), fifth day of fifth lunar month
Wind Festival, February-March, first day of second lunar month

Korea, Democratic People's Republic of
Independence Day (National Day), September 9

Korea, Republic of
Art Festival, National Foundation, November 1-5
Castle Festival, Moyang, ninth day of ninth lunar month
Children's Day (Urini Nal), May 5
Chunhyang Festival, three days from the eighth day of fourth lunar month
Constitution Day, July 17
Foundation Day, October 3
Independence Day (Samiljol), March 1
Liberation Day, August 15
Memorial Day, June 6
Republic Day, August 15

Kortrijk, Belgium
Flanders, Festival of (Festival van Vlaanderen), April to October

Koryak people in Russia
Horns, Festival of (Kil'vey), spring

Koryak people in the USSR
Seal Festival, November, end of seal-hunting season

Kos, Greece
Hippokrateia, August

Kosovo, Serbia, Yugoslavia
Kosovo, Village Festivities of, June
Theatre Groups, Provincial Festival of Kosovo Amateur, June
Theatre Groups, Regional Review of Kosovo Amateur, April

Kosovska Mitrovica, Kosovo, Serbia, Yugoslavia
Theatre Groups, Regional Review of Kosovo Amateur, April

Kota Bharu, Kelantan, Malaysia
Sultan's Birthday Celebration, July

Kotohira, Kagawa, Japan
Kotohira Kompira Festival, October

Kotor, Montenegro, Yugoslavia
South, Festival of the, July-August

Kovacica, Vojvodina, Yugoslavia
Folklore in Vojvodina, Slovakian, May

Kraków, Poland
Horse Festival (Lejkonik), May-June, second Thursday
    after Corpus Christi
Juvenalia, late May or early June

Kralendijk, Bonaire, Netherlands Antilles
Regatta, International, four days in October

Krems, Lower Austria, Austria
Krems Outdoor Festival (Sommerspiele Krems), June-July

'Ksan Indians in Canada: Hazelton, British Columbia
'Ksan Celebrations, Friday evenings in July and August

Ksar El Badi Palace, Marrakech, Morocco
Folklore, Festival of, ten days in May

Kuala Lumpur, Selangor, Malaysia
Independence Day (Merdeka), August 31

Kuala Lumpur to Cave Temple at Batu Caves, Malaysia
Thaipusam, one day in January-February

Kuba people in Congo: Mushenge
Itul, on or near December 7-8, but date varies and festival
    occurs according to king's authorization

Kucevo, Serbia, Yugoslavia
Homolje Motifs, May

Kuchipudi, Andhra Pradesh, India
Dance Festival, Kuchipudi, three days in August-September

Kuhmo, Finland
Music Festival, Kuhmo Chamber (Kuhmon Kamarmusiikki),
    ten days in late July or early August

**Kuksu secret society of North American Indians in
central California**
Hesi Ceremony

Kula, Serbia, Yugoslavia
Theatres of Serbia, Festival of Amateur, first half of June

Kule Loklo Miwok Indian Village, California
Acorn Festival, usually weekend after fourth Friday in
    September
Kule Loklo Celebration, July or August
Strawberry Festival, spring

Kulu, India
Mother Goddess, Festival of Durga, the, first ten days of
    waxing half of Hindu month of Asvina

Kumano Nachi Shrine, Nachi No Falls, Wakayama, Japan
Fire Festival, July 13

Kumaon region of India
Nanda Deven, August-September

Kumbakonam, India
Masi Magham, February-March, two-day festival during
    full moon of Masi; larger festival every twelve years

Kuopio, Finland
Dance and Music Festival, Kuopio, June

Kurdistan
Shavuot, the Feast of Weeks, sixth day of Jewish month
    of Sivan
Simhat Torah (Rejoicing in the Law), 23rd of Jewish month
    of Tishri

Kuromori Village, Sakata City, Yamagata, Japan
Shrine Festival, Kuromori Hie, mid-February

Kusadasi, Turkey
Kusadasi, Festival of, June-July

Kushiki-machi, Higishitagawa-gun, Yamagata, Japan
Kurokowa Noh, early February

Kusinagar near Gorakhpur, India
Buddha's Birthday, Enlightenment, and Salvation (Buddha
    Jayanti), full moon day of Hindu month of Vaisakha

Kutztown, Pennsylvania
Folk Festival, Pennsylvania Dutch, nine days in July,
    including July 4

Kuwait
Independence or Republic Day, June 19
Mecca, Pilgrimage to, eighth through 13th days of Islamic
    month of Dhu'l-Hijjah
National Day, February 25
Sacrifice, Feast of ('Id al-Adha), tenth-twelfth days of
    Islamic month of Dhu'l-Hijjah

Kwangali people in Namibia
Rain-Calling Ceremony (Nyambinyambi), spring

Kwantung Province, China
Martyrs' Day, Canton, March 29

Kyongju, Korea
Shilla Cultural Festival, three days in October during even-numbered years

Kyoto, Japan
Adults Day (Seijin-no-hi), January 15
Ages, Festival of the (Jidai Matsuri), October 22
Gion Matsuri, July
Hollyhock Festival (Aoi Matsuri), May 15
Mibu Dainembutsu Kyogen, end of April
Takigi Noh, two days in early June

Labrador, Newfoundland, Canada
Epiphany, January 6

Lac Courte Oreilles Ojibwa Indians in Wisconsin: Hayward
Powwow, Honor the Earth, July

Lac du Flambeau, Wisconsin
Powwow, Bear River, July

La Chaux-de-Fonds, Neuchatel, Switzerland
La Chaux-de-Fonds, Biennial of, even-numbered years usually in May-June, sometimes autumn

La Coruna, Spain
St. Roch's Day (San Roque Festival), August

La Côte-Saint-André, France
Berlioz International Festival (Internationales Festival Hector Berlioz), one week in mid-September

Ladakh
Harvest (Mandela Ceremony), harvest season

Ladakh, India
Hemis Festival, three days in June or July

La Defense, Paris, France
Music at La Defense, month of June

Lafayette, Indiana
Hunters' Moon, Feast of the, October

Lafayette, Louisiana
Acadiens, Festivals, third week in September
Mardi Gras, February-March

Lagos, Nigeria
Eyo Masquerade, August

La Goulette, North Tunis Region, Tunisia
El Karraka International Festival, July-August

Laguna Beach, California
Arts and Pageant of the Masters, Festival of the, 45 days in July and August

Laguna Pueblo, New Mexico
All Souls' Day, November 2
Nativity of the Virgin, Feast of the, September 8
St. Elizabeth, Feast of, September 25
St. Mary Margaret, Feast of, October 17

Lahore, Pakistan
Data Ganj Baksh Death Festival, 18-19 days of Islamic month of Safar

Lake Balaton area, Hungary
Summer Concerts, Lake Balaton, summer

Lake District, England
Grasmere Sports, third Thursday in August

Lake Havasu City, Arizona
London Bridge Days, first two weekends in October

Lakewood, California
Pan American Festival Week, two days in late April or early May

Lame Deer, Montana
Powwow, Northern Cheyenne, July

Lamego, Viseu, Portugal
Pilgrimage to the Sanctuary of Our Lady of the Remedies (Pardon of Nossa Senhora dos Remédios) and Festival of Lamego, early September

Lamu, Kenya
Muhammad's Birthday (Maulidi), twelfth day of Islamic month of Rabi al-Awwal

Lanark, England
Landimere's or Lanimer Day, the Thursday which falls between June 6-12

Lanark, Lanarkshire, Scotland
Whuppity Scoorie Day, March 1

Lanarkshire, Scotland
Monklands Festival, June
Whuppity Scoorie Day, March 1

Lancashire, England
Keaw Yed Wakes Festival, Sunday of or after August 24

Landshut, Bavaria, Federal Republic of Germany
Landshut Wedding, three weeks, including four Sundays in June-July, every third year

Lawton, Oklahoma
Easter (Oberammergau Sunrise Service), March-April, first Sunday after first full moon after the vernal equinox

Lavagna, Genoa, Italy
Torta dei Fieschi, August 14

Leadville, Buena Vista, and Fairplay, Colorado
Burro Races, Triple Crown Pack, last weekend in July through August

Lealul Knoll, Mongu, Western Province, Zambia
Kuomboka, February-March, when Zambezi River rises

Lebanese-Americans at Bridgeport, Connecticut
Soul, Festival of the (Mahrajan), September 1

Lebanese people in North and South America
St. Maron's Day, February 9

Lebanon
Anjar Festival, first two weeks in September
Baalbek Festival, mid-July to mid-August
Byblos Festival, May-September
Evacuation Day, December 31
Flower Festival, Bikfaya, one day in mid-August
Husayn or Husain Day, tenth day of Islamic month of Muharram
Independence Day, November 22
Lent, February-March, forty-day season preceding Easter
Night of Power (Lailat alqadr), one of the last ten days of Islamic month of Ramadan; usually observed on the 27th
Ramadan, ninth Islamic month
St. Maron's Day, February 9
Springtime Festival, March-April, four successive Thursdays before Orthodox Easter
Wine Festival, Zahle, early September

Leech Lake Reservation, Cass Lake, Minnesota
Powwows, Ojibwa, first Monday in September, last Monday in May, and in winter, spring, and midsummer

Leh, Tibet
New Year (Dosmoche Festival), five days including 28th day of twelfth lunar month

Leicestershire, England
Bottle Kicking and Hare Pie Scramble, Annual, March-April, Easter Monday

Le Kef, Le Kef Region, Tunisia
Sidi-Bou-Makhlouf, Festival, July

Le Kef Region, Tunisia
M'Hamed Ben Khelifa Festival, October
Sidi-Bou-Makhlouf, Festival, July

Leiden, Netherlands
Leiden Day (Leiden Ontzet), October 3

Lela, Volta
New Year Purification before Planting, April, just before planting

Le Mans, Sarthe, France
Le Mans Grand Prix, June

Lenape Delaware Indians in Oklahoma: near Copan
Powwow, Lenape Delaware, late May or early June

Lengua Indians in Gran Chaco, South American
Harvest Dance (Kyaiya), spring, summer, and autumn

Leningrad, Russia, USSR (now St. Petersburg, Russia)
White Night Festival, nine days in June
See also **St. Petersburg, Russia**

Lennoxville, Quebec, Canada
Lennoxville, Festival, July-August

Lenox, Massachusetts
Music, Festival of Contemporary, August
Music Festival, Berkshire, July-September

Leonardtown, Maryland
Oyster Festival, St. Mary's County Maryland, second weekend in October

Lérida, Spain
San Ermengol Retaule Festival, August
San Macario, Festival of, January 2

Lerwick, Shetland Islands, Scotland
Up-Helly-Aa, last Tuesday in January

Leskovac, Serbia, Yugoslavia
Folklore Festival of the Socialist Republic of Serbia, June
Stage, Classics on the Yugoslav, October

Lesotho
Family Day, first Monday in July
Independence Day, October 4
Moshoeshoe Day, March 12
Tree Planting Day, March 21 or 22

Les Saintes-Maries-de-la-Mer, Provence, France
Holy Maries, Feast of (La Fête des Saintes Maries), May 24-25

Letterkenny, County Donegal, Ireland
Folk Festival, Letterkenny International, five days in late August

Leuven, Belgium
Flanders, Festival of (Festival van Vlaanderen), April to October

Lewiston, New York
Artpark, last week in June to mid-August

Lexington, Oklahoma
Oklahoma Day, April 22

Leyden Street to the Fort-Meetinghouse, now the church of the Pilgrimage on Main Street on Burial Hill in Plymouth, Massachusetts
Pilgrim Progress Pageant, every Friday in August

Lhasa, Tibet
Butter Sculpture Festival (Mönlam or Prayer Festival), usually February, two to three weeks during first month of Tibetan calendar
Lights, Festival of (Sang-joe), October-November, 25th day of tenth Tibetan month
New Year (Dosmoche Festival), five days including 28th day of twelfth lunar month

Liberal, Kansas
Mardi Gras (Pancake Day), February-March, Tuesday before Ash Wednesday

Liberia
Africa Day, May 25
Armed Forces Day, February 11
Fast and Prayer Day, April 9
Flag Day, August 24
Independence Day, July 26
Newport Day, Matilda, December 1
Pioneers' Day, January 7
Thanksgiving Day, first Thursday in November

Libya
Evacuation Day, American Bases, June 11
Fast, Feast of Breaking the (Eid al Fitr), first day of Islamic month of Shawwal
Independence Day, December 24
Maimona or Maimonides, evening of last day of Passover and day after Passover
Muhammad's Birthday (Ma'ulid Annabi), twelfth day of Islamic month of Rabi al-Awwal
National Day, September 1
New Year, Jewish (Rosh Hashanah), first day of Jewish month of Tishri
Passover (Pesach), eight days beginning 15th of Jewish month of Nisan
Shavuot, the Feast of Weeks, sixth day of Jewish month of Sivan

Liechtenstein
Annunciation, Feast of the, March 25
Candlemas, February 2
Prince's Birthday, August 15
St. Joseph of Arimathea, Feast Day of, March 19

Liège, Belgium
Theatre, Liège Festival of Young (Le Festival du Jeune Theatre de Liège), October
Wallonia, Festival of (Festival de Wallonie), June-September or October

Liguria, Italy
Ballet, International Festival of, July during even-numbered years

Lille, France
Whit Monday (Procession of Giants of Belgium and France), May-June, Monday after Pentecost

Lima, Peru
St. Francis of Assisi, Feast of (San Francisco's Day), October 4
Santo Domingo Promenade, August 4

Limassol, Cyprus
Art Festival, International, ten days in July
Curium Festival, June-July
Kataklysmos (Flood Festival), May-June, three to five days including fiftieth day after Greek Orthodox Easter (Pentecost)
Mardi Gras (Carnival), February-March, twelve days ending Ash Wednesday
Wine Festival, Limassol, September 15-30

Limburg, Belgium
Assumption, Feast of the (Festival of Virga Jesse), third and fourth Sundays in August every seven years
Flanders, Festival of (Festival van Vlaanderen), April to October
Game of St. Evermaire (Spel van Sint Evermarus), May 1

Lindi, Tanzania
Midimu Ceremony, June through October; begins night during the period when the moon moves from the quarter to its half phase for three days

Lindsborg, Kansas
Messiah Festival, March-April, eight days during Easter week
Swedish Homage Festival, three days during second week in October every odd-numbered year

Lingaraja Temple, Bhubaneswar, India
Ashokashtami, eighth day of waxing half of Hindu month of Chaitra

Linville, North Carolina
Highland Games and Gathering of Scottish Clans, Grandfather Mountain, second full weekend in July
Singing on the Mountain, fourth Sunday in June

Linz, Austria
Bruckner Festival, International (Internationales Brucknerfest), four weeks in September

Lisboa District, Ribatejo, Portugal
Red Waistcoat Festival (Festival of the Colete Encarnado), July

Lisbon, Maine
Moxie Festival, second Saturday in July

Lisbon, Portugal
St. Anthony of Padua, Feast of, June 13

Lisse, South Holland, Netherlands
Flower Show, Keukenhof, March-May
Tulip Festival, last week in April and first week in May

Listowel, County Kerry, Ireland
Writers' Week Listowel, June

Litchfield Park, Goodyear, and Avondale, Arizona
Moore Days, Billy, second weekend in October

Lithuania
Binding of Wreaths (Vainkinas), July
Christmas (Kalēdos), December 25
Christmas Eve (Kūčios), December 24
Easter (Velykos), March-April, first Sunday after first full moon after the vernal equinox
Easter Monday (Velyku Antra Diena), March-April, Monday after Easter
Epiphany (Triju Karaliu Šventē), January 6
Harvest Celebration, Grain (Nubaigai), end of harvest
Holy Innocents' Day (Nekaltuju Šventē), December 28
Independence Day, March 11
Mardi Gras (Užgavenēs), February-March, Tuesday before Ash Wednesday
Midsummer, June 23-24
New Year's Day (Nauju Metu Diena), January 1
Pentecost, May-June, the Sunday fifty days after Easter
Song Festival, every five years in summer
Song Festival (Skamba Kankliai), May

Lithuania (ancient)
July, Feast of (Vainikinas; also known as the Binding of the Wreaths), July
Spring, Feast of (Pavasario Svente), March 16

Lithuanian-Americans
Independence Day, Lithuania, February 16

Little Eagle, South Dakota
Powwow, Sioux, usually in July

Little Italy, New York
St. Januarius's Feast Day, two weeks, including September 19

Little Tokyo, Los Angeles, California
Nisei Week, August

Liverpool, England
Grand National Day, March-April

Ljubljana, Slovenia, Yugoslavia
Ballet Biennial, June-July during odd-numbered years
Summer Festival, Ljubljana International (Festivala Ljubljana), eleven weeks from mid-June to end of August
Youth Culture Week, May

Llanerfyl, Wales
Fool's Fair (Ffair Ffyliaid), first Tuesday in May

Llanes, Oviedo, Spain
St. Roch's Day (San Roque Festival), August

Llangollen, Denbighshire, Wales
Eisteddfod, International Musical (Gerddorol Gydwladol Llangollen), six days during first week in July

Llantilio Crossenny, Wales
Music and Drama, Llantilio Crossenny Festival of, first weekend in May

Lloret de Mar, Gerona, Spain
St. Christina's Day (Festival of Santa Cristina), July 24; festival held in July

Lobamba, Swaziland
New Year (Newala Ceremonies, First Fruits Festival), six days in December-January

Lobi people in Ivory Coast
New Yam Festival (Odwira), October

Lochristi, Belgium
Begonia Festival, three days in August

Lodz, Poland
Ballet Biennial, International, May during even-numbered years
Theatre Encounters, Lodz, spring

Logan, Utah
American West, Festival of, nine days in July-August

Logrono, Spain
St. Mary Magdalene, Feast of (Dance of the Stilts), July

Loiret, France
Musical Weeks of Orleans, International (Semaines Musicales Internationale d'Orleans), two weeks in November-December

Loir-et-Cher, France
Art and History, Festival of, Thursdays, Saturdays, and Sundays in August

Loíza, Puerto Rico
St. James the Greater's Day (Fiesta of Santiago), July 25

Lombardy, Italy
Mardi Gras (Carnevale), February-March, one week
Milan Trade Fair, ten days in April
Vittoriale, Festival of, July-August

London, England
Bach Festival, English, April and May
Bartholomew Fair, August 24
Camden Festival, two weeks in March
Flower Show, Chelsea, last full week in May
Grotto Day, August 5
Last Night, a Saturday in mid-September
Lilies and Roses Day, May 21
London, Festival of the City of, July during even-numbered years
Mime Festival, January-February
Mind and Body, Festival of, March-April
National Anti-Drugs Day, March 11
Oranges and Lemons Day, March 31
Parliament Day, early November
Payment of Quit Rent, September 29
Queen Elizabeth II, Official Birthday of, June 12 or second Saturday in June
Royal Tournament, July
St. Charles's Day, January 30; observed on or near February 2 at Trafalgar Square, London
Thamesday, early September
Theatre Season, Open-Air, May-August
Trafalgar Day (Horatio Nelson Day), October 21
Universal Week of Prayer, first through second Sunday in January
Wood Promenade Concerts, Henry, nine weeks from mid-July to mid-September
Young Writers' Festival, February-May

London, England (medieval)
Christmas Eve, December 24

London Borough of Brent, Middlesex, England
Brent Festival, January-February

London Borough of Ealing, England
Theatre Weeks, International and English Amateur-, alternate years in April

London Borough of Greenwich, England
Greenwich Festival, last two weeks in June

London Borough of Islington, England
Theatre, St. George's Elizabethan, summer through autumn

London Borough of Merton, England
Merton Festival, May

London Borough of Southwark, England
Bankside Globe Festival, July-August

London to Westminster, England
Lord Mayor's Show, November 9; observed second Saturday in November (procession)

Long Island, New York
Belmont Stakes, June, fifth Saturday after Kentucky Derby

Lopen and Hinton St. George, Somerset, England
Punky Night, October 28 or 29 or last Thursday in October

Lorient, Morbihan, France
Lorient Festival, ten days at beginning of August

Los Angeles, California
All Souls' Day, November 2
Christmas Eve, December 24
Cinco de Mayo, May 5
Holy Saturday (Blessing of the Animals), March-April, Saturday before Easter Sunday
Nisei Week, August
Our Lady of Guadalupe, December 12
St. Anthony the Abbot of Egypt, Feast of (Blessing of the Animals), January 17
Transpac Race from Los Angeles to Honolulu, Hawaii, July during odd-numbered years

Lot, France
Music Festival, International, July-August

Lot-et-Garonne, France
Folklore Festival, International, about one week in August

Louisburg, North Carolina
Whistlers Convention, National, second or third weekend in April

Louisiana
Acadiens, Festivals, third week in September
Admission Day, April 30
All Saints' Day, November 1
Bastille Day, July 14
Battle of New Orleans or Hickory's Day, January 8
Blessing of the Fleet (Louisiana Shrimp and Petroleum
  Festival), first weekend in September
Christmas, December 25
Christmas Eve, December 24
Confederate Memorial Day, June 3
Crawfish Festival, first weekend in May
Dance, Calinda, June 23
Epiphany (King's Day), January 6
Halloween, October 31
Jazz and Heritage Festival, New Orleans, ten days in mid-
  April to early May
Long Day, Huey P., August 30
Mardi Gras, begins no later than January 6, Epiphany, and
  ends Fat Tuesday, the day before Ash Wednesday
McDonogh Day, first Friday in May
Music, Louisiana State University Festival of Contemporary,
  one week in early spring
St. Joan of Arc, Feast of, May 9
St. Médardus's Day, June 8
St. Ursula's Day, October 21
Sugar Bowl Classic, January 1 (January 2, if New Year's Day
  falls on a Sunday)
Twelfth Night (Epiphany Eve), January 5

Louisville, Kentucky
Kentucky Derby Day, 15-day festival precedes race, which
  occurs on the first Saturday in May

Lourdes, Hautes-Pyrénées, France
Easter Festival of Sacred Music, March-April, 10 days
  beginning Good Friday
Our Lady of Lourdes, Feast of, February 11; festival
  between February 11-18

Lousa, Beira Baixa, Portugal
Pilgrimage to Nossa Senhora dos Altos Ceus

Louth (County), Ireland
Maytime Festival, International, third week in May

Lovedu people in South Africa
Rainmaking Ceremony, prior to rainy season

Lower Austria, Austria
Carnuntum Festival, July-August
Castle Neulengbach Festival (Schloss Neulengbach), July
Krems Outdoor Festival (Sommerspiele Krems), June-July
Melk, Festival of (Melker Festspiele), July-August
Nestroy Festival (Nestroy-Spiele), July

Stockerau Outdoor Festival (Stockerau Festspiele),
  July-August

Lower Rhine, Germany
Martinsfest, November 10-11

Lower Saxony, Federal Republic of Germany
Mardi Gras (Kopenfahrt, Kope Procession or Festival),
  February-March, Tuesday before Ash Wednesday
Music and Theatre in Herrenhausen, June-August
Plays Festival, Gandersheim Cathedral, May-June
Plays in the Town Hall, May-June to September for two
  consecutive years followed by two-year interim
Puppet Play Week, International, one week in March
  during odd-numbered years

Lower Saxony, Germany
Boundary Walk (Grenzumgang), every ten years, 1951, 1961,
  etc.

Lozithehlezi to Gunundvwini, and Lobamba, Swaziland
New Year (Newala Ceremonies, First Fruits Festival), six days
  in December-January

Luarca, Oviedo, Spain
Vaqueiros de Alzada Festival, July

Lubang, Mindoro, Luzon Island, Philippines
Panunuluyan, December 24

**Lubbecke, North Rhine-Westphalia, Federal Republic of
Germany**
Theatre Nettelstedt, Open-Air, Saturdays and Sundays
  from May to September

Luberon and surrounding towns, Vauclude, France
Musical Weeks of Luberon (Semaines Musicales du Luberon),
  two weeks in July-August

Lublin, Poland
Theatre Confrontations, Young, November

Lucban, Quezon, Luzon Island, Philippines
Water Buffalo Festival (Carabao), May 14 or 15

Lucerne, Switzerland
Music, Lucerne International Festival of (Luzern
  Internationale Musikfestwochen), mid-August to
  mid-September
Pentecost (Pfingsten), May-June, the Sunday fifty days after
  Easter

Ludlow, Shropshire, England
Summer Festival, Ludlow, last week in June and first week
  in July

Lugo, Spain
St. Lawrence of Rome, Feast of (Festival of San Lorenzo), August

Lummi Indians in Washington: Bellingham
Warrior or Veteran Festival, Stommish, month of June

Lund, Sweden
Walpurgis Night (Valborgsmässoafton), April 30

Lüneburg, Lower Saxony, Germany
Mardi Gras (Kopenfahrt, Kope Procession or Festival), February-March, Tuesday before Ash Wednesday

Luxembourg
Burgsonndeg, February or March
Candlemas (Lîchtmesdâg), February 2
Christmas Eve (Chreshdagôvend), December 24
Dancing Procession (Sprangprozessio'n), May-June, Tuesday after Pentecost
Easter (O'schtersonndeg), March-April, first Sunday after first full moon after the vernal equinox
Easter Monday, March-April, Monday after Easter
Flower Festival, Broom (Genzefest), May-June, Whit Monday, Monday after Pentecost
Good Friday (Charfreudeg), March-April, Friday preceding Easter Sunday
Grand Duke, or National, Day, June 23
Holy Saturday (Charsamsdeg), March-April, Saturday before Easter Sunday
Mardi Gras (Fetten Donneschdeg), February-March, Thursday before the beginning of Lent
Mid-Lent Sunday (Bretzelsonndeg, Pretzel Sunday), March, fourth Sunday in Lent
Music Festival, International Classical, mid-June to mid-July
New Year's Day (Neitjorsdâg), January 1
Our Lady, Consoler of the Afflicted, Octave of, eight to 15 days beginning fifth Sunday after Easter
Our Lady of Bildchen, Procession to (Muttergottesprozessio'n Op d'Bildchen), Sunday following August 15
Palm Sunday (Pellemsonndeg), March-April, the Sunday preceding Easter
Pentecost, May-June, the Sunday fifty days after Easter
Pottery Festival, Easter Monday
Remembrance Day, July 6
Shepherd's Fair (Schueberfo'er), two weeks beginning last Sunday in August
St. Hubert, Feast Day of, November 3
St. Nicholas's Day (Neklosdag), December 6
Theatre and Music Festival, International, July-August

Luxembourg, Belgium
Wallonia, Festival of (Festival de Wallonie), June-September or October

Luxembourg City, Luxembourg
Pottery Festival, March-April, Easter Monday

Luxembourg-Ville, Luxembourg
Our Lady, Consoler of the Afflicted, Octave of, eight to 15 days beginning fifth Sunday after Easter

Luxeuil-les-Bains, Haute-Saone, France
Hauts-de-Saone Festival, last weekend in June and first weekend in July

Luxor, Egypt
Nile, Festival of the, spring

Luzon Island, Philippines
Ballet Festival, National, May
Black Nazarene Fiesta, January 1-9
Dances of Obando, three days in mid-May
Moro-Moro Play, April or May
Panunuluyan, December 24
Passion Play, Cenaculo, March-April, Holy Week

Lyon, France
Berlioz International Festival (Internationales Festival Hector Berlioz), one week in mid-September
Lyon International Festival (Festival International de Lyon), June-July
Theatre for Children and Young People, International Encounter of, first two weeks in June during odd-numbered years

Macao
A-Ma, Feast of, April
Double Fifth (Dragon Boat Festival and Festival of the Five Poisonous Creatures), fifth day of fifth lunar month
Double Ninth Day, ninth day of ninth lunar month
Macao Grand Prix, ten days in mid-November
Mid-Autumn Festival, 15th, or full moon, day of eighth lunar month
Our Lord of Passos, Procession of, February-March

Macaracas, Panama
Folklore Festival, Canajacua, four days including Epiphany, January 6

Macedonia
April Fools' Day, April 1
Easter, March-April, first Sunday after first full moon after the vernal equinox
First of March (Drymiais), March 1
Good Friday, March-April, Friday preceding Easter Sunday
Holy Saturday, March-April, Saturday before Easter Sunday
Holy Thursday, March-April, Thursday preceding Easter
Holy Week, March-April, week preceding Easter
Mardi Gras (Cheesefare Sunday), February-March, Sunday before Lent begins

Macedonia *(cont.)*
May Day, May 1
Midsummer, June 23-24
New Year's Eve, December 31
Progress of the Precious and Vivifying Cross, Feast of the, August 1
St. Dominique's Day, January 22
St. Elias Day, August 2
St. George's Day, April 23
St. Plato the Martyr, Feast of, November 18
St. Thomas's Day, March-April, first Sunday after Easter

Macedonia, Yugoslavia
Folk Songs and Dances, Balkan Festival of, July 3-8
Galicnik Wedding, July 12
Ilinden Days Festival, July-August
Summer Festival, Ohrid, July-August
Theatre Festival, "Vojdan Cernodrinski," early June
Theatres for Yugoslav Children and Youth, Festival of Professional, second half of November

Macedonian-Canadians
First of March, March 1

Mackeral Cove, Jamestown, Rhode Island
Penguin Plunge, January 1

Macon, Georgia
Cherry Blossom Festival, Macon, mid-March

Madagascar
Fandroana, June 30
Independence Day, June 26
Memorial Day (Commemoration Day), March 29
Republic Day, December 30

Madeira Island, Portugal
Bach Festival, International, June
St. Sylvester's Day, December 31

Madeiran-Americans in Massachusetts: New Bedford
Blessed Sacrament, Feast of, four days beginning last Thursday in August

Madhya Pradesh, India
Drama Festival, Kalidasa, first week in November

Madras, Tamil Nadu, India
Arts Festival, Kalakshetra, December-January
Chitra Gupta, full moon day of Hindu month of Chaitra

Madrid, Spain
St. Isidore the Husbandman or Farmer, Feast of, May 10-17
St. Lawrence of Rome, Feast Day of, August 10

Madura, India
Avani Mulam, August or September

Madurai, India
Floating Festival, full moon day of Hindu month of Magha
Harvest Festival (Jellikattu Festival), three days during Hindu month of Pausha
Marriage of Meenakshi and Shiva, Festival of the (Chaitra Purnima or Meenakshi Kalyanam), ten days during Hindu months of Chaitra or Vaisakha

Magdalena, Colombia
Cumbia Festival, June

Magna Gracia, Greece
Carnea, August, Greek month of Carneus

Magoaja, Commune of Chiuesti, Cluj, Romania
Pintea the Brave Day, first Sunday in September

Magog, Quebec, Canada
Music Festival, Orford International, eight weeks in July and August

Magura Priei, Commune of Cizer, Salaj, Romania
Weighing Festival, second Sunday in May

Maharashtra, India
Agricultural Festival, during Hindu month of Ashadha
Agricultural Festival (Hadaga), during Hindu month of Asvina
Agricultural Festival (Pola), during Hindu month of Sravana
Agricultural Festival (Pola), during Hindu month of Bhadrapada
Dattatreya's Birthday (Dattatreya Jayanti), full moon day of Hindu month of Margashirsha
Drama Festival, Bombay, January
Elephant God, Festival of the (Ganesha Chaturthi), fourth day of Hindu month of Bhadrapada
Lights, Festival of (Dewali), one week during waning half of Hindu month of Karthika, including 15th day
New Year (Gudi Parva), first day of Hindu month of Chaitra
Sacred Thread Festival (Raksha Bandhan), full moon day of Hindu month of Sravana
Tamasha Festival, November-December (location rotates)

Mahdia, Mahdia Region, Tunisia
Mahdia, Festival of, July-August

Mahdia Region, Tunisia
El Djem Festival, June
Mahdia, Festival of, July-August

Maidu Indians in California: Indian Grinding Rock State Park near Pine Grove
Chaw-Se Big Time Celebration, usually last weekend in September

Maidu Indians in California: Janesville and Greenville
Dance, Bear, dates vary

Maine
Admission Day, March 15
Bay Chamber Concerts, nine Thursday evenings in July and August
Bastille, Festival de la, weekend closest to July 14
Ceremonial Day, usually August 1
Dump Week, National, Thursday after the Fourth of July through Labor Day, first Monday in September
Egg Festival, Central Maine, fourth Saturday in July
Greenwood Day, Chester, first Saturday in December
Kneisel Hall, seven weeks from last week in June to mid-August
Maine Lobster or Seafoods Festival, three days in late July-early August
Maine Memorial Day, February 15
Mollyockett Day, third Saturday in July
Moxie Festival, second Saturday in July
Music, Gamper Festival of Contemporary, one week in late July
Music, Mount Desert Festival of Chamber, five Tuesday evenings from mid-July to August
Music Festival, Bar Harbor, mid-July to mid-August
Music Festival, Bowdoin Summer, last week in June to first week in August
Native American Day, late July
Patriots' Day, April 19; observed third Monday in April
Schooner Days, weekend after July 4
Symphony Concerts, Monteux Conducting School, late June to late July
Windjammer Days, three days in mid-July

Maine-et-Loire, France
Anjou Festival, July-August

Mairang Village, Manipur, India
Lai Haroba Festival, April-May

Majorca, Spain
St. Anthony the Abbot of Egypt, Feast of, January

Makaha Beach, Oahu, Hawaii
Surfing Classic, Buffalo's Big Board, two days in February

Makkovik, Labrador, Newfoundland, Canada
Epiphany, January 6

Makonde people in Tanzania: Newala, Mtwara, and Lindi
Midimu Ceremony, June through October; begins night

during the period when the moon moves from the quarter to its half phase for three days

Malabon, Rizal, Luzon Island, Philippines
Passion Play, Cenaculo, March-April, Holy Week

Malacca, Malaya
Masi Magham, February-March, two-day festival during full moon of Masi

Malacca, Malaysia
Mandi Safar, during Islamic month of Safar
Thaipusam, one day in January-February

Malawi (formerly Nyasaland)
Independence Day, July 6
Martyr's Day, March 3
Midimu Ceremony, June through October; begins night during the period when the moon moves from the quarter to its half phase for three days
Mothers' Day, two days beginning October 17
See also **Nyasaland**

Malaya
Harvest Festival (Pongal), three days during Hindu month of Pausha
Lights, Festival of (Deepavali), one week during waning half of Hindu month of Karthika, including 15th day
Masi Magham, February-March, two-day festival during full moon of Masi
New Year, mid-April, when Sun is in Aries
New Year (Vaisakhi), first day of Hindu month of Vaisakha
Panguni Uttiram, ten days, including the full moon day of Hindu month of Chaitra
Ramadan (Hari Raya), ninth Islamic month

Malay people in Malaysia: Endau
Běla Kampong, annual

Malay people in Philippines: Kalibo, Akland, Panay Island
Ati-Atihan Festival, three days in January, including feast day of Santo Nino (Holy Child Jesus) and ending on a Sunday

Malay people in Thailand
Ramadan, ninth Islamic month

Malaysia
Bachok Festival of Culture, two weeks in May
Běla Kampong, annual
Christmas, December 25
Dayak Festival Day (Gawai Dayak), June 1-2
Double Seventh (Festival of the Seven Sisters), seventh day of seventh lunar month

Malaysia *(cont.)*
Goddess of Mercy, Birthday of, 19th day of third lunar month
Harvest Festival (Bungan), February
Harvest Festival (Padi), May 30-31
Independence Day (Merdeka), August 31
Independence Day, September 16
Lantern Festival, 13th-15th days of first lunar month
Lights, Festival of (Dewali), one week during waning half of Hindu month of Karthika, including 15th day
Mandi Safar, during Islamic month of Safar
Mid-Autumn Festival, 15th, or full moon, day of eighth lunar month
New Year (Vaisakhi), first day of Hindu month of Vaisakha
Panguni Uttiram, ten days, including the full moon day of Hindu month of Chaitra
Puja Ketek Celebrations, October
Ramadan (Lebaran or Hari Raya), ninth Islamic month
Sultan's Birthday Celebration, July
Thaipusam, one day in January-February
Top-Spinning Competitions, June-July, after harvest of rice

Malda, Lérida, Spain
San Macario, Festival of, January 2

Maldives
Independence Day, July 26
Republic Day, November 11; observed November 11-12

Mali
Africa Day, May 25
Army Day, January 20
Independence Day, September 22
Tyi Wara, planting season in April, May, sometimes the entire summer

Malinalco, Mexico
Passion Play, March-April, Holy Week

Malo Crnice, Serbia, Yugoslavia
Theatre Amateurs of the Villages of Serbia, October

Malozi people in Zambia: Lealul Knoll, Mongu, Western Province
Kuomboka, February-March, when Zambezi River rises

Malta
Christmas, December 25
Easter, March-April, first Sunday after first full moon after the vernal equinox
Festa Season, May to October, peaking in July
Good Friday, March-April, Friday preceding Easter Sunday
Harvest Festival (Imnarja or Mnarja), last week in June, including June 29
Independence Day, September 21

Mardi Gras (Carnival), February-March, before Ash Wednesday
Regatta Day, observed on or near September 5
Republic Day, December 13
St. Joseph the Worker, Feast of, May 1
St. Paul's Shipwreck, Feast of, February 10

Maluku, Moluccas, Indonesia
Panas Pela (Cuci Baileo Ceremony), every three years in May

Malvern, Worcestershire, England
Malvern Festival, May-June

Mamaia, Constanta County, Romania
Folklore Festival, National, month of August

Mamoiada, Sardinia, Italy
Carnival of Mamoiada, March-April, Sunday and Tuesday preceding Ash Wednesday

Manchester, England
Lifeboat Day, March

Manchester, Vermont
Arts, Festival of the, early June through mid-October

Mandan Indians in North Dakota: Mandaree
Mandaree Celebration, third weekend in July

Mandan Indians in the Great Plains of the United States
Dance, Sun, usually during summer solstice, June 21

Mandaree, North Dakota
Mandaree Celebration, third weekend in July

Mande-Dyula people in Upper Volta: Dagomba
Muhammad's Birthday (Damba Festival), twelfth day of Islamic month of Rabi al-Awwal

Mandigo people in Sierra Leone
New Year, one and one-half days in late April or early May

Manheim, Pennsylvania
Rose Day, June 10; observed second Sunday in June

Mani, Yucatan, Mexico
Chickaban (Feast of the Storm God Kukulcan), end of October, Mayan month of Xul

Manila, Luzon Island, Philippines
Ballet Festival, National, May
Black Nazarene Fiesta, January 1-9
Panunuluyan, December 24
People Power Anniversary, February 25

Manipur, India
Dance Festival, Ras, three times yearly: full moon of March-April (Basant Ras), September-October, during Dasahara, Festival of Durga, the Mother Goddess (Kunj Ras), and full moon night of December (Maha Ras)
Drama Festival, Manipur Academy, five days in February-March
Jatra Festival, two weeks in December-January
Lai Haroba Festival, April-May
Rasa Leela Festival, one month during August-September

Manitoba, Canada
Arts, Holiday Festival of the, July
Arts, International Festival of the, six weeks during June and July
Arts Week, Creative, last full week in August
Folk Festival, Winnipeg, three or four days during second weekend in July
Folklorama, one week in mid-August
Icelandic Festival (Islendingadagurinn), during last week in July or first week in August
Interlake Festival, June-August
Musical Theatre, Summer, July-August
Sunflower Festival, last weekend in July
Trappers' Festival, Northern Manitoba, nearly one week in mid-February
Ukrainian Festival, National, four days in July or August
Voyageur, Festival du, about one week in February

Mannheim, Baden-Wurttemberg, Federal Republic of Germany
Schiller Days, May

Mansia, Turkey
Mesir Festival, May

Manx people in Isle of Man
Midsummer, June 23-24

Maramures, Romania
Dance Festival, Hora at Prislop (Prislop Round), second Sunday in August
Folklore Festival, Maramuresean, last weekend in December
Tinjaua, early May

Marathon to Athens, Greece
Marathon, International Open, mid-October

Marblehead, Massachusetts
Music Festival, Marblehead Summer, five or six Sunday concerts beginning mid-July

Marches, Italy
Equestrian Tournament of the Quintain, first Sunday in August

Marchóstica, Italy
Living Chess Game (La Partita a Scácchi Viventi), second weekend in September during even-numbered years

Marianas
St. Isidore the Husbandman or Farmer, Feast of, May 15

Maribor, Slovenia, Yugoslavia
Theatres, Borstnik Encounter of Slovenian, October

Maricopa, Arizona
St. Francis of Assisi, Feast of, October 4

Maricopa Indians
Gila River Festival, second weekend in March
St. Francis of Assisi, Feast of, October 4

Marietta, Ohio
Sternwheel Festival, Ohio River, weekend after Labor Day, first Monday in September

Marinduque Island, Philippines
Moriones Festival, March-April, Good Friday to Easter Sunday

Maritime Provinces, Canada
Acadian Festivals, usually three to four days at the end of June; sometimes in July or August
Assumption, Feast of the, and Tintamarre celebration, August 15 and Sunday nearest August 15
Candlemas, February 2

Markgrönigen, Swabia, Germany
St. Bartholomew's Day, August 24
Shepherds' Race (Schäferlauf), August 23-25

Marlboro, Vermont
Music Festival, Marlboro, twelve weekend concerts from mid-July to mid-August

Marlborough, New Zealand
Provincial Anniversary, November 4

Marmaris, Turkey
Marmaris Festival, May-June

Marrakech, Morocco
Fast, Feast of Breaking the (Iid el Sageer), first day of Islamic month of Shawwal
Folklore, Festival of, ten days in May
New Year (Muharram Celebrations), first day of Islamic month of Muharram

Marriamman Teppakulam, Sarovar, India
Floating Festival, full moon day of Hindu month of Magha

Matamoros, Tamaulipas, Mexico
Charro Days Fiesta, February-March, four days beginning
Thursday of the weekend before Lent
St. Isidore, Festival of, mid-May

Mathura, India
Fire Festival (Holi), begins 14th day of Hindu month of
Phalguna and lasts 16 days

Mauritania
Africa Day, May 25
Independence Day, November 28
Women's Day, International, March 8

Mauritanian women
Women's Day, March 8

Mauritius
Fire Festival (Holi), begins 14th day of Hindu month of
Phalguna or Dol; length varies
Independence Day, March 12
Lights, Festival of (Divali), one week during waning half of
Hindu month of Karthika, including 15th day
New Year, ten-day to two-week long celebration at the first
new moon after sun enters Aquarius; one to 15 days of first
month
Pilgrimage to Shrine of Father Laval, September 8
Shiva, Night of (Maha Shivaratree), 13th night and 14th day
of waning half of Hindu month of Phalguna
Thaipusam, one day in January-February
United Nations Day, October 24

Mausoleum of Data Ganj Baksh, Lahore, Pakistan
Data Ganj Baksh Death Festival, 18-19 days of Islamic month
of Safar

Maxville, Ontario, Canada
Highland Games, Glengarry, Saturday before the first
Monday in August

Mayan people
Chickaban (Feast of the Storm God Kukulcan), end of
October, Mayan month of Xul
Dinner of the Milpa (u hanli col), every four years when corn
ripens
Easter, March-April, first Sunday after first full moon after
the vernal equinox
Little Angels (Los Angelitos), October 30

Mayan people in Mexico: Mani, Yucatan
Chickaban (Feast of the Storm God Kukulcan), end of
October, Mayan month of Xul

Mayan people in Mexico: Cancún
Little Angels (Los Angelitos), October 30

Mayan people in Mexico: Chan Kom, Yucatan
Dinner of the Milpa (u hanli col), every four years when corn
ripens

Mayan people in Mexico: Quintana Roo
Patron Crosses, Fiesta of the, late April

Mayo (County), Ireland
Reek Sunday, last Sunday in July (pilgrimage)

Mayo Indians in southern Arizona
Cruz, Fiesta de la
Holy Saturday, March-April, Saturday before Easter Sunday
Our Lady of Guadalupe, December 12

Mayo Indians in Mexico
Cruz, Fiesta de la
Holy Saturday, March-April, Saturday before Easter Sunday
Our Lady of Guadalupe, December 12

Mayo Indians in Mexico: Sonora
Lent, February-March, forty-day season preceding Easter

Mayurbhanj, Orissa, India
Dance Festival, Mayurbhanj Chhau (Chaitra Parva, Spring
Festival), April 11-13

Mbaise area of Nigeria
Road Building Festival, around April

McAlester, Oklahoma
Italian Festival, late May

McCall, Idaho
Music Festival, McCall Summer, third weekend in July

McClure, Pennsylvania
McClure Bean Soup Festival, five days in September

Meadela, Viana do Castelo, Portugal
Meadela, International Festival of, August

Meath, Ireland
Lúgnasad (First Fruits Festival), August 1

Mecca, Saudi Arabia
Mecca, Pilgrimage to, eighth through 13th days of Islamic
month of Dhu'l-Hijjah
Ramadan, ninth Islamic month

Mechelen, Belgium
Flanders, Festival of (Festival van Vlaanderen), April to
October
Folklore Festival, International, four days in
August

Medan, North Sumatra, Sumatra, Indonesia
Medan Anniversary, April 1

Medellin, Antioquia, Colombia
Teatro Custombrista, Regional and National Festivals of,
September; regional and national festivals alternate

Medora, North Dakota
Musical, Medora, mid-June to Labor Day, first Monday in
September
Poetry Gathering, Dakota Cowboy, last weekend in May

Meenakshi Temple, Madurai, India
Floating Festival, full moon day of Hindu month of Magha
Marriage of Meenakshi and Shiva, Festival of the (Chaitra
Purnima or Meenakshi Kalyanam), ten days during Hindu
months of Chaitra or Vaisakha

Meggenhofen, Upper Austria, Austria
Theatre Festival, Farmstead (Theater auf dem Bauernof),
June-August

Meghalaya, India
Drums Festival, Hundred (Wangala), several days during late
autumn, after harvest

Mekkelhorst, Overijssel, Netherlands
Fields, Going to the (Veldgang), May-June, Monday
preceding Ascension Thursday

Meknes, Morocco
Fantasia (Horse Festival), October

Melattur, Tamil Nadu, India
Bhagavatha Mela Festival, one week in May

Melbourne, Victoria, Australia
Australian Open Tennis, January
Drama Festival, Catholic School, June
Free Entertainment in the Parks, year-round
Melbourne Cup Day, first Tuesday in November
Moomba ("let's get together and have fun") Festival, ten
days in March

Melk, Lower Austria, Austria
Melk, Festival of (Melker Festspiele), July-August

Memphis, Tennessee
Cotton Carnival and Musicfest, May-June
Elvis International Tribute Week, week including
August 16
May International Festival, Memphis in, month of May

Mendocino, California
Music Festival, Mendocino, two weeks in mid-July

Mendocino, Fort Bragg, and Gualala, California
Whale Festival, March

Mendoza, Argentina
Grape Harvest, National Festival of the, first week in March

Menominee Indians
Dance, Green Corn
Powwow, Land of the Menominee, first weekend in August

Menton, France
Music Festival, Menton (Festival de Musique de Menton),
month of August

Meridian, Mississippi
Rodgers Festival, Jimmie, last full week in May

Mescalero Apache Indians in New Mexico: Mescalero
Apache Maidens' Puberty Rites, July 4
Mescalero Apache Gahan Ceremonial, July 1-4

Mesilla, New Mexico
All Saints' Day, November 1

Mesquakie Algonquian Indians in Iowa: Tama
Powwow, Mesquakie Celebration, second weekend in August,
Thursday-Sunday

Messina, Sicily
Assumption, Feast of the, two weeks, including
August 15

Messina, Sicily, Italy
Pentecost, May-June, the Sunday fifty days after Easter

Meta, Colombia
Joropo Festival, International, December
St. Martin's Day (Quadrilles of San Martin),
November 11

Metepec, Mexico
St. Isidore, Festival of, mid-May

Metz, France
Music Festival, Metz International Contemporary
(Rencontres Internationales de Musique Contemporaine),
five days in mid-November

Meursault, Nuits-St. Georges, and Beaune in Cote-d'Or, France
Three Glorious Days (Les Trois Glorieuses), twice annually:
July 27-29 and third Saturday through Monday in November

Meurthe-et-Moselle, France
Theatre, World Festival of, two weeks in April-May during
odd-numbered years

Mexican-Americans in Arizona: Tucson
Tucson Meet Yourself Festival, second weekend in October

Mexican-Americans in California: Los Angeles
All Souls' Day, November 2
Holy Saturday (Blessing of the Animals), March-April, Saturday before Easter Sunday

Mexican-Americans in Brownsville, Texas, and Matamoros, Mexico
Charro Days Fiesta, February-March, four days beginning Thursday of the weekend before Lent

Mexico
All Fools' Day, December 28
All Saints' Day (El Día de los Santos), November 1
All Souls' Day (Día de Muertos, Day of the Dead or Festival of Hungry Ghosts), October 30-November 2
Artisans, Day of the, December 4
Candlemas (Día de la Candelaria), February 2, also Aztec New Year
Cervantes Festival, International, three weeks in April-May, sometimes October-November
Charro Days Fiesta, February-March, four days beginning Thursday of the weekend before Lent
Chiapa de Corzo, Fiesta of, January 20
Chickaban (Feast of the Storm God Kukulcan), end of October, Mayan month of Xul
Christmas (Navidad), December 25
Christmas, Twelve Days of, December 25-January 6
Christmas Eve (Noche Buena), December 24, part of Posadas season
Christmas Festival (Night of the Radishes and Nativity Festival), December 23-24
Christmas Festival (Posadas, Feast of the Lodgings), December 16-24 or 25
Cinco de Mayo, May 5
Corpus Christi, May-June
Cruz, Fiesta de la
Cuauhtemoc, Homage to (Homenaje a Cuauhtemoc), August 21
Dance, Peyote (Híkuli), October and November
Dinner of the Milpa (u hanli col), every four years when corn ripens
Easter (Domingo de Resurrección), March-April, first Sunday after first full moon after the vernal equinox
Epiphany (Día de los Reyes Magos), January 5-6
Exaltation of the Cross (Día de la Santa Cruz), May 3
Good Friday (Viernes Santo), March-April, Friday preceding Easter Sunday
Green Squash Festival (Wima'kwari), October
Holy Innocents' Day (Día de los Inocentes), December 28
Holy Saturday (Sábato de Gloria, Saturday of Glory), March-April, Saturday before Easter Sunday

Holy Thursday (Jueves Santo), March-April, Thursday preceding Easter
Holy Week, March-April, week preceding Easter
Independence, Festival of Mexico, September 15-16
Juárez Day (Day of the Indian Chief), March 21
Lent, February-March, forty-day season preceding Easter
Little Angels (Los Angelitos), October 30
Mardi Gras (Carnaval), February-March
Mardi Gras (Carnaval, Fiesta of Games), February-March, one week ending Ash Wednesday
Mardi Gras (Fiesta de Febrero), February-March, Tuesday before Ash Wednesday
Mardi Gras (Tahimoltik, Festival of the Games), February-March, five days, coinciding with lost days of Mayan calendar
Midsummer (Diade de San Juan), June 23-24
Monday on the Hill (Lunes del Cerro, Guelaguetza offering ritual), third and fourth Mondays in July
Nativity of the Virgin, Feast of the (Virgin of the Remedies), one week beginning September 8
Nativity Plays, mid-December to January
New Year's Day, January 1
New Year's Eve (Noche de Pedimento, Wishing Night), December 31
October Fair (Fiestas de Octubre), month-long, October-November
Our Lady of Guadalupe (Nuestra Señora de Guadalupe), December 12
Palm Sunday (Domingo de Palmas), March-April, the Sunday preceding Easter
Passion Play, March-April, Good Friday
Passion Play, March-April, Holy Week
Patron Crosses, Fiesta of the, late April
Pilgrimage to Chalma, first week of January; also held in February, August, September, and during Holy Week
Running of the Bulls, Sunday following August 15
St. Anthony's Day (San Antonio Abad), January 17
St. Anthony the Abbot of Egypt, Feast of (Blessing of the Animals), January 17
St. Francis of Assisi, Festival of, early October
St. Isidore, Festival of, mid-May
St. John the Baptist's Day, June 24
St. Lawrence of Rome, Feast Day of (Día de San Lorenzo), August 10
St. Mark, Fair of (Feria de San Marcos), ten days beginning April 25
St. Michael, Festival of, September 28-29
St. Sebastian, Festival of (Fiesta de San Sebastian), January 20
St. Sebastian's Day (Día de San Sebastián), January 20; observed for nine days, from January 17 to January 25
Santo Isobel, Fiesta of, July 4
Virgen del Rosario, Fiesta for the, October 7
Virgin of Carmen, Fiesta of, July 15
Volador Fiesta, during Corpus Christi or Holy Week

Mexico *(cont.)*
Washington's Birthday, mid-February
Wíikita Festivals, winter festival at Archie, Arizona;
summer festival at Quitovaca, Sonora, Mexico

Mexico, Valley of
New Fire Ceremony, every 52 years

Mexico City, Mexico
Cuauhtemoc, Homage to (Homenaje a Cuauhtemoc),
August 21
Independence, Festival of Mexico, September 15-16
(procession from the Zocolo to the Independence
Monument on Paseo de la Reforma)
Our Lady of Guadalupe (Nuestra Señora de Guadalupe),
December 12

Miami, Florida
Carnaval Miami, first two full weeks in March
Orange Bowl Football Classic, January 1

Miami, Oklahoma
Dance, Green Corn, July or August

Miami Indians in Oklahoma
Indian Heritage Days Celebration, Oklahoma, late May

Miami Indians in Oklahoma: Quapaw
Powwow, Quapaw, second weekend in July

Mibu Temple, Kyoto, Japan
Mibu Dainembutsu Kyogen, end of April

Miccosukee Indians
Arts Festival, week after Christmas

Michigan
Admission Day, January 26
Alpenfest, third week in July
Ann Arbor May Festival, four days in late April or early May
Cherry Festival, National, first full week after July 4
Devil's Night, October 30
Frankenmuth Bavarian Festival, second weekend and third
week in June
Freedom Festival, International, mid-June to July 4
Highland Festival and Games, last weekend in May
Music Camp, National, eight weeks from last week in June
to mid-August
Music Festival, Meadowbrook, twelve weeks from mid-June
to last week in August
Renaissance Festival, Michigan, August-September
St. Joseph of Arimathea, Feast Day of, March 19
Tulip Time, four days beginning Wednesday nearest May 15
White Shirt Day, February 11

Michoacán, Mexico
Candlemas, February 2
Passion Play, March-April, Holy Week

Micronesia
New Year, April, month of Ceuta

Middlesex, England
Brent Festival, January-February

Middletown, Ohio
Middfest International, three days in late September-early
October

Midwest City, Oklahoma
Oklahoma Day, April 22

Mie, Japan
Shrine Kagura Festival, Ise, April and September

Miercurea Ciuc, Baile Jigodin Commune, Harghita, Romania
Spring, Harghita, third Sunday in May

Mihintale, Sri Lanka
Poson (Dhamma Vijaya, Full Moon Day), full moon day
of Hindu month of Jyeshta

Milan, Lombardy, Italy
Mardi Gras (Carnevale), February-March, one week
Milan Trade Fair, ten days in April

Mille Lacs Reservation, Onamia, Minnesota
Powwow, Ojibwa, mid-August

Millsboro, Delaware
Powwow, Nanticoke Indian, second weekend in
September

Milner Park, Johannesburg, South Africa
Rand Show, April-May

Milton Keynes, Buckinghamshire, England
Wavendon Season, May-July

Milwaukee, Wisconsin
Arts, Lakefront Festival of the, June
Folk Fair, Holiday, three days in November
Indian Summer Festival, second weekend in September
Music under the Stars, eight weeks from early July to
mid-August
Summerfest, 11 days, including July 4

Minatogawa, Okinawa
Boat Race Day (Gods of the Sea Festival in Minatogawa),
14th day of fifth lunar month

Minden, Nebraska
Nebraska Danish Days (Danish Ethnic Festival),
May-June

Mindoro, Luzon Island, Philippines
Panunuluyan, December 24

Minehead, Somerset, England
Minehead & Exmoor Festival, last two weeks in July
Minehead Hobby Horse Parade, May

Minho, Portugal
St. Walter, Festivals of (Festas Gualterianas), four days
beginning first Sunday in August

Minnesota
Admission Day, May 11
Assumption, Feast of the, August 15
Belgian-American Days, four days in August
Constitution Day, Norway (Syttende Mai Fest), May 17
Earls Court Day, May 9
Logging Days, Buena Vista, last Saturday in February
Nations, Festival of, last weekend in April
New Year's Day (Kissing Day), January 1
Ni-Mi-Win Celebration, third weekend in August
Powwow, Fond du Lac, July
Powwow, Ojibwa, first weekend in June
Powwow, Ojibwa, mid-August
Powwow, White Earth Chippewa, weekend of or before
June 14
Powwows, Ojibwa, first Monday in September, last weekend
in May, and in winter, spring, and midsummer
Rendezvous Days, second weekend in August
St. Barbara's Day, December 4
St. Wenceslaus's Day, September 28
Sled Dog Races, All American Championships, third
weekend in January
Sliding Festival, Finnish, two days in February
Song of Hiawatha Pageant, last two weeks in July and first
week in August
Stiftungsfest, last weekend in August
Swedes' Day (Svenskarnas Dag), fourth Sunday in June
Watermelon Day, mid-July
Winter Carnival, St. Paul, ten days including last week in
January

Minot, North Dakota
Norsk Høstfest, five days in October
Winterfest, seven to ten days in February

Miranda do Douro, Braganca, Portugal
St. Barbara's Festival, August

Mission of San Antonio de Pala, San Diego County, California
St. Francis of Assisi, Feast of, October 4

Mission San Xavier del Bac, Arizona
Easter, March-April, first Sunday after first full moon after
the vernal equinox; ceremony observed Friday after Easter
Sunday

Mississippi
Admission Day, December 10
Confederate Memorial Day, fourth Monday in April
Davis's Birthday, Jefferson, June 3
Fishing Rodeo, Deep Sea, July fourth weekend
Gum Tree Festival, usually second weekend in May or
sometime in June
Indian Fair, Choctaw, four days in July beginning the
Wednesday after July 4
Landing of d'Iberville, last weekend in April
Natchez Spring (Fall Pilgrimage), month-long program from
early March to early April and for 15 days in October
Rodgers Festival, Jimmie, last full week in May

Missouri
Admission Day, August 10
Clown Festival, Emmett Kelly, early May
Founding of the Church of Jesus Christ of the Latter Day
Saints, April 6
Jour de Fête a Sainte Genevieve Days of Celebration, second
weekend in August
Kewpiesta, third weekend in April
Kingdom Days, last weekend in June
Livestock, Horse Show, and Rodeo, American Royal, two
weeks in November
Mayfest (Maifest), third weekend in May
Missouri Day, third Wednesday in October
Muny, The, mid-June to end of August
Mushroom Festival, first weekend in May
Opera Theatre of Saint Louis, late May to end of June
Ragtime and Traditional Jazz Festival, Annual National, five
days in mid-June
Tom Sawyer Days, National, week of July 4
Truman's Birthday, Harry S., May 8

Mitchell, South Dakota
Corn Palace Festival, four days in September

Mitla, Oaxaca, Mexico
New Year's Eve (Noche de Pedimento, Wishing Night),
December 31

Miura, Kanagawa, Japan
Chakkirako Festival, mid-January

Mix Run, Driftwood, and Sinnemahoning, Pennsylvania
Mix Roundup, Tom, three days in July

Mobile, Alabama
Mardi Gras, February-March, the two weeks before Ash
Wednesday

Moche, Peru
Palm Sunday (La Fiesta de Ramos), March-April, the
Sunday preceding Easter

Moers, North Rhine-Westphalia, Federal Republic of Germany
Castle Play Festival, Moers, five weeks in summer

Mogpog, Marinduque Island, Philippines
Moriones Festival, March-April, Good Friday to Easter
Sunday

Moguerinha, Portugal
Epiphany (Dia dos Reis, Day of the Kings), January 6

Mohave Indians in Arizona: Heard Museum, Phoenix
Indian Fair, Heard Museum Guild, two days in late February

Mohegan Indians in Connecticut: Farmington
Powwow, Connecticut River, weekend before Labor Day, first
Monday in September

Mohegan Indians in Connecticut: Norwich
Mohegan Homecoming, third Sunday in August

Mojo Indians in eastern Bolivia
New Year's Day, when the Pleiades appear

Moldavia, Romania
Comedy, Week of, autumn

Molde, Norway
Jazz Festival, Molde International (Jazzfestpillene i Molde),
one week in late July

Molnlycke, Sweden
NVB (Nykterhetsrorelsens Bildningsversamhet) Festival,
two weeks in June

Moluccas, Indonesia
Panas Pela (Cuci Baileo Ceremony), every three years
in May

Monaco
Arts, International Festival of, July-August
Ballet Festival, Monte Carlo Winter, ten days in late
December-early January
Circus Festival, International, five days in December
Fête Nationale, November 19
Monaco Grand Prix, four days in late May-June
Music Festival, Monte Carlo, July-August
St. Devota's Day, January 27
Theatre, Summer Season at the Fort-Antoine, June-August
Theatre, World Festival of Amateur, every four years in
August-September

Monastery of the Virgin at Saidnaya near Damascus, Syria
Assumption, Feast of the ('Id Rakad-ai-Sayyidah), August
15, Gregorian calendar (N.S.); August 28, Julian calendar
(O.S.)

Monastir, Monastir Region, Tunisia
Theatre, Regional Festival of, June

Monastir Region, Tunisia
Cultural Festival of Oum Ezzine, end of September
Theatre, Regional Festival of, June

Moncada, Valencia, Spain
Mystery of the Passion, March-April, Easter Week

Moneasa, Arad, Romania
Folklore Festival, Arad, August 24

Mongolia
Constitution Day, June 30
New Year (Tsagan Sara, White Moon celebration), around
February
Revolution Day (Nadam), July 11

Mongu, Western Province, Zambia
Kuomboka, February-March, when Zambezi River rises

Mons, Belgium
Golden Chariot and Battle of the Lumecon, Procession of
the, May-June, Trinity Sunday
Wallonia, Festival of (Festival de Wallonie), June-September
or October

Monsanto, Castelo Branco, Portugal
Monsanto, National Festival of, every Sunday in September

Montana
Admission Day, November 8
Crow Fair, at least six days in mid-August
Custer's Last Stand, June 25; observed with a pageant in
late June
Indian Celebration, Badlands, fourth weekend in June
Indian Celebration, Red Bottom, third weekend in June
Indian Days, North American, second week in July
Indian Days, Rocky Boy, usually first weekend in August
Nations, Festival of, nine days in early August
New Year's Day, January 1
Powwow, Northern Cheyenne, July
Powwow, Standing Arrow, third weekend in July
Union Day, Miners', June 13

Montauban, Tarn-et-Garonne, France
Occitanie Festival, one week from late June to
early July

Montauroux and surrounding towns in Var, France
East Var, Festival of, six weeks in July-August

Monte Carlo, Monaco
Arts, International Festival of, July-August

Monte Carlo, Monaco *(cont.)*
  Ballet Festival, Monte Carlo Winter, ten days in late
    December-early January
  Circus Festival, International, five days in December
  Monaco Grand Prix, four days in late May-June
  Music Festival, Monte Carlo, July-August
  Theatre, Summer Season at the Fort-Antoine, June-August
  Theatre, World Festival of Amateur, every four years in
    August-September

Montego Bay, Jamaica
  Reggae Sunsplash, four nights in August

Montenegro (formerly in Yugoslavia)
  Fasinada, July 22

Montenegro, Yugoslavia
  Drama Amateurs of Montenegro, Festival of, June
  South, Festival of the, July-August

Monterey, California
  Jazz Festival, Monterey, third weekend in September

Monteux, Provence, France
  St. Gens, Festival of (La Fête de St. Gens), twice yearly:
    Sunday following May 15 at Monteux and first weekend
    in September at Beaucet

Montevideo, Uruguay
  Mardi Gras, January-February, about one month before Ash
    Wednesday
  Summer Festival of the Lake of Rodo Park, three months,
    January-March

Montreal, Quebec, Canada
  Jazz Festival, Montreal, June-July

Montreal, Quebec, and other parts of French Canada
  St. John the Baptist's Day, June 24

Montreux, Vaud, Switzerland
  Jazz Festival, Montreux International (Montreux Festival
    Internacional de Jazz), two weeks beginning first week in
    July
  Music Festival, Montreux-Vevey (Festival de Musique
    Montreux-Vevey), six weeks beginning in late August

Moore Park Showground, Sydney, New South Wales, Australia
  Easter Show, Royal, during the Easter holidays

Moravia (now part of Czechoslovakia)
  Easter, March-April, first Sunday after first full moon after
    the vernal equinox
  Low Sunday, March-April, Sunday following Easter
  St. John the Baptist's Day, June 24

Moravia, Czechoslovakia
  Folklore Festival of Straznice, three days in June
  Mimes, International Festival of Deaf, odd-numbered years
    during second half of November
  Music Festival, Brno International, October
  Znojmo Feast, every Friday and Saturday in June-September

Moravian-Americans
  Easter, March-April, first Sunday after first full moon after
    the vernal equinox

Moravian-Americans in North Carolina
  Christmas Eve, December 24

Moravian-Americans in Pennsylvania
  Christmas Eve, December 24

Moravian Czech-Americans
  Christmas, December 25
  Christmas Eve, December 24

Morbihan, France
  Lorient Festival, ten days at beginning of August

Morbisch am See, Burgenland, Austria
  Lake Festival (Seespiele), August

Morelos, Mexico
  Mardi Gras, February-March
  St. Isidore, Festival of, May

Morgan City, Louisiana
  Blessing of the Fleet (Louisiana Shrimp and Petroleum
    Festival), first weekend in September

Morocco
  Ashura, tenth day of Islamic month of Muharram
  Camel Market, usually in July
  Fantasia (Horse Festival), October
  Fast, Feast of Breaking the (Iid el Sageer), first day of Islamic
    month of Shawwal
  Folklore, Festival of, ten days in May
  Independence Day (Anniversary of the Throne), March 2
  Maimona or Maimonides, evening of last day of Passover
    and day after Passover
  Marriage Fair, September
  New Year (Muharram Celebrations), first day of Islamic
    month of Muharram
  Passover (Pesach), eight days beginning 15th of Jewish month
    of Nisan
  Pilgrimage to Moulay Idriss, late August or September
  Purim, second day of Jewish month of Kislev
  Ramadan, ninth Islamic month
  Sacrifice, Feast of ('Id al-Kabir), tenth-twelfth days of Islamic
    month of Dhu'l-Hijjah

Munich, Bavaria, Federal Republic of Germany *(cont.)*
Opera Festival, Munich (Münchner Opernfestspiele), 25 days in July-August
Theatre, International Festival of Free, April-May

Munster, North Rhine-Westphalia, Federal Republic of Germany
Theatre Festival, International Arena, May during even-numbered years

Munteni de Jos, Vaslui, Romania
Nation of Heroes, first Sunday in July

Muri, Aargau, Switzerland
Easter Play of Muri, every five or six years in June

Murter by Sibenik, Croatia, Yugoslavia
Drama Amateurs of Croatia, Festival of, May

Muscle Shoals area, Alabama
Music Festival, W.C. Handy, first full week in August

Mushenge, Congo
Itul, on or near December 7-8, but date varies and festival occurs according to king's authorization

Mushio Village, Hikari-machi, Sosa-gun, Chiba, Japan
Nembutsu Kyogen, mid-July

Muskogee-Creek Indians in Oklahoma: Okmulgee
Dance, Green Corn, late summer

Myanmar (formerly Burma)
Buddha's Birthday, Enlightenment, and Salvation (Kason Festival of Watering the Banyon Tree), February-March, full moon day
Lenten Season (Paung-daw-U Pagoda Festival), July-October, begins during Wazo, the fourth month, and ends on the 15th or full moon day of Thadingyut, the seventh month
See also **Burma**

Myrtle Beach, South Carolina
Sun Fun Festival, four days in June

Mysore, India
Mother Goddess, Festival of Durga, the (Dussehra), first ten days of waxing half of Hindu month of Asvina

Mystic Seaport Museum, Mystic, Connecticut
Boat Rendezvous, Antique and Classic, last weekend in July
Music Festival, Sea, first weekend in June

Nabeul Region, Tunisia
Hammamet, International Festival of, July-August

Nachi No Falls, Wakayama, Japan
Fire Festival, July 13

Naga City, Philippines
Our Lady of Peñafrancia, Feast of (Nuestra Senora de Peñafrancia), third week in September

Nagahama, Shiga, Japan
Nagahama Yamakyogen, two days in mid-April

Nagasaki, Japan
Kite-Flying Contest (Nagasaki Takoage), late April
Memorial Day, August 9

Nagoya, Japan
Nagoya City Festival, October 10-20

Nairobi, Kenya
Safari Rally, March-April, Easter weekend

Nambe Pueblo, New Mexico
Nambe Falls Ceremonial, July 4
St. Francis of Assisi, Feast of, October 4

Namibia
Family Day, December 26
Rain-Calling Ceremony (Nyambinyambi), spring

Namur, Belgium
Wallonia, Festival of (Festival de Wallonie), June-September or October

Namwon, North Jeolla, Republic of Korea
Chunhyang Festival, three days from the eighth day of fourth lunar month

Nancy, Meurthe-et-Moselle, France
Theatre, World Festival of, two weeks in April-May during odd-numbered years

Nandgaon, India
Fire Festival (Holi), begins 14th day of Hindu month of Phalguna and lasts 16 days

Naples, Italy
Opera, Naples Open-Air Festival of Summer, July-August
St. Januarius's Feast Day, September 19 (shrine at)

Nara, Japan
Gagaku Festival, early November
Kashihara Shinto Festival, April 3
Lily Festival, June 17
Shrine Festival, Kasuga Wakamiya, December 13-18
Takigi Noh, mid-May
Water Drawing Festival (Omizutori Matsuri), two weeks in March

Nemea (Valley of), Greece (ancient)
Nemean Games, probably August

Nemi (now a village in Italy)
Nemoralia (Festival of Diana Jana), August 13

Nenana, Alaska
Ice Classic, Nenana, late February and early spring

Neapolitan people in Italy
New Year's Eve, December 31

Nepal
Chariot Festival of Macchendranath (Festival of the God of Rain), begins first day of waning half of Hindu month of Vaisakha and lasts two months
Constitution Day, December 16
Cows, Procession of Sacred (Gai Jatra), first day of waning half of Hindu month of Sravana
Elephant God, Festival of the (Ganesha Chaturthi), fourth day of Hindu month of Bhadrapada
Father's Day (Gokarna Aunsi), last day of waning half of Hindu month of Bhadrapada
Fire Festival (Holi or Rung Khelna, Playing with Color), begins 14th day of Hindu month of Phalguna or Dol; length varies
Ghanta Karna, 14th day of waning half of Hindu month of Sravana
Harvest Festival (Makara or Magh Sankranti), three days during Hindu month of Pausha
Independence Day, December 21
Indra Jatra and Kumari Jatra, Festival of the Child Goddess, eight days during Hindu months of Bhadrapada-Asvina
King, Birthday of His Majesty the, December 29
Krishna's Birthday (Krishna Jayanti), eighth day of waning half of Hindu month of Bhadrapada
Lights, Festival of (Diwali or Tihar), one week during waning half of Hindu month of Karthika, including 15th day
Marya, third day of waning half of Hindu month of Sravana
Mother Goddess, Festival of Durga, the (Dasain), first ten days of waxing half of Hindu month of Asvina
National Day (Tribhuvan Jayanti), February 18
National Unity Day (Prithvi Jayanti), January 11
New Year (Bisket Jatra), first day of Hindu month of Vaisakha
New Year (Losar), three days, usually in February
Panchadaan, third day of waning half of Hindu month of Bhadrapada in Kathmandu and Bhadgaon, and eighth day of waxing half of Hindu month of Sravana in Patan and the rest of Nepal
Queen's Birthday, November 8
Shiva, Night of (Mahashivaratri), 13th night and 14th day of waning half of Hindu month of Phalguna

Sithinakha (Kumar Sasthi), sixth day of waxing half of Hindu month of Jyeshta
Snake Festival (Naag Panchami), fifth day of waxing half of Hindu month of Sravana
Teej, third day of waxing half of Hindu month of Sravana
United Nations Day, October 24
Women's Day, International, March 8

Nepalese women
Woman's Day (Tij Day), March 8

Nervi, Liguria, Italy
Ballet, International Festival of, July during even-numbered years

Nesquehaning, Pennsylvania
St. Christopher's Day, July 25

Netherlands
Airborne Operations Day, September 20
Art and Antiques Fair, Old, October-November
Ascension Day, May-June, fortieth day after Easter Sunday
Christmas (Eerste and Tweede Kerstdag), December 25-26
Christmas Eve, December 24
Dew Treading (Dauwtrappen), May-June, Ascension Day
Easter (Paschen or Paasch Zonday), March-April, first Sunday after first full moon after the vernal equinox
Easter Monday (Paasch Maandag), March-April, Monday after Easter
Easter Monday (Vlöggelen, Winging Ceremony), March-April, Easter Sunday and Monday
Eleven Cities Race (Elfstedentocht), January 22
Fields, Going to the (Veldgang), May-June, Monday preceding Ascension Thursday
Floriade, every ten years in April-October
Flower Show, Keukenhof, March-May
Fools, Festival of, three weeks in June
Holland Festival, 23 days in June
Independence Day, July 25
Kallemooi, May-June, Saturday preceding Pentecost
Leiden Day (Leiden Ontzet), October 3
Liberation Day, May 5
Luilak (Lazybones Day or Sluggard's Feast), May-June, Saturday preceding Pentecost or Whit Sunday
Mardi Gras (Vastenavond), February-March, Tuesday before Ash Wednesday
Martinmas, November 11; in Hoorn, observed fourth Monday in August
Midwinter Horn, Blowing the (Midwinterhoorn Blazen), December-January, from beginning of Advent to Sunday following Epiphany
Netherlands University Festival, every four years in December
New Year's Day (Nieuwjaarsdag), January 1
New Year's Eve (Oudejaars Avond), December 31

Netherlands *(cont.)*
Palm Sunday (Palm Zondag), March-April, the Sunday preceding Easter
Pentecost, May-June, the Sunday fifty days after Easter
Pentecost (Merchants' Flower Market), May-June, the Sunday fifty days after Easter
Pinkster Bruid or Pinksterbloem (Whitsun Bride or Whitsun Flower Festival), May-June, Whit Tuesday, the Tuesday after Pentecost Sunday
Prinsjesdag, third Tuesday in September
Queen Juliana's Birthday, April 30
St. Martin's Day, November 11
St. Thomas the Apostle, Feast of, December 21
Twelfth Night (Dreikoningenavond, Three Kings' Eve), January 5
Vlaggetjesdag, anytime from middle to late May
Whistle Making (Fluitjes Maken), about May 1
Windmill Day, second Saturday in May

Netherlands Antilles
Kingdom or Statute Days, December 15
Regatta, International, four days in October

Nett Lake Reservation, Minnesota
Powwow, Ojibwa, first weekend in June

Neuchatel, Switzerland
La Chaux-de-Fonds, Biennial of, even-numbered years usually in May-June, sometimes autumn

Nevada
Admission Day, October 31
Air Races, National Championship, three or four days ending second weekend after Labor Day, first Monday in September
Basque Festival, National, first or second weekend in July
Butler Days, Jim, last weekend in May
Camel Races, International, weekend after Labor Day, first Monday in September
Indian Rodeo and Stampede Days, All, third or fourth weekend in July
Pinenut Festival, October
Poetry Gathering, Cowboy, six days in January
Powwow, La Ka Le'l Ba, annual

Nevada City, California
Music in the Mountains, two weeks in mid-June

Nevada Indians from Canada and the United States in Nevada: Fallon
Indian Rodeo and Stampede Days, All, third or fourth weekend in July

Neves, Viana do Castelo, Portugal
Lady of Neves, Festival of the, August

Nevis
Christmas, December 25
Nevis Tea Meeting, a full moon night in summer

Newala, Tanzania
Midimu Ceremony, June through October; begins night during the period when the moon moves from the quarter to its half phase for three days

New Bedford, Massachusetts
Blessed Sacrament, Feast of, four days beginning last Thursday in August

New Braunfels, Texas
Sausage Festival (Wurstfest), end of October through first week in November

New Brunswick, Canada
Acadian Festival, August 5-15
Bitowa Outdoor Festival, third full weekend in June
Folk Song Festival, Miramichi, three days in late June
Lobster Festival, six days in July

Newbury, New Hampshire
Craftsmen's Fair, six days beginning first Tuesday in August

Newburyport, Massachusetts
Fawkes Day, Guy, November 5

New Caledonia
Bastille Day, July 14

New Canaan, Connecticut
Music Series, Silvermine Chamber, four Sunday evening concerts from mid-June to mid-August

Newcastle, New South Wales, Australia
Folk Festival, Newcastle, mid-June

Newcastle, New Brunswick, Canada
Folk Song Festival, Miramichi, three days in late June

New Castle, New Hampshire
Fawkes Day, Guy, November 5

Newcastle upon Tyne, Northumberland, England
Folk Festival, Newcastle, June-July

New College, Oxford, England
Mint Julep Day, June 1

New Delhi, India
Ballet Festival, Bharatiya Kala Kendra, September-October, three weeks during Durga Puja, Festival of the Mother Goddess

New Delhi, India *(cont.)*
Ballet Festival, Kathak Kendra, annual, date varies
Ballet Festival, Triveni Kala Sangam, annual, date varies
Drama Festival, National School of, February-March
Drama Festival, Sri Ram Center, 15 days beginning second
 week in February
Folk-Dance Festival, Republic Day, January 27-28
Republic Day, January 26

Newfoundland, Canada
Arts, Summer Festival of the, month of July
Bonfire Night, November 5
Burns Night, January 25
Candlemas, February 2
Christmas, December 25
Christmas Eve, December 24
Discovery Day, on or near June 24
Drama Festival, Newfoundland, March-April, six days
 during Easter holidays (location varies)
Epiphany, January 6
St. George's Day, April 23

New Glarus, Wisconsin
William Tell Pageant, first weekend in September

New Glasgow, Nova Scotia, Canada
Tartans, Festival of the, August

New Hampshire
Admission Day, June 21
Craftsmen's Fair, six days beginning first Tuesday in August
Fast Day, fourth Monday in April
Fawkes Day, Guy, November 5
Music Festival, Monadnock, seven weeks from mid-July to
 end of August
Music Festival, New Hampshire, six weeks from early June
 to late August
Muster Day, sometime in June
Winter Carnival, Dartmouth, a weekend in February

New Jersey
Admission Day, December 18
Baby Parade, second Thursday in August
Big Sea Day, second Saturday in August
Boston Massacre Day (Crispus Attucks Day), March 5
Flemington Fair, one week from late August through Labor
 Day, first Monday in September
Hambletonian Harness Racing Classic, first Saturday in
 August
Hollybush Festival, May and June
Miss America Pageant, third Saturday in September
Music Festival, Waterloo Summer, six weeks from late June
 through July
New Jersey Offshore Grand Prix (Benihana Grand Prix
 Power Boat Regatta), four days in mid-July

Poetry Festival, Geraldine R. Dodge, three days in September
St. Patrick's Day Encampment, weekend nearest March 17
Salt Water Day, August
Washington, Crossing of the Delaware, December 25

New Jersey (southern coast)
Wings 'n Water Festival, third weekend in September

New London, Connecticut
Music Festival, Connecticut Early, first three weeks in June
Regatta, Yale-Harvard, usually first Sunday in June

New Mexico
Admission Day, January 6
All Saints' Day, November 1
All Souls' Day (Their Grandfathers Arrive from the West,
 or from the Dead, Feast), November 2
Apache Maidens' Puberty Rites, July 4
Arts and Crafts Show, Annual Eight Northern Indian
 Pueblos, July 18-20
Arts and Crafts Show, Eight Northern Indian Pueblos
 Spring, April 19-20
Balloon Fiesta, Albuquerque International, nine days in early
 October
Bat Flight Breakfast, second Thursday in August
Blessing of the Fields with Corn or Flag Dance, May, date
 varies
Candlemas, February 2
Christmas Eve, December 24
Dance, Basket, January 27
Dance, Corn, May 13
Dance, Deer
Dance, Deer, February, date varies
Dance, Deer and Buffalo, February, date varies
Dance, Eagle, early spring
Dance, Evergreen, February, date varies
Dance, Green Corn
Dance, Los Comanches, February 4-5
Dance, Matchina, December 24-25
Dance, Matchina or Deer, December 25
Dance, Red Paint Kachina, September 12
Dance, Turtle, December 26
Dances, Matchina, December 24-25
Dances, Old Pecos Bull and Corn, August 2
Duck Race, Great American, fourth weekend in August
Enchilada Fiesta, Whole, first full weekend in October
Good Friday, March-April, Friday preceding Easter Sunday
Governor's Feast, first week in February
Harvest Dance, last week in September
Hermit, Feast of the, September 1
Holy Innocents' Day, December 28
Indian Ceremonial, Intertribal, mid-August
Indian Ceremonial Dancing, American, September 29-30
Indian Dances, Traditional, Memorial Day, last Monday in
 May, through Labor Day, first Monday in September

New Mexico *(cont.)*

Indian Market, third weekend in August
Jicarilla Apache Fair, September 14-15
Kokochi, summer solstice
Mescalero Apache Gahan Ceremonial, July 1-4
Music Festival, Santa Fe Chamber, seven weeks in July and August
Nambe Falls Ceremonial, July 4
Nativity of the Virgin, Feast of the, September 8
Navajo Nation Festival, Shiprock (Northern Navajo Fair), usually first weekend in October
New Year's Day, January 1
Opera Festival, Santa Fe, eight weeks in July and August or September
Pope Foot Race, Annual, July 20
Powwow, Little Beaver Rodeo and, late July
Puye Cliff Ceremonial, last weekend in July
St. Anne's Day, July 26
St. Anthony of Padua, Feast of, June 13
St. Augustine, Feast of and Harvest Dance, September 4
St. Bonaventura, Feast of and Corn Dance, July 14
St. Clare of Assisi, Feast of, August 11; observed August 12 with Corn, Harvest, Comanche or Buffalo dances
St. Dominic, Feast of, and Corn Dance, August 4
St. Elizabeth, Feast of, September 25
St. Francis of Assisi (Feast of Forgiveness), August 2
St. Francis of Assisi, Feast of, October 4
St. Ildephonsus, Feast Day of, January 23
St. James the Greater's Day, July 25
St. James the Greater's Day (Fiestas de Santiago y Santa Ana), July 25-26 or nearest weekend
St. Jerome's Day, observed September 29-30
St. John the Baptist's Day (San Juan Pueblo Feast Day), June 24
St. Mary Margaret, Feast of, October 17
St. Peter's Day, June 29
St. Philip, Feast of and Green Corn Dance, May 1
St. Stephen, Feast of and Harvest Dance, September 2
San Diego, Feast of and Corn Dance, November 12
San Estevan, Feast of, September 2
Santa Cruz Days (Coming of the Rivermen), May 3
Santa Fe Fiesta, three to four days over second weekend in September
Shalako Ceremonial (koko awia, the kachina come), late November or early December
Spanish and Indian Fiestas, August 28
Spruce Ceremony
Sundown Torchlight Procession of the Virgin with Deer or Matchina dance, December 24-25

New Mexico pueblos

Assumption, Feast of the, August 15
Candlemas, February 2
Christmas, December 25
Christmas Eve, December 24
Dance, Eagle, early spring
Dance, Green Corn
Easter, March-April, first Sunday after first full moon after the vernal equinox
Epiphany (King's Day with Deer, Buffalo, Eagle, Elk Dances), January 6
Lent, February-March, forty-day season preceding Easter
Nativity of the Virgin, Feast of the, September 8
New Year's Day, January 1
Our Lady of Guadalupe, December 12
St. Anthony of Padua, Feast of, June 13; observed August 15 at Laguna Pueblo
St. James the Greater's Day, July 25
St. John the Baptist's Day (San Juan Pueblo Feast Day), June 24
St. Lawrence of Rome, Feast Day of, August 10
St. Peter's Day, June 29
Symbolic Relay Run, August 5-10

New Orleans, Louisiana

All Saints' Day, November 1
Dance, Calinda, June 23
Epiphany (King's Day), January 6
Halloween, October 31
Jazz and Heritage Festival, New Orleans, ten days in mid-April to early May
Mardi Gras, begins no later than January 6, Epiphany, and ends Fat Tuesday, the day before Ash Wednesday
McDonogh Day, first Friday in May
St. Joan of Arc, Feast of, May 9
St. Ursula's Day, October 21
Sugar Bowl Classic, January 1 (January 2, if New Year's Day falls on a Sunday)
Twelfth Night (Epiphany Eve), January 5

Newport, Rhode Island

America's Cup, August 22, whenever a challenger comes forth
Black Ship Day, last weekend in July
Christmas in Newport, month of December
Independence Day, May 4
Jazz Festival, JVC, three days in mid-August
Music Festival, Newport, two weeks in July
Newport to Bermuda Race, June during even-numbered years

Newport Beach, California

Christmas Boat Parade, Newport Harbor, December 17-23

New Providence Island, Bahama Islands

Fox Hill Day, second Tuesday in August
Goombay Festival, July and August
Junkanoo Festival, December 26-January 1

New River Gorge Bridge, Fayetteville, West Virginia

Bridge Day, third Saturday in October

New River Gorge National River near Oakville, West Virginia
Whitewater Wednesday, third Wednesday in June

New South Wales, Australia
Arts, Big River Festival of, one week in May-June
Arts, Orange Festival of the, one week in April during even-numbered years
Australia Day at the Rocks, January 26; observed late January
Bathurst Carillon City Tourist Festival, September-October
Drama Festival, New South Wales, August-October
Drama Festival, New South Wales High Schools, May-August
Easter Show, Royal, during the Easter holidays
Folk Festival, Newcastle, mid-June
Folk Festival, Numeralla, end of January, including Australia Day, January 26
Folk Festival, Wagga, three days in October
Folklore, Sydney Festival of, two weeks in January, coincides with Festival of Sydney
Foundation Week Celebrations, two weeks in October-November
Music Festival, Carcoar Folk and Traditional Bush, a weekend in April
Performing Arts for Young People, The Leap-Festival of, last week in February
Plays, Wagga Wagga School of Arts Annual Festival of, two consecutive weekends in August-September
Sydney, Festival of, December 31 through January

New Town, North Dakota
Little Shell Celebration, second weekend in August

New York
Admission Day, July 26
Armed Forces Day, third Saturday in May
Artpark, last week in June to mid-August
Arts Festival, Summerscape-Huntington Summer, late June to late August
Arts Series, Wave Hill Performing, September to May
Assumption, Feast of the (Our Lady of the Flowers), August 15
Bastille Day, July 14
Belmont Stakes, June, fifth Saturday after Kentucky Derby
Binghamton Festival, July and August
Bluegrass Festival, Winterhawk, three days during third week in July
Burgoyne's Surrender Day, October 17
Caramoor Festival, nine weeks from mid-June to mid-August
Christmas Season (Festival of Lights), late November-early January
Constitution Day, Norway, May 17
Evacuation Day, November 25
French Festival (French Day), Saturday before Bastille Day, July 14
German Alps Festival, 18 days in July
Groundhog Day, February 2

Harbor Festival, late June to July 4
Hill Cumorah Pageant, nine days (excluding Sunday and Monday) beginning third weekend in July
Holy Saturday, March-April, Saturday before Easter Sunday
Independence Day, Greece, Sunday nearest March 25
Indian Festival, Iroquois, first weekend in September, including Labor Day
Indian Festival, Katari
Indian Festival, Mountain Eagle
Lincoln Center Out-of-Doors Festival, three weeks from mid-August into September
Loyalty Day, May 1 parade
Mardi Gras (Vastenavond), February-March, Tuesday before Ash Wednesday
Maverick Sunday Concerts, Sunday afternoons from July to early September
Mozart Festival, Mostly, seven weeks from mid-July to last week in August
Music Festival, Spring, two days during last week in April
Music Program, Chautauqua Summer, late June to late August
Native American Day, September
Naumburg Orchestral Concerts, four concerts between Memorial Day, last Monday in May, and Labor Day, first Monday in September
New Year (Tet Nguyenden), several days beginning first day of first lunar month
New York City Marathon, first Sunday in November
New York Philharmonic Free Outdoor Park Concerts, three weeks in August
Opera, Glimmerglass, late June to Labor Day, first Monday in September
Opera Festival, Lake George, six weeks from mid-July to last week in August
Our Lady of Flowers, Harvest Festival for, August 15
Pentecost (Pinkster Day), May-June, the Sunday fifty days after Easter
Poetry Day, Black, October 17
Polka Festival, International, three to four days in early August
Powwow, Shinnecock, first weekend in September
Regatta, General Clinton Canoe, last weekend in May
St. Anne's Day, July 26
St. Anthony of Padua, Feast of, June 13
St. Blaise's Day, February 3
St. Januarius's Feast Day, two weeks, including September 19
St. John the Baptist's Day (San Juan Fiesta), Sunday nearest June 24
St. Joseph of Arimathea, Feast Day of, March 19
St. Jude's Day, October 28
St. Nicholas's Day, December 6
St. Patrick's Day (Parade in New York, New York), March 17
St. Paul, Feast of the Conversion of, January 25
Saratoga Festival (Saratoga Performing Arts Center), early June to early September

New York *(cont.)*
Shaker Festival, August
Shakespeare Festival, New York, summer
Simhat Torah (Rejoicing in the Law), 23rd day of Jewish month of Tishri
Stone Day, Lucy, August 13
Strawberry Festival, usually June
Summergarden, July and August
Tulip Time, second Thursday, Friday and Saturday in May
United States Open Tennis Championships, September
Verrazano Day, April 17

New York, New York
Armed Forces Day, third Saturday in May
Bastille Day, July 14
Evacuation Day, November 25
Harbor Festival, late June to July 4
Independence Day, Greece, Sunday nearest March 25
Lincoln Center Out-of-Doors Festival, three weeks from mid-August into September
Loyalty Day, May 1 parade
Mozart Festival, Mostly, seven weeks from mid-July to last week in August
Naumburg Orchestral Concerts, four concerts between Memorial Day, last Monday in May, and Labor Day, first Monday in September
New York City Marathon, first Sunday in November
New York Philharmonic Free Outdoor Park Concerts, three weeks in August
St. Anne's Day, July 26
St. Anthony of Padua, Feast of, June 13
St. John the Baptist's Day (San Juan Fiesta), Sunday nearest June 24
St. Patrick's Day (Parade in New York, New York), March 17
St. Paul, Feast of the Conversion of, January 25
Shakespeare Festival, New York, summer
Summergarden, July and August

New York Mills, New York
Holy Saturday, March-April, Saturday before Easter Sunday

New Zealand
Agricultural Field Days, three days during second week in June
Anzac Day, April 25
April Fools' Day, April 1
Arts Festival, Christchurch, even-numbered years in March
Arts Festival, Maidment, April-May
Auckland Festival, March-April during even-numbered years
Fawkes Day, Guy, November 5
Labour Day, last Monday in October
Mischief Night, November 4
New Zealand Day (Waitangi), February 6
Provincial Anniversary, January 28

Theatre Federation One-Act Play Festival, New Zealand, July-September
Victoria Day (Empire Day), Monday nearest May 24
Wellington Day, January 18

Nez Perce Indians in Idaho: Kamiah
Powwow, Chief Looking Glass, August
Powwow and Root Feast, Mat-Al-YM'A, third weekend in May

Nez Perce Indians in Idaho: Lapwai
Powwow, Epethes, first weekend in March
Powwow, Four Nations, October
Powwow, Warriors Memorial, third weekend in June

Nganasan people in USSR: Siberia
Clean Tent Ceremony, February

Niagara Falls, New York
Christmas Season (Festival of Lights), late November-early January

Niagara-on-the-Lake, Ontario, Canada
Performance Season, Canadian Experimental, month of July
Shaw Festival, 22 weeks from May to October

Nicaragua
Christmas, December 25
Independence Day, September 15
Revolution Day, Sandinista, July 19

Nice, France
Jazz, Nice Grand Parade of (Grande Parade du Jazz), eleven days beginning first week in July
Mardi Gras (Carnival and Battle of the Flowers), February-March, twelve days ending Ash Wednesday

Nicosia, Cyprus
Cyprus International Fair, two weeks in May-June
Nicosia Festival, two to four weeks in May or June

Niger
Bianou, first new moon in February
Black Spirit Festival (Genji Bi Hori), April
Eating the New Millet Ceremony, after harvest
Geerewol Celebrations, June-September, one week during rainy season
Independence Day, August 3
Rain-Bringing Ceremony (Yenaandi), end of the hot-dry season, usually on a Thursday
Republic Day, December 18
Salted Cure (Cure Salée), September or October

Nigeria
Agwunsi Festival, August-September

586

Nigeria *(cont.)*

Argungu Fishing Festival, February

Children's Day, May 27

Christmas, December 25

Dead, Return of the (Odo Festival), every other year in April (Awuru Odo celebration for departure of the dead) and sometime between September and November (arrival of the dead)

Easter, March-April, first Sunday after first full moon after the vernal equinox

Egungun Festival, June

Emume Ala, on or near March 20

Eyo Masquerade, August

Gelede, occasional: end of dry season (March-May); August; and during emergencies and funerals

Imechi Festival, July-August

Independence Day, October 1

Ndok Ceremony, every other year in November-December

New Yam Festival, around end of June

New Yam Festival, two-day festival in August

New Yam Festival, October 12

New Yam Festival (Egbodo Oba Ooni), late June

New Yam Festival (Eje), two-day festival

New Yam Festival (Igun Efon Festival)

New Yam Festival (Igun Ekun Ajinida Festival), annual

New Yam Festival (Igun Luwo Festival)

New Yam Festival (Ilaja Isu Titun)

New Yam Festival (Iri ji Ohuru), August-September

New Yam Festival (Ogijan Festival), annual

New Yam Festival (Onwasato), around August

New Year (Ibu Afo Festival), March, first day of first month, Onwa Izizi, of the Ibu calendar, or determined by council of elders

New Year's Day, end of Ndok season

New Year's Eve, December 31

Okere Juju, five weeks from May to July; height of rainy season

Okpesi or Itensi Festival, around September

Olojo (Ogun Festival), around July

Ramadan (Azumi), ninth Islamic month

Road Building Festival, around April

Sallah, tenth day of Islamic month of Dhu'l-Hijjah

Sango Festival, early November, seven days near end of rainy season

Uhola Festival, new moon in December-January

Washing the Hands (Issa Aka), during yam festivals held in August, September, or October

Yoruba Ibeji Ceremony, at least once monthly

Niigata, Japan

Kite Battles, June 5-12

Nikko, Tochigi, Japan

Dance, Longevity (Ennen-no-mai), June

Dance, Waraku, August

Spring Festival of the Toshogu Shrine, Great (Toshogu Haru-No-Taisai), May 17-18

Nipawin, Saskatchewan, Canada

Pike Festival, Northern, June to August

Nogales, Arizona

Cinco de Mayo, May 5

Nogales, Sonora, Mexico

Cinco de Mayo, May 5

Nola, Campania, Italy

St. Paulinus of Nola, Feast of (Lily Festival), fourth Sunday in June or Sunday following June 22

Nome, Alaska

Ice Golf Classic, Bering Sea, mid-March

Norfolk, Connecticut

Music Festival, Norfolk Chamber, late June to mid-August on weekends

Norfolk, England

Music and the Arts, King's Lynn Festival of, nine days in July

Norfolk, Virginia

Harborfest Norfolk, four days in June

Norman, Oklahoma

Oklahoma Day, April 22

Normandy, France

D-Day (Allied Landing Observances Day), June 6

Michaelmas, September 29

Northam, Western Australia, Australia

Arts, Northam Festival of the, June-July

North America

Dance, Green Corn, date varies

Earth Day (Vernal Equinox), March 20

Pan American Day, April 14

North American southwest

Coronado Day, February 25

North Cape, Norway

Sun Days, Midnight, mid-May through July

North Carolina

Admission Day, November 21

Cherokee of Hoke Intertribal Festival, fourth Saturday in July

Christmas Eve, December 24

Coca Cola 600, last weekend in May

North Carolina *(cont.)*
Confederate Memorial Day, May 10
Dance and Folk Festival, Asheville Mountain, first
 Thursday, Friday, and Saturday in August
Easter Monday, March-April, Monday after Easter
Fiddler's and Bluegrass Festival, Old Time, three days over
 last weekend in May
Halifax Day, April 12
Highland Games and Gathering of Scottish Clans,
 Grandfather Mountain, second full weekend in July
Hollerin' Contest, National, third Saturday in June
Lee-Jackson Day, January 18; observed third Monday in
 January
Mecklenburg Day, May 20
Music Center, Brevard, seven weeks from late June to
 mid-August
Music Festival, Eastern, six weeks from late June to early
 August
Music Festival and Seminar, Moravian, one week in mid-
 June every two or three years; location alternates
Singing on the Mountain, fourth Sunday in June
Unto These Hills Festival
Whistlers Convention, National, second or third weekend
 in April
Wolfe Festival, Thomas, October 3
Wright Brothers Day, December 17

North Coast Islands, Netherlands
Kallemooi, May-June, Saturday preceding Pentecost

North Dakota
Admission Day, November 2
Arikara Celebration, second weekend in July
Arts, International Festival of the, six weeks during June
 and July
Little Shell Celebration, second weekend in August
Mandaree Celebration, third weekend in July
Musical, Medora, mid-June to Labor Day, first Monday in
 September
Norsk Høstfest, five days in October
Poetry Gathering, Dakota Cowboy, last weekend in May
Twin Buttes Celebration, third weekend in August
Winterfest, seven to ten days in February

North Dartmouth, Massachusetts
Eisteddfod Festival of Traditional Music and Crafts, three-
 day festival over third weekend in September

North Dravidian people in India
Fire Festival (Holi), begins 14th day of Hindu month of
 Phalguna or Dol; length varies

Northeast Harbor, Maine
Music, Mount Desert Festival of Chamber, five Tuesday
 evenings from mid-July to August

Northern Hemisphere
Summer Solstice, June 21-22
Winter Solstice, December 21-22

Northern Ireland
Belfast Festival, two and one half weeks in November
Easter Monday, March-April, Monday after Easter
Harvest Festival
Labour Day, first Monday in May
Orange Day, July 12

Northern Marianas
All Souls' Day, November 2

Northern Territory, Australia
Darwin Youth Festival, August (during school holidays)
Folk Festival, Top Half, weekend in June
Picnic Day, first Monday in August

Northern Ute Indians in Utah
Dance, Sun, July and August

North Jeolla, Republic of Korea
Chunhyang Festival, three days from the eighth day of fourth
 lunar month

North Jutland, Denmark
Independence Day (Rebild Festival), July 4

North Korea
See **Korea, Democratic People's Republic of**

North Moldavia, Romania
Theatre, Festival of Youth, odd-numbered years
 in autumn

North Platte, Nebraska
NEBRASKAland DAYS, third week in June

North Pole, Alaska
Winter Carnival, North Pole, a weekend in early March

North Rhine-Westphalia, Federal Republic of Germany
Beethoven Festival, September-October
Castle Play Festival, Moers, five weeks in summer
Castle Theatre Hohenlimburg, June-July
Dance Workshop, Bonn International, July
Duisburg Trends, May during odd-numbered years
Pantomime Festival (Gaukler Festival), October
Plays '78, '79, etc., one week in May
Puppet Theatre of the Nations, International Festival Week,
 one week in May or June
Ruhr Festival, May-June
Summer Academy of Dance, International, two weeks in
 June-July

North Rhine-Westphalia, Federal Republic of Germany *(cont.)*
Theatre Festival, International Arena, May during even-numbered years
Theatre Festival, Open-Air, Saturdays in July and August
Theatre Nettelstedt, Open-Air, Saturdays and Sundays from May to September

Northside Beach, Sheboygan, Wisconsin
Polar Bear Swim Day, January 1

North Sumatra, Sumatra, Indonesia
Medan Anniversary, April 1

North Tunis Region, Tunisia
Art, International Festival of Popular, odd-numbered years in July-August
Carthage, International Festival of, July and August
El Karraka International Festival, July-August
Ezzahra, Festival, July-August

Northumberland, England
Folk Festival, Newcastle, June-July
Hexham Abbey Festival, last two weeks in October

North Vietnam
See **Vietnam, Democratic Republic of**

Northwest Territories, Canada
Caribou Carnival and Championship Dog Derby, one week in March
Christmas, December 25
Northern Games, four days in mid-July
Toonik Time, one week from late April to early May
Top of the World Ski Meet, March-April, Easter weekend

North Yorkshire, England
Richmondshire Festival, May-June during odd-numbered years

Norwalk, Connecticut
Oyster Festival, the weekend after Labor Day, first Monday in September

Norway
April Fools' Day, observed April 1 and 30
Bergen International Festival (Festspillene i Bergen), 15 days beginning last week in May
Christmas (Juledag), December 25
Christmas Eve (Julaften), December 24
Constitution Day, May 17
Easter (Paske), March-April, first Sunday after first full moon after the vernal equinox
Good Friday (Langfredag, Long Friday), March-April, Friday preceding Easter Sunday

Jazz Festival, Molde International (Jazzfestpillene i Molde), one week in late July
Leif Eriksson Day, October 9
Mardi Gras (Fastelavn), February-March, Monday before Ash Wednesday
May Day, May 1
Michaelmas (Mikkelsmesse), September 29
Midsummer (Jonsok), June 23-24
Moving Day (Flyttedag), autumn and April 14
New Year's Day (Nyttårsdag), January 1
New Year's Eve (Nytaarsaften), December 31
Norway, Festival of Northern, June
Olsok, July 29; observed last week in July
Peer Gynt Festival Days, begins August 4
Pentecost (Pinse), May-June, the Sunday fifty days after Easter
Potato Days (Potetserie), October
St. Brictiva's Day, January 11
St. Lucy's Day, December 13
St. Thomas the Apostle, Feast of, December 21
Ski Festival, Holmenkollen, one week in March; second Sunday in March
Sun Days, Midnight, mid-May through July
Sun Pageant Day, end of January-beginning of February
Sun Pageant Day, Narvik, February 8
Twentieth Day (Tyvendedagen), January 13

Norwegian-Americans
Fyr-Bål Fest, two days on weekend nearest June 24
Leif Eriksson Day, October 9
Olsok, July 29; observed last week in July

Norwegian-Americans in Colorado: Breckenridge
Ullr Fest, third week in January

Norwich, Connecticut
Mohegan Homecoming, third Sunday in August

Norwich, Norfolk, England
Music and the Arts, Norfolk and Norwich Triennial Festival of, every three years in October

Norfolk, England
Music and the Arts, Norfolk and Norwich Triennial Festival of, every three years in October

Notre Dame, Indiana
Great Lakes Festival, three weekends in mid-June

Nottingham, Nottinghamshire, England
Nottingham Festival, June

Nottinghamshire, England
Nottingham Festival, June

Nova Gorica, Slovenia, Yugoslavia
Theatres, Nova Gorica Meeting of Small, January

Nova Scotia, Canada
Annapolis Valley Blossom Festival, last week in May
Apple Blossom Festival, five days in late May or early June
Christmas, December 25
Christmas Eve, December 24
Fiddling Contest, Maritime Old Time, two days in July
Gaelic Mod, first full week in August
Gathering of the Clans, July 1
Kipawo Showboat Company, July-August
Summer Carnival, Whycocomagh, July
Tartans, Festival of the, August

Novi Sad, Vojvodina, Yugoslavia
Theatre Games, Yugoslav (Yugoslav Theatre Festival), second half of April
Theatres of Vojvodina, Encounter of, May

Nsukka, Nigeria
Dead, Return of the (Odo Festival), every other year in April (Awuru Odo celebration for departure of the dead) and sometime between September and November (arrival of the dead)

Nuevo Laredo, Mexico, and Laredo, Texas
Washington's Birthday, mid-February

Nuits-St. Georges, Beaune, and Meursault in Cote-d'Or, France
Three Glorious Days (Les Trois Glorieuses), twice annually: July 27-29 and third Saturday through Monday in November

Nulato, Alaska
Stickdance, one week in spring

Numeralla, New South Wales, Australia
Folk Festival, Numeralla, end of January, including Australia Day, January 26

Nuoro, Sardinia, Italy
Redeemer, Feast of the (Festa del Redentore), last Sunday in August

Nupe, West Africa
Muhammad's Birthday (Game Festival), twelfth day of Islamic month of Rabi al-Awwal

Nuremberg, Bavaria, Germany
Christkindlesmarkt (Kriss Kringle's Fair), early December until Christmas, December 25

Nyasaland (now Malawi)
Christmas, December 25
See also **Malawi**

Oahu Island, Hawaii
Cherry Blossom Festival, mid-February through April
Dead, Festival of the (Toro Nagashi, Floating Lantern Ceremony), observed August 15
Kamehameha Day, June 11
New Year (Narcissus Festival), early January to early February
Surfing Classic, Buffalo's Big Board, two days in February

Oakland, California
Cowboys Parade, Black, first Saturday in October

Oakville, California
Jazz Festival, Summer, five weekend concerts over July and August

Oakville, Washington
Tribal Day Celebration, late May

Oakville, West Virginia
Whitewater Wednesday, third Wednesday in June

Oaxaca, Mexico
Christmas Festival (Night of the Radishes and Nativity Festival), December 23-24
Monday on the Hill (Lunes del Cerro, Guelaguetza offering ritual), third and fourth Mondays in July
New Year's Eve (Noche de Pedimento, Wishing Night), December 31

Obando, Bulacan, Luzon Island, Philippines
Dances of Obando, three days in mid-May

Obanos, Navarra, Spain
Mystery of San Guillen and Santa Felicia, August

Oberammergau, Bavaria, Federal Republic of Germany
Passion Play, Oberammergau, every ten years from May to September

Oberndorf, Salzburg, Austria
"Silent Night, Holy Night" Celebration, December 24

Ocean City, New Jersey
Baby Parade, second Thursday in August

Oceanside, California
All Souls' Day (Night of the Candle Ceremony), November 2

Ocean Springs, Mississippi
Landing of d'Iberville, last weekend in April

Ocu, Panama
Country Fair, during January, including Feast of San Sebastian, January 20

Odanah, Wisconsin
Rice Celebration, Wild (Manomin), usually weekend before Labor Day, first Monday in September

Odense, Denmark
Andersen Festival, Hans Christian, month-long, July-August

Odori Park, Sapporo, Hokkaido, Japan
Snow Festival (Yuki Matsuri), February 8-12

Offaly (County) and other northern areas of Ireland
Harvest Festival

Ohio
Admission Day, March 1
Bach Festival, Baldwin-Wallace, two days in mid-May
Brady Day, Captain, July-August
Buzzard Day, first Sunday after March 15
Cincinnati May Festival, Friday and Saturday evenings for two weeks in mid-May
Dulcimer Days, third weekend in May
Gable Birthday Celebration, Clark, Saturday nearest February 1
International Festival, third weekend in May
Johnny Appleseed Week, last week in September
Kent State Memorial Day, May 3-4
Middfest International, three days in late September-early October
Music Center, Blossom, first week in June to second week in September
Oakley Festival, Annie, last full week in July
Opera Festival, Cincinnati Summer, mid-June to mid-July
Paul Bunyan Show, first full weekend in October
Pike Festival, National, May-June (along Route 40)
Pottery Festival, three days during weekend nearest July 20
St. Andrew's Eve (Andrzejki), November 29-30
Soap Box Derby, All American, six days in August
Sternwheel Festival, Ohio River, weekend after Labor Day, first Monday in September

Ohrid, Macedonia, Yugoslavia
Folk Songs and Dances, Balkan Festival of, July 3-8
Summer Festival, Ohrid, July-August

Ojai, California
Ojai Festival, three days in late May

Ojibwa Indians in Minnesota: Cloquet
Powwow, Fond du Lac, July

Ojibwa Indians in Minnesota: Duluth
Ni-Mi-Win Celebration, third weekend in August

Ojibwa Indians in Minnesota: Grand Portage
Rendezvous Days, second weekend in August

Ojibwa Indians in Minnesota: Leech Lake Reservation, Cass Lake
Powwows, Ojibwa, first Monday in September, last weekend in May, and in winter, spring, and midsummer

Ojibwa Indians in Minnesota: Mille Lacs Reservation, Onamia
Powwow, Ojibwa, mid-August

Ojibwa Indians in Minnesota: Nett Lake Reservation
Powwow, Ojibwa, first weekend in June

Ojibwa Indians in Wisconsin: Lac du Flambeau
Powwow, Bear River, July

Ojibwa Indians in Wisconsin: Red Cliff Indian Reservation near Bayfield
Powwow, Ojibwa, August or September

Okeechobee, Florida
Brighton Field Day and Rodeo, third weekend in February

Okinawa
Autumnal Equinox (Jugowa), on or near September 21-22, full moon day of eighth lunar month
Boat Race Day (Gods of the Sea Festival in Minatogawa), 14th day of fifth lunar month
Chrysanthemum Festival (Choyo), ninth day of ninth lunar month
Fifth Month Festival (Gogatsu Matsuri), 15th day of fifth lunar month
Jurokunichi, 16th day of first lunar month
Mochi No Matsuri, eighth day of twelfth lunar month
New Year (Shogatsu), ten-day to two-week long celebration at the first new moon after sun enters Aquarius; one to 15 days of first month
Vernal Equinox, on or near March 21
Winter Solstice (Toji), December 21

Oklahoma
Admission Day, November 16
Arts, Festival of the, six days in late April
Bluegrass and Old-Time Music Festival, Grant's Annual, five days in early August
Cherokee National Holiday, Thursday-Sunday of first weekend in September
Cherokee Strip Day, September 16
Chickasaw Nation Annual Day, first Saturday in October
Dance, Green Corn, July or August
Dance, Green Corn, late summer (Muskogee-Creek Indians)
Dances, Osage Tribal Ceremonial, June
Dance, Sun
Easter (Oberammergau Sunrise Service), March-April, first Sunday after first full moon after the vernal equinox
Fall Festival, October

Oklahoma *(cont.)*
Happy Hunting Party, Festival of the Forest (Kiamichi Owa Chito), late June
Horse, Festival of the, nine days in October
Indian Exposition, American, six days beginning second Monday of August
Indian Heritage Days Celebration, Oklahoma, late May
Indian Memorial Stampede Rodeo, summer
Indian or Native American Day, first Saturday after full moon in September
Italian Festival, late May
Labor Day, three days, including first Monday in September
Labor Day Festivities, Choctaw Nation of Oklahoma, first weekend and Monday in September
Labor Day Powwow, first weekend and Monday in September
Little Pony Society Dances, April
Mayfest, International, five days in May
Native American Cultural Festival, Red Earth, first or second weekend in June
Oklahoma Day, April 22
Oklahoma Historical Day, October 10
Powwow, Citizen Band of Potawatomi Indians of Oklahoma, last weekend in June
Powwow, Comanche Annual, July
Powwow, Kihekah Steh Club Annual, August
Powwow, Lenape Delaware, late May or early June
Powwow, Otoe-Missouri, July
Powwow, Ottawa, one in August and one in September
Powwow, Pawnee Fourth of July, weekend nearest July 4
Powwow, Quapaw, second weekend in July
Powwow, Sac and Fox, second weekend in July
Red Bird Smith Ceremony, August 17
Rogers Day, Will, November 4
Seminole Nation Days, September
Senior Citizens Day, June 9

Oklahoma City, Oklahoma
Arts, Festival of the, six days in late April
Horse, Festival of the, nine days in October
Native American Cultural Festival, Red Earth, first or second weekend in June

Okmulgee, Oklahoma
Dance, Green Corn, late summer

Old Chatham, New York
Shaker Festival, August

Old Saybrook, Connecticut
Christmas Torchlight Parade and Muster, Old Saybrook, second Saturday night in December

Old Town, Maine
Native American Day, late July

O'Leary, Prince Edward Island, Canada
Potato Blossom Festival, last week in July

Olney, England
Mardi Gras (Pancake Day), February-March, Tuesday before Ash Wednesday

Oloron-Sainte-Marie, Lot-et-Garonne, France
Folklore Festival, International, about one week in August

Olt, Romania
Oltenian Ballad, first weekend in October
Romanian "Calus," last weekend in August

Olvera Street, Los Angeles, California
Christmas Eve, December 24
Our Lady of Guadalupe, December 12

Omaha, Nebraska
Ak-Sar-Ben Livestock Exposition and Rodeo, nine days from late September to early October

Omaha Indians in Nebraska: Omaha Reservation
Dance of Thanksgiving (Whe'wahchee), first full moon in August

Omak, Washington
Stampede Days, second week in August

Onamia, Minnesota
Powwow, Ojibwa, mid-August

Ondo's shrine in Pobe, Benin, Nigeria
New Yam Festival, two-day festival in August

Oneida, Wisconsin
Powwow, Oneida, weekend nearest July 4

Oneida Indians in Wisconsin: Oneida
Powwow, Oneida, weekend nearest July 4

Ontario, Canada
Arts Festival, New Directions in the Performing, even-numbered years in summer or autumn
Canadian National Exhibition, three weeks in August and September
Caribana, one week ending the first Monday in August
A Day to Remember, July-August
Folk Arts Festival, May-June
Freedom Festival, International, mid-June to July 4
Grape and Wine Festival, Niagara, ten days in late September
Highland Games, Brantford, second Saturday in July
Highland Games, Fergus, second Saturday in August
Highland Games, Glengarry, Saturday before the first Monday in August

Ontario, Canada *(cont.)*
Music, Mariposa-the Festival of Roots, last weekend in June
Oktoberfest, nine days in early October, beginning the
   Friday before Thanksgiving Monday
Opera Plus, Festival Ottawa, three weeks in July
Performance Season, Canadian Experimental, month of July
Shaw Festival, 22 weeks from May to October
Spring, Festival of, nine days in mid-May
Spring Festival, Guelph, two to three weeks in April-May
Summer Festival, Blyth, July-August
Theatre Festival, Ontario, May
Theatre Festival, Stratford, May-June to October
Winterlude, ten days in February

Onteniente, Valencia, Spain
Battle of the Moors and Christians, August

Oodi people in Botswana
World Environment Day, June 5

Oostduinkerke, Belgium
Shrimp Festival, early July

Ootmarsum, Overijssel, Netherlands
Easter Monday (Vlöggelen, Winging Ceremony),
   March-April, Easter Sunday and Monday
Whistle Making (Fluitjes Maken), about May 1

Opatija, Croatia, Yugoslavia
Summer Festival, Opatija, June-September

Opole, Poland
Puppet Theatres, All-Poland Festival of, odd-numbered years
   in November
Theatre Encounters, Opole, March-April

Oporto, Porto, Portugal
St. Bartholomew's Festival, August
Theatres of Iberian Expression, International Festival of,
   November

Oradea, Transylvania, Romania
Plays, Festival of Short, one week in February

Orange, New South Wales, Australia
Arts, Orange Festival of the, one week in April during even-
   numbered years

Orange, France
Orange Festival (Chorégies d'Orange), four productions in
   late July to early August

Orange County, New York
Assumption, Feast of the (Our Lady of the Flowers),
   August 15

Oranjestad, Aruba
Mardi Gras (Carnival), February-March, Sunday-Tuesday
   before Ash Wednesday

Orasac, Yugoslavia
St. George's Day, April 23

Orastioara de Sus Commune, Hunedoara, Romania
Encounter with History, first Sunday in May

Oregon
Admission Day, February 14
Bach Festival, Oregon, late June to second week in
   July
Britt Festival, June-September
Indian Celebration, Tygh Valley, May
Music Northwest, Chamber, mid-June to late July
Pendleton Round-Up, second full week in September
Poetry Day, Black, October 17
Powwow, Chief Schonchin Days, last weekend in May
Powwow, Nesika Illahee, second weekend in August
Powwow, Warm Springs, June
Restoration Day, November 18 or following Saturday
Root Festival, mid-April
Rose Festival, Portland, June
Shakespeare Festival, Oregon, February through
   October

Orense, Spain
Showcase of Rivadavia, May

Orissa, India
Bathing Festival (Snan Yatra), full moon day of Hindu month
   of Jyeshta
Chaitra Parb, eight days prior to full moon day of Hindu
   month of Chaitra
Chandan Yatra, 21 days beginning third day of waxing half
   of Hindu month of Vaisakha
Dance Festival, Kala Vikash Kendra, twice yearly: three days
   in October-November and on August 10
Dance Festival, Mayurbhanj Chhau (Chaitra Parva, Spring
   Festival), April 11-13
Drama Festival, Orissa Academy, five days in March-April
Jhulan Latra, full moon day of Hindu month of
   Sravana
Juggernaut (Rath Yatra, Festival of Jagannatha), second day
   of waxing half of Hindu month of Ashadha

Orkney Islands, Scotland
St. Magnus Festival, five days over third weekend
   in June

Orkney Springs, Virginia
Music Festival, Shenandoah Valley, four weekends from mid-
   July to early September

Orleans, Loiret, France
Musical Weeks of Orleans, International (Semaines
Musicales Internationale d'Orleans), two weeks in
November-December
St. Joan of Arc, Feast of (Féte de Jeanne d'Arc), second
Sunday in May

Orofino, Idaho
Lumberjack Days, Clearwater County Fair and, third
weekend in September

Oruru, Bolivia
Mardi Gras (Carnival Week), February-March, week before
Lent begins

Osaka, Japan
Osaka International Festival, 18 days in April-May
Shrine Rice Festival, Sumiyashi, June 14

Osijek, Croatia, Yugoslavia
Opera and Ballet, Annual Festival of Chamber, May-June

Osnabruck, Lower Saxony, Federal Republic of Germany
Plays in the Town Hall, May-June to September for two
consecutive years followed by two-year interim

Ossiach, Carinthia, Austria
Summer Festival, Carinthian (Carinthischer Sommer), eight
weeks from late June to late August

Ostend, Belgium
Mardi Gras (Bal du Rat Mort, Dead Rat's Ball), January-
March, usually the weekend before Lent
Summer Festival, International, July-August

Ostfildern, Baden-Wurttemberg, Federal Republic of Germany
Puppet Play Encounter, three days in October during odd-
numbered years

Otago and Southland, New Zealand
Provincial Anniversary, March 23

Ottawa, Ontario, Canada
Opera Plus, Festival Ottawa, three weeks in July
Spring, Festival of, nine days in mid-May
Winterlude, ten days in February

Ouray, Randlett, Whiterocks, Utah
Dance, Ute Bear (Ma'makoni-ni'tkap), three to five days in
April

Our Lady of Guadalupe Church, San Diego, California
Our Lady of Guadalupe, December 12

Our Lady of Guadalupe Church, San Antonio, Texas
Our Lady of Guadalupe (Festival Guadalupaño), Sunday
nearest December 12

Overijssel, Netherlands
Easter Monday (Vlöggelen, Winging Ceremony), March-
April, Easter Sunday and Monday
Fields, Going to the (Veldgang), May-June, Monday
preceding Ascension Thursday
Midwinter Horn, Blowing the (Midwinterhoorn Blazen),
December-January, from beginning of Advent to Sunday
following Epiphany
Pinkster Bruid or Pinksterbloem (Whitsun Bride or
Whitsun Flower Festival), May-June, Whit Tuesday, the
Tuesday after Pentecost Sunday
Whistle Making (Fluitjes Maken), about May 1

Oviedo, Spain
Asturias Day, first Sunday in August
St. Roch's Day (San Roque Festival), August
Vaqueiros de Alzada Festival, July

Owensboro, Kentucky
Bar-B-Q Festival, International, mid-May
Bluegrass Fan Fest, third weekend in September
Summer Festival, July 4

Oxford, England
Bach Festival, English, April and May
Mallard Ceremony, once every hundred years
Mint Julep Day, June 1
Oxford Festival, July-August

Oxfordshire, England
Egg Saturday, February-March, Saturday before Ash
Wednesday

Oxford University, England
Encaenia Day, June

Oxford University, Putney to Martlake, England
Boat Race Day, March-April

Oyo, Nigeria
New Yam Festival (Egbodo Oba Ooni), late June
New Yam Festival (Igun Efon Festival)
New Yam Festival (Igun Ekun Ajinida Festival),
annual
New Yam Festival (Igun Luwo Festival)
New Yam Festival (Ilaja Isu Titun)
New Yam Festival (Ogijan Festival), annual
Olojo (Ogun Festival), around July

Oyo people in Nigeria
Sango Festival, early November, seven days near end of rainy
season

Ozora, Hungary
Pentecost and Whit Monday, May-June, the seventh
Sunday and Monday after Easter

Pacarigtambo, Peru
Assumption, Feast of the, August 15
Exaltation of the Cross (Cruz Velakuy), May 3, alternate
years
St. Andrew's Day (Día de San Andrés), November 30
St. John the Baptist's Day (San Juan Day), June 24
St. Peter's Day (San Pedro), June 29

Pades, Gorj, Romania
In the Sunlit Plain, first week in June

Padova, Veneto, Italy
Theatre Review, Summer, July-August

Padua, Italy
Purim, eleventh day of Jewish month of Sivan

Pago Pago, American Samoa
Flag Day, April 17

Paguate Village, Laguna Pueblo, New Mexico
St. Elizabeth, Feast of, September 25

Pakistan
Chaomos, December 21, winter solstice
Data Ganj Baksh Death Festival, 18-19 days of Islamic month
of Safar
Fast, Feast of Breaking the (Id-ul-Fitr or Eid), first day of
Islamic month of Shawwal
Fire Festival (Holi), begins 14th day of Hindu month of
Phalguna or Dol; length varies
Husayn or Husain Day, tenth day of Islamic month of
Muharram
Independence Day, August 14
Jinnah Day, September 11
Mecca, Pilgrimage to, eighth through 13th days of Islamic
month of Dhu'l-Hijjah
New Year (Muharram Celebrations), first day of Islamic
month of Muharram
Night of Forgiveness (Shab-i-Barat), 15th of Islamic month
of Shaban
Pakistan Day, March 23
Ramadan (Ramazan), ninth Islamic month
Sacrifice, Feast of (Bakrid or Id-ul-Bakr, Sacrifice of the
Ram), tenth-twelfth days of Islamic month of Dhu'l-Hijjah
Shah Abdul Latif Death Festival, 14-16 days during Islamic
month of Safar

Pala Indian Reservation near Oceanside, California
All Souls' Day (Night of the Candle Ceremony),
November 2

Palatinate (Federal Republic of Germany)
Mid-Lent Sunday, March, fourth Sunday in Lent

Palermo, Sicily, Italy
Palermo Festival, first week in October
Theatres, International Meeting of Experimental, April

Palestine
Holy Week, March-April, week preceding Easter
Lent, February-March, forty-day season preceding Easter
Passover (Pesach), eight days beginning 15th day of Jewish
month of Nisan
Springtime Festival, March-April, four successive Thursdays
before Orthodox Easter

Palma del Condado, Huelva, Andalusia, Spain
Wine Harvest, Festival of the, September

Palm Beach, Florida
Palm Beach Festival, two weeks in December

Palmyra, New York
Hill Cumorah Pageant, nine days (excluding Sunday and
Monday) beginning third weekend in July

Pampanga, Philippines
Christmas Season (Giant Lantern Festival), December 24-25

Pamplona, Navarre, Spain
Running of the Bulls (San Fermín Festival), July 6-20

Panama
Black Christ, Festival of the, October 21
Coffee Fair and Flower Festival, four days in late April
Columbus Day (Dia de la Hispanidad), October 12
Country Fair, during January, including Feast of San
Sebastian, January 20
Flag Day, November 4
Folklore Festival, Canajacua, four days including Epiphany,
January 6
Foundation of Panama, August 15
Independence Day, November 3
Independence Day, November 28
Mardi Gras (Carnival and Burial of the Sardine on Ash
Wednesday), February-March, Saturday-Ash Wednesday
Mothers' Day, December 8
St. Joseph's Day (International Fair of San José), ten days,
including March 19

Panama City, Panama
Foundation of Panama, August 15

Panay Island, Philippines
Ati-Atihan Festival, three days in January, including feast
day of Santo Nino (Holy Child Jesus) and ending on a
Sunday

Panay Island, Philippines *(cont.)*
Dinagyand, last weekend in January

Pandaan, East Java, Indonesia
Ballet Festival, Javanese, two nights each month during full
moon from June to November

Pangandaran, West Java, Java
Offering Ceremony, January

Panjim, India
Drama Festival, Goa Academy, five to ten days in November-
December or February-March
Drama Festival, Marathi, February-March

Pantai Charita, Java
Offering Ceremony, July

Papago Indians in Arizona: Casa Grande
Indian Celebration, O'Odham Tash, February

Papago Indians in Arizona: the Mission San Xavier del Bac
Easter, March-April, first Sunday after first full moon after
the vernal equinox; ceremony observed Friday after Easter
Sunday

Papago Indians in Arizona: Sells
St. Francis of Assisi, Feast of, October 4

Papago Indians in Arizona: Tucson
Tucson Festival, two weeks following Easter

**Papago Indians in southern Arizona and northern Sonora,
Mexico**
Wíikita Festivals, winter festival at Archie, Arizona;
summer festival at Quitovaca, Sonora, Mexico

Paphos, Cyprus
Anthestiria Flower Festival, early May
Drama, Paphos Festival of Ancient, June-July
Folk Art Festival: Pampaphia, four days in early August
Kataklysmos (Flood Festival), May-June, three to five days
including fiftieth day after Greek Orthodox Easter
(Pentecost)
Poetry Festival, Palamas, early March

Papua New Guinea
Pig Festival
Pig Festival (Juwo)
Thanksgiving (Waratambar), August, dates vary according
to province

Paraguay
Columbus Day (Day of the Race), October 12
Constitution Day, August 25

Epiphany (Fiesta of the Three Kings), January 5-6
Exaltation of the Cross (La Adoracion de la Cruz), May 2-3
Independence and Flag Day, May 14; observed May 14-15
Midsummer, June 23-24
New Year's Day, January 1
Peace with Bolivia Day, June 12
St. Blaise's Day (St. Blas's Day), February 3
St. John the Baptist's Day (Fiesta de San Juan), June 24
Sts. Peter and John Festival (San Pedro and San Juan),
June 24-29

Paraje Village, Laguna Pueblo, New Mexico
St. Mary Margaret, Feast of, October 17

Parang Kusuma, Jogjakarta District, Java
Offering Ceremony, April

Paraty, Brazil
Divino, Festo do, May-June, Saturday before Pentecost

Paris, France
Autumn Festival, Paris (Festival d'Automne), mid-September
through end of December
Dance Festival of Paris, International, October-December
Lammas (formerly a feast for the Society of the Trade of
Cobblers), August 1
Marais Festival, June-July
Mardi Gras (Carnival), February-March
Music at La Defense, month of June
Napoleon's Day, May 5
Paris Air and Space Show, 11 days in June during odd-
numbered years
Paris Festival Estival (Festival Estival de Paris), mid-July to
mid-September
Paris Marathon, third Saturday in May

Paris, Tennessee
Fish Fry, World's Biggest, usually last full week in April

Parma, Emilia-Romagna, Italy
Theatre, International Festival of University, October

Paro, Bhutan
Paro Tshechu, tenth to 15th days of second lunar month

Parramatta, New South Wales, Australia
Foundation Week Celebrations, two weeks in
October-November

The Pas, Manitoba, Canada
Trappers' Festival, Northern Manitoba, nearly one week in
mid-February

Pasadena, California
Rose Bowl Game, January 1
Tournament of Roses, January 1

Peru *(cont.)*
St. Francis of Assisi, Feast of (San Francisco's Day),
October 4
St. James the Greater's Day, July 25
St. John the Baptist's Day (San Juan Day), June 24
St. Peter's Day (San Pedro), June 29
St. Rose of Lima Day, August 23; observed August 30
Sts. Peter and Paul Day (Dia de San Pedro y San Pablo),
June 29
Santo Domingo Promenade, August 4
Situa, September
Sun Festival (Inti Raymi or Raimi Fiesta), about one week,
including June 24, the winter solstice

Perugia, Italy
Music Festival, Umbria Sacred (Sagra Musicale Umbra), two
weeks in mid-September

Peruvian Inca people
Crow Fair, at least six days in mid-August

Peterborough, New Hampshire
Music Festival, Monadnock, seven weeks from mid-July to
end of August

Petrel, Alicante, Spain
Battle of the Moors and Christians, April 22-24

Pharaohs in ancient Egypt
Heb-sed

Philadelphia, Mississippi
Indian Fair, Choctaw, four days in July beginning the
Wednesday after July 4

Philadelphia, Pennsylvania
Elfreth's Alley Fete Days, two days in early June
Fall Festival, Fairmount Park, 22 days in September-October
Folk Festival, Philadelphia, three days over last weekend in
August
Jazz Festival, Mellon, ten days in mid-June
Music Center, Mann, mid-June to first week in August
New Year's Day (Mummers Parade), January 1
Franklin's Birthday, Benjamin, January 17
Pennsylvania Relay Carnival, University of, one week
beginning Sunday before last weekend in April
Shakespeare's Birthday, April 23

Philippi, Greece
Drama, Festival of Ancient, July-August

Philippines
All Saints' Day, November 1
Ati-Atihan Festival, three days in January, including feast day
of Santo Nino (Holy Child Jesus) and ending on a Sunday

Ballet Festival, National, May
Bataan Day (Araw ng Kagitingan), April 9
Black Nazarene Fiesta, January 1-9
Christmas and Cock's Mass (Misa de Gallo), December 25
Christmas Season (Giant Lantern Festival), December 24-25
Constitution Day, May 14
Dances of Obando, three days in mid-May
Dinagyand, last weekend in January
Exaltation of the Cross (Santacruzan Festival), nine days
in May
Fast, Feast of Breaking the (Hari-Raya Poasa), first day of
Islamic month of Shawwal
Flores de Mayo, month of May
Ginem, at least one day in December
Halloween, October 31
Immaculate Conception, Feast of the, December 8
Independence Day, June 12
May Day, May 1
Moriones Festival, March-April, Good Friday to Easter
Sunday
Moro-Moro Play, April or May
Our Lady of Peñafrancia, Feast of (Nuestra Senora de
Peñafrancia), third week in September
Panunuluyan, December 24
Passion Play, Cenaculo, March-April, Holy Week
Passion Plays
People Power Anniversary, February 25
Philippine-American Friendship Day, July 4
Rizal Day, December 30
Sinulog Festival, third weekend in January
Water Buffalo Festival (Carabao), May 14 or 15

Philopappou Hill, Athens, Greece
Folk Dances, Greek, May-September

Phnom Penh, Cambodia
Water Festival, late October or early November

Phoenix, Arizona
Indian Fair, Heard Museum Guild, two days in late February

Phra Buddha Bat temple near Saraburi, Thailand
Phra Buddha Bat Fair, March

Phuket, Thailand
Vegetarian Festival, first nine days of ninth lunar month

Phum Thuy, Cambodia
Harvest Feast

Piatra-Neamt, North Moldavia, Romania
Theatre, Festival of Youth, odd-numbered years in autumn

Picuris Pueblo, New Mexico
Dances, Matchina, December 24-25

Poland *(cont.)*
  Horse Festival (Lejkonik), second Thursday after Corpus
    Christi
  Independence Day, November 11
  Juvenalia, late May or early June
  Lajkonik, May-June, first Thursday after Corpus Christi
  Liberation Day, July 22
  Mardi Gras (Zapusty, Fat Thursday), February-March,
    Thursday before Lent, which begins on Friday
  Marzanna Day, March 21; observed Saturday or Sunday
    nearest March 21
  May Day (Święto Pierwszego Maja), May 1
  Mimes, International Creative Workshop of,
    September-October
  Music of Warsaw, International Festival of Contemporary
    and Warsaw Autumn Festival (Warszawka), nine days in
    mid-September
  New Year's Day, January 1
  One-Man Shows, National Festival of, November
  Our Lady of Czestochowa, Feast of, May 3
  Our Lady of Czestochowa, Feast of (Feast of the Black
    Madonna of Jasna Gora), August 15
  Plays, Festival of Contemporary Polish, May
  Plays, Festival of Russian and Soviet, November
  Puppet Theatre, International Festival of, May-June during
    even-numbered years
  Puppet Theatre Festival, International, March during odd-
    numbered years
  Puppet Theatres, All-Poland Festival of, November during
    odd-numbered years
  St. Andrew's Day, November 30
  St. Andrew's Eve, November 29
  St. Barbara's Day, December 4
  St. Stephen, Feast of, December 26
  Theatre, International Festival of Open, September-October
    during even-numbered years
  Theatre Confrontations, Young, November
  Theatre Debuts, Start: National Festival of Student, February
    or March
  Theatre Encounter, Jelenia Gora, September
  Theatre Encounters, Lodz, spring
  Theatre Encounters, Opole, March-April
  Theatre Meetings, Kalisz, May
  Theatre Meetings, Rzeszow, April
  Theatre Meetings, Warsaw, December
  Theatres, Biennial of Amateur, September during even-
    numbered years
  Theatres of Northern Poland, Festival of, June
  Theatre Spring, Silesian, May
  Theatrical Forms, Festival of Small, March
  Turon, currently observed the week after Christmas
  Winter Sleigh Party (Kulig), during a heavy snowfall after
    Christmas and before Easter
  Wratislavia Cantans-International Oratorio Festival
    (Miedzynarodowy Festiwal Oratoryjno-Kantatowy), six

days during first week in September
  Wreaths, Wianki Festival of, June 23

Polish-Americans
  Kosciuszko Day, February 4
  Polish Solidarity Day, November 10

Polish-Americans in Indiana: South Bend
  Easter Monday (Paas Festival), March-April, Monday after
    Easter

Polish-Americans in New York: New York Mills
  Holy Saturday, March-April, Saturday before Easter Sunday

Polish-Americans in New York: Orange County
  Assumption, Feast of the (Our Lady of the Flowers),
    August 15

Polish-Americans in Ohio
  St. Andrew's Eve (Andrzejki), November 29-30

**Polish-Americans in Pennsylvania: National Shrine of Our
Lady of Czestochowa, Doylestown**
  Polish Festival, first weekend in September

Polish-Americans in Washington, D.C.
  Wreaths, Wianki Festival of, June 23

Polish National Shrine of Czestochowa, Poland
  Our Lady of Czestochowa, Feast of, May 3

Polynesia
  New Year's Day, when the Pleiades appear

Pomo Indians in California: Cotati
  Indian Day, August

**Pomo Indians in California: Indian Grinding Rock State Park
near Pine Grove**
  Chaw-Se Big Time Celebration, usually last weekend in
    September

Pomo Indians in California: Kule Loklo Miwok Indian Village
  Acorn Festival, usually weekend after fourth Friday in
    September
  Kule Loklo Celebration, July or August
  Strawberry Festival, spring

Ponca City, Oklahoma
  Cherokee Strip Day, September 16

Ponca Indians in the Great Plains of the United States
  Dance, Sun, usually during summer solstice,
    June 21

Ponape Island, Eastern Caroline Islands
Ponape Feast, winter months

Ponce, Puerto Rico
Our Lady of Guadalupe, December 12

Ponta Delgada, Sao Miguel Island, Azores, Portugal
Holy Ghost, Feast of the (Altura Do Espírito Santo), August

Pont du Fahs, Zaghouan Region, Tunisia
Ceres, Festival, May

Pontevedra, Spain
Exaltation of the Shellfish, fourth Sunday in October
San Benitino de Lerez Festival, July
Vigo Days, October or November

Poole, Dorset, England
Theatre Festival, Brownsea Open Air, last week in July and first week in August

Poona, Maharashtra, India
Agricultural Festival (Pola), during Hindu month of Bhadrapada
Elephant God, Festival of the (Ganesha Chaturthi), fourth day of Hindu month of Bhadrapada
Tamasha Festival, November-December (location rotates)

Popayan, Colombia
Holy Week, March-April, week preceding Easter

Pori, Finland
Jazz Festival, Pori International, four days in mid-July

Porotobelo, Panama
Black Christ, Festival of the, October 21

Portalegre, Portugal
Castelo de Vide, National Festival of, August

Port-au-Prince, Haiti
Independence Day, January 1

Porterville, California
Lemoore Celebration, late August

Porthcurno, Penzance, Cornwall, England
Theatre Festival, Minack, end of June to mid-September

Portland, Oregon
Music Northwest, Chamber, mid-June to late July
Rose Festival, Portland, June

Port Louis, Mauritius
Pilgrimage to Shrine of Father Laval, September 8

Porto, Portugal
Famalicao, International Festival of, August
Gondomar, International Festival of, August
Gulpilhares, International Festival of, July
St. Bartholomew's Festival, August
Theatres of Iberian Expression, International Festival of, November

Porto Alegere, Brazil
Candlemas, February 2

Port of Spain, Trinidad and Tobago
Folklore, Prime Minister's Best Village Trophy Competition and Festival of, three weeks beginning first Saturday in November

Portozelo, Viana do Castelo, Portugal
Folklore Festival of St. Martha of Portozelo, International, August

Portsmouth, Hampshire, England
Portsmouth Festival, mid-May

Portsmouth, New Hampshire
Fawkes Day, Guy, November 5

Portugal
Algarve, National Festival of the, two days in August or September
All Saints' Day, November 1
All Souls' Day (Día de Finados, Day of the Dead), November 2
April Fools' Day, April 1
Ascension Day (Ear of Wheat Thursday, Quinta-Feira da Espiga), May-June, fortieth day after Easter Sunday
Assumption, Feast of the (Dia da Nussa Senhora da Assumçao, Day of Our Lady of the Angels), August 15
Bach Festival, International, June
Castelo de Vide, National Festival of, August
Christmas (Día de Natal; also Día da Familia, Day of the Family), December 25
Christmas Eve (Vespera de Natal), December 24
Corpus Christi (Dia de Corpo de Deus), May-June
Easter (Paschoa), March-April, first Sunday after first full moon after the vernal equinox
Epiphany (Dia dos Reis, Day of the Kings), January 6
Famalicao, International Festival of, August
Folklore, Gouveia International Festival of, August
Folklore Festival, Briteiros, August
Folklore Festival, Sao Torcato International, July
Folklore Festival of St. Martha of Portozelo, International, August
Gondomar, International Festival of, August
Guarda, National Festival of, summer
Gulpilhares, International Festival of, July

Portugal *(cont.)*

Holy Ghost, Feast of the (Altura Do Espírito Santo),
   March-August
Holy Queen, Festival of the (Festa da Rainha Santa Isabel),
   first two weeks in July during even-numbered years
Holy Week (Semana Santo), processions in Covilha and Vila
   do Conde during March-April, week preceding Easter
Immaculate Conception, Feast of the (Festa da Imaculada
   Conceição), December 8
Independence Day, December 1
Lady of Neves, Festival of the, August
Liberty Day, April 25
Maiorga, International Festival of, September
Mardi Gras (Carnaval), February-March, Sunday-Tuesday
   before Ash Wednesday
Martinmas (Feast of Sao Martinho), November 11
Meadela, International Festival of, August
Midsummer (Véspera de São João), June 23-24
Monsanto, National Festival of, every Sunday in September
National Day (Camões Memorial Day), June 10
New Year's Day (Anno Novo), January 1
New Year's Eve (Véspera de Ano Novo), December 31
October Fair, nine days in October
Our Lady of Agony, Festival of, three days in August
Our Lady of Fátima Day, July 13
Our Lady of Miracles (Nossa Senhora dos Milagres or Festa
   de Serreta), September 8-15
Our Lady of Mount Carmel (Senhora do Monte do Carmo),
   October
Our Lady of Nazaré Festival, September 8-18
Palm Sunday (Domingo de Ramos), March-April, the
   Sunday preceding Easter
Pentecost (Pentecoste), May-June, the Sunday fifty days after
   Easter
Pilgrimage at Cercio to Santa Barbara, last Sunday in August
Pilgrimage of Castelejo, September
Pilgrimage to Nossa Senhora dos Altos Ceus
Pilgrimage to Our Lady of Nazo, September
Pilgrimage to the Sanctuary of Our Lady of the Remedies
   (Pardon of Nossa Senhora dos Remédios) and Festival of
   Lamego, early September
Red Waistcoat Festival (Festival of the Colete Encarnado),
   July
St. Anthony of Padua, Feast of, June 13
St. Barbara's Festival, August
St. Bartholomew's Festival, August
St. Iria Fair, October
St. John the Baptist's Day, June 24
St. Peter's Day, June 29
St. Sylvester's Day, December 31
St. Vicente, Feast Day of (São Vicente), January 22
St. Walter, Festivals of (Festas Gualterianas), four days
   beginning first Sunday in August
Santarém, International Festival of, second week in June
Santiago Fair and Festival of Setubal, July-August

Tabuleiros Festival (Festa dos Tabuleiros), three or four days
   in mid-July every third year during odd-numbered years
Theatre, International Festival of, June-August
Theatre Competition of Figueira da Foz, Amateur,
   February-April
Theatre Meeting, Viseu Amateur, one week in December
Theatres, Algarve Meeting of Amateur, summer
Theatres of Iberian Expression, International Festival of,
   November
Torredeita, International Festival of, one day in September
Twelfth Night (Epiphany Eve), January 5
Vila Praia de Ancora, International Festival of, June or
   August
Vizela Festival, one week in August

Portuguese-Americans in California: Point Loma
Pentecost, May-June, the Sunday fifty days after Easter

Portuguese-Americans in Massachusetts: Plymouth
Holy Ghost, Festival of the, three days in mid-July

Portuguese-Americans in Rhode Island
Labor Day, first Monday in September

Portuguese Guinea (now Guinea-Bissau)
Mocidade Day, December 1
See also **Guinea-Bissau**

Potam, Sonora, Mexico
Holy Week, March-April, week preceding Easter

Potsdam, New York
Music Festival, Spring, two days during last week in April

Povoa, Braganca, Portugal
Pilgrimage to Our Lady of Nazo, September

Poznan, Poland
Art, Biennial of Children's, June during odd-numbered years

Prague, Czechoslovakia
Spartakiade, eight days in June every five years
Spring Festival, Prague, May 12-June 4

Prahova, Romania
Pages of History, last weekend in July
Red Inn Festival, last Sunday in June

Prambanan near Jogjakarta, Java, Indonesia
Ballet Festival, Ramayana, May-October, four consecutive
   nights during each full moon

Prayag, India
Mauni Amavasya, 15th day of waning half of Hindu month
   of Magha

Pretoria, South Africa
Republic Day (Union Day), May 31

Prilep, Macedonia, Yugoslavia
Theatre Festival, "Vojdan Cernodrinski," early June

Prince Edward Island, Canada
Charlottetown Festival, June-September
Potato Blossom Festival, last week in July

Prince George, British Columbia, Canada
Snowgolf Championship, three days in February

Prizren, Serbia, Yugoslavia
Theatre Amateurs, Encounter of Yugoslav, October

Provence, France
Holy Maries, Feast of (La Fête des Saintes Maries), May 24-25
St. Gens, Festival of (La Fête de St. Gens), twice yearly:
Sunday following May 15 at Monteux and first weekend in
September at Beaucet
St. Martha, Feast of (Fête de la Tarasque), last Sunday in
June and July 29

Providence, Rhode Island
Carberry Day, every Friday the 13th
Independence Day, May 4

Provins, France
Harvest Festival of Provins, France, last weekend in August

Puebla, Mexico
Cinco de Mayo, May 5
St. Francis of Assisi, Festival of, early October

Puebla de Guaman, Huelva, Andalusia, Spain
Pilgrimage of the Virgen de la Pena (Romería of the Virgen
de la Pena), last Sunday in April

Pueblo Indians in northeastern Arizona
New Year (Wüwüchim), four days, including eve of new moon
in November

Puerto Rico
All Saints' Day, November 1
Candlemas (Virgin de la Candelaria), February 2
Casals Festival, 16 days in June
Christmas, December 25
Columbus Day (Discovery Day), October 12
Constitution Day (Commonwealth Day), July 25
Craft's Fair, three days in July, including July 17
Emancipation of the Slaves Day, March 22
Epiphany, January 6
Hostos, Birthday of, Eugenio Maria de (Hostos Day),
January 11

Immaculate Conception, Feast of the (Fiesta de la
Inmaculada Concepción de María), December 8
Jayuya Festival of Indian Lore (Jayuya Indian Festival),
mid-November
Mardi Gras, February-March, before Ash Wednesday
Midsummer, June 23-24
Our Lady of Guadalupe, December 12
Rivera Day, July 17
St. Anthony of Padua, Feast of, June 13
St. James the Greater's Day (Fiesta of Santiago),
July 25
St. John the Baptist's Day (San Juan Bautista), one week,
including June 24
St. Michael's Day, end of September

Pugwash, Nova Scotia, Canada
Gathering of the Clans, July 1

Pulilan, Quezon, Luzon Island, Philippines
Water Buffalo Festival (Carabao), May 14 or 15

Punjab (now a state in India and a province of Pakistan)
Harvest Festival (Lohri), three days during Hindu month of
Pausha
Lights, Festival of (Dewali and Tika Festival), one week
during waning half of Hindu month of Karthika, including
15th day
Mother Goddess, Festival of Durga, the (Navaratri), first
ten days of waxing half of Hindu month of Asvina
New Year (Vaisakhi or Baisakha), first day of Hindu month
of Vaisakha

Puno, Peru
Puno, Día del, November 5

Punxsutawney, Pennsylvania
Groundhog Day, February 2

Pura Besakih temple, Bali, Indonesia
Eka Dasa Rundra, once every hundred years

Puri, Orissa, India
Chandan Yatra, 21 days beginning third day of waxing half
of Hindu month of Vaisakha
Jhulan Latra, full moon day of Hindu month of
Sravana
Juggernaut (Rath Yatra, Festival of Jagannatha), second day
of waxing half of Hindu month of Ashadha

Purilia District, West Bengal, India
Purilia Chhau Festival, April 11-13

Pushkar Lake, Pushkar, Rajasthan, India
Pushkar Fair, begins night before full moon of Hindu month
of Karthika

Putney, Vermont
Music Festival, Yellow Barn, five weeks in July and August

Qatar
Independence Day, September 3

Qingdao, Shandong, China
Sugar Ball Show, 16th day of first lunar month

Quapaw, Oklahoma
Powwow, Ottawa, one in August and one in September
Powwow, Quapaw, second weekend in July

Quapaw Indians in Oklahoma: Quapaw
Powwow, Quapaw, second weekend in July

Quebec, Canada
Carnaval, Quebec, ten days in February
Chicoutimi Olden-Days Carnival, ten days in February
Dollard des Ormeaux, Fête de, May 24
Lennoxville, Festival, July-August
Mardi Gras (Carnaval), February-March
Music Festival, Orford International, eight weeks in July
  and August
Pilgrimage to St. Anne d'Auray, July 26
St. Anne's Day, July 26
St. John the Baptist's Day, June 24
Summer Festival, ten days in July
Western Festival, September

Quebec City, Quebec, Canada
Carnaval, Quebec, ten days in February
Mardi Gras (Carnaval), February-March
Summer Festival, ten days in July

Quechua Indians in Peru: Puno
Puno, Día del, November 5

Quechua Indians in South America
St. James's the Greater's Day (Fiesta of the Llamas), July 25

Queens, New York
United States Open Tennis Championships, September

Queensland, Australia
Arts, North Queensland Festival of, three weeks in December
Carnival of Flowers, end of September-early October
Drama Festival, Warana (Blue Skies), two weeks in
  September-October
Joy of Living, one week in September-early October
Labour Day, May 3
Outback Festival, ten days in August during odd-numbered
  years
Spring Festival, Warana (Blue Skies), September-
  October

Queven, France
Assumption, Feast of the, August 15

Quezon, Luzon Island, Philippines
Ballet Festival, National, May
Black Nazarene Fiesta, January 1-9
People Power Anniversary, February 25
Water Buffalo Festival (Carabao), May
  14 or 15

Quileute Indians in Washington: Quinault Nation, Taholah
Taholah Days, Chief, July fourth weekend

Quimper, Finistere, France
Cornwall, Festival of, one week in July

Quinault Indians in Washington: Quinault Nation, Taholah
Taholah Days, Chief, July fourth weekend

Quintana Roo, Mexico
Patron Crosses, Fiesta of the, late April

Quitovaca, Sonora, Mexico
Wíikita Festivals, winter festival at Archie, Arizona;
  summer festival at Quitovaca, Sonora, Mexico

Rajasthan, India
Bharatiya Lok Kala Festival, annual, date varies
Drama Festival, Rajasthan Academy, usually February or
  March
Pushkar Fair, begins night before full moon of Hindu month
  of Karthika
Teej, third day of waxing half of Hindu month of Sravana

Rajasthan and elsewhere in northern India
Gangaur, Gauri, or Parvati Tritiya, 18-day festival during
  Hindu month of Chaitra

Rajputanan women in India: Bengal
Shasti, Festival of (Aranya Shasti)

Rakuhoji Temple, Yamatomura, Ibaraki, Japan
Demon-God Festival, one day in April

Rama Nagar, Uttar Pradesh, India
Rama Leela Festival, between seven and 31 days in
  September-October

Randlett, Whiterocks, Utah
Dance, Ute Bear (Ma'makoni-ni'tkap), three to five days
  in April

Rapid City, South Dakota
Powwow and Expo, Black Hills and Northern Plains Indian,
  July 10-11

Rasinari, Sibiu, Romania
Pastoral Album, third Sunday in April

Rättvik, Sweden
Folk Dance and Music, International Festival of
(Rattviksdansen), one week in July-August
Midsummer (Midsommer Day), begins Friday evening before
June 24

Ravello, Italy
Music Festival, Ravello (Festival Musicale di Ravello), four
to five days during first week in July

Rawalpindi, Pakistan
Pakistan Day, March 23

Razboieni, Neamt, Romania
Razboieni, Festival of, last Sunday in July

Realmonte, Italy
St. Roch's Day (San Rocco), August 16

Rebild, North Jutland, Denmark
Independence Day (Rebild Festival), July 4

**Recklinghausen, North Rhine-Westphalia, Federal Republic
of Germany**
Ruhr Festival, May-June

Red Bird Smith Ceremonial Grounds near Vian, Oklahoma
Smith Ceremony, Red Bird, August 17

Red Cliff Indian Reservation near Bayfield, Wisconsin
Powwow, Ojibwa, August or September

Redlands, California
Music Festival, Redlands Bowl Summer, Tuesday and
Friday evenings from late June to late August

Red Lodge, Montana
Nations, Festival of, nine days in early August

Red Rock, Oklahoma
Powwow, Otoe-Missouri, July

Regina, Saskatchewan, Canada
Buffalo Days, six days in July-August
Riel, Trial of, Tuesdays, Wednesdays and Fridays in
June-August

Rennes, Ille-et-Vilaine, France
Arts, Festival of Traditional, March
Theatre, Festival of Cafe, November

Reno, Nevada
Air Races, National Championship, three or four days

ending second weekend after Labor Day, first Monday in
September

Resita, Caras-Severin, Romania
Spring Pageant, first weekend in April

Rethymon, Crete, Greece
Wine Festival, two weeks in July

Reykjavik, Iceland
Arts Festival, Reykjavik, 16 days in June during even-
numbered years

Rhineland, Germany
Linden Tree Festival (Lindenfest), second weekend in July

Rhode Island
Admission Day, May 29
America's Cup, August 22, whenever a challenger comes
forth
Black Ship Day, last weekend in July
Cajun and Bluegrass Festival, first weekend in September,
including Labor Day
Carberry Day, every Friday the 13th
Christmas in Newport, month of December
Gaspee Days, 16 days in May-June
Heritage Month, May
Independence Day, May 4
Jazz Festival, JVC, three days in mid-August
Labor Day, first Monday in September
Music Festival, Newport, two weeks in July
Newport to Bermuda Race, June during even-numbered
years
Penguin Plunge, January 1
Powwow, Narragansett, August
Victory Day, second Monday in August

Rhodes, Greece
Cronia
Folk Dance Theatre of Rhodes, June-October

Rhodesia (now divided into Zambia and Zimbabwe)
Easter, March-April, first Sunday after first full moon after
the vernal equinox
Independence Day, November 11

Rhymney Valley District, Wales
Arts Festival, Rhymney Valley, last two weeks in October

Ribatejo, Portugal
Red Waistcoat Festival (Festival of the Colete Encarnado),
July
Tabuleiros Festival (Festa dos Tabuleiros), three or four days
in mid-July every third year during odd-numbered
years

Ribe, Denmark
Stork Day, May 8

Ribeauvillé, France
Flutes, Day of the (Pffiferdaj), first Sunday of September

Richmond, North Yorkshire, England
Richmondshire Festival, May-June during odd-numbered years

Richmond, Missouri
Mushroom Festival, first weekend in May

Richterswil, Switzerland
Turnip Lantern Festival (Rebenlichter), November 10-11

Ricon Indian Reservation near Oceanside, California
All Souls' Day (Night of the Candle Ceremony), November 2

Rijeka, Croatia, Yugoslavia
Rijeka Summer, July-August

Rio de Janeiro, Brazil
Foundation Day, January 20
Mardi Gras (Carnival), February-March, the four days before Ash Wednesday
Mambembao, January-March
St. Sebastian's Day, January 20

Rio Dulce in Argentina
Sumamao, Fiesta de, December 26

Río Frío, Colombia
St. Isidore of Seville, Feast of (San Isidro), April 4

Rio Grande pueblos
Dance, Buffalo, November to January

Rio Vermelho, Brazil
Iemanj Festival, February

Riva, Austria
Good Friday (Kar Freitag), March-April, Friday preceding Easter Sunday

Rivadavia, Orense, Spain
Showcase of Rivadavia, May

River Kwai Bridge, Kanchanaburi, Thailand
River Kwai Bridge Week, last week in November

Riverside, California
Easter (Sunrise Service), March-April, first Sunday after first full moon after the vernal equinox

Rizal, Luzon Island, Philippines
Moro-Moro Play, April or May
Passion Play, Cenaculo, March-April, Holy Week

Rjukan, Norway
Pageant Day, Sun, end of January-beginning of February

Rochester, Michigan
Music Festival, Meadowbrook, twelve weeks from mid-June to last week in August

Rockfish, North Carolina
Cherokee of Hoke Intertribal Festival, fourth Saturday in July

Rockland, Maine
Maine Lobster or Seafoods Festival, three days in late July-early August

Rockland and Thomaston, Maine
Schooner Days, weekend after July 4

Rockport, Maine
Bay Chamber Concerts, nine Thursday evenings in July and August

The Rocks, Sydney, New South Wales, Australia
Australia Day at the Rocks, January 26; observed late January

Romania
Acacia Day, first Sunday in May
All Souls' Day, November 2
Ascension Day, May-June, fortieth day after Easter Sunday
Blajini or the Meek, Feast of the (Sarbatoarea Blajinilor), April, second Monday after Easter
Christmas (Crăciun), December 25
Christmas Eve (Noaptea de Crăciun, Ajunul Crăciunului), December 24
Citadel Festival, second Sunday in June
Comedy, Week of, autumn
Dance Festival, Hora at Prislop (Prislop Round), second Sunday in August
Dance of Transylvania, Men's (Caluser or Caluseri), third week in January
Dionysiad, first Sunday in October
Easter (Duminica Paştilor), March-April, first Sunday after first full moon after the vernal equinox
Easter Monday (Lunia Paştilor), March-April, Monday after Easter
Encounter with History, first Sunday in May
Eternal Heroes, Festival of, second weekend in July
Folklore Festival, Arad, August 24
Folklore Festival, "Hercules," first week in August
Folklore Festival, Maramuresean, last weekend in December
Folklore Festival, National, month of August

Romania *(cont.)*

Gala of One-Man Shows, ten to 12 days in October or November

Good Friday (Vinerea Mare), March-April, Friday preceding Easter Sunday

Harvest, Wheat, late summer

Holy Saturday (Sâmbăta Mare), March-April, Saturday before Easter Sunday

Holy Week (Saptamînapatimilor), March-April, week preceding Easter

In the Sunlit Plain, first week in June

Kalojan or Caloian Ceremony (Kalos Johannes or Kalos Adonis), Monday preceding Assumption, August 25

Liberation Day, August 23

Lime-Tree Day, last Sunday in June

Maidens' Fair on Mount Gaina (Tirgul de fete de pe muntele Gaina), third Sunday in July

Martyrs' Day, Forty, March 9

May Day (Armindini), May 1

Memorial Day (Day of the Dead), May 31

Mountains, Festival of the (Nedeia Muntilor), last weekend in June

Mount Ceahlau Feast, second Sunday in August

National Day, December 1

Nation of Heroes, first Sunday in July

New Year's Day (Anul Nou), January 1

New Year's Eve, December 31

Oltenian Ballad, first weekend in October

Pages of History, last weekend in July

Pastoral Album, third Sunday in April

Pentecost (Rusalii), May-June, the Sunday fifty days after Easter, one week beginning Pentecost Eve

Peony Day, second Sunday in May

Pintea the Brave Day, first Sunday in September

Plays, Festival of Short, one week in February

Razboieni, Festival of, last Sunday in July

Red Inn Festival, last Sunday in June

Republic Day, December 30

Romanian ''Calus,'' last weekend in August

Ropotine, 28th day after Easter

St. Basil's Day (Sfântul Vasile), January 1, Gregorian calendar (N.S.); January 14, Julian calendar (O.S.)

St. George's Day, April 23

St. Lazarus's Day, March-April, Saturday before Palm Sunday

Silvas Festival, second Sunday in June

Song to Romania, June during odd-numbered years

Spring, Harghita, third Sunday in May

Spring Pageant, first weekend in April

Sunrise Festival, last Sunday in April during even-numbered years

Theatre, Festival of Contemporary, one week in January

Theatre, Festival of Youth, odd-numbered years in autumn

Theatres, Festival of National, one week in September or October

Tinjaua, early May

Tismana Garden Festival, August 15

Trinity Sunday, May-June, observed first Sunday after Pentecost

Weighing Festival, second Sunday in May

Winter Traditions, Festival of, last week in December

Yule, December 22

Romania (seashore resorts)

Sea Celebrations, one week ending first Sunday in August

Romanian Romany and Slavic people

Green George Festival, April 24

Roman people

Ides, first day of any month in the Roman calendar

Romans, Drome, France

Music Weeks in Drome, Contemporary, two weeks in June-July

Romany and others' pilgrimage to Les Saintes-Maries-de-la-Mer, Provence, France

Holy Maries, Feast of (La Féte des Saintes Maries), May 24-25

Romany people

Green George Festival, April 24

Romany people in southern Europe

Palm Sunday, March-April, the Sunday preceding Easter

Rome, Georgia

Heritage Holidays, mid-October

Rome, Italy

Baths of Caracalla (Terme di Caracalla), first week in July to second week in August

Candlemas, February 2

Holy Thursday, March-April, Thursday preceding Easter

Holy Week, March-April, week preceding Easter

Mardi Gras, February-March, eight days

Opera, Rome Open-Air Festival of Summer, July-August

Palm Sunday, March-April, the Sunday preceding Easter

Robigalia, April 25

St. Agnes Eve, January 20

St. Anthony of Padua, Feast of, June 13

St. Cecilia's Day, November 22

St. Frances of Rome, Feast Day of, March 9

St. John Lateran's Dedication, November 9

St. Peter's Chair, Festival of, January 18

Rome (ancient)

Agonalia or Agonia (Feast of Janus), January 9

Rome (ancient) *(cont.)*
Bacchanalia, spring
Bean Calends, June 1
Blood, Day of, March 24, climax of six-day festival
Bona Dea (Great Mother Festival), May 1
Castor and Pollux, Festival of, July 8
Cerealia, beginning of April
Compitalia
Consualia, August 21 and December 15
Dog Days, early July-early August
Faunalia, February 13 and December 15
Feralia, February 21
Floralia, April 28-May 3
Fontalia (Festival of Fountains), October 13
Fornacalia (Fornax or Feast of Ovens), one week beginning about February 17
Forum Boarium, the Temple of Hercules
Furrinalia, July 25
Hilaria, March 15
Horse Sacrifice, October, October 15
Juno Caprotina, July 7
Juturnalia, January 11
Larentalia
Lemuralia or Lemuria, Festival of the Dead, 9th, 11th, and 15th of May
Liberalia, March 17
Ludi, dates varied
Lupercalia, mid-February
Magna Mater, April 4
Matralia, June 11
Opalia, December 19
Opiconsivia, August 25
Parentalia, February 13-21
Parilia or Palilia (Festival of Pales), April 21
Quirinalia, February 17
Saturnalia, December 17-23
Terminalia, February 23
Vestalia, June 7-15
Volcanalia, August 23

Roncesvalles, Navarre, Spain
Penitents, Procession of the (La Procesion De La Penitencia), May-June, week preceding Pentecost

Ronne, Bornholm, Denmark
Music Festival, Ronne, Wednesdays and Fridays in July and August

Rosebud, South Dakota
Powwow Days, Rosebud, August
Rosebud Tribal Fair, August

Roseville, Ohio
Pottery Festival, three days during weekend nearest July 20

Rothernburg on the Tauber, Bavaria, Federal Republic of Germany
Master Draught Pageant (Meistertrunk Pageant), May-June, Pentecost, fifty days after Easter

Rotterdam, Netherlands
Holland Festival, 23 days in June

Rouen, France
St. Joan of Arc, Feast of (Fête de Jeanne d'Arc), second Sunday in May

Rouergue, Aveyron, France
Folkloric Festival of Rouergue, International, one week in August

Round Top, Texas
Festival-Institute at Round Top, late May to mid-July

Rovaniemi, Finland
Winter Games, Ounasvaara International, two days in mid-March

Rovinj, Croatia, Yugoslavia
Rovinj Festival, end of August

Roxbury, Virginia
Chickahominy Fall Festival, usually weekend over fourth Saturday in September

Royal Albert Hall, London, England
Last Night, a Saturday in mid-September
Wood Promenade Concerts, Henry, nine weeks from mid-July to mid-September

Ruski Krstur, Vojvodina, Yugoslavia
Drama Memorial, Riznic-Djadja, April
"Red Rose" Festival of Culture, June-July

Russia
Assumption, Feast of the (Uspeniye Presvyato or Bogoroditzy), August 15, Gregorian calendar (N.S.); August 28, Julian calendar (O.S.)
Boat or Baydar, Festival of the, early spring
Christmas (Rozhdestvo Khristovo), December 25
Christmas Eve (Sochelnik), December 24
Easter (Paskha), March-April, first Sunday after first full moon after the vernal equinox
Easter Monday, March-April, Monday after Easter
Epiphany (Bogoyavleniye and Blessing of the Waters), January 6, Gregorian calendar (N.S.); January 19, Julian calendar (O.S.)
Exaltation of the Cross (Vozdvizheniye), September 14
Good Friday (Velikaya Pyatnitza, Great Friday), March-April, Friday preceding Easter Sunday

Russia *(cont.)*
Holy Saturday (Velikaya Subbota, Great Saturday), March-
  April, Saturday before Easter Sunday
Holy Thursday (Votjak or Udmurt), March-April,
  Thursday preceding Easter
Honey Day, August 1
Horns, Festival of (Kil'vey), spring
Lenin, Anniversary of the Death of, January 21
Lent, February-March, forty-day season preceding Easter
Mardi Gras (Maslyanitza, Butter Week), February-March,
  the week before Ash Wednesday
Moscow Stars Festival, nine days in May
New Year's Day (Novyi God), January 1
New Year's Eve, December 31
Pentecost, May-June, the Sunday fifty days after Easter
Plow, Festival of the (Saban Tuy), June 25
St. Andrew's Day, November 30
St. Basil's Day (Den' Svyatovo Vasil'ya), January 1,
  Gregorian calendar (N.S.); January 14, Julian calendar
  (O.S.)
St. George's Day (Jerjew Den), April 23 and November 26
St. Lazarus's Day, March-April, Saturday before Palm
  Sunday
St. Nicholas's Day, December 6
Sts. Peter and Paul Day, June 29
Transfiguration, Feast of the, August 6
Trinity Sunday, May-June, observed first Sunday after
  Pentecost by Western Church; observed the Monday after
  Pentecost by Eastern Orthodox Church
Winter Festival, Russian, three weeks in December-January
White Night Festival, nine days in June

Russia (prerevolutionary)
Semik, seventh Thursday after Easter

Russian-Americans
Christmas, December 25

Russian-Americans in Kansas: Ellis County
St. Nicholas's Day, December 6

Rutten, Limburg, Belgium
Game of St. Evermaire (Spel van Sint Evermarus), May 1

Rwanda
Democracy Day, January 28
Independence Day, July 1
Kamarampaka Day, September 25
Peace and National Unity Day, July 5

Rye, Sussex, England
Rye Festival, first week in September

Rzeszow, Poland
Theatre Meetings, Rzeszow, April

Sabac, Serbia, Yugoslavia
Ljubisa Jovanovic, Festivities in Honor of, October

Sabah, Malaysia
Harvest Festival, Padi, May 30-31

Sac and Fox Indians in Oklahoma: Stroud
Indian Memorial Stampede Rodeo, summer

Sacaton, Arizona
Gila River Festival, second weekend in March

Sacramento, California
Jazz Jubilee, Sacramento Dixieland, four days over last
  weekend in May

Saidnaya near Damascus, Syria
Assumption, Feast of the ('Id Rakad-ai-Sayyidah),
  August 15, Gregorian calendar (N.S.); August 28, Julian
  calendar (O.S.)

Saint-Aignan, Loir-et-Cher, France
Art and History, Festival of, Thursdays, Saturdays, and
  Sundays in August

St. Albans, Vermont
Vermont Maple Festival, three days in April

St. Andrews, Fife, Scotland
St. Andrew's Festival, ten days in February during odd-
  numbered years

St. Andrew's University, Scotland
Raisin Monday, November

St. Ann's, Cape Breton, Nova Scotia, Canada
Gaelic Mod, first full week in August

St. Boniface, Winnipeg, Manitoba, Canada
Voyageur, Festival du, about one week in February

St. Catharines, Ontario, Canada
Folk Arts Festival, May-June
Grape and Wine Festival, Niagara, ten days in late September

St. Croix, Virgin Islands
Christmas Festival, Caribbean, two weeks beginning
  December 23
Epiphany, January 6; Christmas Festival ends January 6

Saint-Denis, Seine, France
Music Festival of Saint-Denis, May-June

Sainte-Baume, France
Musical Festival of La Sainte-Baume, two weeks in
  July-August

Saint-Baume, France *(cont.)*
St. Mary Magdalene, Feast of, July 22 (pilgrimage to holy cave)

Ste. Genevieve, Missouri
Jour de Fête a Sainte Genevieve Days of Celebration, second weekend in August

Saintes, France
Music, Saintes Festival of Ancient (Saintes Festival de Musique Ancienne), one week in early July

St. Helier, Jersey, Channel Islands, Great Britain
Battle of Flowers, second Thursday in August

Saint-Hubert, Belgium
Wallonia, Festival of (Festival de Wallonie), June-September or October

St. Ives, Cornwall, England
Silver Ball, Hurling the, Sunday nearest or Monday after February 3

St. John's, Antigua
Police Week Festival, August-September

St. John's, Newfoundland, Canada
Arts, Summer Festival of the, month of July

St. Kitts
Christmas, December 25

St. Kitts-Nevis
Statehood Day, February 27

St.-Léonard-de-Noblat, France
Quintane, La, second Sunday of November

Saint-Lô, Burgundy, France
Mardi Gras (Carnival), February-March

Saint Louis, Missouri
Muny, The, mid-June to end of August
Opera Theatre of Saint Louis, late May to end of June
Ragtime and Traditional Jazz Festival, Annual National, five days in mid-June

Saint Louis Municipal Opera, Saint Louis, Missouri
Muny, The, mid-June to end of August

St. Lucia
Independence Day, February 22

St. Maarten
Concordia Day, November 11

St. Margarethen, Burgenland, Austria
Passion Play, May-September; every five years

St. Märgen, Black Forest, Germany
Nativity of the Virgin, Feast of the (Pferdeweihe, Blessing of Horses), September 8

St. Paul, Minnesota
Nations, Festival of, last weekend in April
Winter Carnival, St. Paul, ten days including last week in January

St. Petersburg, Russia (formerly Leningrad, Russia, USSR)
Lent, February-March, forty-day season preceding Easter
See also **Leningrad, Russia, USSR**

Saint Pierre and Miquelon
Armistice Day, November 11

Saint-Tite, Quebec, Canada
Western Festival, September

St. Vincent
Caricom Day, observed on or near July 4
Columbus Day (Discovery Day), January 22
Independence and Thanksgiving Day, October 27
Mardi Gras (Carnival), February-March, before Ash Wednesday

Saipan, Marianas
St. Isidore the Husbandman or Farmer, Feast of, May 15

Saitama, Japan
Chichibu Yamaburi, three days in early December

Sakata City, Yamagata, Japan
Shrine Festival, Kuromori Hie, mid-February

Salaj, Romania
Weighing Festival, second Sunday in May

Salé, Morocco
Fast, Feast of Breaking the, first day of Islamic month of Shawwal
Sacrifice, Feast of ('Id al-Kabir), tenth-twelfth days of Islamic month of Dhu'l-Hijjah
Wax Festival, November

Salina, Oklahoma
Oklahoma Historical Day, October 10

Salisbury, Wiltshire, England
Arts, Salisbury Festival of the, September

Salish Indians in Vermont: Arlee
Powwow, Arlee Fourth of July Celebration, first weekend in July

Salley, South Carolina
Chitlin' Strut, Saturday or Sunday after fourth Thursday in November, Thanksgiving

Salt Lake City, Utah
Arts Festival, Utah, five days in late June
Pioneer Day, July 24

Salvador, Bahia, Brazil
Bonfim Festival, ten days beginning second Thursday in January
Jesus dos Navegantes, Bom, January 1

Salzburg, Austria
Easter Festival (Osterfestspiele), March-April, from Palm Sunday to Easter Monday
Hellbrunn Festival (Fest in Hellbrunn), first two weekends in August
Mozart Week (Mozartwoche), nine days at end of January
Salzburg Festival (Salzburger Festspiele), five weeks in July and August
"Silent Night, Holy Night" Celebration, December 24
Theatre Festival, Street (Strassentheater), July-August

Samal, Bataan, Luzon Island, Philippines
Passion Play, Cenaculo, March-April, Holy Week

Sami people
See **Lapp people**

Sanam Luang in front of the Grand Palace, Bangkok, Thailand
Kite Flying Season, February-April on weekday afternoons

San Antonio, New Mexico
St. Anthony of Padua, Feast of, June 13

San Antonio, Texas
Alamo Day, March 6
Cinco de Mayo, May 5
Folklife Festival, Texas, four days during first week in August
Our Lady of Guadalupe (Festival Guadalupaño), Sunday nearest December 12
San Antonio, Fiesta, ten days in April, including April 21
San Jacinto Day, April 21

San Carlos, Arizona
Apache Fair, weekend nearest November 11

Sanchi near Vidisha, India
Buddha's Birthday, Enlightenment, and Salvation (Buddha Jayanti), full moon day of Hindu month of Vaisakha

San Cristóbal Totonicapán, Guatemala
Burning the Devil (La Quema del Diablo), December 7

Sandia Pueblo, New Mexico
New Year's Day, January 1

San Diego, California
Cabrillo Day, six days in September
Cinco de Mayo, May 5
Our Lady of Guadalupe, December 12
Primavera, Fiesta de la, three days in May
Shakespeare Festival, San Diego National, early June through mid-September

San Diego County, California
St. Francis of Assisi, Feast of, October 4

San Dionisio, Rizal, Luzon Island, Philippines
Moro-Moro Play, April or May

San Felipe Pueblo, New Mexico
Candlemas, February 2
Dance, Green Corn
St. Peter's Day, June 29
St. Philip, Feast of and Green Corn Dance, May 1

San Fernando, Pampanga, Philippines
Christmas Season (Giant Lantern Festival), December 24-25

San Francisco, California
Beethoven Festival, three weeks beginning mid-June
Cherry Blossom Festival, one week in April
Music Festival, Stern Grove Midsummer, mid-June to mid-August for ten Sundays
Symphony Pops, San Francisco, three weeks beginning mid-July

Sangli, Maharashtra, India
Tamasha Festival, November-December (location rotates)

San Ildefonso Pueblo, New Mexico
Dances, Matchina, December 25
Jicarilla Apache Fair, September 14-15
St. Ildephonsus, Feast Day of, January 23

San Isidro, Quezon, Luzon Island, Philippines
Water Buffalo Festival (Carabao), May 14 or 15

San Jacinto, Texas
San Jacinto Day, April 21

San Juan, Puerto Rico
Casals Festival, 16 days in June
Mardi Gras, February-March, before Ash Wednesday

San Juan Bautista, California
St. John the Baptist's Day (Fiesta de San Juan Bautista), June 24

San Juan Capistrano Mission, San Juan Capistrano, California
Swallows of San Juan Capistrano, swallows arrive March 19 and depart October 23

San Juan de los Lagos, Jalisco, Mexico
Candlemas, February 2

San Juan Pueblo, New Mexico
Arts and Crafts Show, Annual Eight Northern Indian Pueblos, July 18-20
Dance, Basket, January 27
Dance, Deer, February, date varies
Dance, Matchina, December 24-25
Dance, Turtle, December 26
Harvest Dance, last week in September
Pope Foot Race, Annual, July 20
St. John the Baptist's Day (San Juan Pueblo Feast Day), June 24

Sanjusangendo, Kyoto, Japan
Adults Day (Seijin-no-hi), January 15

San Luis Obispo, California
Mozart Festival, San Luis Obispo, six days in late July and early August

San Marcos, Texas
Chilympiad, Republic of Texas Chili Cookoff, third weekend in September

San Marino
St. Agatha Festival, February 5
St. Marinus Day, September 3
San Marino, Founding of, September 3

San Martin, Meta, Colombia
St. Martin's Day (Quadrilles of San Martin), November 11

San Pablo de los Montes, Toledo, Spain
Cow, Festival of the (Fiesta de la Vaca), January 25

San Pedro de Casta, Peru
Agua, La Fiesta de, first Sunday in October

Santa Ana Pueblo, New Mexico
Puye Cliff Ceremonial, last weekend in July
St. Anne's Day, July 26
St. James the Greater's Day, July 25
St. Peter's Day, June 29

Santa Barbara, California
Music Academy of the West Summer Festival, eight weeks from last week in June to third week in August
Old Spanish Days, five days during full moon in August
Street Painting Festival, I Madonnari Italian, last weekend in May

Santa Clara Pueblo, New Mexico
Dance, Deer and Buffalo, February, date varies
Dances, Matchina, December 25
Holy Innocents' Day, December 28
St. Clare of Assisi, Feast of, August 11; observed August 12 with Corn, Harvest, Comanche or Buffalo dances

Santa Cruz, Mexico
All Saints' Day (El Día de los Santos), November 1

Santa Cruz de la Palma, Santa Cruz de Tenerife, Spain
Virgen Lustral Festival, Bajada de la, every five years in June

Santa Cruz de Tenerife, Spain
Virgen Festival, Bajada de la, every four years in June
Virgen Lustral Festival, Bajada de la, every five years in June

Santa Cruz Etla, Mexico
Virgin of Carmen, Fiesta of, July 15

Santa Eulalia, Guatemala
Sealing the Frost, April-early May

Santa Fe, New Mexico
Arts and Crafts Show, Eight Northern Indian Pueblos Spring, April 19-20
Indian Market, third weekend in August
Music Festival, Santa Fe Chamber, seven weeks in July and August
Opera Festival, Santa Fe, eight weeks in July and August or September
St. Francis of Assisi, Feast of, October 4
Santa Fe Fiesta, three to four days over second weekend in September

Santa Fe Indian Market Plaza, Santa Fe, New Mexico
Indian Market, third weekend in August

Santander, Spain
Music and Dance, Santander International Festival of (Festival Internacional de Musica y Danza de Santander), July-August

Sant'Arcangelo di Romagna, Emilia-Romagna, Italy
Theatre Festival in the Square, July-August

Santarém, Portugal
Santarém, International Festival of, second week in June

Santarém Portugal (cont.)
Theatre, International Festival of, June-August

Santiago de Compostela, Galicia, Spain
St. James the Greater's Day (Fiesta de Santiago Appostol), July 25, during holy years, when St. James's Day falls on a Sunday

Santiago del Estero Province, Argentina
Exaltation of the Cross, May 3

Santo Domingo Pueblo, New Mexico
All Souls' Day, November 2
Dance, Green Corn
St. Dominic, Feast of, and Corn Dance, August 4
St. Peter's Day, June 29

San Vicente, El Salvador
Flores de Mayo, month of May

Sao Miguel Island, Azores, Portugal
Holy Ghost, Feast of the (Altura Do Espírito Santo), August

São Paulo, Brazil
Assumption, Feast of the (Nossa Senhora dos Navegantes), August 15
Mambembao, January-March

Sao Tomé and Principe
Family Day, December 25
Martyrs Day, February 3
National Day, July 12

Sao Torcato, Braga, Portugal
Folklore Festival, Sao Torcato International, July

Sapporo, Hokkaido, Japan
Snow Festival (Yuki Matsuri), February 8-12

Saraburi, Thailand
Phra Buddha Bat Fair, March

Saragossa, Spain
Virgin of the Pillar, Feast of the (Virgen del Pilar), ten days in October

Sarajevo, Bosnia and Herzegovina, Yugoslavia
October Days of Culture, October
Theatres of Yugoslavia, Festival of Small and Experimental, March 27-April 6

Sarasota, Florida
Circus Festival and Parade, Sarasota, first week in January
Music Festival of Florida, three weekends in June

Saratoga, California
Summer Series, Paul Masson, first weekend in June to last weekend in September

Saratoga Springs, New York
Saratoga Festival (Saratoga Performing Arts Center), early June to early September

Sarawak, Malaysia
Dayak Festival Day (Gawai Dayak), June 1-2
Harvest Festival (Bungan), February

Sarawak people in Malaysia
Christmas, December 25

Sardinia, Italy
All Saints' Day, November 1
Carnival of Mamoiada, February-March, Sunday and Tuesday preceding Ash Wednesday
Redeemer, Feast of the (Festa del Redentore), last Sunday in August
St. Efisio, Festival of, May 1-4
Sardinian Cavalcade (Cavalcata Sarda), last Sunday in May or on Ascension Day

Sariaya, Quezon, Luzon Island, Philippines
Water Buffalo Festival (Carabao), May 14 or 15

Sarlat, Dordogne, France
Theatre, Festival of Plays for the, July-August

Sarnath at Deer Park near Varanasi, India
Buddha's Birthday, Enlightenment, and Salvation (Buddha Jayanti), full moon day of Hindu month of Vaisakha

Sarovar, India
Floating Festival, full moon day of Hindu month of Magha

Sarthe, France
Le Mans Grand Prix, June

Saskatchewan, Canada
Battleford Chautauqua, July
Buffalo Days, six days in July-August
Pike Festival, Northern, June to August
Pioneer Days, July
Riel, Trial of, Tuesdays, Wednesdays and Fridays in June-August
Vesna Festival, six days in May

Saskatoon, Saskatchewan, Canada
Pioneer Days, July
Vesna Festival, six days in May

Sassari, Sardinia, Italy
Sardinian Cavalcade (Cavalcata Sarda), last Sunday in May or on Ascension Day

Sassenheim, Holland
Tulip Festival, last week in April and first week in May

Satara District, Maharashtra, India
Agricultural Festival, during Hindu month of Ashadha

Satawal, Micronesia
New Year, April, month of Ceuta

Saudi Arabia
King's Coronation, November 12
Mecca, Pilgrimage to, eighth through 13th days of Islamic month of Dhu'l-Hijjah
National Day, September 12
Ramadan, ninth Islamic month

Sauk Indians in the United States
Veterans' Day, November 11

Savannah, Georgia
Georgia Week Celebrations, one week in February, including February 12
St. Patrick's Day, March 17

Savoie, France
Dullin Prize Competition, May-June, Thursday to Sunday evening of Ascension Day during even-numbered years

Savonlinna, Finland
Opera Festival, Savonlinna (Savonlinnan Oopperajuhlat), first three weeks in July

Saxon people (ancient)
Yule, December 22

Saxony
Trinity Sunday, May-June, observed first Sunday after Pentecost

Scandinavia
April Fools' Day, April 1
Christmas, December 25
Christmas Eve, December 24
May Day, May 1
Midsummer, June 23-24
New Year's Eve, December 31
Twelfth Night (Epiphany Eve), January 5
Yule, December 22

Scandinavia (ancient)
Juul, Feast of (Winter Solstice Festival), December

Scandinavian-Americans
Fyr-Bal Fest, two days on weekend nearest June 24
Leif Eriksson Day, October 9
St. Lucy's Day, December 13
Walpurgis Night, April 30

Scandinavian-Americans in North Dakota: Minot
Norsk Høstfest, five days in October

Schaghiticoke Indians in Connecticut: Farmington
Powwow, Connecticut River, weekend before Labor Day, first Monday in September

Scheveningen, Netherlands
Holland Festival, 23 days in June
Vlaggetjesdag, anytime from middle to late May

Schiermonnikoog, North Coast Islands, Netherlands
Kallemooi, May-June, Saturday preceding Pentecost

Schleswig, Schleswig-Holstein, Federal Republic of Germany
Castle Gottorf, Festival at, July-August

Schleswig-Holstein, Federal Republic of Germany
Castle Gottorf, Festival at, July-August
Kiel Week, one week in June
May Festival, July-August

Schoten, Belgium
Folk-Dance Festival, International (International Volksdansfestival), one week beginning first weekend after first Sunday in July

Schurz, Nevada
Pinenut Festival, October

Schwechat, Lower Austria, Austria
Nestroy Festival (Nestroy-Spiele), July

Schwenksville, Pennsylvania
Folk Festival, Philadelphia, three days over last weekend in August

Schwetzingen, Baden-Wurttemberg, Federal Republic of Germany
Schwetzingen Festival, April-May

Schwyz, Switzerland
Pilgrimage of the Black Madonna, September 14
Theatre, Great World, every five years in June-September

Scotland
All Saints' Day, November 1
April Fools' Day (Huntigowk Day), April 1
Arts, Perth Festival of the, last two weeks in May

Scotland *(cont.)*

Bank Holiday, first Monday in May
Bannockburn Day, June 24
Beltane, April 30
Bonfire Night, Monday nearest May 24
British Open Golf Tournament, summer
Burns Night, January 25
Burry Man's Walk, second week of August
Candlemas, February 2
Christmas (Yule Day), December 25
Christmas Eve, December 24
Common Ridings Day, June
Craigmillar Festival, June or August
Easter (Pace or Pasch Day), March-April, first Sunday after
  first full moon after the vernal equinox
Easter Monday, March-April, Monday after Easter
Edinburgh Fringe Festival, August-September
Edinburgh International Festival, three weeks beginning third
  week in August
Epiphany, January 6
Exaltation of the Cross (Holyrood or Rude Day),
  September 14
Flitting Day, May 25
Gaelic Mod, two weeks in September-October
Glorious Twelfth, August 12
Good Neighbours Festival, one week in late June
Halloween, October 31
Handsel Monday, January, first Monday of the year
Harvest Home Festival (Kern or Kirn Supper), September 24
Highland Games, on or near August 1 into September
Highland Gathering, Braemar, first Saturday in September
Labour Day, first Monday in May
Lammas, August 1
Leap Year Privilege (Bachelors' Day), February 29
Mardi Gras (Fastern's E'en), February-March, Tuesday before
  Ash Wednesday
Martinmas, November 11
Marymass Fair, third or fourth Monday in August
May Day, May 1
Michaelmas, September 29
Midsummer, June 23-24
Monklands Festival, June
New Year's Day, January 1
Nippy Lug Day, Friday after Ash Wednesday
Operatic Society Festival, Haddo House Choral and,
  late summer
Pentecost, May-June, the Sunday fifty days after Easter
Pitlochry Festival, April-October
Plough Monday, first Monday after Epiphany or Twelfth
  Day, January 6
Quarter Days, February 2, May 15, August 1, and
  November 11
Raisin Monday, November
St. Agnes Eve, January 20
St. Andrew's Day, November 30

St. Andrew's Festival, ten days in February during odd-
  numbered years
St. Bridget's Day, February 1
St. Crispin's Day, October 25
St. Luke's Day (Lukesmas), October 18
St. Magnus Festival, five days over third weekend in June
St. Michael's Eve
Samhain (Summer's End), October 31
Stirling District Festival, May-June
Twelfth Night (Epiphany Eve or Four an' Twenty Day),
  January 5
Up-Helly-Aa, last Tuesday in January
Valentine's Day, February 14
Whit Monday, May-June, Monday after Pentecost
Whuppity Scoorie Day, March 1

Scotland (northern)

New Year's Eve (Hogmanay), December 31

Scottish-Americans

Burns Night, January 25
St. Andrew's Day, November 30

Scottish-Americans in Michigan: Alma

Highland Festival and Games, last weekend in May

**Scottish-Americans in North Carolina: Grandfather Mountain
near Linville**

Highland Games and Gathering of Scottish Clans,
  Grandfather Mountain, second full weekend in July

Scottish-Canadians in Canada: Brantford, Ontario

Highland Games, Brantford, second Saturday in July

Scottish-Canadians in Canada: Pugwash, Nova Scotia

Gathering of the Clans, July 1

**Scottish-Canadians in Canada: St. Ann's, Cape Breton,
Nova Scotia**

Gaelic Mod, first full week in August

Scottish people

Glorious Twelfth, August 12

Sea Islands, Georgia

Music Festival, Golden Isles Chamber, nine days in early May

Seattle, Washington

Bumbershoot, September, four days during first weekend
  in September
Constitution Day, Norway, May 17
Folklife Festival, Northwest, four days over last weekend
  in May
Pacific Northwest Festival, last week in July and first week
  in August
Seafair, 16 days in July-August

Sebei people in Uganda
Christmas (Mukutanik), December 25
Misisi Beer Feast, around October and at Christmas; after
millet harvest, during month of Twamo

Sebring, Florida
Sebring 12 Hours (Automobile Hall of Fame Week), third
week in March

Seetal District, Aargau, Switzerland
Meitlisunntig, second Sunday in January

Seinajoki, Finland
Theatre Summer, Amateur, four days in August

Seine, France
Music Festival of Saint-Denis, May-June

Selangor, Malaysia
Independence Day (Merdeka), August 31

Selcuk, Turkey
Ephesus, Festival of, May

Selkirk, Scotland
Common Ridings Day, June

Sells, Arizona
St. Francis of Assisi, Feast of, October 4

Seminole Indians in Florida
Dance, Green Corn, spring or summer

Seminole Indians in Florida: Okeechobee
Brighton Field Day and Rodeo, third weekend in
February

Seminole Indians in Florida: Seminole Reservation
Seminole Fair, fourth weekend in December

**Seminole Indians in Florida: Seminole Reservation
near Hollywood**
Powwow, Seminole, February

Seminole Indians in Oklahoma: Seminole
Seminole Nation Days, September

Seminole Reservation near Hollywood, Florida
Powwow, Seminole, February

Seminole Reservation, Florida
Seminole Fair, fourth weekend in December

Seminole, Oklahoma
Seminole Nation Days, September

Semite people (ancient)
Puruli, seasonal festival

Sendai, Japan
Double Seventh, August 6-8

Seneca Iroquois Indians
Dance, Green Corn
Midwinter Bear Society Dance
New Year's Day, February

Seneca Iroquois Indians in Canada and the United States
Iroquois White Dog Feast (New Year or Midwinter Festival),
several days, including first quarter moon in January

Senegal
Ashura, first ten days of Islamic month of Muharram
Christmas, December 25
Fast, Feast of Breaking the (Korité Feast), first day of Islamic
month of Shawwal
Independence Day, April 4
New Year (Tabaski), first day of Islamic month of Muharram
Ramadan, ninth Islamic month
Sacrifice, Feast of (Tabaski), tenth-twelfth days of Islamic
month of Dhu'l-Hijjah

Senoufo people in Ivory Coast
New Yam Festival (Odwira), October

Seo de Urgel, Lerida, Spain
San Ermengol Retaule Festival, August

Seoul, Korea
Music Festival, Seoul International, first two weeks in May
Shrine Rite, Royal (Chongmyo Taeje), first Sunday in May

Sequim, Washington
Irrigation Festival, first full weekend in May

Seraikalla, Bihar, India
Dance Festival, Chhau Mask, Chaitra-Parva, April 11-13

Serbia, Yugoslavia
Amateur Stages, Belgrade Review of Experimental, mid-May
Amateurs to Their City, October 20
Christmas, December 25
Comedy Festival, Days of, March
Dances and Songs of Crnorecje, May
Dragacevo Assembly of Village Trumpeters, end of August
First of May Is Our Day, May 1-2
Folklore Festival of the Socialist Republic of Serbia, June
Harvest Festivities, Duzijanca, July
Homolje Motifs, May
Kosovo, Village Festivities of, June
Jovanovic, Festivities in Honor of, October

Serbia, Yugoslavia *(cont.)*
Marble and Sound, July-September
Monodrama and Pantomime, Festival of, April
Mother's Day (Materice), December, second Sunday before
  Christmas
New Year's Eve, December 31
Puppet Theatres of Serbia, September-October
Stage, Classics on the Yugoslav, October
Theatre Amateurs, Encounter of Yugoslav, October
Theatre Amateurs of the Villages of Serbia,
  October
Theatre Community Festival, early September
Theatre Festival, Belgrade Amateur, April
Theatre Festival, Belgrade International, September
Theatre Groups, Regional Review of Kosovo Amateur, April
Theatres, Regional Festival of Serbian Amateur, May-June
Theatres of Serbia, Festival of Amateur, first half of June
Theatres of Serbia, Vujic Encounter of Professional,
  May-June
Vintage Festival, September
Young May, April-May

Serbian people in Yugoslavia
Good Friday (Veliki Petak), March-April, Friday preceding
  Easter Sunday
St. Sava's Day, January 14

Serres, Greece
Gynaecocratia, January 8

Setubal, Portugal
Santiago Fair and Festival of Setubal, July-August

Setumaa, Estonia
Peko, Feast of, October 1

Seville, Spain
Good Friday (Viernes Santo), March-April, Friday preceding
  Easter Sunday
Pilgrimage of Our Lady of Valme (Romario of Our Lady
  of Valme), October 17
Seville Fair (April Fair), one week in March or April,
  usually following Easter

Sewanee, Tennessee
Music Center, Sewanee Summer, last week in June to last
  week in July

Seychelles
Liberation Day, June 5
Republic Day, June 29

Sfax, Sfax Region, Tunisia
Music and Popular Arts, Regional Festival of,
  June

Shahaptian Indians in Oregon: Warm Springs
Powwow, Warm Springs, June
Root Festival, mid-April

Shaitli, Dagestan, USSR
Midwinter Festival (Igbi), usually observed on Sunday nearest
  February 5

Shandong, China
Sugar Ball Show, 16th day of first lunar month

Shau Kei Wan, Hong Kong Island
Tam Kung Festival, eighth day of fourth lunar month

Shawnee, Oklahoma
Powwow, Citizen Band of Potawatomi Indians of Oklahoma,
  last weekend in June

Shawnee Indians in Oklahoma: Quapaw
Powwow, Quapaw, second weekend in July

Sheboygan, Wisconsin
Polar Bear Swim Day, January 1

Shediac, New Brunswick, Canada
Lobster Festival, six days in July

Shelbyville, Tennessee
Tennessee Walking Horse National Celebration, ten days
  in August

Sheridan, Wyoming
Indian Days, All American, last weekend in July or first
  in August

Shetland Islands, Scotland
Up-Helly-Aa, last Tuesday in January

Shiga, Japan
Nagahama Yamakyogen, two days in mid-April
Shrine Festival, Gokoku, October-November

Shimmeisha Shrine, Toyohashi, Aichi, Japan
Shimmeisha Oni Festival, mid-February

Shimoda, Japan
Black Ship Day, May-July, dates vary

Shinnecock Indians in New York: Southampton
Powwow, Shinnecock, first weekend in
  September

Shiprock, New Mexico
Navajo Nation Festival, Shiprock (Northern Navajo Fair),
  usually first weekend in October

Shiraz, Iran (formerly Persopolis, Persia)
Arts, Shiraz Festival of, August-September

Shirone, Niigata, Japan
Kite Battles, June 5-12

Shizuoka, Japan
Children's Day (Kodomo-no-hi; formerly Boys' Festival, Tango No Sekku), May 1-5
Kite Battles of Hamamatsu, May 3-5

Sholapur, Maharashtra, India
Agricultural Festival (Pola), during Hindu month of Bhadrapada

Shoshone Indians in the Great Plains of the United States
Dance, Sun, usually during summer solstice, June 21

Shoshone Indians in Wyoming
Christmas Dances, December
Dance, Sun, July or August
Indian Fair, August

Shoshone Indians in Wyoming: Fort Washakie
Indian Days, late June

Show Low, Arizona
Apache Tribal Fair, first weekend in September, including Labor Day

Shrine Church of St. Anthony of Padua, New York, New York
St. Anthony of Padua, Feast of, June 13

Shrine of Badrinath, Himalayas (pilgrimage to)
New Year (Vaisakhi), first day of Hindu month of Vaisakha

Shrine of St. Anne at Church of St. Jean Baptiste, New York, New York
St. Anne's Day, July 26

Shropshire, England
All Souls' Day, November 2
Summer Festival, Ludlow, last week in June and first week in July
Wrekin and Telford Festival, five or six weeks in April-May

Shumen, Bulgaria
Poetry of Friendship, even-numbered years in March
Theatre Days Named after Drumev, during even-numbered years, date varies

Sibenik, Croatia, Yugoslavia
Child, Yugoslav Festival of the, June-July

Siberia, USSR
Archery Festival (Sur-Kharban), spring

Boat or Baydar, Festival of the, early spring
Clean Tent Ceremony, February

Sibiu, Romania
Pastoral Album, third Sunday in April

Sichuan, China
Torch Festival, 24th-26th days of sixth lunar month

Sicilian-Americans in southern California, Detroit, Michigan, Buffalo, New York, and elsewhere in the United States
St. Joseph of Arimathea, Feast Day of, March 19

Sicily
All Souls' Day (Il Giorno dei Morti), November 2
Ascension Day, May-June, fortieth day after Easter Sunday
Assumption, Feast of the, two weeks including August 15
Assumption, Feast of the (Bowing Procession), August 15
Befana Festival, January 5-6
Easter, March-April, first Sunday after first full moon after the vernal equinox
Exaltation of the Cross, September 14
Holy Thursday (Giovedi Santo), March-April, Thursday preceding Easter
Holy Week, March-April, week preceding Easter
New Year's Day, January 1
St. Agatha Festival, February 5; observed February 3-5
St. Agnes Eve, January 20; five-day festival in February
St. Lucy's Day, December 13
St. Joseph of Arimathea, Feast Day of, March 19

Sicily, Italy
Drama, Cycle of Classical, May-June during even-numbered years
Folklore Festival, International, February
Palermo Festival, first week in October
Pentecost, May-June, the Sunday fifty days after Easter
Theatre Festival, July-September
Theatres, International Meeting of Experimental, April

Sidi-Ali-El Hattab, Zaghouan Region, Tunisia
Popular Festival of Sidi-Ali-El Hattab, April

Siena, Tuscany, Italy
Madonna del Voto Day, August 16
Palio, Festival of the (Festa del Palio, Corso del Palio, or Palio of the Contrade), held twice during the summer: July 2 and August 16

Sieradz, Poland
St. Andrew's Day, November 30

Sierra Leone
Ashura, first ten days of Islamic month of Muharram

Sierra Leone *(cont.)*
Christmas (Boys' Alikali Devils in Bo), December 25
Independence Day, April 27
New Year, one and one-half days in late April or early May
New Year (Tabaski), the first day of Islamic month of Muharram
Night of Power (Lai-Lai-Tu-Gadri, Day of Light), 30th day of Islamic month of Ramadan
Ramadan, ninth Islamic month
Republic Day, April 19
Thanksgiving (Awoojoh), may occur on special occasions and during such holidays as Christmas, Easter, Good Friday, and New Year's Day

Sighetu Marmatiei, Maramures, Romania
Folklore Festival, Maramuresean, last weekend in December

Sigmaringen, Baden-Württemberg, Germany
Wooing a Bride (Brauteln), February-March, Tuesday preceding Ash Wednesday

Silesia
Christmas, December 25
May Day, May 1
Mid-Lent Sunday, March, fourth Sunday in Lent

Siletz, Oregon
Powwow, Nesika Illahee, second weekend in August
Restoration Day, November 18 or following Saturday

Siletz Indian tribes in Oregon: Siletz
Powwow, Nesika Illahee, second weekend in August
Restoration Day, November 18 or following Saturday

Siliana, Siliana Region, Tunisia
Ibnou Abi Dhiaf Festival, July

Silifke, Turkey
Folk Dance and Music Festival, Silifke, May

Silvasul de Jos Commune, Hunedoara, Romania
Silvas Festival, second Sunday in June

Sinala, Constanta County, Romania
Folklore Festival, National, month of August

Sind, Pakistan
Shah Abdul Latif Death Festival, 14-16 days during Islamic month of Safar

Singapore
Arts Festival, Singapore, three weeks in December
Kite Festival, Singapore, three to four weekends in January

Mid-Autumn Festival, 15th, or full moon, day of eighth lunar month
Monkey's Festival (Birthday of Ts'oi, T'in Tai Seng Yeh), 16th day of eighth lunar month
National Day, August 9
Nine Imperial Gods, Festival of, ninth day of ninth lunar month
Panguni Uttiram, two days, including the full moon day of Hindu month of Chaitra
Prince, Birthday of the Third, eighth and ninth days of fourth lunar month
Thaipusam, one day in January-February

Sinhalese people in Sri Lanka
New Year (Sinhala Avurudu), two days in April, first of Sinhala month of Bak and Tamil month of Chittrai

Sinj, Croatia, Yugoslavia
Sinj Iron-Ring Chivalric Tournament, first Sunday in August

Sinnemahoning, Driftwood, and Mix Run, Pennsylvania
Mix Roundup, Tom, three days in July

Sioux Indians
Dance, Sun, one to four days at end of June, during summer solstice
Powwow, Sioux, July
Powwow, Sioux, usually in July
Powwow, Sioux, usually in August
Powwow Days, Rosebud, August
Rosebud Tribal Fair, August

Sioux-Lake Village, Sisseton, South Dakota
Powwow, Sioux, July

Siracusa, Sicily, Italy
Drama, Cycle of Classical, May-June during even-numbered years

Sisseton, South Dakota
Powwow, Sioux, July

Sitka, Alaska
Alaska Day, three days in October
Music Festival, Sitka Summer, three consecutive Tuesdays, Fridays, and Saturdays in early June
New Year's Day, January 1

Skagafjordur, Iceland
Horse Meet Show and Races, National, four days in July every four years

Skiatook, Oklahoma
Powwow, Kihekah Steh Club Annual, August

Skopje, Macedonia, Yugoslavia
Theatres for Yugoslav Children and Youth, Festival of Professional, second half of November

Slatina, Olt, Romania
Romanian "Calus," last weekend in August

Slavic people
Christmas Eve, December 24
Easter Monday, March-April, Monday after Easter
Green George Festival, April 24
Mid-Lent Sunday, March, fourth Sunday in Lent
St. Lazarus Day, March-April, Saturday before Palm or Easter Sunday

Slavonski Brod, Croatia, Yugoslavia
Theatres of Croatia, Encounter of Professional, October

Sliven, Bulgaria
Theatre, Holidays of Amateur, April during even-numbered years

Slovakia, Czechoslovakia
Music Festival, Bratislava, October 1-15

Slovakian-Americans
Independence Day, Czechoslovakia, October 28

Slovakian people
Independence Day, Czechoslovakia, October 28

Slovenia, Yugoslavia
Ballet Biennial, June-July during odd-numbered years
Bled Evenings (Bled na Gorenjskem), July-August
Puppet Theaters of Slovenia, Encounter of, February
Summer Festival, Ljubljana International (Festivala Ljubljana), eleven weeks from mid-June to end of August
Theatre Groups of Slovenia, Encounter of, May-June
Theatres, Borstnik Encounter of Slovenian, October
Theatres, Nova Gorica Meeting of Small, January
Youth Culture Week, May

Slovenska Gorica, Slovenia, Yugoslavia
Puppet Theaters of Slovenia, Encounter of, February

Slunchev Bryag, Bulgaria
Golden Orpheus, ten days in June

Smederevska Palanka, Serbia, Yugoslavia
Theatres, Regional Festival of Serbian Amateur, May-June

Smithfield, London, England
Bartholomew Fair, August 24

Smithville, Tennessee
Fiddlers Jamboree and Crafts Festival, Old Time, weekend nearest July 4

Sofia, Bulgaria
Drama, National Review of Modern Bulgarian, every five years in June
Puppet Theatres, National Review of Professional, every five years in October
Theatre, International Festival of Children's and Youth's, every four years, date varies

Solomon Islands
Independence Day, July 7

Somalia
Independence Day, June 26 and July 1

Somerset, England
Minehead & Exmoor Festival, last two weeks in July
Minehead Hobby Horse Parade, May
Miracles at Glastonbury, end of June through end of first week in August
Punky Night, October 28 or 29 or last Thursday in October

Somerton, Arizona
Cocopah Festivities Day, March or April

Sonderborg, Denmark
Tilting Tournament, Sonderborg, three days in July

Songhay people in Niger
Black Spirit Festival (Genji Bi Hori), April
Eating the New Millet Ceremony, after harvest
Rain-Bringing Ceremony (Yenaandi), end of the hot-dry season, usually on a Thursday

Songhay people in West Africa
New Year (Muharram Celebrations), first day of Islamic month of Muharram

Sonoma, California
Vintage Festival, Valley of the Moon, last full weekend in September

Sonora, Mexico
Cinco de Mayo, May 5
Easter, March-April, first Sunday after first full moon after the vernal equinox
Holy Week, March-April, week preceding Easter
Lent, February-March, forty-day season preceding Easter

Sonora (northern), Mexico
Wiikita Festivals, winter festival at Archie, Arizona; summer festival at Quitovaca, Sonora, Mexico

Sonqo, Bolivia
Llama Ch'uyay, July 31-August 1

Sopocachi Alto barrio of La Paz, Bolivia
Immaculate Conception, Feast of the (Fiesta of Concepción),
December 8

Sosa (or Sosa-gun), Chiba, Japan
Nembutsu Kyogen, mid-July
Plays, Oni-Mai, mid-August

South Africa
Boxing Day, December 26
Christmas, December 25
Coon Carnival, January 1
Covenant, Day of the (Braaiveleis), December 16
Easter Monday, March-April, Monday after Easter; begins
Family Week
Fast, Feast of Breaking the (Lebaran), first day of Islamic
month of Shawwal
First Fruits Festival
Founder's Day, April 6
Kruger Day, October 10
Majuba Day (Hill of Doves), February 27
Minstrels' Carnival, Annual, January 2
Muhammad's Birthday (Moulidi-n-nabi), twelfth day of
Islamic month of Rabi al-Awwal
New Year's Day, when Pleiades appear
Rainmaking Ceremony, prior to rainy season
Rand Show, April-May
Republic Day (Union Day), May 31
Thaipusam, one day in January-February
Zulu/Shembe Festival, July 1 through last Sunday
in July

South Africans in South Africa
Christmas, December 25

South America
Christmas Novena, nine days beginning December 16
Pan American Day, April 14
St. James's the Greater's Day (Fiesta of the Llamas), July 25

Southampton, New York
Powwow, Shinnecock, first weekend in September

South Australia, Australia
Adelaide Cup Day, May
Arts, Festival of the, February-March during even-
numbered years
Eight Hour Day, October 11
Performing Arts for Young People, Come Out—Festival of,
first two weeks in May during odd-numbered years
Proclamation Day, December 28; observed on December 28
or nearest Monday

Vintage Festival, Barossa Valley, March-April, seven days
beginning Easter Monday during odd-numbered years

South Bend, Indiana
Easter Monday (Paas Festival), March-April, Monday
after Easter

South Carolina
Admission Day, May 23
All Saints' Day, November 1
Chitlin' Strut, Saturday or Sunday after fourth Thursday
in November, Thanksgiving
Confederate Memorial Day, May 10
Davis's Birthday, Jefferson, June 3
Fawkes Day, Guy, November 5
Houses and Gardens, Festival of, 26 days in
March-April
New Year (Muharram Celebrations), first day of Islamic
month of Muharram
Peach Festival, South Carolina, ten days in mid-July
Spoleto Festival of Two Worlds/U.S.A., two weeks from last
week in May to early June
St. Cecilia's Day, November 22
Southern 500 Stock Car Race, first Monday in September
Sun Fun Festival, four days in June

South Carver, Massachusetts
Cranberry Harvest Festival, two days in late September or
early October

South Dakota
Admission Day, November 2
Borglum Day, Gutzon, August 10
Corn Palace Festival, four days in September
Custer's Last Stand, June 25; observed in late July
Custer's Last Stand (Chief Crazy Horse Pageant), mid-June
to late August
Motor Classic, Black Hills, first Monday in August through
following Sunday
Passion Play, Black Hills, June-August
Pioneers Day, October
Powwow, Santee Sioux, July
Powwow, Sioux, usually in July
Powwow, Sioux, July
Powwow, Sioux, usually in August
Powwow and Expo, Black Hills and Northern Plains Indian,
July 10-11
Powwow Days, Rosebud, August
Rosebud Tribal Fair, August
Seventy-Six, Days of, first full weekend in August

**Southeastern Massachusetts University, North Dartmouth,
Massachusetts**
Eisteddfod Festival of Traditional Music and Crafts, three-
day festival over third weekend in September

Southern Arapaho Indians in Oklahoma
Labor Day Powwow, first weekend and Monday in September

Southern Cheyenne Indians in Oklahoma
Dance, Sun

Southern Cheyenne Indians in Oklahoma: Anadarko
Indian Exposition, American, six days beginning second Monday of August

Southern Hemisphere
Summer Solstice, December 21-22
Winter Solstice, June 21-22

Southern Vermont Art Center, Manchester, Vermont
Arts, Festival of the, early June through mid-October

Southern Yemen (now People's Democratic Republic of Yemen)
Independence Day, November 29

South Fulton, Tennessee
Banana Festival, International, mid-September
See also **Fulton, Kentucky**

South Holland, Netherlands
Flower Show, Keukenhof, March-May
Tulip Festival, last week in April and first week in May

South Korea
See **Korea, Republic of**

South Queensferry, Scotland
Burry Man's Walk, second week of August

South Sahara Region, Tunisia
Sahara National Festival, one week in November-December, depending on the weather and the harvest

South Sulawesi, Celebes, Indonesia
Ujung Pandang Anniversary, April 1

South Union, Kentucky
Shaker Festival, ten days beginning second Thursday in July

South Vietnam
See **Vietnam, Republic of**

South Wales
Christmas Season (Mari Lwyd)

Spa, Belgium
Spa, Festival of, August

Spain
All Saints' Day, November 1

April Fools' Day, April 1
Ash Wednesday, February-March, fortieth day before Easter Sunday
Assumption, Feast of the, August 15
Assumption, Feast of the (Mystery Play of Elche, El Misterio de Elche), August 14-15
Asturias Day, first Sunday in August
Battle of the Moors and Christians, February
Battle of the Moors and Christians, April 22-24
Battle of the Moors and Christians, June
Battle of the Moors and Christians, July
Battle of the Moors and Christians, August
Battle of the Moors and Christians, September
Burial of the Sardine (Entierro de la Sardina), March-April, four to five days beginning Easter Monday
Candlemas, February 2
Caudillo, Day of the, October 1
Christmas (Navidad), December 25
Christmas Eve (Noche Buena), December 24
Cock Festival (Fiesta del Gallo), usually on February 2, Candlemas
Columbus Day (Hispanity Day or Day of Spanish Consciousness), October 12
Corpus Christi (Corpus Cristi), May-June
Cow, Festival of the (Fiesta de la Vaca), January 25
Cuenca Encounter, March
Danzantes y Pecados Festival, June
Easter (Domingo de Resurreccion), March-April, first Sunday after first full moon after the vernal equinox
Endiablada Festival, early February
Epiphany (Dia de los Reyes Magos), January 5-6
Exaltation of the Shellfish, fourth Sunday in October
First of March (Marzas), last night of February and first of March
Good Friday (Viernes Santo), March-April, Friday preceding Easter Sunday
Halloween, October 31
Holy Innocents' Day, December 28
Holy Saturday (Sabado de Gloria), March-April, Saturday before Easter Sunday
Holy Week (Semana Santa; processions in Seville and Murcia), March-April, week preceding Easter
Horse Fair, May
Human Towers of Valls (Xiquets de Valls), June 24
Immaculate Conception, Feast of the, December 8
Mardi Gras (Carnaval), February-March, Sunday-Tuesday before Ash Wednesday
May Day, May 1
Mid-Lent Sunday (Mezza Quaresima), March, fourth Sunday in Lent
Midsummer (La Vispera de San Juan), June 23-24
Mother's Day, December 8
Music, Barcelona International Festival of (Festival Internacional de Musica de Barcelona), month of October

Sparta (ancient)
Carnea, August, Greek month of Carneus
Hyacinthia, July

Spearfish, South Dakota
Passion Play, Black Hills, June-August

Spiez, Bern, Switzerland
Play, Spiez Castle, three times per week in August

Spittal an der Drau, Carinthia, Austria
Comedy Festival at Porcia Castle, July-August

Spivey's Corner, North Carolina
Hollerin' Contest, National, third Saturday in June

Split, Croatia, Yugoslavia
Summer Festival, Split, July-August

Spokan Indians in Washington: Wellpinit
Labor Day Celebration, first Monday in September

Spoleto, Umbria, Italy
Spoleto Festival of Two Worlds (Festival dei Due Mondi),
late June to mid-July

Springe Deister, Lower Saxony, Germany
Boundary Walk (Grenzumgang), every ten years, 1951,
1961, etc.

Springfield, Illinois
Carillon Festival, International, one weeks in mid-June

Spring Grove, Minnesota
Constitution Day, Norway (Syttende Mai Fest), May 17

Sri Lanka (formerly Ceylon)
Buddha's Birthday, Enlightenment, and Salvation (Wesak),
eighth day of Hindu month of Vaisakha
Esala Perahera (Mahanuwara Esala Dalada Perahera), July-
August, nine nights during annual festival, full moon day
of eighth month, Esala
Heroes Day, May 22
Independence Day, February 4
Kataragama Festival, June-July
New Year (Sinhala Avurudu), two days in April, first of
Sinhala month of Bak and Tamil month of Chittrai
Poson (Dhamma Vijaya, Full Moon Day), full moon day
of Hindu month of Jyeshta
Sangamitta Day, full moon day of first month
See also **Ceylon**

Sri Mariamman Temple at Bukit Mertajam, Malaysia
Panguni Uttiram, ten days, including the full moon day of
Hindu month of Chaitra

Srinigar, Jammu and Kashmir, India
Drama Festivals, Academy, February in Jammu; August
in Srinagar

Sri Veeramakaliamman Temple in Singapore
Panguni Uttiram, March-April, two days, including the full
moon day of Chaitra

Staffordshire, England
Dance, Horn, Monday after September 4
Vic Festival, four weeks in May-June

Stanhope, New Jersey
Music Festival, Waterloo Summer, six weeks from late June
through July

Stara Pazova, Vojvodina, Yugoslavia
Theatres of Vojvodina, Encounter of Slovak Amateur,
February

Stara Zagora, Bulgaria
Oral Interpretation, Competition in, even-numbered years,
date varies

State House, Annapolis, Maryland
Ratification Day, January 14

State University of New York in Cobleskill, New York
Indian Festival, Iroquois, first weekend in September,
including Labor Day

Stavelot, Belgium
Theatre Festival of Stavelot, Vacation (Les Vacances-Theatre
de Stavelot), July
Wallonia, Festival of (Festival de Wallonie), June-September
or October

Stirling, Stirlingshire, Scotland
Stirling District Festival, May-June

Stockerau, Lower Austria, Austria
Stockerau Outdoor Festival (Stockerau Festspiele),
July-August

Stockholm, Sweden
Music Festival, Stockholm, six weeks in June-July
Ship's Island, Festival of, July
Theatre, Drottningholm Court, June to August-September
Walpurgis Night (Valborgsmässoafton), April 30

Stoke-on-Trent, Staffordshire, England
Vic Festival, four weeks in May-June

Stoke Prior, Worcestershire, England
Arts Festival, L.G. Harris, second week in October during
even-numbered years

Stone City-Anamosa, Iowa
Art Festival, Grant Wood, second Sunday in June

Stone Mountain, Georgia
Yellow Daisy Festival, second weekend in September

Stoughton, Wisconsin
Constitution Day, Norway (Syttende Mai Fest), weekend nearest May 17

Strasbourg, Alsace, Bas-Rhin, France
Music Festival, Strasbourg International (Festival International de Musique de Strasbourg), 16 days beginning first week in June

Stratford, Ontario, Canada
Theatre Festival, Stratford, May-June to October

Stratford, Connecticut
Shakespeare Festival, American

Stratford-upon-Avon, Warwickshire, England
Shakespeare Company Festival, Royal, April-December
Shakespeare's Birthday, April 23

Straznice, Moravia, Czechoslovakia
Folklore Festival of Straznice, three days in June

Stresa, Italy
Musical Weeks, Stresa (Settimane Musicali di Stresa Festival Internazionale), late August to late September

Stroud, Gloucestershire, England
Stroud Festival, second and third weeks in October

Stroud, Oklahoma
Indian Memorial Stampede Rodeo, summer
Powwow, Sac and Fox, second weekend in July

Stroumbi Village near Paphos, Cyprus
Wine Festival, Stroumbi Village, several days in early September

Sturgis, South Dakota
Motor Classic, Black Hills, first Monday in August through following Sunday

Stuttgart, Arkansas
Duck Calling Contest and Wings over the Prairie Festival, World Championship, November, Tuesday through Friday of Thanksgiving week

Styria, Austria
Autumn, Styrian (Steirischer Herbst), eight weeks in October-November

Subotica, Serbia, Yugoslavia
Harvest Festivities, Duzijanca, July
Vintage Festival, September

Sudan
Fast, Feast of Breaking the (Eid Saghir), first day of Islamic month of Shawwal
Independence Day, January 1
Revolution Day, May 25
Unity Day, March 3

Suffolk, England
Music and the Arts, Aldeburgh Festival of, ten to 17 days in June or July

Suffolk County, Massachusetts
Bunker Hill Day, June 17
Evacuation Day, March 17

Sulawesi, Indonesia
See Celebes, Indonesia

Sultan Park, Walters, Oklahoma
Powwow, Comanche Annual, July

Sumatra, Indonesia
Fast, Feast of Breaking the (Urou Raja Puasa or Idulfitri), first day of Islamic month of Shawwal
Medan Anniversary, April 1

Sumerian people (ancient)
Vernal Equinox, on or near March 21

Sun Prairie, Wisconsin
Groundhog Day, February 2

Supai, Arizona
Peach Festival, August

Suquamish, Washington
Art Fair, Native American, mid-April
Seattle Days, August 18-20 or third weekend in August

Suquamish Indians in Washington: Suquamish
Art Fair, Native American, mid-April
Seattle Days, August 18-20 or third weekend in August

Surakarta, Central Java, Java
Sultan's Coronation, May

Surin, Thailand
Elephant Round-Up, third week of November

Surinam
Christmas, December 25; two-day holiday

Surinam *(cont.)*
Fast, Feast of Breaking the (Idul Fitre), first day of Islamic month of Shawwal
Fire Festival (Holi Phagwa), begins 14th day of Hindu month of Phalguna or Dol; length varies
Freedom, Day of, July 1
Independence Day, November 25
New Year's Day, January 1

Surrey, England
Derby Day, late May or early June
Dicing for the Maid's Money Day, January
Theatre, Polesden Lacey Open Air, end of June to beginning of July

Sursee, Switzerland
Gansabhauet, November 11

Sussex, England
Brighton Festival, April-May
Rye Festival, first week in September

Sussex and other parts of England
Doleing Day (Gooding Day), December 21

Sussex County, Delaware
Return Day, Thursday after Presidential Election Day, every leap year

Susu people in West Africa
New Year (Muharram Celebrations), first day of Islamic month of Muharram

Svetozarevo, Serbia, Yugoslavia
Comedy Festival, Days of, March

Swabia, Germany
St. Bartholomew's Day, August 24
Shepherds' Race (Schäferlauf), August 23-25

Swansea, Wales
Music and the Arts, Swansea Festival of, three weeks in October

Swaziland
Flag Day, National, April 25
Incwala, three weeks to one month-long ceremony: Little Incwala lasts two days beginning at the summer solstice and new moon; the Big Incwala takes place for six days after the full moon
Independence Day (Somhlolo Day), September 6
King's Birthday, July 22
New Year (Newala Ceremonies, First Fruits Festival), six days in December-January

Reed Dance (Umhlanga), one week in late August-early September
United Nations Day, October 24

Sweden
Advent, four-week season beginning Sunday nearest November 30 and ending December 24
Annunciation, Feast of the (Varfrudagen or Marie Bebådelsedag; also known as Lady Day and Våffla or Waffle Day), March 25
April Fools' Day, April 1
Ascension Day (Kristi Himmelsfärdsdag), May-June, fortieth day after Easter Sunday
Boxing Day, December 26
Christmas (Juldagen), December 25
Christmas Eve (Julafton), December 24
Constitution and Flag Day, June 6
Easter (Paskdagen), March-April, first Sunday after first full moon after the vernal equinox
Easter Monday (Annandag Påsk), March-April, Monday after Easter
Epiphany (Trettondag Jul), January 6
Folk Dance and Music, International Festival of (Rattviksdansen), one week in July-August
Good Friday (Langfredagen, Long Friday), March-April, Friday preceding Easter Sunday
Gustafus Adolphus Day, November 6
Holy Saturday, March-April, Saturday before Easter Sunday
Holy Thursday (Skärtorsdag), March-April, Thursday preceding Easter
King's Birthday, November 11, observed June 2
Lent (Fastlagen), February-March, forty-day season preceding Easter
Mardi Gras (Fastlagsafton), February-March
Martinmas (Mårten Gås), November 11
May Day (Första Maj), May 1
Midsummer (Midsommer Day), begins Friday evening before June 24
Music Festival, Stockholm, six weeks in June-July
New Year's Day (Nyårsdagen), January 1
NVB (Nykterhetsrorelsens Bildningsversamhet) Festival, two weeks in June
Pentecost (Pingst), May-June, the Sunday fifty days after Easter; two-day festival
St. Eric's Day, May 18
St. Knut's Day (Tjugondag Knut), January 13
St. Lucy's Day (Luciadagen), December 13
St. Martin's Day, November 11
St. Stephen, Feast of, December 26
Ship's Island, Festival of, July
Theatre, Drottningholm Court, June to August-September
Vasaloppet, first Sunday in March
Visby Festival, July-August
Walpurgis Night (Valborgsmässoafton), April 30
Winter Fair, Great Lapp, four days in February

Swedish-Americans
St. Eric's Day, May 18
St. Lucy's Day, December 13

Swedish-Americans in California: Kingsburg
Swedish Festival, Kingsburg, third weekend in May

Swedish-Americans in Illinois: Bishop Hill
Agricultural Days (Jordoruksdagarna), two days in
late September

Swedish-Americans in Illinois: Chicago
Swedes' Day (Svenskarnas Dag), June 24

Swedish-Americans in Kansas: Lindsborg
Swedish Homage Festival, three days during second week
in October every odd-numbered year

Swedish-Americans in Minnesota
Swedes' Day (Svenskarnas Dag), fourth Sunday in June

Sweetwater, Texas
Rattlesnake Roundup, Sweetwater, second weekend in March

Swinouscie, Poland
Art Festival, Academic Youth, month-long, June

Swiss-Americans
Homstrom, first Sunday in February

Swiss-Americans in Wisconsin: New Glarus
William Tell Pageant, first weekend in September

Switzerland
Alpabfahrten, September-October
Alps, Procession to the (Alpaufzug), late April or May
Ascension Day (Banntag), May-June, fortieth day
after Easter
Berchtold's Day (Berchtoldstag), January 2
Boys' Rifle Match (Knabenschiessen), second weekend
in September
Christmas (Weihnachten), December 25
Christmas Eve (Heiliger Abend), December 24
Confederation Day, August 1
Corpus Christi (Fronleichnamsfest), May-June
Cow Fights (Kuhkämpfe), April
Dividing of the Cheese (Käseteilet), September
Easter (Ostern), March-April, first Sunday after first full
moon after the vernal equinox
Easter Monday, March-April, Monday after Easter
Easter Play of Muri, every five or six years in June
Epiphany, January 6
Escalade, December 11
First Fruits of the Alps Sunday (Les Prémices des Alpes),
fourth Sunday in August

First of March (Chalanda Marz), March 1
Fish Carnival (Groppenfasnacht), third Sunday before Easter,
every three years
Gansabhauet, November 11
Glarus Festival, first Thursday in April
Good Friday (Ceremony of Pleureuses), March-April,
Friday before Easter
Guardian Angel, Festival of the (Schutzengelfest), second
Sunday in July
Homstrom, first Sunday in February
Interlaken Festival, June-August
Jazz Festival, Montreux International (Montreux Festival
Internacional de Jazz), two weeks beginning first week
in July
June Festival, International, May-early June
Konigsfelden Festival, even-numbered years during weekends
in August-September
La Chaux-de-Fonds, Biennial of, even-numbered years
usually in May-June, sometimes autumn
Landsgemeinden, last Sunday in April
Lausanne, Festival of the City of, June
Lausanne International Festival (Festival International de
Lausanne), thirty concerts from May to first week in July
Mardi Gras (Carnival), February-March
Mardi Gras (Fastnacht), February-March, sometimes
celebrated before, and sometimes after, Ash Wednesday
May Day, May 1
May Day Eve (Maitag Vorabend), April 30
Meitlisunntig, second Sunday in January
Menuhin Festival, three weeks in August
Midsummer (Mitsommer Fest), June 24
Music, Lucerne International Festival of (Luzern
Internationale Musikfestwochen), mid-August to
mid-September
Music Festival, Montreux-Vevey (Festival de Musique
Montreux-Vevey), six weeks beginning in late August
New Year's Day (Neujahrstag), January 1
New Year's Eve (Silversterabend), December 31
Onion Market (Zibelemarit or Zybelemärit), fourth
Monday in November
Opera Festival, Italian, October
Pentecost (Pfingsten), May-June, the Sunday fifty days
after Easter
Pilgrimage of the Black Madonna, September 14
Play, Spiez Castle, three times per week in August
Play at Altdorf, Wilhelm Tell, even-numbered years on
weekends in August-September
Plays at Interlaken, Wilhelm Tell Pastoral, July-August
St. Anthony the Abbot of Egypt, Feast of (Festa di Sant'
Antonio), January 17
St. George's Day, April 23
St. Nicholas's Day (Samichlaus Abend, Santa Claus Night),
December 6
St. Placidus Festival, July 11
St. Sylvester's Day (Silversterklause), December 31

Switzerland *(cont.)*

Shepherd Sunday (Schäfer Sonntag), second Sunday
in September

Six O'Clock Ringing Festival (Sechselauten), third Sunday
and Monday in April

Summer-Nights Festival, Basel, June

Summer Season, Geneva, June-August

Theatre, Great World, every five years in June-September

Theatres, Bern International Festival of Small, three weeks
in June

Turnip Lantern Festival (Rebenlichter), November 10-11

Twelfth Night (Epiphany Eve), January 5

Wine Growers' Festival (Fête des Vignerons), 16 days in
August every 25 years

Yodeling Festivals (Jodlerfests), end of May through
September during odd-numbered years

Sydney, New South Wales, Australia

Australia Day at the Rocks, January 26; observed late
January

Australian Open Tennis, January

Easter Show, Royal, during the Easter holidays

Folklore, Sydney Festival of, two weeks in January, coincides
with Festival of Sydney

Performing Arts for Young People, The Leap-Festival of,
last week in February

Sydney, Festival of, December 31 through January

Sylhet, Bangladesh

Sun Festival (Suryapuja), spring

Syracuse, Sicily

St. Lucy's Day, December 13

Syria

Artistic Festival of the Damascus International Fair,
20 days in July

Assumption, Feast of the ('Id Rakad-ai-Sayyidah),
August 15, Gregorian calendar (N.S.); August 28, Julian
calendar (O.S.)

Candlemas (Dukkul al-Sayyid ila-l-Haykal), February 2

Christmas ('Id al Milad), December 25

Christmas Eve (Beiramun 'Id al Milad), December 24

Circumcision, Feast of the ('Id al-Khitan), January 1,
Gregorian calendar (N.S.); January 14, Julian calendar
(O.S.)

Easter (Al-'Id al-Kabir), March-April, first Sunday after first
full moon after the vernal equinox

Epiphany (Lailat al-Ghitās) and Epiphany Eve (Lailat
al-Qadr), January 5-6

Evacuation Day, April 17

Exaltation of the Cross ('Id Raf'al-Salīb), September 14,
Gregorian calendar (N.S.); September 27, Julian calendar
(O.S.)

Good Friday (Al-Jum'ah al-Hazinah, Sorrowful Friday),
March-April, Friday preceding Easter Sunday

Holy Thursday (Khamis al-Jasad), March-April, Thursday
preceding Easter

Liberation Anniversary, October War of, October 6

Mardi Gras (al-Marfa, Carnival, and Khamis al-Marfa,
Carnival Thursday), February-March, the week before Lent,
especially Thursday

Martyrs Day, April 6

Martyrs' Day, Forty ('Id al-Arba 'in Shahid), March 9

Mecca, Pilgrimage to, eighth through 13th days of Islamic
month of Dhu'l-Hijjah

New Year's Day ('Id Ras al-Sanah), January 1

Ramadan, ninth Islamic month

Republics Day, United Arab, September 1

Revolution Day, March 8

St. Barbara's Day, December 4

St. George's Day ('Id Marjurjus), April 23 at monastery
at Humeira

St. Nicholas's Day (St. Nicholas Thaumaturgus, the Wonder-
Worker), December 6

Sts. Peter and Paul Day, June 29

Soul, Festival of the (Mahrajan), September 1

Springtime Festival, March-April, four successive Thursdays
before Orthodox Easter

Transfiguration, Feast of the ('Id al-Tajalli), August 6

Szczecin, Poland

Theatrical Forms, Festival of Small, March

Szeged, Hungary

Folk Dance, International Festival of, July during odd-
numbered years

Summer Festival, Szeged, third week in July to third week
in August

Szekszard, Hungary

Folklore, Danube Festival of, every three years
in July

Szombathely, Hungary

Savaria Festival, August

Tabarka, Jendouba Region, Tunisia

Tabarka, Festival of, July-August

Tabasco, Mexico

St. Sebastian, Festival of (Fiesta de San Sebastian),
January 20

Tahiti

Armistice Day, November 11

Bastille Day (Tiurai), July 14

Tahlequah, Oklahoma

Cherokee National Holiday, September, Thursday-Sunday
of first weekend in September

Taholah, Washington
Taholah Days, Chief, July fourth weekend

Taira, Okinawa
Boat Race Day (Gods of the Sea Festival in Minatogawa), 14th day of fifth lunar month

Taiwan
Arbor Day, March 12
Chiang Kai-shek Day, October 31 or November 1
Confucius's Birthday (Teachers' Day), 27th day of eighth lunar month
Constitution Day, December 25
Double Fifth (Tuan Wu; Dragon Boat Festival and Festival of the Five Poisonous Creatures), fifth day of fifth lunar month
Double Ninth Day (Tiong-iong Choeh or Double Yang), ninth day of ninth lunar month
Double Seventh (Festival of the Weaving Maid and the Herd Boy or Chhit Sek, Seventh Evening and Birthday of the Chhit-niu-ma, or Seven Old Maids), seventh day of seventh lunar month
Double Tenth Day, October 10
Foundation Days, January 1-2
Grave-Sweeping and Cold Food Festival (Han Shih, Cold Food Feast), fourth or fifth day of third lunar month, 105 or 106 days after the winter solstice
Hungry Ghosts, Festival of, 15th day of seventh lunar month
Lantern Festival (Yaun Shaw), 13th-15th days of first lunar month
Making Happiness Festival (Tso-Fu), ninth day of first lunar month
Matsu, Birthday of (Matsu Festival), 23rd day of third lunar month
Mid-Autumn Festival, 15th, or full moon, day of eighth lunar month
New Year, ten-day to two-week long celebration at the first new moon after sun enters Aquarius; one to 15 days of first month
Sun Yat-sen Day, November 12
Winter Solstice (Tang choeh î), December 21
Youth Day, March 29

Talladega Speedway, Alabama
Winston 500, first Sunday in May

Tallinn, Estonia
Singing Festival (Laulipidu), every fifth year on June 25

Tama, Iowa
Powwow, Mesquakie Celebration, second weekend in August, Thursday-Sunday

Tamaulipas, Mexico
Charro Days Fiesta, February-March, four days beginning Thursday of the weekend before Lent
St. Isidore, Festival of, mid-May

Tamil Nadu, India
Arts Festival, Kalakshetra, December-January
Bhagavatha Mela Festival, one week in May
Harvest Festival (Pongal), three days during Hindu month of Pausha
Mother Goddess, Festival of Durga, the, first ten days of waxing half of Hindu month of Asvina
Vaikunth Ekadashi, twenty-day pilgrimage over 11th days of waxing and waning halves of Hindu month of Margashirsha

Tamil people in Malaya
Harvest Festival (Pongal), three days during Hindu month of Pausha

Tamil people in southern India
Skanda Shashti, October-November, Tamil month of Tulam
Thaipusam, one day in January-February

Tamil people in Sri Lanka
New Year (Sinhala Avurudu), two days in April, first of Sinhala month of Bak and Tamil month of Chittrai

Tam Kung Temple, Shau Kei Wan, Hong Kong Island
Tam Kung Festival, May, eighth day of fourth lunar month

Tampa, Florida
Gasparilla Pirate Festival and Invasion, six days beginning the Monday after the first Tuesday in February

Tampere, Finland
Pispalan Sottiisi, June during even-numbered years
Theatre Summer, Tampere, August

Tanglewood, Lenox, Massachusetts
Music Festival, Berkshire, July-September

Tanjore, India
Harvest Festival (Jellikattu Festival), three days during Hindu month of Pausha

Tanosu, Ghana
Apo Festival

Tanunda, South Australia, Australia
Vintage Festival, Barossa Valley, March-April, seven days beginning Easter Monday during odd-numbered years

Tanzania
Farmer's Day (Saba Saba Day), July 7

Tanzania *(cont.)*
First Fruits Festival, March
Independence and Republic Day, December 9
Midimu Ceremony, June through October; begins night
during the period when the moon moves from the quarter
to its half phase for three days
Revolution Day, Zanzibar, January 12
Union Day, April 26

Taormina, Sicily, Italy
Theatre Festival, July-September

Taos Pueblo, New Mexico
All Souls' Day, November 2
Christmas Eve, December 24
Dance, Deer
Dance, Los Comanches, February 4-5
Indian Ceremonial Dancing, American, September
29-30
New Year's Day, January 1
Our Lady of Guadalupe, December 12
St. Anne's Day, July 26
St. Francis of Assisi, Feast of, October 4
St. James the Greater's Day (Fiestas de Santiago y Santa
Ana), July 25-26 or nearest weekend
St. Jerome's Day, observed September 29-30
Santa Cruz Days (Coming of the Rivermen), May 3
Sundown Torchlight Procession of the Virgin with Deer or
Matchina dance, December 24-25

Tarahumara Indians in Mexico: eastern Chihuahua
Dance, Peyote (Híkuli), October and November

Taranaki, New Zealand
Provincial Anniversary, March 11

Tarascon, Provence, France
St. Martha, Feast of (Fête de la Tarasque), last Sunday in
June and July 29

Tarn-et-Garonne, France
Occitanie Festival, one week from late June to early
July

Tarpon Springs, Florida
Epiphany, January 6
St. Michael's Day, November 8
St. Nicholas's Day, December 6

Tarragona, Spain
Passion, Sacred Drama of the, February-May, Sundays
during Lent until month after Easter

Tasikmalaya, Java
Offering Ceremony, July

Tasmania, Australia
Blue Gum Festival of Tasmania, March
Drama Festival, Burnie Youth, last week in July
Drama Festival, Deloraine Youth, one week in July
Eight Hour Day or Labour Day, March 5
Eisteddfod, Eastern Shore, October
Eisteddfod, Hobart, June
Eisteddfod Society Festival, August-September
Hobart Cup Day, on or near January 23
Launceston Cup Day, February
Recreation Day, first Monday in November
Regatta Day, Hobart, February 9-10

Tatar Republic, Russia, USSR
Plow, Festival of the (Saban Tuy), June 25

Taureg people in Niger: Ingal
Salted Cure (Cure Salée), September or October

Taypi, Bolivia
St. Michael's Day (Fiesta de San Miguel), September 29

Tegal, Central Java, Java
Offering Ceremony, August

Tehran, Iran
Plays from Iranian Provinces, ten days in April
Summer Festival for Children, mid-June to mid-August

Tel Aviv, Israel
Israel Festival, dates vary, some time between May
and September

Telford, Shropshire, England
Wrekin and Telford Festival, five or six weeks in April-May

Tell Toqaan, Syria
Ramadan, ninth Islamic month

Telluride, Colorado
Bluegrass and Country Music Festival, Telluride, three days
in late June
Film Festival, International, first weekend in September,
including Labor Day
Hang Gliding Festival, Telluride, second week in September
Jazz Festival, Telluride, three days in mid-August
Music Festival, Telluride Chamber, two weekends in
mid-August

Teltown on River Boyne in Meath, Ireland
Lúgnasad (First Fruits Festival), August 1

Tenby, Wales
Christmas Eve, December 24; three-week Mumming Drama
during Christmas season

Tenby, Wales *(cont.)*
St. Crispin's Day, October 25

Tengger Mountains, East Java, Indonesia
Kassada, January, 14th of Kassada, 12th month of
Tenggerese year

Tennessee
Admission Day, June 1
Arts Festival, Dogwood, 17 days in April
Banana Festival, International, mid-September
Cherokee Days of Recognition, first weekend in August
Cotton Carnival and Musicfest, May-June
Country Music Fan Fair, International, one week in
early June
Davis's Birthday, Jefferson, June 3
Dulcimer and Harp Convention, second weekend in June
Elvis International Tribute Week, week including August 16
Fiddlers Jamboree and Crafts Festival, Old Time, weekend
nearest July 4
Fish Fry, World's Biggest, usually last full week in April
Graveyard Cleaning and Decoration Day, July
Jackson's Birthday, Andrew, March 15
May International Festival, Memphis in, month of May
Music Center, Sewanee Summer, last week in June to last
week in July
Ramp Festival, Cosby, first Sunday in May
Storytelling Festival, National, three days in October
Tennessee Walking Horse National Celebration, ten days
in August

Tenosique, Tabasco, Mexico
St. Sebastian, Festival of (Fiesta de San Sebastian),
January 20

Terlingua, Texas
Chili Cookoff, Terlingua, first full weekend in November

Tesuque Pueblo, New Mexico
Blessing of the Fields with Corn or Flag Dance, May,
date varies
Dance, Eagle, early spring
Dance, Matchina or Deer, December 25
San Diego, Feast of and Corn Dance, November 12

Teton Village, Wyoming
Music Festival, Grand Teton, early July to last week
in August

Texas
Admission Day, December 29
Alamo Day, March 6
Buccaneer Days, last weekend in April through first weekend
in May
Cactus Jack Festival, second weekend in October

Charro Days Fiesta, February-March, four days beginning
Thursday of the weekend before Lent
Chili Cookoff, Terlingua, first full weekend in November
Chilympiad, Republic of Texas Chili Cookoff, third weekend
in September
Cinco de Mayo, May 5
Confederate Memorial Day, January 19
Cotton Bowl Classic, January 1
Davis's Birthday, Jefferson, June 3
Father of Texas Day, November 3
Festival-Institute at Round Top, late May to mid-July
Folklife Festival, Texas, four days during first week in August
Graveyard Cleaning and Decoration Day, July
Holy Saturday (Easter Fires Pageant), March-April,
Saturday before Easter Sunday
Independence Day, March 2
Johnson's Birthday, Lyndon B., August 27
Juneteenth (Emancipation Day), June 19
Livestock Show and Rodeo, Southwestern Exposition and,
last two weeks in January
Mardi Gras, February-March
Mother-in-law Day, March 5
Opera Festival, Spring, May
Our Lady of Guadalupe (Festival Guadalupaño), Sunday
nearest December 12
Rattlesnake Roundup, Sweetwater, second weekend in March
Rose Festival, Texas, five days in October
San Antonio, Fiesta, ten days in April, including April 21
San Jacinto Day, April 21
Sausage Festival (Wurstfest), end of October through first
week in November
State Fair of Texas, 17 days in October
Washington's Birthday, mid-February

Thailand
Buddha's Birthday, Enlightenment, and Salvation (Visakha),
eighth day of fourth lunar month
Buddhist Priesthood, Admission to the (Buart Nark),
April-May
Chakkri Day, April 6
Christmas, December 25
Chulalongkorn Day, October 23
Constitution Day, December 10
Coronation Day (Chulalongkorn's Day), May 5
Elephant Round-Up, third week of November
Fast, Feast of Breaking the (Hari Raya Puasa), first day of
Islamic month of Shawwal
Four Miracles Assembly (Magha Puja), full moon day of
third lunar month
Kite Flying Season, February-April on weekday afternoons
Lenten Season (Vassa), July-October, begins during Wazo,
the fourth month, and ends on the 15th or full moon day
of Thadingyut, the seventh month
Lights, Festival of (Loy Krathong), full moon day of twelfth
lunar month

Tirol, Austria *(cont.)*
Mardi Gras (Schemenlauf, Running of the Spectres),
  January-March, week before Ash Wednesday
Passion Play, June-September
Passion Play, every six years from June to September
Perchtenlauf, usually January 6
Tirolese Summer, mid-July to mid-August

Tiruchirapalli, Tamil Nadu, India
Harvest Festival (Jellikattu Festival), three days during
  Hindu month of Pausha
Vaikunth Ekadashi, twenty-day pilgrimage over 11th days
  of waxing and waning halves of Hindu month of
  Margashirsha

Tirumala hills shrine, Tirupati, India
Tirupati Festival, ten days during Hindu month
  of Bhadrapada

Tirupati, India
Tirupati Festival, ten days during Hindu month
  of Bhadrapada

Tismana, Gorj, Romania
Tismana Garden Festival, August 15

Tivat, Montenegro, Yugoslavia
South, Festival of the, July-August

Tlaxcala, Mexico
Mardi Gras, February-March

Tobati, Paraguay
Epiphany (Fiesta of the Three Kings), January
  5-6

Tochigi, Japan
Dance, Longevity (Ennen-no-mai), June
Dance, Waraku, August
Spring Festival of the Toshogu Shrine, Great (Toshogu
  Haru-No-Taisai), May 17-18

Todaiji Temple in Nara, Japan
Water Drawing Festival (Omizutori Matsuri), two weeks
  in March

Togo
Habye Festival, small festival every third year, larger festival
  every fifth year in November
Independence Day, April 27
Liberation Day, January 13
Planting Ceremony

Tohono O'Odham Indians in Arizona: Tucson
San Xavier Pageant and Fiesta, April

Tok, Alaska
Sled Race, Tok Race of Champions Dog, late March

Tokyo, Japan
Neri-Kuyo, August 16, every three years
Pickle-Market or Sticky-Sticky Fair (Bettara-Ichi),
  October 19
Shrine Festival, Kanda Myojin, two days in mid-May
Shrine Festival, Yushima, two days in late May
Shrines Festival, Three (Sanja Matsuri), second
  weekend in May
Shrine Rice Festival, Suwa, January
Takigi Noh, summer
Yasukini Matsuri, four-day observance in April; also in
  summer, autumn, and winter

Toledo, Ohio
International Festival, third weekend in May

Toledo, Spain
Cow, Festival of the (Fiesta de la Vaca), January 25
Danzantes y Pecados Festival, June

Tomah, Wisconsin
Wisconsin Dells Stand Rock Ceremonials, nightly from
  mid-June to Labor Day, first Monday in September

Tomar, Ribatejo, Portugal
Tabuleiros Festival (Festa dos Tabuleiros), three or four days
  in mid-July every third year during odd-numbered years

Tonawanda, New York
Strawberry Festival, usually June

Tonga
Emancipation Day, June 4
New Year's Day (Ta'u Fo'ou), January 1
Sunday School Day (Faka Me), first Sunday in May

Tonopah, Nevada
Butler Days, Jim, last weekend in May

Toowoomba, Queensland, Australia
Carnival of Flowers, end of September-early October
Joy of Living, one week in September-early October

Topeka, Kansas
Admission Day, January 29

Toronto, Ontario, Canada
Canadian National Exhibition, three weeks in August
  and September
Caribana, one week ending the first Monday in August
Music, Mariposa-the Festival of Roots, last weekend
  in June

Torredeita, Viseu, Portugal
Torredeita, International Festival of, one day in September

Tortola, British Virgin Islands
Tortola Festival, begins first week in August

Tortugas Indians in New Mexico
Our Lady of Guadalupe, December 12

Torun, Poland
One-Man Shows, National Festival of, November
Theatres of Northern Poland, Festival of, June

Tottori, Japan
Spring Festival, one day in mid-April

Toulon, Var, France
Chateauvallon Festival, July-August
Music Festival, Toulon (Festival de Musique de Toulon),
   June-July

Tours, France
Music Festival, Touraine (Fêtes Musicales en Touraine),
   one week in late June or early July

Tower of London, London, England
Lilies and Roses Day, May 21

Toyohashi, Aichi, Japan
Shimmeisha Oni Festival, mid-February

Tracadie, New Brunswick, Canada
Bitowa Outdoor Festival, third full weekend in June

Tralee, County Kerry, Ireland
Rose of Tralee International Festival, six days in
   August-September

Transylvania, Romania
Harvest, Wheat, late summer
Maidens' Fair on Mount Gaina (Tirgul de fete de pe muntele
   Gaina), third Sunday in July
Pentecost, May-June, the Sunday fifty days after Easter
Plays, Festival of Short, one week in February
Theatre, Festival of Contemporary, one week in January
Theatres, Festival of National, one week in September
   or October
Yule, December 22

Transylvanian Romany and Slavic people
Green George Festival, April 24

Traunstein, Upper Bavaria, Germany
St. George's Day (Georgiritt Parade), April 23

Traverse City, Michigan
Cherry Festival, National, first full week after July 4

Trebinje, Bosnia and Herzegovina, Yugoslavia
Drama Amateurs, Yugoslav, end of June-beginning of July

Trichur, India
Pooram, during Hindu month of Vaisakha

Trinidad
All Saints' Day, November 1
Husayn or Husain Day (Hosay), tenth day of Islamic month
   of Muharram
New Year's Day, January 1
Sts. Peter and Paul Day, June 29

Trinidad and Tobago
Emancipation Day, August 1
Fire Festival (Phagwa), full moon day in March
Folklore, Prime Minister's Best Village Trophy Competition
   and Festival of, three weeks beginning first Saturday
   in November
Independence Day, August 31
Kiddies' Carnival, February, week preceding Carnival
Labour Day, June 19
Mardi Gras (Carnival), February-March, Monday and
   Tuesday before Ash Wednesday

Trivandrum, Kerala, India
Dance Festivals, Kathakali, March-April and
   October-November

Tsezy people in USSR: Shaitli, Dagestan
Midwinter Festival (Igbi), usually observed on Sunday nearest
   February 5

Tuaran Dusun people in Borneo
Mobog, annual

Tuchi Yokut Indians in California: Porterville
Lemoore Celebration, late August

Tucson, Arizona
Easter, March-April, first Sunday after first full moon after
   the vernal equinox
Our Lady of Guadalupe, December 12
San Xavier Pageant and Fiesta, April
Tucson Festival, two weeks following Easter
Tucson Meet Yourself Festival, second weekend in
   October
Vaqueros, Fiesta de los, four days beginning last Thursday
   in February

Tulsa, Oklahoma
Mayfest, International, five days in May

Tunbridge, Vermont
Vermont's World's Fair, four days in mid-September

Tunduru, Mozambique
Midimu Ceremony, June through October; begins night during the period when the moon moves from the quarter to its half phase for three days

Tunis, Tunisia
Passover (Pesach), eight days beginning 15th day of Jewish month of Nisan

Tunisia
Arbor Day or Tree Festival Day, second Sunday in November
Art, International Festival of Popular, July-August during odd-numbered years
Carthage, International Festival of, July and August
Ceres, Festival, May
Constitution and National Day, June 1; two-day holiday
Cultural Days, March
Cultural Festival of Oum Ezzine, end of September
Dougga, Festival of, July
El Djem Festival, June
El Karraka International Festival, July-August
Evacuation Day, October 15
Ezzahra, Festival, July-August
Hammamet, International Festival of, July-August
Hanukkah, eight days beginning 25th day of Jewish month of Kislev
Ibnou Abi Dhiaf Festival, July
Independence Day, March 20
Mahdia, Festival of, July-August
M'Hamed Ben Khelifa Festival, October
Music and Popular Arts, Regional Festival of, June
Passover (Pesach), eight days beginning 15th day of Jewish month of Nisan
Popular Festival of Sidi-Ali-El Hattab, April
Republic Day, July 25
Revolution Day, January 18
Sahara National Festival, one week in November-December, depending on the weather and the harvest
Sidi-Bou-Makhlouf, Festival, July
Summer Festival, July-August
Tabarka, Festival of, July-August
Theatre, Regional Festival of, June
Tisha B'Av, ninth day of Jewish month of Av
Tree Festival Day, second Sunday in November
Women's Day, August 13
Yom Kippur, tenth day of Jewish month of Tishri
Youth Day, June 2

Tuolumne Indian Rancheria, Tuolumne, California
Indian Acorn Festival, Mi-Wuk, annual

Tupelo, Mississippi
Gum Tree Festival, usually second weekend in May or sometime in June

Turgovishte, Bulgaria
Theatre, National Review of Children's and Youth's, every three years, date varies

Turkey
Ashura, tenth day of Islamic month of Muharram
Bodrum Festival, September
Bursa Festival, July
Children's Day, April 23
Ephesus, Festival of, May
Fast, Feast of Breaking the (Seker Bayram, Sugar Feast), first day of Islamic month of Shawwal
Folk Dance and Music Festival, Silifke, May
Golden Orange Festival, August-September
Holy Thursday, March-April, Thursday preceding Easter
Husayn or Husain Day, tenth day of Islamic month of Muharram
Istanbul Festival, International, June-July
Izmir International Fair, August-September
Kusadasi, Festival of, June-July
Marmaris Festival, May-June
May Day, May 1
Mecca, Pilgrimage to, eighth through 13th days of Islamic month of Dhu'l-Hijjah
Mediterranean Festival, June
Mesir Festival, May
Mevlana (Whirling Dervishes), Festival of, nine days to two weeks in December
Muhammad's Birthday, twelfth day of Islamic month of Rabi al-Awwal
Nasreddin Hoca Festival, July
New Year (Yevmi Ashurer, Day of Sweet Soup), first day of Islamic month of Muharram
Night Journey of Muhammad (Lélé-I-Mirach), 27th day of Islamic month of Rajab
Night of Forgiveness (Berat Kandili or Lélé-Bereat), 15th day of Islamic month of Shaban
Night of Power or Destiny (Lélé-I-Kadir), observed on the 27th day of Islamic month of Ramadan
Pamukkale, Festival of, May
Pergamum, Festival of, May
Ramadan (Ramazan), ninth Islamic month
Republic Day, October 29; two-day holiday
Sacrifice, Feast of (Kurban Bayram or Kourban Bairam), tenth-twelfth days of Islamic month of Dhu'l-Hijjah
Troy at Hisarlik, Festival of, August
Wrestling Games of Kirkpinar, one week in June
Youth and Sports Day, May 19

Turkey (on the shores of the Bosporus)
Epiphany, January 6

Turtmann, Valais, Switzerland
St. George's Day, April 23

Tus, Mashhad, Iran
Tus, Festival of, July

Tuscany, Italy
Ascension Day (Cricket Festival, Festa del Grillo), May-June,
fortieth day after Easter Sunday
Easter (Scoppio del Carro, Ceremony of the Car), March-
April, first Sunday after first full moon after the
vernal equinox
Holy Saturday (Scoppia del Carro, Explosion of the Car),
March-April, Saturday before Easter Sunday
Holy Week, March-April, week preceding Easter
Impruneta, Festa del, late October
Madonna del Voto Day, August 16
Mardi Gras, February-March, Tuesday before
Ash Wednesday
Musical May, Florence (Maggio Musicale Fiorentino), eight
weeks in May and June
Nativity of the Virgin, Feast of the, September 8
Palio, Festival of the (Festa del Palio, Corso del Palio, or
Palio of the Contrade), held twice during the summer:
July 2 and August 16
St. Roch's Day (San Rocco), August 16
Theatre Review, International, April-May

Tuscarora Indians in North Carolina: Rockfish
Cherokee of Hoke Intertribal Festival, fourth Saturday
in July

Tuscumbia, Alabama
Keller Festival, Helen, last weekend in June

Tuskahoma, Oklahoma
Labor Day Festivities, Choctaw Nation of Oklahoma, first
weekend and Monday in September

Twin Buttes, North Dakota
Twin Buttes Celebration, third weekend
in August

Tyler, Texas
Rose Festival, Texas, five days in October

Tyrol, Austria
See **Tirol, Austria**

Tzintzuntzan, Mexico
Mardi Gras (Fiesta de Febrero), February-March, Tuesday
before Ash Wednesday

Tzintzuntzan, Michoacán, Mexico
Passion Play, March-April, Holy Week

Ube Shrine, Iwami, Tottori, Japan
Spring Festival, one day in mid-April

Udaipur, Rajasthan, India
Bharatiya Lok Kala Festival, annual, date varies
Drama Festival, Rajasthan Academy, usually February
or March

Uganda
Christmas (Mukutanik), December 25
Harvest Season (Lara)
Independence Day, October 9
Liberation Day, April 11
Misisi Beer Feast, around October and at Christmas; after
millet harvest, during month of Twamo

Uhashi Shrine, Komatsu, Ishikawa, Japan
Komatsu Otabi Festival, mid-May

Ujung Pandang, South Sulawesi, Celebes, Indonesia
Ujung Pandang Anniversary, April 1

Ukrainian-Americans
Easter, March-April, first Sunday after first full moon after
the vernal equinox
Midsummer (Kupalo), June 24

Ukrainian-Americans in Canada: Dauphin, Manitoba
Ukrainian Festival, National, four days in July or August

Ukrainian-Canadians
Epiphany (Old Christmas), January 7

Ukrainian-Canadians in Canada: Dauphin, Manitoba
Ukrainian Festival, National, four days in July or
August

Ukrainian-Canadians in Canada: Saskatoon, Saskatchewan
Vesna Festival, six days in May

Ukrainian Republic, USSR
Easter, March-April, first Sunday after first full moon after
the vernal equinox
Midsummer (Kupalo), June 24
Republic Day, January 22
Spring, Kiev, second half of May

Ulldecona, Tarragona, Spain
Passion, Sacred Drama of the, February-May, Sundays
during Lent until month after Easter

Umbria, Italy
Joust of the Quintain, second weekend in September
Spoleto Festival of Two Worlds (Festival dei Due
Mondi), late June to mid-July

Union Grove, North Carolina
Fiddler's and Bluegrass Festival, Old Time, May, three days over last weekend in May

Union of Soviet Socialist Republics (USSR)
Boys' Day, February 22
Clean Tent Ceremony, February
Granddad Frost Day, January 1
May Day, May 1
Midwinter Festival (Igbi), usually observed on Sunday nearest February 5
Mushroom Harvest, late September or early October
October Socialist Revolution Day, November 7; observed November 7-8 in Moscow
Plow, Festival of the (Saban Tuy), June 25
Reindeer Slaughtering, autumn
St. George's Day, observed February 25
Seal Festival, November, end of seal-hunting season
Seal Festival (Keretkun Festival), two to three days in late autumn
Simhat Torah (Rejoicing in the Law), 23rd day of Jewish month of Tishri
Spring, Kiev, second half of May
Sun Celebration, Midnight (Ysyakh), on or near December 21
Victory Day, May 7; observed May 9
White Night Festival, nine days in June
Woman's Day, International (Mezhdunarodnyi Zhenski Den'), March 8
Youth Day, International (Internatzional'nyi Den' Komsomola), first Sunday in September

United Arab Emirates
National Day, December 2
Ramadan, ninth Islamic month

United Nations member nations
World Environment Day, June 5

United Nations-sponsored
World Food Day, October 16

United States
Advent, four-week season beginning Sunday nearest November 30 and ending December 24
Allen, Birthday of Richard, February 11
Anthony Day, Susan B., February 15 or August 26
April Fools' Day, April 1
Arbor Day, April 22 in Nebraska; usually observed last Friday in April elsewhere in the U.S.
Armed Forces Day (formerly Army Day), third Saturday in May
Ascension Day, May-June, fortieth day after Easter Sunday
Ash Wednesday, February-March, fortieth day before Easter Sunday
Assumption, Feast of the, August 15

Audubon Day, John James, April 26
Author's Day, November 1 (reading clubs)
Bastille Day, July 14
Beltane, April 30
Bible Sunday, last Sunday in November or Sunday before Thanksgiving
Bible Week, National, third week in October
Big House Ceremony, annual twelve-night ceremony
Black History Month, February
Blessing the Sun (Birchat Hahamah), every 28 years on the first Wednesday of Jewish month of Nisan
Boy Scouts Day, February 8
Brotherhood Week, week which contains February 22
Burns Night, January 25
Candlewalk, The, December 31
Children's Day, second Sunday in June
Children's Day (Kodomo-no-hi; formerly Boys' Festival, Tango No Sekku), May 5
Christmas, December 25
Christmas, Twelve Days of, December 25-January 6
Christmas Eve, December 24
Christmas Festival (Posadas, Feast of the Lodgings), December 16-24 or 25
Circumcision, Feast of the, January 1
Citizenship Day, September 17
Columbus Day, October 12; observed second Monday in October
Constitution Day, Norway, May 17
Corpus Christi, May-June, the Sunday following Trinity Sunday
Czech Festival, first weekend in August
Dance, Hopi Niman, third or fourth Saturday in July
Dance, Sun, usually during summer solstice, June 21
Davis Cup, November-December
Daytona 500, February
Dead, Festival of the (Bon Odori or Obon Matsuri), observed July 12-16
Devil's Night, October 30
Doctors' Day, March 30
Double Fifth (Dragon Boat Festival and Festival of the Five Poisonous Creatures), fifth day of fifth lunar month
Easter, March-April, first Sunday after first full moon after the vernal equinox
Edison's Birthday, Thomas, February 11
Election Day, the Tuesday after the first Monday in November
Emancipation Proclamation Day, January 1
Epiphany, January 6, Gregorian calendar (N.S.); January 19, Julian calendar (O.S.)
Exaltation of the Cross (Recovery of the True Cross), September 14
Exaltation of the Cross (Holy Cross Day), May 3
Family Week, National, begins first Sunday in May
Father's Day, third Sunday in June
Fire Prevention Week, observed week including October 9
Flag Day, June 14

United States *(cont.)*

French Festival (French Day), Saturday before Bastille Day, July 14

Fyr-Bål Fest, two days on weekend nearest June 24

German Day, October 6

Girl Scout Day, March 12

Girls' Doll Festival (Hina Matsuri; also known as Hina-No-Sekku, Peach Blossom Festival), observed March 3

Gold Star Mothers Day, last Sunday of September

Good Friday, March-April, Friday preceding Easter Sunday

Great American Smokeout, third Thursday in November

Groundhog Day, February 2

Halloween, October 31

Hanukkah, eight days beginning 25th day of Jewish month of Kislev

Holy Innocents' Day, December 28

Holy Saturday, March-April, Saturday before Easter Sunday

Holy Thursday, March-April, Thursday preceding Easter

Holy Week, March-April, week preceding Easter

Homstrom, first Sunday in February

Hospital Day and Week, National, week including May 12

Hostos, Birthday of (Hostos Day), January 11

Humane Sunday, first Sunday in May

Human Rights Day, December 10

Hunting and Fishing Day, fourth Saturday in September

Inauguration Day, January 20

Independence Day (Fourth of July), July 4

Independence Day (Rebild Festival), July 4

Independence Day, Czechoslovakia, October 28

Independence Day, Greek, March 25

Independence Day, Hungary, October 23

Independence Day, Lithuania, February 16

Inventors Day, February 8

Iroquois White Dog Feast (New Year or Midwinter Festival), several days, including first quarter moon in January

Jamestown Day, observed Sunday nearest May 13

Jefferson's Birthday, Thomas, April 13

Job's Birthday, February 30

Johnny Appleseed, Birthday of, September 26

Johnny Appleseed Day, March 11

Jour de Fête a Sainte Genevieve Days of Celebration, second weekend in August

Juneteenth (Emancipation Day), June 19

King, Jr.'s Birthday, Martin Luther, January 15, observed third Monday in January

Kosciuszko Day, February 4

Kwanzaa, December 26 through January 1

Labor Day, first Monday in September

Lammas, August 1

Law Day, May 1

Leif Eriksson Day, October 9

Lights, Festival of (Dewali), one week during waning half of Hindu month of Karthika, including 15th day

Lincoln's Birthday, Abraham, February 12, observed first Monday in February

Loyalty Day, May 1

Lúgnasad (First Fruits Festival), August 1

Mardi Gras (Fasnacht), February-March, Tuesday before Ash Wednesday

Mardi Gras (Rosemontag, Rose Monday), February-March, Monday preceding Lent

Martinmas, November 11

Martyrs of North America, Feast of, September 26

May Day, May 1

Mayfest (Maifest), third weekend in May

Memorial Day (formerly Decoration Day), May 30; observed last Monday in May

Mid-Lent Sunday (Mothering Sunday), March, fourth Sunday in Lent

Midsummer, June 23-24

Mother-in-law Day, fourth Sunday in October

Mother's Day, second Sunday in May

National Aviation Day, August 19

National Boss Day, October 16

National Finals Rodeo, nine days in early December

National Freedom Day, February 1

National Grandparents Day, first Sunday after Labor Day, first Monday in September

National Magic Day, October 31

National Maritime Day and Merchant Marine Week, May 22

Native American Day, usually fourth Friday of September; date varies according to state

New Year, ten-day to two-week long celebration at the first new moon after sun enters Aquarius; one to 15 days of first lunar month

New Year (Jamshed Navaroz or Patati, Day of Repentance), March 21

New Year, Jewish (Rosh Hashanah), first day of Jewish month of Tishri

New Year's Day, January 1

New Year's Eve, December 31

New Year's Eve (Watch Night Service), December 31

Olsok, July 29; observed last week in July

Our Lady of Carmel (La Madonna del Carmine), July 16

Palm Sunday, March-April, the Sunday preceding Easter

Passover (Pesach), eight days beginning 15th day of Jewish month of Nisan

Peace, International Day of, third Tuesday in September

Pearl Harbor Day, December 7

Pentecost, May-June, the Sunday fifty days after Easter

Police Memorial Day, May 15

Polish Solidarity Day, November 10

Presidents Day, third Monday in February

Pulaski Day, October 11

Purim, 14th day of Jewish month of Adar

Quadragesima Sunday, February-March, first Sunday in Lent

Queen Isabella Day, April 22

Race Relations Sunday, February, Sunday nearest February 12

Reformation Day, observed Sunday preceding October 31

United States *(cont.)*
Rural Life Sunday (Soil Stewardship Sunday), May, fifth
 Sunday after Easter
Secretaries' Day and Week, last full week in April;
 Wednesday of Secretaries' Week is Secretaries' Day
Shavuot, the Feast of Weeks, sixth day of Jewish month
 of Sivan
St. Anne's Day, July 26
St. Anthony the Abbot of Egypt, Feast of (Blessing of
 the Animals), January 17
St. Barbara's Day, December 4
St. Bartholomew's Day, August 24
St. Benedict's Day, March 21
St. Bridget's Day, February 1
St. Charles's Day, January 30
St. David's Day, March 1
St. Dismas's Day, second Sunday in October
St. Elizabeth Ann Seton, Feast of, January 4; observed as
 Mother Seton Day, December 1 by the Sisters of Charity
 of St. Vincent De Paul
St. Eric's Day, May 18
St. Frances Cabrini, Feast of, November 13
St. Francis of Assisi, Feast of, October 4
St. George's Day, April 23
St. Joseph of Arimathea, Feast Day of, March 19
St. Lucy's Day, December 13
St. Médardus's Day, June 8
St. Michael's Day, November 8
St. Nicholas's Day, December 6
St. Patrick's Day, March 17
St. Stephen's Day, August 20
St. Tammany's Day, May 1
St. Urho's Day, March 16
St. Wenceslaus's Day, September 28
Samhain (Summer's End), October 31
Senior Citizens Day, May 1
Stewardship Sunday, second Sunday in November
Sukkot (Feast of Booths or Feast of the Tabernacles),
 15th-21st or 22nd of Jewish month of Tishri
Summer Solstice, June 21-22
Super Bowl Sunday, last Sunday in January
Sweetest Day, third Saturday in October
Tellabration, November, the Friday before Thanksgiving
Thanksgiving, fourth Thursday in November
Thanksgiving, Schwenkfelder, September 24
Tucson Festival, two weeks following Easter
Twelfth Night (Epiphany Eve), January 5
United Service Organizations (USO), Founding of,
 February 4
United States Grand Prix, first Sunday in October
United States Open Championship in Golf, four days
 ending third Sunday in June
United States Open Tennis Championships, September
Universal Week of Prayer, first through second Sunday
 in January

Up-Helly-Aa, last Tuesday in January
Valentine's Day, February 14
Veterans' Day, November 11
Volunteers of America, Founder of, July 28
Von Steuben Day, September 17; often observed fourth
 Sunday in September
Walpurgis Night, April 30
Washington's Birthday, George, February 22, observed third
 Monday in February
Waygoose Feast, (Beanfest, or Beano in England;
 Fastnachtsschmaus, Lichtschmaus, or Martinschmaus),
 near St. Bartholomew's Day, August 24
Whit Monday, May-June, Monday after Whit Sunday
Williams Day, Roger, February 5
Woman's Equality Day, August 26
World Peace Day, September 19
World Series, mid-October
Yom Kippur, tenth day of Jewish month of Tishri
Yule, December 22

United States (southeastern)
Dance, Green Corn, weekend ceremonies in May-September
 lead up to festival

United States (southern)
Lee Day, Robert E., January 19; may be observed third
 Monday in January

United States military installations
Armed Forces Day, third Saturday in May

United States Naval Station, Adak, Alaska
Oklahoma Day, April 22; observed early autumn

University of Pennsylvania, Philadelphia, Pennsylvania
Pennsylvania Relay Carnival, University of, one week
 beginning Sunday before last weekend in April

Upper Austria, Austria
Operetta Weeks (Operettenwochen), eight weeks from early
 July to first week in September
Summer Festival, Grein (Sommerspiele Grein), July-August
Theatre Festival, Farmstead (Theater auf dem Bauernof),
 June-August

Upper Bavaria, Germany
St. George's Day (Georgiritt Parade), April 23

Upper Mattaponi Indians in Virginia: Walkerton
Spring Festival, Upper Mattaponi, fourth Saturday in May

Upper Volta (now Burkina Faso)
Bega Ceremonies, one week opening the planting season
Christmas, December 25
Independence Day, August 5

Upper Volta (now Burkina Faso) *(cont.)*
Muhammad's Birthday (Damba Festival), twelfth day of
Islamic month of Rabi al-Awwal
Ramadan, ninth Islamic month
Republic Day, December 11
Youth Day, November 30
See also **Burkina Faso**

Upsala, Sweden
Walpurgis Night (Valborgsmässoafton), April 30

Uri, Switzerland
Play at Altdorf, Wilhelm Tell, even-numbered years on
weekends in August-September

Urosevac, Kosovo, Yugoslavia
Theatre Groups, Provincial Festival of Kosovo Amateur, June

Uruguay
Artigas Day, June 19
Battle of Las Piedras Day, May 17
Blessing of the Waters or Family Day, December 8
Children's Day, January 6
Christmas, December 25
Constitution Day, July 18
Creole Week (Semana Criolla), March-April, Holy Week
Folklore, National Festival of, three days in January
Independence Day, August 25
Mardi Gras, January-February, about one month before
Ash Wednesday
Summer Festival of the Lake of Rodo Park, three months,
January-March

Utah
Admission Day, January 4
American West, Festival of, nine days in July-August
Arts Festival, Utah, five days in late June
Bonneville Speed Week, third week in August
Dance, Sun, July and August
Dance, Ute Bear (Ma'makoni-ni'tkap), three to five days
in April
Golden Spike Day, May 10
Pioneer Day, July 24

Utah State University, Logan, Utah
American West, Festival of, nine days in July-August

Ute Indians in Colorado: Ignacio
Dance, Southern Ute Sun, first weekend after
July 4
Dance, Ute Bear, first weekend in May

Ute Indians in the Great Plains of the United States
Dance, Sun, usually during summer solstice,
June 21

Ute Indians in Utah: Ouray, Randlett, Whiterocks
Dance, Ute Bear (Ma'makoni-ni'tkap), three to five days
in April

Uttar Pradesh, India
Mother Goddess, Festival of Durga, the, first ten days of
waxing half of Hindu month of Asvina
Rama Leela Festival, between seven and 31 days in
September-October
Rasa Leela Festival, one month during August-September
Teej (Hariyali Teej or Hari Tritiya), third day of waxing half
of Hindu month of Sravana

Uvalde, Texas
Cactus Jack Festival, second weekend in October

Vaison-la-Romaine, Vauclude, France
Vaison-la-Romaine and Carpentras, Festival of, July-August

Valais, Switzerland
Cow Fights (Kuhkämpfe), April
First Fruits of the Alps Sunday (Les Prémices des Alpes),
fourth Sunday in August
St. George's Day, April 23
Shepherd Sunday (Schäfer Sonntag), second Sunday
in September

Val d'Anniviers, Valais, Switzerland
First Fruits of the Alps Sunday (Les Prémices des Alpes),
fourth Sunday in August

Valencay, Indre, France
Art and History, Festival of, Sundays in July and August

Valencia, Spain
Assumption, Feast of the (Mystery Play of Elche, El Misterio
de Elche), August 14-15
Battle of the Moors and Christians, February
Battle of the Moors and Christians, August
Mystery of the Passion, March-April, Easter Week
St. Joseph's Day Bonfires (Fallas de San José), March 12-19
Valencia Fair Days (Battle of Flowers), July 24

Valenciennes, France
St. Veronica, Feast of, July 12; observed the following
Monday

Valley Forge National Historical Park, Pennsylvania
Continental Army, Departure of, Sunday nearest
June 19
Washington's Birthday (Cherries Jubilee), several days
in February

Valley of Mexico
See **Mexico, Valley of**

Valley of Nemea, Greece (ancient)
See **Nemea (Valley of), Greece (ancient)**

Valls, Catalonia, Spain
Human Towers of Valls (Xiquets de Valls), June 24

Valparaiso, Chile
Sts. Peter and Paul Day, June 29

Valreas, Vaucluse, France
Nights of the Enclave (Nuits de l'Enclave des Papes),
July-August

Vancouver, British Columbia, Canada
Polar Bear Swim Day, January 1
Vancouver Heritage Festival, May-June
Vancouver International Festival, late May to late June

Vanuatu (formerly New Hebrides)
Independence Day, July 30

Var, France
Arts and Music, Frejus Forum of (Forum des Arts et de la
Musique), July
Chateauvallon Festival, July-August
East Var, Festival of, six weeks in July-August
Music Festival, Toulon (Festival de Musique de Toulon),
June-July

Varanasi, India
Buddha's Birthday, Enlightenment, and Salvation (Buddha
Jayanti), full moon day of Hindu month of Vaisakha

Varna, Bulgaria
Golden Dolphin, every three years in October

Vaslui, Romania
Dionysiad, first Sunday in October
Nation of Heroes, first Sunday in July

Vauclude, France
Musical Weeks of Luberon (Semaines Musicales du Luberon),
two weeks in July-August
Vaison-la-Romaine and Carpentras, Festival of, July-
August

Vaucluse, France
Nights of the Enclave (Nuits de l'Enclave des Papes),
July-August

Vaud, Switzerland
Jazz Festival, Montreux International (Montreux Festival
Internacional de Jazz), two weeks beginning first week
in July
Lausanne, Festival of the City of, June

Lausanne International Festival (Festival International de
Lausanne), thirty concerts from May to first week in July
Music Festival, Montreux-Vevey (Festival de Musique
Montreux-Vevey), six weeks beginning in late August
Wine Growers' Festival (Fête des Vignerons), 16 days in
August every 25 years

Vedda people in Ceylon
New Year (Vaisakhi), first day of Hindu month of Vaisakha

Veliko Turnovo, Bulgaria
Drama, Review of Historical, every three years, date varies

Veneto, Italy
Opera and Ballet Festival, July-September
Opera Festival, Verona (Arena di Verona), second week in
July to first week in September
Shakespeare Festival, June-September
Theatre Review, Summer, July-August

Venezuela
Bolívar Day, July 24
Christmas, December 25
Christmas Carol Mass (Misa de Aguinaldo), December 16-24
Christmas Eve, December 24
Easter, March-April, first Sunday after first full moon after
the vernal equinox
Epiphany (Día de los Tres Reyes), January 6
Exaltation of the Cross, May 3
Independence Day, July 5
Puppet Festival of Venezuela, National, one week usually
between August and November
Teachers' Day (Día Del Maestro), January 15
Theater, Eastern Festival of, ten days annually, date varies
Theatre, Festival of Popular, annual, date varies
Theater Festival, International, date varies during even-
numbered years

Venice, Italy
Mardi Gras, February-March, ending Tuesday before
Ash Wednesday
Music, Venice International Festival of Contemporary,
second and third weeks in April
Redeemer, Feast of the (Festa del Redentore), third Sunday
in July
Venice Biennial, May-December during odd-numbered years

Verges, Gerona, Spain
Verges Festival, March-April, Thursday before Easter

Vermont
Admission Day, March 4
Arts, Festival of the, early June through mid-October
Bennington Battle Day, August 16
Coolidge, Birthday Celebration of Calvin, July 4

Vietnam, Democratic Republic of
Independence Day, September 2; official independence on
March 8

Vietnam, Republic of
Republic Day, October 26

Vietnamese-Americans in New York
New Year (Tet Nguyenden), several days beginning first day
of first lunar month

Vigo, Pontevedra, Spain
Vigo Days, October or November

Vila Franca de Xira, Lisboa District, Ribatejo, Portugal
Red Waistcoat Festival (Festival of the Colete
Encarnado), July

Vila Moura, Faro, Portugal
Algarve, National Festival of the, two days in August
or September

Vila Praia de Ancora, Viana do Castelo, Portugal
Vila Praia de Ancora, International Festival of, June
or August

Villach, Carinthia, Austria
Summer Festival, Carinthian (Carinthischer Sommer), eight
weeks from late June to late August

Villafranca del Panades, Barcelona, Spain
San Felix Martyr, Feast of, August

Villajoyosa, Alicante, Spain
Battle of the Moors and Christians, July

Villavicencio, Meta, Colombia
Joropo Festival, International, December

Ville-Bonheur, Haiti
Pilgrimage to Saut d'Eau, early July-July 16

Villena, Alicante, Spain
Battle of the Moors and Christians, September

Villeneuve-lez-Avignon, Gard, France
Summer Meetings, International, month-long, July-August

Vilnius, Lithuania
Song Festival (Skamba Kankliai), May

Virginia
Admission Day, June 25
Apple Blossom Festival, Shenandoah, Thursday through
Saturday nearest May 1

Appomattox Day, April 9
Boomerang Festival, usually October
Chickahominy Fall Festival, usually weekend over fourth
Saturday in September
Confederate Memorial Day, last Monday in May
Earls Court Day, May 9
Fiddler's Convention, Old, four days during second week
in August
Harborfest Norfolk, four days in June
Jousting Tournament, third Saturday in June and second
Sunday in October
Lee-Jackson Day, January 18; observed third Monday
in January
Music Festival, Shenandoah Valley, four weekends from mid-
July to early September
New Year's Eve (First Night), December 31
Pony Penning on Chincoteague Island, late July
Scottish Games, Virginia, fourth weekend in July
Spring Festival, Upper Mattaponi, fourth Saturday in May
Summer Festival, Wolf Trap Farm Park, 13 weeks from June
to first week in September
Washington's Birthday, George, third weekend in February
Yorktown Day, October 19

Virginia City, Nevada
Camel Races, International, weekend after Labor Day, first
Monday in September

Virgin Islands
Christmas Festival, Caribbean, two weeks beginning
December 23
Epiphany, January 6; Christmas Festival ends January 6
Hurricane Supplication Day, fourth Monday in July and
second or third Monday in October
Liberty Day, November 4; observed first Monday in
November
Mardi Gras (Carnival), follows Easter, usually last two weeks
in April
Roosevelt Day, Franklin D., January 30
St. Ursula's Day, October 21
Tortola Festival, begins first week in August
Transfer Day, March 31; observed last Monday in March
Virgin Islands Donkey Races Day, February 22

Visby, Gotland Island, Sweden
Visby Festival, July-August

Viseu, Portugal
Folklore, Gouveia International Festival of, August
Pilgrimage to the Sanctuary of Our Lady of the Remedies
(Pardon of Nossa Senhora dos Remédios) and Festival of
Lamego, early September
Theatre Meeting, Viseu Amateur, one week in December
Torredeita, International Festival of, one day in
September

Vissoie, Val d'Anniviers, Valais, Switzerland
First Fruits of the Alps Sunday (Les Prémices des Alpes),
fourth Sunday in August

Vistula River, Poland
Marzanna Day, March 21; observed Saturday or Sunday
nearest March 21

Vitoria, Alava, Spain
Vitoria Encounter, October or December

Vjatka, Russia
Holy Thursday (Votjak or Udmurt), March-April,
Thursday preceding Easter

Vlaardingen, Netherlands
Vlaggetjesdag, anytime from middle to late May

Vojvodina, Yugoslavia
Autumn of Culture, second half of October
Drama Memorial, Riznic-Djadja, April
Folklore Groups of Vojvodina, Encounter of Hungarian,
June
Folklore in Vojvodina, Slovakian, May
Games of May, May
Music and Folklore of Romanians Living in Vojvodina,
May
"Red Rose" Festival of Culture, June-July
Sterija, Days of, October
Theatre Days of Romanians in Vojvodina, April
Theatre Games, Yugoslav (Yugoslav Theatre Festival),
second half of April
Theatres, Encounter of Slovak Amateur Children's,
April-May
Theatres of Vojvodina, Encounter of, May
Theatres of Vojvodina, Encounter of Amateur, May
Theatres of Vojvodina, Encounter of Slovak Amateur,
February

Volta
New Year Purification before Planting, April, just before
planting

Vorarlberg, Tirol, Austria
Bregenz Festival (Bregenzer Festspiele), four weeks in
July-August
Easter, March-April, first Sunday after first full moon after
the vernal equinox

Vratsa, Bulgaria
Theatre, National Review of Pocket, every five years,
date varies

Vrsac, Vojvodina, Yugoslavia
Sterija, Days of, October

Wagga Wagga, New South Wales, Australia
Folk Festival, Wagga, three days in October
Plays, Wagga Wagga School of Arts Annual Festival of, two
consecutive weekends in August-September

Wagrain, Salzburg, Austria
"Silent Night, Holy Night" Celebration, December 24

Wakayama, Japan
Fire Festival, July 13

Wales
Arts Festival, Rhymney Valley, last two weeks in October
Bank Holiday, first Monday in May
Bank Holiday, last Monday of August
Beltane, April 30
Christmas, December 25
Christmas Eve, December 24, three-week Mumming Drama
during Christmas season
Easter Monday, March-April, Monday after Easter
Eisteddfod, International Musical (Gerddorol Gydwladol
Llangollen), six days during first week in July
Eisteddfod of Wales, Royal National (Eisteddfod
Genedlaethol Frenhinol Cymru), first full week in August
Fool's Fair (Ffair Ffyliaid), first Tuesday in May
Halloween (Apple and Candle Night), October 31
Labour Day, first Monday in May
Literature, Hay-on-Wye Festival of, ten days in late May
Music and Drama, Llantilio Crossenny Festival of, first
weekend in May
Music and the Arts, Swansea Festival of, three weeks
in October
New Year's Day, January 1
Old New Year's Day, January 12 or 13
St. Crispin's Day, October 25
St. David's Day, March 1
St. Stephen, Feast of (Hunting the Wren), December 26
Whit Monday, May-June, Monday after Pentecost

Walker River Paiute Indians in Nevada: Schurz
Pinenut Festival, October

Walkerton, Virginia
Spring Festival, Upper Mattaponi, fourth Saturday
in May

Walpi Pueblo, Arizona
Sky-God Festival (Powamû Festival), February, nine-day
kachina ceremony

Walters, Oklahoma
Powwow, Comanche Annual, July

Wangford, East Suffolk, England
Wangford Festival, eight days in July

Waraku Pond, Nikko, Tochigi, Japan
Dance, Waraku, August

Warm Springs, Oregon
Powwow, Warm Springs, June
Root Festival, mid-April

Warm Springs (north of), Oregon
Indian Celebration, Tygh Valley, May

Warsaw, Poland
Theatre Meetings, Warsaw, December

Warwick, Rhode Island
Gaspee Days, 16 days in May-June

Warwickshire, England
Shakespeare Company Festival, Royal, April-December
Shakespeare's Birthday, April 23

Washington
Admission Day, November 11
Apple Blossom Festival, Washington State, April or May
Art Fair, Native American, mid-April
Bumbershoot, four days during first weekend in September
Constitution Day, Norway, May 17
Folklife Festival, Northwest, four days over last weekend
  in May
Irrigation Festival, first full weekend in May
Labor Day Celebration, first Monday in September
Pacific Northwest Festival, last week in July and first week
  in August
Powwow, Yakima, September
Rodeo, Ellensburg, first weekend in September
Seafair, 16 days in July-August
Seattle Days, August 18-20 or third weekend in August
Stampede Days, second week in August
Taholah Days, Chief, July fourth weekend
Tribal Day Celebration, late May
Warrior or Veteran Festival, Stommish, month of June
White Swan Celebrations, July fourth weekend

Washington, Arkansas
Jonquil Festival, third weekend in March

Washington, D.C.
Admission Day, Oklahoma, November 16
Cherry Blossom Festival, six days in late March-April
Christmas Tree, Lighting of the National, mid-December
  through January 1
Easter Monday (Easter Egg Roll), March-April, Monday
  after Easter
Equal Opportunity Day, November 19
Folklife, Festival of American, two weeks in late June
  and early July

Frisbee Festival, National, first weekend in September
Kite Festival, Smithsonian, late March-early April
Malcolm X Day, third Sunday in May
Music Festival, American, Sunday evenings in April and May
Wreaths, Wianki Festival of, June 23

Washington Cathedral, Washington, D.C.
Admission Day, Oklahoma, November 16

Washington Crossing, New Jersey
Washington's Crossing of the Delaware, December 25

Washington Crossing, Pennsylvania
Washington's Crossing of the Delaware, December 25

Washo Indians in Nevada: Carson City
Powwow, La Ka Le'l Ba, annual

Waterfall Temple, Penang, Malaysia
Thaipusam, one day in January-February

Waterford, County Waterford, Ireland
Opera, International Festival of Light, September

Waterloo, Ontario, Canada
Oktoberfest, nine days in early October, beginning the
  Friday before Thanksgiving Monday

Waterloo, New Jersey
Poetry Festival, Geraldine R. Dodge, three days in September

Waynesboro, Virginia
New Year's Eve (First Night), December 31

Weimar, German Democratic Republic
Shakespeare Days, April

Weiser, Idaho
Fiddlers' Contest, National Old-Time, third full week
  in June

Weissenburg, Bavaria, Federal Republic of Germany
Theatre, Summer Festival at the Bergwald, weekends in
  June-July

Wellington, New Zealand
Fawkes Day, Guy, November 5
Provincial Anniversary, January 21
Wellington Day, January 18

Wellpinit, Washington
Labor Day Celebration, first Monday in September

Welsh-Americans
St. David's Day, March 1

Welsh-Americans in Pennsylvania
Eisteddfod, Cynonfardd, last Saturday in April

Welsh people
Christmas Eve, December 24

Wenatchee, Washington
Apple Blossom Festival, Washington State, April or May

West Africa
Ashura, first ten days of Islamic month of Muharram
Fast, Feast of Breaking the (Salla or 'Id-al-Fitr), first day of Islamic month of Shawwal
Muhammad's Birthday, twelfth day of Islamic month of Rabi al-Awwal
Muhammad's Birthday (Game Festival), twelfth day of Islamic month of Rabi al-Awwal
New Year (Muharram Celebrations), first day of Islamic month of Muharram
New Year (Tabaski or Ashura), first day of Islamic month of Muharram
New Year Harvest Festivals
Night of Power or Destiny (Lailat al-Qadr), one of the last ten days of Islamic month of Ramadan; usually observed on the 27th
Ramadan, ninth Islamic month
Sacrifice, Feast of (al-'id al-kabir), tenth-twelfth days of Islamic month of Dhu'l-Hijjah

West Bengal, India
Jatra Festivals of Calcutta, ten to 15 days in winter
Purilia Chhau Festival, April 11-13
Tagore, Birthday of Rabindranath, May 7
Theatre Festivals, Children's Little, second week in May and three weeks in December

West Berlin, Federal Republic of Germany
Horizon '79, '81, etc., three to four weeks in June-July during odd-numbered years
Metamusik Festival, even-numbered years in October
Pantomime-Music-Dance-Theatre, April-June
Theatre Rally, May

West Bohemia, Czechoslovakia
Puppet Theatres, Skupa Festival of Professional, May

Western Australia, Australia
Arts, Northam Festival of the, June-July
Arts for Young People, Festival of Performing—Round Up, five days in February
Australia Day, on or near June 1
Eight Hour Day or Labour Day, March 5
Foundation Day, State, June 1
Fremantle Week, late October-early November
Perth, Festival of, February-March

Western Europe
Earth Day (Vernal Equinox), March 20

Western Province, Zambia
Kuomboka, February-March, when Zambezi River rises

Western Samoa
Anzac Day, April 25
Independence Day, January 1; observed first three days in June
White Sunday, second Sunday in October

West Flanders, Belgium
Flanders, Festival of (Festival van Vlaanderen), April to October
Holy Blood, Procession of the (Processie van het Heilig Bloed), observed first Monday after May 2
Penitents, Procession of the (Boetprocessie van Veurne), last Sunday in July

West Germany
See **Germany, Federal Republic of**

Westhoughton, Lancashire, England
Keaw Yed Wakes Festival, Sunday of or after August 24

West Indians in Canada: Toronto, Ontario
Caribana, one week ending the first Monday in August

West Java, Java
Offering Ceremony, January

Westland, New Zealand
Provincial Anniversary, December 1

Westmeath (County), Ireland
Drama Festival, All-Ireland Amateur, April-May

Westminster, England
Lord Mayor's Show, November 9; observed second Saturday in November (procession starts in London)

Westminster, Maryland
Fall Harvest Day, second Saturday in October

West Moldavia, Romania
Gala of One-Man Shows, ten to 12 days in October or November

Westmorland and other areas in northern England; Scotland
Nippy Lug Day, February, Friday after Ash Wednesday

Westphalia, Germany
St. Crispin's Day, observed June 20
St. Peter's Day, February 22

West Sussex, England
Chichester '900' Festivities, two weeks beginning second week in July
Theatre, Chichester Festival, May-September

West Virginia
Admission Day, June 20
Bridge Day, third Saturday in October
Italian Heritage Festival, West Virginia, first weekend in September
Lights, Winter Festival of, early November through late January
Mountain State Forest Festival, first Wednesday through Sunday in October
New Year's Eve (First Night), December 31
Pike Festival, National, May-June (along Route 40)
Regatta, Charleston Sternwheel, August-September; ten days ending Labor Day, first Monday in September
Vandalia Gathering, last weekend in May
Whitewater Wednesday, third Wednesday in June
Winter Festival, Alpine, six days in early January

West Yorkshire, England
Literature Festival, Ilkley, June during odd-numbered years
Thornton Festival, last week in June

Wetzlar, Hesse, Federal Republic of Germany
Industry Festival of Wetzlar, mid-June to mid-July

Wexford, County Wexford, Ireland
Opera, Wexford Festival, two weeks in late October

Wexford (County), Ireland
Arts Festival, Gorey, summer
Opera, Wexford Festival, two weeks in late October

Wheeling, West Virginia
Lights, Winter Festival of, early November through late January

White Earth, Minnesota
Powwow, White Earth Chippewa, weekend of or before June 14

White House lawn, Washington, D.C.
Christmas Tree, Lighting of the National, mid-December through January 1
Easter Monday (Easter Egg Roll), March-April, Monday after Easter

White Mountain Apache Indians in Arizona
Dance, Sunrise, four days including Labor Day, first Monday in September

Whiterocks, Utah
Dance, Ute Bear (Ma'makoni-ni'tkap), three to five days in April

White Shield, North Dakota
Arikara Celebration, second weekend in July

White Springs, Florida
Folk Festival, Florida, two to three days in late May
Foster Memorial Day, January 13

Whittlesey, Cambridgeshire, England
Straw Bear Day, December-January, Saturday preceding Plough Monday

Whycocomagh, Nova Scotia, Canada
Summer Carnival, Whycocomagh, July

Wichita, Kansas
Powwow, Mid-America All-American Indian Center, last full weekend in July

Wichita Mountains Wildlife Refuge in Lawton, Oklahoma
Easter (Oberammergau Sunrise Service), March-April, first Sunday after first full moon after the vernal equinox

Wickenburg, Arizona
Gold Rush Days, second weekend in February

Wicklow (County), Ireland
Irish Houses Festival, Great, first two weeks in June

Wiesbaden, Hesse, Federal Republic of Germany
May Festival, Wiesbaden International (Internationale Maifestspiele), month of May

Wigene, Belgium
Bruegel Feesten, second Sunday in September every other year

Wilber, Nebraska
Czech Festival, first weekend in August

Williamsport, Pennsylvania
Little League World Series, late August

Wilmington, Delaware
African Methodist Quarterly Meeting Day, last Saturday in August

Wilton, Connecticut
St. Nicholas's Day, December 6

Wiltshire, England
Arts, Salisbury Festival of the, September

Wiltz, Luxembourg
Flower Festival, Broom (Genzefest), May-June, Whit
  Monday, Monday after Pentecost
Theatre and Music Festival, International, July-August

Winchester, Hampshire, England
Arts, Winchester Festival of the, July

Winchester, Virginia
Apple Blossom Festival, Shenandoah, Thursday through
  Saturday nearest May 1

Window Rock, Arizona
Navajo Nation Fair, second week in September, usually
  Wednesday or Thursday through Sunday
Navajo Nightway and Mountain Topway Ceremonials,
  December, date varies

Windsor, Ontario, Canada
Freedom Festival, International, mid-June to
  July 4

Windsor, Berkshire, England
Windsor Festival, two weeks in mid-September

Winnebago Indians in Nebraska: Winnebago
Powwow, Winnebago, usually late July

Winnebago Indians in Wisconsin: Tomah
Wisconsin Dells Stand Rock Ceremonials, nightly from mid-
  June to Labor Day, first Monday in September

Winnipeg, Manitoba, Canada
Folk Festival, Winnipeg, three or four days during second
  weekend in July
Folkorama, one week in mid-August
Interlake Festival, June-August
Musical Theatre, Summer, July-August
Voyageur, Festival du, about one week in
  February

Winston-Salem, North Carolina
Music Festival and Seminar, Moravian, one week in mid-
  June every two or three years; location alternates

Winter Park, Florida
Bach Festival of Winter Park, three days in late February
  or early March

Winterthur, Switzerland
Turnip Lantern Festival (Rebenlichter), November 10-11

Winton, Queensland, Australia
Outback Festival, ten days in August during odd-
  numbered years

Wisconsin
Admission Day, May 29
Arts, Lakefront Festival of the, June
Birkebeiner, American (the Birkie), three days in late
  February
Constitution Day, Norway (Syttende Mai Fest), weekend
  nearest May 17
Folk Fair, Holiday, three days in November
Groundhog Day, February 2
Indian Summer Festival, second weekend in September
Lumberjack World Championships, three days in July
Mardi Gras, February-March
Music Festival, Peninsula, two weeks in mid-August
Music under the Stars, eight weeks from early July to
  mid-August
Polar Bear Swim Day, January 1
Powwow, Bear River, July
Powwow, Honor the Earth, July
Powwow, Land of the Menominee, first weekend in August
Powwow, Ojibwa, August or September
Powwow, Oneida, weekend nearest July 4
Rice Celebration, Wild (Manomin), usually weekend before
  Labor Day, first Monday in September
Summerfest, 11 days, including July 4
William Tell Pageant, first weekend in September
Wisconsin Dells Stand Rock Ceremonials, nightly from mid-
  June to Labor Day, first Monday in September

Wiyot Indians in northwestern California
World Renewal Ceremony, July and August

Wobe people in Ivory Coast
New Yam Festival (Odwira), October

Wodaabe people in Niger
Geerewol Celebrations, June-September, one week during
  rainy season

Wolfville, Nova Scotia, Canada
Kipawo Showboat Company, July-August

Woodland Bowl, Keshena, Wisconsin
Powwow, Land of the Menominee, first weekend in
  August

Woodstock, New York
Maverick Sunday Concerts, Sunday afternoons from July
  to early September

Worcester, England
Three Choirs Festival, seven to ten days in mid-August;
  location alternates annually

Worcester, Massachusetts
Music Festival, Worcester, October and November

Worcestershire, England
Arts Festival, L.G. Harris, second week in October during even-numbered years
Malvern Festival, May-June
Pershore Festival, last two weeks in June

Worthington, Massachusetts
Music Festival, Sevenars, five Sundays from mid-July to mid-August

Wroclaw, Poland
Plays, Festival of Contemporary Polish, May
Theatre, International Festival of Open, even-numbered years in September-October
Wratislavia Cantans-International Oratorio Festival (Miedzynarodowy Festiwal Oratoryjno-Kantatowy), six days during first week in September

Wunsiedel, Bavaria, Federal Republic of Germany
Luisenburg Festival, June-August

Würzburg, Germany
Mozart Festival (Mozartfest), three weeks in June

Wyoming
Admission Day, July 10
Christmas Dances, December
Dance, Sun, July or August
Dance and Ethete Celebration, Sun, July
Earls Court Day, May 9
Frontier Day, observed last full week in July
Gift of the Waters Pageant, first weekend in August
Green River Rendezvous, second Sunday in July
Indian Days, late June
Indian Days, All American, last weekend in July or first in August
Indian Fair, August
Jackalope Days, late June
Labor Day Powwow, first Monday in September
Mountain Man Rendezvous, first weekend in September
Music Festival, Grand Teton, early July to last week in August
Powwow, Arapaho Community, June
Powwow, Northern Arapaho, August
Powwow, Wyoming Indian High School, May
Powwow, Yellow Calf Memorial, May
Wyoming Day, December 10

Xanten/Birten, North Rhine-Westphalia, Federal Republic of Germany
Theatre Festival, Open-Air, Saturdays in July and August

Xanthi, Greece
Gynaecocratia, January 8

Xinan, China
Buddha's Birthday, Enlightenment, and Salvation, eighth day of fourth lunar month

Yakima Indians in Washington: Yakima Reservation
Powwow, Yakima, September
White Swan Celebrations, July fourth weekend

Yakutsk, USSR
Sun Celebration, Midnight (Ysyakh), on or near December 21

Yamagata, Japan
Kurokowa Noh, early February
Shrine Festival, Kuromori Hie, mid-February

Yamatomura, Ibaraki, Japan
Demon-God Festival, one day in April

Yamuna River (along the), India
Karthika Snan, during Hindu month of Karthika

Yaounde, Federal Republic of Cameroon
Independence Day, January 1

Yaqui Indians in Arizona
Holy Saturday, March-April, Saturday before Easter Sunday
Holy Week (Deer Dance and Lenten Ceremonies), March-April, week before Easter
Lent, February-March, forty-day season preceding Easter; observances every Friday from Ash Wednesday through Holy Week
Palm Sunday, March-April, the Sunday preceding Easter
San Xavier Pageant and Fiesta, April
Tucson Festival, two weeks following Easter

Yaqui Indians in Arizona: near Tucson
Easter, March-April, first Sunday after first full moon after the vernal equinox
San Xavier Pageant and Fiesta, April
Tucson Festival, two weeks following Easter

Yaqui Indians in Mexico: Potam, Sonora
Holy Week, March-April, week preceding Easter

Yaqui Indians in Mexico: Sonora
Easter, March-April, first Sunday after first full moon after the vernal equinox
Lent, February-March, forty-day season preceding Easter

Yaqui Indians in southern Arizona and Mexico
Cruz, Fiesta de la
Holy Saturday, March-April, Saturday before Easter Sunday
Our Lady of Guadalupe, December 12
Santo Isobel, Fiesta of, July 4

Yarmouth Port, Massachusetts
Music Festival, Cape and Islands Chamber, three weeks from end of July to mid-August

Yasukini Shrine, Tokyo, Japan
Yasukini Matsuri, four-day observance in April; also in summer, autumn, and winter

Yatenga Region of Upper Volta
Bega Ceremonies, one week opening the planting season

Ybor City, Florida
Garbanzo, Fiesta Sopa de, begins Sunday nearest February 9 and ends Saturday
Guavaween, last Saturday in October

Yellowknife, Northwest Territories, Canada
Caribou Carnival and Championship Dog Derby, one week in March

Yemen
Passover (Pesach), eight days beginning 15th day of Jewish month of Nisan
Purim, 14th day of Jewish month of Adar
Shavuot, the Feast of Weeks, sixth day of Jewish month of Sivan
Simhat Torah, 23rd day of Jewish month of Tishri
Sukkot (Feast of Booths or Feast of the Tabernacles), 15th-21st or 22nd of Jewish month of Tishri
Tisha B'Av, ninth day of Jewish month of Av
Yom Kippur, tenth day of Jewish month of Tishri

Yemen, People's Democratic Republic of
Independence Day, November 30
National Day, September 26
National Day, October 14

Yemen Arab Republic
National Day, September 26
Reform Movement Day, June 13

Yokosuka, Japan
Anjin Matsuri, April
Black Ship Day, May-July, dates vary

York, Yorkshire, England
Mystery Plays, York Festival and, every three years in June

Yorkshire, England
Christmas Eve (Tolling the Devil's Knell), December 24
Clipping the Church Day, August 5
Mystery Plays, York Festival and, every three years in June

Yorktown, Virginia
Yorktown Day, October 19

Yoruba people
Gelede, occasional: end of dry season (March-May); August; and during emergencies and funerals
Iro Festivals, five festivals annually
New Yam Festival, two-day festival in August
New Yam Festival (Egbodo Oba Ooni), late June
New Yam Festival (Eje, two-day festival)
New Yam Festival (Igun Efon Festival)
New Yam Festival (Igun Ekun Ajinida Festival), annual
New Yam Festival (Igun Luwo Festival)
New Yam Festival (Ilaja Isu Titun)
New Yam Festival (Ogijan Festival), annual
Olojo (Ogun Festival), around July
Sango Festival, early November, seven days near end of rainy season
Thanksgiving (Awoojoh), may occur on special occasions and during such holidays as Christmas, Easter, Good Friday, and New Year's Day

Yoruba people in Nigeria: Ede
Egungun Festival, June

Yoruba people in Nigeria: Oyo
Olojo (Ogun Festival), around July

Yoshida, Japan
Mount Fuji Climbing Season, July 1-August 26

Young America, Minnesota
Stiftungsfest, last weekend in August

Ypres, Belgium
Cat Festival (Kattestoet), second Sunday in May every three years

Yucatan, Mexico
Chickaban (Feast of the Storm God Kukulcan), end of October, Mayan month of Xul
Dinner of the Milpa (u hanli col), every four years when corn ripens
Mardi Gras, February-March

Yuchi Indians
Dance, Green Corn

Yugoslavia
Amateur Stages, Belgrade Review of Experimental, mid-May
Amateurs to Their City, October 20
Autumn of Culture, second half of October
Ballet Biennial, June-July during odd-numbered years
Bled Evenings (Bled na Gorenjskem), July-August
Child, Yugoslav Festival of the, June-July
Children's Day (Dechiyi Dan), December, a Sunday before Christmas
Christmas (Božic), December 25

651

Yugoslavia *(cont.)*
Theatres of Vojvodina, Encounter of, May
Theatres of Vojvodina, Encounter of Amateur, May
Theatres of Vojvodina, Encounter of Slovak Amateur,
February
Theatres of Yugoslavia, Festival of Small and Experimental,
March 27-April 6
Vintage Festival, September
Young May, April-May
Youth Culture Week, May
Youth Day (Marshall Tito's Birthday), May 25
Zagreb Evenings, June-September

Yukon, Canada
Asking Festival (Ai-yá-g'ûk)
Discovery Days, observed in August
Klondike Gold Discovery Day, observed the Monday nearest
August 17

Yuma Indians in Arizona
Dead, Observance for the (Keruk), seven nights annually

Yuma Indians in California
Dead, Observance for the (Keruk), seven nights annually

Yunnan, China
Torch Festival, 24th-26th days of sixth lunar month

Yuriria, Guanajuato, Mexico
Nativity Plays, mid-December to January

Yurok Indians in northwestern California
World Renewal Ceremony, July and August

Zaandam, Netherlands
Luilak (Lazybones Day or Sluggard's Feast), May-June,
Saturday preceding Pentecost or Whit Sunday

Zacatecas, Mexico
St. Anthony's Day (San Antonio Abad), January 17

Zaghouan Region, Tunisia
Ceres, Festival, May
Popular Festival of Sidi-Ali-El Hattab, April

Zagreb, Croatia, Yugoslavia
Folklore Review, International, July
Puppet Festival, International, September-October
Theatre, Days of Young, December
Theatres for Children and Youth, Encounter of Professional,
May
Zagreb Evenings, June-September

Zahle, Lebanon
Wine Festival, Zahle, early September

Zaire (Democratic Republic of the Congo; formerly Belgian Congo)
Christmas, December 25
Fisherman's Day, June 24
Founders Day and Youth Day, October 14
Independence Day, June 30
Martyrs' Day, January 4
Parents' Day, July 31, two-day holiday

Zajecar, Serbia, Yugoslavia
Young May, April-May

Zambia (formerly Northern Rhodesia)
Africa Day, May 25
Farmers' Day, August 2
Heroes' Day, observed first Monday in July
Independence Day, October 24, two-day holiday
Kuomboka, February-March, when Zambezi River rises
Labour Day, May 3, observed first Monday in May
Midimu Ceremony, June through October; begins night
during the period when the moon moves from the quarter
to its half phase for three days
Unity Day, July 6; observed first Tuesday in July
Youth Day; March 13 or first Monday in August

Zapotec Indians in Mexico: Oaxaca
Monday on the Hill (Lunes del Cerro, Guelaguetza offering
ritual), third and fourth Mondays in July

Zealand, Denmark
Viking Festival, three days to two weeks in June-July

Zemun, Serbia, Yugoslavia
Monodrama and Pantomime, Festival of, April

Zgorzelec, Poland
Amateur One-Man Shows, National Meeting of, October

Zimbabwe (formerly Southern Rhodesia)
Africa Day, May 25
Christmas, December 25
Heroes Days, two-day holiday, including August 11
Independence Day, April 18
Midimu Ceremony, June through October; begins night
during the period when the moon moves from the quarter
to its half phase for three days

Zinacantan, Mexico
Mardi Gras (Carnaval, Fiesta of Games), February-March,
one week ending Ash Wednesday
St. Lawrence of Rome, Feast Day of (Día de San Lorenzo),
August 10
St. Sebastian's Day (Día de San Sabastián), January 20;
observed for nine days, from January 17 to January 25
Virgen del Rosario, Fiesta for the, October 7

Zinza, Tanzania
First Fruits Festival, March

Znojmo, Moravia, Czechoslovakia
Znojmo Feast, every Friday and Saturday in June-September

Zululand, South Africa
Christmas, December 25

Zulu people in South Africa
First Fruits Festival

Zuni Indians in New Mexico: Santa Fe Indian Market Plaza, Santa Fe
Indian Market, third weekend in August

Zuñi Pueblo, New Mexico
All Souls' Day, November 2
Dance, Red Paint Kachina, September 12
Kokochi, summer solstice
Shalako Ceremonial (koko awia, the kachina come), late
    November or early December

Zurich, Switzerland
Boys' Rifle Match (Knabenschiessen), second weekend
    in September
June Festival, International, May-early June
Six O'Clock Ringing Festival (Sechselauten), third Sunday
    and Monday in April
Turnip Lantern Festival (Rebenlichter), November 10-11

Name Index

The Name Index is an alphabetical listing of persons with whom holidays and festivals are associated, according to the sources indexed.

Abbott, Robert S. (1868-1940)
Bud Billiken Day, August 14

'Abdu'l-Bahá (Abbas Effendi, 1844-1921)
'Abdu'l-Bahá, Ascension of, November 28
'Abdu'l-Bahá, Birth of, May 23

Adams, William (1564-1620)
Anjin Matsuri, April

Alexandra, queen of King Edward VII of Great Britain (1844-1925)
Alexandra Rose Day, a Saturday in June

Ali Muhammad, Mirza (1819-1850)
Báb, Birth of the, October 20
Báb, Declaration of the, May 23
Báb, Martyrdom of the, July 9

Allen, Richard (1760-1831)
Allen Day, Richard, February 11

Alvarez Pineda, Alonzo (fl. 1519)
Buccaneer Days, last weekend in April through first
  weekend in May

Andersen, Hans Christian (1805-1875)
Andersen Festival, Hans Christian, July-August
Children's Book Day, International, April 2

Anthony, Susan B. (1820-1906)
Anthony Day, Susan B., February 15 or August 24

Artigas, José Gervasio (1764-1850)
Artigas Day, June 19

Audubon, John James (1785-1851)
Audubon Day, April 26

Aung San (1914-1947)
Martyrs Day, Burma, July 19

Austin, Stephen Fuller (1793-1836)
Father of Texas Day, November 3

Bach, Johann Sebastian (1685-1750)
Bach Festival, Baldwin-Wallace, two days in mid-May
Bach Festival, Carmel, mid-July to early August
Bach Festival, English, April and May
Bach Festival, International, June
Bach Festival, Oregon, late June to second week in July
Bach Festival (Bachwoche Ansbach), ten days in late July
  during odd-numbered years

Bach Festival of Winter Park, three days in late February
  or early March
Bach Music Festival, two weekends in May

Baden-Powell, Robert (1857-1941)
Girl Guides Thinking Day, February 22
Thinking Day, February 22

Bahá'u'lláh (Mirza Husayn Ali Nuri, 1817-1892)
Bahá'u'lláh, Ascension of, May 29
Bahá'u'lláh, Birth of the, November 12
Bahá'u'lláh, Declaration of, April 21-May 2

Balfour, Arthur J. (1848-1930)
Balfour Declaration Day, November 2

Barca, Calderon de la (1600-1681)
Calderon Festival in the Old Courtyard, June-July

Barnum, Phineas Taylor (1810-1891)
Barnum Festival, 17 days from late June to July 4

Baudoin III, count of Flanders (fl. 10th century)
Cat Festival, second Sunday in May

Beethoven, Ludwig van (1770-1827)
Beethoven Concerts, Martonvásár, summer
Beethoven Festival, September-October
Beethoven Festival, three weeks beginning mid-June

Beiderbecke, Bix (1903-1931)
Jazz Festival, Bix Beiderbecke Memorial, three days during
  last weekend in July

Berchtold (late 12th-early 13th century)
Berchtold's Day, January 2

Berlioz, Hector (1803-1869)
Berlioz International Festival, one week in mid-
  September

Bhumibol Adulyadej, king of Thailand (b. 1927)
Coronation Day (Chulalongkorn's Day), May 5
National Day, Thailand, December 5

Birendra Bir Bikram Shah Dev, king of Nepal (b. 1945)
King, Birthday of His Majesty the, December 29

Blavatsky, Helena Petrovna (1831-1891)
Blavatsky, Death of, May 9

Bliss, Henry Edward Ernest Victor (1869-1926)
Baron Bliss Day, March 9

Bodhidharma (fl. sixth century)
Ta Mo's Day, fifth day of tenth lunar month

Boganda, Barthélémy (1910-1959)
Boganda Day, March 29

Bolívar, Simon, president of Peru (1783-1830)
Bolívar Day, July 24

Boone, Daniel (c. 1734-1820)
Boone Festival, first through second Saturdays in October

Booth, Ballington (1857-1940)
Volunteers of America, Founder of, July 28

Booth, William (1829-1912)
Salvation Army Founder's Day, April 10

Borglum, Gutzon (John Gutzon de la Mothe Borglum, 1867-1941)
Borglum Day, Gutzon, August 10

Botev, Khristo (1848-1876)
Botev Day, May 20

Bowles, William Augustus (d. 1803)
Billy Bowlegs Festival, first full weekend in June

Brady, Samuel (1758-1795)
Brady Day, Captain, July-August

Brightwell, Dr. W.T. (b. 1916)
Blueberry Festival, Alabama, third Saturday in June

Britt, Peter (1819-1905)
Britt Festival, June-September

Bronte, Anne (1820-1849)
Thornton Festival, last week in June

Bronte, Charlotte (1816-1855)
Thornton Festival, last week in June

Bronte, Emily (1818-1848)
Thornton Festival, last week in June

Brown, John (1800-1859)
Brown Day, John, May 9

Bruckner, Anton (1824-1896)
Bruckner Festival, International, four weeks in September

Bruegel, Pieter (c. 1525 or 1530-1569)
Bruegel Feesten, second Sunday in September every other year

Buddha
See **Gautama, Siddhartha**

Burbank, Luther (1849-1926)
Burbank Day, March 7

Burgoyne, John (1722-1792)
Burgoyne's Surrender Day, October 17

Burk, Calamity Jane (Cannary) (1852?-1903)
Seventy-Six, Days of, first full weekend in August

Burns, Robert (1759-1796)
Burns Night, January 25

Butler, Jim (1855-1923)
Butler Days, last weekend in May

Cabot, John (c. 1450- c. 1499)
Discovery Day, on or near June 24

Cabrillo, Juan Rodríguez (d. 1543)
Cabrillo Day, six days in September

Camões, Luiz Vaz de (1524?-1580)
National Day (Camões Memorial Day), June 10

Canute the Great (c. 995-1035)
St. Knut's Day, January 13

Capp, Al (Alfred Gerald Caplin, 1909-1979)
Sadie Hawkins Day, first Saturday in November

Casals, Pablo (1876-1973)
Casals Festival, 16 days in June

Castellano, Juan Maria de (fl. late 19th-early 20th century)
Hermit, Feast of the, September 1

Cervantes, Miguel de (1547-1616)
Cervantes Festival, International, three weeks in April-May

Chapman, John (1774-1845)
Johnny Appleseed, Birthday of, September 26
Johnny Appleseed Day, March 11
Johnny Appleseed Festival, third week in September
Johnny Appleseed Week, last week in September

Charlemagne, king of the Franks (742-814)
St. Charlemagne's Day, January 28

Charles I, king of Great Britain (1600-1649)
St. Charles's Day, January 30

Charles II, king of Great Britain (1630-1685)
Shick-Shack Day, May 29

Chiang Kai-shek, president of China (1887-1975)
Chiang Kai-shek Day, October 31 or November 1

Chouteau, Jean Pierre (1758-1849)
Oklahoma Historical Day, October 10

Ch'ü Yüan (328-298 B.C.)
Double Fifth, fifth day of fifth lunar month

Clark, George Roger (1752-1818)
Vincennes Day, February 24

Clinton, General George (1739-1812)
Regatta, General Clinton Canoe, last weekend in May

Columbus, Christopher (1451-1506)
Columbus Day in Haiti (Discovery Day), December 5
Columbus Day in St. Vincent (Discovery Day), January 22
Columbus Day in the Cayman Islands (Discovery Day),
  May 17
Columbus Day in the United States and elsewhere, October
  12; observed second Monday in October
Jayuya Festival of Indian Lore (Jayuya Indian Festival),
  mid-November

Confucius (551-479 B.C.)
Confucius's Birthday, 27th day of eighth lunar month

Coolidge, Calvin, president of the United States (1872-1933)
Coolidge, Birthday Celebration of Calvin, July 4

Coronado, Francisco Vásquez de (c. 1510-1554)
Coronado Day, February 25

Crandall, Prudence (1803-1890)
Crandall Day, Prudence, Saturday before Labor Day, first
  Monday in September

Crispin (d. c. 287)
St. Crispin's Day, October 25

Crispinian (d. c. 287)
St. Crispin's Day, October 25

Cromwell, Oliver (1599-1658)
Cromwell Day, September 3

Cuauhtemoc (c. 1495-1522)
Cuauhtemoc, Homage to (Homenaje a Cuauhtemoc),
  August 21

Custer, George Armstrong (1839-1876)
Custer's Last Stand, late June or early July

Davis, Dwight F. (1879-1945)
Davis Cup, November-December

Davis, Jefferson, president of the Confederate States (1808-1889)
Davis's Birthday, Jefferson, June 3

Dédé, Sanité (fl. 1820s)
Dance, Calinda, June 23

Desgranges, Henri (1865-1940)
Tour de France, four weeks in July

Dessalines, Jean-Jacques (1758?-1806)
Independence Day, Haiti, January 1

Devanamipiya, king of Ceylon (fl. second half of third century B.C.)
Sangamitta Day, full moon day of first lunar month or full
  moon day of Hindu month of Jyeshta

Dickens, Charles (1812-1870)
Broadstairs Dickens Festival, eight days in June

Disraeli, Benjamin, earl of Beaconsfield (1804-1881)
Primrose Day, April 19

Dodge, Geraldine Rockefeller (1882-1973)
Poetry Festival, Geraldine R. Dodge, three days in September

Douglas, Frederick (1817-1895)
Black History Month, February

Drumev, Vasil (c. 1840-1901)
Theatre Days Named after Drumev, date varies during even-
  numbered years

Duarte, Juan Pablo (1813-1876)
Duarte Day, January 26

Dullin, Charles (1885-1949)
Dullin Prize Competition, May-June, Thursday-Sunday
  evening of Ascension Day during even-numbered years

Eddy, Mary Baker (1821-1910)
Eddy, Birthday of Mary Baker, July 16

Edison, Thomas Alva (1847-1931)
Edison Pageant of Light, second Wednesday-third Saturday
  in February, including February 11
Edison's Birthday, Thomas, February 11

Elijah (c. 1000 years before Christian era)
Elijah Day, July 20

Elizabeth I, queen of England (1533-1603)
Queen's Day, November 17

Elizabeth II, queen of England (b. 1926)
Queen Elizabeth II, Birthday of, June 12 or second Saturday
  in June

Fawkes, Guy (1750-1606)
Fawkes Day, Guy, November 5

Ferdowsi of Tus (c. 935-c. 1020 or 1026)
Tus, Festival of, July

Fieschi of Lavagna, Count (fl. 1240)
Torta dei Fieschi, August 14

Foster, Stephen (1826-1864)
Foster Memorial Day, January 13

Fox, George (1624-1691)
Fox, Death of George, January 13

Franco, Francisco (1892-1975)
Caudillo, Day of the, October 1

Franklin, Benjamin (1706-1790)
Franklin's Birthday, Benjamin, January 17

Franz Joseph II, prince of Liechtenstein (b. 1905)
Prince's Birthday, August 15

Frederick IX, king of Denmark (1899-1972)
King's Birthday, March 11

Gable, Clark (1901-1960)
Gable Birthday Celebration, Clark, Saturday nearest February 1

Gandhi, Mohandas Karamchand (1869-1948)
Gandhi's Birthday (Gandhi Jayanti), October 2

Garner, John Nance, vice president of the United States (1868-1967)
Cactus Jack Festival, second weekend in October

Gasparilla, José (d. 1820s)
Gasparilla Pirate Festival and Invasion, six days beginning second Monday in February

Gauranga (Chaitanya Mahaprabhu, 1485-1533)
Fire Festival (Holi), 14th day of Hindu month of Phalguna or Dol

Gautama, Siddhartha (c. 563- c. 483 B.C.)
Buddha's Birthday, Enlightenment, and Salvation, eighth day of fourth lunar month

Gedaliah ben Ahikam (fl. 586 B.C.)
Gedaliah, Fast of, September-October, the days following Jewish New Year (Rosh Hashanah)

George, prince of Bavaria (d. 1503)
Landshut Wedding, three weeks, including four Sundays in June-July, every third year

George III, king of England (1738-1820)
Fourth of June, on or near June 4

George V, king of England (1865-1936)
King's Birthday, a Monday in early June

Go-Yozei, emperor of Japan (1586-1611)
Martyr Day, February 5

Greenwood, Chester (1858-1937)
Greenwood Day, Chester, first Saturday in December

Gregory the Theologian (fl. fourth century)
Three Hierarchs or Archbishops, Holiday of the, January 30

Grillparzer, Franz (1791-1872)
Castle Plays Festival, June-July

Gruber, Franz Xaver (1787-1863)
"Silent Night, Holy Night" Celebration, December 24

Gustafus Adolphus II, king of Sweden (1594-1632)
Gustafus Adolphus Day, November 6

Gustav I, king of Sweden (1496?-1560)
Constitution and Flag Day, June 6
Vasaloppet, first Sunday in March

Gustav IV Adolph, king of Sweden (1778-1837)
King's Birthday, November 11; observed June 2

Handel, George Friedrich (1685-1759)
Handel Festival, six days in summer

Handsome Lake (fl. 1799)
Strawberry Festival, usually June

Handy, William Christopher (1873-1958)
Music Festival, W.C. Handy, first full week in August

Hassan II, king of Morocco (b. 1929)
Throne Day, Morocco, March 3

Haydn, Franz Joseph (1732-1809)
Haydn Memorial Concerts, summer

Hedwig, princess of Poland (1457-1502)
Landshut Wedding, three weeks, including four Sundays in June-July, every third year

Hemingway, Ernest (1899-1961)
Hemingway Days, week including July 21

Henry VI, king of England (1421-1471)
Lilies and Roses Day, May 21

Hickok, Wild Bill (1837-1876)
Seventy-Six, Days of, first full weekend in August

Hippocrates (c. 460- c. 377 B.C.)
Hippokrateia, August

Hirohito, emperor of Japan (1901-1989)
Hirohito's Birthday, April 29

Horia, Nicolas (alternate spelling Horea, 1735?-1785)
Weighing Festival, second Sunday in May

Hostos, Eugenio Maria de (1839-1903)
Hostos, Birthday of (Hostos Day), January 11

Houdini, Harry (1874-1926)
National Magic Day, October 31

Houston, Sam (1793-1863)
Independence Day, Texas, March 2

Hujwiri, Ali (Syed Ali Abdul Hasan Bin Usman
Hajwiri, d. 1072)
Data Ganj Baksh Death Festival, 18-19 days of Islamic
month of Safar

Husayn, Imam (624-680)
Husayn or Husain Day, tenth day of Islamic month
of Muharram

Husayn Ali Nuri, Mirza
See **Bahá'u'lláh**

Hussein, king of Jordan (b. 1935)
Hussein Day, November 14

Ibsen, Henrik (1828-1906)
Peer Gynt Festival Days, begins August 4

Isabel de Flores (1586-1617)
St. Rose of Lima, Feast of, August 23

Isabella, queen of Spain (1451-1504)
Queen Isabella Day, April 22

Jackson, Andrew, president of the United States (1767-1845)
Jackson's Birthday, Andrew, March 15

Jackson, Thomas Jonathan "Stonewall" (1824-1863)
Lee-Jackson Day, January 18, observed third Monday
in January

Jalāl ad-Dīn ar-Rūmī (c. 1207-1273)
Mevlana (Festival of Whirling Dervishes), nine days to two
weeks in December

James IV, king of Scotland (1473-1513)
Common Ridings Day, June

Jefferson, Thomas, president of the United States (1743-1826)
Jefferson's Birthday, Thomas, April 13

Jesus of Nazareth (c. 6 B.C.-c. 30 A.D.)
Ascension Day, May-June, fortieth day after Easter Sunday
Baptism of the Lord, Feast of the, Sunday after January 6
Black Christ, Festival of the, October 21
Black Nazarene Fiesta, January 1-9
Candlemas, February 2
Christmas, December 25
Christ the King, Feast of, last Sunday in October; mid-
November in Guam/Northern Marianas
Circumcision, Feast of the, January 1
Corpus Christi, May-June, the Sunday after Trinity Sunday
Easter, March-April, first Sunday after the first full moon
after the vernal equinox
Epiphany, January 6
Exaltation of the Cross, September 14
Good Friday, March-April, Friday before Easter
Holy Family, Feast of the, Sunday after January 6
Holy Thursday, March-April, Thursday before Easter
Palm Sunday, March-April, the Sunday before Easter Sunday
Precious Blood, Feast of the Most, July 1
Sacred Heart of Jesus, Feast of the, May-June, the Friday
after Corpus Christi
Transfiguration, Feast of the, August 6

Je-Tsong-Kha-Pa (1357-1419)
Lights, Festival of (Sang-joe), 25th day of tenth
Tibetan month

Jimmu Tenno, emperor of Japan (fl. 660 B.C.)
Foundation Day, Japanese National, February 11

Jinnah, Muhammed Ali (1876-1948)
Jinnah Day, September 11

John Chrysostum (fl. fourth century)
Three Hierarchs or Archbishops, Holiday of the, January 30

Johnson, Lyndon Baines, president of the United States
(1908-1973)
Johnson's Birthday, Lyndon B., August 27

Joseph, Chief (In-mut-too-yah-lat-lat, c. 1840-1904)
Powwow, Warriors Memorial, third weekend in June

Jovanovic, Ljubisa (b. 1936)
Jovanovic, Festivities in Honor of, October

Joyce, James (1882-1941)
Bloomsday, June 16

Juárez, Benito Palbo (1806-1872)
Juárez Day (Day of the Indian Chief), March 21

Juliana, queen of the Netherlands (b. 1909)
Queen Juliana's Birthday, April 30

Kalakaua, David, king of Hawaii (1836-1891)
Merrie Monarch Festival, March-April, several days
beginning Easter Sunday

Kalidasa (fl. fifth century)
Drama Festival, Kalidasa, first week in November

Kamehameha I, king of Hawaii (1758?-1819)
Kamehameha Day, June 11

Karenga, Maulana (b. 1941)
Kwanzaa, December 26 through January 1

Kartini, Raden Adjeng (1879-1904)
Kartini Day, April 21

Keaulana, "Buffalo" (n.d.)
Surfing Classic, Buffalo's Big Board, two days in
February

Keller, Helen (1880-1968)
Keller Festival, Helen, last weekend in June

Kelly, Emmett (1898-1979)
Clown Festival, Emmett Kelly, early May

**Kennedy, John F., president of the United States
(1917-1963)**
Kennedy Day, John F., November 24; observed last
Sunday in November

Key, Francis Scott (1779-1843)
National Anthem Day, September 14

Khomeini, Ayatollah (1901-1989)
Khomeini Day, February 1

King, Jr., Martin Luther (1929-1968)
King's Birthday, January 15; observed third Monday
in January

Kirillovich, Bartholomew (1314-1392)
St. Sergius of Radonezh, September 25

Kivi, Aleksis (pseud. for Aleksis Stenvall, 1834-1872)
Kivi Day, October 10

Komensky, Jan Amos (1592-1670)
Teacher's Day, March 28

Kosciuszko, Tadeusz (1746-1817)
Kosciuszko Day, February 4

Kossuth, Lajos (1802-1894)
Kossuth Day, March 20

Kruger, Stephanus Johannes Paulus (1825-1904)
Kruger Day, October 10

Kuhio Kalanianaole, Jonah, prince of Hawaii (1871-1921)
Kuhio Kalanianaole Day, one week in March, including
March 26

Lak, Piet (fl. 1672)
Luilak (Lazybones Day or Sluggard's Feast), May-June,
Saturday before Pentecost

Latif, Shah Abdul (1689-1752)
Shah Abdul Latif Death Festival, 14-16 days of Islamic month
of Safar

Laval, Father Jacques Désiré (1803-1884)
Pilgrimage to Shrine of Father Laval, September 8

Lee, Ann (1736-1784)
Lee, Birthday of Ann, February 29

Lee, Robert E. (1807-1870)
Lee Day, Robert E., January 19; may be observed third
Monday in January
Lee-Jackson Day, January 18; third Monday in January

Leif Eriksson (fl. 1000)
Leif Eriksson Day, Iceland, Norway, and United States,
October 9

Le Moyne, Pierre, sieur d'Iberville (1661-1706)
Landing of d'Iberville, last weekend in April

Lenin, Vladimir Ilich (1870-1924)
Lenin, Anniversary of the Death of, January 21

Leo, emperor of Constantinople (n.d.)
Life-Bearing Spring (Zoodochos Pege), March-April,
Friday after Easter

Leopold I, king of Belgium (1790-1865)
Independence Day, Belgium, July 21

**Lincoln, Abraham, president of the United States
(1809-1865)**
Black History Month, February
Equal Opportunity Day, November 19
Lincoln's Birthday, Abraham, February 12; observed first
Monday in February

Long, Huey P. (1893-1935)
Long Day, Huey P., August 30

Longfellow, Henry Wadsworth (1807-1882)
Song of Hiawatha Pageant, last two weeks in July and
first week in August

Lönnrot, Elias (1802-1884)
Kalevala Päivä Day, February 28

Looking Glass, Chief (d. 1877)
Powwow, Looking Glass, August

Lubbock, Sir John (1843-1913)
St. Lubbock's Day, first Monday in August

Ludwig I of Bavaria (1786-1868)
Oktoberfest, 16 days beginning first Sunday in October

Lu Pan (b. 606 B.C.)
Lu Pan, Birthday of, July 18

Luther, Martin (1483-1546)
Martinsfest, November 10-11
Reformation Day, October 31; observed Sunday
before October 31

MacArthur, Douglas (1880-1964)
MacArthur Day, Douglas, January 26

Magellan, Ferdinand (c. 1480-1521)
Magellan or Discovery Day, March 6

Mahavira, Lord Vardhamana (c. 599-527 B.C.)
Lights, Festival of (Dewali), one week during Hindu
month of Karthika
Mahavira's Birthday, 13th day of waxing half of Hindu
month of Chaitra
Pajjusana, eight-day penance in August

Maimon, Moses Ben (1135-1204)
Maimona or Maimonides, March-April, evening of last
day of Passover and day after

Malcolm X (Malcolm Little, 1925-1965)
Malcolm X Day, third Sunday in May

Margrethe II, queen of Denmark (b. 1940)
Queen Margrethe's Birthday, April 16

Marley, Bob (1945-1981)
Reggae Sunsplash, four nights in August

Mary, mother of Jesus (first century B.C.-first century A.D.)
Annunciation, Feast of the, March 25

Assumption, Feast of the, August 15
Holy Family, Feast of the, Sunday after January 6
Immaculate Conception, Feast of the, December 8
Mary, Month of (Mois de Marie), May
Nativity of the Virgin, September 8
Presentation of the Blessed Virgin Mary, November 21
Queenship of Mary, August 22
Visitation of the Blessed Virgin Mary, Feast of the,
July 2 (Anglican); May 31 (Roman Catholic and Protestant)

Massasoit (d. 1661)
Thanksgiving, fourth Thursday in November

May, Karl (1842-1912)
May Festival, July-August

McDonogh, John (1779-1850)
McDonogh Day, first Friday in May

Meiji Setsu, emperor of Japan (ruled 1864-1911)
Meiji Setsu, November 3

Menuhin, Yehudi (b. 1916)
Menuhin Festival, three weeks in August

Milagrous, Señor de los (fl. before 1655)
Purple Spring, month of October

Mix, Tom (1880-1940)
Mix Roundup, Tom, three days in July

Modestus (patriarch of Jerusalem from 631-34)
St. Modesto's Day, December 18

Mohr, Father Josef (1792-1848)
"Silent Night, Holy Night" Celebration, December 24

Mollyockett (fl. 18th century)
Mollyockett Day, third Saturday in July

Monroe, Bill (b. 1912)
Bluegrass Fan Fest, third weekend in September

Moore, Billy (d. 1934)
Moore Days, Billy, second weekend in October

Morton, J. Sterling (1832-1902)
Arbor Day, April 22 in Nebraska; last Friday in April in
the rest of the United States

Moshoeshoe (c. 1790-1870)
Moshoeshoe Day, March 12

Moulay Idriss I (fl. eighth century)
Pilgrimage to Moulay Idriss, late August or September

Mozart, Wolfgang Amadeus (1756-1791)
  Mozart, Birthday of, January 27
  Mozart Festival, German, eight days during second week
    in June
  Mozart Festival, Mostly, seven weeks in mid-July to last week
    in August
  Mozart Festival, San Luis Obispo, six days late July-
    early August
  Mozart Festival, Vermont, three weeks mid-July to first week
    in August
  Mozart Festival (Mozartfest), three weeks in June
  Mozart Week, nine days at end of January

Muhammad (c. 570-632)
  Muhammad's Birthday, 12th day of Islamic month of
    Rabi al-Awwal
  New Year (Muharram Celebrations), first day of Islamic
    month of Muharram
  Night Journey of Muhammad, 27th day of Islamic
    month of Rajab
  Night of Power, usually 27th day of Islamic month
    of Ramadan

Munoz Rivera, Luis (1859-1916)
  Craft's Fair, three days in July, including July 17
  Munoz Rivera Day, July 17

Nanak, Guru (1469-1539)
  Nanak's Day (Nanak Parab), full moon day of Hindu
    month of Karthika

Napoleon Bonaparte (1761-1821)
  Napoleon's Day, May 5

Nayak, Tirumala (fl. 17th century)
  Floating Festival, full moon day of Hindu month
    of Magha

Nelson, Horatio (1758-1805)
  Trafalgar Day (Nelson Day), October 21

Nestroy, Johann (1801-1862)
  Nestroy Festival (Nestroy-Spiele) July

Newport, Matilda (fl. 1822)
  Matilda Newport Day, December 1

**Ngouabi, Marien, president of the People's Republic of
Congo (1938-1977)**
  Sacrifice, Day of the Supreme, March 18

Nightingale, Florence (1820-1910)
  Hospital Day and Week, National, week including
    May 12
  Nurses' Week, first or second week of May

Oakley, Annie (Phoebe Ann Moses, 1860-1926)
  Oakley Festival, Annie, last full week in July

Oglethorpe, James Edward (1696-1785)
  Georgia Week Celebrations, one week in February, including
    February 12

O'Neill, Rose (1874-1944)
  Kewpiesta, third weekend in April

**Oranmiyan, King (fl. sometime between the late 12th and
15th centuries)**
  Olojo (Ogun Festival), around July

Padmasambhava (Guru Rinpoche, fl. eighth century)
  Hemis Festival, three days in June or July
  Paro Tshechu, March-April, 10th-15th days of second
    lunar month

Pahlevi, Shah Mohammed Riza (1919-1980)
  National Day, Iran, October 26

Paine, Thomas (1737-1809)
  Paine Day, Thomas (Common Sense Day), Sunday nearest
    January 29

Palamas, Costis (1859-1943)
  Palamas Poetry Festival, early March

Parnell, Charles Stewart (1846-1891)
  Ivy Day, October 6

Patton, George Jr. (1885-1945)
  Remembrance Day, Luxembourg, July 6

Penn, William (1644-1718)
  Pennsylvania Day, October 24

Perry, Matthew (1794-1858)
  Black Ship Day, May-July, dates vary

Phillip, Arthur (1738-1814)
  Australia Day, January 26 or following Monday
  Australia Day at the Rocks, late January

Pinkerton, J.G. "Paw Paw" (b. 1926)
  Tellabration, November, Friday before Thanksgiving

Pintea the Brave (fl. 18th century)
  Pintea the Brave Day, first Sunday in September

Ponce de León (1460-1521)
  Pascua Florida Day, April 2

Presley, Elvis (1935-1977)
  Elvis International Tribute Week, week including August 16

St. Peter (d. c. 64)
St. Peter's Chains, Feast of, August 1
St. Peter's Chair, Festival of, January 18
St. Peter's Day, June 29
Sts. Peter and Paul Day, June 29

St. Peter Baptist (d. 1597)
Martyr Day, February 5

St. Philibert (c. 608-c. 685)
St. Philibert's Day, August 20

St. Philip (fl. first century)
St. Philip, Feast of and Green Corn Dance,
   May 1
Sts. Philip and James, Feast of, May 3

St. Philip of Moscow (1507-1569)
St. Philip of Moscow's Day, January 9

St. Piran (d. c. 480)
St. Piran's Day, March 5

St. Placidus (fl. 614)
St. Placidus Festival, July 11

St. Plato or Plane-tree (d. c. 306)
St. Plato the Martyr, Feast of, November 18

St. Polycarp, bishop of Smyrna (c. 69-c. 155)
St. Polycarp's Day, January 26

St. Roch (c. 1350-c. 1380)
St. Roch's Day, August 16

St. Sava (c. 1174-1235)
St. Sava's Day, January 14

St. Sebastian (d. c. 288)
St. Sebastian's Day, January 20

St. Servatus (d. 384)
Frost, or Ice, Saints Day, May 11-14

St. Sidi Abdallah Ben Hassoun (n.d.)
Wax Festival, November

St. Simon Stylites (c. 390-459)
St. Simon Stylites's Day, January 5

St. Spyridon, bishop of Tremithus (d. c. 348)
St. Spyridon, Feast Day of, December 14

St. Stanislaus of Kracow (1030-1079)
St. Stanislaus, Feast of, April 11

St. Stephen (d. c. 35)
Boxing Day, December 26
Floral Carnival, National, August 20
St. Stephen, Feast of, December 26

St. Stephen, king of Hungary (c. 975-1038)
St. Stephen's Day, August 20

St. Swithin, bishop of Winchester (c. 800-862)
St. Swithin's Day, July 15

St. Sylvester (314-335)
St. Sylvester's Day, December 31

St. Teresa of Avila (1515-1582)
St. Teresa of Avila, Feast of, October 15

St. Therese of Lisieux (1873-1897)
St. Therese of Lisieux, Feast of, October 1

St. Thomas á Becket of Canterbury (c. 1118-1170)
St. Thomas of Canterbury, Feast of, December 29

St. Thomas Aquinas (c. 1225-1274)
St. Thomas Aquinas, Feast of, January 28

St. Thomas More (1478-1535)
St. Thomas More, Feast Day of, June 22

St. Thomas the Apostle (d. 53)
Doleing Day, December 21
St. Thomas the Apostle, Feast of, December 21

St. Thorlak Thorhalli, bishop of Skalholt (1133-1193)
St. Thorlak's Day, December 23

St. Ursula (fl. fourth century)
St. Ursula's Day, October 21

St. Vartan (d. 451)
Sts. Vartan and Ghevont Day, February-March, Thursday
before Lent

St. Vicente (d. 1173)
St. Vicente, Feast Day of, January 22

St. Vincent de Paul (1581-1660)
St. Vincent de Paul, Feast of, September 27

St. Vincent of Sargossa (d. 304)
St. Vincent of Sargossa, Feast Day of, January 22

St. Vitus (d. c. 303)
St. Vitus's Day, June 15

St. Walpurgis, Walpurga, or Walburga (c. 710-779)
Walpurgis Night (Feast of Valborg), April 30

St. Wenceslaus, duke of Bohemia (c. 907-929)
St. Wenceslaus's Day, September 28

St. Willibrod (Wilfred, 658?-739)
Dancing Procession (Sprangprozessio'n), May-June,
Tuesday after Pentecost

Sakanoue-no-Tamuramora (758-811)
Nebuta Matsuri, August 2-7

Sangamitta, princess of India (fl. 288 B.C.)
Sangamitta Day, full moon day of first lunar month or
full moon day of Hindu month of Jyeshta

**Sango, third Alafin of Oyo (possible historical figure who
lived during the 15th century)**
Sango Festival, early November, seven days near end of
rainy season

San Isidro Labrador (1070-1130)
St. Isidore the Husbandman or Farmer, Feast of, May 15

San Martín, José Francisco de (1778-1850)
San Martin Day, August 17

Santo Cristo (c. third century)
Santo Cristo and San Vicente Ferrer, Festival of, September

San Vicente Ferrer (c. 1350-1419)
Santo Cristo and San Vicente Ferrer, Festival of, September

Schiller, Friedrich von (1759-1805)
Schiller Days, May

Schonchin, Chief (1790s-1892)
Powwow, Schonchin Days, last weekend in May

Schubert, Franz (1797-1828)
Schubertiade Hohenems, 16 days in June

Schwenkfeld, Kaspar (1490-1561)
Thanksgiving, Schwenkfelder, September 24

Seatlh, Chief (1786?-1866)
Seattle Days, August 18-20, or third weekend
in August

Seiwa, emperor of Japan (850-880)
Gion Matsuri, July

Sejong, king of Korea (1397-1450)
Alphabet Day (Han-gul), early October

Selassie, Haile, emperor of Ethiopia (Ras Tafari, 1892-1975)
National Day, Ethiopia, September 12
Selassie's Birthday, Haile, July 23
Selassie's Coronation Day, Haile, on or near
November 15

Seward, William Henry (1801-1872)
Seward's Day, March 30; observed last Monday in March

Shakespeare, William (1564-1616)
Shakespeare Company Festival, Royal, April-December
Shakespeare Days, April
Shakespeare Festival, June-September
Shakespeare Festival, American
Shakespeare Festival, New York, summer
Shakespeare Festival, Oregon, February through October
Shakespeare Festival, San Diego National, early June-mid
September
Shakespeare's Birthday, April 23

Shankarachaya, Adi (788-820)
Shankarachaya Jayanti or Birthday, fifth or tenth day
during waxing half of Hindu month of Vaisakha

Shaw, George Bernard (1856-1950)
Shaw Festival, 22 weeks from May to October

Shembe, Isaiah (fl. 1911)
Zulu/Shembe Festival, July 1 through last Sunday in July

Sibelius, Jean (1865-1957)
Helsinki Festival (Helsinen Juhlaviikot), 18 days beginning
August 24

Sigurdsson, Jón (1811-1879)
Independence Day, Iceland, June 17

Sirikit, queen of Thailand (b. 1932)
Queen's Birthday, Thailand, August 12

Smith, Hyrum (1800-1844)
Smith, Martyrdom of Joseph and Hyrum, June 27

Smith, Joseph (1805-1844)
Smith, Birthday of Joseph, April 24
Smith, Martyrdom of Joseph and Hyrum, June 27

Smith, Red Bird (1850-1918)
Red Bird Smith Ceremony, August 17

Somhlolo or Subhuza, founder of Swaziland (fl. 19th century)
Independence Day, Swaziland (Somhlolo Day), September 6

Soto, Hernando De (c. 1500-1542)
(De) Soto Celebration, one week in March or early April

Squanto (d. 1622)
Thanksgiving, fourth Thursday in November

Stanton, Elizabeth Cady (1815-1902)
Stanton Day, Elizabeth Cady, November 12

Stephen the Great, prince of Moldavia (1435-1504)
Nation of Heroes, first Sunday in July
Razboieni, Festival of, last Sunday in July

Stone, Lucy (1818-1893)
Stone Day, Lucy, August 13

Subhuza II, king of Swaziland (1899-1982)
King's Birthday, July 22

Sun Yat-sen, leader of China (1866-1925)
Arbor Day, March 12
Double Tenth Day, October 10
Sun Yat-sen Day, November 12

Swedenborg, Emmanuel (1688-1772)
New Church Day, June 19

Tagore, Rabindranath (1861-1941)
Tagore, Birthday of Rabindranath, May 7

Taholah, Chief (late 18th century-early 19th century)
Taholah Days, July fourth weekend

Tamanend (fl. 1685)
St. Tammany's Day, May 1

Tekakwitha, Kateri (1656-1680)
Indian Celebration, American, July 17

Tenchi, emperor of Japan (626-671)
Time Observance Day, June 10

Therese of Saxony-Hildburghausen (1792-1854)
Oktoberfest, 16 days beginning first Sunday in October

Thierry of Alsace (1100-1168)
Holy Blood, Procession of the, first Monday after May 2

Tito, Marshall (Josip Broz Tito, 1892-1980)
Youth Day (Marshall Tito's Birthday), May 25

Tokugawa Ieyasu, Shogun (1543-1616)
Spring Festival of the Toshogu Shrine, May 17-18

Tombalbaye, Nagarta Francois, president of Chad (1918-1975)
National Day, Chad, April 13

Toyotami Hideyoshi (1537-1598)
Ages, Festival of the (Jidai Matsuri), October 22

Truman, Harry S., president of the United States (1884-1972)
Truman's Birthday, Harry, May 8

Tulsidas (1543?-1623)
Tulsidas Jayanti, seventh day of waxing half of Hindu month of Sravana

Twain, Mark (pseud. for Samuel Langhorne Clemens, 1835-1910)
Calaveras County Fair & Frog Jumping Jubilee, May 13-16
Tom Sawyer Days, National, week of July 4

Urban I, Pope (d. 230)
St. Urban's Day, May 25

Valdemar II (1170-1241)
Valdemar's Day, June 15

Valentine, bishop of Terni (d. 270)
Valentine's Day, February 14

Valentine of Rome (fl. third century)
Valentine's Day, February 14

Valmiki, Ai Kavi (fl. between 500-300 B.C.)
Valmiki's Jayanti or Birthday, full moon day of Hindu month of Asvina

Verrazano, Giovanni da (1485?-1528?)
Verrazano Day, April 17

Vladimirescu, Tudor (c. 1780-1821)
In the Sunlit Plain, first week in June

Von Steuben, Friedrich (1730-1794)
Von Steuben Day, September 17; often observed fourth Sunday in September

Wagner, Richard (1813-1883)
Bayreuth Festival, Bayreuther Festspiele & Richard Wagner Festival, five weeks during July-August

Wangchuk, Jigme Singye (b. 1955)
King's Birthday, November 11

Washington, George, president of the United States (1732-1799)
Continental Army, Departure of, Sunday nearest June 19
Washington's Birthday, February 22
Washington's Birthday (Cherries Jubilee), several days in February
Washington's Crossing of the Delaware, December 25

Wesley, John (1703-1791)
Aldersgate Experience, Sunday nearest May 24

Williams, Roger (c. 1603-1683)
Williams Day, February 5

Wisdom, John (fl. 1860s)
Heritage Holidays, mid-October

Wise, Rabbi Isaac Mayer (1819-1900)
Wise, Sabbath of, last Sabbath in March

Wolfe, Thomas (1900-1938)
Wolfe Festival, Thomas, October 3

Wood, Grant (1892-1942)
Art Festival, Grant Wood, second Sunday in June

Wood, Henry (1869-1944)
Wood Promenade Concerts, Henry, nine weeks from mid
July-mid September

Wright, Orville (1871-1948)
National Aviation Day, August 19
Wright Brothers Day, December 17

Wright, Wilbur (1867-1912)
National Aviation Day, August 19
Wright Brothers Day, December 17

Xavier, Joaquim José da Silva (1748-1792)
Tiradentes or Inconfidência Week (Tooth Puller Day), April

Yi Sun-shin (fl. 16th century)
Cherry Blossom Festival, Chinhae, early April

Young, Brigham (1801-1877)
Young, Birthday of, June 1

Zarathustra or Zoroaster, Spitaman (c. 628-c. 551 B.C.)
Khordad Sal, sixth day of Hindu month of Bhadrapada
Zarthastno Diso, April 30 by Fasli sect, May 29 by Kadmi
sect, and June 1 by Shahenshai sect

Religion Index

The Religion Index lists, by major religion and denomination, religious holidays and festivals, as well as secular events with partial or former religious significance, when given by the sources indexed.

BAHÁ'Í
'Abdu'l-Bahá, Ascension of, November 28
'Abdu'l-Bahá, Birth of, May 23
Ayyam-i-Ha, February 26-March 1
Báb, Birth of the, October 20
Báb, Declaration of the, May 23
Báb, Martyrdom of the, July 9
Bahá'u'lláh, Ascension of, May 29
Bahá'u'lláh, Birth of the, November 12
Bahá'u'lláh, Declaration (Feast of Ridvan), April 21-May 2
Covenant, Day of the, November 26 or 27
New Year's Day (Nawruz), March 21
Nineteen-Day Feast, first day of each of 19 months in Bahá'í calendar
Race Unity Day, June 13, observed second Sunday in June
World Peace Day, September 19
World Religion Day, third Sunday in January

BALINESE
Eka Dasa Rundra, once every hundred years, Pura Besakih temple, Bali, Indonesia
Temple Festivals, annual, date varies according to temple, Bali, Indonesia

BUDDHIST
Airing the Classics, sixth day of sixth lunar month, China
Autumnal Equinox Day (Higan Ritual), September 23 or 24, Japan
Boun Phan Vet, twelfth lunar month, Laos
Buddha's Birthday, Enlightenment, and Salvation (Wesak), eighth day of fourth lunar month
Buddha's Birthday, Enlightenment, and Salvation (Buddha Jayanti), full day of Hindu month of Vaisakha, India
Buddha's Birthday, Enlightenment, and Salvation (Kason Festival of Watering the Banyon Tree), eighth day of fourth lunar month, Myanmar (formerly Burma)
Buddha's Birthday, Enlightenment, and Salvation (Vixakha Bouxa or Festival of Rockets, Boun Bang Fay), full moon day of Hindu month of Vaisakha, Laos
Buddha's Birthday, Enlightenment, and Salvation (Hana Matsuri, Flower Festival), April 8, Japan
Buddhist Priesthood, Admission to the (Buart Nark), April-May, Thailand
Butter Sculpture Festival (Mönlam or Prayer Festival), two to three weeks during first Tibetan month
Chariot Festival of Macchendranath (Festival of the God of Rain), begins first day of waning half of Hindu month of Vaisakha and lasts two months, Nepal
Dalai Lama, Birthday of, July 6, Tibetan exiles in India

Dead, Festival of the (Bon or Obon Matsuri), 15th day of seventh lunar month; July 12-16 in Japan
Dead, Festival of the (Toro Nagashi, Floating Lantern Ceremony), August 15, Hawaii
Esala Perahera (Mahanuwara Esala Dalada Perahera), nine nights including full moon day of eighth lunar month, Sri Lanka
Four Miracles Assembly (Magha Puja), full moon day of third lunar month
Ghanta Karna, 14th day of waning half of Hindu month of Sravana, Nepal
Goddess of Mercy, Birthday of, 19th day of third lunar month; 19th day of tenth lunar month in Hong Kong
Harvest (Mandela Ceremony), during harvest season, Ladakh
Hemis Festival, three days in June or July, Ladakh
Hungry Ghosts, Festival of (Ullambana), 15th day of seventh lunar month
Kataragama Festival, June-July, Sri Lanka
Jizo-Ennichi or Jiso Kshitigarba, 24th of each month, China and Japan
Lenten Season (Vassa), July-October, begins during Wazo, fourth lunar month, and ends on the 15th or full moon day of Thadingyut, seventh lunar month
Lights, Festival of (Loy Krathong), full moon day of twelfth lunar month, Thailand
Lotus, Birthday of, 24th day of sixth lunar month, China
Matsu, Birthday of (Matsu Festival), 23rd day of third lunar month, Taiwan
Memorial to Broken Dolls Day, June 3, Japan
Mibu Dainembutsu Kyogen, end of April, Japan
Mystery Play of Tibet, last day of the year
Neri Kuyo, every three years on August 16, Joshinji Temple, Tokyo, Japan
New Year (Losar), three days, usually in February; date annually determined by Tibetan astrologers in Dharmsala
New Year (Sinhala Avurudu), two days in April, first days of Sinhala month of Bak and Tamil month of Chittrai, Sri Lanka
New Year (Songkran), mid-April, when Sun is in Aries; observed April 13-15, Thailand
Panchadaan, third day of waning half of Hindu month of Bhadrapada in Kathmandu and Bhadgaon, and eighth day of waxing half of Hindu month of Sravana in Patan and the rest of Nepal
Paro Tshechu, 10th-15th days of second lunar month, Paro, Bhutan
Phra Buddha Bat Fair, March, Phra Buddha temple near Saraburi, Thailand
Poson or Dhamma Vijaya, Full Moon Day, full moon day of Hindu month of Jyeshta, Sri Lanka

BUDDHIST *(cont.)*

Prayer Day, Universal (Dzam Ling Chi Sang), 14th-16th days of fifth Tibetan lunar month, Tibet

Robe Offering Month (Kathin Season or Tod Kathin), full moon day of 11th lunar month to full moon day of 12th lunar month, Thailand

Sangamitta Day, full moon day of the first month or full moon day of Hindu month of Jyeshta, Sri Lanka

Shinbyu, summer, Burma (now Myanmar)

Shrine Festival, Chusonji, May, Chusonji, Iwate, Japan

Shrines Festival, Three (Sanja Matsuri), second weekend in May, Asakusa Kannon Temple, Tokyo, Japan

Sugar Ball Show, 16th day of first lunar month, Haiyun Buddhist Convent, Qingdao, Shandong, China

Ta Mo's Day, fifth day of tenth lunar month, China and Japan

Tazaungdaing, full moon day of Burmese month of Tazauungmon

Vernal Equinox, on or near March 21, Okinawa

Water Drawing Festival (Omizutori Matsuri), two weeks in March, Todaiji Temple, Nara, Japan

Yen Lo's Birthday, eighth day of first lunar month, China

Tenggerese Buddha Dharma

Kassada, January, 14th of Kassada, 12th month of Tenggerese year, East Java, Indonesia

CHRISTIAN

Advent, four-week season beginning Sunday nearest November 30 and ending December 24

Advent Sunday, Sunday nearest November 30

All Saints' Day, November 1

All Souls' Day, November 2

Annunciation, Feast of the, March 25

Ascension Day, May-June, fortieth day after Easter Sunday

Ash Wednesday, February-March, fortieth day before Easter Sunday

Assumption, Feast of the, August 15

Baptism of the Lord, Feast of the, Sunday following January 6

Battles of the Moors and Christians, various dates and locations in Spain

Befana Festival, January 5-6, Italy and Sicily

Black Christ, Festival of the, January 15, Esquipulas, Guatemala

Black Nazarene Fiesta, January 1-9, Manila and Quezon, Luzon Island, Philippines

Blessed Sacrament, Feast of, four days beginning last Thursday in August, Madeiran-Americans in Bedford, Massachusetts

Blessing of Seeds and Tools, start of the planting season, Mozambique

Candlemas, February 2

Christmas, December 25

Christmas Eve, December 24

Christmas Festival (Night of the Radishes and Nativity Festival), December 23-24, Oaxaca, Mexico

Christmas Festival (Posadas, Feast of the Lodgings), December 16-24 or 25, Hispanic-Americans, Mexico, and the Philippines

Circumcision, Feast of the, January 1, Gregorian calendar (N.S.); January 14, Julian calendar (O.S.)

Clipping the Church Day, August 5, Guiseley, Yorkshire, England

Common Prayer Day, April-May, fourth Friday after Easter, Denmark

Corpus Christi, May-June, the Sunday following Trinity Sunday (Roman Catholic and in the United States); the Thursday following Trinity Sunday (other Christian)

Dancing Procession (Sprangprozessio'n), May-June, Tuesday after Pentecost, Echternach, Luxembourg

Dom Fair, November through Christmas, December 25, Germany

Easter, March-April, first Sunday after first full moon after the vernal equinox

Epiphany, January 6, Gregorian calendar (N.S.); January 19, Julian calendar (O.S.)

Exaltation of the Cross, September 14 (formerly May 3, Roman Catholic)

Fields, Going to the (Veldgang), Monday preceding Ascension Thursday, Netherlands

Folklore Festival, Canajacua, four days including January 6, Macaracas, Panama

Good Friday, March-April, Friday preceding Easter Sunday

Guardian Angel, Festival of the (Schutzengelfest), second Sunday in July, Appenzell, Switzerland

Holy Innocents' Day, December 28

Holy Saturday, March-April, Saturday before Easter Sunday

Holy Spirit, Festival of the Divine, one week in May, Diamantina and other cities in Brazil

Holy Thursday, March-April, Thursday preceding Easter

Holy Week, March-April, week preceding Easter

Honey Day, August 1, Russia

Hurricane Supplication Day, fourth Monday in July and second or third Monday in October, Virgin Islands

Immaculate Conception, Feast of the, December 8

Jamestown Day, Sunday nearest May 13, United States

Lent, February-March, forty-day season preceding Easter

Lost Sunday, third Sunday before Lent

Low Sunday, March-April, Sunday following Easter

Martyrs' Day, Forty ('Id al-Arba 'in Shahid), March 9, Greece, Romania, and Syria

Michaelmas, September 29 (Western Church); November 8 (Eastern Church)

Mid-Lent Sunday, March, fourth Sunday in Lent

Miracles at Glastonbury, June-August, Glastonbury, Somerset, England

Moro-Moro Play, April or May, Luzon Island, Philippines

CHRISTIAN *(cont.)*

Mystery of San Guillen and Santa Felicia, August, Obanos, Navarra, Spain

Mystery of the Passion, March-April, Easter week, Moncada, Valencia, Spain

Mystery Plays, York Festival and, every three years in June, York, Yorkshire, England

Nativity of the Virgin, Feast of the, September 8

Nativity Plays, mid-December to January, Guanajuato, Mexico

Olsok, last week in July in Norway and United States; July 29-30 in Faroe Islands

Oranges and Lemons Day, March 31

Our Lady, Consoler of the Afflicted, Octave of, eight to 15 days beginning fifth Sunday after Easter, Luxembourg-Ville, Luxembourg

Our Lady Aparecida, Festival of, May 11, Aparecida, Brazil

Our Lady of Agony, Festival of, three days in August, Viana do Castelo, Portugal

Our Lady of Bildchen, Procession to (Muttergottesprozessio'n Op d'Bildchen), Sunday after August 15, Vianden, Luxembourg

Our Lady of Czestochowa, Feast of, May 3, Polish National Shrine of Czestochowa, Poland

Our Lady of Czestochowa, Feast of (Feast of the Black Madonna of Jasna Gora), August 15, Jasna Gora monastery, Czestochowa, Poland

Our Lady of Mercy, Festival of, September, Barcelona, Spain

Our Lady of Miracles (Nossa Senhora dos Milagres or Festa de Serreta), September 8-5, Azores, Portugal

Our Lady of Mount Carmel (Senhora do Monte do Carmo), October, Moura, Beja, Portugal

Our Lady of Nazaré Festival, September 8-18, Nazaré, Estremadura, Portugal

Our Lady of Peñafrancia, Feast of (Feast of Nuestra Senora de Peñafrancia), third week in September, Naga City, Philippines

Our Lady of the Angels, August, Cartego, Costa Rica

Our Lord of Passos, Procession of, February-March, Macao

Palm Sunday, March-April, the Sunday preceding Easter

La Passio Festival, February-March, during Lent, Esparraguera, Barcelona, Spain

Passion, Sacred Drama of the, Sundays during Lent until Sunday after Easter, Ulldecona, Tarragona, Spain

Passion Play, Black Hills, June-August, Spearfish, South Dakota

Passion Plays, dates vary, Austria, Mexico, Philippines, Federal Republic of Germany, Spain

Passion Sunday, March, Sunday preceding Palm Sunday

Passiontide, March, last two weeks of Lent

Penitents, Procession of the (Boetprocessie van Veurne), last Sunday in July, Furnes, West Flanders, Belgium

Penitents, Procession of the (La Procesion De La Penitencia), week before Pentecost, Roncesvalles, Navarra, Spain

Pentecost, May-June, the Sunday fifty days after Easter

Pilgrimage of Castelejo, September, Portugal

Pilgrimage of La Dandelada (Romería of La Dandelada), second Sunday in September, Ávila, Spain

Pilgrimage of Our Lady of the Cabeza (Romería of the Virgen de la Cabeza), end of April, Andujar, Jaen, Andalusia, Spain

Pilgrimage of Our Lady of Valme (Romario of Our Lady of Valme), October 17, Dos Hermanas, Spain

Pilgrimage of Pedro Bervardo (Romería of Pedro Bervardo), September 5-17, Ávila, Spain

Pilgrimage of the Black Madonna, September 14, Einseideln, Switzerland

Pilgrimage of the Dew (Romería Del Rocío), Thursday or Friday before Pentecost Sunday through Monday or Tuesday after Pentecost, Spain

Pilgrimage of the Virgen de la Pena (Romería of the Virgen de la Pena), last Sunday in April, Puebla de Guaman, Huelva, Andalusia, Spain

Pilgrimage to Chalma, first week of January; also held in February, August, September, and during Holy Week, Mexico

Pilgrimage to Our Lady of Nazo, September, Povoa, Braganca, Portugal

Pilgrimage to St. Anne d'Auray, July 26

Pilgrimage to the Sanctuary of Our Lady of the Remedies (Pardon of Nossa Senhora dos Remédios and Festival of Lamego), early September, Lamego, Viseu, Portugal

Quadragesima Sunday (Firebrand Sunday), February, first Sunday in Lent

Quinquagesima Sunday, February, Sunday before Lent

Redeemer, Feast of the, third Sunday in July, Giudecca Island and Venice, Veneto, Italy

Relic Sunday, third Sunday after June 24

Rogation Days, May, fifth Sunday through Wednesday after Easter

Running of the Bulls, Sunday following August 15

St. Agnes Eve, January 20

St. Agnes of Assisi, Feast of, November 16

St. Alban's Day, June 22

St. Andrew Corsini, Feast Day of, February 4

St. Andrew's Day, November 30

St. Anne's Day, July 26

St. Anthony of Padua, Feast of, June 13

St. Anthony the Abbot of Egypt, Feast of (Blessing of the Animals), January 17; observed Sunday nearest January 17

St. Apollonia's Day, February 9

St. Augustine of Canterbury, Feast of, May 26 (Anglican and Episcopalian); May 27 (Roman Catholic)

St. Augustine of Hippo, Feast Day of, August 28

St. Barbara's Day, December 4

St. Barnabas's Day, June 11

St. Bartholomew's Day, August 24

St. Basil's Day, January 1, Gregorian calendar (N.S.); January 14, Julian calendar (O.S.)

CHRISTIAN *(cont.)*
St. Benedict's Day, March 21
St. Bernard of Montjoux, May 28
St. Blaise's Day, February 3
St. Bonaventura, Feast of, July 14
St. Brendan's Day, May 16
St. Brictiva's Day, January 11
St. Bridget's Day, February 1
St. Catherine's Day, November 25
St. Cecilia's Day, November 22
St. Christina's Day (Festival of Santa Cristina), July 24; festival in July
St. Christopher's Day, July 25
St. Clare of Assisi, Feast of, August 11
St. Clement's Day, November 23
St. Crispin's Day, October 25
St. Daniel's Day, December 11
St. David's Day, March 1
St. Demetrius, Festival of, October 26
St. Denis's Day, October 9
St. Devota's Day, January 27
St. Dismas's Day, March 25
St. Dominic, Feast of, August 4
St. Dominique's Day, January 22
St. Dorothy, Feast of, February 6
St. Dunstan's Day, May 19
St. Dymphna's Day, May 15
St. Edmund Campion, Feast Day of, December 1
St. Edward the Confessor's Day, October 13
St. Elias Day, August 2
St. Elizabeth, Feast of, July 8
St. Elizabeth of Hungary, Feast of, November 19
St. Elmo's Day, June 2
St. Eric's Day, May 18
St. Frances of Rome, Feast Day of, March 9
St. Francis de Sales, Feast of, January 24
St. Francis of Assisi, Feast of, October 4
St. Francis Xavier, Feast Day of, December 3
St. Gall, Feast of, October 16
St. George's Day, April 23
St. Giles's Day, September 1
St. Gregory I the Great, Feast of, September 3
St. Gregory's Day, March 12
St. Helena's Day, August 18
St. Honoratus's Day, January 16
St. Hubert, Feast Day of, November 3
St. Isidore of Seville, Feast of, April 4
St. Isidore the Husbandman or Farmer, Feast of, May 15
St. Ivo, Pardon of, May 19
St. James the Greater's Day, July 25
St. Januarius's Feast Day, September 19
St. Jerome's Day, September 30
St. Joan of Arc, Feast of, May 31
St. John, Apostle and Evangelist, Feast of, December 27
St. John Damascene, Feast of, December 4

St. John Lateran's Dedication, November 9
St. John the Baptist's Day, June 24
St. Joseph of Arimathea, Feast Day of, March 19
St. Joseph the Worker, Feast of, May 1, Malta
St. Jude's Day, October 28
St. Julian the Hospitaler, Feast of, January 9 or February 12
St. Lambert's Day, September 17
St. Lawrence of Rome, Feast Day of, August 10
St. Lazarus's Day, March-April, Saturday preceding Palm Sunday, Eastern Orthodox and Russian Orthodox; Saturday before Palm or Easter Sunday, Slavic people in Bulgaria
St. Leo III, Feast of, June 12
St. Leonard's Day, November 6
St. Leopold, Feast Day of, November 15
St. Lucy's Day, December 13
St. Luke, Feast Day of, October 18
St. Mark, Feast of, April 25
St. Martha, Feast of, July 29
St. Martin's Day, November 11
St. Mary Magdalene, Feast of, July 22
St. Matthew's Day, September 21
St. Médardus or Médard's Day, June 8
St. Mennas's Day, November 11
St. Michael's Day, November 8 (Eastern Church); September 29 (Western Church)
St. Modesto's Day, December 18
St. Nicholas's Day, December 6, Gregorian calendar (N.S.); December 19, Julian calendar (O.S.)
St. Oswald's Day, February 28
St. Patrick's Day, March 17
St. Paul, Feast of the Conversion of, January 25
St. Paulinus of Nola, Feast of, June 22
St. Peter's Day, June 29
St. Philibert's Day, August 20
St. Piran's Day, March 5
St. Placidus Festival, July 11
St. Plato the Martyr, Feast of, November 18
St. Polycarp's Day, January 26
St. Roch's Day, August 16
St. Rose of Lima, Feast of, August 23
St. Sarkis's Day, January 21
St. Sava's Day, January 14
St. Sebastian's Day, January 20
St. Simon Stylites's Day, January 5
St. Sofia's Day, May 15
St. Spyridon, Feast Day of, December 14
St. Stanislaus, Feast of, April 11
St. Stephen, Feast of, December 26
St. Stephen Day, Crown of, January 6
St. Stephen of Hungary's Day, August 2
St. Swithin's Day, July 15
St. Sylvester's Day, December 31
St. Teresa of Avila, Feast of, October 15
St. Therese of Lisieux, Feast of, October 1

CHRISTIAN *(cont.)*
St. Thomas Aquinas, Feast of, January 28
St. Thomas More, Feast Day of, June 22
St. Thomas of Canterbury, Feast of, December 29
St. Thomas the Apostle, Feast of, December 21
St. Thorlak's Day, December 23
St. Urban's Day, May 25
St. Ursula's Day, October 21
St. Veronica, Feast of, July 12
St. Vicente, Feast Day of, January 22
St. Vincent de Paul, Feast of, September 27
St. Vincent of Sargossa, Feast Day of, January 22
St. Vitus's Day, June 15
St. Vlasio's Day, February 11
St. Wenceslaus's Day, September 28
Sts. Cosmas and Damian Day, September 27
Sts. Joachim and Anne, Feast of, July 26
Sts. Peter and John Festival, June 24-29, Paraguay
Sts. Peter and Paul Day, June 29
Sts. Philip and James, Feast of, May 1
San Ermengol Retaule Festival, August, Seo de Urgel, Lerida, Spain
San Macario, Festival of, January 2, Malda, Lerida, Spain
Septuagesima Sunday, third Sunday before Lent
Tabuleiros Festival (Festa dos Tabuleiros), three or four days in mid-July every third year during odd-numbered years
Thanksgiving (Awoojoh), may occur on special occasions and during such holidays as Christmas, Easter, Good Friday, and New Year's Day, Sierra Leone
Thanksgiving (Waratambar), August, dates vary according to province, Papua New Guinea
Transfiguration, Feast of the, August 6
Trinity Sunday, May-June, observed first Sunday after Pentecost by Western church; observed the Monday after Pentecost by Eastern Orthodox Church
Verges Festival, March-April, Thursday before Easter, Verges, Gerona, Spain
Virgen del Rosario, Fiesta for the, October 7, Zinacantan, Mexico
Virgen Festival, Bajada de la, every four years in June, El Hierro, Santa Cruz de Tenerife, Spain
Virgin of Carmen, Fiesta of, July 15, Santa Cruz Etla, Mexico
Virgin of the Pillar, Feast of the (Virgen del Pilar), ten days in October, Saragossa, Spain
Visitation of the Blessed Virgin Mary, Feast of the, July 2 (Anglican), May 31 (Roman Catholic and Protestant)
Water Buffalo Festival (Carabao), May 14 or 15, Angona, Lucban, Pulilan, San Isidro, and Sariaya, Quezon, Luzon Island, Philippines
White Sunday, second Sunday in October, American Samoa and Western Samoa
Whit Monday, May-June, Monday after Pentecost
World Day of Prayer, first Friday in March

African Methodist Episcopal Church
Allen Day, Richard, February 11

African Union Methodist Church
African Methodist Quarterly Meeting Day, last Saturday in August

Amish Church
Folk Festival, Pennsylvania Dutch, nine days in July, including July 4, Kutztown, Pennsylvania

Anglican
All Saints' Day, November 1
All Souls' Day, November 2
Annunciation, Feast of the, March 25
Ash Wednesday, February-March, fortieth day before Easter Sunday
Brotherhood Sunday, Sunday nearest February 22
Christmas, December 25
Ember Days, Wednesday, Friday and Saturday of the weeks following first Sunday in Lent; Pentecost; September 14, Holy Cross Day; and December 13, St. Lucy's Day
Epiphany, January 6
Holy Innocents' Day, December 28
Holy Saturday, March-April, Saturday preceding Easter Sunday
Immaculate Conception, Feast of the, December 8
Michaelmas, September 29
Mid-Lent Sunday (Mothering Sunday), March, fourth Sunday in Lent
Pentecost (Whitsunday or White Sunday), May-June, the Sunday fifty days after Easter
St. Agnes Eve, January 20
St. Boniface, Feast Day of, June 5
St. Charles's Day, January 30; observed on or near February 2 at Trafalgar Square, London, England
St. Hilary's Day, January 13
St. Patrick's Day, March 17
St. Paul, Feast of the Conversion of, January 25
St. Stephen, Feast of, December 26
St. Swithin's Day, July 15
Sts. Philip and James, Feast of, May 1
Saints, Doctors, Missionaries, and Martyrs Day, November 8
Stir-Up Sunday, late November, Sunday preceding Advent Sunday
Transfiguration, Feast of the, August 6

Armenian Church
Candlemas (Dyarntarach), February 14

Baptist
New Year's Eve (Watch Night Service), December 31
Williams Day, Roger, February 5

Brethren Church (Dunkards)
Folk Festival, Pennsylvania Dutch, nine days in July, including July 4, Kutztown, Pennsylvania

675

Calvinist
  St. Mark's Day (Szent Márk Napja and Buza-Szentelo, Blessing of Wheat), April 25, Hungary

Christian Science
  Eddy, Birthday of Mary Baker, July 16

Church of England
  All Saints' Day, November 1
  Ash Wednesday, February-March, fortieth day before Easter Sunday
  Candlemas, February 2
  Ember Days, Wednesday, Friday and Saturday of the weeks following first Sunday in Lent; Pentecost; September 14, Holy Cross Day; and December 13, St. Lucy's Day
  Harvest Home Festival (Ingathering or Inning), September 24
  Holy Innocents' Day, December 28
  Holy Thursday, May, Ascension Day, fortieth day after Easter Sunday
  Immaculate Conception, Feast of the, December 8
  Michaelmas, September 29
  Rogation Days, May, fifth Sunday through Wednesday after Easter
  St. Etheldreda's Day, October 17

Church of Jesus Christ of the Latter Day Saints (Mormon)
  Founding of the Church of Jesus Christ of the Latter Day Saints, April 6
  Hill Cumorah Pageant, nine days (excluding Sunday and Monday) beginning third weekend in July, Palmyra, New York
  Pioneer Day, July 24, Idaho and Utah
  Smith, Birthday of Joseph, April 24
  Smith, Martyrdom of Joseph and Hyrum, June 27
  Young, Birthday of Brigham, June 1

Church of the New Jerusalem (Swedenborgians)
  New Church Day, June 19

Church Women United
  World Community Day, first Friday in November

Congregationalists
  Easter, March-April, first Sunday after first full moon after the vernal equinox

Coptic Orthodox Church
  Assumption, Feast of the, August 15
  Christmas, December 25, Iraq
  Christmas (Ganna or Genna; officially Leddat), January 7, Ethiopia
  Exaltation of the Cross (Meskel, Finding of the True Cross), September 27; end of the rainy season, Ethiopia
  New Year, September 11, Egypt and Egyptian-Canadians

Council of Churches
  Stewardship Sunday, second Sunday in November, Canada and the United States

Dunkards
  See Brethren Church

Eastern Orthodox
  Advent, four-week season beginning Sunday nearest November 30 and ending December 24
  All Souls' Day, November 2
  Annunciation, Feast of the, March 25, Gregorian calendar (N.S.); April 7, Julian calendar (O.S.)
  Ascension Day, May-June, fortieth day after Easter Sunday
  Ash Wednesday, February-March, fortieth day before Easter Sunday; Lent begins Monday before Ash Wednesday
  Assumption, Feast of the, August 15
  Baptism of the Lord, Feast of the, Sunday following Epiphany, January 6
  Candlemas, February 2
  Christmas, January 6
  Christmas Eve, December 24
  Circumcision, Feast of the, January 1, Gregorian calendar (N.S.); January 14, Julian calendar (O.S.)
  Easter, March-April, first Sunday after first full moon after the vernal equinox (using the Julian calendar)
  Epiphany, January 6, Gregorian calendar (N.S.); January 19, Julian calendar (O.S.)
  Exaltation of the Cross (Invention of the Cross), September 14
  Good Friday, March-April, Friday preceding Easter Sunday
  Holy Innocents' Day, December 29
  Holy Saturday, March-April, Saturday before Easter Sunday
  Holy Thursday, March-April, Thursday preceding Easter
  Immaculate Conception, Feast of the, December 9
  Lent (Meat Fare Sunday), February-March, eight days before Lent begins
  Michaelmas, November 8
  Nativity of the Virgin, Feast of the (Nativity of Our Most Holy Lady, the Theotokas or Nativity of the Theotokas), September 8; some churches observe on September 21
  Palm Sunday, March-April, the Sunday preceding Easter
  Pentecost, May-June, the Sunday fifty days after Easter
  St. Agnes Eve, January 20
  St. Andrew's Day, November 30
  St. Anthony the Abbot of Egypt, Feast of (Blessing of the Animals), January 17
  St. Basil's Day, January 1, Gregorian calendar (N.S.); January 14, Julian calendar (O.S.)
  St. Christopher's Day, July 25
  St. George's Day, April 23, Gregorian calendar (N.S.); May 6, Julian calendar (O.S.)
  St. James the Greater's Day, April 30
  St. John, Apostle and Evangelist, Feast of, May 8

Eastern Orthodox *(cont.)*

St. John the Baptist's Day, June 24 and August 29, the martyrdom of St. John

St. Lazarus's Day, March-April, Saturday preceding Palm Sunday

St. Matthew's Day, November 16

St. Matthias, Feast of, August 9

St. Michael's Day, November 8

St. Modesto's Day, December 18

St. Nicholas's Day, December 6, Gregorian calendar (N.S.); December 19, Julian calendar (O.S.)

St. Paul, Feast of the Conversion of, January 25

St. Stephen, Feast of, December 27

St. Thomas the Apostle, Feast of, October 6

Transfiguration, Feast of the, August 6, Gregorian calendar (N.S.); August 19, Julian calendar (O.S.)

Episcopalian

All Saints' Day, November 1

Annunciation, Feast of the, March 25

Ascension Day, May-June, fortieth day after Easter Sunday

Ash Wednesday, February-March, fortieth day before Easter Sunday

Candlemas, February 2

Christmas Eve, December 24

Circumcision, Feast of the, January 1

Easter, March-April, first Sunday after first full moon after the vernal equinox

Good Friday, March-April, Friday preceding Easter Sunday

Holy Innocents' Day, December 28

Holy Saturday, March-April, Saturday before Easter Sunday

Michaelmas (Feast of St. Michael and All Angels), September 29

Mid-Lent Sunday (Mothering Sunday), March, fourth Sunday in Lent, United States

Palm Sunday, March-April, the Sunday preceding Easter

Pentecost (Whitsunday), May-June, the Sunday fifty days after Easter

St. Agnes Eve, January 20

St. Andrew's Day, November 30

St. Charles's Day, January 30, United States

St. Clare of Assisi, Feast of, August 11

St. Francis of Assisi, Feast of, October 4

St. James the Greater's Day, July 25

St. John the Baptist's Day, June 24

St. Matthias, Feast of, February 24

St. Patrick's Day, March 17

St. Peter's Day, June 29

St. Stephen, Feast of, December 26

St. Thomas the Apostle, Feast of, December 21

Sts. Philip and James, Feast of, May 1

Transfiguration, Feast of the, August 6

Ethiopian Church

Exaltation of the Cross (Meskel, Finding of the True Cross), September 27; end of the rainy season, Ethiopia

Transfiguration, Feast of the (Buhé), August 19, Ethiopia

Greek Orthodox

Assumption, Feast of the, begins August 6 and lasts nine days

Easter, March-April, first Sunday after first full moon after the vernal equinox (using the Julian calendar)

Elijah Day, July 20

Epiphany, January 6, Gregorian calendar (N.S.); January 19, Julian calendar (O.S.)

Exaltation of the Cross, September 14

Good Friday, March-April, Friday preceding Easter Sunday

Holy Innocents' Day, December 28

Holy Thursday, March-April, Thursday preceding Easter

Holy Week, March-April, week preceding Easter

Lammas, August 1

Lent, February-March, forty-day season preceding Easter

Presentation of Blessed Virgin Mary, Feast of the, November 21

St. Basil's Day, January 1, Gregorian calendar (N.S.); January 14, Julian calendar (O.S.)

St. Mark, Feast of, April 25

St. Nikephoros's Day, March 13, Greece

Lutheran

All Saints' Day, November 1

Annunciation, Feast of the, March 25

Ascension Day, May-June, fortieth day after Easter Sunday

Ash Wednesday, February-March, fortieth day before Easter Sunday

Candlemas, February 2

Circumcision, Feast of the, January 1

Easter, March-April, first Sunday after first full moon after the vernal equinox

Epiphany, January 6

Good Friday, March-April, Friday preceding Easter Sunday

Holy Innocents' Day, December 28

Holy Saturday, March-April, Saturday before Easter Sunday

Michaelmas (Feast of St. Michael and All Angels), September 29

Palm Sunday, March-April, the Sunday preceding Easter

Pentecost, May-June, the Sunday fifty days after Easter

Reformation Day, October 31; observed Sunday preceding October 31

Rose Day, June 10; observed second Sunday in June, Pennsylvania

St. Andrew's Day, November 30

St. John the Baptist's Day, June 24

St. Lucy's Day, December 13

St. Matthias, Feast of, February 24

St. Patrick's Day, March 17

St. Paul, Feast of the Conversion of, January 25

St. Stephen, Feast of, December 26

Lutheran *(cont.)*
St. Thomas the Apostle, Feast of, December 21
Transfiguration, Feast of the, August 6

Malabar Christians
St. Thomas the Apostle, Feast of, December 21, Kerala, India

Maronite Christians
St. Maron's Day, February 9, Lebanon and North and South America

Mennonite Church
Folk Festival, Pennsylvania Dutch, nine days in July, including July 4, Kutztown, Pennsylvania
Sunflower Festival, last weekend in July, Manitoba, Canada

Methodist
Aldersgate Experience, Sunday nearest May 24
New Year's Eve (Watch Night Service), December 31, United States
Sunday School Day (Faka Me), first Sunday in May, Tonga

Missouri Synod Lutheran
Easter, March-April, first Sunday after first full moon after the vernal equinox

Mormon
See **Church of Jesus Christ of the Latter Day Saints**

National Catholic Prison Chaplains Association, United States
St. Dismas's Day, second Sunday in October, prisons in the United States

National Council of Churches, United States
Children's Day, second Sunday in June

National Council of Churches, United States, and World Evangelical Alliance, London, England
Universal Week of Prayer, first through second Sunday in January

National Laymen's Committee, United States
Bible Week, National, third week in October

Nazareth Baptist Church
Zulu/Shembe Festival, July 1 through last week in July, Ekuphakemeni Shembe's Shrine, Inanda, South Africa

Penitentes in New Mexico
Good Friday, March-April, Friday preceding Easter Sunday

Presbyterian churches in the United States
New Year's Eve (Watch Night Service), December 31

Protestant
All Saints' Day, November 1
Ash Wednesday, February-March, fortieth day before Easter Sunday
Bastille Day, July 14, French-Americans in New York, New York
Bible Sunday, last Sunday in November or Sunday before Thanksgiving, United States
Candlemas, February 2
Christmas, December 25
Christmas Eve, December 24
Christ the King, Feast of, last Sunday in August
Easter, March-April, first Sunday after first full moon after the vernal equinox
Epiphany, January 6
Family Week, National, begins first Sunday in May, United States
Footwashing Day, a Sunday in early summer or Holy Thursday, Kentucky
Good Friday, March-April, Friday preceding Easter Sunday
Holy Innocents' Day, December 28
Holy Thursday, March-April, Thursday preceding Easter
Holy Week, March-April, week preceding Easter
Lent, February-March, forty-day season preceding Easter
Martinmas, November 11
Martinsfest, November 10-11, Erfurt and Thuringia, Germany
Nativity of the Virgin, Feast of the, September 8
New Year's Eve (Silversterabend), December 31, Switzerland
Orange Day, July 12, Northern Ireland
Palm Sunday, March-April, the Sunday preceding Easter
Pentecost, May-June, the Sunday fifty days after Easter
Race Relations Sunday, Sunday nearest February 12, United States
Reformation Day, October 31; observed Sunday preceding October 31
Rogation Days, May, fifth Sunday through Wednesday after Easter
St. George's Day, April 23
St. John, Apostle and Evangelist, Feast of, December 27
St. Nicholas's Day, December 6
St. Stephen, Feast of, December 26

Religious Society of Friends (Quakers)
Fox, Death of George, January 13

Roman Catholic
All Saints' Day, November 1
All Souls' Day, November 2
All Souls' Day (Día de Muertos, Day of the Dead or Festival of Hungry Ghosts), October 30-November 2, Mexico
Annunciation, Feast of the, March 25
Ascension Day, May-June, fortieth day after Easter Sunday

Roman Catholic *(cont.)*

Ash Wednesday, February-March, fortieth day before Easter Sunday

Assumption, Feast of the, August 15

Baptism of the Lord, Feast of the, Sunday following Epiphany, January 6

Bastille Day, July 14, French-Americans in New York, New York

Black Christ, Festival of the, October 21, Porotobelo, Panama

Blessing of the Fishing Fleet and Biloxi Shrimp Festival and Fais Do Do, first weekend in June, Biloxi, Alabama

Blessing of the Fleet (Louisiana Shrimp and Petroleum Festival), first weekend in September, Morgan City, Louisiana

Blessing of the Shrimp Fleet, last weekend in June, Bayou La Batre, Alabama

Brotherhood Sunday, Sunday nearest February 22

Candlemas, February 2

Christmas, December 25

Christmas, Nine Days Before, December 16

Christmas Eve, December 24

Christmas Festival (Posadas, Feast of the Lodgings), December 16-24 or 25, Philippines

Christ the King, Feast of, last Sunday in October

Circumcision, Feast of the, January 1

Cooks' Festival (Fête de Cuisinieres), Saturday nearest August 10, Pointe-a-Pitre, Guadeloupe

Corpus Christi, May-June, the Sunday following Trinity Sunday

Easter, March-April, first Sunday after first full moon after the vernal equinox

Easter Festival of Sacred Music, March-April, 10 days beginning Good Friday, Lourdes, Hautes-Pyrénées, France

Elijah Day, July 20

Ember Days, Wednesday, Friday and Saturday of the weeks following first Sunday in Lent; Pentecost; September 14, Holy Cross Day; and December 13, St. Lucy's Day

Epiphany, January 6

Exaltation of the Cross (Holyrood Day), September 14

Family Week, National, begins first Sunday in May, United States

Frost, or Ice, Saints Day, May 12-14, Ellis County, Kansas

Frost, or Ice, Saints Day (Eisheiligan), May 11-14, France and Germany

Furry Day, May 8, Helston, Cornwall, England

Good Friday, March-April, Friday preceding Easter Sunday

Guardian Angels, Festival of, October 2

Hermit, Feast of the, September 1, Hot Springs, New Mexico

Holy Blood, Procession of the (Processie van het Heilig Bloed), observed first Monday after May 2, Bruges, West Flanders, Belgium

Holy Family, Feast of the, January, Sunday after Epiphany

Holy Ghost, Feast of the (Altura Do Espírito Santo), March-August, Ponta Delgada, Sao Miguel Island, Azores, Portugal

Holy Ghost, Festival of the, three days in mid-July, Plymouth, Massachusetts

Holy Innocents' Day, December 28

Holy Saturday, March-April, Saturday before Easter Sunday

Holy Thursday, March-April, Thursday preceding Easter

Holy Week, March-April, week preceding Easter

Holy Years, every 25 years

Immaculate Conception, Feast of the, December 8

Immaculate Heart of Mary, Feast of the, Saturday following the second Sunday after Pentecost

Jubilate Sunday, third Sunday after Easter

Lent, February-March, forty-day season preceding Easter

Martinmas, November 11

Martinsfest, November 10-11, Düsseldorf and Lower Rhine, Germany

Martyrs of North America, Feast of, September 26, Canada and United States

Michaelmas (Feast of SS. Michael, Gabriel, and Raphael, Archangels), September 29

Mid-Lent Sunday (Laetare Sunday), March, fourth Sunday in Lent

Midsummer, June 23-24 through June 29, Brazil

Nativity of the Virgin, Feast of the, September 8

Our Lady of Carmel (La Madonna del Carmine), mid-July, Guam/Northern Marianas

Our Lady of Carmel (La Madonna del Carmine), July 16, Italian-Americans and Italy

Our Lady of Czestochowa, Feast of (Feast of the Black Madonna of Jasna Gora), August 15, Jasna Gora monastery, Czestochowa, Poland

Our Lady of Fátima Day, July 13, Fátima, Estremadura, Portugal

Our Lady of Guadalupe, December 12

Our Lady of Lourdes, Feast of, February 11; festival between February 11-18, Lourdes, France

Our Lady of Miracles (Nossa Senhora dos Milagres or Festa de Serreta), September 8-15, Gustine, California

Our Lady of Sorrows, Festival of Mary, September 15

Our Lady of the Happy Ending, January, Brazil

Palm Sunday, March-April, the Sunday preceding Easter

Patron Crosses, Fiesta of the, late April, Quintana Roo, Mexico

Pentecost, May-June, the Sunday fifty days after Easter

Pilgrimage at Cercio to Santa Barbara, last Sunday in August, Portugal

Pilgrimage to Saut d'Eau, early July-July 16, Ville-Bonheur, Haiti

Pilgrimage to Shrine of Father Laval, September 8, Port Louis, Mauritius

Plough Monday, first Monday after Epiphany or Twelfth Day, January 6

Precious Blood, Feast of the Most, July 1

Presentation of Blessed Virgin Mary, Feast of the, November 21

Queenship of Mary, August 22

Roman Catholic *(cont.)*

Reek Sunday, last Sunday in July, Ireland

Reformation Day, October 31, observed Sunday preceding October 31

Rogation Days, May, fifth Sunday through Wednesday after Easter

Rosary, Festival of the, first Sunday in October

Rose Sunday, fourth Sunday in Lent

Sacred Heart of Jesus, Feast of the, May-June, the Friday following Corpus Christi

St. Agnes Eve, January 20

St. Andrew's Day, November 30

St. Anthony of Padua, Feast of, June 13

St. Anthony the Abbot of Egypt, Feast of (Blessing of the Animals), January 17

St. Bede the Venerable, Feast of, May 25

St. Blaise's Day, February 3

St. Boniface, Feast Day of, June 5

St. Bridget's Day, February 1, Ireland

St. Christopher's Day, July 25

St. Clare of Assisi, Feast of, August 11

St. Columba's Day, June 9

St. Elizabeth Ann Seton, Feast of, January 4; observed as Mother Seton Day, December 1 by the Sisters of Charity of St. Vincent De Paul, United States

St. Etheldreda's Day, June 23

St. Fiacre's Day, August 30

St. Frances Cabrini, Feast of, November 13, United States

St. Francis of Assisi, Feast of, October 4

St. Geneviève's Day, January 3

St. George's Day, April 23

St. Gregory I the Great, Feast of, September 3

St. Gudula's Day, January 8, Belgium

St. Hilary's Day, January 14

St. Ignatius Loyola, Feast of, July 31

St. Ildephonsus, Feast Day of, January 23, San Ildefonso Pueblo, New Mexico

St. Isidore the Husbandman or Farmer, Feast of, May 15, Marianas

St. James the Greater's Day, July 25

St. Januarius's Feast Day, two weeks, including September 19, Little Italy, New York

St. Jerome's Day, September 30

St. John, Apostle and Evangelist, Feast of, December 27; May 6, festival in Rome

St. John Lateran's Dedication, November 9, Rome

St. John Nepomucene Neumann, Feast of, January 5

St. John the Baptist's Day, June 24 and August 29, the martyrdom of St. John

St. Joseph of Arimathea, Feast Day of, March 19

St. Joseph's Day (International Fair of San José), ten days, including March 19, David, Panama

St. Jude's Day, October 28, Buffalo, New York

St. Lucy's Day, December 13

St. Mark, Feast of, April 25

St. Matthias, Feast of, May 14

St. Michael's Day, September 29

St. Nicholas's Day, December 6

St. Patrick's Day, March 17

St. Peter's Chains, Feast of, August 1

St. Peter's Chair, Festival of, January 18, Rome

St. Peter's Day, June 29

St. Stephen, Feast of, December 26

St. Stephen, Feast of, and Harvest Dance (San Estevan, Feast of), September 2, Acoma Pueblo, New Mexico

St. Swithin's Day, July 15, England

St. Thomas the Apostle, Feast of, July 3

Sts. Philip and James, Feast of, May 3

Sumamao, Fiesta de, December 26, Argentina

Transfiguration, Feast of the, August 6

Volador Fiesta, during Corpus Christi or Holy Week, Guatemala and Mexico

Russian Orthodox

St. Lazarus's Day, March-April, Saturday preceding Palm Sunday

St. Philip of Moscow's Day, January 9

St. Sergius of Radonezh, September 25

Shakers

See **United Society of Believers in Christ's Second Appearing, the Millennial Church**

Swedenborgians

See **Church of the New Jerusalem**

United Society of Believers in Christ's Second Appearing, the Millennial Church (Shakers)

Lee, Birthday of Ann, February 29

Shaker Festivals: mid-July, Auburn, Kentucky; ten days beginning second Thursday in July, South Union, Kentucky; and August, Old Chatham, New York

CONFUCIANISM

Confucius's Birthday, 27th day of eighth lunar month

Grave-Sweeping and Cold Food Festival (Qing Ming, Clear and Bright Festival), fourth or fifth day of third lunar month

Shrine Rite, Royal (Chongmyo Taeje), first Sunday in May, Seoul, Korea

HINDU

Amalaka Ekadashi, 11th day of waxing half of Phalguna

Ashokashtami, eighth day of waxing half of Chaitra, Bhubaneshwar, India

Avani Mulam, August or September, Madura, India

Bhairava Ashtami, eighth day of waning half of Margashirsha

Bhima or Bhima-sena, Festival of, near time of monsoon, India

HINDU *(cont.)*

Bhishma Ashtami, eighth day of waxing half of Magha or during Karthika, India

Brother and Sister Day (Bhai-Dooj, Bhaiya Duj, or Bhratri Dwitya), second day of waxing half of Karthika, India

Chaitra Parb, eight days prior to full moon day of Chaitra, Orissa, India

Chandan Yatra, 21 days beginning third day of waxing half of Vaisakha, India

Chariot Festival of Macchendranath (Festival of the God of Rain), begins first day of waning half of Vaisakha and lasts two months, Nepal

Chitra Gupta, full moon day of Chaitra, Madras, India

Cow Holiday (Gopastami), India

Cows, Procession of Sacred (Gai Jatra), first day of waning half of Sravana, Nepal

Dattatreya's Birthday (Dattatreya Jayanti), full moon day of Margashirsha, Maharashtra, India

Dead, Feast of the (Pitra Pasksha or Pitra Visarjana and Amavasya), waning half of Asvina

Dhan Teras or Dhanvantri Trayodashi, 13th day of waning half of Karthika

Elephant God, Festival of the (Ganesha Chaturthi), fourth day of Bhadrapada

Eleventh (Ekadashi), 11th day of each waxing and waning moon

Esala Perahera (Mahanuwara Esala Dalada Perahera), July-August, nine nights during annual festival, full moon day of eighth month, Sri Lanka

Fire Festival (Holi), begins 14th day of Phalguna or Dol; length varies

Floating Festival, full moon day of Magha, India

Fourteenth Day of Bhadra, Eternal Anniversary of (Anant Chaturdashi), 14th day of waxing half of Bhadrapada

Gangaur, Gauri, or Parvati Tritiya, 18-day festival in Chaitra, northern India

Ganges River Festival (Ganga Dussehra), tenth day of waxing half of Jyeshta

Gita Jayanti, 11th day of waxing half of Margashirsha

Goddess of Fortune, Festival of the (Lukshmi or Laksmi Puja), during month of Asvina

Govardhan Puja and Annakut, first day of waxing half of Karthika, northern India

Guru Purnima, full moon day of Ashadha, India

Halashasti or Balarama Shashti, sixth day of waning half of Bhadrapada, northern India

Hari-Shayana Ekadashi, 11th day of Karthika

Harvest Festival (Kojagara), full moon of Asvina, India

Harvest Festival (Makara Sankranti in northern India, Pongal in southern India), three days during Pausha

Indra Jatra and Kumari Jatra, Festival of the Child Goddess, eight days during Bhadrapada-Asvina, Nepal

Janaki Navami, ninth day of waxing half of Vaisakha

Jhulan Latra, full moon day of Sravana, Orissa, India

Juggernaut (Rath Yatra, Festival of Jagannatha), second day of waxing half of Ashadha, Orissa, India

Jyeshta Ashtami, eighth day of waxing half of Jyeshta, Kashmir

Karthika Purnima, full moon day of Karthika

Karthika Snan, month of Karthika, India

Karwachoth or Karwa Chauth, fourth day of waning half of Karthika, married Hindu women in India

Kataragama Festival, June-July, Sri Lanka

Kati Bihu, September 21-22, Assam, India

Krishna's Birthday (Janmashtami), eighth day of waning half of Bhadrapada

Kumbh Mela Festival, every twelfth year in January; every six years at Hardvar, Ujjain, and Nasik, Allahabad, India

Lights, Festival of (Dewali), one week during waning half of Karthika, including 15th day

Magha Purnima, full moon day of Magha, India

Marriage of Meenakshi and Shiva, Festival of the (Chaitra Purnima or Meenakshi Kalyanam), ten days during Chaitra or Vaisakha, Madurai, India

Masi Magham, February-March, two-day festival during full moon of Masi; larger festival every twelve years, Kumbakonam, India

Mauni Amavasya, 15th day of waning half of Magha, India

Monkey God Festival (Hanuman Jayanti), full moon day of Chaitra

Mother Goddess, Festival of Durga, the, first ten days of waxing half of Asvina

Nanda Deven, August-September, Kumaon region of India

Narak Chaturdashi, 14th day of waning half of Karthika

Narieli Purnima, full moon day of Sravana, southern India

Narsimha Jayanti, 14th day of waxing half of Vaisakha

New Year, mid-April, when Sun is in Aries, Malaya

New Year (Gudi Parva), first day of Chaitra, Maharashtra, India

New Year (Sinhala Avurudu), two days in April, first of Sinhala month of Bak and Tamil month of Chittrai

New Year (Ugadi Parva), first day of Chaitra, Andhra, India

New Year (Vaisakhi), first day of Vaisakha

New Year's Celebration (Kuningen, Feast of All Souls), final day of ten-day New Year's celebration, Galungan; every 210 days, Bali

Nirjala Ekadashi, eleventh day of waxing half of Jyeshta

Panguni Uttiram, two days, including the full moon day of Chaitra, Malaysia and Singapore; ten days, including the full moon day of Chaitra, Malaya

Parshurama Jayanti, third day of waxing half of Vaisakha

Pooram, during month of Vaisakha, Trichur, India

Protection, Festival to Pledge (Rakhim), during month of Sravana, India

Pushkar Fair, begins night before full moon of Karthika, Rajasthan, India

Putrada Ekadashi, 11th day of waxing half of Sravana

Radha Ashtami, eighth day of waning half of Bhadrapada

HINDU *(cont.)*

Rama, Festival of (Rama-Navami), ninth day of waning half of Chaitra, India

Rasa Leela Festival, one month during August-September, Manipur and Uttar Pradesh, India

Rishi Panchami, fifth day of waxing half of Bhadrapada

Sacred Thread Festival (Raksha Bandhan), full moon day of Sravana

Sakata Chauth, fourth day of waning half of Magha

Shankarachaya Jayanti or Birthday, fifth day (southern India) or tenth day (northern India) of waxing half of Vaisakha

Sharad Purnima, full moon day of Asvina

Shasti, Festival of (Aranya Shasti), Rajputanan women in Bengal, India

Shitala Ashtami, eighth day of waxing half of Chaitra

Shiva, Gajan of, during month of Chaitra, Bengal, India

Shiva, Night of (Mahashivaratri), 13th night and 14th day of waning half of Phalguna

Sithinakha (Kumar Sasthi), sixth day of waxing half of Jyeshta, Nepal

Skanda Shashti, October-November, month of Tulam, Tamils in southern India

Snake Festival (Naag Panchami), fifth day of waxing half of Sravana

Spring Festival (Vasant or Basant Panchami), fifth day of waxing half of Magha

Sravani Mela, during month of Sravana, Bihar, India

Sun Festival (Suryapuja), spring, Bangladesh

Surya Shashti, sixth day of waxing half of Karthika, married Hindu women with children

Swarupa Dwadashi, 12th day of waning half of Pausha, Hindu women

Teej, third day of waxing half of Sravana, Hindu women in India

Teej (Haritlika Teej), third day of waxing half of Bhadrapada, Hindu women

Teej (Hariyali Teej or Hari Tritiya), third day of waxing half of Sravana, Hindu women in Uttar Pradesh, India

Thaipusam, one day in January-February

Tirupati Festival, ten days during Bhadrapada, Tirupati, India

Tools, Festival of (Visvakarma Puja), end of Bhadrapada

Tulsidas Jayanti, seventh day of waxing half of Sravana

Undecaying Third (Akshya Tritiya), third day of waxing half of Vaisakha

Vaitarani, 11th day of waning half of Margashirsha

Vata Savitri (Savitri Vrata or Vow), 13th day or full moon day of waning half of Jyeshta, married Hindu women

Vishnu's Awakening (Devathani Ekadashi), 11th day of waxing half of Karthika

Wish-Fulfilling Eleventh (Kamada Ekadashi), 11th day of waning half of Sravana

Vaishnavite

Monkey God Festival (Hanuman Jayanti), full moon day of Chaitra

Narsimha Jayanti, 14th day of waxing half of Vaisakha

Rama, Festival of (Rama-Navami), ninth day of waning half of Chaitra

Rukmani Ashtami, eighth day of waning half of Pausha

ISLAMIC

Ashura, tenth day of month of Muharram; often, first ten days of Muharram

Data Ganj Baksh Death Festival, 18th and 19th days of month of Safar, Mausoleum of Data Ganj Baksh, Lahore, Pakistan

Fast, Feast of Breaking the ('Id al-Fitr or 'Id as-saghîr), first day of month of Shawwal

Mandi Safar, during month of Safar, Malacca, Malaysia

Mecca, Pilgrimage to, eighth through 13th days of month of Dhu'l-Hijjah

Muhammad's Birthday (Mawlid al-Nabi), twelfth day of month of Rabi al-Awwal

Nebi Mousa, Feast of, March-April, Saturday before Easter, Jerusalem

New Year (Muharram Celebrations), first day of month of Muharram

Night of Forgiveness (Laylat al-Bar 'ah), 15th day of month of Shaban

Night Journey of Muhammad (Laylat al-Mi'raj), 27th day of month of Rajab

Night of Power or Destiny (Laylat al-Qadr), one of the last ten days of month of Ramadan; usually observed on the 27th

Pilgrimage to Moulay Idriss, late August or September, Moulay Idriss, Morocco

Ramadan, ninth month of Islamic year, month of fasting

Sacrifice, Feast of ('Id al-Adha), tenth-twelfth days of month of Dhu'l-Hijjah

Thanksgiving (Awoojoh), may occur on special occasions and during such holidays as Christmas, Easter, Good Friday, and New Year's Day, Sierra Leone

Wax Festival, November, Salé, Morocco

Mevlana Muslims

Mevlana (Festival of Whirling Dervishes), nine days to two weeks in December, Konya, Turkey

Shiite Muslims

Husayn or Husain Day, tenth day of month of Muharram

Sufis and other Muslims

Muhammad's Birthday (Maulid), twelfth day of month of Rabi al-Awwal, Egypt

Sunni Muslims

Ashura, tenth day of month of Muharram

JAIN

Lights, Festival of (Dewali), one week during waning half of Karthika, including 15th day, India and Malaysia

Mahavira's Birthday (Mahavira Jayanti), 13th day of waxing half of Chaitra, India

Pajjusana, eight-day penance in August

Paryushana or Partyshana Parva, during month of Bhadrapada, India

Digambara (sky-clad) Jaina

Paryushana or Partyshana Parva, during month of Bhadrapada

Svetambar (white-clad) Jaina

Paryushana or Partyshana Parva, during month of Bhadrapada

JEWISH

April Fools' Day, April 1

Asarah be-Tevet (Fast of Tevet), tenth day of month of Tevet

Balfour Declaration Day, November 2, Israel

Blessing the Sun (Birchat Hahamah), every 28 years on the first Wednesday of month of Nisan, Israel and United States

Brotherhood Sunday, Sunday nearest February 22

Deliverance, Day of, prior to Passover

Family Week, National, begins first Sunday in May, United States

Fifteenth of Av (Hamishah Asar be-Av), 15th day of month of Av

First-Born, Fast of the, 14th day of month of Nisan

Gedaliah, Fast of, day following Jewish New Year (Rosh Hashanah)

Hagodol (Great Sabbath), festival preceding Passover

Hanukkah, eight days beginning 25th day of month of Kislev

Holocaust Day (Yom Hashoah), 27th day of month of Nisan

Hoshana Rabbah (Great Salvation), seventh day of Sukkot on 21st day of month of Tishri

Lag b'Omer, 18th day of month of Iyar, the 33rd day in the fifty-day period between Passover and Shavuot, in addition to the fifty-day period itself

Maimona or Maimonides, evening of last day of Passover and day after Passover

New Year, Jewish (Rosh Hashanah), first day of month of Tishri

New Year of Trees (B'Shevat; also known as Hamishah Assar Bi-Shebat), 15th day of month of Shevat, Israel

Passover (Pesach), seven or eight days beginning 15th day of month of Nisan

Purim, 14th day of month of Adar

Rosh Chodesh, first day of every Jewish month; day of new moon and last day of each month with 30 days

Shavuot (Feast of Weeks), sixth day of month of Sivan

Shemini Atzeret, eighth day of the Festival of Sukkot, observed on 22nd day of month of Tishri

Simhat Torah (Rejoicing in the Law), 23rd day of month of Tishri

Sukkot (Feast of Booths or Feast of the Tabernacles), 15th-21st or 22nd of month of Tishri

Ta'anit Esther, 13th day of month of Adar

Tammuz, Fast of the 17th of, 17th day of month of Tammuz

Tisha B'Av, ninth day of month of Av

Trumpets, Feast of, first day of seventh month (post-Exilic)

Water-Drawing Festival (Simhat bet Ha-sho'evah), night after first day of Sukkot and every night of Sukkot thereafter, Israel

Yom ha-Zikkaron (Day of Remembrance), fourth day of month of Iyar, Israel

Yom Kippur, tenth day of month of Tishri

Conservative Jews

Passover (Pesach), eight days beginning 15th day of month of Nisan

Simhat Torah (Rejoicing in the Law), 23rd day of month of Tishri

Orthodox Jews

Passover (Pesach), eight days beginning 15th day of month of Nisan

Simhat Torah (Rejoicing in the Law), 23rd day of month of Tishri

Sukkot (Feast of Booths or Feast of the Tabernacles), 15th-21st or 22nd of month of Tishri

Reform Jews

Passover (Pesach), seven days beginning 15th day of month of Nisan

Simhat Torah (Rejoicing in the Law), 22nd or 23rd day of month of Tishri in Israel

Sukkot (Feast of Booths or Feast of the Tabernacles), 15th-21st or 22nd of month of Tishri

Wise, Sabbath of, last Sabbath in March

KONKO-KYO

Kawate Bunjiro, Festival of, observed on or near October 25, Japan

Tenchi Kane no Kami, Festival of, on or near April 25, Japan

NEO-PAGAN (United States)

Holy Saturday, March-April, Saturday before Easter Sunday

Lammas, August 1

Lúgnasad (First Fruits Festival), August 1

Midsummer, June 23-24

Quadragesima Sunday, February, first Sunday in Lent

St. Bridget's Day, February 1

Samhain (Summer's End), October 31

Saturnalia

Twelfth Night (Epiphany Eve), January 5

NEO-PAGAN (United States) *(cont.)*
  Up-Helly-Aa, last Tuesday in January
  Walpurgis Night, April 30
  Yule, December 22

Gardnerian Witches (United States)
  Beltane, April 30
  Lúgnasad (First Fruits Festival), August 1

Wicca
  Imbolc (Brigit's Day), February 2

RASTAFARIANS
  Selassie's Coronation Day, Haile, on or near November 15,
  Jamaica

SHINTO
  Kashihara Shinto Festival, April 3, Kashihara Shrine,
  Kashihara, Nara, Japan
  Kotohira Kompira Festival, October, Kotohira, Kagawa,
  Japan
  Lily Festival, June 17, Nara, Japan
  Shrine Festival, Kasuga Wakamiya, December 13-18, Nara,
  Japan
  Shrine Kagura Festival, Ise, April and September, Ise, Mie,
  Japan
  Tori-no-ichi, November, Japan
  Water Drawing Festival (Omizutori Matsuri), two weeks in
  March, Todaiji Temple in Nara, Japan

SIKH
  Hola Mohalla, March 8, Anandpur Sahib, India
  Lights, Festival of (Dewali), one week during waning half
  of Karthika, including 15th day, India
  Nanak's Day (Nanak Parab), full moon day of
  Karthika
  New Year (Vaisakhi), first day of Vaisakha

TAOIST
  Bun Festival, four to five days in May, Cheung Chau Island,
  Hong Kong
  Hungry Ghosts, Festival of, 15th day of seventh lunar
  month
  Ta Chiu, several days during 11th and 12th lunar months
  at three-, five-, ten-year, or longer, intervals, Hong
  Kong
  Tam Kung Festival, eighth day of fourth lunar month,
  Tam Kung Temple, Shau Kei Wan, Hong Kong
  Island
  Vegetarian Festival, first nine days of ninth lunar month,
  Phuket, Thailand

TAOIST (CHINESE)
  Prince, Birthday of the Third, eighth and ninth days of fourth
  lunar month, Singapore
  Yü Huang Shang Ti, Jade or Pearly Emperor, eighth day of
  first lunar month

YORUBA
  Gelede, occasional: end of dry seasons (March-May); August;
  and during emergencies and funerals, Nigeria
  Iro Festivals, five festivals annually
  New Yam Festival, two days in August, Ondo's shrine in Pobe,
  Benin, Nigeria
  New Yam Festival (Egbodo Oba Ooni), late June, Oyo,
  Nigeria
  New Yam Festival (Eje), two-day festival, Nigeria
  New Yam Festival (Igun Efon Festival), Oyo, Nigeria
  New Yam Festival (Igun Ekun Ajinida Festival), annual,
  Oyo, Nigeria
  New Yam Festival (Igun Luwo Festival), Oyo, Nigeria
  New Yam Festival (Ilaja Isu Titun), Oyo, Nigeria
  Olojo, around July, Oyo, Nigeria
  Sango Festival, early November, seven days near end of rainy
  season, Ede, Nigeria
  Yoruba Ibeji Ceremony, at least once monthly, Nigeria

ZOROASTRIAN
  Fravashi Festivals, 19th of each month and during last
  ten days of the year
  Khordad Sal, March 21 (Fasli sect); July 13 (Kadmi sect);
  August 13 (Shahenshai sect)
  New Year (Jamshed Navaroz or Patati, Day of Repentance),
  March 21
  Zarthastno Diso, April 30 (Fasli sect); May 29 (Kadmi sect);
  June 1 (Shahenshai sect)

Parsi
  Khordad Sal, March 21 (Fasli sect); July 13 (Kadmi sect);
  August 13 (Shahenshai sect)
  New Year (Jamshed Navaroz or Patati, Day of Repentance),
  March 21
  Remembrance of the Departed Days, March, last ten days
  of the Parsi year, the ten days preceding the vernal equinox;
  March (Fasli sect); July (Kadmi sect); August (Shahenshai
  sect)
  Zarthastno Diso, April 30 (Fasli sect); May 29 (Kadmi sect);
  June 1 (Shahenshai sect)

Chronological Indexes

The indexes below list entries from the *Holidays and Festivals Index* that are observed according to various ethnic, religious, and geographical calendars. The entries indexed under **Gregorian Calendar Index** are organized by month—first, by those holidays which fall on fixed days within the month, then by those observed according to the Gregorian calendar, but not on the same date every year (for example, "the last weekend in January" or "three days in April"). Entries indexed under **Christian Movable Days Index** are Christian festivals that occur as part of the Christian liturgical year, as well as secular events whose dates are determined by the date of Easter. Jewish holidays are indexed in **Jewish Calendar Index**, and Islamic days in **Islamic Calendar Index**. **Chinese Calendar Index** lists holidays celebrated in several Asian countries which follow the lunar calendar traditionally used in China. **Hindu Calendar Index** lists events whose dates are determined by the Hindu lunar calendar and also includes some festivals observed according to the Buddhist calendar. Entries begin with the month in which the new year occurs. **Other Movable Days Index** lists events that fall into various other chronological categories, including holidays observed either annually or once during a given cycle of years, festivals observed according to various seasonal or agricultural criteria, and events for which no dates were provided in the source materials or whose dates are according to other calendars than those noted above.

Gregorian Calendar Index

January

January
Dicing for the Maid's Money Day • Guildford, Surrey, England
Drama Festival, Bombay • Bombay, Maharashtra, India
Offering Ceremony • Ambar Ketawang, Jogjakarta, Java
Offering Ceremony • Pangandaran, West Java, Java
Our Lady of the Happy Ending • Brazil
St. Anthony the Abbot of Egypt, Feast of • La Puebla, Majorca, Spain
Shrine Rice Festival, Suwa • Tokyo, Japan
Theatres, Nova Gorica Meeting of Small • Nova Gorica, Slovenia, Yugoslavia

January 1
Australian Open Tennis • Sydney and Melbourne, Australia
Bank Holiday • England (also Good Friday, Easter Monday, December 25, and December 26)
Circumcision, Feast of the • Christian
Coon Carnival • Cape Town, South Africa
Cotton Bowl Classic • Dallas, Texas
Emancipation Proclamation Day • United States
Granddad Frost Day • USSR
Independence Day • Yaounde, Federal Republic of Cameroon
Independence Day • Port-au-Prince, Haiti
Independence Day • Sudan
Jesus dos Navegantes, Bom • Salvador, Brazil
Liberation Day • Cuba
New Year's Day
Orange Bowl Football Classic • Miami, Florida
Penguin Plunge • Mackerel Cove, Jamestown, Rhode Island
Polar Bear Swim Day • English Bay, Vancouver, British Columbia, Canada
Polar Bear Swim Day • Northside Beach, Sheboygan, Wisconsin
Rose Bowl Game • Pasadena, California
St. Basil's Day • Christian

Singing to Rings (Ladouvane) • west Bulgaria (June 24 in the rest of the country)
Sugar Bowl Classic • New Orleans, Louisiana (January 2, if New Year's Day falls on a Sunday)
Tournament of Roses • Pasadena, California

January 1-2
Foundation Days • Taiwan

January 1-9
Black Nazarene Fiesta • Manila and Quezon, Luzon Island, Philippines

January 2
Admission Day • Georgia
Ancestry Day • Haiti
Beginning of Work Day (Shigoto Hajime) • Japan
Berchtold's Day (Berchtoldstag) • Switzerland
First Writing of the Year (Kakizome) • Japan
Minstrels' Carnival, Annual • Cape Town, South Africa
San Macario, Festival of • Malda, Lérida, Spain

January 3
Admission Day • Alaska
Genshi-Sai • Japan
St. Geneviève's Day • Roman Catholic

January 4
Admission Day • Utah
Independence Day • Burma (now Myanmar)
Martyrs' Day • Zaire
St. Elizabeth Ann Seton, Feast of • Roman Catholic; United States

January 5
Christmas Eve • Armenia
St. John Nepomucene Neumann, Feast of • Roman Catholic
St. Simon Stylites's Day • Christian
Twelfth Night (Epiphany Eve)

January 5-6
Befana Festival • Christians in Italy and Sicily
Epiphany • Christian (Gregorian calendar)

January 5-February 5
Ice & Snow Festival, Harbin • Harbin, China

January 6
Admission Day • New Mexico
Army Day • Iraq
Children's Day • Uruguay
Christmas • Eastern Orthodox
Christmas (Dznoont) • Armenia
Epiphany • Christian (Gregorian calendar)
Haxey Hood Game • Haxey, England
Maroon Festival • Jamaica
St. Stephen Day, Crown of • Christian
Winter Solstice Festival • Egypt

Usually January 6
Perchtenlauf • Imst and Thaur in Tirol, Austria

Four days including Epiphany, January 6
Folklore Festival, Canajacua • Macaracas, Panama

Sunday following Epiphany, January 6
Baptism of the Lord, Feast of the • Christian
Holy Family, Feast of the • Roman Catholic

Sunday following January 6 if Epiphany doesn't fall on a Sunday
Epiphany • Armenian-Americans

Begins no later than January 6, Epiphany, and ends Fat Tuesday, the day before Ash Wednesday
Mardi Gras • New Orleans, Louisiana

Saturday preceding Plough Monday, first Monday after January 6
Straw Bear Day • Whittlesey, Cambridgeshire, England

First Monday after January 6
Plough Monday • Bulgaria and Great Britain

January 6-Ash Wednesday
Mardi Gras (Farsang) • Hungary

January 7
Bullfinch Exchange Festival (Usokae) • Dazaifu, Fukuoka, Japan
Christmas (Ganna or Genna; officially called Leddat) • Coptic Church in Ethiopia
Distaff Day • England
Epiphany (Old Christmas) • Ukrainian-Canadians
Pioneers' Day • Liberia

St. John the Baptist's Day • Greece
Seven Herbs Festival (Nanakusa Matsuri) • Japan

January 7-Tuesday before Ash Wednesday
Mardi Gras (Fasching Carnival) • Munich, Germany

January 8
Battle of New Orleans or Hickory's Day • Louisiana
Battle of New Orleans Day • Massachusetts
Gynaecocratia • Komotini, Xanthi, Kilkis, and Serres, Greece
St. Gudula's Day • Roman Catholics in Belgium
Women's Day (Midwife's Day) • Greece

January 9
Admission Day • Connecticut
Agonalia or Agonia (Feast of Janus) • ancient Rome
St. Philip of Moscow's Day • Russian Orthodox

January 9
St. Julian the Hospitaler, Feast of • Christian (or February 12)

January 11
Hostos, Birthday of (Hostos Day) • Puerto Rico and the United States
Independence Day (August 11) • Chad
Juturnalia • ancient Rome
National Unity Day (Prithvi Jayanti) • Nepal
Republic Day • Albania
St. Brictiva's Day • Norway

January 12
Revolution Day • Zanzibar, Tanzania

January 12 or 13
Old New Year's Day • Wales

January 13
Foster Memorial Day • White Springs, Florida, and Stephen Foster Memorial Association and musical societies
Fox, Death of George • Quaker
Liberation Day • Togo
St. Hilary's Day • Anglican
St. Knut's Day (Tjugondag Knut) • Sweden
Twentieth Day (Tyvendedagen) • Norway

January 14
Ass, Feast of the • medieval northern France
Circumcision, Feast of the • Christian (Julian calendar; January 1, Gregorian calendar)
Ratification Day • State House, Annapolis, Maryland
St. Basil's Day • Christian (Julian calendar; January 1, Gregorian calendar)
St. Hilary's Day • Roman Catholic
St. Sava's Day • Serbian people in Yugoslavia

January 15
Adults Day (Seijin-no-hi) • Sanjusangendo, Kyoto and elsewhere in Japan
Black Christ, Festival of the • Esquipulas, Guatemala
Teachers' Day (Día Del Maestro) • Venezuela

January 16
St. Honoratus's Day • France

January 17
Franklin's Birthday, Benjamin • Philadelphia, Pennsylvania
St. Anthony's Day (San Antonio Abad) • Zacatecas and elsewhere in Mexico
St. Anthony the Abbot of Egypt, Feast of (Blessing of the Animals) • Christian

Sunday nearest January 17
St. Anthony the Abbot of Egypt, Feast of (Blessing of the Animals) • Christian

January 17 to January 25
St. Sebastian's Day (Día de San Sebastián) • Zinacantan, Mexico

January 17-Ash Wednesday
Mardi Gras (Carnevale) • Italy

January 18
Revolution Day • Tunisia
St. Peter's Chair, Festival of • Roman Catholics in Rome
Wellington Day • Wellington, New Zealand

January 19
Confederate Memorial Day • Texas
Epiphany • Christian (Julian calendar; January 6, Gregorian calendar)
Lee Day, Robert E. • southern United States (may be observed third Monday in January)

January 20
Army Day • Mali
Chiapa de Corzo, Fiesta of • Chiapas, Mexico
Foundation Day • Rio de Janeiro, Brazil
Grandmother's Day (Babin Den) • Bulgaria
Heroes Day • Cape Verde
Inauguration Day • United States
St. Agnes Eve • Christian
St. Sebastian's Day • Christian
St. Sebastian's Day • Rio de Janeiro, Brazil
St. Sebastian, Festival of (Fiesta de San Sebastian) • Tenosique, Tabasco, Mexico

January, including Feast of San Sebastian, January 20
Country Fair • Ocu, Panama

January 21
Lenin, Anniversary of the Death of • Moscow, Russia
Provincial Anniversary • Wellington, New Zealand
St. Sarkis's Day • Armenia

January 22
Columbus Day (Discovery Day) • St. Vincent
Eleven Cities Race (Elfstedentocht) • Friesland Province, Netherlands
Republic Day • Ukrainian Republic
St. Dominique's Day (Midwife's Day) • Greece, Macedonia, and Greek refugees from Bulgaria
St. Vicente, Feast Day of (São Vicente) • Portugal
St. Vincent of Sargossa, Feast Day of • Christian; France

January 23
St. Ildephonsus, Feast Day of • Roman Catholics at San Ildefonso Pueblo, New Mexico

On or near January 23
Hobart Cup Day • southern Tasmania, Australia

January 24
Alasita Fair ("Buy from Me" Fair) • Aymara Indians in Bolivia
Paul Pitcher Day • Cornwall, England
St. Francis de Sales, Feast of • Christian

Weekend nearest January 24
California Gold Rush Day • Marshall Gold Discovery State Historical Park, Coloma, California

January 25
Burns Night • Newfoundland, Canada, England, Scotland, and Scottish-Americans
Cow, Festival of the (Fiesta de la Vaca) • San Pablo de los Montes, Toledo, Spain
St. Paul, Feast of the Conversion of • Christian; New York, New York

January 26
Admission Day • Michigan
Duarte Day • Dominican Republic
MacArthur Day, Douglas • Arkansas
Republic Day • New Delhi, India
St. Polycarp's Day • Christian

End of January, including Australia Day, January 26
Folk Festival, Numeralla • Numeralla, New South Wales, Australia

January 26 or following Monday
Australia Day • Australia

January 27
Dance, Basket • San Juan Pueblo, New Mexico

January 27 (cont.)
Mozart, Birthday of • music societies worldwide
St. Devota's Day • Monaco

January 27-28
Folk-Dance Festival, Republic Day • New Delhi, India

January 28
Democracy Day • Rwanda
Provincial Anniversary • Auckland, New Zealand
St. Charlemagne's Day • France
St. Thomas Aquinas, Feast of • Christian

January 29
Admission Day • Kansas, especially Topeka

Sunday nearest January 29
Paine Day, Thomas (Common Sense Day) • Hugenot-Thomas Paine Historical Society

January 30
Roosevelt Day, Franklin D. • Kentucky and Virgin Islands
St. Charles's Day • Anglicans in England and Episcopalians in the United States
Three Hierarchs or Archbishops, Holiday of the • Greece

January 31
Independence Day • Nauru
New Year's Eve • Umbanda religion in Brazil

Three days in January
Folklore, National Festival of • Durazno, Uruguay

Three days in January, including feast day of Santo Nino (Holy Child Jesus) and ending on a Sunday
Ati-Atihan Festival • Negrito and Malay peoples at Kalibo, Akland, Panay Island, Philippines

Six days in January
Poetry Gathering, Cowboy • Elko, Nevada

Several days, including first quarter moon in January
Iroquois White Dog Feast (New Year or Midwinter Festival) • Senaca, Cayuga, and other Iroquois Indians in Canada and the United States

One week in January
Puppet Theatre Week 1978, 1979, etc. • location varies within Federal Republic of Germany
Theatre, Festival of Contemporary • Brasov, Transylvania, Romania

Two weeks in January
Folklore, Sydney Festival of • Sydney, New South Wales, Australia (coincides with Festival of Sydney)

Three to four weekends in January
Kite Festival, Singapore • Singapore

Six days in early January
Winter Festival, Alpine • Davis, West Virginia

First week in January
Circus Festival and Parade, Sarasota • Sarasota, Florida
Pilgrimage to Chalma • Christians at Chalma, Mexico (also held in February, August, September, and during Holy Week)

First through second Sunday in January
Universal Week of Prayer • National Council of Churches, United States, and World Evangelical Alliance, London, England

First Monday in January
Handsel Monday • Scotland

Second Sunday in January
Meitlisunntig • Seetal district of Aargau, Switzerland

Ten days beginning second Thursday in January
Bonfim Festival • Salvador, Bahia, Brazil

Mid-January
Chakkirako Festival • Kainan Temple, Miura, Kanagawa, Japan

Last two weeks in January
Livestock Show and Rodeo, Southwestern Exposition and • Fort Worth, Texas

Third week in January
Dance of Transylvania, Men's (Caluser or Caluseri) • Deva, Hunedoara, Romania
Ullr Fest • Norwegian-Americans at Breckenridge, Colorado

Third weekend in January
Sinulog Festival • Celou, Philippines
Sled Dog Races, All American Championships • Ely, Minnesota

Third Sunday in January
World Religion Day • Bahá'í

Third Monday in January
King, Jr.'s Birthday, Martin Luther (January 15) • United States
Lee-Jackson Day (January 18) • North Carolina and Virginia

Begins third Friday in January and lasts 11 days
Western Stock Show, National • Denver, Colorado

Late January
Australia Day at the Rocks • the Rocks, Sydney, New South Wales, Australia

Ten days including last week in January
Winter Carnival, St. Paul • St. Paul, Minnesota

Last weekend in January
Dinagyand • Iloilo City, Panay Island, Philippines

Last Sunday in January
Mount Cameroon Race • Mount Cameroon, Cameroon
Super Bowl Sunday • United States

Last Tuesday in January
Up-Helly-Aa • Lerwick, Shetland Islands, Scotland and Neo-pagans in the United States

Nine days at end of January
Mozart Week (Mozartwoche) • Salzburg, Austria

Three days in January or February
Cruft's Dog Show • England

January-February
Arts Festival, Hong Kong • Hong Kong
Bermuda Festival • Hamilton, Bermuda
Brent Festival • London Borough of Brent, Middlesex, England
Mime Festival • London, England
Mihr, Festival of • ancient Armenia (forty days after Christmas)

One day in January-February
Thaipusam • Hindus in Malaysia, Mauritius, Singapore, South Africa, and Hindu Tamils in southern India

Early January to early February
New Year (Narcissus Festival) • Honolulu, Oahu Island, Hawaii

Late January to mid-February
Olympic Games (winter games) • location varies

End of January to beginning of February
Sun Pageant Day • Rjukan, Norway

January-March
Mambembao • Brasilia, Rio de Janeiro, and Sao Paulo, Brazil
Mardi Gras (Bal du Rat Mort, Dead Rat's Ball) • Ostend, Belgium (usually the weekend before Lent)
Summer Festival of the Lake of Rodo Park • Montevideo, Uruguay

February

February
Argungu Fishing Festival • Argungu, Nigeria
Battle of the Moors and Christians • Bocairente, Valencia, Spain
Black History Month • United States
Bonten Festival • Akita, Japan
Clean Tent Ceremony • Nganasan people in Siberia, USSR
Dance, Deer • San Juan Pueblo, New Mexico
Dance, Deer and Buffalo • Santa Clara Pueblo, New Mexico
Dance, Evergreen • Isleta Pueblo, New Mexico
Daytona 500 • Daytona International Speedway, Daytona Beach, Florida
Drama Festivals, Academy • Jammu, Jammu and Kashmir, India
Folklore Festival, International • Agrigento, Sicily, Italy
Harvest Festival (Bungan) • Berawan people at Sarawak, Malaysia
Iemanj Festival • Rio Vermelho, Brazil
Indian Celebration, O'Odham Tash • Papago Indians at Casa Grande, Arizona
Launceston Cup Day • northern Tasmania, Australia
New Year (Tsagan Sara, White Moon celebration) • Mongolia
New Year's Day • Seneca Iroquois Indians
Pilgrimage to Chalma • Christians at Chalma, Mexico (also first week in January, August, September, and during Holy Week)
Plum Blossom Festival (Baika-sai) • Japan
Powwow, Seminole • Seminole Indians at Seminole Reservation near Hollywood, Florida
Puppet Theaters of Slovenia, Encounter of • Slovenska Gorica, Slovenia, Yugoslavia
Spring Festival (Li Chun, Spring Is Here) • China
Theatre Groups, Encounter of Andalucian • Granada, Spain
Theatres of Vojvodina, Encounter of Slovak Amateur • Stara Pazova, Vojvodina, Yugoslavia
Verviers, Festival of • Verviers, Belgium

February 1
Khomeini Day • Iran
National Freedom Day • United States
St. Bridget's Day • Great Britain and Neo-pagans in the United States

Saturday nearest February 1
Gable Birthday Celebration, Clark • Cadiz, Ohio

February 2
Candlemas • Christian
Groundhog Day • England, Germany, and the United States
Imbolc (Brigit's Day) • Wiccan
New Year's Day • Aztec
Quarter Days • Scotland (also May 15, August 1, and November 11)

Usually on February 2, Candlemas
Cock Festival (Fiesta del Gallo) • Spain

On or near February 2
St. Charles's Day (January 30) • Anglicans at Trafalgar Square, London, England

February 3
Martyrs Day • Sao Tomé and Principe
St. Blaise's Day • Christian

Sunday nearest or Monday after February 3
Silver Ball, Hurling the • St. Ives, Cornwall, England

February 3-5
St. Agatha Festival • Catania, Sicily

February 4
Armed Struggle Day, Commencement of the • Angola
Independence Day • Sri Lanka
Kosciuszko Day • Polish-American communities in the United States
Provincial Anniversary • Nelson, New Zealand
St. Andrew Corsini, Feast Day of • Christian
United Service Organizations (USO), Founding of • service centers in the United States

February 4-5
Dance, Los Comanches • Taos Pueblo, New Mexico

February 5
Martyr Day • Japan
Runeberg, Birthday of Johann Ludvig • Helsinki, Finland
St. Agatha Festival • San Marino
St. Agatha Festival (Girls' Festival) • France
Williams Day, Roger • Baptists in the United States

Usually Sunday nearest February 5
Midwinter Festival (Igbi) • Tsezy people at Shaitli, Dagestan, USSR

February 6
Admission Day • Massachusetts
New Zealand Day (Waitangi) • New Zealand
St. Dorothy, Feast of • Christian

February 7
Independence Day • Grenada

February 8
Boy Scouts Day • Boy Scouts in the United States
Broken Needles Festival (Hari-Kuyo; also known as the Festival or Mass of the Broken Needles or Needle Day) • Tokyo, Japan
Inventors Day • National Inventors Hall of Fame, United States

Kite Flying Day • Korea
Sun Pageant Day, Narvik • Narvik, Norway

February 8-12
Snow Festival (Yuki Matsuri) • Odori Park, Sapporo, Hokkaido, Japan

February 9
St. Apollonia's Day • Christian
St. Maron's Day • Maronite Christians in Lebanon and in North and South America

Begins Sunday nearest February 9 and ends the next Saturday
Garbanzo, Fiesta Sopa de • Spanish-, Cuban-, and Italian-Americans at Ybor City, Florida

February 9-10
Regatta Day, Hobart • southern Tasmania, Australia

February 10
St. Paul's Shipwreck, Feast of • Malta

February 11
Allen Day, Richard • African Methodist Episcopal Church, United States
Armed Forces Day • Liberia
Edison's Birthday, Thomas • United States
Foundation Day, Japanese National (Kigensetsu) • Japan
Our Lady of Lourdes, Feast of • Christian
St. Vlasios's Day • Greece
White Shirt Day • Flint, Michigan
Youth Day • Cameroon

Second Wednesday through third Saturday in February, including February 11
Edison Pageant of Light • Fort Myers, Florida

February 11-18
Our Lady of Lourdes, Feast of • Roman Catholics at Lourdes, France
Our Lady of Lourdes, Feast of • Chamorros people in Guam/Northern Marianas

February 12
St. Julian the Hospitaler, Feast of • Christian (or January 9)
Union Day • Burma (now Myanmar)

Sunday nearest February 12
Race Relations Sunday • Protestants in the United States

One week in February, including February 12
Georgia Week Celebrations (including Oglethorpe Day) • Savannah, Georgia

February 13
Faunalia • ancient Rome (and December 15)

February 13-21
Parentalia • ancient Rome

February 14
Admission Day • Arizona
Admission Day • Oregon
Candlemas (Dyarntarach) • Armenian Church in Armenia
Fourteenth of February (Fjortende Februar) • Denmark
Valentine's Day
Vinegrower's Day (Trifon Zarezan, Viticulturists' Day) •
Bulgaria

February 15
Anthony Day, Susan B. • United States (or August 26)
Maine Memorial Day (Battleship Day; Remember the
Maine Day; Spanish-American War Memorial Day) •
Connecticut, Maine, and Massachusetts

Around February 15-17
Snowhut or Snowcave Festival (Kamakura Matsuri) •
northern Japan

February 16
Independence Day, Lithuania • Lithuanian-American
communities in the United States

February 17
Quirinalia • ancient Rome

One week beginning about February 17
Fornacalia (Fornax, Feast of Ovens) • ancient Rome

February 18
Independence Day • Gambia
National Day (Tribhuvan Jayanti) • Kathmandu, Nepal

February 21
Feralia • ancient Rome
Shaheel or Shaheed Day or Martyrs Day • Bangladesh

February 22
Abu Simbel Festival • Abu Simbel temple in Egypt
Boys' Day (also Army Day) • USSR
Girl Guides Thinking Day • England and British
Commonwealth countries
Independence Day • St. Lucia
St. Peter's Day • Westphalia, Germany
Thinking Day • England
Virgin Islands Donkey Races Day • Frederiksted and
Christiansted, Virgin Islands

Sunday nearest February 22
Brotherhood Sunday

Week which contains February 22
Brotherhood Week • United States

February 23
Republic Day • Guyana
Terminalia • ancient Rome, along road to Laurentum

February 24
Independence Day • Estonia
St. Matthias, Feast of • Episcopalian and Lutheran
Vincennes Day • Indiana

February 25
Coronado Day • North American southwest
National Day • Kuwait
People Power Anniversary • Quezon City, Manila,
Philippines
St. George's Day • Mtskheta, Georgian Republic, USSR

February 26-March 1
Ayyam-i-Ha • Bahá'í

February 27
Independence Day • Dominican Republic
Majuba Day (Hill of Doves) • Boer people in South Africa
Statehood Day • St. Kitts-Nevis

February 28
Kalevala Päivä Day • Finland
St. Oswald's Day • Christian

February 29
Leap Year Day
Leap Year Privilege (Bachelors' Day) • England, Ireland,
and Scotland
Lee, Birthday of Ann • Shakers (United Society of Believers
in Christ's Second Appearing, the Millennial Church)

February 30
Job's Birthday • African-Americans in Maryland

A weekend in February
Winter Carnival, Dartmouth • Hanover, New Hampshire

Two days in February
Sliding Festival, Finnish • Aurora, Minnesota
Surfing Classic, Buffalo's Big Board • Makaha Beach,
Oahu, Hawaii

Three days in February
New Year (Losar) • Buddhists in Tibet and Buddhist
Tibetan exiles in India and Bodhnath, Nepal (usually
in February; date annually determined by Tibetan
astrologers in Dharmsala, India)
Snowgolf Championship • Prince George, British
Columbia, Canada

Four days in February
Winter Fair, Great Lapp • Lapp people at Jokkmokk, Lappland, Sweden

Five days in February
Arts for Young People, Festival of Performing—Round Up • Perth, Western Australia, Australia
St. Agnes Eve (January 20) • Catania, Sicily

Several days in February
Washington's Birthday, George (Cherries Jubilee) • Valley Forge State Park, Pennsylvania

One week in February
Plays, Festival of Short • Oradea, Transylvania, Romania
Voyageur, Festival du • St. Boniface, Winnipeg, Manitoba, Canada

Seven to ten days in February
Winterfest • Minot, North Dakota

Nine-day kachina ceremony in February
Sky-God Festival (Powamû Festival) • Hopi Indians at Walpi Pueblo, Arizona

Ten days in February
Anchorage Fur Rendezvous • Anchorage, Alaska
Carnaval, Quebec • Quebec City, Quebec, Canada
Chicoutimi Olden-Days Carnival • Chicoutimi, Quebec, Canada
Winterlude • Ottawa, Ontario, Canada

Ten days in February during odd-numbered years
St. Andrew's Festival • St. Andrews, Fife, Scotland

Early February
Endiablada Festival • Almonacid del Marquesado, Cuenca, Spain
Horaiji Temple Dengaku Festival • Horai, Aichi, Japan
Kurokowa Noh • Kushiki-machi, Higishitagawa-gun, Yamagata, Japan

Beginning or end of February
New Year (Losar) • Bhutan

First new moon in February
Bianou • Agadés, Niger

First week in February
Governor's Feast • Acoma Pueblo, New Mexico

First week or weekend in February
Ice Worm Festival • Cordova, Alaska

First Sunday in February
Homstrom • Switzerland and Swiss-Americans

First Monday in February
Lincoln's Birthday, Abraham (February 12) • United States

Monday after the first Tuesday in February
Gasparilla Pirate Festival and Invasion • Tampa, Florida

Five days during second week in February
Drama Festival, Gujarat Academy • Ahmedabad, Gujarat, India

Fifteen days beginning second week in February
Drama Festival, Sri Ram Center • New Delhi, India

Second weekend in February
Gold Rush Days • Wickenburg, Arizona

Mid-February
Lupercalia • ancient Rome
Shimmeisha Oni Festival • Shimmeisha Shrine, Toyohashi, Aichi, Japan
Shrine Festival, Kuromori Hie • Kuromori Village, Sakata City, Yamagata, Japan
Washington's Birthday, George • Laredo, Texas, and Nuevo Laredo, Mexico

Nearly one week in mid-February
Trappers' Festival, Northern Manitoba • The Pas, Manitoba, Canada

Third weekend in February
Brighton Field Day and Rodeo • Seminole Indians at Okeechobee, Florida
Washington's Birthday, George • Alexandria, Virginia

Sunday before third Monday in February
Crab Races, World Championship • Crescent City, California

Third Monday in February
Presidents Day • United States
Washington's Birthday, George (February 22) • United States

Late February
Ice Classic, Nenana • Nenana, Alaska (also early spring)

Two days in late February
Indian Fair, Heard Museum Guild • Hopi, Navajo, Apache, Plains, Pima, and Mohave Indians at the Heard Museum, Phoenix, Arizona

Three days in late February
Arts, Festival of Native • Fairbanks, Alaska
Birkebeiner, American (the Birkie) • Cable, Wisconsin

Last week in February
Performing Arts for Young People, The Leap—Festival of • Sydney, New South Wales, Australia

Four days beginning last Thursday in February
Vaqueros, Fiesta de los • Tucson, Arizona

Last Saturday in February
Logging Days, Buena Vista • Bemidji, Minnesota

Last day of February
Shvod • Armenia

Last night of February and first of March
First of March (Marzas) • Spain

February or March
Burgsonndeg • Luxembourg
Drama Festival, Rajasthan Academy • Jaipur, Udaipur, Jodhpur, and elsewhere in Rajasthan, India
Theatre Debuts, Start: National Festival of Student • Poland

Three days in late February or early March
Bach Festival of Winter Park • Winter Park, Florida

February-March
Drama Festival, Marathi • Goa, Daman, and Diu Union Territory, Panjim, India
Drama Festival, National School of • New Delhi, India
Kiddies' Carnival • Trinidad and Tobago (during week preceding Carnival)
Kuomboka • Malozi people at Lealul Knoll, Mongu, Western Province, Zambia (when Zambezi River rises)
Our Lord of Passos, Procession of • Christians in Macao
Perth, Festival of • Perth, Western Australia, Australia
Xipe, Festival of • Aztec (near Carnival time; during Aztec month of Tlacaxipehualiztli)

Even-numbered years in February-March
Arts, Festival of the • Adelaide, South Australia, Australia

Full moon day in February-March
Buddha's Birthday, Enlightenment, and Salvation (Kason Festival of Watering the Banyon Tree) • Buddhists in Myanmar (formerly Burma)

Saturday before the Saturday before Mardi Gras, nine days before Mardi Gras in February-March
Decoration Day (Psychosavato) • Greece

Five days in February-March
Drama Festival, Manipur Academy • Imphal, Manipur, India

One week in February-March
Mardi Gras (Carnevale) • Milan, Italy

Seven weeks from early February to late March
Old Island Days • Key West, Florida

February-April
Kite Flying Season • Sanam Luang in front of the Grand Palace, Bangkok, Thailand (on weekday afternoons)
Okambondondo, Feast of • Angola
Theatre Competition of Figueira da Foz, Amateur • Figueira da Foz, Coimbra, Portugal

Mid-February through April
Cherry Blossom Festival • Honolulu, Oahu Island, Hawaii

February-May
Young Writers' Festival • London, England

February-October
Shakespeare Festival, Oregon • Ashland, Oregon

March

March
Arts, Festival of Traditional • Rennes, Ille-et-Vilaine, France
Arts Festival, Dublin • Dublin, County Dublin, Ireland
Ballet Festival Week • Munich, Bavaria, Federal Republic of Germany (or May)
Begonia Festival, Ballarat • Ballarat, Victoria, Australia
Blue Gum Festival of Tasmania • Tasmania, Australia
Comedy Festival, Days of • Svetozarevo, Serbia, Yugoslavia
Cuenca Encounter • Cuenca, Spain
Cultural Days • El Alaa, Kairouan Region, Tunisia
Dance, Deer • Hananomaki, Iwate, Japan
Dance Festival, Kerala Kalamandalam • Cheruthuruthy, Kerala, India
First Fruits Festival • Zinza, Tanzania
Lifeboat Day • Manchester, England
Phra Buddha Bat Fair • Phra Buddha Bat temple near Saraburi, Thailand
Remembrance of the Departed Days • Fasli sect of Parsis
Swallow Songs • Greece (return of the swallows)
Theatrical Forms, Festival of Small • Szczecin, Poland
Whale Festival • Mendocino, Fort Bragg, and Gualala, California

Even-numbered years in March
Arts Festival, Christchurch • Christchurch, New Zealand
Poetry of Friendship • Shumen, Bulgaria

Odd-numbered years in March
Puppet Theatre Festival, International • Bialystok, Poland

March 1
Admission Day • Nebraska
Admission Day • Ohio
First of March • Albania, Bulgaria, Cyprus, and Greece (Martenitza); Macedonia (Drymiais); and Macedonian- and Bulgarian-Canadians

March 1 *(cont.)*
First of March (Chalanda Marz) • Engadine, Grisons, Switzerland
Independence Day (Samiljol) • Republic of Korea
St. David's Day • England, Wales, and Welsh-Americans
Whuppity Scoorie Day • Lanark, Lanarkshire, Scotland

March 2
Independence Day • Texas
Independence Day (National Day) • Morocco
Victory of Aduwa Day • Ethiopia

One week, including March 2
Peasants' Day • Burma (now Myanmar)

March 3
Admission Day • Florida
Girls' Doll Festival (Hina Matsuri; also known as Hina-No-Sekku, Peach Blossom Festival) • Japan and Japanese-Americans
Liberation Day • Bulgaria
Martyr's Day • Malawi
Throne Day • Morocco
Unity Day • Sudan

March 4
Admission Day • Vermont
Charter Day • Pennsylvania

March 5
Boston Massacre Day • Boston, Massachusetts
Boston Massacre Day (Crispus Attucks Day) • New Jersey
Eight Hour Day or Labour Day • Western Australia and Tasmania
Mother-in-law Day • Amarillo, Texas
St. Piran's Day • Cornwall, England

On or near March 5
Excited Insects, Feast of • Korea (Kyongchip) and People's Republic of China (Ching Che)

March 6
Alamo Day • Houston and San Antonio, Texas
Independence Day • Ghana
Magellan or Discovery Day • Guam

March 7
Bird and Arbor Day • California
Burbank Day • California

March 8
Hola Mohalla • Sikh people at Anandpur Sahib, India
Labour Day • Victoria, Australia
Revolution Day • Syria
Woman's Day (Tij Day) • women in Nepal
Woman's Day, International

March 9
Baron Bliss Day • Belize
Martyrs' Day, Forty • Greece, Romania, and Christians in Syria ('Id al-Arba'in Shahid)
St. Frances of Rome, Feast Day of • Rome, Italy

March 10
Army Commemoration Day (Rikugun-Kinenbi) • Japan
Jousting the Bear (La Giostra dell'Orso) • Pistoia, Italy

March 11
Independence Day • Lithuania
Johnny Appleseed Day • United States
King's Birthday • Denmark
National Anti-Drugs Day • students at King's College, London, England
National No Smoking Day • Great Britain
Provincial Anniversary • Taranaki, New Zealand

March 12
Arbor Day • Taiwan
Girl Scout Day • United States
Independence Day • Mauritius
Moshoeshoe Day • Lesotho
St. Gregory's Day • Belgium

March 12-19
St. Joseph's Day Bonfires (Fallas de San José) • Valencia, Spain

March 13
National Day • Grenada
St. Nikephoros's Day • Greek Orthodox in Greece

March 13 or first Monday in August
Youth Day • Zambia (formerly Northern Rhodesia)

March 15
Admission Day • Maine
Hilaria • ancient Rome
Jackson's Birthday, Andrew • Tennessee

First Sunday after March 15
Buzzard Day • Hinckley Ridge near Hinckley, Ohio

March 16
St. Urho's Day • Finnish-Americans
Spring, Feast of (Pavasario Svente) • ancient Lithuania

March 17
Camp Fire Founders' Day • Camp Fire Girls and Boys groups
Evacuation Day • Boston and Suffolk County, Massachusetts
Liberalia • ancient Rome
St. Patrick's Day • Christians in Canada, Ireland, and the United States

Weekend nearest March 17
St. Patrick's Day Encampment • Morristown, New Jersey

March 18
Sheelah's Day • Ireland

March 19
St. Joseph of Arimathea, Feast Day of • Roman Catholic
St. Joseph's Day (Dia de San Giuseppe) • Italy
Swallows of San Juan Capistrano • San Juan Capistrano
Mission, San Juan Capistrano, California (swallows arrive;
swallows depart October 23)

Ten days, including March 19
St. Joseph's Day (International Fair of San José) • Roman
Catholics at David, Panama

March 20
Earth Day (Vernal Equinox) • parts of North America and
Western Europe
Independence Day • Tunisia
Kossuth Day • Hungary and Hungarians elsewhere

On or near March 20
Emume Ala • Igbo people in Nigeria

March 21
Back Badge Day • Gloucestershire Regiment of the
British Army
Children's Poetry Day
Juárez Day (Day of the Indian Chief) • Mexico
Khordad Sal • Fasli sect of Parsis in India and elsewhere
National Agriculture Day • Farm bureaus, marketing
associations, and Future Farmers of America in Maryland
and elsewhere
New Year (Jamshed Navaroz or Patati, Day of Repentance) •
Parsis and other Zoroastrians in the United States and
elsewhere
New Year's Day (Nauroz) • Afghanistan
New Year's Day (Nawruz) • Bahá'í
New Year's Day (No Ruz or Naw Roz) • Iran
St. Benedict's Day • Pennsylvania-Dutch people in the
United States

On or near March 21
Vernal Equinox

Saturday or Sunday nearest March 21
Marzanna Day • along the Vistula River, Poland

March 21 or 22
Tree Planting Day • Lesotho

On or near March 21-22
Vernal Equinox, Festival of (Shunki Korei-Sai) • Japan

March 22
Arab League Day • Jordan
Emancipation of the Slaves Day • Puerto Rico
Pakistan Day • Rawalpindi, Pakistan
Provincial Anniversary • Otago and Southland,
New Zealand

March 24, climax of six-day festival
Blood, Day of • Galli, priests of Attis in ancient Rome

March 25
Annunciation, Feast of the • Christian (moves to April 1
if March 25 occurs within Holy Week)
Independence Day • Cyprus
Independence Day • Greece; Greek-Americans
Lady Day (Quarter Day) • England and Ireland
Maryland Day • Maryland
Quarter Days • England and Ireland (also June 24, September
29, and December 25)

Sunday nearest March 25
Independence Day, Greece • New York, New York

March 26
Independence Day • Bangladesh
Tichborne Dole • Alresford, Hampshire, England

One week in March, including March 26
Kuhio Kalanianaole Day • Kauai, Hawaii

March 27
Resistance Day • Burma (Myanmar)

March 27-April 6
Theatres of Yugoslavia, Festival of Small and Experimental •
Sarajevo, Bosnia and Herzegovina, Yugoslavia

March 28
Teacher's Day • Czechoslovakia

March 29
Boganda Day • Central African Republic
Delaware Swedish Colonial Day • Delaware Swedish
Colonial Society and others in Delaware
Martyrs' Day, Canton • China, especially in Kwantung
Province
Memorial Day (Commemoration Day) • Madagascar
Youth Day • Taiwan

March 30
Doctors' Day • United States

March 31
Oranges and Lemons Day • Christians in London,
England

Full moon day in March
Fire Festival (Phagwa) • Trinidad and Tobago

One week in March
Caribou Carnival and Championship Dog Derby • Yellowknife, Northwest Territories, Canada
Jazz Festival, *Boston Globe* • Boston, Massachusetts

One week in March during odd-numbered years
Puppet Play Week, International • Braunschweig, Lower Saxony, Federal Republic of Germany

Ten days in March
Canberra Week (includes Canberra Day) • Canberra, Australian Capital Territory, Australia
Moomba ("let's get together and have fun") Festival • Melbourne, Victoria, Australia

Two weeks in March
Camden Festival • London, England
Water Drawing Festival (Omizutori Matsuri) • Buddhist and Shinto people at Todaiji Temple in Nara, Japan

Early March
Poetry Festival, Palamas • Paphos, Cyprus

Usually a Sunday in early March
Women's Day, International • Great Britain

A weekend in early March
Winter Carnival, North Pole • North Pole, Alaska

First week in March
Grape Harvest, National Festival of the • Mendoza, Argentina
Motorcycle Week • Daytona Beach, Florida

First two full weeks in March
Carnaval Miami • Hispanic-Americans at Miami, Florida

First weekend in March
Powwow, Epethes • Nez Perce Indians at Lapwai, Idaho

First Sunday in March
Vasaloppet • Sweden

First Monday in March
Pulaski Day • Illinois

First Tuesday in March
Town Meeting Day • Vermont

First Friday in March
Friday in Lide • Cornwall, England
World Day of Prayer • Christian

11-32 day-long race begins first Saturday in March
Iditarod Trail Sled Dog Race • Anchorage, Alaska

Second weekend in March
Gila River Festival • Pima and Maricopa Indians at Sacaton, Arizona
Rattlesnake Roundup, Sweetwater • Sweetwater, Texas

One week in March including second Sunday in March
Ski Festival, Holmenkollen • Holmenkollen Hill, Norway

Second Monday in March
Commonwealth Day • Great Britain and Commonwealth countries, including Canada

Mid-March
Cherry Blossom Festival, Macon • Macon, Georgia
Ice Golf Classic, Bering Sea • Nome, Alaska
Storlog • Tibet (one and one-half months after the New Year, Dosmoche Festival)

Two days in mid-March
Kannon Festival • Asakusa Kannon Temple, Japan
Winter Games, Ounasvaara International • Rovaniemi, Finland

Third week in March
Reindeer Driving Competition • Lapp people at Inari, Finland
Sebring 12 Hours (Automobile Hall of Fame Week) • Sebring, Florida
Winter Carnival, Fairbanks • Fairbanks, Alaska

Third weekend in March
Jonquil Festival • Washington, Arkansas

Third Monday in March
Canberra Day • Canberra, Australian Capital Territory, Australia

Four days ending third Saturday in March
Rodeo, National Circuit Finals • Pocatello, Idaho

Late March
Sled Race, Tok Race of Champions Dog • Tok, Alaska

Last Monday in March
Seward's Day (March 30) • Alaska
Transfer Day (March 31) • Virgin Islands

Last Sabbath in March
Wise, Sabbath of • Reform Jews

Spring

March or April
Cocopah Festivities Day • Cocopah Indians at Somerton, Arizona

Early spring
Boat or Baydar, Festival of the • Chukchi people in Siberia, Russia
Dance, Eagle • Tesuque, Jemez, and other New Mexico pueblos
Ice Classic, Nenana • Nenana, Alaska (also late February)

One week in March or early April
(De) Soto Celebration • Bradenton, Florida

One week in early spring
Music, Louisiana State University Festival of Contemporary • Baton Rouge, Louisiana

One week in March or April, usually following Easter
Seville Fair (April Fair) • Seville, Spain

Spring
Archery Festival (Sur-Kharban) • Buryat people in Siberia
Bacchanalia • Rome, Italy
Dionysus • Athens, Greece (and winter)
Harvest Dance (Kyaiya) • Lengua Indians at Gran Chaco, South America (also summer and autumn)
Horns, Festival of (Kil'vey) • Koryak people in Russia
Nile, Festival of the • Luxor, Egypt
Rain-Calling Ceremony (Nyambinyambi) • Kwangali people in Namibia
Strawberry Festival • Pomo Indians at Kule Loklo Miwok Indian Village, California
Sun Festival (Suryapuja) • Hindus in Sylhet, Bangladesh
Theatre Encounters, Lodz • Lodz, Poland

March-April
Boat Race Day • Oxford and Cambridge universities, Putney to Martlake, England
Crane Watch (Wings over the Platte) • Kearney and Grand Island, Nebraska
Dance Festivals, Kathakali • Trivandrum, Kerala, India (and October-November)
Dipri Festival • Abidji people at Gomon, Ivory Coast
Grand National Day • Aintree, Liverpool, England
Mind and Body, Festival of • London, England
Natchez Spring (Fall Pilgrimage) • Natchez, Mississippi
Theatre Encounters, Opole • Opole, Poland

Even-numbered years during March-April
Auckland Festival • Auckland, New Zealand

Five days in spring
Bluegrass Festival, Bean Blossom • Bean Blossom, Indiana

Five days in March-April
Drama Festival, Orissa Academy • Bhubaneswar, Orissa, India

One week in spring
Stickdance • Athapaskan Indians at Kaltag and Nulato, Alaska

Six days in late March-April
Cherry Blossom Festival • Washington, D.C.

First month of spring every second year
Isthmian Games • Corinth, ancient Greece

26 days in March-April
Houses and Gardens, Festival of • Charleston, South Carolina

Every six years in spring
Daedala, Little • ancient Boethia

Four to five weeks in March-April
Bermuda College Weeks • Hamilton, Bermuda

Every sixty years in spring
Daedala, Great • ancient Boethia

Late March-early April
Kite Festival, Smithsonian • the Mall, Washington, D.C.

Spring or summer
Dance, Green Corn • Seminole Indians in Florida

April

March-May
Flower Show, Keukenhof • Lisse, South Holland, Netherlands

April
A-Ma, Feast of • Macao
Anjin Matsuri • Yokosuka, Japan
Black Spirit Festival (Genji Bi Hori) • Songhay people in Niger
Cow Fights (Kuhkämpfe) • Valais, Switzerland

March-August
Holy Ghost, Feast of the (Altura Do Espírito Santo) • Roman Catholics at Ponta Delgada, Sao Miguel Island, Azores, Portugal

April *(cont.)*

Dogwood Festival • Atlanta, Georgia

Drama Memorial, Riznic-Djadja • Ruski Krstur, Vojvodina, Yugoslavia

Folk Dance Festival, Cork International Choral and • Cork, County Cork, Ireland

Little Pony Society Dances • Comanche Indians at Apache Park, Apache, Oklahoma

Monodrama and Pantomime, Festival of • Zemun, Serbia, Yugoslavia

Music Festival, En Gev • En Gev, Israel

New Year (Kalpa Vruksha) • Hindus in rural India

New Year Purification before Planting • Dudulsi, a Gurunsi village in Lela, Volta (just before planting)

Nganja, Feast of • Angola

Offering Ceremony • Parang Kusuma, Jogjakarta District, Java

Offering Ceremony • Pelabuhan Ratu, Java

Popular Festival of Sidi-Ali-El Hattab • Sidi-Ali-El Hattab, Zaghouan Region, Tunisia

Road Building Festival • Igbo people in Mbaise area of Nigeria

San Xavier Pageant and Fiesta • Tohono O'Odham and Yaqui Indians at Tucson, Arizona

Shakespeare Days • Weimar, German Democratic Republic

Shrine Kagura Festival, Ise • Ise, Mie, Japan (and September)

Shrine Rice Festival, Katori • Katori, Chiba, Japan

Theatre Days of Romanians in Vojvodina • Alibunar, Vojvodina, Yugoslavia

Theatre Festival, Belgrade Amateur • Belgrade, Serbia, Yugoslavia

Theatre Groups, Regional Review of Kosovo Amateur • Kosovska Mitrovica, Gnjilane and Pec, Kosovo, Yugoslavia

Theatre Meetings, Rzeszow • Rzeszow, Poland

Theatres, International Meeting of Experimental • Palermo, Sicily, Italy

Tiradentes (Tooth Puller Day or Inconfidência Week) • Brazil

Tyi Wara • Bambara people in Mali (planting season in April, May, sometimes the entire summer)

Even-numbered years in April

Puppet Theatres, Holidays of Amateur • Haskovo, Bulgaria

Theatre, Holidays of Amateur • Sliven, Bulgaria

Every other year in April (Awuru Odo celebration for departure of the dead) and sometime between September and November (arrival of the dead)

Dead, Return of the (Odo Festival) • Igbo people at Nsukka, Nigeria

Alternate years in April

Theatre Weeks, International and English Amateur- • London Borough of Ealing, England

April 1

April Fools' Day

EOKA (Greek National Union of Cypriot Fighters Day) • Cyprus

Medan Anniversary • Medan, North Sumatra, Sumatra, Indonesia

Republic Day, Islamic • Iran

Ujung Pandang Anniversary • Ujung Pandang, South Sulawesi, Sulawesi, Celebes, Indonesia

April 1 and 30

April Fools' Day • Germany and Norway

April 2

Children's Book Day, International

Pascua Florida Day • Florida (Pascua Florida Week is March 27-April 2)

April 3

Kashihara Shinto Festival • Kashihara Shrine, Kashihara, Nara, Japan

April 4

Independence Day • Senegal

Liberation Day • Hungary

Magna Mater • ancient Rome

St. Isidore of Seville, Feast of (San Isidro) • Río Frío, Colombia

Shellfish Gathering (Shiohi-gari) • Japan

April 6

Chakkri Day • Thailand

Founder's Day • South Africa

Founding of the Church of Jesus Christ of the Latter Day Saints • Church of Jesus Christ of the Latter Day Saints and other Mormon churches

Martyrs Day • Syria

April 7

Annunciation, Feast of the • Eastern Orthodox (Julian calendar; March 25, Gregorian calendar)

World Health Day • United Nations-sponsored

April 8

Buddha's Birthday, Enlightenment, and Salvation (Hana Matsuri, Flower Festival) • Buddhists in Japan

April 9

Appomattox Day • Appomattox, Virginia

Bataan Day (Araw ng Kagitingan) • Philippines

Budget Day • Great Britain

Fast and Prayer Day • Liberia

April 10

Salvation Army Founder's Day

April 11
Heroes Day • Costa Rica
Liberation Day • Uganda
St. Stanislaus, Feast of • Christian

April 11-13
Dance Festival, Mayurbhanj Chhau (Chaitra Parva, Spring Festival) • Mayurbhanj, Orissa, India
Purilia Chhau Festival • Bagmundi Village, Purilia District, West Bengal, India

April 11-13 (Chaitra-Parva)
Dance Festival, Chhau Mask • Seraikalla, Bihar, India

April 12
Halifax Day • North Carolina

April 13
Jefferson's Birthday, Thomas • United States
National Day • Chad

April 13-15
New Year (Songkran) • Buddhists in Thailand

April 14
Pan American Day • Central, North, and South America

April 16
Queen Margrethe's Birthday • Copenhagen, Denmark

April 17
Children's Protection Day • Japan
Evacuation Day • Syria
Flag Day • Pago Pago, American Samoa
Verrazano Day • New York

April 18
Independence Day • Zimbabwe (formerly Southern Rhodesia)

April 19
Boston Marathon (Patriot's Day) • Boston, Massachusetts (or nearest Monday)
Primrose Day • England
Republic Day • Sierra Leone

Thursday between April 19 and 25
Summer, First Day of • Iceland

April 19-20
Arts and Crafts Show, Eight Northern Indian Pueblos Spring • DeVargas Mall, Santa Fe, New Mexico

April 21
Kartini Day • Indonesia

Parilia or Palilia (Festival of Pales) • ancient Rome
Queen Elizabeth II, Birthday of (Falkland Islands Day) • Falkland Islands
San Jacinto Day • San Antonio and San Jacinto, Texas

Ten days in April, including April 21
San Antonio, Fiesta • San Antonio, Texas

April 21-May 2
Bahá'u'lláh, Declaration of (Feast of Ridvan) • Bahá'í

April 22
Arbor Day • Nebraska
Earth Day
Oklahoma Day • Guthrie, Lexington, Midwest City, and Norman, Oklahoma
Queen Isabella Day • Spain and parts of the United States

April 22-23
St. George's Day • Alicante, Spain

April 22-24, held over St. George's Day
Battle of the Moors and Christians • Alcoy and Petrel, Alicante, Spain

April 23
Children's Day • Turkey
St. George's Day • Christian (in Russia, also November 26)
Shakespeare's Birthday • Stratford-upon-Avon, Warwickshire, England
Shakespeare's Birthday • Philadelphia, Pennsylvania

On or near April 23
Peppercorn Day • Bermuda
Spring, Feast of • Latvia

April 24
Children's Day • Iceland
Green George Festival • Romanian and Transylvanian Romanies and Slavs
Martyrs' Day • Armenians
Smith, Birthday of Joseph • Mormon

April 24-25
St. Mark, Feast of (Toro de San Marcos, Bull of St. Mark) • Spain

April 25
Anzac Day • Australia, New Zealand, and Western Samoa
Flag Day, National • Swaziland
Liberation Day • Italy
Liberty Day • Portugal
River Kwai Bridge commemorative service • Kanchanaburi War Cemetery, Kanchanaburi, Thailand
Robigalia • Rome

April 25 *(cont.)*
St. Mark, Feast of • Christian
St. Mark's Day (Szent Márk Napja and Buza-Szentelo, Blessing of Wheat) • Calvinists in Hungary

Ten days beginning April 25
St. Mark, Fair of (Feria de San Marcos) • Aguascalientes, Mexico

On or near April 25
Tenchi Kane no Kami, Festival of • Konko-kyo religion, Japan

April 26
Audubon Day • United States
Confederate Memorial Day • Florida and Georgia
Union Day • Tanzania

April 27
Independence Day • Sierra Leone
Independence Day • Togo
Republic Day, Second • Austria
Revolution Day, Saur • Afghanistan

April 28
Admission Day • Maryland

April 28-May 3
Floralia • ancient Rome

April 29
Hirohito's Birthday (Tencho Setsu) • Japan

April 30
Admission Day • Louisiana
April Fools' Day • Germany and Norway (also April 1)
Beltane
May Day Eve
Queen Juliana's Birthday • Amsterdam and The Hague, Netherlands
St. James the Greater's Day • Eastern Orthodox
Walpurgis Night (Feast of Valborg) • northern Europeans and United States
Zarthastno Diso • Fasli sect of Parsis

April 30-May 1
May Day Eve

One day in April
Demon-God Festival • Rakuhoji Temple, Yamatomura, Ibaraki, Japan

A weekend in April
Music Festival, Carcoar Folk and Traditional Bush • Carcoar, New South Wales, Australia

Three days in April
Vermont Maple Festival • St. Albans, Vermont

Three to five days in April
Dance, Ute Bear (Ma'makoni-ni'tkap) • Ute Indians at Ouray, Randlett, Whiterocks, Utah

Four-day observance in April
Yasukini Matsuri • Yasukini Shrine, Tokyo, Japan (also in summer, autumn, and winter)

One week in April
Cherry Blossom Festival • Japantown, San Francisco, California

One week in April during even-numbered years
Arts, Orange Festival of the • Orange, New South Wales, Australia

Ten days in April
Milan Trade Fair • Milan, Lombardy, Italy
Plays from Iranian Provinces • Tehran, Iran

17 days in April
Arts Festival, Dogwood • Knoxville, Tennessee

Beginning of April
Cerealia • ancient Rome

Early April
Cherry Blossom Festival, Chinhae • Chinhae, Japan
Geranium Day • England
Thirteenth Day Out (Sizdar-Bedah) • Iran (13th day after Noruz; on or near March 21)

First full week in April
Master's Golf Tournament • Augusta National Golf Club, Georgia

First weekend in April
Spring Pageant • Resita, Caras-Severin, Romania

First Thursday in April
Glarus Festival • Switzerland

First Friday in April
Student Government Day • Massachusetts

Second or third weekend in April
Whistlers Convention, National • Louisburg, North Carolina

Mid-April
Art Fair, Native American • Suquamish Indians at Suquamish, Washington

Mid-April *(cont.)*

New Year • Kampuchea and Khmer Republic (now Cambodia), Laos (Boun Pimay), Hindus in Cambodia and Malaya (when Sun is in Aries)

New Year (Thingyan; Pwe) • Burma (when Sun is in Aries; first-fourth days of month of Tagu)

Root Festival • Shahaptian and Chinookan Indians at Warm Springs, Oregon

One day in mid-April

Spring Festival • Ube Shrine, Iwami, Tottori, Japan

Two days in mid-April

Nagahama Yamakyogen • Hachiman Shrine, Nagahama, Shiga, Japan

Shrine Festival, Itsukushima • Itsukushima Island, Hiroshima, Japan

Second half of April

Theatre Games, Yugoslav (Yugoslav Theatre Festival) • Novi Sad, Vojvodina, Yugoslavia

Second and third weeks in April

Music, Venice International Festival of Contemporary • Venice, Veneto, Italy

Third weekend in April

Folk Festival, Arkansas • Mountain View, Arkansas

Folk Festival, New England • Natick, Massachusetts

Kewpiesta • Branson, Missouri

Third Sunday in April

Pastoral Album • Rasinari, Sibiu, Romania

Third Sunday and Monday in April

Six O'Clock Ringing Festival (Sechselauten) • Zurich, Switzerland

Third Monday in April

Patriots' Day (April 19) • Connecticut, Maine, and Massachusetts

Last two weekends in April

Romantic Festival • Clowes Memorial Hall, Butler University, Indianapolis, Indiana

Fourth Monday in April

Confederate Memorial Day • Mississippi

Fast Day • New Hampshire

Late April

Gula, Feast of • Babylonia

Kite-Flying Contest (Nagasaki Takoage) • Nagasaki, Japan

Patron Crosses, Fiesta of the • Roman Catholic Mayan people at Quintana Roo, Mexico

Four days in late April

Coffee Fair and Flower Festival • Boquete, Panama

Six days in late April

Arts, Festival of the • Oklahoma City, Oklahoma

One week in late April

Rose Festival • Thomasville, Georgia

Last full week in April

Secretaries' Week (Wednesday is Secretaries' Day) • United States

Usually last full week in April

Fish Fry, World's Biggest • Paris, Tennessee

Two days during last week in April

Music Festival, Spring • Potsdam, New York

One week beginning Sunday before the last weekend in April

Pennsylvania Relay Carnival, University of • University of Pennsylvania, Philadelphia, Pennsylvania

Last weekend in April

Landing of d'Iberville • Ocean Springs, Mississippi

Nations, Festival of • St. Paul, Minnesota

Last Sunday in April

Landsgemeinden • Appenzell, Switzerland

Pilgrimage of the Virgen de la Pena (Romeria of the Virgen de la Pena) • Puebla de Guaman, Huelva, Spain

Last Sunday in April during even-numbered years

Sunrise Festival • Timisoara, Timis, Romania

Last Monday in April

Confederate Memorial Day • Alabama

Last Friday in April

Arbor Day • United States

Last Saturday in April

Eisteddfod, Cynonfardd • Welsh-Americans in Pennsylvania

Kite Festival, Maryland • Baltimore, Maryland

Maryland Hunt Club • Glyndon, Maryland

End of April

Mibu Dainembutsu Kyogen • Buddhists at Mibu Temple, Kyoto, Japan

Pilgrimage of Our Lady of the Cabeza (Romeria of the Virgen de la Cabeza) • Andujar, Jaen, Andalusia, Spain

April or May

Apple Blossom Festival, Washington State • Wenatchee, Washington

April or May *(cont.)*
  Bobo Masquerade • Burkina Faso (before the first rain)
  Moro-Moro Play • San Dionisio, Rizal, Luzon Island,
    Philippines
  Puppets, International Festival of • Barcelona, Spain

Every five years in April or May
  Flower Festival (Ghent Floralies) • Ghent, Belgium

One day in late April or early May
  Shark Angling Competition, International • waters off
    City Wharf, Gibraltar

One and one-half days in late April or early May
  New Year • Mandigo people in Sierra Leone

Two days in late April or early May
  Pan American Festival Week • Lakewood, California

Three days in late April or early May
  Music Festival, Cornell College Spring • Mount Vernon, Iowa

Four days in late April or early May
  Ann Arbor May Festival • Ann Arbor, Michigan

Two weeks in April or May
  Cherry Blossom Festival • Japan

Late April or May
  Alps, Procession to the (Alpaufzug) • Switzerland

April-May
  Arts Festival, Maidment • Auckland, New Zealand
  Bach Festival, English • Oxford and London, England
  Brighton Festival • Brighton, Sussex, England
  Brussels International Fair • Brussels, Belgium
  Buddhist Priesthood, Admission to the (Buart Nark) •
    Buddhists in Thailand
  Deer-Hunting Festival (Aboakyer) • Effutu people in Ghana
  Drama Festival, All-Ireland Amateur • Athlone, County
    Westmeath, Ireland
  Lai Haroba Festival • Mairang Village, Manipur, India
  Ploughing Ceremony • Brahman people in Thailand
  Rand Show • Milner Park, Johannesburg, South Africa
  Schwetzingen Festival • Schwetzingen, Baden-Wurttemberg,
    Federal Republic of Germany
  Theatre, International Festival of Free • Munich, Bavaria,
    Federal Republic of Germany
  Theatre Review, International • Florence, Tuscany, Italy
  Theatres, Encounter of Slovak Amateur Children's • Backi
    Petrovac, Vojvodina, Yugoslavia
  Young May • Zajecar, Serbia, Yugoslavia

Sunday evenings in April and May
  Music Festival, American • Washington, D.C.

One week from late April to early May
  Toonik Time • Inuit people at Frobisher Bay, Northwest
    Territories, Canada

Ten days in mid-April to early May
  Jazz and Heritage Festival, New Orleans • New Orleans,
    Louisiana

Two weeks in April-May
  Arts, Birmingham Festival of the • Birmingham,
    Alabama

Two weeks in April-May during odd-numbered years
  Theatre, World Festival of • Nancy, Meurthe-et-Moselle,
    France

Two to three weeks in April-May
  Spring Festival, Guelph • Guelph, Ontario, Canada

18 days in April-May
  Osaka International Festival • Osaka, Japan

Three weeks in April-May
  Cervantes Festival, International • Guanajuato, Mexico
    (sometimes October-November)

**Month-long in April-May, including May 12, Jerusalem
Reunification Day**
  Spring in Jerusalem Festival • Jerusalem, Israel

Five or six weeks in April-May
  Wrekin and Telford Festival • Telford, Shropshire,
    England

Six weeks in April-May
  Arts Festival, Braintree District • Braintree, Essex,
    England

April-early May
  Sealing the Frost • Cuchumatan Indians at Santa Eulalia,
    Guatemala

Last week in April and first week in May
  Tulip Festival • Hillegom, Lisse, and Sassenheim, South
    Holland, Netherlands

Last weekend in April through first weekend in May
  Buccaneer Days • Corpus Christi, Texas

April-June
  Pantomime-Music-Dance-Theatre • West Berlin, Federal
    Republic of Germany

Early April-late July
  Olympic Games (summer games) • location varies

Every Thursday from April-September

Korcula, Festival of (Moreska) • Korcula, Croatia, Yugoslavia (and July 27, Croatia's Insurrection Day)

April-October

Flanders, Festival of (Festival van Vlaanderen) • Antwerp, Bruges, Brussels, Ghent, Kortrijk, Leuven, Limburg, and Mechelen, Belgium

Pitlochry Festival • Pitlochry, Perthshire, Scotland

Every ten years from April to October

Floriade • Amsterdam, Netherlands

April-December

Shakespeare Company Festival, Royal • Stratford-upon-Avon, Warwickshire, England

May

May

Adelaide Cup Day • South Australia

Ballet Festival, National • Manila, Quezon, Luzon Island, Philippines

Ballet Festival Week • Munich, Bavaria, Federal Republic of Germany (or March)

Blessing of the Fields with Corn or Flag Dance • Tesuque Pueblo, New Mexico (date varies)

Ceres, Festival • Pont du Fahs, Zaghouan Region, Tunisia

Cup Final Day • Great Britain

Dances and Songs of Crnorecje • Boljevac, Serbia, Yugoslavia

Drama Amateurs of Croatia, Festival of • Murter by Sibenik, Croatia, Yugoslavia

Drama Festival, Okanagan Zone • Vernon, British Columbia, Canada

Ephesus, Festival of • Selcuk, Turkey

Film Festival, Cannes • Cannes, France

Folk Dance and Music Festival, Silifke • Silifke, Turkey

Folklore in Vojvodina, Slovakian • Kovacica, Vojvodina, Yugoslavia

Games of May • Becej, Vojvodina, Yugoslavia

Heritage Month • Rhode Island

Homolje Motifs • Kucevo, Serbia, Yugoslavia

Horse Fair • Jerez de la Frontera, Cádiz, Spain

Indian Celebration, Tygh Valley • north of Warm Springs, Oregon

Mad Sunday • Isle of Man (Sunday preceding the Tourist Trophy Motorcycle Races)

Merton Festival • London Borough of Merton, England

Mesir Festival • Mansia, Turkey

Minehead Hobby Horse Parade • Minehead, England

Music and Folklore of Romanians Living in Vojvodina • location varies within Vojvodina, Yugoslavia

Music Competition, Queen Elisabeth International (Concours Musical International Reine Elisabeth) • Brussels, Belgium

Opera Festival, Spring • Houston, Texas

Pamukkale, Festival of • Denizli, Turkey

Patios Festival • Cordoba, Spain

Pergamum, Festival of • Bergama, Turkey

Plays, Festival of Contemporary Polish • Wroclaw, Poland

Powwow, Wyoming Indian High School • Arapaho Indians at Ethete, Wyoming

Powwow, Yellow Calf Memorial • Arapaho Indians at Ethete, Wyoming

Puppet Theatres, Skupa Festival of Professional • Plzen, West Bohemia, Czechoslovakia

Puppet Theatres of Bosnia and Herzegovina, Meeting of • location varies within Bosnia and Herzegovina, Yugoslavia

St. Isidore, Festival of • Acapantzingo, Morelos, Mexico

Schiller Days • Mannheim, Baden-Wurttemberg, Federal Republic of Germany

Showcase of Rivadavia • Rivadavia, Orense, Spain

Shrine Festival, Chusonji • Chusonji, Iwate, Japan

Song Festival (Skamba Kankliai) • Vilnius, Lithuania

Sultan's Coronation • Surakarta, Central Java, Java

Thargelia • ancient Greece

Theatre Festival, Ontario • locations vary within Ontario, Canada

Theatre Meetings, Kalisz • Kalisz, Poland

Theatre Rally • West Berlin, Federal Republic of Germany

Theatres for Children and Youth, Encounter of Professional • Zagreb, Croatia, Yugoslavia

Theatres of Vojvodina, Encounter of • Novi Sad, Vojvodina, Yugoslavia

Theatres of Vojvodina, Encounter of Amateur • Kikinda, Vojvodina, Yugoslavia

Theatre Spring, Silesian • Katowice, Poland

Tyi Wara • Bambara people in Mali (also April; sometimes the entire planting season)

World Cup (soccer; four weeks of playoffs could also be held in June or July)

Youth Culture Week • Ljubljana, Slovenia, Yugoslavia

Month of May

Flores de Mayo • San Vicente, El Salvador

Flores de Mayo • Philippines

Indianapolis 500 • Indianapolis, Indiana (ending with race on Memorial Day, last Monday in May)

Mary, Month of (Mois de Marie) • France

May Festival, Wiesbaden International (Internationale Maifestspiele) • Wiesbaden, Hesse, Federal Republic of Germany

May International Festival, Memphis in • Memphis, Tennessee

Even-numbered years in May

Ballet Biennial, International • Lodz, Poland

Theatre Festival, International Arena • Munster, North Rhine-Westphalia, Federal Republic of Germany

Odd-numbered years in May
Duisburg Trends • Duisburg, North Rhine-Westphalia, Federal Republic of Germany

Every three years in May
Panas Pela (Cuci Baileo Ceremony) • Pelau versi Ulilima, Maluku, Moluccas, Indonesia

May 1
Anthesteria (Day of Flowers) • Greece
Bona Dea (Great Mother Festival) • ancient Rome
Dipping Day • Cornwall, England
Game of St. Evermaire (Spel van Sint Evermarus) • Rutten, Limburg, Belgium
Labor Day, International
Law Day • American Bar Association in the United States
Lei Day • Hawaii
Loyalty Day • Cooch's Bridge, Delaware; U.S. Veterans of Foreign Wars in New York City
May Day
St. Joseph's Day • Chamorros people in Guam/Northern Marianas
St. Joseph the Worker, Feast of • Malta
St. Philip, Feast of and Green Corn Dance • San Felipe Pueblo, New Mexico
St. Tammany's Day • United States
Sts. Philip and James, Feast of • Anglican and Episcopalian
Senior Citizens Day • Massachusetts and other United States
Spring, Bringing of the (Kevad Püha) • Estonia

Thursday through Saturday nearest May 1
Apple Blossom Festival, Shenandoah • Winchester, Virginia

May 1 through mid-September
Tivoli Concerts (Tivolis Koncertsal) • Copenhagen, Denmark

On or near May 1
Whistle Making (Fluitjes Maken) • Ootmarsum, Overijssel, Netherlands

May 1-2
First of May Is Our Day • Belgrade, Serbia, Yugoslavia

May 1-4
St. Efisio, Festival of • Cagliari, Sardinia, Italy

May 1-5 kite-flying contest
Children's Day (Kodomo-no-hi; formerly Boys' Festival, Tango No Sekku) • Hamamatsu, Japan

First Monday after May 2
Holy Blood, Procession of the (Processie van het Heilig Bloed) • Roman Catholics in Bruges, West Flanders, Belgium

May 2-3
Exaltation of the Cross • Dominican Republic
Exaltation of the Cross (La Adoracion de la Cruz) • Paraguay

May 2-June 27
Filipina, Fiesta • Hawaii

May 3
Constitution Day • Japan
Constitution Day (Swieto Trzeciego Majo) • Poland
Exaltation of the Cross • Christian
Labour Day • Queensland, Australia
Our Lady of Czestochowa, Feast of • Polish National Shrine of Czestochowa, Poland
Sts. Philip and James, Feast of • Roman Catholic
Santa Cruz Days (Coming of the Rivermen) • Cochiti and Taos pueblos, New Mexico

May 3, alternate years
Exaltation of the Cross (Cruz Velakuy) • Pacarigtambo, Peru

May 3-4
Hakata Dontaku • Fukuoka City, Japan
Kent State Memorial Day • Kent State University, Ohio

May 3-5
Kite Battles of Hamamatsu • Hamamatsu, Shizuoka, Japan

May 4
Independence Day • Anthony, Newport, and Providence, Rhode Island

May 5
Children's Day (Kodomo-no-hi; formerly Boys' Festival, Tango No Sekku) • Japan
Children's Day (Kodomo-no-hi, also known as Festival of Flags or Banners; formerly Boys' Festival, Tango No Sekku) • Japanese-Americans
Children's Day • Korea
Children's Day (Urini Nal) • Republic of Korea
Cinco de Mayo
Coronation Day (Chulalongkorn's Day) • Thailand
Liberation Day • Denmark
Liberation Day • Netherlands
Napoleon's Day • the Invalides in Paris, France

May 6
St. George's Day • Eastern Orthodox (Julian calendar; April 23, Gregorian calendar)
St. John, Apostle and Evangelist, Feast of • Roman Catholics in Rome

May 7
Tagore, Birthday of Rabindranath • Calcutta, India

May 7-8

St. Nicholas's Day • Bari, Apulia, Italy

May 8

Furry Day • Roman Catholics in Helston, Cornwall, England

Liberation Day • German Democratic Republic

St. John, Apostle and Evangelist, Feast of • Eastern Orthodox

Stork Day • Ribe, Denmark

Truman's Birthday, Harry S. • Missouri

V-E Day

May 9

Blavatsky, Death of Helena • Theosophical Society

Brown Day, John • civil rights groups

Earls Court Day • Iowa, Kansas, Minnesota, Virginia, and Wyoming

Liberation Day • Czechoslovakia

Liberation Day • Jersey, Channel Islands, Great Britain

St. Joan of Arc, Feast of • New Orleans, Louisiana

Victory Day • USSR

May 9, 11, and 15

Lemuralia or Lemuria, Festival of the Dead • ancient Rome

May 10

Confederate Memorial Day • North and South Carolina

Golden Spike Day • Golden Spike Historical Monument at Corrine, Utah

Begins May 10

Bird Week • Japan

May 10-17

St. Isidore the Husbandman or Farmer, Feast of • Madrid, Spain

May 11

Admission Day • Minnesota

Constitution Day • Laos

Holy Day of Letters • Bulgaria and Yugoslavia (Julian calendar; May 24, Gregorian calendar)

Our Lady of Aparecida, Festival of • Aparecida, Brazil

May 11-14

Frost, or Ice, Saints Day (Eisheiligan) • Roman Catholics in France and Germany

Week including May 12

Hospital Day and Week, National • hospitals and hospital associations in the United States

First or second week of May; usually includes Nurses' Day, May 12

Nurses' Week

May 12 or 13

Garland Day • Abbotsbury, Dorsetshire, England

May 12-14

Frost, or Ice, Saints Day • Roman Catholic German-Russians in Ellis County, Kansas

May 12-June 4

Spring Festival, Prague • Prague, Czechoslovakia

May 13

Dance, Corn • Cochiti Pueblo, New Mexico

Kuan Ti, Festival of • China

Sunday nearest May 13

Jamestown Day (May 13) • Christians in the United States

May 13-16

Calaveras County Fair and Frog Jumping Jubilee • Calaveras Fairgrounds, Angels Camp, California

May 14

Constitution Day • Philippines

St. Matthias, Feast of • Roman Catholic

May 14 or 15

Water Buffalo Festival (Carabao) • Angono, Lucban, Pulilan, San Isidro, and Sariaya, Quezon, Luzon Island, Philippines

May 14-15

Independence and Flag Day • Paraguay

May 15

Austrian State Treaty Day

Hollyhock Festival (Aoi Matsuri) • Kyoto, Japan

Police Memorial Day • United States

Quarter Days • Scotland (also August 1, November 11, and February 2)

St. Dymphna's Day • Geel, Antwerp, Belgium

St. Isidore the Husbandman or Farmer, Feast of • Roman Catholic Carolinians in Saipan, Marianas, Philippines

St. Sofia's Day • Czechoslovakia

Four days beginning Wednesday nearest May 15

Tulip Time • Holland, Michigan

Sunday following May 15

St. Gens, Festival of (La Fête de St. Gens) • Monteux, Provence, France (also first weekend in September at Beaucet)

May 16

St. Brendan's Day • Ireland

May 16-17
Black Ship Day • Yokosuka, Shimoda, and other port cities in Japan

May 17
Battle of Las Piedras Day • Uruguay
Columbus Day (Discovery Day) • Cayman Islands
Constitution Day • Nauru
Constitution Day, Norway • Seattle, Washington; Brooklyn, New York
Constitution Day, Norway (Syttende Mai Fest) • Spring Grove, Minnesota
Summer, First Day of (Mut l-ard, the Death of the Ground) • Morocco

Weekend nearest May 17
Constitution Day, Norway (Syttende Mai Fest) • Stoughton, Wisconsin

May 17-18
Spring Festival of the Toshogu Shrine, Great (Toshogu Haru-No-Taisai) • Nikko, Tochigi, Japan

May 18
St. Eric's Day • Sweden and Swedish-Americans

May 19
Flag Day of the Army • Finland
St. Dunstan's Day • Christian
St. Ivo, Pardon of • pilgrimage in France
Youth and Sports Day • Turkey

May 20
Botev Day • Bulgaria
Constitution Day • Cameroon
Independence Day • Cuba
Mecklenburg Day • North Carolina

May 21
Battle of Iquique or Navy Day • Chile
Lilies and Roses Day • Tower of London, London, England

May 21-23
Anastenaria • Agia Serres and Langada, Greece

May 22
Heroes Day • Sri Lanka
National Maritime Day and Merchant Marine Week • United States
Sovereignty and Thanksgiving Day • Haiti

May 23
Abdu'l-Bahá , Birth of • Bahá'í
Admission Day • South Carolina

Báb, Declaration of the • Bahá'í
Labour Day • Jamaica

May 24
Dollard des Ormeaux, Fête de • Quebec, Canada
Holy Day of Letters • Bulgaria and Yugoslavia (Gregorian calendar; May 11, Julian calendar)

Sunday nearest May 24
Aldersgate Experience • Methodist

Monday nearest May 24
Bonfire Night • Scotland
Victoria Day (Empire Day) • England and British Commonwealth countries

May 24-25
Holy Maries, Feast of (La Fête des Saintes Maries) • Romanies and others' pilgrimage to Les Saintes-Maries-de-la-Mer, Provence, France

May 25
Africa Day • Chad, Liberia, Mali, Mauritania, Zambia, and Zimbabwe
Flitting Day • Scotland
Independence Day • Argentina (and July 9)
Independence Day • Jordan
National Day • Argentina
Organization of African Unity (OAU) Day • Equatorial Guinea
Revolution Day • Sudan
St. Bede the Venerable, Feast of • Roman Catholic
St. Urban's Day • Germany
Youth Day (Marshall Tito's Birthday) • Yugoslavia

May 26
Independence Day • Guyana
St. Augustine of Canterbury, Feast of • Anglican and Episcopalian

May 27
Children's Day • Nigeria
Independence Day (Jeshn) • Afghanistan (observed in late August)
St. Augustine of Canterbury, Feast of • Roman Catholic

May 28
St. Bernard of Montjoux • French Alps

May 29
Admission Day • Rhode Island
Admission Day • Wisconsin
Bahá'u'lláh, Ascension of • Bahá'í
Shick-Shack Day • northern England
Zarthastno Diso • Kadmi sect of Parsis

May 30-31
Harvest Festival, Padi • Kadazan or Dusun people at Sabah,
Malaysia

May 31
Memorial Day (Day of the Dead) • Romania
Republic Day (Union Day) • Capetown, Pretoria, and
Bloemfontein, South Africa
St. Joan of Arc, Feast of • Christian
Visitation of the Blessed Virgin Mary, Feast of the •
Protestant and Roman Catholic

Three days in May
Primavera, Fiesta de la • San Diego, California

Four days in May
Mountain Laurel Festival, Kentucky • Pineville, Kentucky
Theatre of Hvar, Days of the • Hvar, Croatia, Yugoslavia

Four to five days in May
Bun Festival • Chinese Taoists at Cheung Chau Island, Hong
Kong

Five days in May
Mayfest, International • Tulsa, Oklahoma

Six days in May
Banderesi, Festival of the • Bucchianico, Abruzzi, Italy
Vesna Festival • Ukrainian-Canadians at Saskatoon,
Saskatchewan, Canada

One week in May
Bhagavatha Mela Festival • Melattur, Tamil Nadu, India
Holy Spirit, Festival of the Divine • Diamantina and other
cities in Brazil
Plays '78, '79, etc. • Mulheim, North Rhine-Westphalia,
Federal Republic of Germany

Nine days in May
Arts Festival • Atlanta, Georgia
Exaltation of the Cross (Santacruzan Festival) • Christians
in the Philippines
Horse Show and Country Fair, Devon • Devon, Pennsylvania
Moscow Stars Festival • Moscow, Russia, USSR

Ten days in May
Folklore, Festival of • grounds of Ksar El Badi Palace,
Marrakech, Morocco

Two weeks in May
Bachok Festival of Culture • Bachok, Kelantan,
Malaysia

Two weekends in May
Bach Music Festival • Bethlehem, Pennsylvania

Early May
Anthestiria Flower Festival • Paphos, Cyprus
Clown Festival, Emmett Kelly • Houston, Missouri
Tinjaua • Maramures, Romania

Three days in early May
Mille Miglia • race through Italy

Nine days in early May
Music Festival, Golden Isles Chamber • Sea Islands, Georgia

First days of May
Maytime Fairies • Ireland

First two weeks in May
Music Festival, Seoul International • Seoul, Korea

First two weeks in May during odd-numbered years
Performing Arts for Young People, Come Out-Festival of •
Adelaide, South Australia, Australia

16 days beginning first week in May
Musical, Bordeaux International May (Mai Musical
International) • Bordeaux, Gironde, France

First weekend in May
Crawfish Festival • Breaux Bridge, Louisiana
Mushroom Festival • Richmond, Missouri
Music and Drama, Llantilio Crossenny Festival of •
Llantilio Crossenny, Wales

First full weekend in May
Irrigation Festival • Sequim, Washington

First Sunday in May
Acacia Day • Hanu-Conachi forest, Fundeni, Galati,
Romania
Encounter with History • Costesti, Orastioara de Sus
Commune, Hunedoara, Romania
Humane Sunday • American Humane Society-sponsored;
United States
Ramp Festival, Cosby • Kineauvista Hill near Cosby,
Tennessee
Shrine Rite, Royal (Chongmyo Taeje) • Confucians in Seoul,
Korea
Sunday School Day (Faka Me) • Methodists in Tonga
Winston 500 • Talladega Speedway, Alabama

Begins first Sunday in May
Family Week, National • Jewish, Protestant, and Roman
Catholic people in the United States

First Monday in May
Bank Holiday • England, Ireland, Scotland, and Wales
Labour Day • England, Northern Ireland, Scotland, and Wales

First Monday in May *(cont.)*
Labour Day (May 3) • Zambia (formerly Northern Rhodesia)
May Day • Great Britain and Northern Ireland

First Tuesday in May
Fool's Fair (Ffair Ffyliaid) • Llanerfyl, Wales

First Friday in May
McDonogh Day • New Orleans, Louisiana

15-day festival precedes race, which occurs on the first Saturday in May
Kentucky Derby Day • Churchill Downs, Louisville, Kentucky

Second week in May
Theatre Festivals, Children's Little • Calcutta, West Bengal, India (also three weeks in December)

Second weekend in May
Shrines Festival, Three (Sanja Matsuri) • Asakusa Kannon Temple, Tokyo, Japan

Second Sunday in May
Mother's Day • United States
Peony Day • Baneasa, Galati, Romania
St. Joan of Arc, Feast of (Fête de Jeanne d'Arc) • Rouen and Orleans, France
Weighing Festival • Magura Priei, Commune of Cizer, Salaj, Romania

Second Sunday in May every three years
Cat Festival • Ypres, Belgium

Week of second Monday in May
Feis Ceoil • Dublin, County Dublin, Ireland

Second Thursday, Friday and Saturday in May
Tulip Time • Dutch-Americans at Pella, Iowa

Second Saturday in May
Preakness Stakes • Baltimore, Maryland (nine-day event)
Windmill Day • Netherlands

Mid-May
Amateur Stages, Belgrade Review of Experimental • Belgrade, Serbia, Yugoslavia
Bar-B-Q Festival, International • Owensboro, Kentucky
Komatsu Otabi Festival • Uhashi and Hiyoshi shrines, Komatsu, Ishikawa, Japan
Portsmouth Festival • Portsmouth, Hampshire, England
St. Isidore, Festival of • Metepec, Mexico
St. Isidore, Festival of • Matamoros, Tamaulipas, Mexico
Takigi Noh • Kofukuji Temple, Nara, Japan

Two days in mid-May
Bach Festival, Baldwin-Wallace • Berea, Ohio
Shrine Festival, Kanda Myojin • Tokyo, Japan

Three days in mid-May
Dances of Obando • Obando, Bulacan, Luzon Island, Philippines

One week in mid-May
Theatre Rally, North Germany • location varies within Federal Republic of Germany

Nine days in mid-May
Spring, Festival of • Ottawa, Ontario, Canada

Friday and Saturday evenings for two weeks in mid-May
Cincinnati May Festival • Cincinnati, Ohio

Anytime from middle to late May
Vlaggetjesdag • Ijmuiden, Katwijk, Scheveningen, and Vlaardingen, Netherlands

Second half of May
Spring, Kiev • Kiev, Ukraine, USSR

Third week in May
Maytime Festival, International • Dundalk, County Louth, Ireland

Third weekend in May
Dulcimer Days • Coshocton, Ohio
International Festival • Toledo, Ohio
Mayfest (Maifest) • German-Americans at Hermann, Missouri
Powwow and Root Feast, Mat-Al-YM'A • Nez Perce Indians at Kamiah, Idaho
Swedish Festival, Kingsburg • Swedish-Americans at Kingsburg, California
Tea Party Festival, Chestertown • Chestertown, Maryland

Third Sunday in May
Malcolm X Day • Washington, D.C.
Spring, Harghita • Miercurea Ciuc, Baile Jigodin Commune, Harghita, Romania

Third Saturday in May
Armed Forces Day • United States military installations and in New York, New York
Paris Marathon • Paris, France

Fourth Saturday in May
Spring Festival, Upper Mattaponi • Upper Mattaponi Indians near Walkerton, Virginia

Late May

Humor and Satire Festival, National • Gabrovo, Bulgaria

Indian Heritage Days Celebration, Oklahoma • Miami and
Peoria Indians in Oklahoma

Italian Festival • Italian-Americans at McAlester, Oklahoma

Mayoring Day • Great Britain

Tribal Day Celebration • Chehalis Salishan Indians at
Oakville, Washington

Two days in late May

Shrine Festival, Yushima • Tokyo, Japan

Two to three days in late May

Folk Festival, Florida • White Springs, Florida

Three days in late May

Ojai Festival • Ojai, California

A Thursday through Sunday in late May

Jazz Festival, Barbados/Caribbean • Barbados

Ten days in late May

Literature, Hay-on-Wye Festival of • Hay-on-Wye, Wales

**Last weekend in May (Memorial Day weekend in the United
States)**

Butler Days, Jim • Tonopah, Nevada

Coca Cola 600 • Charlotte Motor Speedway, Charlotte,
North Carolina

Dance, Ute Bear • Ute Indians at Ignacio, Colorado

Highland Festival and Games • Scottish-Americans at
Alma, Michigan

Malki Museum Fiesta • Cahuilla Indians in California

Mule Days • Bishop, California

Poetry Gathering, Dakota Cowboy • Medora, North Dakota

Powwow, Schonchin Days • Klamath Indians at Klamath
Falls, Oregon

Regatta, General Clinton Canoe • Cooperstown to
Bainbridge, New York

Street Painting Festival, I Madonnari Italian • Santa
Barbara, California

Vandalia Gathering • Charleston, West Virginia

Three days over last weekend in May

Fiddler's and Bluegrass Festival, Old Time • Union Grove,
North Carolina

Four days over last weekend in May

Folklife Festival, Northwest • Seattle, Washington

Jazz Jubilee, Sacramento Dixieland • Sacramento, California

Last two weeks in May

Arts, Perth Festival of the • Perth, Perthshire, Scotland

Ballet and Music Festival, Copenhagen Royal Danish •
Copenhagen, Denmark

Last week in May

Annapolis Valley Blossom Festival • Nova Scotia, Canada

Last full week in May

Flower Show, Chelsea • London, England

Rodgers Festival, Jimmie • Meridian, Mississippi

15 days beginning last week in May

Bergen International Festival (Festspillene i Bergen) •
Bergen, Norway

Last Sunday in May or on Ascension Day

Sardinian Cavalcade (Cavalcata Sarda) • Sassari,
Sardinia, Italy

Last Monday in May

Confederate Memorial Day • Virginia

Memorial Day (May 30) • United States

May or June

Bath Festival • Bath, Avon, England

Five days in late May or early June

Apple Blossom Festival • Annapolis Valley Region, Nova
Scotia, Canada

One week in May or June

Ille Festival • Betton, Ille-et-Vilaine, France

Puppet Theatre of the Nations, International Festival Week •
Bochum, North Rhine-Westphalia, Federal Republic of
Germany

Two to four weeks in May or June

Nicosia Festival • Nicosia, Cyprus

Usually second weekend in May or sometime in June

Gum Tree Festival • Tupelo, Mississippi

Late May or early June

Derby Day • Epsom Racecourse, Surrey, England

Juvenalia • Kraków, Poland

Powwow, Lenape Delaware • Lenape Delaware Indians near
Copan, Oklahoma

May-June

Cotton Carnival and Musicfest • Memphis, Tennessee

Dance Festival, Alberta • Edmonton, Alberta, Canada

Fleadh Nua • Ennis, County Clare, Ireland

Folk Arts Festival • St. Catharines, Ontario, Canada

French Open Tennis Championships • Auteil, France

Hollybush Festival • Glassboro, New Jersey

Malvern Festival • Malvern, Worcestershire, England

Marmaris Festival • Marmaris, Turkey

Music Festival of Saint-Denis • Saint-Denis, Seine,
France

May-June *(cont.)*
Nebraska Danish Days (Danish Ethnic Festival) • Danish-Americans at Minden, Nebraska
Opera and Ballet, Annual Festival of Chamber • Osijek, Croatia, Yugoslavia
Pike Festival • along Route 40 through Pennsylvania, Maryland, West Virginia, and Ohio
Plays Festival, Gandersheim Cathedral • Bad Gandersheim, Lower Saxony, Federal Republic of Germany
Ruhr Festival • Recklinghausen, North Rhine-Westphalia, Federal Republic of Germany
Stirling District Festival • Stirling, Stirlingshire, Scotland
Theatre Groups of Slovenia, Encounter of • location varies within Slovenia, Yugoslavia
Theatre of Silence, Carte Blanche at the (Carte Blanche au Theatre du Silence) • La Rochelle, Charente-Maritime, France
Theatres, Regional Festival of Serbian Amateur • Smederevska Palanka, Serbia, Yugoslavia
Theatres of Serbia, Vujic Encounter of Professional • Serbia, Yugoslavia (location varies within)
Vancouver Heritage Festival • Vancouver, British Columbia, Canada

Even-numbered years in May-June
Drama, Cycle of Classical • Siracusa, Sicily, Italy
La Chaux-de-Fonds, Biennial of • La Chaux-de-Fonds, Neuchatel, Switzerland (sometimes in autumn)
Puppet Theatre, International Festival of • Bielsko-Biala, Poland

Odd-numbered years in May-June
Richmondshire Festival • Richmond, North Yorkshire, England

Four days in late May-June
Monaco Grand Prix • Monte Carlo, Monaco

One week in May-June
Arts, Big River Festival of • Grafton, New South Wales, Australia

Ten days from late May to early June
Rose Festival • Kazanluk, Bulgaria

Two weeks in May-June
Cyprus International Fair • Nicosia, Cyprus

Two weeks from last week in May to early June
Spoleto Festival of Two Worlds/U.S.A. • Charleston, South Carolina

16 days in May-June
Gaspee Days • Cranston, Warwick, Rhode Island

Four weeks in May-June
Vic Festival • Stoke-on-Trent, Staffordshire, England

Six weeks from mid-May to June
Vienna Weeks (Wiener Festwochen) • Vienna, Austria

Eight weeks in May and June
Musical May, Florence (Maggio Musicale Fiorentino) • Florence, Tuscany, Italy

May-early June
June Festival, International • Zurich, Switzerland

Late May to late June
Vancouver International Festival • Vancouver, British Columbia, Canada

Late May to end of June
Opera Theatre of Saint Louis • Saint Louis, Missouri

May-June to September for two consecutive years followed by two-year interim
Plays in the Town Hall • Osnabruck, Lower Saxony, Federal Republic of Germany

May-June to October
Theatre Festival, Stratford • Stratford, Ontario, Canada

May-July
Wavendon Season • Milton Keynes, Buckinghamshire, England

Several days between May and July
Arts Festival, Jyvaskyla • Jyvaskyla, Finland

Five weeks from May to July; height of rainy season
Okere Juju • Itsekiri people in Nigeria

Thirty concerts from May to first week in July
Lausanne International Festival (Festival International de Lausanne) • Lausanne, Vaud, Switzerland

First week in May to middle of July
Boston Pops • Boston, Massachusetts

Mid-May through July
Sun Days, Midnight • North Cape, Norway

Late May to mid-July
Festival-Institute at Round Top • Round Top, Texas

May-August
Drama Festival, New South Wales High Schools • New South Wales, Australia
Theatre Season, Open-Air • London, England

Ten to eleven weeks from late May to early August
Opera, Glyndebourne Festival • Glyndebourne, East Sussex, England

May-September
Byblos Festival • Byblos, Lebanon
Folk Dances, Greek • Philopappou Hill, Athens, Greece
Theatre, Chichester Festival • Chichester, West Sussex, England

End of May through September during odd-numbered years
Yodeling Festivals (Jodlerfests) • Switzerland

Every five years from May to September
Passion Play • St. Margarethen, Burgenland, Austria

Every ten years from May to September
Passion Play, Oberammergau • Oberammergau, Bavaria, Federal Republic of Germany

Saturdays and Sundays from May to September
Theatre Nettelstedt, Open-Air • Lubbecke, North Rhine-Westphalia, Federal Republic of Germany

Weekend ceremonies in May-September lead up to festival
Dance, Green Corn • Creek Indians in the southeastern United States

Mid-May to September
Folk Dancing at Corfu, Greek • Kerkyra, Corfu, Greece

May-September, Memorial Day through Labor Day
Indian Dances, Traditional • Gallup, New Mexico
Naumburg Orchestral Concerts • New York, New York (four concerts)

Some time between May and September
Israel Festival • Caesarea, Haifa, Jerusalem, and Tel Aviv, Israel

Four consecutive nights during each full moon from May to October
Ballet Festival, Ramayana • Prambanan near Jogjakarta, Java, Indonesia

May to October, peaking in July
Festa Season • towns in Gozo and Malta

22 weeks from May to October
Shaw Festival • Niagara-on-the-Lake, Ontario, Canada

Odd-numbered years from May to December
Venice Biennial • Venice, Veneto, Italy

June

June
Arts, Lakefront Festival of the • Milwaukee, Wisconsin
Bach Festival, International • Funchal, Madeira Island, Portugal
Bambuco, Festival of • Neiva, Huila, Colombia
Battle of the Moors and Christians • Penalsordo, Badajoz, Spain
Common Ridings Day • Selkirk and Haywick, Scotland
Craigmillar Festival • Craigmillar, Edinburgh, Scotland (or August)
Cumbia Festival • El Banco, Magdalena, Colombia
Dance, Longevity (Ennen-no-mai) • Nikko, Tochigi, Japan
Dance and Music Festival, Kuopio • Kuopio, Finland
Dances, Osage Tribal Ceremonial • Greyhorse, Homin, and Pawhuska, Oklahoma
Danzantes y Pecados Festival • Camunas, Toledo, Spain
Drama Amateurs of Montenegro, Festival of • Bijelo Polje, Montenegro, Yugoslavia
Drama Festival, Catholic School • Melbourne, Victoria, Australia
Egungun Festival • Yoruba people at Ede, Nigeria
Eisteddfod, Hobart • Hobart, Tasmania, Australia
El Djem Festival • El Djem (formerly Thysdrus), Mahdia Region, Tunisia
Encaenia Day • Oxford University, England
Folklore Festival of the Socialist Republic of Serbia • Leskovac, Serbia, Yugoslavia
Folklore Groups of Vojvodina, Encounter of Hungarian • location varies within Vojvodina, Yugoslavia
Franconian Festival Week • Bayreuth, Bavaria, Federal Republic of Germany
Kosovo, Village Festivities of • Klina by Pec, Kosovo, Yugoslavia
Lausanne, Festival of the City of • Lausanne, Vaud, Switzerland
Le Mans Grand Prix • Le Mans, Sarthe, France
Mediterranean Festival • Izmir, Turkey
Monklands Festival • Airdrie and Coatbridge, Lanarkshire, Scotland
Music and Popular Arts, Regional Festival of • Sfax, Sfax Region, Tunisia
Norway, Festival of Northern • Harstad, Norway
Nottingham Festival • Nottingham, Nottinghamshire, England
Performance '78,'79, etc. • location varies within British Columbia, Canada
Powwow, Arapaho Community • Arapaho Indians at Arapahoe, Wyoming
Powwow, Warm Springs • Shahaptian and Chinookan Indians at Warm Springs, Oregon
Rose Festival, Portland • Portland, Oregon
Summer-Nights Festival, Basel • Basel, Switzerland
Theatre, Regional Festival of • Monastir, Monastir Region, Tunisia

June *(cont.)*
Theatre Festival of Bosnia and Herzegovina • Jajce, Bosnia and Herzegovina, Yugoslavia
Theatre Groups, Provincial Festival of Kosovo Amateur • Urosevac, Kosovo, Yugoslavia
Theatres of Northern Poland, Festival of • Torun, Poland
Vila Praia de Ancora, International Festival of • Vila Praia de Ancora, Viana do Castelo, Portugal (or August)
Wimbledon, Lawn Tennis Championships at • England
World Cup (soccer; four weeks of playoffs could also be held in May or July)
Writers' Week Listowel • Listowel, County Kerry, Ireland
Xilónen, Festival of • Aztec

Usually June
Strawberry Festival • Iroquois Indians at Tonawanda, New York

Month of June
Art Festival, Academic Youth • Swinouscie, Poland
Music at La Defense • La Defense, Paris, France
Warrior or Veteran Festival, Stommish • Lummi Indians at Bellingham, Washington

Even-numbered years in June
Newport to Bermuda Race • Newport, Rhode Island, to Bermuda
Pispalan Sottiisi • Tampere, Finland

Odd-numbered years in June
Art, Biennial of Children's • Poznan, Poland
Literature Festival, Ilkley • Ilkley, West Yorkshire, England
Song to Romania • Bucharest, Romania

Every three years in June
Mystery Plays, York Festival and • York, Yorkshire, England

Every four years in June
Virgen Festival, Bajada de la • El Hierro, Santa Cruz de Tenerife, Spain

Every five years in June
Drama, National Review of Modern Bulgarian • Sofia, Bulgaria
Virgen Lustral Festival, Bajada de la • Santa Cruz de la Palma, Santa Cruz de Tenerife, Spain

Every five or six years in June
Easter Play of Muri • Muri, Aargau, Switzerland

June 1
Admission Day • Kentucky
Admission Day • Tennessee
Bean Calends • ancient Rome
Children's Day • Cape Verde

Foundation Day, State • Western Australia
Madaraka Day (also known as Responsibility Day and Self-Government Day) • Kenya
Mint Julep Day • New College, Oxford, England
Young, Birthday of Brigham • Mormon
Zarthastno Diso • Shahenshai sect of Parsis

On or near June 1
Australia Day • Western Australia

June 1; two-day holiday
Constitution and National Day • Tunisia

June 1-2
Dayak Festival Day (Gawai Dayak) • Dayak people at Sarawak, Malaysia

June 1-3
Independence Day (January 1) • Western Samoa

June 1 through August 15
Pilgrimage, Lough Derg • Pilgrimage of St. Patrick's Purgatory in Ireland

June 2
King's Birthday (November 11) • Sweden
Republic Day • Federal Republic of Germany
Republic Day (Constitution Day) • Italy
St. Elmo's Day • Christian
Seaman's Day • Iceland (or first Sunday in June)
Youth Day • Tunisia

June 3
Confederate Memorial Day • Kentucky
Confederate Memorial Day • Louisiana
Davis's Birthday, Jefferson
Memorial to Broken Dolls Day • Buddhists in Japan

June 4
Emancipation Day • Kingdom of Tonga
Labour Day • Bahama Islands

On or near June 4
Fourth of June • England

June 5
Constitution Day • Denmark
Liberation Day • Seychelles
St. Boniface, Feast Day of • Anglican and Roman Catholic
World Environment Day • United Nations member nations; Oodi people in Botswana; Czechoslovakia

June 5-12
Kite Battles • Shirone, Niigata, Japan

June 6
Constitution and Flag Day • Sweden
D-Day (Allied Landing Observances Day) • Normandy, France
Memorial Day • Republic of Korea

Thursday which falls between June 6-12
Landimere's or Lanimer Day • Lanark, England

June 7-15
Vestalia • ancient Rome

June 8
St. Médardus's Day • French-Americans in Louisiana; Belgium

June 9
St. Columba's Day • Roman Catholic
Senior Citizens Day • Oklahoma

June 10
National Day (Camões Memorial Day) • Portugal
Time Observance Day • Japan

June 11
Evacuation Day, American Bases • Libya
Kamehameha Day • Iolani Palace, Honolulu, Oahu Island, Hawaii
Matralia • Forum Boarium, the Temple of Hercules, ancient Rome
St. Barnabas's Day • England

June 12
Helsinki Day • Finland
Independence Day • Philippines
Peace with Bolivia Day • Paraguay
St. Leo III, Feast of • Christian

June 12 or second Saturday in June
Queen Elizabeth II, Official Birthday of • London, England and throughout Great Britain

June 13
Reform Movement Day • Yemen Arab Republic
St. Anthony of Padua, Feast of • Christian
Union Day, Miners' • Butte, Montana

June 13-29
Juninas, Festas (Bumba-meu-Boi folk drama) • Brazil

Weekend of or before June 14
Powwow, White Earth Chippewa • White Earth, Minnesota

June 14
Flag Day • United States

Shrine Rice Festival, Sumiyashi • Osaka, Japan

June 15
Admission Day • Arkansas
Farmer's Day • Korea
Magna Charta Day • England
Pioneer Day • Franklin, Idaho
St. Vitus's Day • Christian
Valdemar's Day • Denmark

June 16
Bloomsday • Dublin, Ireland

June 17
Bunker Hill Day • Boston and Suffolk County, Massachusetts
Children's Day, National • Indonesia
Independence Day • Iceland
Lily Festival • Shinto religion at Nara, Japan

June 18
Evacuation Day • Egypt

June 19
Artigas Day • Uruguay
Independence Day • Laos
Independence or Republic Day • Kuwait
Juneteenth (Emancipation Day) • African-Americans in Texas and other southern United States
Labour Day • Trinidad and Tobago
New Church Day • Swedenborgians, or Church of the New Jerusalem

Sunday nearest June 19
Continental Army, Departure of • Valley Forge National Historical Park, Pennsylvania

June 20
Admission Day • West Virginia
St. Crispin's Day • Westphalia, Germany

June 21
Admission Day • New Hampshire
Summer Solstice • Germany
Sun Festivals, Midnight • Alaska

June 21-22
Summer Solstice • northern hemisphere
Winter Solstice • southern hemisphere

June 22
St. Alban's Day • Christian
St. Paulinus of Nola, Feast of • Christian
St. Paulinus of Nola, Feast of (Lily Festival) • Nola, Italy (or fourth Sunday in June)
St. Thomas More, Feast Day of • Christian

June 23
Dance, Calinda • African and Creole peoples at New Orleans, Louisiana
Grand Duke, or National, Day • Luxembourg
St. Etheldreda's Day • Roman Catholic
Wreaths, Wianki Festival of • Poland and Polish-Americans in Washington, D.C.

Begins Friday evening before June 24
Midsummer (Midsommer Day) • Sweden

June 23-24
Midsummer

June 23-24, St. John the Baptist's Day, until June 29, St. Peter's Day
Midsummer • Roman Catholics in Brazil

June 24
Bannockburn Day • Scotland
Fisherman's Day • Zaire
Human Towers of Valls (Xiquets de Valls) • Valls, Catalonia, Spain
Indian, Day of the (Día del Indio) • Peru and other Latin American countries
Quarter Days • England and Ireland (also September 29, December 25, and March 25)
St. John the Baptist's Day • Christian
Singing to Rings (Ladouvane) • Bulgaria (January 1 in west Bulgaria)
Swedes' Day (Svenskarnas Dag) • Swedish-Americans at Chicago, Illinois

Three days, including June 24
Midsummer • Latvia (Ligo Feast)

About one week, including June 24
Sun Festival (Inti Raymi or Raimi Fiesta) • Inca people at Cuzco, Peru

June 24-29
Sts. Peter and John Festival (San Pedro and San Juan) • Paraguay

On or near June 24
Discovery Day • Newfoundland, Canada

Sunday nearest June 24
St. John the Baptist's Day (San Juan Fiesta) • New York, New York

Saturday nearest to June 24
Midsummer (Juhannus Day, St. John the Baptist's Day) • Finland

Two days on weekend nearest June 24
Fyr-Bal Fest • Norwegian- and Swedish-Americans at Ephraim, Wisconsin

One week, including June 24
St. John the Baptist's Day (San Juan Bautista) • Puerto Rico

Third Sunday after Midsummer Day, June 24
Relic Sunday • Christian

June 25
Admission Day • Virginia
Independence Day • Mozambique
Plow, Festival of the (Saban Tuy) • Kazan, Tatar Republic, USSR

Every fifth year on June 25
Singing Festival (Laulipidu) • Tallinn, Estonia

June 26
Independence Day • Madagascar
Independence Day • Somalia (also July 1)

June 27
National Day • Djibouti
Smith, Martyrdom of Joseph and Hyrum • Church of Jesus Christ of the Latter Day Saints and smaller Mormon churches

June 28-29
Goose and River Festival, Palio of the • Pavia, Italy

June 29
Republic Day • Seychelles
St. Peter's Day • Christian
Sts. Peter and Paul Day • Christian

Sunday following June 29
Sts. Peter and Paul Day (ceremony of Blessing of the Sea) • Ostend, Blankenberge, and other seaport towns in Belgium

June 30
Army Day • Guatemala
Burning of the Three Firs • Thann, France
Constitution Day • Mongolia
Fandroana • Madagascar
Independence Day • Democratic Republic of the Congo

One day in June
Muster Day • New Hampshire

A Saturday in June
Alexandra Rose Day • Great Britain
Belmont Stakes • Long Island, New York (fifth Saturday after the Kentucky Derby)

One weekend in June, coincides with Queen Elizabeth II's Birthday
Folk Festival, Top Half • location varies: Alice Springs, Darwin, or Mount Isa, Northern June Territory, Australia

Three days in June
Folklore Festival of Straznice • Straznice, Moravia, Czechoslovakia

Four days in June
Harborfest Norfolk • Norfolk, Virginia
Sun Fun Festival • Myrtle Beach, South Carolina

Last day of four-day race in June
Gold Cup Day • England

One week in June
Kiel Week • Kiel, Schleswig-Holstein, Federal Republic of Germany
Pau Festival • Pau, Basses-Pyrenees, France
Wrestling Games of Kirkpinar • Kirkpinar, Edirne, Turkey

Eight days in June
Broadstairs Dickens Festival • Broadstairs, Kent, England

Eight days in June every five years
Spartakiade • Prague, Bohemia, Czechoslovakia

Nine days in June
White Night Festival • Leningrad (now St. Petersburg), Russia, USSR

Ten days in June
Golden Orpheus • Slunchev Bryag, Bulgaria

11 days in June during odd-numbered years
Paris Air and Space Show • Paris, France

Two weeks in June
NVB Festival (Nykterhetsrorelsens Bildningsversamhet) • Molnlycke, Sweden

16 days in June
Casals Festival • San Juan, Puerto Rico
Schubertiade Hohenems • Hohenems, Austria

16 days in June during even-numbered years
Arts Festival, Reykjavik • Reykjavik, Iceland

17 days in June
Arts Festival, Three Rivers • Pittsburgh, Pennsylvania

18 days in June
Music, Anchorage Festival of • Anchorage, Alaska

Three weeks in June
Fools, Festival of • Amsterdam, Netherlands

Mozart Festival (Mozartfest) • Würzburg, Germany
Theatres, Bern International Festival of Small • Bern, Switzerland

Three weekends in June
Music Festival of Florida • Sarasota, Florida

23 days in June
Holland Festival • Amsterdam, Rotterdam, Scheveningen, the Hague, and other cities in Netherlands

Early June
Theatre Festival, "Vojdan Cernodrinski" • Prilep, Macedonia, Yugoslavia

A Monday in early June
King's Birthday • most states in Australia

Two days in early June
Capital Expo • Frankfort, Kentucky
Elfreth's Alley Fete Days • Philadelphia, Pennsylvania
Takigi Noh • Heian Shrine, Kyoto, Japan

Three consecutive Tuesdays, Fridays, and Saturdays in early June
Music Festival, Sitka Summer • Sitka, Alaska

One week in early June
Country Music Fan Fair, International • Nashville, Tennessee

First week in June
In the Sunlit Plain • Pades, Gorj, Romania

16 days beginning first week in June
Music Festival, Strasbourg International (Festival International de Musique de Strasbourg) • Strasbourg, Alsace, Bas-Rhin, France

First or second week in June
Native American Cultural Festival, Red Earth • Oklahoma City, Oklahoma

First weekend in June
Blessing of the Fishing Fleet and Biloxi Shrimp Festival and Fais Do Do • Biloxi, Alabama
Folk Festival, Pittsburgh • David L. Lawrence Convention Center, Pittsburgh, Pennsylvania
Music Festival, Sea • Mystic Seaport Museum, Mystic, Connecticut
Powwow, Ojibwa • Ojibwa Indians at Nett Lake Reservation, Minnesota

First full weekend in June
Billy Bowlegs Festival • Fort Walton Beach, Florida

715

First Sunday in June
Regatta of the Great Maritime Republics • Pisa, Italy

Usually first Sunday in June
Regatta, Yale-Harvard • New London, Connecticut

First Saturday in June
Caricom Day • Antigua and Barbuda

First half of June
Theatres of Serbia, Festival of Amateur • Kula, Serbia, Yugoslavia

First two weeks in June
Irish Houses Festival, Great • County Wicklow, Ireland

First two weeks in June during odd-numbered years
Theatre for Children and Young People, International Encounter of • Lyon, Rhone, France

First three weeks in June
Music Festival, Connecticut Early • New London, Connecticut

Second week in June
Santarém, International Festival of • Santarém, Portugal

Three days during second week in June
Agricultural Field Days • New Zealand

Eight days during second week in June
Mozart Festival, German (Deutsches Mozartfest) • Augsburg, Federal Republic of Germany, and other German cities (location alternates)

Second weekend in June
Dulcimer and Harp Convention • Cosby, Tennessee
Rattlesnake Roundup, Morris • Morris, Pennsylvania

Second weekend and third week in June
Frankenmuth Bavarian Festival • German-Americans at Frankenmuth, Michigan

Second Sunday in June
Art Festival, Grant Wood • Stone City-Anamosa, Iowa
Children's Day • sponsored by National Council of Churches, United States
Citadel Festival • Cetatea Ica, Cernat, Covasna, Romania
Race Unity Day (June 13) • Bahá'í
Rose Day (June 10) • Lutherans at Manheim, Pennsylvania
Silvas Festival • Hateg, Silvasul de Jos Commune, Hunedoara, Romania

Second Saturday in June
Trooping the Colour • Great Britain

Mid-June
Brass Band Festival, Great American • Centre College, Danville, Kentucky
Folk Festival, Newcastle • Newcastle, New South Wales, Australia

Four days in mid-June
Ascot, Royal • Berkshire, England

Five days in mid-June
Ragtime and Traditional Jazz Festival, Annual National • Saint Louis, Missouri

One week in mid-June
Carillon Festival, International • Springfield, Illinois

One week in mid-June every two or three years
Music Festival and Seminar, Moravian • Winston-Salem, North Carolina (location alternates)

Ten days in mid-June
Jazz Festival, Mellon • Philadelphia, Pennsylvania

Two weeks in mid-June
Music in the Mountains • Nevada City, California

Three weeks beginning mid-June
Beethoven Festival • San Francisco, California
Music and Dance Festival, Granada International (Festival Internacional de Musica y Danza de Granada) • Granada, Spain

Three weekends in mid-June
Great Lakes Festival • Notre Dame, Indiana

Last two weeks in June
Arts Festival, Dawlish • Dawlish, Devonshire, England
Greenwich Festival • London Borough of Greenwich, England
Pershore Festival • Pershore, Worcestershire, England

Third week in June
NEBRASKAland DAYS • North Platte, Nebraska

Third full week in June
Fiddlers' Contest, National Old-Time • Weiser, Idaho

Third weekend in June
Country Music and Bluegrass Festival • Payson, Arizona
Indian Celebration, Red Bottom • Frazer, Montana
Jazz Festival, Playboy • Hollywood, California
Powwow, Warriors Memorial • Nez Perce Indians at Lapwai, Idaho

Five days over third weekend in June
St. Magnus Festival • Kirkwall, Orkney Islands, Scotland

716

Third full weekend in June
Bitowa Outdoor Festival • Tracadie, New Brunswick, Canada

Four days ending third Sunday in June
United States Open Championships in Golf • location varies

Third Sunday in June
Father's Day • Canada and the United States

Saturday before the third Monday of June
Children's Reckoning (Kinderzeche) • Dinkelsbühl, Bavaria, Federal Republic of Germany

Third Wednesday in June
Whitewater Wednesday • New River Gorge National River near Oakville, West Virginia

Third Saturday in June
Blueberry Festival, Alabama • Brewton, Alabama
Hollerin' Contest, National • Spivey's Corner, North Carolina
Jousting Tournament • Mount Solon, Virginia (also second Sunday in October)
Lou Bunch Day • Central City, Colorado

Fourth weekend in June
Indian Celebration, Badlands • Brockton, Montana

Fourth Sunday in June
St. Paulinus of Nola, Feast of (Lily Festival) • Nola, Italy (or Sunday following June 22)
Singing on the Mountain • Linville, North Carolina
Swedes' Day (Svenskarnas Dag) • Swedish-Americans in Minnesota

Late June
Custer's Last Stand • Crow Indians at the Crow Reservation in Montana
Happy Hunting Party, Festival of the Forest (Kiamichi Owa Chito) • Choctaw Indians at Beavers Bend State Park, Broken Bow, Oklahoma
Indian Days • Shoshone Indians at Fort Washakie, Wyoming
Jackalope Days • Douglas, Wyoming
New Yam Festival (Egbodo Oba Ooni) • Yoruba people at Oyo, Nigeria

Three days in late June
Bluegrass and Country Music Festival, Telluride • Telluride, Colorado
Folk Song Festival, Miramichi • Newcastle, New Brunswick, Canada

Five days in late June
Arts Festival, Utah • Salt Lake City, Utah

One week in late June
Good Neighbours Festival • Dumfries, Scotland

Last week in June
Harvest Festival (Imnarja or Mnarja) • Buskett Gardens, Malta
Thornton Festival • Thornton, Bradford, West Yorkshire, England

Last weekend in June
Blessing of the Shrimp Fleet • Roman Catholics at Bayou La Batre, Alabama
Keller Festival, Helen • Tuscumbia, Alabama
Kingdom Days • Fulton, Missouri
Mountains, Festival of the (Nedeia Muntilor) • Fundata, Brasov, Romania
Music, Mariposa-the Festival of Roots • Toronto, Ontario, Canada
Powwow, Citizen Band of Potawatomi Indians of Oklahoma • Shawnee, Oklahoma
Regatta, Idaho • Burley, Idaho

Last Sunday in June
Lime-Tree Day • Buciumeni, Galati, Romania
Red Inn Festival • Gura Vitioarei, Prahova, Romania
St. Martha, Feast of (Fête de la Tarasque) • Tarascon, Provence, France (also July 29)

End of June
New Yam Festival • Nigeria
Theatre Festival, Medieval • Hita, Guadalajara, Spain

One to four days at end of June, during summer solstice
Dance, Sun • Sioux Indians

Usually three to four days at end of June; sometimes July or August
Acadian Festivals • Maritime Provinces, Canada

Three days in June or July
Hemis Festival • Buddhists at Hemis Gompa monastery, Ladakh, India

One week in late June or early July
Music Festival, Touraine (Fêtes Musicales en Touraine) • Tours, France

Ten to 17 days in June or July
Music and the Arts, Aldeburgh Festival of • Aldeburgh, Suffolk, England

Late June or early July
Bawming the Thorn Day • Appleton, Cheshire, England

June-July

Arts, Northam Festival of the • Northam, Western Australia, Australia

Bellac Festival • Bellac, Haute-Vienne, France

Calderon Festival in the Old Courtyard • Bamberg, Bavaria, Federal Republic of Germany

Castle Plays Festival • Forchtenstein, Burgenland, Austria

Castle Theatre Hohenlimburg • Hagen and Hohenlimburg, North Rhine-Westphalia, Federal Republic of Germany

Chester Festival • Chester, England

Child, Yugoslav Festival of the • Sibenik, Croatia, Yugoslavia

Common Ridings Day • Scotland

Curium Festival • Curium near Limassol, Cyprus

Drama, Paphos Festival of Ancient • Paphos, Cyprus

European Festival Weeks • Passau, Bavaria, Federal Republic of Germany

Folk Festival, Newcastle • Newcastle upon Tyne, Northumberland, England

Istanbul Festival, International • Istanbul, Turkey

Jazz Festival, Montreal • Montreal, Canada

Kataragama Festival • Buddhists and Hindus at Kataragama, Sri Lanka

Krems Outdoor Festival (Sommerspiele Krems) • Krems, Lower Austria, Austria

Kusadasi, Festival of • Kusadasi, Turkey

Lyon International Festival (Festival International de Lyon) • Lyon, Rhone, France

Marais Festival • Paris, France

Music Festival, Toulon (Festival de Musique de Toulon) • Toulon, Var, France

Puppeteers, National Festival of Amateur • Chrudim, East Bohemia, Czechoslovakia

"Red Rose" Festival of Culture • Ruski Krstur, Vojvodina, Yugoslavia

Rice Festival • Japan (date varies)

Top-Spinning Competitions • Malaysia (after harvest of rice)

Odd-numbered years in June-July

Ballet Biennial • Ljubljana, Slovenia, Yugoslavia

Nights of Bourgogne, Festival of the (Festival des Nuits de Bourgogne) • Dijon, Cote-d'Or, France

Every three years in June-July

Theatre Days, Summer • Vidin, Bulgaria

Every five years in June-July

Puppeteers, International Festival of Amateur • Chrudim, East Bohemia, Czechoslovakia

Weekends in June-July

Theatre, Summer Festival at the Bergwald • Weissenburg, Bavaria, Federal Republic of Germany

Three days to two weeks in June-July

Viking Festival • Frederikssund, Calf Island, Zealand, Denmark

One week from late June to early July

Occitanie Festival • Montauban, Tarn-et-Garonne, France

Two weeks in June-July

Music Weeks in Drome, Contemporary • Romans, Drome, France

Summer Academy of Dance, International • Cologne, North Rhine-Westphalia, Federal Republic of Germany

Two weeks in late June and early July

Folklife, Festival of American • Washington, D.C.

Three weeks from late June to early July

Opera, Des Moines Metro Summer Festival of • Indianola, Iowa

Three weeks, including four Sundays in June-July, every third year

Landshut Wedding • Landshut, Bavaria, Federal Republic of Germany

Three to four weeks in June-July during odd-numbered years

Horizon '79, '81, etc. • West Berlin, Federal Republic of Germany

Last three weeks in June through first week in July

Crop Over • Bridgetown and all over Barbados

Six weeks in June-July

Arts, International Festival of the • International Peace Garden, Dunseith, North Dakota, and Manitoba, Canada

Music Festival, Stockholm • Stockholm, Sweden

Six weeks from late June through July

Music Festival, Waterloo Summer • Stanhope, New Jersey

June to second week in July

Arts Colony, Inspiration Point Fine • Eureka Springs, Arkansas

Mid-June to July 4

Freedom Festival, International • Windsor, Ontario, Canada, and Detroit, Michigan

Mid-June to mid-July

Industry Festival of Wetzlar • Wetzlar, Hesse, Federal Republic of Germany

Music Festival, International Classical • Echternach, Luxembourg

Opera Festival, Cincinnati Summer • Cincinnati, Ohio

Mid-June to late July
Music Northwest, Chamber • Portland, Oregon

Late June to July 4
Harbor Festival • New York, New York

17 days from late June to July 4
Barnum Festival • Bridgeport, Connecticut

Late June to second week in July
Bach Festival, Oregon • Eugene, Oregon

Late June to mid-July
Spoleto Festival of Two Worlds (Festival dei Due Mondi) • Spoleto, Umbria, Italy

Late June to late July
Symphony Concerts, Monteux Conducting School • Hancock, Maine

Last week in June and first week in July
Summer Festival, Ludlow • Ludlow, Shropshire, England

Last week in June to last week in July
Music Center, Sewanee Summer • Sewanee, Tennessee

Last weekend in June and first week in July
Gettysburg Civil War Heritage Days • Gettysburg, Pennsylvania

Last weekend in June and first weekend in July
Hauts-de-Saone Festival • Luxeuil-les-Bains, Haute-Saone, France

End of June-beginning of July
Drama Amateurs, Yugoslav • Trebinje, Bosnia and Herzegovina, Yugoslavia
Theatre, Polesden Lacey Open Air • Great Bookham, Surrey, England

June-August
Castle Festival at Jagsthausen • Jagsthausen, Baden-Wurttemberg, Federal Republic of Germany
Cloister Festival • Feuchtwangen, Bavaria, Federal Republic of Germany
Interlake Festival • Winnipeg, Manitoba, Canada
Interlaken Festival • Interlaken, Bern, Switzerland
Luisenburg Festival • Wunsiedel, Bavaria, Federal Republic of Germany
Music and Theatre in Herrenhausen • Hannover, Lower Saxony, Federal Republic of Germany
Passion Play, Black Hills • Spearfish, South Dakota
Pike Festival, Northern • Nipawin, Saskatchewan, Canada
Summer Season, Geneva • Geneva, Switzerland
Theatre, International Festival of • Santarém, Portugal

Theatre, Summer Season at the Fort-Antoine • Monte Carlo, Monaco
Theatre Festival, Dinkelsbühl Open-Air • Dinkelsbühl, Bavaria, Federal Republic of Germany
Theater Festival, Epidauros • Epidauros, Peloponnese, Greece
Theatre Festival, Farmstead (Theater auf dem Bauernof) • Meggenhofen, Upper Austria, Austria
Theatre Festival in Schwabisch-Hall, Open-Air • Baden-Wurttemberg, Federal Republic of Germany
Vienne Festival • Vienne en Dauphine, Isere, France

Four Sunday evening concerts from mid-June to mid-August
Music Series, Silvermine Chamber • New Canaan, Connecticut

Tuesday and Friday evenings from late June to late August
Music Festival, Redlands Bowl Summer • Redlands, California

Tuesdays, Wednesdays and Fridays in June-August
Riel, Trial of • Regina, Saskatchewan, Canada

Six weeks from early June to late August
Music Festival, New Hampshire • Center Harbor, New Hampshire

Six weeks from late June to early August
Music Festival, Eastern • Greensboro, North Carolina

Seven weeks from late June to mid-August
Music Center, Brevard • Brevard, North Carolina

Seven weeks from last week in June to mid-August
Kneisel Hall • Blue Hill, Maine

Eight weeks from late June to late August
Summer Festival, Carinthian (Carinthischer Sommer) • Ossiach and Villach, Austria

Eight weeks from last week in June to mid-August
Music Camp, National • Interlochen, Michigan

Eight weeks from last week in June to third week in August
Music Academy of the West Summer Festival • Santa Barbara, California

Nine weeks from mid-June to mid-August
Caramoor Festival • Katonah, New York

Nine weeks from last week in June to last week in August
Music Festival, Aspen • Aspen, Colorado

Ten weeks from last week in June to last week in August
Grant Park Concerts • Chicago, Illinois

Eleven weeks from mid-June to end of August
Summer Festival, Ljubljana International (Festivala Ljubljana) • Ljubljana, Yugoslavia

Twelve weeks from mid-June to last week in August
Music Festival, Meadowbrook • Rochester, Michigan

Early June to late August
Arts, Banff Festival of the • Banff, Alberta, Canada

Mid-June to early August
Music Festival, Colorado • Boulder, Colorado

Mid-June to first week in August
Music Center, Mann • Philadelphia, Pennsylvania

Mid-June to mid-August
Summer Festival for Children • Tehran, Iran

Mid-June to mid-August for ten Sundays
Music Festival, Stern Grove Midsummer • San Francisco, California

Mid-June to late August
Custer's Last Stand (Chief Crazy Horse Pageant) • Hot Springs, South Dakota

Mid-June to end of August
Muny, The • Saint Louis Municipal Opera, Saint Louis, Missouri

Late June to mid-August on weekends
Music Festival, Norfolk Chamber • Norfolk, Connecticut

Late June to late August
Arts Festival, Summerscape-Huntington Summer • Huntington, New York
Music Program, Chautauqua Summer • Chautauqua, New York
Opera and Ballet, Budapest Concerts and Open-Air • Budapest, Hungary

Last week in June to first week in August
Music Festival, Bowdoin Summer • Brunswick, Maine

Last week in June to mid-August
Artpark • Lewiston, New York

End of June through end of first week in August
Miracles at Glastonbury • Glastonbury, Somerset, England

June to August-September
Theatre, Drottningholm Court • Stockholm, Sweden

June-September
Britt Festival • Jacksonville, Oregon

Charlottetown Festival • Charlottetown, Prince Edward Island, Canada
Opera, Ballet and Music Festival, Vichy • Vichy, France
Passion Play • Thiersee, Tirol, Austria
Roche-Jagu, Festival of • Ploezal-Runan, Cotes-du-Nord, France
Shakespeare Festival • Verona, Veneto, Italy
Summer Festival, Opatija • Opatija, Croatia, Yugoslavia
Zagreb Evenings • Zagreb, Croatia, Yugoslavia

Every five years in June-September
Theatre, Great World • Einsiedeln, Schwyz, Switzerland

Every six years from June to September
Passion Play • Erl, Tirol, Austria

Nightly from mid-June to Labor Day, first Monday in September
Wisconsin Dells Stand Rock Ceremonials • Winnebago Indians at Tomah, Wisconsin

Every Friday and Saturday in June-September
Znojmo Feast • Znojmo, Moravia, Czechoslovakia

Saturday evenings and Sunday afternoons from mid-June to early September
Music Mountain • Falls Village, Connecticut

One week sometime between June and September, during rainy season
Geerewol Celebrations • Wodaabe people in Niger

Eight weeks from June to September
Dance Festival, Jacob's Pillow • Becket, Massachusetts

13 weeks from June to first week in September
Summer Festival, Wolf Trap Farm Park • Vienna, Virginia

June through last week in September
Athens Festival • Athens, Greece

Early June to early September
Saratoga Festival (Saratoga Performing Arts Center) • Saratoga Springs, New York

Early June through mid-September
Shakespeare Festival, San Diego National • San Diego, California

First week in June to second week in September
Music Center, Blossom • Cuyahoga Falls, Ohio

First weekend in June to last weekend in September
Summer Series, Paul Masson • Saratoga, California

Mid-June to Labor Day, first Monday in September
Musical, Medora • Medora, North Dakota

Mid-June to early September
Music at Gretna • Mount Gretna, Pennsylvania

Late June to Labor Day, first Monday in September
Opera, Glimmerglass • Cooperstown, New York

Last week in June to second week in September
Ravinia Festival • Chicago or Highland Park, Illinois

End of June to mid-September
Theatre Festival, Minack • Porthcurno, Penzance,
Cornwall, England

June-September or October
Wallonia, Festival of (Festival de Wallonie) • Brabant
Wallon, Brussels, Chimay, Hainaut, Huy, Liège,
Luxembourg, Mons, Namur, Saint-Hubert, and
Stavelot, Belgium

June-October
Folk Dance Theatre of Rhodes • Rhodes, Greece

**June through October; begins night during the period when
the moon moves from the quarter to its half phase for
three days**
Midimu Ceremony • Makonde people; Newala, Mtwara, and
Lindi, Tanzania; Tunduru, Mozambique; Malawi; Zambia;
Zimbabwe

Early June through mid-October
Arts, Festival of the • Southern Vermont Art Center,
Manchester, Vermont

**Two nights each month during full moon from June
to November**
Ballet Festival, Javanese • Pandaan, East Java, Indonesia

Summer

Early summer
Thargelia • ancient Greece (also during May)

A Sunday in early summer or on Holy Thursday
Footwashing Day • Protestants in Kentucky

Summer
Arts Festival, Gorey • Gorey, County Wexford, Ireland
Battle of Flowers, Vienna • Vienna, Austria
Beethoven Concerts, Martonvásár • Martonvásár, Hungary
British Open Golf Tournament • England and Scotland
Dance, Green Corn • Seminole Indians in Florida (or spring)
Fairhope Jubilee • Fairhope, Alabama

Guarda, National Festival of • Guarda, Portugal
Harvest Dance (Kyaiya) • Lengua Indians at Gran Chaco,
South America (also autumn and spring)
Haydn Memorial Concerts • Eszterháza Palace,
Fertöd, Hungary
Indian Memorial Stampede Rodeo • Sac and Fox Indians
at Stroud, Oklahoma
Olympic Games • location varies for summer games
Shakespeare Festival, New York • Central Park, New York,
New York
Shinbyu • Buddhists in Burma (now Myanmar)
Summer Concerts, Lake Balaton • Lake Balaton area,
Hungary
Takigi Noh • Hie Shrine, Tokyo, Japan
Takigi Noh • Hachiman Shrine, Kamakura City,
Kanagawa, Japan
Theatre of Nations • location varies
Theatres, Algarve Meeting of Amateur • Faro, Portugal
Wíikita Festival • Papago Indians at Quitovaca, Sonora,
Mexico
Yasukini Matsuri • Yasukini Shrine, Tokyo, Japan (also
four days in April and during autumn and winter)

Even-numbered years in summer or autumn
Arts Festival, New Directions in the Performing •
Hamilton, Ontario, Canada

Every fourth summer
Pythian Games • ancient Greece

Every five years during the summer
Folk Art, National Festival of • Koprivshtitsa, Bulgaria
Song Festival • Latvia
Song Festival • Lithuania

Summer solstice
Kokochi • Zuñi Pueblo, New Mexico

Usually during summer solstice
Dance, Sun • Blackfeet Indians
Dance, Sun • Great Plains Indians, including Ponca,
Kiowa, Bûngi, Mandan, Hidatsa, Arapaho, Cheyenne,
Crow, Shoshone, Ute, Comanche and others

A full moon night in summer
Nevis Tea Meeting • Nevis

Every Sunday at noon during the summer
Pied Piper of Hamelin Festival • Hamelin, Federal
Republic of Germany

Six days in summer
Handel Festival • Halle, German Democratic
Republic

Three weeks to one month-long ceremony: Little Incwala lasts two days beginning at the summer solstice and new moon; the Big Incwala takes place for six days after the full moon
Incwala • Swaziland

Five weeks in summer
Castle Play Festival, Moers • Moers, North Rhine-Westphalia, Federal Republic of Germany

Midsummer
Bicycle Ride Across Iowa (Ragbrai) • Iowa
Panathenaea • Athens, Greece

Late summer
Dance, Green Corn • Muskogee-Creek Indians at Okmulgee, Oklahoma
Folk-Art Festival • Bourgas, Bulgaria
Harvest, Wheat • Transylvania, Romania
Operatic Society Festival, Haddo House Choral and • Aberdeen, Scotland

Summer through autumn
Theatre, St. George's Elizabethan • London Borough of Islington, England

July

July
Arts, Holiday Festival of the • Neepawa, Manitoba, Canada
Arts, Winchester Festival of the • Winchester, Hampshire, England
Arts and Music, Frejus Forum of (Forum des Arts et de la Musique) • Frejus, Var, France
Ballet Days, Hamburg • Hamburg, Federal Republic of Germany
Battleford Chautauqua • Battleford, Saskatchewan, Canada
Battle of the Moors and Christians • Villajoyosa, Alicante, Spain
Binding of Wreaths (Vainikinas; also known as Feast of July) • Lithuania
Bridge Fair and International Equestrian Festival, Hortobágy • Hortobágy, Hungary
Bursa Festival • Bursa, Turkey
Calgary Exhibition and Stampede • Calgary, Alberta, Canada
Castle Kobersdorf Festival • Kobersdorf, Burgenland, Austria
Castle Neulengbach Festival (Schloss Neulengbach) • Neulengbach, Lower Austria, Austria
Dance and Ethete Celebration, Sun • Arapaho Indians at Ethete, Wyoming
Dance Workshop, Bonn International • Bonn, North Rhine-Westphalia, Federal Republic of Germany
Darwin Show Day • Australia

Diamond Day • Ascot, England (day of the King George VI and Queen Elizabeth Diamond Stakes race)
Dougga, Festival of • Dougga, Beja Region, Tunisia
Folklore Festival, Sao Torcato International • Sao Torcato, Braga, Portugal
Folklore Review, International • Zagreb, Croatia, Yugoslavia
Fur Trade Days • Chadron, Nebraska
Gion Matsuri • Kyoto, Japan
Graveyard Cleaning and Decoration Day • Kentucky, Tennessee, and Texas
Gulpilhares, International Festival of • Gulpilhares, Porto, Portugal
Harvest Festivities, Duzijanca • Subotica, Serbia, Yugoslavia
Hyacinthia • ancient Sparta
Ibnou Abi Dhiaf Festival • Siliana, Siliana Region, Tunisia
Katherine Show Day • Australia
Klondike Days Exposition • Edmonton, Alberta, Canada
Nasreddin Hoca Festival • Aksehir, Turkey
Nestroy Festival (Nestroy-Spiele) • Schwechat, Lower Austria, Austria
Offering Ceremony • Tasikmalaya and Pantai Charita, Java
Olojo (Ogun Festival) • Ife and Yoruba peoples at Oyo, Nigeria
Pioneer Days • Saskatoon, Saskatchewan, Canada
Powwow, Bear River • Ojibwa Indians at Lac du Flambeau, Wisconsin
Powwow, Comanche Annual • Sultan Park, Walters, Oklahoma
Powwow, Fond du Lac • Ojibwa Indians at Cloquet, Minnesota
Powwow, Honor the Earth • Lac Courte Oreilles Ojibwa Indians at Hayward, Wisconsin
Powwow, Northern Cheyenne • Lame Deer, Montana
Powwow, Otoe-Missouri • Red Rock, Oklahoma
Powwow, Santee Sioux • Flandreau, South Dakota
Powwow, Sioux • Sioux Indians at Sioux-Lake Village, Sisseton, South Dakota
Red Waistcoat Festival (Festival of the Colete Encarnado) • Vila Franca de Xira, Lisboa District, Ribatejo, Portugal
Remembrance of the Departed Days • Kadmi sect of Parsis
Royal Tournament • London, England
St. Christina's Day (Festival of Santa Cristina) • Lloret de Mar, Gerona, Spain
St. Mary Magdalene, Feast of (Dance of the Stilts, Procession of St. Mary Magdalene) • Anguiano, Logrono, Spain
San Benitino de Lerez Festival • Pontevedra, Spain
Ship's Island, Festival of • Stockholm, Sweden
Sidi-Bou-Makhlouf, Festival • Le Kef, Le Kef Region, Tunisia
Sultan's Birthday Celebration • Kota Bharu, Kelantan, Malaysia
Summer Carnival, Whycocomagh • Whycocomagh, Nova Scotia, Canada
Tennant Creek Show Day • Australia

July *(cont.)*

Theatre Festival of Stavelot, Vacation (Les Vacances-Theatre de Stavelot) • Stavelot, Belgium

Theatrical, Musical and Artistic Encounters of Grasse, Rithma: International • Grasse, Alpes-Maritimes, France

Tus, Festival of • Tus, Mashhad, Iran

Vaqueiros de Alzada Festival • Brana de Aristebano, Luarca, Oviedo, Spain

World Cup (soccer; four weeks of playoffs may also be in May or June)

Usually in July

Camel Market • Huelmime, Morocco

Powwow, Sioux • Sioux Indians at Little Eagle, South Dakota

Sandcastle Days • Imperial Beach, California

Month of July

Arts, Summer Festival of the • St. John's, Newfoundland, Canada

Performance Season, Canadian Experimental • Niagara-on-the-Lake, Ontario, Canada

Even-numbered years in July

Ballet, International Festival of • Nervi, Liguria, Italy

Dramatic Groups, "Istvan Horvath Cadet" Festival of • Kazincbarcika, Hungary

London, Festival of the City of • London, England

Odd-numbered years in July

Folk Dance, International Festival of • Szeged, Hungary

Transpac Race • Los Angeles, California, to Honolulu, Hawaii

Every three years in July

Folklore, Danube Festival of • Kalocsa, Baja, and Szekszard, Hungary

July 1

Freedom, Day of • Surinam

Gathering of the Clans • Scottish-Canadians at Pugwash, Nova Scotia, Canada

Gettysburg Day • Gettysburg, Pennsylvania

Half-Year Day • Hong Kong

Independence Day • Burundi

Independence Day • Rwanda

Independence Day • Somalia (and June 26)

Precious Blood, Feast of the Most • Roman Catholic

Republic Day • Ghana

July 1-2

Canada Day • Canada

July 1-4

Mescalero Apache Gahan Ceremonial • Mescalero Apache Indians at Mescalero, New Mexico

July 1 through last Sunday in July

Zulu/Shembe Festival • Ekuphakemeni Shembe's Shrine, Inanda, South Africa

July 1-August (seven weeks)

Summer Festival, Copenhagen • Copenhagen, Denmark

July 1-August 26

Mount Fuji Climbing Season • Yoshida, Japan

July 2

Palio, Festival of the (Festa del Palio; also known as Corso del Palio or Palio of the Contrade) • Siena, Tuscany, Italy (also on August 16)

Visitation of the Blessed Virgin Mary, Feast of the • Christian

July 3

Admission Day • Idaho

Independence Day • Algeria

St. Thomas the Apostle, Feast of • Roman Catholic

July 3-6

Devil's Promenade • Comanche, Kiowa, and Creek Indians

July 3-8

Folk Songs and Dances, Balkan Festival of • Ohrid, Macedonia, Yugoslavia

July 4

Apache Maidens' Puberty Rites • Mescalero Apache Indians at Mescalero, New Mexico

Coolidge, Birthday Celebration of Calvin • Plymouth Notch, Vermont

Flag Day • Alaska

Flag Day • Hawaii

Independence Day (Fourth of July) • United States

Independence Day (Rebild Festival) • United States and Aalborg, Rebild, North Jutland, Denmark

Nambe Falls Ceremonial • Nambe Pueblo, New Mexico

Old Midsummer Eve • England

Philippine-American Friendship Day • Philippines

Santo Isobel, Fiesta of • Yaqui Indians in southern Arizona and Mexico

Summer Festival • Owensboro, Kentucky

On or near July 4

Caricom Day • Barbados, Guyana, and St. Vincent

Weekend nearest July 4

Fiddlers Jamboree and Crafts Festival, Old Time • Smithville, Tennessee

Fishing Rodeo, Deep Sea • Gulfport, Mississippi

Powwow, Oneida • Oneida Indians at Oneida, Wisconsin

Powwow, Pawnee Fourth of July • Pawnee, Oklahoma

Weekend nearest July 4 *(cont.)*
Taholah Days • Hoh, Quinault, and Quileute Indians at Quinault Nation, Taholah, Washington
White Swan Celebrations • Yakima Indians at Yakima Reservation, Washington

Week including July 4
Tom Sawyer Days, National • Hannibal, Missouri

Nine days, including July 4
Folk Festival, Pennsylvania Dutch • Pennsylvania Dutch, Amish, Dunkards, and Mennonites at Kutztown, Pennsylvania

11 days, including July 4
Summerfest • Milwaukee, Wisconsin

Four days in July beginning the Wednesday after July 4
Indian Fair, Choctaw • Choctaw Indians at Pearl River Indian Community near Philadelphia, Mississippi

Thursday after the Fourth of July through Labor Day, first Monday in September
Dump Week, National • Kennebunkport, Maine

Weekend after July 4
Dance, Southern Ute Sun • Ute Indians at Ignacio, Colorado
Schooner Days • Rockland and Thomaston, Maine

First full week after July 4
Cherry Festival, National • Traverse City, Michigan

July 5
Fighter's or Warrior's Day • Yugoslavia
Independence Day • Cape Verde
Independence Day • Venezuela
Peace and National Unity Day • Rwanda

Three days beginning Sunday after July 5
Giants, Festival of the (Fête des Géants) • Douai, France

July 6
Dalai Lama, Birthday of • Tibetan exiles in India
Independence Day • Comoros
Independence Day • Malawi
Remembrance Day • Luxembourg

July 6-20
Running of the Bulls (San Fermín Festival) • Pamplona, Navarre, Spain

July 7
Double Seventh (Festival of the Weaving Maid and the Herd Boy or Tanabata Matsuri, the Weaver Princess Festival; also known as Star Festival) • Japan

Farmer's Day (Saba Saba Day) • Tanzania
Independence Day • Solomon Islands
Juno Caprotina • ancient Rome

July 8
Castor and Pollux, Festival of • ancient Rome
St. Elizabeth, Feast of • Huyalas, Peru

July 9
Báb, Martyrdom of the • Bahá'í
Independence Day • Argentina (and May 25)

July 10
Admission Day • Wyoming
Independence Day • Bahama Islands

July 10-11
Powwow and Expo, Black Hills and Northern Plains Indian • Rapid City, South Dakota

July 11
Revolution Day (Nadam) • Mongolia
St. Placidus Festival • Disentis, Grisons, Switzerland

July 12
Galicnik Wedding • Galicnik, Macedonia, Yugoslavia
Independence Day • Kiribati
National Day • São Tomé and Principe
Orange Day • Protestants in Northern Ireland

Monday after July 12
St. Veronica, Feast of • Valenciennes, France

July 12-16
Dead, Festival of the (Bon Odori or Obon Matsuri) • Buddhist Japanese-Americans in the United States

July 13
Fire Festival • Kumano Nachi Shrine, Nachi No Falls, Wakayama, Japan
Khordad Sal • Kadmi sect of Parsis in India and elsewhere
Night Watch (La Retraite aux Flambeaux) • France
Our Lady of Fátima Day • Roman Catholics at Fátima, Estremadura, Portugal

Saturday before Bastille Day, July 14
French Festival (French Day) • French-Americans at Cape Vincent, New York

July 14
Bastille Day
Revolution Day • Iraq
St. Bonaventura, Feast of • Christian
St. Bonaventura, Feast of and Corn Dance • Cochiti Pueblo, New Mexico

Weekend closest to July 14
Bastille, Festival de la • Acadian people at Augusta, Maine

July 15
St. Swithin's Day • Anglicans in Great Britain; Pennsylvania
Virgin of Carmen, Fiesta of • Santa Cruz Etla, Mexico

Early July to July 16
Pilgrimage to Saut d'Eau • Ville-Bonheur, Haiti

July 16
Eddy, Birthday of Mary Baker • Christian Science
Our Lady of Carmel (La Madonna del Carmine) • Italy and Italian-Americans

July 17
Constitution Day • Republic of Korea
Indian Celebration, American (Feast of Kateri Tekakwitha) • Belleville, Illinois
Munoz Rivera Day • Puerto Rico
Revolution Day, July (Peaceful Revolution Day) • Iraq

Three days in July, including July 17
Craft's Fair • Barranquitas, Puerto Rico

July 18
Constitution Day • Uruguay
Lu Pan, Birthday of • Hong Kong
National Day • Spain

July 18-20
Arts and Crafts Show, Annual Eight Northern Indian Pueblos • San Juan Pueblo, New Mexico

July 19
Martyrs Day • Burma (now Myanmar)
Revolution Day, Sandinista • Nicaragua

July 20
Elijah Day • Roman Catholic and Greek Orthodox
Independence Day • Colombia
Pope Foot Race, Annual • San Juan Pueblo, New Mexico

Three days during weekend nearest July 20
Pottery Festival • Crooksville and Roseville, Ohio

July 21
Independence Day • Belgium
Liberation Day • Guam

Week including July 21
Hemingway Days • Key West, Florida

July 22
Fasinada • Gospa od Skrpjelo, Montenegro (formerly Yugoslavia)

King's Birthday • Swaziland
Liberation Day • Poland
St. Mary Magdalene, Feast of • pilgrimage to holy cave in Sainte Baume, Provence, France

July 23
National Day • Egypt
Selassie's Birthday, Haile • Addis Ababa, Ethiopia

July 24
Bolívar Day • Venezuela
Pioneer Day • Mormon
Pioneer Day • Mormons at Bloomington, Idaho, and Salt Lake City, Utah
Valencia Fair Days (Battle of Flowers) • Valencia, Spain

July 25
Constitution Day (Commonwealth Day) • Puerto Rico
Furrinalia • ancient Rome
Guanacaste Day • Costa Rica
Independence Day • Netherlands
Republic Day • Tunisia
St. Christopher's Day • Christian
St. James the Greater's Day • Christian

July 25, during holy years, when St. James's Day falls on a Sunday
St. James the Greater's Day (Fiesta de Santiago Appostol) • Santiago de Compostela, Galicia, Spain

July 25-26 or nearest weekend
St. James the Greater's Day (Fiestas de Santiago y Santa Ana) • Taos Pueblo, New Mexico

July 26
Admission Day • New York
Independence Day • Liberia
Independence Day • Maldive Islands
Pilgrimage to St. Anne d'Auray • Beaupré, Quebec, Canada
St. Anne's Day • Christian
Sts. Joachim and Anne, Feast of • Christian

July 27
Korcula, Festival of (Moreska) • Korcula, Croatia, Yugoslavia (and every Thursday from April-September)

July 27-29
Three Glorious Days (Les Trois Glorieuses) • Nuits-St. Georges, Beaune, and Meursault in Cote-d'Or, France (and third Saturday through Monday in November)

July 28
Independence Day • Peru
Volunteers of America, Founder of • Volunteers of America

July 29
St. Martha, Feast of (Fête de la Tarasque) • Tarascon, Provence, France (also last Sunday in June)

July 29-30
Olsok • Faroe Islands

July 30
Independence Day • Vanuatu (formerly New Hebrides)

July 31
St. Ignatius Loyola, Feast of • Christian

July 31, two-day holiday
Parents' Day • Zaire

July 31-August 1
Llama Ch'uyay • Sonqo, Bolivia

Two days in July
Fiddling Contest, Maritime Old Time • Dartmouth, Nova Scotia, Canada

Three days in July
Lumberjack World Championships • Hayward, Wisconsin
Mix Roundup, Tom • Sinnemahoning, Driftwood, and Mix Run, Pennsylvania
Tilting Tournament, Sonderborg • Sonderborg, Denmark

Four days in July every four years
Horse Meet Show and Races, National • Skagafjordur, Iceland

Six days in July
Lobster Festival • Shediac, New Brunswick, Canada

One week in July
Cornwall, Festival of • Breton people at Quimper, Finistere, France
Drama Festival, Deloraine Youth • Deloraine, Tasmania, Australia
Folklore, World Festival of • Gannat, Allier, France
Opera Festival, Colorado • Colorado Springs, Colorado

Eight days in July
Wangford Festival • Wangford, East Suffolk, England

Nine days in July
Music and the Arts, King's Lynn Festival of • King's Lynn, Norfolk, England

Ten days in July
Art Festival, International • Limassol, Cyprus
Summer Festival • Quebec City, Quebec, Canada

11 days in July
Summer Festival, Bavarian • German-Americans at Barnesville, Pennsylvania

Two weeks in July
Carcassone, Festival of • Carcassone, Aude, France
Music Festival, Newport • Newport, Rhode Island
Wine Festival • Rethymon, Crete, Greece

18 days in July
German Alps Festival • Hunter Mountain Ski Bowl, Hunter, New York

20 days in July
Artistic Festival of the Damascus International Fair • Damascus, Syria

Three weeks in July
Opera Plus, Festival Ottawa • Ottawa, Ontario, Canada

Three and one-half weeks in July
Aix-en-Provence International Festival of Opera and Music (Festival International d'Art Lyrique et de Musique d'Aix-en-Provence) • Aix-en-Provence, France
Buxton Festival • Buxton, England

Four weeks in July
Arts, Flagstaff Festival of the • Flagstaff, Arizona
Tour de France • France

Early July
Esplanade Concerts • Boston, Massachusetts
Grain, Festival of Ears of (Schrulblha) • Tibet
Shrimp Festival • Oostduinkerke, Belgium

Two days in early July
Djakovo Embroidery • Djakovo, Croatia, Yugoslavia

Three consecutive Saturday evenings in early July
Aston Magna Festival • Great Barrington, Massachusetts

One week in early July
Music, Saintes Festival of Ancient (Saintes Festival de Musique Ancienne) • Saintes, France

Ten days in early July
Arts, Festival of International Contemporary (Recontres Internationales d'Art Contemporain) • La Rochelle, France

Six weeks beginning in early July
Victoria International Festival • Victoria, British Columbia, Canada

Four to five days during first week in July
Music Festival, Ravello (Festival Musicale di Ravello) • Ravello, Italy

Six days during first week in July
Eisteddfod, International Musical (Gerddorol Gydwladol Llangollen) • Llangollen, Denbighshire, Wales

Nine days beginning first week in July
Music, Cheltenham International Festival of • Cheltenham Spa, England

Eleven days beginning first week in July
Jazz, Nice Grand Parade of (Grande Parade du Jazz) • Nice, France

Two weeks beginning first week in July
Jazz Festival, Montreux International (Montreux Festival Internacional de Jazz) • Montreux, Vaud, Switzerland

First two weeks in July during even-numbered years
Holy Queen, Festival of the (Festa da Rainha Santa Isabel) • Coimbra, Beira Litoral, Portugal

First three weeks in July
Opera Festival, Savonlinna (Savonlinnan Oopperajuhlat) • Savonlinna, Finland

First weekend in July
Powwow, Arlee Fourth of July Celebration • Salish Indians at Arlee, Vermont

First or second weekend in July
Basque Festival, National • Basque-Americans at Elko, Nevada

First Sunday in July
Nation of Heroes • Munteni de Jos, Vaslui, Romania

One week beginning first Sunday in July
Folk Dance Festival of Ireland, International • Cobh, County Cork, Ireland

One week beginning first weekend after first Sunday in July
Folk-Dance Festival, International (International Volksdansfestival) • Schoten, Belgium

First Monday in July
Family Day • Lesotho
Heroes' Day • Zambia (formerly Northern Rhodesia)

First Tuesday in July
Unity Day (July 6) • Zambia (formerly Northern Rhodesia)

First Thursday in July
Ommegang Pageant • Brussels, Belgium

Second week in July
Indian Days, North American • Indians from Canada and the United States at the Blackfeet Reservation at Browning, Montana

Two weeks beginning second week in July
Chichester '900' Festivities • Chichester, West Sussex, England

Second weekend in July
Arikara Celebration • White Shield, North Dakota
Eternal Heroes, Festival of • Mosna, Jassy, Romania
Linden Tree Festival (Lindenfest) • Geisenheim, Rhineland, Germany
Powwow, American Indian • Bedford, Pennsylvania
Powwow, Quapaw • Shawnee, Miami, and Quapaw Indians at Quapaw, Oklahoma
Powwow, Sac and Fox • Stroud, Oklahoma

Second full weekend in July
Highland Games and Gathering of Scottish Clans, Grandfather Mountain • Scottish-Americans at Grandfather Mountain near Linville, North Carolina

Three or four days during second weekend in July
Folk Festival, Winnipeg • Winnipeg, Manitoba, Canada

Second Sunday in July
Green River Rendezvous • Pinedale, Wyoming
Guardian Angel, Festival of the (Schutzengelfest) • Appenzell, Switzerland

Ten days beginning second Thursday in July
Shaker Festival • South Union, Kentucky

Second Saturday in July
Highland Games, Brantford • Scottish-Canadians at Brantford, Ontario, Canada
Moxie Festival • Lisbon, Maine

Mid-July
Chugiak-Eagle River Bear Paw Festival • Chugiak and Eagle River, Alaska
Nembutsu Kyogen • Mushio Village, Hikari-machi, Sosa-gun, Chiba, Japan
Our Lady of Carmel (La Madonna del Carmine) • Chamorros people in Guam/Northern Marianas
Shaker Festival • Auburn, Kentucky
Watermelon Day • Iowa and Minnesota

Three days in mid-July
Holy Ghost, Festival of the • Roman Catholic Portuguese-Americans at Plymouth, Massachusetts
Windjammer Days • Boothbay Harbor, Maine

Three or four days in mid-July every third year during odd-numbered years
  Tabuleiros Festival (Festa dos Tabuleiros; Feast of the Holy Ghost) • Christians at Tomar, Ribatejo, Portugal

Four days in mid-July
  Jazz Festival, Pori International • Pori, Finland
  New Jersey Offshore Grand Prix (Benihana Grand Prix Power Boat Regatta) • Point Pleasant Beach, New Jersey
  Northern Games • Inuit people and Indians of Alaska, Yukon, Labrador and the Northwest territories at Inuvik area, Northwest Territories, Canada

Five or six Sunday concerts beginning mid-July
  Music Festival, Marblehead Summer • Marblehead, Massachusetts

Ten days in mid-July
  Peach Festival, South Carolina • Gaffney, South Carolina

Two weeks in mid-July
  Music Festival, Mendocino • Mendocino, California

Three weeks beginning mid-July
  Symphony Pops, San Francisco • San Francisco, California

Third week in July
  Alpenfest • Gaylord, Michigan
  Folk Music Festival Kaustinen • Kaustinen, Finland
  Golden Days • Fairbanks, Alaska

Three days during third week in July
  Bluegrass Festival, Winterhawk • Hillsdale, New York

Monday through Thursday during third full week in July
  Swan Upping • Thames River, from Blackfriars to London, England

Third weekend in July
  Mandaree Celebration • Arikara, Hidatsa, and Mandan Indians at Mandaree, North Dakota
  Music Festival, McCall Summer • McCall, Idaho
  Powwow, Standing Arrow • Kootenai Indians at Elmo, Montana

About the third weekend in July
  Dance, Green Corn • Kickapoo Indians near Horton, Kansas

Nine days (excluding Sunday and Monday) beginning third weekend in July
  Hill Cumorah Pageant • Mormons at Cumorah Hill, near Palmyra, New York

Third or fourth weekend in July
  Indian Rodeo and Stampede Days, All • Nevada and other Indians from Canada and the United States at Fallon, Nevada

Third Sunday in July
  Maidens' Fair on Mount Gaina (Tirgulde fete de pe muntele Gaina) • Mount Gaina, Transylvania, Romania
  Redeemer, Feast of the (Festa del Redentore) • Venice and Giudecca Island, Venetis, Italy

Third and fourth Mondays in July
  Monday on the Hill (Lunes del Cerro; Guelaguetza offering ritual) • Zapotec Indians at Oaxaca, Mexico

Third Saturday in July
  Mollyockett Day • Bethel, Maine

Third or fourth Saturday in July
  Dance, Hopi Niman • Hopi Indians in the United States

Last two weeks in July
  Cambridge Festival • Cambridge, England
  Minehead & Exmoor Festival • Minehead, Somerset, England

Fourth weekend in July
  Scottish Games, Virginia • Alexandria, Virginia

Fourth Monday in July
  Hurricane Supplication Day • Virgin Islands (also second or third Monday in October)

Fourth Saturday in July
  Cherokee of Hoke Intertribal Festival • Cherokee and Tuscarora Indians at Rockfish, North Carolina
  Egg Festival, Central Maine • Pittsfield, Maine

Late July
  Custer's Last Stand • Custer, South Dakota (during Gold Discovery Days)
  Native American Day • Penobscot Reservation near Old Town, Maine
  New Year's Day • northwest California Indians
  Pony Penning on Chincoteague Island • Chincoteague Island, Virginia
  Powwow, Little Beaver Rodeo and • Jicarilla Apache Indians at Dulce, New Mexico

Usually late July
  Powwow, Winnebago • Winnebago Indians at Winnebago, Nebraska

Six days in late July
  Dodge City Days • Dodge City, Kansas

One week in late July

Jazz Festival, Molde International (Jazzfestpillene i Molde)
• Molde, Norway

Music, Gamper Festival of Contemporary • Brunswick,
Maine

Ten days in late July

Music Festival, Cabrillo • Aptos, California

Ten days in late July during odd-numbered years

Bach Festival (Bachwoche Ansbach) • Ansbach, Federal
Republic of Germany

Last week in July

Dinosaur Days • Dinosaur National Monument near Grand
Junction, Colorado

Drama Festival, Burnie Youth • Burnie, Tasmania, Australia

Olsok (July 29) • Norway; Norwegian-Americans in the
United States

Potato Blossom Festival • O'Leary, Prince Edward Island,
Canada

Last full week in July

Cheyenne Frontier Days • Cheyenne, Wyoming

Oakley Festival, Annie • Greenville, Ohio

Last weekend in July

Black Ship Day • Rhode Island

Boat Rendezvous, Antique and Classic • Mystic Seaport
Museum, Mystic, Connecticut

Pages of History • Brebu, Prahova, Romania

Pilgrimage to St. Anne d'Auray • Auray, Brittany, France

Puye Cliff Ceremonial • Santa Ana Pueblo, New Mexico

Sunflower Festival • Mennonites at Manitoba, Canada

Last full weekend in July

Nordic Fest • Decorah, Iowa

Powwow, Mid-America All-American Indian Center •
Wichita, Kansas

Three days during last weekend in July

Jazz Festival, Bix Beiderbecke Memorial • Davenport,
Iowa

Last Sunday in July

Penitents, Procession of the (Boetprocessie van Veurne) •
Furnes, West Flanders, Belgium

Razboieni, Festival of • Razboieni, Neamt, Romania

Reek Sunday • Roman Catholics' pilgrimage to Croagh
Patrick Mountain in County Mayo, Ireland

Witches, Procession of the • Beselare, Belgium

July or August

Acadian Festivals • Acadian people in Maritime Provinces,
Canada (usually three to four days at the end of June)

Dance, Green Corn • Cayuga Indians at Miami, Oklahoma

Dance, Sun • Shoshone Indians in Wyoming

Kule Loklo Celebration • Pomo Indians at Kule Loklo Miwok
Indian Village, California

Three days in July or August

Horse Festival, Wild (Nomaoi Matsuri) • Honshu, Japan

Three days in late July or early August

Olympics, World Eskimo Indian • Fairbanks, Alaska

Four days in July or August

Ukrainian Festival, National • Ukrainian-Canadians and
Ukrainian-Americans at Dauphin, Manitoba, Canada

Ten days in late July or early August

Hot Air Balloon Championships, United States National •
Indianola, Iowa

Music Festival, Kuhmo Chamber (Kuhmon Kamarmusiikki)
• Kuhmo, Finland

Last week in July or first week in August

Icelandic Festival (Islendingadagurinn) • Icelandic-
Canadians at Gimli, Manitoba, Canada

Last weekend in July or first in August

Indian Days, All American • Sheridan, Wyoming

July-August

Anjou Festival • Angers, Maine-et-Loire, France

Arles Festival • Arles, Bouches-du-Rhone, France

Arts, International Festival of • Monte Carlo, Monaco

Bad Hersfeld in the Monastery Ruins, Festival of • Bad
Hersfeld, Hesse, Federal Republic of Germany

Bankside Globe Festival • London Borough of Southwark,
England

Binghamton Festival • Binghamton, New York

Bled Evenings (Bled na Gorenjskem) • Slovenia, Yugoslavia

Brady Day, Captain • Brady Lake, Ohio

Carnuntum Festival • Deutsch-Altenburg, Lower Austria,
Austria

Carthage, International Festival of • Carthage, North
Tunis Region, Tunisia

Castle Gottorf, Festival at • Schleswig, Schleswig-Holstein,
Federal Republic of Germany

Chateauvallon Festival • Toulon/Ollioules, Var, France

Comedy Festival at Porcia Castle • Spittal an der Drau,
Carinthia, Austria

Dance, Sun • Northern Ute Indians in Utah

A Day to Remember • Morrisburg, Ontario, Canada

Drama, Festival of Ancient • Philippi, Greece

Drama, Festival of Ancient • Thasos, Greece

El Karraka International Festival • La Goulette, North Tunis
Region, Tunisia

Ezzahra, Festival • Ezzahra, North Tunis Region, Tunisia

July-August *(cont.)*

Goombay Festival • Freeport, Grand Bahama Island, and Nassau, New Providence Island, Bahama Islands

Hammamet, International Festival of • Hammamet, Nabeul Region, Tunisia

Ilinden Days Festival • Bitola, Macedonia, Yugoslavia

Imechi Festival • Igbo people in Nigeria

Kipawo Showboat Company • Wolfville, Nova Scotia, Canada

La Meuse Festival • Dinant, Belgium

Lantern-Floating Festival • rural Japan (after harvest)

Lennoxville, Festival • Lennoxville, Quebec, Canada

Mahdia, Festival of • Mahdia, Mahdia Region, Tunisia

Marksmen's Festival (Schützenfeste) • Germany (date varies according to location)

May Festival • Bad Segeberg, Schleswig-Holstein, Federal Republic of Germany

Melk, Festival of (Melker Festspiele) • Melk, Lower Austria, Austria

Musical Theatre, Summer • Winnipeg, Manitoba, Canada

Music and Dance, Santander International Festival of (Festival Internacional de Musica y Danza de Santandar) • Santander, Spain

Music Festival, International • Gourdon-en-Quercy, Lot, France

Music Festival, Monte Carlo • Monte Carlo, Monaco

Music, Opera and Theatre, Durbuy Festival of • Durbuy, Belgium

Nights of the Enclave (Nuits de l'Enclave des Papes) • Valreas, Vaucluse, France

Olympus Festival • Katerini, Greece

Opera, Naples Open-Air Festival of Summer • Naples, Italy

Opera, Rome Open-Air Festival of Summer • Rome, Italy

Oxford Festival • Oxford, England

Play at Interlaken, Tell Pastoral • Interlaken, Bern, Switzerland

Regatta Week • Crowes, Isle of Wight, Great Britain

Rijeka Summer • Rijeka, Croatia, Yugoslavia

Santiago Fair and Festival of Setubal • Setubal, Portugal

South, Festival of the • Budva, Kotor, Tivat, and Hercegnovi, Montenegro, Yugoslavia

Stockerau Outdoor Festival (Stockerau Festspiele) • Stockerau, Lower Austria, Austria

Summer Festival • Kairouan, Kairouan Region, Tunisia

Summer Festival, Blyth • Blyth, Ontario, Canada

Summer Festival, Friesach • Friesach, Carinthia, Austria

Summer Festival, Grein (Sommerspiele Grein) • Grein im Strudengau, Upper Austria, Austria

Summer Festival, International • Ostend, Belgium

Summer Festival, Ohrid • Ohrid, Macedonia, Yugoslavia

Summer Festival, Split • Split, Croatia, Yugoslavia

Summergarden • New York, New York

Tabarka, Festival of • Tabarka, Jendouba Region, Tunisia

Theatre, Festival of Plays for the • Sarlat, Dordogne, France

Theatre and Music Festival, International • Wiltz, Luxembourg

Theatre Festival, Street (Strassentheater) • Salzburg, Austria

Theatre Festival in the Square • Sant'Arcangelo di Romagna, Emilia-Romagna, Italy

Theatre on Margaret Island, Open-Air • Budapest, Hungary

Theatre Review, Summer • Padova, Veneto, Italy

Vaison-la-Romaine and Carpentras, Festival of • Vaison-la-Romaine and Carpentras, Vauclude, France

Visby Festival • Visby, Gotland Island, Sweden

Vittoriale, Festival of • Gardone Riviera, Lombardy, Italy

World Renewal Ceremony • Yurok, Karok, Hupa, and Wiyot Indians in northwestern California

Odd-numbered years in July-August

Art, International Festival of Popular • Carthage, North Tunis Region, Tunisia

Four productions in late July to early August

Orange Festival (Chorégies d'Orange) • Orange, France

Sundays in July and August

Art and History, Festival of • Valencay, Indre, France

Five Sundays from mid-July to mid-August

Music Festival, Sevenars • Worthington, Massachusetts

Five Tuesday evenings from mid-July to August

Music, Mount Desert Festival of Chamber • Northeast Harbor, Maine

Wednesdays and Fridays in July and August

Music Festival, Ronne • Ronne, Bornholm, Denmark

Nine Thursday evenings in July and August

Bay Chamber Concerts • Rockport, Maine

Friday evenings in July and August

'Ksan Celebrations • 'Ksan Indians at Hazelton, British Columbia, Canada

Saturdays in July and August

Theatre Festival, Open-Air • Xanten/Birten, North Rhine-Westphalia, Federal Republic of Germany

Weekends from early July to mid-August

Castle Hill Festival • Ipswich, Massachusetts

Weekends from mid-July to mid-August

Mohawk Trail Concerts • Charlemont, Massachusetts

Five weekend concerts over July and August

Jazz Festival, Summer • Oakville, California

Twelve weekend concerts from mid-July to mid-August
Music Festival, Marlboro • Marlboro, Vermont

Three days in late July-early August
Maine Lobster or Seafoods Festival • Rockland, Maine

Five days in late July ending first Monday in August, Jamaican Independence Day
Jamaica Festival • Jamaica, especially Kingston, Montego Bay

Six days in July-August
Buffalo Days • Regina, Saskatchewan, Canada

Six days in late July and early August
Mozart Festival, San Luis Obispo • San Luis Obispo, California

One week in July-August
Folk Dance and Music, International Festival of (Rattviksdansen) • Rattvik, Sweden

Nine days in July-August
American West, Festival of • Utah State University, Logan, Utah

Two weeks in July-August
Musical Festival of La Sainte-Baume • Sainte-Baume, Var, France
Musical Weeks of Luberon (Semaines Musicales du Luberon) • Luberon and surrounding towns, Vauclude, France

16 days in July-August
Seafair • Seattle, Washington

Three weeks from mid-July to first week in August
Mozart Festival, Vermont • Burlington, Vermont

Three weeks from end of July to mid-August
Music Festival, Cape and Islands Chamber • Yarmouth Port, Massachusetts

Three and one-half weeks in July-August
Avignon Festival (Festival d'Avignon) • Avignon, France

25 days in July-August
Opera Festival, Munich (Münchner Opernfestspiele) • Munich, Bavaria, Federal Republic of Germany

Four weeks in July-August
Bregenz Festival (Bregenzer Festspiele) • Bregenz, Vorarlberg, Austria

One month in July-August
Andersen Festival, Hans Christian • Odense, Denmark

Summer Meetings, International • Villeneuve-lez-Avignon, Gard, France

Five weeks in July and August
Music Festival, Yellow Barn • Putney, Vermont
Salzburg Festival (Salzburger Festspiele) • Salzburg, Austria

Five weeks from first week in July to mid-August
Summer Festival, Central City • Central City, Colorado

Five weeks in late July and August
Bayreuth Festival (Bayreuther Festspiele and Richard Wagner Festival) • Bayreuth, Bavaria, Federal Republic of Germany

Six weeks in July-August
East Var, Festival of • Montauroux and surrounding towns in Var, France

Six weeks from mid-July to last week in August
Opera Festival, Lake George • Glen Falls, New York

45 days in July-August
Arts and Pageant of the Masters, Festival of the • Laguna Beach, California

Seven weeks in July and August
Music Festival, Santa Fe Chamber • Santa Fe, New Mexico

Seven weeks from second week in July to third week in August
Dubrovnik Festival (Dubrovacke Ljetne Igre) • Dubrovnik, Croatia, Yugoslavia

Seven weeks from mid-July to end of August
Music Festival, Monadnock • Peterborough, New Hampshire

Seven weeks from mid-July to last week in August
Mozart Festival, Mostly • New York, New York

Eight weeks in July and August
Music Festival, Orford International • Magog, Quebec, Canada

Eight weeks from early July to mid-August
Music under the Stars • Milwaukee, Wisconsin

Early July-early August
Dog Days • ancient Rome

Early July to last week in August
Music Festival, Grand Teton • Teton Village, Wyoming

First week in July to second week in August
Baths of Caracalla (Terme di Caracalla) • Rome, Italy

Mid-July to early August
Bach Festival, Carmel • Carmel, California

Mid-July to mid-August
Baalbek Festival • Baalbek, Lebanon
Music Festival, Bar Harbor • Bar Harbor, Maine
Tirolese Summer • Innsbruck, Tirol, Austria

Third week in July to third week in August
Summer Festival, Szeged • Szeged, Hungary

Last two weeks in July and first week in August
Song of Hiawatha Pageant • Dakota Indians at Pipestone,
Minnesota

Last week in July and first week in August
Pacific Northwest Festival • Seattle, Washington
Theatre Festival, Brownsea Open Air • Poole, Dorset,
England

Last week in July to second week in August
Music from Bear Valley • Bear Valley, California

Last weekend in July through August
Burro Races, Triple Crown Pack • Fairplay, Leadville,
and Buena Vista, Colorado

Eight weeks in July-August or September
Opera Festival, Santa Fe • Santa Fe, New Mexico

July-September
Marble and Sound • Arandjelovac, Serbia, Yugoslavia
Music Festival, Berkshire • Tanglewood, Lenox,
Massachusetts
Opera and Ballet Festival • Verona, Veneto, Italy
Theatre Federation One-Act Play Festival, New Zealand •
various locations within New Zealand
Theatre Festival • Taormina, Sicily, Italy

Sunday afternoons from July to early September
Maverick Sunday Concerts • Woodstock, New York

Four weekends from mid-July to early September
Music Festival, Shenandoah Valley • Orkney Springs,
Virginia

Eight weeks from early July to first week in September
Operetta Weeks (Operettenwochen) • Bad Ischl, Upper
Austria, Austria

Nine weeks from mid-July to mid-September
Wood Promenade Concerts, Henry • Royal Albert Hall,
London, England

Eleven weeks from first week in July to late September
Summer Series, Hollywood Bowl • Hollywood, California

Second week in July to first week in September
Opera Festival, Verona (Arena di Verona) • Verona,
Veneto, Italy

Mid-July to mid-September
Paris Festival Estival (Festival Estival de Paris) • Paris,
France

August

August
Battle of the Moors and Christians • Onteniente,
Valencia, Spain
Carnea • Cyrene, Magna Græcia, Peloponnesus, and
Sparta, Greece (Greek month of Carneus)
Castelo de Vide, National Festival of • Castelo de Vide,
Portalegre, Portugal
Craigmillar Festival • Craigmillar, Edinburgh, Scotland
(or June)
Dance, Waraku • near Waraku Pond, Nikko, Tochigi, Japan
Darwin Youth Festival • Darwin, Northern Territory,
Australia (during school holidays)
Discovery Days • Dawson City, Yukon, Canada
Drama Festivals, Academy • Srinigar, Jammu and
Kashmir, India
Eyo Masquerade • Lagos, Nigeria
Famalicao, International Festival of • Famalicao, Porto,
Portugal
Festidanza • Arequipa, Peru
Folk Festival • Arequipa, Peru
Folklore, Gouveia International Festival of • Gouveia,
Viseu, Portugal
Folklore Festival, Briteiros • Briteiros, Braga, Portugal
Folklore Festival of St. Martha of Portozelo, International
• Portozelo, Viana do Castelo, Portugal
Gondomar, International Festival of • Gondomar, Porto,
Portugal
Hippokrateia • Kos, Greece
Hooting at Hunger (Homowo) • Ga people in Ghana
Indian Day • Pomo Indians at Cotati, California
Indian Days, Fort Hall • Bannock Shoshone Indians at
Fort Hall, Idaho
Indian Fair • Shoshone Indians in Wyoming
Lady of Neves, Festival of the • Neves, Viana do Castelo,
Portugal
Lake Festival (Seespiele) • Morbisch am See, Burgenland,
Austria
Meadela, International Festival of • Meadela, Viana do
Castelo, Portugal
Music, Festival of Contemporary • Lenox, Massachusetts
Mystery of San Guillen and Santa Felicia • Obanos,
Navarra, Spain
New Yam Festival (Onwasato) • Ibo people in Nigeria
Nisei Week • Japanese-Americans at Little Tokyo, Los
Angeles, California

August *(cont.)*

Offering Ceremony • Tegal, Central Java, Java

Our Lady of the Angels • pilgrimage to basilica in Cartago, Costa Rica

Peach Festival • Havasupai Indians at Supai, Arizona

Pennsylvania Dutch Days • Hershey, Pennsylvania

Pilgrimage to Chalma • Christians at Chalma, Mexico (also held during first week in January, in February, September, and March-April, during Holy Week)

Powwow, Kihekah Steh Club Annual • Skiatook, Oklahoma

Powwow, Looking Glass • Nez Perce Indians at Kamiah, Idaho

Powwow, Narragansett • Narragansett Indians at Charlestown, Rhode Island

Powwow, Northern Arapaho • Arapaho, Wyoming

Powwow, Ottawa • Quapaw, Oklahoma (also one in September)

Powwow Days, Rosebud • Sioux Indians at Rosebud, South Dakota

Remembrance of the Departed Days • Shahenshai sect of Parsis

Rosebud Tribal Fair • Sioux Indians at Rosebud, South Dakota

St. Barbara's Festival • Miranda do Douro, Braganca, Portugal

St. Bartholomew's Festival • Oporto, Porto, Portugal

St. Lawrence of Rome, Feast of (Festival of San Lorenzo) • Foz, Lugo, Spain

St. Roch's Day (San Roque Festival) • Betanzos, La Coruna, Spain, and Llanes, Oviedo, Spain

Salt Water Day • New Jersey

San Ermengol Retaule Festival • Seo de Urgel, Lerida, Spain

San Felix Martyr, Feast of • Villafranca del Panades, Barcelona, Spain

Savaria Festival • Szombathely, Hungary

Shaker Festival • Old Chatham, New York

Spa, Festival of • Spa, Belgium

Tartans, Festival of the • New Glasgow, Nova Scotia, Canada

Thanksgiving (Waratambar) • Christians in Papua New Guinea (dates vary according to province)

Theatre Summer, Tampere • Tampere, Finland

Troy at Hisarlik, Festival of • Canakkale, Turkey

Vila Praia de Ancora, International Festival of • Vila Praia de Ancora, Viana do Castelo, Portugal

Washing the Hands (Issa Aka) • Ibo people in Nigeria (may also be held during yam festivals in September or October)

Probably August

Nemean Games • valley of Nemea, ancient Greece

Usually in August

Powwow, Sioux • Sioux Indians in South Dakota

Month of August

Folklore Festival, National • Mamaia, Efore, and Sinala, Constanta County and the Black Sea Coast, Romania

Music Festival, Menton (Festival de Musique de Menton) • Menton, France

August 1

Army Day, Peking • Peking, China

Confederation Day • Switzerland

Emancipation Day • Trinidad and Tobago

Honey Day • Christians in Russia

Independence Day • Benin

Lammas

Lúgnasad (First Fruits Festival)

Progress of the Precious and Vivifying Cross, Feast of the • Macedonia

Quarter Days • Scotland (also November 11, February 2, and May 15)

St. Peter's Chains, Feast of • Roman Catholic

Wattle Day • Australia (or September 1)

Usually August 1

Ceremonial Day • Passamaquoddy Indians between Perry and Eastport, Maine

On or near August 1

Doggett's Coat and Badge Race • Thames River, England

On or near August 1 into September

Highland Games • Scotland

August 2

Dances, Old Pecos Bull and Corn • Jemez Pueblo, New Mexico

Farmers' Day • Zambia (formerly Northern Rhodesia)

Freedom Day • Guyana

St. Elias Day • Macedonia

St. Francis of Assisi (Feast of Forgiveness) • Arroyo Hondo, New Mexico and southern Colorado

August 2-7

Nebuta Matsuri • Aomori, Japan

August 3

Independence Day • Niger

August 4

St. Dominic, Feast of • Christian

St. Dominic, Feast of, and Corn Dance • Jemez and Santo Domingo pueblos, New Mexico

Santo Domingo Promenade • Lima, Peru

Begins August 4

Peer Gynt Festival Days • Norway

August 5
Clipping the Church Day • Guiseley, Yorkshire, England
Grotto Day • London, England
Independence Day • Upper Volta

Saturday nearest St. Oswald's Day, August 5
Rush-Bearing Day • Grasmere, England

August 5-6
Transfiguration, Feast of the (Del Mundo Festival or Fiesta Agostinas) • El Salvador

August 5-10
Symbolic Relay Run • New Mexico pueblos

August 5-15, ending on the Feast of the Assumption
Acadian Festival • Acadian people at Caraquet, New Brunswick, Canada

August 6
Hiroshima Day
Peace Festival • Peace Memorial Park in Hiroshima, Japan
Transfiguration, Feast of the • Christian

August 6, two-day festival
Independence Day • Bolivia

August 6-8
Double Seventh (Festival of the Weaving Maid and the Herd Boy or Tanabata Matsuri, the Weaver Princess Festival; also known as Star Festival) • Sendai, Japan

Begins August 6 and lasts nine days
Assumption, Feast of the • Greek Orthodox

August 9
Memorial Day • Nagasaki, Japan
National Day • Singapore
St. Matthias, Feast of • Eastern Orthodox

August 10
Admission Day • Missouri
Borglum Day, Gutzon • Mount Rushmore, South Dakota
Dance Festival, Kala Vikash Kendra • Cuttack, Orissa, India (also during three days in October-November)
Independence Day • Ecuador
St. Lawrence of Rome, Feast Day of • Christian

Saturday nearest August 10, Feast of St. Lawrence
Cooks' Festival (Fête de Cuisinieres) • Roman Catholics at Pointe-a-Pitre, Guadeloupe

August 10-12
Puck's Fair • Killorglin, County Kerry, Ireland

August 11
Night of the Shooting Stars (The Perseids Meteor Shower) • observers everywhere but at the South Pole
St. Clare of Assisi, Feast of • Christian

Two-day holiday, including August 11
Heroes Days • Zimbabwe (formerly Southern Rhodesia)

August 12
Glorious Twelfth (opening of grouse-hunting season) • Scotland and Scots elsewhere
Native American Day • Massachusetts
Queen's Birthday • Thailand
St. Clare of Assisi, Feast of, with Corn, Harvest, Comanche or Buffalo dances (August 11) • Santa Clara Pueblo, New Mexico

August 13
Khordad Sal • Shahenshai sect of Parsis in India and elsewhere
Nemoralia (Festival of Diana Jana) • Nemi (now a village in Italy)
Stone Day, Lucy • many organizations, including the Lucy Stone League in New York
Women's Day • Tunisia

August 14
Bud Billiken Day • Chicago, Illinois (observed second Saturday in August)
Independence Day • Pakistan
Liberty Tree Day • Massachusetts
Torta dei Fieschi • Lavagna, Genoa, Italy
V-J Day
V-J Day (World War II Memorial Day) • Arkansas

August 14-15
Assumption, Feast of the (Mystery Play of Elche, El Misterio de Elche) • Elche, Valencia, Spain

August 15
Assumption, Feast of the, Christian (Gregorian calendar; August 28, Julian calendar)
Dead, Festival of the (Toro Nagashi, Floating Lantern Ceremony) • Buddhists at Honolulu, Hawaii
Dozynki (Pod Debami) Festival (Okrezne; Harvest Festival) • Poland
Foundation of Panama • Panama City, Panama
Independence Day • Republic of Congo
Independence Day • India
Liberation Day • Republic of Korea
Mother's Day • Costa Rica
Our Lady of Czestochowa, Feast of (Feast of the Black Madonna of Jasna Gora) • Jasna Gora monastery, Czestochowa, Poland
Our Lady of Flowers, Harvest Festival for • Polish-Americans in Orange County, New York

August 15 *(cont.)*
Prince's Birthday • Liechtenstein
Republic Day • Republic of Korea
St. Anthony of Padua, Feast of • Laguna Pueblo, New Mexico
Tismana Garden Festival • Tismana, Gorj, Romania

Three days, including Congo Independence Day, August 15
Three Glorious Days • Republic of Congo

Two weeks, including August 15
Assumption, Feast of the • Messina, Sicily

August 15 and Sunday nearest August 15
Assumption, Feast of the (Tintamarre celebration) • Acadian people in the Maritime Provinces, Canada

Sunday nearest August 15
Assumption, Feast of the (Blessing of the Grapes, Haghoghy Ortnovtyoon or Navasard Armenian Grape Festival) • Armenia

Sunday following August 15
Our Lady of Bildchen, Procession to (Muttergottes-prozessio'n Op d'Bildchen) • Vianden, Luxembourg
Running of the Bulls • Aztecs and Christians at Huamantla, Mexico

August 15-18
Dance, Fools' (Awa Odori) • Japan

August 16
Bennington Battle Day • Bennington, Vermont
Madonna del Voto Day • Siena, Italy
Palio, Festival of the (Festa del Palio; also known as Corso del Palio or Palio of the Contrade) • Siena, Tuscany, Italy (also on July 2)
Political Restitution Day • Dominican Republic
St. Roch's Day (San Rocco) • Florence and Realmonte, Italy

August 16 every three years
Neri-Kuyo • Buddhists at Joshinji Temple, Tokyo, Japan

Week including August 16
Elvis International Tribute Week • Graceland, Memphis, Tennessee

August 17
Independence Day • Gabon
Independence Day • Indonesia
Red Bird Smith Ceremony • Red Bird Smith Ceremonial Grounds near Vian, Oklahoma
San Martín Day • Argentina

Monday nearest August 17
Klondike Gold Discovery Day • Yukon

August 18
St. Helena's Day • Christian

August 18-20 or third weekend in August
Seattle Days • Suquamish Indians at Suquamish, Washington

August 19
National Aviation Day • United States
Transfiguration, Feast of the • Eastern Orthodox (Julian calendar; August 6, Gregorian calendar)
Transfiguration, Feast of the (Buhé) • Ethiopian Church in Ethiopia

August 20
Constitution Day • Hungary
Floral Carnival, National • Debrecen, Hungary
St. Philibert's Day • Christian
St. Stephen's Day • Hungary and the United States

August 21
Consualia • ancient Rome (and December 15)
Cuauhtemoc, Homage to (Homenaje a Cuauhtemoc) • Mexico City, Mexico

August 22
America's Cup • Newport, Rhode Island (whenever a challenger comes forth, usually every three to four years)
Queenship of Mary • Roman Catholic

August 23
Liberation Day • Romania
St. Rose of Lima, Feast of • Christian
Volcanalia • ancient Rome

August 23-25
Shepherds' Race (Schäferlauf) • Markgrönigen, Swabia, Germany

August 24
Bartholomew Fair • Smithfield, London, England
Flag Day • Liberia
Folklore Festival, Arad • Moneasa, Arad, Romania
St. Bartholomew's Day • Christian

On or near St. Bartholomew's Day, August 24
Waygoose Feast (Beanfest, or Beano in England; Fastnachtsschmaus, Lichtschmaus, or Martinschmaus) • printers in England, Germany, and the United States

Sunday of or after August 24
Keaw Yed Wakes Festival • Westhoughton, Lancashire, England

18 days beginning August 24
Helsinki Festival (Helsingin Juhlaviikot) • Helsinki, Finland

Monday before Assumption, August 25
Kalojan or Caloian Ceremony (Kalos Johannes or Kalos Adonis) • Romania

August 25
Constitution Day • Paraguay
Independence Day • Uruguay
Liberation Day • France
Opiconsivia • ancient Rome

August 26
Anthony Day, Susan B. • United States (or February 15)
Woman's Equality Day • United States

August 27
Johnson's Birthday, Lyndon B. • Texas

August 28
Assumption, Feast of the • Christian (Julian calendar; August 15, Gregorian calendar)
St. Augustine of Hippo, Feast Day of • Christian
Spanish and Indian Fiestas • Isleta Pueblo, New Mexico

August 29
St. John the Baptist's Day (Martyrdom of St. John) • Eastern Orthodox and Roman Catholic

August 30
Long Day, Huey P. • Louisiana
St. Fiacre's Day • Roman Catholic
St. Rose of Lima Day • Peru

August 31
Independence Day • Trinidad and Tobago
Independence Day (Merdeka) • Kuala Lumpur, Selangor, Malaysia

Thursdays, Saturdays, and Sundays in August
Art and History, Festival of • Saint-Aignan, Loir-et-Cher, France

Every Friday in August
Pilgrim Progress Pageant • up Leyden Street to the Fort-Meetinghouse on Main Street, now the church of the Pilgrimage on Burial Hill in Plymouth, Massachusetts

Three times per week in August
Play, Spiez Castle • Spiez, Bern, Switzerland

One day in August
Green Bean Festival • Iroquois Indians

First full moon in August
Dance of Thanksgiving (Whe'wahchee) • Omaha Indians at the Omaha Reservation in Nebraska

Two days in August
Pony Express Ride • Pennsylvania
New Yam Festival • Yoruba people at Ondo's shrine in Pobe, Benin, Nigeria

One weekend in August
Dodonea Festival • Ioannina, Greece
Jazz Festival, Concord • Concord, California

Three days in August
Air Show, International • Abbotsford, British Columbia, Canada
Begonia Festival • Lochristi, Belgium
Hobo Convention • Britt, Iowa
Our Lady of Agony, Festival of • Viana do Castelo, Portugal

Four days in August
Belgian-American Days • Belgian-Americans at Ghent, Minnesota
Folklore Festival, International • Mechelen, Belgium
Theatre Summer, Amateur • Seinajoki, Finland

Four nights in August
Reggae Sunsplash • Montego Bay, Jamaica

Five days during full moon in August
Old Spanish Days • Santa Barbara, California

Six days in August
Horse Show, Dublin • Dublin, County Dublin, Ireland
Soap Box Derby, All American • Akron, Ohio

One week in August
Confolens Festival • Confolens, Charente, France
Folklore, Central American Congress of (Congreso Centroamericano de Folclorologia Nicoya) • Costa Rica
Folkloric Festival of Rouergue, International • Rouergue, Aveyron, France
Play Festival, Act Five • Canberra, Australian Capital Territory, Australia
Vizela Festival • Caldas de Vizela, Braga, Portugal

About one week in August
Folklore Festival, International • Oloron-Sainte-Marie, Lot-et-Garonne, France
Hede Festival • Hede, Ille-et-Vilaine, France

Eight days in August
Folklore Festival, Billingham International • Billingham, Cleveland, England
Pajjusana • Jaina religion

736

Nine days in August
Jerash Festival • Jerash, Jordan

Ten days in August
Tennessee Walking Horse National Celebration • Shelby-ville, Tennessee

Ten days in August during odd-numbered years
Outback Festival • Winton, Queensland, Australia

16-day fast in August
Assumption, Feast of the • Ethiopia

16 days in August every 25 years
Wine Growers' Festival (Fête des Vignerons) • Vevey, Vaud, Switzerland

Three weeks in August
Menuhin Festival • Gstaad-Saanen, Switzerland
New York Philharmonic Free Outdoor Park Concerts • New York, New York

Two days in early August
Abbey Fair • Bethlehem, Connecticut

Three days in early August
Pjodhatid • Vestmannaeyjar, Iceland

Three to four days in early August
Polka Festival, International • Hunter Mountain, Hunter, New York

Four days in early August
Folk Art Festival: Pampaphia • Paphos, Cyprus

Five days in early August
Bluegrass and Old-Time Music Festival, Grant's Annual • Hugo, Oklahoma

Nine days in early August
Nations, Festival of • Red Lodge, Montana

Ten days at beginning of August
Lorient Festival • Gaelic people at Lorient, Morbihan, France

First week in August
Folklore Festival, "Hercules" • Baile Herculane, Caras Severin, Romania

Begins first week in August
Tortola Festival • Tortola, British Virgin Islands

Four days during first week in August
Folklife Festival, Texas • HemisFair grounds of the Institute of Texan Cultures, San Antonio, Texas

First full week in August
Eisteddfod of Wales, Royal National (Eisteddfod Genedlaethol Frenhinol Cymru) • alternates between North and South Wales each year
Gaelic Mod • Scottish-Canadians at St. Ann's, Cape Breton, Nova Scotia, Canada
Music Festival, W.C. Handy • Muscle Shoals area, Alabama

First weekend in August
Cherokee Days of Recognition • Cherokee Indians at Cleveland, Tennessee
Czech Festival • Czech-Americans at Wilber, Nebraska
Gift of the Waters Pageant • Thermopolis, Wyoming
Navajo Trails Fiesta • Durango, Colorado
Powwow, Land of the Menominee • Menominee Indians at Woodland Bowl, Keshena, Wisconsin

Usually first weekend in August
Indian Days, Rocky Boy • Chippewa and Cree Indians at Box Elder, Montana

First full weekend in August
Seventy-Six, Days of • Deadwood, South Dakota

First two weeks in August
Harrogate International Festival • Harrogate, England

First two weekends in August
Hellbrunn Festival (Fest in Hellbrunn) • Salzburg, Austria

One week ending first Sunday in August, Navy Day
Sea Celebrations • Constanta and resorts on the seashore, Romania

First Sunday in August
Asturias Day • Gijon, Oviedo, Spain
Cromm Dub's Sunday • Mount Callen, County Clare, Ireland
Equestrian Tournament of the Quintain • Ascoli Piceno, Marches, Italy
Sinj Iron-Ring Chivalric Tournament • Sinj, Croatia, Yugoslavia

Four days beginning first Sunday in August
St. Walter, Festivals of (Festas Gualterianas) • Guimarães, Minho, Portugal

One week ending the first Monday in August
Caribana • West Indians at Toronto, Ontario, Canada

Saturday before the first Monday in August
Highland Games, Glengarry • Maxville, Ontario, Canada

First Monday in August
Admission Day (August 1) • Colorado
Emancipation Day • Bahama Islands

First Monday in August *(cont.)*
Independence Day (August 2) • Jamaica
Nut Monday • Great Britain
Picnic Day • Northern Territory, Australia
St. Lubbock's Day • England
Youth Day • Zambia (or March 13)

First Monday in August through following Sunday
Motor Classic, Black Hills • Sturgis, South Dakota

Six days beginning first Tuesday in August
Craftsmen's Fair • Mount Sunapee State Park, Newbury, New Hampshire

First Thursday, Friday, and Saturday in August
Dance and Folk Festival, Asheville Mountain • Asheville, North Carolina

First Saturday in August
Hambletonian Harness Racing Classic • East Rutherford, New Jersey

Second week in August
Burry Man's Walk • South Queensferry, Scotland
Rendezvous Days • Ojibwa Indians at Grand Portage, Minnesota
Stampede Days • Colville Indians at Omak, Washington

Four days during second week in August
Fiddler's Convention, Old • Galax, Virginia

Second weekend in August
Jour de Fête a Sainte Genevieve Days of Celebration • French-, German-, and Spanish-Americans at Ste. Genevieve, Missouri
Little Shell Celebration • New Town, North Dakota
Powwow, Mesquakie Celebration • Mesquakie Algonquian Indians at Tama, Iowa (Thursday-Sunday)
Powwow, Nesika Illahee • Siletz Indian tribes at Siletz, Oregon

Second Sunday in August
Dance Festival, Hora at Prislop (Prislop Round) • Mount Prislop, Borsa, Maramures County, Romania
Mount Ceahlau Feast • Durau, Romania

Second Monday in August
Victory Day • Rhode Island

Six days beginning second Monday of August
Indian Exposition, American • Southern Cheyenne and other Indians at Anadarko, Oklahoma

Second Tuesday in August
Fox Hill Day • Nassau, New Providence Island, Bahama Islands

Second Thursday in August
Baby Parade • Ocean City, New Jersey
Bat Flight Breakfast • Carlsbad Caverns, New Mexico
Battle of Flowers • St. Helier, Jersey, Channel Islands, Great Britain

Second Friday and Saturday in August
Folk Festival, Goschenhoppen Historians' • Pennsylvania Dutch people at Goschenhoppen Park, East Greenville, Pennsylvania

Second Saturday in August
Big Sea Day • New Jersey
Bud Billiken Day (August 14) • Chicago, Illinois
Highland Games, Fergus • Fergus, Ontario, Canada

Mid-August
Dragon, Spearing the (Drachenstich) • Fürth, Germany
Indian Ceremonial, Intertribal • Gallup, New Mexico
Plays, Oni-Mai • Sosa, Chiba, Japan
Powwow, Ojibwa • Ojibwa Indians at Mille Lacs Reservation, Onamia, Minnesota

One day in mid-August
Flower Festival, Bikfaya • Bikfaya, Lebanon

Two days in mid-August
Poetry Festival • Bisbee, Arizona

Three days in mid-August
Jazz Festival, JVC • Newport, Rhode Island
Jazz Festival, Telluride • Telluride, Colorado
Rodeo, Payson • Payson, Arizona

At least six days in mid-August
Crow Fair • Crow Indians, northwest Canadian Indians, Plains States Indians, Inca Peruvian Indians, and Alaskan Eskimos at Crow Agency near Hardin, Montana

One week in mid-August
Folklorama • Winnipeg, Manitoba, Canada

Seven to ten days in mid-August
Three Choirs Festival • Gloucester, Hereford, and Worcester, England (location alternates)

Two weekends in mid-August
Music Festival, Telluride Chamber • Telluride, Colorado

Two weeks in mid-August
Music Festival, Peninsula • Fish Creek, Wisconsin

Second half of August
Harvest Festival • Daruvar, Croatia, Yugoslavia

Third week in August
Bonneville Speed Week • Bonneville Salt Flats, Utah

Three weeks beginning third week in August
Edinburgh International Festival • Edinburgh, Scotland

Third weekend in August
Indian Market • Southwestern Indians, including Hopi, Navajo, and Zuni Indians at Santa Fe Plaza, Santa Fe, New Mexico
Ni-Mi-Win Celebration • Ojibwa Indians at Duluth, Minnesota
Twin Buttes Celebration • Twin Buttes, North Dakota

Third Sunday in August
Mohegan Homecoming • Mohegan Indians at Norwich, Connecticut

Third and fourth Sundays in August every seven years
Assumption, Feast of the (Festival of Virga Jesse) • Hasselt, Limburg, Belgium

Third or fourth Monday in August
Marymass Fair • Irvine, Ayrshire, Scotland

Third Thursday in August
Grasmere Sports • Lake District, England

Third Friday in August
Admission Day (August 21) • Hawaii

Fourth weekend in August
Duck Race, Great American • Deming, New Mexico
Marriage of Goliath (Les Vêpres de Gouyasse) • Ath, Hainaut, Belgium

Fourth Sunday in August
First Fruits of the Alps Sunday (Les Prémices des Alpes) • Vissoie, Val d'Anniviers, Valais, Switzerland

Fourth Monday in August
Martinmas • Hoorn, Netherlands

Late August
Independence Day (Jeshn) • Afghanistan (May 27)
Lemoore Celebration • Tuchi Yokuts Indians near Porterville, California
Little League World Series • Williamsport, Pennsylvania
Rice Celebration, Wild (Manomin) • Bad River Ojibwa Indians at Odanah, Wisconsin (usually weekend before Labor Day, first Monday in September)

Five days in late August
Folk Festival, Letterkenny International • Letterkenny, County Donegal, Ireland

Six weeks beginning in late August
Music Festival, Montreux-Vevey (Festival de Musique Montreux-Vevey) • Montreux and Vevey, Vaud, Switzerland

Last full week in August
Arts Week, Creative • Gimli, Manitoba, Canada

Last two weeks in August
Music Festival, Idyllwild • Idyllwild, California

Last weekend in August
Harvest Festival of Provins, France • Provins, France
Romanian "Calus" • Slatina, Olt, Romania
Stiftungsfest • German-Americans at Young America, Minnesota

Three days over last weekend in August
Folk Festival, Philadelphia • Philadelphia/Schwenksville, Pennsylvania

Eleven days through last Sunday in August
Iowa State Fair • Des Moines, Iowa

Last Sunday in August
Christ the King, Feast of • Protestant
Pilgrimage at Cercio to Santa Barbara • Roman Catholics from Cercio to Santa Barbara, Portugal
Plague Sunday • Eyam, Derbyshire, England
Redeemer, Feast of the (Festa del Redentore) • Nuoro, Sardinia, Italy

Two weeks beginning last Sunday in August
Shepherd's Fair (Schueberfo'er) • Luxembourg

Last Monday in August
Bank Holiday • England, Ireland, and Wales

Last Tuesday in August
Lammas Fair Day • Ballycastle, Ireland

Four days beginning last Thursday in August
Blessed Sacrament, Feast of • Christian Madeiran-Americans at New Bedford, Massachusetts

Last Saturday in August
African Methodist Quarterly Meeting Day • African Union Methodist Church, Wilmington, Delaware

End of August
Dragacevo Assembly of Village Trumpeters • Guca, Serbia, Yugoslavia
Rovinj Festival • Rovinj, Croatia, Yugoslavia

Sunday before Donnybrook Fair begins at the end of August
Walking Sunday • Ireland

August or September
  Avani Mulam • Hindus in Madura, India
  Powwow, Ojibwa • Ojibwa Indians at Red Cliff Indian
    Reservation near Bayfield, Wisconsin

Two days in August or September
  Algarve, National Festival of the • Vila Moura, Faro,
    Portugal

Five days in late August or early September
  Jazz Festival, Chicago • Chicago, Illinois

Late August or September
  Pilgrimage to Moulay Idriss • Moulay Idriss, Morocco

Late August or early September
  Harvest Celebration (Obzinky; Posviceni) • Czechoslovakia

August-September
  Agwunsi Festival • Igbo people in Nigeria
  Arts, Shiraz Festival of • Shiraz (formerly Persepolis), Iran
  Edinburgh Fringe Festival • Edinburgh, Scotland (coincides
    with Edinburgh International Festival)
  Eisteddfod Society Festival • Devonport, Tasmania,
    Australia
  Freeing the Insects Festival • Japan
  Golden Orange Festival • Antalya, Turkey
  Harvest Festival (Onam) • Kerala, India (four to ten days
    in Malyalam month of Chingam)
  Izmir International Fair • Izmir, Turkey
  Nanda Deven • Hindus in the Kumaon region of India
  New Yam Festival (Iri ji Ohuru) • Igbo people in Nigeria
  Police Week Festival • St. John's, Antigua
  Prachum Ben • Cambodia (12th day of waning moon
    of Photrobot)
  Renaissance Festival, Michigan • Holly, Michigan

Even-numbered years during weekends in August-September
  Konigsfelden Festival • Brugg/Windisch, Aargau,
    Switzerland
  Play at Altdorf, Tell • Altdorf, Uri, Switzerland

Every other year in August-September
  Dance, Hopi Snake • Hopi Indians in Arizona

Every four years in August-September
  Theatre, World Festival of Amateur • Monte Carlo,
    Monaco

Some Saturday and Sunday concerts in August and September
  South Mountain Concerts • Pittsfield, Massachusetts

Two consecutive weekends in August-September
  Plays, Wagga Wagga School of Arts Annual Festival of •
    Wagga Wagga, New South Wales, Australia

Three days in August-September
  Dance Festival, Kuchipudi • Kuchipudi, Andhra Pradesh,
    India

Six days in August-September
  Rose of Tralee International Festival • Tralee, County
    Kerry, Ireland

One week from late August through Labor Day, first Monday in September
  Flemington Fair • Flemington, New Jersey

One week in late August-early September
  Reed Dance (Umhlanga) • Swaziland

Three weeks in August and September
  Canadian National Exhibition • Toronto, Ontario, Canada

Three weeks from mid-August into September
  Lincoln Center Out-of-Doors Festival • New York, New York

One month during August-September
  Rasa Leela Festival • Manipur and Uttar Pradesh, India
    (during Janmashtami, Krishna's birthday celebration)

Mid-August to mid-September
  Music, Lucerne International Festival of (Luzern Inter-
    nationale Musikfestwochen) • Lucerne, Switzerland

Late August to late September
  Musical Weeks, Stresa (Settimane Musicali di Stresa
    Festival Internazionale) • Stresa, Italy

End of August-beginning of September
  September in the Town • Casertavecchia, Caserta,
    Compania, Italy

August-October
  Drama Festival, New South Wales • New South Wales,
    Australia

One week usually between August and November
  Puppet Festival of Venezuela, National • Venezuela

September

September
  Arts, Salisbury Festival of the • Salisbury, Wiltshire,
    England
  Battle of the Moors and Christians • Caudete, Albacete,
    and Villena, Alicante, Spain
  Bodrum Festival • Bodrum, Turkey
  Dijon Festival • Dijon, Cote-d'Or, France
  Dividing of the Cheese (Käseteilet) • Justis Valley area,
    Switzerland

September *(cont.)*

Gathering of the Fruits • Albania

Killing the Pigs, Festival of (Seatapmise Päev) • Estonia

Maiorga, International Festival of • Figueira da Foz, Coimbra, Portugal

Marriage Fair • Ait Hadiddou Berber people at Imilchil, Morocco

Mountain Pasture, Return from (Almabtrieb) • German Alps

Native American Day • New York

New Yam Festival (Odwira) • Ewe people in Ghana

Okpesi or Itensi Festival • Igbo people in Nigeria

Opera, International Festival of Light • Waterford, County Waterford, Ireland

Our Lady of Mercy, Festival of • Barcelona, Spain

Pilgrimage of Castelejo • Christians at Castelejo, Castelo Branco, Portugal

Pilgrimage of the Black Madonna • Einseideln, Switzerland

Pilgrimage to Chalma • Christians at Chalma, Mexico (also in February, August, first week in January and during Holy Week)

Pilgrimage to Our Lady of Nazo • Povoa, Braganca, Portugal

Powwow, Ottawa • Quapaw, Oklahoma (and in August)

Powwow, Yakima • Yakima Indians at Yakima Reservation, Washington

Santo Cristo and San Vicente Ferrer, Festival of • Graus, Huesca, Spain

Seminole Nation Days • Seminole Indians at Seminole, Oklahoma

Shrine Kagura Festival, Ise • Ise, Mie, Japan (and April)

Situa • Inca people in Peru

Teatro Custombrista, Regional and National Festivals of • Medellin, Antioquia, Colombia (regional and national festivals alternate)

Theatre Encounter, Jelenia Gora • Jelenia, Gora, Poland

Theatre Festival, Belgrade International • Belgrade, Serbia, Yugoslavia

United States Open Tennis Championships • Queens, New York

Ute Fair, Southern • Ignacio, Colorado

Vintage Festival • Subotica, Serbia, Yugoslavia

Washing the Hands (Issa Aka) • Ibo people in Nigeria (or in August or October, during yam festivals)

Western Festival • Saint-Tite, Quebec, Canada

Wine Festival, Jerez • Jerez de la Frontera, Cádiz, Spain

Wine Harvest, Festival of the • Palma del Condado, Huelva, Spain

Even-numbered years in September

Theatres, Biennial of Amateur • Poland

September 1

Hermit, Feast of the • Roman Catholic Hispanic-Americans at Hot Springs, New Mexico

National Day • Libya

Partridge Day • England

Republics Day, United Arab • Syria

St. Giles's Day • Christian

Soul, Festival of the (Mahrajan) • Syria and Lebanese-Americans in Bridgeport, Connecticut

Wattle Day • Australia (or August 1)

Two weeks beginning September 1

Besançon International Festival (Festival International de Besançon) • Besançon, Doubs, France

September 2

Independence Day • Democratic Republic of Vietnam

St. Stephen, Feast of and Harvest Dance (Feast of San Estevan) • Acoma Pueblo, New Mexico

September 3

Cromwell Day • England

Independence Day • Qatar

Path Clearing Festival (Akwambo) • Ghana

St. Gregory I the Great, Feast of • Roman Catholic

St. Marinus Day • San Marino

San Marino, Founding of • San Marino

September 4

St. Augustine, Feast of and Harvest Dance • Isleta Pueblo, New Mexico

Monday after September 4

Dance, Horn • Abbots Bromley, Staffordshire, England

Observed on or near September 5

Regatta Day • Malta

September 5-17

Pilgrimage of Pedro Bervardo (Romería of Pedro Bervardo) • Ávila, Spain

September 6

Independence Day (Somhlolo Day) • Swaziland

September 7

Independence Day • Brazil

Six days beginning on or near September 7

Mithra, Feast of (Mihrajan) • Persia (now Iran)

September 8

Andorra National Festival • Andorra

Literacy Day, International • U.N./UNESCO-sponsored

Nativity of the Virgin, Feast of the • Christian

Pilgrimage to Shrine of Father Laval • Roman Catholics at Port Louis, Mauritius

Thanksgiving (Evamelunga, the Taking Away of Burden and Sin) • Cameroon

One week beginning September 8
Nativity of the Virgin, Feast of the (Virgin of the Remedies) • Mexico

September 8-15
Our Lady of Miracles (Nossa Senhora dos Milagres or Festa de Serreta) • Roman Catholic Azorean Portuguese people at Gustine, California, and Azores, Portugal

September 8-18
Our Lady of Nazaré Festival • Nazaré, Estremadura, Portugal

September 9
Admission Day • California
Independence Day (National Day) • Democratic People's Republic of Korea
National Day • Bulgaria

September 10
Air Force Day • Canada
National Day • Belize

September 11
Jinnah Day • Pakistan
New Year • Coptic Orthodox Egyptian-Canadians and in Egypt
New Year (Enkutatash) • Ethiopia

September 12
Dance, Red Paint Kachina • Zuñi Pueblo, New Mexico
Defenders' Day • Baltimore, Maryland
National Day • Ethiopia
National Day • Saudi Arabia

September 14
Exaltation of the Cross • Christian
National Anthem Day • Maryland

Sunday following September 14
Pig Face Sunday • Avening, Gloucestershire, England

September 14-15
Jicarilla Apache Fair • San Ildefonso Pueblo, New Mexico

September 15
Battle of Britain Day • England
Independence Day • Costa Rica
Independence Day • El Salvador
Independence Day • Guatemala
Independence Day • Honduras
Independence Day • Nicaragua
Our Lady of Sorrows, Festival of Mary • Roman Catholic
Respect for the Aged Day (Keiro-no-ki) • Japan

Sunday nearest September 15
Exaltation of the Cross (Kud Khach) • Armenia

September 15-16
Independence, Festival of Mexico • procession from the Zocolo to the Independence Monument on Paseo de la Reforma in Mexico City, Mexico

September 15-30
Wine Festival, Limassol • Limassol, Cyprus

September 16
Cherokee Strip Day • Ponca City, Enid, and Perry, Oklahoma
Independence Day • Malaysia

September 17
Citizenship Day • United States
Hero, Day of the National • Angola
St. Lambert's Day • Christian
Von Steuben Day • United States (often observed fourth Sunday in September)

September 18
Independence Day • Chile

September 19
St. Januarius's Feast Day • shrine at Naples, Italy
World Peace Day • Bahá'í religion in the United States

Two weeks, including September 19
St. Januarius's Feast Day • Roman Catholic Italian-Americans at Little Italy, New York

September 20
Airborne Operations Day • Netherlands

September 21
Independence Day • Belize
Independence Day • Malta
Nativity of the Virgin, Feast of the (Nativity of Our Most Holy Lady, the Theotokas or Nativity of the Theotokas) • some Eastern Orthodox churches
St. Matthew's Day • Carpathian Mountains

September 21-22
Kati Bihu • Hindus at Assam, India

On or near September 21-22
Autumnal Equinox (Jugowa) • Okinawa (full moon day of the eighth month)

September 22
Independence Day • Mali

September 22-23
Autumnal Equinox

September 23 or 24
Autumnal Equinox Day (Higan Ritual) • Buddhists in Japan

September 24
Harvest Home Festival • northern England and
  Scotland
Independence Day (September 8) • Guinea-Bissau
Thanksgiving, Schwenkfelder • Pennsylvania Dutch people
  in the United States

September 25
Kamarampaka Day • Rwanda
Liberation Forces Day, Popular • Mozambique
St. Elizabeth, Feast of • Paguate Village, Laguna Pueblo,
  New Mexico
St. Sergius of Radonezh • Russian Orthodox

September 26
Johnny Appleseed, Birthday of • United States
Martyrs of North America, Feast of • Roman Catholics in
  Canada and the United States
National Day • People's Democratic Republic of Yemen
  (formerly Southern Yemen)
National Day • Yemen Arab Republic

September 27
Exaltation of the Cross • Christian (Julian calendar;
  September 14, Gregorian calendar)
Exaltation of the Cross (Meskel, Finding of the True
  Cross) • Coptic and Ethiopian churches in Ethiopia
  (end of rainy season)
St. Vincent de Paul, Feast of • Christian
Sts. Cosmas and Damian Day • Christian

September 28
St. Wenceslaus's Day • Czech-Americans in Iowa and
  Minnesota, and in Czechoslovakia

September 28-29
St. Michael, Festival of • Jesus Maria, Nayarit, Mexico

September 29
Constitution Day • Brunei
Michaelmas • Western Church (November 8, Eastern
  Church)
Payment of Quit Rent • London, England
Quarter Days • England and Ireland (also December 25,
  March 25, and June 24)
St. Michael's Day • Christian

September 29-30
Indian Ceremonial Dancing, American • Taos, New
  Mexico (including San Geronimo Day)
St. Jerome's Day • Taos Pueblo, New Mexico

September 30
Independence Day • Botswana
St. Jerome's Day • Roman Catholic

Every Sunday in September
Monsanto, National Festival of • Monsanto, Castelo
  Branco, Portugal

One day in September
Torredeita, International Festival of • Torredeita,
  Viseu, Portugal

Three days in September
Caruaru Roundup • Pernambuco, Brazil
Poetry Festival, Geraldine R. Dodge • Waterloo, New Jersey

Four days in September
Corn Palace Festival • Mitchell, South Dakota

Five days in September
McClure Bean Soup Festival • McClure, Pennsylvania

Six days in September
Cabrillo Day • San Diego area, California

One week in September
Theatres, National Festival of Youth • location varies
  within England
Water Festival at Menjer Lake • Garung Village, Central
  Java, Java

Four weeks in September
Bruckner Festival, International (Internationales
  Brucknerfest) • Linz, Austria

Early September
Pilgrimage to the Sanctuary of Our Lady of the Remedies
  (Pardon of Nossa Senhora dos Remédios and Festival of
  Lamego) • Lamego, Viseu, Portugal
Thamesday • London, England
Theatre Community Festival • Belgrade, Serbia,
  Yugoslavia
Wine Festival, Zahle • Zahle, Lebanon

Several days in early September
Wine Festival, Stroumbi Village • Stroumbi Village near
  Paphos, Cyprus

First week in September
Rye Festival • Rye, Sussex, England

Six days during first week in September
Wratislavia Cantans-International Oratorio Festival
  (Miedzynarodowy Festiwal Oratoryjno-Kantatowy) •
  Wroclaw, Poland

First two weeks in September
Anjar Festival • Anjar, Lebanon

Four weeks beginning first week in September
Berlin Festival Weeks (Berliner Festwochen) • Berlin,
Federal Republic of Germany

**First weekend in September (Labor Day weekend in the
United States)**
Blessing of the Fleet (Lousiana Shrimp and Petroleum
Festival) • Morgan City, Louisiana
Cherokee National Holiday • Cherokee Indians at Tahlequah,
Oklahoma (Thursday-Sunday of Labor Day weekend)
Country Music Contest and Festival, National Old-Time •
Avoca, Iowa
Crab Derby, Hard National • Crisfield, Maryland
Frisbee Festival, National • the Mall near the National
Air and Space Museum, Washington, D.C.
Grape Festival (Wedding of the Wine and Cheese Pageant)
• Nauvoo, Illinois
Italian Heritage Festival, West Virginia • Clarksburg,
West Virginia
Mountain Man Rendezvous • Fort Bridger, Wyoming
Polish Festival • Polish-Americans at National Shrine of
Our Lady of Czestochowa, Doylestown, Pennsylvania
Powwow, Connecticut River • Schaghiticoke, Paucatuck
Pequot, Mashantucket Pequot, Mohegan, and Golden
Hill Paugussett Indians at Farmington, Connecticut
Powwow, Shinnecock • Shinnecock Indians at
Southampton, New York
Rodeo, Ellensburg • Ellensburg, Washington
St. Gens, Festival of (La Fête de St. Gens) • Beaucet,
Provence, France (also Sunday following May 15
at Monteux)
William Tell Pageant • Swiss-Americans at New Glarus,
Wisconsin

Four days during first weekend in September
Bumbershoot • Seattle, Washington

First weekend and Monday in September
Apache Tribal Fair • Apache Indians near Show Low,
Arizona
Cajun and Bluegrass Festival • Escoheag, Rhode Island
Film Festival, International • Telluride, Colorado
Indian Festival, Iroquois • Iroquois Indians at State
University of New York in Cobleskill
Labor Day • Caddo Indians at Binger, Oklahoma
Labor Day Festivities, Choctaw Nation of Oklahoma •
Tuskahoma, Oklahoma
Labor Day Powwow • Southern Arapaho Indians in
Oklahoma

Four days including Labor Day, first Monday in September
Dance, Sunrise • White Mountain Apache Indians in
Arizona

First Sunday in September
Flutes, Day of the (Pffiferdaj) • Ribeauvillé, France

Pintea the Brave Day • Magoaja, Commune of Chiuesti,
Cluj, Romania
Youth Day, International (Internatzional'nyi Den'
Komsomola) • USSR

Ten days ending first Monday in September
Regatta, Charleston Sternwheel • Charleston, West
Virginia

First Monday in September
Labor Day • Bucks County, Pennsylvania, and Portuguese-
Americans in Rhode Island
Labor Day • Canada and the United States
Labor Day Celebration • Spokan Indians at Wellpinit,
Washington
Labor Day Powwow • Arapaho Indians at Ethete, Wyoming
Powwows, Ojibwa • Ojibwa Indians at Leech Lake
Reservation, Cass Lake, Minnesota (also in winter,
spring, midsummer, and Memorial Day, last Monday
in May)
Skipjack Races, Labor Day • Deal Island, Maryland
Southern 500 Stock Car Race • Darlington, South Carolina

On or near Labor Day, first Monday in September
Dance, Green Corn • Iroquois Indians

Weekend after Labor Day, first Monday in September
Camel Races, International • Virginia City, Nevada
Oyster Festival • Norwalk, Connecticut
Sternwheel Festival, Ohio River • Marietta, Ohio

First Sunday after first Monday in September
National Grandparents Day • United States

**First Saturday in September (during Labor Day weekend
in the United States)**
Crandall Day, Prudence • Canterbury, Connecticut
Highland Gathering, Braemar • Braemar, Scotland

**Nine days from first Saturday through second Sunday in
September**
Århus Festival Week (Århus Festuge) • Århus, Denmark

First Saturday after full moon in September
Indian Day (Native American Day) • Oklahoma

**Three or four days ending second weekend after first
Monday in September**
Air Races, National Championship • Reno, Nevada

Second week in September
Hang Gliding Festival, Telluride • Telluride, Colorado
Navajo Nation Fair • Window Rock, Arizona (usually
Wednesday or Thursday through Sunday)

Second full week in September
Pendleton Round-Up • Pendleton, Oregon

Second weekend in September
Boys' Rifle Match (Knabenschiessen) • Zurich, Switzerland
Indian Summer Festival • Milwaukee, Wisconsin
Joust of the Quintain • Foligno, Umbria, Italy
Powwow, Nanticoke Indian • Millsboro, Delaware
Sausage Fair (Bad Durkheim Wurstmarkt) • Bad Durkheim,
  Germany (Saturday through Tuesday; also Friday
  through Monday during third weekend in September)
Yellow Daisy Festival • Stone Mountain, Georgia

Second weekend in September during even-numbered years
Living Chess Game (La Partita a Scácchi Viventi) •
  Marchóstica, Italy

Three to four days over second weekend in September
Santa Fe Fiesta • Santa Fe, New Mexico

Second Sunday in September
Pilgrimage of La Dandelada (Romería of La Dandelada) •
  Ávila, Spain
Shepherd Sunday (Schäfer Sonntag) • Belalp, Valais,
  Switzerland

Second Sunday in September every other year
Bruegel Feesten • Wigene, Belgium

Mid-September
Banana Festival, International • Fulton, Kentucky, and
  South Fulton, Tennessee
Vintage Feast (Fiesta de la Vendimia) • Jerez de la
  Frontera, Cádiz, Spain

A Saturday in mid-September
Last Night • Royal Albert Hall, London, England

Four days in mid-September
Oyster Festival, Galway • Galway, County Connemara,
  Ireland
Vermont's World's Fair • Tunbridge, Vermont

One week in mid-September
Berlioz International Festival (Internationales Festival
  Hector Berlioz) • Lyon and La Côte-Saint-André, France

Nine days in mid-September
Music of Warsaw, International Festival of Contemporary
  and Warsaw Autumn Festival (Warszawka) • Jesien
  Warsaw, Poland

Two weeks in mid-September
Music Festival, Umbria Sacred (Sagra Musicale Umbra) •
  Perugia, Italy
Windsor Festival • Windsor, Berkshire, England

Third week in September
Johnny Appleseed Festival • Fort Wayne, Indiana
Our Lady of Peñafrancia, Feast of (Nuestra Senora de
  Peñafrancia, Feast of) • Naga City, Philippines

Third weekend in September
Acadiens, Festival • Lafayette, Louisiana
Bluegrass Fan Fest • Owensboro, Kentucky
Chilympiad, Republic of Texas Chili Cookoff • San
  Marcos, Texas
Jazz Festival, Monterey • Monterey, California
Lumberjack Days, Clearwater County Fair and • Orofino,
  Idaho
Sausage Fair (Bad Durkheim Wurstmarkt) • Bad Durkheim,
  Germany (Friday through Monday; also Saturday through
  Tuesday during second weekend in September)
Wings 'n Water Festival • southern New Jersey coast

Three-day festival over third weekend in September
Eisteddfod Festival of Traditional Music and Crafts •
  Southeastern Massachusetts University, North
  Dartmouth, Massachusetts

Third Tuesday in September
Peace, International Day of • U.N.-sponsored; United
  States
Prinsjesdag • The Hague, Netherlands

Third Saturday in September
Miss America Pageant • Atlantic City, New Jersey

Fourth Friday in September
Native American Day • Arizona, California, Connecticut,
  and Illinois

Usually fourth Friday in September
Native American Day • United States (date varies
  according to state)

Usually weekend after fourth Friday in September
Acorn Festival • Pomo Indians at Kule Loklo Miwok
  Indian Village, California

Fourth Saturday in September
Hunting and Fishing Day • United States
Kids' Day • Kiwanis International-sponsored

Usually weekend over fourth Saturday in September
Chickahominy Fall Festival • Chickahominy Indians near
  Roxbury, Virginia

Two days in late September
Agricultural Days (Jordoruksdagarna) • Swedish-Americans
  at Bishop Hill, Illinois

Ten days in late September
Grape and Wine Festival, Niagara • St. Catharines, Ontario, Canada

Last week in September
Harvest Dance • San Juan Pueblo, New Mexico
Johnny Appleseed Week • Ohio

Last weekend in September
Patriots' Weekend, Annual • Bethel/Redding area of Connecticut

Usually last weekend in September
Chaw-Se Big Time Celebration • Pomo Indians and Maidu Indians at Indian Grinding Rock State Park near Pine Grove, California

Last full weekend in September
Vintage Festival, Valley of the Moon • Sonoma, California

Two days over last weekend in September
Fiddler's Contest and Festival, Old Time • Payson, Arizona

Last Sunday in September
Gold Star Mothers Day • United States

End of September
Cultural Festival of Oum Ezzine • Jamel, Monastir Region, Tunisia
St. Michael's Day • Puerto Rico

September or October
Salted Cure (Cure Salée) • Taureg people at Ingal, Niger

Two days in late September or early October
Cranberry Harvest Festival • South Carver, Massachusetts

One week during September or October
Nairobi Show • Kenya
Theatres, Festival of National • Cluj-Napoca, Transylvania, Romania

Late September or early October
Mushroom Harvest • Byelorussia, USSR

September-October
Aloha Week • Hawaii
Alpabfahrten • Switzerland
Artistic Weeks, Budapest • Budapest, Hungary
Bathurst Carillon City Tourist Festival • Bathurst, New South Wales, Australia
Beethoven Festival • Bonn, Federal Republic of Germany
Dance Festival, Krishnattam • Guruvayur, Kerala, India
Film and Song Festival, International Trade Fair • Thessaloniki, Greece
Mimes, International Creative Workshop of • Poland
Music Weeks, Budapest • Budapest, Hungary
New Yam Festival (Odwira) • Abron, Aburi, Akan, and Asante peoples in Ghana (varies in length from several days to forty days)
Puppet Festival, International • Zagreb, Croatia, Yugoslavia
Puppet Theatres of Serbia • location varies within Serbia, Yugoslavia
Spring Festival, Warana (Blue Skies) • Brisbane, Queensland, Australia

Even-numbered years in September-October
Theatre, International Festival of Open • Wroclaw, Poland

Three days in late September-early October
Middfest International • Middletown, Ohio

One week in September-early October
Joy of Living • Toowoomba, Queensland, Australia

Between seven and 31 days in September-October
Rama Leela Festival • Rama Nagar, Uttar Pradesh, India

Nine days from late September to early October
Ak-Sar-Ben Livestock Exposition and Rodeo • Ak-Sar-Ben Field, Omaha, Nebraska

Two weeks in September-October
Drama Festival, Warana (Blue Skies) • Brisbane, Queensland, Australia
Gaelic Mod • Scotland

22 days in September-October
Fall Festival, Fairmount Park • Philadelphia, Pennsylvania

End of September-early October
Carnival of Flowers • Toowoomba, Queensland, Australia

September-November
Dead, Return of the (Odo Festival) • Igbo people at Nsukka, Nigeria (also every other year in April)

Mid-September through end of December
Autumn Festival, Paris (Festival d'Automne) • Paris, France

September to May
Arts Series, Wave Hill Performing • Bronx, New York

Autumn

Early autumn
Oklahoma Day • U.S. Naval Station, Adak, Alaska

Autumn
Comedy, Week of • Galati, Moldavia, Romania

Autumn *(cont.)*

Dead, Feast for the (Ohgíwe) • Iroquois women (also during spring or occasional, during Iroquois White Dog Feast)

Dead, Time of the (Velu Laiks) • Latvia

Folklore and Amateur Work in Culture and Arts • Bihac, Bosnia and Herzegovina, Yugoslavia

Haloa, Festival of • ancient Greek women

Harvest Dance (Kyaiya) • Lengua Indians at Gran Chaco, South America (also spring and summer)

Moving Day (Flyttedag) • Bergen and other large towns in Norway (and April 14)

New Year's Day • Eskimo

Reindeer Slaughtering • Chukchi, USSR

Sedna, Feast of • Central Eskimos

Yasukini Matsuri • Yasukini Shrine, Tokyo, Japan (also summer, winter, and four days in April)

Even-numbered years in autumn

Arts Festival, New Directions in the Performing • Hamilton, Ontario, Canada (or summer)

Ballet, International Festival of (Festival Internacional de Ballet de La Habana) • Havana, Cuba

Odd-numbered years in autumn

Theatre, Festival of Youth • Piatra-Neamt, North Moldavia, Romania

Every other autumn

Arts en Belgique, Europalia Festival des • Brussels, Belgium

Two to three days in late autumn

Seal Festival (Keretkun Festival) • Chukchi people in Siberia, USSR

Several days in late autumn, after harvest

Drums Festival, Hundred (Wangala) • Garo Hills, Meghalaya, India

October

October

Amateur One-Man Shows, National Meeting of • Zgorzelec, Poland

Dance, Hupa Autumn (Tunchitdilya) • Hupa Indians in northern California

Eisteddfod, Eastern Shore • Hobart, Tasmania, Australia

Fall Festival • Cherokee Indians at Jay, Oklahoma

Fantasia (Horse Festival) • Fez, Morocco

Fantasia (Horse Festival) • Meknes, Morocco

Gold Rush Days, Dahlonega • Dahlonega, Georgia

Green Squash Festival (Wima'kwari) • Huichol, Mexico

Han Lu (the Dew Grows Cold) • China

Hunters' Moon, Feast of the • Lafayette, Indiana

Jovanovic, Festivities in Honor of • Sabac, Serbia, Yugoslavia

Kotohira Kompira Festival • Shinto religion in Kotohira, Kagawa, Japan

M'Hamed Ben Khelifa Festival • El Kaalaa El Khasba, Le Kef Region, Tunisia

Misisi Beer Feast • Sebei people in Uganda (and at Christmas; after millet harvest, during month of Twamo)

Music Festival, Brno International • Brno, Moravia, Czechoslovakia

New Yam Festival (Odwira) • Dan, Wobe, Senoufo, Baoule, Bete, and Lobi peoples in Ivory Coast

October Days of Culture • Sarajevo, Bosnia and Herzegovina, Yugoslavia

Opera Festival, Italian • Théâtre de Beaulieu, Lausanne, Switzerland

Our Lady of Mount Carmel (Senhora do Monte do Carmo) • Moura, Beja, Portugal

Pinenut Festival • Walker River Paiute Indians at Schurz, Nevada

Pioneers Day • South Dakota

Popular Traditions, Festival of • Isfahan, Iran

Potato Days (Potetserie) • Norway

Powwow, Four Nations • Nez Perce Indians at Lapwai, Idaho

Puja Ketek Celebrations • Bachok, Kelantan, Malaysia

St. Iria Fair • Faro, Portugal

Skulls, Ceremony for the • Aymara Indians

Stage, Classics on the Yugoslav • Leskovac, Serbia, Yugoslavia

Sterija, Days of • Vrsac, Vojvodina, Yugoslavia

Theatre, International Festival of University • Parma, Emilia-Romagna, Italy

Theatre, Liège Festival of Young (Le Festival du Jeune Theatre de Liège) • Liège, Belgium

Theatre Amateurs, Encounter of Yugoslav • Prizren, Serbia, Yugoslavia

Theatre Amateurs of the Villages of Serbia • Malo Crnice, Serbia, Yugoslavia

Theatre and Music, Berlin Festival Days of • East Berlin, German Democratic Republic

Theatre Festival, Dublin • Dublin, County Dublin, Ireland

Theatres, Borstnik Encounter of Slovenian • Maribor, Slovenia, Yugoslavia

Theatres of Bosnia and Herzegovina, Encounter of Professional • Brcko, Bosnia and Herzegovina, Yugoslavia

Theatres of Croatia, Encounter of Professional • Slavonski Brod, Croatia, Yugoslavia

Washing the Hands (Issa Aka) • Ibo people in Nigeria (also in August and September during yam festivals)

Usually October

Boomerang Festival • Hampton, Virginia

Month of October
Music, Barcelona International Festival of (Festival Internacional de Musica de Barcelona) • Barcelona, Spain
Purple Spring • Peru

Even-numbered years in October
Metamusik Festival • West Berlin, Federal Republic of Germany

Every three years in October
Golden Dolphin • Varna, Bulgaria
Music and the Arts, Norfolk and Norwich Triennial Festival of • Norwich, Norfolk, England

Every five years in October
Puppet Theatres, National Review of Professional • Sofia, Bulgaria

October 1
Caudillo, Day of the • Spain
Independence Day • Cyprus
Independence Day • Nigeria
Peko, Feast of • Estonians at Setumaa, Estonia
St. Therese of Lisieux, Feast of • Christian
Unification Day • Cameroon

October 1, two-day holiday
National Days • People's Republic of China

October 1-15
Music Festival, Bratislava • Bratislava, Slovakia, Czechoslovakia

October 2
Gandhi's Birthday (Gandhi Jayanti) • India
Guardian Angels, Festival of • Roman Catholic
Independence Day • Guinea
Old Man's Day • Braughing, Hertfordshire, England

October 3
Foundation Day • Republic of Korea
Leiden Day (Leiden Ontzet) • Leiden, Netherlands, and Holland Society of New York
Wolfe Festival, Thomas • Asheville, North Carolina

October 3-4
St. Francis of Assisi, Feast of • Assisi, Italy, and the United States

October 4
Independence Day • Lesotho
St. Francis of Assisi, Feast of • Christian

October 6
Armed Forces Day • Egypt

German Day • German-American communities in the United States
Ivy Day
Liberation Anniversary, October War of • Syria
St. Thomas the Apostle, Feast of • Eastern Orthodox

October 7
Republic Day (Foundation Day) • German Democratic Republic
Virgen del Rosario, Fiesta for the • Zinacantan, Mexico

Three days, including October 7
Riley Festival, James Whitcomb • Greenfield, Indiana

October 9
Independence Day • Uganda
Leif Eriksson Day
St. Denis's Day • Christian

Week including October 9
Fire Prevention Week • United States

October 10
Double Tenth Day • Taiwan
Founding of the Republic • China
Kivi Day • Finland
Kruger Day • South Africa
Oklahoma Historical Day • Salina, Oklahoma
Physical Education or Sports Day • Japan

On or near October 10
Fiji Day • Fiji

October 10-20
Nagoya City Festival • Nagoya, Japan

October 11
Eight Hour Day • South Australia
Pulaski Day • United States

October 12
Columbus Day
Independence Day • Equatorial Guinea
New Yam Festival • Nigeria

October 13
Fontalia (Festival of Fountains) • ancient Rome
St. Edward the Confessor's Day • Christian

October 14
Founders Day and Youth Day • Zaire
National Day • People's Democratic Republic of Yemen (formerly Southern Yemen)

October 15
Chong Jiu Festival • China
Ether Day • Massachusetts General Hospital in Boston
Evacuation Day • Tunisia
Horse Sacrifice, October • ancient Rome
St. Teresa of Avila, Feast of • Christian

October 16
National Boss Day • United States
St. Gall, Feast of • Christian
World Food Day • United Nations-sponsored; Barbados

October 17
Burgoyne's Surrender Day • New York
Pilgrimage of Our Lady of Valme (Romario of Our Lady
of Valme) • Dos Hermanas near Sevilla, Spain
Poetry Day, Black • New York and Oregon
St. Etheldreda's Day • Church of England at Ely, England
St. Mary Margaret, Feast of • Paraje Village, Laguna
Pueblo, New Mexico

Two days beginning October 17
Mothers' Day • Malawi

October 18
Heroes Day • Jamaica
St. Luke, Feast Day of • Christian

October 19
Pickle-Market or Sticky-Sticky Fair (Bettara-Ichi) • near
Ebisu Shrine, Tokyo, Japan
Yorktown Day • Massachusetts and Yorktown, Virginia

October 20
Amateurs to Their City (Liberation Day of Belgrade) •
Belgrade, Serbia, Yugoslavia
Báb, Birth of the • Bahá'í

October 21
Black Christ, Festival of the • Roman Catholics at
Porotobelo, Panama
St. Ursula's Day • British Virgin Islands and New Orleans,
Louisiana
Trafalgar Day (Nelson Day) • London, England

October 22
Abu Simbel Festival • Abu Simbel temple in Egypt
Ages, Festival of the (Jidai Matsuri) • Kyoto, Japan

October 23
Chulalongkorn Day • Thailand
Independence Day, Hungary • observed by Hungarian-
Americans
Swallows of San Juan Capistrano • San Juan Capistrano
Mission, San Juan Capistrano, California (swallows
depart; swallows arrive March 19)

October 24
Pennsylvania Day • Pennsylvania
United Nations Day • member nations; a holiday in Haiti,
Mauritius, Nepal, and Swaziland

October 24, two-day holiday
Independence Day • Zambia (formerly Northern Rhodesia)

October 24-26
Thesmophoria • ancient Greece

October 25
St. Crispin's Day • Christian

On or near October 25
Kawate Bunjiro, Festival of • Konko-kyo religion in
Japan and among Japanese elsewhere

October 26
National Day • Iran
Republic Day • Republic of Vietnam
St. Demetrius, Festival of • Thessaloniki, Greece, and
Thrace, Greece

October 27
Independence and Thanksgiving Day • St. Vincent

Begins October 27
Book Reading Week • Japan

October 28
Independence Day • Czechoslovakia and Czechs and
Slovaks in the United States and elsewhere outside
Czechoslovakia
St. Jude's Day • Roman Catholics at Buffalo, New York
Thanksgiving • Czechoslovakia

October 29; two-day holiday
Republic Day • Turkey

October 30
Devil's Night • Detroit, Michigan
Little Angels (Los Angelitos) • Mayan people at
Cancún, Mexico

October 30-November 2
All Souls' Day (Día de Muertos, Day of the Dead or Festival
of Hungry Ghosts) • Roman Catholics in Mexico

Sunday before October 31
Reformation Day • Christian

Saturday before October 31
Halloween (Halloween parade) • Anaheim, California

October 31
Admission Day • Nevada, especially Carson City
Halloween
National Magic Day • United States
Samhain (Summer's End)

October 31 or November 1
Chiang Kai-shek Day • Taiwan

Saturday nearest full moon in October
Ironman Triathlon Championships • Kailua-Kone, Hawaii

Three days in October
Alaska Day • Sitka, Alaska
Folk Festival, Wagga • Wagga Wagga, New South Wales, Australia
Storytelling Festival, National • Jonesboro, Tennessee

Three days in October during even-numbered years
Shilla Cultural Festival • Kyongju, Korea

Three days in October during odd-numbered years
Puppet Play Encounter • Ostfildern, Baden-Wurttemberg, Federal Republic of Germany

Four days in October
Regatta, International • Kralendijk, Bonaire, Netherlands Antilles

Five days in October
Norsk Hostfest • Scandinavian-Americans at Minot, North Dakota
Rose Festival, Texas • Tyler, Texas

One week in October
Music Series, Contemporary • Hungary

Nine days in October
Horse, Festival of the • Oklahoma City, Oklahoma
October Fair • people from Alentejo and Algarve regions at Castro Verde-Beja, Portugal

Ten days in October
Virgin of the Pillar, Feast of the (Virgen del Pilar) • Saragossa, Spain

15 days in October
Natchez Spring (Fall Pilgrimage) • Natchez, Mississippi (also March-April)

17 days in October
State Fair of Texas • Dallas, Texas

Three weeks in October
Music and the Arts, Swansea Festival of • Swansea, Wales

Early October
Alphabet Day (Han-gul) • Korea
St. Francis of Assisi, Festival of • Cuetzalan, Puebla, Mexico

Two days in early October
Catoctin Colorfest • Thurmont, Maryland

Four days in early October
Shrimp Festival, National • Gulf Shores, Alabama

Nine days in early October
Balloon Fiesta, Albuquerque International • Albuquerque, New Mexico
Oktoberfest • German-Canadians at Kitchener, Waterloo, Ontario, Canada (beginning the Friday before Thanksgiving Monday)

First week in October
Palermo Festival • Palermo, Sicily, Italy

Five days during first week in October
Dance Festival, Darpana • Ahmedabad, Gujarat, India

First weekend in October
Locomotive Chase Festival, Great • Adairsville, Georgia
Oltenian Ballad • Corabia, Olt, Romania

Usually first weekend in October
Navajo Nation Festival, Shiprock (Northern Navajo Fair) • Navajo Indians at Shiprock, New Mexico

First full weekend in October
Enchilada Fiesta, Whole • Las Cruces, New Mexico
Paul Bunyan Show • Nelsonville, Ohio

First two weekends in October
London Bridge Days • Lake Havasu City, Arizona

First Sunday in October
Agua, La Fiesta de • San Pedro de Casta, Peru
Dionysiad • Husi, Vaslui, Romania
Rosary, Festival of the • Roman Catholic
St. Michael's Day • Finland
United States Grand Prix • United States

16 days, usually beginning first Sunday in October
Oktoberfest • Munich, Bavaria, Germany

First Wednesday through Sunday in October
Mountain State Forest Festival • Elkins, West Virginia

First Saturday in October
Battle of Germantown, Reenactment of • Germantown, Pennsylvania

First Saturday in October *(cont.)*
Chickasaw Nation Annual Day • Byng School near Ada,
Oklahoma
Cowboys Parade, Black • Oakland, California

First through second Saturdays in October
Boone Festival, Daniel • Barbourville, Kentucky

Second and third weeks in October
Stroud Festival • Stroud, Gloucestershire, England

Second week in October during even-numbered years
Arts Festival, L.G. Harris • Stoke Prior, Worcestershire,
England

**Three days during second week in October every odd-
numbered year**
Swedish Homage Festival • Swedish-Americans at
Lindsborg, Kansas

Second weekend in October
Cactus Jack Festival • Uvalde, Texas
Marimo Festival • Ainu people at Akan Lake, Hokkaido,
Japan
Moore Days, Billy • Avondale, Goodyear, and Litchfield
Park, Arizona
Oyster Festival, St. Mary's County Maryland •
Leonardtown, Maryland
Tucson Meet Yourself Festival • Czech-, German-, Indian-,
Italian-, and Mexican-Americans at Tucson, Arizona

Second Sunday in October
Círio de Nazaré • Brazil
Jousting Tournament • Mount Solon, Virginia (also third
Saturday in June)
St. Dismas's Day • National Catholic Prison Chaplains
Association and prisons in the United States
White Sunday • American Samoa and Western Samoa

Second Monday in October
Columbus Day • United States
Thanksgiving Day • Canada

Second or third Monday in October
Hurricane Supplication Day • Virgin Islands (and fourth
Monday in July)

Second Tuesday in October
Fraternal Day • Alabama

Second Saturday in October
Fall Harvest Day • Westminster, Maryland

Mid-October
Heritage Holidays • Rome, Georgia

Marathon, International Open • Marathon to Athens,
Greece
World Series • Canada and the United States

Last two weeks in October
Arts, Festival of Asian • Hong Kong
Arts Festival, Rhymney Valley • Rhymney Valley District,
Wales
Hexham Abbey Festival • Hexham, Northumberland,
England

Second half of October
Autumn of Culture • Backi Petrovac, Vojvodina,
Yugoslavia

Third week in October
Bible Week, National • National Laymen's Committee,
United States
Pirate Week Festival • George Town, Grand Cayman,
Cayman Islands

Third Wednesday in October
Missouri Day • Missouri

Third Saturday in October
Bridge Day • New River Gorge Bridge, Fayetteville,
West Virginia
Sweetest Day • United States

Fourth Sunday in October
Exaltation of the Shellfish • grove in Pontevedra
Province, Spain
Mother-in-law Day • United States

Late October
Harvest of Grapes (Szüret) • Hungary
Impruneta, Festa del • Florence, Tuscany, Italy

Two weeks in late October
Opera, Wexford Festival • Wexford, County Wexford,
Ireland

Last weekend in October
Chesapeake Appreciation Days • Annapolis, Maryland

Last Sunday in October
Christ the King, Feast of • Roman Catholic
Rose Festival, Saffron • Consuegra, Spain

Last Monday in October
Labour Day • New Zealand

Last Saturday in October
Guavaween • Cuban-Americans at Ybor City, Florida

End of October

Chickaban (Feast of the Storm God Kukulcan) • Mayan people in Mani, Yucatan, Mexico (during month of Xul)

October or November

Mother's Day (Antrosht) • Gurage province, Ethiopia (after rainy season ends)

Vigo Days • Vigo, Pontevedra, Spain

10-12 days in October or November

Gala of One-Man Shows • Bacau, West Moldavia, Romania

Late October or early November

Water Festival • Phnom Penh, Cambodia

October-November

AN tOIREACHTAS • Gaelic (location varies within Ireland)

Art and Antiques Fair, Old • Delft, Netherlands

Dance, Peyote (Hikuli) • Tarahumara and Huichol Indians in eastern Chihuahua, Mexico

Dance Festivals, Kathakali • Trivandrum, Kerala, India (also March-April)

Kite Flying Competition • Indonesia (during weeks preceding the rainy season, which begins in November)

Music Festival, Worcester • Worcester, Massachusetts

Shrine Festival, Gokoku • Hikone City, Shiga, Japan

Skanda Shashti • Hindu Tamils in southern India (Tamil month of Tulam)

Three days in October-November

Dance Festival, Kala Vikash Kendra • Cuttack, Orissa, India (also August 10)

Two weeks in October-November

Foundation Week Celebrations • Parramatta, New South Wales, Australia

One month during October-November

October Fair (Fiestas de Octubre) • Guadalajara, Mexico

Eight weeks in October-November

Autumn, Styrian (Steirischer Herbst) • Graz, Austria

Late October-early November

Fremantle Week • Fremantle, Western Australia, Australia

Late October through November

Dances, Basket • Hopi Indians in northeastern Arizona

End of October through first week in November

Sausage Festival (Wurstfest) • German-Americans at New Braunfels, Texas

October or December

Vitoria Encounter • Vitoria, Alava, Spain

October-December

Dance Festival of Paris, International • Paris, France

November

November

New Year's Day • Hopi Indians

One-Man Shows, National Festival of • Torun, Poland

Plays, Festival of Russian and Soviet • Katowice, Poland

Raisin Monday • St. Andrew's University, Scotland

Seal Festival • Koryak people in the USSR (end of seal-hunting season)

Theatre, Festival of Cafe • Rennes, Ille-et-Vilaine, France

Theatre Confrontations, Young • Lublin, Poland

Theatres of Iberian Expression, International Festival of • Oporto, Porto, Portugal

Tori-no-ichi • Shinto religion in Japan

Wax Festival • Salé, Morocco

Odd-numbered years in November

Puppet Theatres, All-Poland Festival of • Opole, Poland

Small festival every third year, larger festival every fifth year in November

Habye Festival • Habye people in Togo

November 1

All Saints' Day • Christian

Author's Day • reading clubs in the United States

Awakeners, Day of the (Den na Buditelite) • Bulgaria

Independence Day • Antigua

National Day • Algeria

November 1-5

Art Festival, National Foundation • Chinju, Republic of Korea

November 2

Admission Day • North Dakota

Admission Day • South Dakota

All Souls' Day • Christian

Balfour Declaration Day • Jews in Israel

Memorial Day • Brazil

November 3

Culture Day (Bunka-no-hi) • Japan

Father of Texas Day • Austin, Texas

Independence Day • Panama

Meiji Setsu • Japan

St. Hubert, Feast Day of • Belgium and Luxembourg

November 3, two-day celebration

Independence Day • Dominica

November 4
Flag Day • Panama
Mischief Night • England, Australia and New Zealand
Provincial Anniversary • Marlborough, New Zealand
Rogers Day, Will • Oklahoma

November 5
Bonfire Night • Newfoundland, Canada
Fawkes Day, Guy
Independence Day, First Call for • El Salvador
Puno, Día del • Andean, Quechua, and Aymara Indians
at Puno, Peru
Ringing Day • England

November 6
Gustafus Adolphus Day • Sweden
St. Leonard's Day • Austria and Germany
St. Leonard's Ride (Leonhardiritt) • Bad Tölz, Bavaria,
Germany

November 7-8
October Socialist Revolution Day (November 7) • Moscow,
Russia, USSR

November 8
Admission Day • Montana
Michaelmas • Eastern Church (September 29, Western
Church)
Queen's Birthday • Nepal
St. Michael's Day • Eastern Orthodox in Ethiopia
Saints, Doctors, Missionaries, and Martyrs Day • Anglicans
and Church of England in England

November 9
Independence Day • Cambodia
St. John Lateran's Dedication • Roman Catholic Church
of St. John the Baptist, Rome

November 9-10
Kristallnacht

November 10
Polish Solidarity Day • Polish-Americans

November 10-11
Martinsfest • Protestants in Erfurt and Thuringia,
Germany, and Roman Catholics in Düsseldorf and Lower
Rhine, Germany
Turnip Lantern Festival (Rebenlichter) • Richterswil,
Winterthur, and Zurich, Switzerland

November 11
Admission Day • Washington
Armistice Day
Gansabhauet • Sursee, Switzerland

Independence Day • Angola
Independence Day • Poland
Independence Day • Rhodesia
King's Birthday • Bhutan
Martinmas • Christian
Quarter Days • Scotland (also February 2, May 15, and
August 1)
Remembrance Day • Bermuda
Remembrance Day • Canada
St. Martin's Day • Christian
St. Mennas's Day • Greece
Veterans' Day • United States

Weekend nearest November 11
Apache Fair • Apache Indians at San Carlos, Arizona

November 11-12
Republic Day (November 11) • Maldives

November 12
Bahá'u'lláh, Birth of the • Bahá'í
King's Coronation • Saudi Arabia
Republic Day • Austria
San Diego, Feast of and Corn Dance • Jemez and Tesuque
pueblos, New Mexico
Stanton Day, Elizabeth Cady • women's organizations
Sun Yat-sen Day • Taiwan

November 13
St. Frances Cabrini, Feast of • Roman Catholics in the
United States

November 14
Children's Day • India
Hussein Day, King • Jordan

November 15
Dynasty Day (Fête de la Dynastie) • Belgium
St. Leopold, Feast Day of (Fasslrutschen or Gaense Tag,
Goose Day) • Austria
Seven-Five-Three Festival Day (Shichi-Go-San) • Japan

On or near November 15
Selassie's Coronation Day, Haile • Ras Tafarians in Jamaica

November 16
Admission Day, Oklahoma • Washington Cathedral,
District of Columbia, and Oklahoma
St. Agnes of Assisi, Feast of • Christian
St. Matthew's Day • Eastern Orthodox

November 17
Penance Day (Buss and Bettag Day) • Federal Republic
of Germany
Queen's Day • Great Britain

November 18
Independence Day • Latvia
St. Plato the Martyr, Feast of • Macedonia
World Fellowship Day • YWCAs in 69 countries

November 18 or following Saturday
Restoration Day • Siletz Indian tribes at Siletz, Oregon

November 19
Equal Opportunity Day • National Cemetery, Washington, D.C.
Fête Nationale • Monaco
St. Elizabeth, Feast of • Peru

November 21
Admission Day • North Carolina
Presentation of Blessed Virgin Mary, Feast of the • Greek Orthodox and Roman Catholic

November 22
Independence Day • Lebanon
St. Cecilia's Day • England, Rome, Italy, and Charleston, South Carolina

November 23
Labor Thanksgiving Day • Japan
Niiname-Sai, Festival of • Japan
Repudiation Day • Frederick County, Maryland
St. Clement's Day • England

November 25
Evacuation Day • New York, New York
Independence Day • Surinam
St. Catherine's Day • Christian

November 26
St. George's Day (Jerjew Den) • Russia (and April 23)

November 26 or 27
Covenant, Day of the • Bahá'í

November 28
'Abdu'l-Bahá, Ascension of • Bahá'í
Independence Day • Mauritania
Independence Day • Panama
Republic Day • Chad

November 28-29
Independence Day • Albania

November 29
Independence Day • Southern Yemen (now People's Democratic Republic of Yemen)
Martinmas • Estonia
St. Andrew's Eve • Poland

November 29-30
Republic Day • Yugoslavia
St. Andrew's Eve (Andrzejki) • Polish-Americans in Ohio

November 30
Independence Day • Barbados
Independence Day • People's Democratic Republic of Yemen (formerly Southern Yemen)
St. Andrew's Day • Christian
Youth Day • Republic of Upper Volta

Sunday before Sunday nearest November 30
Stir-Up Sunday • Anglicans in England

Sunday nearest November 30
Advent Sunday • Christian

Four-week season beginning Sunday nearest November 30-December 24
Advent • Christian

Friday before Thanksgiving
Telleration • Bermuda, Canada, and United States

Three days in November
Folk Fair, Holiday • Milwaukee, Wisconsin

Four days, including eve of new moon in November
New Year (Wüwüchim) • Hopi and Pueblo Indians in northeastern Arizona

Five days in November
Dance and Drama, Festival of • Hyderabad, Andhra Pradesh, India

One week in November
Sigma Festival • Bordeaux, Gironde, France

Two weeks in November
Livestock, Horse Show, and Rodeo, American Royal • Kansas City, Missouri

Two and one-half weeks in November
Belfast Festival • Belfast, Northern Ireland

Early November
Gagaku Festival • Kasuga Shrine, Nara, Japan
Parliament Day • London, England
Theatre Festival, Children's • Copenhagen, Denmark

Two to three days in early November
Folk Festival, Ozark • Eureka Springs, Arkansas

Seven days in early November, near end of rainy season
Sango Festival • Oyo and Yoruba peoples at Ede, Nigeria

First week in November
Drama Festival, Kalidasa • Bhopal, Madhya Pradesh, India

First full weekend in November
Chili Cookoff, Terlingua • Terlingua, Texas

First Sunday in November
New York City Marathon • New York, New York

First Monday in November
Liberty Day (November 4) • Virgin Islands
Recreation Day • northern Tasmania, Australia

First Tuesday in November
Melbourne Cup Day • Melbourne, Victoria, Australia

The Tuesday after the first Monday in November
Election Day • United States

Thursday after Tuesday after the first Monday in November every leap year
Return Day • Delaware, especially Sussex County

First Thursday in November
Thanksgiving Day • Liberia

First Friday in November
World Community Day • Church Women United

First Saturday in November
Sadie Hawkins Day

Three weeks beginning first Saturday in November
Folklore, Prime Minister's Best Village Trophy Competition and Festival of • Port of Spain, Trinidad and Tobago

Second Sunday in November
Arbor Day or Tree Festival Day • Tunisia
Poppy Day (November 11) • Great Britain
Quintane, La • St.-Léonard-de-Noblat, France
Remembrance Day (November 11) • England
Stewardship Sunday • Council of Churches in Canada and the United States
Tree Festival Day • Tunisia

Second Saturday in November
Lord Mayor's Show (November 9) • procession through London to Westminster, England

Mid-November
Christ the King, Feast of • Chamorros people in Guam/ Northern Marianas
Grey Cup Day • Canada
Jayuya Festival of Indian Lore (Jayuya Indian Festival) • Jayuya, Puerto Rico

Five days in mid-November
Music Festival, Metz International Contemporary (Rencontres Internationales de Musique Contemporaine) • Metz, France

Ten days in mid-November
Macao Grand Prix • Macao

Second half of November
Theatres for Yugoslav Children and Youth, Festival of Professional • Skopje, Macedonia, Yugoslavia

Odd-numbered years during second half of November
Mimes, International Festival of Deaf • Brno, Moravia, Czechoslovakia

Third week of November
Elephant Round-Up • Surin, Thailand

Third Thursday in November
Great American Smokeout • United States

Third Saturday through Monday in November
Three Glorious Days (Les Trois Glorieuses) • Nuits-St. Georges, Beaune, and Meursault in Cote-d'Or, France (and July 27- 29)

Fourth Monday in November
Onion Market (Zibelemarit or Zybelemärit) • Bern, Switzerland

Fourth Tuesday through Friday in November
Duck Calling Contest and Wings Over the Prairie Festival, World Championship • Stuttgart, Arkansas

Fourth Thursday in November
Powwow, Poarch Creek Indian Thanksgiving Day • Poarch Creek Indians at Atmore, Alabama
Thanksgiving • United States

Saturday or Sunday after fourth Thursday in November
Chitlin' Strut • Salley, South Carolina

Last week in November
River Kwai Bridge Week • River Kwai Bridge, Kanchanaburi, Thailand

Last Sunday in November
Kennedy Day, John F. (November 24) • Massachusetts

Last Sunday in November or Sunday before Thanksgiving
Bible Sunday • many Protestant churches in the United States

Late November or early December
Shalako Ceremonial (koko awia, the kachina come) • Zuñi Pueblo, New Mexico

November-December
Davis Cup • United States
Tamasha Festival • Aurangabad, Bombay, Poona, and Sangli, Maharashtra, India (location rotates)
Theatre, National Festival of New (Festival Nacional del Nuevo Teatro) • Bogota, Cundinamarca, Colombia

Every other year in November-December
Ndok Ceremony • Nigeria

Five to ten days in November-December
Drama Festival, Goa Academy • Goa, Daman, and Diu Union Territory, Panjim, India (or February-March)

One week in November-December, depending on the weather and the harvest
Sahara National Festival • Douz, South Sahara Region, Tunisia

Ten days in November-December during odd-numbered years
Hong Kong, Festival of • Hong Kong

Two weeks in November-December
Musical Weeks of Orleans, International (Semaines Musicales Internationale d'Orleans) • Orleans, Loiret, France

November through Christmas, December 25
Dom Fair • Christians at Hamburg, Germany

November to January
Dance, Buffalo • Rio Grande pueblos

Early November through late January
Lights, Winter Festival of • Wheeling, West Virginia

Late November through early January
Christmas Around the World • Chicago, Illinois
Christmas Season (Festival of Lights) • Niagara Falls, New York

November-February
Midwinter Rites, Bella Coola (Kusiut) • Bella Coola, Kimsquit, and other Indians in coastal British Columbia, Canada

December

December
Christmas Dances • Shoshone Indians in Wyoming
Joropo Festival, International • Villavicencio, Meta, Colombia
Navajo Nightway and Mountain Topway Ceremonials • Navajo Indians at Window Rock, Arizona (date varies)
Santon Fair • Marseille, France

Theatre, Days of Young • Zagreb, Croatia, Yugoslavia
Theatre Meetings, Warsaw • Warsaw, Poland

Month of December
Christmas in Newport • Newport, Rhode Island

Every four years in December
Netherlands University Festival • Amsterdam, Netherlands

December 1
Independence Day (August 13) • Central African Republic
Independence Day • Portugal
Mocidade Day • Portuguese Guinea
National Day • Romania
Newport Day, Matilda • Liberia
Provincial Anniversary • Chatham and Westland, New Zealand
St. Edmund Campion, Feast Day of • Christian
St. Elizabeth Ann Seton, Feast of (Mother Seton Day) • Sisters of Charity of St. Vincent De Paul in the United States

December 2
National Day • United Arab Emirates
Republic Day • Laos

December 3
Admission Day • Illinois
St. Francis Xavier, Feast Day of • Christian

December 4
Artisans, Day of the • Mexico
St. Barbara's Day • Christian
St. John Damascene, Feast of • Christian

December 5
Columbus Day (Discovery Day) • Haiti
Kriss Kringle Day • Austria and Germany (or December 24)
National Day • Thailand

December 5 or 6 or December 24
Knecht Ruprecht • northern Germany

December 6
Constitution Day • Republic of Ireland
Independence Day • Bophuthatswana
Independence Day • Finland
St. Nicholas's Day • Christian (Gregorian calendar; December 19, Julian calendar)

December 7
Admission Day • Delaware
Burning the Devil (La Quema del Diablo) • San Cristóbal Totonicapán and Guatemala City, Guatemala
Independence Day (August 7) • Ivory Coast
Pearl Harbor Day • United States

Usually on or near December 7-8, but date varies and festival occurs according to king's authorization
Itul • Kuba people at Mushenge, Congo

Begins several days before December 8
Immaculate Conception, Feast of the (La Immaculada Concepción) • Juticalpa, Honduras

December 8
Blessing of the Waters or Family Day • Uruguay
Broken Needles Festival (Hari-Kuyo; also known as the Festival or Mass of the Broken Needles or Needle Day) • Kyoto, Japan
Immaculate Conception, Feast of the • Christian
Mothers' Day • Panama and Spain
St. Bartholomew's Day • Armenia
School Reunion Day • Spain

December 9
Immaculate Conception, Feast of the • Eastern Orthodox
Independence and Republic Day • Tanzania

December 10
Admission Day • Mississippi
Constitution Day • Thailand
Human Rights Day • United Nations-sponsored; observed in Equatorial Guinea and the United States
National Day • Burma (now Myanmar)
Wyoming Day • Wyoming

December 11
Admission Day • Indiana
Escalade • Geneva, Switzerland
Republic Day • Upper Volta
St. Daniel's Day • Christian

December 12
Admission Day • Pennsylvania
Independence Day (Jamhuri Day) • Kenya
Our Lady of Guadalupe (Nuestra Señora de Guadalupe) • Basilica of Our Lady of Guadalupe, Mexico City, Mexico, and elsewhere

Sunday nearest December 12
Our Lady of Guadalupe (Festival Guadalupaño) • Our Lady of Guadalupe Church, and throughout San Antonio, Texas

Twelve days beginning December 12
Yuletide Lads • Iceland

December 13
Republic Day • Malta
St. Lucy's Day • Christian

December 13-18
Shrine Festival, Kasuga Wakamiya • Nara, Japan

December 14
Admission Day • Alabama
St. Spyridon, Feast Day of • Corfu, Greece

December 14-28
Halcyon Days

December 15
Consualia • ancient Rome (and August 21)
Faunalia • ancient Rome (and February 13)
Kingdom or Statute Days • Netherlands Antilles

December 16
Christmas, Nine Days Before • Roman Catholic
Constitution Day • Nepal
Covenant, Day of the (Braaiveleis) • Afrikaaners in South Africa
Independence Day • Bahrain
Victory Day • Bangladesh

Nine days beginning December 16
Christmas Novena • South America

December 16-24
Christmas Carol Mass (Misa de Aguinaldo) • Caracas, Venezuela

December 16-24 or 25
Christmas Festival (Posadas, Feast of the Lodgings) • Hispanic-Americans and in Mexico

December 16-January 6
Christmas Season and Cock's Mass (Misa de Gallo) • Philippines

December 17
Wright Brothers Day • Kitty Hawk and Dayton, North Carolina

December 17-23
Christmas Boat Parade, Newport Harbor • Newport Beach, California
Saturnalia • ancient Rome

December 18
Admission Day • New Jersey
Republic Day • Niger
St. Modesto's Day (Oxen's Feast) • Greece

December 19
Opalia • ancient Rome
St. Nicholas's Day • Eastern Orthodox (Julian calendar; December 6, Gregorian calendar)

December 21
Capac Raimi • Inca people at Huanacaurí, Peru
(summer solstice)
Chaomos • Kafir Kalash people near Chitral, Pakistan
Doleing Day (Gooding Day) • Sussex and other parts
of England
Forefathers' Day • Plymouth, Massachusetts
Independence Day • Nepal
St. Thomas the Apostle, Feast of • Christian
Winter Solstice • northern hemisphere

On or near December 21
Juul, Feast of • ancient Scandinavia (winter solstice
festival)
Sun Celebration, Midnight (Ysyakh) • Yakutsk, USSR

December 21-22
Summer Solstice • southern hemisphere
Winter Solstice • northern hemisphere
Winter Solstice Celebration • Hopi Indians in northeastern
Arizona

December 21-25
Nativity of the Sun • northern Europe

December 22
Yule

December 23
St. Thorlak's Day • Iceland

Begins December 23
Christmas Eve (Juleaftgen) • Denmark

December 23-24
Christmas Festival (Night of the Radishes and Nativity
Festival) • Oaxaca, Mexico

Two weeks beginning December 23
Christmas Festival, Caribbean • Christiansted, St. Croix,
Virgin Islands

December 23-January 23
Junkanoo Festival • Jamaica

December 24
Christmas Eve • Christian
Independence Day • Libya
Panunuluyan • Lubang, Mindoro, Luzon Island, and
Manila, Philippines
"Silent Night, Holy Night" Celebration • Hallein,
Oberndorf, Wagrain, all of Salzburg, Austria

December 24-January 6
Christmas (Boże Narodzenie) • Poland

**December 24, three-week Mumming Drama during
Christmas season**
Christmas Eve • Tenby, South Wales

December 24-25
Christmas Season (Giant Lantern Festival) • San Fernando,
Pampanga, Philippines
Dance, Matchina • San Juan Pueblo, New Mexico
Dances, Matchina • Picuris Pueblo, New Mexico
Sundown Torchlight Procession of the Virgin with Deer or
Matchina Dance • Taos Pueblo, New Mexico

Second Sunday before Christmas, December 25
Mother's Day (Materice) • Serbia, Yugoslavia

December 25
Bank Holiday • England (also January 1, Good Friday,
Easter Monday, and December 26)
Children's Day • Congo
Christmas • Christian
Constitution Day • Taiwan
Dance, Matchina or Deer • Tesuque Pueblo, New Mexico
Dances, Matchina • San Ildefonso Pueblo, New Mexico
Dances, Matchina • Santa Clara Pueblo, New Mexico
Family Day • Angola
Family Day • Sao Tomé and Principe
Misisi Beer Feast • Sebei people in Uganda (also in October)
Nativity of the Sun (Mithraic Festival) • Persia (now Iran)
Quarter Days • England and Ireland (and March 25,
June 24, September 29)
Washington's Crossing of the Delaware • Washington
Crossing, Pennsylvania, and Washington Crossing,
New Jersey

December 25, two-day holiday
Christmas • Surinam

December 25-26
Christmas (Eerste and Tweede Kerstdag) • Netherlands/
Holland
Christmas (Juledag) • Denmark
Christmas (Weihnachten) • Germany
Christmas (Ziemas Svētku Diena) • Latvia

Between Christmas, December 25, and January 1
Fools, Feast of • medieval Europe

December 25-January 6
Christmas, Twelve Days of
Lord of Misrule • medieval western Europe (or October 31-
November 1 to February 2)

Week after Christmas, December 25
Arts Festival • Miccosukee Indians in Florida
Turon • Poland

December 26
Bank Holiday • England (also January 1, Good Friday, Easter Monday, and December 25)
Boxing Day
Dance, Turtle • San Juan Pueblo, New Mexico
Family Day • Namibia
St. Stephen, Feast of • Christian
Sumamao, Fiesta de • Roman Catholics at an arroyo of the Rio Dulce in Argentina

Several days beginning December 26
Sydney to Hobart Yacht Race • Australia

December 26-January 1
Junkanoo Festival • Nassau, Bahama Islands
Kwanzaa • African-Americans and African-Canadians

December 27
St. John, Apostle and Evangelist, Feast of • Christian
St. Stephen, Feast of • Eastern Orthodox

December 28
Admission Day • Iowa
All Fools' Day • Mexico
Holy Innocents' Day • Christian

December 28 or nearest Monday
Proclamation Day • South Australia

December 29
Admission Day • Texas
Holy Innocents' Day • Eastern Orthodox
King, Birthday of His Majesty the • Nepal
St. Thomas of Canterbury, Feast of • Christian

December 30
Republic Day • Madagascar
Republic Day • Romania
Rizal Day • Philippines

December 31
Candlewalk, The • England and the United States
Evacuation Day • Lebanon
New Year's Eve
Republic Day • Congo
St. Sylvester's Day • Christian

December 31 through January
Sydney, Festival of • Sydney, New South Wales, Australia

December 31 until Ash Wednesday (February-March)
Mardi Gras (Karneval) • Cologne, Germany

Full moon night of December
Dance Festival, Ras • Manipur, India (also during full moon of March-April and September-October, during Festival of Durga, the Mother Goddess)

At least one day in December
Ginem • Bagobo people in Philippines

A Sunday in December
Mother's Day • Yugoslavia

A Sunday before Christmas, December 25
Children's Day (Dechiyi Dan) • Yugoslavia

The three Thursday evenings before Christmas, December 25
Knocking Nights (Klöpfelnächte or Klöpfleinsnächte) • Germany

Five days in December
Circus Festival, International • Monte Carlo, Monaco

One week in December
Theatre Meeting, Viseu Amateur • Viseu, Portugal

Nine days to two weeks in December
Mevlana (Whirling Dervishes, Festival of) • Mevlana Muslims in Konya, Turkey

Two weeks in December
Palm Beach Festival • Palm Beach, Florida

Three weeks in December
Arts, North Queensland Festival of • Innisfail, Queensland, Australia
Arts Festival, Singapore • Singapore
Theatre Festivals, Children's Little • Calcutta, West Bengal, India (and second week in May)

Early December
Bear Festival • Ainu people in Japan

Three days in early December
Chichibu Yamaburi • Chichibu Shrine, Chichibu City, Saitama, Japan

Nine days in early December
National Finals Rodeo • location varies within the United States

Early December until Christmas, December 25
Christkindlesmarkt (Kriss Kringle's Fair) • Nuremberg, Bavaria, Germany

First Saturday in December
Greenwood Day, Chester • Farmington, Maine

Second Saturday night in December
Christmas Torchlight Parade and Muster, Old Saybrook •
Old Saybrook, Connecticut

Third Sunday in December
Father's Day (Ochichi, or Očevi) • Yugoslavia

Fourth weekend in December
Seminole Fair • Seminole Indians at Seminole
Reservation, Florida

Last week in December
Winter Traditions, Festival of • Botosani, Romania

Last weekend in December
Folklore Festival, Maramuresean • Sighetu Marmatiei,
Maramures, Romania

December or early January during the dry season
Nja Festival • Bamum people in Cameroon

December-January
Arts Festival, Kalakshetra • Madras, Tamil Nadu, India

New moon in December-January
Uhola Festival • Dakkarkari people in Nigeria

Six days in December-January
New Year (Newala Ceremonies, First Fruits Festival) •
Lozithehlezi to Gunundvwini, and Lobamba, Swaziland

Ten days in late December-early January
Ballet Festival, Monte Carlo Winter • Monte Carlo,
Monaco

Two weeks in December-January
Jatra Festival • Imphal, Manipur, India

Three weeks in December-January
Winter Festival, Russian • Moscow, Russia, USSR

Mid-December through January 1
Christmas Tree, Lighting of the National • White House
Lawn, Washington, D.C.

Mid-December to January
Nativity Plays • Celaya and Yuriria, Guanajuato, Mexico

**December-April, during a heavy snowfall after Christmas and
before Easter**
Winter Sleigh Party (Kulig) • Poland

Winter

Winter
Dionysus • Athens, Greece (also May)
Wíikita Festival • Papago Indians at Archie, Arizona
Yasukini Matsuri • Yasukini Shrine, Tokyo, Japan (also
summer, autumn, and four days in April)

Nine-day winter solstice ceremony
Soyal or Soyala • Hopi Indians

10-15 days in winter
Jatra Festivals of Calcutta • Calcutta, West Bengal, India

Twenty days during winter
Dance, Hupa Winter (Haichitdilya) • Hupa Indians in
northern California

Winter months
Ponape Feast • Ponape Island, Eastern Caroline Islands

Christian Movable Days Index

This list includes Christian holidays as well as secular festivals whose dates are based on Christian calendar dates. Advent Sunday (the first Sunday in Advent) begins the Christian liturgical calendar. Dates for most movable holidays in the Christian year are defined by the date of Easter, which is set at the first Sunday after the first full moon after the vernal equinox (March 21).

Late November, Sunday before Advent Sunday
Stir-Up Sunday • Anglicans in England

Sunday nearest November 30
Advent Sunday

Four-week season beginning Sunday nearest November 30-December 24
Advent

Beginning of Advent to Sunday following Epiphany (December-January)
Midwinter Horn, Blowing the (Midwinterhoorn Blazen) • Overijssel, Netherlands

About 76 days before Easter (about one month before Ash Wednesday, January-February)
Mardi Gras • Montevideo, Uruguay

About 67 days before Easter (the three weeks before Ash Wednesday)
Mardi Gras (Apokreos, Carnival) • Greece (last week is called Cheese Week)

Nine weeks before Easter (third Sunday before Lent)
Lost Sunday
Septuagesima Sunday

About 60 days before Easter (the two weeks before Ash Wednesday)
Mardi Gras • Mobile, Alabama

58 days before Easter (twelve days ending Ash Wednesday)
Mardi Gras (Carnival) • Limassol, Cyprus
Mardi Gras (Carnival; Battle of the Flowers) • Nice, France

Eight weeks before Easter (second Sunday before Lent)
Sexagesima Sunday

54 days before Easter (eight days before Lent begins)
Lent (Meat Fare Sunday) • Eastern Orthodox

About 53 days before Easter (week before Ash Wednesday)
Mardi Gras (Carnival Week) • Oruro, Bolivia
Mardi Gras (Fasching, Carnival) • Austria
Mardi Gras (Maslyanitza, Butter Week) • Russia
Mardi Gras (Schemenlauf, Running of the Spectres) • Imst, Tirol, Austria
Mardi Gras (Sirna Sedmitza, Cheese Week) • Bulgaria

About 53rd through 46th days before Easter (the week before Lent, especially Thursday)
Mardi Gras (al-Marfa, Carnival, and Khamis al-Marfa, Carnival Thursday) • Syria

About 53rd through 46th days before Easter (one week ending Ash Wednesday)
Mardi Gras (Carnaval, Fiesta of Games) • Zinacantun, Mexico

52 days before Easter (Thursday before Ash Wednesday)
Mardi Gras (Fetten Donneschdeg) • Luxembourg
Mardi Gras (Tincunaco Ceremony) • Calchaqui Valley, Argentina
Sts. Vartan and Ghevont Day • Armenia
Vartanantz Day • Armenians worldwide

52nd through 55th days before Easter (four days beginning Thursday of the weekend before Ash Wednesday)
Charro Days Fiesta • Brownsville, Texas, and Matamoros, Mexico

51st through 47th days before Easter (Friday-Tuesday before Ash Wednesday)
Mardi Gras (Carnival) • Barranquilla, Atlántico, Colombia

50th day before Easter (Saturday before Ash Wednesday)
Egg Saturday • Oxfordshire, England

50th through 47th days before Easter (the four days before Ash Wednesday)
Mardi Gras (Carnival) • Rio de Janeiro, Brazil

50th through 46th days before Easter (Saturday before Ash Wednesday through Ash Wednesday)
Mardi Gras (Carnival and Burial of the Sardine on Ash Wednesday) • Panama
Mardi Gras (Intruz, Carnival) • Goa, India

49 days before Easter (Sunday before Ash Wednesday)
Mardi Gras (Cheesefare Sunday) • Macedonia
Mardi Gras (Të Lidhurat, Carnival Sunday) • Albania
Quinquagesima Sunday

49th and 47th days before Easter (Sunday and Tuesday before Ash Wednesday)
Carnival of Mamoiada • Mamoiada, Sardinia, Italy

49th through 47th days before Easter (Sunday-Tuesday before Ash Wednesday)
Mardi Gras (Carnaval) • Portugal
Mardi Gras (Carnaval) • Spain
Mardi Gras (Carnival) • Oranjestad, Aruba
Mardi Gras (Carnival of the Gilles, or Clowns) • Binche, Belgium

49th through 46th days before Easter (Sunday before Ash Wednesday through Ash Wednesday)
Mardi Gras (Carnival) • Martinique and Guadeloupe

48 days before Easter (Monday before Ash Wednesday)
Mardi Gras (Fastelavn) • Norway
Mardi Gras (Fastelavn or Fastelavan) • Denmark
Mardi Gras (Rosemontag, Rose Monday) • German-Americans

48th and 47th days before Easter (Monday and Tuesday before Ash Wednesday)
Mardi Gras (Tuesday is Bursting Day and Bun Day) • Iceland
Mardi Gras (Carnival) • Trinidad and Tobago
Mardi Gras (Collop Monday and Shrove or Pancake Tuesday) • England
Mardi Gras (Fastnacht and Rosemontag, Rose Monday) • Germany

47th day before Easter (ends Tuesday before Ash Wednesday)
Mardi Gras • Venice, Veneto, Italy

47th day before Easter (Tuesday before Ash Wednesday)
Mardi Gras • France
Mardi Gras • Tuscany, Italy
Mardi Gras (Fasnacht) • Pennsylvania Dutch people in the United States
Mardi Gras (Fastern's E'en) • Scotland
Mardi Gras (Fiesta de Febrero) • Tzintzuntzan, Mexico
Mardi Gras (Kopenfahrt, Kope Procession or Festival) • Lüneburg, Lower Saxony, Germany
Mardi Gras (Laskiaispäivä) • Finland
Mardi Gras (Pancake Day) • Olney, England, and Liberal, Kansas
Mardi Gras (Shrove Tuesday) • Ireland
Mardi Gras (Užgavenės) • Lithuania
Mardi Gras (Vastenavond) • Netherlands and Dutch-Americans in New York
Mardi Gras (Vastla Päev) • Estonia
Wooing a Bride (Brauteln) • Sigmaringen, Baden-Württemberg, Germany

47th and 46th days before Easter (Tuesday before Ash Wednesday and Ash Wednesday)
Mardi Gras (Carnival) • Carriacou, Grenada

Sometimes celebrated before, and sometimes after, Ash Wednesday
Mardi Gras (Fastnacht) • Switzerland

40 days before Easter (begins Lent)
Ash Wednesday

40-day season preceding Easter
Lent (in Eastern Orthodox churches, Lent begins the Monday before Ash Wednesday)
Passio Festival, La • Esparraguera, Barcelona, Spain

40-day season preceding Easter (observances every Friday from Ash Wednesday through Holy Week)
Lent • Yaqui Indians in Arizona

Sundays during Lent until month after Easter
Passion, Sacred Drama of the • Ulldecona, Tarragona, Spain

Thursday before Lent, which begins on Friday
Mardi Gras (Zapusty, Fat Thursday) • Poland

44th day before Easter (Friday after Ash Wednesday)
Nippy Lug Day • Westmorland and other areas in northern England and in Scotland

40th day before Easter (first Sunday in Lent)
Chalk Sunday • Ireland
Quadragesima Sunday (Firebrand Sunday)

37th, 35th, and 34th days before Easter (Wednesday, Friday and Saturday of the week following first Sunday in Lent)
Ember Days • Anglican (also of the weeks during Pentecost, September 14, and December 13)

21st day before Easter (three weeks before Easter, fourth Sunday in Lent)
Mid-Lent Sunday
Rose Sunday • Roman Catholic

21st day before Easter every three years (three weeks before Easter, third Sunday before Easter every three years)
Fish Carnival (Groppenfasnacht) • Ermatingen, Switzerland

14th day before Easter (Sunday preceding Palm Sunday, fifth Sunday in Lent)
Carling Sunday • Czechoslovakia, Germany, and Great Britain
Passion Sunday • England and Italy (Domenica delle Passione)

Two weeks before Easter (last two weeks of Lent)
Passiontide

Eight days before Easter (Saturday before Palm Sunday)
St. Lazarus's Day • Eastern and Russian Orthodox in Greece, Romania, and Russia

Eighth day before or day before Easter (Saturday before Palm or Easter Sunday)
St. Lazarus's Day • Slavic people in Bulgaria

Seventh day before Easter (Sunday before Easter)
Palm Sunday

Weekend before Easter (Palm Sunday weekend)
Calico Pitchin', Cookin', and Spittin' Hullabaloo • Calico, California

Week before Easter
Creole Week (Semana Criolla) • Uruguay
Holy Week
Holy Week (Deer Dance and Lenten Ceremonies) • Yaqui Indians in Arizona
Passion Play • Malinalco, Mexico
Passion Play • Tzintzuntzan, Michoacán, Mexico
Passion Play, Cenaculo • Cainta, Malabon, and Navota, Rizal, Luzon Island, Philippines
Passion Play, Cenaculo • Samal, Bataan, Luzon Island, Philippines
Pilgrimage to Chalma • Chalma, Mexico
Volador Fiesta • Guatemala and Mexico (or during Corpus Christi)

One week before Easter through day after Easter (Palm Sunday to Monday after Easter)
Easter Festival (Osterfestspiele) • Salzburg, Austria

Fourth day before Easter (Wednesday before Easter)
Spy Wednesday

Four successive Thursdays before Eastern Orthodox Easter
Springtime Festival • Bekáa Valley, throughout Syria, Lebanon, and former Palestine

Third day before Easter (Thursday before Easter)
Holy Thursday
Verges Festival • Verges, Gerona, Spain

Second day before Easter (Friday before Easter)
Bank Holiday • England (also Easter Monday, December 25, and December 26)
Good Friday
Passion Play • Ixtapalapa, Federal District, Mexico

Second day before Easter through Easter (Good Friday to Easter Sunday)
Moriones Festival • Boac, Gasan, and Mogpog, Marinduque Island, Philippines

Ten days beginning Friday before Easter
Easter Festival of Sacred Music • Roman Catholics in Lourdes, Haute-Pyrénées, France

Day before Easter (Saturday before Easter)
Holy Saturday
Nebi Mousa, Feast of • Muslims in Jerusalem

First Sunday after first full moon after the vernal equinox (Eastern Orthodox churches use Julian calendar)
Easter

Easter weekend
Safari Rally • Nairobi, Kenya
Top of the World Ski Meet • Eskimos, Canadians, and Canadian-Indians at Inuvik, Northwest Territories, Canada

Easter week
Mystery of the Passion • Moncada, Valencia, Spain

During the Easter holidays
Easter Show, Royal • Moore Park Showground, Sydney, New South Wales, Australia
Young People's Festival • Plymouth, Devonshire, England

Several days beginning Easter
Merrie Monarch Festival • Hilo, Hawaii

Six days during Easter holidays
Drama Festival, Newfoundland • location varies annually within Newfoundland, Canada

Eight days during Easter week
Messiah Festival • Lindsborg, Kansas

Easter Sunday and Monday after Easter
Easter Monday (Vlöggelen, Winging Ceremony) • Ootmarsum, Netherlands

Monday after Coptic Easter
Spring Day, Smell the (Sham al-Neseem) • Egypt

Monday after Easter
Bank Holiday • England (also Good Friday, December 25, and December 26)
Bottle Kicking and Hare Pie Scramble, Annual • Hallaton, Leicestershire, England
Easter Monday
Pottery Festival • Luxembourg City, Luxembourg

Monday and Tuesday after Easter
Easter Monday • Estonia
Easter Monday (Hocktide, Hock Monday, Hock Tuesday or Tutti Day) • England

Four to five days beginning Monday after Easter
Burial of the Sardine (Entierro de la Sardina) • Spain

Seven days beginning Monday after Easter during odd-numbered years
Vintage Festival, Barossa Valley • Barossa Valley, Tanunda, South Australia, Australia

Usually week before or after Easter Week
Drama Festival, National Student • location varies within England

Thursday after Easter
Dead Remembrance Thursday (Khamis al-Amwat) • Jordan

Friday after Easter
Life-Bearing Spring (Zoodochos Pege) • Greece

Two weeks following Easter
Tucson Festival • Hispanic-Americans and Papago and Yaqui Indians in Tucson, Arizona

After Easter; usually last two weeks in April
Mardi Gras (Carnival) • Virgin Islands

Seventh day after Easter (Sunday after Easter)
Low Sunday (also known as Close Sunday, Low Easterday, Quasimodo Sunday) • Moravia, Germany, and Brazil
St. Thomas's Day • Greece and Macedonia

Eight days after Easter (second Monday after Easter)
Blajini (Meek), Feast of the (Sarbatoarea Blajinilor) • Romania

21st day after Easter (third Sunday after Easter)
Jubilate Sunday • Roman Catholic

25th day after Easter
Rousa, Feast of • Greece

26th day after Easter (fourth Friday after Easter)
Common Prayer Day (Store Bededag) • Denmark

28th day after Easter
Ropotine • Romania

35th day after Easter
Rural Life Sunday (Soil Stewardship Sunday) • United States

Begins 35th day after Easter (fifth Sunday through Wednesday after Easter)
Rogation Days

Begins 35th day after Easter (eight to 15 days beginning fifth Sunday after Easter)
Our Lady, Consoler of the Afflicted, Octave of • Luxembourg-Ville, Luxembourg

37th day after Easter (Monday before Ascension Thursday)
Fields, Going to the (Veldgang) • Mekkelhorst, Overijssel, Netherlands

Before 40th day after Easter (before Ascension Day)
Well Dressing • England

40th day after Easter
Ascension Day
Dew Treading (Dauwtrappen) • Netherlands
Holy Thursday • Church of England in England

40th through 43rd days after Easter during even-numbered years (Thursday to Sunday evening of Ascension Day)
Dullin Prize Competition • Aix-les-Bains, Savoie, France

Sixth week after Easter (week before Pentecost)
Penitents, Procession of the (La Procesion De La Penitencia) • Roncesvalles, Navarre, Spain

47th or 48th day after Easter through 51st or 52nd day after Easter (Thursday or Friday before Pentecost Sunday through Monday or Tuesday after Pentecost)
Pilgrimage of the Dew (Romería Del Rocío) • Almonte, Huelva, Andalusia, Spain

48th through 51st days after Easter (Friday to Monday evening of Pentecost during odd-numbered years)
Theatre, Biennial of International • Vichy, Allier, France

49th day after Easter (Saturday before Pentecost)
Divino, Festo do • Alcântara and Paraty, Brazil
Kallemooi • Schiermonnikoog, North Coast Islands, Netherlands
Luilak (Lazybones Day or Sluggard's Feast) • Zaandam, Haarlem, Amsterdam, and other western towns in the Netherlands

49th through 56th days after Easter (one week beginning Pentecost Eve)
Pentecost (Rusalii) • Romania

Seventh Thursday after Easter
Semik • prerevolutionary Russia

The Sunday 50 days after Easter
Ember Days (also first Sunday in Lent, September 14, and December 13)
Master Draught Pageant (Meistertrunk Pageant) • Rothernburg on the Tauber, Bavaria, Federal Republic of Germany
Pentecost

Three to five days including the 50th day after Greek Orthodox Easter (Pentecost)
   Kataklysmos Festival (Flood Festival) • Larnaca, Limassol, Paphos, and other towns, Cyprus

50th and 51st days after Easter (Pentecost Sunday and the following Monday)
   Marins, Fête des • Honfleur, France
   Pentecost and Whit Monday • Ozora, Hungary

51st day after Easter (Monday after Pentecost)
   Flower Festival, Broom (Genzefest) • Wiltz, Luxembourg
   Trinity Sunday • Eastern Orthodox Church
   Whit Monday

52nd day after Easter (Tuesday after Pentecost)
   Dancing Procession (Sprangprozessio'n) • Echternach, Luxembourg
   Pinkster Bruid (Pinksterbloem or Whitsun Bride or Whitsun Flower Festival) • Overijssel, Netherlands

Eighth to ninth weeks after Easter (Corpus Christi week)
   La Patum Festival • Berga, Barcelona, Spain

57th day after Easter (first Sunday after Pentecost)
   Golden Chariot and Battle of the Lumecon, Procession of the • Mons, Belgium
   Trinity Sunday

61st day after Easter (the Thursday following Trinity Sunday; non-Catholic Christians)
   Corpus Christi

64th day after Easter (the Sunday following Trinity Sunday, first Sunday after Pentecost)
   Corpus Christi • Roman Catholics and in the United States
   Volador Fiesta • Guatemala and Mexico (or during Holy Week)

68th day after Easter (first Thursday after Corpus Christi)
   Lajkonik • Poland

69th day after Easter (the Friday after Corpus Christi)
   Sacred Heart of Jesus, Feast of the • Roman Catholic

70 days after Easter (Saturday following the second Sunday after Pentecost)
   Immaculate Heart of Mary, Feast of the • Roman Catholic

75th day after Easter (second Thursday after Corpus Christi)
   Horse Festival (Lejkonik) • Kraków, Poland

99 days after Easter
   Transfiguration, Feast of the • Armenia

Jewish Calendar Index

First day of every Jewish month; day of new moon and last day of each month with 30 days
Rosh Chodesh

Tishri
(corresponds to Gregorian September-October)

First day of Tishri
New Year, Jewish (Rosh Hashanah; also known as Day of Blowing the Shofar)
Trumpets, Feast of • post-Exilic Jews

Second day of Tishri
Gedaliah, Fast of

Tenth day of Tishri
Yom Kippur (also known as Day of Atonement; High Holiday)

15th-21st or 22nd days of Tishri
Sukkot (Feast of Booths or Feast of the Tabernacles)

15th night of Tishri, night after first day of Sukkot, and every night of Sukkot thereafter
Water-Drawing Festival (Simhat bet ha-sho'evah) • Israel

21st day of Tishri, seventh day of Sukkot
Hoshana Rabbah (Great Salvation)

22nd day of Tishri, eighth day of Sukkot
Shemini Atzeret

23rd day of Tishri
Simhat Torah (Rejoicing in the Law)

Heshvan
(corresponds to Gregorian October-November)

29th day of Heshvan
Seged • Falasha Jews in Ethiopia

Kislev
(corresponds to Gregorian November-December)

Second day of Kislev
Purim • Casablanca, Morocco

Eight days beginning 25th day of Kislev
Hanukkah

Tevet
(corresponds to Gregorian December-January)

Tenth day of Tevet
Asarah be-Tevet (Fast of Tevet)

Shevat
(corresponds to Gregorian January-February)

15th day of Shevat
New Year of Trees (B'Shevat or Hamishah Assar Bi-Shebat) • Jewish people in Israel

Adar
(corresponds to Gregorian February-March)

13th day of Adar
Ta'anit Esther

14th day of Adar
Purim • Iran, United States, and Yemen

Nisan
(corresponds to Gregorian March-April)

Every 28 years on the first Wednesday of Nisan
Blessing the Sun (Birchat Hahamah) • Jews in Israel and the United States

Festival preceding Passover, which begins 15th day of Nisan
Hagodol (Great Sabbath)

Before Passover, which begins 15th day of Nisan
Deliverance, Day of

14th day of Nisan
First-Born, Fast of the

Seven days beginning 15th of Nisan
Passover (Pesach)

Evening of last day of Passover and the day after
Maimona or Maimonides • Jews in Libya and Morocco

27th day of Nisan
Holocaust Day (Yom Hashoah)

Iyar
(corresponds to Gregorian April-May)

Fourth day of Iyar
Yom ha-Zikkaron (Day of Remembrance) • Israel

Iyar *(cont.)*
(corresponds to Gregorian April-May)

15th day of Iyar
Independence Day • Israel

18th day of Iyar, the 33rd day in the fifty-day period between Passover and Shavuot, in addition to the fifty-day period itself
Lag b'Omer

Sivan
(corresponds to Gregorian May-June)

Sixth day of Sivan
Shavuot (Feast of Weeks; also known as Jewish Feast
of Pentecost)

11th day of Sivan
Purim • Padua, Italy

Tammuz
(corresponds to Gregorian June-July)

17th day of Tammuz
Tammuz, Fast of the 17th of

Av
(corresponds to Gregorian July-August)

Ninth day of Av
Tisha B'Av

15th day of Av
Fifteenth of Av (Hamishah Asar be-Av)

Islamic Calendar Index

Chinese Calendar Index

24th day of each month
Jizo—Ennichi or Jiso Kshitigarba • Buddhists in China and Japan

**First Month
(corresponds to Gregorian January-February)**

Ten-day to two-week long celebration at the first new moon after sun enters Aquarius, during the first month (length varies)
New Year

Several days beginning first day of the first month
New Year (Tet Nguyenden) • Vietnam and Vietnamese-Americans in New York

Last day of winter in lunar calendar
Bean-Throwing Festival (Setsubun) • Japan

Second day of the first month
Pilgrimage to Shrines of Tsai Shên • China (also 15th day of ninth month)

Seventh day of the first month
Mankind, Birthday of • China

Eighth day of the first month
Yen Lo's Birthday • Buddhists in China
Yü Huang Shang Ti, Jade or Pearly Emperor • Chinese Taoists

Ninth day of the first month
Making Happiness Festival (Tso-Fu) • Taiwan

13th day of the first month
Hoi Lim Festival, Ha Bac Province • Vietnam

13th-15th days of the first month
Lantern Festival (Yaun Shaw) • Taiwan, China, Hong Kong, and Penang, Malaysia

15th day of the first month
Burning the Moon House (Dal-jip-tae-u-gee or Viewing the First Full Moon; Dal-ma-ji) • Kyungsang Province, Korea
Great Fifteenth • Korea

Full moon day of the first month or full moon day of Hindu month of Jyeshta
Sangamitta Day • Sri Lanka

16th day of the first month
Jurokunichi • Hanashiro, Okinawa
Sugar Ball Show • Haiyun Buddhist Convent, Qingdao, Shandong, China

18th day of the first month
Star Festival • China

19th day of the first month
Rat's Wedding Day • China

**Second Month
(corresponds to Gregorian February-March)**

First day of the second month
Wind Festival • Korea

Second day of the second month
Bok Kai Festival • Chinese-Americans at Marysville, California

10th-15th days of the second month
Paro Tshechu • Buddhists in Paro, Bhutan (or on a date in early spring determined by lamas)

18th day of the second month
Wu Kuan's Day • China

**Third Month
(corresponds to Gregorian March-April)**

Fourth or fifth day of the third month, 105 or 106 days after the winter solstice
Grave-Sweeping and Cold Food Festival (Qing Ming, Clear and Bright) • China and elsewhere

Fifth day of the third month
Grave-Sweeping and Cold Food Festival (Thanh-Minh, Pure and Bright) • Vietnam

Full moon day of the third month
Four Miracles Assembly (Magha Puja) • Buddhists in Laos (Makha Bouxa) and Thailand (Magha Puja)

19th day of the third month
Goddess of Mercy, Birthday of • Buddhists in China, Japan, Korea, Malaysia, and Tibet (or between March-April; observed on 19th day of tenth month in Hong Kong)

23rd day of the third month
Matsu, Birthday of (Matsu Festival) • Buddhists in Taiwan
Tin Hau Festival • Hong Kong

Fourth Month
(corresponds to Gregorian April-May)

Eighth day of the fourth month
Buddha's Birthday, Enlightenment, and Salvation •
Buddhist (observed April 8 in Japan)
Tam Kung Festival • Tam Kung Temple, Shau Kei Wan,
Hong Kong Island

Eighth and ninth days of the fourth month
Prince, Birthday of the Third • Chinese Taoists in Singapore

Three days from the eighth day of the fourth month, to coincide with Buddha's birthday
Chunhyang Festival • Namwon, North Jeolla, Republic
of Korea

Fifth Month
(corresponds to Gregorian May-June)

Fifth day of the fifth month
Double Fifth (Dragon Boat Festival and Festival of the
Five Poisonous Creatures)
Summer Solstice Day (Doan Ngu) • Vietnam
Swing Festival (Tano) • Korea

14th day of the fifth month
Boat Race Day • Minatogawa and Taira, Okinawa (Gods
of the Sea Festival in Minatogawa)

15th day of the fifth month
Fifth Month Festival (Gogatsu Matsuri) • Okinawa

Sixth Month
(corresponds to Gregorian June-July)

Sixth day of the sixth month
Airing the Classics (Double Sixth Day) • Buddhists in
China

15th day of the sixth month
Shampoo Day (Yoodoonal) • Korea

Full moon day of the sixth month
Buddha's Birthday, Enlightenment, and Salvation (Vixakha
Bouxa; Festival of Rockets, Boun Bang Fay) • Buddhists
in Laos

24th day of the sixth month
Lotus, Birthday of • Buddhists in Peking, China

24th-26th days of the sixth month
Torch Festival • Yunnan and Sichuan, China

Seventh Month
(corresponds to Gregorian July-August)

Seventh day of the seventh month
Double Seventh (Festival of the Weaving Maid and the
Herd Boy)

15th day of the seventh month
Dead, Festival of the • Buddhists
Hungry Ghosts, Festival of (Ullambana) • Buddhists
and Taoist

Eighth Month
(corresponds to Gregorian August-September)

15th day of the eighth month
Trung-Thu • Vietnam (or in September-October; full
moon after new moon in Virgo)

15th, or full moon, day of the eighth month
Mid-Autumn Festival

16th day of the eighth month
Monkey's Festival (Birthday of Ts'oi, T'in Tai Seng Yeh)
• Hong Kong and Singapore

27th day of the eighth month
Confucius's Birthday • Taiwan (Teachers' Day), Hong
Kong, China

Ninth Month
(corresponds to Gregorian September-October)

Ninth month
Dead, Feast of the (Ho Khao Padap Dinh) • Laos

First nine days of the ninth month
Vegetarian Festival • Phuket, Thailand

Ninth day of the ninth month
Castle Festival, Moyang • Gochang, Republic of Korea
Chrysanthemum Festival (Choyo) • Japan, Korea,
and Okinawa
Double Ninth Day
Nine Imperial Gods, Festival of • Singapore

15th day of the ninth month
Pilgrimage to Shrines of Tsai Shên • China (and second
day of first month)

Tenth Month
(corresponds to Gregorian October-November)

First day of the tenth month
Sending the Winter Dress • China

Tenth Month *(cont.)*
(corresponds to Gregorian October-November)

Fifth day of the tenth month
Ta Mo's Day • China and Japan

19th day of the tenth month
Goddess of Mercy, Birthday of • Buddhists in Hong Kong

Eleventh Month
(corresponds to Gregorian November-December)

Eleventh month
Winter Solstice (Tung Chih) • China

Full moon day of the eleventh month to full moon day of twelfth month
Robe Offering Month (Kathin Season or Tod Kathin) • Buddhists in Thailand

Several days during the eleventh and twelfth months at 3-, 5-, 10-year, or longer, intervals
Ta Chiu • Taoists in Hong Kong

Twelfth Month
(corresponds to Gregorian December-January)

Eighth day of the twelfth month
Mochi No Matsuri • Okinawa

20th day of the twelfth month
Sweeping Floors, Day for • Hong Kong

23rd or 24th day of the twelfth month and New Year's Eve and Day
Kitchen God Celebration (Tsao Chün) • China

28th day of the twelfth month for five days
New Year (Dosmoche Festival) • Leh and Lhasa, Tibet

29th day of the twelfth month
Thirtieth, Night of the (Ch'u Hsi) • China

Hindu Calendar Index
(includes some holidays observed according to the Buddhist calendar)

11th day of each waxing and waning moon (24 times yearly)
Eleventh (Ekadashi)

Vaisakha
(corresponds to Gregorian April-May)

Vaisakha
Pooram • Hindus in Trichur, India

First day of Vaisakha
New Year • Bangladesh, India, Malaysia, Nepal, Punjab, and Sri Lanka

Third day of waxing half of Vaisakha
Parshurama Jayanti • Hindu
Undecaying Third (Akshya Tritiya) • Hindu

21 days beginning third day of waxing half of Vaisakha
Chandan Yatra • Hindus in Puri, Orissa, Bhubaneshwar, Baripada, and Balanga, India

Fifth day of waxing half of Vaisakha
Shankarachaya Jayanti or Birthday • Hindus in southern India

Ninth day of waxing half of Vaisakha
Janaki Navami • Hindu

Tenth day of waxing half of Vaisakha
Shankarachaya Jayanti or Birthday • Hindus in northern India

14th day of waxing half of Vaisakha
Narsimha Jayanti • Hindu and Vaishnavite

Full moon day of Vaisakha
Buddha's Birthday, Enlightenment, and Salvation (Buddha Jayanti) • Buddhists in India, Laos, and Sri Lanka

Begins first day of waning half of Vaisakha and lasts two months
Chariot Festival of Macchendranath (Festival of the God of Rain) • Buddhist Newars and Hindus in Patan and Kathmandu, Nepal

Jyeshta
(corresponds to Gregorian May-June)

Sixth day of waxing half of Jyeshta
Sithinakha (Kumar Sasthi) • Hindus in Nepal

Eighth day of waxing half of Jyeshta
Jyeshta Ashtami • Hindus in Khir Bhawani, Kashmir

Tenth day of waxing half of Jyeshta
Ganges River Festival (Ganga Dussehra) • Hindus along the Ganges River, India

Eleventh day of waxing half of Jyeshta
Nirjala Ekadashi • Hindu

Full moon day of Jyeshta
Bathing Festival (Snan Yatra) • Orissa, India
Poson or Dhamma Vijaya (Full Moon Day) • Buddhists in Sri Lanka, especially Anuradhapura and Mihintale

13th day of waning half or full moon day of Jyeshta
Vata Savitri (Savitri Vrata or Vow) • married Hindu women

Ashadha
(corresponds to Gregorian June-July)

Ashadha
Agricultural Festival • Satara District, Maharashtra, India
Esala Perahera (Mahanuwara Esala Dalada Perahera) • Buddhists and Hindus in Kandy, Sri Lanka (or nine nights during annual festival, full moon day of Esala, eighth month)

Second day of waxing half of Ashadha
Juggernaut (Rath Yatra, Festival of Jagannatha) • Hindus at Jagannatha temple at Puri, Orissa, India

Full moon day of Ashadha
Guru Purnima (also known as Ashadha Purnima; Guru Vyas Purnima) • Hindus in India

Sravana
(corresponds to Gregorian July-August)

Sravana
Agricultural Festival (Pola) • Maharashtra, India
Protection, Festival to Pledge (Rakhi) • Hindus in India
Sravani Mela • Hindus in Deogarh, Bihar, India

Begins during Wazo, the fourth Buddhist month, and ends on the 15th or full moon day of Thadingyut, the seventh Buddhist month
Lenten Season • Buddhist

Sravana *(cont.)*
(corresponds to Gregorian July-August)

Third day of waxing half of Sravana
Teej • Hindu women in India and Kathmandu, Nepal
Teej (Hariyali Teej or Hari Tritiya) • Hindu women in
Uttar Pradesh, India

Fifth day of waxing half of Sravana
Snake Festival (Naag Panchami in northern India and
Nepal; Nagarapanchami in southern India)

Seventh day of waxing half of Sravana
Tulsidas Jayanti • Hindu

Eighth day of waxing half of Sravana
Panchadaan • Buddhists in Patan and elsewhere in Nepal
see also **Eighth Day of waning half of Bhadrapada**

11th day of waxing half of Sravana
Putrada Ekadashi • Hindu

Full moon day of Sravana
Amarnath Yatra • Amarnath cave with sacred ice lingam
in the Kashmir Himalayas
Jhulan Latra • Hindus at Jagannath Temple at Puri,
Orissa, India
Narieli Purnima • Hindus in southern India
Sacred Thread Festival (Raksha Bandhan in northern
India; Avani Avittam in southern India) • Hindu

First day of waning half of Sravana
Cows, Procession of Sacred (Gai Jatra) • Hindus in Nepal

Third day of waning half of Sravana
Marya • Patan, Nepal

11th day of waning half of Sravana
Wish-Fulfilling Eleventh (Kamada Ekadashi) • Hindu

14th day of waning half of Sravana
Ghanta Karna • Buddhists in Nepal

Bhadrapada
(corresponds to Gregorian August-September)

Bhadrapada
Agricultural Festival (Pola) • Poona and Sholapur,
Maharashtra, India
Paryushana or Partyshana Parva • Digambar Jaina and
Svetambar Jaina people in India

Ten days during Bhadrapada
Tirupati Festival • Hindus at shrine on Tirumala hills,
Tirupati, India

Third day of waxing half of Bhadrapada
Teej (Haritlika Teej) • Hindu women

Fourth day of waxing half of Bhadrapada
Elephant God, Festival of the (Ganesha Chaturthi) • India
and Nepal (one-week festival in Bombay, Maharashtra,
India)

Fifth day of waxing half of Bhadrapada
Rishi Panchami • Hindu

14th day of waxing half of Bhadrapada
Fourteenth Day of Bhadra, Eternal Anniversary of (Anant
Chaturdashi) • Hindu

Third day of waning half of Bhadrapada
Panchadaan • Buddhists in Kathmandu and Bhadgaon,
Nepal

Sixth day of waning half of Bhadrapada
Halashasti or Balarama Shashti • Hindus in northern
India

Eighth day of waning half of Bhadrapada
Krishna's Birthday • Hindus in India and Nepal (twelve-
day celebration in Manipur, India)
Radha Ashtami • Hindu
see also **Eighth day of waxing half of Sravana**

Last day of waning half of Bhadrapada
Father's Day (Gokarna Aunsi) • Nepal

End of Bhadrapada
Tools, Festival of (Visvakarma Puja) • Hindu

Eight days during Bhadrapada-Asvina
Indra Jatra and Kumari Jatra, Festival of the Child Goddess
• Hindus in Kathmandu, Nepal (12th day of waxing moon
is Kumari Jatra)

Asvina
(corresponds to Gregorian September-October)

Asvina
Agricultural Festival (Hadaga) • Maharashtra, India
Goddess of Fortune, Festival of the (Lukshmi or Laksmi
Puja) • Hindus in Bengal, India

First ten days of waxing half of Asvina
Dance Festival, Ras • Manipur, India (also during full
moon of March-April and full moon night of December)
Mother Goddess, Festival of Durga, the • India and Nepal

Asvina *(cont.)*
(corresponds to Gregorian September-October)

Three weeks during Festival of Durga, the Mother Goddess, beginning first ten days of waxing half of Asvina
Ballet Festival, Bharatiya Kala Kendra • New Delhi, India

Full moon day of Asvina
Harvest Festival (Kojagara) • Hindus in India
Sharad Purnima • Hindu
Valmiki's Jayanti or Birthday • India

Waning half of Asvina
Dead, Feast of the (Pitra Pasksha or Pitra Visarjana and Amavasya) • Hindus in Gaya, India

Karthika
(corresponds to Gregorian October-November)

Karthika
Bhishma Ashtami • India
Karthika Snan • Hindus along the Ganges and Yamuna rivers, India

First day of waxing half of Karthika
Govardhan Puja and Annakut • Hindus in Mount Govardhan and elsewhere in northern India

Second day of waxing half of Karthika
Brother and Sister Day (Bhai-Dooj, Bhaiya Duj, or Bhratri Dwitya; also known as Yama Dvitiya) • Hindus in India

Sixth day of waxing half of Karthika
Surya Shashti • married Hindu women with children

11th day of waxing half of Karthika
Hari-Shayana Ekadashi • Hindu
Vishnu's Awakening (Devathani Ekadashi) • Hindu

Begins night before full moon of Karthika
Pushkar Fair • Hindus at Pushkar Lake, Pushkar, Rajasthan, India

Full moon day of Karthika
Karthika Purnima • Hindu
Nanak's Day (Nanak Parab) • Sikh people
Varuna, Festival of • eastern Bengal, India

Fourth day of waning half of Karthika
Karwachoth or Karwa Chauth • married Hindu women in India

13th day of waning half of Karthika
Dhan Teras or Dhanvantri Trayodashi • Hindu

14th day of waning half of Karthika
Narak Chaturdashi • Hindu

One week during waning half of Karthika, including 15th day
Lights, Festival of (Dewali) • Hindu, Jaina, and Sikh peoples in India and elsewhere

Margashirsha
(corresponds to Gregorian November-December)

11th day of waxing half of Margashirsha
Gita Jayanti • Hindu

Twenty-day pilgrimage over 11th days of waxing and waning halves of Margashirsha
Vaikunth Ekadashi • Tiruchirapalli, Madras, India

Full moon day of Margashirsha
Dattatreya's Birthday (Dattatreya Jayanti) • Hindus in Maharashtra, India

Eighth day of waning half of Margashirsha
Bhairava Ashtami • Hindu

11th day of waning half of Margashirsha
Vaitarani • Hindu

Pausha
(corresponds to Gregorian December-January)

Pausha
Kite Festival, International • Ahmedabad, Gujarat, India

Three days during Pausha
Harvest Festival • India, Malaya, and Nepal; first day is called Bhogi or Bogi Pongal, Day of Joy; second day is Pongal (literally, *it boils*); and third day is Mattu Pongal, Festival of the Cows

Eighth day of waning half of Pausha
Rukmani Ashtami • Vaishnavite Hindu

12th day of waning half of Pausha
Swarupa Dwadashi • Hindu women

Magha
(corresponds to Gregorian January-February)

Fifth day of waxing half of Magha
Spring Festival (Vasant or Basant Panchami) • Hindus in Bengal, India

Other Movable Days Index

Every Friday the 13th
Carberry Day • Brown University, Providence, Rhode Island

Monthly
St. Michael's Feast • Amhara, Ethiopia

At least once monthly
Yoruba Ibeji Ceremony • Nigeria

First day of each of 19 months in Bahá'í calendar
Nineteen-Day Feast • Bahá'í

First day of any month in the Roman calendar
Ides • Roman

Twelfth day of every month
Michaelmas • Abyssinia

19th of each month and during last ten days of the year
Fravashi Festivals • Zoroastrian

14th of Kassada, 12th month of Tenggerese year (January)
Kassada • Tenggerese Buddha Dharma religion at Mount Bromo, Tengger Mountains, East Java, Indonesia

Three days, usually in February
New Year (Losar) • Buddhist Tibetan exiles in India and Bodhnath, Nepal (date determined by Tibetan astrologers in Dharmsala, India)

Two to three weeks during first month of Tibetan calendar (usually February)
Butter Sculpture Festival (Mönlam or Prayer Festival) • Buddhists in Lhasa, Tibet

Five days in February-March, coinciding with lost days of Mayan calendar
Mardi Gras (Tahimoltik, Festival of the Games) • Chamula Mayan people in Chamula, Mexico

11th-13th day of Greek month of Anthesterion (February-March)
Anthesteria • Athens, Greece

Last ten days of the Parsi year, the ten days preceding the vernal equinox (March)
Remembrance of the Departed Days • Parsi

First day of first month, Onwa Izizi, of the Ibu calendar (March), or determined by council of elders
New Year (Ibu Afo Festival) • Ibo people in Nigeria

Month of Ceuta (April)
New Year • Satawal, Micronesia

Month of Huey Tozoztli (April)
Chicomecoatl • Aztec
Cinteotl, Festival for • Aztec

First of Sinhala month of Bak and Tamil month of Chittrai (two days in April)
New Year (Sinhala Avurudu) • Buddhist and Hindu Sinhalese and Tamil peoples in Sri Lanka

First through fourth days of month of Tagu (mid-April, when Sun is in Aries)
New Year (Thingyan; Pwe) • Burma (now Myanmar)

14th-16th days of fifth Tibetan lunar month (usually June or July)
Prayer Day, Universal (Dzam Ling chi Sang) • Buddhists in Tibet

Greek month of Carneus (August)
Carnea • Cyrene, Magna Græcia, Peloponnesus, and Sparta, Greece

12th day of waning moon of Photrobot (August-September)
Prachum Ben • Cambodia

Four to ten days in Malyalam month of Chingam (August-September)
Harvest Festival (Onam) • Kerala, India

Month of Xul (end of October)
Chickaban (Feast of the Storm God Kukulcan) • Mayan people in Mani, Yucatan, Mexico

Around October and at Christmas; after millet harvest, during month of Twamo
Misisi Beer Feast • Sebei people in Uganda

Full moon day of Burmese month of Tazauungmon (October-November)
Tazaungdaing • Buddhist people in Burma (now Myanmar)

Month of Tulam (October-November)
Skanda Shashti • Hindu Tamil people in southern India

25th day of tenth Tibetan month
Lights, Festival of (Sang-joe) • Lhasa, Tibet

Twelfth month (November)
Boun Phan Vet • Buddhists in Vientiane, Laos

Two days before full moon day of twelfth month (November)
Wat Simouang Festival • Vientiane, Laos

Last day of the Tibetan year
Mystery Play of Tibet • Buddhists in Tibet

Occasional: Saturdays and before major festivals
Fravashi Festivals • Armenia

Occasional: end of dry seasons (March-May), August, and during emergencies and funerals
Gelede • Yoruba people in Nigeria

May occur on special occasions and during such holidays as Christmas, Easter, Good Friday, and New Year's Day
Thanksgiving (Awoojoh) • Yoruba, Christian Creole, and Muslim Aku people in Sierra Leone

Final day of ten-day New Year's celebration, Galungan; every 210 days
New Year's Celebration (Kuningen, Feast of All Souls) • Hindu people in Bali, Indonesia

Ten-day celebration (according to Wauku calendar of 210 days per year)
New Year (Galungan) • Bali, Indonesia

280th day of the year (14th day, counting by twenties, from February)
Quecholli, Feast of Mixcoatl • Aztec

End of Ndok season
New Year's Day • Ibibio people in Nigeria

Formerly in autumn; now held irregularly
Oaqöl • Hopi women

Prior to rainy season
Rainmaking Ceremony • Lovedu people in South Africa

End of the hot-dry season, usually on a Thursday
Rain-Bringing Ceremony (Yenaandi) • Songhay people in Niger

Five-day New Year feast
Sacaea • Babylonia (later Persia)

Monday nearest to official date proclaimed in England
Queen Elizabeth's Day • Australia and Fiji

Seasonal festival
Puruli • ancient Semite

When the Pleiades appear
New Year's Day • Polynesia; Mojo Indians in eastern Bolivia; and Kaffir people in South Africa

Year-round
Free Entertainment in the Parks • Melbourne, Victoria, Australia

Annually
Artemis Karyatis, Feast of • ancient Greece at Karyai
Ballet Festival, Kathak Kendra • New Delhi, India
Ballet Festival, Triveni Kala Sangam • New Delhi, India
Běla Kampong • Malay people at Endau, Malaysia
Bharatiya Lok Kala Festival • Udaipur, Rajasthan, India
Indian Acorn Festival, Mi-Wuk • Tuolumne Indian Rancheria near Tuolumne, California
Mobog • Tuaran Dusun people in Borneo
Music, International Society of Contemporary • location varies; London-based
New Yam Festival (Igun Ekun Ajinida Festival) • Yoruba people at Oyo, Nigeria
New Yam Festival (Ogijan Festival) • Yoruba people at Oyo, Nigeria
Offering Day • Christian (date determined by the Christian Church)
Powwow, La Ka Le'l Ba • Washo Indians at Carson City, Nevada
Temple Festivals • date varies according to temples throughout Bali
Theatre, Festival of Popular • Guayana City, Bolivar, Venezuela
Theatre Festival, International Street (Internationales Strassentheaterfestspiele) • Vienna, Austria
Theatres, Showcase of Independent • Las Palmas, Canary Islands, Spain

Two nights annually
Heshwash Ceremony • California Yokuts Indians

Seven nights annually
Dead, Observance for the (Keruk) • Diegueño and Yuma Indians in California and Yuma Indians in Arizona

Ten days annually
Theater, Eastern Festival of • Barcelona, Estado Anzoategui, Venezuela

Annual twelve-night ceremony
Big House Ceremony • Delaware Indians in the United States

Five festivals annually
Iro Festivals • Yoruba people

Annual, near time of monsoon
Bhima or Bhima-sena, Festival of • Hindu Gond people in Central Provinces of India

Observed on variable dates *(cont.)*

782

Title Codes and Call Numbers for Sources

The following list contains the books indexed in *Holidays and Festivals Index*, the abbreviations used throughout the *Index* to refer to them, and the Dewey Decimal and Library of Congress (LC) classification numbers for each book.

AmerBkDays-1978
Dewey: 394.2
LC: GT4803.H36

Hatch, Jane M. *American Book of Days.* 3rd ed., H.W. Wilson, 1978.

AnnivHol-1983
Dewey: 394.26
LC: GT3930.G822

Gregory, Ruth W. *Anniversaries and Holidays.* American Library Association, 1983.

BkDays-1864
Dewey: 394
LC: DA110.C445

Chambers, Robert. *Book of Days.* 1862-64. Reprinted by Omnigraphics, 1990.

BkFest-1937
Dewey: 394.26
LC: GT3930.S75

Spicer, Dorothy Gladys. *Book of Festivals.* 1937. Reprinted by Omnigraphics, 1990.

BkFestHolWrld-1970
Dewey: 394.26
LC: GT3932.I17

Ickis, Marguerite. *The Book of Festivals and Holidays the World over.* Dodd, Mead & Co., 1970.

BkHolWrld-1986
Dewey: 394.26
LC: GT3933.V36

Van Straalen, Alice. *Book of Holidays around the World.* E.P. Dutton, 1986.

Chases-1993
Dewey: 394.26
LC: D11.5.C49

Chase's Annual Events. 1993.

DaysCustFaith-1957
Dewey: 291.36
LC: GR930.H29

Harper, Howard V. *Days and Customs of All Faiths.* 1957. Reprinted by Omnigraphics, 1990.

DictDays-1988
Dewey: 394.26
LC: GT3925.D861

Dunkling, Leslie. *Dictionary of Days.* Facts on File, 1988.

DictFolkMyth-1984
Dewey: 398
LC: GR35.F98

Leach, Maria, ed. *Funk & Wagnalls Standard Dictionary of Folklore, Mythology & Legend.* Funk & Wagnall, 1984.

DictMyth-1962
Dewey: 398.03
LC: GR35.J62

Jobes, Gertrude. *Dictionary of Mythology, Folklore and Symbols.* Scarecrow, 1962.

DictWrldRel-1989
Dewey: 291.03
LC: BL31.A24

Crim, Keith. *Perennial Dictionary of World Religions.* Harper & Row, 1989.

FestSaintDays-1915
Dewey: 263.9
LC: BV43.U77

Urlin, Ethel L. *Festivals, Holy Days, and Saints' Days.* 1915. Reprinted by Omnigraphics, 1992.